Lecture Notes in Computer Science 1119
Edited by G. Goos, J. Hartmanis and J. van Leeuwen

Springer
Berlin
Heidelberg
New York
Barcelona
Budapest
Hong Kong
London
Milan
Paris
Santa Clara
Singapore
Tokyo

Ugo Montanari Vladimiro Sassone (Eds.)

CONCUR '96: Concurrency Theory

7th International Conference
Pisa, Italy, August 26-29, 1996
Proceedings

Springer

Series Editors

Gerhard Goos, Karlsruhe University, Germany

Juris Hartmanis, Cornell University, NY, USA

Jan van Leeuwen, Utrecht University, The Netherlands

Volume Editors

Ugo Montanari
Vladimiro Sassone
Università di Pisa, Dipartimento di Informatica
Corso Italia 40, I-56125 Pisa, Italy

Cataloging-in-Publication data applied for

Die Deutsche Bibliothek - CIP-Einheitsaufnahme

Concurrency theory : 7th international conference ; proceedings / CONCUR '96, Pisa, Italy, August 26 - 29, 1996. Ugo Montanari ; Vladimiro Sassone (ed.). - Berlin ; Heidelberg ; New York ; Barcelona ; Budapest ; Hong Kong ; London ; Milan ; Paris ; Santa Clara ; Singapore ; Tokyo : Springer, 1996
(Lecture notes in computer science ; Vol. 1119)
ISBN 3-540-61604-7
NE: Montanari, Ugo [Hrsg.]; CONCUR <7, 1996, Pisa>; GT

CR Subject Classification (1991): F.3, F.1, D.3, D.1, C.2

ISSN 0302-9743
ISBN 3-540-61604-7 Springer-Verlag Berlin Heidelberg New York

Typesetting: Camera-ready by author
SPIN 10513437 06/3142 – 5 4 3 2 1 0 Printed on acid-free paper

Preface

The purpose of the *CONCUR* conferences is to bring together researchers, developers and students in order to advance the science of concurrency theory and promote its applications. Interest in the conference is continuously growing, as a consequence of the importance and ubiquity of concurrent systems and applications, and of the scientific relevance of their foundations. The first two meetings were held in *Amsterdam* in 1990 and 1991, the following meetings in *Stony Brook*, *Hildesheim*, *Uppsala*, and *Philadelphia*. The proceedings have appeared in Springer LNCS, as Vols. 458, 527, 630, 715, 836 and 962. The *Steering Committee* of *CONCUR* is composed of

Jos Baeten (chair, Eindhoven),
Eike Best (Hildesheim),
Kim Larsen (Aalborg),
Ugo Montanari (Pisa),
Scott Smolka (Stony Brook),
Pierre Wolper (Liège).

The conference *CONCUR'96* will be held in Pisa on August 26–29, 1996. This volume contains 37 papers, selected out of 133 submitted papers; seven invited papers (four invited talks and three tutorials) are also included. The selected papers are grouped into sessions on

Process Algebras, Categorical Approaches, The π-Calculus, Decidability & Complexity, Probability, Functional & Constraint Programming, Petri Nets, Verification, Automata & Causality, Practical Models, Shared-Memory Systems.

The invited talks are by *Samson Abramsky* (Edinburgh), *José Meseguer* (SRI), *Faron Moller* (Uppsala), *Wolfgang Reisig* (Berlin); the tutorials are by *Andrea Corradini* (Pisa), *Vijay Saraswat* (Xerox PARC), and *Bent Thomsen* (ICL/IC-PARC). In connection with the conference, some sessions devoted to demonstrations of (semi-)automatic academic tools for the analysis and verification of concurrent systems are organized. A satellite workshop on *Verification of Infinite State Systems* (*VISS*) will be held on Friday, August 30.

The members of the *Program Committee* of *CONCUR'96* are

Luca Aceto (Aalborg and Sussex),
Jan Bergstra (Utrecht),
Rance Cleaveland (NCSU),
Mads Dam (SICS),
Philippe Darondeau (Rennes),
Rocco De Nicola (Firenze),
Javier Esparza (München),
Ursula Goltz (Hildesheim),
Bob Harper (Pittsburgh),
Tom Henzinger (Berkeley),
Ugo Montanari (Pisa, chair),
Luis Monteiro (Lisboa),
Mogens Nielsen (Aarhus),
Amir Pnueli (Rehovot),
Jan Rutten (CWI),
Davide Sangiorgi (Sophia Ant.),
Scott Smolka (Stony Brook),
Bernhard Steffen (Passau),
Colin Stirling (Edinburgh),
Frits Vaandrager (Nijmegen),
Walter Vogler (Augsburg),
David Walker (Warwick).

The program committee meeting was held electronically in the week from April 29 to May 4, 1996.

The members of the *Organizing Committee* of ***CONCUR'96*** are

Pierpaolo Degano (chair, Pisa),
Roberto Gorrieri (Bologna), Corrado Priami (Pisa),
Stefania Gnesi (IEI-CNR, Pisa), Vladimiro Sassone (Pisa).

The conference has received support from *Gruppo Nazionale Informatica Matematica – CNR, Office of Naval Research European Office, U.S. Air Force European Office*, and the *University of Pisa.*

Pisa, June 1996
Ugo Montanari
Program Committee Chair

concur 96
7th International Conference on Concurrency Theory
26-29 August, 1996, Pisa, Italy

Referees

P. Aziz Abdulla
L. Aceto
R. Alur
R. Amadio
J. Hedegaard Andersen
S. Anderson
A. Arnold
A. Asperti
P. Azema
E. Badouel
C. Baier
M. Baldamus
J. Baptista
T. Basten
M. von der Beeck
J. Bergstra
K. Bernstein
G. Berthelot
B. Berthomieu
E. Best
G. Bhat
N. Bhatt
G. Blelloch
B. Bloom
F. de Boer
M. Boreale
A. Bouajjani
A. Bouali
G. Boudol
F. Boussinot
J. Bradfield
F. van Breugel
S. Brookes
O. Burkart
B. Caillaud
L. Caires
L. Capra
I. Castellani
G. Cattani
D. Caucal
M. Chaudron
A. Cheng
A. Chizzoni
E. Clarke
R. Cleaveland
C. Colby
F. Corradini
P.-L. Curien
S. Dal-Zilio
M. Dam
D. Dams
Ph. Darondeau
Z. Dayar
F. De Cindio
R. De Nicola
P. Degano
J. Desel
A. van Deursen
R. Devillers
P. Di Blasio
V. Diekert
M. Droste
U. Engberg
J. Esparza
G. Ferrari
W. Ferreira
J. Fiadeiro
M. Fiore
W. Fokkink
T. Franzen
L. Fredlund
F. Gadducci
P. Gardner
T. Gehrke
T. Gelsema
A. Geser
C. Girault
R. van Glabbeek
S. Gnesi
R. Gorrieri
E. Goubault
S. Graf
B. Grahlmann
B. Graves
W. Griffioen
J.-F. Groote
V. Gupta
R. Harper
D. Hauschildt
M. Hennessy
J. Gulmann Henriksen
T. Henzinger
C. Hermida
T. Hildebrandt
G. Holzmann
K. Honda
E. Horita
M. Huhn
H. Hungar
H. Huttel
A. Ingolfsdottir
P. Inverardi
P. Iyer
B. Jacobs
R. Jagadeesan
D. Janin
M. Jantzen
L. Jenner
O. Jensen
M. Jerrum
H. Jifeng
J. Bæk Jørgensen
B. Jonsson
S. Kahrs
R. Kaivola
Y. Kesten
A. Kiehn
E. Kindler
J. Kleijn
J. Kleist
J.-W. Klop
P. Kopke
M. Koutny
L. Kristensen
K. Kristoffersen
R. Kuiper
K. Narayan Kumar
O. Kupferman
M. Kwiatkowska
A. Labella
R. Langerak
D. Latella
P. Lee
F. Levi
H. Lin

B. Lisper
X. Liu
A. Lopes
G. Lüttgen
A. Mader
A. Maggiolo-Schettini
F. Maraninchi
T. Margaria
W. Marrero
S. Mauw
R. Mayr
K. McMillan
S. Melzer
M. Mendler
D. Miller
E. Moggi
F. Moller
L. Monteiro
B. Mott
M. Mukund
V. Natarajan
U. Nestmann
P. Niebert
J. Niehren
M. Nielsen
O. Nierstrasz
F. Orava
G. Overgaard
P. Paczkowski
C. Palamidessi
P. Pananagden
J. Parrow
D. Pavlovic
J. Pearson
E. Pelz
L. Moniz Pereira
P. Pettersson
F. Pfenning
A. Philippou
B. Pierce
S. Pinchinat
G. Pinna
A. Piperno
M. Pistore
A. Pitts
A. Pnueli
A. Porto
J. Power
S. Prasad
C. Priami
L. Priese
R. Pugliese
P. Quaglia
F. van Raamsdonk
Y. Ramakrishna
R. Ramanujam
J.-C. Raoult
J. Rathke
A. Rensink
P. Resende
M. de Rijke
G. Ristori
P. Rodenburg
S. Roemer
J. Romijn
A. Roscoe
F. Rossi
J. Rutten
M. Ryan
A. Sandholm
D. Sands
D. Sangiorgi
V. Sassone
A. Schalk
I. Schiering
K. Schmidt
Ph. Schnoebelen
P. Scott
R. Segala
P. Sewell
E. Shahar
R. de Simone
A. Simpson
A. Skou
S. Smolka
O. Sokolsky
B. Sprick
J. Springintveld
I. Stark
G. Stefanescu
P. Stevens
C. Stirling
K. Stølen
K. Sunesen
H. van Thienen
W. Thomas
P. Kumar Tiwari
C. Tofts
D. Turi
D. Turner
I. Ulidowski
A. Uselton
F. Vaandrager
R. Valk
V. Vasconcelos
C. Verhoef
T. Verhoeff
B. Victor
E. de Vink
W. Vogler
H. Volzer
K. Wagner
D. Walker
F. Wallner
R. Walter
I. Walukiewicz
S. Weeks
M. Weichert
C. Weise
M. Wermelinger
J. Winkowski
G. Winskel
S.-H. Wu
D. Yankelevich
S. Yovine
J. Zwiers

Contents

Invited Talk

Retracing Some Paths in Process Algebra 1
Samson Abramsky

Process Algebras

Process Calculus Based Upon Evaluation to Committed Form 18
Andrew Pitts and Joshua Ross

A Process Algebra with Distributed Priorities 34
Rance Cleaveland, Gerald Lüttgen, and Vaidhyanathan Natarajan

Symbolic Transition Graph with Assignment 50
Huimin Lin

Tutorial

Models for Concurrent Constraint Programming 66
Vineet Gupta, Radha Jagadeesan, and Vijay Saraswat

Categorical Approaches

Comparing Transition Systems with Independence and Asynchronous Transition Systems 84
Thomas Hildebrandt and Vladimiro Sassone

A Presheaf Semantics of Value-Passing Processes 98
Glynn Winskel

Elementary Control Structures 115
John Power

The π-Calculus

On Transformations of Concurrent Object Programs 131
Anna Philippou and David Walker

On Bisimulations for the Asynchronous π-Calculus 147
Roberto Amadio, Ilaria Castellani, and Davide Sangiorgi

On the Expressiveness of Internal Mobility in Name-Passing Calculi 163
Michele Boreale

Decoding Choice Encodings 179
Uwe Nestmann and Benjamin Pierce

Invited Talk

Infinite Results 195
Faron Moller

Decidability & Complexity

Decidability of Bisimulation Equivalence for Normed Pushdown Processes 217
Colin Stirling

The Modal mu-Calculus Alternation Hierarchy is Strict 233
Julian Bradfield

Bisimulation Collapse and the Process Taxonomy 247
Olaf Burkart, Didier Caucal, and Bernhard Steffen

On the Expressive Completeness of the Propositional mu-Calculus with Respect to the Monadic Second Order Logic 263
David Janin and Igor Walukiewicz

Tutorial

A Facile Tutorial 278
Bent Thomsen, Lone Leth, and Tsung-Min Kuo

Probability

Testing Probabilistic Automata 299
Roberto Segala

Extended Markovian Process Algebra 315
Marco Bernardo and Roberto Gorrieri

Invited Talk

Rewriting Logic as a Semantic Framework for Concurrency: A Progress Report 331
José Meseguer

Functional & Constraint Programming

Truly Concurrent Constraint Programming 373
Vineet Gupta, Radha Jagadeesan, and Vijay Saraswat

Constraints as Processes 389
Björn Victor and Joachim Parrow

A Calculus of Mobile Agents 406
Cédric Fournet, Georges Gonthier, Jean-Jacques Lévy, Luc Maranget, and Didier Rémy

Algebraic Interpretation of Lambda Calculus with Resources 422
Carolina Lavatelli

Tutorial

Concurrent Graph and Term Graph Rewriting 438
Andrea Corradini

Petri Nets

Petri Boxes and Finite Precedence 465
Raymond Devillers

Constrained Properties, Semilinear Systems, and Petri Nets 481
Ahmed Bouajjani and Peter Habermehl

Linear Constraint Systems as High-Level Nets 498
Eike Best and Catuscia Palamidessi

Verification

A Space-Efficient On-the-fly Algorithm for Real-Time Model Checking . . 514
Thomas Henzinger, Orna Kupferman, and Moshe Vardi

State Equivalences for Rectangular Hybrid Automata 530
Thomas Henzinger and Peter Kopke

Verifying Abstractions of Timed Systems 546
Serdar Taşıran, Rajeev Alur, Robert Kurshan, and Robert Brayton

Towards Automatic Temporal Logic Verification of Value Passing Process Algebra Using Abstract Interpretation 563
Alessandro Fantechi, Stefania Gnesi, and Diego Latella

Invited Talk

Modelling and Verification of Distributed Algorithms 579
Wolfgang Reisig

Automata & Causality

An Algorithmic Approach for Checking Closure Properties of ω-Regular Languages 596
Doron Peled, Thomas Wilke, and Pierre Wolper

Towards Automata for Branching Time and Partial Order 611
Michaela Huhn and Peter Niebert

Asynchronous Cellular Automata for Pomsets without Auto-Concurrency 627
Manfred Droste and Paul Gastin

Action Refinement and Property Inheritance in Systems of Sequential Agents 639
Michaela Huhn

Practical Models

A Calculus for Concurrent Objects 655
Paolo Di Blasio and Kathleen Fisher

Refinement in Interworkings 671
Sjouke Mauw and Michel Reniers

Equivalences of Statecharts 687
Andrea Maggiolo-Schettini, Adriano Peron, and Simone Tini

Shared-Memory Systems

Modular Verification for Shared-Variable Concurrent Programs 703
Jürgen Dingel

The Impact of Hardware Models on Shared Memory Consistency Conditions 719
Jerry James and Ambuj Singh

Synchronous Development of Asynchronous Systems 735
Clemens Fischer and Wil Janssen

Author Index 751

Retracing Some Paths in Process Algebra

Samson Abramsky
Laboratory for the Foundations of Computer Science
University of Edinburgh

1 Introduction

The very existence of the CONCUR conference bears witness to the fact that "concurrency theory" has developed into a subject unto itself, with substantially different emphases and techniques to those prominent elsewhere in the semantics of computation.

Whatever the past merits of this separate development, it seems timely to look for some convergence and unification. In addressing these issues, I have found it instructive to trace some of the received ideas in concurrency back to their origins in the early 1970's. In particular, I want to focus on a seminal paper by Robin Milner [Mil75][1], which led in a fairly direct line to his enormously influential work on CCS [Mil80, Mil89]. I will take (to the extreme) the liberty of applying hindsight, and show how some different paths could have been taken, which, it can be argued, lead to a more unified approach to the semantics of computation, and moreover one which may be better suited to modelling today's concurrent, object-oriented languages, and the type systems and logics required to support such languages.

2 The semantic universe: transducers

Milner's starting point was the classical automata-theoretic notion of *transducers*, *i.e.* structures

$$(Q, X, Y, q_0, \delta)$$

where Q is a set of states, $q_0 \in Q$ the initial state, X the set of inputs, Y the set of outputs, and

$$\delta : Q \times X \rightharpoonup Y \times Q$$

[1]Similar ideas appeared independently in the work of Hans Bekić [Bek71].

is the transition function (here a partial function). If we supply a sequence of inputs $x_0, \ldots, x_k$ to such a transducer, we obtain the orbit

$$q_0 \xrightarrow{x_0} y_0, q_1 \xrightarrow{x_1} y_1, q_2 \xrightarrow{x_2} \cdots \xrightarrow{x_k} y_k, q_{k+1}$$

if $\delta(q_i, x_i) = y_i, q_{i+1}$, $0 \leq i \leq k$. This generalizes to non-deterministic transducers with transition function

$$\delta : Q \times X \longrightarrow \mathcal{P}(Y \times Q)$$

in an evident fashion.

The key idea in [Mil75] is to give a denotational semantics for concurrent programs as *processes*, which were taken to be extensional versions of transducers. There are two ingredients to this idea:

1. Instead of modelling programs by functions or relations, to model them by entities with more complex behaviours, taking account of the possible interactions between a program and its environment during the course of a computation.

   "The meaning of a program should express its history of access to resources which are not local to it." [Mil75]

2. Instead of modelling concurrent programs by automata, with all the intensionality this entails, to look for a more extensional description of the *behaviours* of transducers.

To obtain this extensional view of transducers, consider the recursive definition

$$R = X \rightharpoonup Y \times R.$$

This defines a mathematical space of "resumptions" in which the states of transducers are "unfolded" into their observable behaviours. Milner solved equations such as this over a category of domains in [Mil75], but in fact it can be solved in a canonical fashion over **Set**—in modern terminology, the functor

$$T_{X,Y} : \mathbf{Set} \longrightarrow \mathbf{Set}$$

$$T_{X,Y}(S) = X \rightharpoonup Y \times S$$

has a final coalgebra $R \xrightarrow{\cong} T_{X,Y}(R)$. Indeed, Milner defined a notion $\sim$ of behavioural equivalence between transducers, and for any transducer

(Q, X, Y, q_0, δ) a map $h_\delta : Q \longrightarrow R$ which is in fact the final coalgebra homomorphism from the coalgebra

$$\hat{\delta} : Q \longrightarrow T_{X,Y}(Q)$$

to R (where $\hat{\delta}$ is the exponential transpose of δ), and proved that

$$(Q, X, Y, q_0, \delta) \sim (Q', X, Y, q_0', \delta') \iff h_\delta(q_0) = h_{\delta'}(q_0').$$

From a modern perspective, we can also make light of a technical problem which figured prominently in [Mil75], namely how to model non-determinism. Historically, this called forth Plotkin's work on powerdomains [Plo76], but for the specific application at hand, the equation

$$R = X \longrightarrow \mathcal{P}(Y \times R)$$

has a final coalgebra in the category of classes in Peter Aczel's non-well-founded set theory [Acz88], and if we are content to bound the cardinality of subsets by an inaccessible cardinable κ, then the equation

$$R = X \longrightarrow \mathcal{P}^{<\kappa}(Y \times R)$$

has a final coalgebra in **Set** [Bar93b]. Moreover, the equivalence induced by this model coincides with strong bisimulation [Acz88].

However, this is not central to our concerns here. Rather, we want to focus on three important choices in the path followed by Milner from this starting point:

- Type-free *vs.* typed
- Extrinsic *vs.* intrinsic interaction
- Names *vs.* information paths.

We want to examine the consequences of making different choices on these issues.

2.1 Typed vs. type-free

Rather than looking at a single type-free space of resumptions as above, and trying to invent some plausible operations on this space, we will focus instead on the *category* of resumptions, and try to identify the structure naturally present in this category.

The category $\mathcal{R}$ of resumptions (we will for simplicity confine ourselves to the deterministic resumptions) has as objects sets, and as morphisms

$$\mathcal{R}(X,Y) = X \rightharpoonup Y \times \mathcal{R}(X,Y)$$

i.e. the space of resumptions parameterized by the sets of "inputs" X and "outputs" Y. The composition of resumptions $f \in \mathcal{R}(X,Y)$ and $g \in \mathcal{R}(Y,Z)$ is defined (coinductively [Acz88]) by:

$$f;g(x) = \begin{cases} (z, f';g') & f(x) = (y, f'), g(y) = (z, g') \\ \text{undefined} & \text{otherwise.} \end{cases}$$

The identity resumption $\mathtt{id}_X \in \mathcal{R}(X,X)$ is defined by

$$\mathtt{id}_X(x) = (x, \mathtt{id}_X).$$

We can picture this composition as sequential (or "series") composition of transducers.

We can define a monoidal structure on $\mathcal{R}$ by

$$X \otimes Y = X + Y \quad \text{(disjoint union of sets)}$$

and if $f \in \mathcal{R}(X,Y)$, $g \in \mathcal{R}(X',Y')$, $f \otimes g \in \mathcal{R}(X \otimes X', Y \otimes Y')$ is defined by:

$$f \otimes g(\mathtt{inl}(x)) = \begin{cases} (\mathtt{inl}(y), f' \otimes g), & f(x) = (y, f') \\ \text{undefined} & \text{otherwise} \end{cases}$$

$$f \otimes g(\mathtt{inr}(x')) = \begin{cases} (\mathtt{inr}(y'), f \otimes g'), & g(x') = (y', g') \\ \text{undefined} & \text{otherwise.} \end{cases}$$

This is (asynchronous) parallel composition of transducers: at each stage, we respond to an input on the X "wire" according to f, with output appearing on the Y wire, and to an input on the X' wire according to g, with output appearing on the Y' wire.

The remaining definitions to make this into a symmetric monoidal structure on $\mathcal{R}$ are straightforward, and left to the reader. Note that the associativity and symmetry isomorphisms, like the identities, have just one state; they are "history-free".

Finally, there is a feedback operator: for each X, Y, U a function

$$\mathtt{Tr}^U_{X,Y} : \mathcal{R}(X \otimes U, Y \otimes U) \longrightarrow \mathcal{R}(X,Y)$$

defined by

$$\mathtt{Tr}^U_{X,Y}(f)(x) = \begin{cases} (y, f'), & \exists k.\, f(x) = (u_0, f_0), \\ & f_0(u_0) = (u_1, f_1), \\ & \vdots \\ & f_k(u_k) = (y, f') \\ \text{undefined} & \text{otherwise.} \end{cases}$$

One should picture a token entering at the X wire, circulating k times around the feedback loop at the U wire, and exiting at Y.

This feedback operator satisfies a number of algebraic properties (to simplify the statement of these properties, we elide associativity isomorphisms, *i.e.* we pretend that $\mathcal{R}$ is *strict* monoidal):

Naturality in X

$$\mathtt{Tr}^U_{X,Y}((g \otimes \mathtt{id}_U); f) = g; \mathtt{Tr}^U_{X',Y}(f)$$

where $f : X' \otimes U \longrightarrow Y \otimes U$, $g : X \longrightarrow X'$.

Naturality in Y

$$\mathtt{Tr}^U_{X,Y}(f; (g \otimes \mathtt{id}_U)) = \mathtt{Tr}^U_{X,Y'}(f); g$$

where $f : X \otimes U \longrightarrow Y' \otimes U$, $g : Y' \longrightarrow Y$.

Naturality in U

$$\mathtt{Tr}^U_{X,Y}(f; (\mathtt{id}_Y \otimes g)) = \mathtt{Tr}^{U'}_{X,Y}((\mathtt{id}_X \otimes g); f)$$

where $f : X \otimes U \longrightarrow Y \otimes U'$, $g : U' \longrightarrow U$.

Vanishing

$$\mathtt{Tr}^I_{X,Y}(f) = f$$

where $f : X \longrightarrow Y$, and

$$\mathtt{Tr}^{U \otimes V}_{X,Y}(f) = \mathtt{Tr}^U_{X,Y}(\mathtt{Tr}^V_{X \otimes U, Y \otimes U}(f))$$

where $f : X \otimes U \otimes V \longrightarrow Y \otimes U \otimes V$.

Superposing

$$\mathtt{Tr}^U_{X \otimes Z, Y \otimes W}((\mathtt{id}_X \otimes \mathtt{sym}_{Z,U}); (f \otimes g); (\mathtt{id}_Y \otimes \mathtt{sym}_{U,W})) = \mathtt{Tr}^U_{X,Y}(f) \otimes g$$

where $f : X \otimes U \longrightarrow Y \otimes U$, $g : Z \longrightarrow W$.

Yanking

$$\mathtt{Tr}^{X}_{X,X}(\mathtt{sym}_{X,X}) = \mathtt{id}_X.$$

This says that $\mathcal{R}$ is a *traced (symmetric) monoidal category* in the sense of [JSV95] (*cf.* also [Has96] for the symmetric and cartesian cases, and [BE93] for related axioms).

2.2 Intrinsic vs. extrinsic interaction: paths vs. names

Why this apparent digression into the structure of the category of resumptions? Our aim is to address the question of how to model *interaction between processes*, which is surely the key notion in concurrency theory, and arguably in the semantics of computation as a whole. Resumptions as they stand model a single process in terms of its potential interactions with its environment. To quote Robin Milner again:

> "A crucial feature is the ability to define the operation of *binding* together two processes (which may represent two cooperating programs, or a program and a memory, or a computer an an input/output device) to yield another process representing the composite of the two computing agents, with their mutual communications internalized." [Mil75]

The route Milner followed to define this binding was in terms of the use of "names" or "labels": in terms of resumptions, one modifies their defining equation to

$$R(X,Y) = X \rightharpoonup Y \times L \times R(X,Y)$$

where L is a set of labels, so that output is tagged with a label, which can then be used by some "routing combinator" to dispatch the output to its destination process. This led in a fairly direct line of descent to the action names α, β, γ of CCS [Mil80, Mil89], and the names of the π-calculus [MPW92] and action structures [MMP95]. Clearly a great deal has been achieved with this approach. Nevertheless, we wish to lodge some criticisms of it.

- interaction becomes extrinsic: we must add some additional structure, typically a "synchronization algebra" on the labels [Win83], which implicitly refers to some external agency for matching up labels and generating communication events, rather than finding the meaning of interaction in the structure we already have.

- interaction becomes ad hoc: because it is an "invented" additional structure, many possibilities arise, and it is hard to identify any as canonical.

- interaction becomes global: using names to match up communications implies some large space in which potential communications "swim", just as the use of references in imperative languages implies some global heap. Although the scope of names may be delimited, as in the π-calculus, the local character of particular interactions is not immediately apparent, and must be laboriously verified. This appears to account for many of the complications encountered in reasoning about concurrent object-oriented languages modelled in the π-calculus, as reported in [Jon93, Jon96].

We will now describe a construction which appears in [JSV95], and which can be seen as a general form of the "Geometry of Interaction" [Gir88], and also as a general but basic form of game semantics [Abr96b]. This construction applies to any traced monoidal category $\mathcal{C}$, *i.e.* to any calculus of boxes and wires closed under series and parallel composition and feedback, and builds a compact closed category $\mathcal{G}(\mathcal{C})$, into which $\mathcal{C}$ fully and faithfully embeds. (It is in fact the unit of a (bi)adjunction between the categories of traced monoidal and compact closed categories.) Its significance in the present context is that it gives a general way of introducing a symmetric notion of interaction which addresses the issues raised above:

- interaction is intrinsic: it is found from the basic idea that processes are modelled in terms of their interactions with their environment. Building in the distinction between "process" and "environment" at a fundamental level makes interaction inherent in the model, rather than something that needs to be added.

- interaction is modelled as composition in the category $\mathcal{G}(\mathcal{C})$. Thus interaction is aligned with the computation-as-cut-elimination paradigm, and hence a unification of concurrency with other work in denotational semantics, type theory, categorical logic etc. becomes possible. See [AGN96a, Abr93, Abr95b] for a detailed discussion of this point.

- interaction is local. The dynamics of composition traces out "information paths", which are closely related to the types of the processes which interact. There is no appeal to a global mechanism for matching names. As we will see, this is general enough to model λ-calculus, state and concurrency, but, we believe, carries much more structure than the use of names to mediate interactions.

3 The $\mathcal{G}$ construction

Given a traced monoidal category $\mathcal{C}$, we define a new category $\mathcal{G}(\mathcal{C})$ as follows:

- The objects of $\mathcal{G}(\mathcal{C})$ are pairs (A^+, A^-) of objects of $\mathcal{C}$. The idea is that A^+ is the type of "moves by Player (the System)", while A^- is the type of "moves by Opponent (the Environment)".
- A morphism $f : (A^+, A^-) \longrightarrow (B^+, B^-)$ in $\mathcal{G}(\mathcal{C})$ is a morphism

$$f : A^+ \otimes B^- \longrightarrow A^- \otimes B^+$$

  in $\mathcal{C}$.
- Composition is defined by symmetric feedback (*cf.* [AJ94b, AJ94a]):

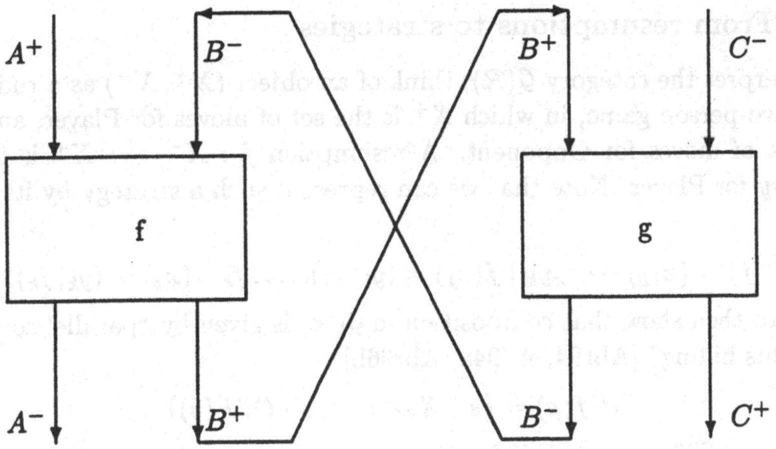

If $f : (A^+, A^-) \longrightarrow (B^+, B^-)$ and $g : (B^+, B^-) \longrightarrow (C^+, C^-)$ then $f;g : (A^+, A^-) \longrightarrow (C^+, C^-)$ is defined by

$$f;g = \mathrm{Tr}^{B^- \otimes B^+}_{A^+ \otimes C^-, A^- \otimes C^+}(\alpha; f \otimes g; \gamma)$$

where

$$\alpha : A^+ \otimes C^- \otimes B^- \otimes B^+ \xrightarrow{\cong} A^+ \otimes B^- \otimes B^+ \otimes C^-$$

and

$$\gamma : A^- \otimes B^+ \otimes B^- \otimes C^+ \xrightarrow{\cong} A^- \otimes C^+ \otimes B^- \otimes B^+$$

are the canonical isomorphisms defined using the symmetric monoidal structure. (Again, we have elided associativity isomorphisms.)

- The identities are given by the symmetry isomorphisms in $\mathcal{C}$:
$$\mathbf{id}_{(A^+,A^-)} = \mathbf{sym}_{A^+,A^-} : A^+ \otimes A^- \xrightarrow{\cong} A^- \otimes A^+.$$

There is an evident involutive duality on this category, given by

$$(A^+, A^-)^* = (A^-, A^+).$$

There is also a tensor structure, given by

$$(A^+, A^-) \otimes (B^+, B^-) = (A^+ \otimes B^+, A^- \otimes B^-).$$

$\mathcal{G}(\mathcal{C})$ is a compact-closed category [KL80], with internal homs given by

$$(A^+, A^-) \multimap (B^+, B^-) = (A^- \otimes B^+, A^+ \otimes B^-).$$

4 Examples

4.1 From resumptions to strategies

To interpret the category $\mathcal{G}(\mathcal{R})$, think of an object (X^+, X^-) as a rudimentary two-person game, in which X^+ is the set of moves for Player, and X^- the set of moves for Opponent. A resumption $f : X^- \longrightarrow X^+$ is then a *strategy* for Player. Note that we can represent such a strategy by its set of *plays*:

$$P(f) = \{x_1 y_1 \cdots x_k y_k \mid f(x_1) = (y_1, f_1), \ldots, f_{k-1}(x_k) = (y_k, f_k)\}.$$

One can then show that composition in $\mathcal{G}(\mathcal{R})$ is given by "parallel composition plus hiding" [Abr94, AJ94a, Abr96b]:

$$P(f;g) = \{s \upharpoonright X, Z \mid s \in P(f) \| P(g)\}$$

$$S \| T = \{s \in \mathcal{L}(X, Y, Z) \mid s \upharpoonright X, Y \in S \wedge s \upharpoonright Y, Z \in T\}$$

where $X = X^+ + X^-$, $Y = Y^+ + Y^-$, $Z = Z^+ + Z^-$, and

$$\mathcal{L}(S_1, S_2, S_3) = \{s \in (S_1 + S_2 + S_3)^* \mid s_i \in S_j \wedge s_{i+1} \in S_k \implies |j - k| \leq 1\}.$$

The identities are the "copycat" strategies as in [AJ94a, Abr96b]. We can then obtain the simple category of games described in [Abr96b] by applying a specification structure in the sense of [AGN96b] to $\mathcal{G}(\mathcal{R})$, in which the properties over (X^+, X^-) are the prefix-closed subsets of $(X^- X^+)^*$, *i.e.* the "safety properties" [AP93], which in this context are the game trees.

4.2 Some geometries of interaction

Suppose we begin with the simpler category **Pfn** of sets and partial functions (which is a lluf sub-category of $\mathcal{R}$). This is easily seen to be a sub-traced-monoidal category of $\mathcal{R}$, with tensor as disjoint union, and the trace given by a sum-of-paths formula (*cf.* [AM82]). That is, if

$$f : X + U \rightharpoonup Y + U$$

is a partial function, then

$$\mathtt{Tr}^{U}_{X,Y}(f) = \bigvee_{k \in \omega} f_k,$$

where $f_k(x)$ is defined and equal to y iff starting from x we perform exactly k iterations of the feedback loop around U before exiting at Y with result y:

$$f_k = \mathtt{inl}_{X,U}; (f; [0, \mathtt{inr}_{X,U}])^k; f; [\mathtt{id}_Y, 0]$$

where 0 is the everywhere undefined partial function. We can think of this sub-category of $\mathcal{R}$ as the "one-state resumptions", so that, applying the $\mathcal{G}$ construction to **Pfn** we get a category of history-free strategies [AJ94a].

As a minor variation, we could start with the category **PInj** of sets and partial injective maps. Then $\mathcal{G}(\mathbf{PInj})$ is essentially the original Geometry of Interaction construction of Girard, as explained in [AJ94a, AJM96]. In particular, the composition in $\mathcal{G}(\mathbf{PInj})$ corresponds exactly to the Execution Formula. This category can be lifted to the setting of Hilbert spaces by applying the free construction described in [Bar93a], which sends a set X to the Hilbert space $l_2(X)$ of square summable families $\{a_x \mid x \in X\}$.

As a final variation, we could start with **Rel**, the category of sets and relations. This yields a non-deterministic version of the Geometry of Interaction, which can be generalized via non-deterministic resumptions to a category of non-deterministic strategies. $\mathcal{G}(\mathbf{Rel})$ is the example mentioned at the end of [JSV95].

4.3 Stochastic interaction

As a more substantial variation of the above, consider the following category of *stochastic kernels* [Law62, Gir81]. Objects are structures $(X, \mathcal{M}(X))$, where $\mathcal{M}(X)$ is a σ-algebra of subsets of X. A morphism $f : X \longrightarrow Y$ is a function

$$f : X \times \mathcal{M}(Y) \longrightarrow [0, 1]$$

such that for each $x \in X$ $f(x,\cdot) : \mathcal{M}(Y) \longrightarrow [0,1]$ is a measure, and for each $M \in \mathcal{M}(Y)$, $f(\cdot, M) : X \longrightarrow [0,1]$ is a measurable function. One can think of stochastic kernels as "probabilistic transition functions". Note that we do not require that each $f(x,\cdot)$ is a probability measure, *i.e.* that $f(x,Y) = 1$, since we wish to allow for "partial" transition functions.

Composition is by integration: if $f : X \to Y$ and $g : Y \to Z$, then

$$f;g(x,M) = \int_Y g(\cdot, M) df(x,\cdot).$$

Identities are given by point measures:

$$\mathtt{id}_X(x,M) = \begin{cases} 1, & x \in M \\ 0, & x \notin M. \end{cases}$$

Tensor product is given by disjoint union; note that $\mathcal{M}(X+Y) \cong \mathcal{M}(X) \times \mathcal{M}(Y)$.

Feedback is given by a sum-over-paths formula. Given $f : X \otimes U \longrightarrow Y \otimes U$, and $x \in X$, we define for each $k \in \omega$ a measure μ_k on $\mathcal{M}(U)$ which gives the probability that we will end up in M starting from x after exactly k traversals of the feedback loop:

$$\mu_0(M) = f(\mathtt{inl}(x), (\varnothing, M))$$

$$\mu_{k+1}(M) = \int_U f(\mathtt{inr}(\cdot), (\varnothing, M)) d\mu_k.$$

The probability that we will end up in $M \in \mathcal{M}(Y)$ starting from x after exactly k iterations of the feedback loop is given by:

$$f_0(x,M) = f(\mathtt{inl}(x), (M, \varnothing))$$

$$f_{k+1}(x,M) = \int_U f(\mathtt{inr}(\cdot), (M, \varnothing)) d\mu_k.$$

Finally, the trace is defined by summing over all paths:

$$\mathtt{Tr}^U_{X,Y}(f)(x,M) = \Sigma_{k \in \omega} f_k(x,M).$$

4.4 From particles to waves: the "New Foundations" version of Geometry of Interaction

All the above models can be thought of as dynamical systems in which an information "token" or "particle" traces some path around a network. This particulate interpretation of diagrams of boxes and wires is supported by the "additive" (disjoint union) interpretation of the tensor. It is also possible to give an interpretation in which an information "wave" travels through the network; formally, this will be supported by a "multiplicative" (cartesian product) interpretation of the tensor.

Specifically, we can define a traced monoidal structure on the category **Cpo** of cpo's and continuous functions, in which the tensor is given by the cartesian product, and feedback by the least fixpoint operator: that is, if $f : D \times A \longrightarrow E \times A$, then

$$\mathtt{Tr}^{A}_{D,E}(f) = \lambda d : D.\, f(d, \mathbf{Y}(f(d, \cdot); \mathtt{snd})); \mathtt{fst}.$$

The category $\mathcal{G}(\mathbf{Cpo})$ is then exactly the category $\mathcal{GI}(\mathfrak{C})$ described in [AJ94b].

A sub-category of this category will consist of dataflow networks, built up from objects which are domains of streams. The symmetric feedback operator giving the composition in $\mathcal{G}(\mathbf{Cpo})$ has been used in this context [SDW96, GS96], *inter alia* in developing assumption/commitment style proof rules for dataflow networks.

4.5 The continuous case?

One final "example" should be mentioned, although we have not as yet succeeded in working out the details. The operations of series and parallel composition and feedback are standard in continuous-time control systems, electronic circuits and analogue computation. In particular, feedback is interpreted by solving a differential equation. There should then presumably be a traced monoidal category $\mathfrak{C}$ of manifolds and smooth maps, for which $\mathcal{G}(\mathfrak{C})$ would give an "infinitesimal" model of interaction. Such a category might be relevant to the study of hybrid systems [PS95].

5 Consequences

We shall, very briefly, sketch some further developments from this point.

5.1 Correctness issues

We can associate correctness properties with the rudimentary types of $\mathcal{G}(\mathfrak{C})$, in the setting of specification structures [AGN96b]. Types can then carry strong correctness information, and the type inference rule for composition

$$\frac{f : A \to B \quad g : B \to C}{f; g : A \to C}$$

becomes a compositional proof rule for process interaction. See [Abr93, Abr95b, AGN96a, AGN96b] for further discussion and applications.

We shall mention some particular cases for the examples described above.

Resumptions In this case, we can get the structure of games as safety properties, and of winning strategies as liveness properties, as described in [AJ94a, Abr96b]. In particular, the fact that winning strategies are closed under composition corresponds to a guarantee that there is no "infinite chattering" [Hoa85] in interaction.

Geometry of Interaction In this case, we can focus on nilpotency as a semantic analogue of normalization, as in [Gir88], or instead proceed as in the previous example, as in [AJ94a], where a Full Completeness Theorem for Multiplicative Linear Logic is obtained.

5.2 Modelling types and functions

The divide between concurrency theory and denotational semantics, type theory and categorical logic is bridged in our approach, since the categories we construct, or derivatives thereof, have the right structure to model typed, higher-order programming languages. The key point is that we are now modelling functions as processes, and function application as a particular form of process interaction, as advocated in [Mil92], but in a highly structured, syntax-free and compositional fashion.

Moreover, the quality of these process models of functional computation is high: the models based on games yielded the first syntax-independent constructions of fully abstract models for PCF [AJM96, HO96], and this has been followed by a number of further results [AM95, McC96b, McC96a]. The degree of mathematical structure in these models is also witnessed by the axiomatic treatment of full abstraction it has been possible to extract from them [Abr96a].

5.3 State and concurrency

It has also proved possible to give a game semantics for Idealized Algol [Abr95a], which is a clean integration of higher-order functional programming with imperative features and block structure [Rey81, Ten94]. Again, this has led to the first syntax-independent construction of a fully abstract model [AM96]. The treatment of local variables is process-based, following the line of [Mil75, Mil80, Red96]; but with the the right mathematical tools now available, a more definitive treatment can be given, as confirmed by the results on full abstraction.

This model of Idealized Algol extends smoothly to incorporate concurrency [Abr95a]. It remains to be seen how accurate the model of the concurrent language is, but the situation looks quite promising: moreover, Idealized Parallel Algol is rich enough to represent rather directly many of the features of today's concurrent object-oriented languages.

References

[Abr93] S. Abramsky. Interaction categories (extended abstract). In *Theory and Formal Methods '93*, Workshops in Computer Science, pages 57–70. Springer-Verlag, 1993.

[Abr94] S. Abramsky. Proofs as processes. *Theoretical Computer Science*, 135:5–9, 1994.

[Abr95a] S. Abramsky. A game semantics for Idealized Parallel Algol. Unpublished lecture, 1995.

[Abr95b] S. Abramsky. Interaction categories and communicating sequential processes. In A. W. Roscoe, editor, *A Classical Mind: Essays in Honour of C. A. R. Hoare*, pages 1–15. Prentice Hall International, 1995.

[Abr96a] S. Abramsky. Axioms for full abstraction and full completeness. Submitted for publication, 1996.

[Abr96b] S. Abramsky. Semantics of interaction. In *Proceedings of 1995 CLiCS Summer School, Isaac Newton Institute.* Cambridge University Press, 1996. To appear.

[Acz88] P. Aczel. *Non-well-founded sets.* CSLI, 1988.

[AGN96a] S. Abramsky, S. Gay, and R. Nagarajan. Interaction categories and the foundations of typed concurrent programming. In *Deductive program design: Proceedings of the 1994 Marktoberdorf International Summer School.* Springer-Verlag, 1996. To appear.

[AGN96b] S. Abramsky, S. Gay, and R. Nagarajan. Specification structures and propositions-as-types for concurrency. In *Logics for Concurrency: Structure vs. Automata*, Lecture Notes in Computer Science. Springer-Verlag, 1996.

[AJ94a] S. Abramsky and R. Jagadeesan. Games and full completeness for multiplicative linear logic. *Journal of Symbolic Logic*, 59(2):543–574, 1994.

[AJ94b] S. Abramsky and R. Jagadeesan. New foundations for the geometry of interaction. *Information and Computation*, 111(1):53–119, 1994. Conference version appeared in LiCS '92.

[AJM96] S. Abramsky, R. Jagadeesan, and P. Malacaria. Full abstraction for PCF. Submitted for publication, 1996.

[AM82] M. A. Arbib and E. G. Manes. The pattern-of-calls expansion is the canonical fixpoint for recursive definitions. *Journal of the ACM*, 29(2):577–602, 1982.

[AM95] S. Abramsky and G. McCusker. Games and full abstraction for the lazy λ-calculus. In *Tenth Annual Symposium on Logic in Computer Science*, pages 234–243, 1995.

[AM96] S. Abramsky and G. McCusker. Full abstraction for Idealized Algol. To appear, 1996.

[AP93] M. Abadi and G. Plotkin. A logical view of composition and refinement. *Theoretical Computer Science*, 114(1):3–30, 1993.

[Bar93a] M. Barr. Algebraically compact functors. Technical report, 1993.

[Bar93b] M. Barr. Terminal coalgebras for endofunctors on sets. Technical Report, 1993.

[BE93] S. Bloom and Z. Esik. *Iteration Theories*. Springer-Verlag, 1993.

[Bek71] H. Bekić. Towards a mathematical theory of processes. Technical Report TR25.125, IBM Laboratory, Vienna, 1971.

[Gir81] M. Giry. A categorical approach to probability theory. In *Categorical Aspects of Topology and Analysis*, volume 915 of *Lecture Notes in Mathematics*. Springer-Verlag, 1981.

[Gir88] J.-Y. Girard. Geometry of interaction I: interpretation of System F. In R. Ferro, editor, *Logic Colloquium '88*, pages 221–260. North Holland, 1988.

[GS96] R. Grosu and K. Stølen. A model for mobile point-to-point dataflow networks without channel sharing. Technical report, 1996.

[Has96] M. Hasegawa. Traced computational models. Technical report, 1996.

[HO96] M. Hyland and C.H. L. Ong. On full abstraction for PCF. Submitted for publication, 1996.

[Hoa85] C. A. R. Hoare. *Communicating Sequential Processes.* Prentice Hall International, 1985.

[Jon93] C. B. Jones. Process-algebraic foundations for an object-based design notation. Technical Report UMCS-93-10-1, University of Manchester, 1993.

[Jon96] C. B. Jones. Some practical problems and their influence on semantics. In Hanne Riis Nielson, editor, *Programming Languages and Systems—ESOP '96*, volume 1058 of *Lecture Notes in Computer Science*, pages 1–17. Springer-Verlag, 1996.

[JSV95] A. Joyal, R. Street, and D. Verity. Traced monoidal categories. Technical report, 1995.

[KL80] G. M. Kelly and M. Laplaza. Coherence for compact closed categories. *Journal of Pure and Applied Algebra*, 19:193–213, 1980.

[Law62] F. W. Lawvere. The category of probabilistic mappings. Unpublished manuscript, 1962.

[McC96a] G. McCusker. *Games and Full Abstraction for a functional metalanguage with recursive types.* PhD thesis, Imperial College, University of London, 1996. to appear.

[McC96b] G. McCusker. Games and full abstraction for FPC. In *International Symposium on Logic in Computer Science*, 1996.

[Mil75] R. Milner. Processes: a mathematical model of computing agents. In *Logic Colloquium '73*, pages 157–173. North Holland, 1975.

[Mil80] R. Milner. *A Calculus of Communicating Systems.* Springer-Verlag, 1980.

[Mil89] R. Milner. *Communication and Concurrency*. Prentice Hall International, 1989.

[Mil92] R. Milner. Functions as processes. *Mathematical Structures in Computer Science*, 2(2):119–142, 1992.

[MMP95] A. Mifsud, R. Milner, and J. Power. Control structures. In *Tenth Annual Symposium on Logic in Computer Science*, pages 188–198, 1995.

[MPW92] R. Milner, J. Parrow, and D. Walker. A calculus of mobile processes. *Information and Computation*, 100(1):1–77, 1992.

[Plo76] G. Plotkin. A powerdomain construction. *SIAM Journal on Computing*, 5(3):452–487, 1976.

[PS95] A. Pnueli and J. Sifakis, editors. *Special issue on hybrid systems*, 1995. Theoretical Computer Science vol. 138 no. 1.

[Red96] U. Reddy. Global state considered unncessary: an object-based semantics for Algol. *Lisp and Functional Programming*, 1996.

[Rey81] J. C. Reynolds. The essence of Algol. In J. W. de Bakker and J. C. van Vliet, editors, *Algorithmic Languages*, pages 345–372. North Holland, 1981.

[SDW96] K. Stølen, F. Dederichs, and R. Weber. Assumption/commitment rules for networks of asynchronously communicating agents. *Formal Aspects of Computing*, 1996.

[Ten94] R. D. Tennent. Denotational semantics. In S. Abramsky, D. M. Gabbay, and T. S. E. Maibaum, editors, *Handbook of Logic in Computer Science*, volume 3, pages 169–322. Oxford University Press, 1994.

[Win83] G. Winskel. Synchronization trees. In *Automata, Languages and Programming: 10th International Colloquium*, pages 695–711. Springer-Verlag, 1983.

Process Calculus Based upon Evaluation to Committed Form

Andrew M. Pitts and Joshua R. X. Ross

Cambridge University Computer Laboratory, Cambridge CB2 3QG, UK

Abstract. An approach to the semantics of CCS-like communicating processes is proposed that is based upon evaluation of processes to input- or output-committed form, with no explicit mention of silent actions. This leads to a co-inductively defined notion of *evaluation bisimilarity*—a form of weak equivalence which is shown to be a congruence, even in the presence of summation. The relationship between this evaluation-based approach and the more traditional, labelled transition semantics is investigated. In particular, with some restriction on sums, CCS observation equivalence is characterised purely in terms of evaluation to committed form, and evaluation bisimilarity is characterised as a weak delay equivalence. These results are extended to the higher order case, where evaluation bisimilarity coincides with Sangiorgi's weak context bisimilarity. An evaluation-based approach to π-calculus and the relationship with Milner and Sangiorgi's reduction-based notion of barbed bisimulation are also examined.

1 Introduction

Beginning with Milner's CCS [13], it has become commonplace to specify the operational semantics of languages for concurrent, communicating processes by means of an action-labelled transition relation between process expressions—ideally one that is inductively defined by rules following the structure of expressions [20]. In particular this provides the means for defining notions of process equivalence in terms of various kinds of bisimulation relation derived from the labelled transition system, with associated co-induction proof techniques. This approach to process calculi has been very fruitful. So before proposing an alternative approach, as we do in this paper, it is necessary to examine the weak points of the status quo. We identify two which influenced the worked presented here.

First, the construction of *weak* bisimulation congruences is not as simple as one might wish. The gap between CCS observation equivalence and observation congruence in the presence of summation is the best known example of the difficulties we have in mind. The use of a transition system in which externally unobservable behaviour is represented *explicitly* (by τ-transitions) does not always fit well with defining equivalences that both abstract from such behaviour and are congruences for the language constructs.

Secondly and perhaps more significantly, for languages that have higher-order features [16, 24], or which combine concurrent communication with higher order functions [5, 21], it has proved difficult to devise labelled transition semantics that are both simple and give rise to weak bisimilarities with expected properties. For example, witness the difficulties caused by the combination of (higher order) value-passing actions with static restriction discussed by Sangiorgi in [23].

Milner and Sangiorgi were partly addressing this second kind of problem when they introduced the notion of barbed bisimulation [17], defined in terms of a reduction relation and a convergence predicate. This approach is both simple (especially when combined with the use of 'chemistry' [2], *i.e.* a structural congruence relation) and uniform—in the sense that one can easily apply it to some quite different-looking calculi. It has certainly been applied successfully: see [15, 22, 4]. Yet there remain difficulties of the first kind mentioned above, to do with factoring out reduction ($= \tau$-transition) in weak equivalences; and the 'barbed' approach usually involves quite heavy use of closure under contexts in order to obtain a congruence relation.

For sequential languages, the use of a reduction relation to specify operational semantics usually comes along with some fixed strategy for reducing configurations, including a notion of which configurations are in final, or *canonical*, form. Therefore, for many purposes one can abstract away from the single steps of reduction and just consider an *evaluation relation* between configurations and the canonical forms to which they give rise (if any). As for one-step reduction relations, so for 'big-step' evaluation relations, the ideal situation is where evaluation to canonical form is inductively defined by rules that follow the syntactical structure of the language. For programming languages, the best known example of a large scale operational semantics in this style is the definition of Standard ML [18]. In a somewhat purer vein, evaluation to canonical form is a key part of Martin-Löf's type-theoretic foundation for constructive mathematics [11].

This paper attempts to demonstrate that process calculi can be based upon evaluation to canonical form and that some of the problems mentioned above are solved thereby; in particular, in this approach there is no mention of τ-transitions *a priori*. At first it might seem unlikely that the interactive nature of process communication can be adequately captured by an evaluation relation. But note that canonical forms may well contain unevaluated subexpressions that get 'activated' in bisimulation equivalences based upon evaluation. The paradigmatic example is Abramsky's 'lazy' lambda calculus [1], in which evaluation does not take place 'under the lambda'—canonical forms are lambda abstractions, $\lambda x.E$, with E unevaluated. Abramsky's *applicative bisimulation* is the greatest symmetric relation $\mathcal{R}$ between closed lambda terms such that if $M_1 \mathrel{\mathcal{R}} M_2$ and $M_1 \Downarrow \lambda x.E_1$, then $M_2 \Downarrow \lambda x.E_2$ holds for some E_2 with $E_1[N/x] \mathrel{\mathcal{R}} E_2[N/x]$ for all closed N. Here $\Downarrow$ denotes the (call-by-name) evaluation relation. The 'interaction' embodied in this definition is one of evaluating to a lambda abstraction versus supplying an argument for the parameter in the body of the abstraction.

To develop a similar style of semantics for processes, the crucial question is of course: "what are the canonical forms?" For CCS-like calculi, a natural answer is to take processes like $a(x).P(x)$ and $\bar{a}v.Q$ which are committed to input and output actions respectively. (We consider other answers in Section 4.2.) We develop this 'evaluation to committed form' approach in Section 2 (for the non value-passing case, for simplicity). As is the case for the reduction-based approach leading to barbed bisimilarity, we work modulo a structural congruence relation. In fact this seems to be necessary for the evaluation-based approach to yield a sufficiently rich theory (see Remark 2.4). We define an associated notion of *evaluation bisimilarity* and adapt Howe's work [9] on congruence properties of applicative bisimilarity to show that it is a congruence. (Although we put restrictions on summation in Section 2, the congruence property holds without them: see

Section 4.4.) Besides being a congruence, evaluation bisimilarity seems a reasonable 'weak, branching-time' process equivalence whose definition is completely τ-free. In Section 3 we investigate its relationship to existing, transition-based equivalences.

To do that we first have to examine the relationship between our notion of evaluation to committed form, $P \Downarrow \ell.P'$, and the usual labelled transition relation. Roughly speaking, $P \Downarrow \ell.P'$ means that P can do some number of τ-transitions followed by an ℓ-transition to become a process strongly equivalent to P': see Lemma 3.1 and Theorem 3.3. These results permit one to characterise CCS observation equivalence purely in terms of evaluation to committed form (at least in the case that summation is restricted to action-guarded summands). Moreover, they lead to a characterisation of evaluation bisimilarity as *delay bisimilarity* [25]—which is like CCS observation equivalence except that $\xrightarrow{\tau^*\ell}$ is used in place of $\xrightarrow{\tau^*\ell\tau^*}$: see Theorem 3.6. Such delay equivalences have occurred recently in work on higher order process calculi [23] and on integrations of functions and processes [3]. Pleasingly, the evaluation-based approach extends smoothly to higher order processes and we obtain a coincidence between evaluation bisimilarity and Sangiorgi's *weak context bisimilarity* (Theorem 4.1). This is described briefly in Section 4 along with a number of other topics: a treatment of asynchronous-output π-calculus in terms of evaluation to input-committed form, the relationship between our evaluation-based approach and the 'barbed' approach, and the apparent mismatch between evaluation and transition in the presence of unrestricted summation.

2 Evaluation Bisimilarity

We illustrate the use of an evaluation relation to specify the behaviour of communicating processes with respect to a variant of CCS [13] which we call *normal* CCS (NCCS). It has operators for composition, restriction, recursion, and synchronous input and output, but has summation restricted to *normal* processes—which by definition are (finite) sums of processes committed to input or output actions. NCCS process expressions are given by the grammar

$$\begin{array}{rl} \text{processes} & E ::= X \mid N \mid E|E \mid (\nu x)E \mid (\mathit{rec}X)E \\ \text{normal processes} & N ::= \mathbf{0} \mid K \mid N+N \\ \text{committed processes} & K ::= x.E \mid \bar{x}.E \end{array}$$

where X ranges over a countably infinite set of process *variables* and x ranges over a countably infinite set of channel *names*. Name restriction is written $(\nu x)E$, rather than $E \setminus x$ as in CCS, and we prefer to make it a binding operation: free occurrences in E of the name x become bound in $(\nu x)E$. The other binding operation is for recursively defined processes: free occurrences in E of the process variable X become bound in $(\mathit{rec}X)E$. Throughout *we identify expressions up to α-conversion of bound names and variables*, and write $E =_\alpha E'$ to indicate that E and E' are syntactically identical modulo α-conversion. We use $\mathit{fv}(E)$ and $\mathit{fn}(E)$ to indicate respectively the finite set of free variables and free names of E. An NCCS process expression E is *closed* if $\mathit{fv}(E)$ is empty and *open* otherwise. Most of the time we will refer to closed process expressions simply as *processes*, and use letters like $P, Q, R, \ldots$ to denote them. For simplicity we have omitted any relabelling operator from NCCS. Instead we make do with name substitution as an operation on syntax: $E[x'/x]$ denotes the result (well-defined up to α-conversion) of substituting the name x' for all free occurrences of the name x in E. Similarly $E[E'/X]$ denotes the result of substituting the process expression E' for all free occurrences of the variable X in E. Following usual CCS practice, we write a typical committed process as $\ell.P$ where ℓ ranges over *labels*, which are either names (x) or *co-names* ($\bar{x}$):

$$\ell ::= x \mid \bar{x}.$$

As usual, $\bar{\ell} = \bar{x}$ if $\ell = x$ is a name, and $\bar{\ell} = x$ if $\ell = \bar{x}$ is a co-name.

Before defining an evaluation semantics for NCCS processes, we have to give a notion of structural congruence that turns out to be an essential ingredient of the definition.

Definition 2.1. An NCCS *congruence relation*, $\mathcal{E}$, is an equivalence relation between NCCS process expressions which is closed under the following rules.

$$\text{(cr1)}\ \frac{E_1\ \mathcal{E}\ E_2 \quad E_1'\ \mathcal{E}\ E_2'}{E_1|E_1'\ \mathcal{E}\ E_2|E_2'} \qquad \text{(cr2)}\ \frac{E_1\ \mathcal{E}\ E_2}{(\nu x)E_1\ \mathcal{E}\ (\nu x)E_2}$$

$$\text{(cr3)}\ \frac{E_1\ \mathcal{E}\ E_2}{(\mathit{rec}X)E_1\ \mathcal{E}\ (\mathit{rec}X)E_2} \qquad \text{(cr4)}\ \frac{E_1\ \mathcal{E}\ E_2}{\ell.E_1\ \mathcal{E}\ \ell.E_2} \qquad \text{(cr5)}\ \frac{N_1\ \mathcal{E}\ N_2 \quad N_1'\ \mathcal{E}\ N_2'}{N_1 + N_1'\ \mathcal{E}\ N_2 + N_2'}$$

Structural congruence, $\equiv$, is the smallest such relation containing the following pairs of processes:

$$P_1|(P_2|P_3) \equiv (P_1|P_2)|P_3, \quad N_1 + (N_2 + N_3) \equiv (N_1 + N_2) + N_3,$$
$$(\nu x)(P_1|P_2) \equiv ((\nu x)P_1)|P_2 \quad \text{if } x \notin \mathit{fn}(P_2),$$
$$P_1|P_2 \equiv P_2|P_1, \quad N_1 + N_2 \equiv N_2 + N_1, \quad (\nu x_1)(\nu x_2)P \equiv (\nu x_2)(\nu x_1)P,$$
$$P|\mathbf{0} \equiv P, \quad N + \mathbf{0} \equiv N, \quad (\nu x)\mathbf{0} \equiv \mathbf{0}.$$

Notions of structural congruence are an extremely useful way to simplify the specification of the operational semantics of reactive systems. They were first popularised by the 'chemical abstract machine' of Berry and Boudol [2]. The form we are using is like that used in Milner's presentation of reduction for π-calculus processes in [15]. In one sense the identifications made by such congruences just take us one step further up the path abstracting away from inessential choices in the concrete representation of syntax. Although there is some choice as to which identities should be 'structural' (for example, we have not included any identities for recursive processes), those relating to composition and restriction seem essential for evaluation to committed form to lead to a sufficiently rich theory of process evaluation and equivalence. (See Remark 2.4 below.)

Definition 2.2 (Evaluation to committed form). The *evaluation relation* for NCCS takes the form $P \Downarrow K$, where P and K are processes and K is in 'committed form', *i.e.* is of the form $\ell.P'$ for some name or co-name ℓ and some process P'. It is inductively generated by the following axiom and rules.

$$(\Downarrow 0)\ \frac{P_1 \Downarrow \ell.P_1'}{P_2 \Downarrow \ell.P_2'} \text{ if } P_1 \equiv P_2 \text{ and } P_1' \equiv P_2' \qquad (\Downarrow 1)\ (N + \ell.P)|Q \Downarrow \ell.(P|Q)$$

$$(\Downarrow 2)\ \frac{P_1 \Downarrow \ell.P_1' \quad P_2 \Downarrow \bar{\ell}.P_2' \quad P_1'|P_2' \Downarrow K}{P_1|P_2 \Downarrow K}$$

$$(\Downarrow 3)\ \frac{P \Downarrow \ell.P'}{(\nu x)P \Downarrow \ell.(\nu x)P'} \text{ if } x \notin \{\ell, \bar{\ell}\} \qquad (\Downarrow 4)\ \frac{E[(recX)E/X]|Q \Downarrow K}{((recX)E)|Q \Downarrow K}$$

For readers familiar with the usual labelled transition semantics of CCS, the above rules should suggest that $P \Downarrow \ell.P'$ means that P can do some number of τ-transitions followed by an ℓ-transition to become P'. This intuition is roughly correct: we will make the relationship between evaluation and transition precise in Section 3 (see Corollary 3.4). Manifestly Definition 2.2 is a 'τ-free' description of how processes execute. Here is a simple example to illustrate a distinctive feature of the evaluation rule ($\Downarrow$2) for synchronised communication—namely that the effects of such synchronisations (*i.e.* 'τ-transitions') are only observable if there is some externally observable (input or output) action that the process can offer.

Example 2.3. Let $P = x.\mathbf{0}|\bar{x}.\mathbf{0}$. Then rule ($\Downarrow$2) cannot be applied and $P \Downarrow K$ holds just for $K \equiv x.\bar{x}.\mathbf{0}$ and $K \equiv \bar{x}.x.\mathbf{0}$. For $P|y.\mathbf{0}$ however, in addition to evaluations committing to x and $\bar{x}$, the evaluation $P|y.\mathbf{0} \Downarrow y.\mathbf{0}$ can be deduced using rule ($\Downarrow$2) together with rules ($\Downarrow$0) and ($\Downarrow$1).

Remark 2.4. Note that evaluation to committed form takes place modulo structural congruence—this is the force of rule ($\Downarrow$0). Not only does this permit a simpler presentation of the rules, it appears to be *necessary* for the notion of evaluation bisimilarity given below to have the expected structural properties. For example without ($\Downarrow$0), in 2.3 one could only deduce $(x.\mathbf{0}|\bar{x}.\mathbf{0})|y.\mathbf{0} \Downarrow y.P'$ for $P' = (x.\mathbf{0}|\bar{x}.\mathbf{0})|\mathbf{0}$, whereas $x.\mathbf{0}|(\bar{x}.\mathbf{0}|y.\mathbf{0}) \Downarrow y.(\mathbf{0}|(\mathbf{0}|\mathbf{0}))$ would still hold. Therefore, without structural congruence, the definition of evaluation bisimilarity given below would fail to make composition associative.

Since one is working modulo structural congruence, in trying to construct the proof of an evaluation from the bottom up, one cannot deduce the last rule used in the proof merely from the syntactic structure of the process expression on the left hand side of $\Downarrow$. In this respect the situation is similar to that for reduction in the π-calculus as formulated in [15]. Note that rules ($\Downarrow$1)–($\Downarrow$4) explain how the various NCCS syntactic constructs evaluate, *but only in the context of some parallel process*, Q (which of course may be $\mathbf{0}$). Given that one is working modulo structural congruence anyway, the presence of such contexts is not much of a further complication to the business of constructing proofs of evaluation. Note that there is no need to use a context $[-]|Q$ in rules ($\Downarrow$2) and ($\Downarrow$3) since the apparently more general rules

$$\frac{P_1 \Downarrow \ell.P_1' \quad P_2 \Downarrow \bar{\ell}.P_2' \quad (P_1'|P_2')|Q \Downarrow K}{(P_1|P_2)|Q \Downarrow K} \qquad \frac{P|Q \Downarrow \ell.P'}{((\nu x)P)|Q \Downarrow \ell.(\nu x)P'} \text{ if } x \notin \{\ell, \bar{\ell}\} \cup fn(Q)$$

are derivable. Here are some further derived properties of evaluation that we will need. They are easily established by induction on the proofs of evaluation.

Lemma 2.5. *(i) If $P \Downarrow \ell.P'$, then $P|Q \Downarrow \ell.(P'|Q)$ for any Q.*
(ii) If $(\nu x)P \Downarrow \ell.P''$, then $P \Downarrow \ell.P'$ for some P' with $(\nu x)P' \equiv P''$.
(iii) Evaluation is name equivariant, *in the sense that for any permutation σ of the set of channel names, if $P \Downarrow K$ then $P[\sigma] \Downarrow K[\sigma]$. ($P[\sigma]$ indicates the substituted expression $P[\sigma(x)/x \mid x \in dom(\sigma)]$.)*

Definition 2.6 (Evaluation bisimilarity). A binary relation $\mathcal{R}$ between NCCS processes is an *evaluation simulation* if $P_1 \mathcal{R} P_2$ implies for all Q that

$$P_1|Q \Downarrow \ell.P_1' \Rightarrow \exists P_2' \,(P_2|Q \Downarrow \ell.P_2' \;\&\; P_1' \mathcal{R} P_2').$$

If the reciprocal relation $\mathcal{R}^{-1} \stackrel{\text{def}}{=} \{(P_1, P_2) \mid P_2 \mathcal{R} P_1\}$ is also an evaluation simulation, we say that $\mathcal{R}$ is an *evaluation bisimulation*. Finally, two NCCS processes are *evaluation bisimilar*, written $P_1 \simeq_\Downarrow P_2$, if $P_1 \mathcal{R} P_2$ holds for some evaluation bisimulation $\mathcal{R}$.

Here are some simple properties of $\simeq_\Downarrow$, proved using Lemma 2.5.

Lemma 2.7. *Evaluation bisimilarity is the greatest evaluation bisimulation. It is an equivalence relation and contains structural congruence. Moreover, if $P_1 \simeq_\Downarrow P_2$ then $P_1|Q \simeq_\Downarrow P_2|Q$, $(\nu x)P_1 \simeq_\Downarrow (\nu x)P_2$, and $P_1[\sigma] \simeq_\Downarrow P_2[\sigma]$ (for any process Q, name x, and permutation of names σ).*

The definition of evaluation bisimilarity for NCCS is analogous to the notion of *applicative bisimilarity* for functional languages introduced by Abramsky [1] and studied by Howe [9] and others—so much so, that we can adapt Howe's method [10] for proving congruence properties of applicative bisimilarity in the presence of non-determinism to the case in point. However, there is one important complication compared with applicative bisimilarity—namely the quantification over contexts $[-]|Q$ which occurs in Definition 2.6. Here is an example to show that such contexts are necessary to obtain congruence properties of bisimilarity in this setting. The example uses $Q = y.\mathbf{0}$, with y a fresh name. We will see in the next section (Theorem 3.8) that this is in fact the *only* instance of Q one needs to consider.

Example 2.8. Suppose that $\mathcal{R}$ satisfies

$$\begin{array}{l} P_1 \mathcal{R} P_2 \;\&\; P_1 \Downarrow \ell.P_1' \Rightarrow \exists P_2' \,(P_2 \Downarrow \ell.P_2' \;\&\; P_1' \mathcal{R} P_2') \\ P_1 \mathcal{R} P_2 \;\&\; P_2 \Downarrow \ell.P_2' \Rightarrow \exists P_1' \,(P_1 \Downarrow \ell.P_1' \;\&\; P_1' \mathcal{R} P_2') \end{array} \tag{1}$$

Then it is not necessarily the case that $\mathcal{R} \subseteq \simeq_\Downarrow$, and hence in particular $\simeq_\Downarrow$ cannot be defined as the greatest relation satisfying (1). For example, let $\mathcal{R}$ be $\{(x.\bar{x}.\mathbf{0} + \bar{x}.x.\mathbf{0}, x.\mathbf{0}|\bar{x}.\mathbf{0})\} \cup \equiv$. If P is either $x.\bar{x}.\mathbf{0} + \bar{x}.x.\mathbf{0}$ or $x.\mathbf{0}|\bar{x}.\mathbf{0}$, then $P \Downarrow K$ holds just for $K = x.\bar{x}.\mathbf{0}$ and $K = \bar{x}.x.\mathbf{0}$. Therefore $\mathcal{R}$ certainly satisfies (1). However $x.\bar{x}.\mathbf{0} + \bar{x}.x.\mathbf{0}$ is not evaluation bisimilar to $x.\mathbf{0}|\bar{x}.\mathbf{0}$. For $(x.\mathbf{0}|\bar{x}.\mathbf{0})|y.\mathbf{0} \Downarrow y.\mathbf{0}$, whereas $(x.\bar{x}.\mathbf{0} + \bar{x}.x.\mathbf{0})|y.\mathbf{0} \Downarrow y.P$ only holds for $P = x.\bar{x}.\mathbf{0} + \bar{x}.x.\mathbf{0}$ and clearly $x.\bar{x}.\mathbf{0} + \bar{x}.x.\mathbf{0} \not\simeq_\Downarrow \mathbf{0}$. The greatest $\mathcal{R}$ satisfying (1) is indeed an equivalence relation, but not a congruence since this example shows that it relates $x.\bar{x}.\mathbf{0} + \bar{x}.x.\mathbf{0}$ to $x.\mathbf{0}|\bar{x}.\mathbf{0}$, but does not relate $(x.\bar{x}.\mathbf{0} + \bar{x}.x.\mathbf{0})|y.\mathbf{0}$ to $(x.\mathbf{0}|\bar{x}.\mathbf{0})|y.\mathbf{0}$. In contrast, we now show that $\simeq_{\Downarrow}$ is indeed a congruence for NCCS.

Extend evaluation bisimilarity from closed to open process expressions by taking closed instantiations: we write $E_1 \simeq^{\circ}_{\Downarrow} E_2$ to mean that $E_1[\vec{P}/\vec{X}] \simeq_{\Downarrow} E_2[\vec{P}/\vec{X}]$ holds for all substitutions of processes $\vec{P}$ for the free variables $\vec{X}$ of E_1, E_2.

Theorem 2.9. *$\simeq^{\circ}_{\Downarrow}$ is an NCCS congruence relation* (cf. *Definition 2.1*).

Proof. That $\simeq^{\circ}_{\Downarrow}$ is an equivalence relation satisfying (cr1) and (cr2) follows from Lemma 2.7. To establish the other properties, the first proof strategy that comes to mind is to take the smallest relation containing $\simeq_{\Downarrow}$ and closed under (cr3)–(cr5), and show that it is an evaluation bisimulation. It is hard to see how to do this directly, because in an evaluation $P \Downarrow \ell.P'$, P' may be structurally quite different from P. Instead we use an indirect approach adapted from [9, 10]. Let $\simeq^{*}_{\Downarrow}$ be the binary relation between process expressions inductively defined by rules (cr1)–(cr5) together with

$$(\simeq^{*}_{\Downarrow}1)\ \frac{E_1 \simeq^{*}_{\Downarrow} E_2}{E_1' \simeq^{*}_{\Downarrow} E_2'} \text{ if } E_1 \equiv E_1' \text{ and } E_2 \simeq^{\circ}_{\Downarrow} E_2' \qquad (\simeq^{*}_{\Downarrow}2)\ X \simeq^{*}_{\Downarrow} X \qquad (\simeq^{*}_{\Downarrow}3)\ \mathbf{0} \simeq^{*}_{\Downarrow} \mathbf{0}$$

To show that $\simeq^{\circ}_{\Downarrow}$ satisfies (cr3)–(cr5), clearly it suffices to prove that $\simeq^{\circ}_{\Downarrow}$ coincides with $\simeq^{*}_{\Downarrow}$. Although being an equivalence relation is not part of the definition of $\simeq^{*}_{\Downarrow}$, it is not hard to see that it is at least reflexive. Hence by rule $(\simeq^{*}_{\Downarrow}1)$ we have $\simeq^{\circ}_{\Downarrow} \subseteq \simeq^{*}_{\Downarrow}$. For the reverse inclusion, it suffices just to prove for *closed* process expressions that $P_1 \simeq^{*}_{\Downarrow} P_2 \Rightarrow P_1 \simeq_{\Downarrow} P_2$, since the general case follows from the easily verified fact that $\simeq^{*}_{\Downarrow}$ is preserved under substituting process expressions for process variables. To prove this implication, one can exploit the fact that $\simeq_{\Downarrow}$ is the largest evaluation bisimulation. First one proves

$$P_1 \Downarrow \ell.P_1' \ \&\ P_1 \simeq^{*}_{\Downarrow} P_2 \Rightarrow \exists P_2' \, (P_2 \Downarrow \ell.P_2' \ \&\ P_1' \simeq^{*}_{\Downarrow} P_2') \tag{2}$$

by induction on the proof of $P_1 \Downarrow \ell.P_1'$. This induction over proofs of evaluation lies at the heart of the whole proof of the theorem and is quite delicate. To carry through each induction step one needs decomposition properties of $P \simeq^{*}_{\Downarrow} Q$ that follow the structure of P *modulo structural congruence*, such as

$$P_1|P_2 \equiv P \ \&\ P \simeq^{*}_{\Downarrow} Q \Rightarrow \exists Q_1, Q_2 \, (P_1 \simeq^{*}_{\Downarrow} Q_1 \ \&\ P_2 \simeq^{*}_{\Downarrow} Q_2 \ \&\ Q_1|Q_2 \simeq_{\Downarrow} Q).$$

Thus structural congruence introduces an extra complication compared with [9, 10]. We omit the details of the proof of (2) here. Since by definition $\simeq^{*}_{\Downarrow}$ is closed under rule (cr1), it follows from (2) that $\simeq^{*}_{\Downarrow}$ restricted to closed processes is an evaluation simulation. Since the definition of $\simeq^{*}_{\Downarrow}$ is not symmetric (because of $(\simeq^{*}_{\Downarrow}1)$), one cannot immediately conclude that it is also an evaluation bisimulation. However, it is not hard to show that the reciprocal relation $(\simeq^{*}_{\Downarrow})^{-1}$ is contained in $(\simeq^{*}_{\Downarrow})^{tc}$, the transitive closure of $\simeq^{*}_{\Downarrow}$. Thus $(\simeq^{*}_{\Downarrow})^{tc}$ is a symmetric relation and an evaluation simulation on closed process expressions (because $\simeq^{*}_{\Downarrow}$ is), hence is an evaluation bisimulation. Therefore it is contained in $\simeq_{\Downarrow}$ and hence so is $\simeq^{*}_{\Downarrow}$, as required. □

Quite possibly there are other, more direct ways of proving this theorem for a calculus as simple as NCCS. However, the above adaptation of 'Howe's method' [9, 10] has the distinct advantage of *robustness*: our experience shows that the same method can be used for more complicated calculi, such as those considered in Sections 4.1 and 4.2.

We believe that evaluation to committed form and the associated notion of evaluation bisimilarity have a certain naturalness for the type of interaction embodied in CCS. The fact that $\simeq_{\Downarrow}$ yields a congruent notion of process equivalence for NCCS is at least some evidence in favour of this belief. But two interrelated questions immediately arise. What equational laws are validated by $\simeq_{\Downarrow}$, and what is its relationship to other, known process equivalences? We address both questions in the next section.

3 Evaluation versus Transition

The standard *labelled transition system* for CCS [13], adapted to the syntax of NCCS, takes the form $P \xrightarrow{\alpha} P'$, where P and P' are NCCS processes and the action α is either a label or the distinguished, internal action τ. Labelled transitions are inductively generated by the following axiom and rules.

$$(\to 1)\ \ell.P \xrightarrow{\ell} P \qquad (\to 2)\ \frac{P_1 \xrightarrow{\alpha} P_1'}{P_1|P_2 \xrightarrow{\alpha} P_1'|P_2} \quad \frac{P_2 \xrightarrow{\alpha} P_2'}{P_1|P_2 \xrightarrow{\alpha} P_1|P_2'}$$

$$(\to 3)\ \frac{P_1 \xrightarrow{\ell} P_1' \quad P_2 \xrightarrow{\bar{\ell}} P_2'}{P_1|P_2 \xrightarrow{\tau} P_1'|P_2'} \qquad (\to 4)\ \frac{P \xrightarrow{\alpha} P'}{(\nu x)P \xrightarrow{\alpha} (\nu x)P'}\ \text{if } \alpha \notin \{x, \bar{x}\}$$

$$(\to 5)\ \frac{E[(recX)E/X] \xrightarrow{\alpha} P}{(recX)E \xrightarrow{\alpha} P} \qquad (\to 6)\ \frac{N_1 \xrightarrow{\ell} P}{N_1 + N_2 \xrightarrow{\ell} P} \quad \frac{N_2 \xrightarrow{\ell} P}{N_1 + N_2 \xrightarrow{\ell} P}$$

We write $\xrightarrow{\tau^*}$ for the reflexive-transitive closure of the relation $\xrightarrow{\tau}$, and write $P \xrightarrow{\tau^*\ell} P'$ (respectively $P \xrightarrow{\tau^*\ell\tau^*} P'$) to mean that $P \xrightarrow{\tau^*} P'' \xrightarrow{\ell} P'$ (respectively $P \xrightarrow{\tau^*\ell} P'' \xrightarrow{\tau^*} P'$) holds for some P''. Finally, recall from [13] that two processes are *strongly equivalent*, $P_1 \sim P_2$, if they are related by some symmetric binary relation $\mathcal{R}$ satisfying

$$\forall P_1, P_2, P_1', \alpha\, (P_1\ \mathcal{R}\ P_2\ \&\ P_1 \xrightarrow{\alpha} P_1' \Rightarrow \exists P_2'\, (P_2 \xrightarrow{\alpha} P_2'\ \&\ P_1\ \mathcal{R}\ P_2'))\ .$$

Lemma 3.1. *For all NCCS processes P, P', Q, and all labels ℓ*

(i) If $P \xrightarrow{\ell} P'$ then $P \Downarrow \ell.P'$
(ii) If $P \xrightarrow{\tau} P'$ and $P'|Q \Downarrow K$, then $P|Q \Downarrow K$.
(iii) If $P \Downarrow \ell.P'$, then $P \xrightarrow{\tau^*\ell} P''$ for some P'' with $P'' \sim P'$.

Proof. Properties (i) and (ii) are proved by induction on the proof of transitions from the rules ($\to$1)–($\to$6). Property (iii) is proved by induction on the proof of the evaluation $P \Downarrow \ell.P'$ from the rules ($\Downarrow$0)–($\Downarrow$4). We omit the details. □

Remark 3.2. In fact the proof of part (iii) of the lemma shows that it is valid with $\sim$ replaced by any relation $\mathcal{E}$ satisfying:

- $\mathcal{E}$ is a congruence relation (for the NCCS syntax) containing structural congruence and satisfying a 'back-and-forth' property with respect to actions of the form $\tau^*\ell$, *i.e.* if $P_1 \mathrel{\mathcal{E}} P_2$ and $P_1 \xrightarrow{\tau^*\ell} P_1'$, then $P_2 \xrightarrow{\tau^*\ell} P_2'$ for some P_2' with $P_1' \mathrel{\mathcal{E}} P_2'$;
- recursive processes are related to their unfoldings: $(recX)E \mathrel{\mathcal{E}} E[(recX)E/X]$.

Structural congruence itself possesses the first of these properties. However, it does not possess the second since we have not chosen to regard the unfolding of recursive process expressions as 'structural'—because of the use of substitution involved. (This is in contrast to the unfolding of *replicated* processes, $!P \equiv !P|P$, present in the π-calculus structural congruence [15].) Consequently, in part (iii) we have to make do with the next best thing to $\equiv$, namely strong equivalence. For example, one has $((recX)x.X)|y.0 \Downarrow y.P$ for $P = x.(recX)x.X$, but $((recX)x.X)|y.0 \xrightarrow{\tau^* y} P'$ holds only with $P' = ((recX)x.X)|0$ which is strongly equivalent, but not structurally congruent to P.

Theorem 3.3. *For all NCCS processes P, P', labels ℓ, and names $x \notin fn(P)$*

(i) $\exists P''\,(P \xrightarrow{\tau^*\ell} P'' \;\&\; P'' \sim P') \Leftrightarrow \exists P''\,(P \Downarrow \ell.P'' \;\&\; P'' \sim P')$.
(ii) $\exists P''\,(P \xrightarrow{\tau^*} P'' \;\&\; P'' \sim P') \Leftrightarrow \exists P''\,(P|x.0 \Downarrow x.P'' \;\&\; P'' \sim P')$.
(iii) $\exists P''\,(P \xrightarrow{\tau^*\ell\tau^*} P'' \;\&\; P'' \sim P') \Leftrightarrow \exists P''\,(P|\bar{\ell}.x.0 \Downarrow x.P'' \;\&\; P'' \sim P')$.

Proof. Combine Lemma 3.1 with the following simple properties of the labelled transition system:

$$P \xrightarrow{\ell} P' \Rightarrow \ell \in fn(P) \cup \overline{fn(P)}$$

$$P|x.0 \xrightarrow{\tau^* x} P' \Rightarrow \exists P''\,(P \xrightarrow{\tau^*} P'' \;\&\; P''|0 =_\alpha P')$$

$$P|\bar{\ell}.x.0 \xrightarrow{\tau^* x} P' \Rightarrow \exists P''\,(P \xrightarrow{\tau^*\ell\tau^*} P'' \;\&\; P''|0 =_\alpha P')$$

where $x \notin fn(P)$ and $\ell \neq x$. □

Note that modulo strong equivalence, part (i) of the theorem characterises evaluation to committed form in terms of transition, whereas part (ii) characterises NCCS *reduction*—*i.e.* zero or more τ-transitions—in terms of evaluation. The theorem also yields the following characterisation of the restriction to NCCS of CCS *observation equivalence*, $\approx$ (which coincides with the restriction of CCS observation congruence, because of the limited form of summation in NCCS). Recall from [13] that two processes are observation equivalent if they are related by some *weak bisimulation*—a relation $\mathcal{R}$ such that both $\mathcal{R}$ and $\mathcal{R}^{-1}$ satisfy: for all P_1, P_2 if $P_1 \mathrel{\mathcal{R}} P_2$ then

$$P_1 \xrightarrow{\tau} P_2 \Rightarrow \exists P_2'\,(P_2 \xrightarrow{\tau^*} P_2' \;\&\; P_1' \mathrel{\mathcal{R}} P_2') \qquad \text{(wb1)}$$

$$P_1 \xrightarrow{\ell} P_1' \Rightarrow \exists P_2'\,(P_2 \xrightarrow{\tau^*\ell\tau^*} P_2' \;\&\; P_1' \mathrel{\mathcal{R}} P_2') \qquad \text{(wb2)}$$

Corollary 3.4. *Observation equivalence is the largest symmetric binary relation $\mathcal{R}$ on NCCS processes satisfying that if $P_1 \mathcal{R} P_2$ then*

$$P_1|x.\mathbf{0} \Downarrow x.P_1' \Rightarrow \exists P_2' \,(P_2|x.\mathbf{0} \Downarrow x.P_2' \;\&\; P_1' \mathcal{R} P_2')$$
$$P_1|\bar{\ell}.x.\mathbf{0} \Downarrow x.P_1' \Rightarrow \exists P_2' \,(P_2|\bar{\ell}.x.\mathbf{0} \Downarrow x.P_2' \;\&\; P_1' \mathcal{R} P_2')$$

hold for any label ℓ and any name $x \notin fn(P_1P_2)$ (or equivalently, for some such x, by the equivariance properties of evaluation with respect to permuting free names).

Proof. Since strong equivalence is contained in $\approx$, it follows easily from Theorem 3.3 that $\approx$ is such an $\mathcal{R}$. Conversely, one can also use the theorem to show that for any such $\mathcal{R}$, the composition $\sim\mathcal{R}\sim$ is a weak bisimulation and hence $\mathcal{R} \subseteq \sim\mathcal{R}\sim \subseteq \approx$. □

Part (i) of Theorem 3.3 immediately suggests a way to modify the notion of observation equivalence in order to obtain a transition-based bisimilarity coinciding with the notion of evaluation bisimilarity introduced in the previous section—namely change clause (wb2) to

$$P_1 \xrightarrow{\ell} P_1' \Rightarrow \exists P_2' \,(P_2 \xrightarrow{\tau^*\ell} P_2' \;\&\; P_1' \mathcal{R} P_2') \qquad \text{(wb2}'\text{)}$$

Definition 3.5 (Delay bisimilarity). A binary relation $\mathcal{R}$ between (NCCS) processes is a *delay simulation* if $P_1 \mathcal{R} P_2$ implies that both (wb1) and (wb2′) hold. If $\mathcal{R}^{-1}$ is also a delay simulation, we say $\mathcal{R}$ is a *delay bisimulation*. Two processes are *delay bisimilar*, written $P_1 \simeq_{\text{dl}} P_2$, if $P_1 \mathcal{R} P_2$ holds for some delay bisimulation $\mathcal{R}$.

This notion of process equivalence is studied by Weijland [25] who credits its formulation to Milner (see [12] for example). It is also the specialisation to first order processes of Sangiorgi's notion of *weak context bisimilarity* for higher order process calculi, studied in [23].

Theorem 3.6. *For NCCS processes, evaluation bisimilarity coincides with delay bisimilarity.*

Proof. We will need the following facts about delay bisimilarity which can easily be proved from the definition.

(a) $\simeq_{\text{dl}}$ is the greatest delay bisimulation, is an equivalence relation, and contains strong equivalence

(b) If $P_1 \simeq_{\text{dl}} P_2$, then $P_1|Q \simeq_{\text{dl}} P_2|Q$. (In fact delay bisimilarity is an NCCS congruence.)

These facts, together with part (i) of Theorem 3.3, imply that $\simeq_{\text{dl}}$ is an evaluation bisimulation. Thus $P_1 \simeq_{\text{dl}} P_2$ implies $P_1 \simeq_{\Downarrow} P_2$. For the converse implication it suffices to show that $\simeq_{\Downarrow}$ is a delay (bi)simulation. So suppose $P_1 \simeq_{\Downarrow} P_2$. There are two cases to consider.

Case $P_1 \xrightarrow{\tau} P_1'$: we have to show $P_2 \xrightarrow{\tau^*} P_2'$ for some P_2' with $P_1' \simeq_{\Downarrow} P_2'$. Picking any $x \notin fn(P_1P_2)$, $P_1|x.\mathbf{0} \Downarrow x.P_1''$ holds for some $P_1'' \sim P_1'$ by Theorem 3.3(ii). Since $P_1 \simeq_{\Downarrow} P_2$ we also have $P_1|x.\mathbf{0} \simeq_{\Downarrow} P_2|x.\mathbf{0}$ (by Lemma 2.7), so $P_2|x.\mathbf{0} \Downarrow x.P_2''$ for some P_2'' with $P_1'' \simeq_{\Downarrow} P_2''$. By 3.3(ii) again, $P_2 \xrightarrow{\tau^*} P_2'$ for some $P_2' \sim P_2''$. By (a), since $P_i' \sim P_i''$ $(i = 1, 2)$, we also have that $P_i' \simeq_{\mathrm{dl}} P_i''$; and hence by the first part of the proof we have that $P_i' \simeq_{\Downarrow} P_i''$. So by transitivity of $\simeq_{\Downarrow}$, we do indeed have $P_1' \simeq_{\Downarrow} P_2'$, as required.

Case $P_1 \xrightarrow{\ell} P_1'$: we have to show $P_2 \xrightarrow{\tau^*\ell} P_2'$ for some P_2' with $P_1' \simeq_{\Downarrow} P_2'$. The proof is like the previous case, but using part (i) of Theorem 3.3. □

Example 3.7 (τ-Laws). Although we did not include an operation $\tau.P$ for prefixing by a silent action in the NCCS syntax, as one might expect it is definable up to evaluation bisimilarity as $(\nu x)(x.P|\bar{x}.0)$, where $x \notin fn(P)$. Similarly, one can extend summation to include τ-guarded summands: given a normal process N and processes $P_1, \ldots, P_n$ define $N + \tau.P_1 + \cdots + \tau.P_n$ to be $(\nu x)((N + x.P_1 + \cdots + x.P_n)|\bar{x}.0)$, where x is not free in $N, P_1, \ldots, P_n$. It is easy to prove that the following τ-laws are valid up to delay bisimilarity and hence by the theorem, up to evaluation bisimilarity:

$$P \simeq_{\Downarrow} \tau.P \qquad N + \tau.N' \simeq_{\Downarrow} (N + N') + \tau.N' . \tag{3}$$

Such laws, together with the structural congruence laws, idempotence of $+$ and an Expansion Law provide a complete axiomatisation of the equational theory of evaluation bisimilarity on the finite (*rec*-free) part of NCCS: the details will appear in the second author's thesis. Note that notwithstanding the first law in (3) and Theorem 2.9, in general $N + \tau.N'$ is *not* evaluation bisimilar to $N + N'$. For example, $x.0 + \tau.y.0 \not\simeq_{\Downarrow} x.0 + y.0$. (This does not contradict the congruence property of $\simeq_{\Downarrow}$, because $N + [-]$ is only an operator on normal processes, not on all processes.) Of course, by virtue of Theorem 3.6 not all τ-laws valid for the restriction of CCS observation equivalence to NCCS hold for evaluation bisimilarity. For example $x.(N + \tau.P)$ and $x.(N + \tau.P) + x.P$ are not delay bisimilar in general, but they are observation equivalent.

We can also use Theorem 3.6 to resolve the question raised in the previous section about the extent to which quantification over contexts $[-]|Q$ in the definition of evaluation bisimulation can be avoided. As the following result shows, we need only consider a single context $[-]|x.0$, with x fresh. This result is in the same spirit as Sangiorgi's characterisation of his weak context bisimilarity in terms of 'normal bisimulations': see [23, Theorem 7.4]. However, the reduction in context quantification we are dealing with here is much less subtle than that involved in going from context bisimilarity to normal bisimilarity. We have more to say about a higher order version of evaluation bisimilarity in Section 4.1.

Theorem 3.8. *Evaluation bisimilarity is the largest symmetric binary relation $\mathcal{R}$ on NCCS processes satisfying that if $P_1 \;\mathcal{R}\; P_2$, then for any name $x \notin fn(P_1P_2)$ (or equivalently, for some such x)*

$$P_1|x.0 \Downarrow \ell.P_1' \Rightarrow \exists P_2' \, (P_2|x.0 \Downarrow \ell.P_2' \;\&\; P_1' \;\mathcal{R}\; P_2') \ . \tag{4}$$

Proof. It follows from the definition of $\simeq_{\Downarrow}$ that it is a symmetric relation satisfying (4). Conversely given such an $\mathcal{R}$, let $\bar{\mathcal{R}}$ be the least relation containing $\sim\mathcal{R}\sim$ and such that $P_1|x.0 \sim Q_1 \;\bar{\mathcal{R}}\; Q_2 \sim P_2|x.0$ with $x \notin fn(P_1P_2)$ implies $P_1 \;\bar{\mathcal{R}}\; P_2$. Using Theorem 3.3, it is not hard to prove that $\bar{\mathcal{R}}$ is a delay bisimulation. Therefore by Theorem 3.6 it is contained in $\simeq_{\Downarrow}$ and hence so is $\mathcal{R}$. □

4 Further Topics

In this section we briefly outline some further developments of the approach to process calculi based upon evaluation to committed form.

4.1 Evaluation bisimilarity for higher order calculi

Consider a higher order version of NCCS in which synchronised communication involves passing process expressions. Input-committed processes now take the form $x.F$ where $F = (X)E$ is an *abstraction* (and free occurrences of the process variable X in E are bound in F); such a process is ready to receive a process P on channel x and then continue with $E[P/X]$. Output-committed processes take the form $\bar{x}.C$ where $C = (\nu\vec{x})\langle P_1\rangle P_2$ is a *concretion* (free occurrences of the names $\vec{x}$ in P_1 or P_2 are bound in C); such a process is ready to send P_1 on channel x and then continue with P_2, all within a scope in which the names $\vec{x}$ are restricted. See for example Sangiorgi [23] for further syntactic details and a labelled transition system formalising the intended input/output behaviour. Transitions now take the form $P \xrightarrow{\tau} P'$ and $P \xrightarrow{\ell} A$, where in the second case if ℓ is a name then A is an abstraction, and if ℓ is a co-name then A is a concretion. First order prefixing can be regarded as a special case of higher order prefixing if we define $x.P$ to mean $x.(X)P$ where $X \notin fv(P)$, and define $\bar{x}.P$ to mean $\bar{x}.\langle \mathbf{0}\rangle P$. (Sangiorgi also considers τ prefixing, but as we noted in Example 3.7, this is definable in terms of label prefixing, composition and restriction.)

In *loc. cit.* Sangiorgi considers the problem of defining a suitable bisimilarity which, unlike previous attempts, identifies some pairs of processes (such as $\bar{y}.\langle\mathbf{0}\rangle\mathbf{0}$ and $(\nu x)\bar{y}.\langle x.\mathbf{0}\rangle\mathbf{0}$) which one can argue should be behaviourly equivalent in the presence of statically bound restrictions. He develops a congruent notion of bisimilarity, called *(weak) context bisimilarity*, and shows that it has the desired properties. Weak context bisimilarity is a generalisation to higher order of the notion of delay bisimilarity. Indeed the form of the definition is exactly as in Definition 3.5, except that in clause (wb2′) P_1' and P_2' are now abstractions or concretions (according to whether ℓ is a name or a co-name). So one has to extend the relation $\mathcal{R}$ from processes to these syntactic categories in order to assert in (wb2′) that P_1' and P_2' are related by $\mathcal{R}$. This is done by defining

$$F_1 \mathrel{\mathcal{R}} F_2 \overset{\text{def}}{\Leftrightarrow} \forall C\,(F_1 \bullet C \mathrel{\mathcal{R}} F_2 \bullet C) \qquad C_1 \mathrel{\mathcal{R}} C_2 \overset{\text{def}}{\Leftrightarrow} \forall F\,(C_1 \bullet F \mathrel{\mathcal{R}} C_2 \bullet F) \quad (5)$$

where $F \bullet C \overset{\text{def}}{=} (\nu\vec{x})(E[P_1/X] \| P_2)$ if $F = (X)E, C = (\nu\vec{x})\langle P_1\rangle P_2$, and $\vec{x} \cap fn(E) = \emptyset$; $C \bullet F$ is defined symmetrically.

Interestingly, it turns out that Theorem 3.6 easily extends to a coincidence of a higher order version of evaluation bisimilarity with Sangiorgi's weak context bisimilarity, as we now indicate. First, evaluation to committed form extends very naturally to the higher order case. We replace ($\Downarrow$2) by

$$\frac{P_1 \Downarrow \ell.A_1 \quad P_2 \Downarrow \bar{\ell}.A_2 \quad A_1 \bullet A_2 \Downarrow K}{P_1 | P_2 \Downarrow K}$$

The other evaluation rules remain essentially as in Definition 2.2, but one also has to suitably extend the notion of structural congruence to abstractions and concretions. Secondly, evaluation bisimilarity extends naturally to the higher order calculus: $\simeq_{\Downarrow}$ is the greatest symmetric relation $\mathcal{R}$ on higher order processes such that if $P_1 \mathcal{R} P_2$ then for all Q, if $P_1|Q \Downarrow \ell.A_1$ then $P_2|Q \Downarrow \ell.A_2$, for some A_2 with $A_1 \mathcal{R} A_2$ (where $\mathcal{R}$ is extended to abstractions and concretions as in (5)).

Theorem 4.1. *Higher order evaluation bisimilarity coincides with Sangiorgi's weak context bisimilarity [23, Definition 3.11].*

The proof is very much as for Theorem 3.6, once one has established the higher order analogue of Theorem 3.3. We omit the details here. The proof of Theorem 3.8 also extends: *one can replace the quantification over Q with the use of a single process $Q = x.\mathbf{0}$ without affecting the relation of higher order evaluation bisimilarity.* We expect that the quantification implicit in the use of (5) can also be reduced along the lines of [23, Section 7] using Sangiorgi's 'Factorisation Theorem' (*loc. cit.*, Theorem 4.7).

4.2 Evaluation to input-committed form

If parallel composition in process calculus plays a role analogous to application in functional languages, then input-committed processes $x(X).E$ are somewhat like lambda abstractions $\lambda X.E$ 'located' at x. (The analogy can be made more precise, as in [14].) Experience with applicative bisimilarity for functional calculi [1, 9] suggests considering an evaluation-based approach to process calculi in which the only canonical forms are input-committed processes. For variety, we illustrate how this looks for the π-calculus [15] with asynchronous output and no summation—the 'essence' of the language to judge by recent results [7, 19, 4]. The syntax of such processes is

$$P ::= x.(x)P \mid \bar{x}.\langle x\rangle \mid \mathbf{0} \mid P|P \mid (\nu x)P \mid !P$$

where x ranges over names. One works modulo a structural congruence relation, $\equiv$, generated by the relevant identities in Definition 2.1 together with an identity for unfolding replicated processes: $!P \equiv P|!P$. This identity means that we will not need an explicit evaluation rule for replicated processes. Similarly, by building restrictions into the other rules, we can do without an explicit rule for restriction (in other words ($\Downarrow$3) will become derivable). Altogether we arrive at the following remarkably compact evaluation semantics for this variety of π-calculus.

$$\frac{P_1 \Downarrow y.(x)P_1'}{P_2 \Downarrow y.(x)P_2'} \text{ if } P_1 \equiv P_2 \text{ and } \forall x\,(P_1' \equiv P_2') \qquad \frac{Q \Downarrow y_1.(x)Q' \quad (\nu\vec{x})Q'[y_2/x] \Downarrow K}{(\nu\vec{x})((\bar{y}_1.\langle y_2\rangle)|Q) \Downarrow K}$$

$$(\nu\vec{x})((y.(x)P)|Q) \Downarrow y.(x)(\nu\vec{x})(P|Q) \text{ if } y \notin \vec{x}$$

Then define *evaluation bisimilarity*, $\simeq_{\Downarrow}$, for this calculus to be the largest symmetric binary relation $\mathcal{R}$ between processes such that if $P_1 \mathcal{R} P_2$, then for all Q

$$P_1|Q \Downarrow y.(x)P_1' \Rightarrow \exists P_2'\,(P_2|Q \Downarrow y.(x)P_2' \;\&\; \forall x\,(P_1' \mathcal{R} P_2'))\ .$$

One can adapt the method outlined in the proof of Theorem 2.9 to show that $\simeq_{\Downarrow}$ *is a congruence for this* π*-calculus.* We have not yet investigated the relationship between $\simeq_{\Downarrow}$ and other notions of weak congruence that have been proposed in the literature. However, the work of Honda and Yoshida [8], Fournet and Gonthier [4] and others, suggests that for this kind of asynchronous-output calculus one should observe outputs rather than inputs. It is possible to give a congruent notion of evaluation bisimilarity based on evaluation to output-committed form (which would be $\bar{x}.C$, with C a concretion of the form $(\nu\vec{x})(\langle y\rangle|P)$ in this case), but we do not give the details here.

4.3 Barbed bisimulation

Milner and Sangiorgi [17] introduced the notion of barbed bisimulations for process calculi, based upon a reduction-oriented approach to process semantics. It has proved useful for defining equivalences in the π-calculus and related systems (see [4], for example). The motivations for the evaluation-based approach we have introduced in this paper are quite similar to those expressed in [17]. Technically, the evaluation-to-committed-form approach seems more elegant: barbed bisimilarities are defined using a reduction relation and a convergence predicate and these usually have to be defined from a labelled transition system; whereas evaluation bisimilarity is defined using a single, inductively defined evaluation relation. More tellingly, the 'barbed' approach usually involves quite heavy use of closure under contexts in order to obtain a congruence relation; whereas we have seen that evaluation bisimilarities are already congruences. On the other hand, the evaluation-to-committed-form approach is very much tied to defining equivalences that ignore internal actions (*i.e.* weak rather than strong equivalences); and it imposes a harder discipline than the reduction-based approach, since it may be easier to find reasonable notions of reduction and convergence for some 'new' process calculus which may arise.

Whatever the *pros* and *cons* of each approach, observe that for NCCS at least, the results of Section 3 mean that weak barbed bisimilarities can be defined starting just from the evaluation relation. For we saw in Theorem 3.3(ii) that reduction can be defined in terms of evaluation (modulo strong equivalence). And if we follow [17, Section 5.1] and define $P\Downarrow$ to mean $\exists P', \ell\,(P \xrightarrow{\tau^*\ell\tau^*} P')$, then by Lemma 3.1 we have that $P\Downarrow \Leftrightarrow \exists K\,(P \Downarrow K)$ (fortunately, from a notational point of view). Here for example, is a characterisation of observation equivalence for NCCS as a barbed congruence whose definition is phrased in terms of evaluation. It seems unlikely that NCCS evaluation bisimilarity (*i.e.* delay bisimilarity) can be given a 'barbed' characterisation.

Theorem 4.2. *Observation equivalence,* $\approx$, *is the largest symmetric binary relation* $\mathcal{R}$ *on NCCS processes satisfying that if* $P_1\ \mathcal{R}\ P_2$ *then for any NCCS context* $C[-]$ *and any name* $x \notin fn(C[P_1], C[P_2])$

$$C[P_1]|x.\mathbf{0} \Downarrow x.P_1' \Rightarrow \exists P_2'\,(C[P_2]|x.\mathbf{0} \Downarrow x.P_2' \;\&\; P_1'\ \mathcal{R}\ P_2')$$
$$C[P_1]\Downarrow \Rightarrow C[P_2]\Downarrow$$

Proof. Let $\approx_b$ denote the greatest such relation. It is not hard to see from the results in Section 3 that $\approx$ is contained in $\approx_b$. Moreover it is clear from its definition that $\approx_b$ is a congruence. Using this together with careful use of contexts to track $\xrightarrow{\tau^*\ell\tau^*}$ in terms of convergence, one can show the reverse inclusion. The details will appear in the second author's thesis. □

4.4 Unrestricted summation

Extend NCCS with unrestricted binary sums of processes, $P_1 + P_2$, with evaluation rules

$$(\Downarrow 5)\ \frac{P_1 \Downarrow \ell.P}{(P_1+P_2)|Q \Downarrow \ell.(P|Q)} \qquad \frac{P_2 \Downarrow \ell.P}{(P_1+P_2)|Q \Downarrow \ell.(P|Q)}$$

Note that these rules conservatively extend NCCS evaluation: if P_1 and P_2 are normal processes, then the rules do not give any new evaluations for the NCCS process $P_1 + P_2$. The method for proving congruence outlined in Theorem 2.9 works just as well for this extended language and so we obtain:

Theorem 4.3. *Evaluation bisimilarity (defined just as in Definition 2.6) is a congruence for NCCS extended with sums satisfying* ($\Downarrow$*5).*

The problem comes when one tries to find labelled transition rules for + which permit the results of Section 3 to go through. Two possibilities come to mind: ordinary *CCS summation* [13] and *external non-deterministic choice* (see Hennessy [6, Chapter 5]). (Note that *internal* non-deterministic choice $P_1 \oplus P_2$ is already definable in NCCS as $(\nu x)(x.P_1|\bar{x}.\mathbf{0}|x.P_2)$, where $x \notin fn(P_1 P_2)$.) For either of these choices of transition rules properties (i) and (iii) of Lemma 3.1 continue to hold, but for neither choice does property (ii) still hold. As a consequence one can give examples (which we omit here for lack of space) showing that in neither case does delay bisimilarity agree with evaluation bisimilarity in the presence of rule ($\Downarrow$5). Whether or not $\simeq_\Downarrow$ can be given a transition-based characterisation, it seems from the above theorem that it is a reasonable notion of weak equivalence for the language with unrestricted summation.

5 Conclusions

We feel the results described here vindicate evaluation to committed form as a promising approach to the topic of 'weak' equivalence in process calculi, both in its own right and in the way it relates and sheds light on existing approaches. In conclusion, we mention two aspects which may bear further investigation. First, evaluation seems at a slightly higher level of abstraction than labelled transition; moreover it places the emphasis upon composition and restriction as fundamental operations (indeed in some cases as purely structural ones—*cf.* Section 4.2). Maybe these considerations can suggest new avenues in the rather under-developed subject of denotational semantics for communicating processes up to weak equivalence. Secondly, since evaluation relations are already a convenient way to specify the structural operational semantics of functional languages, our approach may aid in developing theories of equivalence for languages integrating functional and process-theoretic features. To that end, an evaluation-based approach to CML [21] and a comparison with the transition-based theory developed by Ferreira *et al* in [3] will appear in the second author's thesis.

References

1. S. Abramsky. The lazy λ-calculus. In D. A. Turner, ed., *Research Topics in Functional Programming*, 65–117. Addison Wesley, 1990.
2. G. Berry and G. Boudol. The chemical abstract machine. *Theoretical Computer Science*, 96:217–248, 1992.
3. W. Ferreira, M. Hennessy, and A. Jeffrey. A theory of weak bisimulation for core CML. Technical Report 05/95, Computer Science, University of Sussex, 1995.
4. C. Fournet and G. Gonthier. The reflexive CHAM and the join-calculus. In *Proc. 23rd POPL*, 372–385. ACM Press, 1996.
5. A. Giacalone, P. Mishra, and S. Prasad. Facile: A Symmetric Integration of Concurrent and Functional Programming. *Int. J. Parallel Programming*, 18(2):121–160, 1989.
6. M. Hennessy. *Algebraic Theory of Processes*. MIT Press, 1988.
7. K. Honda and M. Tokoro. On asynchronous communication semantics. In M. Tokoro and O. Nierstrasz, editors, *Proc. ECOOP'91*, *Lecture Notes in Computer Science*, 612:21–51. Springer-Verlag, 1991.
8. K. Honda and N. Yoshida. On reduction-based process semantics. In *Proc. 13th Conf. on Foundations of Software Technology and Theoretical Computer Science*, *Lecture Notes in Computer Science*, 761:371–387. Springer-Verlag, 1993.
9. D. J. Howe. Equality in lazy computation systems. In *Proc. 4th LICS*, 198–203. IEEE Computer Society Press, 1989.
10. D. J. Howe. Proving congruence of bisimulation in functional programming languages. *Information and Computation*, 124(2):103–112, 1996.
11. P. Martin-Löf. Constructive mathematics and computer programming. In *Proc. 6th Int. Cong. for Logic, Methodology, and Philosophy of Science*, 153–175. North-Holland, 1982.
12. R. Milner. A modal characterisation of observable machine-behaviour. In *Proc. CAAP'81*, *Lecture Notes in Computer Science*, Vol. 112. Springer-Verlag, 1981.
13. R. Milner. *Communication and Concurrency*. Prentice Hall, 1989.
14. R. Milner. Functions as processes. In *Proc. 17th ICALP*, *Lecture Notes in Computer Science*, 443:167–180. Springer-Verlag, 1990.
15. R. Milner. The polyadic π-calculus: A tutorial. In F. L. Bauer *et al*, ed., *Logic and Algebra of Specification*. Springer-Verlag, 1993.
16. R. Milner, J. Parrow, and D. Walker. A calculus of mobile processes (parts I and II). *Information and Computation*, 100:1–77, 1992.
17. R. Milner and D. Sangiorgi. Barbed bisimulation. In W. Kuich, ed., *Proc. 19th ICALP*, *Lecture Notes in Computer Science*, 623:685–695. Springer-Verlag, 1992.
18. R. Milner, M. Tofte, and R. Harper. *The Definition of Standard ML*. MIT Press, 1990.
19. B. C. Pierce and D. N. Turner. Pict: A programming language based on the pi-calculus. To appear.
20. G. D. Plotkin. A structural approach to operational semantics. Technical Report DAIMI FN-19, Aarhus University, 1981.
21. J. Reppy. CML: A higher-order concurrent language. In *Proc. PLDI*, 293–259. ACM Press, 1991.
22. D. Sangiorgi. *Expressing Mobility in Process Algebras: First-Order and Higher-Order Paradigms*. PhD thesis, Dept. Computer Science, University of Edinburgh, 1992.
23. D. Sangiorgi. Bisimulation for higher-order process calculi. Technical Report RR-2508, INRIA, 1995.
24. B. Thomsen. Plain CHOCS. A second generation calculus for higher order processes. *Acta Informatica*, 30(1):1–59, 1993.
25. W. P. Weijland. *Synchrony and Asynchrony in Process Algebra*. PhD thesis, University of Amsterdam, 1989.

A Process Algebra with Distributed Priorities

Rance Cleaveland[1] Gerald Lüttgen[2] V. Natarajan[1]

[1] Department of Computer Science, North Carolina State University, Raleigh, NC 27695-8206, USA, e-mail: {rance,nvaidhy}@eos.ncsu.edu. Research supported by NSF grant CCR-9120995, ONR Young Investigator Award N00014-92-J-1582, NSF Young Investigator Award CCR-9257963, NSF grant CCR-9402807, and AFOSR grant F49620-95-1-0508.

[2] Fakultät für Mathematik und Informatik, Universität Passau, 94030 Passau, Germany, e-mail: luettgen@fmi.uni-passau.de. Research support partly provided by the German Academic Exchange Service under grant D/95/09026 (Doktorandenstipendium HSP II/ AUFE).

Abstract. This paper presents a process algebra for distributed systems in which some actions may take precedence over others. In contrast with existing approaches to priorities, our algebra only allows actions to preempt others at the same "location" and therefore captures a notion of *localized precedence*. Using Park's and Milner's notion of strong bisimulation as a basis, we develop a behavioral congruence and axiomatize it for finite processes; we also derive an associated observational congruence. Simple examples highlight the utility of the theory.

1 Introduction

Process algebras [11, 13] provide widely studied frameworks for modeling and verifying concurrent systems [9]. Such theories typically consist of a simple language with a well-defined operational semantics given in terms of labeled transition systems; a behavioral equivalence is then used to relate implementations and specifications, which are both given as terms in the language. In order to facilitate compositional reasoning, in which systems are verified on the basis of the behavior of their components, researchers have devoted great attention to the definition of behavioral congruences, which allow the substitution of "equals for equals" inside larger systems. Traditional process algebras focus on modeling the potential nondeterminism that concurrent processes may exhibit; approaches have also been suggested for introducing sensitivity to other aspects of system behavior, including *priority* [1, 2, 4, 5, 6, 12, 15] and *true concurrency* [3, 14]. The latter work presents theories in which parallelism is treated as a primitive notion that is not reducible to nondeterminism, while the former enables the modeling of systems in which some system transitions (e.g. interrupts) may take precedence over others.

In this paper, we develop an algebraic theory of action priority for *distributed* systems. As in existing work, our aim is to model systems in which some transitions have precedence over others. Our point of departure is that the priority scheme should be localized within individual sites in the system; actions should only be able to pre-empt actions being performed at the "same location." This constraint reflects an essential intuition about distributed systems, which is that the execution of a process on one processor should not affect the behavior of a process on another processor unless the designer explicitly builds in an interaction (e.g. synchronization) between them. Technically, we begin with a theory of priority that includes a notion of global precedence [6, 15] and show how its semantics may be altered using ideas from true concurrency [3] to localize capabilities for pre-emption. We then define a strong congruence for this language, axiomatize it for finite processes, and derive an observational congruence along the lines of [13].

Organization of the Paper. In the next section we present a generic example illustrating the need for local pre-emption in modeling systems. The following three sections present our language and derive the technical results discussed above, while Sect. 6 presents an example showing the application of our theory. Sect. 7 discusses related work, and the last section presents our conclusions and directions for future work. Due to space constraints we refer the reader to [7] for the proofs of our main theorems.

2 Motivating Example

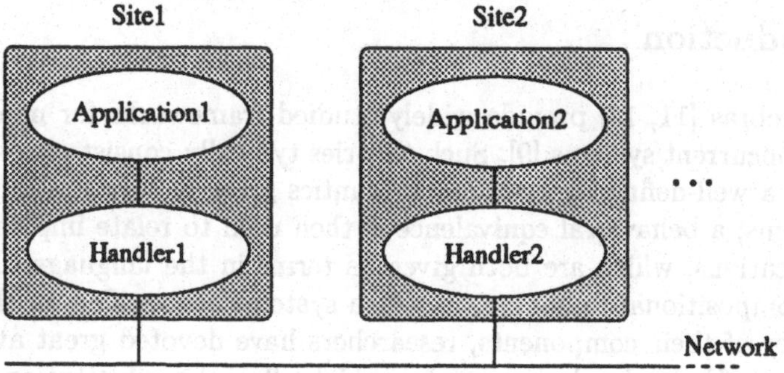

Fig. 1. Standard distributed system

The example depicted in Fig. 1 motivates the need for considering a local notion of pre-emption when dealing with priorities in distributed systems. It consists of two sites, `Site1` and `Site2`, e.g. two computers, that are connected via the network `Network`. Each site runs an application, `Application1` and `Application2`, respectively, which may send or receive information from the application at the other site via its (interrupt-)handler, `Handler1` or `Handler2`. A handler delivers the message to the network or receives a message for its site from the network and notifies the application by sending an interrupt. Now, we have the following intuitive requirements which the semantics of our language CCS^{prio} should satisfy in order to reflect the behavior of the system correctly. First, an interrupt of a handler should pre-empt the normal work of the application at its site, i.e. the application should immediately respond to an interrupt request. Second, both sites should be able to perform internal computations that are local to their site without interference from the other site. In particular, internal activities of `Handler1` should not pre-empt those of `Handler2`, and vice versa. While traditional process-algebraic treatments [6, 15] of priority satisfy the first requirement, they typically violate the second, since they allow `Application1` to pre-empt `Application2` if the former has higher priority, even though they are running on different sites. In general, one would expect priorities at different sites to be incomparable. The semantics given in [6, 15], however, do not permit this distinction to be made; the net effect is that some computations that one would expect to find in a distributed system are improperly suppressed. We propose to remedy this shortcoming in this paper by introducing a notion of *local pre-emption*.

3 Syntax and Semantics of CCS^{prio}

In this section we define the syntax and semantics of our language CCS^{prio}, which is based on CCS [13].

3.1 Syntax of CCS^{prio}

The syntax of CCS^{prio} differs from CCS in the structure of the action set which exhibits a priority scheme. For the sake of simplicity, we restrict ourselves to a two-level priority scheme. However, all results presented in this paper can be generalized to multi-level priority schemes in a straightforward fashion. Intuitively, actions represent potential synchronizations that a process may be willing to engage in with its environment. Given a choice between a synchronization on a high priority action and one on a low priority action, a process should choose the former.

Formally, let Λ be a countable set of action labels, not including the *internal* or *silent* action τ. For every *input action* $a \in \Lambda$, there exists a *complementary action* $\overline{a}$, the corresponding *output action*. Let $\overline{\Lambda} =_{\text{df}} \{\overline{a} \mid a \in \Lambda\}$, and let us denote the set of all actions $\Lambda \cup \overline{\Lambda} \cup \{\tau\}$, where $\tau \notin \Lambda$, by A. Intuitively, an action indicates that a process is willing to perform a synchronization on the *port* associated with the action name, i.e. action a means that the process wants to receive a message from port a whereas $\overline{a}$ means that the process wants to send a message via port a. The action τ represents either an internal action of a process or the synchronization of two processes on some port in order to communicate with each other. Finally, we let $a, b, \ldots$ range over Λ and $\alpha, \beta, \ldots$ over A.

In order to define *prioritized actions*, let $\underline{\Delta}$ be a countable set of prioritized action labels disjoint from Λ. Then $\underline{A} =_{\text{df}} \underline{\Delta} \cup \overline{\underline{\Delta}} \cup \{\underline{\tau}\}$ is the set of *prioritized actions*, where $\underline{\tau}$ is the prioritized *internal* or *silent* action. We use $\mathcal{A} =_{\text{df}} A \cup \underline{A}$

to denote the set of all actions. Intuitively, prioritized actions are considered to be names for "important" channels. Therefore, communications on a prioritized action should be preferred over communications on unprioritized actions. In the remainder of the paper, let $\underline{a}, \underline{b}, \ldots$ range over $\underline{\Lambda}$, the symbols $\underline{\alpha}, \underline{\beta}, \ldots$ over $\underline{A}$, and γ, δ over $\mathcal{A}$. Additionally, we extend $\bar{\ }$ by $\bar{\bar{\gamma}} = \gamma$, and if $L \subseteq \mathcal{A} \setminus \{\tau, \underline{\tau}\}$ then $\overline{L} =_{\text{df}} \{\overline{\gamma} \mid \gamma \in L\}$. A mapping f on $\mathcal{A}$ is a ***relabeling*** if f preserves priorities (i.e. $f(\Lambda) \subseteq \Lambda$ and $f(\underline{\Lambda}) \subseteq \underline{\Lambda}$), is such that the set $\{\gamma \mid f(\gamma) \neq \gamma\}$ is finite, and satisfies the following: $f(\overline{a}) = \overline{f(a)}$ $f(\overline{\underline{a}}) = \overline{f(\underline{a})}$, $f(\tau) = \tau$, and $f(\underline{\tau}) = \underline{\tau}$.

The syntax of our language is defined by the BNF

$$P \quad ::= \quad \mathbf{0} \mid \gamma.P \mid P + P \mid P|P \mid P[f] \mid P \setminus L \mid C \stackrel{\text{def}}{=} P$$

where f is a relabeling, $L \subseteq \mathcal{A} \setminus \{\tau, \underline{\tau}\}$, and C is a process constant. We use the standard definitions for ***sort*** of a process, ***free*** and ***bound variables***, ***open*** and ***closed terms***, ***guarded recursion***, and ***contexts***. We refer to closed and guarded terms as ***processes*** and denote syntactic equality by $\equiv$. Let $P, Q, R, \ldots$ range over the set $\mathcal{P}$ of processes.

3.2 Locations

We now introduce the notion of ***location***, which will be used in the next section in the operational semantics for CCS^{prio} as a basis for deciding when one transition pre-empts another. Intuitively, a location is a string representing the "address" of a subterm inside a larger term; when a system performs an action, our semantics will also note the location of the subterm that "generates" this action. Our account of locations closely follows that of [14].

Formally, let $\mathcal{A}_{\text{loc}} =_{\text{df}} \{L, R, l, r\}$ be the ***location alphabet***, and let $\mathcal{L}oc$ denote the set of all words over $\mathcal{A}_{\text{loc}}$ concatenated with the special symbol $\bullet$ to the left, i.e. $\mathcal{L}oc$ is the set of all ***locations***. As usual, $\cdot$ denotes the concatenation operator as e.g. in $\bullet \cdot L \cdot l \in \mathcal{L}oc$. Further, we write $M \cdot \zeta$ for $\{m \cdot \zeta \mid m \in M\}$ where $M \subseteq \mathcal{L}oc$ and $\zeta \in \mathcal{A}_{\text{loc}}$. As noted above, a location represents the address of a subterm, with $\bullet$ denoting the current term, l (r) representing the left (right) subterm of a $+$, and L (R) the left (right) component of a $|$. For example, the process $(a.\mathbf{0} \mid b.\mathbf{0}) + c.\mathbf{0}$ can perform action a from location $\bullet \cdot L \cdot l$, action b from location $\bullet \cdot R \cdot l$, and action c from location $\bullet \cdot r$. For simplicity, we often write m instead of $\bullet \cdot m$ for $m \in \mathcal{L}oc$.

As mentioned in the introduction, we want to adopt the view that processes on different sides of the parallel operator are (logically) executed on different processors, i.e. at different locations. Thus, priorities on different sides of the parallel operator are distributed and, therefore, should be incomparable. However, processes on different sides of the summation operator, which models non-deterministic choice, are scheduled on a single processor, i.e. they should be comparable. We formalize this intuition in the following ***comparability relation*** on locations which is adapted from [10].

Definition 1. The comparability relation $\bowtie$ on locations is the smallest reflexive and symmetric subset of $\mathcal{L}oc \times \mathcal{L}oc$ such that for all $v, w \in \mathcal{L}oc$.

1. $(v \cdot l, w \cdot r) \in \bowtie$, and
2. $(v, w) \in \bowtie$ implies $(v \cdot \zeta, w \cdot \zeta) \in \bowtie$ for $\zeta \in \mathcal{A}_{\mathrm{loc}}$.

We write $v \bowtie w$ instead of $(v, w) \in \bowtie$.

Note that the comparability relation is not transitive, e.g. we have $L \cdot l \bowtie r$ and $r \bowtie R \cdot l$ but $L \cdot l \not\bowtie R \cdot l$ since $L \not\bowtie R$. Considering our example $(a.0 \mid b.0) + c.0$ above, the locations of the actions a and c and the locations of the actions b and c are comparable since they are just on different sides of the summation operator. In contrast, the locations of the actions a and b are incomparable since they are on different sides of the parallel operator.

In the following, let $m, n, o, \ldots$ range over $\mathcal{Loc}$ and let $[m]$ denote the set $\{o \in \mathcal{Loc} \mid o \bowtie m\}$. Moreover, we close $\mathcal{Loc}$ with respect to pairing; that is, if $m, n \in \mathcal{Loc}$ then we let $\langle m, n \rangle \in \mathcal{Loc}$ also. Allowing pairs of locations is necessary because communications in a CCS-based framework take place between two processes offering complementary actions. The result of a communication is an internal action which is assigned with the two locations of the complementary actions. Finally, we define $\langle m, n \rangle \cdot \zeta =_{\mathrm{df}} \langle m \cdot \zeta, n \cdot \zeta \rangle$ and $[\langle m, n \rangle] =_{\mathrm{df}} [m] \cup [n]$ where $m, n \in \mathcal{Loc}$ and $\zeta \in \mathcal{A}_{\mathrm{loc}}$.

3.3 Semantics of CCS^{prio}

The *(operational) semantics* of a CCS^{prio} process $P \in \mathcal{P}$ is given by a labeled transition system $\langle \mathcal{P}, \mathcal{A}, \longrightarrow, P \rangle$ where $\mathcal{P}$ is the set of states, $\mathcal{A}$ the alphabet, $\longrightarrow$ the transition relation, and P the start state. The transition relation $\longrightarrow \subseteq \mathcal{P} \times (\mathcal{Loc} \times \mathcal{A}) \times \mathcal{P}$ is defined in Table 2 using Plotkin-style operational rules. We write $P \xrightarrow{m,\gamma} P'$ instead of $\langle P, m, \gamma, P' \rangle \in \longrightarrow$. We say that P *may engage in action γ offered from location m and thereafter behaves like process P'*. Moreover, if $\gamma \in \underline{\mathcal{A}}$ then we abbreviate $P \xrightarrow{m,\underline{\gamma}} P'$ by $P \xrightarrow{\underline{\gamma}} P'$ since it turns out that the location m is not important when reasoning about prioritized transitions, i.e. transitions labeled by a prioritized action.

The presentation of the operational rules requires ***prioritized initial action sets*** which are defined as the least relations satisfying the rules in Table 1. Intuitively, $\underline{\mathbb{I}}_m(P)$ denotes the set of all prioritized initial actions of P from location m. Note that those sets are either empty or contain exactly one initial transition. $\underline{\mathbb{I}}_m(P) = \emptyset$ means that either m is not a location of P or P wants to perform an unprioritized action at location m. Additionally, let us denote the set of all prioritized initial actions of process P from locations $M \subseteq \mathcal{Loc}$ by $\underline{\mathbb{I}}_M(P)$, and the set of all prioritized initial actions of process P by $\underline{\mathbb{I}}(P)$. We also define analogous initial action sets ignoring internal actions and denote them by $\underline{\mathbb{II}}_m(P)$, $\underline{\mathbb{II}}_M(P)$, and $\underline{\mathbb{II}}(P)$, respectively.

Note that the set of actions is defined independently from the transition relation $\longrightarrow$. Therefore, $\longrightarrow$ is well-defined. The side conditions of the operational semantic rules guarantee that a process does not perform an unprioritized action if it can engage in a prioritized synchronization or internal computation, i.e. a $\underline{\tau}$-transition, from a comparable location. Therefore, $\underline{\tau}$-actions have pre-emptive

Table 1. Initial action sets

$\underline{I}_m(C) =_{\mathrm{df}} \underline{I}_m(P)$ where $C \stackrel{\mathrm{def}}{=} P$	$\underline{I}_{\bullet}(\underline{\alpha}.P) =_{\mathrm{df}} \{\underline{\alpha}\}$
$\underline{I}_{m \cdot l}(P+Q) =_{\mathrm{df}} \underline{I}_m(P)$	$\underline{I}_{n \cdot r}(P+Q) =_{\mathrm{df}} \underline{I}_n(Q)$
$\underline{I}_m(P[f]) =_{\mathrm{df}} \{f(\underline{\alpha}) \mid \underline{\alpha} \in \underline{I}_m(P)\}$	$\underline{I}_m(P \setminus L) =_{\mathrm{df}} \underline{I}_m(P) \setminus (L \cup \overline{L})$
$\underline{I}_{m \cdot L}(P \mid Q) =_{\mathrm{df}} \underline{I}_m(P)$	$\underline{I}_{n \cdot R}(P \mid Q) =_{\mathrm{df}} \underline{I}_n(Q)$
$\underline{I}_{\langle m \cdot L, n \cdot R \rangle}(P \mid Q) =_{\mathrm{df}} \underline{I}_m(P) \cup \underline{I}_n(Q) \cup \{\underline{\tau} \mid \underline{\mathbb{I}}_m(P) \cap \overline{\underline{\mathbb{I}}}_n(Q) \neq \emptyset\}$	
$\underline{I}_M(P) =_{\mathrm{df}} \bigcup \{\underline{I}_m(P) \mid m \in M\}$	$\underline{\mathbb{I}}_M(P) =_{\mathrm{df}} \underline{I}_M(P) \setminus \{\underline{\tau}\}$
$\underline{I}(P) =_{\mathrm{df}} \underline{I}_{\mathcal{L}oc}(P)$	$\underline{\mathbb{I}}(P) =_{\mathrm{df}} \underline{I}(P) \setminus \{\underline{\tau}\}$

power over unprioritized actions. The reason that prioritized visible actions do *not* have priority over unprioritized actions is that visible actions only indicate the potential of a synchronization, i.e. the potential of progress, whereas internal actions describe *real* progress in our model.

The semantics of CCS^{prio} for prioritized transitions is the same as the usual CCS semantics. The difference arises by the side conditions of the rules for unprioritized transitions. The process $\gamma.P$ may engage in action γ and then behaves like P. The *summation operator* $+$ denotes *nondeterministic choice*. The process $P+Q$ may behave like process P (Q) if Q (P) does not pre-empt unprioritized actions by performing a $\underline{\tau}$-action. Note that priorities arising from different sides of the summation operator are comparable. The *restriction operator* $\setminus L$ prohibits the execution of actions in $L \cup \overline{L}$. Thus, the restriction operator permits the *scoping* of actions. $P[f]$ behaves exactly as the process P where the actions are renamed with respect to the relabeling f. The process $P|Q$ stands for the *parallel composition* of P and Q according to an *interleaving semantics* with *synchronized communication* on complementary actions resulting in the internal action τ or $\underline{\tau}$. Since locations on different sides of a parallel operator are incomparable, $\underline{\tau}$'s arising from a location of P (Q) cannot pre-empt the execution of an action, even an unprioritized one, of Q (P). Only if P (Q) engages in a prioritized synchronization with Q (P) can unprioritized actions of P and Q be pre-empted. Finally, $C \stackrel{\mathrm{def}}{=} P$ denotes a *constant definition*, i.e. C is a recursively defined process which behaves as a distinguished solution of the equation $C = P$.

Table 2. Operational semantics for CCS^{prio}

Act	$\dfrac{}{\underline{\alpha}.P \xrightarrow{\underline{\alpha}} P}$	Act	$\dfrac{}{\alpha.P \xrightarrow{\bullet,\alpha} P}$
Sum1	$\dfrac{P \xrightarrow{\underline{\alpha}} P'}{P+Q \xrightarrow{\underline{\alpha}} P'}$	Sum1	$\dfrac{P \xrightarrow{m,\alpha} P'}{P+Q \xrightarrow{m\cdot l,\alpha} P'}\ \underline{\tau} \notin \underline{\mathrm{I}}(Q)$
Sum2	$\dfrac{Q \xrightarrow{\underline{\alpha}} Q'}{P+Q \xrightarrow{\underline{\alpha}} Q'}$	Sum2	$\dfrac{Q \xrightarrow{n,\alpha} Q'}{P+Q \xrightarrow{n\cdot r,\alpha} Q'}\ \underline{\tau} \notin \underline{\mathrm{I}}(P)$
Rel	$\dfrac{P \xrightarrow{\underline{\alpha}} P'}{P[f] \xrightarrow{\underline{f(\alpha)}} P'[f]}$	Rel	$\dfrac{P \xrightarrow{m,\alpha} P'}{P[f] \xrightarrow{m,f(\alpha)} P'[f]}$
Res	$\dfrac{P \xrightarrow{\underline{\alpha}} P'}{P \setminus L \xrightarrow{\underline{\alpha}} P' \setminus L}\ \underline{\alpha} \notin L \cup \overline{L}$	Res	$\dfrac{P \xrightarrow{m,\alpha} P'}{P \setminus L \xrightarrow{m,\alpha} P' \setminus L}\ \alpha \notin L \cup \overline{L}$
Com1	$\dfrac{P \xrightarrow{\underline{\alpha}} P'}{P\|Q \xrightarrow{\underline{\alpha}} P'\|Q}$	Com1	$\dfrac{P \xrightarrow{m,\alpha} P'}{P\|Q \xrightarrow{m\cdot L,\alpha} P'\|Q}\ \underline{\mathbb{I}}_{[m]}(P) \cap \overline{\underline{\mathbb{I}}}(Q) = \emptyset$
Com2	$\dfrac{Q \xrightarrow{\underline{\alpha}} Q'}{P\|Q \xrightarrow{\underline{\alpha}} P\|Q'}$	Com2	$\dfrac{Q \xrightarrow{n,\alpha} Q'}{P\|Q \xrightarrow{n\cdot R,\alpha} P\|Q'}\ \underline{\mathbb{I}}_{[n]}(Q) \cap \overline{\underline{\mathbb{I}}}(P) = \emptyset$
Com3	$\dfrac{P \xrightarrow{\underline{a}} P' \quad Q \xrightarrow{\overline{\underline{a}}} Q'}{P\|Q \xrightarrow{\underline{\tau}} P'\|Q'}$	Com3	$\dfrac{P \xrightarrow{m,a} P' \quad Q \xrightarrow{n,\overline{a}} Q'}{P\|Q \xrightarrow{\langle m\cdot L,n\cdot R\rangle,\tau} P'\|Q'}$ $\underline{\mathbb{I}}_{[m]}(P) \cap \overline{\underline{\mathbb{I}}}(Q) = \emptyset$ and $\underline{\mathbb{I}}_{[n]}(Q) \cap \overline{\underline{\mathbb{I}}}(P) = \emptyset$
Con	$\dfrac{P \xrightarrow{\underline{\alpha}} P'}{C \xrightarrow{\underline{\alpha}} P'}\ C \stackrel{\text{def}}{=} P$	Con	$\dfrac{P \xrightarrow{m,\alpha} P'}{C \xrightarrow{m,\alpha} P'}\ C \stackrel{\text{def}}{=} P$

4 Prioritized Strong Bisimulation

In this section we present an equivalence relation for CCS^{prio} processes that is based on bisimulation [17]. Our aim is to characterize the largest congruence contained in the "naive" adaption of strong bisimulation [13] to our framework.

Definition 2 Naive Prioritized Strong Bisimulation. A symmetric relation $\mathcal{R} \subseteq \mathcal{P} \times \mathcal{P}$ is called *naive prioritized strong bisimulation* if for every $\langle P, Q\rangle \in \mathcal{R}$, $\gamma \in \mathcal{A}$, and $m \in \mathcal{L}oc$ the following condition holds.

$$P \xrightarrow{m,\gamma} P' \text{ implies } \exists Q', n.\ Q \xrightarrow{n,\gamma} Q' \text{ and } \langle P', Q'\rangle \in \mathcal{R}\ .$$

We write $P \simeq Q$ if there exists a naive prioritized strong bisimulation $\mathcal{R}$ such that $\langle P, Q\rangle \in \mathcal{R}$.

It is straightforward to establish that $\simeq$ is the *largest* naive prioritized strong bisimulation and that $\simeq$ is an equivalence relation. Unfortunately, $\simeq$ is *not* a congruence, which is a necessary requirement for an equivalence to be suitable for compositional reasoning. The lack of compositionality is demonstrated by the following example, which presents the traditional view of process algebras that "parallelism = nondeterminism." We have $a.\underline{b}.0 + \underline{b}.a.0 \simeq a.0 \,|\, \underline{b}.0$ but $(a.\underline{b}.0 + \underline{b}.a.0) \,|\, \overline{\underline{b}}.0 \not\simeq (a.0 \,|\, \underline{b}.0) \,|\, \overline{\underline{b}}.0$ since the latter can perform an a-transition while the corresponding a-transition of the former process is pre-empted because the right process in the summation can engage in a $\underline{\tau}$-transition.

The above observation is not surprising since the distribution of processes influences the pre-emption of transitions and, consequently, the bisimulation. Thus, in order to find the largest congruence relation $\simeq^+$ contained in $\simeq$ we have to take the *local* pre-emption of processes into account. In the following, we define ***prioritized strong bisimulation*** $\simeq^+$, which is indeed the largest congruence contained in $\simeq$.

Definition 3 Prioritized Strong Bisimulation. A symmetric relation $\mathcal{R} \subseteq \mathcal{P} \times \mathcal{P}$ is a ***prioritized strong bisimulation*** if for every $\langle P, Q \rangle \in \mathcal{R}$, $\alpha \in A$, $\underline{\alpha} \in \underline{A}$, and $m \in \mathcal{L}oc$ the following conditions hold.

1. $P \xrightarrow{\underline{\alpha}} P'$ implies $\exists Q'.\, Q \xrightarrow{\underline{\alpha}} Q'$ and $\langle P', Q' \rangle \in \mathcal{R}$.
2. $P \xrightarrow{m,\alpha} P'$ implies $\exists Q', n.\, Q \xrightarrow{n,\alpha} Q'$, $\underline{\mathbb{I}}_{[n]}(Q) \subseteq \underline{\mathbb{I}}_{[m]}(P)$, and $\langle P', Q' \rangle \in \mathcal{R}$.

We write $P \simeq^+ Q$ if there exists a prioritized strong bisimulation $\mathcal{R}$ such that $\langle P, Q \rangle \in \mathcal{R}$.

The difference between this definition and the definition of $\simeq$ is the additional requirement concerning the initial action sets, parameterized with the appropriate locations, in the condition for unprioritized transitions. Intuitively, the prioritized initial action set of a process with respect to some location, and not the location itself, is a measure of the pre-emptive power of the process relative to that location. Thus, the second condition of Definition 3 states that an unprioritized action α from some location m of the process P has to be matched by the same action from some location n of Q and that the pre-emptive power of Q with respect to n is at most as strong as the pre-emptive power of P with respect to m.

Proposition 4. *The relation $\simeq^+$ is a congruence, i.e. for all* $\mathsf{CCS}^{\mathsf{prio}}$ *contexts $C[X]$ we have: $P \simeq^+ Q$ implies $C[P] \simeq^+ C[Q]$.*

Theorem 5. *The congruence $\simeq^+$ is the* largest *congruence contained in $\simeq$.*

Axiomatization of $\simeq^+$

In this section we give an axiomatization of $\simeq^+$ for *finite* processes, i.e. processes that do not contain recursion. In order to develop the axiomatization, we add a new, binary summation operator $\oplus$ to the process algebra $\mathsf{CCS}^{\mathsf{prio}}$. This operator is called ***distributed summation*** and needed for giving an expansion axiom (cf. Axiom (E)). Its semantics is similar to + except that priorities on different sides of the operator are considered as incomparable.

Definition 6 Distributed Summation. The semantics of the new binary operator $\oplus$ on processes is defined by the following operational rules.

$$\underline{\text{iSum1}}\ \frac{P \xrightarrow{\alpha} P'}{P \oplus Q \xrightarrow{\underline{\alpha}} P'} \qquad \text{iSum1}\ \frac{P \xrightarrow{m,\alpha} P'}{P \oplus Q \xrightarrow{m\cdot L,\alpha} P'}$$

$$\underline{\text{iSum2}}\ \frac{Q \xrightarrow{\alpha} Q'}{P \oplus Q \xrightarrow{\underline{\alpha}} Q'} \qquad \text{iSum2}\ \frac{Q \xrightarrow{n,\alpha} Q'}{P \oplus Q \xrightarrow{n\cdot R,\alpha} Q'}$$

Table 3. Axiomatization of $\simeq^+$ (Part I)

(A1)	$x + y = y + x$	(iA1)	$x \oplus y = y \oplus x$
(A2)	$x + (y + z) = (x + y) + z$	(iA2)	$x \oplus (y \oplus z) = (x \oplus y) \oplus z$
(A3)	$x + x = x$	(iA3)	$x \oplus x = x$
(A4)	$x + 0 = x$	(iA4)	$x \oplus 0 = x$

(P) $\underline{\tau}.x + \alpha.y = \underline{\tau}.x$

(E) $P \equiv \bigoplus_i \sum_j \gamma_{ij}.P_{ij}$ and $Q \equiv \bigoplus_k \sum_l \delta_{kl}.Q_{kl}$ implies

$$\begin{aligned} P\,|\,Q = {} & \\ & \textstyle\bigoplus_i \sum_j (\gamma_{ij}.(P_{ij}\,|\,Q) + \sum_k \sum_l \{\tau.(P_{ij}\,|\,Q_{kl}) \mid \gamma_{ij} = \overline{\delta}_{kl},\ \gamma_{ij}, \delta_{kl} \in A\} \\ & \qquad\qquad + \textstyle\sum_k \sum_l \{\underline{\tau}.(P_{ij}\,|\,Q_{kl}) \mid \gamma_{ij} = \overline{\delta}_{kl},\ \gamma_{ij}, \delta_{kl} \in \underline{A}\}) \oplus \\ & \textstyle\bigoplus_k \sum_l (\delta_{kl}.(P\,|\,Q_{kl}) + \sum_i \sum_j \{\tau.(P_{ij}\,|\,Q_{kl}) \mid \gamma_{ij} = \overline{\delta}_{kl},\ \gamma_{ij}, \delta_{kl} \in A\} \\ & \qquad\qquad + \textstyle\sum_i \sum_j \{\underline{\tau}.(P_{ij}\,|\,Q_{kl}) \mid \gamma_{ij} = \overline{\delta}_{kl},\ \gamma_{ij}, \delta_{kl} \in \underline{A}\}) \end{aligned}$$

(Res1)	$0 \setminus L = 0$		(Rel1)	$0[f] = 0$
(Res2)	$(\gamma.x) \setminus L = 0$	$(\gamma \in L \cup \overline{L})$	(Rel2)	$(\gamma.x)[f] = f(\gamma).(x[f])$
(Res3)	$(\gamma.x) \setminus L = \gamma.(x \setminus L)$	$(\gamma \notin L \cup \overline{L})$	(Rel3)	$(x + y)[f] = x[f] + y[f]$
(Res4)	$(x + y) \setminus L = (x \setminus L) + (y \setminus L)$		(iRel3)	$(x \oplus y)[f] = x[f] \oplus y[f]$
(iRes4)	$(x \oplus y) \setminus L = (x \setminus L) \oplus (y \setminus L)$			

Now, we turn to the axiom system for prioritized strong bisimulation. We write $\vdash P = Q$ if P can be rewritten to Q using the axioms in the Tables 3 and 4. Axioms (S2) and (S3) involve side conditions. The relation $\sqsubseteq_i$ is the precongruence on finite processes generated from the axioms (iC1), (iC2), and (iC3) using the laws of inequational reasoning. The axioms in Table 3 are basically those presented in [6] augmented with the corresponding axioms for the incomparable summation operator. Moreover, the expansion axiom has been adapted for our

Table 4. Axiomatization of $\simeq^+$ (Part II) and axiomatization of $\sqsubseteq_{\mathrm{i}}$

(D1) $(x \oplus \alpha.y) + \beta.z = (x + \beta.z) \oplus \alpha.y$	(iC1) $\underline{\alpha}.x \sqsubseteq_{\mathrm{i}} \underline{\alpha}.y$
(D2) $(x \oplus \underline{\alpha}.y) + \beta.z = x \oplus (x + \underline{\alpha}.y + \beta.z)$	(iC2) $\mathbf{0} \sqsubseteq_{\mathrm{i}} \nu.x \quad (\nu \in \mathcal{A} \setminus \{\underline{\tau}\})$
(D3) $(x \oplus y) + \underline{\alpha}.z = (x + \underline{\alpha}.z) \oplus (y + \underline{\alpha}.z)$	(iC3) $\alpha.x \sqsubseteq_{\mathrm{i}} \mathbf{0}$
(Ic1) $\underline{\alpha}.x + \underline{\beta}.y = \underline{\alpha}.x \oplus \underline{\beta}.y$	
(Ic2) $\underline{\alpha}.x + y = (\underline{\alpha}.x + y) \oplus \underline{\alpha}.x$	
(S1) $(x + \underline{\alpha}.y) \oplus (x' + \underline{\alpha}.y') = (x + \underline{\alpha}.y + \underline{\alpha}.y') \oplus (x' + \underline{\alpha}.y + \underline{\alpha}.y')$	
(S2) $(x + \alpha.z) \oplus (y + \alpha.z) = (x + \alpha.z) \oplus y$	$(\vdash x \sqsubseteq_{\mathrm{i}} y)$
(S3) $x \oplus y = x + y$	$(\vdash x =_{\mathrm{i}} y)$

algebra (cf. Axiom (E) where $\sum$ is the indexed version of $+$ and $\bigoplus$ the indexed version of the new summation operator $\oplus$). The axioms in Table 4 are new and show how we may "restructure" locations. They deal with the ***distributivity*** of the summation operators (Axioms (D1), (D2), and (D3)), the ***interchangeability*** of the summation operators (Axioms (Ic1) and (Ic2)), and the ***saturation*** of locations (Axioms (S1), (S2), and (S3)), respectively.

Lemma 7. *Let $\vdash P \sqsubseteq_{\mathrm{i}} Q$ for some processes $P, Q \in \mathcal{P}$. Then, $\mathbb{I}(P) \subseteq \mathbb{I}(Q)$ holds. Moreover, $\underline{\tau} \in \mathrm{I}(P)$ if and only if $\underline{\tau} \in \mathrm{I}(Q)$.*

We write $\vdash P =_{\mathrm{i}} Q$ iff $\vdash P \sqsubseteq_{\mathrm{i}} Q$ and $\vdash Q \sqsubseteq_{\mathrm{i}} P$. Considering the meaning of the side conditions as made precise in Lemma 7, it is immediately clear that the Axioms (S2) and (S3) are sound. In order to prove our axiomatization complete, we introduce a notion of *normal form* of processes that is based on the following definition.

Definition 8 Summation Form. A process $P \in \mathcal{P}$ is in ***summation form*** if it has the form $P \equiv \bigoplus_{i=1}^{m} \sum_{j=1}^{n_i} \gamma_{ij}.P_{ij}$ where $m, n_i \in \mathbb{N}$ and the processes P_{ij} are again in summation form. Per definition, $\mathbf{0}$ is in summation form.

Intuitively, P is distributed throughout m incomparable locations which themselves consist of n_i comparable locations, $1 \leq i \leq m$. Now, we are able to define *normal forms*.

Definition 9 Normal Form. Let $P \equiv \bigoplus_{i=1}^{m} \sum_{j=1}^{n_i} \gamma_{ij}.P_{ij}$ be in summation form. We define $\underline{\gamma}_{i*} =_{\mathrm{df}} \{\gamma_{ij} \mid 1 \leq j \leq n_i\} \cap \underline{A}$. The process P is said to be in *normal form* if the following properties hold.

1. $\emptyset \subset L \subseteq \mathbb{I}(P)$ implies $\exists i. \underline{\gamma}_{i*} = L$.
2. $\gamma_{ij} = \underline{\tau}$ and $\gamma_{kl} \in A$ imply $i \neq k$.
3. $\gamma_{ij} = \gamma_{kl} = \underline{\alpha}$ implies $\exists j'. P_{ij'} \equiv P_{kl}$ and $\gamma_{ij'} = \underline{\alpha}$.

4. $i \neq k$ implies $\underline{\gamma}_{i*} \neq \underline{\gamma}_{k*}$.
5. $\gamma_{ij}.P_{ij} \equiv \gamma_{kl}.P_{kl}$, $\gamma_{ij} \in A$, and $i \neq k$ imply $\underline{\gamma}_{i*} \not\subset \underline{\gamma}_{j*}$.

Proposition 10. *If P is a finite process, then there exists a normal form N such that $\vdash N = P$.*

Rewriting a process in its normal form requires restructuring its locations. After this is done, standard techniques used in CCS (cf. [13]) can be applied in order to show our axiomatization complete.

Theorem 11 Soundness & Completeness. *For finite processes $P, Q \in \mathcal{P}$ we have $\vdash P = Q$ if and only if $P \simeq^{+} Q$.*

5 Prioritized Observational Congruence

The behavioral congruence developed in the previous section is too strong for verifying systems in practice, as it requires that two equivalent terms match each other's transitions exactly, even those labeled by internal actions. In this section we remedy this problem by developing a semantic congruence that abstracts away from internal transitions. Our approach follows the lines of [15, 13]. We start off with the definition of a naive prioritized weak bisimulation which abstracts from internal actions. This relation is an adaption of observational equivalence [13].

Definition 12 Naive Weak Transition Relation. We define:

1. $\hat{\gamma} =_{\mathrm{df}} \epsilon$ if $\gamma \in \{\underline{\tau}, \tau\}$ and $\hat{\gamma} =_{\mathrm{df}} \gamma$, otherwise.
2. $\stackrel{\epsilon}{\Longrightarrow}_{\times} =_{\mathrm{df}} (\stackrel{\underline{\tau}}{\rightarrow} \cup \{\stackrel{m,\tau}{\longrightarrow} \mid m \in \mathcal{L}oc\})^{*}$
3. $\stackrel{\underline{\alpha}}{\Longrightarrow}_{\times} =_{\mathrm{df}} \stackrel{\epsilon}{\Longrightarrow}_{\times} \circ \stackrel{\underline{\alpha}}{\rightarrow} \circ \stackrel{\epsilon}{\Longrightarrow}_{\times}$
4. $\stackrel{m,\alpha}{\Longrightarrow}_{\times} =_{\mathrm{df}} \stackrel{\epsilon}{\Longrightarrow}_{\times} \circ \stackrel{m,\alpha}{\longrightarrow} \circ \stackrel{\epsilon}{\Longrightarrow}_{\times}$

Definition 13 Naive Prioritized Weak Bisimulation. A symmetric relation $\mathcal{R} \subseteq \mathcal{P} \times \mathcal{P}$ is a *naive prioritized weak bisimulation* if for every $\langle P, Q \rangle \in \mathcal{R}$, $\gamma \in \mathcal{A}$, and $m \in \mathcal{L}oc$ the following condition holds.

$$P \stackrel{m,\gamma}{\longrightarrow} P' \text{ implies } \exists Q', n.\, Q \stackrel{n,\hat{\gamma}}{\Longrightarrow}_{\times} Q' \text{ and } \langle P', Q' \rangle \in \mathcal{R}\,.$$

We write $P \approx_{\times} Q$ if there exists a naive prioritized weak bisimulation $\mathcal{R}$ such that $\langle P, Q \rangle \in \mathcal{R}$.

It is fairly easy to see that $\approx_{\times}$ is not a congruence for CCS^{prio}. On the other hand, it reflects an intuitive approach to abstracting away from internal computation, and consequently we devote the rest of this section to characterizing the largest congruence contained in this relation. To do so, we first redefine the weak transition relation as follows.

Definition 14 Prioritized Weak Transition Relation. For $L, M \subseteq \underline{A} \setminus \{\underline{\tau}\}$ we define the following notations.

1. $\hat{\underline{\tau}} =_{\mathrm{df}} \underline{\epsilon}$, $\hat{\underline{a}} =_{\mathrm{df}} \underline{a}$, $\hat{\tau} =_{\mathrm{df}} \epsilon$, and $\hat{a} =_{\mathrm{df}} a$.
2. $P \overset{m,\alpha}{\underset{L}{\longrightarrow}} P'$ iff $P \xrightarrow{m,\alpha} P'$ and $\mathbb{I}_{[m]}(P) \subseteq L$.
3. $\overset{\underline{\epsilon}}{\Longrightarrow} =_{\mathrm{df}} (\overset{\underline{\tau}}{\rightarrow} \cup \{\overset{m,\tau}{\underset{\bullet}{\longrightarrow}} \mid m \in \mathcal{L}oc\})^*$
4. $\overset{\underline{\alpha}}{\Longrightarrow} =_{\mathrm{df}} \overset{\underline{\epsilon}}{\Longrightarrow} \circ \overset{\underline{\alpha}}{\rightarrow} \circ \overset{\underline{\epsilon}}{\Longrightarrow}$
5. $\overset{\epsilon}{\underset{L}{\Longrightarrow}} =_{\mathrm{df}} (\overset{\underline{\tau}}{\rightarrow} \cup \{\overset{m,\tau}{\underset{L}{\longrightarrow}} \mid m \in \mathcal{L}oc\})^*$
6. $P \overset{m,\alpha}{\underset{L,M}{\Longrightarrow}} P'$ iff $\exists P'', P'''. P \overset{\epsilon}{\underset{L}{\Longrightarrow}} P'' \overset{m,\alpha}{\underset{L}{\longrightarrow}} P''' \overset{\underline{\epsilon}}{\Longrightarrow} P'$ and $\mathbb{I}(P'') \subseteq M$.

Intuitively, $P \overset{m,\alpha}{\underset{L}{\longrightarrow}} P'$ means that P can evolve to P' by performing action α from location m and the pre-emptive power of P at location m is at most L. Recall that the prioritized initial action set of a process (with respect to a location) is a measure of its pre-emptive power. Actually, there are two slightly different views of pre-emption which are encoded in the sets L and M in the definition of $P \overset{m,\alpha}{\underset{L,M}{\Longrightarrow}} P'$, respectively. Whereas L is concerned with the influence of the environment, i.e. a parallel context, on actions performed on the path from P to P''', the set M reflects the impact of P'' on potential synchronization partners (cf. Rule Com3). Note that the definition of $P \overset{\epsilon}{\underset{L}{\Longrightarrow}} P'$ corresponds with our intuition that internal actions, and, therefore, their locations are unobservable. Additionally, a parallel context of P is not influenced by internal actions performed by P since priorities arising from different sides of the parallel operator are incomparable. Therefore, the parameter M is unnecessary in the definition of the relation $\overset{\epsilon}{\underset{L}{\Longrightarrow}}$.

Definition 15 Prioritized Weak Bisimulation. A symmetric relation $\mathcal{R} \subseteq \mathcal{P} \times \mathcal{P}$ is a ***prioritized weak bisimulation*** if for every $\langle P, Q \rangle \in \mathcal{R}$, $\alpha \in A$, $\underline{\alpha} \in \underline{A}$, and $m \in \mathcal{L}oc$ the following conditions hold.

1. $\exists Q', Q''. Q \overset{\underline{\epsilon}}{\Longrightarrow} Q'' \overset{\underline{\epsilon}}{\Longrightarrow} Q'$, $\mathbb{I}(Q'') \subseteq \mathbb{I}(P)$, and $\langle P, Q' \rangle \in \mathcal{R}$.
2. $P \overset{\underline{\alpha}}{\rightarrow} P'$ implies $\exists Q'. Q \overset{\hat{\underline{\alpha}}}{\Longrightarrow} Q'$ and $\langle P', Q' \rangle \in \mathcal{R}$.
3. $P \xrightarrow{m,\alpha} P'$ implies $\exists Q', n. Q \overset{n,\hat{\alpha}}{\underset{L,M}{\Longrightarrow}} Q'$, $L = \mathbb{I}_{[m]}(P)$, $M = \mathbb{I}(P)$, and $\langle P', Q' \rangle \in \mathcal{R}$.

We write $P \underset{\sim}{\approx} Q$ if there exists a prioritized weak bisimulation $\mathcal{R}$ such that $\langle P, Q \rangle \in \mathcal{R}$.

From this definition, we may directly conclude that $\underset{\sim}{\approx}$ is the *largest* prioritized weak bisimulation, and that $\underset{\sim}{\approx}$ is an equivalence relation. The first condition of Definition 15 guarantees that prioritized weak bisimulation is compositional with respect to the parallel operator. Its necessity is best illustrated by the following example. The processes $P \overset{\mathrm{def}}{=} \underline{\tau}.\underline{a}.0$ and $Q \overset{\mathrm{def}}{=} \underline{a}.0$ would be considered as equivalent if the first condition would be absent. However, the context $C[X] \overset{\mathrm{def}}{=} X \mid (\overline{\underline{a}}.0 + b.0)$ is able to distinguish them.

Proposition 16. *The equivalence relation $\underline{\approx}$ is a congruence with respect to all* CCS^{prio} *operators except the summation operator* $+$, *the distributed summation operator* $\oplus$, *and recursion.*

In contrast to [15], the summation fix presented in [13] is not sufficient in order to achieve a congruence relation. E.g., let $C \stackrel{\text{def}}{=} \underline{\tau}.D$ and $D \stackrel{\text{def}}{=} \tau.C$. Now, define $P \stackrel{\text{def}}{=} \tau.C$ and $Q \stackrel{\text{def}}{=} \underline{\tau}.D$. By Definition 15 we may observe $P \underline{\approx} Q$, but $P + a.0 \not\underline{\approx} Q + a.0$ since the former can perform an a-action whereas the latter cannot. It turns out that we have to require that observationally congruent processes must have the same initial actions. This requirement is stronger than the first condition of Definition 15.

Definition 17 Prioritized Observational Congruence. We define $P \underline{\approx}^+ Q$ if for all $\alpha \in A$, $\underline{\alpha} \in \underline{A}$, and $m \in \mathcal{L}oc$ the following conditions hold.

1. $\underline{\mathbb{I}}(P) = \underline{\mathbb{I}}(Q)$
2. $P \xrightarrow{\underline{\alpha}} P'$ implies $\exists Q'.\, Q \stackrel{\underline{\alpha}}{\Longrightarrow} Q'$ and $P' \underline{\approx} Q'$.
3. $P \xrightarrow{m,\alpha} P'$ implies $\exists Q', n.\, Q \stackrel{n,\alpha}{\underset{L,M}{\Longrightarrow}} Q'$, $L = \mathbb{I}_{[m]}(P)$, $M = \mathbb{I}(P)$, and $P' \underline{\approx} Q'$.
4. $Q \xrightarrow{\underline{\alpha}} Q'$ implies $\exists P'.\, P \stackrel{\underline{\alpha}}{\Longrightarrow} P'$ and $P' \underline{\approx} Q'$.
5. $Q \xrightarrow{m,\alpha} Q'$ implies $\exists P', n.\, P \stackrel{n,\alpha}{\underset{L,M}{\Longrightarrow}} P'$, $L = \mathbb{I}_{[m]}(Q)$, $M = \mathbb{I}(Q)$, and $P' \underline{\approx} Q'$.

Theorem 18. *The relation $\underline{\approx}^+$ is the largest congruence contained in $\approx_\times$.*

The proof of this theorem makes use of the presence of the distributed summation operator in CCS^{prio}.

6 Example

In this section we demonstrate the utility of CCS^{prio} for the verification of distributed systems using an example involving an architecture scheme found in many of today's computers.

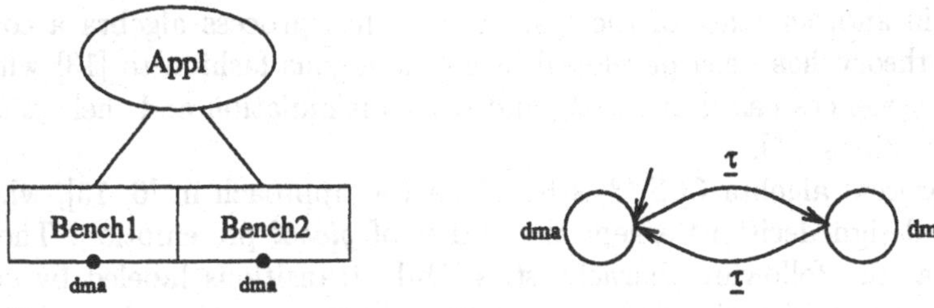

Fig. 2. Example system and its semantics

Our example system consists of an application which receives and writes data from two memory benches (cf. Fig. 2, left hand side). In order to improve the efficiency in a computer system each bench is connected to a direct-memory-access (DMA) controller. To overcome the low speed of most memory modules, the application Appl works alternately with each memory bench. We model Appl in CCS^{prio} by $\texttt{Appl} \stackrel{\text{def}}{=} \underline{\texttt{fetch1}}.\underline{\texttt{fetch2}}.\texttt{Appl}$. Each memory bench Bench1 and Bench2 is continuously able to serve the application or to allow the external DMA controller to access the memory via the channel dma. However, if a memory bench has to decide between both activities, then it chooses the former since the progress of the application is considered as more important. Consequently, we define $\texttt{Bench1} \stackrel{\text{def}}{=} \overline{\underline{\texttt{fetch1}}}.\texttt{Bench1} + \texttt{dma}.\texttt{Bench1}$ and $\texttt{Bench2} \stackrel{\text{def}}{=} \overline{\underline{\texttt{fetch2}}}.\texttt{Bench2} + \texttt{dma}.\texttt{Bench2}$. The overall system Sys is given by $\texttt{Sys} \stackrel{\text{def}}{=} (\texttt{Appl} \,|\, \texttt{Bench1} \,|\, \texttt{Bench2}) \setminus \{\texttt{fetch1}, \texttt{fetch2}\}$. Since the application uses the memory cells alternately, the DMA is expected to be allowed to access the free memory bench. Therefore, the specification is simply $\texttt{Spec} \stackrel{\text{def}}{=} \texttt{dma}.\texttt{Spec}$. The CCS^{prio} semantics of Sys is given in Fig. 2, right hand side, where we abstract from the locations of the action dma. It is easy to see that the symmetric closure of

$$\{\langle \texttt{Spec}, \texttt{Sys}\rangle, \langle \texttt{Spec}, (\underline{\texttt{fetch2}}.\texttt{Appl} \,|\, \texttt{Bench1} \,|\, \texttt{Bench2}) \setminus \{\texttt{fetch1}, \texttt{fetch2}\}\rangle\}$$

is a prioritized weak bisimulation. Note that Condition (1) of Definition 15 is trivially satisfied since Spec and Sys do not contain any visible prioritized actions. Therefore, we obtain $\texttt{Spec} \approx \texttt{Sys}$ as expected. However, in the traditional approach [6, 15] the dma-loops in the labeled transition system of Sys would be missing, and Sys would not be observationally equivalent to Spec.

7 Discussion and Related Work

Several proposals have been made for extending traditional process algebras with priorities. They differ in the aspects of computation, such as interrupts [1], programming constructs like the PRIALT construct of occam [5, 12], or real-time [4], that they aim to capture.

An extension of CCS [13] with priorities has been proposed in [6], where priorities are assigned to actions in a *globally dynamic* way, i.e. in one state of a system action α may have priority over action β while the situation may be converse in another state of the system. For that process algebra a complete semantic theory has been developed in an analogous fashion to [13] which includes congruences based on strong and weak bisimulation and their axiomatic characterizations [15].

Our process algebra CCS^{prio} is based on the approach in [6, 15], where we adopt all design decisions except the notion of *global* pre-emption. Therefore, CCS^{prio} has the following characteristics. Only transitions labeled by complementary actions with the same priority may engage in a synchronization. As in [6], we consider actions with different priorities as *different* channels. This is sufficient for most cases occurring in practice [8] and avoids that priorities values have to be adjusted in case of communication (cf. [4, 10]). The strong relation of CCS^{prio} to the process algebra proposed in [6, 15] can be made precise by the following fact. If we globalize pre-emption in our framework by defining $[m] =_{df} \mathcal{Loc}$ for all $m \in \mathcal{Loc}$, our operational semantics and our behavioral relations reduce to the corresponding notions presented in [6, 15].

For a comparison with our work it is of importance that all the above mentioned traditional approaches are provided with a semantics which deals with *global* pre-emption. In contrast, we consider a notion of *local* pre-emption. This idea is also presented in [10], where a CSP-based language is extended with priorities. However, this process algebra suffers from a complicated semantics, especially for the hiding operator. The authors only conjecture that their strong bisimulation is a congruence. They do not provide an axiomatization for their equivalence and do not present a theory for observational congruence. Also Prasad's *Calculus of Broadcasting Systems with Priorities* (PCBS) [18] deals with a distributed notion of priorities. For PCBS a nice semantic theory based on bisimulation has been developed. However, our process algebra CCS^{prio} is concerned with a different model for communication.

We close this section with some remarks about our notion of strong and weak bisimulation. Since our semantic theory reflects local pre-emption, locations are implicitly occurring in our semantic equivalences. However, in contrast to [3] locations are not explicitly considered in our bisimulations. Our objective is not to observe locations but to observe local pre-emption which is necessary for causal reasoning in process algebras with priorities.

8 Conclusions and Future Work

In this paper we have presented a process algebra, CCS^{prio}, with distributed priorities. The key idea for this algebra is to take the distribution of the considered system into account for defining a notion of *local* pre-emption. We have developed a semantic theory for this algebra and have shown its suitability by an example. However, it remains to show how our prioritized bisimulations can be computed before implementing CCS^{prio} in an automated verification tool [9]. In order to apply standard algorithms [16] the bisimulations have to be characterized using a transition relation that is not parameterized with prioritized initial action sets. Moreover, we intend to axiomatize prioritized observational congruence.

References

1. J.C.M. Baeten, J.A. Bergstra, and J.W. Klop. Syntax and defining equations for an interrupt mechanism in process algebra. *Fundamenta Informaticae IX*, pages 127–168, 1986.
2. E. Best and M. Koutny. Petri net semantics of priority systems. *Theoretical Computer Science*, 96:175–215, 1992.

3. G. Boudol, I. Castellani, M. Hennessy, and A. Kiehn. Observing localities. *Theoretical Computer Science*, 114(1):31–61, June 1993.
4. P. Brémonde-Grégoire, I. Lee, and R. Gerber. ACSR: An algebra of communicating shared resources with dense time and priorities. In E. Best, editor, *CONCUR '93*, volume 715 of *Lecture Notes in Computer Science*, pages 417–431, Hildesheim, Germany, August 1993. Springer-Verlag.
5. J. Camilleri and G. Winskel. CCS with priority choice. *Information and Computation*, 116(1):26–37, January 1995.
6. R. Cleaveland and M.C.B. Hennessy. Priorities in process algebra. *Information and Computation*, 87(1/2):58–77, July/August 1990.
7. R. Cleaveland, G. Lüttgen, and V. Natarajan. A process algebra with distributed priorities. Technical Report TR-96-02, North Carolina State University, March 1996.
8. R. Cleaveland, G. Lüttgen, V. Natarajan, and S. Sims. Priorities for modeling and verifying distributed systems. In T. Margaria and B. Steffen, editors, *Second International Workshop on Tools and Algorithms for the Construction and Analysis of Systems (TACAS '96)*, volume 1055 of *Lecture Notes in Computer Science*, pages 278–297, Passau, Germany, March 1996. Springer-Verlag.
9. R. Cleaveland, J. Parrow, and B. Steffen. The Concurrency Workbench: A semantics-based tool for the verification of finite-state systems. *ACM Transactions on Programming Languages and Systems*, 15(1):36–72, January 1993.
10. H. Hansson and F. Orava. A process calculus with incomparable priorities. In *Proceedings of the North American Process Algebra Workshop*, Workshops in Computing, pages 43–64, Stony Brook, New York, August 1992. Springer-Verlag.
11. C.A.R. Hoare. *Communicating Sequential Processes*. Prentice-Hall, London, 1985.
12. C.-T. Jensen. *Prioritized and Independent Actions in Distributed Computer Systems*. PhD thesis, Aarhus University, August 1994.
13. R. Milner. *Communication and Concurrency*. Prentice-Hall, London, 1989.
14. U. Montanari and D. Yankelevich. A parametric approach to localities. In W. Kuich, editor, *Automata, Languages and Programming (ICALP '92)*, volume 623 of *Lecture Notes in Computer Science*, pages 617–628, Vienna, July 1992. Springer-Verlag.
15. V. Natarajan, L. Christoff, I. Christoff, and R. Cleaveland. Priorities and abstraction in process algebra. In P.S. Thiagarajan, editor, *Foundations of Software Technology and Theoretical Computer Science*, volume 880 of *Lecture Notes in Computer Science*, pages 217–230, Madras, India, December 1994. Springer-Verlag.
16. R. Paige and R.E. Tarjan. Three partition refinement algorithms. *SIAM Journal of Computing*, 16(6):973–989, December 1987.
17. D.M.R. Park. Concurrency and automata on infinite sequences. In *Proceedings of 5th G.I. Conference on Theoretical Computer Science*, volume 104 of *Lecture Notes in Computer Science*, pages 167–183. Springer-Verlag, 1980.
18. K. V. S. Prasad. Broadcasting with priority. In *Proceedings of the 5th European Symposium on Programming*, volume 788 of *Lecture Notes in Computer Science*, pages 469–484, Edinburgh, U.K., April 1994. Springer-Verlag.

Symbolic Transition Graph with Assignment*

Huimin Lin
Laboratory for Computer Science
Institute of Software, Chinese Academy of Sciences
P.O Box 8718, Beijing 100080
E-mail: lhm@ios.ac.cn

Abstract

A new model for message–passing processes is proposed which generalizes the notion of symbolic transition graph as introduced in [HL95], by allowing *assignments* to be carried in transitions. The main advantage of this generalization is that a wider class of processes can be represented as finite state graphs. Two kinds of operational semantics, ground and symbolic, are given to such graphs. On top of them both ground and symbolic bisimulations are defined and are shown to agree with each other. An algorithm is also presented which computes bisimulation formulae for finite state symbolic transition graphs with assignments, in terms of the greatest solutions of *predicate equation systems*.

1 Introduction

Transition graphs are a popular semantic model for concurrency. The theory of bisimulation for such graphs has been well developed [Mil89]. Efficient bisimulation checking algorithms for finite state graphs have been proposed and are at the hearts of many existing verification tools for concurrency ([CPS89, GLZ89, SV89], among others). Traditional transition graphs use unstructured atomic actions as labels and, as a consequence, when non-trivial data domains are involved even very simple processes would generate infinite state graphs, thus beyond the scope of the existing tools. For example consider the process C defined by

$$C \Leftarrow c?x.d!x.C$$

where c, d are channel names and x ranges over integers. The standard transition graph for such a simple process is in fact infinite branching, because C has a transition $c?n$ for each integer n (Figure 1, left). This is somehow counter-intuitive, since all C can do is repeatedly read (input) an integer from c then send (output) it along d, so conceptually only *two* actions are needed in the description of its behaviour. Of course these actions are more complex in nature

*Supported by grants from the President Fund of Chinese Academy of Sciences, the National Science Foundation of China, and EU KIT 119 project SYMSEM.

Figure 1: Traditional and symbolic graphs for C

as they bear internal structures: an input action should indicate the channel to read from as well the variable to store the received value, and similarly for an output action.

With such intuition in mind the notion of *symbolic transition graph* (STG for short) was advocated in [HL95]. In a STG each node is associated with a set of free (data) variables and each transition is labeled by an abstract action guarded by a boolean "trigger". Many processes with infinite state transition graphs are indeed symbolically finite state. For example the STG for the process C has only two states, as pictured in the right of Figure 1 where the trivial boolean guard *true* has been omitted. Based on such symbolic transition systems a theory of *symbolic bisimulation* has been developed which precisely captures the standard notion of bisimulation. An algorithm is also presented which, when given two finite state symbolic graphs, computes a characteristic boolean formula for them, namely they are bisimilar if and only if the formula evaluates to *true*.

But still many intuitively simple processes can not be pictured as finite STGs. For example given the following definition

$$P(x) \Leftarrow c!x.P(x+1)$$

the process $P(0)$ can first output, along channel c, the integer 0, then 1, 2, , 3 .... The STG for $P(x)$ has countably many states representing $P(x+1)$, $P(x+2)$, $P(x+3)$, ..., with edges $P(x+n) \overset{true,c!x+n}{\longmapsto} P(x+n+1)$ for $n \geq 0$.

The main purpose of this paper is to generalize the notion of symbolic transition graph so that processes like $P(x)$ above can be associated with finite state graphs. This is achieved by introducing *assignments* into labels. An edge now takes the form $n \overset{b,\overline{x}:=\overline{e},\alpha}{\longmapsto} n'$, where, besides a boolean condition b and an abstract action α, there is also an assignment $\overline{x} := \overline{e}$. Roughly it means if b is evaluated to *true* at node n then the action α can be fired, and, after the transition, the free variables $\overline{x}$ at node n' will have the values of $\overline{e}$ *evaluated at* n. With such extension the graph for $P(0)$ has only two nodes, as depicted in the left of Figure 2 (where the trivial boolean condition *true* has been omitted from the edges). We call such a graph *symbolic transition graph with assignment* (STGA for short). Note that STG is a special case of STGA with trivial assignment (identity mapping).

In a traditional transition graph each node denotes a unique process (closed

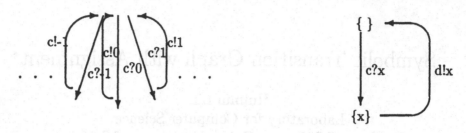

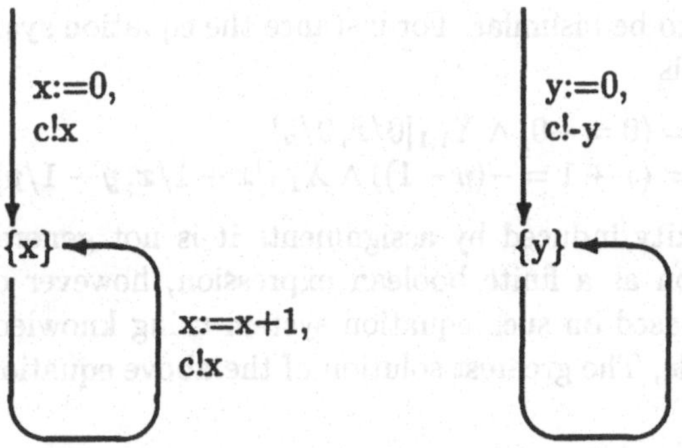

Figure 2: Symbolic transition graphs with assignments

term). But a node in a STGA has a set of free variables, leaving room for different interpretations. Given a STGA a *state* consists of a node n together with an evaluation (or *environment*) ρ mapping variables to values. At a state n_ρ one can use ρ to evaluate the outgoing edges at n, resulting a ground transition. As an example let us call m the node with free variable $\{x\}$ in the left graph of Figure 2 and let $\rho_i(x) = i$ for integer i. Then we have the following ground transitions:

$$m_{\rho_0} \xrightarrow{c!1} m_{\rho_1} \xrightarrow{c!2} m_{\rho_2} \xrightarrow{c!3} m_{\rho_3} \xrightarrow{c!4} \cdots$$

Note that here the changes of states are caused not only by performing actions $c!1$ and $c!2 \ldots$, but also by *modifying the value of the state variable x*: in the first transition the value of x changes from 0 to 1, and in the second from 1 to 2, *etc.* In this way a STGA is interpreted as a traditional transition graph whose nodes are the states of the STGA and edges the ground transitions, so the notion of (ground) bisimulation can be defined over states in the standard way.

A STGA can also be given a more abstract interpretation using *terms*. A *term* is a pair n_σ where n is a node in the graph and σ is a substitution. Accordingly, an edge can be interpreted as symbolic transitions between terms. For example, the edge $m \overset{true,x:=x+1,c!x}{\longmapsto} m$ gives rise to the symbolic transitions $m_{[x/x]} \xrightarrow{true,c!x+1} m_{[x+1/x]}$, $m_{[x+1/x]} \xrightarrow{true,c!x+1+1} m_{[x+1+1/x]}$, *etc.* In this way a STGA can be interpreted as a symbolic transition system between open terms. In the sequel we will often write (n, σ) more succinctly as n_σ. On top of the symbolic interpretation the notion of symbolic bisimulation can be defined in the spirit of [HL95]. One of the main results of this paper shows that these two notions of bisimulation in fact coincide.

By introducing assignments into edges many (even symbolically) infinite state transition systems can be represented by finite state STGAs, which opens the possibility of computing (symbolic) bisimulations for such systems. In this paper we present an algorithm which, when given a pair of STGAs, returns a predicate equation system whose greatest solution characterizes the most general condition for the two STGAs to be bisimilar. For instance the equation system for the two STGAs in Figure 2 is

$$X_{0,0} = (0 = -0) \wedge X_{1,1}[0/x, 0/y]$$
$$X_{1,1} = (x+1 = -(y-1)) \wedge X_{1,1}[x+1/x, y-1/y]$$

Due to the complexity induced by assignments it is not generally possible to compute the solution as a finite boolean expression, however one can reason about bisimilarity based on such equation system using knowledge about data domain. For example, The greatest solution of the above equations amounts to: for any $n \geq 0$

$$(x\underbrace{+1+\ldots+1}_{n} = -(y\underbrace{-1-\ldots-1}_{n}))[0,0/x,y],$$

which can be easily verified using elementary knowledge about integers.

The rest of this section is devoted to the discussion of related work. STGA is formally defined in the next section. Section 3 gives operational semantics and defines both ground and symbolic bisimulations. In section 4 the notion of predicate equation systems is introduced, followed by an algorithm for generating such equation systems from STGAs. Finally, concluding remarks are drawn in Section 5 where further research directions are also outlined.

Related Work Symbolic transition graph with assignment is a direct generalization of symbolic transition graph, first advocated in [HL95]. The notion of symbolic bisimulation is inherited from that paper. Ground bisimulation is defined on terms there, while it is defined over *states* in this paper which reflects more closely the intuition of computation.

Data independent processes are studies in [JP92] where tests on data are not allowed and data expressions are restricted to single data values or variables. With the help of "schematic variables" checking (early) bisimulation for finite state data independent processes can be reduced to that for finite state pure processes. In [CR94] a theory of *abstract interpretations* is developed for value–passing processes, the idea being to map (large or infinite) value spaces down to (small) "abstract value" spaces and instantiate data variables over the abstract value space. This approach relies on the existence of such abstraction functions. [DHG95] proposes techniques for model checking a class of problems with (small) control parts and (large) data parts, by instantiating the control variables to obtain an intermediate description of the systems and perform model checking at such intermediate level. [HI93] considers a process language with assignment and builds a denotational model for testing equivalence. [Sch94] proposes *parameterised graphs* and contains separate algorithms for calculating each of the iterative approximations to strong bisimulation.

2 Symbolic Transition Graph with Assignment

Let ι range over a set of *base types*. We presuppose the following syntactic categories:

$v, \ldots \in Val_\iota$: a set of data values
$x, \ldots \in DVar_\iota$: a countable set of data variables
$e, \ldots \in DExp_\iota$: a set of data expressions
$b, \ldots \in BExp$: a set of boolean expressions
$c, \ldots \in Chan$: a set of channel names

It is assumed that both Val_ι and $DVar_\iota$ are included in $DExp_\iota$, and that $e = e' \in BExp$ for any $e, e' \in DExp_\iota$. $BExp$ is equipped with the usual operators $\wedge, \vee, \neg, \Rightarrow$ and $\forall$.

An *evaluation* $\rho \in Eval$ is a type-respecting mapping from *Var* to *Val* and we use the standard notation $\rho\{x \mapsto v\}$ to denote the evaluation which differs from ρ only in that it maps x to v. An application of ρ to a data expression e, denoted $\rho(e)$, always yields a value from *Val* and similarly for boolean expressions; $\rho(b)$ is either true or false. We use $\rho \models b$ to indicate that $\rho(b) = true$, and $b \models b'$ to mean for any ρ if $\rho(b)$ is true then so is $\rho(b')$. We will also write $b = b'$ for $b \models b'$ and $b' \models b$. A finite set of boolean expressions B is called a b-partition if $\bigvee B = b$.

A *substitution* σ is a type-respecting mapping from data variables to expressions and we use $e\sigma$ to denote the result of applying σ to the expression e. We will write $[\overline{e}/\overline{x}]$ for the substitution sending $\overline{x}$ to $\overline{e}$. If $\sigma \equiv [\overline{e}/\overline{x}]$ then $dom(\sigma) = \{\overline{x}\}$ and $cod(\sigma) = fv(\overline{e})$. Composition of substitutions is denoted by juxtaposition, and $\emptyset$ is the (polymorphic) empty substitution. $\sigma[x \mapsto e]$ denotes the substitution which differs from σ only in that it sends x to e. If $\sigma \equiv [\overline{e}/\overline{x}]$ then the application of σ to ρ is defined by $\sigma\rho = \rho\{\overline{x} \mapsto \rho(\overline{e})\}$. It is easy to see that $(\sigma\rho)(e) = \rho(e\sigma)$ when $fv(e) \subseteq dom(\sigma)$.

An *assignment* θ has the form $\overline{x} := \overline{e}$, with $\overline{x}$ and $\overline{e}$ having the same length and type. We will often take the liberty to identify an assignment $\overline{x} := \overline{e}$ with the substitution $[\overline{e}/\overline{x}]$.

An *action* is either a silent action τ, an input action $c?x$, or an output action $c!e$, where $c \in Chan$. Actions are ranged over by α. The sets of free and bound variables of actions are given by $fv(c!e) = fv(e)$, $bv(c?x) = \{x\}$, and empty otherwise. The set of channel names used in an action is defined by $chan(c?x) = chan(c!e) = \{c\}$ and $chan(\tau) = \emptyset$. Two actions are *equal over* b, written $\alpha =^b \alpha'$, if when α has the form $c!e$ then α' has the form $c!e'$ and $b \models e = e'$, otherwise $\alpha \equiv \alpha'$. A *guarded action with assignment* is a triple (b, θ, α) where b is a boolean expression, θ an assignment, and α an action.

Definition 2.1 A symbolic transition graph with assignments (STGA for short) is a rooted directed graph where each node n has an associated finite set of free variables $fv(n)$ and each edge is labeled by a guarded action with assignment. A STGA is *well-formed* if whenever $(b, \overline{x} := \overline{e}, \alpha)$ is the label of an edge from n to m, written $n \overset{b,\overline{x}:=\overline{e},\alpha}{\longmapsto} m$, then $fv(b, \overline{e}) \subseteq fv(n)$, $fv(\alpha) \subseteq \{\overline{x}\}$, and $fv(m) \subseteq \{\overline{x}\} \cup bv(\alpha)$. □

We will often simply write $n \overset{\theta,\alpha}{\longmapsto} m$ for $n \overset{true,\theta,\alpha}{\longmapsto} m$, and will also omit θ when it is the identity assignment on $fv(n)$.

Two STGAs can be composed using parallel composition operator $\parallel$ and restriction operator $\backslash$. When composing two STGAs it is required that they use disjoint name spaces for data variables (so the only way for them to cooperate is through communication). The nodes of the parallel composition $(\mathcal{G}\|\mathcal{H})\backslash R$, with R a set of channel names, are pairs of those of $\mathcal{G}$ and $\mathcal{H}$ with $fv(<n,m>) = fv(n) \cup fv(m)$, and the edges are created by the following rules (where the symmetric rule of par has been omitted):

$$\text{par} \quad \frac{n \overset{b,\overline{x}:=\overline{e},\alpha}{\longmapsto} n'}{<n,m> \overset{b,\overline{x},\overline{y}:=\overline{e},\overline{y},\alpha}{\longmapsto} <n',m>} \quad \begin{array}{l} chan(\alpha) \cap R = \emptyset \\ fv(m) = \{\overline{y}\} \end{array}$$

$$\text{com} \quad \frac{n \overset{b_1,\overline{x}:=\overline{e}_1,c?z}{\longmapsto} n', \quad m \overset{b_2,\overline{y}:=\overline{e}_2,c!\overline{e}}{\longmapsto} m'}{<n,m> \overset{b_1 \wedge b_2,\overline{x},\overline{y},z:=\overline{e}_1,\overline{e}_2,e[\overline{e}_2/\overline{y}],\tau}{\longmapsto} <n',m'>}$$

Proposition 2.2 *1. The STGA for $(\mathcal{G}\|\mathcal{H})\backslash R$ as defined above is well-formed.*

2. $(\mathcal{G}\|\mathcal{H})\backslash R = (\mathcal{H}\|\mathcal{G})\backslash R$ and $((\mathcal{G}\|\mathcal{H})\|\mathcal{F})\backslash R = (\mathcal{G}\|(\mathcal{H}\|\mathcal{F}))\backslash R$.

As an example of how to generate symbolic graphs from a process description language let us consider regular value–passing *CCS* given by the following BNF grammar:

$$t \ ::= \ \mathbf{0} \mid \alpha.t \mid b \rightarrow t \mid t+t \mid P(\overline{e})$$

where for each process identifier P there is a definition $P(\overline{x}) \Leftarrow t$ which satisfies $fv(t) \subseteq \{\overline{x}\}$ and is *guarded*, *i.e.* every identifier in t is within the scope of an action prefixing α. .. Given a term t in this language a STGA can be generated using the following rules:

$$\frac{}{\alpha.t \overset{true,\emptyset,\alpha}{\longmapsto} t} \qquad \frac{t \overset{b,\theta,\alpha}{\longmapsto} t'}{t+u \overset{b,\theta,\alpha}{\longmapsto} t'} \qquad \frac{t \overset{b,\theta,\alpha}{\longmapsto} t'}{u+t \overset{b,\theta,\alpha}{\longmapsto} t'}$$

$$\frac{t \overset{b,\theta,\alpha}{\longmapsto} t'}{b' \rightarrow t \overset{b \wedge b',\theta,\alpha}{\longmapsto} t'} \qquad \frac{t \overset{b,\theta,\alpha}{\longmapsto} t'}{P(\overline{e}) \overset{b[\overline{e}/\overline{x}],\theta[\overline{x}:=\overline{e}],\alpha}{\longmapsto} t'} \ P(\overline{x}) \Leftarrow t \text{ is a definition}$$

The conventional way to infer moves from a recursively defined process term $P(\overline{e})$ with definition clause $P(\overline{x}) \Leftarrow t$ is to substitute $\overline{e}$ for $\overline{x}$ in t and look for moves from the resulted term:

$$\frac{t[\overline{e}/\overline{x}] \overset{b,\alpha}{\longmapsto} t'}{P(\overline{e}) \overset{b,\alpha}{\longmapsto} t'}$$

This is an *eager* approach: substitutions are performed when moves are inferred. A disadvantage with this approach is that very often it results in infinite state graphs. An example is the process $P(0)$ where $P(x) \Leftarrow c!x.P(x+1)$. Though simple, using this rule the symbolic graph for $P(0)$ will have infinite number of nodes representing $P(0)$, $P(0+1)$, $P(0+1+1)$, ...

$$\frac{m \overset{b,\theta,\tau}{\longmapsto} n}{m_\rho \overset{\tau}{\longrightarrow} n_{\theta\rho}} \ \rho \models b \qquad \frac{m \overset{b,\theta,c!e}{\longmapsto} n}{m_\rho \overset{c!\rho(e\theta)}{\longrightarrow} n_{\theta\rho}} \ \rho \models b \qquad \frac{m \overset{b,\theta,c?y}{\longmapsto} n}{m_\rho \overset{c?y}{\longrightarrow} n_{\theta\rho}} \ \rho \models b$$

Figure 3: Late Operational Semantics

Here we adopt a rather *lazy* approach: the substitutions necessary in inferring moves from recursively defined terms are postponed. They are carried in the transitions and will be performed later when processes are compared for bisimulation, as we shall see below. For regular value–passing *CCS* it is not difficult to see that graphs generated with the new rules are always *finite*, because any process term involves only finite many recursive definition clauses and each such clause gives rise to a finite subgraph. In the Introduction we have already seen how the process $P(0)$ can be pictured as a finite graph with assignments.

3 Operational Semantics and Bisimulations

Given a STGA a *state* n_ρ is a pair consisting of a node n together with an evaluation ρ supplying values for free variables of n (it is understood that ρ is restricted to $fv(n)$). The late (ground) operational semantics is defined as the least relation over states generated by the rules in Figure 3. Late (ground) bisimulation can then be defined in the standard way:

Definition 3.1 A late (ground) bisimulation is a symmetric relation R over states such that: if $(m_\rho, n_\varrho) \in R$ then

1. $m_\rho \overset{c?y}{\longrightarrow} m'_{\rho'}$ implies there exists $n_\varrho \overset{c?z}{\longrightarrow} n'_{\varrho'}$ and $(m'_{\rho'\{y\mapsto v\}}, n'_{\varrho'\{z\mapsto v\}}) \in R$ for all $v \in Val$.
2. for any other actions $m_\rho \overset{a}{\longrightarrow} m'_{\rho'}$ implies there exists $n_\varrho \overset{a}{\longrightarrow} n'_{\varrho'}$ and $(m'_{\rho'}, n'_{\varrho'}) \in R$.

We write $m_\rho \sim n_\varrho$ if there is a late bisimulation R such that $(m_\rho, n_\varrho) \in R$. Two graphs $\mathcal{G}$ and $\mathcal{G}'$ are bisimilar with respect to ρ and ρ' if $r_\rho \sim r'_{\rho'}$ where r and r' are the roots of the two graphs, respectively. □

We can also give a more abstract operational semantics to STGAs without referring to evaluations. This semantics is defined on *terms*. Given a symbolic transition graph $\mathcal{G}$, a term n_σ consists of a node and a substitution with $dom(\sigma) = fv(n)$. The set of free variables of the term $t \equiv n_\sigma$ is $fv(t) = fv(fv(n)\sigma)$. t is called *closed* when $fv(t) = \emptyset$.

The *symbolic* operational semantics is defined as the least relation generated by the rules in Figure 4. It is called "symbolic" because boolean and data expressions do not get evaluated, instead they are symbolically carried in transitions.

$$\frac{m \overset{b,\theta,\tau}{\longmapsto} n}{m_\sigma \overset{b\sigma,\tau}{\longrightarrow} n_{\theta\sigma}} \qquad \frac{m \overset{b,\theta,c!e}{\longmapsto} n}{m_\sigma \overset{b\sigma,c!(e\theta\sigma)}{\longrightarrow} n_{\theta\sigma}} \qquad \frac{m \overset{b,\theta,c?x}{\longmapsto} n}{m_\sigma \overset{b\sigma,c?z}{\longrightarrow} n_{\theta\sigma[x\mapsto z]}} \; z \notin \begin{array}{l} dom(\theta)\cup \\ fv(cod(\theta)\sigma) \end{array}$$

Figure 4: Symbolic Operational Semantics

The semantic rules only perform the assignments (as substitutions) and rename input variables if necessary, when passing through edges.

With symbolic operational semantics (late) *symbolic bisimulation* can then be defined as in [HL95]:

Definition 3.2 Let $\mathbf{S} = \{ S^b \mid b \in BExp \}$ be a *BExp*-indexed family of symmetric relations over terms. Define the functional $\mathcal{B}$ by letting $\mathcal{B}(\mathbf{S})$ be the *BExp*-indexed family of symmetric relations such that $(t, u) \in \mathcal{B}(S)^b$ if and only if

> whenever $t \overset{b_1,\alpha}{\longrightarrow} t'$ then there is a $b \wedge b_1$-partition B with $fv(B) \cap bv(\alpha) = \emptyset$ and for each $b' \in B$ there exists a $u \overset{b_2,\alpha'}{\longrightarrow} u'$ such that $b' \models b_2$, $\alpha =^{b'} \alpha'$, and $(t', u') \in S^{b''}$ for some b'' with $b' \models b''$.

$\mathbf{S}$ is a late symbolic bisimulation if $\mathbf{S} \subseteq \mathcal{B}(\mathbf{S})$. We write $t \simeq^b u$ if there is a late symbolic bisimulation $\mathbf{S}$ such that $(t, u) \in S^b$. Two graphs $\mathcal{G}$ and $\mathcal{G}'$ are symbolic bisimilar over b if $r_\emptyset \simeq^b r'_\emptyset$ where r and r' are the roots of the two graphs. □

The following theorem states that symbolic bisimulation captures ground bisimulation. It's proof follows the line of Theorem 4.5 in [HL95].

Theorem 3.3 $n_\sigma \simeq^b m_{\sigma'}$ *if and only if* $n_{\sigma\rho} \sim m_{\sigma'\rho}$ *for every* ρ *such that* $\rho \models b$.

4 Computing Bisimulation for STGA

If a graph is finite, i.e. without loops, the presence of substitutions in the edges is superficial: they can be removed by travelling from the root to the leaves, starting from the empty substitution, applying symbolic interpretation (Figure 4) when passing through an edge and computing new free variables when encountering a node, resulting in a symbolic transition graph without assignments. For such graphs algorithms for computing bisimulation formulae already exist ([HL95]).

Substitutions make real differences for graphs with loops. For example, suppose we are trying to match symbolic transitions for the two graphs in Figure 2, starting at the pair of loop entrances with empty substitutions. The first time we pass the loop body the matching condition is $x{+}1 = -(y{-}1)$, but the second time it becomes $x{+}1{+}1 = -(y{-}1{-}1)$, and the third time $x{+}1{+}1{+}1 = -(y{-}1{-}1{-}1)$ ..., due to the substitutions $x := x + 1$ and $y := y - 1$ in the edges. Instead of attempting to compute a single bisimulation formula for a given pair of STGAs, here we present an algorithm which returns a *predicate equation system* over a set of *predicate variables.* The meaning of these predicate variables are taken as the greatest solution of the equation system.

4.1 Predicate Equation Systems

Formally let the sets of *predicate types* be given by

$$\pi ::= prop \mid \iota_1 \ldots \iota_n \rightarrow prop$$

For each predicate type π we assume a set of *predicate variables* PV_π, ranged over by X, Y,.... Then the set of well-formed propositions and predicates are generated by the following rules:

$$\frac{b \in BExp}{b : prop} \qquad \frac{b \in BExp,\ \Phi : prop}{b \Rightarrow \Phi : prop}$$

$$\frac{x \in DVar,\ \Phi : prop}{\forall x \Phi : prop} \qquad \frac{\Phi, \Psi : prop}{\Phi \wedge \Psi : prop}$$

$$\frac{\Phi, \Psi : prop}{\Phi \vee \Psi : prop} \qquad \frac{\overline{e} \in DExp_{\iota_1} \times \ldots \times DExp_{\iota_n},\ \Lambda : \iota_1 \ldots \iota_n \rightarrow prop}{\Lambda \overline{e} : prop}$$

$$\frac{X \in PV_{\iota_1 \ldots \iota_n \rightarrow prop}}{X :\ \iota_1 \ldots \iota_n \rightarrow prop} \qquad \frac{\overline{x} \in DVar_{\iota_1} \times \ldots \times DVar_{\iota_n},\ \Phi : prop}{(\overline{x})\Phi : \iota_1 \ldots \iota_n \rightarrow prop}$$

Note that predicate variables always appear in positive positions. As usual the universal qualification $\forall x \Phi$ binds x in Φ. Functional abstraction $(\overline{x})\Phi$ is another binder: here each $x_i \in \overline{x}$ is a bound variable with scope Φ. The set of free data variables of Φ is denoted $fv(\Phi)$. Φ is *data closed* if $fv(\Phi) = \emptyset$.

Let **Bool** be the set of truth values $\{false, true\}$ with the natural ordering $false \prec true$. A (groud) *valuation* $\mathcal{V}$ maps each $X \in PV_{\iota_1 \ldots \iota_n \rightarrow prop}$ to a function from $Val_{\iota_1} \times \ldots \times Val_{\iota_n}$ to **Bool**. The **Bool** ordering $\prec$ can be extended pointwise to truth valued functions by letting $f \prec g$ *iff* $f(\overline{v}) \prec g(\overline{v})$ for all vectors of values $\overline{v}$ with appropriate type, and to valuations by letting $\mathcal{V} \prec \mathcal{V}'$ *iff* $\mathcal{V}(X) \prec \mathcal{V}'(X)$ for all X. Propositions and predicates are interpreted with respect to an evaluation ρ and a valuation $\mathcal{V}$ inductively thus

$$\begin{aligned}
&\|b\|_{\rho,\mathcal{V}} = \rho(b) \\
&\|b \Rightarrow \Phi\|_{\rho,\mathcal{V}} = \rho(b) \Rightarrow \|\Phi\|_{\rho,\mathcal{V}} \\
&\|\forall x \Phi\|_{\rho,\mathcal{V}} = \forall v \in Val\ \|\Phi\|_{\rho\{x \mapsto v\},\mathcal{V}} \\
&\|\Phi_1 \wedge \Phi_2\|_{\rho,\mathcal{V}} = \|\Phi_1\|_{\rho,\mathcal{V}} \wedge \|\Phi_2\|_{\rho,\mathcal{V}} \\
&\|\Phi_1 \vee \Phi_2\|_{\rho,\mathcal{V}} = \|\Phi_1\|_{\rho,\mathcal{V}} \vee \|\Phi_2\|_{\rho,\mathcal{V}} \\
&\|\Lambda \overline{e}\|_{\rho,\mathcal{V}} = \|\Lambda\|_{\rho,\mathcal{V}}(\rho(\overline{e})) \\
&\|X\|_{\rho,\mathcal{V}} = \mathcal{V}(X) \\
&\|(\overline{x})\Phi\|_{\rho,\mathcal{V}} = \lambda \overline{v} :\ Val\ \|\Phi\|_{\rho\{\overline{x} \mapsto \overline{v}\},\mathcal{V}}
\end{aligned}$$

The operators $\Rightarrow$, $\wedge$, $\vee$ and $\forall$ on the right hand sides are semantic.

A ***predicate equation system*** E is of the form

$$\{ X_i = \Lambda_i \mid i \in I \}$$

where X_i and Λ_i are of the same type and $X_i \neq X_j$ for $i \neq j$. E is ***predicate closed*** if all predicate variables in its right hand sides are included in $\{ X_i \mid i \in I \}$. E is ***closed*** if it is predicate closed and all its right hand sides are data closed. In an equation $X = (\overline{x})\Phi$, $\overline{x}$ is the ***formal parameter*** of X. In the algorithm below we will write the formal and actual parameters of predicate variables together, in the form of substitutions. For instance, the equation system

$$\begin{aligned} X_{0,0} &= (0 = -0) \wedge X_{1,1}(0,0) \\ X_{1,1} &= (x,y)((x+1 = -(y-1)) \wedge X_{1,1}(x+1, y-1)) \end{aligned}$$

will be written as

$$\begin{aligned} X_{0,0} &= (0 = -0) \wedge X_{1,1}[0/x, 0/y] \\ X_{1,1} &= (x+1 = -(y-1)) \wedge X_{1,1}[x+1/x, y-1/y]. \end{aligned}$$

Given a valuation $\mathcal{V}$ and an evaluation ρ, a ***solution*** of E is a fix-point of the right hand sides of E, *i.e.* a function ζ mapping $X_i : \iota_1 \dots \iota_n \rightarrow \textit{prop}$ to $\textit{Val}_{\iota_1} \times \dots \times \textit{Val}_{\iota_n} \rightarrow \mathbf{Bool}$ such that

$$\zeta(X_i) = \|\Lambda_i\|_{\rho, \mathcal{V}\{\zeta\}} \qquad i \in I$$

where $\mathcal{V}\{\zeta\}$ denotes the obvious modification to $\mathcal{V}$ by ζ.

It is straightforward to check that, with respect to a valuation $\mathcal{V}$ and an evaluation ρ, the meaning of right hand sides of E defines a monotonic functional $\lambda\zeta\|\overline{\Lambda}\|_{\rho,\mathcal{V}\{\zeta\}}$. Therefore by a standard result due to Tarski [Tar55] it has both the least and the greatest solutions, and it is the latter that we are interested in (since we are dealing with strong bisimulation here). If E is closed then its solutions do not depend on any valuation and evaluation, and we shall simply say "ζ is a solution of E".

Propositions and predicates can also be interpreted symbolically. A ***symbolic valuation*** $\mathcal{U}$ is a function mapping each $X \in PV_{\iota_1 \dots \iota_n \rightarrow prop}$ to a function $f : \textit{DExp}_{\iota_1} \times \dots \times \textit{DExp}_{\iota_n} \rightarrow \textit{BExp}$ which is consistent with respect to evaluation in the sense that $\rho(\overline{e}) = \rho(\overline{e}')$ implies $\rho(f(\overline{e})) = \rho(f(\overline{e}'))$ for any ρ. Then a symbolic meaning can be assigned to propositions and predicates with respect to a symbolic valuation by the following rules:

$$\begin{aligned} &[\![b]\!]_{\mathcal{U}} = b \\ &[\![b \Rightarrow \Phi]\!]_{\mathcal{U}} = b \Rightarrow [\![\Phi]\!]_{\mathcal{U}} \\ &[\![\forall x \Phi]\!]_{\mathcal{U}} = \forall x [\![\Phi]\!]_{\mathcal{U}} \\ &[\![\Phi_1 \wedge \Phi_2]\!]_{\mathcal{U}} = [\![\Phi_1]\!]_{\mathcal{U}} \wedge [\![\Phi_2]\!]_{\mathcal{U}} \\ &[\![\Phi_1 \vee \Phi_2]\!]_{\mathcal{U}} = [\![\Phi_1]\!]_{\mathcal{U}} \vee [\![\Phi_2]\!]_{\mathcal{U}} \\ &[\![\Lambda \overline{e}]\!]_{\mathcal{U}} = [\![\Lambda]\!]_{\mathcal{U}}(\overline{e}) \\ &[\![X]\!]_{\mathcal{U}} = \mathcal{U}(X) \\ &[\![(\overline{x})\Phi]\!]_{\mathcal{U}} = \lambda \overline{x} [\![\Phi]\!]_{\mathcal{U}} \end{aligned}$$

where $\Rightarrow$, $\wedge$, $\vee$ and $\forall$ on the right hand sides are operators on *BExp*.

The set of all boolean expressions *BExp* can be ordered by letting $b \sqsubset b'$ *iff* $b \models b'$. With this ordering *BExp* forms a complete lattice. $\sqsubset$ agrees with $\prec$ on **Bool** in the sense that $b \sqsubset b'$ *iff* $b\rho \prec b'\rho$ for any ρ. This ordering can be extended pointwise to functions from $DExp_{\iota_1} \times \ldots \times DExp_{\iota_n}$ to *BExp* in a standard way.

Given an evaluation ρ a symbolic valuation $\mathcal{U}$ can be "evaluated" to a (ground) valuation $\mathcal{U}_\rho$ by letting, for each X,

$$\mathcal{U}_\rho(X)(\overline{v}) = \rho(\mathcal{U}(X)(\overline{v})) \qquad \text{for all } \overline{v}$$

Then we have the following lemma:

Lemma 4.1 *For any proposition Φ and abstraction Λ, $\rho([\![\Phi]\!]_\mathcal{U}) = \|\Phi\|_{\rho,\mathcal{U}_\rho}$ and $\rho([\Lambda]_\mathcal{U}) = \|\Lambda\|_{\rho,\mathcal{U}_\rho}$ for any evaluation ρ.*

Proof: By mutual induction on the structures of Φ and Λ. □

A *symbolic solution* of a predicate equation system $E: \ \{X_i = \Lambda_i \mid i \in I\}$, with respect to $\mathcal{U}$, is a function η mapping $X_i : \iota_1 \ldots \iota_n \rightarrow prop$ to $DExp_{\iota_1} \times \ldots \times DExp_{\iota_n} \rightarrow BExp$ for each $i \in I$ such that

$$\eta(X_i) = [\Lambda_i]_{\mathcal{U}\{\eta\}} \qquad i \in I$$

where $\mathcal{U}\{\eta\}$ denotes the obvious modification to $\mathcal{U}$ by η. When E is closed then its symbolic solutions do not depend on any $\mathcal{U}$. Again as the symbolic meaning of the right hand sides of E is a monotonic functional with respect to $\sqsubset$, E has both the least and the greatest symbolic solutions.

Proposition 4.2 *For a closed equation system E, η is a symbolic solution of E iff η_ρ is a solution of E for any ρ. In particular η is the greatest symbolic solution of E iff η_ρ is the greatest solution of E for any ρ.*

4.2 The Algorithm

A *path* in a graph is a sequence of connected edges. Given two graphs $\mathcal{G}$ and $\mathcal{H}$, a *matching path* is a pair consisting of a path p in $\mathcal{G}$ and a path q in $\mathcal{H}$:

$$p = n_0 \overset{b_0,\theta_0,\alpha_0}{\longmapsto} n_1 \overset{b_1,\theta_1,\alpha_1}{\longmapsto} \ldots \overset{b_{k-1},\theta_{k-1},\alpha_{k-1}}{\longmapsto} n_k$$
$$q = m_0 \overset{b'_0,\theta'_0,\alpha'_0}{\longmapsto} m_1 \overset{b'_1,\theta'_1,\alpha'_1}{\longmapsto} \ldots \overset{b'_{k-1},\theta'_{k-1},\alpha'_{k-1}}{\longmapsto} m_k$$

such that α and α' are of the same type, i.e., either $\alpha \equiv \tau \equiv \alpha'$, or $\alpha \equiv c!e$ and $\alpha' \equiv c!e'$, or $\alpha \equiv c?x$ and $\alpha \equiv c?y$. A *matching loop* is a matching path such that $n_0 = n_k$, $m_0 = m_k$ and (n_0, m_0), called the *entry* of the matching loop, is in a matching path from the roots of $\mathcal{G}$ and $\mathcal{H}$. We will simply write "loop" for "matching loop" and "loop entry" for "matching loop entry".

$$bisim(\mathcal{G},\mathcal{H}) = \text{for each } (n,n') \in loopEntries \text{ return } X_{n,n'} = match(n,\emptyset,n',\emptyset)$$

$$match(n,\sigma,n',\sigma') = \bigwedge_{\gamma} match_{\gamma}(n,\sigma,n',\sigma')$$

$$\begin{aligned}
&match_{\tau}(n,\sigma,n',\sigma') = \\
&\text{let } B_{ij} = close(n_i,\theta_i\sigma,n'_j,\theta'_j\sigma') \\
&\qquad\qquad \text{for } n \overset{b_i,\theta_i,\tau}{\longmapsto} n_i,\; n' \overset{b'_j,\theta'_j,\tau}{\longmapsto} n'_j \\
&\text{in } \bigwedge_i (b_i\sigma \Rightarrow \bigvee_j (b'_j\sigma' \wedge B_{ij})) \wedge \bigwedge_j (b'_j\sigma' \Rightarrow \bigvee_i (b_i\sigma \wedge B_{ij}))
\end{aligned}$$

$$\begin{aligned}
&match_{c!}(n,\sigma,n',\sigma') = \\
&\text{let } B_{ij} = close(n_i,\theta_i\sigma,n'_j,\theta'_j\sigma') \\
&\qquad\qquad \text{for } n \overset{b_i,\theta_i,c!e_i}{\longmapsto} n_i,\; n' \overset{b'_j,\theta'_j,c!e'_j}{\longmapsto} n'_j \\
&\text{in } \bigwedge_i (b_i\sigma \Rightarrow \bigvee_j (b'_j\sigma' \wedge e_i\theta_i\sigma = e'_j\theta'_j\sigma' \wedge B_{ij})) \wedge \\
&\quad \bigwedge_j (b'_j\sigma' \Rightarrow \bigvee_i (b_i\sigma \wedge e_i\theta_i\sigma = e'_j\theta'_j\sigma' \wedge B_{ij}))
\end{aligned}$$

$$\begin{aligned}
&match_{c?}(n,\sigma,n',\sigma') = \\
&\text{let } B_{ij} = \text{let } z = newVar() \\
&\qquad\qquad B'_{ij} = close(n_i,\theta_i\sigma[x\mapsto z],n'_j,\theta'_j\sigma'[y\mapsto z]) \\
&\qquad\qquad\qquad \text{for } n \overset{b_i,\theta_i,c?x}{\longmapsto} n_i,\; n' \overset{b'_j,\theta'_j,c?y}{\longmapsto} n'_j \\
&\qquad\quad \text{in } \forall z B'_{ij} \\
&\text{in } \bigwedge_i (b_i\sigma \Rightarrow \bigvee_j (b'_j\sigma' \wedge B_{ij})) \wedge \bigwedge_j (b'_j\sigma' \Rightarrow \bigvee_i (b_i\sigma \wedge B_{ij}))
\end{aligned}$$

$$\begin{aligned}
close(n,\sigma,n',\sigma') = {} & \text{if } (n,n') \in loopEntries \text{ then return } X_{n,n'}(\sigma,\sigma') \\
& \text{else } match(n,\sigma,n',\sigma'))
\end{aligned}$$

Figure 5: The Algorithm for Late Symbolic Bisimulation

The algorithm for late strong bisimulation is presented in Figure 5, where γ ranges over $\{\tau, c!, c?\}$. It takes as input a pair of finite symbolic transition graphs, $\mathcal{G}$ and $\mathcal{H}$, with disjoint name spaces for data variables and uses the set *loopEntries* of their matching loop entries which also includes the pair of the root nodes of $\mathcal{G}$ and $\mathcal{H}$. The output is a predicate equation system. The function *bisim* introduces a predicate variable for each matching loop entry and creates an equation for each matching loop. At each pair of matching nodes it calls function *match* to generate a proposition which embodies a partition as required by the definition of symbolic bisimulation.

The correctness of the algorithm is a direct consequence of the following theorem:

Theorem 4.3 *Let $E = \{X_{n,n'} = \Lambda_{n,n'}\}$ be the equation system returned by the algorithm on $\mathcal{G}$ and $\mathcal{H}$.*

1. *If η is a symbolic solution of E and $\eta(X_{n,n'})(\overline{e},\overline{e}') = b$ then $n_{[\overline{e}/\overline{x}]} \simeq^b n'_{[\overline{e}'/\overline{x}']}$.*

2. *If η is the greatest symbolic solution of E and $n_{[\overline{e}/\overline{x}]} \simeq^b n'_{[\overline{e}'/\overline{x}']}$ then $b \models \eta(X_{n,n'})(\overline{e},\overline{e}')$.*

where $\overline{x}$ and $\overline{x}'$ are the free variables of n and n', respectively.

Proof: *1.* Let $S^b = \{(n_{[\overline{e}/\overline{x}]}, n'_{[\overline{e}'/\overline{x}']})\}$ where $b = \eta(X_{n,n'})(\overline{e},\overline{e}')$. Then it can be shown that $\mathbf{S} = \{S^b\}$ is a symbolic bisimulation.

2. Suppose $\mathbf{S} = \{S^b\}$ is a symbolic bisimulation between terms of $\mathcal{G}$ and $\mathcal{H}$ such that $(n_{[\overline{e}/\overline{x}]}, n'_{[\overline{e}'/\overline{x}']}) \in S^b$ for some $S^b \in \mathbf{S}$. For each $X_{n,n'}$ set $\eta'(X_{n,n'})(\overline{e},\overline{e}') = \begin{cases} b & \text{if } (n_{[\overline{e}/\overline{x}]}, n'_{[\overline{e}'/\overline{x}']}) \in S^b \text{ for some } S^b \in \mathbf{S}. \\ \mathit{false} & \text{otherwise.} \end{cases}$ Then it can be shown that η' is a symbolic solution of E. Hence $\eta'(X_{n,n'})(\overline{e},\overline{e}') \models \eta(X_{n,n'})(\overline{e},\overline{e}')$. □

The algorithm reduces the problem of deciding bisimulation of two STGAs to the problem of checking validity for the greatest solution of a closed equation system. Unlike boolean equation systems which can be effectively solved [Lar92, Liu92], a predicate equation system may involve arbitrary data and boolean expressions and it is in general not possible to automatically compute its greatest solution, except for some special cases (see **Remark** below). However one can reason with the greatest solution using data domain knowledge. For instance the equation system returned by the algorithm for the two STGAs in Figure 2 is

$$\begin{aligned} X_{0,0} &= (0 = -0) \wedge X_{1,1}[0/x, 0/y] \\ X_{1,1} &= (x+1 = -(y-1)) \wedge X_{1,1}[x+1/x, y-1/y]. \end{aligned}$$

It spells out, for any $n \geq 0$

$$(x \underbrace{+1 + \ldots + 1}_{n} = -(y \underbrace{-1 - \ldots - 1}_{n}))[0,0/x,y],$$

which can be easily proved by mathematical induction using elementary knowledge on integers.

As another example let us consider the two STGAs in Figure 6 which can be written in *CCS* syntax as

$$\begin{aligned} M &\Leftarrow r?x.c!x.M_1(x) \\ M_1(x) &\Leftarrow r?u.\mathit{if}\ u > 0\ \mathit{then}\ M_1(x+u)\ \mathit{else}\ M_1(x-u) \\ N &\Leftarrow r?y.c!y.N_1(y) \\ N_1(y) &\Leftarrow r?v.N_1(y+|v|) \end{aligned}$$

where $|v|$ denotes the absolute value of v. Both processes accumulate the inputs received via r and output the sums along c. Running the algorithm generates the following result:

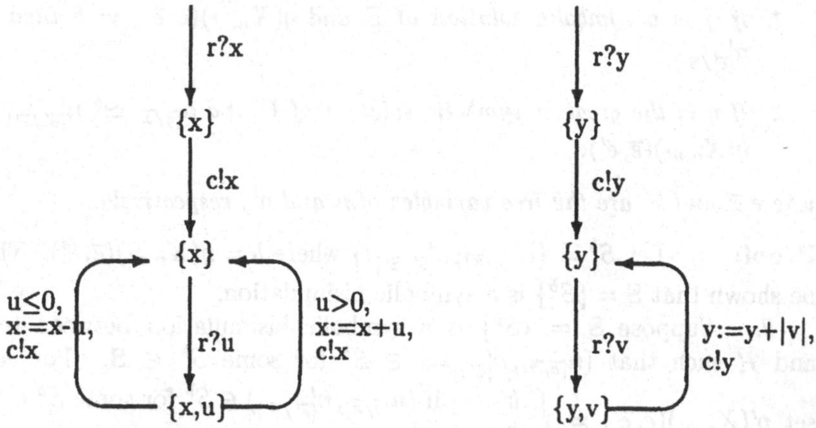

Figure 6: Processes which accumulate inputs

$$\begin{aligned}X_{0,0} &= \forall z_1 X_{2,2}[z_1/x, z_1/y]\\ X_{2,2} &= \forall z_2\ (\neg z_2 > 0 \Rightarrow x - z_2 = y + |z_2| \wedge X_{2,2}[x - z_2/x, y + |z_2|/y]) \wedge\\ &\quad (z_2 > 0 \Rightarrow x + z_2 = y + |z_2| \wedge X_{2,2}[x + z_2/x, y + |z_2|/y]) \wedge\\ &\quad (\neg z_2 > 0 \wedge x - z_2 = y + |z_2| \wedge X_{2,2}[x - z_2/x, y + |z_2|/y] \vee\\ &\quad z_2 > 0 \wedge x + z_2 = y + |z_2| \wedge X_{2,2}[x + z_2/x, y + |z_2|/y])\end{aligned}$$

Using laws of propositional calculus the second equation can be simplified to

$$\begin{aligned}X_{2,2} = \forall z_2\ &(\neg z_2 > 0 \Rightarrow x - z_2 = y + |z_2| \wedge X_{2,2}[x - z_2/x, y + |z_2|/y]) \wedge\\ &(z_2 > 0 \Rightarrow x + z_2 = y + |z_2| \wedge X_{2,2}[x + z_2/x, y + |z_2|/y])\end{aligned}$$

So $\forall z_1 X_{2,2}[z_1/x, z_1/y]$ means, for any $n > 1$,

$$\begin{aligned}\forall z_1 \forall z_2\ (z_2 > 0 \Rightarrow \ldots \forall z_n\ &(z_n > 0 \Rightarrow z_1 + \ldots + z_{n-1} + z_n = z_1 + \ldots + |z_n|) \wedge\\ &\neg z_n > 0 \Rightarrow z_1 + \ldots + z_{n-1} - z_n = z_1 + \ldots + |z_n|) \wedge\\ &\vdots\\ \neg z_2 > 0 \Rightarrow \ldots \forall z_n\ &(z_n > 0 \Rightarrow z_1 - \ldots - z_{n-1} + z_n = z_1 + \ldots + |z_n|) \wedge\\ &\neg z_n > 0 \Rightarrow z_1 - \ldots - z_{n-1} - z_n = z_1 + \ldots + |z_n|).\end{aligned}$$

These booleans can be easily shown to be *true* by mathematical induction using simple facts about integers.

Note that the greatest solutions of the above two equation systems amount to infinite conjunctions, and mathematical induction is essential in establishing their truth.

Remark An important special case is simple STGAs where edges do not carry assignments (more accurately all assignments are identity mappings). For such graphs the only substitutions in the resulting equation systems are simply renamings generated when matching input actions. So if we try to compute the greatest fixpoint of such an equation system by iteration, starting from the constant function mapping every data expression to *true*, then this process will converge after at most n iterations where n is the maximum number of times that data variables are bound. Hence the greatest solutions of the equation systems for simple STGAs *can* be computed automatically. [HL95] presents an algorithm which computes bisimulation formulae for such graphs, without referring to predicate equations. This is achieved by ordering data variables and always using the smallest unused variable when matching an input action, so that the algorithm will visit each matching loop n times if the active variables in the loop are bound by n input actions.

5 Conclusions and Future Work

We have introduced the notion of symbolic transition graphs in which edges are labeled by boolean conditions, actions, as well as assignments. The presence of assignments as part of labels makes it possible to represent state transitions not only caused by communication actions, but also by changing values of state variables. As a consequence many traditional transition graphs which are infinite state can be represented as finite STGAs. A theory of symbolic bisimulation for such STGAs has been developed, and it is shown that this notion of symbolic bisimulation precisely captures the standard notion of bisimulation when STGAs are interpreted as traditional transition systems over states. Thus STGAs are mathematically tractable. We have also presented an algorithm which, when given two STGAs, computes a predicate equation system whose greatest solution characterizes the condition under which the two STGAs are bisimilar. The algorithm has been implemented (in Standard ML) and tested on some small problems, including all of the examples used in this paper.

We have only developed the theory of symbolic bisimulation and the algorithm for the late version of bisimulation equivalence. The same can be done for early bisimulation as well, but due to space limitation these have to be omitted from this extended abstract.

The algorithm reduces the problem of checking bisimulation for STGAs to the problem of reasoning about the greatest solutions of predicate equation systems over data domain. As future work we would like to investigate techniques for verifying properties concerning such solutions. The STGA model is very general and it would be interesting to identify some subclasses for which the greatest solutions are computable (one such case is STGs as discussed in the remark of the previous section). Another topic for further research is to extend the current framework to deal with weak equivalences.

Acknowledgments: Thanks to Matthew Hennessy and Julian Rathke for discussions on this subject. Comments from two anonymous referees have led to several improvements. The main body of this work was carried out during a visit to Sussex University in 1995, and I am grateful to the EU KIT project for financial support.

References

[CPS89] R. Cleaveland, J. Parrow, and B. Steffen. A semantics based verification tool for finite state systems. In *Proceedings of the 9th International Symposium on Protocol Specification, Testing and Verification*, North Holland, 1989.

[CR94] R. Cleaveland and J. Riely. Testing-based abstractions for value-passing systems. In *CONCUR'94*, number 836 in Lecture Notes in Computer Science, pages 417 – 432. Springer–Verlag, 1994.

[DHG95] W. Damn, H. Hungar, and O. Grumberg. What if model checking must be truly symbolic? In *Proceedings of the Workshop on Tools and Algorithms for the Construction and Analysis of Systems*, 1995. Aarhus, Denmark.

[GLZ89] J. Godskesen, K. Larsen, and M. Zeeberg. Tav user manual. Report R89-19, Aalborg University, 1989.

[HI93] M. Hennessy and A. Ingolfsdottir. Communicating processes with value-passing and assignment. *Formal Aspects of Computing*, 3:346 – 366, 1993.

[HL95] M. Hennessy and H. Lin. Symbolic bisimulations. *Theoretical Computer Science*, 138:353 – 389, 1995.

[JP92] B. Jonsson and J. Parrow. Deciding bisimulation equivalences for a class of non-finite-state programs. *Information and Computation*, 1992. to appear. Also available as SICS research Report R-89/8908.

[Lar92] K.G. Larsen. Efficient local correctness checking. In *Computer Aided Verification*, Lecture Notes in Computer Science. Springer–Verlag, 1992.

[Liu92] X. Liu. *Specification and Decomposition in Concurrency*. Ph.d. thesis, Aalborg University, 1992.

[Mil89] R. Milner. *Communication and Concurrency*. Prentice-Hall, 1989.

[Sch94] M.Z. Schreiber. *Value-passing Process Calculi as a Formal Method*. Ph.D. thesis, Imperial College, 1994.

[SV89] R. De Simone and D. Vergamimi. Aboard auto. Report RT111, INRIA, 1989.

[Tar55] A. Tarski. A lattice-theoretical fixpoint theorem and its applications. *Pacific Journal of Mathematics*, 5, 1955.

Models for Concurrent Constraint Programming

Vineet Gupta * Radha Jagadeesan ** Vijay Saraswat*

Abstract. Concurrent constraint programming is a simple but powerful framework for computation based on four basic computational ideas: *concurrency* (multiple agents are simultaneously active), *communication* (they interact via the monotonic accumulation of constraints on shared variables), *coordination* (the presence or absence of information can guard evolution of an agent), and *localization* (each agent has access to only a finite, though dynamically varying, number of variables, and can create new variables on the fly). Unlike other foundational models of concurrency such as CCS, CSP, Petri nets and the π-calculus, such flexibility is already made available within the context of *determinate* computation. This allows the development of a rich and tractable theory of concurrent processes within the context of which additional computational notion such as indeterminacy, reactivity, instantaneous interrupts and continuous (dense-time) autonomous evolution have been developed.

We survey the development of some of these extensions and the relationships between their semantic models.

1 Introduction

Concurrent Constraint Programming (CCP) arose as a generalization of work in dataflow and concurrent logic programming languages. The central idea is to view processes as independent agents communicating by imposing constraints on shared variables. Constraints are taken to be pieces of partial information — they *constrain* the values that variables can take rather than, as in imperative languages, *fixing* the value.

The importance of the idea of constraint-based communication for computation lies in the methodology of *compositional computing* that it enables. Hitherto, the only principled method for the construction of large computational systems has been *decomposition* or modularization. The system is broken into smaller pieces, with interface variables serving as the boundary between computation internal to the module and external computation. In many settings it is desirable to have a *reusable* collection of such modules — therefore it becomes necessary to construct rather general components that capture some interesting set of aspects of the behavior, and then allow for several ways in which such components can be combined to achieve a range of desired functionality. For instance, when modeling a circuit one may desire to have models for components (voltage and current sources, resistors, wires, lamps) constructed independent of their context of

* Xerox PARC, 3333 Coyote Hill Road, Palo Alto Ca 94304; {vgupta, saraswat}@parc.xerox.com

** Dept. of Mathematical Sciences, Loyola University-Lake Shore Campus, Chicago, Il 60626; radha@math.luc.edu

use (the no-function-in-structure principle of [dKB85]). For this to work, it must be possible for the internal structure of the component to represent the effect of all the possible networks that it may be placed in. One desires modularity, and yet *sensitivity* to the environment.

Constraint-based communication offers one such means for achieving the desired flexibility. A component $p(X, Y, Z)$ may share an interface (X) with another component $q(X, A)$ and a different interface (Y, Z) with yet another $r(Y, Z, B)$. The influence p may have with q (via X) is *symmetric*: the constraints imposed by both p and q on X are jointly visible to both p and q (and to other agents with access to X, i.e. sharing this unit of interface). Furthermore constraints are *additive*: the constraints c that p may impose on X could combine with the constraints d that q may impose on X to enable the presence of another constraint e which is not separately entailed by either c or d. This allows a component to have *non-local* influences on other components: p may impose a constraint on Y which could combine with a constraint imposed by r on (Y, B) that could affect another component s that shares B. In this way a component may have an affect on other components with which it is not connected directly and with which it even does not share any interface. Further, constraints support *dynamic interfaces* (c.f. "mobility" in the π-calculus): as p evolves it may introduce another interface variable T which may be communicated via its previous interface to a new component thus establishing a new interface. Similarly, shared interface variables may be dropped. Finally, such concurrent communication between components is *determinate* and *timing-independent* ("Church -Rosser") — what matters is not *when* a constraint is added to the shared store, but that it is.

These ideas have led to the development of several concrete modeling/programming notations e.g.cc(FD)[HSD92], Oz [SHW94], and notations in model-based computing (see http://www.parc.xerox.com/mbc). Underlying them, over the last several years we have developed mathematical models for programming combinators involved. The purpose of this review is to collect together in one place and summarize the basic development of these models.

In outline, the basic ideas are as follows. Communication in CCP is based on a generic, parametric notion of first-order pieces of partial information: first-order because the constraints involve *variables* over some underlying domain of discourse, partial because constraints do not necessarily completely determine the values that variables take. The development of the control constructs within CCP proceeds uniformly, given a particular choice of a constraint system. The basic paradigm is formalized by means of the language of *determinate CCP*:

$P ::= a$	*Tell* the constraint a to the store.
$\mid$ **if** a **then** P	If a can be deduced from the store, reduce to P.
$\mid$ **new** X **in** P	Introduce a new variable X in P.
$\mid P, P$	Run in parallel.

In this setup, recursive procedure calls with parameters can also be supported. Denotations of program are taken to be the "fixed points" of the program: those stores in which the program can run to quiescence without adding any more information. Thus the denotations are sets of constraints with certain properties.

Reactive computation is introduced by means of the notion that a program may interact with its environment in a sequence of discrete time steps [SJG94a]. At each time step, a determinate cc program is executed to quiescence. Two new concepts are introduced:

P ::= **hence** P	Run P at every step from the next instant.
| **if** a **else next** P	Unless a can be deduced from the store, reduce to P at the next instant.

Recursion is now allowed to happen only across time instants. Denotations are taken to be sets of sequences of constraints with certain properties.

Instantaneous interrupts cannot be supported in the above model of concurrent computation: one can only detect the *absence* of information, or negative information, at the current instant and act on it at the *next* instant. Supporting the detection of negative information instantaneously requires extending the untimed language cc, since cc itself does not allow the detection of such unstable information — any information detected by a cc program is never invalidated, something which is not true of negative information. We did this by adding *defaults*, which allow us to detect stable negative information:

P ::= **if** a **else** P	Unless a can be deduced from the store, reduce to P.

Introducing defaults poses the problem of non-monotonicity: a constraint that could be produced in the presence of a may not be produced in the presence of additional information $a \wedge b$. Nevertheless we showed [SJG] that a remarkably simple model was possible for this language that took a process to be a set of *pairs* of constraints.

Extending Default cc over discrete time provides a framework for reactive computing that supports instantaneous interrupts.

In order to model physical systems, it becomes necessary to extend these ideas to allow for continuously varying agents. This is done by extending the notion of a constraint system to a *continuous constraint system*: essentially this allows for the specification of constraints (such as those involving differential equations) which vary continuously over (real) time. No new constructs are needed – just the interpretation of time has to be taken now to be the reals rather than the integers. Denotations now become functions from the non-negative reals to Default cc observations, similar to the Timed Default cc observations which were functions from natural numbers to Default cc observations.

The embeddings between these languages are summarized in Figure 1. Note that we have systematically ignored the dimension of indeterminacy (e.g. guarded nondeterministic choice). This leads to an orthogonal development of all these ideas, which is outside the scope of this paper.

2 The cc languages

We will first give brief accounts of the various languages mentioned in Figure 1. For detailed information, we refer the reader to the appropriate papers.

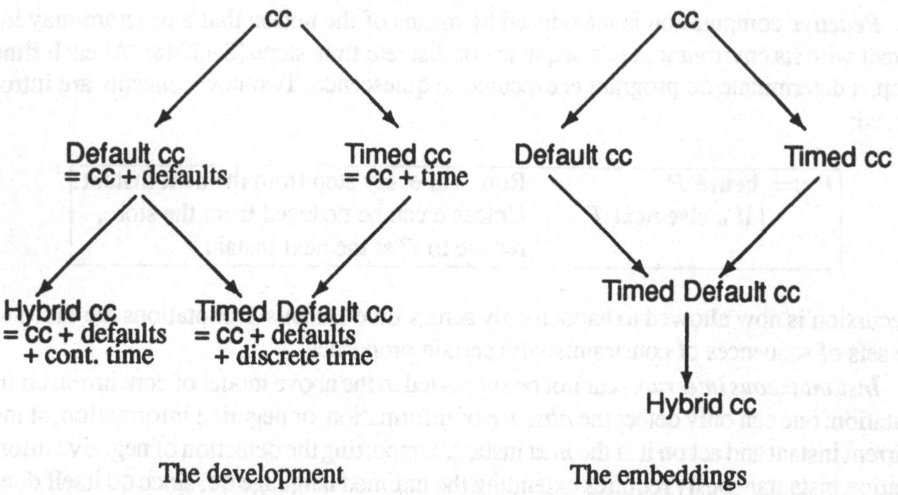

Fig. 1. The relations between the cc languages.

2.1 Constraint Systems.

All cc languages are built generically over constraint systems [Sar92, SRP91]. A constraint system $\mathcal{D}$ is a system of partial information, consisting of a set of primitive constraints (first-order formulas) or *tokens* D, closed under conjunction and existential quantification, and an inference relation (logical entailment), denoted by $\vdash$, that relates tokens to tokens. We use $a, b, \ldots$ to range over tokens. Logical entailment induces through symmetric closure the logical equivalence relation, $\approx$.

Definition 1. A *constraint system* is a structure $\langle D, \vdash, \mathbf{Var}, \{\exists_X \mid X \in \mathbf{Var}\}\rangle$ such that:

1. D is closed under conjunction($\wedge$); $\vdash \subseteq D \times D$ satisfies:
   (a) $a \vdash a$
   (b) $a \vdash a'$ and $a' \wedge a'' \vdash b$ implies that $a \wedge a'' \vdash b$
   (c) $a \wedge b \vdash a$ and $a \wedge b \vdash b$
   (d) $a \vdash b_1$ and $a \vdash b_2$ implies that $a \vdash b_1 \wedge b_2$.
2. **Var** is an infinite set of *variables*, such that for each variable $X \in \mathbf{Var}$, $\exists_X : D \to D$ is an operation satisfying usual laws on existentials:
   (a) $a \vdash \exists_X a$
   (b) $\exists_X(a \wedge \exists_X b) \approx \exists_X a \wedge \exists_X b$
   (c) $\exists_X \exists_Y a \approx \exists_Y \exists_X a$
   (d) $a \vdash b$ implies that $\exists_X a \vdash \exists_X b$.
3. $\vdash$ is decidable.

The last condition is necessary to have an effective operational semantics.

A *constraint* is an entailment closed subset of D. The set of constraints, written $|D|$, ordered by inclusion($\subseteq$), forms a complete algebraic lattice with least upper bounds induced by $\wedge$, least element $\texttt{true} = \{a \mid \forall b \in D.\, b \vdash a\}$ and greatest element $\texttt{false} = D$. Reverse inclusion is written $\supseteq$. $\exists, \vdash$ lift to operations on constraints. Examples of such systems are the system Herbrand (underlying logic programming), FD [HSD92], and Gentzen [SJG94b].

Example 1. **The Herbrand constraint system.** Let L be a first-order language L with equality. The tokens of the constraint system are the atomic propositions. Entailment is specified by Clark's Equality Theory, which include the usual entailment relations that one expects from equality. Thus, for example, $f(X,Y) = f(A, g(B,C))$ must entail $X = A$ and $Y = g(B,C)$.

Example 2. **The FD constraint system.** Variables are assumed to range over finite domains. In addition to tokens representing equality of variables, there are tokens that that restrict the range of a variable to some finite set.

Example 3. **The Gentzen constraint system.** For real-time computation we have found the simple constraint system ($\mathcal{G}$) to be very useful. Gentzen provides the very simple level of functionality that is needed to represent signals, *e.g.* as in ESTEREL and LUSTRE. The primitive tokens a_i of Gentzen are atomic propositions $X, Y, Z \ldots$. These can be thought of as signals in a computing framework. The entailment relation is trivial, i.e. $a_1 \wedge \ldots \wedge a_n \vdash_{\mathcal{G}} a$ iff $a = a_i$ for some i. Finally $\exists_X(a_1 \wedge \ldots \wedge a_n) = b_1 \wedge \ldots \wedge b_n$ where $b_i = a_i$ if $a_i \neq X$ and $b_i = \texttt{true}$ otherwise.

In the rest of this paper we will assume that we are working in some constraint system $\langle D, \vdash, \mathbf{Var}, \{\exists_X \mid X \in \mathbf{Var}\}\rangle$. We will let $a, b \ldots$ range over D. We use $u, v, w \ldots$ to range over constraints.

2.2 Concurrent constraint programming

The model for determinate cc [SRP91] is based on observing for each agent A those stores u in which it is quiescent, that is those stores u in which executing A does not result in the generation of any more information. Define the predicate $A\downarrow^u$ (read: "A converges on u" or "A quiesces on u"). The intended interpretation is: A when executed in u does not produce any information that is not entailed by u. We then have the evident axioms for the combinators:

Tell The only inputs on which a can converge are those that already contain the information in a:

$$\frac{a \in u}{a \downarrow^u}$$

Ask The first corresponds to the case in which the ask is not answered, and the second in which it is:

$$\frac{a \notin u}{(\textbf{if } a \textbf{ then } A)\downarrow^u} \quad \frac{A\downarrow^u}{(\textbf{if } a \textbf{ then } A)\downarrow^u}$$

Parallel Composition To converge on u, both components must converge on u:

$$\frac{A_1 \downarrow^u A_2 \downarrow^u}{(A_1, A_2) \downarrow^u}$$

Hiding Information about the variable X is local to A.

$$\frac{A \downarrow^v \exists_X .u = \exists_X .v}{(\textbf{new } X \textbf{ in } A) \downarrow^u}$$

Note that these axioms for the relation are "compositional": whether an agent converges on u is determined by some conditions involving whether its sub-agents converge on u. This suggests taking the denotation of an agent A to be the set of all u such that $A \downarrow^u$ — thus the denotation of an agent is the set of all its quiescent stores. Because of the axioms above, the denotation is compositional.

Conversely, we would like to obtain the sets of observations which can be the denotations of agents. Such a set should have the property that above every (input) token a, there is a unique minimal element (the output) in the denotation. We can say this generally by requiring that the sets of constraints representing denotations be closed under glbs of arbitrary non-empty subsets.

The following definitions are evident —

$$\begin{aligned}
[\![a]\!] &= \{u \in |D| \mid a \in u\}\\
[\![\textbf{if } a \textbf{ then } B]\!] &= \{u \in |D| \mid a \in u \Rightarrow u \in [\![B]\!]\}\\
[\![A, B]\!] &= [\![A]\!] \cap [\![B]\!]\\
[\![\textbf{new } X \textbf{ in } A]\!] &= \{u \in |D| \mid \exists v \in [\![A]\!], \exists_X u = \exists_X v\}
\end{aligned}$$

Recursion is handled via least fixed points on the domain of processes ordered by reverse inclusion.

The output of a process Z on a given input i is the least o in Z that is above i.

$$Z(i) = \{o \in |D| \mid o \in Z, \forall j \in Z, j \supseteq i \Rightarrow j \supseteq o\}$$

The determinacy of cc is reflected in the fact that $Z(i)$ is always a singleton set.

2.3 The Timed cc programming language

Our first extension of cc for specifying reactive systems was Timed cc [SJG94a]. The necessity for this arose from the fact that cc does not allow the detection of negative information, *i.e.* the absence of information. However, this information is frequently needed in a reactive system — we often want to take some action because a certain event did not occur within a certain time.

Timed cc arises from combining cc with work on the synchronous languages ([BG92], [HCP91], [GBGIM91], [Har87], [CLM91]). These languages are based on the hypothesis of Perfect Synchrony: *Program combinators are determinate primitives that respond instantaneously to input signals. At any instant the presence* and *the absence of signals can be detected.* In synchronous languages, physical time has the same status as any other external event, *i.e.* time is multiform. So combination of programs with different notions of time is allowed. Programs that operate only on "signals" can be compiled into finite state automata with simple transitions. Thus, the single step execution time of the program is bounded and makes the synchrony assumption realizable in practice.

Integrating cc with synchronous languages yields Timed cc: at each time step the computation executed is a cc program. Computation progresses in cycles: input a constraint from the environment, compute to quiescence, generating the constraint to be output at this time instant, and the program to be executed at subsequent time instants. There is no relation between the store at one time instant and the next—constraints that persist, if any, must explicitly be part of the program to execute at subsequent time instants.

The addition of time allows the detection of negative information as follows—if a has not happened at time t, we can take action based on that information at time $t+1$, since no further information could contradict the fact that a was not true at time t. Thus time-steps naturally allow us to detect and act upon such negative information. The syntax of Timed cc is built as follows:

$$P ::= a \mid P, P \mid \textbf{if } a \textbf{ then } P \mid \textbf{new } X \textbf{ in } P \mid \textbf{if } a \textbf{ else next } P \mid \textbf{hence } P$$

The cc combinators behave as before. The agent **if** a **else next** P, when executed at time t, checks if a becomes true at time t. If it does, then nothing happens, otherwise P is set up to execute at the next time instant. **hence** P executes a copy of P at each time step *after* the time step at which it was activated.

Notation. Let s, s' be sequences over some domain *Dom*, and let d be an element of the domain. $s \cdot s'$ denotes sequence concatenation. d can be considered a one element sequence for this purpose. Given a set of sequences Z, we use Z **after** s to denote the set of sequences $\{s' \mid s \cdot s' \in Z\}$, and $Z(0)$ to be $\{u \in Dom \mid \exists s.\ u \cdot s \in Z\}$. $|s|$ denotes the length of s. s^i denotes the prefix of s of length i, while $s(i)$ denotes the i'th element. $\exists_X s$ is the string s', where $s'(k) = \exists_X s(k)$, for all $k < |s|$. ϵ denotes the empty sequence.

Model for Timed cc. Execution of a Timed cc program can be seen as a sequence of executions of cc programs. Thus an observation is a sequence of quiescent stores of each of these programs. So observations are finite sequences of constraints, and the set of all observations is denoted **TccObs**. A process Z is a set of observations satisfying the following conditions:

- ϵ, the empty sequence, is in Z.
- If $s \in Z$, then every prefix of s is also in Z.
- For every $s \in Z$, the set (Z **after** s)(0) is a cc process.

The last condition is due to the fact that we have a cc process at each step, so after any sequence of interactions with the environment, we have a cc process left to execute, to determine the result of the next interaction.

The definitions of the combinators are as expected:

$$\begin{aligned}
\mathcal{T}[\![a]\!] &= \{\epsilon\} \cup \{u \cdot s \in \mathbf{TccObs} \mid a \in u\} \\
\mathcal{T}[\![\mathbf{if}\ a\ \mathbf{then}\ B]\!] &= \{\epsilon\} \cup \{u \cdot s \in \mathbf{TccObs} \mid a \in u \Rightarrow u \cdot s \in \mathcal{T}[\![B]\!]\} \\
\mathcal{T}[\![A, B]\!] &= \mathcal{T}[\![A]\!] \cap \mathcal{T}[\![B]\!] \\
\mathcal{T}[\![\mathbf{new}\ X\ \mathbf{in}\ A]\!] &= \{s \in \mathbf{TccObs} \mid \exists s' \in \mathcal{T}[\![A]\!], \exists_X s = \exists_X s', \\
&\qquad \forall i < |s|. s(i) \in \mathbf{new}\ X\ \mathbf{in}\ (\mathcal{T}[\![A]\!]\ \mathbf{after}\ s'^{i-1})(0)\} \\
\mathcal{T}[\![\mathbf{if}\ a\ \mathbf{else\ next}\ B]\!] &= \{\epsilon\} \cup \{u \cdot s \in \mathbf{TccObs} \mid a \notin u \Rightarrow s \in \mathcal{T}[\![B]\!]\} \\
\mathcal{T}[\![\mathbf{hence}\ A]\!] &= \{\epsilon\} \cup \{u \cdot s \in \mathbf{TccObs} \mid \forall s_1, s_2. [s = s_1 \cdot s_2 \Rightarrow s_2 \in \mathcal{T}[\![A]\!]]\}
\end{aligned}$$

Note that we did not need to add recursion explicitly to the language, as the construct **hence** A enables us to define guarded parameterless recursion.

The output of a Timed cc process Z on a sequence of inputs i is a sequence o with $|i| = |o|$ and $o(k) \in ((Z\ \mathbf{after}\ o^{k-1})(0))(i(k))$.

2.4 Default cc

While the extension of cc to Timed cc allowed us to detect negative information, there was still an asymmetry between positive and negative information — negative information could not be acted upon until the next time instant. This is not acceptable in several situations, since the delays could cascade, rendering the model useless. So it is necessary to detect negative information immediately, and this requires extending the basic monotonic model of cc.

The fundamental move we now make is to allow the expression of *defaults*, after [Rei80]. We allow agents of the form **if** a **else** A, which intuitively mean that *in the absence of* information a, reduce to A. Note however that A may itself cause further information to be added to the store; and indeed, several other agents may simultaneously be active and adding more information to the store. Therefore requiring that information a be absent amounts to making an *assumption* about the future evolution of the system: not only does it not entail a now, but also it will not entail a in the future. Such a demand on "stability" of negative information is inescapable if we want a computational framework that does not produce results dependent on vagaries of the differences in speeds of processors executing the program. We call the resulting language Default cc [SJG].

The critical question in building a model for Default cc then is: how should the notion of observation be extended? Intuitively, the answer seems obvious: observe for each agent A those stores u in which they are quiescent, *given the guess v about the final result*, since once the negative information is detected with respect to the final result, it cannot be voided. Note that the guess v must always be stronger than u — it must contain at least the information on which A is being tested for quiescence.

We define a predicate $A \downarrow_v^u$ (read as: "A converges on u under the guess v"). We then have the evident axioms for the primitive combinators:

Tell The information about the guess v is not needed:

$$\frac{a \in u}{a \downarrow_v^u}$$

Positive Ask The first two rules cover the case in which the ask is not answered, and the third the case in which it is:

$$\frac{a \notin v}{(\textbf{if } a \textbf{ then } A) \downarrow^u_v} \quad \frac{a \notin u, A \downarrow^v_v}{(\textbf{if } a \textbf{ then } A) \downarrow^u_v} \quad \frac{A \downarrow^u_v}{(\textbf{if } a \textbf{ then } A) \downarrow^u_v}$$

Parallel Composition Note that a guess v for A_1, A_2 is propagated down as the guess for A_1 and A_2:

$$\frac{A_1 \downarrow^u_v \; A_2 \downarrow^u_v}{(A_1, A_2) \downarrow^u_v}$$

Negative Ask In the first case, the default is disabled, and in the second it can fire:

$$\frac{a \in v}{(\textbf{if } a \textbf{ else } A) \downarrow^u_v} \quad \frac{A \downarrow^u_v}{(\textbf{if } a \textbf{ else } A) \downarrow^u_v}$$

Hiding Hiding becomes considerably more complicated in this model, we refer the reader to [SJG] for details.

Again, note that these axioms for the relation are "compositional": whether an agent converges on (u, v) is determined by some conditions involving whether its sub-agents converge on (u, v). This suggests taking the denotation of an agent A to be the set of all (u, v) such that $A \downarrow^u_v$; because of the axioms above, the denotation is compositional. Formally, we define observations as a pair of constraints (u, v), where $u \subseteq v$. The intended interpretation is: (u, v) is an observation of A if when the guess v is used to resolve defaults, then executing A in u does not produce any information not entailed by u, and executing A in v does not produce any information not entailed by v.

Define **DObs** $\stackrel{d}{=} \{(u, v) \in |D| \times |D| \mid v \supseteq u\}$. A process Z is a collection of observations that satisfies the following conditions:

1. Guess convergence — $(v, v) \in Z$ if $(u, v) \in Z$. We will only make those guesses v under which a process can actually quiesce, *i.e.* executing the process in v does not produce any information not entailed by v.
2. Local determinacy — the idea is that once a guess is made, every process behaves like a cc agent. Thus, for each v such that $(v, v) \in Z$, the set $\{u \in |D| \mid (u, v) \in Z\}$ is a cc process.

The denotational definitions now follow from the model given above.

$$\mathcal{D}[\![a]\!] \stackrel{d}{=} \{(u, v) \in \textbf{DObs} \mid a \in u\}$$

$$\mathcal{D}[\![\textbf{if } a \textbf{ then } A]\!] \stackrel{d}{=} \{(u, v) \in \textbf{DObs} \mid a \in v \Rightarrow (v, v) \in \mathcal{D}[\![A]\!], \; a \in u \Rightarrow (u, v) \in \mathcal{D}[\![A]\!]\}$$

$$\mathcal{D}[\![\textbf{if } a \textbf{ else } A]\!] \stackrel{d}{=} \{(u, v) \in \textbf{DObs} \mid a \notin v \Rightarrow (u, v) \in \mathcal{D}[\![A]\!]\}$$

$$\mathcal{D}[\![A, B]\!] \stackrel{d}{=} \mathcal{D}[\![A]\!] \cap \mathcal{D}[\![B]\!]$$

For the formal definition of hiding, we refer the reader to [SJG]. Recursion is modeled by least fixed points on the domain of processes ordered by reverse inclusion, however we will consider Default cc without recursion. Here are some examples illustrating some denotations.

Example 4.

$$\mathcal{D}[\![\mathbf{if}\ a\ \mathbf{else}\ a]\!] = \{(u,v) \in \mathbf{DObs} \mid a \in v\}$$

This is an example of a default theory which does not have any extensions ([Rei80]). However, it does provide some information, it says that the quiescent points must be greater than a, and it is necessary to keep this information to get a compositional semantics. It is different from **if** b **else** b, whereas in default logic and synchronous languages both these agents are considered the same, *i.e.* meaningless, and are thrown away.

Example 5.

$$\mathcal{D}[\![\mathbf{if}\ a\ \mathbf{then}\ b, \mathbf{if}\ a\ \mathbf{else}\ b]\!] = \\ \{(u,v) \in \mathbf{DObs} \mid b \in v, ((a \notin v) \vee (a \in u)) \Rightarrow b \in u\}$$

This agent is "almost" like "if a then b else b", and illustrates the basic difference between positive and negative information. In most semantics, one would expect it to be identical to the agent b. However, **if** a **else** b is not the same as **if** $\neg a$ **then** b, in the second case some agent must explicitly write $\neg a$ in the store, but in the first case merely the fact that no agent can write a is sufficient to trigger b. This difference is demonstrated by running both b and **if** a **then** b, **if** a **else** b in parallel with **if** b **then** a — (b, **if** b **then** a) produces $a \sqcup b$ on $true$, while **if** a **then** b, **if** a **else** b, **if** b **then** a produces no output.

The output of a Default cc process Z on input i is some resting point o, such that there is no stopping point between i and o. Thus

$$Z(i) = \{o \in |D| \mid (o,o) \in Z, \forall (j,o) \in Z, j \supseteq i \Rightarrow j \supseteq o\}$$

Note that the i/o relation may not be monotone, for example $(\mathcal{D}[\![\mathbf{if}\ a\ \mathbf{else}\ b]\!])(\mathtt{true}) = \{b\}$, while $(\mathcal{D}[\![\mathbf{if}\ a\ \mathbf{else}\ b]\!])(a) = \{a\}$. Note also that Default cc programs can have no outputs or multiple outputs on an input. For example **if** a **else** a has no output on `true`, while both a and b are possible outputs of **if** a **else** b, **if** b **else** a on `true`. Default cc programs which have unique outputs for all inputs are called *determinate*. In [SJG], we describe an algorithm for determinacy detection.

2.5 Timed Default cc

Default cc can be extended to yield a timed language just as cc was extended to Timed cc. At each time step, a Default cc program is executed to determine the output on the given input, then the program for the next step is set up, and the system becomes dormant until the next step is triggered by an input from the environment. Thus we get a reactive programming language in the family of synchronous programming languages ([BB91]), called Timed Default cc [SJG].

We need to add one more combinator to Default cc, **hence** A, which executes a new copy of A at each step after the current one.

Just as Timed cc observations were finite sequences of cc observations, similarly Timed Default cc observations are finite sequences of Default cc observations. However notice from the input-output relation of Default cc that only Default cc observations of the form (v, v) can be seen as the result of an execution. Since at any time step the previous time steps are completed, their observations must be of the form (v, v). So a Timed Default cc observation is a sequence of Default cc observations in which all elements but the last must be of the form (v, v). The definition of a process remains the same as Timed cc, with cc changed to Default cc.

The denotational definitions of processes are as before, we repeat them here for completeness.

$$\begin{aligned}
\mathcal{P}[\![a]\!] &= \{\epsilon\} \cup \{(u,v)\cdot s \in \textbf{TDObs} \mid a \in u\} \\
\mathcal{P}[\![\textbf{if } a \textbf{ then } B]\!] &= \{\epsilon\} \cup \{(u,v)\cdot s \in \textbf{TDObs} \mid a \in u \Rightarrow (u,v)\cdot s \in \mathcal{P}[\![B]\!] \\
&\qquad\qquad\qquad\qquad\qquad\qquad\quad a \in v \Rightarrow (v,v) \in \mathcal{P}[\![B]\!]\} \\
\mathcal{P}[\![A,B]\!] &= \mathcal{P}[\![A]\!] \cap \mathcal{P}[\![B]\!] \\
\mathcal{P}[\![\textbf{if } a \textbf{ else } B]\!] &= \{\epsilon\} \cup \{(u,v)\cdot s \in \textbf{TDObs} \mid a \notin v \Rightarrow (u,v)\cdot s \in \mathcal{P}[\![B]\!]\} \\
\mathcal{P}[\![\textbf{hence } A]\!] &= \{\epsilon\} \cup \{(u,v)\cdot s \in \textbf{TDObs} \mid \forall s_1, s_2.\, s = s_1 \cdot s_2 \Rightarrow s_2 \in \mathcal{P}[\![A]\!]\}
\end{aligned}$$

The definition of hiding is similar to the definition in Timed cc, we refer the reader to [SJG] for details.

The input output relation is similar to that for Timed cc— the output of a Timed Default cc process Z on a sequence of inputs $i = \langle i_0, i_1, \ldots i_n\rangle$ is a sequence $o = \langle o_0, o_1, \ldots o_n\rangle$, where $o_k \in ((Z \textbf{ after } o'^{k-1})(0))(i_k)$, where $o'(k) = (o_k, o_k)$ for all $k < |o|$.

We demonstrate the expressiveness of Timed Default cc by defining a few combinators in terms of the basic ones given above.

Example 6. We can define the **next** A combinator to start a copy of A at the next time instant, in terms of **hence** A —

$$\textbf{next } A = \textbf{new } \texttt{stop} \textbf{ in hence } [\textbf{if } \texttt{stop} \textbf{ else } A, \textbf{hence } \texttt{stop}]$$

Thus if **next** A is called at time 1, then from time 2 onwards **if** `stop` **else** A is executed. At time 2, no `stop` is generated (as it is local and **hence** `stop` does not start generating it till time 3), so A is started. From 3 onwards, `stop` is generated. Thus the net effect is the execution of a copy of A at time 2.

Example 7. A useful variant of **hence** A is **always** $A \stackrel{d}{=} A$, **hence** A, it simply starts a new copy of A every time, instead of from the next time instant.

Example 8. Parameterless guarded recursion can also be defined using **hence**. Consider a Timed Default cc program as a set of declarations $g :: A$ along with an agent. (Here g names a parameterless procedure.) These declarations can be replaced by the construct **always if** g **then** A. The names of the agents g can now occur in the program, and will be treated as simple propositional constraints. Note that only one call of an agent may be made at one time instant.

Example 9. Another useful combinator is **first** a **do** B, which starts the process B at the first time instant that a becomes true. It can be defined as

$$\begin{aligned}
\textbf{first } a \textbf{ do } B = \textbf{new } \texttt{stop} \textbf{ in always } [&\textbf{if } \texttt{stop} \textbf{ else if } a \textbf{ then } B \\
&\textbf{if } a \textbf{ then hence } \texttt{stop}]
\end{aligned}$$

This program keeps on executing **if** a **then** A, unless it receives the signal `stop`. The `stop` is produced in all instants after a is true. Note the fact that this definition is identical to the definition for the continuous language Hybrid cc [GJS], this will also be the case for the other definitions given below.

Example 10. The agent **time** A **on** a denotes a process whose notion of time is the occurrence of the tokens a — A evolves only at the time instants at which the store entails a. This is definable as follows:

Given a token a and a sequence $s \in \mathbf{TDObs}$, define the subsequence of s in which $a \in \pi_1(s(i))$ as s_a. Formally, this subsequence is defined by induction on the length as follows:

$$\epsilon_a = \epsilon$$

$$(s \cdot (u,v))_a = \begin{cases} s_a \cdot (u,v), & \text{if } a \in u \\ s_a, & \text{otherwise} \end{cases}$$

Now define $\mathcal{P}[\![\mathbf{time}\ A\ \mathbf{on}\ a]\!] \stackrel{d}{=} \{s \in \mathbf{TDObs} \mid s_a \in \mathcal{P}[\![A]\!]\}$.

This combinator satisfies the following equational laws, which can be used to remove its occurrences from any program.

$$\begin{aligned}
\mathbf{time}\ b\ \mathbf{on}\ a &= \mathbf{first}\ a\ \mathbf{then}\ b \\
\mathbf{time}\ (\mathbf{if}\ b\ \mathbf{then}\ B)\ \mathbf{on}\ a &= \mathbf{first}\ a\ \mathbf{then}\ \mathbf{if}\ b\ \mathbf{then}\ \mathbf{time}\ B\ \mathbf{on}\ a \\
\mathbf{time}\ (\mathbf{if}\ b\ \mathbf{else}\ B)\ \mathbf{on}\ a &= \mathbf{first}\ a\ \mathbf{then}\ \mathbf{if}\ b\ \mathbf{else}\ \mathbf{time}\ B\ \mathbf{on}\ a \\
\mathbf{time}\ (A,B)\ \mathbf{on}\ a &= (\mathbf{time}\ A\ \mathbf{on}\ a), (\mathbf{time}\ B\ \mathbf{on}\ a) \\
\mathbf{time}\ \mathbf{new}\ x\ \mathbf{in}\ A\ \mathbf{on}\ a &= \mathbf{new}\ x\ \mathbf{in}\ \mathbf{time}\ A\ \mathbf{on}\ a, (x \text{ not free in } a) \\
\mathbf{time}\ (\mathbf{hence}\ B)\ \mathbf{on}\ a &= \mathbf{first}\ a\ \mathbf{do}\ [\mathbf{hence}\ (\mathbf{if}\ a\ \mathbf{then}\ \mathbf{time}\ B\ \mathbf{on}\ a)]
\end{aligned}$$

time A **on** a can be used to construct various other combinators that manipulate the notion of time ticks being fed to a process. The general schema is to time the process A on some signal `go`. Now another process is set up to generate `go` whenever one wants A to proceed. The next few examples illustrate this.

Example 11. **do** A **watching** a is an interrupt primitive related to *strong abortion* in ESTEREL ([Ber93]). **do** A **watching** a behaves like A until a time instant when a is entailed; when a is entailed A is killed instantaneously. Using **time** this is definable as:

$$\begin{aligned}
\mathbf{do}\ A\ \mathbf{watching}\ a = \mathbf{new}\ \mathtt{stop}, \mathtt{go}\ \mathbf{in}\ [&\mathbf{time}\ A\ \mathbf{on}\ \mathtt{go}, \\
&\mathbf{first}\ a\ \mathbf{do}\ \mathbf{always}\ \mathtt{stop}, \\
&\mathbf{always}\ \mathbf{if}\ \mathtt{stop}\ \mathbf{else}\ \mathtt{go}]
\end{aligned}$$

Example 12. There is a related weak abortion construct ([Ber93]) —**do** A **trap** a behaves like A until a time instant when a is entailed; when a is entailed A is killed from the *next* time instant. It can be defined as

$$\begin{aligned}
\mathbf{do}\ A\ \mathtt{trap}\ a = \mathbf{new}\ \mathtt{stop}, \mathtt{go}\ \mathbf{in}\ [&\mathbf{time}\ A\ \mathbf{on}\ \mathtt{go}, \\
&\mathbf{first}\ a\ \mathbf{do}\ \mathbf{hence}\ \mathtt{stop}, \\
&\mathbf{always}\ \mathbf{if}\ \mathtt{stop}\ \mathbf{else}\ \mathtt{go}]
\end{aligned}$$

Note that the signal `stop` is generated from the time instant *after* a is seen.

Example 13. The Suspension-Activation primitive, $\mathbf{S}_a\mathbf{A}_b(A)$, is a preemption primitive that is a variant of *suspension* in ESTEREL ([Ber93]). $\mathbf{S}_a\mathbf{A}_b(A)$ behaves like A until a time instant when a is entailed; when a is entailed A is suspended immediately (hence the S_a). A is reactivated in the time instant when b is entailed (hence the A_b). The familiar (`control` – `Z`, `fg`) is a construct in this vein. This can be expressed as:

$$\mathbf{S}_a\mathbf{A}_b(A) = \textbf{new}\ \texttt{stop}, \texttt{go}\ \textbf{in}\ [\textbf{time}\ A\ \textbf{on}\ \texttt{go},\ \textbf{always if}\ \texttt{stop}\ \textbf{else}\ \texttt{go},\ \textbf{first}\ a\ \textbf{do do (always}\ \texttt{stop}\textbf{)}\ \textbf{watching}\ b]$$

2.6 Hybrid cc

Timed Default cc was obtained by extending Default cc across the natural numbers. Similarly, extending Default cc across the real numbers yields Hybrid cc [GJS, GJSB95, GJS96]. Hybrid cc is intended to be a language for describing hybrid systems, which are systems that can evolve discretely as well as continuously [BG90, NSY92, MMP92, GNRR93].

We model hybrid systems that evolve in a piecewise continuous manner. Thus a run of a hybrid system consists of an alternating sequence of points and open intervals — open intervals of continuous evolution connected by points of discrete change where discontinuities can occur. The "extension" of Default cc over continuous time proceeds in two stages. First, we introduce the notion of a *continuous* constraint system — a real-time extension of constraint systems — to describe the continuous evolution of system trajectories alluded to above. Next, the Default cc model of processes is extended over continuous time to describe Hybrid cc processes.

Continuous constraint systems(ccs) are described in detail in [GJS]. Informally, continuous constraint systems are obtained by incorporating intuitions from real analysis into constraint systems. Intuitively, continuous constraint systems express the information content of initial value problems in integration. Continuous constraint systems support an integration operation, $\int^r \texttt{init}(a) \wedge \texttt{cont}(b)$[3], which determines the effect at time r of b holding continuously in the interval $(0, r)$, if a held at time 0. For example, $\int^7 \texttt{init}(x = 3) \wedge \texttt{cont}(dot(x) = 4) \vdash x = 31$. [GJS] describes a set of axioms for continuous constraint systems — these include intuitive properties of integration such as the monotonicity and continuity of integration, and some computability axioms to enable finite description and implementation. A continuous evolution of the ccs is a function from some prefix of the reals to $|D|$, such that $\exists a.\forall r > 0.f(r) = \int^r a$.

Example 14. A trivial continuous constraint system can be described as follows: Let $\langle D, \vdash_D, \mathbf{Var}, \{\exists_X \mid X \in \mathbf{Var}\}\rangle$ be a constraint system. Define the trivial ccs on it via the integration operations $\int^r \texttt{init}(a) \wedge \texttt{cont}(b) = b, r > 0$. The for $r > 0$ this the integral is independent of the initial conditions, so it does not allow any continuously varying temporal evolution. All continuous evolutions of the ccs are constant over $(0, \infty)$. We will use it later to embed Timed Default cc in Hybrid cc.

[3] `cont` and `init` may be thought of as labels which distinguish the constraints which hold continuously from those which hold at the initial points.

Example 15. The simplest non-trivial ccs is defined on a constraint system $\langle D, \vdash_D, \emptyset, \emptyset \rangle$, where D contains tokens of the form $dot(x,m) = r$, which is intended to mean that the m'th derivative of x is r. The inference relation is defined to conform to this intuition. Now we can define the integration relation to mean usual integration — note that the continuous evolutions of this ccs are all polynomial functions of one variable. No existential quantification is allowed for computability reasons.

Now, we are ready to describe informally what Hybrid cc observations should be. First, note that we intend the execution at every time instant to be modeled by the execution in Default cc. So, we choose observations to be functions with domain a prefix of the non-negative reals and range Default cc observations[4]. Secondly, every function f satisfies *piecewise continuity* — *i.e.* for any point in the interior of its domain, both components of the behavior of f on some open interval to the right arise from continuous evolutions of the ccs. For such a function, we can partition its domain into a (possibly infinite) alternating sequence of points and open intervals, called *phases* of the observation — the point phases indicate discontinuities and the open interval phases are continuous behaviors of the ccs. Finally, as in Timed Default cc, we intend the functions to satisfy observability — *i.e.* the computation in any phase but the last is a completed Default cc computation. We use **HObs** for the set of Hybrid cc observations.

Processes are sets of observations that satisfy similar conditions as in Timed cc— the empty observation is in every process, and all processes are prefix closed. In addition, if every proper prefix of an observation is in a process, then the observation must be in the process. Finally we wish to be able to execute Default cc programs in each phase, so as before the process **after** any observation must form a Default cc process. These definitions are stated precisely in [GJS].

The only new combinator we need to add to the set of Default cc combinators is again **hence** A, which executes a new copy of A at every real time point in the *open* interval starting at the time it was called. The denotational definitions are similar to Timed Default cc. We use $\pi_1(z)$ and $\pi_2(z)$ to denote the first and second components of a pair z.

$$\begin{aligned}
\mathcal{H}[\![a]\!] &= \{\epsilon\} \cup \{f \in \mathbf{HObs} \mid a \in \pi_1(f(0))\} \\
\mathcal{H}[\![\mathbf{if}\ a\ \mathbf{then}\ B]\!] &= \{\epsilon\} \cup \{f \in \mathbf{HObs} \mid a \in \pi_1(f(0)) \Rightarrow f \in \mathcal{H}[\![B]\!] \\
&\qquad a \in \pi_2(f(0)) \Rightarrow (\pi_2(f(0)), \pi_2(f(0))) \in \mathcal{H}[\![B]\!]\} \\
\mathcal{H}[\![A, B]\!] &= \mathcal{H}[\![A]\!] \cap \mathcal{H}[\![B]\!] \\
\mathcal{H}[\![\mathbf{if}\ a\ \mathbf{else}\ B]\!] &= \{\epsilon\} \cup \{f \in \mathbf{HObs} \mid a \notin \pi_2(f(0)) \Rightarrow f \in \mathcal{H}[\![B]\!]\} \\
\mathcal{H}[\![\mathbf{hence}\ A]\!] &= \{\epsilon\} \cup \{f \in \mathbf{HObs} \mid \forall t > 0, f\restriction[t,\infty) \in \mathcal{H}[\![A]\!]\}
\end{aligned}$$

where $f\restriction[t,\infty)(r) = f(t+r), 0 \leq r$. Again, we omit the definition of hiding. Guarded parameterless recursion can again be coded using **hence** . The input-output relation for a process on a piecewise continuous input trace is defined as for Timed Default cc.

Combinators. The hybrid analogs of the defined combinators given above can be defined in Hybrid cc also. In fact, none of the definitions change. For details, see [GJS].

[4] Contrast this against the observations of Timed Default cc, which were functions from a prefix of the natural numbers to Default cc observations.

3 The relationships between the languages

As pointed out in the introduction, the languages given above are successively more general. We will now give the embeddings that establish the partial order shown in Figure 1. Note that while we have omitted the definition of hiding in some of the above languages, all the embeddings hold for programs with hiding also.

3.1 Embedding cc in Default cc

cc embeds conservatively in Default cc. The embedding of cc into Default cc is immediate, since Default cc is a strictly larger language. Denotationally, given a cc process Q, the Default cc process corresponding to it is given by $\{(u, v) \in \mathbf{DObs} \mid u, v \in Q\}$.

The partial converse exploits a characterization of a large class of "monotone" Default cc processes — intuitively, this class captures the processes that do not exploit the ability to detect negative information. For any determinate Default cc process P, the input output relation $P(i)$ is the graph of a monotone function, if P satisfies:

1. If $(u, v) \in P$ then $(u, u) \in P$.
2. If $(u, v) \in P, (v', v') \in P, v' \supseteq v$ then $(u, v') \in P$.

Note that the embedding of any cc process satisfies both the properties given above, and thus is monotone. For a Default cc process P satisfying the conditions of the above lemma, the fixed point set of the corresponding cc process is just $\{u \mid (u, u) \in P\}$.

Furthermore, all the definitions of Default cc (including hiding) for the cc combinators also commute with this embedding, so if we take the embedding first and then use the Default cc definitions, we get the same results as using the cc definitions and then embedding in Default cc.

3.2 Embedding cc in Timed cc

Timed cc allows a different embedding of cc. This embedding exploits the time structure of Timed cc to reveal some of the operational structure of the cc program.

We can define **first** a **then next** A as

new `stop` **in always if** a **then** [**if** `stop` **else next** A, **hence** `stop`]

The embedding is as follows:

$$\begin{aligned}\mathcal{E}(a) &= a, \mathbf{hence}\ a\\ \mathcal{E}(\mathbf{if}\ a\ \mathbf{then}\ A) &= \mathbf{first}\ a\ \mathbf{then\ next}\ \mathcal{E}(A)\\ \mathcal{E}(A, B) &= \mathcal{E}(A), \mathcal{E}(B)\\ \mathcal{E}(\mathbf{new}\ X\ \mathbf{in}\ A) &= \mathbf{new}\ X\ \mathbf{in}\ \mathcal{E}(A)\end{aligned}$$

Recursive calls can be spread across time by adding **next** before them — **next** A = **first** `true` **then next** A. An interesting feature of this embedding is that at any time-step, the cc program to be executed is a tell process. This embedding reveals a lot more of the operational structure of the program than the usual cc semantics — informally it represents a step semantics to cc programs obtained by stratifying the addition of constraints to the store. Note that the embedding is not fully abstract — two equivalent cc programs may be embedded differently. For example a, b will be embedded differently from a, **if** a **then** b.

It is also possible to construct a partial converse to the above embedding. Consider the monotone observations of Timed cc— those sequences s where for all $1 < i < |s|$, $s(i) \supseteq s(i-1)$. Consider any Timed cc process containing only such observations, we will call it a monotone process if it also satisfies the following condition: If $s \cdot u$ and $s \cdot u'$ are in Z, and $u' \supseteq u$, then Z **after** $(s \cdot u') \subseteq Z$ **after** $(s \cdot u)$. This is similar to the second condition in the above subsection. Then, we have:

Lemma 2. *Let Z be a monotone Timed cc process. Define $Z' = \{u \in |D| \mid \exists s \in Z, s(|s|-1) = u, \forall k > 0 \exists s'.(s \cdot s') \in Z, |s'| = k, \forall i < k.s'(i) = u\}$. Then Z' is a cc process.*

The Z' in this lemma consists of all those u under which Z reaches quiescence — that is, unless there is some input from the environment, Z will not add anything to the store. It can be alternatively defined as $\{u \in |D| \mid \exists s \in |D|^\omega, Fin(s) \subseteq Z, u = \bigsqcup_i s(i)\}$, where $Fin(s)$ is the set of finite prefixes of s.

Let A be a cc program. Let $Z = T[\![\mathcal{E}(A)]\!]$ be the process obtained by embedding it in Timed cc. Let Z' be the cc process defined in Lemma 2. Then $Z' = [\![A]\!]$.

Embedding Timed cc and Default cc in Timed Default cc. Since Default cc is conservative over cc, Timed cc directly embeds in Timed Default cc. Also, since a recursion-free Default cc program embeds in any one instant of the Timed Default cc program, every recursion-free Default cc program can be understood as a Timed Default cc program, embedding Default cc in Timed Default cc.

3.3 Embedding Timed Default cc in Hybrid cc

Since Timed Default cc is a discrete language with no autonomous behavior, the continuous constraint system over which Hybrid cc is built is the one described in Example 14.

In order to encode the **hence** A of Timed Default cc, we need to know when the next input comes in from the environment. Following the discrete time synchronous languages such as `Esterel`, we attach to each discrete input a special token `tick`. Thus `tick` is a discrete signal, and whenever any input comes in from the environment, `tick` is always present. Now we can embed Timed Default cc in Hybrid cc. The only non-trivial case is **hence** of Timed Default cc. The embedding of **hence** A becomes **hence if** `tick` **then** $E(A)$, where $E(A)$ is the embedding of A. Thus at every `tick` after the current one, a copy of A is started. Since all agents to be executed later are in the scope of a **if** `tick` **then** ..., computation occurs only when `tick` occurs, otherwise the system is dormant, which is exactly what we would expect for a reactive system.

As with the earlier embeddings, a partial converse can be described. Consider the subset **DHObs** of Hybrid cc observations built upon the constraint system of Example 14, which have the property that `tick` is true in every point phase, and the pair of constraints at any point in any interval phase are (`true`, `true`). Each such observation obviously corresponds to a Timed Default cc observation, so every Timed Default cc process can be embedded into a Hybrid cc process. The following lemma states the connection between these embeddings.

Lemma 3. *Given a* Timed Default cc *program P, let its embedding in* Hybrid cc *be P'. Then the denotation $\mathcal{P}[\![P]\!]$ when embedded in* **DHObs** *is exactly* $\mathcal{H}[\![P']\!] \cap$ **DHObs**.

Acknowledgements. This work was supported by grants from ARPA and ONR, and the second author was supported by a grant from the NSF.

References

[BB91] A. Benveniste and G. Berry, editors. *Another Look at Real-time Systems*, September 1991. Special issue of the Proceedings of the IEEE.

[Ber93] G. Berry. Preemption in concurrent systems. In *Proc. of FSTTCS*. Springer-Verlag, 1993. LNCS 781.

[BG90] A. Benveniste and P. Le Guernic. Hybrid dynamical systems and the signal language. *IEEE Transactions on Automatic control*, 35(5):535–546, 1990.

[BG92] G. Berry and G. Gonthier. The ESTEREL programming language: Design, semantics and implementation. *Science of Computer Programming*, 19(2):87 – 152, November 1992.

[CLM91] E. M. Clarke, D. E. Long, and K. L. McMillan. A language for compositional specification and verification of finite state hardware controllers. In Benveniste and Berry [BB91]. Special issue of the Proceedings of the IEEE.

[dBHdRR92] J. W. de Bakker, C. Huizing, W. P. de Roever, and G. Rozenberg, editors. *REX workshop "Real time: Theory in Practice"*, volume 600 of *Lecture Notes in Computer Science*. Springer Verlag, 1992.

[dKB85] Johan de Kleer and John Seely Brown. *Qualitative Reasoning about Physical Systems*, chapter Qualitative Physics Based on Confluences. MIT Press, 1985. Also published in AIJ, 1984.

[GBGlM91] P. Le Guernic, M. Le Borgne, T. Gauthier, and C. le Maire. Programming real time applications with SIGNAL. In Benveniste and Berry [BB91]. Special issue of the Proceedings of the IEEE.

[GJS] Vineet Gupta, Radha Jagadeesan, and Vijay Saraswat. Computing with continuous change. *Science of Computer Programming*. To appear.

[GJS96] Vineet Gupta, Radha Jagadeesan, and Vijay Saraswat. Hybrid cc, hybrid automata and program verification. In Alur, Henzinger, and Sontag, editors, *Hybrid Systems III*, Lecture Notes in Computer Science. Springer Verlag, 1996. To appear.

[GJSB95] Vineet Gupta, Radha Jagadeesan, Vijay Saraswat, and Daniel Bobrow. Programming in hybrid constraint languages. In Panos Antsaklis, Wolf Kohn, Anil Nerode, and Sankar Sastry, editors, *Hybrid Systems II*, volume 999 of *Lecture Notes in Computer Science*, pages 226–251. Springer Verlag, November 1995.

[GNRR93] Robert Grossman, Anil Nerode, Anders Ravn, and Hans Rischel, editors. *Hybrid Systems*, volume 736 of *Lecture Notes in Computer Science*. Springer Verlag, 1993.

[Har87] D. Harel. Statecharts: A visual approach to complex systems. *Science of Computer Programming*, 8:231 – 274, 1987.

[HCP91] N. Halbwachs, P. Caspi, and D. Pilaud. The synchronous programming language LUSTRE. In Benveniste and Berry [BB91]. Special issue of the Proceedings of the IEEE.

[HSD92] Pascal Van Hentenryck, Vijay A. Saraswat, and Yves Deville. Constraint processing in cc(fd). Technical report, Computer Science Department, Brown University, 1992.

[MMP92] O. Maler, Z. Manna, and A. Pnueli. From timed to hybrid systems. In de Bakker et al. [dBHdRR92], pages 447–484.

[NSY92] X. Nicollin, J. Sifakis, and S. Yovine. From ATP to timed graphs and hybrid systems. In de Bakker et al. [dBHdRR92].

[Rei80] Ray Reiter. A logic for default reasoning. *Artificial Intelligence*, 13:81 – 132, 1980.

[Sar92] Vijay A. Saraswat. The Category of Constraint Systems is Cartesian-closed. In *Proc. 7th IEEE Symp. on Logic in Computer Science, Santa Cruz*, 1992.

[SHW94] Gert Smolka, Henz, and J. Werz. *Constraint Programming: The Newport Papers*, chapter Object-oriented programming in Oz. MIT Press, 1994.

[SJG] V. A. Saraswat, R. Jagadeesan, and V. Gupta. Timed Default Concurrent Constraint Programming. *Journal of Symbolic Computation*. To appear. Extended abstract appeared in the *Proceedings of the 22nd ACM Symposium on Principles of Programming Languages*, San francisco, January 1995.

[SJG94a] V. A. Saraswat, R. Jagadeesan, and V. Gupta. Foundations of Timed Concurrent Constraint Programming. In Samson Abramsky, editor, *Proceedings of the Ninth Annual IEEE Symposium on Logic in Computer Science*, pages 71–80. IEEE Computer Press, July 1994.

[SJG94b] V. A. Saraswat, R. Jagadeesan, and V. Gupta. Programming in timed concurrent constraint languages. In B.Mayoh, E.Tougu, and J.Penjam, editors, *Constraint Programming*, volume 131 of *NATO Advanced Science Institute Series F: Computer and System Sciences*, pages 367–413. Springer-Verlag, 1994.

[SRP91] V. A. Saraswat, M. Rinard, and P. Panangaden. Semantic foundations of concurrent constraint programming. In *Proceedings of Eighteenth ACM Symposium on Principles of Programming Languages, Orlando*, January 1991.

Comparing Transition Systems with Independence and Asynchronous Transition Systems

*Thomas T. Hildebrandt**   *Vladimiro Sassone**,⋆

* **BRICS** – Computer Science Dept., University of Aarhus
⋆ Dipartimento di Informatica, Università di Pisa

Abstract. Transition systems with independence and asynchronous transition systems are *noninterleaving* models for concurrency arising from the same simple idea of decorating transitions with events. They differ for the choice of a *derived* versus a *primitive* notion of event which induces considerable differences and makes the two models suitable for different purposes. This opens the problem of investigating their mutual relationships, to which this paper gives a fully comprehensive answer.
In details, we characterise the category of *extensional* asynchronous transitions systems as the largest full subcategory of the category of (labelled) asynchronous transition systems which admits TSI, the category of transition systems with independence, as a *coreflective* subcategory. In addition, we introduce *event-maximal* asynchronous transitions systems and we show that their category is *equivalent* to TSI, so providing an exhaustive characterisation of transition systems with independence in terms of asynchronous transition systems.

Introduction

Following the leading idea of CCS [11] and related process calculi [10, 2, 12, 9], the behaviour of concurrent systems is often specified *extensionally* by describing their 'state-transitions' and the observable behaviours that such transitions produce. The simplest formal model of computation able to express naturally this idea is that of *labelled transition systems*, where the labels on the transitions are thought of as the actions of the system at its 'external ports', or, more generally, the observable part of its behaviour.

Transition systems are an *interleaving* model of concurrency, which means that they do not allow to draw a natural distinction between interleaved and concurrent execution of actions. More precisely, transition systems do not model the fact that concurrent actions can overlap in time and reduce concurrency to a nondeterministic choice of action interleavings, so loosing track of the casual dependencies between actions and, consequently, of the fact that computations that differ only for the order of independent actions represent, actually, the same behaviour. In other words, interleaving models abstract away from the difference between the factual *temporal* occurrence order and the more conceptual *causal* ordering of actions. The simplest exemplification of this situation is provided by the CCS terms $a \mid b$ and $a.b + b.a$, both described by the following transition system.

---

* Basic Research in Computer Science, Centre of the Danish National Research Foundation.
⋆ This author was supported by EU Human Capital and Mobility grant ERBCHBGCT920005.

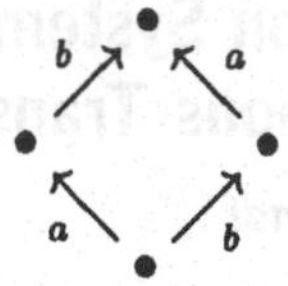

(1)

Although for many applications this level of abstraction is appropriate, for several other kinds of analysis a model may be desirable that takes full account of concurrency. For instance, apart from any philosophical consideration about the semantic relevance of cause/effect relationships, knowing that different interleavings represent the same behaviour can reduce considerably the state-space explosion problem when checking system properties such as safety properties and fairness [8, 20, 16].

Several efforts have been devoted to the search of transition-based *noninterleaving* models, e.g., transition systems enriched with additional features that make expressing concurrency explicitly possible (cf., e.g., [17, 4, 6, 7, 5, 3]). The present paper focuses on two such models, namely *asynchronous transition systems*, introduced independently by Bednarczyk [1] and Shields [19], and *transitions systems with independence*, proposed by Winskel and Nielsen [21]. These two competing approaches are, among the others, those building on the simplest idea: endow transition systems with some formal notion of 'similarity' of transitions that enables to distinguish whether or not the opposite edges in diagrams such as (1) represent the same action. Intuitively, this is achieved in both approaches by thinking of transitions as *occurrences* of *events*, two transitions representing the same event if they correspond to the same action. However, the differences induced on the models by the different choices of how to assign events to transitions are definitely not trivial. And so are the relationships that these models bear to each other.

Getting to the details, asynchronous transition systems assign events to transitions explicitly and enrich the structure further by adding an *independence relation* on the events which describes their causal relationships. This clearly makes distinguishing nondeterminism and concurrency possible; $a.b+b.a$ and $a|b$ can be represented respectively by, e.g., the following *labelled* asynchronous transition systems, where $\sim$ indicates whether or not the events e and e' (labelled by a and b) are independent.

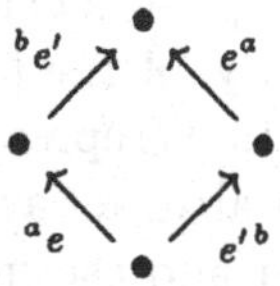

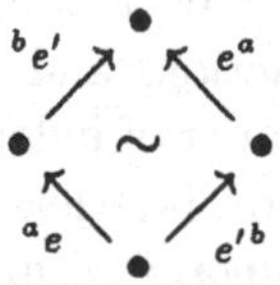

Observe that here and in the rest of the paper we consider *labelled* asynchronous transition systems [1, 21], i.e., asynchronous transition systems with a further labelling of events, as the proper extension of labelled transition systems.

The expressive power of asynchronous transition systems is clearly not limited to the example above; for instance, Bednarczyk [1] and Mukund and Nielsen [14] have shown that noninterleaving related issues for CCS processes—such as *localities*—can be modelled faithfully using this model. However, it can be argued that assigning both the independence relation and the decoration of transitions with events explicitly means assigning too much. In fact, this obviously introduces some *redundancies* in the model: there are, for instance, many non-isomorphic variations of the asynchronous transitions systems above which can still be reasonably thought as models of $a|b$ and $a.b + b.a$. Moreover, although it is usually easy to tell about independence of transitions, in many important cases it is at least *not* immediate to assign events to transitions: it might very well be the goal of the entire semantic analysis to understand what the events of the system and their mutual relationships are. This consideration seems to indicate that asynchronous transitions systems cannot have a significant impact in Plotkin's SOS style semantics, unless the independence relation is promoted to a greater role.

Transition systems with independence are an attempt to answer to the previous observation. Here events are *not* introduced explicitly. They are rather *derived* from the structure of the 'simply-labelled' transitions, upon which the independence relation is directly layered. In such a model, each of the CCS terms discussed above admits only one transition system which can faithfully represent it, viz., respectively,

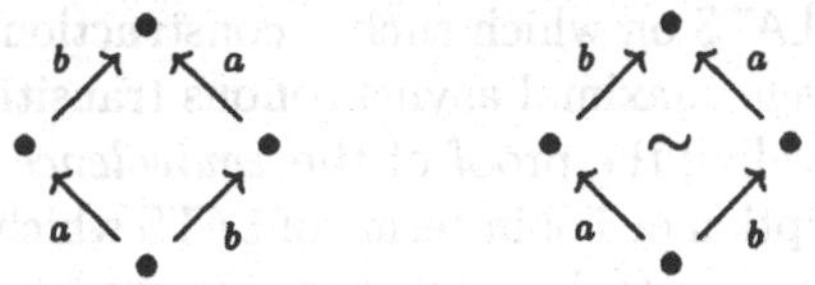

The implicit information about events can be easily deduced from the presence (or the absence) of $\sim$, making the achieved expressive power comparable to that of asynchronous transition systems. Moreover, avoiding a primitive notion of event makes providing a *'noninterleaving'* operational semantics in the SOS style a relatively simple task (cf. [21]).

However, in order to be consistent with the computational intuition, the axiomatics of transition systems with independence involves (apparently necessarily [18]) *one* condition expressed 'globally' in terms of all the transitions representing occurrences of the same event. This contrasts with the 'local' conditions defining asynchronous transition systems and can make hard checking that a given structure is a transitions system with independence. Thus, the differences induced on the two models by the choice of a *primitive* versus a *derived* notion of event are far-reaching and seem to make them suitable for different applications. This indicates that it is not wise to choose *once and for all* between asynchronous transition systems and transition systems with independence, which, in turn, opens the issue of investigating *formally* their analogies and differences. The contribution of this paper is to answer exhaustively such a question, which, actually, escaped the thorough analysis of models for concurrency carried out in [21, 15, 18]. Precisely, we prove that transition systems with independence besides being nicely related to a class of asynchronous transition systems that we call *extensional*, are *equivalent* to the so-called *event-maximal* asynchronous transition systems. These latter can be seen at the same time as those transition systems that make as few identifications of transitions as possible, i.e., contain no confusion about event identities, and as those in which such identities are derivable from the independence relation, i.e., reduce the redundancy. It is worth mentioning that the converse does not hold: the asynchronous transitions systems for which the independence relation is in turn derivable from the structure of events, and therefore redundant, are slightly less general. They correspond to the transitions systems with independence for which 'independence is concurrency' considered in [15, 18].

Concerning the organization of the paper and its technical contributions, after recalling in Section 1 the definitions of LATS and TSI, respectively the categories of labelled asynchronous transitions systems and of transitions systems with independence, in Section 2 we look for a functor adjoint to the obvious embedding TSI ↪ LATS. In particular, we identify the category of extensional asynchronous transitions systems, eLATS, as the largest subcategory of LATS which admits TSI as a *coreflective* subcategory. It is worth noticing here that *at*: eLATS → TSI, the right adjoint of the coreflection, complements and corrects a non-well-defined construction sketched in [21]: as a matter of fact, due to the greater generality of asynchronous transition systems, eLATS happens to be the largest subcategory of LATS on which such a construction makes sense. Finally, Section 3 introduces event-maximal asynchronous transitions systems and their category meLATS, providing the proof of the *equivalence* TSI ≅ meLATS. This yields a complete description of TSI in terms of LATS which can be useful in practise to translate back and forth between the two models when the application one has in mind requires it.

Summing up our results, this paper presents the following commutative diagram, which makes completely formal and precise the relationships between transition systems with independence and asynchronous transition systems.

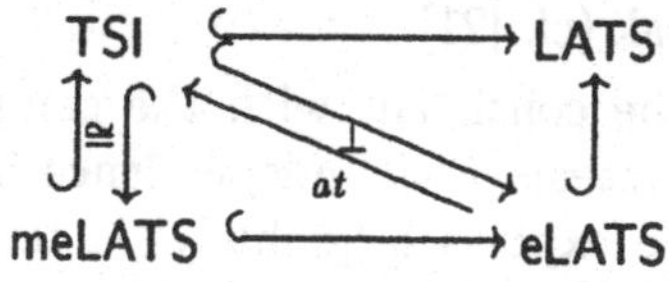

1 Preliminaries

In this section we recall briefly the definitions of asynchronous transition systems, transition systems with independence, and their respective categories [1, 21].

As discussed in the introduction, asynchronous transition systems are simply transition systems whose transitions are decorated by events equipped with an independence relation. Four axioms (A1–A4) are needed to guarantee the intended meaning for the events and the independence relation.

Definition 1.1 (*Labelled Asynchronous Transition Systems*)
*A labelled asynchronous transition system (*lats *for short) is a structure*

$$A = (S_A, i_A, E_A, Tran_A, I_A, L_A, \ell_A),$$

where $(S_A, i_A, E_A, Tran_A)$ is a transition system with set of states S_A, initial state $i_A \in S_A$, and transitions $Tran_A \subseteq S_A \times E_A \times S_A$, and where E_A is a set of events, L_A a set of labels, $\ell_A: E_A \to L_A$ a labelling function, and $I_A \subseteq E_A \times E_A$, the independence relation, is an irreflexive, symmetric relation such that

A1. $e \in E_A \quad \Rightarrow \quad \exists s_1, s_2 \in S_A.\ (s_1, e, s_2) \in Tran_A$;

A2. $(s, e, s_1), (s, e, s_2) \in Tran_A \quad \Rightarrow \quad s_1 = s_2$;

A3. $e_1\ I_A\ e_2\ \&\ (s, e_1, s_1), (s, e_2, s_2) \in Tran_A \quad \Rightarrow$
$\exists u.\ (s_1, e_2, u), (s_2, e_1, u) \in Tran_A$;

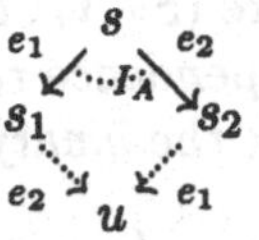

A4. $e_1\ I_A\ e_2\ \&\ (s, e_1, s_1), (s_1, e_2, u) \in Tran_A \quad \Rightarrow$
$\exists s_2.\ (s, e_2, s_2), (s_2, e_1, u) \in Tran_A$.

In the rest of the paper we shall let $I(e)$ denote the set $\{e' \mid e\ I_A\ e'\}$ and, for convenience, use (s, e^a, s') as a shorthand for a transition (s, e, s') with $\ell_A(e) = a$.

The following is the standard definition of morphisms for lats, which essentially captures the idea of *simulation* (cf. [1, 21]).

Definition 1.2 (*Asynchronous Transition System Morphisms*)
For A and A' lats, a morphism from A to A' is a triple of (partial) functions[1] *$(\sigma: S_A \to S_{A'}, \eta: E_A \rightharpoonup E_{A'}, \lambda: L_A \rightharpoonup L_{A'})$, where (σ, η) is a morphism of labelled transition systems, i.e.,*

▷ $\sigma(i_A) = i_{A'}$;

▷ $(s_1, e, s_2) \in Tran_A\ \&\ \eta(e){\downarrow} \quad \Rightarrow \quad (\sigma(s_1), \eta(e), \sigma(s_2)) \in Tran_{A'}$;
$(s_1, e, s_2) \in Tran_A\ \&\ \eta(e){\uparrow} \quad \Rightarrow \quad \sigma(s_1) = \sigma(s_2)$;

which preserves the labelling, i.e., makes the following diagram commutative

$$\begin{array}{ccc} E_A & \xrightarrow{\eta} & E_{A'} \\ {\scriptstyle \ell_A}\downarrow & & \downarrow{\scriptstyle \ell_{A'}} \\ L_A & \xrightarrow[\lambda]{} & L_{A'}; \end{array}$$

and the independence, i.e.,

$$e_1\ I_A\ e_2\ \&\ \eta(e_1){\downarrow},\ \eta(e_2){\downarrow} \quad \Rightarrow \quad \eta(e_1)\ I_{A'}\ \eta(e_2).$$

[1] We use, respectively, $f: A \to B$ and $f: A \rightharpoonup B$ to indicate total and partial functions. For f a partial function, $f(x){\downarrow}$ ($f(x){\uparrow}$) means that f is (un)defined at x.

It is immediate to see that lats and their morphisms form a category, which we shall refer as LATS.

Starting from Definition 1.1, transition systems with independence attempt to simplify the structure retaining explicitly only the independence, now layered directly on the transitions. As already mentioned, the notion of event becomes implicit, determined by the independence relation through the equivalence $\sim$.

Definition 1.3 (*Transition Systems with Independence*)
A transition system with independence (tsi for short) is a structure

$$T = (S_T, i_T, L_T, \mathit{Tran}_T, I_T),$$

where $(S_T, i_T, L_T, \mathit{Tran}_T)$ *is a transition system and* $I_T \subseteq \mathit{Tran}_T \times \mathit{Tran}_T$, *the independence relation, is an irreflexive, symmetric relation, such that, denoting by* $\prec$ *the binary relation on transitions given as*

$$\begin{aligned}(s,a,s_1) \prec (s_2,a,u) \quad &\Leftrightarrow \\ &\exists b \in L_T.\ (s,a,s_1)\ I_T\ (s,b,s_2)\ \& \\ &\quad (s,a,s_1)\ I_T\ (s_1,b,u)\ \&\ (s,b,s_2)\ I_T\ (s_2,a,u)\end{aligned}$$

and by $\sim$ *the least equivalence on transitions which includes it, we have*

T1. $(s,a,s_1) \sim (s,a,s_2) \Rightarrow s_1 = s_2$;

T2. $(s,a,s_1)\ I_T\ (s,b,s_2) \Rightarrow \exists u.\ (s,a,s_1)\ I_T\ (s_1,b,u)\ \&\ (s,b,s_2)\ I_T\ (s_2,a,u)$;

T3. $(s,a,s_1)\ I_T\ (s_1,b,u) \Rightarrow \exists s_2.\ (s,a,s_1)\ I_T\ (s,b,s_2)\ \&\ (s,b,s_2)\ I_T\ (s_2,a,u)$;

T4. $(s,a,s_1) \prec\cup\succ (s_2,a,u)\ I_T\ (w,b,w') \Rightarrow (s,a,s_1)\ I_T\ (w,b,w')$.

The $\sim$-equivalence classes, in the following denoted by $[(s,a,s')]$, for (s,a,s') a representative of the class, are to be thought of as events, i.e., $t_1 \prec t_2$ means that t_1 and t_2 are part of a 'concurrency diamond', whilst $t_1 \sim t_2$ means that they are occurrences of the same event. Concerning the axioms, notice then that T1 (the global condition mentioned earlier) corresponds to A2 and axioms T2 and T3 correspond, respectively, to A3 and A4. The role of T4 is to ensure that the independence relation is actually well defined as a relation on events. In the rest of the paper we shall see that this view of $[(s,a,s')]$ agrees with the notion of events for lats and that, in fact, it identifies an interesting subclass of them.

Using $I(t)$ to denote the set $\{t' \mid t\ I_T\ t'\}$, we can state the following lemma which will be useful later on. As a matter of notations, we shall use π_i to denote projections, i.e., if t is (s,a,s'), then $\pi_1(t) = s$, $\pi_2(t) = a$ and $\pi_3(t) = s'$.

Lemma 1.4
Axiom T4 *is equivalent to*

$$t_1 \sim t_2 \quad \Rightarrow \quad I(t_1) = I(t_2). \qquad \text{(T4')}$$

Proof. Easy, by induction. ✓

The following definition of morphisms for transition systems with independence resembles closely that given earlier for lats.

Definition 1.5 (*Transition System with Independence Morphisms*)
For T and T' tsi, a morphism from T to T' consists of a pair of (partial) functions $(\sigma\colon S_T \to S_{T'}, \lambda\colon L_T \rightharpoonup L_{T'})$ which is a morphism of transition systems and, in addition, preserves independence, i.e.,

$$(s_1, a, s_2)\ I_T\ (s'_1, b, s'_2)\ \&\ \lambda(a)\downarrow, \lambda(b)\downarrow \quad \Rightarrow$$
$$(\sigma(s_1), \lambda(a), \sigma(s_2))\ I_{T'}\ (\sigma(s'_1), \lambda(b), \sigma(s'_2)).$$

We shall use TSI to denote the category of tsi and their morphisms.

The following lemma states that tsi morphisms are well defined as maps of events, an easy consequence of the fact that they preserve independence that we shall use in order to embed TSI into LATS.

Lemma 1.6 (*Morphisms map Events to Events*)
For $(\sigma, \lambda)\colon T \to T'$ a morphism of tsi and $(s_1, a, s_2) \sim (s'_1, a, s'_2)$ equivalent transitions of T, if $\lambda(a)\downarrow$, then $(\sigma(s_1), \lambda(a), \sigma(s_2)) \sim (\sigma(s'_1), \lambda(a), \sigma(s'_2))$, i.e., lats morphisms preserve $\sim$.

2 From LATS to TSI: a coreflection

The scene is now set to expose the adjunction between TSI and a full subcategory of LATS. First, we define an inclusion $ta\colon \mathsf{TSI} \hookrightarrow \mathsf{LATS}$ in the obvious way.

On the objects, ta acts by decorating each transition with the event identified by the $\sim$-class the transition belongs to. The label of such an event is, of course, the label originally carried in the tsi by the transition. Observe that, in force of Definition 1.3 of $\sim$, this labelling is well defined. Finally, the independence relation of $ta(T)$ is inherited directly from the one of T. The formal definition is as follows.

Definition 2.1 (TSI $\hookrightarrow$ LATS)
For T a tsi, let $ta(T)$ be the structure $(S_T, i_T, E, Tran, I, L_T, \ell)$, where, denoting by $\sim$ the equivalence relation induced by I_T as in Definition 1.3,

- ▷ *$E = Tran_T/\!\sim$, the set of $\sim$-classes of $Tran_T$;*
- ▷ *$Tran = \{(s_1, [(s_1, a, s_2)], s_2) \mid (s_1, a, s_2) \in Tran_T\}$;*
- ▷ *$[(s_1, a, s_2)]\ I\ [(s'_1, a, s'_2)]$ if and only if $(s_1, a, s_2)\ I_T\ (s'_1, a, s'_2)$;*
- ▷ *$\ell([(s_1, a, s_2)]) = a$.*

It follows from Lemma 1.4 that the definition of the independence on the events of $ta(T)$ is well given. It is now easy to verify the following.

Proposition 2.2
The transition system $ta(T)$ is a lats.

Proof. Axiom A1 is trivially satisfied. Axiom A2 is satisfied because of T1, for, by definition of *ta*, two transitions carry the same event if and only if they belong to the same $\sim$-class in T. Concerning A3 and A4, they correspond directly to T2 and T3. ✓

In order to define *ta* as a functor, we need to assign its action on the morphisms in TSI.

Definition 2.3 (TSI $\hookrightarrow$ LATS)
For $(\sigma, \lambda)\colon T \to T'$ *a morphism of tsi, let* $ta\big((\sigma,\lambda)\big)$ *be* (σ, η, λ)*, where*

$$\eta\big([(s,a,s')]\big) = \begin{cases} [(\sigma(s), \lambda(a), \sigma(s'))] & \textit{if } \lambda(a)\!\downarrow, \\ \textit{undefined} & \textit{if } \lambda(a)\!\uparrow. \end{cases}$$

That Definition 2.3 is well given follows from Lemma 1.6; it is then easy to check that *ta* is a *full* and *faithful* functor, i.e., an embedding of TSI in LATS.

The obvious idea for a map *at* left inverse to *ta*, as hinted also in [21], is to forget the events and bring the independence from the events down to the transitions, i.e., for A a lats, to take $at(A)$ to be $(S_A, i_A, L_A, \mathit{Tran}, I)$, where

- ▷ $(s,a,s') \in \mathit{Tran}$ if and only if $(s, e^a, s') \in \mathit{Tran}_A$,
- ▷ $(s,a,s_1)\ I\ (s_2,b,s_3)$ if and only if $(s, e_1^a, s_1), (s_2, e_2^b, s_3) \in \mathit{Tran}_A\ \&\ e_1\ I_A\ e_2$.

This construction, however, contrarily to the claims of [21], is not well defined on the whole LATS, since the interplay between the explicitly given independence and events in lats allows rather complicated situations—of dubious computational significance—which cannot be expressed with tsi. A counterexample is illustrated by the following lats.

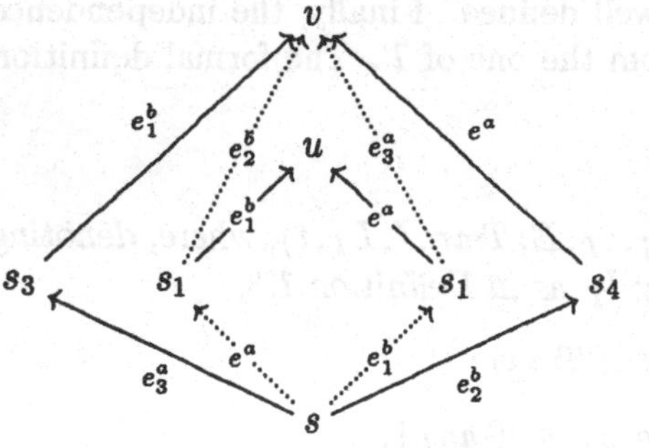

The independent events are $e\ I_A\ e_1$, $e_3\ I_A\ e_1$, $e\ I_A\ e_2$, and $e_2\ I_A\ e_3$, i.e., the system consists of three independency diamonds 'on top of each other'. It is easy to check that this is an object of LATS. However, by applying *at* we create a 'ghost' independency diamond (the one highlighted by the dotted lines), so violating condition T1. In fact, $(s,a,s_3) \sim (s,a,s_1)$ with $s_1 \neq s_3$. This demonstrates that the combination of independence and events makes it hard to define 'uniformly' a map from LATS to TSI to act as left inverse to $ta\colon$ TSI $\hookrightarrow$ LATS.

However, it is not hard to check that things go smoothly for those lats belonging to the *image* of *ta*. In such a case, *at* lands in TSI and, of course, we have the following result.

Lemma 2.4
For any T *in* TSI*, we have* $at \circ ta(T) = T$.

At this point, the issue arises of identifying suitable conditions which, imposed on lats, constrain them down to a category which bears good relationships with TSI. Possibly, one should also like to find a nice characterisation of the image of *ta* in LATS. We shall do so next, by focusing on *extensional* asynchronous transition systems.

We start by considering lats A satisfying

$$(s_1, e_1^a, s_2) \neq (s_1, e_2^b, s_2) \in \mathit{Tran}_A \quad \Rightarrow \quad a \neq b. \qquad \text{(Ex)}$$

In words, these are lats where no two transitions between the same states can carry the same label. This is a kind of extensionality condition that, in view of Definition 1.3, is clearly necessary for our purposes. In fact, without (Ex), the one-to-one correspondence between morphisms of the kinds $ta(T) \to A$ and $T \to at(A)$—required by the adjointness conditions—would not exist. Next, we let the counterexample discussed above guide us to identify two simple additional conditions—strengthening A3 and A4 with uniqueness criteria—that we shall prove to be *necessary* and *sufficient* in order for *at* to be well defined on lats satisfying (Ex). As a notation, for $(s, e^a, s') \in \mathit{Tran}_A$, we shall use $at(s, e^a, s')$ to refer to the (unique) transition $(s, a, s') \in \mathit{Tran}_{at(A)}$ it corresponds to.

Proposition 2.5
For A a lats satisfying (Ex), *at(A) belongs to* TSI *if and only if*

i) for $e_1 \; I_A \; e_2$ *and* $(s, e_1^a, s_1), (s, e_2^b, s_2) \in \mathit{Tran}_A$, *there exists a* ***unique*** *pair* $(s_1, x_2^b, u), (s_2, x_1^a, u) \in \mathit{Tran}_A$ *such that* $e_1 \; I_A \; x_2$, $e_2 \; I_A \; x_1$, *and* $x_1 \; I_A \; x_2$.

ii) for $e_1 \; I_A \; e_2$ *and* $(s, e_1^a, s_1), (s_1, e_2^b, u) \in \mathit{Tran}_A$, *there exists a* ***unique*** *pair* $(s, x_2^b, s_2), (s_2, x_1^a, u) \in \mathit{Tran}_A$ *such that* $e_1 \; I_A \; x_2$, $e_2 \; I_A \; x_1$, *and* $x_1 \; I_A \; x_2$.

Proof. If $at(A) \in$ TSI, the pairs of transitions in *i)* and *ii)* exist because of axioms A3 and A4. Their uniqueness is needed in order for $at(A)$ to satisfy axiom T1. Suppose that, on the contrary, in case *ii)* there are two pairs $(s_1, x_2^b, u), (s_2, x_1^a, u)$ and $(s_1, y_2^b, w), (s_2, y_1^a, w)$ satisfying the condition. Since A satisfies (Ex), we have $w \neq u$, which implies that $at(s, e_2^b, s_2) \prec at(s_1, y_2^b, w)$ and $at(s, e_2^b, s_2) \prec at(s_1, x_2^b, u)$, i.e., that $at(s_1, x_2^b, u) \sim at(s_1, y_2^b, w)$, which contradicts T1. The case for *ii)* can be proved along the same lines, thus showing the necessity of the conditions.

Concerning their sufficiency, the extensionality guarantees that $I_{at(A)}$ is irreflexive, whilst the property of symmetry for $I_{at(A)}$ is inherited from I_A. It remains check that the axioms T1–T4 defining tsi hold for $at(A)$. Axioms A3, A4 and conditions *i)* and *ii)* above ensure that if $at(t) \prec at(t')$, then $\pi_2(t) = \pi_2(t')$, i.e., t and t' represent the same event. It follows then by induction that $at(t) \sim at(t')$ implies $\pi_2(t) = \pi_2(t')$, for all $at(t), at(t') \in \mathit{Tran}_{at(A)}$. If in addition $\pi_1(at(t)) = \pi_1(at(t'))$, then also $\pi_1(t) = \pi_1(t')$ and axiom A2 implies that $\pi_3(at(t)) = \pi_3(at(t'))$. So T1 is satisfied. Actually, this also implies that T4 holds. For, since the independence in $at(A)$ is inherited from that on the events in A, and t and t' carry the same event, we have that $at(t) \sim at(t')$ implies $I(at(t)) = I(at(t'))$. This, as proved by Lemma 1.4, is equivalent to T4. Finally, T2 and T3 hold because of the corresponding A3 and A4. ✓

We call *extensional* the lats satisfying (Ex) and the conditions of Proposition 2.5, and we denote by **eLATS** the full subcategory of **LATS** they determine.

Clearly, *at* can be extended to a functor from **eLATS** to **TSI** which simply 'forgets' the event component of **LATS** morphisms, i.e., for $(\sigma,\eta,\lambda)\colon A \to A'$, take $at\big((\sigma,\eta,\lambda)\big)$ to be (σ,λ). We shall see next that such a functor is right adjoint to ta: **TSI** $\hookrightarrow$ **eLATS**.

Proposition 2.6 ($ta \dashv at$: **TSI** $\rightharpoonup$ **eLATS**)
*For any $A \in$ **eLATS** and any morphism $m\colon T \to at(A)$ in **TSI**, there exists a unique morphism $m^T\colon ta(T) \to A$ such that $at(m^T) = m$.*

Proof. Let m be (σ,λ). Clearly, by definition of at, m^T must be of the form (σ,γ,λ) for some $\gamma\colon E_{ta(T)} \to E_A$. It is easy to realize that the only possible choice for γ is the following: for $(s,a,s') \in Tran_T$ and $\lambda(a)\!\downarrow$, let $\gamma([(s,a,s')])$ be the event $e \in E_A$ of the unique transition $(\sigma(s), e^{\lambda(a)}, \sigma(s')) \in Tran_A$. This is a well given definition, for Lemma 1.6 ensures that m maps all transitions in $[(s,a,s')]$ to the same $\sim$-class of $Tran_{at(A)}$, and the proof of Proposition 2.5 shows that if two transitions belong to the same $\sim$-class of $Tran_{at(A)}$, they originate from transitions in $Tran_A$ carrying the same event. This proves both existence and uniqueness of m^T. ✓

Proposition 2.6 proves that the identity natural transformation

$$\eta = \big\{ id_T\colon T \to at \circ ta(T) \big\}_{T \in \mathsf{TSI}}$$

is the *unit* of an adjunction involving ta and at. Moreover, since η is an isomorphism, by standard results in category theory, we have that the adjunction $ta \dashv at$: **TSI** $\rightharpoonup$ **eLATS** is a coreflection, i.e., **TSI** is *coreflective* in **eLATS**. This, together with Proposition 2.5 and the discussion at the beginning of the present section, shows that **eLATS** is the largest subcategory of **LATS** on which at can be defined as a functor to **TSI**, yielding a right adjoint to ta.

3 meLATS: A category of LATS equivalent to TSI

In this section we identify the *replete* image of ta in **LATS**, i.e., the full subcategory **meLATS** of **eLATS** consisting of the objects isomorphic to $ta(T)$, for some $T \in$ **TSI**. In addition, we characterise those lats for which the independence can be recovered from the structure of events, and relate them to a relevant subcategory of **TSI** considered in [15, 18].

Recall from basic category theory that **meLATS** is determined by the coreflection: it consists of those $A \in$ **eLATS** for which the corresponding component ϵ_A of the *counit* of $ta \dashv at$ is iso. Applying standard categorical results to derive ϵ from $(-)^T$ and η, we find that it is the natural transformation

$$\epsilon = \big\{ (id_{S_A}, \gamma, id_{L_A})\colon ta \circ at(A) \to A \big\}_{A \in \mathsf{eLATS}},$$

where for $(s,a,s') \in Tran_{at(A)}$, $\gamma([(s,a,s')]) =_{def} e$, for $e \in E_A$ the event of the unique $(s,e^a,s') \in Tran_A$. Clearly, ϵ_A is iso if and only if γ is such, i.e.,

$$\forall t,t' \in Tran_A,\ \pi_2(t) = \pi_2(t') \quad\Rightarrow\quad at(t) \sim at(t'),$$

which means that two transitions carry the same event if and only if they belong to the same $\sim$-class of A (viewed as a tsi). Although this characterises meLATS $\subset$ LATS equivalent to TSI, it would of course be better to find a more direct description of it, one not referring to $at(A)$. This is the purpose of the notion of *event-maximal* asynchronous transitions systems introduced next.

Intuitively, a lats is *event-maximal* if its events and independence are 'tightly coupled', so that one cannot 'split' events without destroying the global lats structure. More precisely, A is event-maximal if for any $\bar{e} \in E_A$ and any subset T of transitions carrying $\bar{e}$, the structure resulting from replacing $\bar{e}$ on the transitions in T by a *fresh* event $\tilde{e}$ is *no* longer a lats.

Definition 3.1 (*Event-Maximal Asynchronous Transition Systems*)
For A a LATS*, $\bar{e} \in E_A$, and $T \subset T_{\bar{e}} = \{t \in Tran_A \mid \pi_2(t) = \bar{e}\}$, let $A[T]$ denote the replacement of $\bar{e}$ on the transitions in T for a fresh event $\tilde{e} \notin E_A$, i.e., $A[T] = (S_A, i_A, E_A \cup \{\tilde{e}\}, Tran, I, L_A, \ell)$, where*

- ▷ $Tran = (Tran_A \setminus T) \cup \{(s_1, \tilde{e}, s_2) \mid (s_1, \bar{e}, s_2) \in T\}$;
- ▷ $I = I_A \cup \{(\tilde{e}, e) \mid \bar{e}\, I_A\, e\}$;
- ▷ $\ell(e) = \begin{cases} \ell_A(e) & \text{if } e \in E_A, \\ \ell_A(\bar{e}) & \text{if } e = \tilde{e}. \end{cases}$

A lats A is event-maximal if for each $\bar{e} \in E_A$ and each nonempty $T \subset T_{\bar{e}}$, the transition systems $A[T]$ is not a lats.
The category meLATS *is the full subcategory of* LATS *consisting of the extensional, event-maximal lats.*

Observe that the interesting, nontrivial choices for T are those such that $\emptyset \subset T \subset T_{\bar{e}}$, i.e., those in which at least one $\tilde{e}$-transition is added and at least one $\bar{e}$-transition is kept in $A[T]$. The definition above, stating that any such structure must fail to be a lats, is our way to express that—as remarked in the introduction—the identity of the events in event-maximal lats is forced by the independence relation. This provides us with the direct characterisation of TSI in terms of LATS that we sought.

Proposition 3.2 (meLATS $\cong$ TSI)
meLATS *is equivalent to* TSI.

Proof. Let A be an extensional lats. We prove that the counit ϵ_A is iso if and only if A belongs to meLATS. To this purpose, let γ be the event component of ϵ_A.

If γ is iso, i.e., for all $t, t' \in Tran_A$ we have that $\pi_2(t) = \pi_2(t')$ implies $at(t) \sim at(t')$, for any choice of $\bar{e} \in E_A$ and any $\emptyset \subset T \subset T_{\bar{e}}$, then the condition in Definition 3.1 is satisfied, since, by the extensionality of A, either A3 or A4 must fail for $A[T]$. In fact, in order for $A[T]$ to be a LATS, extensionality implies that $t' \in T$ whenever a $at(t') \sim at(t)$ for some $t \in T$, i.e., by the hypothesis on γ, T should be $T_{\bar{e}}$. So A is event-maximal.

If γ is not iso, i.e., if there exist t and t' such that which $at(t) \not\sim at(t')$ but $\pi_2(t) = \pi_2(t')$, then $T = \{t'' \mid at(t'') \sim at(t)\} \subset T_{\pi_2(t)}$ is a nonempty set for which the 'splitting' of $\pi_2(t)$ yields a lats, i.e., A is not event-maximal. ✓

To conclude this exposition, we observe that the independence relation in event-maximal lats is *not* uniquely determined by rest of the structure. This is due to the fact that the independence on events is still rather *intensional* notion: events may be independent and still never occur in the same path, i.e., intuitively, be mutually exclusive. Observing that such situations have little computational relevance, one may consider on lats the property

$$e_1 \, I_A \, e_2 \quad \Rightarrow \quad \exists (s, e_1, s_1), (s, e_2, s_2) \in Tran_A, \tag{E}$$

which can be seen as an extensionality condition on I_A. It is easy to prove that, if $A \in$ meLATS satisfies (E), then $e_1 \, I_A \, e_2$ if and only if there exists a square in A involving e_1 and e_2, i.e.,

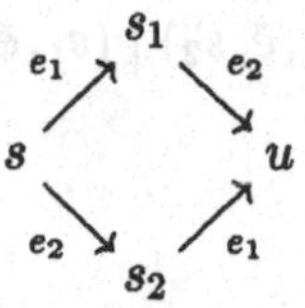

Thus, for such lats the independence is completely redundant and can be omitted: all the information is already contained in $(S_A, i_A, E_A, Tran_A, L_A, \ell_A)$.

It is worth remarking here that a condition corresponding to (E) for TSI—viz., whenever $t \, I_T \, t'$, there exist $(s, a, s') \sim t$ and $(s, b, s'') \sim t'$ in $Tran_T$—was identified in [15, 18] while investigating the tight relationships between tsi and event structures. Such a condition yields $\mathsf{TSI_E}$, a very good-behaved full subcategory of TSI for which we can state the following corollary of Proposition 3.2, which concludes the paper. Here we use $\mathsf{meLATS_E}$ to denote the full subcategory of meLATS consisting of the structures satisfying (E).

Proposition 3.3 ($\mathsf{meLATS_E} \cong \mathsf{TSI_E}$)
$\mathsf{meLATS_E}$ *is equivalent to* $\mathsf{TSI_E}$.

References

[1] M.A. Bednarczyk. Categories of asynchronous systems PhD thesis in Computer Science, University of Sussex (1988), report no. 1/88.

[2] J.M.C. Baeten and W.P. Weijland. Process Algebra Cambridge Tracts in Theoretical Computer Science, 18 (1990), Cambridge University Press.

[3] G-L. Cattani and V. Sassone. Higher Dimensional Transition Systems, To appear in Proceedings of LICS 96 (1996), IEEE Computer Society Press.

[4] R. van Glabbeek. *Bisimulations for higher dimensional automata*, email message sent to the *Concurrency* mailing list on July 7, 1991. Available at `http://theory.stanford.edu/people/rvg/hda`.

[5] R. VAN GLABBEEK AND G. PLOTKIN. Configuration Structures. In *Proceedings of LICS'95*, D. Kozen (Ed.), IEEE Computer Society Press (1995), 99–109.

[6] E. GOUBAULT. Domains of Higher-Dimensional Automata. In *Proceedings of CONCUR'93*, E. Best (Ed.), LNCS 715 (1993), Springer-Verlag, 293–307.

[7] E. GOUBAULT AND T. JENSEN. Homology of Higher-Dimensional Automata. In *Proceedings of CONCUR'92*, W.R. Cleaveland (Ed.), LNCS 630 (1992), Springer-Verlag, 254–268.

[8] P. GODEFROID AND P. WOLPER. Using Partial Orders for the Efficient Verification of Deadlock Freedom and Safety Properties, In *Proceedings of CAV'91*, K.G. Larsen *et al.* (Eds.), LNCS 575 (1991), Springer-Verlag, 332–342.

[9] M. HENNESSY. *Algebraic Theory of Processes.* Series in the Foundations of Computing (1988), The MIT Press.

[10] C.A.R. HOARE. *Communicating Sequential Processes.* Series in Computer Science (1985), Prentice-Hall.

[11] R. MILNER. *Communication and Concurrency.* Series in Computer Science (1989), Prentice Hall.

[12] R. MILNER. *The polyadic π-calculus: a tutorial.* In *Logic and Algebra of Specification*, F.L. Bauer *et al.* (Eds.), Springer-Verlag, (1993).

[13] M. MUKUND. Petri Nets and Step Transition Systems. *International Journal of Foundations of Computer Science*, vol. 3, n. 4 (1992), 443–478.

[14] M. MUKUND AND M. NIELSEN. CCS, Locations and Asynchronous Transition Systems In *Proceedings of FST & TCS'92*, R. Shyamasundar (Ed.), LNCS n. 652 (1992), Springer-Verlag, 328–341.

[15] M. NIELSEN, V. SASSONE AND G. WINSKEL. Relationships between Models of Concurrency, In *Proceedings of REX'93. A Decade of Concurrency: Reflections and Perspectives*, LNCS n. 803, (1994), J.W. de Bakker *et al.* (Eds.), Springer-Verlag, 425–476.

[16] D. PELED. All from One, One for All: On Model Checking Using Representatives, In *Proceedings of CAV'93*, C. Courcoubetis (Ed.), LNCS n. 697 (1993), Springer-Verlag, 409–423.

[17] V. PRATT. Modelling Concurrency with Geometry. In *Proceedings of 18th ACM Symposium on Principles of Programming Languages*, ACM Press, (1991), 311–322.

[18] V. SASSONE, M. NIELSEN, AND G. WINSKEL. Models for Concurrency: Towards a Classification. To appear in *Theoretical Computer Science.* An extended abstract appears as 'A Classification of Models for Concurrency' in *Proceedings of CONCUR'93*, E. Best (Ed.), LNCS 715 (1993), Springer-Verlag, 82–96.

[19] M.W. SHIELDS. Concurrent machines Theoretical Computer Science n .28 (1985), 449–465.

[20] A. VALMARI. A Stubborn attack on state explosion, In Proceedings of CAV'90, DIMACS Series n. 3 (1991), 25–42.

[21] G. WINSKEL AND M. NIELSEN. Models for Concurrency In *Handbook of Logic and the Foundations of Computer Science*, vol. IV, S. Abramsky *et al.* (Eds.), Oxford University Press, 1995.

A Presheaf Semantics of Value-Passing Processes

(Extended Abstract)

Glynn Winskel

BRICS* – Computer Science Dept., University of Aarhus

Abstract. This paper investigates presheaf models for process calculi with value passing. Denotational semantics in presheaf models are shown to correspond to operational semantics in that bisimulation obtained from open maps is proved to coincide with bisimulation as defined traditionally from the operational semantics. Both "early" and "late" semantics are considered, though the more interesting "late" semantics is emphasised. A presheaf model and denotational semantics is proposed for a language allowing process passing, though there remains the problem of relating the notion of bisimulation obtained from open maps to a more traditional definition from the operational semantics. A tentative beginning is made of a "domain theory" supporting presheaf models.

Introduction

The papers [12, 4] explore presheaf models for concurrency. Here begins an investigation of the use of presheaves to model higher-order features, most dramatic in the situation of process calculi where processes can be communicated as values.

Something of higher-order appears even in value-passing process calculi where values lie in some discrete datatype like integers or booleans. As is customary, for value-passing calculi, we draw a distinction between "early" and "late" semantics. *Early* semantics coincides with that presented in [14] where a value-passing calculus is reduced to a value-free one by immediately instantiating the variable in an input action to its possible values, the resulting processes being set together in a nondeterministic sum. According to *late* semantics input actions contain bound variables which only become instantiated when a communication is made. Generally (see e.g. [15, 6, 16]), a late semantics for value passing represents the result of input communication as an abstraction, denoting a function from values to processes. Whereas the usual models for concurrency, transition systems, labelled Petri nets and event structures and the like, accommodate early semantics for value-passing directly, following [14, 7, 8], the late semantics seems accomplished most smoothly in domain-theoretic settings, which readily support abstractions.

Two ways seem open to extending models for concurrency to higher-order features. One is to take existing models, most of these transitions systems in one disguise or another, and essentially decorate them with extra structure. Another is to develop a new class of models, some of which can be seen to correspond to existing models, and which at the same time are rich enough to support

* Basic Research in Computer Science, Centre of the Danish National Research Foundation.

constructions of the kind we are used to seeing in domain theory. This paper follows the latter course in investigating presheaf models.

Presheaf models for concurrency have the advantage of including interleaving models like synchronisation trees and independence models like labelled event structures, as well as contributing a general definition of bisimulation based on open maps. As we will see, they also extend to higher-order, though presently many questions remain, chief among them being the problem of simultaneously combining higher-order features with independence of the kind seen in event structures and Petri nets. A more specific problem is that of obtaining a characterisation in terms of the operational semantics of the bisimulation obtained from open maps for a process-passing calculus. On the positive side, the usual definition of "late bisimulation" and "early bisimulation" for ordinary value-passing is reconciled with the definition of bisimulation obtained on presheaves via open maps.

1 The language VProc

VProc is a process language for passing values along channels, inspired by CCS. Its syntax:

$$t ::= nil \mid \tau.t \mid a!e.t \mid a?x.t \mid t_1 \mid t_2 \mid t_1 + t_2 \mid [e_1 = e_2]t \mid X \mid recX.t$$

where x merges over value-variables Var, X over process-variables $Pvar$, a over channel names C, and e, e_1, e_2 over value-expressions. We will not go into the details of the form of value-expressions beyond remarking that they may contain free value-variables and when evaluated yield values in a set V. For simplicity we assume that recursive definitions of processes $recX.t$ are guarded in the sense that all free occurrences of X in t lie under, though not necessarily immediately under, a prefix $\tau.$-, $a!e.$- or $a?x.$-.

1.1 Late transition semantics for VProc

We specify the transitions a closed term can perform. A transition $t \xrightarrow{\alpha} t'$, where t is a closed term, is understood to mean that the process t can perform action α to become t'; actions α range over τ-actions τ, output actions $a!v$, where $a \in C$ and $v \in V$, and input actions $a?x$, where $a \in C$ and $x \in Var$.

τ rule: $\tau.t \xrightarrow{\tau} t$

Output rule: $a!e.t \xrightarrow{a!v} t$

where e, necessarily closed, evaluates to value v.

Input rule: $a?x.t \xrightarrow{a?y} t[y/x]$

where $y \in Var$ is assumed not captured by its substitution for x in t.

Parallel rules:

$$\frac{t_1 \xrightarrow{\alpha} t_1'}{t_1|t_2 \xrightarrow{\alpha} t_1'|t_2} \qquad \frac{t_2 \xrightarrow{\alpha} t_2'}{t_1|t_2 \xrightarrow{\alpha} t_1|t_2'}$$

In the first parallel rule t_2 must have no free variables in common with action α; a symmetric condition is enforced for the second parallel rule.

$$\frac{t_1 \xrightarrow{a!v} t_1' \quad t_2 \xrightarrow{a?y} t_2'}{t_1|t_2 \xrightarrow{\tau} t_1'|t_2'[v/y]} \qquad \frac{t_1 \xrightarrow{a?y} t_1' \quad t_2 \xrightarrow{a!v} t_2'}{t_1|t_2 \xrightarrow{\tau} t_1'[v/y]|t_2'}$$

Sum rules:

$$\frac{t_1 \xrightarrow{\alpha} t_1'}{t_1 + t_2 \xrightarrow{\alpha} t_1'} \qquad \frac{t_2 \xrightarrow{\alpha} t_2'}{t_1 + t_2 \xrightarrow{\alpha} t_2'}$$

Condition rule:

$$\frac{t \xrightarrow{\alpha} t'}{[e_1 = e_2]t \xrightarrow{\alpha} t'}$$

provided e_1 and e_2 evaluate to the same value.
Recursion rule:

$$\frac{t[recX.t/X] \xrightarrow{\alpha} t'}{recX.t \xrightarrow{\alpha} t'}$$

1.2 Late bisimulation

Definition 1. A *late bisimulation* is a binary relation R between closed process terms such that whenever $t_1 R t_2$
(i) $t_1 \xrightarrow{\tau} t_1' \Rightarrow \exists t_2'.\ t_2 \xrightarrow{\tau} t_2' \ \&\ t_1' \ R\ t_2'$ and $t_2 \xrightarrow{\tau} t_2' \Rightarrow \exists t_1'.\ t_1 \xrightarrow{\tau} t_1' \ \&\ t_1' \ R\ t_2'$
(ii) $t_1 \xrightarrow{a!v} t_1' \Rightarrow \exists t_2'.\ t_2 \xrightarrow{a!v} t_2' \ \&\ t_1' \ R\ t_2'$ and $t_2 \xrightarrow{a!v} t_2' \Rightarrow \exists t_1'.\ t_1 \xrightarrow{a!v} t_1' \ \&\ t_1' \ R\ t_2'$
(iii) $t_1 \xrightarrow{a?y} t_1' \Rightarrow \exists t_2', z.\ t_2 \xrightarrow{a?z} t_2' \ \&\ \forall v \in V.\ t_1'[v/y] \ R\ t_2'[v/z]$ and
$t_2 \xrightarrow{a?y} t_2' \Rightarrow \exists t_1', z.\ t_1 \xrightarrow{a?z} t_1' \ \&\ \forall v \in V.\ t_1'[v/y] \ R\ t_2'[v/z]$.

Say closed process terms t_1, t_2 are *late bisimilar* iff there is a late bisimulation R such that $t_1 R t_2$.

2 Open maps and bisimulation on presheaves

Let $\mathbf{P}$ be a small category. It is to be thought of as a category of path objects (or path shapes) in which morphisms stand for an extension of one path by another. Let $\widehat{\mathbf{P}} = [\mathbf{P}^{op}, \mathbf{Set}]$, the category of presheaves over $\mathbf{P}$. Recall, a morphism $h : X \to Y$, between presheaves X, Y, is *open* iff for all morphisms $m : P \to Q$ in $\mathbf{P}$, the square

$$\begin{array}{ccc} X(P) & \xleftarrow{Xm} & X(Q) \\ {\scriptstyle h_P}\downarrow & & \downarrow{\scriptstyle h_Q} \\ Y(P) & \xleftarrow{Ym} & Y(Q) \end{array}$$

is a quasi-pullback, i.e. whenever $p \in X(P)$ and $q \in Y(Q)$ satisfy $h_P(p) = (Ym)(q)$, then there exists $p' \in X(Q)$ such that $(Xm)(p') = p$ and $h_Q(p') = q$. (This definition of open map, translates via the Yoneda Lemma to an equivalent path-lifting property of h—see [12].)

Say presheaves X, Y are *bisimilar* iff there is a span of surjective open maps between them, equivalently, iff there is $R \hookrightarrow X \times Y$ such that the compositions with the projections $R \hookrightarrow X \times Y \stackrel{\pi_1}{\to} X$ and $R \hookrightarrow X \times Y \stackrel{\pi_2}{\to} Y$ are surjective open.

In [12, 4] we defined bisimulation between *rooted* presheaves, presheaves X, over a category assumed to have an initial object I, for which $X(I)$ is a singleton. For rooted presheaves bisimulation is defined merely through the presence of a open maps (not requiring surjectivity). This is because open maps between rooted presheaves are necessarily surjective.

We can cast further light on rooted presheaves with the help of a "lifting" construction which will be important later, as is to be expected from traditional domain theory. For $\mathbf{P}$, a small category, define its *lifting* $\mathbf{P}_\perp$ to consist of $\mathbf{P}$ with a new initial object (called $\perp$) adjoined freely. Given $X \in \widehat{\mathbf{P}}$, define $\text{lift}(X) \in \widehat{\mathbf{P}}_\perp$ to be the rooted presheaf which acts as X on copies of $P \in \mathbf{P}$ and yields a singleton, $\{*\}$ say, on $\perp$. The lift operation extends in the obvious way to a functor which gives an equivalence between $\widehat{\mathbf{P}}$ and the subcategory of rooted presheaves over $\mathbf{P}_\perp$; on maps h in $\widehat{\mathbf{P}}$, $\text{lift}(h)$ is open iff h is surjective open. These remarks are useful in another context, that of algebraic set theory—see [10], p. 72.

3 A domain-theoretic setting

In proposing categories of presheaves as our "domains" of processes we are leaving domain theory as traditionally understood; processes are denoted by presheaves, objects in a category rather than elements of a partial order. This is not new; several proposals have been made for generalisation of powerdomains that leave the category of partial orders, for instance [13, 1, 18], and presheaves, being a way to introduce nondeterministic branching to computation paths, have much in common with powerdomains.

We sketch a setting, generalising traditional domain theory, in which we can place the work on presheaf models. The category analogue of algebraic cpo's is finitely accessible categories [2] in which the role of the basis of finite/isolated/compact elements is replaced by that of a small subcategory of finitely presentable objects; every object of a finitely accessible category is a directed colimit of finitely presentable objects. This is analogous to the fact that an algebraic cpo is the ideal completion of its finite elements. Morphisms between finitely accessible categories are functors preserving directed colimits, the analogue of continuous functions.

A way to introduce nondeterminism to a finitely accessible category $\mathcal{C}$ is via a construction on the "basis" of finitely presentable objects $\mathcal{C}^0$: Freely close $\mathcal{C}^0$ under all finite colimits to get a new basis (in which nondeterministic branching has been introduced). The finitely accessible category with this new category as basis, got by closing under directed colimits, can be thought of as the nondeterministic computations of $\mathcal{C}$. This "ideal completion" is equivalent to the category of presheaves over $\mathcal{C}^0$ (by results of [9], ch.VI). So taking presheaves combines two operations, adding branching to a basis (the part that takes us outside partial orders), and then completing to a finitely accessible category. Viewed in this way, taking presheaves over the basis of a finitely accessible category yields a "monad" on finitely accessible categories, reminiscent of powerdomain monads.[1]

The Kleisli category of the monad associated with taking presheaves is **Prof**, the bicategory of *profunctors* (see e.g. [3] where they are called *distributors*). Profunctors and their categorical constructions provide a convenient setting in which to provide semantics to process calculi with value and process passing. The bicategory **Prof** has small categories as objects and as morphisms $F : \mathbf{P} \nrightarrow \mathbf{Q}$, where **P** and **Q** are small categories, we take functors $F : \mathbf{P} \to \widehat{\mathbf{Q}}$. Composition in **Prof**, say of $F : \mathbf{P} \nrightarrow \mathbf{Q}$ and $G : \mathbf{Q} \nrightarrow \mathbf{R}$, is given to within isomorphism by $G^\dagger \circ F : \mathbf{P} \nrightarrow \mathbf{R}$—here $G^\dagger$ is the left Kan extension $\mathrm{Lan}_{y_Q} G$ of G with respect to the Yoneda embedding $y_Q : \mathbf{Q} \to \widehat{\mathbf{Q}}$. Left Kan extensions and so composition are only determined up to isomorphism; thus the fact that **Prof** is really a bicategory, and not a category. Note that profunctors, or more properly their left Kan extensions, preserve (surjective) open maps and so bisimulation by [4] Lemma 3—the extra preservation of surjectivity is easy to show. **Cat** the category of small categories embeds in **Prof**: A functor $F : \mathbf{P} \to \mathbf{Q}$ is sent to the composition $y_Q \circ F$ with the Yoneda embedding $y_Q : \mathbf{Q} \to \widehat{\mathbf{Q}}$. The embedding **Cat** $\to$ **Prof** preserves small colimits.

Prof forms a model of classical linear logic. To see its monoidal closed structure, for small categories $\mathbf{P}, \mathbf{Q}$, define

$$\mathbf{P} \multimap \mathbf{Q} = \mathbf{P}^{op} \times \mathbf{Q} \quad \text{and} \quad \mathbf{P} \otimes \mathbf{Q} = \mathbf{P} \times \mathbf{Q}\,,$$

where product $\times$ on the right is the usual product of categories, and observe the natural bijection:

$$\mathbf{Prof}(\mathbf{P}, [\mathbf{Q} \multimap \mathbf{R}]) \cong \mathbf{Prof}(\mathbf{P} \otimes \mathbf{Q}, \mathbf{R})$$

The unit of $\otimes$ is **1**, the category with a single object and morphism. **Prof** has products and coproducts which coincide on objects, where both are given by coproduct in **Cat**. As a model of classical linear logic there is the same kind of degenerary familiar from the category of relations; par ($\wp$) coincides with tensor ($\otimes$), and $\perp$ with **1** (so **Prof** is compact-closed). Linear involution $\mathbf{P}^\perp$ is isomorphic to $\mathbf{P} \multimap \mathbf{1}$ and so to $\mathbf{P}^{op}$.

Morphisms $\mathbf{1} \nrightarrow (\mathbf{P} \multimap \mathbf{Q})$ correspond to presheaves over $\mathbf{P}^{op} \times \mathbf{Q}$ and so to profunctors $\mathbf{P} \nrightarrow \mathbf{Q}$. They correspond to colimit-preserving functors from $\widehat{\mathbf{P}}$ to $\widehat{\mathbf{Q}}$.

When we attend to presheaf semantics we are involved with various sorts of functors. Certainly we quickly encounter functors from **P** to $\widehat{\mathbf{Q}}$ corresponding, to within isomorphism, to colimit-preserving functors from $\widehat{\mathbf{P}}$ to $\widehat{\mathbf{Q}}$, between presheaves. We also meet more general "continuous" functors $\widehat{\mathbf{P}} \to \widehat{\mathbf{Q}}$, for example to cope with processes which can receive processes as values. As usual

[1] In this motivational section, we won't be distracted by the constructions more properly taking place in a 2-category/bicategory—thus the quotes around "monad".

in linear logic we can recover these with the help of an exponential (!). Define $!\mathbf{P}$, to be a completion of $\mathbf{P}$ under finite colimits; more precisely we can take $!\mathbf{P}$ to be a skeletal subcategory of the subcategory of $\widehat{\mathbf{P}}$ consisting of finitely presentable objects. Then profunctors $!\mathbf{P} \nrightarrow \mathbf{Q}$ correspond, to within isomorphism, to functors $\widehat{\mathbf{P}} \to \widehat{\mathbf{Q}}$ which are continuous in the sense that they preserve directed colimits.

Prof provides us with a rich repertoire of constructions on categories of presheaves. We pause to ask how the constructions are reflected in notions of open maps and bisimulation.

It is clear when a map is (surjective) open in a coproduct $\mathbf{P} + \mathbf{Q}$ in **Prof**: $h : X \to Y$ is (surjective) open in $\widehat{\mathbf{P} + \mathbf{Q}}$ iff the two components $h_1 : X_1 \to Y_1$ and $h_2 : X_2 \to Y_2$ are (surjective) open in $\widehat{\mathbf{P}}$ and $\widehat{\mathbf{Q}}$ respectively. Because products in **Prof** are given by the same construction on objects, the same holds for products.

Let $h : X \to Y$ be a map in $\widehat{\mathbf{P} \otimes \mathbf{Q}}$. For $P \in \mathbf{P}$, define h^P to be the natural transformation $h^P : X(P, -) \to Y(P, -)$ with component $(h^P)_Q = h_{P,Q}$ at $Q \in \mathbf{Q}$. In a similar way, define $h^Q : X(-, Q) \to Y(-, Q)$ for any $Q \in \mathbf{Q}$. Now, we can observe: $h : X \to Y$ is (surjective) open in $\widehat{\mathbf{P} \otimes \mathbf{Q}}$ iff
$\forall P \in \mathbf{P}.\, h^P$ is (surjective) open in $\widehat{\mathbf{Q}}$ and $\forall Q \in \mathbf{Q}.\, h^Q$ is (surjective) open in $\widehat{\mathbf{P}}$.

There is a similar characterisation of open maps in $\widehat{\mathbf{P} \multimap \mathbf{Q}}$ because $\mathbf{P} \multimap \mathbf{Q} = \mathbf{P}^{op} \times \mathbf{Q}$. A map $h : X \to Y$ in $\widehat{\mathbf{P} \multimap \mathbf{Q}}$ is (surjective) open iff
$\forall P \in \mathbf{P}.\, h^P$ is (surjective) open in $\widehat{\mathbf{Q}}$ and $\forall Q \in \mathbf{Q}.\, h^Q$ is (surjective) open in $\widehat{\mathbf{P}^{op}}$.
Note openness and bisimilarity in $\mathbf{P} \multimap \mathbf{Q}$ involves openness and bisimilarity in $\widehat{\mathbf{P}^{op}}$! However, in the situation where $\mathbf{P}$ is a discrete category, h is open iff h^P is open for all $P \in \mathbf{P}$.

This proposal of a domain theoretic framework in which to understand presheaf models cannot be definitive at present. We would, for instance, expect to work within some cartesian-closed subcategory of finitely accessible categories. But, more importantly, until the aim of bringing independence models within a domain-theoretic framework is carried out fully we should remain open-minded.

4 A late path category

We seek a path category $\mathbf{P}$ with respect to which closed process terms of **VProc** denote presheaves. Its objects should reflect that a compution path of a process may begin with a τ-action, an output action $a!v$ or an input action $a?$, when it may either resume with a computation path, or, in the case where it has first performed an input action, input a value before resuming the computation path. This guides us to wishing to denote closed terms of **VProc** by presheaves over path category $\mathbf{P}$, which is an initial solution to

$$\mathbf{P} \cong \mathbf{P}_\perp + \sum_{(a,v) \in C \times V} \mathbf{P}_\perp + \sum_{a \in C} (V \multimap \mathbf{P})_\perp$$

in **Prof**—here we treat the set V as a discrete category. The solution is easy to construct, firstly because it is sufficient to find an initial solution to

$$\mathbf{P} \cong \mathbf{P}_\perp + \sum_{(a,v)\in C\times V} \mathbf{P}_\perp + \sum_{a\in C} (V^{op} \times \mathbf{P})_\perp$$

in **Cat** (where $V^{op} = V$ as V is discrete), and secondly because all the operations used preserve the property that the category is a partial order. This means an initial solution has the form of a partial order

$$\mathbf{P} = \mathbf{P}_\perp + \sum_{(a,v)\in C\times V} \mathbf{P}_\perp + \sum_{a\in c} (V^{op} \times \mathbf{P})_\perp$$

whose path objects are given inductively by:
- $\tau. \in \mathbf{P}$, and $\tau.P \in \mathbf{P}$ if $P \in \mathbf{P}$,
- $a!v. \in \mathbf{P}$, and $a!v.P \in \mathbf{P}$ if $P \in \mathbf{P}$,
- $a? \in \mathbf{P}$, and $a?(v \mapsto P) \in \mathbf{P}$ if $P \in \mathbf{P}$,

where $a \in C$ and $v \in V$, and whose morphisms (the partial order) are given inductively by the following clauses, where $P, P' \in \mathbf{P}, a \in C$ and $v \in V$:
- $P \leq P$,
- $\tau. \leq \tau.P$, and $\tau.P \leq \tau.P'$ if $P \leq P'$,
- $a!v. \leq a!v.P$, and $a!v.P \leq a!v.P'$ if $P \leq P'$,
- $a? \leq a?(v \mapsto P)$, and $a?(v \mapsto P) \leq a?(v \mapsto P')$ if $P \leq P'$.

Notation: We use (P, Q) to name the unique morphism from P to Q in $\mathbf{P}$ when $P \leq Q$.

We are using suggestive names for the objects of $\mathbf{P}$ to pick out to which component of a sum they belong:
- $\tau.$ is the least element of the leftmost summand of $\mathbf{P}$, other elements of this component being of the form $\tau.P$.
- $a!v.$ is the least element of the output summand associated with outputting value v on channel a; other elements of this component have the form $a!v.P$.
- $a?$ is the least element of the summand associated with a commitment to input on channel a; its other elements take the form $a?(v \mapsto P)$ and correspond to resuming a computation path after inputting value v.

We could have derived the above constructions on path objects systematically from operations associated with sums, lifting and product of categories.

5 Late presheaf semantics

We introduce operations on presheaves which capture the meaning of operations in **VProc**.

5.1 Prefixing

Let $X \in \widehat{\mathbf{P}}$. We define $\tau.X \in \widehat{\mathbf{P}}$ by taking $\tau.X = In_\tau \circ \mathrm{lift}(X)$. where $In_\tau : \widehat{\mathbf{P}_\perp} \to \widehat{\mathbf{P}}$ takes a presheaf over $\mathbf{P}_\perp$ to the corresponding presheaf over the left summand $\mathbf{P}_\perp$ in

$$\mathbf{P} = \mathbf{P}_\perp + \sum_{(a,v)\in C\times V} \mathbf{P}_\perp + \sum_{a\in C} (V^{op} \times \mathbf{P})_\perp . \qquad (\dagger)$$

Recalling our notation for path objects it follows that for $X \in \widehat{\mathbf{P}}$ and a path object $Q \in \mathbf{P}$

$$\tau.X(Q) = \begin{cases} X(P) & \text{if } Q = \tau.P, \\ \{*\} & \text{if } Q = \tau., \\ \emptyset & \text{otherwise.} \end{cases}$$

Similarly, for $X \in \widehat{\mathbf{P}}, a \in C$ and $v \in V$, we define $a!v.X \in \widehat{\mathbf{P}}$ so that on a path object $Q \in \mathbf{P}$

$$a!.X(Q) = \begin{cases} X(P) & \text{if } Q = a!v.P, \\ \{*\} & \text{if } Q = a!v., \\ \emptyset & \text{otherwise.} \end{cases}$$

Let $F : V \to \widehat{\mathbf{P}}$ and $a \in C$. We define $a?F \in \widehat{\mathbf{P}}$ as follows. First notice that F corresponds to a presheaf X over $V^{op} \times \mathbf{P}$, and now define $a?F = In_{a?} \circ \mathrm{lift}(X)$ where $In_{a?} : \widehat{\mathbf{P}_\perp} \to \widehat{\mathbf{P}}$ takes a presheaf over $(V^{op} \times \mathbf{P})_\perp$ to the corresponding presheaf over the a-summand in $\mathbf{P}$ (see (†) above). Now, for $F : V \to \widehat{\mathbf{P}}, a \in C$ and a path object $Q \in \mathbf{P}$ we obtain

$$a?F(Q) = \begin{cases} (Fv)(P) & \text{if } Q = a?(v \mapsto P), \\ \{*\} & \text{if } Q = a?, \\ \emptyset & \text{otherwise.} \end{cases}$$

Notation: If $G(v) \in \widehat{\mathbf{P}}$, for any $v \in V$, we can as usual write $\lambda v.G(v)$ for the associated function $V \to \widehat{\mathbf{P}}$. We write $a?v.G(v)$ for $a?(\lambda v.G(v))$.

5.2 Sums

Coproducts of presheaves provide nondeterministic sums of processes.
If $X_1, X_2, \cdots, X_n \in \widehat{\mathbf{P}}$, we use $X_1 + \cdots + X_n$ to denote the presheaf which at a path object $P \in \mathbf{P}$ takes the set-value

$$(X_1 + \cdots + X_n)(P) = X_1(P) + \cdots + X_n(P),$$

the disjoint union of sets $X_1(P), \cdots, X_n(P)$. For a morphism (P, Q) of $\mathbf{P}$, where $P \leq Q$,

$$(X_1, + \cdots + X_n)(P, Q) = X_1(P, Q) + \cdots + X_n(P, Q),$$

making use of the functorial nature of disjoint union (= coproduct) of sets.

Similarly, if $X_i, i \in I$, is an indexed family of presheaves $X_i \in \widehat{\mathbf{P}}$, we use $\sum_{i\in I} X_i$ to denote their coproduct. If $I = \emptyset$ this is the empty presheaf $\emptyset$, with empty set as value at each path object.

5.3 A decomposition result

We will now observe that every presheaf $X \in \widehat{\mathbf{P}}$ decomposes into a sum of disjoint components rooted at one of the minimal path objects $\tau., a!v., a?$ where $a \in C, v \in V$. The notion of *rooted component* will play a key role. Let M be a minimal object in $\mathbf{P}$, Let $X \in \widehat{\mathbf{P}}$. Any $m \in X(M)$ determines a sub-presheaf C of X as follows. Letting $m \in X(M)$, define

$$C(P) = \begin{cases} \{p \in X(P) \mid X(M,P)(p) = m\} & \text{if } M \leq P, \\ \emptyset & \text{otherwise} \end{cases}$$

for $P \in \mathbf{P}$, and when $P \leq Q$ define the function $C(P,Q) : C(Q) \to C(P)$ by

$$C(P,Q)(q) = X(P,Q)(q) \text{ for } q \in C(Q)$$

— because X is a contravariant functor it follows that

$$X(M,P)(X(P,Q)(q) = X(M,Q)(q) = m$$

so that $X(P,Q)(q) \in C(P)$. It is easily checked that C is a presheaf and indeed a sub-presheaf of X because its action on morphisms (P,Q), when $P \leq Q$, restricts that of X.

Notation: In this situation, we shall say C is a *rooted component* of X at m.

Rooted components of X are pairwise disjoint in the sense that if M, M' are minimal objects of $\mathbf{P}$ and C is a rooted component at $m \in X(M)$ and C' is a rooted component at $m' \in C(M')$, then if at $P \in \mathbf{P}$, $C(P) \cap C'(P) \neq \emptyset$ then $M = M'$ and $m = m'$. Thus, for any path object $P \in \mathbf{P}$,

$$X(P) = \bigcup_{M} \bigcup_{m \in X(M)} C_m(P)\,, \qquad (1)$$

a disjoint union, where M ranges over minimal objects of $\mathbf{P}$. Consequently, X is isomorphic to a sum of its rooted components:

$$X \cong \sum_{M} \sum_{m \in X(M)} C_m \qquad (2)$$

where M ranges over minimal objects of $\mathbf{P}$ and C_m is the rooted component of X at m.

We analyse further the form of rooted components of $X \in \widehat{\mathbf{P}}$.

A rooted component C_i at $i \in X(\tau.)$ is isomorphic to $\tau.X_i$ where $X_i \in \widehat{\mathbf{P}}$ is given by

$$X_i(P) = C_i(\tau.P), \text{ on objects } P \in \mathbf{P}, \text{ and}$$
$$X_i(P,Q) = C_i(\tau.P, \tau.Q) : X_i(Q) \to X_i(P), \text{ on morphisms } P \leq Q \text{ of } \mathbf{P}.$$

We write $X \xrightarrow{\tau} X'$ when there is $i \in X(\tau.)$ such that $X' = X_i$. The assignment $i \mapsto X_i$ is a bijection between the sets $X(\tau.)$ and $\{X' \mid X \xrightarrow{\tau} X'\}$.

A rooted component C_i at $i \in X(a!v)$, for $a \in Ch$ and $v \in V$, is isomorphic to $a!v.X_j$, where $X_j \in \widehat{\mathbf{P}}$ is given by

$$X_j(P) = C_j(a!v.P), \text{ on objects } P \in \mathbf{P}, \text{ and}$$
$$X_j(P,Q) = C_j(a!v.P, a!v.Q), \text{ on morphisms } P \leq Q \text{ of } \mathbf{P}.$$

We write $X \xrightarrow{a!v} X'$ when there is $j \in X(a!v)$ such that $X' = X_j$. The assignment $j \mapsto X_j$ is a bijection between the sets $X(a!v.)$ and $\{X' \mid X \xrightarrow{a!v} X'\}$.

Let C_k be a rooted component at $K \in X(a?)$. Define

$$X_k(v)(P) = C_k(a?(v \mapsto P)), \text{ and}$$
$$X_k(v)(P,Q) = C_k(a?(v \mapsto P), a?(v \mapsto Q)) : X_k(v)(Q) \to X_k(v)(P).$$

Then X_k is a function from values $v \in V$ to presheaves $X_k(v) \in \widehat{\mathbf{P}}$ such that C_k is isomorphic to $a?X_k$. We write $X \xrightarrow{a?} F$ when there is $k \in X(a?)$ such that F is isomorphic to X_k. The assignment $k \mapsto X_k$ is a bijection between the sets $X(a?)$ and $\{F \mid X \xrightarrow{a?} F\}$.

Recalling (1) above and the definition of X_i for $j \in X(a!v)$ and X_k for $k \in X(a?)$ we deduce:

$$X(\tau.P) = \bigcup_{i \in X(\tau.)} X_i(P)$$
$$X(a!v.P) = \bigcup_{j \in X(a!v.)} X_j(P)$$
$$X(a?(v \mapsto P)) = \bigcup_{k \in X(a?)} X_k(v)(P)$$

with unions which are disjoint, where $a \in C$ and $v \in V$.

Recalling the decomposition (2) above, we obtain the following decomposition result:

Proposition 2. *Let $X \in \widehat{\mathbf{P}}$. Then*

$$X \cong \sum_{i \in X(\tau.)} \tau.X_i + \sum_{(a,v) \in C \times V} \sum_{j \in X(a!v.)} a!v.X_j + \sum_{a \in C} \sum_{k \in X(a?.)} a?X_k\ .$$

5.4 Guarded recursive definitions

Presheaf categories possess all colimits and so in particular ω-colimits for building denotations of recursive definitions. In fact, because all our definitions have been given concretely as operations on sets, we are able to show that they are all continuous with respect to the sub-presheaf relation, and the solution of recursive definitions reduces to finding fixed points of a continuous function on cpo's; we obtain solutions up to equality and not just isomorphism.

There is clearly a well-founded relation $\prec$ on path objects $\mathbf{P}$ given by their inductive definition. If a presheaf X say is a solution to a guarded recursive definition then X will be equal to an expression in which each occurrence of X lies under a prefix operation. Hence by the results of Section 5.3, $X(P)$ is given in terms of $X(Q)$ where $Q \prec P$. Thus, by well-founded induction any solution is uniquely determined. A similar argument applies to an operation on presheaves, like parallel composition defined below, whose values on presheaves is defined recursively in terms of the operation under prefixes—it too is uniquely determined.

5.5 Parallel composition

Let $X, Y \in \widehat{\mathbf{P}}$ have the decompositions :

$$X \cong \sum_{i \in I} \tau.X_i + \sum_{(a,v) \in C \times V} \sum_{j \in J_{a,v}} a!v.X_j + \sum_{a \in C} \sum_{k \in K_a} a?X_k$$

$$Y \cong \sum_{l \in L} \tau.Y_l + \sum_{(a,v) \in C \times V} \sum_{m \in M_{a,v}} a!v.Y_m + \sum_{a \in C} \sum_{n \in N_a} a?Y_n$$

Their parallel composition $X \mid Y$ is defined recursively to be

$$\sum_{i \in I} \tau.(X_i \mid Y) + \sum_{(a,v) \in C \times V} \sum_{j \in J_{a,v}} a!v.(X_j \mid Y) + \sum_{a \in C} \sum_{k \in K_a} a?v.(X_k(v) \mid Y)$$

$$+ \sum_{l \in L} \tau.(X \mid Y_l) + \sum_{(a,v) \in C \times V} \sum_{m \in M_{a,v}} a!v.(X \mid Y_m) + \sum_{a \in C} \sum_{n \in N_a} a?v.(X \mid Y_n(v))$$

$$+ \sum_{(a,v) \in C \times V} \sum_{j \in J_{a,v}} \sum_{n \in N_a} \tau.(X_j \mid Y_n(v) + \sum_{(a,v) \in C \times V} \sum_{m \in M_{a,v}} \sum_{k \in K_a} \tau.(X_k(v) \mid Y_m) \,.$$

5.6 Late denotational semantics

Suppose t is a process term with free process-variables within $U_1, \cdots, U_m$ and free value-variables within $x_1, \cdots, x_n$ (possibly empty lists). The denotation of t in this context, written $[\![t[U_1, \cdots, U_m; x_1, \cdots, x_n]]\!]$, is a function (extendable to a functor) $\widehat{\mathbf{P}}^m \times V^n \to \widehat{\mathbf{P}}$, given by structural induction on t in the usual fashion, matching syntactic constructs with the appropriate semantics operations:

$$[\![nil[\vec{U};\vec{x}]]\!]\,\vec{X}\,\vec{v} = \emptyset, \text{ the empty presheaf.}$$

$$[\![\tau.t[\vec{U};\vec{x}]]\!]\,\vec{X}\,\vec{v} = \tau.([\![t[\vec{U};\vec{x}]]\!]\,\vec{X}\,\vec{v})$$

$$[\![a!e.t[\vec{U};\vec{x}]]\!]\,\vec{X}\,\vec{v} = a!w.([\![t[\vec{U};\vec{x}]]\!]\,\vec{X}\,\vec{v})$$

where e evaluates to w in environment $\vec{v}\,/\,\vec{x}$.

$$[\![a?y.t[\vec{U};\vec{x}]]\!]\,\vec{X}\,\vec{v} = a?w.([\![t[\vec{U};\vec{x},y]]\!]\,\vec{X}\,\vec{v}\,w)$$

$$[\![t_1 \mid t_2[\vec{U};\vec{x}]]\!]\,\vec{X}\,\vec{v} = [\![t_1[\vec{U};\vec{x}]]\!]\,\vec{X}\,\vec{v} \mid [\![t_2[\vec{U};\vec{x}]]\!]\,\vec{X}\,\vec{v}$$

$$[\![t_1 + t_2[\vec{U};\vec{x}]]\!]\,\vec{X}\,\vec{v} = [\![t_1[\vec{U};\vec{x}]]\!]\,\vec{X}\,\vec{v} + [\![t_2[\vec{U};\vec{x}]]\!]\,\vec{X}\,\vec{v}$$

$$[\![[e_1 = e_2]t[\vec{U};\vec{x}]]\!]\,\vec{X}\,\vec{v} = \begin{cases} [\![t[\vec{U};\vec{x}]]\!]\,\vec{X}\,\vec{v} & \text{if } e_1, e_2 \text{ evaluate to a common value in } \vec{v}\,/\,\vec{x}. \\ \emptyset, & \text{the empty presheaf, otherwise.} \end{cases}$$

$$[\![U_i[\vec{U};\vec{x}]]\!]\,\vec{X}\,\vec{v} = X_i$$

$$[\![recY.t[\vec{U};\vec{x}]]\!]\,\vec{X}\,\vec{v} = R, \text{ the unique solution of } R = [\![t[\vec{U},Y;\vec{x}]]\!]\,\vec{X}\,R\,\vec{v}\,.$$

Lemma 3. *Let t be a process term with free process-variables among $U_1, \cdots, U_m$ and free value-variables among $x_1, \cdots, x_n$. Suppose $s_1, \cdots, s_m$ are closed process-terms and that $v_1, \cdots, v_n$ are values in V. Then,*

$$[\![t[\vec{U};\vec{x}]]\!][\![\vec{s}]\!] = [\![t[\vec{s}\,/\,\vec{U}][\vec{v}\,/\,\vec{x}]]\!].$$

The decomposition result and the preparatory discussion suggest that we view a presheaf over **P** as a transition system. In particular, it is sensible to view a relation $X \xrightarrow{\tau} X'$ holding between presheaves X, X' as meaning that the process represented by the presheaf X can make a τ-transition to a process represented by the presheaf X'. There is a similar reading of $X \xrightarrow{a!v} X'$, while $X \xrightarrow{a?} F$ means X can receive a value on channel a when, depending on the value v received, it will resume as process $F(v)$.

6 The late semantics related

A closed process term is associated with two transition systems, one from the transition semantics and one from its denotation as a presheaf. The next lemma asserts, essentially, that the relation

$$\{([\![t]\!], t) \mid t \text{ a closed process term}\}$$

is a late-bisimulation between the two transition systems.

Lemma 4. *Let t be a closed process term. Then,*

$$[\![t]\!] \xrightarrow{\tau} X \textit{iff} \exists t'.\ t \xrightarrow{\tau} t' \ \&\ [\![t']\!] = X\ ,$$
$$[\![t]\!] \xrightarrow{a!v} X \textit{iff} \exists t'.\ t \xrightarrow{a!v} t' \ \&\ [\![t']\!] = X\ ,$$
$$[\![t]\!] \xrightarrow{a?} F \textit{iff} \exists t', y.\ t \xrightarrow{ay} t' \ \&\ [\![t'[y]]\!] = F\ .$$

Proof. For $W \in \widehat{\mathbf{P}}$ and t a closed process term define $W \approx t$ iff

$$\forall Z.\ W \xrightarrow{\tau} Z \Leftrightarrow \exists t'.\ t \xrightarrow{\tau} t' \ \&\ [\![t']\!] = Z,$$
$$\forall Z, a, v.\ W \xrightarrow{a!v} Z \Leftrightarrow \exists t'.\ t \xrightarrow{a!v} t' \ \&\ [\![t']\!] = Z, \text{ and}$$
$$\forall F, a.\ W \xrightarrow{a?} F \Leftrightarrow \exists t', y.\ t \xrightarrow{a?y} t' \ \&\ [\![t'[y]]\!] = F.$$

The proof proceeds by structural induction an process terms t with induction hypothesis:

If t has free process-variables within $X_1, \cdots, X_n$, free value-variables within $x_1, \cdots, x_n$, and $S_1, \cdots, S_n$ are closed process-terms such that

$$X_i \text{ is guarded in } t \text{ or } [\![S_i]\!] \approx S_i, \text{ whenever } 1 \leq i \leq m,$$

then for all $v_1, \cdots, v_n \in V$,

$$[\![t[\vec{X}; \vec{x}]]\!]\ [\![\vec{s}]\!]\ \vec{v} \approx t[\vec{s} \ / \vec{X}; \vec{v} \ / \vec{x}]$$

—using an obvious vector notation.

Clearly, when t is closed the induction hypothesis amounts to $[\![t]\!] \approx t$, as required. □

As will be seen, the bisimilarity induced by spans of open maps in $\widehat{\mathbf{P}}$ coincides with the natural translation of late bisimulation to presheaves.

Definition 5. A *late bisimulation on presheaves* consists of a binary relation R on presheaves $\widehat{\mathbf{P}}$ such that whenever $X\,R\,Y$,

$$X \xrightarrow{\tau} X' \Rightarrow \exists Y'.\ Y \xrightarrow{\tau} Y' \ \&\ X'\ R\,Y',$$
$$Y \xrightarrow{\tau} Y' \Rightarrow \exists X'.\ X \xrightarrow{\tau} X' \ \&\ X'\ R\,Y',$$

$$X \xrightarrow{a!v} X' \Rightarrow \exists Y'.\ Y \xrightarrow{a!v} Y' \ \&\ X'\ R\,Y',$$
$$Y \xrightarrow{a!v} Y' \Rightarrow \exists X'.\ X \xrightarrow{a!v} Y \ \&\ X'\ R\,Y',$$

$$X \xrightarrow{a?} F \Rightarrow \exists G.\ Y \xrightarrow{a?} G \ \&\ \forall v \in V.\ F(v)\ R\,G(v),$$
$$Y \xrightarrow{a?} G \Rightarrow \exists F.\ X \xrightarrow{a?} F \ \&\ \forall v \in V.\ F(v)\ R\,G(v).$$

Say $X, Y \in \widehat{\mathbf{P}}$ are *late bisimilar* iff $X\ \ R\ \ Y$ for some late bisimulation on presheaves R.

That surjective open maps induce late bisimulations on presheaves follows directly from the next lemma.

Lemma 6. *Assume $f : X \to Y$ is an open map $\widehat{\mathbf{P}}$.*

Let M be a minimal object of $\widehat{\mathbf{P}}$. If C is a rooted component of X at $m \in X(M)$ then the image fC is a rooted component of Y at $f_M(m)$; the restriction f_C of f to C is an open map $f_C : C \to fC$.

Moreover, if f is surjective then any rooted component of Y is the image of a rooted component of X under f, and each restriction f_C, where C is a rooted component of X, is a surjective open map.

Proof. Direct consequence of the definition of open map. □

Corollary 7 *If $h : X \to Y$ is a surjective open map in $\widehat{\mathbf{P}}$, then X, Y are late bisimilar.*

Proof. Define R a relation on presheaves by:

$$W \; R \; Z \text{ iff } \exists f : W \to Z \text{ surjective and open in } \widehat{\mathbf{P}}.$$

Then R is a late bisimulation on presheaves by Lemma 6. □

Corollary 8 *If X, Y are bisimilar in $\widehat{\mathbf{P}}$, i.e. they are related by an span of surjective open maps, then X, Y are late bisimilar as presheaves.*

Proof. From Corollary 7, as late bisimilarity on presheaves is easily seen to be an equivalence relation. □

Thus a span of surjective open maps yields a late bisimulation between presheaves. We now show the converse. For the presheaves X, Y and a late-bisimulation R which relates them we construct a sub-presheaf of $R_{XY} \subseteq X \times Y$ whose projections to X and Y are surjective open maps.

For $X \in \widehat{\mathbf{P}}$, recall from Section 5.3, the bijections between

- $i \in X(\tau.)$ and transitions $X \xrightarrow{\tau} X_i$,
- $j \in X(a!v)$ and transitions $X \xrightarrow{a!v} X_j$,
- $k \in X(a?)$ and transitions $X \xrightarrow{a?} X_k$.

They are used in the next definition.

Definition 9. Let R be a late bisimulation. Define, by induction on the structure of path objects $P \in \mathbf{P}$, sets $R_{XY}(P)$ whenever XRY:

$$\begin{aligned}
R_{XY}(\tau.) &= \{(i,l) \in X(\tau.) \times Y(\tau.) \mid X_i \; R \, Y_l\} \\
R_{XY}(\tau.P) &= \bigcup\{R_{X_i Y_l}(P) \mid (i,l) \in R_{XY}(\tau.)\} \\
\\
R_{XY}(a!v.) &= \{(j,m) \in X(a!v.) \times Y(a!v.) \mid X_j \; R \, Y_m\} \\
R_{XY}(a!v.P) &= \bigcup\{R_{X_j Y_m}(P) \mid (j,m) \in R_{XY}(a!v.)\} \\
\\
R_{XY}(a?) &= \{(k,n) \in X(a?) \times Y(a?) \mid \forall v \in V.\; X_k(v) \; R \, Y_n(v)\} \\
R_{XY}(a?(v \mapsto P)) &= \bigcup\{R_{X_{k}(v) Y_{n}(v)}(P) \mid (k,n) \in R_{XY}(a?)\}
\end{aligned}$$

Lemma 10. *Let R be a late bisimulation on presheaves. If $X \; R \; Y$, then*
(i) R_{XY} extends to a sub-presheaf of $X \times Y$.

(ii) The compositions $R_{XY} \hookrightarrow X \times Y \xrightarrow{\pi_1} X$ *and* $R_{XY} \hookrightarrow X \times Y \xrightarrow{\pi_2} Y$ *are surjective open, where* π_1, π_2 *are the projections associated with the product* $X \times Y$.

Proof. (i) It is first necessary to show that $R_{XY}(P) \subseteq X(P) \times Y(P)$. This follows by induction on the structure of $P \in \widehat{\mathbf{P}}$. For instance consider a path object of the form $a?(v \mapsto P)$. Suppose $X \xrightarrow{a?} X_k, k \in X(a?)$, and $Y \xrightarrow{a?} Y_n, n \in Y(a?)$, with $\forall v \in V.\ X_k(v)\ R\ Y_n(v)$. Now,

$$\begin{aligned} R_{X_k(v)Y_n(v)}(P) &\subseteq X_k(v)(P) \times Y_n(v)(P) && \text{by induction,} \\ &\subseteq X(a?(v \mapsto P)) \times Y(a?(v \mapsto P)) && \text{by Section 5.3.} \end{aligned}$$

Thus

$$R_{XY}(a?(v \mapsto P)) \subseteq X(a?(v \mapsto P)) \times Y(a?(v \mapsto P)).$$

An induction on the clauses for deriving morphisms $P \leq Q$ in $\widehat{\mathbf{P}}$ (see Section 4) shows $X(P,Q) \times Y(P,Q)$ restricts to a function $R_{XY}(Q) \to R_{XY}(P)$, making R_{XY} a sub-presheaf of $X \times Y$.

(ii) Write ρ_1, ρ_2 for the restriction of the projections $R_{XY} \hookrightarrow X \times Y \xrightarrow{\pi_1} X$ and $R_{XY} \hookrightarrow X \times Y \xrightarrow{\pi_2} Y$. That each component ρ_{1P}, ρ_{2P} is surjective is proved by induction on the structure of path objects P. The quasi-pullback conditions providing the openness of ρ_1 and ρ_2 are shown to hold by induction on the clauses for deriving morphisms $P \leq Q$ in $\widehat{\mathbf{P}}$. □

Hence :

Theorem 11. *Presheaves* $X, Y \in \widehat{\mathbf{P}}$ *are late-bisimilar iff they are related by a span of surjective open maps.*

The next lemma links late-bisimilation on presheaves and late-bisimulation on closed terms of **VProc**, and yields the main result of this section—the equivalence of the operational and denotational formulations of bisimilarity.

Lemma 12. *Let* t_1, t_2 *be closed process terms. The denotations* $[\![t_1]\!], [\![t_2]\!]$ *are late bisimilar as presheaves iff* t_1, t_2 *are late bisimilar.*

Proof. Assuming R is a late-bisimulation on presheaves, it is claimed we obtain a late-bisimulation S on (closed) process terms by defining

$$S = \{(t_1, t_2) \mid [\![t_1]\!]\ R\ [\![t_2]\!]\}.$$

Conversely, assuming S is a late-bisimulation on (closed) process terms, it is claimed we obtain a late bisimulation on presheaves by defining

$$R = \{([\![t_1]\!], [\![t_2]\!]) \mid t_1 S t_2\}.$$

The proof of those two claims rests on Lemma 4, with recourse to the Substitution Lemma 3. □

Theorem 13. *Closed process terms* t_1, t_2 *of* **VProc** *are late-bisimilar iff their denotations* $[\![t_2]\!], [\![t_2]\!]$ *are related by a span of surjective open maps.*

Proof. Directly from Theorem 11 and Lemma 12. □

7 Variations

A transition semantics and bisimulation for **VProc** with early value passing can be obtained easily on the lines of [14]. An appropriate presheaf semantics is obtained with a path category a partial order which is an initial solution to:

$$\mathbf{P} = \mathbf{P}_\perp + \sum_{(a,v)\in C\times V} \mathbf{P}_\perp + \sum_{(a,v)\in C\times V} \mathbf{P}_\perp$$

In fact $\widehat{\mathbf{P}}$ is isomorphic to rooted presheaves over $\mathbf{P}_\perp$ which is readily seen to be isomorphic to a category of synchronisation trees in which labels have the form τ, $a!v$ or $a?v$ where $a \in C$ and $v \in V$, a category $\mathbf{ST}_{C\times V}$ in the notation of [12, 4]. For such categories bisimulation obtained from open maps has been shown to coincide with Park and Milner's strong bisimulation [12]. Furthermore, denotational semantics is given in [19] in which denotations of terms as synchronisation trees are strong bisimilar to the transition systems from an operational semantics. Thus there is no difficulty in producing a denotational semantics so that the denotation of closed terms in $\widehat{\mathbf{P}}$ are connected by a span of open surjections iff the terms are strong bisimilar.

A much greater challenge is provided by a process-passing language with a syntax similar to that of **VProc**

$$t ::= nil \mid \tau.t \mid a!t_1.t_2 \mid a?X.t \mid (t_1 \mid t_2) \mid t_1 + t_2 \mid X \mid recX.t$$

but where in contrast to **VProc** a process t_1 can be sent along a channel a by a process $a!t_1.t_2$ and an arbitrary process can be received on a and bound to process-variable X in a process $a?X.t$. A transition semantics can be found, for instance, in [16]. A path category for process-passing with late semantics is reasonably taken to be an initial solution to the following isomorphism in **Prof**

$$\mathbf{P} \cong \mathbf{P}_\perp + \sum_{a\in C} (\mathbf{P}\times\mathbf{P})_\perp + \sum_{a\in C} (!\mathbf{P} \multimap \mathbf{P})_\perp$$

or sufficiently an initial solution to

$$\mathbf{P} \cong \mathbf{P}_\perp + \sum_{a\in C} (\mathbf{P}+\mathbf{P})_\perp + \sum_{a\in C} ((!\mathbf{P})^{op} \times \mathbf{P})_\perp$$

in **Cat**—the constructions one is led to by Section 3. There is little trouble in giving a denotational semantics to a term with n free variables as a functor $\widehat{\mathbf{P}}^n \to \widehat{\mathbf{P}}$. So closed terms, denoting presheaves in $\widehat{\mathbf{P}}$, inherit a notion of bisimulation from open maps in presheaf categories. But there is a problem in understanding the bisimulation that arises, for example as a coinductive definition based on a transition semantics, along the usual lines. The difficulties are due to the function space component $(!\mathbf{P} \multimap \mathbf{P})$.

On the other hand, there seem to be no fundamental difficulties in presenting a presheaf model of the Pi-calculus, where following the lead of [17, 5] we (Cattani,Stark,Winskel) move to $\mathbf{Prof}^{\mathbf{I}}$, indexed by a category of name-sets $\mathbf{I}$.

Acknowledgements

I especially thank Martin Hyland for very helpful discussions during my stay at the Isaac Newton Institute, Cambridge University. Thanks also to Jaap van Oosten for useful remarks.

References

1. Abramsky, S., On semantic foundations of applicative multiprogramming. Proc. ICALP'83, Barcelona, LNCS 154, 1983.
2. Adamek, J., and Rosicky J., Locally presentable and accessible categories. LMS Lecture Notes Series 189, 1994.
3. Borceux, F., Handbook of categorical logic, 1. Cambridge University Press, 1994.
4. Cattani, G.L., and Winskel, G., Presheaf models for concurrency. Manuscript, 1996.
5. Fiore, M., Moggi, E., and Sangiori, D., A fully abstract model for the Pi-calculus. Proc. of LICS'96.
6. Hennessy, M., and Ingolfsdottir, A., A theory of communicating processes with value passing. Information and Computation, 107(2), 1993.
7. Hennessy, M., and Plotkin, G., A term model for CCS. Proc. 9th MFCS, Poland, LNCS 88, 1980.
8. Ingolfsdottir, A., A semantic theory for value-passing processes, late appraoch—Parts I and II. BRICS reports RS–95–3/22, 1995.
9. Johnstone, P.T., Stone Spaces. Cambridge University Press, 1982.
10. Joyal, A., and Moerdijk, I., Algebraic set theory. LMS Lecture Notes Series 220, Cambridge University Press, 1995.
11. Joyal, A., and Moerdijk, I., A completeness theorem for open maps. In Annals of Pure and Applied Logic 70, 51-86, 1994.
12. Joyal, A., Nielsen, M., and Winskel, G., Bisimulation from open maps. Report Series RS-94-7, BRICS, University of Aarhus, Denmark, May 1994. Accepted for a LICS 93 special issue of Information and Computation.
13. Lehman, D., Categories for fixed point semantics. FOCS 17, 1976.
14. Milner, A.R.G., Communication and concurrency, Prentice Hall, 1989.
15. Milner, R., Parrow, J., and Walker, D., A calculus of mobile processes, Parts I and II. Information and Computation, 100:1-77, 1992.
16. Sangiori, D., Bisimulation for higher-order process calculi. INRIA Report, Sophia-Antipolis, RR-2508, 1995.
17. Stark, I.,A fully abstract domain model for the Pi-calculus. Proc. of LICS'96, 1996.
18. Vickers, S., Geometric theories and databases. In LMS Lecture Notes Series 177, 1992.
19. Winskel, G., and Nielsen, M., Models for concurrency. In the Handbook of Logic in Computer Science, vol.IV, ed. Abramsky, Gabbay and Maibaum, Oxford University Press, 1995.

Elementary Control Structures

John Power*

Department of Computer Science, University of Edinburgh, King's Buildings, Edinburgh EH9 3JZ, Scotland

Abstract. We define the notion of elementary control structure, and prove that, for fixed sets of names and prime arities, assignment of arities to names, and fixed set of controls, the category of elementary control structures is equivalent to the category of control structures, modulo two mild conditions. We further demonstrate that a mildly special case of closed action calculus forms a calculus for elementary control structures, providing the initial object in the category. Finally, we prove the category of elementary control structures is equivalent to that of fibrational control structures.

1 Introduction

Control structures were introduced by Milner and colleagues in [MMP] (see also [G], [HP] and [Mil]) as a proposed general setting for the study of semantics, in particular semantics for concurrency, allowing a unified account of many current models of concurrency, such as variants of the π-calculus and Petri nets. This extends the work of Meseguer and Montanari [MM] who used a monoidal category to account for the algebraic structure of processes associated with a Petri net.

First, one has a symmetric monoidal category, whose arrows are regarded as actions, with domain and codomain representing input and output arities. The composition of the category represents dataflow composition, and the monoidal structure represents parallel composition. The category is locally preordered, i.e., each homset is endowed with the structure of a preorder, and this is respected by both sorts of composition: the preorders represent reaction relations. There is a functorial parametrization of actions on a name: one has a set X of names, each name x having an arity p, and for each name, there is an endofunctor ab_x. In addition, to each name x of arity p is assigned an action $< x >: 1 \longrightarrow p$; for each arity p, there is a discard action $\omega : p \longrightarrow 1$; and the structure is parametric on a set of controls $\mathcal{K}$, determined by the particular calculus being modelled. This is all subject to a string of axioms, which we detail in Sect. 2. Given fixed sets of names and prime arities, an assignment of arities to names, and a fixed set of controls, one has a category of control structures.

---

* I acknowledge the support of ESPRIT Basic Research Action 6453: Types for proofs and programs and EPSRC grant GR/J84205: Frameworks for programming language semantics and logic, and a visit to the Isaac Newton Institute for a month while this paper was being written.

The definition of a control structure has much data and many axioms. So it is not clear from the definition whether the data and axioms are definitive or somewhat arbitrary. Moreover, several people have noted that the definition looks close to that of the π-calculus, so have wondered whether control structures are largely restricted to modelling variants of the π-calculus. Finally, the definition is somewhat unusual as a category theoretic definition for use in semantics, as the use of names is distinctive: they are remarkably similar to variables, in that one binds over them, one may substitute names for names, and two actions are equal if they are α-convertible with respect to names; so it is surprising to see a set of names explicitly as part of a semantics. Thus we ask whether one can characterize control structures in terms of a simpler structure that is more definitive, more obviously general, and does not include the unusual role of names.

Here, we define elementary control structures. If one restricts control structures to what we call locally finite control structures, all known control structures of interest being such, then we can prove that, for fixed sets of names and prime arities, assignment of arities to names, and fixed set of controls, the category of locally finite control structures is equivalent to a full subcategory of the category of elementary control structures. The definition of elementary control structure is simpler than that of control structure and more obviously general; it has no set of names; and we identify precisely those elementary control structures that arise from control structures. The latter were formally justified by two criteria: if one fixes the set of names and their arities, they are closed under congruence; and the corresponding action calculus [MMP] is an initial object in the category of control structures. The same apply for elementary control structures: the first is trivial, and the second follows from Gardner's reformulation of action calculi as closed action calculi [G]. Moreover, elementary control structures fit into a general semantic theory of notions of computation [PR].

Further, we prove the category of elementary control structures is equivalent to the category of fibrational control structures introduced in [HP]. This strengthens the status of both structures: elementary control structures are simpler with more obviously complete and natural axioms, whereas fibrational control structures allow a more direct account of open communication. The main result of this paper also allows a mildly simplified proof of the main result of [HP], which relates control structures with fibrational control structures.

In fact, there is a more general and more natural phenomenon implicit here. In order to obtain the equivalence we seek, we define an elementary control structure for fixed set P of prime arities, and fixed set $\mathcal{K}$ of controls, to consist of a strict symmetric monoidal category C_0 and an identity on objects, strict symmetric monoidal functor from $\mathcal{M}$, the free category with strictly associative finite products on P, to C_0, together with some preorder structure and operators to model reaction and controls respectively. However, there is no strong reason in developing semantics to remain so close to the orginal definition of control structure; and some of the structure of elementary control structures is both unnecessary and unnatural for an elegant, general semantics. More natural would be to consider an arbitrary category $\mathcal{M}$ with finite products, a symmetric monoidal category C_0, and a strong symmetric monoidal functor from $\mathcal{M}$ to C_0, together with preorder structure and operators as above to model reaction and controls. Then, one would model prime arities by a function from the set of prime arities to the set of objects of $\mathcal{M}$, and model the rest of the structure as before. This added generality has several advantages. For instance, one immediately has a notion of map of such models that allows the arity monoid to vary. One also immediately fits into a general theory of semantics of notions of computation [PR], for which a semantics for nondeterminism has already been seen as a special case [AP], and in terms of which other notions of computation are gradually being modelled. In this paper, we do not develop this more general, more natural semantics, but restrict attention to establishing the equivalence outlined above: we leave it to the reader educated in modern denotational semantics to appreciate the implicit, more natural, more general setting for these semantics.

The paper is organized as follows: first, in Sect. 2, we recall the definition of control structure and some relevant facts. Then, in Sect. 3, we define elementary control structures; in Sect. 4, we make precise and prove the equivalence. In Sect. 5, we define an elementary action calculus as a mildly special case of Gardner's closed action calculus, and show that it is the initial object of the category of elementary control structures. Finally, in Sect. 6, we recall the definition of fibrational control structures, and prove the category of elementary control structures equivalent to the category of fibrational control structures.

2 Control Structures

In this section, we recall from [MMP] the definition of control structure. An *action structure* consists of a strict monoidal preordered category A, whose objects $k, l, m, n, \cdots$ are called *arities* and whose morphisms $a, b, c, \cdots$ are called *actions*. The underlying monoid of A is denoted $(M, \otimes, 1)$, and we denote the composite of $a : l \longrightarrow m$ with $b : m \longrightarrow n$ by $a \cdot b$. The identity id_m is maximal in the preorder $A(m, m)$ for all m. An action structure is also equipped with a countable set X of *names*; each name x is assigned an arity k, denoted $x : k$, and a preordered functor $ab_x : A \longrightarrow A$ such that if $x : k$ and $a : m \longrightarrow n$, then $ab_x a : k \otimes m \longrightarrow k \otimes n$.

The name-set X is assumed fixed, as is the arity monoid M and the assignment of arities to names. Moreover, M is assumed to be the free monoid on a set P of *prime* arities, and the arity of each name is assumed to be prime, and infinitely many names are associated with each prime arity. Note that this implies that P is countable.

A *symmetric action structure* is an action structure with a symmetry c on the underlying strict monoidal category, such that

- $ab_x c = id \otimes c$,
- $ab_x(ab_x a) = id \otimes ab_x a$,
- $ab_x(a \otimes id) = ab_x a \otimes id$, and

- $(c_{k,l} \otimes id_m) \cdot ab_y ab_x a = ab_x ab_y a \cdot (c_{k,l} \otimes id_n)$ if $x \neq y$.

A *control* K is an operator that allows the construction of an action $K(\mathbf{a})$ from a sequence $\mathbf{a}$ of actions, subject to a rule of arity of the form that given a vector $(a_i : m_i \longrightarrow n_i)$ of length r, we have $K(\mathbf{a}) : m \longrightarrow n$ subject to a side-condition constraining the values of r, m_i, n_i, m and n. A *control structure* consists of a signature $\mathcal{K}$ and a symmetric action structure A equipped with

- a *datum* $< x >: 1 \longrightarrow p$ for each $x : p \in X$,
- a *discard* operation $\omega : p \longrightarrow 1$ for each prime p, and
- a *control* operation K for each $K \in \mathcal{K}$, obeying the arity rules for $\mathcal{K}$,

such that

- $ab_x < y >= id \otimes < y >$ if $x \neq y$,
- $ab_x \omega = id \otimes \omega$,
- $(x) < x >= id$,
- $[x/x]a = a$,
- $[y/x](< x > \otimes < x >) =< y > \otimes < y >$, and
- $[y/x]K(a_1, \cdots, a_n) = K([y/x]a_1, \cdots, [y/x]a_n)$,

where for all $a : m \longrightarrow n$ and $x, y : p \in X$, $(x)a$ is defined to be $(ab_x a).(\omega_p \otimes id_n)$ and $[y/x]a$ is defined to be $(< y > \otimes id_m) \cdot (x)a$. The action $[y/x]a$ should be thought of as renaming x to y in a. The expression $< xy >$ shall sometimes be used as an abbreviation for $< x > \otimes < y >$, and similarly for binding.

We recall from [MMP] the notion of *surface* of actions, i.e., those names through which an action can interact. For an action a, let $surf(a) = \{x \in X \mid ab_x(a) \neq id \otimes a\}$. Informally, these are the names that occur freely in the action.

A morphism of control structures from the structure $(A, \otimes, c, ab, < >, \omega, \mathcal{K})$ to $(A', \otimes', c', ab', < >', \omega', \mathcal{K}')$ (with the same control signature, sets P and X and arity assignments) is a strict symmetric monoidal functor $f : A \longrightarrow A'$ which is the identity on objects and preserves the additional structure, i.e., ab, $< >$, ω and the controls. It follows that for any action a in A, $surf(f(a)) \subseteq surf(a)$. Given P, X, the arity function, and $\mathcal{K}$, control structures and morphisms between them form a category we denote by $CS(\mathcal{K})$.

For an example, the initial control structure (= action calculus) for a version of the π-calculus without replication has actions generated by controls $\boldsymbol{\nu} : 1 \longrightarrow p$ (a new name of arity p), $\mathbf{out} : p \otimes m \longrightarrow 1$ (output through a port) and for each $a : m \longrightarrow n$, $\mathbf{box}(a) : p \longrightarrow n$. This can be used to model input by means of $\mathbf{box}(id_m)$. There is one axiom which expresses communication through matching input/output ports. The remaining preorder structure is freely induced by this axiom and the preorder-enriched monoidal category structure.

3 Elementary Control Structures

In this section, we define the notion of elementary control structure. We then give a functor from the category of control structures, for given P and $\mathcal{K}$, to that of elementary control structures.

The definition of an elementary control structure includes reference to the free category with strictly associative finite products on a set P. So, before defining an elementary control structure, we will give an explicit description of that category. The idea is that P will be the set of primes used in the definition of control structure, or equivalently, that of elementary control structure, and our main constructions are based upon the free category with strictly associative finite products built from it. This really is an unnecessary complication if one's aim is to provide an elegant natural semantics for Milner's action calculi, but it is one forced upon us if we are to obtain an equivalence between control structures and elementary control structures.

Proposition 1. *Given a set P, the free category $\mathcal{M}$ with strictly associative finite products on P may be described as follows:*

- *an object of $\mathcal{M}$ is a finite sequence $(p_1, \cdots, p_m)$ of elements of P*
- *an arrow from $(p_1, \cdots, p_m)$ to $(q_1, \cdots, q_n)$ is a function $\phi : \{1, \cdots, n\} \longrightarrow \{1, \cdots, m\}$ such that for all i, $q_i = p_{\phi(i)}$*
- *composition is given by composition of functions.*

Proof. Routine calculation. ∎

We assume the set P is fixed, M is the free monoid on it, and $\mathcal{M}$ is the free category with strictly associative finite products on the set P. So M is the set of objects of $\mathcal{M}$. A *projection* is a map in $\mathcal{M}$ such that ϕ is an order preserving injection.

We now move to the definition of elementary control structure. First, we need a little notation. A *control signature* $\mathcal{K}$ is a family of tuples of arbitrary finite length, each of the form $K : ((m_1, n_1), \cdots, (m_r, n_r)) \mapsto (m, n)$. The idea, as in Sect. 2, is that each K is to be modelled by an operator that allows the construction of an action $K(\mathbf{a})$ from a sequence $\mathbf{a}$ of actions, subject to the arity rule that given a vector $(a_i : m_i \longrightarrow n_i)$ of length r, we have $K(\mathbf{a}) : m \longrightarrow n$. We assume $\mathcal{K}$ is fixed, and we let C_0 denote the underlying ordinary category of a locally preordered category C.

Definition 2. An *elementary control structure* consists of a strict symmetric monoidal locally preordered category C and an identity on objects strict symmetric monoidal functor $J : \mathcal{M} \longrightarrow C_0$ such that each projection $\pi_2 : k \times m \longrightarrow m$ is maximal in $C(k \otimes m, m)$, together with, for each control K with arity information $((m_1, n_1), \cdots, (m_r, n_r)) \mapsto (m, n)$ and each k, a function $C_0(k \otimes m_1, n_1) \times \cdots \times C_0(k \otimes m_r, n_r) \longrightarrow C_0(k \otimes m, n)$, natural with respect to maps $f : k \longrightarrow k'$ in $\mathcal{M}$.

We call an arrow of C an *action*. This definition of elementary control structure places it immediately as an instance of the structures described for denotational semantics in [PR]. It is routine to verify that the naturality condition on controls may be expressed in the form that the given family of functions forms a natural transformation between two functors from $\mathcal{M}$ to *Set*.

To understand the definition of elementary control structure in computational terms, the composition corresponds to dataflow and the tensor to parallel composition, as with control structures; the category $\mathcal{M}$ and functor J assert that one has basic actions of copying, discarding and permuting names (although not explicitly having a set of names), *cf* [G] and [HP]; the controls are as in control structures, and the parametrization of the controls is as in [G]: it is needed to account for controls on actions with non-empty surface, the parametrization being equivalent to parametrizing over all possible surfaces. The computational significance of the naturality in $\mathcal{M}$ of the controls is not entirely clear yet: one could ask, for instance, for naturality with respect to C, and it is unclear what is the computational significance of either choice. The development of further examples should make that clearer in due course.

The leading examples of elementary control structures are still being developed, so it is premature to say much about them. However, a simple way to generate examples at present is by use of the equivalence we will establish between control structures and elementary control structures: given a control structure, we obtain an elementary control structure by restricting to those actions with empty surface. In particular, given any action calculus, those actions with empty surface form an elementary control structure. For a particular example,

Example 1. Consider the action calculus mentioned at the end of Sect. 2 for a version of the π-calculus: it had controls

$$\nu : 1 \to p \qquad \textbf{out} : p \otimes m \to 1 \qquad \frac{a : m \to n}{\textbf{box}(a) : p \to n}$$

and one axiom to express communication through matching input/output ports. So one has the elementary control structure freely generated by these controls, with the preorder relation also freely generated, subject to the axiom. The actions of this elementary control structure consist of the closed terms for a fragment of the π-calculus, together with some closed formulae that have no computational meaning but which are generated by the syntax of the π-calculus. For more detail of this and other variants of the π-calculus as action calculi and hence as elementary control structures, see [Mil].

For another example, Mifsud's thesis [Mif] contains an account of reflexive control structures, in order to account for recursion. To do this,

Example 2. For each arity k, have a control which, to each action from $k \otimes m$ to $k \otimes n$, yields an action from m to n. Subject these to axioms for naturality and coherence in k, m and n, with respect to both categorical composition and the tensor product. Controls for a control structure are equally controls for an elementary control structure. So the equivalent version of Mifsud's reflexive control structures in terms of elementary control structures amounts to elementary control structures with what is called a *trace* on the strict symmetric monoidal category C_0. The concepts of reflexion and trace are studied in detail in Mifsud's thesis.

One can similarly describe higher order elementary control structures by use of controls too, and that is part of the thesis work of Hasegawa. The notion of higher order action calculus, with the higher order structure expressed using controls, appears in [G] and [Mil]; and that notion readily give rises to a notion of higher order elementary control structure.

The general theory of notions of computation of Power and Robinson [PR] is intimately related to the notion of elementary control structure, and many examples of the former may be seen as examples of the latter. For instance,

Example 3. One obtains a semantics for nondeterminism by giving a control for a binary operator: given two actions from m to n, one has a control to give a nondeterministic choice of the two, and one subjects it to equations for associativity, commutativity, and idempotence. That is the setting for the Anderson and Power's semantics for nondeterminism [AP].

Given the definition of elementary control structure, there is an evident definition of *morphism* of elementary control structures: it is a functor that strictly preserves all the structure. For given P and $\mathcal{K}$, this yields a category $ECS(\mathcal{K})$ of elementary control structures. It is immediate that, with P and $\mathcal{K}$ fixed, the category $ECS(\mathcal{K})$ is defined by operations and universally defined equations, so we have

Proposition 3. *$ECS(\mathcal{K})$ is closed under congruences.*

We can immediately start to make precise the relationship between control structures and elementary control structures by observing

Proposition 4. *The following data gives a functor $(\ )_e : CS(\mathcal{K}) \longrightarrow ECS(\mathcal{K})$. The elementary control structure A_e is given as follows:*

- *the underlying category of A_e is given by those actions with empty surface.*
- *The functor $J : \mathcal{M} \longrightarrow A_e$ sends the projections to ω's and the diagonals to actions of the form $(x) < xx >$.*
- *Given a control K, the function $A_{e0}(k \otimes m_1, n_1) \times \cdots \times A_{e0}(k \otimes m_r, n_r) \longrightarrow A_{e0}(k \otimes m, n)$ is given by $(\mathbf{x})K((< \mathbf{x} > \otimes id_{m_1}) \cdot a_1, \cdots, (< \mathbf{x} > \otimes id_{m_r}) \cdot a_r)$ for a choice of vector $\mathbf{x}$ of disjoint names.*

The behaviour of $(\ )_e$ on morphisms is given by restriction.

Proof. It was shown in [MMP] that each of the operations in the definition of a control structure reduces surface, so for instance $surf(a \otimes b) \subseteq surf(a) \cup surf(b)$. So A_e is closed under the strict symmetric monoidal structure of A. The functions for the controls are well defined for the same reason, and their naturality follows since for any control K, vector of actions $\mathbf{a}$, and names x and y, all of appropriate arity, one has $[x/y]K(\mathbf{a}) = K([x/y]\mathbf{a})$. ■

We now seek to use the above construction to derive an equivalence between the category of control structures, for fixed sets of names and arities, arity assignment, and set of controls, and the category of elementary control structures. In order to do that, we need mild restrictions of the definitions.

Definition 5. We call a control structure *locally finite* if every action has finite surface.

Every control structure studied to date has been locally finite, and it is unclear whether there exists any non locally finite control structure of any interest. So at present, there is no known natural example of such. The restriction of $(\ )_e$ to locally finite control structures is fully faithful, thus exhibiting the category of locally finite control structures as a full subcategory of the category of elementary control structures. It is easy to see this result as a corollary of the stronger result we prove in the next section: there we identify those elementary control structures that arise from locally finite control structures, thus showing the definitions of locally finite control structure and elementary control structure equivalent modulo a mild condition on the latter.

4 Recovering Control Structures from Elementary Control Structures

In this section, we identify those elementary control structures that arise from locally finite control structures. We believe the definition of elementary control structure should be taken as more primitive, and this result shows how an older construction relates to it.

Definition 6. An elementary control structure is *strong* if given actions $a : k_1 \otimes k_3 \otimes k_4 \otimes k_5 \longrightarrow n$ and $a' : k_1 \otimes k_2 \otimes k_3 \otimes k_5 \longrightarrow n$ such that the evident two composites from $k_1 \otimes k_2 \otimes k_3 \otimes k_4 \otimes k_5$ to n agree, there is a unique action $b : k_1 \otimes k_3 \otimes k_5 \longrightarrow n$ that, composed with the evident projections, yields a and a'.

Definition 7. Given an elementary control structure and a pair of arities (m, n), an action $a : k \otimes m \longrightarrow n$ is called a *weakening* of $a' : k' \otimes m \longrightarrow n$ if $a = (\pi \otimes id_m) \cdot a'$, where π is a projection.

Lemma 8. *In any strong elementary control structure, for all (k, m, n) and $a : k \otimes m \longrightarrow n$, there exists a unique action $b : k' \otimes m \longrightarrow n$ such that a is a weakening of b, but b is not a weakening of any other action.*

Proof. Consider the family of all actions of which a is a weakening. It is necessarily finite, since each k is a product of primes. Now apply the condition finitely often to obtain b. ∎

We will call such b the *strong* action determined by a.

Now, to construct a locally finite control structure from a strong elementary control structure, we assume as in Sect. 2 that we have a fixed set X of names together with an arity function $ar : X \longrightarrow P$, with each $p \in P$ assigned countably many names. We will denote the preimage of p by X_p. For simplicity of exposition, we will assume that X is well ordered: it is not essential to our constructions, but it allows us to speak of sequences rather than sets, which is convenient. The ordering is not of computational significance: the names merely yield contexts, and we need a precise way to speak of contexts in order to establish our theorem; assuming a well order on the set of names, then respecting the well order in all our constructions, is a convenient, relatively simple way to do so.

Construction 9. Given a strong elementary control structure E, we give the data for a control structure $F(E)$ as follows: an arrow in $F(E)$ from m to n is a sequence $[x_1, \cdots, x_r]$ of distinct names of X, respecting the well order of X, together with a strong action $a : k \otimes m \longrightarrow n$, such that $k = p_1 \otimes \cdots \otimes p_r$, where $x_i \in X_{p_i}$. We define $\otimes$, $\cdot$, c, $< x >$, ω, $(x)a$ and K, then define $ab_x a = (x)(< x > \otimes a)$. For tensors, define $([\mathbf{x}], a) \otimes_{F(E)} ([\mathbf{y}], b)$ as follows:

- first juxtapose $\mathbf{x}$ and $\mathbf{y}$, then reorder the juxtaposed sequence and delete repetitions so that it is ordered consistently with the order on X, giving, say, $\mathbf{z}$ with corresponding sequence of arities $p_1 \cdots p_r$
- then take the strong copy of $f \cdot (a \otimes b) : p_1 \otimes \cdots \otimes p_r \otimes m \otimes m' \longrightarrow n \otimes n'$, where f is determined by the construction of $\mathbf{z}$ from $\mathbf{x}$ and $\mathbf{y}$
- take the corresponding subsequence of $\mathbf{z}$ as the required sequence of distinct names, and take the strong copy as above as the strong action.

Composition and controls are done similarly, c and ω are evident, and $< x >$ is given by $([x], id)$ if the latter is strong, and the trivial strengthening otherwise. The construction $(x)-$ is defined by two cases:

1. if $x = x_j$ lies in $\mathbf{x}$, then put $(x)([\mathbf{x}], a) = ([x_1 \cdots \hat{x_j} \cdots x_r], (id \otimes c_{p_{j+1} \cdots p_r, p_j}) \cdot a)$
2. if not, $(x)([\mathbf{x}], a) = ([\mathbf{x}], \pi \cdot a)$, where π projects out the arity of x.

■

Observe that $(x)-$ is well defined, as a is strong. Moreover, it follows immediately from the definition, specifically by inspection of the first components, that once we have proved $F(E)$ is a control structure, $surf([\mathbf{x}], a) = |\mathbf{x}|$.

We first seek to prove that this construction gives us a control structure. The proof is largely routine, taking care whether an action in E is strong or not. The main lemma one needs is

Lemma 10. *In $F(E)$, $[x/y]([y], a)$, which is defined to be $(< x > \otimes id).(y)([y], a)$, is equal to $([x], a)$.*

One can then deduce by routine calculation

Proposition 11. *$F(E)$ is a locally finite control structure.*

Since A_e for a control structure A is given by the actions of A with empty surface, it follows easily that

Proposition 12. *For any strong elementary control structure E, the elementary control structure $F(E)_e$ is isomorphic to E.* ■

Proposition 13. *Let $A = (A, \otimes, c, ab, <>, \omega, \mathcal{K})$ be a locally finite control structure. Then A is isomorphic to $F(A_e)$.*

Proof. First observe that for each m and n, the set of actions from m to n in A is in bijection with the set of actions from m to n in $F(A_e)$: given $a : m \longrightarrow n$ in A, it has a surface, which is uniquely ordered to be consistent with the order on X, say $[x_1, \cdots, x_r]$, with corresponding arity $k = p_1 \otimes \cdots \otimes p_r$. The action $(\mathbf{x})a$ is strong. So send a to $([x_1, \cdots, x_r], (\mathbf{x})a)$. The inverse is given by sending $([x_1, \cdots, x_r], a)$ to $(< x_1 \cdots x_r > \otimes id_m) \cdot a$. It is routine to verify that this construction respects the structure of a control structure. Observe in doing so that some $< x >$ has empty surface if and only if all of that arity do: our mapping from a control structure A to $F(A_e)$ takes $< x >$ to $([x], id)$ if the surface of all $< x >$ are non-empty, and to the trivial stengthening otherwise. ∎

Propositions 11, 12 and 13 allow us to deduce

Theorem 14. *For fixed sets of names and prime arities, assignment of arities to names, and family of controls, the functor $(\ )_e : CS(\mathcal{K}) \longrightarrow ECS(\mathcal{K})$ induces an equivalence of categories between the category of locally finite control structures and that of strong elementary control structures.*

5 Elementary Action Calculi

In this section, we define elementary action calculi: these are essentially Gardner's closed action calculi [G]. We prove that the action calculus for a given set of controls provides an initial object in the category of elementary control structures; and we observe that it follows from Gardner's work that the functor from the category of control structures to that of elementary control structures sends the action calculus to the elementary action calculus.

Given a monoid $(M, \otimes, 1)$ and a set $\mathcal{K}$ of controls, each with arity information $((m_1, n_1), \cdots, (m_r, n_r)) \mapsto (m, n)$, the *elementary action calculus* EAC($\mathcal{K}$) is a quotient of a term algebra, given by the closed action calculus CAC($\mathcal{K}'$) of [G].

Terms have the form $t : m \to n$, for $m, n \in (M, \otimes, 1)$, where t is constructed from basic operators $\mathbf{id}_m, \omega_m, \Delta_m, \mathbf{i}_{m,n}, \cdot, \otimes$ and the controls $K \in \mathcal{K}$. The operators ω_m, Δ_m and $\mathbf{i}_{m,n}$ correspond to the data making $\mathcal{M}$ have finite products, as is apparent from the axioms accompanying these operators. The other operators are self-explanatory.

Definition 15. The set of *elementary terms* over $\mathcal{K}$, denoted by ET($\mathcal{K}$), is generated by the following rules:

$$\mathbf{id}_m : m \to m$$

$$\frac{s : k \to l \qquad t : l \to m}{s \cdot t : k \to m}$$

$$\frac{s : k \to m \qquad t : l \to n}{s \otimes t : k \otimes l \to m \otimes n}$$

$$\Delta_m : m \to m \otimes m$$

$$\mathbf{i}_{m,n} : m \otimes n \to n \otimes m$$

$$\omega_m : m \to \epsilon$$

$$\frac{t_1 : k \otimes m_1 \to n_1 \quad \ldots \quad t_r : k \otimes m_r \to n_r}{K_k(t_1, \ldots, t_r) : k \otimes m \to n}$$

for each control $K \in \mathcal{K}$ with arity information $((m_1, n_1), \cdots, (m_r, n_r)) \mapsto (m, n)$ and each arity k.

We shall omit the arity subscripts on the basic operators when they are apparent.

Definition 16. The equational theory EAC is the set of equations upon terms generated by the action structure axioms except those for ab_x:

$$\begin{aligned}
A1 &: \quad s \cdot \mathbf{id} = s = \mathbf{id} \cdot s \\
A2 &: \quad s \otimes \mathbf{id}_\epsilon = s = \mathbf{id}_\epsilon \otimes s \\
A3 &: \quad \mathbf{id} \otimes \mathbf{id} = \mathbf{id} \\
A4 &: \quad s \cdot (t \cdot u) = (s \cdot t) \cdot u \\
A5 &: \quad s \otimes (t \otimes u) = (s \otimes t) \otimes u \\
A6 &: \quad (s \cdot t) \otimes (u \cdot v) = (s \otimes u) \cdot (t \otimes v)
\end{aligned}$$

those for a symmetry and to make $\mathcal{M}$ have finite products:

$$\begin{aligned}
B1 &: \quad \Delta_m \cdot (\omega_m \otimes \mathbf{id}) = \mathbf{id} \\
B2 &: \quad \Delta_m \cdot \mathbf{i}_{m,m} = \Delta_m \\
B3 &: \quad \mathbf{i}_{k,m} \cdot (s \otimes t) = (t \otimes s) \cdot \mathbf{i}_{l,n} \\
B4 &: \quad \mathbf{i}_{m,n} \cdot \mathbf{i}_{n,m} = \mathbf{id} \\
B5 &: \quad \mathbf{i}_{m \otimes n,k} = (\mathbf{id} \otimes \mathbf{i}_{n,k}) \cdot (\mathbf{i}_{m,n} \otimes \mathbf{id}) \\
B6 &: \quad \omega_{m \otimes n} = \omega_m \otimes \omega_n \\
B7 &: \quad \Delta_{m \otimes n} = (\Delta_m \otimes \Delta_n) \cdot (\mathbf{id} \otimes \mathbf{i}_{m,n} \otimes \mathbf{id}) \\
B8 &: \quad \Delta_m \cdot (\Delta_m \otimes \mathbf{id}) = \Delta_m \cdot (\mathbf{id} \otimes \Delta_m)
\end{aligned}$$

and the following *control axioms*:

$$\begin{aligned}
C1 &: \quad K_{p \otimes k}(\omega_p \otimes t_1, \ldots, \omega_p \otimes t_r) = \omega_p \otimes K_k(t_1, \ldots, t_r) \\
C2 &: \quad K_{k \otimes p \otimes q}((\mathbf{id} \otimes \mathbf{i}_{p,q} \otimes \mathbf{id}) \cdot t_1, \ldots, (\mathbf{id} \otimes \mathbf{i}_{p,q} \otimes \mathbf{id}) \cdot t_r) = \\
&\quad (\mathbf{id} \otimes \mathbf{i}_{p,q} \otimes \mathbf{id}) \cdot K_{k \otimes q \otimes p}(t_1, \ldots, t_r) \\
C3 &: \quad K_{k \otimes p}((\mathbf{id} \otimes \Delta_p \otimes \mathbf{id}) \cdot t_1, \ldots, (\mathbf{id} \otimes \Delta_p \otimes \mathbf{id}) \cdot t_r) = \\
&\quad (\mathbf{id} \otimes \Delta_p \otimes \mathbf{id}) \cdot K_{k \otimes p \otimes p}(t_1, \ldots, t_r)
\end{aligned}$$

We write $s = t \in \mathrm{EAC}$ if $s, t \in \mathrm{ET}(\mathcal{K})$ and $s = t$ is in the equational theory EAC.

We have defined $\mathbf{id}_m$, ω_m, Δ_m and $\mathbf{i}_{m,n}$ for arbitrary arities and included the axioms B5–B7 following Gardner [G] in order to make clear that this is her construction $\mathrm{CAC}(\mathcal{K}')$. The alternative was to define them only for prime arities.

Definition 17. The elementary action calculus $\mathrm{EAC}(\mathcal{K})$ is defined to be the quotient $\mathrm{ET}(\mathcal{K})/\mathrm{EAC}$.

We can adopt Gardner's result [G] Section 4 to the effect

Proposition 18. *$(\,)_e$ sends the action calculus $AC(\mathcal{K})$ to* $\mathrm{EAC}(\mathcal{K})$.

Moreover, it is immediate from the definition that

Theorem 19. $\mathrm{EAC}(\mathcal{K})$ *is the initial object in $ECS(\mathcal{K})$.*

6 Fibrational Control Structures

In this section, we recall the definition of fibrational control structure from [HP], and we prove that elementary control structures are equivalent to fibrational control structures. In fact, strong elementary control structures are equivalent to what were there called abstract control structures, which are fibrational control structures subject to a condition. We could have proved our main result of this paper by appeal to the main result of [HP], which relates control structures with fibrational control structures, then by invoking the result of this section: but the approach of this paper is more direct, and in fact gives a mildly easier proof of the result of [HP]. A fibrational formulation of control structures seemd likely to be helpful in the study of dynamics, specifically in modelling open communication.

For the purposes of this section, we continue the same notational conventions as in previous sections unless clear otherwise from the context.

Notation 20. Given any category $\mathcal{M}$ with finite products, we can define another category $s(\mathcal{M})$ as follows:

- an object is a pair (k, m) of objects of $\mathcal{M}$
- an arrow from (k, m) to (k', m') is a pair (f, g) of arrows in $\mathcal{M}$ with $f : k \longrightarrow k'$ and $g : k \times m \longrightarrow m'$
- composition is evident.

Proposition 21. *The category $s(\mathcal{M})$ has finite products. Moreover, if $\mathcal{M}$ has strictly associative finite products, so does $s(\mathcal{M})$.*

Proposition 22. *In $s(\mathcal{M})$, every map $(f, g) : (k, m) \longrightarrow (k', m')$ factors uniquely as a map of the form (id, h) followed by one of the form (j, π_2).*

Proof. For the existence, put $h = g$ and $j = f$. It is evident that these are the only possibilities, so we have unicity. ∎

Definition 23. A *fibrational control structure* consists of

1. a functor $h : s(\mathcal{M})^{op} \times M \longrightarrow Preord$. The functor h determines a locally preordered graph G_h with vertex set M and with edge preorder from m to n given by the disjoint union over k of $h(k, m, n)$. We denote the underlying ordinary graph by G_{h0}.
2. a strict monoidal locally preordered category structure on G_h such that
   - composition restricts to a family of maps $\cdot : h(k, m, n) \times h(k', n, p) \longrightarrow h(k \times k', m, p)$ natural in the first variable with respect to $s(\mathcal{M})$, meaning that for all $(f, g) : (k, m) \longrightarrow (k'', m'')$ in $s(\mathcal{M})$, the evident diagram commutes, and natural in the second variable with respect to maps of the form $(f', \pi_2) : (k', n) \longrightarrow (k'', n)$
   - the tensor product restricts to a family $\otimes : h(k, m, n) \times h(k', m', n') \longrightarrow h(k \times k', m \times m', n \times n')$, natural in $s(\mathcal{M})$ in both variables, meaning that for all $(f, g) : (k, m) \longrightarrow (k'', m'')$ in $s(\mathcal{M})$, the evident diagram commutes, and the dual
   - id_m (which necessarily lies in $h(1, m, m)$) is maximal in the preorder, as are its weakenings
3. the family $c_{m,n} \in h(1, m \times n, n \times m)$ given by $h(id, c)id_{n \times m}$ provides a symmetry for this strict monoidal structure, modulo the evident composition with $h(c_{k,k'}, \pi_2)$
4. for each control K with arity information $((m_1, n_1), \cdots, (m_r, n_r)) \mapsto (m, n)$ and each $(k_1, \cdots, k_r)$, a function $G_{h0}(k_1, m_1, n_1) \times \cdots \times G_{h0}(k_r, m_r, n_r) \longrightarrow G_{h0}(k_1 \times \cdots \times k_r, m, n)$, natural in each variable with respect to maps of the form $(f_i, \pi_2) : (k_i, m_i) \longrightarrow (k_i', m_i)$

such that $h(\pi_1, \pi_{k \times m}) : h(j, k \times m, n) \longrightarrow h(j \times k, m, n)$ is invertible for all j, k, m, n. We denote the inverse by $(\ )^{-}$. ∎

Theorem 24. *Given a fibrational control structure* $(h, \cdot, \otimes, \mathcal{K})$,

1. *the locally preordered subcategory of* G_h *consisting of object set* M *and homs given by* $h(1, m, n)$ *for all* m *and* n, *is a strict symmetric monoidal subcategory of* G_h, *which we denote* C_h
2. *the function sending* $g : m \longrightarrow n$ *to* $h(id_1, g)id_n$ *forms an identity on objects strict symmetric monoidal functor* $J_h : \mathcal{M} \longrightarrow C_{h0}$
3. *for each control* K *with arity information* $((m_1, n_1), \cdots, (m_r, n_r)) \mapsto (m, n)$, *the family* $C_{h0}(k_1 \times m_1, n_1) \times \cdots \times C_{h0}(k_r \times m_r, n_r) \longrightarrow C_{h0}(k_1 \times \cdots \times k_r \times m, n)$ *of functions given by applying the final condition in the definition of fibrational control structure, and using the control data supplied by* K *and* $(k_1, \cdots, k_r)$, *is natural in each variable with respect to maps* $f_i : k_i \longrightarrow k_i'$ *in* $\mathcal{M}$.

Proof. This all follows by routine checking, largely using the naturality axioms of fibrational control structures. ∎

Observe that the third part of Theorem 24 does not immediately agree with the data for an elementary control structure, because the controls here are parametrized by sequences of arites $(k_1, \cdots, k_r)$, whereas in elementary control structures, they are parametrized by a single arity k. It is routine to verify that the two are equivalent, by use of diagonals, symmetries, and projections. So we freely use whichever is convenient in the following. We chose to parametrize elementary control structures by a single arity as that yields a more direct relationship with other semantic work, specifically on operator algebras, especially in the presence of higher order controls.

Corollary 25. *Given a fibrational control structure* $(h, \cdot, \otimes, \mathcal{K})$, *the functor given by* $J_h : \mathcal{M} \longrightarrow C_{h0}$ *and the control data of Theorem 24 form an elementary control structure.*

We remark that it is routine, given the definition of abstract control structure appearing in [HP], to see that a fibrational control structure forms an abstract control structure if and only if the constructed elementary control structure is strong. For the construction of a fibrational control structure from an elementary control structure,

Theorem 26. *Given an elementary control structure* $(C, \otimes, c, J : \mathcal{M} \longrightarrow C_0, \mathcal{K})$, *the following data form a fibrational control structure:*

1. $h_C : s(\mathcal{M})^{op} \times M \longrightarrow$ *Preord, defined by* $h_C(k, m, n) = C(k \times m, n)$, *with* $h_C(f, g)$ *given by precomposition with* $J(<\pi_1 \cdot f, g>) : (k, m) \longrightarrow (k', m')$
2. *composition* $\cdot_C : h_C(k, m, n) \times h_C(k', n, p) \longrightarrow h_C(k \times k', m, p)$, *defined by applying* $id_{k'} \otimes -$ *to* $C(k \times m, n)$, *then using the composition and symmetry of* C
3. *tensor* $\otimes_C : h_C(k, m, n) \times h_C(k', m', n') \longrightarrow h_C(k \times k', m \times m', n \times n')$, *defined by the tensor and symmetry of* C
4. *for each control* K *with arity information* $((m_1, n_1), \cdots, (m_r, n_r)) \mapsto (m, n)$ *and each* $(k_1, \cdots, k_r)$, *the function* $h_{C0}(k_1, m_1, n_1) \times \cdots \times h_{C0}(k_r, m_r, n_r) \longrightarrow h_{C0}(k_1 \times \cdots \times k_r, m, n)$ *defined by the corresponding parametrized control function composed with the evident projections, symmetries and diagonals* $C_0(k_1 \times m_1, n_1) \times \cdots \times C_0(k_r \times m_r, n_r) \longrightarrow C_0(k_1 \times \cdots \times k_r \times m, n)$.

Proof. This is routine calculation, with no surprises. ∎

It is a triviality that, starting with an elementary control structure, applying the construction of Theorem 26, then applying the construction of Theorem 24, we regain an elementary control structure that is isomorphic to the original one, because $h_C(1, m, n)$ is defined to be $C(m, n)$, etcetera. It is not quite as obvious, but still follows by routine checking, that starting with a fibrational control structure and applying the two constructions also returns an isomorphic copy of the original fibrational control structure: the key point is that $h(k, m, n)$ is naturally isomorphic to $h(1, k \times m, n)$, so h is fully determined by its naturality and its behaviour on the full subcategory of $s(\mathcal{M})^{op} \times M$ determined by triples of the form $(1, m, n)$; similarly for the rest of the data. So we conclude

Corollary 27. *The categories of fibrational control structures and elementary control structures determined by a set P and control signature $\mathcal{K}$ are equivalent.*

The equivalence of course is given by the constructions of Theorems 24 and 26.

7 Further Work

There has been some study of higher order action calculi, for instance in [Mil], and in particular by Gardner and Hasegawa, in order to investigate such calculi as the λ-calculus. There is no definition of higher order control structure, but one might investigate higher order elementary control structures as a next step, in conjunction with the development of higher order action calculi. This seems likely to be pursued in the thesis of Hasegawa.

Alex Mifsud [Mif] has defined reflexive control structures to model recursion. So, in addition to and in conjunction with higher order, one would like to extend the equivalence between control structures and elementary control structures to reflexive versions.

Elementary control structures do not directly account for open communication, as the emphasis is on actions with empty surface, and open communication is about communication on the surface of an action. However, fibrational control structures [HP] are equivalent to elementary control structures and allow the study of openness, so further development of a fibrational version of elementary control structures seems important. This should certainly be done with an eye to and led by a desire for appropriate dynamic structures.

One delicacy with control structures has been the two axioms with side condition $x \neq y$. This delicacy makes it difficult to define a notion of map of control structures that allows the arity monoid to vary. However, in passing to elementary control structures, one no longer has such a side condition. So in particular, the notion of map between elementary control structures extends readily to one in which the arity monoid is allowed to vary. So we ask what is the significance of that for models of action calculi. An alternative possibility for generalising maps of control structures has been broached, and it retains names: it involves adding a separation structure on the monoid of names, and asking a map to preserve that; so one wonders how the two possible approaches to this question relate.

Finally, elementary control structures are an instance of structures considered by Power and Robinson [PR] in semantics. They consider a base category B, typically with finite products, and an identity on objects strict symmetric premonoidal functor from B to some other category. A typical base category is *Set*. In this paper, we have as base category the free category with strictly associative finite products on a set. We may see our example as a *theory*, which may be modelled in *Set* together with an extension. For some of the most important control structures, actions are freely generated by the controls, then factored by an equivalence such as weak bisimulation. The factoring amounts to the category theoretic factoring of a congruence on a category with structure, cf [AP], which accounts for nondeterminism in the setting of [PR] in similar fashion. So one would like to use that fact to integrate elementary control structures into modern denotational semantics. One would immediately have access to the tools of modern denotational semantics such as linear type theory and the corresponding logics. Also, it suggests a classification of several of the more fundamental controls, and might shed some light on classification of reaction relations too.

References

[AP] Anderson, S.O., Power, A.J.: A representable approach to nondeterminism. (submitted)

[G] Gardner, P.: A name-free account of action calculi. Proc. MFPS 95. Electronic Notes in Theoretical Computer Science **1** (1995)

[HJ] Hermida, C., Jacobs, J.: Fibrations with indeterminates: contextual and functional completeness for polymorphic lambda calculi. Math. Structures in Computer Science **5** (1995) 501–531

[HP] Hermida, C., Power, A.J.: Fibrational control structures. Proc. CONCUR 95. LNCS **962** (1995) 117–129

[M] Mac Lane, S.: Categories for the working mathematician. Springer-Verlag (1971)

[MM] Meseguer, J., Montanari, U.: Petri nets are monoids. Information and Computation **88** (1990) 105–155

[MMP] Mifsud, A., Milner, R., Power, A.J.: Control structures. Proc. 10th LICS (1995) 188–198

[Mif] Mifsud, A.: Reflexive control structures. Edinburgh Ph.D. thesis (submitted)

[Mil] Milner, R.: Calculi for interaction. Acta Informatica (to appear)

[PR] Power, A.J., Robinson, E.P.: Premonoidal categories and notions of computation (submitted)

On Transformations of Concurrent Object Programs

Anna Philippou and David Walker

Department of Computer Science, University of Warwick
Coventry CV4 7AL, U.K.

Abstract. Transformation rules which increase the scope for concurrent activity within systems prescribed by programs of concurrent object languages are given. The correctness of the rules is proved using a semantic definition by translation to a mobile-process calculus. The main theoretical development concerns the notions of confluence and partial confluence.

1 Introduction

The main aim of this paper is to enunciate and prove the soundness of transformation rules for programs of a concurrent object language. Its starting point is work of C B Jones [5, 8] on formal development of concurrent programs utilizing ideas from object-oriented programming. A central part of that development process is the use of transformations to increase the scope for concurrent activity within systems of objects prescribed by programs without altering their observable behaviours. Our interest here is not in formal development of concurrent programs *per se*, but rather in the elaboration of theoretical concepts and techniques useful in proving the correctness of such transformations. The results of the paper concern a specific concurrent object programming language, a variant of the $\pi o \beta \lambda$ language [5] which in turn is derived from the POOL family [1]. This small language is rich enough for the problems to be interesting and difficult and for the concepts and techniques to be illustrated to good effect. The concepts and techniques are, however, widely applicable. We build on work using calculi of mobile processes as semantic bases for concurrent object languages, for instance [18, 20, 6, 10, 14, 15]. In our view these general models of concurrent systems with changing structure are very well suited to giving natural and direct semantic definitions of such languages. This method of semantic definition has two additional, related, benefits. First, the process-calculus theory may be used to reason rigorously about classes of systems and individual systems prescribed by programs. Secondly, the general models act as a unifying and simplifying framework, not only by providing a single arena for the semantic definition of different languages, but also by connecting systems expressed in them with other kinds of mobile systems, thereby enabling concepts and techniques originating in different domains to be generalized and applied in others.

The main theoretical development concerns the notions of *confluence* and *partial confluence* of processes. To quote Milner [12], the essence of confluence is that "of any two possible actions, the occurrence of one will never preclude the other". A key observation is that in reasoning about the behaviour of a confluent system it is often sufficient to examine in detail only a part of that behaviour: from this and the fact of the system's confluence it may be possible to deduce properties of the remaining behaviour. In [14] confluence was the basis for a proof that certain syntactic conditions prohibiting sharing of references guarantee determinacy of concurrent object programs. Generalizations of these conditions play a rôle in the transformation rules we consider. Moreover the key observation above is central to the proofs of their correctness. As shown in [10], partial confluence is useful in reasoning about classes of non-confluent systems in which interaction between possibly non-confluent components is of a certain disciplined kind. Here the theory of partial confluence is extended to accommodate divergence. This is necessary as in considering the correctness of the transformation rules, the possibility of non-termination of method invocations must be taken into account. It turns out that the extension of the theory of partial confluence to accommodate divergence is quite complicated.

This paper is a summary of a fairly large body of work. To make best use of the space available the emphasis is on explaining the problems tackled and the main ideas used and results obtained, rather than giving a detailed technical account [13]. In the next section background material is presented and in section 3 the transformations are introduced. Section 4 outlines the theory of partial confluence while in section 5 the correctness of the transformations is sketched. The paper ends with a discussion of related research.

2 Background

The programming language is statically typed with types bool (Booleans), int (integers), unit (the one-element type) and ref(A) for A a class name. A value of type ref(A) is a reference to an object of class A; classes are explained below. In the abstract syntax definitions below we use A to range over class names, m over method names, X, Y over variable names, f over constants and operators of the Boolean, integer and unit types, E over expressions, and S over commands, and we write $\widetilde{Z}$ for a tuple $Z_1, \ldots, Z_n$ of syntactic entities. The expressions and commands are the well-typed phrases given as follows:

$$E \ ::= \ X \ | \ X^{\dagger} \ | \ \mathsf{new}(A) \ | \ f(\widetilde{E}) \ | \ E!m(\widetilde{E})$$

$$\begin{aligned} S \ ::= \ & X := E \ | \ \mathsf{output}\, E \ | \ \mathsf{return}\, E \ | \ E!m(\widetilde{E}) \ | \ \mathsf{commit}\, E!m(\widetilde{E}) \\ | \ & S_1; S_2 \ | \ \mathsf{if}\, E \,\mathsf{then}\, S_1 \,\mathsf{else}\, S_2 \,. \end{aligned}$$

Declarations are given as follows where T ranges over types. First, variable declarations are given by

$$Vdec \ ::= \ \mathsf{var}\, X_1 : T_1, \ldots, X_p : T_p \,.$$

Then method declarations are given by

$$Mdec \ ::= \ \mathsf{method}\, m(\widetilde{Y} : \widetilde{T}) : T, \ Vdec, \ S$$

where $\widetilde{Y}$ of types $\widetilde{T}$ are the formal parameters, T is the result type, and S is the body of the method with *Vdec* declaring variables local to it. Sequences of method declarations are given by

$$Mdecs \ ::= \ Mdec_1, \ldots, Mdec_q$$

and class declarations by

$$Cdec \ ::= \ \mathsf{class}\ A,\ Vdec,\ Mdecs\ .$$

Finally, program declarations are given by

$$Pdec \ ::= \ Cdec_1, \ldots, Cdec_r,\ \mathsf{trigger}\ E_0$$

where E_0 is of the form $\mathsf{new}(A)!m()$.

Pdec above prescribes the possible computations of a system of concurrent objects each of which is an instance of one of the classes declared in it. The expression E_0 acts as a trigger to initiate computation by creating and activating an object of one of the classes A. Arbitrarily-many objects may be created during computation, and references to objects (and simple values) may be passed in interactions between objects. Each object of class A as in *Cdec* above has private variables as declared in *Vdec*. On creation it assumes a quiescent state in which each of its private variables has the value nil (representing a reference to no object for variables of ref type and the undefined value for variables of type bool, int and unit), and any one of its methods as declared in *Mdecs* may be invoked. When an object α invokes in an object β its method m as in *Mdec* above (with some parameters), the activity of α is suspended until the result of the invocation is returned to it. On invocation β executes the body S of m. It may return a result to α by executing a return command. Alternatively, β may, via a commit command, delegate to another object γ the responsibility for returning a result to α, thereby freeing itself to continue with some other activity. On completing execution of the method body S, β resumes its quiescent state; only then may another method be invoked in β. Objects may enjoy concurrent activity as the return of a result or the delegation of the responsibility for returning a result need not be the last action in a method body.

An informal account of the meanings of expressions and commands follows. Evaluation of X involves reading the value of the private variable X. That of $X^{\dagger}$ is similar except that the value of X becomes nil when it is read. Evaluation of $\mathsf{new}(A)$ results in the creation of an object of class A; the value of the expression is a reference to that object. f ranges over constants (0, true, nil etc.) and simple operators (+, = etc.). The evaluation of $E!m(\widetilde{E})$ involves the evaluation of E and then the expressions in the tuple $\widetilde{E}$ followed by the invocation of method m with parameters the values of $\widetilde{E}$ in the object to which the value of E is a reference. The value of the expression $E!m(\widetilde{E})$ is the simple value or reference returned to the object as the result of the method invocation. The result type of a command of the form $E!m(\widetilde{E})$ is unit. The assignment, sequence and conditional commands are standard. Execution of output E involves evaluation of E and the output of its (integer) value to the environment. The return and commit commands, which have been explained above, are illustrated in the example class declarations below from [5]. Both may be used to construct binary tree-structured symbol tables. The first is as follows:

```
class T
var K:int, V:ref(A), L:ref(T), R:ref(T)
method insert(X:int, W:ref(A)):unit
     if K=nil then (K:=X ; V:=W ; L:=new(T) ; R:=new(T))
     else if X=K then V:=W
          else if X<K then L!insert(X,W)
               else R!insert(X,W) ;
     return nil
method search(X:int):ref(A)
     if K=nil then return nil
     else if X=K then return V
          else if X<K then return L!search(X)
               else return R!search(X)
```

An object of this class represents a node which stores in its variables K, V, L, R an integer key, a value (a reference to an object of some class A), and references to two instances of the class (its left and right children in the tree structure of which it is a component). It has two actions: the method **insert** which allows a key-value pair to be inserted, and the method **search** which returns the value associated with its key parameter (or nil if there is none). Note that when a method is invoked in the root of a tree of T-nodes, the entire tree becomes blocked until the root returns the result of the invocation to the caller. Contrast this with the following variation of T:

```
class T
var K:int, V:ref(A), L:ref(T), R:ref(T)
method insert(X:int, W:ref(A)):unit
     return nil ;
     if K=nil then (K:=X ; V:=W ; L:=new(T) ; R:=new(T))
     else if X=K then V:=W
          else if X<K then L!insert(X,W)
               else R!insert(X,W)
method search(X:int):ref(A)
     if K=nil then return nil
     else if X=K then return V
          else if X<K then commit L!search(X)
               else commit R!search(X)
```

In this case, when a node's **insert** method is invoked it releases the caller from the rendezvous *before* proceeding to deal with the insertion. Also, if its **search** method is invoked with a key smaller (resp. larger) than that stored in the node, it will *commit* the search to its left (resp. right) child, thereby freeing itself to respond to another invocation while the search is in progress. Thus within a tree of objects of this second class, many insertions and searches may proceed concurrently.

We may view the second class as being obtained from the first by the application of three transformations: in the `insert` method a command of the form S; return E is transformed to return $E; S$, and in the `search` method two commands of the form return $E!m(\widetilde{E})$ are transformed to commit $E!m(\widetilde{E})$. Our aim is to find syntactic conditions under which such transformations may be safely applied and to prove that this is the case.

In the available space we can not give the semantic definition on which the proofs are based. It takes the form of a structural translation in which each phrase Z of the language is mapped to an agent $[\![Z]\!]$ of a mobile-process calculus. Several calculi have been used in this way, for instance π-calculus [18, 6, 20], Higher-Order π-calculus [21], CHOCS [16], π-calculus with simple values [19], and an extension of π-calculus with higher-order abstractions and data other than names but with only first-order interaction [11]; see also [15] for Pict, an experimental programming language based on π-calculus in which one may express concurrent objects. We outline very briefly the form of the semantic definition. An important factor not explained in detail here is that extensive use is made of the type system of the calculus, both in structuring the definition and in reasoning about agents representing programs.

The encoding of a program declaration *Pdec* as above takes the form

$$[\![Pdec]\!] \stackrel{\mathrm{def}}{=} (\nu\tilde{n})\,([\![Cdec_1]\!] \mid \ldots \mid [\![Cdec_r]\!] \mid [\![E_0]\!])$$

where with $Cdec_i$ declaring class A_i, $[\![Cdec_i]\!]$ is a replicator of the form

$$!\,(\nu a)\,\overline{n_{A_i}}\langle a\rangle.\,\mathrm{Obj}_{A_i}\langle a,\ldots\rangle$$

which may emit via n_{A_i} arbitrarily-many object 'names': $\mathrm{Obj}_{A_i}\langle a,\ldots\rangle$ represents an object of class A_i with 'name' a in its initial quiescent state. A derivative of $[\![Pdec]\!]$ has the form

$$Q \equiv (\nu\tilde{q})(P_1 \mid \ldots \mid P_n \mid [\![Cdec_1]\!] \mid \ldots \mid [\![Cdec_r]\!] \mid T)$$

where each P_i, representing an object, is a derivative of some Obj_{A_j} and T is a derivative of $[\![E_0]\!]$. The only free name of Q is *out*: an agent of the form $[\![\mathsf{output}\,E]\!]$ uses it to emit the value of E. The form of Q is preserved under derivation, although the number of P-components (the number of objects in the represented system) may grow.

Writing $\approx_b$ for branching bisimilarity, the following result is proved in [10] (for a language extending the one studied here).

Theorem 1. Let *Pdec* be an arbitrary program of the language in which the first class `T` above is declared. Let *Pdec'* be the program obtained from it by replacing the declaration of that class by that of the second class `T` above. Then $[\![Pdec]\!] \approx_b [\![Pdec']\!]$.

Central to the proof is a notion of *partial confluence* of agents. In section 4 we generalize that notion and its associated theory. First, however, we examine the transformations more closely.

3 Transformations

Our aim is to enunciate syntactic conditions under which transformations of the forms

$$S;\mathsf{return}\,E \;\rightsquigarrow\; \mathsf{return}\,E;S \qquad \text{and} \qquad \mathsf{return}\,E!m(\widetilde{E}) \;\rightsquigarrow\; \mathsf{commit}\,E!m(\widetilde{E})$$

may be safely applied, and to prove that this is the case. To begin to do this we first note that we must take account of the possibility of non-termination of method invocations. For consider the following program declaration *Pdec*:

```
class A
method m():unit
   new(A)!m() ; return nil ; output 3

trigger new(A)!m()
```

Pdec prescribes a single non-terminating computation in which nothing is output to the environment. If, however, the first transformation is applied to the body of method **m**, so that it becomes `return nil ; new(A)!m() ; output 3`, the resulting program has computations in which output is produced. Moreover, if instead in *Pdec* the body of method **m** is changed to `return new(A)!m() ; output 3` to obtain *Pdec′* and the second transformation is then applied so that the body becomes `commit new(A)!m() ; output 3`, the resulting program again has computations in which output is produced although nothing is output in the single non-terminating computation of *Pdec′*.

The criterion of correctness we will adopt will in fact consider the transformations *not* to alter the observable behaviours of *Pdec* and *Pdec′*. The reason for this is that both they and their respective transformed variants prescribe *divergent* systems which may proceed indefinitely without interacting with the environment. Thus rather than using branching bisimilarity as the criterion of indistinguishability of behaviour as in the theorem cited above, we will use a variant of it which is sensitive to divergence. This is introduced in section 4; for systems which are free from divergence it coincides with branching bisimilarity. This regime allows us also to give an account of run-time errors, for instance when one object attempts to invoke a method in another using a nil reference, by treating them as engendering divergence.

To move towards the syntactic conditions we first examine why the transformations can not be applied arbitrarily. Consider the following program declaration *Pdec*:

```
class A
var X:ref(A), Y:ref(B)
method m():unit
   X:=new(A) ; Y:=new(B) ; Y!init() ; return X!inca(Y) ;
   output Y!read()
method inca(Z:ref(B)):unit
   Z!incb() ; return nil

class B
var W:int
method init():unit
   W:=0 ; return nil
method incb():unit
   W:=W+1 ; return nil
method read():int
   return W

trigger new(A)!m()
```

The single computation of *Pdec* results in the trigger creating an object α of class `A` which creates objects β of class `A` and γ of class `B`, and 1 being output to the environment. Suppose *Pdec'* is obtained from it by applying the first transformation to the body of method `inca` of class `A`, resulting in `return nil ; Z!incb()`. The output on executing *Pdec'* could be either 1 or 0, the latter if α invokes `read` in γ before β invokes `incb` in γ, something which is not possible in *Pdec* as in that case β must invoke `incb` in γ before freeing α to invoke `read` in γ. Further, if *Pdec''* is obtained from *Pdec* by applying the second transformation to the body of method `m` of class `A`, resulting in `return X!inca(Y)` being replaced by `commit X!inca(Y)`, then again the output could be either 1 or 0 as by committing to β the responsibility for returning a result to the trigger, α frees itself to invoke method `read` in γ before β invokes `incb`.

These simple examples strongly suggest that syntactic conditions sufficient to guarantee safety of the transformations should prohibit sharing of references to some extent. In [14] conditions of that nature were identified and shown to guarantee confluence of programs conforming to them. In the following definition we generalize these conditions.

Definition 2. The classes $A_1, \ldots, A_n$ form a *community* if for each method body S of each A_i:

1. S does not contain $X := Y$ where X, Y are of type $\mathsf{ref}(A_j)$,
2. S does not contain $E_0!m(\widetilde{E}, X, \widetilde{E'})$ or return X where X is of type $\mathsf{ref}(A_j)$,
3. if E contains $X!m(E_1, \ldots, E_n)$ where $X : \mathsf{ref}(A_j)$, then for no $h \in [1..n]$ does E_h have a subexpression $F_0!m'(\widetilde{F}, X^{\dagger}, \widetilde{F'})$, and
4. S is *responsible* (see below).

The intention is that objects of a community are not directly responsible for the creation of shared references to objects of that community. Condition 1 prevents a reference to an object of the community being copied. Note that assignments of the form $X := Y$ where X, Y are of other ref types and of the form $X := Y^\dagger$ may appear in a community. Communication of a reference from one object to another can take place in two ways: as an argument or as a result of a method invocation. Condition 2 ensures that if an object of a community sends a reference to an object of that community then it relinquishes it. Note that a community may contain phrases similar to those prohibited by condition 2 but which differ in that $X^\dagger$ appears in the place of X. Moreover, in an expression of the form $X!m(E_1, \ldots, E_n)$, where a method is to be invoked in the object of the community to which the value of X is a reference, evaluation of $E_1, \ldots, E_n$ should not result in that reference being communicated to another object: this is the purpose of condition 3. The purpose of condition 4 is to ensure that no confusion occurs about returning the result of an invocation. A command is *return/commit free*, *rcf*, if it contains no return command and no commit command.

Definition 3. The set of *responsible* commands is given as follows:

1. return E and commit $E!m(\tilde{E})$ are responsible;
2. $S_1; S_2$ is responsible if exactly one of S_1, S_2 is responsible and the other is *rcf*;
3. if E then S_1 else S_2 is responsible if S_1, S_2 are responsible.

While objects of a community may not be directly responsible for the creation of shared references to objects of that community, other objects may be. The following definition strengthens the notion of 'community' to prevent this latter possibility.

Definition 4. Let *Pdec* be a program declaration whose classes are G, $\tilde{A}$, $\tilde{N}$. In *Pdec* the classes G, $\tilde{A}$ form a *guarded community* with *guard* G if:

1. the classes $G, \tilde{A}$ form a community;
2. no method body of a class in $\tilde{N}$ contains new(A_i);
3. no method of class G has result type ref(A_i);
4. if $E!m(\tilde{E})$ occurs in a method body of the classes $G, \tilde{A}$, then E is of type ref(A_i);
5. no method body of the classes $G, \tilde{A}$ contains an output command.

The intention is that within a system prescribed by such a program, references to $\tilde{A}$-objects can not be shared although other references may be. Condition 1 ensures that objects within the guarded community are not directly responsible for the creation of sharing of $\tilde{A}$-references. Conditions 2–4 prevent $\tilde{A}$-references being acquired by $\tilde{N}$-objects (which might otherwise act in such ways as to share them): $\tilde{N}$-objects are unable to create references to $\tilde{A}$-objects (condition 2); $\tilde{N}$-objects can interact with $\tilde{A}$-objects only by invoking methods in G-objects, and G-objects do not return $\tilde{A}$-references (condition 3); no G-object or $\tilde{A}$-object can invoke a method in a G-object or an $\widetilde{N}$-object (condition 4), necessary as G-objects and $\widetilde{A}$-objects can share references to $\widetilde{N}$-objects, and references to G-objects can be shared. Finally, no G-object or $\widetilde{A}$-object can interact with the program's environment. To see why this is necessary consider, for example, a variant of the second symbol-table class T in the previous section in which method bodies contain output commands.

The subsystem generated by a guarded community within a program is a region of particularly orderly behaviour. (This will be expressed more formally later.) One might wonder if the transformations can always be applied safely within classes comprising a guarded community. In fact this is not the case as can be seen by considering the following program declaration *Pdec*:

```
class N
method m():unit
   new(G)!m0() ; return nil ; output 3

class G
var X:ref(A)
method m0():unit
   X:=new(A) ; X!m1(X†) ; return nil

class A
method m1(Y:ref(A)):unit
   new(A)!m2(Y†) ; return nil
method m2(Y:ref(A)):unit
   return Y!m3()
method m3():unit
   return nil

trigger new(N)!m()
```

Execution results in the trigger creating an object α of class N which creates an object β of class G which creates an object γ of class A which creates an object δ of class A. The system deadlocks without producing output: δ can only invoke method m3 in γ, but γ can only receive the result of its invocation of method m2 in δ. However, if the first transformation is applied to the body of method m1, yielding `return nil ; new(A)!m2(Y†)`, the resulting program outputs 3. If instead *Pdec'* is obtained from *Pdec* by replacing the body of m1 with `return new(A)!m2(Y†)`, again the program deadlocks without output, while if the second transformation is applied to the body of m1 of *Pdec'*, yielding `commit new(A)!m2(Y†)`, again 3 is output. This motivates the following condition.

Definition 5. Let *Pdec* be a program declaration in which the classes $G, \widetilde{A}$ form a guarded community. $G, \widetilde{A}$ form a *society* if no method body in $G, \widetilde{A}$ contains an expression $X!m(\widetilde{E}, X^{\dagger}, \widetilde{E'})$.

It is in fact the case, though it is not obvious, that a system generated by a society (which for convenience we refer to also as a 'society') can not have 'cycles' of references or return links of a certain kind and hence that a method invocation in a society can not fail because of deadlock. This will be explained further in section 5. Finally we can state the transformation rules.

Transformation 6 Suppose $G, \widetilde{A}$ form a society in a program *Pdec*.

1. A command of the form S; return E may be replaced by return $E; S$ in a method body of $G, \widetilde{A}$ provided no variable X occurs (as X or $X^\dagger$) in both S and E.
2. A command of the form return $E!M(\widetilde{E})$ may be replaced by commit $E!M(\widetilde{E})$ in a method body of $G, \widetilde{A}$.

We now turn to proving their correctness.

4 Partial confluence

In [12] a refined form of determinacy of agents, *confluence*, was introduced and studied. Among the results established was that certain forms of restricted composition of agents preserve confluence; see also [2] for work on confluence. The study of partial confluence of agents was initiated by Milner and pursued in [17]. The emphasis there was on showing that restricted compositions of possibly non-confluent agents may themselves be confluent if the constraints the agents place on one another's behaviour are sufficiently strong. In [10] a new notion of partial confluence, useful in reasoning about classes of systems in which a subsystem interacts in a disciplined manner with a possibly non-confluent environment, was introduced. Its basic theory was developed and it was used to prove the indistinguishability in an arbitrary program context of the symbol-table classes described in section 2. Here we outline an extension of that theory to accommodate divergence. This turns out to be quite complicated. In the space available we can only outline the main definitions and results; see [13] for a full account.

Let $\mathcal{V}$ be the set of visible actions and $Act = \mathcal{V} \cup \{\tau\}$ the set of actions. First recall that an agent P *diverges*, written $P\uparrow$, if P can perform an infinite sequence of τ actions; otherwise P *converges*, $P\downarrow$. Letting α range over Act we say further that $P\downarrow\alpha$ if $P\downarrow$ and whenever $P \Longrightarrow P'' \xrightarrow{\alpha} P'$ then $P'\downarrow$. Moreover letting s range over $\mathcal{V}^*$ we write $P\downarrow s$ if whenever $P \stackrel{t}{\Longrightarrow} P'$ with t a prefix of s, $P'\downarrow$. The divergence-sensitive variant of branching bisimilarity is the following.

Definition 7. The relation *db-bisimilarity* is the largest symmetric relation $\simeq$ such that if $P \simeq Q$ then for all α, if $P\downarrow\alpha$, then $Q\downarrow\alpha$ and whenever $P \xrightarrow{\alpha} P'$ then (a) $Q \Longrightarrow Q'' \xrightarrow{\alpha} Q'$ with $P \simeq Q''$ and $P' \simeq Q'$, or (b) $\alpha = \tau$ and $P' \simeq Q$.

Consistently with the use of db-bisimilarity we modify the definitions of 'determinacy' and 'confluence' from [12] as follows. An agent P is *determinate* if for any $s \in \mathcal{V}^*$, if $P\downarrow s$, $P \stackrel{s}{\Longrightarrow} P_1$ and $P \stackrel{s}{\Longrightarrow} P_2$, then $P_1 \simeq P_2$. If $r, s \in \mathcal{V}^*$, the *excess of r over s*, r/s, is defined by setting $\varepsilon/s = \varepsilon$ where ε is the empty sequence and $(ar)/s = a(r/s)$ if $a \notin s$ and $r/(s/a)$ otherwise. Then an agent P is *confluent* if for all sequences $r, s \in \mathcal{V}^*$, if $P \downarrow rs$, $P \stackrel{r}{\Longrightarrow} P_1$ and $P \stackrel{s}{\Longrightarrow} P_2$ then $P \downarrow sr$ and there are P_1', P_2' such that $P_1 \stackrel{s/r}{\Longrightarrow} P_1'$, $P_2 \stackrel{r/s}{\Longrightarrow} P_2'$ and $P_1' \simeq P_2'$. The following notion is useful.

Definition 8. The *convergent core* of an agent P is

$$\mathrm{cc}(P) = \{Q \mid \text{for some } s \in \mathcal{V}^*,\ P \downarrow s \text{ and } P \stackrel{s}{\Longrightarrow} Q\}.$$

The following abbreviation is convenient: $P \Longrightarrow\stackrel{\alpha}{\longrightarrow} P'$ means that $P \Longrightarrow P'' \stackrel{\alpha}{\longrightarrow} P'$ for some P'' with $P'' \simeq P$ and moreover if $\alpha = \tau$ then $P' \not\simeq P$. Now we can define the appropriate notion of partial confluence.

Definition 9. Let $R \subseteq \mathcal{V}$. An agent P is *R-confluent* if whenever $Q \in \mathrm{cc}(P)$, $\rho \in R$ and $\alpha \in Act$,

1. if $Q \downarrow \rho$, $Q \stackrel{\rho}{\longrightarrow} Q_1$ and $Q \Longrightarrow\stackrel{\rho}{\longrightarrow} Q_2$, then $Q_1 \simeq Q_2$, and
2. if $Q \downarrow \rho\alpha$, $Q \stackrel{\rho}{\longrightarrow} Q_1$ and $Q \Longrightarrow\stackrel{\alpha}{\longrightarrow} Q_2$ then $Q \downarrow \alpha\rho$ and for some Q_1', Q_2', $Q_2 \Longrightarrow\stackrel{\rho}{\longrightarrow} Q_2'$, $Q_1 \Longrightarrow\stackrel{\alpha}{\longrightarrow} Q_1'$ and $Q_1' \simeq Q_2'$.

It is required of an R-confluent agent that each agent in its convergent core (1) be $\simeq$-determinate under R-actions which do not introduce divergence and (2) enjoy a confluence property with respect to R-actions and arbitrary actions which do not together introduce divergence. It is quite easy to see that db-bisimilarity preserves R-confluence. The use of a *branching* variant of bisimilarity is important here as the theory is concerned with agents whose behaviour is not invariant under τ-transitions; see [10] for further discussion. In analysing the transformation rules, care is required in handling the possibility that a divergent system may evolve to a convergent state. The following refinement handles this in a satisfactory way.

Definition 10. An agent P is *fully R-confluent* if it is R-confluent and for every derivative Q of P and $\rho \in R$, if $Q \uparrow \rho$ and $Q \stackrel{\rho}{\longrightarrow} Q'$ then $Q' \uparrow$.

Thus if a derivative of a fully R-confluent agent diverges on an R-action, it may not perform that action and reach a convergent state.

Now suppose $\widetilde{\mathsf{M}} = \mathsf{M}_1, \ldots, \mathsf{M}_q$ and $\widetilde{\mathsf{R}} = \mathsf{R}_1, \ldots, \mathsf{R}_q$ are distinct sorts and that the sorting λ is such that $\lambda(\mathsf{M}_i) = (\xi_i, \mathsf{R}_i)$ for some ξ_i not containing any $\mathsf{M}_j, \mathsf{R}_j$ and that R_i occurs in no other object sort. Let M^-, resp. M^+, be the set of all actions with negative, resp. positive, subject in $\widetilde{\mathsf{M}}$ and similarly for R^- and R^+; let $M = M^- \cup M^+$ and $R = R^- \cup R^+$.

It is convenient to introduce a further abbreviation. For $s = \alpha_1 \ldots \alpha_n \in Act^*$ we write $\stackrel{s}{\longrightarrow}_{\simeq}$ for the composite relation $\simeq\stackrel{\alpha_1}{\longrightarrow}\simeq \ldots \simeq\stackrel{\alpha_n}{\longrightarrow}\simeq$. The significance of the following theorem is that the $\simeq$-state of a restricted composition of R-confluent agents is not altered by intra-actions via actions in R, provided that all $\widetilde{\mathsf{R}}$-names are restricted.

Theorem 11. Suppose P, I are fully R-confluent, $P \xrightarrow{s}_{\simeq} P'$ and $I \xrightarrow{\overline{s}}_{\simeq} I'$ with $s, \overline{s} \in R^*$ sequences of complementary actions, and $\widetilde{p}$ contains all $\widetilde{\mathsf{R}}$-names free in P, I. Then $(\nu\widetilde{p})(P \mid I) \simeq (\nu\widetilde{p})(P' \mid I')$.

We continue with a rather long definition.

Definition 12. A derivation-closed set $\mathcal{S}$ of fully R-confluent agents is (M^-, R^+)-*tidy* if there is a partition $\{\mathcal{S}^{\widetilde{r}} \mid \widetilde{r}$ a finite set of $\widetilde{\mathsf{R}}$-names$\}$ of $\mathcal{S}$, an (M^-, R^+)-*tidy partition*, such that

1. if $P \in \mathcal{S}^{\widetilde{r}}$ and $P \xrightarrow{\alpha} P'$ where $\alpha \notin M^- \cup R^+$ then $P' \in \mathcal{S}^{\widetilde{r}}$;
2. if $P \in \mathcal{S}^{\widetilde{r}}$ and $P \xrightarrow{\mu} P'$ where $\mu = \overline{m}(\widetilde{v}, \nu r) \in M^-$ then $P' \in \mathcal{S}^{\widetilde{r}, r}$;
3. if $P \in \mathcal{S}^{\widetilde{r}}$ and $P \xrightarrow{\rho} P'$ where $\rho \in R^+$ then $r = \mathsf{subj}(\rho) \in \widetilde{r}$ and $P' \in \mathcal{S}^{\widetilde{r}-r}$.

Further, $\mathcal{S}$ is (M^-, R^+)-*ready* if it is (M^-, R^+)-tidy and

4a. if $P \in \mathcal{S}^{\widetilde{r}}$ and $\rho \in R^+$ with $\mathsf{subj}(\rho) \in \widetilde{r}$, then $P \xrightarrow{\rho}$.

The notions (M^+, R^-)-*tidy* and (M^+, R^-)-*tidy partition* are defined dually. We say that $\mathcal{S}$ is (M^+, R^-)-*disciplined* if it is (M^+, R^-)-tidy and

4b. if $P \in \mathcal{S}^r$ (where r is a singleton), $P \downarrow$ and $P \xrightarrow{\mu}$ where $\mu \in M^+$, then $P \Longrightarrow \xrightarrow{\rho}$ where $\mathsf{subj}(\rho) = \overline{r}$.

To grasp the motivation for this definition consider a program declaration in which $G, \widetilde{A}$ form a society. Think of I (with state space $\mathcal{I}$) as $(\nu n_{\widetilde{A}})[\![G, \widetilde{A}]\!]$ and of P (with state space $\mathcal{P}$) as the encoding of the remaining classes and the trigger. Neglecting creation of G-objects, interaction between derivatives of P and derivatives of I involves method invocations, represented here by M-actions, and returns of results, represented by R-actions. An (M^-, R^+)-tidy partition of $\mathcal{P}$ divides its agents, all of which are required to be fully R-confluent, into classes whose indices record the free $\widetilde{\mathsf{R}}$-names of their elements; conditions 1–3 ensure that this interpretation is accurate. Condition 4a stipulates that an agent must be able to receive any value via any of its free $\widetilde{\mathsf{R}}$-names. This corresponds to the property of the language that when an object invokes a method, other than by a commit command, its activity is suspended as it awaits the return of the result of that invocation. An (M^+, R^-)-tidy partition of $\mathcal{I}$ divides its agents in a complementary way. Condition 4b requires that if a convergent agent has one free $\widetilde{\mathsf{R}}$-name r and it may initiate another activity via an M^+-action, then it may also return a result via r, possibly after some τ-actions which, however, do not change its $\simeq$-state.

Now let $\mathcal{I}^\flat$ be the transition graph obtained from $\mathcal{I}$ by deleting all points not in an $\mathcal{I}^{\widetilde{r}}$ with $|\widetilde{r}| \leq 1$ (i.e. all points in which there is more than one outstanding method invocation) and all arrows incident on such points. Let $Q^\flat$ be the point in $\mathcal{I}^\flat$ corresponding to Q in $\mathcal{I}$ (if it exists). Then we have:

Theorem 13. Suppose $\mathcal{P}$ is (M^-, R^+)-ready with (M^-, R^+)-tidy partition $\{\mathcal{P}^{\widetilde{r}}\}_{\widetilde{r}}$, and $\mathcal{I}$ is (M^+, R^-)-disciplined with (M^+, R^-)-tidy partition $\{\mathcal{I}^{\widetilde{r}}\}_{\widetilde{r}}$. Suppose $P \in \mathcal{P}^{\emptyset}$, $I \in \mathcal{I}^{\emptyset}$ and no derivative of $(\nu\widetilde{p})(P \mid I)$ contains a free occurrence in subject position of a name of sort $\widetilde{\mathsf{R}}$ or of sort $\widetilde{\mathsf{M}}$. Then $(\nu\widetilde{p})(P \mid I) \simeq (\nu\widetilde{p})(P \mid I^{\flat})$.

5 Correctness

Let *Pdec* be a program declaration in which $G, \widetilde{A}$ form a society. Let *Pdec'* be obtained from it by applying a single transformation to one of the method bodies of $G, \widetilde{A}$. Then $[\![Pdec]\!]$ is of the form $(\nu\widetilde{p})(P \mid I)$ where $I = (\nu n_{\widetilde{A}})[\![G, \widetilde{A}]\!]$ with P encoding the remaining classes and the trigger, and $[\![Pdec']\!]$ is $(\nu\widetilde{p})(P \mid I')$ where I' is the encoding of the transformed society. Let the transition graphs $\mathcal{P}$ of P and $\mathcal{I}$ of I be partitioned as described above. It can be shown that these partitions meet the appropriate 'tidiness' requirements. Moreover, $\mathcal{P}$ is ready. Further, it can be shown that $\mathcal{I}$ is disciplined. This follows from:

Theorem 14. Suppose $G, \widetilde{A}$ form a society.

1. The agent $(\nu n_{\widetilde{A}})[\![G, \widetilde{A}]\!]$ is confluent.
2. Let Q be a derivative of $(\nu n_{\widetilde{A}})[\![G, \widetilde{A}]\!]$ which contains a single $\widetilde{\mathsf{R}}$-name r, representing that exactly one method invocation originating outside the society has not yet been returned and that r is the name via which the return is to be made. Suppose that $Q\downarrow$. Then $Q \stackrel{\overline{r}(v)}{\Longrightarrow} Q'$ for some Q' and v. Moreover, if also $Q \downarrow r$ then $Q \stackrel{\overline{r}(v)}{\Longrightarrow} Q^q$ where each object-agent component of Q^q represents an object in its quiescent state.

The first part gives a precise sense in which a society is, as stated earlier, a region of 'particularly orderly behaviour'. The import of the second part is that if Q is a derivative of $(\nu n_{\widetilde{A}})[\![G, \widetilde{A}]\!]$ representing a state in which exactly one method invocation originating outside the society has not yet been returned, then either Q is divergent, because it has a non-terminating computation or because it has a computation in which a run-time error occurs, or it can return the result of the outstanding invocation, *the* result because the agent is confluent. Moreover if the system is convergent after returning the result, it may reach a state in which each object has become quiescent.

The final hypothesis of Theorem 13, on free names in subject position, follows easily from the sorting respected in the semantic definition. Hence by the theorem,

$$[\![Pdec]\!] \simeq (\nu\widetilde{p})(P \mid I^{\flat}) \qquad \text{and} \qquad [\![Pdec']\!] \simeq (\nu\widetilde{p})(P \mid I'^{\flat}).$$

Thus to prove $[\![Pdec]\!] \simeq [\![Pdec']\!]$ it suffices to show that the agents $I^{\flat}$ and $I'^{\flat}$ are indistinguishable in an arbitrary program context. This would be most directly achieved if we could show that $I^{\flat} \simeq I'^{\flat}$: the result would follow as $\simeq$ is preserved by the operators. In fact this does hold if the agents are *strongly convergent*, i.e. such that each of their derivatives is convergent, but not in general.

Theorem 15. If $I^\flat$ and $I'^\flat$ are strongly convergent then $I^\flat \simeq I'^\flat$.

Before sketching the proof, to understand why the result does not hold unconditionally suppose the first transformation is applied to S; return E where S is the only source of divergence (consider for instance a minor variation of the class A in the first example of section 3). Then $I^\flat \uparrow$ but $I'^\flat \downarrow$ as the result will be returned via r before the diverging computation begins. Note, however, that $I'^\flat \uparrow r$. Dually, if the second transformation is applied in a body of the form return $E!m(\widetilde{E})$; S where S is the only source of divergence, then this time $I^\flat \downarrow$ (but $I^\flat \uparrow r$) while $I'^\flat \uparrow$ as the replacement of return by commit unguards the divergence. Although $I^\flat \not\simeq I'^\flat$ in such cases, the slight differences in divergent behaviour are lost in a program context which, being ready, can contribute R^+-actions to turn any r-divergence of $I^\flat$ into divergence of $(\nu\widetilde{p})(P \mid I^\flat)$, and similarly for $I'^\flat$. Given that this small difficulty can be overcome it remains to outline how the theorem is proved.

Suppose *Pdec'* results from *Pdec* by an application of the second transformation in the body of method m of class A, return $E!m'(\widetilde{E})$ being changed to commit $E!m'(\widetilde{E})$. Suppose Q is a derivative of $I^\flat$ in which the name r is to be used for the return of the result of a method invocation originating outside the society. Then $I'^\flat$ has a derivative Q' which differs from Q only in that in Q' some object-agents of class A are in an active state or a quiescent state while the corresponding object-agents in Q are blocked awaiting the return of an invocation. To see how this may come about suppose that in reaching Q an object α has invoked m in an object β and that β has invoked m' (via the command in question) in an object γ and is waiting for the result to be returned to it so it can return it to α. In the computation from $I'^\flat$, the agent corresponding to β would have committed to γ the responsibility for returning a result to α, thus freeing itself to continue with other activity. $I'^\flat$ can thus mirror the computation of $I^\flat$ very closely, except that the return of a result from γ to α is made via β in $I^\flat$ but directly in $I'^\flat$. By a rigorous analysis a close correspondence between the (possibly many and possibly long) chains of return links arising in the two derivations can be shown. Since $I^\flat \downarrow r$, by the previous theorem $Q \stackrel{\overline{r}(v)}{\Longrightarrow} Q^q$ where each object-agent in Q^q is quiescent. Hence $Q' \stackrel{\overline{r}(v)}{\Longrightarrow} Q'^q$ for the same v and for a similar Q'^q. Of course, $I'^\flat$ is capable of activity which can not be mirrored directly by $I^\flat$: for instance β above, having committed its responsibility to γ, may make another method invocation or may resume its quiescent state and have one of its methods invoked. But because $I'^\flat$ is confluent and it *can* return the result v via r, it can not also return a different result. These observations, together with the fact that if P is confluent and convergent and $P \Longrightarrow P'$, $P' \simeq P$, can be used to show that there is a db-bisimulation relating $I^\flat$ and $I'^\flat$. The proof for the first transformation uses similar ideas but is more complicated.

Having established that a single transformation may be safely applied the main result follows:

Theorem 16. Let *Pdec* be a program declaration in which the classes $G, \widetilde{A}$ form a society. Let *Pdec'* be obtained from it by applying the transformations an arbitrary number of times to method bodies of $G, \widetilde{A}$. Then $[\![Pdec]\!] \simeq [\![Pdec']\!]$.

6 Related work

The problem of the correctness of transformations of the kinds considered here was posed by C B Jones and has been studied by him in a number of papers [5, 6, 7, 8] within a broad programme concerned with formal development methods for concurrent programs. The following definition and rules are quoted from [8] (note that there are some significant differences in notation between that paper and the present one).

> A unique reference is defined to be one which is never 'copied' nor which has general (unshared) references passed over it – neither in nor out (since one can't pass unique references, this restricts arguments to be references to 'immutable' objects).
>
> S; **return** e is equivalent to **return** e; S providing
> – S contains no **return** or **delegate** statements and always terminates;
> – e is a simple expression (i.e. no method calls: compare [the transformation below]) and is not affected by S; and
> – every method invoked by S belongs to objects reached by unique references.
>
> **return** $l.m(x)$ is equivalent to **delegate** $l.m(x)$ providing
> – $l.m(x)$ terminates; and
> – l is a unique reference.

In [3] Jones and Hodges give an operational semantics for $\pi o\beta\lambda$ and use it to argue for the correctness of these transformations.

As stated earlier, our interest here is not in formal development of concurrent programs *per se*, but rather in the elaboration of concepts and techniques useful in proving the correctness of such transformations (and for other purposes). The rules studied in the present paper differ from those quoted above in that they enunciate syntactic conditions under which the transformations may be applied. In [8, 3] termination of method invocations is a hypothesis of the rules. Here we use a notion of equivalence sensitive to divergence and thereby treat explicitly diverging computations and run-time errors. Further, we exclude the possibility of deadlock by analysing in detail how 'cycles' can arise and imposing a condition to prevent this. The conditions enunciated here differ from those of [8, 3] also in that, in contrast to unique references as defined above, objects of a society may pass references to non-society objects and also references to society objects. A destructive-read expression similar to that used here was considered, from a different stance, in the somewhat difficult paper [4] in which the word 'island' was used with a connotation somewhat similar to that of 'society' here. In [9] a type system for a fragment of π-calculus in which a discipline in the use of names similar to that observed by agents representing society objects is presented.

Acknowledgment We are indebted to C B Jones whose related research provided an important stimulus to the present work and to Xinxin Liu for earlier joint work on partial confluence.

References

1. P. America. Issues in the design of a parallel object-oriented language. *Formal Aspects of Computing*, 1:366–411, 1989.
2. J. F. Groote and M. Sellink. Confluence for process verification. In *Proceedings of CONCUR'95*, pages 204–218. Springer, 1995.
3. S. Hodges and C. B. Jones. Fixing the semantics of some concurrent object-oriented concepts: SOS and proofs. In *Proceedings of the Schloß Dagstuhl workshop on 'Object-orientation with Parallelism and Persistence'*, to appear.
4. J. Hogg. Islands: aliasing protection in object-oriented languages. In *Proceedings of OOPSLA'91*, pages 271–285. ACM Press, 1991.
5. C. B. Jones. Constraining interference in an object-based design method. In *Proceedings of TAPSOFT'93*, pages 136–150. Springer, 1993.
6. C. B. Jones. A pi-calculus semantics for an object-based design notation. In *Proceedings of CONCUR'93*, pages 158–172. Springer, 1993.
7. C. B. Jones. Process algebra arguments about an object-based design method. In *Essays in Honour of C. A. R. Hoare*. Prentice-Hall, 1994.
8. C. B. Jones. Accommodating interference in the formal design of concurrent object-based programs. *Formal Methods in System Design*, to appear.
9. N. Kobayashi, B. Pierce, and D. Turner. Linearity and the pi-calculus. *Principles of Programming Languages*, 1996.
10. X. Liu and D. Walker. Confluence of processes and systems of objects. In *Proceedings of TAPSOFT'95*, pages 217–231. Springer, 1995.
11. X. Liu and D. Walker. Partial confluence of processes and systems of objects. *submitted for publication*, 1995.
12. R. Milner. *Communication and Concurrency*. Prentice-Hall, 1989.
13. A. Philippou and D.Walker. Technical report, University of Warwick, forthcoming.
14. A. Philippou and D. Walker. On sharing and determinacy in concurrent systems. In *Proceedings of CONCUR'95*, pages 456–470. Springer, 1995.
15. B. Pierce and D. Turner. Concurrent objects in a process calculus. In *Theory and Practice of Parallel Programming, Sendai, Japan*, pages 187–215. Springer, 1994.
16. B. Thomsen. Plain CHOCS: a second generation calculus for higher order processes. *Acta Informatica*, 30(1):1–59, 1993.
17. C. Tofts. *Proof methods and pragmatics for parallel programming*. PhD thesis, University of Edinburgh, 1990.
18. D. Walker. π-calculus semantics for object-oriented programming languages. In *Proceedings of TACS'91*, pages 532–547. Springer, 1991.
19. D. Walker. Algebraic proofs of properties of objects. In *Proceedings of ESOP'94*, pages 501–516. Springer, 1994.
20. D. Walker. Objects in the π-calculus. *Information and Computation*, 116:253–271, 1995.
21. D. Walker. Process calculus and parallel object-oriented programming lanaguages. In P. Tvrdik T. Casavant and F. Plasil, editors, *Parallel Computers: Theory and Practice*, pages 369–390. Computer Society Press, 1995.

On Bisimulations for the Asynchronous π-Calculus *

Roberto M. Amadio
CNRS, Sophia-Antipolis

Ilaria Castellani
INRIA, Sophia-Antipolis

Davide Sangiorgi
INRIA, Sophia-Antipolis

Abstract

The *asynchronous π-calculus* is a variant of the π-calculus where message emission is non-blocking. Honda and Tokoro have studied a semantics for this calculus based on bisimulation. Their bisimulation relies on a modified transition system where, at any moment, a process can perform any input action.

In this paper we propose a new notion of bisimulation for the asynchronous π-calculus, defined on top of the standard labelled transition system. We give several characterizations of this equivalence including one in terms of Honda and Tokoro's bisimulation, and one in terms of *barbed equivalence*. We show that this bisimulation is preserved by name substitutions, hence by input prefix. Finally, we give a complete axiomatization of the (strong) bisimulation for finite terms.

1 Introduction

Process interaction in a distributed system without global clock is usually modelled by message passing. In this context, one often distinguishes between *synchronous* and *asynchronous* message passing. In the former, the send and receive events can be regarded as happening at the same time. In the latter, one can imagine that messages are sent and travel in the ether till they reach their destination, while the sending process accomplishes other tasks.

In the *distributed algorithms* community the distinction synchronous vs. asynchronous communication is not considered a very important issue. For instance [Tel95], pp 44 says:

> Messages in distributed systems can be passed either synchronously or asynchronously. (...) For many purposes synchronous message passing can be regarded as a special case of asynchronous message passing (...)

Indeed one can simulate a synchronous communication with two asynchronous ones. On the other hand in the *language design* community the distinction seems

*The authors were partially supported by France Télécom, CTI-CNET 95-1B-182 Modélisation de Systèmes Mobiles.

to be quite relevant. Basically, asynchronous communication is easier to implement than the synchronous one as it is closer to the communication primitives offered by available distributed systems. In particular, asynchronous communication has become a popular choice in the design of languages for the programming of distributed applications. An early proposal is Agha's actors model [Agh86], while more recent contributions based on the theory of the π-calculus include Pict [PT96] and the join calculus [FG96].

A second community where the distinction synchronous vs. asynchronous is gaining momentum is that concerned with the *semantics of programs*. In this community one is often interested in comparing calculi. Certain translations turn out to be fully abstract in an asynchronous setting, where the observer has less power. Examples include the encoding of input-guarded choice [NP96] into the asynchronous π-calculus and the encoding of the asynchronous π-calculus into the join calculus [FG96].

A way to restrict a process calculus to asynchronous communications is to remove output prefixing. In other terms, an asynchronous output $\overline{a}$ followed by a process P is the same as the parallel composition $\overline{a} \mid P$. If the calculus has a non-deterministic sum, then we also disallow output guards. We can justify this decision as follows: (i) An output on a choice point forces synchronizations at the implementation level, this seems to contradict the very essence of asynchronous communication (we are not aware of any programming language which allows this). (ii) At the semantic level a calculus with output guards is more discriminating, in particular certain desirable equations such as (2) in section 4 fail to hold.

The resulting calculus is still quite expressive when working in a framework where channel names are transmissible values, e.g. the π-calculus [MPW92]. Indeed it is quite easy to simulate the synchronous π-calculus in the asynchronous one: the sending process waits for an acknowledgment from the receiving process on a private channel. Basic results on the expressiveness of the asynchronous π-calculus can be found in the works by Honda and Tokoro, and Boudol [HT91, Bou91], where the asynchronous π-calculus was first proposed.

When communications are asynchronous, the sender of an output message does not know when the message is actually consumed. In other words, an asynchronous observer, as opposed to a synchronous one, cannot directly detect the input actions of the observed process. Consequently, the asynchronous calculus requires the development of an appropriate semantic framework.

In this paper we develop a theory of bisimulation for the asynchronous π-calculus both in the strong and in the weak case. Our starting point is an original notion of asynchronous bisimulation over the standard labelled transition system. As a first contribution, we provide several characterizations of this bisimulation, and in particular we study under which conditions it coincides with *barbed equivalence*. We also show that our asynchronous bisimulation coincides with that proposed by Honda and Tokoro, which is based on a modified transition system for the π-calculus, on the sublanguage that they consider. As a second result, we observe that asynchronous bisimulation is preserved by the input prefix of the π-calculus (a similar property is proved in [HT92]) and coincides with *ground* bisimulation (a bisimulation where only *one* fresh name is considered in the input clause). Finally, we give a complete axiomatization of asynchronous bisimulation in the strong case for finite terms.

Insensitivity to name instantiation (and hence the possibility of using ground forms of bisimulation) appears to depend on having no output prefixing. It does not depend on having asynchronous, rather than synchronous, bisimulation (see [BS96] for a study of insensitivity to name instantiation for various forms of synchronous bisimulations).

Forms of asynchronous π-calculus have also been studied in [HKH95], but the bisimilarity used is the standard (synchronous) one. Part of our theory, in particular axioms and normal forms, is related to that in [HKH95]. Our formulation of asynchronous bisimulation has been recently used by Nestmann and Pierce [NP96] to prove the full abstraction of the above-mentioned encoding of input-guarded choice.

The paper is organized as follows. In section 2 we provide the basic definitions. In section 3 we present various characterizations and properties of *strong* asynchronous bisimulation. In section 4 we study an equational theory which characterizes strong asynchronous bisimulation for finite terms. In section 5 we adapt some of the results in section 3 to the *weak* case. In this short version of the paper, most of the proofs are omitted; they can be found in [ACS96].

2 Asynchronous π-calculus

The *asynchronous* π-calculus is defined as a subset of the π-calculus where: (i) There is no output prefixing, and (ii) outputs cannot be on a choice point (formally sums are allowed only on input prefixes and τ's). Our language differs from the one proposed in [HT91, Bou91] for the presence of a form of choice. This will be important in the axiomatisation (section 4).

We assume a countable collection Ch of channel names, say $a, b, \ldots$ We distinguish between general processes $P, Q, \ldots$ and guards $G, H, \ldots$ as specified in the following grammars:

$$P ::= \overline{a}b \mid P \mid P \mid \nu a\, P \mid !G \mid G \qquad G ::= 0 \mid a(b).P \mid \tau.P \mid G + G$$

In figure 1 we define a labelled transition system with early instantiation (rule *(in)*). The actions α are specified as follows: $\alpha ::= \tau \mid \overline{a}b \mid \overline{a}(b) \mid ab$. Conventionally we set $n(\alpha) = fn(\alpha) \cup bn(\alpha)$ where:

$$fn(\tau) = \emptyset \quad fn(\overline{a}(b)) = \{a\} \quad fn(\overline{a}b) = fn(ab) = \{a, b\}$$
$$bn(\tau) = \emptyset \quad bn(\overline{a}(b)) = \{b\} \quad bn(\overline{a}b) = bn(ab) = \emptyset$$

The rules *(sync)*, *(sync$_{ex}$)*, *(comp)*, and *(sum)* have a symmetric version which is omitted. Indeed, parallel composition and sum should be understood as commutative operators. We denote with $\equiv$ syntactic identity modulo α-renaming and with $fn(P)$ the names free in P.

The notion of *weak* transition is defined as usual:

$$P \stackrel{\tau}{\Rightarrow} P' \quad \text{iff} \quad P(\stackrel{\tau}{\rightarrow})^* P'$$
$$P \stackrel{\alpha}{\Rightarrow} P' \quad \text{iff} \quad P \stackrel{\tau}{\Rightarrow} \cdot \stackrel{\alpha}{\rightarrow} \cdot \stackrel{\tau}{\Rightarrow} P' \quad (\text{for } \alpha \neq \tau)$$

We write $\rightarrow$ and $\Rightarrow$ as abbreviations for $\stackrel{\tau}{\rightarrow}$ and $\stackrel{\tau}{\Rightarrow}$, respectively. The relations $\rightarrow$ and $\Rightarrow$ are often called *reduction* relations.

(*cong*)	$\dfrac{P \equiv P' \quad P' \xrightarrow{\alpha} Q' \quad Q' \equiv Q}{P \xrightarrow{\alpha} Q}$	(τ)	$\dfrac{\cdot}{\tau.P \xrightarrow{\tau} P}$
(*in*)	$\dfrac{\cdot}{a(b).P \xrightarrow{ac} [c/b]P}$	(*out*)	$\dfrac{\cdot}{\overline{a}b \xrightarrow{\overline{a}b} 0}$
(*out$_{ex}$*)	$\dfrac{P \xrightarrow{\overline{a}b} P' \quad a \neq b}{\nu b\, P \xrightarrow{\overline{a}(b)} P'}$	(ν)	$\dfrac{P \xrightarrow{\alpha} P' \quad a \notin n(\alpha)}{\nu a\, P \xrightarrow{\alpha} \nu a\, P'}$
(*sync*)	$\dfrac{P \xrightarrow{\overline{a}b} P' \quad Q \xrightarrow{ab} Q'}{P \mid Q \xrightarrow{\tau} P' \mid Q'}$	(*sync$_{ex}$*)	$\dfrac{P \xrightarrow{\overline{a}(b)} P' \quad Q \xrightarrow{ab} Q' \quad b \notin fn(Q)}{P \mid Q \xrightarrow{\tau} \nu b(P' \mid Q')}$
(*comp*)	$\dfrac{P \xrightarrow{\alpha} P' \quad bn(\alpha) \cap fn(Q) = \emptyset}{P \mid Q \xrightarrow{\alpha} P' \mid Q}$	(*sum*)	$\dfrac{G \xrightarrow{\alpha} P}{G + G' \xrightarrow{\alpha} P}$
(*rep*)	$\dfrac{G \xrightarrow{\alpha} P}{!G \xrightarrow{\alpha} P \mid !G}$		

Figure 1: Labelled transition system with early instantiation

The first important technical point arises in the definition of *commitment*. In the asynchronous case it seems natural to restrict the observation to the *output* commitments. The intuition is that an observer has no direct way of knowing if the message he has sent has been received. All the sender can do is to introduce an output particle in the system, unless there is an explicitly programmed acknowledgment mechanism there is no way for him to know when the particle is actually consumed.

Definition 1 (commitment) *The strong commitment of a process on a channel expresses the fact that the process is ready to send a message on that channel. Formally, $P \downarrow \overline{a}$ if P can make an output action whose subject is a, that is if there exist P', b such that $P \xrightarrow{\overline{a}b} P'$ or $P \xrightarrow{\overline{a}(b)} P'$. The weak commitment is then defined as:*

$$P \Downarrow \overline{a} \text{ if } P \Rightarrow P' \text{ and } P' \downarrow \overline{a}$$

From the definition of reduction and commitment the notion of barbed bisimulation is derived in a canonical way.

Definition 2 (barbed bisimulation) *A symmetric relation S on π-terms is a (strong) barbed bisimulation if whenever PSQ the following holds:*

1. *If $P \downarrow \overline{a}$ then $Q \downarrow \overline{a}$.*
2. *If $P \rightarrow P'$ then $Q \rightarrow Q'$ and $P'SQ'$.*

Let $\stackrel{\bullet}{\sim}$ be the largest barbed bisimulation. The notion of weak barbed simulation is obtained by replacing everywhere the commitment $\downarrow$ with $\Downarrow$ and the transition $\rightarrow$ with $\Rightarrow$. We denote with $\stackrel{\bullet}{\approx}$ the largest weak barbed bisimulation.

A more refined notion of bisimulation can be obtained if we also allow observation of output transitions.

Definition 3 ($o\tau$-bisimulation) *A symmetric relation S on π-terms is a (strong) $o\tau$-bisimulation if PSQ, $P \xrightarrow{\alpha} P'$, α is not an input action, and $bn(\alpha) \cap fn(Q) = \emptyset$ implies $Q \xrightarrow{\alpha} Q'$ and $P'SQ'$. Let $\sim_{o\tau}$ be the largest $o\tau$-bisimulation. Again, the notion of weak $o\tau$-bisimulation is obtained by replacing strong transitions with weak transitions. We denote with $\approx_{o\tau}$ the largest weak $o\tau$-bisimulation.*

Both barbed bisimulation and $o\tau$-bisimulation are too rough to distinguish processes such as $a(b).\overline{c}b$ and $a(b).\overline{d}b$. Clearly these processes exhibit different behaviours when they are put in parallel with a process $\overline{a}b$. It is then natural to refine barbed bisimulation to an equivalence which is preserved by parallel composition. Following [MS92], we call it barbed equivalence.

Definition 4 (barbed equivalence) *The relations of strong and weak barbed equivalence are defined as follows:*

$$P \sim_b Q \quad \text{if } \forall R (P \mid R \overset{\bullet}{\sim} Q \mid R)$$
$$P \approx_b Q \quad \text{if } \forall R (P \mid R \overset{\bullet}{\approx} Q \mid R)$$

Another approach consists in looking for a variant of the input clause. This leads to the following notion of asynchronous bisimulation. We will see later (definition 7) that several other equivalent definitions are possible.

Definition 5 (asynchronous bisimulation) *A relation S is an asynchronous bisimulation if it is an $o\tau$-bisimulation and whenever PSQ and $P \xrightarrow{ab} P'$ the following holds:*

- *either $Q \xrightarrow{ab} Q'$ and $P'SQ'$*
- *or $Q \xrightarrow{\tau} Q'$ and $P'S(Q' \mid \overline{a}b)$.*

Let $\sim_a$ be the largest asynchronous bisimulation. The definition of weak asynchronous bisimulation is obtained by replacing the strong labelled transitions with the weak labelled transitions everywhere. We denote with $\approx_a$ the largest weak asynchronous bisimulation.

Since asynchronous bisimulation is the basic bisimulation considered in this paper, we will call it simply bisimulation in what follows.

Remark 1 (comparison with [HT91]) *Definition 5 relies on a standard labelled transition system. Honda and Tokoro [HT91] take a different approach. They modify the labelled transition system by replacing the input rule with the following rule for the $\mathbf{0}$ process (which to some extent allows one to observe the behaviour of a process after an input):*

$$\frac{\cdot}{\mathbf{0} \xrightarrow{ab} \overline{a}b} \qquad (1)$$

Since rules in [HT91] are applied modulo a structural equivalence $\equiv_{HT}$, and $P \equiv_{HT} P \mid 0$, this implies that any process P can perform any input ab.

We think that rule 1 is not so appealing because: (i) it introduces an infinite branching, (ii) it is not obviously compatible with a calculus including choice or other dynamic operators (in particular 0 fails to be a unit for the choice operator, at least with the usual rule for choice), and (iii) it does not reflect the computational content of processes.

Honda and Tokoro's bisimulation coincides with ours; the proof is easy, using the characterisation of our asynchronous bisimulation as 1-bisimulation (definition 7).

The following properties are specific to the asynchronous π-calculus:

Lemma 1

1. *If* $P \xrightarrow{\overline{a}b} P'$ *then* $P \sim_a \overline{a}b \mid P'$.
2. *If* $P \xrightarrow{\overline{a}(b)} P'$ *then* $P \sim_a \nu b\,(\overline{a}b \mid P')$.
3. *If* $P \xrightarrow{\overline{a}b} \cdot \xrightarrow{\alpha} P'$ *then* $P \xrightarrow{\alpha} \cdot \xrightarrow{\overline{a}b} P'$.
4. *If* $P \xrightarrow{\overline{a}(b)} \cdot \xrightarrow{\alpha} P'$ *and* $b \notin n(\alpha)$ *then* $P \xrightarrow{\alpha} \cdot \xrightarrow{\overline{a}(b)} P'$.

3 Asynchronous bisimulation, strong case

In this section we study some properties of strong asynchronous bisimulation (definition 5). In section 5 we will discuss how these results can be lifted to the weak case. Since most proofs for the weak case can be trivially adapted to the strong case we delay all proofs to that section. The contributions of the present section can be summarized as follows:

1. We show that bisimulation is preserved by name substitution.
2. We provide several equivalent definitions of bisimulation.
3. We prove that bisimulation and barbed equivalence coincide.

The definition of bisimulation has been given in an *early* style, and thus contemplates the substitution of the bound name of an input with all possible names. In the *ground*[1] style [San95], on the other hand, *no* name instantiation is needed in the input clause.

Definition 6 (ground bisimulation) *A relation S is a ground bisimulation if it is an $o\tau$-bisimulation and whenever PSQ, $P \xrightarrow{ab} P'$ and $b \notin fn(P \mid Q)$ the following holds:*

[1] We use the adjective ground to emphasize the fact that in this bisimulation the formal parameter of an input prefix is treated as a fresh constant. Note that the terminology ground equivalence was used in [MPW92], pp 28, with quite a different meaning.

- *either* $Q \overset{ab}{\rightarrow} Q'$ *and* $P'SQ'$
- *or* $Q \overset{\tau}{\rightarrow} Q'$ *and* $P'S(Q' \mid \overline{a}b)$.

We denote with $\sim_g$ *the largest ground bisimulation. Weak ground bisimulation is obtained by replacing transitions with weak transitions. We denote with* $\approx_g$ *the largest weak ground bisimulation.*

Theorem 1 *Strong ground bisimulation is preserved by name substitutions.*

An important corollary of theorem 1 is that bisimulation and ground bisimulation coincide.

Corollary 1 *Strong bisimulation and strong ground bisimulation coincide:* $\sim_a = \sim_g$.

A second corollary is that bisimulation is preserved by input prefix (a property which fails in the synchronous calculus). We can then easily conclude as follows.

Corollary 2 *Strong bisimulation is a congruence.*

Besides early and ground, other variants of bisimulation which have been studied in the literature are *late* and *open*. The difference among all these variants is in the requirements on closure under name instantiations. Late bisimulation requires that matching input transitions should be adequate for all instantiations of the bound name. In open [San93] bisimulation the only constraints on equalities among names are those imposed by name extrusion and are recorded as a distinction in the bisimulation clauses. Moreover, in the synchronous π-calculus strong late and early bisimulations are not congruences because they are not preserved by input prefixes, hence the induced congruences, called late and early congruences, have been introduced. In the asynchronous π-calculus, bisimulation is preserved by name instantiations, and therefore all the above forms of bisimulation coincide. We omit the definitions of late and open (which are best defined on a late transition system) and we simply state the result.

Corollary 3 *Late and open variants of strong (asynchronous) bisimulation coincide with the early strong (asynchronous) bisimulation.*

We have thus demonstrated some interesting mathematical properties of our notion of bisimulation. Our next task will be to give an intuitive justification of this notion. First, we introduce three further definitions of bisimulation, which differ in the formulation of the input clause, and we show them all equivalent to definition 5. Roughly, 1-bisimulation requires preservation under parallel composition with an output, while 2,3-bisimulations propose variants of the diagram chasing in the input clause (cf. definition 5).

Definition 7 (variants of bisimulation) *An i-bisimulation* $(i = 1, 2, 3)$ *is an* $o\tau$*-bisimulation S such that:*

- (1-bisimulation) *PSQ implies* $(P \mid \overline{a}b)\, S\, (Q \mid \overline{a}b)$, *for all* $\overline{a}b$.

- (2-bisimulation) *PSQ and* $P \overset{ab}{\rightarrow} P'$ *implies*
  - *either* $Q \overset{ab}{\rightarrow} Q'$ *and* $P'SQ'$
  - *or* $Q \overset{\tau}{\rightarrow} Q'$ *and there is* P'' *s.t.* $P' \overset{\overline{a}b}{\rightarrow} P''$ *and* $P''SQ'$.
- (3-bisimulation) *PSQ and* $P \overset{ab}{\rightarrow} P'$ *implies*
  - *either* $Q \overset{ab}{\rightarrow} Q'$ *and* $P'SQ'$
  - *or there are* P'', P''' *s.t.* $P' \overset{\overline{a}b}{\rightarrow} P''$, $P \overset{\tau}{\rightarrow} P'''$ *and* $P''SP'''$.

We denote with $\sim_i$ *the largest i-bisimulation, for* $i = 1, 2, 3$.

Theorem 2 (characterization) *All definitions of bisimulation are equivalent. That is:* $\sim_a = \sim_1 = \sim_2 = \sim_3$.

Our last result connects bisimulation with barbed equivalence. It should be noted that our definition of barbed equivalence follows [MS92]. Honda and Yoshida [HY95] rely on a stronger notion of barbed equivalence, where the preservation under parallel composition with outputs is required at each step.

Theorem 3 *Let P, Q be processes. Then* $P \sim_b Q$ *iff* $P \sim_a Q$.

4 Equational theory, strong case

We present now an equational theory which characterizes strong asynchronous bisimulation on finite terms. In the rest of this section we shall concentrate on the restricted language without replication. In this case the following equation summarizes the differences between the synchronous and the asynchronous bisimulations:

$$a(b).(\overline{a}b \mid P) + \tau.P = \tau.P \qquad b \notin fn(P) \tag{2}$$

The reader should pause to formally verify this equation according to definition 5. A particular instance of equation 2 is $a(b).\overline{a}b + \tau = \tau$ which intuitively says that the process that emits what it has just received can be "absorbed" in an internal action.

Our axiom system is reported in figure 2. The proof of completeness relies on a non-standard notion of normal form. Let us first observe that, due to the absence of output prefix in the syntax, the parallel operator cannot be completely eliminated via an expansion theorem. Unrestricted outputs will continue to be present as parallel components in normal forms, and their possible communications with the rest of the process will remain potential (that is, they will not give rise to an explicit τ-action in the normal form). A related notion of normal form is introduced in [HKH95]. In this work the equational theory captures strong synchronous, rather than *asynchronous*, bisimulation; the axiom system is essentially the same as that in figure 2 but without equation 2.

We introduce some notation. Let $\prod_{i \in I} \overline{a_i} b_i$ denote a product of outputs, defined up to the laws (P1)–(P3) in figure 2 (monoid laws for $\mid$). We shall use $\vec{c}$ to denote a sequence of names $c_1, \ldots, c_m$. If $\vec{c} = c_1, \ldots, c_m$, we let $\nu\vec{c}P$ stand for $\nu c_1 \ldots \nu c_m P$. If $\vec{c} = \varepsilon$ (the empty sequence), we let by convention $\nu\varepsilon P \equiv P$. With a slight abuse of notation, we will sometimes use $\vec{c}$ also to represent the set $\{c_1, \ldots, c_m\}$. We define now the set $Fire(\nu\vec{c}\prod_{i\in I}\overline{a_i}b_i)$ of indices of firable outputs of $\prod_{i\in I}\overline{a_i}b_i$ when all names in $\vec{c}$ are restricted.

Definition 8 *Let* $P \equiv \nu\vec{c}\prod_{i\in I}\overline{a_i}b_i$. *Then* $Fire(P) = \bigcup_n Fire_{n\in\omega}(P)$, *where* $Fire_n(P)$ *is the set of indices of outputs that can be fired after exactly n steps, given by:*

$$\begin{aligned} Fire_0(P) &= \{i \mid a_i \notin \vec{c}\} \\ Fire_{n+1}(P) &= \{i \mid \exists\, k \in Fire_n(P)\ b_k = a_i\} \setminus \bigcup_{m\le n} Fire_m(P) \end{aligned}$$

Example 1 *Let* $P = \nu b\,\nu c\,\Pi_{i\in I}\overline{a_i}b_i$ *with* $I = \{1,2,3,4\}$ *and* $\overline{a_1}b_1 = \overline{a}b$, $\overline{a_2}b_2 = \overline{a}c$, $\overline{a_3}b_3 = \overline{b}c$, *and* $\overline{a_4}b_4 = \overline{c}b$. *Then* $Fire_0(P) = \{1,2\}$, $Fire_1(P) = \{3,4\}$, *and* $Fire_n(P) = \emptyset$ *for* $n \ge 2$. *Hence* $Fire(P) = I$. *Note that by construction* $Fire_n(P) \cap Fire_m(P) = \emptyset$ *if* $n \ne m$.

Let $=_{SP}$ be the congruence induced by the laws (S1)–(S4), (P1)–(P3) in figure 2 (commutative monoid laws and idempotence for $+$, and commutative monoid laws for $|$).

Definition 9 *A* normal form *is a term defined up to (S1)–(S3) and (P1)–(P3) of the form:*

$$\nu\vec{c}\left(\prod_{i\in I}\overline{a_i}b_i \mid (\sum_{j\in J}\tau.P_j + \sum_{k\in K}a_k(b).P_k)\right)$$

where the sets I, J, K *are pairwise disjoint, each* P_j, P_k *is a normal form, and supposing* $\vec{c} = c_1, \ldots, c_m$, *the following conditions are satisfied:*

1. *(All restricted names are emitted)* $\forall \ell \in \{1, \ldots, m\}\ \exists i \in I\ \ b_i = c_\ell$
2. *(All outputs are firable)* $Fire(\nu\vec{c}\prod_{i\in I}\overline{a_i}b_i) = I$
3. *(Non-redundancy)* $\forall k \forall j\ \ P_k \ne_{SP} (\overline{a_k}b \mid P_j)$.

By convention $\prod_{i\in I}\overline{a_i}b_i \equiv \mathbf{0}$ *if* $I = \emptyset$ *(and similarly for the sums* $\sum_{j\in J}\tau.P_j$ *and* $\sum_{k\in K}a_k(b).P_k$*). Thus* $\mathbf{0}$ *is a normal form, when* $\vec{c} = \varepsilon$ *and* $I = J = K = \emptyset$. *A* guarded normal form *is a normal form such that* $\vec{c} = \varepsilon$ *and* $I = \emptyset$.

We will show that each term P can be reduced to a normal form using axioms $\mathcal{A}$ in figure 2. Most axioms are standard: (EXP) is an instance of the expansion theorem applied to guards, (OABS) is a form of expansion in which the output particles which are not firable are forced to synchronize or to be postponed. Let $=_{\mathcal{A}}$ denote the congruence induced by these axioms. The proof of normalisation uses nested induction on the depth and on the structure of P.

Definition 10 *The* depth *of a process* P, $d(P)$, *is defined inductively by:*

$$\begin{aligned} d(0) &= 0; \quad d(\overline{a}b) = 1; \\ d(a(b).P) &= d(\tau.P) = 1 + d(P); \\ d(P \mid Q) &= d(P) + d(Q); \\ d(\nu a\, P) &= d(P); \\ d(G + F) &= max\{\, d(G), d(F)\, \}. \end{aligned}$$

Remark 2 *$d(P)$ is an upper bound on the length of the transition sequences of P. It is easy to see that if P' is a subterm of P then $d(P') \leq d(P)$.*

Lemma 2 (normalisation lemma) *For any process P there exists a normal form:*

$$\lceil P \rceil \equiv \nu \vec{c} \left(\prod_{i \in I} \overline{a_i} b_i \mid (\sum_{j \in J} \tau.P_j + \sum_{k \in K} a_k(b).P_k) \right)$$

such that $P =_{\mathcal{A}} \lceil P \rceil$ and $d(\lceil P \rceil) \leq d(P)$. In particular, every guarded sum G can be reduced to a guarded normal form $\lceil G \rceil \equiv \sum_{j \in J} \tau.\, P_j + \sum_{k \in K} a_k(b).\, P_k$.

In the proof of our completeness result, we shall use also the following:

Lemma 3 (separation) *Let P and Q be two normal forms:*

$$P \equiv \nu \vec{u} (\prod_{i \in I} \overline{a_i} b_i \mid P_\Sigma) \quad \text{and} \quad Q \equiv \nu \vec{v} (\prod_{h \in H} \overline{c_h} d_h \mid Q_\Sigma)$$

where $P_\Sigma \equiv (\sum_{j \in J} \tau.\, P_j + \sum_{k \in K} a_k(b).\, P_k)$ and $Q_\Sigma \equiv (\sum_{\ell \in L} \tau.\, Q_\ell + \sum_{m \in M} c_m(d).\, Q_m)$. If $P \sim_a Q$ then there exists an injective substitution σ that renames the set $\vec{v}$ into $\vec{u}$ and acts as the identity otherwise, such that:

$$\prod_{i \in I} \overline{a_i} b_i \equiv \sigma \prod_{h \in H} \overline{c_h} d_h \quad \text{and} \quad P_\Sigma \sim_a \sigma\, Q_\Sigma$$

Theorem 4 *On the finite terms, the equivalence $\sim_a$ is the congruence generated by the axioms $\mathcal{A}$.*

5 Asynchronous bisimulation, weak case

In an asynchronous world a process can make an input and then emit it again on the same channel without changing the overall behaviour of the system. Some interesting equations that hold in the weak semantics and that further motivate its study are the following:

$$\begin{aligned} !(a(b).\overline{a}b) &= 0 \\ a(b).(\overline{a}b \mid a(b).P) &= a(b).(P) \\ a(b).(\overline{a}b \mid G) + G &= a(b).G \end{aligned}$$

We present the weak versions of theorems 1 and 2. Our first task is to show that (weak) bisimulation is preserved by substitutions and coincides with ground bisimulation. To this end we first establish some elementary properties whose proof is not completely standard, in particular some work needs to be done to prove transitivity of $\approx_a$. In the following $P, Q, R \ldots$ denote processes.

(S1) $G+\mathbf{0} = G$

(S2) $G+G' = G'+G$

(S3) $G+(G'+G'') = (G+G')+G''$

(S4) $G+G = G$

(P1) $P \mid \mathbf{0} = P$

(P2) $P \mid Q = Q \mid P$

(P3) $P \mid (Q \mid R) = (P \mid Q) \mid R$

(R1) $\nu a\,(\sum_{i\in I} \alpha_i.\, P_i) = \sum\{\alpha_i.\nu a\, P_i \mid i \in I,\ a \notin n(\alpha_i)\}$

(R2) $\nu a\,(P \mid Q) = P \mid \nu a\, Q \quad$ if $a \notin fn(P)$

(R3) $\nu a\, \nu b\, P = \nu b\, \nu a\, P$

(EXP) (*Expansion Theorem*) Let $J \cap K = \emptyset = L \cap M$, $b \notin fn(Q)$, $d \notin fn(P)$.

$$P = (\sum_{j\in J} \tau.\, P_j + \sum_{k\in K} a_k(b).\, P_k) \quad \text{and} \quad Q = (\sum_{\ell\in L} \tau.\, Q_\ell + \sum_{m\in M} c_m(d).\, Q_m). \text{ Then:}$$

$$P \mid Q = \sum_{j\in J} \tau.\, (P_j \mid Q) + \sum_{k\in K} a_k(b).\, (P_k \mid Q) + \sum_{\ell\in L} \tau.\, (P \mid Q_\ell) + \sum_{m\in M} c_m(d).\, (P \mid Q_m)$$

(OABS) (*Output Absorption*) Let I, J, K be disjoint, $F = Fire\,(\nu\vec{u} \prod_{i\in I} \overline{a_i} b_i)$, $\overline{F} = I \backslash F$, $\vec{v} = \{u_l \mid \exists i \in F\, (a_i = u_l \text{ or } b_i = u_l)\}$ and $\vec{w} = \vec{u} \backslash \vec{v}$. If $b \notin \vec{w}$, then:

$$\nu\vec{u} \left(\prod_{i\in I} \overline{a_i} b_i \mid (\sum_{j\in J} \tau.\, P_j + \sum_{k\in K} a_k(b).\, P_k) \right) = \nu\vec{v} \left(\prod_{i\in F} \overline{a_i} b_i \mid S \right) \quad \text{where:}$$

$$S = \sum_{j\in J} \tau.\, \nu\vec{w}\, (\prod_{i\in\overline{F}} \overline{a_i} b_i \mid P_j) + \sum_{\substack{k\in K \\ a_k\notin\vec{w}}} a_k(b).\, \nu\vec{w}\, (\prod_{i\in\overline{F}} \overline{a_i} b_i \mid P_k) + \sum_{\substack{k\in K \\ a_k=a_h, h\in\overline{F}}} \tau.\, \nu\vec{w}\, (\prod_{\substack{i\in\overline{F} \\ i\neq h}} \overline{a_i} b_i \mid [b_h/b] P_k)$$

(IABS) (*Input Absorption*) $\quad a(b).\, (\overline{a}b \mid P) + \tau.\, P = \tau\,.\, P \qquad b \notin fn(P)$

Figure 2: Axioms $\mathcal{A}$

Lemma 4 *Bisimulation is preserved by parallel composition, restriction, replication and guarded sum, and it is included in ground bisimulation:*

1. *If $P \approx_a Q$ then $P \mid R \approx_a Q \mid R$, $\nu a\, P \approx_a \nu a\, Q$, $\alpha.P + R \approx_a \alpha.Q + R$, and $!P \approx_a !Q$.*

2. *If $P \approx_a Q$ then $P \approx_g Q$.*

Let σ denote a name substitution which is almost everywhere the identity. Whenever we apply a substitution to a process or an action we suppose that the bound names have been renamed so that no conflict can arise, in particular σ acts as an identity on bound names and if $\sigma(c) \neq c$ then $\sigma(c)$ is not a bound name either.

Lemma 5 *The transitions of P and σP can be related as follows:*

1. *If $P \xrightarrow{\alpha} P'$ then $\sigma P \xrightarrow{\sigma\alpha} \sigma P'$.*

2. *If $\sigma P \xrightarrow{\alpha'} P''$ and $\alpha' \neq \tau$ then for some P', $P \xrightarrow{\alpha} P'$, $\sigma P' \equiv P''$, and $\sigma\alpha = \alpha'$.*

3. *If $\sigma P \xrightarrow{\tau} P''$ then:*

   (a) *either there is P', $P \xrightarrow{\tau} P'$ and $\sigma P' \equiv P''$.*

   (b) *or $P \xrightarrow{\overline{a}b} \cdot \xrightarrow{dc} P'$ and $[b/c]\sigma P' \sim_a P''$ (c fresh).*

   (c) *or $P \xrightarrow{\overline{a}(b)} \cdot \xrightarrow{dc} P'$ and $\nu b\,([b/c]\sigma P') \sim_a P''$ (c fresh).*

We are now ready to prove the crucial lemma.

Lemma 6 *If $P \approx_g Q$ then $\sigma P \approx_a \sigma Q$.*

PROOF. One shows that the following relation is a bisimulation *up to $\sim_a$ and restriction:*

$$S = \{(\sigma P, \sigma Q) \mid P \approx_g Q, \sigma \text{ substitution }\} \tag{3}$$

Suppose $\sigma P \xrightarrow{\alpha} P'$. If α is a τ or output action then the "up to" means that there are $\vec{d}$, P'', Q'', Q' such that $\sigma Q \stackrel{\alpha}{\Rightarrow} Q'$ and

$$P' \sim_a \nu\vec{d}\,P'' \quad P''SQ'' \quad \nu\vec{d}\,Q'' \sim_a Q' \tag{4}$$

If $\alpha \equiv ab$ is an input action then the "up to" means that there are $\vec{d}$, P'', Q'', Q' such that:

- either $\sigma Q \stackrel{ab}{\Rightarrow} Q'$ and condition 4 holds.

- or $\sigma Q \stackrel{\tau}{\Rightarrow} Q'$ and

$$P' \sim_a \nu\vec{d}\,P'' \quad P''SQ'' \quad \nu\vec{d}\,Q'' \sim_a (Q' \mid \overline{a}b) \tag{5}$$

□

Theorem 5 *Weak ground bisimulation and weak bisimulation coincide and they are preserved by substitution.*

PROOF. From lemma 4(2) and lemma 6 applied with the identity substitution we know that $P \approx_g Q$ iff $P \approx_a Q$. From lemma 6 we can conclude that both bisimulations are preserved by substitution. □

It follows that weak bisimulation is preserved by all operators but sum (as usual) and that late and open variants of the weak bisimulation coincide with the early bisimulation studied here.

Corollary 4 *If $P \approx_a Q$ then $a(b).P \approx_a a(b).Q$.*

We can generalise the characterization of asynchronous bisimulation in terms of 1-bisimulation to the weak case.

Definition 11 *Let S be a weak $o\tau$-bisimulation. We say that S is a* weak 1-bisimulation *if PSQ implies $(P \mid \bar{a}b)\, S\, (Q \mid \bar{a}b)$. We denote with $\approx_1$ the largest weak 1-bisimulation.*

Theorem 6 (characterization) *The 1-bisimulation coincides with (asynchronous) bisimulation. That is: $\approx_a = \approx_1$.*

We now relate barbed equivalence and bisimulation. In the weak case our results rely crucially on the matching operator which we introduce next (in the strong case matching is not needed). We suppose that the grammar of the calculus is extended by the clause: $P ::= \cdots \mid [a = b]P$. The rule associated to matching in the labelled transition system is:

$$(match)\quad \frac{P \xrightarrow{\alpha} P'}{[c = c]P \xrightarrow{\alpha} P'}$$

We concentrate on the weak case first; the strong case is easier.

Proposition 1 *Let P, Q, R be processes. Then:*

1. *If σ is an injective substitution on $fn(P \mid Q)$ then $P \approx_a Q$ iff $\sigma P \approx_a \sigma Q$.*

2. *If $P \approx_a Q$ then $P \mid R \approx_a Q \mid R$, for any process R.*

3. *If $P \approx_a Q$ then $P \approx_b Q$.*

PROOF. The proof of (1) is standard. The proof of (2) is shaped upon the one for lemma 4 (we cannot use directly this lemma because we have extended the calculus with matching). The proof of (3) follows by:

$$\begin{aligned} P \approx_a Q &\Rightarrow \forall R (P \mid R \approx_a Q \mid R) \\ &\Rightarrow \forall R (P \mid R \approx_b Q \mid R) \\ &\Rightarrow P \overset{\bullet}{\approx} Q \end{aligned}$$

□

We recall that a lts $(Pr, Act, \mapsto)$ is *image finite* if for any process P and action α the set $\{P' \mid P \overset{\alpha}{\mapsto} P'\}$ is finite. We say that a process P is image finite if the lts generated by P is image finite. Image finite processes form an interesting class: w.r.t. strong reduction all processes are image finite (up to renaming of bound names), and w.r.t. weak reduction all finite control processes (cf. [Dam93]) are image finite modulo the equation $\nu a\, P = P$ for $a \notin fn(P)$.

Theorem 7 *If P and Q are image finite processes, and $P \approx_b Q$ then $P \approx_a Q$.*

PROOF. Let $\mathcal{F}$ be the monotone operator over $\mathcal{P}(Pr \times Pr)$ associated with the definition of asynchronous bisimulation. Suppose $\approx_a^0 = Pr \times Pr$, $\approx_a^{k+1} = \mathcal{F}(\approx_a^k)$, and $\approx_a^\omega = \bigcap_{k<\omega} \approx_a^k$. It is well-known that on an image finite lts the operator $\mathcal{F}$ preserves co-directed sets. In particular, $\mathcal{F}(\approx_a^\omega) = \approx_a^\omega$. It follows that on image finite processes $\approx_a = \approx_a^\omega$. We show that $P \approx_b Q$ implies $P \approx_a^\omega Q$. From the previous remark the theorem follows.

More precisely, we define a collection of tests $R(n, L)$ depending on $n \in \omega$ and L finite set of channel names, and show by induction on n that:

$$\exists L, L' \,(L \supseteq fn(P \mid Q), L' \subseteq L \text{ and } \nu L' \,(P \mid R(n,L)) \overset{\bullet}{\approx} \nu L' \,(Q \mid R(n,L))))$$
$$\text{implies } P \approx_a^n Q.$$

If the property above holds then we can conclude the proof by observing:

$$\begin{aligned} P \approx_b Q &\Rightarrow \forall R (P \mid R \overset{\bullet}{\approx} Q \mid R) \\ &\Rightarrow \forall n \in \omega \,(P \mid R(n,L) \overset{\bullet}{\approx} Q \mid R(n,L)) \quad \text{with } L = fn(P \mid Q),\ L' = \emptyset \\ &\Rightarrow \forall n \in \omega \,(P \approx_a^n Q) \\ &\Rightarrow P \approx_a^\omega Q \end{aligned}$$

Full definitions of the tests $R(n, L)$ can be found in [ACS96] □

Remark 3 *(1) In the proof for the strong case one can achieve the effect of matching with synchronization. Therefore theorem 7 holds also for a calculus without matching. In the weak case matching plays an essential role, for instance the terms $\overline{a}b$ and $\overline{a}c$ cannot be separated when put in parallel with the process $!(b(d).\overline{c}d) \mid !(c(d).\overline{b}d)$ (which is an equalizer in Honda-Tokoro terminology).*

(2) The definition of the tests $R(n, L)$ does not *involve the guarded sum. This implies that the characterization theorem still holds for an asynchronous calculus without guarded sum.*

(3) In the asynchronous calculus with matching *the various notions of bisimulation do not collapse. For instance consider $P \equiv a(c).\overline{b}e + a(c).\mathbf{0}$ and $Q \equiv P + a(c).[c = d]\overline{b}e$. The processes P and Q are early equivalent but late distinct. Moreover asynchronous bisimulation and barbed equivalence fail to be congruences. If we refine asynchronous bisimulation to an asynchronous congruence (by asking invariance under substitution) and if we refine barbed equivalence to barbed congruence (by considering contexts including the input prefix) then we can show that asynchronous congruence coincides with barbed congruence.*

Strong case (without matching):

- $\overset{\bullet}{\sim} \supset \sim_{o\tau} \supset \sim_a = \sim_g = \sim_1 = \sim_2 = \sim_3 = \sim_b$.
- $\sim_a$ is a congruence.
- Axiom which distinguishes asynchronous from synchronous bisimulation: $a(b).(\overline{a}b \mid P) + \tau.P = \tau.P$, if $b \notin fn(P)$.

Weak case:

- $\overset{\bullet}{\approx} \supset \approx_{o\tau} \supset \approx_a = \approx_1$.
- Without matching: $\approx_g = \approx_a$ is a congruence and $\approx_a \subset \approx_b$.
- With matching on image finite processes: $\approx_a = \approx_b$.

Figure 3: Summary of results

6 Conclusion

Our contributions are summarized in figure 3. We leave open the problem of finding an axiomatization of weak asynchronous bisimulation (with or without matching), and the problem of determining the counterpart in the weak case of the characterisations of strong asynchronous bisimulation in terms of $\sim_2$ and $\sim_3$. In another direction, it would be worth investigating the applications of theorem 5 (bisimulation equals ground bisimulation) to automatic verification. For instance, one may wonder if it is possible to speed up current verification techniques by compiling into the asynchronous π-calculus and applying ground bisimulation. For this, it would be useful to find syntactic conditions under which asynchronous and synchronous bisimulations coincide.

Acknowledgements
We would like to thank David N. Turner for interesting initial discussions and Marco Pistore and the anonymous referees for helpful comments.

References

[ACS96] R. Amadio, I. Castellani, and D. Sangiorgi. On bisimulations for the asynchronous π-calculus. Research Report To appear, INRIA, Sophia-Antipolis, 1996. Available at `http://wwwi3s.unice.fr/~amadio/`.

[Agh86] G. Agha. *Actors: a model of concurrent computation in distributed systems.* MIT-Press, 1986.

[Bou91] G. Boudol. Asynchrony and the π-calculus. Research Report 1702, INRIA, Sophia-Antipolis, 1991.

[BS96] M. Boreale and D. Sangiorgi. Some congruence properties for π-calculus bisimilarities. Research Report 2870, INRIA, Sophia-Antipolis, 1996.

[Dam93] M. Dam. Model checking mobile processes. In *Proc. CONCUR'93*, Lecture Notes in Computer Science, 715:22–36, 1993. Full version in SICS report RR94:1, 1994.

[FG96] C. Fournet and G. Gonthier. The reflexive CHAM and the join-calculus. *Proc. ACM-POPL*, 1996.

[HKH95] M. Hansen, J. Kleist, and H. Hüttel. Bisimulations for asynchronous mobile processes. In *Proceedings of the Tbilisi Symposium on Language, Logic, and Computation*, 1995. Research paper HCRC/RP-72, Human Communication Research Centre, University of Edinburgh.

[HT91] K. Honda and M. Tokoro. An object calculus for asynchronous communication. *Proc. ECOOP 91, Geneve*, 1991.

[HT92] K. Honda and M. Tokoro. On asynchronous communication semantics. *Object-based concurrent computing, SLNCS 612*, 1992.

[HY95] K. Honda and N. Yoshida. On reduction based process semantics. *Theoretical Computer Science*, 151:437–486, 1995.

[MPW92] R. Milner, J. Parrow, and D. Walker. A Calculus of Mobile Process, Parts 1-2. *Information and Computation*, 100(1):1–77, 1992.

[MS92] R. Milner and D. Sangiorgi. Barbed bisimulation. In *Proc. ICALP 92, SLNCS 623*, 1992.

[NP96] U. Nestmann and B. Pierce. Decoding choice encodings. In *CONCUR 96, SLNCS to appear*, Pisa, 1996.

[PT96] B. Pierce and D. Turner. Pict: a programming language based on the π-calculus. U. Cambridge, 1996.

[San93] D. Sangiorgi. A theory of bisimulation for the π-calculus. in *Proc. CONCUR'93* Lecture Notes in Computer Science, 715:127–142, 1993.

[San95] D. Sangiorgi. Lazy functions and mobile processes. Research Report RR-2515, INRIA, Sophia-Antipolis, 1995. Available via anonymous ftp from `cma.cma.fr` as `pub/papers/davide/RR-2515.ps`.

[Tel95] G. Tel. *Introduction to distributed algorithms*. Cambridge University Press, 1995.

On the Expressiveness of Internal Mobility in Name-Passing Calculi*

Michele Boreale

Dipartimento di Scienze dell'Informazione

Università di Roma "La Sapienza"

Abstract

We consider the language πI, a name-passing calculus introduced by Sangiorgi, where only private names can be exchanged among processes (internal mobility). The calculus πI has simple mathematical theory, very close to that of CCS. We provide an encoding from (an asynchronous variant of) the π-calculus to πI, which is fully abstract on the reduction relations of the two calculi. The result shows that, in name-passing calculi, internal mobility is the essential ingredient as far as expressiveness is concerned.

1 Introduction

By now, the π-calculus [13] is generally recognized as *the* prototypical algebraic language for describing concurrent systems with dynamically evolving communication linkage. The latter phenomenon, known as *mobility*, is modelled through the passing of channel names among processes (name-passing). The expressive power of the π-calculus is demonstrated by the existence of simple and fully abstract translations into it for a variety of computational formalisms, including λ-calculus [12], higher-order process calculi [15] and calculi which permits reasoning on the causal or spatial structure of the systems [4, 17].

The price to pay for this expressiveness is a rather complex mathematical theory of the π-calculus. A source of complications is, above all, the need to take *name instantiation* (otherwise called substitution) into account. Input and output at a of a tuple of names $\tilde{b}$ are written, respectively, as $a(\tilde{b}).P$ (input prefix) and $\overline{a}\langle\tilde{b}\rangle.P$ (output prefix), with P representing the continuation of the prefix. An input and an output prefix can be consumed in a communication, where a tuple of names is passed and used to instantiate the formal parameters of the input prefix, thus:

$$a(\tilde{c}).P \mid \overline{a}\langle\tilde{b}\rangle.Q \stackrel{\tau}{\longrightarrow} P\{\tilde{b}/\tilde{c}\} \mid Q \qquad (*)$$

with $\{\tilde{b}/\tilde{c}\}$ denoting the instantiation of names in $\tilde{c}$ with names in $\tilde{b}$. Name instantiation is a central aspect in the mathematical treatment of certain behavioural relations.

*Work partially supported by EEC, HCM Project Express and by CNR within the project "Specifica ad Alto Livello e Verifica di Sistemi Digitali". Author's e-mail address: `michele@dsi.uniroma1.it`

E.g., bisimilarity in the π-calculus comes in several different forms (early, late and open), depending on the name instantiation strategy chosen for matching input actions [13, 14, 16], and it is not clear which one should be preferred. Name instantiation also complicates the pragmatics of the π-calculus, since any implementation has to keep track, explicitly (e.g. using environments) or implicitly, of the bindings among names created by communications like (*) as the computation proceeds (see e.g. [8]).

It is therefore natural to try to isolate fragments of the π-calculus enjoying a simpler treatment of name instantiation, while retaining non-trivial expressive power. In this paper, we examine the calculus πI, a sub-language of the π-calculus proposed in [19]. A prominent feature of πI is that it avoids using name instantiation (other than α-conversion). This makes its mathematical treatment and its pragmatics much simpler than those of the π-calculus: indeed the only extra ingredient of πI over CCS is α-conversion of names (see [19]). We show that an "asynchronous" variant of the π-calculus [10, 3, 18] can be translated, in a simple and compositional fashion, into πI. There is a precise operational correspondence, on the reduction relations of the two calculi, between the source process and translated process. The correspondence can be also concisely stated as full abstraction of the translation w.r.t. the *barbed bisimulation* equivalence of [15]. A more precise account of our work follows.

The language πI is obtained from the π-calculus by imposing the constraint that only *private* names be communicated among processes. Output at a of a tuple of private names $\tilde{b}$ is written as $(\nu\,\tilde{b})(\overline{a}\langle\tilde{b}\rangle.P)$, where $(\nu\,\tilde{b})$ is the *restriction* operator of the π-calculus. After the interaction, the communicated names remain private:

$$a(\tilde{c}).P \mid (\nu\,\tilde{b})\overline{a}\langle\tilde{b}\rangle.Q \xrightarrow{\tau} (\nu\,\tilde{b})(P\{\tilde{b}/\tilde{c}\} \mid Q) \qquad (**)$$

Since both $a(\tilde{c})$. and $(\nu\,\tilde{b})$ act as binders for the names $\tilde{c}$ and $\tilde{b}$, respectively, up to α-conversion it is possible to assume in (**) that $\tilde{b} = \tilde{c}$: thus no name instantiation is needed in πI. The kind of dynamic reconfiguration corresponding to the passing of private names is called *internal mobility* in [19].

In πI it is impossible to directly describe *external* mobility, i.e., output of public names (or *free output*), as given by (*). In [19], it has been shown that πI is expressive enough to encode in a fully abstract way λ-calculus and certain forms of *strictly* higher-order process calculi. However, neither of these formalisms exhibits external mobility. In particular, in strictly higher- order calculi, no name-passing feature is present, since only processes (or abstraction of processes) can be passed around. It is therefore natural to wonder whether external mobility, at least in some limited form, can be "programmed" via the internal one.

In the paper, we consider asynchronous π-calculus, π_a, a language with external mobility introduced by Honda [10] and, independently, by Boudol [3]. This is a variant of the π-calculus where the continuation of a free output prefix is always the empty process (*asynchronous free output*), and the *matching* operator [13], used to test for equalities between names, is omitted. The limitation to asynchronous output prefix is not serious, since it has been shown that the full output prefix can be, in a reasonable sense, programmed in π_a [3]. On the other hand, matching plays a secondary role, as far as expressiveness is concerned (e.g. it is not necessary to encode the λ-calculus, higher-order calculi etc.), and its omission leads to a nicer mathematical treatment of many behavioural relations (e.g. on π_a, unlike the π-calculus, bisimulation is a full congruence [10, 9, 5]).

We define a compositional encoding, $[\![\,.\,]\!]$, from π_a to πI. The basic idea is that the output of a free name b at a, $\overline{a}b$, is replaced, in πI, by the output of a private name x, which acts as a pointer to a *link* process from x to b, written $x \rightarrow b$. Intuitively, $x \rightarrow b$ behaves like a buffer with entrance at x and exit at b: however, names transmitted at b are not the same as names received at x (this would require free output), but are, in turn, linked to them (the definition of link processes will be indeed recursive). Since a link $x \rightarrow b$ transforms outputs at x into outputs at b, a process owing x can trigger an output at b by interacting with $x \rightarrow b$.

Thus link processes can be used to naturally encode those π_a-processes in which any receiver, say $a(x).P$, can only use x in P as an output channel. We call π_a^i the subset of π_a obeying this "inversion of polarity" syntactical condition. We show that the full π_a can be faithfully encoded in the fragment π_a^i. Thus the encoding $[\![\,.\,]\!]$ is actually obtained as the composition of two simple translations: one ($\{\![\,.\,]\!\}$) from π_a to π_a^i, and the other ($(\![\,.\,]\!)$) from π_a^i to πI. Each of these two encodings is proven to be fully abstract w.r.t. barbed bisimilarity, a behavioural equivalence which focuses on the reduction relations of process calculi. The meaning of this result is that whatever can be programmed in the π-calculus, it can be programmed in πI. This strengthens the claim of [19], that, in the π-calculus, internal mobility is responsible for most of the expressive power, whereas external mobility is responsible for most of the mathematical complications.

The encoding $\{\![\,.\,]\!\}$ is also interesting on its own. The underlying idea is that, whenever a name b is passed, the sender keeps for himself the right of using name b as an input. In the translated process, the receiver is hence passed two things: a "polarized" b, which can be only used for output, *plus* the private address of a channel manager, to which all requests of using b as an input channel must be addressed. Thus, all subsequent communications along b will have the channel manager as a receiver. This suggests that, without loosing expressive power, it should be possible to further refine the channel discipline of π_a^i to get a calculus in which each channel, once created, has a single, statically localized receiver; the latter could be understood as an *object*, in the sense of object-oriented programming. This "unique receiver" property is particularly desirable for distributed implementation of concurrent languages: it is, for example, one of the motivations behind the *join-calculus* of Fournet and Gonthier [7].

The rest of the paper is organized as follows. Section 2 contains some background material on π_a, πI and on the behavioural relations used throughout the paper. Section 3 presents the encoding from π_a to π_a^i. Section 4 presents the encoding from π_a^i to πI. The paper ends with a few conclusive remarks in Section 5.

2 Background

In this section we introduce the languages π_a, π_a^i and πI, their basic operational semantics and some behavioural relations on them.

2.1 The languages π_a, π_a^i and πI

The name-passing languages π_a, π_a^i and πI can be regarded as fragments of a common π-calculus subset, which we call $\mathcal{P}$. Below, we shall first describe $\mathcal{P}$ and then isolate out of it the fragments of our interest, by constraining the output constructs.

The countable set $\mathcal{N}$ of *names* is ranged over by $a, b, \ldots, x, y, \ldots$. A countable set of *agent identifiers*, each having a non-negative integer arity, is ranged over by $A, A', \ldots$. *Processes* are ranged over by P, Q and R. The subset of the π-calculus syntax we shall consider is built from the operators of guarded summation, restriction, parallel composition, replication and agent identifier:

$$P \;:= \textstyle\sum_{i\in I} S_i \;\mid\; \nu\, a\, P \;\mid\; P_1 \,|\, P_2 \;\mid\; !P \;\mid\; A(a_1,\ldots,a_k)$$
$$S \;:= a(\tilde{b}).P \;\mid\; \overline{a}(\tilde{b}).P \;\mid\; \overline{a}\langle\tilde{b}\rangle.\mathbf{0}\,.$$

where k is the arity of A. The prefixes $a(\tilde{b}).$, $\overline{a}(\tilde{b}).$ and $\overline{a}\langle\tilde{b}\rangle.$ are called, respectively, input prefix, bound output prefix and (asynchronous) free output prefix; in the input prefix $a(\tilde{b})$ and in the bound output prefix $\overline{a}(\tilde{b})$, the components of $\tilde{b}$ are pairwise distinct. In the free output $\overline{a}\langle\tilde{b}\rangle$, we omit the surrounding brackets $\langle\rangle$ when $\tilde{b}$ has one or zero components. In summations, the index-set I is finite; for $\sum_{i\in\emptyset} \alpha_i.P_i$ the symbol $\mathbf{0}$ is also used, while binary summation $\sum_{i\in\{1,2\}} P_i$ is often written as $P_1 + P_2$. We abbreviate $\alpha.\mathbf{0}$ as α and $\nu\, a\, \nu\, b\, P$ as $(\nu\, a, b\,)P$.

We only admit *guarded* summation, since, by contrast with full summation, it preserves bisimilarity even for weak relations, where silent moves are partially ignored. Following [19], we have also introduced explicitly the bound output prefix $\overline{a}(\tilde{b}).P$, that in in the full π-calculus would only be syntactic sugar for $\nu\,\tilde{b}\,(\overline{a}\langle\tilde{b}\rangle.P)$.

Input prefix $a(\tilde{b})$. and restriction $\nu\, a$ act as *binders* for names $\tilde{b}$ and a, respectively. *Free names, bound names* of a process P, written $\mathrm{fn}(P)$ and $\mathrm{bn}(P)$ respectively, arise as expected; the *names* of P, written $\mathrm{n}(P)$ are $\mathrm{fn}(P) \cup \mathrm{bn}(P)$. *Substitutions*, ranged over by $\sigma, \sigma' \ldots$ are functions from $\mathcal{N}$ to $\mathcal{N}$; for any expression E, we write $E\sigma$ for the expression obtained from applying σ to E. Composition of two substitutions σ and σ' is written $\sigma\sigma'$. We assume the following decreasing order of precedence when writing process expressions: substitution, prefix, replication, restriction, parallel composition, summation.

Each agent identifier has an associated defining equation, $A(x_1, \ldots, x_k) \Leftarrow P$, where k is the arity of A, the x_i's are all distinct and $\mathrm{fn}(P) \subseteq \{x_1, \ldots, x_k\}$.

The transition rules for the language operators are given in Table 1. *Actions*, ranged over by μ, can be of four forms: τ (interaction), $a(\tilde{b})$ (input), or $\nu\,\tilde{b}'\,\overline{a}\langle\tilde{b}\rangle$ (output), $\overline{a}(\tilde{b})$ (bound output). By convention, we shall identify actions $\nu\,\tilde{b}\,\overline{a}\langle\tilde{b}\rangle$ and $\overline{a}(\tilde{b})$. Functions $\mathrm{bn}(\cdot)$, $\mathrm{fn}(\cdot)$ and $\mathrm{n}(\cdot)$ are extended to actions as expected, once we set $\mathrm{bn}(a(\tilde{b})) = \tilde{b}$ and $\mathrm{bn}(\nu\,\tilde{b}'\,\overline{a}\langle\tilde{b}\rangle) = \tilde{b}'$.

Throughout the paper, we work up to α-conversion on names — that is, we implicitly take an underlying representation of names based on de Bruijn indices [6] — so to avoid tedious side conditions in transition rules and bisimulation clauses. Therefore, for instance, in a process bound names are assumed different from each other and from the free names, and α-equivalent processes are assumed to have the same transitions. All our notations are extended to tuples componentwise.

Following Milner [11], we only admit *well-sorted processes*: the sorting prevents arity mismatching in communications, like in $\overline{a}\langle b, c\rangle.\, P \,|\, a(x).\, Q$. Moreover, substitutions must map names onto names of the same sort. We do not present the sorting system because it is not essential to understand the contents of this paper.

We say that a name a occurs in P in *input- (resp. output-) subject position* if P contains a prefix $a(\tilde{b})$ (resp. $\overline{a}\langle\tilde{b}\rangle$ or $\overline{a}(\tilde{b})$) not inside the scope of a binder for a. We

$$\textbf{Sum}: \sum_{i\in I}\alpha_i.P_i \xrightarrow{\alpha_j} P_j,\ j\in I \qquad \textbf{Rep}: \frac{P \mid !P \xrightarrow{\mu} P'}{!P \xrightarrow{\mu} P'}$$

$$\textbf{Par}: \frac{P_1 \xrightarrow{\mu} P_1'}{P_1 \mid P_2 \xrightarrow{\mu} P_1' \mid P_2} \qquad \textbf{Com}: \frac{P_1 \xrightarrow{(\nu \tilde{b}')\overline{a}(\tilde{b})} P_1' \quad P_2 \xrightarrow{a(\tilde{c})} P_2'}{P_1 \mid P_2 \xrightarrow{\tau} \nu\tilde{b}'(P_1' \mid P_2'\{\tilde{b}/\tilde{c}\})}$$

$$\textbf{Res}: \frac{P \xrightarrow{\mu} P'}{\nu c P \xrightarrow{\mu} \nu c P'},\ c \notin \mathrm{n}(\mu) \qquad \textbf{Open}: \frac{P \xrightarrow{(\nu \tilde{b}')\overline{a}(\tilde{b})} P'}{\nu c P \xrightarrow{(\nu \tilde{b}' c)\overline{a}(\tilde{b})} P'},\ c \neq a, c \in \tilde{b} - \tilde{b}'$$

$$\textbf{Ide}: \frac{P\{\tilde{b}/\tilde{x}\} \xrightarrow{\mu} P'}{A(\tilde{b}) \xrightarrow{\mu} P'}\ \text{if } A(\tilde{x}) \Leftarrow P$$

Table 1: Operational semantics of $\mathcal{P}$ (symmetric versions of Par, Com, Close omitted).

call:

- $\mathcal{P}$ the above defined set of π-calculus processes;
- π_{a} the subset of $\mathcal{P}$ with no bound output prefixes and no agent identifiers;
- $\pi_{\mathrm{a}}^{\mathrm{i}}$ the subset of π_{a} in which, for terms of the form $a(\tilde{b}).P$, no $b_i \in \tilde{b}$ occurs in P in input subject position;
- πI the subset of $\mathcal{P}$ without free output prefix.

Note that the language πI contains both replication and agent identifiers: contrary to what happens in the π-calculus, these two primitives are not equivalent (see [19]) in πI. Even though replication can be derived from identifiers, we decided to keep it for notational convenience.

2.2 Barbed bisimilarity, standard bisimilarity and expansion preorder

Weak barbed bisimilarity [15] is the relation we are most interested in. We will, however, use in some of the proofs a few auxiliary relations: standard (strong and weak) bisimilarities and the expansion preorder.

In the sequel, we let $\Longrightarrow$ be the reflexive and transitive closure of $\xrightarrow{\tau}$, let $\xRightarrow{\mu}$ be $\Longrightarrow\xrightarrow{\mu}\Longrightarrow$, and let $P \xRightarrow{\hat{\mu}} Q$ be $P \xRightarrow{\mu} Q$, if $\mu \neq \tau$, and $P \Longrightarrow Q$, if $\mu = \tau$.

2.2.1 Barbed bisimilarity

Barbed bisimilarity [15] represents a uniform mechanism for defining behavioural equivalences, which focuses on two concepts common to different process calculi: the *reduction relation* $\xrightarrow{\tau}$ and an *observability predicate* $\downarrow a$. In π-calculus, we say that P *commits* to a, and write $P \downarrow a$, if P contains a prefix $a(\tilde{b})$, or $\overline{a}\langle\tilde{b}\rangle$ or $\overline{a}(\tilde{b})$ which is not underneath another prefix or in the scope of a νa restriction operator. This means that P is capable of interacting immediately on channel a. We write $P \Downarrow a$ if P is capable of interacting on a possibly after a few invisible steps, i.e. if $P \Longrightarrow \downarrow a$.

Definition 2.1 (weak barbed bisimilarity) *A symmetric binary relation $\mathcal{R}$ on $\mathcal{P} \times \mathcal{P}$ is a* weak barbed bisimulation *if and only if, whenever $P \mathcal{R} Q$:*

1. *$P \xrightarrow{\tau} P'$ implies there exists Q' s.t. $Q \Longrightarrow Q'$ and $P' \mathcal{R} Q'$, and*

2. *$P \downarrow a$ implies $Q \Downarrow a$, for any a.*

We say that P and Q are barbed bisimilar, *written $P \simeq Q$ if and only if $P \mathcal{R} Q$ for some barbed bisimulation $\mathcal{R}$.*

2.2.2 Standard bisimilarities

A few forms of (standard) bisimilarity have been proposed for the π-calculus, notably the *late, early* and *open* bisimilarities [13, 16], depending on the specific name instantiation strategy adopted for input actions. Here, we take advantage of the fact that, over the subsets of the π-calculus we are interested in (πI, π_a and hence π_a^i), these forms coincide with each other and with another, simpler form of bisimilarity, called *ground* bisimilarity (see [9, 10, 18, 5]). In the latter, no name instantiation of the input formal parameter is required, apart from α-conversion. We recall its definition below.

Definition 2.2 (strong ground bisimilarity) *A symmetric relation $\mathcal{R} \subseteq \mathcal{P} \times \mathcal{P}$ is a* strong ground bisimulation *if $P \mathcal{R} Q$ and $P \xrightarrow{\mu} P'$ imply that there exists Q' s.t. $Q \xrightarrow{\mu} Q'$ and $P' \mathcal{R} Q'$. Two processes P and Q are* strongly ground bisimilar, *written $P \sim Q$, if $P \mathcal{R} Q$ for some strong bisimulation $\mathcal{R}$.*

The weak versions of this bisimulation, where one ignores silent steps in matching transitions, is obtained in the usual way: weak ground bisimilarity is defined by replacing in Definition 2.2 the transition $Q \xrightarrow{\mu} Q'$ with $Q \stackrel{\widehat{\mu}}{\Longrightarrow} Q'$. We use $\approx$ for weak ground bisimilarity.

Since we are only interested in the π_a and πI fragments of $\mathcal{P}$, where all mentioned forms of standard bisimilarity coincide, in the sequel we shall omit the adjective 'ground' when referring to $\sim$ and $\approx$.

2.2.3 Expansion preorder

The expansion relation $\lesssim$ [1, 20] is an asymmetric variant of $\approx$ which allows us to count the number of τ-actions performed by the processes. Thus, $P \lesssim Q$ holds if $P \approx Q$ but also Q has at least as many τ-moves as P. As for standard bisimilarities, different (ground, early, late, open) forms of expansion can be defined on the π-calculus, depending on the chosen name instantiation strategy. Again, it is easily seen that all these forms coincide on the subsets of the π-calculus of our interest, π_a and πI (the proof parallels that given in [9, 10, 18] for standard bisimilarities). We give below the definition of ground expansion preorder, omitting the adjective 'ground'.

Definition 2.3 (expansion preorder) *A relation $\mathcal{R} \subseteq \mathcal{P} \times \mathcal{P}$ is an* expansion *if $P \mathcal{R} Q$ implies:*

1. *Whenever $P \xrightarrow{\mu} P'$, there exists Q' s.t. $Q \overset{\mu}{\Longrightarrow} Q'$ and $P' \mathcal{R} Q'$;*

2. *whenever $Q \xrightarrow{\mu} Q'$, there exists P' s.t. $P \xrightarrow{\hat{\mu}} P'$ and $P' \mathcal{R} Q'$.*

We say that Q expands *P, written $P \lesssim Q$, if $P \mathcal{R} Q$, for some expansion $\mathcal{R}$.*

We often write $Q \gtrsim P$ in place of $P \lesssim Q$. The following proposition summarizes a few properties of the behavioural relations considered in the paper, and some relationships between them:

Proposition 2.4

a) Over the languages π_a and πI, the relations $\sim$, $\approx$ and $\lesssim$ are preserved by all operators and by name instantiations.

b) The following is a chain of strict inclusions between relations: $\sim$, $\lesssim$, $\approx$, $\simeq$.

3 From π_a to π_a^i

Let us illustrate informally how a π_a process can be translated in π_a^i. The basic idea is that whenever a name b is passed, the receiver, say R, is also passed the (private) address z of an "input manager" process, $z \hookrightarrow b$. The latter serves all requests of using b as an input channel. In particular, whenever activated at z, $z \hookrightarrow b$ performs the requested input and then gives the control and the result of the input operation back at a private return address, h. Hence, all input actions of R at b are transformed, via the encoding, into interactions at z with $z \hookrightarrow b$.

For notational simplicity, we only present below the encoding for the monadic fragment of π_a. The polyadic case will be easily accommodated afterward. First, the formal definition of the input manager process:

Definition 3.1 (input manager process) *Let z and b be two names. An* input manager *for b at z is the π_a^i process:*

$$z \hookrightarrow b \stackrel{\mathrm{def}}{=} !\, z(h).b(x,y).\overline{h}\langle x,y\rangle\,.$$

The encoding $\{\!|\,.\,|\!\}$ from (monadic) π_a to π_a^i is defined in Table 2. The definition makes use of an auxiliary parameter, ρ, which is a finite partial function from $\mathcal{N}$ to $\mathcal{N}$. It is used in the input clause $(a(x).P)$ to record the transformation of input actions at x into interactions at z with links of the form $z \hookrightarrow b$. The notation $\rho[^x\!/_y]$ denotes the partial function which yields y on x and behaves like ρ elsewhere. Furthermore, ran(ρ) denotes the set $\{y : \rho(x) = y$, for some $x\}$. When, in some statement, we declare a name to be *fresh* we mean it is different from any name occurring in any process or in any function ρ previously mentioned in the statement. Bound names are always assumed to be fresh.

Before proving full abstraction of $\{\!|\,.\,|\!\}$ we need to fix a basic property of it. In the following lemma, part 1 is a well-known distributivity law for $!$, due to Milner [11]. Part 2 shows that, under certain conditions, an input manager process $z \hookrightarrow a$ somehow acts as a substitution of z with a, if z is hidden.

Let ρ be a finite partial function from $\mathcal{N}$ to $\mathcal{N}$. $\{\!|P|\!\}\rho$ is defined as:

$$\{\!|a(x).P|\!\}\rho \stackrel{\mathrm{def}}{=} \begin{cases} a(x,z).\{\!|P|\!\}\rho[{}^{z}\!/\!_{x}] & \text{if } \rho \text{ is undefined on } a \text{, with } z \text{ fresh} \\ \nu\, h\left(\overline{z}h \mid h(x,y).\{\!|P|\!\}\rho[{}^{y}\!/\!_{x}]\right) & \text{if } \rho(a)=z\text{, with } h,y \text{ fresh} \end{cases}$$

$$\{\!|\overline{a}b|\!\}\rho \stackrel{\mathrm{def}}{=} \nu\, z\left(\overline{a}\langle b,z\rangle \mid z \hookrightarrow b\right) \text{ with } z \text{ fresh} \qquad \{\!|\nu\, x\, P|\!\}\rho \stackrel{\mathrm{def}}{=} \nu\, x\, \{\!|P|\!\}\rho$$

$$\{\!|\textstyle\sum_{i\in I} S_i|\!\}\rho \stackrel{\mathrm{def}}{=} \textstyle\sum_{i\in I}\{\!|S_i|\!\}\rho \qquad \{\!|\,!\,P|\!\}\rho \stackrel{\mathrm{def}}{=} \,!\,\{\!|P|\!\}\rho$$

$$\{\!|P \mid Q|\!\}\rho \stackrel{\mathrm{def}}{=} \{\!|P|\!\}\rho \mid \{\!|Q|\!\}\rho \qquad \text{Define: } \{\!|P|\!\} \stackrel{\mathrm{def}}{=} \{\!|P|\!\}\emptyset\,.$$

Table 2: Definition of the encoding $\{\!|\,.\,|\!\}$ from π_{a} to $\pi^{\mathrm{i}}_{\mathrm{a}}$.

Lemma 3.2 *Let P, P_1 and P_2 be processes in π_{a}.*

1. $\nu\, y\left(!\,y(x).P \mid P_1 \mid P_2\right) \sim \nu\, y\,(!\,y(x).P \mid P_1) \mid \nu\, y\,(!\,y(x).P \mid P_2)$, *provided that y may occur free in P, P_1 and P_2 only in output-subject position.*
2. $\nu\, z\left(z \hookrightarrow a \mid \{\!|P|\!\}\rho[{}^{z}\!/\!_{a}]\right) \gtrsim [\![P]\!]\rho$, *where ρ is undefined in a, and z is fresh.*

PROOF: Part 1 is shown by exhibiting the appropriate bisimulation (see e.g. [11]). Part 2 is proven by induction on P, exploiting part 1. The most interesting case is when $P = a(x).P'$. Then we have:

$$\begin{array}{rl}
\nu\, z\left(z \hookrightarrow a \mid \{\!|P|\!\}\rho[{}^{z}\!/\!_{a}]\right) & = \\
& \text{(definition of } \{\!|\,.\,|\!\}) \\
\nu\, z\left(z \hookrightarrow a \mid \nu\, h\left(\overline{z}\langle h\rangle \mid h(x,y).\{\!|P'|\!\}\rho[{}^{z}\!/\!_{a}][{}^{y}\!/\!_{x}]\right)\right) & \sim \\
& \text{(laws for } \nu\, h \text{ and part 1)} \\
\nu\, h\left(\nu\, z\left(z \hookrightarrow a \mid \overline{z}\langle h\rangle\right) \mid \nu\, z\left(z \hookrightarrow a \mid h(x,y).\{\!|P'|\!\}\rho[{}^{z}\!/\!_{a}][{}^{y}\!/\!_{x}]\right)\right) & \gtrsim \\
& \text{(laws for } \gtrsim\,,\ \mid \text{ and } \nu\, z) \\
\nu\, h\left(a(x,y).\overline{h}\langle x,y\rangle \mid h(x,y).\nu\, z\left(z \hookrightarrow a \mid \{\!|P'|\!\}\rho[{}^{z}\!/\!_{a}][{}^{y}\!/\!_{x}]\right)\right) & \gtrsim \\
& \text{(induction hyp., laws for } \mid,\ \nu\, h) \\
a(x,y).\nu\, h\left(\overline{h}\langle x,y\rangle \mid h(x,y).\{\!|P'|\!\}\rho[{}^{y}\!/\!_{x}]\right) & \gtrsim \\
& \text{(a simple law for } \gtrsim) \\
a(x,y).\{\!|P'|\!\}\rho[{}^{y}\!/\!_{x}] & = \\
& \text{(definition of } \{\!|\,.\,|\!\}). \\
\{\!|P|\!\}\rho\,. &
\end{array}$$

□

The following proposition shows the tight correspondence between transitions of P and transitions of $\{\!|P|\!\}\rho$.

Proposition 3.3 (strong operational correspondences) *Let ρ and P be s.t.* $\mathrm{fn}(P) \cap \mathrm{ran}(\rho) = \emptyset$.

a) Suppose that $P \stackrel{\mu}{\longrightarrow} P'$. Then we have:

1. $\mu = a(x)$ *implies* $\{\!|P|\!\}\rho \stackrel{a(x,y)}{\longrightarrow}\ \gtrsim \{\!|P'|\!\}\rho[{}^{y}\!/\!_{x}]$;

2. $\mu = \overline{a}b$ *implies* $\{\!|P|\!\}\rho \stackrel{\nu y \overline{a}\langle b,y\rangle}{\longrightarrow} \gtrsim y \hookrightarrow b \mid \{\!|P'|\!\}\rho$*, with* $y \notin \mathrm{fn}(P')$*;*

3. $\mu = \nu\, b \overline{a}b$ *implies* $\{\!|P|\!\}\rho \stackrel{(\nu\, b,y)\overline{a}\langle b,y\rangle}{\longrightarrow} \gtrsim y \hookrightarrow b \mid \{\!|P'|\!\}\rho$*, with* $y \notin \mathrm{fn}(P')$*;*

4. $\mu = \tau$ *implies* $\{\!|P|\!\}\rho \stackrel{\tau}{\longrightarrow} \gtrsim \{\!|P'|\!\}\rho$.

b) The converse of part a), i.e.: Suppose that $\{\!|P|\!\}\rho \stackrel{\mu}{\longrightarrow} P_1$*. Then there is* $P' \in \pi_a$ *s.t.:*

1. $\mu = a(x,y)$ *implies* $P \stackrel{a(x)}{\longrightarrow} P'$ *with* $P_1 \gtrsim \{\!|P'|\!\}\rho[y/x]$*;*

2. $\mu = \nu\, y\, \overline{a}\langle b,y\rangle$ *implies* $P \stackrel{\overline{a}b}{\longrightarrow} P'$ *with* $y \notin \mathrm{fn}(P')$ *and* $P_1 \gtrsim y \hookrightarrow b \mid \{\!|P'|\!\}\rho$*;*

3. $\mu = (\nu\, b, y)\overline{a}\langle b,y\rangle$ *implies* $P \stackrel{\nu\, b \overline{a}b}{\longrightarrow} P'$ *with* $y \notin \mathrm{fn}(P')$ *and* $P_1 \gtrsim y \hookrightarrow b \mid \{\!|P'|\!\}\rho$*;*

4. $\mu = \tau$ *implies* $P \stackrel{\tau}{\longrightarrow} P'$*, with* $P_1 \gtrsim \{\!|P'|\!\}\rho$.

PROOF: Each part is proven by transition induction. The only subtle points arise in the proof of parts a)(4) and b)(4), where also Lemma 3.2(2) is used. As an example, we show part a)(4). The only non-trivial case is when the last rule applied for deriving $P \stackrel{\tau}{\longrightarrow} P'$ is a communication rule (we suppose for simplicity that the communicated name is free; the case when it is restricted can be easily accommodated):

$$\texttt{Com}: \quad \frac{P_1 \stackrel{\overline{a}b}{\longrightarrow} P_1',\ P_2 \stackrel{a(x)}{\longrightarrow} P_2'}{P_1 \mid P_2 \stackrel{\tau}{\longrightarrow} P_1 \mid P_2\{b/x\}}.$$

where we suppose that $x \notin \mathrm{fn}(P_1')$. By induction hypothesis, we have that:

$$\{\!|P_1|\!\}\rho \stackrel{\nu y \overline{a}\langle b,y\rangle}{\longrightarrow} \gtrsim y \hookrightarrow b \,|\, \{\!|P_1'|\!\}\rho \text{ with } y \notin \mathrm{fn}(P_1') \text{ and } \{\!|P_2|\!\}\rho \stackrel{a(x,y)}{\longrightarrow} \gtrsim \{\!|P_2'|\!\}\rho[y/x]. \quad (1)$$

Then we have:

$$\begin{array}{rcl}
\{\!|P_1 \mid P_2|\!\}\rho & \stackrel{\tau}{\longrightarrow} \gtrsim & \nu y \big(y \hookrightarrow b \mid \{\!|P_1'|\!\}\rho \mid \{\!|P_2'|\!\}\rho[y/x]\{b/x\} \big) \\
 & & \text{(from (1) and interaction)} \\
 & = & \nu y \big(y \hookrightarrow b \mid \{\!|P_1' \mid P_2'|\!\}\rho[y/x] \big)\{b/x\} \\
 & & \text{(since } x, y \notin \mathrm{fn}(P_1') \text{ and by def. of } \{\!|\,.\,|\!\}) \\
 & \gtrsim & \{\!|P_1' \mid P_2'|\!\}\rho\{b/x\} \quad \text{(Lemma 3.2(2))} \\
 & = & \{\!|P_1' \mid P_2'\{b/x\}|\!\}\rho \\
 & & \text{(by a simple property of the encoding and the fact} \\
 & & \text{that } x \notin \mathrm{fn}(P_1')).
\end{array}$$

□

As a consequence of the previous proposition, we get the following correspondence on commitments and weak invisible transitions:

Proposition 3.4

a) $P \downarrow a$ *if and only if* $\{\!|P|\!\} \downarrow a$.

b) $P \Longrightarrow P'$ *implies* $\{\!|P|\!\} \Longrightarrow \gtrsim \{\!|P'|\!\}$*;*

c) $\{\!|P|\!\} \Longrightarrow P_1$ *implies that there is* P' *s.t.* $P \Longrightarrow P'$ *and* $P_1 \gtrsim \{\!|P'|\!\}$.

d) $P \Downarrow a$ *if and only if* $\{\!|P|\!\} \Downarrow a$.

PROOF: Part a) is a trivial consequence of the previous lemma. Part d) is a consequence of parts a), b) and c). Part b) and c) are shown by exploiting Proposition 3.3, parts a(4) and b(4), and the properties of $\lesssim$. As an example, we show part c).

For some $n \geq 0$ it holds that $\{\!|P|\!\} \xrightarrow{\tau^n} P_1$. We proceed by induction on n. The case $n = 0$ is trivial. If $n > 0$, the for some Q, we have $\{\!|P|\!\} \xrightarrow{\tau^{n-1}} Q \xrightarrow{\tau} P_1$. By the induction hypothesis, we have, for some P'' in π_a,

$$P \Longrightarrow P'' \quad \text{with } Q \gtrsim \{\!|P''|\!\}.$$

From this and $Q \xrightarrow{\tau} P_1$, we deduce that, for some R in π_a^i,

$$\{\!|P''|\!\} \xrightarrow{\hat{\tau}} R \quad \text{with } P_1 \gtrsim R.$$

Now, by Proposition 3.3(b)(4), there is P' in π_a s.t.

$$P'' \xrightarrow{\hat{\tau}} P' \quad \text{with } R \gtrsim \{\!|P'|\!\}.$$

Thus, we have found P' s.t. $P \Longrightarrow P'$ and $P_1 \gtrsim \{\!|P'|\!\}$, and proved the thesis. □

Remark 3.5 In the proof of item (c) of the above proposition the use of the expansion relation turns out to be necessary to close up the induction. Had we used weak bisimilarity $\approx$ in place of $\gtrsim$ in the above proof, from $Q \approx \{\!|P''|\!\}$ and $Q \xrightarrow{\tau} P_1$, we could have only inferred $\{\!|P''|\!\} \Longrightarrow R$ (in place of the stronger $\{\!|P''|\!\} \xrightarrow{\hat{\tau}} R$); as a consequence, we could not have applied Proposition 3.3(b)(4) to close up the induction. □

A simple proof technique for barbed bisimilarity:

Definition 3.6 *A symmetric binary relation* $\mathcal{R}$ *over* π_a *is a* barbed bisimulation up to expansion *if, whenever* $P \mathcal{R} Q$ *it holds:*

a) $P \xrightarrow{\tau} P'$ *implies that there exist* P_1, Q' *and* Q_1 *s.t.:* $P' \gtrsim P_1$ *and* $Q \Longrightarrow Q' \gtrsim Q_1$ *and* $P_1 \mathcal{R} Q_1$.

b) $P \downarrow a$ *implies* $Q \Downarrow a$.

Lemma 3.7 *If* $\mathcal{R}$ *is a barbed bisimulation up to expansion then* $\mathcal{R} \subseteq \simeq$.

We arrive at the main theorem of the section:

Theorem 3.8 (full abstraction of $\{\!|\,.\,|\!\}$ w.r.t. barbed bisimilarity) *Let* P *and* Q *be processes in* π_a. *Then* $P \simeq Q$ *if and only if* $\{\!|P|\!\} \simeq \{\!|Q|\!\}$.

Proof: Exploiting the above Proposition 3.4 and Proposition 3.3, it is easy to show that the relation:

$$\mathcal{R} = \{(\{\!|P|\!\}, \{\!|Q|\!\}) : P \simeq Q\}$$

is a barbed bisimulation up to expansion in π_a^i: this establishes the 'if' part.

For the 'only if' part, again exploiting the above Proposition 3.4 and Proposition 3.3, it is easy to see that the relation:

$$\mathcal{R} = \{(P, Q) : \{\!|P|\!\} \simeq \{\!|Q|\!\}\}$$

is a barbed bisimulation up to expansion in π_a. □

We indicate now the modifications necessary to extend $\{\!|\,.\,|\!\}$ to the full polyadic π_a. We use the following notations: for $\tilde{u} = (u_1, \ldots, u_k)$ and $\tilde{v} = (v_1, \ldots, v_k)$, $[\tilde{v}/\tilde{u}]$ stands for $[v_1/u_1] \cdots [v_k/u_k]$ and $\tilde{u} \hookrightarrow \tilde{v}$ stands for $u_1 \hookrightarrow v_1 \mid \cdots \mid u_k \hookrightarrow v_k$. The clauses for input and output prefixes of Table 2 are replaced by the two clauses:

$$\{\!|a(\tilde{x}).P|\!\}\rho \stackrel{\text{def}}{=} \begin{cases} a(\tilde{x}, \tilde{z}).\{\!|P|\!\}\rho[\tilde{z}/\tilde{x}] & \text{if } \rho \text{ is undefined on } a, \text{ with } \tilde{z} \text{ fresh} \\ \nu h \left(\overline{z}h \mid h(\tilde{x}, \tilde{y}).\{\!|P|\!\}\rho[\tilde{y}/\tilde{x}]\right) & \text{if } \rho(a) = z, \text{ with } h \text{ and } \tilde{y} \text{ fresh} \end{cases}$$

$$\{\!|\overline{a}\langle\tilde{b}\rangle|\!\}\rho \stackrel{\text{def}}{=} (\nu\,\tilde{z})\left(\overline{a}\langle\tilde{b}, \tilde{z}\rangle \mid \tilde{z} \hookrightarrow \tilde{b}\right) \quad \tilde{z} \text{ fresh}$$

with the obvious requirements on the number of components of $\tilde{z}$ and $\tilde{y}$, which must furthermore be all distinct. The proofs carry over with some straightforward (mostly notational) changes. We omit the details.

4 From π_a^i to πI

Let us explain informally the second step of our translation, from π_a^i to πI. The basic idea is that the output of a free name b is replaced by the output of a bound name x plus a *link* from x to b, $x \to b$. The latter transforms outputs at x into outputs at b. Intuitively, $x \to b$ behaves like a buffer with entrance at x and exit at b: however, the name transmitted at b is not the same as the one received at x, but just, recursively, *linked* to it. Link processes have been introduced in [19], where they have been used to encode the lazy λ-calculus into πI.

Definition 4.1 (link processes, [19]) *Let a and b be two names. A* link from a to b *is the recursively defined* πI *process:*

$$a \to b \;\Leftarrow\; !\,a(x).\overline{b}(y).\,y \to x\;.$$

The encoding $(\!|\,.\,|\!)$ from π_a^i to πI is defined in Table 3. Again, we present the encoding for the monadic fragment of π_a^i. The polyadic calculus will be accommodated afterward.

In order to prove full abstraction of $(\!|\,.\,|\!)$, we need to fix a few properties of link processes. In the next lemma, part 1 says that whenever the exit point of one link coincides with the entrance point of another one, and this common point is hidden, then the two links are, so to speak, connected. This means that they behave as a single link. Part 2 of the lemma states then, under certain conditions, a link acts as a substitution.

$(\!|P|\!)$ is defined as:

$$
\begin{array}{llll}
(\!|a(x).P|\!) \stackrel{\text{def}}{=} a(x).(\!|P|\!) & (\!|\overline{a}b|\!) \stackrel{\text{def}}{=} \overline{a}(x).\, x \to b \;\; x \text{ fresh} \\
(\!|\sum_{i\in I} S_i|\!) \stackrel{\text{def}}{=} \sum_{i\in I}(\!|S_i|\!) & (\!|\nu\, x\, P|\!) \stackrel{\text{def}}{=} \nu\, x\,(\!|P|\!) \\
(\!|P \mid Q|\!) \stackrel{\text{def}}{=} (\!|P|\!) \mid (\!|Q|\!) & (\!|\,!P|\!) \stackrel{\text{def}}{=} \,!(\!|P|\!).
\end{array}
$$

Table 3: Definition of the encoding $(\!|\,.\,|\!)$, from $\pi^{\mathrm{i}}_{\mathrm{a}}$ to πI.

Lemma 4.2

1. *Let x and y be different from z. Then $\nu\, y\,(x \to y \mid y \to z) \gtrsim x \to z$.*

2. *Let P be a process in π_{a} and suppose that y does not occur free in P in input-subject position. Then $\nu\, y\,\big(y \to a \mid (\!|P|\!)\big) \gtrsim (\!|P\{a/y\}|\!)$.*

PROOF: Part 1 is proven by exhibiting the appropriate expansion relation.

Part 2 is proven by induction on P and exploiting part 1. The most interesting case is when $P = \overline{y}c$, for some c. Then we have:

$$
\begin{array}{rcl}
\nu\, y\,(y \to a \mid (\!|P|\!)) & = & \nu\, y\,\big(y \to a \mid \overline{y}(x).\, x \to c\big) \\
& & \text{(def. of } (\!|\,.\,|\!)) \\
& \sim & \nu\, y\,\big(y(x).(a(w).\, w \to x \mid y \to a) \mid \overline{y}(x).\, x \to c\big) \\
& & \text{(def. of } y \to a \text{ and laws for } !) \\
& \gtrsim & (\nu\, y, x)\big(a(w).\, w \to x \mid y \to a \mid x \to c\big) \\
& & \text{(a simple law for } \gtrsim) \\
& \sim & a(w).(\nu\, y, x)\big(w \to x \mid x \to c \mid y \to a\big) \\
& & \text{(laws for } \mid \text{ and } (\nu\, y, x)) \\
& \sim & a(w).\nu\, x\,\big(w \to x \mid \nu\, y\,(x \to c \mid y \to a)\big) \\
& & \text{(laws for } \nu\, y) \\
& \stackrel{\text{def}}{=} & P_1\,.
\end{array}
$$

Now, we have to distinguish whether $c = y$ or $c \neq y$. Suppose that $c = y$ (the case $c \neq y$ can be easily accommodated). Then applying part 1 of the lemma we get $\nu\, y\,(x \to c \mid y \to a) \gtrsim x \to a$, by which we have:

$$
\begin{array}{rcll}
P_1 & \gtrsim & a(w).\nu\, x\,(w \to x \mid x \to a) & \\
& \gtrsim & a(w).\, w \to a & \text{(applying part 1 again)} \\
& = & (\!|\overline{x}x\{a/x\}|\!) & \text{(def. of } (\!|\,.\,|\!)).
\end{array}
$$

□

The following proposition shows the tight correspondence between transitions of P and transitions of $(\!|P|\!)$.

Proposition 4.3 (strong operational correspondences) *Let P be a process in $\pi^{\mathrm{i}}_{\mathrm{a}}$.*

a) Suppose that $P \xrightarrow{\mu} P'$. Then we have:

1. $\mu = a(x)$ *implies* $(\!|P|\!) \xrightarrow{a(x)} \gtrsim (\!|P'|\!)$;

2. $\mu = \overline{a}b$ *implies* $(\!|P|\!) \xrightarrow{\overline{a}(x)} \gtrsim x \to b \mid (\!|P'|\!)$, *with* $x \notin \mathrm{fn}(P')$;

3. $\mu = \overline{a}(b)$ *implies* $(\!|P|\!) \xrightarrow{\overline{a}(x)} \gtrsim \nu b(x \to b \mid (\!|P'|\!))$, *with* $x \notin \mathrm{fn}(P')$;

4. $\mu = \tau$ *implies* $(\!|P|\!) \xrightarrow{\tau} \gtrsim (\!|P'|\!)$.

b) The converse of part a), i.e.: Suppose that $(\!|P|\!) \xrightarrow{\mu} P_1$. *Then there is* $P' \in \pi^{\mathrm{i}}_{\mathrm{a}}$ *s.t.:*

1. $\mu = a(x)$ *implies* $P \xrightarrow{a(x)} P'$ *with* $P_1 \gtrsim (\!|P'|\!)$;

2. $\mu = \overline{a}(x)$ *implies either:*

   2.a) $P \xrightarrow{\overline{a}b} P'$, *with* $x \notin \mathrm{fn}(P')$ *and* $P_1 \gtrsim x \to b \mid (\!|P'|\!)$, *or*

   2.b) $P \xrightarrow{\overline{a}(b)} P'$, *with* $x \notin \mathrm{fn}(P')$ *and* $P_1 \gtrsim \nu b(x \to b \mid (\!|P'|\!))$;

3. $\mu = \tau$ *implies* $P \xrightarrow{\tau} P'$, *with* $P_1 \gtrsim (\!|P'|\!)$.

Proof: Each part of the lemma is proven by transition induction. The only subtle points arise in the proof of parts a)(4) and b)(3), where also Lemma 4.2(2) is used. As an example, we show part a)(4). The only non-trivial case is when the last rule applied for deriving $P \xrightarrow{\tau} P'$ is a communication rule (we suppose for simplicity that the communicated name is free; the case when it is restricted can be easily accommodated):

$$\mathtt{Com}: \frac{P_1 \xrightarrow{\overline{a}b} P_1',\ P_2 \xrightarrow{a(x)} P_2'}{P_1 \mid P_2 \xrightarrow{\tau} P_1 \mid P_2\{b/x\}}.$$

By induction hypothesis, we have that:

$$(\!|P_1|\!) \xrightarrow{\overline{a}(x)} \gtrsim x \to b \mid (\!|P_1'|\!) \text{ with } x \notin \mathrm{fn}(P_1'), \text{ and } (\!|P_2|\!) \xrightarrow{a(x)} \gtrsim (\!|P_2'|\!). \qquad (2)$$

Then we have that:

$$\begin{array}{llll} (\!|P_1 \mid P_2|\!) & \xrightarrow{\tau} \gtrsim & \nu x\big(x \to b \mid (\!|P_1' \mid P_2'|\!)\big) & \text{(from (2) and interaction)} \\ & \gtrsim & (\!|(P_1' \mid P_2')\{b/x\}|\!) & \text{(Lemma 4.2(2)).} \\ & = & (\!|P_1' \mid P_2'\{b/x\}|\!) & \text{(since } x \notin \mathrm{fn}(P_1')\text{).} \end{array}$$

□

Remark 4.4 Note in the above proof that, since P_2 is a $\pi^{\mathrm{i}}_{\mathrm{a}}$ process, name x does not appear in P_2' in input-subject position: this fact permits applying Lemma 4.2(2). This is the point in the technical development where the "inversion of polarity" property of $\pi^{\mathrm{i}}_{\mathrm{a}}$ turns out to be essential.

The proof of the next tworesults is similar to the corresponding proofs for $\{\!|\,.\,|\!\}$.

Proposition 4.5

a) $P \downarrow a$ *if and only if* $(\!|P|\!) \downarrow a$.

b) $P \Longrightarrow P'$ *implies* $(\!|P|\!) \Longrightarrow \gtrsim (\!|P'|\!)$;

c) $(\!|P|\!) \Longrightarrow P_1$ *implies that there is* P' *s.t.* $P \Longrightarrow P'$ *and* $P_1 \gtrsim (\!|P'|\!)$.

d) $P \Downarrow a$ *if and only if* $(\!|P|\!) \Downarrow a$.

Theorem 4.6 (full abstraction of $(\!|\,.\,|\!)$ w.r.t. barbed bisimilarity) *Let P and Q be any two processes in* π_a^i. *Then* $P \simeq Q$ *if and only if* $(\!|P|\!) \simeq (\!|Q|\!)$.

In order to extend the encoding $(\!|\,.\,|\!)$ to polyadic π_a^i, it is enough to replace the input prefix and output prefix clauses of Table 3 with the following two:

$$(\!|a(\tilde{x}).P|\!) \stackrel{\text{def}}{=} a(\tilde{x}).(\!|P|\!), \quad (\!|\overline{a}\langle\tilde{b}\rangle|\!) \stackrel{\text{def}}{=} \overline{a}(\tilde{x}).\,\tilde{x} \to \tilde{b}$$

where, for $\tilde{x} = (x_1, \ldots, x_k)$ and $\tilde{b} = (b_1, \ldots, b_k)$, $\tilde{x} \to \tilde{b}$ stands for $x_1 \to b_1 \mid \cdots \mid x_k \to b_k$. Again, the proofs are easily extended. We omit the details.

One might wonder whether our encoding is fully abstract w.r.t. weak bisimilarity. The answer is negative, as shown by the following counter-example.

Counterexample 4.7 (non-full abstraction of $(\!|\,.\,|\!)$ w.r.t. weak bisimilarity) Consider the processes in π_a^i: $P \stackrel{\text{def}}{=} Eq(a,b) \mid \overline{c}a$ and $Q \stackrel{\text{def}}{=} Eq(a,b) \mid \overline{c}b$, where $Eq(a,b) \stackrel{\text{def}}{=} !\,a(x).\overline{b}x \mid !\,b(x).\overline{a}x$ is Honda's *equalizer* [10]. Of course, $P \not\simeq Q$, but $(\!|P|\!) \approx (\!|Q|\!)$. The proof proceeds by first showing that for any z different from a and b, the relation $\mathcal{R}$ defined as:
$\{\,((\!|Eq(a,b)|\!) \mid z \to b, (\!|Eq(a,b)|\!) \mid z \to a\,), ((\!|Eq(a,b)|\!) \mid z \to a, (\!|Eq(a,b)|\!) \mid z \to b\,)\}$
is a weak bisimulation *up to expansion and up to context* and hence is contained in $\approx$ [4, 19]. From this fact, it easily follows that the relation $\{((\!|P|\!),(\!|Q|\!)),((\!|Q|\!),(\!|P|\!))\} \cup \approx$ is a weak bisimulation up to context [4], and hence $(\!|P|\!) \approx (\!|Q|\!)$.

Note that, from an observational point of view, in the absence of matching it is perfectly reasonable to regard the processes P and Q as equivalent, because the equalizer $Eq(a,b)$ makes a and b indistinguishable under any context. Indeed, P and Q are barbed congruent, i.e. they are barbed bisimilar under any context. This leaves open the possibility that $(\!|\,.\,|\!)$ be fully abstract for barbed congruence as well: but the proof or disproof of this fact seems to be quite difficult.

Let us define now the encoding $[\![\,.\,]\!]$ from π_a to πI as the composition of $\{\!|\,.\,|\!\}$ and $(\!|\,.\,|\!)$, thus: $[\![P]\!] \stackrel{\text{def}}{=} (\!|\{\!|P|\!\}|\!)$. As an easy consequence of Theorems 3.8 and 4.6, we get the result we were most interested in:

Corollary 4.8 (full abstraction of $[\![\,.\,]\!]$ for barbed bisimilarity) *Let P and Q be two processes in* π_a. *Then* $P \simeq Q$ *if and only if* $[\![P]\!] \simeq [\![Q]\!]$.

5 Conclusions

In this paper, we have provided an encoding from asynchronous π-calculus to πI which is fully abstract on the reductions relations of the two calculi, thus proving that external mobility can be programmed via internal mobility.

For future work, it would be interesting to investigate full abstraction of (variations of) our encoding w.r.t. relations finer than barbed bisimilarity, such as barbed congruence or weak bisimilarity. The existence of these encodings would give evidence that it is possible to *reason* (not only program) on the π-calculus using the simpler theory of πI.

Relationships between πI and the join-calculus should be investigated. Indeed, the join-calculus naturally enjoys the "inversion of polarity" condition on input actions that makes it possible to define a simple encoding from π_a^i to πI. This suggests that a translation of the join-calculus into πI might be even simpler than the translation of π_a presented in this work. Also, the first of our encodings suggests that it might be possible to recast, in a traditional name-passing setting, some features of the join-calculus (like the unique-receiver property), by imposing to π_a^i natural syntactic limitations and/or typing disciplines, without loosing (much) expressive power. Similar work in this direction is independently being made by R. Amadio [2].

Acknowledgments

I am grateful to Davide Sangiorgi for having pointed to me the research direction pursued in the paper. Three anonymous referees provided valuable comments.

References

[1] Arun-Kumar and M. Hennessy. An efficiency preorder for processes. *Acta Informatica*, 29:737–760, 1992.

[2] R. Amadio. A note on objects and localities. Technical report, INRIA-Sophia Antipolis, 1996.

[3] G. Boudol. Asynchrony and the π-calculus (note). Technical Report RR-1702, INRIA-Sophia Antipolis, 1992.

[4] M. Boreale and D. Sangiorgi. A fully abstract semantics for causality in the π-calculus. Technical Report ECS-LFCS-94-297, Dept. of Comp. Sci., Edinburgh University, 1994. An extract appeared in *Proc. of STACS'95*, LNCS 900, Springer Verlag.

[5] M. Boreale and D. Sangiorgi. Some congruence properties for π-calculus bisimilarities. Technical Report RR-2870, INRIA-Sophia Antipolis, 1996.

[6] N. G. de Bruijn. Lambda-calculus notation with nameless dummies: a tool for automatic formula manipulation with application to the Church-Rosser theorem. *Indag. Math.*, 5(34):381–392, 1972.

[7] C. Fournet and G. Gonthier. The reflexive CHAM and the join-calculus. 1996. To appear in the *Proc. of POPL'96*.

[8] G. Ferrari, U. Montanari, and P. Quaglia. π-calculus with explicit substitutions. Technical report, Università di Pisa, 1994. Extended abstract appeared in *Proc. of MFCS'94*.

[9] M. Hansen, J. Kleist, and H. Hüttel. Bisimulations for asynchronous mobile processes. In *Proceedings of the Tbilisi Symposium on Language, Logic, and Computation.*, 1995. Research paper HCRC/RP-72, Human Communication Research Centre, University of Edinburgh.

[10] K. Honda. Two bisimilarities for the ν-calculus. Technical Report 92-002, Departement of Computer Science, Keio University, 1992.

[11] R. Milner. The polyadic π-calculus: A tutorial. Technical Report ECS-LFCS-91-180, LFCS, Dept. of Computer Science, Edinburgh Univ., 1991.

[12] R. Milner. Functions as processes. *Mathematical Structure in Computer Science*, 2(2):119–141, 1992.

[13] R. Milner, J. Parrow, and D. Walker. A calculus of mobile processes, part I and II. *Information and Computation*, 100:1 -41 and 42–78, 1992.

[14] J. Parrow and D. Sangiorgi. Algebraic theories for name-passing calculi. *Information and Computation*, 120(2):174–197, 1995.

[15] D. Sangiorgi. *Expressing Mobility in Process Algebras: First-Order and Higher-Order Paradigms.* PhD thesis, Department of Computer Science, University of Edinburgh, 1992.

[16] D. Sangiorgi. A theory of bisimulation for the π-calculus. In E. Best, editor, *Proceedings of CONCUR '93, LNCS 715.* Springer-Verlag, Berlin, 1993. To appear in *Acta Informatica.*

[17] D. Sangiorgi. Locality and non-interleaving semantics in calculi for mobile processes. Technical Report ECS–LFCS–94–282, LFCS, Dept. of Computer Science, Edinburgh University, 1994. An extract appeared in *Proc. TACS '94, LNCS*, Springer-Verlag.

[18] D. Sangiorgi. Lazy functions and mobile processes. Technical Report RR-2515, INRIA, 1995.

[19] D. Sangiorgi. π-calculus, internal mobility, and agent-passing calculi. Technical Report RR-2539, INRIA, 1995. Extended Abstract in *Proc. of TAPSOFT'95.*

[20] D. Sangiorgi and R. Milner. The problem of "Weak Bisimulation up-to". In W.R. Cleveland, editor, *Proceedings of CONCUR '92*, volume 630, pages 32–46. Springer Verlag, 1992.

Decoding Choice Encodings

Uwe Nestmann[1] * Benjamin C. Pierce[2] **

[1] Friedrich-Alexander-Universität Erlangen-Nürnberg, Informatik VII, Martensstraße 3, D-91058 Erlangen
[2] University of Cambridge, Computer Laboratory, New Museums Site, Pembroke Street, Cambridge CB2 3QG

Abstract. We study two encodings of the ***asynchronous π-calculus*** with ***input-guarded choice*** into its choice-free fragment. One encoding is divergence-free, but refines the atomic commitment of choice into gradual commitment. The other preserves atomicity, but introduces divergence. The divergent encoding is fully abstract with respect to weak bisimulation, but the more natural divergence-free encoding is not. Instead, we show that it is fully abstract with respect to ***coupled simulation***, a slightly coarser — but still coinductively defined — equivalence that does not enforce bisimilarity of internal branching decisions. The correctness proofs for the two choice encodings exploit the properties of ***decodings*** from translations to source terms.

1 Introduction

The problem of implementing the concurrent choice operator in terms of lower-level constructs is interesting from a number of points of view. Theoretically, it contributes new insight on the expressivity of process calculi and the computational content of choice. More practically, it provides correctness arguments supporting the design of high-level concurrent languages on top of process calculi. Furthermore, it is tightly related to the distributed implementation of synchronization [14, 17, 12, 3].

Our interest in the study of choice encodings originates from the design and implementation of the high-level concurrent language Pict [19, 20], an asynchronous choice-free π-calculus [7, 2] enriched with several layers of encoded syntactic sugar. There, choice is provided as a library module by a straightforward encoding. Surprisingly, however, this encoding turns out not to be valid with respect to standard weak bisimulation.

For the formal study, we use standard π-calculus notation for restriction $(\nu x)\,P$ of name x to process P, parallel composition $P_1|P_2$, input $y(x).P$ of a name from channel y for use as x in P, and output $\overline{y}\langle z\rangle$ of name z on channel y. Furthermore, $\prod$ and $\sum$ denote indexed parallel composition and input-guarded choice, respectively. For convenience, we introduce the conditional

---

* `Uwe.Nestmann@informatik.uni-erlangen.de`, supported by the DFG, Sonderforschungsbereich 182, project C2, and by the DAAD-programs ARC and HSPII-AUFE.

** `Benjamin.Pierce@cl.cam.ac.uk`, supported by the British SERC.

form test l then P else Q which performs a case analysis by reading from l one of the special names t or f, and behaving afterwards like P or Q, respectively.

We study two variants of the choice encoding. The non-divergent version, which is more interesting from a pragmatic perspective, will occupy most of our attention. For each choice expression, the translation

$$\mathcal{C}\Big[\!\Big[\sum_{j\in J} y_j(x).P_j \Big]\!\Big] \stackrel{\text{def}}{=} (\nu l)\Big(\bar{l}\langle t\rangle \;\Big|\; \prod_{j\in J} \mathit{Branch}_l\langle\, y_j(x).P_j \,\rangle \Big)$$

runs a mutual exclusion protocol, installing a local lock —a message that carries a special name— on the parallel composition of its branches. The branches

$$\mathit{Branch}_l\langle\, y_j(x).P_j \,\rangle \stackrel{\text{def}}{=} y_j(x) \,.\, \mathsf{test}\ l\ \mathsf{then}\ (\, \mathcal{C}[\![P_j]\!] \mid \bar{l}\langle f\rangle\,)\ \mathsf{else}\ (\, \overline{y_j}\langle x\rangle \mid \bar{l}\langle f\rangle\,)$$

concurrently try to test the lock after reading messages from the environment. Only the first branch managing to interrogate the lock will proceed with its continuation (then) and thereby commit the choice — every other branch will then be forced to resend its message and abort its continuation (else). The resending of messages by non-chosen branches essentially reflects the asynchronous character of the encoding. For an asynchronous observer, who can not detect when a message is consumed by a receptor, the resending of messages is immaterial, and so this encoding seems intuitively to be correct.

However, even for the asynchronous observer, it turns out that source terms and their $\mathcal{C}$-translations are not weakly bisimilar. The reason is that the latter carry out commitments only gradually, resulting in intermediate states which do not correspond any source term. In order to deal with partially committed states, we characterize the correctness of the encoding as a pair of opposite simulations which are *coupled* by requiring that less committed (i.e. simulating) processes can always internally evolve into more committed (i.e. simulated) processes [17].

For comparison, we also study another encoding that introduces an alternate path in each branch of a choice that allows it to "back out" and return to its initial state after it has taken the lock. This encoding avoids gradual commitments and is fully abstract up weak bisimilarity. However, it is pragmatically unsatisfactory since it introduces divergence.

The remainder of the paper is organized as follows. We first introduce the setting of an asynchronous π-calculus (Section 2). Then, we present and compare the divergence-free encoding $\mathcal{C}$ and the divergent encoding $\mathcal{D}$ (Section 3). Based on an intermediate language which lets us factor the $\mathcal{C}$-encoding, we define two *decoding* functions that constitute a coupled simulation (Section 4). This leads to our main result: for all source terms S,

$$S \rightleftarrows \mathcal{C}[\![S]\!]$$

where $\rightleftarrows$ denotes asynchronous coupled simulation equivalence (Section 5). Finally, we discuss some subtleties of our results and sketch related and future work (Section 6). Proofs of technical lemmas are omitted in this summary, but can be found in the full version [16].

2 Technical preliminaries

Many variants of the π-calculus [13] have appeared in the recent process algebra literature. We use here an asynchronous, first-order, monadic π-calculus [7, 2]. Replication is restricted to input processes and evaluated lazily, i.e. spawning copies only by means of communication. For notational convenience, we use a conditional form based on special boolean names. The choice operator is finite, and all the branches of a choice must be guarded by input prefixes.

2.1 Syntax

Let $\mathbf{N}$ be a countable set of *names*. Let the *booleans* $\mathbf{B}$ be $\{t, f\}$ with $\mathbf{B} \cap \mathbf{N} = \emptyset$ and *values* $\mathbf{V}$ be $\mathbf{N} \cup \mathbf{B}$. The set $\mathbb{S}$ of *processes* P is defined by the grammar

$$
\begin{aligned}
R &::= y(x).P \\
P &::= R \;\mid\; !R \;\mid\; \sum_{j \in J} R_j \;\mid\; \textsf{test } y \textsf{ then } P \textsf{ else } P \\
&\quad\;\; \mathbf{0} \;\mid\; \overline{y}\langle z\rangle \;\mid\; (\nu x)\, P \;\mid\; P|P \;\mid
\end{aligned}
$$

where $y, z \in \mathbf{V}$, $x \in \mathbf{N}$, and J ranges over finite sets of indices. We also use the abbreviation $R_1 + R_2$ to denote binary choice. Operator precedence is, in decreasing order of binding strength: (1) prefixing, restriction, replication, (2) substitution, (3) parallel composition, and (4) choice. A term is *guarded* when it occurs as a subterm of an input prefix.

The operational semantics of restriction, parallel composition, input and output is standard. The form $!R$ denotes the replication operator restricted to input-prefixes. In $\overline{y}\langle z\rangle$ and $y(x)$, the name y is called the *subject*, whereas x, z are called *objects*. We refer to outputs as *messages* and to input, replicated input, and choice as *receptors*. An expression test y then P else Q can be seen as abbreviation for $y(b)$. if b then P else Q with the usual meaning of if.

The definitions of name substitution and α-conversion are standard. A name x is *bound* in P if P contains an x-binding operator, i.e. either a restriction (νx) or an input prefix $y(x)$ as a subterm. A name x is *free* in P if it occurs outside the scope of an x-binding operator. We write $bn(P)$ and $fn(P)$ for the sets of P's bound and free names; $n(P)$ is their union. Renaming of bound names by α-conversion $=_\alpha$ is as usual. Substitution $P\{^z/_x\}$ is given by replacing all free occurrences of x in P with z, first α-converting P to avoid capture. Use of the boolean constants t and f as bound variables is forbidden.

2.2 Operational semantics

Let $y \in \mathbf{N}$ and $z \in \mathbf{V}$. The set $\mathbf{L}$ of *labels* μ is generated by

$$\mu \;::=\; \overline{y}\langle \nu z\rangle \;\mid\; \overline{y}\langle z\rangle \;\mid\; y\langle z\rangle \;\mid\; \tau$$

representing the bound and free output, early input, and internal action. The functions bn and fn yield the bound names (those marked by ν in bound outputs) and free names (all others) of a label. Let $n(\mu)$ denote their union $bn(\mu) \cup fn(\mu)$.

The operational semantics for processes is given as a transition system with $\mathbb{S}$ as its set of states. The transition relation $\longrightarrow \subseteq \mathbb{S} \times \mathbf{L} \times \mathbb{S}$ is defined as the smallest relation generated by the set of rules in Table 1. We use an *early* instantiation scheme, as expressed in the three *INP*-rules and the rules *TRUE/FALSE* and *COM/CLOSE*, since it allows us to define bisimulation without clauses for name-instantiation and since it allows for a more intuitive modelling in Section 4. Note that the rules *TRUE/FALSE* follow the intuition of combining input-prefix with a subsequent test for the input value. As usual, rule *OPEN* prepares for scope extrusion, whereas in *CLOSE* the previously opened scope of a bound name is closed upon its reception.

Weak arrows $\Rightarrow$ denote the reflexive and transitive closure of internal transitions; arrows with hats describe that two processes are either related by a particular transition or else equal in the case of an internal transition.

$$\Rightarrow \stackrel{\text{def}}{=} \xrightarrow{\tau}{}^{*} \qquad \xrightarrow{\hat{\mu}} \stackrel{\text{def}}{=} \begin{cases} \xrightarrow{\mu} & \text{if } \mu \neq \tau \\ \xrightarrow{\tau} \cup = & \text{if } \mu = \tau \end{cases} \qquad \begin{array}{l} \stackrel{\hat{\mu}}{\Longrightarrow} \stackrel{\text{def}}{=} \Rightarrow \xrightarrow{\hat{\mu}} \Rightarrow \\ \stackrel{\mu}{\Longrightarrow} \stackrel{\text{def}}{=} \Rightarrow \xrightarrow{\mu} \Rightarrow \end{array}$$

2.3 Asynchronous bisimulation

The concept of asynchronous messages suggests a non-standard way of observing processes. Since sending a message to an observed system is not blocking for the observer, the latter can not immediately detect whether the message was actually received, or not. The only possible observations are messages eventually coming back from the system, maybe caused by the former input. Different formulations of asynchronous bisimulation (inducing the same equivalence) have been proposed in the literature, based on a modified labelled input rule [8], on output-only barbed congruences [9], and on a standard labelled semantics with asynchronous observers [1]. Here, we follow the latter approach.

Definition 2.1 (Simulation, bisimulation). A binary relation $\mathcal{S}$ on $\mathbb{S} \times \mathbb{S}$ is a *strong simulation* if $(P, Q) \in \mathcal{S}$ implies:

- if $P \xrightarrow{\mu} P'$, where μ is either τ or output with $bn(\mu) \cap fn(P|Q) = \emptyset$, then there is Q' such that $Q \xrightarrow{\mu} Q'$ and $(P', Q') \in \mathcal{S}$
- $(\,\overline{a}\langle z\rangle|P\,,\,\overline{a}\langle z\rangle|Q\,) \in \mathcal{S}$ for arbitrary messages $\overline{a}\langle z\rangle$.

$\mathcal{B}$ is called a *strong bisimulation* if both $\mathcal{B}$ and $\mathcal{B}^{-1}$ are strong simulations. Let $\sim$ denote the largest strong bisimulation.

Replacing $Q \xrightarrow{\mu} Q'$ with $Q \stackrel{\hat{\mu}}{\Longrightarrow} Q'$ in this definition yields the *weak* versions of the above relations. Q *weakly simulates* P, written $P \preccurlyeq Q$, if $(P, Q) \in \mathcal{S}$ for some weak simulation $\mathcal{S}$. Let $\approx$ denote the largest *weak bisimulation.*

As shown in [6, 1], weak early asynchronous bisimulation is a congruence on $\mathbb{S}$ without test-expressions; it is easy to extend this result to test-expressions, since they behave like input expressions. (This would not be true for if-conditionals, which behave like simple matching operators.)

Lemma 2.2. *$\approx$ is a congruence on $\mathbb{S}$.*

$$\textit{E-INP:} \quad y(x).P \xrightarrow{y\langle z\rangle} P\{z/x\}$$

$$\textit{R-INP:} \quad !\,y(x).P \xrightarrow{y\langle z\rangle} P\{z/x\} \mid !\,y(x).P$$

$$\textit{C-INP:} \quad \sum_{j\in J} y_j(x).P_j \xrightarrow{y_k\langle z\rangle} P_k\{z/x\} \qquad \text{if } k \in J$$

$$\textit{TRUE:} \quad \text{test } l \text{ then } P \text{ else } Q \xrightarrow{l\langle t\rangle} P$$

$$\textit{FALSE:} \quad \text{test } l \text{ then } P \text{ else } Q \xrightarrow{l\langle f\rangle} Q$$

$$\textit{OUT:} \quad \overline{y}\langle z\rangle \xrightarrow{\overline{y}\langle z\rangle} 0$$

$$\textit{COM}^*: \quad \frac{P \xrightarrow{\overline{y}\langle z\rangle} P' \qquad Q \xrightarrow{y\langle z\rangle} Q'}{P \mid Q \xrightarrow{\tau} P' \mid Q'}$$

$$\textit{RES:} \quad \frac{P \xrightarrow{\mu} P'}{(\nu x)\,P \xrightarrow{\mu} (\nu x)\,P'} \qquad \text{if } x \notin n(\mu)$$

$$\textit{OPEN:} \quad \frac{P \xrightarrow{\overline{y}\langle x\rangle} P'}{(\nu x)\,P \xrightarrow{\overline{y}(\nu x)} P'} \qquad \text{if } y \neq x$$

$$\textit{CLOSE}^*: \quad \frac{P \xrightarrow{\overline{y}(\nu z)} P' \qquad Q \xrightarrow{y\langle z\rangle} Q'}{P \mid Q \xrightarrow{\tau} (\nu z)(\,P' \mid Q'\,)} \qquad \text{if } z \notin fn(Q)$$

$$\textit{PAR}^*: \quad \frac{P_1 \xrightarrow{\mu} P_1'}{P_1 \mid P_2 \xrightarrow{\mu} P_1' \mid P_2} \qquad \text{if } bn(\mu) \cap fn(P_2) = \emptyset$$

$$\textit{ALPHA:} \quad \frac{P \xrightarrow{\mu} P'}{Q \xrightarrow{\mu} P'} \qquad \text{if } P =_\alpha Q$$

* *and the evident symmetric rules*

Table 1. Early operational semantics

2.4 When weak bisimulation is still too strong ...

Every bisimulation $\mathcal{B}$ can be regarded as a pair $(\mathcal{S}_1, \mathcal{S}_2)$ of contrary simulations $\mathcal{S}_1$ and $\mathcal{S}_2^{-1}$, where $\mathcal{S}_1$ and $\mathcal{S}_2$ contain exactly the same pairs of processes, i.e. $\mathcal{S}_1 = \mathcal{B} = \mathcal{S}_2$. For some applications, this requirement is too strong, which led Parrow and Sjödin to develop the notion of *coupled simulation* [17].

In this paper, we use a formulation, as suggested in [5, 18], where coupling requires the ability of a simulating process to evolve into a simulated process by internal action. We recapitulate the formal definition:

Definition 2.3 (Coupled simulation). A *coupled simulation* is a pair $(\mathcal{S}_1, \mathcal{S}_2)$, where $\mathcal{S}_1$ and $\mathcal{S}_2^{-1}$ are weak simulations that satisfy

- if $(P, Q) \in \mathcal{S}_1$, then there is some Q' such that $Q \Rightarrow Q'$ and $(P, Q') \in \mathcal{S}_2$;
- if $(P, Q') \in \mathcal{S}_2$, then there is some P' such that $P \Rightarrow P'$ and $(P', Q') \in \mathcal{S}_1$.

Two processes P and Q are *coupled similar*, written $P \rightleftarrows Q$, if they are related by both components of some coupled simulation.

Using dotted lines to represent the simulations, the coupling property of $(\mathcal{S}_1, \mathcal{S}_2)$ may be depicted as an 'internally out-of-step bisimulation' by:

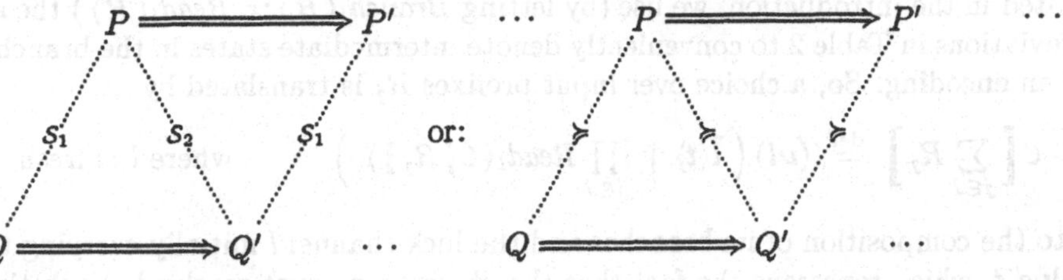

Of two processes contained in one component relation of some coupled simulation, the simulated (more committed) process is always a bit ahead of its simulating (less committed) counterpart. Intuitively, 'Q coupled simulates P' means that 'Q is *at most as committed* as P' with respect to internal choices and that Q may internally evolve to a state Q' where it is *at least as committed* as P, i.e. where P coupled simulates Q'.

Fact 2.4.1. $\approx \;\subset\; \rightleftarrows \;\subset\; \preccurlyeq$.

On processes without infinite τ-sequences, coupled simulation is strictly finer than testing equivalence, so it represents a reasonable (and coinductively defined) candidate in the lattice of process equivalences [5].

Furthermore, the coupled simulation $\rightleftarrows$ is an equivalence and, by similar arguments as for the congruence properties of $\approx$, it constitutes a congruence in our asynchronous setting.

Proposition 2.4. $\rightleftarrows$ *is a congruence on* $\mathbf{S}$.

Later on, we will make use of the following lemma.

Lemma 2.5. *Let* $(\mathcal{S}_1, \mathcal{S}_2)$ *be a coupled simulation and* $\mathcal{B}$ *a weak bisimulation. Then the composite pair* $(\mathcal{S}_1\mathcal{B}, \mathcal{S}_2\mathcal{B})$ *is again a coupled simulation.*

3 Encoding choice

This section contains two simple encodings of $\mathbb{S}$ into its choice-free fragment, $\mathbb{T}$. Both encodings $\mathcal{C}[\![\,]\!], \mathcal{D}[\![\,]\!] : \mathbb{S} \to \mathbb{T}$ map terms of the source language $\mathbb{S}$ inductively into the target language $\mathbb{T}$. Since both functions coincide on all constructors but choice, we use a common homomorphic scheme of definition, where $[\![\,]\!]$ may denote either $\mathcal{C}[\![\,]\!]$ or $\mathcal{D}[\![\,]\!]$:

$$
\begin{array}{rclrcl}
[\![\mathbf{0}]\!] & \stackrel{\text{def}}{=} & \mathbf{0} & [\![P_1|P_2]\!] & \stackrel{\text{def}}{=} & [\![P_1]\!] \mid [\![P_2]\!] \\
[\![\overline{y}\langle z\rangle]\!] & \stackrel{\text{def}}{=} & \overline{y}\langle z\rangle & [\![(\nu x)P]\!] & \stackrel{\text{def}}{=} & (\nu x)[\![P]\!] \\
[\![y(x).P]\!] & \stackrel{\text{def}}{=} & y(x).[\![P]\!] & [\![!P]\!] & \stackrel{\text{def}}{=} & ![\![P]\!]
\end{array}
$$

$$
[\![\mathsf{test}\ y\ \mathsf{then}\ P_1\ \mathsf{else}\ P_2]\!] \stackrel{\text{def}}{=} \mathsf{test}\ y\ \mathsf{then}\ [\![P_1]\!]\ \mathsf{else}\ [\![P_2]\!]
$$

Two slightly different ways of implementing choices will be considered, differing only with respect to the possibility of undoing activities of branches.

Divergence-free protocol. In order to formulate the choice algorithm that we presented in the introduction, we use (by letting $\mathit{Branch}_l\langle R\rangle := \mathit{Read}_l\langle R\rangle$) the abbreviations in Table 2 to conveniently denote intermediate states in the branches of an encoding. So, a choice over input prefixes R_j is translated by

$$
\mathcal{C}\Big[\!\!\Big[\sum_{j\in J} R_j\Big]\!\!\Big] \stackrel{\text{def}}{=} (\nu l)\Big(\,\bar{l}\langle t\rangle \mid \prod_{j\in J} \mathit{Read}_l\langle \mathcal{C}[\![R_j]\!]\rangle\,\Big) \qquad \text{where } l \text{ is fresh}
$$

into the composition of its branches and the lock channel l initially carrying the value t, which represens the fact that the choice is not yet resolved. Each time the lock is read, it is immediately reinstalled with the value f. This guarantees mutual exclusion: at most one branch will ever be chosen.

Protocol with undo-loops. The main difference from the encoding $\mathcal{C}[\![\,]\!]$ is that a supposedly committed branch may still change its mind and deny the commitment, releasing the lock and also the value that it has consumed from the environment. This behavior is realized by modifying the *Test*-abbreviation of the $\mathcal{C}$-encoding as shown in Table 2, where the operator $\oplus$ for internal choice is encoded by a concurrent race for a shared channel. It is crucial to reinstall t in the case that a successfully activated branch undoes its activity. In order to have a fresh copy of the branch in initial state available after having undone an activity, we use replication (by letting $\mathit{Branch}_l\langle R\rangle := !\mathit{Read}_l\langle R\rangle$) and get:

$$
\mathcal{D}\Big[\!\!\Big[\sum_{j\in J} R_j\Big]\!\!\Big] \stackrel{\text{def}}{=} (\nu l)\Big(\,\bar{l}\langle t\rangle \mid \prod_{j\in J} !\,\mathit{Read}_l\langle \mathcal{D}[\![R_j]\!]\rangle\,\Big) \qquad \text{where } l \text{ is fresh}
$$

In their $\mathcal{D}$-translation, convergent branches of a choice term possibly engage in internal loops. In contrast, the $\mathcal{C}$-encoding does not add divergence to the behavior of source terms, as can be observed by inspection of the *Test*-abbreviations in Table 2. (In [16], we provide formal arguments.) However, we shall see that the $\mathcal{D}$-encoding is interesting despite its divergence.

	$Read_l\langle R\rangle$	$\stackrel{\text{def}}{=}$	$y(x).Test_l\langle R\rangle$
$\mathcal{C}[\![\,]\!]:$	$Test_l\langle R\rangle$	$\stackrel{\text{def}}{=}$	test l then $Commit_l\langle R\rangle$ else $Abort_l\langle R\rangle$
$\mathcal{D}[\![\,]\!]:$	$Test_l\langle R\rangle$	$\stackrel{\text{def}}{=}$	test l then $Commit_l\langle R\rangle \oplus Undo_l\langle R\rangle$ else $Abort_l\langle R\rangle$
	$Undo_l\langle R\rangle$	$\stackrel{\text{def}}{=}$	$\bar{l}\langle t\rangle \mid \bar{y}\langle x\rangle$
	$Commit_l\langle R\rangle$	$\stackrel{\text{def}}{=}$	$\bar{l}\langle f\rangle \mid P$
	$Abort_l\langle R\rangle$	$\stackrel{\text{def}}{=}$	$\bar{l}\langle f\rangle \mid \bar{y}\langle x\rangle$
	$P \oplus Q$	$\stackrel{\text{def}}{=}$	$(\nu i)\,(\ \bar{i}\langle i\rangle \mid i(i).P \mid i(i).Q\ )$ with $i \notin fn(P\vert Q)$

Table 2. Abbreviations for encoding functions (with $R = y(x).P$)

Correctness results for encodings into process calculi are naturally based on some way of expressing the operational correspondence between source terms and their translations, i.e. between their transition systems. Since, in general, a single step of a source term is implemented by many steps at the target-level, some of the latter will be of only administrative nature, while some may be considered as *committing* since they correspond to progress at the source-level.

Let us call an encoding *prompt* if every initial step of a translated term is committing. For the operational correspondence of prompt encodings, it suffices to consider initial steps and to relate their derivatives to source term derivatives. In fact, most encodings studied up to now in the literature are prompt. However, our choice encodings are not: initial steps of translations are never committing. Consequently, we must explicitly deal with arbitrary intermediate states and relate them to equivalent source terms.

Since both encodings use a fragment of the source language as target and the labels in their transition systems are identical, we may compare source terms and translations directly. The following example serves to illustrate the difference between the $\mathcal{C}$- and $\mathcal{D}$-encodings as regards correctness. Let

$$S \equiv \overline{y_2}\langle z\rangle \mid N \qquad \textit{where} \qquad N \equiv y_1(x).P_1 + y_2(x).P_2$$

describe a binary choice in the presence of a single message matching the second branch, where P_1, P_2 are arbitrary target terms (i.e. not containing choices).

The transition systems of S and its translations $\mathcal{C}[\![S]\!]$ and $\mathcal{D}[\![S]\!]$ are depicted in Table 3. The dotted lines that are labeled with $\succcurlyeq$ are to be read from left to right; they represent two simulations: one on $\mathbb{S}\times\mathbb{T}$, and one on $\mathbb{T}\times\mathbb{S}$. The dotted lines that are labelled with $\approx$ represent a single bisimulation on $\mathbb{S}\times\mathbb{T}$. In the definition of asynchronous bisimulation, input transitions are only considered by the closure under contexts of arbitrary messages. Therefore, we only mention internal and output transitions in the depicted transitions systems since those are to be simulated literally. The reader is invited to check the simulations.

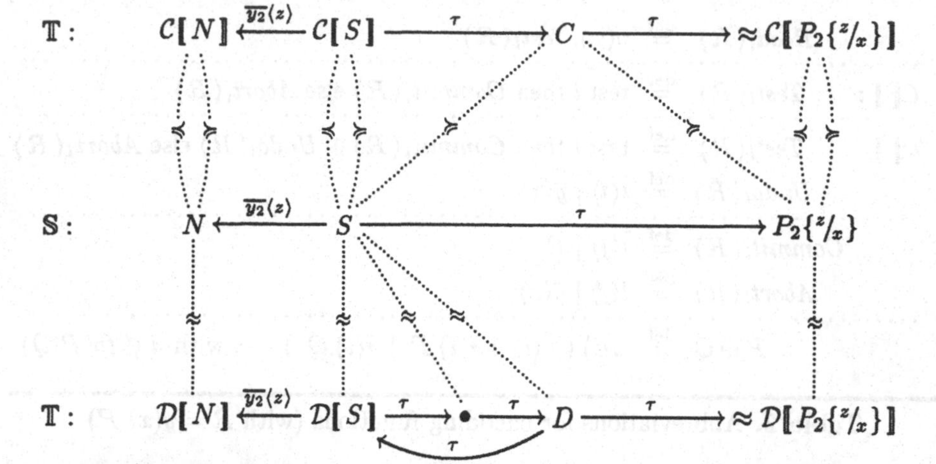

Table 3. Transition systems for the distinguishing example

We highlight C and D since they represent the intermediate states where a committing action is enabled: C may perform an action where the y_2-branch takes the lock; in D, that branch has already taken the lock, and the next step will be to internally decide to commit or to undo. We may phrase C as having *partially committed*: it is guaranteed that *one* of the branches will eventually be chosen, but, at that stage of commitment, it is not yet clear which one. As a consequence, the state C does not directly correspond to any source term with respect to weak bisimulation. In contrast, the state D in the $\mathcal{D}$-translation has not partially committed, since it can always back out, and therefore it directly corresponds to S unless it internally decides to commit.

It is instructive to convince oneself that the successor states of C and D will only be equivalent to $[\![P_2\{^z/_x\}]\!]$ up to asynchronous bisimulation. Both

$$S \not\approx \mathcal{C}[\![S]\!] \quad \text{and} \quad S \approx \mathcal{D}[\![S]\!]$$

hold, which together allow us to conclude that the $\mathcal{C}$-encoding is not fully abstract with respect to weak bisimulation. To be precise, it neither preserves nor reflects weak bisimulation: $\mathcal{C}[\![S_1]\!] \approx \mathcal{C}[\![S_2]\!]$ does not imply $S_1 \approx S_2$, since $S_1 = S$ and $S_2 = \mathcal{C}[\![S]\!]$ give the necessary counterexample. Also $S_1 \approx S_2$ does not imply $\mathcal{C}[\![S_1]\!] \approx \mathcal{C}[\![S_2]\!]$, as $S_1 = S$ and $S_2 = \mathcal{D}[\![S]\!]$ show.

The observation that $S \succcurlyeq C \succcurlyeq P_2\{^z/_x\}$ with $S \Rightarrow P_2\{^z/_x\}$ in the above example suggests *coupled simulation* as an appropriate notion of correctness for the $\mathcal{C}$-encoding. For the proof, we are faced with two technical problems arising from the need of dealing with partially committed intermediate states: (1) the analysis of the operational behavior of target processes that are not immediate derivatives of translations (this problem also applies to the $\mathcal{D}$-encoding); (2) we have to relate states like C to two different source states, one representing its *reset* (S), the other its *completed* commitment ($P_2\{^z/_x\}$).

4 Decoding choice

Associating a derivative of a translation with some source terms amounts to defining a mapping from target terms to source terms, i.e. to providing a decoding function. This is not straightforward since target terms do not provide enough structure to tell from which source terms they come.

We introduce *annotated source terms* as abbreviations for derivatives of translations of source terms. Each occurrence of choice is decorated with annotations that provide the information about which target state the choice inhabits, based on a representation of the choices' derivation history. By building literally upon source terms instead of the expanded target terms, annotated terms exhibit an explicit choice structure. For an arbitrary J-indexed choice with branches $R_j{=}y_j(x).P_j$ for $j \in J$, we use

- a partial function $V : J \rightharpoonup \mathbf{V}$, mapping choice indices to values, and
- a possibly empty set $B \subseteq J$ of choice indices such that $B \cap dom(V) = \emptyset$.

The definedness of $V(j)$ means that a value was read from the environment and is held by branch j. The set B records those branches which have already accessed the boolean lock; $B{=}\emptyset$ indicates that the choice has not yet committed.

Definition 4.1 (Annotated choice). Let $R_j{=}y_j(x).P_j$ for $j \in J$. Let $V : J \rightharpoonup \mathbf{V}$ and $B \subseteq J$ with $B \cap dom(V) = \emptyset$. Then the construct shown to the right is called an *annotated choice*.

$$\Big(\sum_{j\in J} R_j\Big)_B^V$$

Let $+$ and $-$ denote the extension and removal operations for sets and partial functions. Let $\mathbb{P}$ denote the language $\mathbb{S}$ by extending the grammar with a clause for annotated choice; its operational semantics is given by the rules in Tables 1 and 4. Extend the relations $\approx$ and $\rightleftarrows$ to $\mathbb{P}$. We distinguish three cases for choice constructors: *initial* for $V = \emptyset = B$, *partial* for $V \neq \emptyset$ and $B = \emptyset$, and *committed* for $B \neq \emptyset$. Committed choice, describing the behavior of aborted branches, exhibits the particularly useful property that it does not show any asynchronously observable activity (analogous to the *identity receptors* of [8]) but resending all the values that are currently held by its branches.

READ:	$\Big(\sum_{j\in J} R_j\Big)_B^V$	$\xrightarrow{y_k(z)}$	$\Big(\sum_{j\in J} R_j\Big)_B^{V+(k\mapsto z)}$	*if* $k \in J \setminus (V \cup B)$
COMMIT:	$\Big(\sum_{j\in J} R_j\Big)_\emptyset^V$	$\xrightarrow{\tau}$	$\Big(\sum_{j\in J} R_j\Big)_{\{k\}}^{V-(k\mapsto z)} \mid P_k\{^{V(k)}\!/\!_x\}$	*if* $k \in V$
ABORT:	$\Big(\sum_{j\in J} R_j\Big)_{B\neq\emptyset}^V$	$\xrightarrow{\tau}$	$\Big(\sum_{j\in J} R_j\Big)_{B+k}^{V-(k\mapsto z)} \mid \overline{y_k}\langle V(k)\rangle$	*if* $k \in V$

Table 4. Early operational semantics for annotated choice

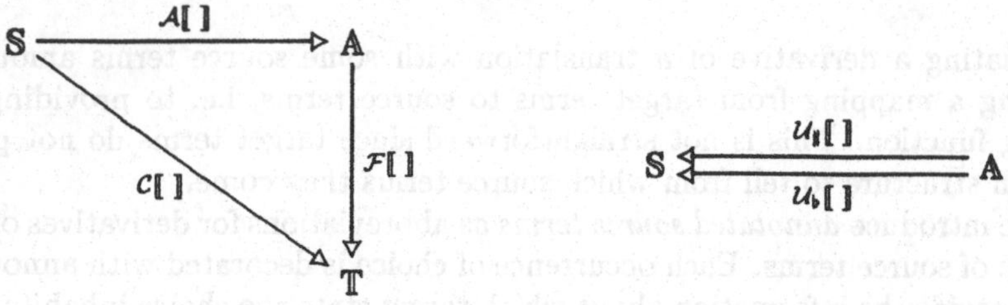

$$\mathcal{A}\Big[\!\!\Big[\sum_{j\in J} R_j\Big]\!\!\Big] \stackrel{\text{def}}{=} \Big(\sum_{j\in J} \mathcal{A}[\![R_j]\!]\Big)_\emptyset^\emptyset$$

$$\mathcal{F}\Big[\!\!\Big[\Big(\sum_{j\in J} R_j\Big)_B^V\Big]\!\!\Big] \stackrel{\text{def}}{=} (\nu l)\Big(\, \bar{l}\langle b\rangle \;\Big|\; \prod_{j\in J\setminus(V\cup B)} Read_l\langle\, \mathcal{F}[\![R_j]\!]\,\rangle \;\Big|\; \prod_{j\in V} Test_l\langle\, \mathcal{F}[\![R_j]\!]\,\rangle\{^{V(j)}/_x\}\Big)$$

where $b = t$ if $B = \emptyset$, and f otherwise

(initial): $$\mathcal{U}\Big[\!\!\Big[\Big(\sum_{j\in J} R_j\Big)_\emptyset^\emptyset\Big]\!\!\Big] \stackrel{\text{def}}{=} \sum_{j\in J} \mathcal{U}[\![R_j]\!]$$

(committed): $$\mathcal{U}\Big[\!\!\Big[\Big(\sum_{j\in J} R_j\Big)_{B\neq\emptyset}^V\Big]\!\!\Big] \stackrel{\text{def}}{=} \prod_{j\in V} \overline{y_j}\langle V(j)\rangle$$

(partial): $$\mathcal{U}_\flat\Big[\!\!\Big[\Big(\sum_{j\in J} R_j\Big)_\emptyset^{V\neq\emptyset}\Big]\!\!\Big] \stackrel{\text{def}}{=} \prod_{j\in V} \overline{y_j}\langle V(j)\rangle \;\Big|\; \sum_{j\in J} \mathcal{U}_\flat[\![R_j]\!]$$

$$\mathcal{U}_\sharp\Big[\!\!\Big[\Big(\sum_{j\in J} R_j\Big)_\emptyset^{V\neq\emptyset}\Big]\!\!\Big] \stackrel{\text{def}}{=} \prod_{j\in V-k} \overline{y_j}\langle V(j)\rangle \;\Big|\; \mathcal{U}_\sharp[\![P_k]\!]\{^{V(k)}/_x\}$$

where k denotes any of the partial commitments in V

Table 5. Factorization and decoding

Lemma 4.2. $\Big(\sum_{j\in J} R_j\Big)_{B\neq\emptyset}^V \approx \prod_{j\in V} \overline{y_j}\langle V(j)\rangle.$

For technical convenience, we use a language $\mathbb{A} \subset \mathbb{P}$ containing exactly those annotated terms that represent derivatives of translated source terms (cf. [16]). This enables inductive definitions of functions on arbitrarily complex abbreviated target terms, which we use for the factorization (with $\mathcal{C}[\![\,]\!] = \mathcal{F}[\![\,]\!] \circ \mathcal{A}[\![\,]\!]$) and decodings (with $\mathcal{U}[\![\,]\!] \circ \mathcal{A}[\![\,]\!] = \mathrm{id}$) in Table 5. All the functions act homomorphically on every constructor but choice according to the scheme in Section 3.

The annotating encoding $\mathcal{A}[\![\,]\!]$ maps source terms to abbreviated target terms. The flattening encoding $\mathcal{F}[\![\,]\!]$ expands abbreviations to target terms. Viewing the flattening as a relation, the correct interplay with the semantics of $\mathbb{A}$ is expressed by:

Proposition 4.3. *$\mathcal{F}$ is a strong bisimulation.*

The two decoding functions $\mathcal{U}$ map abbreviations back to source terms, each by exploiting the structure of terms in $\mathbb{A}$ exhibiting partial commitments explicitly. For non-partial choice constructors, the two decoding functions coincide; for partial choice, they act differently according to the intuition of resetting ($\mathcal{U}_\flat[\![\,]\!]$) and committing ($\mathcal{U}_\sharp[\![\,]\!]$). Viewing the decoding functions as relations, we can state our key proposition.

Proposition 4.4. *$(\mathcal{U}_\sharp^{-1}, \mathcal{U}_\flat^{-1})$ is a coupled simulation.*

5 Main results

In this section, we sketch the direct correspondence between source and target terms up to coupled simulation by exploiting the former results for the $\mathcal{A}$-encoding. In [16], we prove the divergence-freedom of the $\mathcal{C}$-encoding.

Reasoning about the annotated versions of choice allowed us to use their high-level structure for the decoding functions. We argued that we could concentrate on the annotated language $\mathbb{A}$, since its flattening $\mathcal{F}$ expanded the abbreviations correctly into target terms. In order to combine those ideas, let the simulations $\mathfrak{C}$ (completeness) and $\mathfrak{S}^{-1}$ (soundness) be defined by

$$\mathfrak{C} \stackrel{\text{def}}{=} \mathcal{U}_\sharp^{-1}\mathcal{F} \;\subset \mathbb{S}\times\mathbb{T} \qquad \text{and} \qquad \mathfrak{S} \stackrel{\text{def}}{=} \mathcal{U}_\flat^{-1}\mathcal{F} \;\subset \mathbb{S}\times\mathbb{T}.$$

The results for abbreviated target terms in $\mathbb{A}$ carry over to target terms in $\mathbb{T}$.

Theorem 5.1. *$(\mathfrak{C}, \mathfrak{S})$ is a coupled simulation.*

Proof: By Propositions 4.3 and 4.4, and Lemma 2.5. □

Observe that $\mathfrak{C}$ is constructed from the committing decoding $\mathcal{U}_\sharp[\![\,]\!]$, so derivatives of target terms are at most as committed as their $\mathfrak{C}$-related source terms. Analogously, $\mathfrak{S}$ is constructed from the resetting decoding $\mathcal{U}_\flat[\![\,]\!]$, so derivatives of target terms are at least as committed as their $\mathfrak{S}$-related source terms.

The relations $\mathfrak{C}$ and $\mathfrak{S}$ are sufficiently big to contain all source and target terms and, in particular, to relate all source terms and their $\mathcal{C}$-translations.

Lemma 5.2. *For all $S \in \mathbb{S}$: $(S, \mathcal{C}[\![S]\!]) \in \mathfrak{C} \cap \mathfrak{S}$.*

Proof: Due to the factorization of $\mathcal{C}[\![\,]\!]$ into $\mathcal{A}[\![\,]\!]$ and $\mathcal{F}[\![\,]\!]$, we know that, for all $S \in \mathbb{S}$, the translation $\mathcal{A}[\![S]\!]$ yields a witness for $(S, \mathcal{C}[\![S]\!])$ being contained in both $\mathfrak{C}$ and $\mathfrak{S}$. □

The $\mathcal{C}$-encoding is operationally correct since every source term is simulated by its translation (completeness via $\mathfrak{C}$) and also itself simulates its translation (soundness via $\mathfrak{S}$). The result is even stronger since the simulations are coupled.

The $\mathcal{C}$-encoding is also behaviorally correct, in the sense that source terms and their $\mathcal{C}$-translations are semantically equivalent with respect to asynchronous coupled simulation.

Theorem 5.3 (Correctness of $\mathcal{C}$). *For all* $S \in \mathbb{S} : S \rightleftarrows \mathcal{C}[\![S]\!]$.

Proof: By Theorem 5.1 and Lemma 5.2. □

Since coupled simulation is only slightly weaker than weak bisimulation, Theorem 5.3 is a powerful statement of the correctness of the $\mathcal{C}$-encoding: source terms and their $\mathcal{C}$-translations have the same externally visible asynchronous branching behavior in every term context within $\mathbb{S}$.

Similarly, we can prove the correctness of the $\mathcal{D}$-encoding as the weak bisimulation equivalence of source terms and their $\mathcal{D}$-translations.

Theorem 5.4 (Correctness of $\mathcal{D}$). *For all* $S \in \mathbb{S} : S \approx \mathcal{D}[\![S]\!]$.

Although the correctness property for $\mathcal{D}[\![\ ]\!]$ is stronger than the corresponding property for $\mathcal{C}[\![\ ]\!]$, the latter has the advantage of being divergence-free.

Full abstraction, underlining the behavioral correctness of encodings, as

$$S_1 \rightleftarrows S_2 \text{ iff } \mathcal{C}[\![S_1]\!] \rightleftarrows \mathcal{C}[\![S_2]\!] \quad \text{and} \quad S_1 \approx S_2 \text{ iff } \mathcal{D}[\![S_1]\!] \approx \mathcal{D}[\![S_2]\!]$$

for all $S_1, S_2 \in \mathbb{S}$ in our case, can be retrieved from the above correctness statements as simple corollaries by applying transitivity of the congruences.

6 Conclusions

We have investigated two different encodings of the asynchronous π-calculus with input-guarded choice into its choice-free fragment. Several points deserve to be discussed in more detail.

Correctness: For both choice encodings, we provided a framework that allowed us to compare source terms and their translations directly. This enabled us to use a correctness notion that is stronger than the usual full abstraction, which here comes up as a simple corollary. The strength of our results may be compared with the notion of representability in [10, 11], where it was left as an open problem whether some form of summation could be behaviorally represented by concurrent combinators. Our divergent encoding (for theoretical questions like representability, divergence is acceptable) provides a first positive answer for the representability of input-guarded choice up to weak asynchronous bisimulation.

Our results also hold in the setting of value-passing CCS with boolean values and test-expressions. However, in the π-calculus, these additional notions can be encoded by a simple name-passing protocol (as shown in [15]). Furthermore, the results (except for the congruence properties) can be generalized to calculi with polyadic communication, full replication, and matching.

Asynchrony: For both encodings, their correctness proofs cannot be built upon standard (i.e. synchronous) notions of simulation. The reason lies in the inherent asynchrony of the algorithm, which arises from the resending of messages (which must not be kept by a branch when the choice has already committed to a competing branch).

Non-promptness: Most examples of encodings into process calculi known in the literature enjoy the simplifying property of being *prompt*, i.e. initial transitions of translations are committing, by corresponding to some particular computation step of their source. Both of our choice encodings fall in the class of non-prompt encodings that, moreover, can not be dealt with by optimization with administrative normal forms.

Partial commitments: With respect to the different results for the two choice encodings, it is crucial to notice that only $\mathcal{C}[\![\;]\!]$ breaks up the atomicity of committing a choice. The resulting partially committed states are exactly the reason why correctness up to weak bisimulation has to fail, whereas coupled simulation applies successfully.

Divergence: We have not been able to formulate a choice encoding which is divergence-free *and* correct with respect to weak bisimulation. We conjecture that it is impossible.

Decodings: Any operational correctness proof which states that an encoding is *sound* in the sense that each step of a translation is compatible with some source step implicitly uses the idea of mapping back the translation to its source term in order to detect the correspondence. We made this intuition explicit in decoding functions which provide a notation for the proofs that is both compact and intuitive. With prompt encodings, the reconstruction of source terms from target terms is rather simple, since it suffices to deal with literal translations. In contrast, non-prompt encodings require the decoding of *derivatives* of translations.

Annotations: The only way to detect the origin of derivatives of translations is to retrace their derivation histories. As the underlying semantics, one could, for example, use causality-based techniques, but this would introduce extra technical overhead. Instead, we exploit annotated source terms that precisely capture the information that is necessary to perform the backtracking. An intermediate language built from annotated source terms provides the basis for a sound factorization and a proper setting for the definition of decodings.

Related work The $\mathcal{C}$-encoding represents a striking example where weak bisimulation is too strong a criterion to compare process systems. It is similar to the multiway synchronization example of [17]. The latter led to the definition of coupled simulation in order to deal with gradual commitments, which do also appear in the $\mathcal{C}$-encoding. Our encodings differ in that they address the implementation of channel-based choice in the context of an underlying medium supplying asynchronous message-passing; they are thus more closely related to the work of Mitchell [14], Knabe [12], and Busi and Gorrieri [3].

In [14], a divergent choice encoding in the rather restricted setting of Static CCS was proved correct with respect to an adapted ('weak-must') testing equivalence that accepts divergent implementations $(\tau^\omega|P)$ of P as valid, but that lacks a powerful (e.g. coinductive) proof technique.

Future work Axiomatizations of both weak asynchronous bisimulation and asynchronous coupled simulation are not yet known. Alternative formulations of the definitions of asynchronous bisimulation (see [1], also for an axiomatization in the strong case) might prove convenient for finding modal characterizations and also, in general, for establishing bisimulations.

Finally, we are interested in more sophisticated divergence-free choice encodings as they are used in the Pict language, especially with respect to efficiency and garbage collection issues. Further variants might address *events* [21] or mixed guarded choice [12]. All of these encodings have in common that they require channel manager processes in order to run more complicated protocols. Therefore, we cannot expect to be able to compare source terms and target terms directly. Furthermore, a correctness result will have to take into account that translations may only behave well in contexts that respect the protocol which is expected for the free names of the translation. Techniques like "firewalls" [4] may be necessary to protect translations from hostile contexts.

Acknowledgements

We are indebted to David N. Turner for the original asynchronous choice encodings in Pict, on which our encoding $\mathcal{C}[\![\;]\!]$ is based. Ole Jensen, Kohei Honda, Cédric Fournet, Robin Milner, Davide Sangiorgi, Peter Sewell, and the rest of the Edinburgh/Cambridge *Pi Club* and the *Dienstagsclub* at Erlangen joined us in many productive discussions. The anonymous referees provided useful and detailed comments on the paper.

References

1. R. M. Amadio, I. Castellani, and D. Sangiorgi. On Bisimulations for the Asynchronous π-Calculus. In *Proceedings of CONCUR'96 (August 26–29, Pisa, Italy)*, 1996. This volume.
2. G. Boudol. Asynchrony and the π-calculus (note). Rapport de Recherche 1702, INRIA Sophia-Antipolis, May 1992.
3. N. Busi and R. Gorrieri. Distributed Conflicts in Communicating Systems. In P. Ciancarini, O. Nierstrasz, and A. Yonezawa, editors, *Object-Based Models and Languages for Concurrent Systems (Bologna, Italy, July 1994)*, volume 924 of *Lecture Notes in Computer Science*, pages 49–65. Springer, 1995.
4. C. Fournet and G. Gonthier. The Reflexive Chemical Abstract Machine and the Join-Calculus. In *23rd Annual Symposium on Principles of Programming Languages (POPL) (St. Petersburg Beach, Florida)*, pages 372–385. ACM Press, 1996.
5. R. Glabbeek. The Linear Time – Branching Time Spectrum II: The semantics of sequential systems with silent moves (Extended Abstract). In E. Best, editor, *Fourth International Conference on Concurrency Theory (CONCUR '93, Hildesheim)*, volume 715 of *Lecture Notes in Computer Science*, pages 66–81. Springer, 1993.
6. K. Honda. Two Bisimilarities in ν-Calculus. CS report 92-002, Keio University, 1992. Revised on March 31, 1993.
7. K. Honda and M. Tokoro. An Object Calculus for Asynchronous Communication. In P. America, editor, *ECOOP '91*, volume 512 of *Lecture Notes in Computer Science*, pages 133–147. Springer, 1991.

8. K. Honda and M. Tokoro. On Asynchronous Communication Semantics. In M. Tokoro, O. Nierstrasz, and P. Wegner, editors, *Object-Based Concurrent Computing 1991*, volume 612 of *Lecture Notes in Computer Science*, pages 21–51. Springer, 1992.
9. K. Honda and N. Yoshida. On Reduction-Based Process Semantics. *Theoretical Computer Science*, 152(2):437–486, 1995.
10. K. Honda and N. Yoshida. Combinatory Representation of Mobile Processes. In *21st Annual Symposium on Principles of Programming Languages (POPL)*, pages 348–360. ACM Press, January 1994.
11. K. Honda and N. Yoshida. Replication in Concurrent Combinators. In M. Hagiya and J. C. Mitchell, editors, *Theoretical Aspects of Computer Software*, volume 789 of *Lecture Notes in Computer Science*, pages 786–805. Springer, 1994.
12. F. Knabe. A Distributed Protocol for Channel-Based Communication with Choice. *Computers and Artificial Intelligence*, 12(5):475–490, 1993.
13. R. Milner, J. Parrow, and D. Walker. A Calculus of Mobile Processes, Part I/II. *Information and Computation*, 100:1–77, 1992.
14. K. Mitchell. *Implementations of Process Synchronisation and their Analysis.* PhD thesis, LFCS, University of Edinburgh, July 1986.
15. U. Nestmann. PhD thesis. Institut für Mathematische Maschinen und Datenverarbeitung, Friedrich-Alexander-Universität Erlangen-Nürnberg. To appear 1996.
16. U. Nestmann and B. C. Pierce. Decoding Choice Encodings. Interner Bericht IMMD VII–01/96, Friedrich-Alexander-Universität Erlangen-Nürnberg, Apr. 1996. Available from `ftp://ftp.informatik.uni-erlangen.de/local/inf7/papers/Nestmann/`. Also as Technical Report 392, University of Cambridge.
17. J. Parrow and P. Sjödin. Multiway Synchronization Verified with Coupled Simulation. In R. Cleaveland, editor, *Third International Conference on Concurrency Theory (CONCUR '92, Stony Brook, NY)*, volume 630 of *Lecture Notes in Computer Science*, pages 518–533. Springer, 1992.
18. J. Parrow and P. Sjödin. The Complete Axiomatization of cs-Congruence. In P. Enjalbert, E. W. Mayr, and K. W. Wagner, editors, *STACS '94*, volume 775 of *Lecture Notes in Computer Science*, pages 557–568. Springer, 1994.
19. B. C. Pierce and D. N. Turner. Concurrent Objects in a Process Calculus. In T. Ito and A. Yonezawa, editors, *Theory and Practice of Parallel Programming (TPPP, Sendai, Japan, 1994)*, volume 907 of *Lecture Notes in Computer Science*, pages 187–215. Springer, 1995.
20. B. C. Pierce and D. N. Turner. Pict: A programming language based on the pi-calculus. Technical report in preparation; available electronically, 1996.
21. J. Reppy. *Higher-Order Concurrency*. PhD thesis, Cornell University, June 1992. Technical Report TR 92-1285.

Infinite Results

Faron Moller
Computing Science Department
Uppsala University

P.O. Box 311
S-751 05 Uppsala, SWEDEN

Abstract

Recently there has been a spurt of activity in concurrency theory centred on the analysis of infinite-state systems. Much of this work stems from a task dedicated to the study in the recently-concluded ESPRIT BRA Concur2, and much of it has subsequently appeared in the proceedings of the annual CONCUR conference. In this paper, we present an overview of various results obtained regarding expressivity, decidability, and complexity, focussing on the various techniques exploited in each case.

1 Introduction

The study of (sequential) program verification has an inherent theoretical barrier in the form of the halting problem and formal undecidability. The simplest programs which manipulate the simplest infinite data types such as integer variables immediately fall foul of these theoretical limitations. During execution, such a program may evolve into any of an infinite number of states, and knowing if the execution of the program will lead to any particular state, such as the halting state, will typically be impossible. However, this has not prevented a successful attack on the problem of proving program correctness, and there are now elegant and accepted techniques for the semantic analysis of software.

The history behind the modelling of concurrent systems, in particular hardware systems, has followed a different course. Here, systems have been modelled strictly as finite-state systems, and formal analysis tools have been developed for completely exploring the reachable states of any given system, for instance with the goal of detecting whether or not a halting, ie, deadlocked, state is accessible. This abstraction has been warranted up to a point. Real hardware components are indeed finite entities, and protocols typically behave in a regular fashion irrespective of the diversity of messages which they may be designed to deliver.

In specifying concurrent systems, it is not typical to explicitly present the state spaces of the various components, for example by listing out the states and transition function, but rather to specify them using some higher-level modelling language. Such formalisms for describing concurrent systems are not usually so restrictive in their expressive power. For example, the typical process algebra can encode integer registers, and with them compute arbitrary computable functions; and Petri nets constitute a graphical language for finitely presenting typically infinite state systems. However, tools which employ such formalisms generally depend on techniques for first assuring that the state space of the system being specified is semantically, if not syntactically, finite. For example, a given process algebra tool might syntactically check that no static operators such as parallel composition appear within the scope of a recursive definition; and a given Petri net tool might check that a net is safe, that is, that no place may acquire more than one token. Having verified the finiteness of the system at hand, the search algorithm can, at least in principle, proceed.

The problem with the blind search approach, which has thwarted attempts to provide practical verification tools, is of course that of state space explosion. The number of reachable states of a system will typically be on the order of exponential in the number of components which make up the system. Hence a great deal of research effort has been expended on taming this state space, typically by developing intelligent search strategies. Various promising techniques have been developed which make for the automated analysis of extremely large state spaces feasible; one popular approach to this problem is through the use of BDD (binary decision diagram) encodings of automata [5]. However, such approaches are inherently bound to the analysis of finite-state systems.

Recently, interest in addressing the problem of analysing infinite-state spaces has blossomed within the concurrency theory community. The practical motivation for this has been both to provide for the study of parallel program verification, where infinite data types are manipulated, as well as to allow for more faithful representations of concurrent systems. For example, real-time and probabilistic models have come into vogue during the last decade to reflect for instance the temporal and nondeterministic behaviour of asynchronous hardware components responding to continuously-changing analogue signals; and models have been developed which allow for the dynamic reconfiguration of a system's structure. Such enhancements to the expressive power of a modelling language immediately give rise to infinite-state models, and new paradigms not based on state space search need be introduced to successfully analyse systems expressed in such formalisms.

A particularly relevant question here then is deciding when two infinite-state systems are in some semantic sense equal. Such questions are of course not new in the field of theoretical computer science. Since the proof by Moore [42] in 1956 of the decidability of language equivalence for finite-state automata, formal language theorists have been studying the equivalence problem over classes of automata which express languages which are more expressive than the class of regular languages generated by finite-state automata. Bar-Hillel, Perles and Shamir [3] were the first to demonstrate in 1961 that the class of languages defined by context-free grammars was too wide to permit a decidable theory for language equivalence. The search for a more precise dividing line is still active, with the most outstanding open problem concerning the decidability of language equivalence between deterministic push-down automata.

Decidability questions for Petri nets were addressed already two decades ago, with the thesis of Hack [19]. However, it has only been in the much more recent past that a more concerted effort has been focussed on such questions, with the interest driven in part by analogies drawn between classes of concurrent system models and classes of generators for families of formal languages. In [36] Milner exploits the relationship between regular (finite-state) automata as discussed in [46] and regular behaviours to present the decidability and a complete axiomatisation of bisimulation equivalence for finite-state behaviours, whilst in his textbook [38] he demonstrates that the halting problem for Turing machines can be encoded as a bisimulation question for the full CCS calculus thus demonstrating undecidability in general. This final feat is carried out elegantly using finite representations of counters in the thesis of Taubner [49]. These results are as expected; however, real interest was stirred with the discovery by Baeten, Bergstra and Klop [1, 2] that bisimulation equivalence is decidable for a family of infinite-state automata generated by a general class of context-free grammars.

Much of the effort on exploring such decidability issues has taken place within the framework of the recently-concluded ESPRIT BRA Concur2 which included a task dedicated to the study of infinite states. As such, many of the milestones in the field have appeared in the proceedings of the annual CONCUR conferences, as well as in the proceedings of the satellite workshop INFINITY which accompanies the CONCUR'96 conference. In this paper, we present an overview of various results obtained regarding expressivity, decidability, and complexity, with particular emphasis on the bisimulation equivalence problem, focussing on the various techniques exploited in each case.

2 Rewrite Transition Systems

Concurrent systems are modelled semantically in a variety of ways. They may be defined for example by the infinite traces or executions which they may perform, or by the entirety of the properties which they satisfy in some particular process logic, or as a particular algebraic model of some equational specification. In any case, a fundamental unifying view is to interpret such systems as edge-labelled directed graphs, whose nodes represent the states in which a system may exist, and whose transitions represent the possible behaviour of the system originating in the state represented by the node from which the transition emanates; the label on a transition represents an event corresponding to the execution of that transition, which will typically represent an interaction with the environment. The starting point for our study will thus be such graphs, which will for us represent processes.

Definition 2.1 A *labelled transition system* is a tuple $\langle S, \Sigma, \longrightarrow, \alpha_0, F\rangle$ where

- S is a set of *states*.
- Σ is a finite set of *labels*.

- $\longrightarrow \subseteq S \times \Sigma \times S$ is a *transition relation*, written $\alpha \xrightarrow{a} \beta$ for $\langle \alpha, a, \beta \rangle \in \longrightarrow$.
- $\alpha_0 \in S$ is a distinguished *start state*.
- $F \subseteq S$ is a finite set of *final states* which are *terminal*: for each $\alpha \in F$ there is no $a \in \Sigma$ and $\beta \in S$ such that $\alpha \xrightarrow{a} \beta$.

This notion of a labelled transition system differs from the standard definition of a finite state automata (as for example given in [27]) in that the set of states need not be finite, and final states must not have any outgoing transitions. This last restriction is mild and justified in that a final state refers to the successful termination of a concurrent system. This contrasts with unsuccessful termination (ie, deadlock) which is represented by all non-final terminal states. We could remove this restriction, but only at the expense of Theorem 2.3 below which characterises a wide class of labelled transition systems as push-down automata which accept on empty stack. (An alternative approach could be taken to recover Theorem 2.3 based on PDA which accept by final state, but we do not pursue this alternative in this paper.)

In this overview, we follow the example set by Caucal [9] and consider the families of labelled transition systems defined by various rewrite systems. Such an approach provides us with a clear link between well-studied classes of formal languages and transition system generators, a link which is of particular interest when it comes to exploiting process-theoretic techniques in solving problems in classical formal language theory.

Definition 2.2 A *sequential labelled rewrite transition system* is a tuple $\langle V, \Sigma, P, \alpha_0, F \rangle$ where

- V is a finite set of *variables*; the elements of V^* are referred to as *states*.
- Σ is a finite set of *labels*.
- $P \subseteq V^* \times \Sigma \times V^*$ is a finite set of *rewrite rules*, written $\alpha \xrightarrow{a} \beta$ for $\langle \alpha, a, \beta \rangle \in P$, which are extended by the *prefix rewriting rule*: if $\alpha \xrightarrow{a} \beta$ then $\alpha\gamma \xrightarrow{a} \beta\gamma$.
- $\alpha_0 \in V^*$ is a distinguished *start state*.
- $F \subseteq V^*$ is a finite set of *final states* which are *terminal*.

A *parallel labelled rewrite transition system* is defined precisely as above, except that the elements of V^* are read modulo commutativity of catenation, which is thus interpretted as parallel, rather than sequential, composition.

We shall freely extend the transition relation $\longrightarrow$ homomorphically to finite sequences of actions $w \in \Sigma^*$ so as to write $\alpha \xrightarrow{\varepsilon} \alpha$ and $\alpha \xrightarrow{aw} \beta$ whenever $\alpha \xrightarrow{a} \cdot \xrightarrow{w} \beta$. Also, we refer to the set of states α into which the initial state can be rewritten, that is, such that $\alpha_0 \xrightarrow{w} \alpha$ for some $w \in \Sigma^*$, as the *reachable* states. Although we do not insist that all states be reachable, we shall assume that all variables in V are accessible from the initial state, that is, that for all $X \in V$ there is some $w \in \Sigma^*$ and $\alpha, \beta \in V^*$ such that $\alpha_0 \xrightarrow{w} \alpha X \beta$.

This definition is slightly more general than that given by Caucal, which does not take into account final states nor the possibility of parallel rewriting as an alternative to sequential rewriting. By doing this, we expand the study of the classes of transition systems which are defined, and extend some of the results given by Caucal, notably in the characterisation of arbitrary sequential rewrite systems as push-down automata.

The families of transition systems which can be defined by restricted rewrite systems can be classified using a form of Chomsky hierarchy. (Type 1—context-sensitive—rewrite systems do not feature in this hierarchy since the rewrite rules by definition are only applied to the prefix of a composition.) This hierarchy provides an elegant classification of several important classes of transition systems which have been defined and studied independent of their appearance as particular rewrite systems. This classification is presented as follows.

	Restriction on the rules $\alpha \xrightarrow{a} \beta$ of P	Restriction on F	Sequential composition	Parallel composition
Type 0:	*none*	*none*	PDA	PN
Type $1\frac{1}{2}$:	$\alpha \in Q\Gamma$ and $\beta \in Q\Gamma^*$ where $V = Q \uplus \Gamma$	$F = Q$	PDA	PPDA
Type 2:	$\alpha \in V$	$F = \{\varepsilon\}$	BPA	BPP
Type 3:	$\alpha \in V,\ \beta \in V \cup \{\varepsilon\}$	$F = \{\varepsilon\}$	FSA	FSA

In the remainder of this section, we explain the classes of transition systems which are represented in this table, working upwards starting with the most restrictive class.

FSA represents the class of finite-state automata. Clearly if the rules are restricted to be of the form $A \xrightarrow{a} B$ or $A \xrightarrow{a} \varepsilon$ with $A, B \in V$, then the reachable states of both the sequential and parallel transition systems will be a subset of the finite set of variables V. (We assume here that the initial state itself is a member of V.)

Example 0 *In the following we present two type 3 (regular) rewrite systems along with the FSA transition systems which the initial states X and A, respectively, denote.*

$X \xrightarrow{a} Y$

$Y \xrightarrow{b} \varepsilon$

$Y \xrightarrow{c} \varepsilon$

$A \xrightarrow{a} B$

$A \xrightarrow{a} C$

$B \xrightarrow{b} \varepsilon$

$C \xrightarrow{c} \varepsilon$

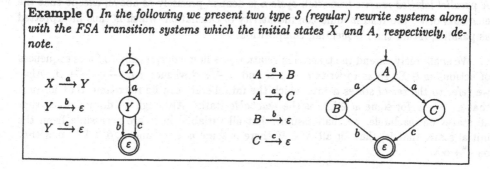

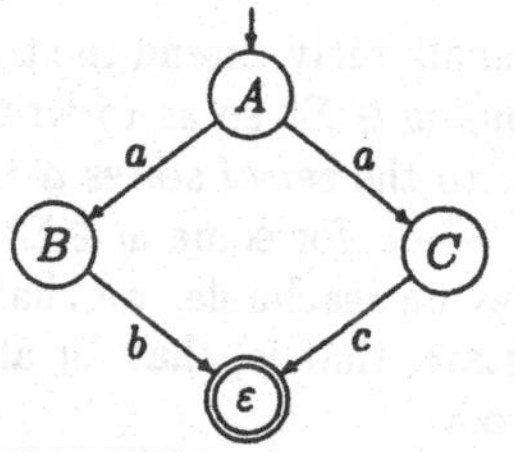

BPA represents the class of Basic Process Algebra processes of Bergstra and Klop [4], which are the transition systems associated with Greibach normal form (GNF) context-free grammars in which only left-most derivations are permitted.

Example 1 *In the following we present a type 2 (GNF context-free grammar) rewrite system along with the BPA transition system which the initial state X denotes.*

$X \xrightarrow{a} XB$

$X \xrightarrow{c} \varepsilon$

$B \xrightarrow{b} \varepsilon$

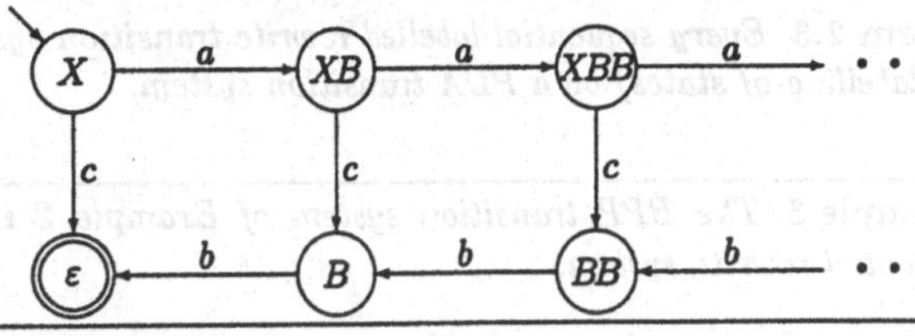

BPP represents the class of Basic Parallel Processes introduced by Christensen [11] as a parallel analogy to BPA, and are defined by the transition systems associated with GNF context-free grammars in which arbitrary grammar derivations are permitted.

Example 2 *The type 2 rewrite system from Example 1 gives rise to the following BPP transition system with initial state X.*

$X \xrightarrow{a} XB$

$X \xrightarrow{c} \varepsilon$

$B \xrightarrow{b} \varepsilon$

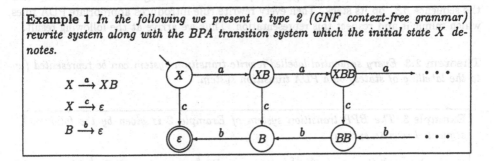

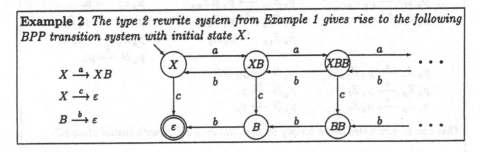

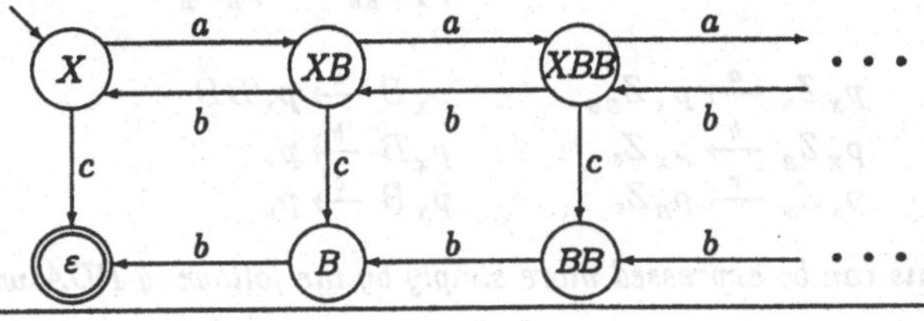

PDA represents the class of push-down automata which accept on empty stack. To present such PDA as a restricted form of rewrite system, we first assume that the variable set V is partitioned into disjoint sets Q (finite control states) and Γ (stack symbols). The rewrite rules are then of the form $pA \xrightarrow{a} q\beta$ with $p, q \in Q$, $A \in \Gamma$ and $\beta \in \Gamma^*$, which represents the usual PDA transition which says that while in control state p with the symbol A at the top of the stack, you may read the input symbol a, move into control state q, and replace the stack element A with the sequence β. Finally, the set of final states is given by Q, which represent the PDA configurations in which the stack is empty.

Caucal [9] demonstrates that, disregarding final states, any unrestricted (type 0) sequential rewrite system can be presented as a PDA, in the sense that the transition systems are isomorphic up to the labelling of states. The stronger result, in which final states are taken into consideration, actually holds as well. The idea behind the encoding is as follows. Given a rewrite system, take n to be at least as large as the length of any sequence appearing on the left hand side of any of its rules, and strictly larger than the length of any final state. Let $Q = \{ p_\alpha \ : \ \alpha \in V^* \text{ and length}(\alpha) < n \}$ and $\Gamma = V \cup \{ Z_\alpha \ : \ \alpha \in V^* \text{ and length}(\alpha) \leq n \}$. Every final transition state α is represented by the PDA state p_α, that is, by the PDA being in control state p_α with an empty stack denoting acceptance; and every non-final transition system state $\alpha\beta\gamma$ with length(α) $< n$, length($\beta\gamma$) > 0 only if length(α) $= n - 1$, and length(β) > 0 only if length(γ) $= n$, is represented in the PDA by $p_\alpha\beta Z_\gamma$, that is, by the PDA being in control state p_α with the sequence βZ_γ on its stack. Then every rewrite rule introduces appropriate PDA rules which mimic it and respect this representation. Thus we arrive at the following result.

Theorem 2.3 *Every sequential labelled rewrite transition system can be represented (up to the labelling of states) by a PDA transition system.*

Example 3 *The BPP transition system of Example 2 is given by the following sequential rewrite system.*

$$X \xrightarrow{a} XB \qquad X \xrightarrow{c} \varepsilon \qquad B \xrightarrow{b} \varepsilon \qquad XB \xrightarrow{b} X$$

By the above construction, this gives rise to the following PDA with initial state $p_X Z_\varepsilon$. (We omit rules corresponding to the unreachable states.)

$$\begin{array}{lll}
p_X Z_\varepsilon \xrightarrow{a} p_X Z_B & p_X Z_{BB} \xrightarrow{a} p_X B Z_{BB} & p_B Z_\varepsilon \xrightarrow{b} p_\varepsilon \\
p_X Z_\varepsilon \xrightarrow{c} p_\varepsilon & p_X Z_{BB} \xrightarrow{b} p_X Z_B & p_B Z_B \xrightarrow{b} p_B Z_\varepsilon \\
 & p_X Z_{BB} \xrightarrow{c} p_B Z_B & p_B Z_{BB} \xrightarrow{b} p_B Z_B \\
 & & p_B B \xrightarrow{b} p_B \\
p_X Z_B \xrightarrow{a} p_X Z_{BB} & p_X B \xrightarrow{a} p_X BB & \\
p_X Z_B \xrightarrow{b} p_X Z_\varepsilon & p_X B \xrightarrow{b} p_X & \\
p_X Z_B \xrightarrow{c} p_B Z_\varepsilon & p_X B \xrightarrow{c} p_B &
\end{array}$$

This can be expressed more simply by the following PDA with initial state pZ.

$$\begin{array}{lll}
pZ \xrightarrow{a} pBZ & pB \xrightarrow{a} pBB & qZ \xrightarrow{c} q \\
pZ \xrightarrow{c} q & pB \xrightarrow{b} p & qB \xrightarrow{b} q \\
 & pB \xrightarrow{c} pBB &
\end{array}$$

Note that, as is reflected in the above construction, every BPA is given by a single-state PDA; the reverse identification is also immediately evident. However, we shall see in Section 2.2 that any PDA presentation of the transition system of Example 2 must have at least 2 control states: this transition system is not represented by any BPA.

PPDA represents the class of 'parallel' push-down automata, which are defined as above except that they have random access capability to the stack.

Example 4 *The BPA transition system of Example 1 is isomorphic to that given by the following PPDA with initial state pX.*

$$pX \xrightarrow{a} pBX \qquad pX \xrightarrow{c} q \qquad qB \xrightarrow{b} q$$

Note that when the stack alphabet has only one element, PDA and PPDA trivially coincide. Also note that BPP coincides with the class of single-state PPDA. We shall see in Section 2.2 that any PPDA presentation of the transition system of Example 1 must have at least 2 control states: this transition system is not represented by any BPP.

PN represents the class of (finite, labelled, weighted place/transition) Petri nets, as is evident by the following interpretation of unrestricted parallel rewrite systems. The variable set V represents the set of places of the Petri net, and each rewrite rule $\alpha \xrightarrow{a} \beta$ represents a Petri net transition labelled a with the input and output places represented by α and β respectively, with the weights on the input and output arcs given by the relevant multiplicities in α and β. Note that a BPP is a communication-free Petri net, one in which each transition has a unique input place.

Example 5 *The following unrestricted parallel rewrite system with initial state X and final state Y*

$$X \xrightarrow{a} XA \qquad XAB \xrightarrow{c} X \qquad YA \xrightarrow{a} Y$$
$$X \xrightarrow{b} XB \qquad X \xrightarrow{d} Y \qquad YB \xrightarrow{b} Y$$

describes the Petri net which in its usual graphical representation net would be rendered as follows. (The weight on all the arcs is 1.)

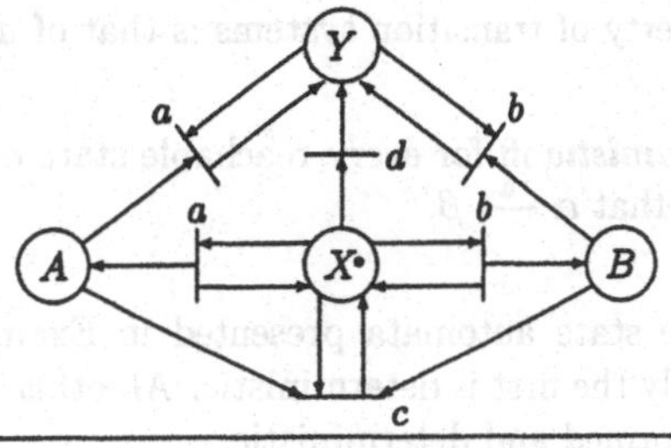

Although in the sequential case, PDA constitutes a normal form for unrestricted rewrite transition systems, it is unlikely that this result holds in the parallel case. For example, we conjecture that there is no PPDA which represents an isomorphic transition system to that of the PN in Example 5.

2.1 Languages and Bisimilarity

Given a labelled transition system T with initial state α_0, we can define its *language* $L(T)$ to be the language generated by its initial state α_0, where the language generated by a state is defined in the usual fashion as the sequences of actions which label rewrite transitions leading from the given state to a final state.

Definition 2.4 $L(s) = \{w \in \Sigma^* : \alpha \xrightarrow{w} \beta$ for some $\beta \in F\}$, and $L(T) = L(\alpha_0)$. α and β are *language equivalent*, written $\alpha \sim_L \beta$, iff they generate the same language: $L(\alpha) = L(\beta)$.

With respect to the languages generated by rewrite systems, if a rewrite system is in the process of generating a word, then the partial word should be extendible to a complete word. That is, from any reachable state of the transition system, a final state should be reachable. If the transition system satisfies this property, it is said to be *normed*.

Definition 2.5 We define the *norm* of any state α of a labelled transition system, written $\mathrm{norm}(\alpha)$, to be the length of a shortest rewrite transition sequence which takes α to a final state, that is, the length of a shortest word in $L(\alpha)$. By convention, we define $\mathrm{norm}(\alpha) = \infty$ if there is no sequence of transitions from α to a final state, that is, $L(\alpha) = \emptyset$. The transition system is *normed* iff every reachable state α has a finite norm.

Note that, due to our assumption following Definition 2.2 on the accessibility of all the variables, if a type 2 rewrite transition system is normed, then all of its variables must have finite norm. The following then is a basic fact about the norms of BPA and BPP states.

Lemma 2.6 *Given any state $\alpha\beta$ of a type 2 rewrite transition systems (BPA or BPP),* $\mathrm{norm}(\alpha\beta) = \mathrm{norm}(\alpha) + \mathrm{norm}(\beta)$.

A further common property of transition systems is that of *determinacy*.

Definition 2.7 T is *deterministic* iff for every reachable state α and every label a there is at most one state β such that $\alpha \xrightarrow{a} \beta$.

For example, the two finite state automata presented in Example 0 are both normed transition systems, while only the first is deterministic. All other examples which we have presented have been both normed and deterministic.

In the realm of concurrency theory, language equivalence is generally taken to be too coarse an equivalence. For example, it equates the two transition systems of Example 0 which generate the same language $\{ ab, ac \}$ yet demonstrate different deadlocking capabilities due to the nondeterministic behaviour exhibitted by the second transition system. Many finer equivalences have been proposed, with *bisimulation equivalence* being perhaps the finest behavioural equivalence studied. (Note that we do not consider here any so-called 'true concurrency' equivalences such as those based on partial orders.) Bisimulation equivalence was define by Park [43] and used to great effect by Milner [37, 38]. Its definition, in the presence of final states, is as follows.

Definition 2.8 A binary relation $\mathcal{R}$ on states of a transition system is a *bisimulation* iff whenever $(\alpha, \beta) \in \mathcal{R}$ we have that

- if $\alpha \xrightarrow{a} \alpha'$ then $\beta \xrightarrow{a} \beta'$ for some β' with $(\alpha', \beta') \in \mathcal{R}$;
- if $\beta \xrightarrow{a} \beta'$ then $\alpha \xrightarrow{a} \alpha'$ for some α' with $(\alpha', \beta') \in \mathcal{R}$;
- $\alpha \in F$ iff $\beta \in F$.

α and β are *bisimulation equivalent* or *bisimilar*, written $\alpha \sim \beta$, iff $(\alpha, \beta) \in \mathcal{R}$ for some bisimulation $\mathcal{R}$.

Lemma 2.9 *$\sim = \bigcup\{\mathcal{R} : \mathcal{R}$ is a bisimulation relation$\}$ is the largest bisimulation relation, and is an equivalence relation.*

Bisimulation equivalence has an elegant characterisation in terms of certain two-player games [47]. Starting with a pair of states $\langle\alpha, \beta\rangle$, the two players alternate moves according to the following rules.

1. If exactly one of the pair of states is a final state, then player I is deemed to be the winner. Otherwise, player I chooses one of the states and makes some transition from that state (either $\alpha \xrightarrow{a} \alpha'$ or $\beta \xrightarrow{a} \beta'$). If this proves impossible, due to both states being terminal, then player II is deemed to be the winner.
2. Player II must respond to the move made by player I by making an identically-labelled transition from the other state (either $\beta \xrightarrow{a} \beta'$ or $\alpha \xrightarrow{a} \alpha'$). If this proves impossible, then player I is deemed to be the winner.
3. The play then repeats itself from the new pair $\langle\alpha', \beta'\rangle$. If the game continues forever, then player II is deemed to be the winner.

The following result is then immediately evident.

Fact 2.10 *$\alpha \sim \beta$ iff Player II has a winning strategy in the bisimulation game starting with the pair $\langle\alpha, \beta\rangle$.*

Conversely, $\alpha \not\sim \beta$ iff Player I has a winning strategy in the bisimulation game starting with the pair $\langle\alpha, \beta\rangle$.

Proof Any bisimulation relation defines a winning strategy for player II for the bisimulation game starting from a pair in the relation: the second player merely has to respond to moves by the first in such a way that the resulting pair is contained in the bisimulation.

Conversely, a winning strategy for player II for the bisimulation game starting from a particular pair of states defines a bisimulation relation containing that pair, namely the collection of all pairs which appear after every exchange of moves during any and all games in which player II uses this strategy. □

Also immediately evident then is the following lemma with its accompanying corollary relating bisimulation equivalence to language equivalence.

Lemma 2.11 *If $\alpha \sim \beta$ and $\alpha \xrightarrow{w} \alpha'$ with $w \in \Sigma^*$, then $\beta \xrightarrow{w} \beta'$ such that $\alpha' \sim \beta'$.*

Corollary 2.12 *If $\alpha \sim \beta$ then $\alpha \sim_L \beta$.*

Apart from being the fundamental notion of equivalence for several process algebraic formalisms, bisimulation equivalence has several pleasing mathematical properties, not least of which being that it is decidable over classes of transition systems for which all other common equivalences, including language equivalence, remain undecidable. Furthermore as given by the following lemma, language equivalence and bisimilarity coincide over the class of normed deterministic processes.

Lemma 2.13 *For states α and β of a normed deterministic transition system, if $\alpha \sim_L \beta$ then $\alpha \sim \beta$. Thus, taken along with Corollary 2.12, $\sim_L$ and $\sim$ coincide.*

Hence it is sensible to concentrate on the more mathematically tractable bisimulation equivalence when investigating decidability results for language equivalence for deterministic language generators. In particular, by studying bisimulation equivalence we can rediscover old theorems about the decidability of language equivalence, as well as provide more efficient algorithms for these decidability results than have previously been presented. We expect that the techniques which can be exploited in the study of bisimulation equivalence will prove useful in tackling other language theoretic problems, notably the problem of deterministic push-down automata.

2.2 Expressivity Results

Our Chomsky hierarchy from above gives us the following classification of processes.

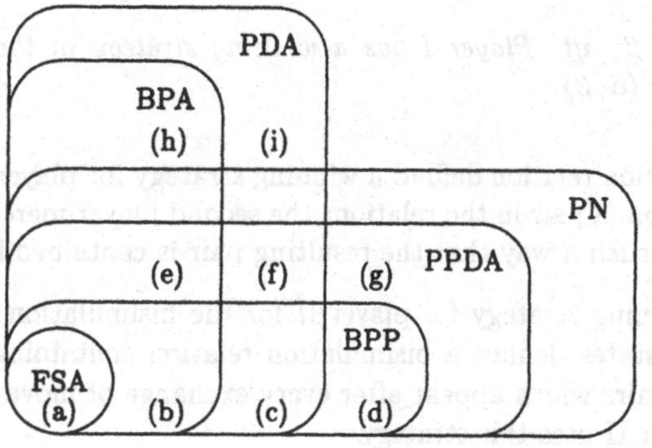

In this section we demonstrate the strictness of this hierarchy by providing example transition systems which lie precisely in the gaps indicated in the classification. (We ignore the question of separating PN and PPDA, due to the uncertainty behind the existence of this gap; see the conjecture at the end of Section 2.) We in fact do more than this by giving examples of normed deterministic transition systems which separate all of these classes up to bisimulation (and hence also language) equivalence. These results complement those presented for the taxonomy described by Burkart, Caucal and Steffen [7].

(a) Example 0 provides a simple normed deterministic FSA.

(b) The rewrite system with the two rules $A \xrightarrow{a} AA$ and $A \xrightarrow{b} \varepsilon$ gives rise to the same rewrite transition system regardless of whether the rewrite system is sequential or parallel. Hence this is an example of a normed deterministic rewrite transition system which is both a BPA and a BPP but not an FSA.

(c) Example 2 provides a transition system which can be described by both a BPP (Example 2) and a PDA (Example 3). However, it cannot be described up to bisimilarity by any BPA. To see this, suppose that we have a BPA which represents this transition system up to bisimilarity, and let m be greater than the norm of any of its variables. Then the BPA state corresponding to XB^m in Example 2 must be of the form $A\alpha$ where $A \in V$ and $\alpha \in V^+$. But then *any* sequence of norm(A) norm-reducing transitions must lead to the BPA state α, while the transition system in Example 2 has two such non-bisimilar derived states, namely XB^{k-1} and B^k where $k = \text{norm}(\alpha)$.

(d) The following BPP with initial state X

$$X \xrightarrow{a} XB \qquad X \xrightarrow{c} XD \qquad X \xrightarrow{e} \varepsilon \qquad B \xrightarrow{b} \varepsilon \qquad D \xrightarrow{d} \varepsilon$$

is not language equivalent to any PDA, as its language is easily confirmed not to be context free. (The words in this language from $a^*c^*b^*d^*e$ are exactly those of the form $a^kc^nb^kd^ne$, which is clearly not a context-free language.)

(e) Example 1 provides a transition system which can be described by both a BPA (Example 1) and a PPDA (Example 4). However, due to a pumping lemma for BPP given by Christensen [11] it is not language equivalent to any BPP.

(f) The following PDA with initial state pX

$$pX \xrightarrow{a} pXX \qquad pX \xrightarrow{b} q \qquad pX \xrightarrow{c} r \qquad qX \xrightarrow{b} q \qquad rX \xrightarrow{c} r$$

coincides with the PPDA which it defines, since there is only one stack symbol. This transition system is depicted as follows.

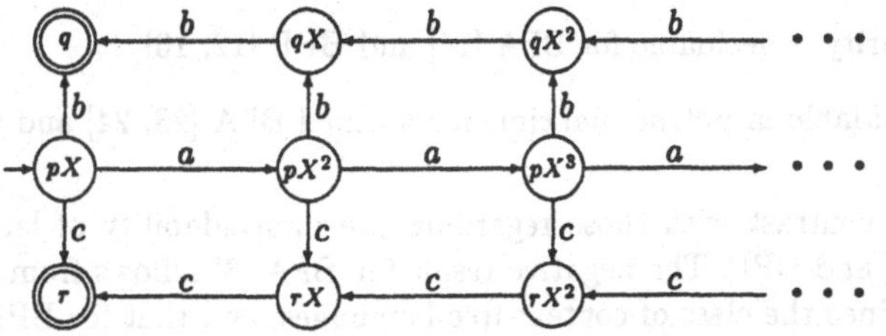

However, this transition system cannot be language equivalent to any BPP, due again to the pumping lemma for BPP [11], nor bisimilar to any BPA, due to a similar argument as for (c).

(g) The following PPDA with initial state pX

$$pX \xrightarrow{a} pA \qquad pA \xrightarrow{a} pAA \quad pA \xrightarrow{b} qB \qquad qA \xrightarrow{b} qB \quad qB \xrightarrow{c} r \qquad rA \xrightarrow{c} r \quad rB \xrightarrow{c} r$$

generates the language $\{ a^n b^k c^n \ : \ 0 < k \leq n \}$, and hence cannot be language equivalent to any BPP, due again to the pumping lemma for BPP [11], nor any PDA, as this language is not context-free.

(h) The following BPA with initial state X

$$X \xrightarrow{a} XA \qquad X \xrightarrow{b} XB \qquad X \xrightarrow{c} \varepsilon \qquad A \xrightarrow{a} \varepsilon \qquad B \xrightarrow{b} \varepsilon$$

generates the language $\{ wcw^R : w \in \{a,b\}^* \}$ and hence is not language equivalent to any PN [44].

(i) The following PDA with initial state pX

$$\begin{array}{lllll} pX \xrightarrow{a} pAX & pA \xrightarrow{a} pAA & pB \xrightarrow{a} pAB & qA \xrightarrow{a} q & rA \xrightarrow{a} r \\ pX \xrightarrow{b} pBX & pA \xrightarrow{b} pBA & pB \xrightarrow{b} pBB & qB \xrightarrow{b} q & rB \xrightarrow{b} r \\ pX \xrightarrow{c} qX & pA \xrightarrow{c} qA & pB \xrightarrow{c} qB & qX \xrightarrow{a} q & rX \xrightarrow{b} r \\ pX \xrightarrow{d} rX & pA \xrightarrow{d} rA & pB \xrightarrow{d} rB & & \end{array}$$

like (h) above is not language equivalent to any PN, and like (c) above is not bisimilar to any BPA.

3 Decidability Results for Type 2 Rewrite Systems

In this section we describe several positive results which have been established regarding the decidability of bisimilarity for type 2 rewrite transition systems. In particular, we shall briefly describe the techniques behind the following results:

1. Bisimilarity is decidable for BPA [14] and BPP [12, 13].
2. It is decidable in polynomial time for normed BPA [23, 24] and normed BPP [25].

These results contrast with those regarding the undecidability of language equivalence for both BPA and BPP. The negative result for BPA [3] follows from the fact that BPA effectively defines the class of context-free languages; and that for BPP [21] follows from a modification by Hirshfeld of a technique of Jančar which is described in Section 4. Both arguments can be shown to hold for the class of normed systems. Also, for both BPA and BPP, this undecidability extends to all equivalences which lie in Glabbeek's spectrum [16] between bisimilarity and language equivalence [31, 18, 28].

Baeten, Bergstra and Klop [1, 2] presented the first such decidability result, that bisimilarity for normed BPA is decidable. Their lengthy proof exploits the periodicity which exists in normed BPA transition systems, and several simpler proofs exploiting structural properties were soon recorded, notably by Caucal [8], Hüttel and Stirling [29], and Groote [17]. Huynh and Tian [30] demonstrated that this problem has a complexity of Σ_2^P by providing a nondeterministic algorithm which relies on an NP oracle; Hirshfeld, Jerrum and Moller [23, 24] refined this result by providing a polynomial algorithm, thus showing the problem to be in P. A generally more efficient, though worst-case exponential, algorithm is presented by Hirshfeld and Moller [26]. Finally, Christensen, Hüttel and Stirling [14, 15] demonstrated the general problem to be decidable, whilst Burkart, Caucal and Steffen [6] demonstrated an elementary decision procedure. For the parallel case, Christensen, Hirshfeld and Moller [12, 13] demonstrated the general decidability result for BPP, whilst Hirshfeld, Jerrum and Moller [25] presented a polynomial algorithm for the normed case.

One direction for decidability results, determining non-bisimilarity, is automatic using the following finite characterisation of bisimulation equivalence over *image-finite* transition systems, those for which there are only a finite number of transitions with a given label from any given reachable state.

Definition 3.1 The ***stratified bisimulation relations*** [38] $\sim_n$ are defined as follows.

- $\alpha \sim_0 \beta$ for all states.
- $\alpha \sim_{k+1} \beta$ iff
  - if $\alpha \xrightarrow{a} \alpha'$ then $\beta \xrightarrow{a} \beta'$ for some β' with $\alpha' \sim_k \beta'$;
  - if $\beta \xrightarrow{a} \beta'$ then $\alpha \xrightarrow{a} \alpha'$ for some α' with $\alpha' \sim_k \beta'$;
  - $\alpha \in F$ iff $\beta \in F$.

Lemma 3.2 *If α and β are image-finite, then $\alpha \sim \beta$ iff $\alpha \sim_n \beta$ for all $n \geq 0$.*

It is clear that rewrite transition systems are image-finite, and that this lemma applies. It is equally clear that each of the relations $\sim_n$ is decidable, and that therefore non-bisimilarity is semi-decidable over rewrite transition systems.

Hence our decidability results would follow from demonstrating the semi-decidability of bisimilarity. For this, we first note the following congruence results which hold for both BPA and BPP.

Fact 3.3 *$\sim$ is a congruence (with respect to catenation) over both BPA and BPP; that is, if $\alpha \sim \beta$ and $\alpha' \sim \beta'$ then $\alpha\alpha' \sim \beta\beta'$.*

Given a binary relation $\mathcal{R}$ on states of a type 2 rewrite transition system, let $\stackrel{\mathcal{R}}{\equiv}$ denote the least congruence containing $\mathcal{R}$; that is, $\stackrel{\mathcal{R}}{\equiv}$ is the least equivalence relation which contains $\mathcal{R}$ and the pair $(\alpha\alpha', \beta\beta')$ whenever it contains each of (α, β) and (α', β').

Definition 3.4 A binary relation $\mathcal{R}$ on states of a type 2 rewrite transition system is a *bisimulation base* iff whenever $(\alpha, \beta) \in \mathcal{R}$ we have that

- if $\alpha \xrightarrow{a} \alpha'$ then $\beta \xrightarrow{a} \beta'$ for some β' with $\alpha' \stackrel{\mathcal{R}}{\equiv} \beta'$;
- if $\beta \xrightarrow{a} \beta'$ then $\alpha \xrightarrow{a} \alpha'$ for some α' with $\alpha' \stackrel{\mathcal{R}}{\equiv} \beta'$.

Caucal [8] introduced the technique of using bisimulation bases for providing the decidability of normed BPA, by noting that the relation $\stackrel{\mathcal{R}}{\equiv}$ is a bisimulation whenever $\mathcal{R}$ is a bisimulation base; hence two states are bisimilar iff they are related by some bisimulation base. More than this we have the following finite base result for both BPA and BPP.

Fact 3.5 $\alpha \sim \beta$ *iff* $(\alpha, \beta) \in \mathcal{R}$ *for some finite bisimulation base* $\mathcal{R}$*, and it is semidecidable if a given finite relation* $\mathcal{R}$ *is a bisimulation base. Hence* $\sim$ *is semi-decidable.*

The statement of the above fact hides the complexity of its proof. The result for BPA is provided by Christensen, Hüttel and Stirling [15] and relies on a weak cancellation property, that $\alpha \sim \beta$ whenever $\alpha\gamma \sim \beta\gamma$ for infinitely many non-bisimilar γ. The result for BPP is most elegantly provided by Hirshfeld [22], though this is a revised proof using Dickson's Lemma [20] of a result of Redie [45] that every congruence on a finitely generated commutative semigroup (such as bisimilarity over BPP) is finitely generated. We note finally the desired result which follows from these finite base results.

Theorem 3.6 $\sim$ *is decidable for both BPA and BPP.*

When we turn our attention towards normed transition systems, we discover a useful unique decomposition result such as those considered by Milner and Moller [39, 40] for finite processes. Given a normed type 2 rewrite transition system, we say that a variable X is *prime* (with respect to bisimilarity) iff $\alpha = \varepsilon$ whenever $X \sim Y\alpha$.

Fact 3.7 *Every state of a normed type 2 rewrite transition system has a unique (up to bisimilarity) prime decomposition.*

Notice that this unique decomposition result immediately gives the finite base result from Fact 3.5 as a corollary. We merely take the finite relation $\mathcal{R}$ to relate each variable to its unique decomposition.

An obvious algorithm for deciding equivalence then is to compute the prime decompositions of the two states being compared and compare these. To compute the prime decompositions, we need first compute which of the variables are prime. This can be done iteratively, by assuming first that only the variables with norm 1 are prime (which they must be, due to Lemma 2.6), and then introducing primes as they are discovered (by deducing that they cannot be expressed in terms of the existing decompositions). By the use of careful bookkeeping this can be accomplished in both cases in polynomial time, thus giving our desired results.

Theorem 3.8 $\sim$ *is polynomial time decidable for both normed BPA and normed BPP.*

Hence the results for BPA and BPP are identical: bisimilarity is decidable in general and decidable in polynomial time for the normed cases, and these results follow from similar results regarding congruence and decomposability. However, this disguises the diversity in the actual details; interestingly, different techniques seem necessary for the two cases. In particular, care must be taken in the sequential case BPA as prime decompositions can be exponentially long.

An interesting corollary of the result for BPA is that language equivalence between simple (ie, deterministic) grammars is decidable in polynomial time. This result follows immediately from Lemma 2.13, and improves on the original doubly exponential algorithm of Korenjak and Hopcroft [34] as well as the singly exponential algorithm of Caucal [10].

As a final point, we note that the basic techniques which the above results rely upon, namely the congruence and decomposition properties, fail immediately for more general rewrite transition systems. As a simple example, if we take the following rewrite rules

$$A \xrightarrow{a} AA \qquad\qquad B \xrightarrow{a} A \qquad\qquad AA \xrightarrow{b} \varepsilon$$

then clearly $A \sim BA$. Hence congruence fails as $AA \not\sim BAA$, and cancellation (and hence any reasonable decomposition result) fails as $\varepsilon \not\sim B$. In this case, even Lemma 2.6 regarding the additivity of the norm fails, as norm$(A) = 2$ while norm$(AA) = 1$. Hence a more delicate analysis is necessary for attacking more general rewrite systems, such as for PDA. However, this can still be possible, as demonstrated by Stirling [48].

4 Undecidability Results for PPDA

In this section we demonstrate Jančar's technique [32] for demonstrating undecidability results for bisimilarity through mimicking Minsky machines in a weak fashion but faithfully enough to capture the halting problem. Jančar first employed his ideas to demonstrate the undecidability of bisimulation equivalence over the class of Petri nets. Hirshfeld [21] modified the argument to demonstrate the undecidability of trace equivalence over BPP. Jančar and Moller [33] then used the technique to demonstrate the undecidability of regularity checking of Petri nets with respect to both simulation and trace equivalence.

In the following we generalize Jančar's result by demonstrating the undecidability of (normed) PPDA. Jančar's technique applies ideally in this case, as PPDA offer precisely the ingredients present in Petri nets which are needed to mimic Minsky machines.

Minsky Machines [41] are simple straight-line programs which make use of only two counters. Formally, a *Minsky machine* is a sequence of labelled instructions

$$\begin{array}{ll} \mathtt{X}_0 & : \mathrm{comm}_0 \\ \mathtt{X}_1 & : \mathrm{comm}_1 \\ & \cdots \\ \mathtt{X}_{n-1} & : \mathrm{comm}_{n-1} \\ \mathtt{X}_n & : \mathtt{halt} \end{array}$$

where each of the first n instructions is either of the form

$$\mathtt{X}_\ell\ :\ \mathtt{c}_0 := \mathtt{c}_0{+}1;\ \mathtt{goto}\ \mathtt{X}_j \qquad \text{or} \qquad \mathtt{X}_\ell\ :\ \mathtt{c}_1 := \mathtt{c}_1{+}1;\ \mathtt{goto}\ \mathtt{X}_j$$

or of the form

$$\begin{array}{ll} \mathtt{X}_\ell\ :\ \mathtt{if}\ \mathtt{c}_0 = 0\ \mathtt{then}\ \mathtt{goto}\ \mathtt{X}_j & \text{or} \quad \mathtt{X}_\ell\ :\ \mathtt{if}\ \mathtt{c}_1 = 0\ \mathtt{then}\ \mathtt{goto}\ \mathtt{X}_j \\ \quad\ \ \mathtt{else}\ \mathtt{c}_0 := \mathtt{c}_0{-}1;\ \mathtt{goto}\ \mathtt{X}_k & \qquad\quad\ \ \mathtt{else}\ \mathtt{c}_1 := \mathtt{c}_1{-}1;\ \mathtt{goto}\ \mathtt{X}_k \end{array}$$

A Minsky machine M starts executing with the value 0 in the counters $\mathtt{c}_0$ and $\mathtt{c}_1$ and the control at the label $\mathtt{X}_0$. When the control is at label $\mathtt{X}_\ell$ $(0 \le \ell < n)$, the machine executes instruction comm_ℓ, modifying the contents of the counters and transferring the control to the appropriate label as directed by the instruction. The machine halts if and when the control reaches the `halt` instruction at label $\mathtt{X}_n$. We recall now the fact that the halting problem for Minsky Machines is undecidable: there is no algorithm which decides whether or not a given Minsky machine halts.

A Minsky machine as presented above gives rise to the following PPDA.

- The input alphabet is $\Sigma = \{i, d, z, \omega\}$.
- The control states are $Q = \{p_0, p_1, \cdots, p_{n-1}, p_n, q_0, q_1, \cdots, q_{n-1}, q_n\}$.
- The stack alphabet is $\Gamma = \{Z, 0, 1\}$.
- For each machine instruction

$$\mathtt{X}_\ell\ :\ \mathtt{c}_b := \mathtt{c}_b{+}1;\ \mathtt{goto}\ \mathtt{X}_j$$

  we have the PPDA rules

$$p_\ell Z \xrightarrow{i} p_j bZ \qquad \text{and} \qquad q_\ell Z \xrightarrow{i} q_j bZ.$$

- For each machine instruction

$$\begin{array}{l} \mathtt{X}_\ell\ :\ \mathtt{if}\ \mathtt{c}_b = 0\ \mathtt{then}\ \mathtt{goto}\ \mathtt{X}_j \\ \quad\ \ \mathtt{else}\ \mathtt{c}_b := \mathtt{c}_b{-}1;\ \mathtt{goto}\ \mathtt{X}_k \end{array}$$

  we have the PPDA rules

$$p_\ell b \xrightarrow{d} p_k \qquad p_\ell Z \xrightarrow{z} p_j Z \qquad p_\ell b \xrightarrow{z} q_j b$$
$$q_\ell b \xrightarrow{d} q_k \qquad q_\ell Z \xrightarrow{z} q_j Z \qquad q_\ell b \xrightarrow{z} p_j b$$

- We have the one final PPDA rule

$$p_n Z \xrightarrow{\omega} p_n$$

The two states p_0Z and q_0Z of this PPDA each mimic the machine M in the following sense.

- When M is at the command labelled X_ℓ with the values x and y in its counters, this is reflected by the PPDA being in state $p_\ell 0^x 1^y Z$ (or $q_\ell 0^x 1^y Z$).
- If this command is an increment, then the PPDA has only one transition available from the control state p_ℓ (q_ℓ), which is labelled by i (for 'increment'), resulting in the PPDA state reflecting the state of the machine upon executing the increment command.
- If this command is a successful test for zero (that is, the relevant counter has the value 0), then the PPDA has only one transition available from the control state p_ℓ (q_ℓ), which is labelled z (for 'zero'), again resulting in the PPDA state reflecting the state of the machine upon executing the test for zero command.
- If this command is a decrement (that is, a failed test for zero), then the PPDA in control state p_ℓ (q_ℓ) has three possible transitions, exactly one of which is labelled d (for 'decrement') which would once again result in the PPDA state reflecting the state of the machine upon executing the decrement command.
- In this last instance, the PPDA has the option to disregard the existence of a relevant counter symbol in the stack and behave as if the program counter was zero. This reflects the weakness of Petri nets (and hence PPDA) in their inability to test for zero (a weakness which works in their favour with respect to several important positive decidability results such as the reachability problem [35]). In this case, the PPDA in control state p_ℓ (q_ℓ) may make a z transition in either of two ways: either by "honestly" cheating using the rule $p_\ell Z \xrightarrow{z} p_j Z$ ($q_\ell Z \xrightarrow{z} q_j Z$), or by "knowingly" cheating using the rule $p_\ell b \xrightarrow{z} q_j b$ ($q_\ell b \xrightarrow{z} p_j b$) thus moving the control state over into the domain of the other PPDA mimicking M.

Fact 4.1 $p_0Z \sim q_0Z$ *iff the Minsky machine M does not halt.*

Proof If M halts, then a winning strategy for player I in the bisimulation game would be to mimic the behaviour of M in either of the two PPDA states. Player II's only option in response would be to do the same with the other PPDA state. Upon termination, the game states will be $p_n 0^x 1^y Z$ and $q_n 0^x 1^y Z$ for some values x and y. Player I may then make the transition $p_n 0^x 1^y Z \xrightarrow{\omega} p_n 0^x 1^y$ which cannot be answered by player II from the state $q_n 0^x 1^y Z$. Hence p_0Z and q_0Z cannot be bisimilar.

If M fails to halt, then a winning strategy for player II would be to mimic player I's moves for as long as player I mimics M, and to cheat knowingly or honestly, respectively, in the instance that player I cheats honestly or knowingly, respectively, so as to arrive at the situation where the two states are identical; from here player II can copy every move of player I verbatim. Hence p_0Z and q_0Z must be bisimilar. □

We thus have undecidability of bisimulation equivalence over a very restricted class of Petri nets: those with only two unbounded places and a minimal degree of nondeterminism. Note that this nondeterminism is essential: Jančar [32] shows that bisimulation equivalence is decidable between two Petri nets when one of them is deterministic up to bisimilarity.

The above PPDA can be made into a normed rewrite transition system by adding a new input symbol n along with the following PPDA rules (one for each $i = 0 \ldots n$ and each $X = Z, 0, 1$).

$$\begin{array}{ll} p_\ell X \stackrel{n}{\longrightarrow} p_\ell & \qquad q_\ell X \stackrel{n}{\longrightarrow} q_\ell \\ p_\ell X \stackrel{n}{\longrightarrow} q_\ell & \qquad q_\ell X \stackrel{n}{\longrightarrow} p_\ell \end{array}$$

These moves allow the PPDA to exhaust its stack at any point during its execution, and continues to allow player II to produce a pair of identical states if player I elects to take one of these non-M-mimicking transitions. The same argument can then be made to show that p_0Z and q_0Z are bisimilar exactly when the Minsky machine M does not halt.

Theorem 4.2 *Bisimilarity is undecidable over the class of normed PPDA.*

This result contrasts interestingly with that of Stirling [48] regarding the decidability of bisimilarity over the class of normed PDA.

References

[1] J.C.M. Baeten, J.A. Bergstra and J.W. Klop (1987). Decidability of bisimulation equivalence for processes generating context-free languages. Proceedings of PARLE'87, *Lecture Notes in Computer Science* **259**:94–113.

[2] J.C.M. Baeten, J.A. Bergstra and J.W. Klop (1993). Decidability of bisimulation equivalence for processes generating context-free languages. *Journal of the ACM* **40**:653–682.

[3] Y. Bar-Hillel, M. Perles and E. Shamir (1961). On formal properties of simple phrase structure grammars. *Zeitschrift für Phonetik, Sprachwissenschaft, und Kommunikationsforschung* **14**:143–177.

[4] J.A. Bergstra and J.W. Klop (1985). Algebra of Communicating Processes with Abstraction. *Theoretical Computer Science* **37**:77–121.

[5] J.R. Burch, E.M. Clarke, K.L. McMillan, D.L. Dill and L.J. Hwang (1990). Symbolic model checking 10^{20} states and beyond. Proceedings of LICS'90:428–439.

[6] O. Burkart, D. Caucal and B. Steffen (1995). An elementary decision procedure for arbitrary context-free processes. Proceedings of MFCS'95. *Lecture Notes in Computer Science* **969**:423–433.

[7] O. Burkart, D. Caucal and B. Steffen (1996). Bisimulation collapse and the process taxonomy. This volume.

[8] D. Caucal (1990). Graphes canoniques des graphes algébriques. *Informatique Théorique et Applications (RAIRO)* **24**(4):339–352.

[9] D. Caucal (1992). On the regular structure of prefix rewriting. *Journal of Theoretical Computer Science* **106**:61–86.

[10] D. Caucal (1993). A fast algorithm to decide on the equivalence of stateless DPDA. *Informatique Théorique et Applications (RAIRO)* **27**(1):23–48.

[11] S. Christensen (1993). *Decidability and Decomposition in Process Algebras*. Ph.D. Thesis ECS-LFCS-93-278, Department of Computer Science, University of Edinburgh.

[12] S. Christensen, Y. Hirshfeld and F. Moller (1993). Decomposability, decidability and axiomatisability for bisimulation equivalence on basic parallel processes. Proceedings of LICS'93:386–396.

[13] S. Christensen, Y. Hirshfeld and F. Moller (1993). Bisimulation equivalence is decidable for basic parallel processes. Proceedings of CONCUR'93, *Lecture Notes in Computer Science* **715**:143–157.

[14] S. Christensen, H. Hüttel and C. Stirling (1992). Bisimulation equivalence is decidable for all context-free processes. Proceedings of CONCUR'92, *Lecture Notes in Computer Science* **630**:138–147.

[15] S. Christensen, H. Hüttel and C. Stirling (1995). Bisimulation equivalence is decidable for all context-free processes. *Information and Computation* **121**(2):143–148.

[16] R.J. van Glabbeek (1990). The linear time-branching time spectrum. Proceedings of CONCUR'90, *Lecture Notes in Computer Science* **458**:278–297.

[17] J.F. Groote (1991). A short proof of the decidability of bisimulation for normed BPA processes. *Information Processing Letters* **42**:167–171.

[18] J.F. Groote and H. Hüttel (1994). Undecidable equivalences for basic process algebra. *Information and Computation* **115**(2):353–371.

[19] M. Hack (1976). *Decidability questions for Petri nets*. Ph.D. Thesis, Technical Report 161, Laboratory for Computer Science, Massachusetts Institute of Technology.

[20] L.E. Dickson (1913). Finiteness of the odd perfect and primitive abundant numbers with distinct factors. *American Journal of Mathematics* **35**:413–422.

[21] Y. Hirshfeld (1993). Petri Nets and the Equivalence Problem. Proceedings of CSL'93, *Lecture Notes in Computer Science* **832**:165–174.

[22] Y. Hirshfeld (1994). Congruences in commutative semigroups. Research report ECS-LFCS-94-291, Department of Computer Science, University of Edinburgh.

[23] Y. Hirshfeld, M. Jerrum and F. Moller (1994). A polynomial-time algorithm for deciding equivalence of normed context-free processes. Proceedings of FOCS'94:623–631.

[24] Y. Hirshfeld, M. Jerrum and F. Moller (1996). A polynomial algorithm for deciding bisimilarity of normed context-free processes. *Theoretical Computer Science* **158**:143–159.

[25] Y. Hirshfeld, M. Jerrum and F. Moller (1996). A polynomial algorithm for deciding bisimulation equivalence of normed basic parallel processes. To appear in *Mathematical Structures in Computer Science.*

[26] Y. Hirshfeld and F. Moller (1994). A fast algorithm for deciding bisimilarity of normed context-free processes. Proceedings of CONCUR'94, *Lecture Notes in Computer Science* **836**:48–63.

[27] J.E. Hopcroft and J.D. Ullman (1979). **Introduction to Automata Theory, Languages, and Computation**. Addison Wesley.

[28] H. Hüttel (1993). Undecidable equivalences for basic parallel processes. Proceedings of FSTTCS'93, *Lecture Notes in Computer Science.*

[29] H. Hüttel and C. Stirling (1991). Actions speak louder than words: proving bisimilarity for context-free processes. Proceedings of LICS'91:376–386.

[30] D.T. Huynh and L. Tian (1994). Deciding bisimilarity of normed context-free processes is in Σ_2^P. *Theoretical Computer Science* **123**:183–197.

[31] D.T. Huynh and L. Tian (1995). On deciding readiness and failure equivalences for processes. *Information and Computation* **117**(2):193–205.

[32] P. Jančar (1993). Decidability questions for bisimilarity of Petri nets and some related problems. Proceedings of STACS'94, *Lecture Notes in Computer Science* **775**:581–592.

[33] P. Jančar and F. Moller (1995). Checking regular properties of Petri nets. Proceedings of CONCUR'95, *Lecture Notes in Computer Science* **962**:348–362.

[34] A. Korenjak and J. Hopcroft (1966). Simple deterministic languages. Proceedings of 7th IEEE Switching and Automata Theory conference:36–46.

[35] E. Mahr (1984). An algorithm for the general Petri net reachability problem. *SIAM Journal of Computing* **13**:441–460.

[36] R. Milner (1984). A complete inference system for a class of regular behaviours. *Journal of Computer and System Science* **28**:439–466.

[37] R. Milner (1980). **A Calculus of Communicating Systems**. *Lecture Notes in Computer Science* **92**.

[38] R. Milner (1989). **Communication and Concurrency**. Prentice-Hall.

[39] R. Milner and F. Moller (1990). Unique decomposition of processes. *Bulletin of the European Association for Theoretical Computer Science* **41**:226–232.

[40] R. Milner and F. Moller (1993). Unique decomposition of processes. *Theoretical Computer Science* **107**:357–363.

[41] M. Minsky (1967). **Computation: Finite and Infinite Machines**. Prentice-Hall.

[42] E.F. Moore (1956). Gedanken experiments on sequential machines. In *Automata Studies*:129–153.

[43] D.M.R. Park (1981). Concurrency and automata on infinite sequences. *Lecture Notes in Computer Science* **104**:168–183.

[44] J.L. Peterson (1981). **Petri Net Theory and the Modelling of Systems**. Prentice-Hall.

[45] L. Redei (1965). **The theory of finitely generated commutative semigroups**. Oxford University Press.

[46] A. Salomaa (1966). Two complete axiom systems for the algebra of regular events. *Journal of the ACM* **13**(1):158–169.

[47] C. Stirling (1995). Local model checking games. Proceedings of CONCUR'95, *Lecture Notes in Computer Science* **962**:1–11.

[48] C. Stirling (1996). Decidability of bisimulation equivalence for normed pushdown processes. This volume.

[49] D. Taubner (1989). **Finite Representations of CCS and TCSP Programs by Automata and Petri Nets**. *Lecture Notes in Computer Science* **369**.

Decidability of Bisimulation Equivalence for Normed Pushdown Processes

Colin Stirling

Department of Computer Science
University of Edinburgh
email: cps@dcs.ed.ac.uk

1 Introduction

In the classical theory of automata the expressive power of pushdown automata is matched by context-free grammars. Both accept the same family of languages, the context-free languages. Concurrency theory requires a more intensional exposition of behaviour (as language equivalence need not be preserved in the presence of communicating abstract machines). Many finer equivalences have been proposed. Bisimulation equivalence, due to Park and Milner, has received much attention.

Baeten, Bergstra and Klop proved that bisimulation equivalence is decidable for irredundant context-free grammars (without the empty production). Within process calculus theory these grammars correspond to normed BPA processes. Their proof relies on isolating a complex periodicity from the transition graphs of these processes. Simpler proofs of the result soon followed which expose algebraic structure.

Caucal and Monfort showed that normed pushdown processes (the process analogue of irredundant pushdown automata without ϵ-transitions) are strictly more expressive than normed BPA with respect to bisimulation equivalence. In this paper we prove that bisimulation equivalence is decidable for this richer family of processes. However the proof is not easy, and does not follow immediately from the techniques used for showing decidability of normed BPA. One indication of this is that the proof of decidability of bisimulation equivalence for BPP (Basic Parallel Processes) is similar to that for BPA. However, bisimulation equivalence is undecidable for the pushdown extension to BPP.

2 Normed pushdown processes

Ingredients for describing pushdown processes are a finite set of states $\mathcal{P} = \{p_1, \ldots, p_k\}$, a finite set of stack symbols $\Gamma = \{X_1, \ldots, X_m\}$, a finite set of actions $\mathcal{A} = \{a_1, \ldots, a_n\}$ and a finite family of basic transitions, each of the form $pX \xrightarrow{a} q\alpha$ where p and q are states, a is an action, X is a stack symbol and α is a sequence of stack symbols. A *pushdown process* is then any expression $p\alpha$, $p \in \mathcal{P}$ and $\alpha \in \Gamma^*$, whose behaviour (transition graph) is determined by the basic transitions together with the following prefix rule, where $\beta \in \Gamma^*$:

$$\text{if } pX \xrightarrow{a} q\alpha \text{ then } pX\beta \xrightarrow{a} q\alpha\beta$$

This account follows the presentation of Caucal [6]. It is a slight redescription of classical pushdown automata (without ϵ-transitions and final states), as for instance in [15], viewing them as generators instead of as acceptors.

Example 1 Let $\mathcal{P} = \{p, q, r, s\}$, $\Gamma = \{X\}$ and $\mathcal{A} = \{a, b, c, d\}$. The family of basic transitions is

$$\{pX \xrightarrow{a} pXX,\ pX \xrightarrow{c} q\epsilon,\ pX \xrightarrow{b} r\epsilon,\ qX \xrightarrow{d} sX,\ sX \xrightarrow{d} q\epsilon,\ rX \xrightarrow{d} r\epsilon\}$$

where ϵ is the empty stack sequence. The transition graph generated by pX is:

$$\begin{array}{ccccc}
q\epsilon \xleftarrow{d} sX \xleftarrow{d} qX & \xleftarrow{d} & sXX \xleftarrow{d} qXX & \xleftarrow{d} & \ldots \\
\uparrow c & & \uparrow c \quad\quad & & \vdots \\
pX \quad \xrightarrow{a} \quad pXX & \xrightarrow{a} & pXXX & \xrightarrow{a} & \ldots \\
\downarrow b & & \downarrow b \quad\quad & & \vdots \\
r\epsilon \quad \xleftarrow{d} \quad rX & \xleftarrow{d} & rXX & \xleftarrow{d} & \ldots
\end{array}$$

For any $n \geq 0$ the transition $qXX^n \xrightarrow{d} sXX^n$ is derived from the basic transition $qX \xrightarrow{d} sX$ using the prefix rule when β is X^n. □

Example 1 illustrates how a pushdown process may generate an infinite state transition graph. In the following we are interested in comparing the behaviour of two pushdown processes. Without loss of generality, we can assume that they are built from the same ingredients $\mathcal{P}$, Γ, $\mathcal{A}$ and basic transitions (as the appropriate disjoint union, with respect to states and stack symbols, of two pushdown descriptions is a pushdown description). One notion of behaviour of $p\alpha$ is the language it generates, which is the set of words $\{w \in \mathcal{A}^* \ : \ \exists q \in \mathcal{P}. p\alpha \xrightarrow{w} q\epsilon\}$ where the extended transitions $\xrightarrow{w}$ are defined in the usual way. Acceptance is by empty stack instead of by final state (see [15]). The process pX of Example 1 generates the language $\{a^n b d^n \ : \ n \geq 0\} \cup \{a^n c d^{2n} \ : \ n \geq 0\}$. Any language generated by a pushdown process is context-free, and for each context-free language without the empty string there is a pushdown process which generates it. This remains true under the following restriction. A process $p\alpha$ is *normed* if every reachable process with a non-empty stack generates a non-empty language. (That is, for every $q\beta$ such that $\beta \neq \epsilon$ and $p\alpha \xrightarrow{v} q\beta$ for some v, there is a w and a state r, such that $q\beta \xrightarrow{w} r\epsilon$.) Normedness amounts to irredundancy in the pushdown automaton. In the rest of the paper we assume this restriction to normed pushdown processes.

Each context-free language without the empty string is also generated by a normed pushdown process whose state set $\mathcal{P}$ contains just one state. In which case $\mathcal{P}$ is superfluous, and the result is a normed context-free or BPA process (in Greibach normal form). The stack symbols Γ are the nonterminals and basic transitions have the form $X \xrightarrow{a} \alpha$. The prefix rule is: if $X \xrightarrow{a} \alpha$ then $X\beta \xrightarrow{a} \alpha\beta$. The language generated by a context-free process α is $\{w : \alpha \xrightarrow{w} \epsilon\}$. There is a standard transformation, see [15], which translates a normed pushdown process into a normed context-free process which generates the same language. With respect to languages, the expressive power of normed context-free processes is the same as normed pushdown processes.

Concurrency theory is built on a more intensional account of behavioural equivalence than that given by languages. A pivotal notion, due to Park and Milner, is bisimilarity which is finer than language equivalence on processes.

Definition 1 A binary relation $\mathcal{R}$ between processes is a bisimulation relation provided that whenever $(E, F) \in \mathcal{R}$, for all a

$$\begin{array}{l} \text{if } E \xrightarrow{a} E' \text{ then } \exists F'.\, F \xrightarrow{a} F' \text{ and } (E', F') \in \mathcal{R}, \text{ and} \\ \text{if } F \xrightarrow{a} F' \text{ then } \exists E'.\, E \xrightarrow{a} E' \text{ and } (E', F') \in \mathcal{R}. \end{array}$$

Two processes E and F are defined to be bisimulation equivalent, or bisimilar, written $E \sim F$, if there is a bisimulation relation $\mathcal{R}$ relating them.

The transformation from pushdown processes to context-free processes does not preserve bisimulation equivalence. In fact, with respect to bisimilarity normed pushdown processes constitute a richer family than normed context-free processes, as shown by Caucal and Monfort [7]. Their proof is very elegant, and utilises the canonical graph of a process which is the quotient of its transition graph with respect to bisimulation equivalence. For instance, the canonical graph for Example 1 fuses together the pairs of vertices labelled qX^n and rX^{2n} for any $n \geq 0$. Normed context-free processes are closed under canonical graphs in the sense that for each such canonical graph there is a normed context-free process whose transition graph is isomorphic to it. Normed pushdown processes fail to have this property. Caucal and Monfort show that Example 1 is a counter-example, as its canonical graph lacks the regular structure (as identified by Muller and Schupp [19]) that the transition graph of a pushdown process must possess. Burkart and Steffen provide additional insight into pushdown processes [3], by showing that, unlike context-free processes, they are closed under Hoare parallel composition with finite state processes (with respect to bisimilarity). Moreover they demonstrate that the family of pushdown processes is the smallest extension of context-free processes with this closure property.

Baeten, Bergstra and Klop proved that bisimulation equivalence is decidable for normed context-free processes [1, 2]. Simpler proofs were developed in [5, 11, 17, 13], and [14] showed that there is even a polynomial time decision procedure. The decidability result was generalized in [10] to encompass unnormed processes, and then refined in [4] to give upper bounds. Groote and Hüttel proved that other standard equivalences on processes (traces, failures, simulation, 2/3-bisimulation etc..,) are all undecidable [12]. Similar results were proved for Basic Parallel Processes, BPP, which are like context-free processes except that a process expression α is a multiset[1]. Christensen, Hirshfeld and Moller showed that bisimulation equivalence is decidable for normed BPP [8], and this result was generalised in [9] to include the unnormed case. Hüttel proved that the other equivalences are undecidable [16].

Decidability of bisimulation equivalence for normed pushdown processes is harder to show than for normed context-free processes. There are many reasons for this. First Baeten, Bergstra and Klop's method is not applicable, as normed pushdown transition graphs need not display the periodicity upon which their proof relies. Secondly, the structural methods in the simplifed proofs of decidability, which appeal to decomposition and congruence, are not immediately applicable, as it is not clear what are the components of a pushdown process: a context-free process $X_1 \ldots X_n$ is built from the subprocesses X_i, but a process $pX_1 \ldots X_n$ does not contain X_i as a pushdown component. Perhaps the clearest indication of the increased difficulty is that for the pushdown extension of BPP[2] bisimulation equivalence is undecidable, a result due to Hirshfeld (utilizing Jančar's technique for showing undecidability of bisimilarity for Petri nets [18]).

The proof presented below of decidability of bisimulation equivalence for normed pushdown processes consists of two semi-decision procedures (for which we are unable to provide a complexity measure). One half of the proof is easy, as bisimilarity is characterizable using approximants when processes, such as pushdown processes, are image-finite[3].

Definition 2 The family $\{\sim_n : n \geq 0\}$ is defined inductively as follows

$$\begin{array}{l} E \sim_0 F \text{ for all processes } E, F \\ E \sim_{n+1} F \text{ iff for each } a \in \mathcal{A} \\ \quad \text{if } E \xrightarrow{a} E' \text{ then } \exists F'. F \xrightarrow{a} F' \text{ and } E' \sim_n F', \text{ and} \\ \quad \text{if } F \xrightarrow{a} F' \text{ then } \exists E'. E \xrightarrow{a} E' \text{ and } E' \sim_n F' \end{array}$$

The following is a standard result.

Proposition 1 *If E and F are image-finite then $E \sim F$ iff $\forall n \geq 0.\ E \sim_n F$.*

For each $n \geq 0$, the relation $\sim_n$ is decidable for pushdown processes, and therefore bisimulation inequivalence is semi-decidable via the simple procedure which seeks the least i such that $p\alpha \not\sim_i q\beta$. Therefore we just need to establish the semi-decidability of bisimulation equivalence. The crux of this part of the proof is that there is a finite tableau proof of $p\alpha \sim q\beta$. As finite proofs can be enumerated, this amounts to a semi-decision procedure. The method generalises the technique developed by the author and Hüttel [17]. It relies upon exposure of structure within normed pushdown processes. We introduce a finer equivalence than bisimilarity to ensure a congruence, and we show that with respect to it

---

[1] The prefix rule becomes: if $X \xrightarrow{a} \alpha$ then $\delta X \beta \xrightarrow{a} \delta\alpha\beta$.

[2] When the prefix rule is: if $pX \xrightarrow{a} q\alpha$ then $p\delta X\beta \xrightarrow{a} q\delta\alpha\beta$.

[3] E is image-finite if for each $w \in A^*$ the set $\{F : E \xrightarrow{w} F\}$ is finite.

pushdown processes can be taken apart, when extra stack symbols are introduced.

3 Congruence and decomposition

Two key properties underpin decidability of bisimulation equivalence on normed context-free processes:

$$\text{Congruence: if } \alpha \sim \beta \text{ then } \alpha\delta \sim \beta\delta$$
$$\text{Decomposition: if } \alpha\delta \sim \beta\delta \text{ then } \alpha \sim \beta$$

Explicit use of these features can be seen in the decidability proof using tableaux [17]. In fact, there is a stronger property of unique prime decomposition due to Hirshfeld [13]. In the more general case, when the restriction to being normed is lifted, the first feature still holds but the second can fail. However bisimulation equivalence is still decidable because a weakened version of decomposition holds: if there are infinitely many different δ (up to $\sim$) such that $\alpha\delta \sim \beta\delta$ then $\alpha \sim \beta$.

Neither property holds for normed pushdown processes. A counterexample to congruence is that although $qX \sim rXX$ in Example 1 of the previous section, $qXX \not\sim rXXX$. Example 1 also furnishes instances of failure of decomposition such as $rX^6 \sim qX^3$ but $rX^5 \not\sim qX^2$.

Congruence fails because bisimilarity of pushdown processes does not imply that they agree on their final states when the stack empties: for instance the bisimulation relation between qX and rXX contains the pair $(q\epsilon, r\epsilon)$. However a congruence can be enforced by strengthening the definition of bisimulation equivalence.

Definition 1 A binary relation $\mathcal{R}$ on pushdown processes is an a-bisimulation provided that whenever $(p\alpha, q\beta) \in \mathcal{R}$, for all $a \in \mathcal{A}$

if $\alpha = \epsilon$ then $\beta = \epsilon$ and $p = q$, and
if $\beta = \epsilon$ then $\alpha = \epsilon$ and $p = q$, and
if $p\alpha \xrightarrow{a} p'\alpha'$ then $\exists q'\beta'.\, q\beta \xrightarrow{a} q'\beta'$ and $(p'\alpha', q'\beta') \in \mathcal{R}$, and
if $q\beta \xrightarrow{a} q'\beta'$ then $\exists p'\alpha'.\, p\alpha \xrightarrow{a} p'\alpha'$ and $(p'\alpha', q'\beta') \in \mathcal{R}$.

The "a" stands for "agreeing", as the first two clauses require final states to be the same when processes terminate. Two pushdown processes $p\alpha$ and $q\beta$ are a-bisimilar, written $p\alpha \equiv q\beta$, if there is an a-bisimulation relating them. Note that the earlier pair qX and rXX are not a-bisimilar. Later we shall relate $\sim$ and $\equiv$.

Not surprisingly a-bisimilarity is an equivalence relation, and it is also a congruence with respect to stacking.

Proposition 1 *The relation $\equiv$ is an equivalence relation.*

Proposition 2 *If $p\alpha \equiv q\beta$ then $p\alpha\delta \equiv q\beta\delta$.*

A-bisimilarity can also be characterized using approximants.

Definition 2 The family $\{\equiv_n : n \geq 0\}$ is defined inductively on pushdown processes as follows:

$$pX\alpha \equiv_0 qY\beta \text{ and } p\epsilon \equiv_0 p\epsilon$$
$$p\alpha \equiv_{n+1} q\beta \text{ iff } p\alpha \equiv_0 q\beta, \text{ and for each } a \in \mathcal{A},$$
$$\text{if } p\alpha \xrightarrow{a} p'\alpha' \text{ then } \exists q'\beta'.\, q\beta \xrightarrow{a} q'\beta' \text{ and } p'\alpha' \equiv_n q'\beta', \text{ and}$$
$$\text{if } q\beta \xrightarrow{a} q'\beta' \text{ then } \exists p'\alpha'.\, p\alpha \xrightarrow{a} p'\alpha' \text{ and } p'\alpha' \equiv_n q'\beta'.$$

Notice that the base relation $\equiv_0$ does not include all pairs of pushdown processes.

Proposition 3 $p\alpha \equiv q\beta$ *iff* $\forall n \geq 0.\ p\alpha \equiv_n q\beta$.

We define an extended pushdown description by augmenting the stack symbols Γ with a finite family of stack constants $\mathcal{W}$. Assume that the state set of the pushdown description is $\mathcal{P} = \{p_1, \ldots, p_k\}$. Each new stack symbol $W \in \mathcal{W}$ has an associated definition

$$W \stackrel{\text{def}}{=} (q_1\delta_1, \ldots, q_k\delta_k)$$

where each $q_i \in \mathcal{P}$, and each δ_i is a sequence of stack elements, possibly including constants. However we assume that if $\delta_i \neq \epsilon$ then its first symbol belongs to Γ. The intention is that for each state $p_j \in \mathcal{P}$ the behaviour of p_jW is that of $q_j\delta_j$, the jth component of the definition of W[4]. An *extended* pushdown process is an expression $p\alpha$ where $\alpha = \epsilon$ or $\alpha \in \Gamma(\Gamma \cup \mathcal{W})^*$. Basic transitions are unaffected, remaining of the form $pX \xrightarrow{a} q\alpha$ where $X \in \Gamma$ and $\alpha \in \Gamma^*$. However the prefix rule is generalised to

$$\text{if } pX \xrightarrow{a} q\alpha \text{ then } pX\beta \xrightarrow{a} [q\alpha\beta]$$

where bracketing [ ] is defined as follows:

$$[p_i\epsilon] = p_i\epsilon, \text{ and}$$
$$[p_iX\beta] = p_iX\beta, \text{ and}$$
$$[p_iW\beta] = [q_i\delta_i\beta] \text{ when } W \stackrel{\text{def}}{=} (q_1\delta_1, \ldots, q_k\delta_k)$$

Therefore it follows that whenever $p\alpha$ is an extended pushdown process and $p\alpha \xrightarrow{w} q\beta$ then $q\beta$ is also an extended pushdown process.

The presence of constants does not affect congruence, and they also provide a handle for composing pushdown processes.

Proposition 4 *If* $pX\alpha \equiv qY\beta$ *then* $pX\alpha W \equiv qY\beta W$.

Proposition 5 *If* $W \stackrel{\text{def}}{=} (q_1\delta_1\beta, \ldots, q_k\delta_k\beta)$ *and* $V \stackrel{\text{def}}{=} (q_1\delta_1, \ldots, q_k\delta_k)$ *then* $pX\alpha W \equiv pX\alpha V\beta$.

[4] This selection notation $(\ldots)$ for pushdown processes is used in [20, 3].

Proposition 6 *If* $W \stackrel{\text{def}}{=} (q_1\delta_1, \ldots, q_k\delta_k)$ *and* $V \stackrel{\text{def}}{=} (r_1\lambda_1, \ldots, r_k\lambda_k)$ *and for each* $i : 1 \le i \le k$, $q_i\delta_i \equiv r_i\lambda_i$ *then* $pX\alpha W \equiv pX\alpha V$.

It is time to examine the condition of being normed more carefully. The *norm* of a process $p\alpha$, when α may contain constants, is a k-tuple $(n_1, \ldots, n_k)$ where each $n_i \in \mathrm{N} \cup \{\perp\}$. The component n_i is either the length of a shortest word w such that $p\alpha \stackrel{w}{\longrightarrow} p_i\epsilon$ or there is no such word and n_i is the undefined element $\perp$. We let $\mathrm{n}(p\alpha)$ be the norm of $p\alpha$, and we let $\mathrm{n}(p\alpha)_i$ be its ith component. The restriction to normed processes implies that at least one entry in a norm is different from $\perp$. Let $\max(p\alpha)$ be the maximum defined entry in $\mathrm{n}(p\alpha)$ and $\min(p\alpha)$ be the least defined entry. Finally we let $\mathrm{D}(p\alpha)$ be the set $\{i : \mathrm{n}(p\alpha)_i \neq \perp\}$. We can now slightly refine the previous Proposition.

Proposition 7 *If* $W \stackrel{\text{def}}{=} (q_1\delta_1, \ldots, q_k\delta_k)$ *and* $V \stackrel{\text{def}}{=} (r_1\lambda_1, \ldots, r_k\lambda_k)$ *and for each* $i \in \mathrm{D}(pX\alpha)$. $q_i\delta_i \equiv r_i\lambda_i$ *then* $pX\alpha W \equiv pX\alpha V$.

We now define two useful measures on a pushdown description. We let M be just greater than the maximum norm of a stack symbol in Γ:

$$M \stackrel{\text{def}}{=} 1 + \max\{\max(pX) : p \in \mathcal{P} \text{ and } X \in \Gamma\}$$

And we let G be the maximum length of a stack sequence in a basic transition, where $|\;|$ means "length of":

$$G \stackrel{\text{def}}{=} \max\{|\alpha| : pX \stackrel{a}{\longrightarrow} q\alpha \text{ is a basic transition}\}$$

The family of finite constants $\mathcal{W}$ is partitioned into two. First are *simple* constants. Each has a definition $U \stackrel{\text{def}}{=} (q_1\delta_1, \ldots, q_k\delta_k)$ where each $\delta_i \in \Gamma^+$ and $|\delta_i| \le MG$: constants are not allowed in their definition, and neither is the empty stack. Up to renaming of constants, there are only finitely many different simple constants, because of the constraint on their length. Their role is to provide a format for decomposition, as the next result shows.

Lemma 1 *If* $pX\alpha \equiv q\beta\delta$ *and* $\beta \in \Gamma^+$ *and* $\max(pX) < \min(q\beta)$ *and* $|\beta| \le M$ *then there is a simple* $U \stackrel{\text{def}}{=} (q_1\gamma_1, \ldots, q_k\gamma_k)$ *such that*

1. $pXU\delta \equiv q\beta\delta$, *and* 2. $\forall i \in \mathrm{D}(pX).\, [p_i\alpha] \equiv q_i\gamma_i\delta$.

Proof: Suppose $pX\alpha \equiv q\beta\delta$ and $\beta \in \Gamma^+$ and $\max(pX) < \min(q\beta)$ and $|\beta| \le M$. For each $i \in \mathrm{D}(pX)$ consider a shortest w_i such that $pX \stackrel{w_i}{\longrightarrow} p_i\epsilon$. Therefore, $pX\alpha \stackrel{w_i}{\longrightarrow} [p_i\alpha]$. Since $pX\alpha \equiv q\beta\delta$ we know that $q\beta\delta \stackrel{w_i}{\longrightarrow} q_i\lambda_i$ and $[p_i\alpha] \equiv q_i\lambda_i$. However, as $\max(pX) < \min(q\beta)$ it follows that $\lambda_i = \gamma_i\delta$ and $q\beta \stackrel{w_i}{\longrightarrow} q_i\gamma_i$ and $\gamma_i \neq \epsilon$, and as $\beta \in \Gamma^+$ this means that $\gamma_i \in \Gamma^+$. Also because $|w_i| < M$ (and $|\beta| \le M$) it follows that $|\gamma_i| \le MG$. Let $U \stackrel{\text{def}}{=} (q_1\gamma_1, \ldots, q_k\gamma_k)$ where for each $i \in \mathrm{D}(pX)$ $q_i\gamma_i$ is determined as above and for each $i \notin \mathrm{D}(pX)$, $q_i\gamma_i = pX$. By definition U is a simple constant, and by construction 2 holds. By induction on n it follows that for any $p'\alpha'$ such that $\alpha' \in \Gamma^+$ and $D(p'\alpha') \subseteq D(pX)$, $p'\alpha'U\delta \equiv_n p'\alpha'\alpha$. Therefore $pXU\delta \equiv pX\alpha$, which implies 1. □

The other constants are *recursive*. Each recursive constant has a definition $V \stackrel{\text{def}}{=} (q_1\lambda_1, \ldots, q_k\lambda_k)$, where each λ_i is either empty or of the form $\lambda_i'V$ where V is the defining constant and λ_i' is a non-empty sequence of stack symbols which may contain simple (but not recursive) constants. The first use of these constants is to relate $\sim$ and $\equiv$. Let I be a special initial constant $I \stackrel{\text{def}}{=} (p_1\epsilon, \ldots, p_1\epsilon)$.

Proposition 8 *$pX\alpha \sim qY\beta$ iff $pX\alpha I \equiv qY\beta I$.*

The starting point is to show that $p\alpha \sim q\beta$ is semi-decidable, and when α and β are both non-empty the problem reduces to $p\alpha I \equiv q\beta I$. When α and β are sufficiently large, Lemma 1 provides a mechanism for further reduction, to an equivalence of the form $pXU\delta \equiv q\beta'\delta$, where there is the common subsequence δ. Simple decomposition, if $p\alpha\delta \equiv q\beta\delta$ then $p\alpha \equiv q\beta$, does not hold in general. However there is a weakened version, which is a little subtle, and should be compared with the general case of context-free processes, as described earlier. This is the second and chief role of recursive constants. We now state the central result, which oils the decidability proof. In it we assume that $\Delta \subseteq (\Gamma \cup \mathcal{W})^*$ is a finite or infinite set of stack sequences.

Lemma 2 *If $pX\alpha\delta \equiv qY\beta\delta$ for all $\delta \in \Delta$, and α and β do not contain recursive constants then there exists a finite family $\mathcal{V}$ of recursive constants such that for each $\delta \in \Delta$ there is a $V \stackrel{\text{def}}{=} (q_1\lambda_1, \ldots, q_k\lambda_k)$ in $\mathcal{V}$ such that*

1. $pX\alpha V \equiv qY\beta V$,
2. $\forall i \in D(pX\alpha) \cup D(qY\beta)$. *if* $\lambda_i = \epsilon$ *then* $[p_i\delta] \equiv [q_i\delta]$,
3. $\forall i$. *if* $\lambda_i = \lambda_i'V$ *then* $[p_i\delta] \equiv q_i\lambda_i'\delta$.

Proof: Suppose $pX\alpha\delta \equiv qY\beta\delta$ for all $\delta \in \Delta$, and α, β do not contain recursive constants. Assume a total ordering on the state set $\{p_1, \ldots, p_k\}$, so that $p_i < p_j$ whenever $i < j$. We say that the recursive constant V is definitionally equivalent to V' if their definitions are the same except for their occurrences of V and V': in which case, for all $n \geq 0$, $pX\alpha V \equiv_n pX\alpha V'$ for any p, X and α.

For each $\delta \in \Delta$ we define the family $\{V_i^\delta : 0 \leq i \leq k^2\}$ iteratively, so that for each i properties 2 and 3 hold for V_i^δ and property 1 holds when $i = k^2$. Furthermore, for each i the set $\{V_i^\delta : \delta \in \Delta\}$ when quotiented by definitional equivalence is finite. From this the result follows by taking $\mathcal{V}$ to be the family $\{V_{k^2}^\delta : \delta \in \Delta\}$ after quotienting by definitional equivalence.

The element $V_0^\delta \stackrel{\text{def}}{=} (p_1\epsilon, \ldots p_k\epsilon)$. Clearly, both 2 and 3 hold, and the set $\{V_0^\delta : \delta \in \Delta\}$ is a singleton up to definitional equivalence. Assume V_i^δ for $0 \leq i < k^2$ has been defined, and that both 2 and 3 hold for it, and that the set $\{V_i^\delta : \delta \in \Delta\}$ is finite up to definitional equivalence. If property 1 is also true then let V_j^δ, for all $j : i \leq j \leq k^2$ be V_i^δ. Otherwise V_{i+1}^δ is constructed as a refinement of V_i^δ.

As 1 fails there is a least $n \geq 0$ such that $pX\alpha V_i^\delta \not\equiv_n qY\beta V_i^\delta$. By definition $n > 0$. However, we also know that $pX\alpha\delta \equiv qY\beta\delta$. Hence $pX\alpha \xrightarrow{a} [p_1'\alpha_1]$ and $qY\beta \xrightarrow{a} [q_1\beta_1]$ for some a and $p_1'\alpha_1$ and $q_1\beta_1$ such that $[p_1'\alpha_1\delta] \equiv [q_1\beta_1\delta]$ and $[p_1'\alpha_1 V_i^\delta] \not\equiv_{n-1} [q_1\beta_1 V_i^\delta]$. The sequences α_1 and β_1 do not contain recursive constants. If both α_1 and β_1 are non-empty then we can obtain a subsequent pair $p_2'\alpha_2$ and $q_2\beta_2$ such that $[p_2'\alpha_2\delta] \equiv [q_2\beta_2\delta]$ and $[p_2'\alpha_2 V_i^\delta] \not\equiv_{n-2} [q_2\beta_2 V_i^\delta]$, and so on. Therefore as n is finite we must reach a pair $p_j'\alpha_j$ and $q_j\beta_j$ such that $[p_j'\alpha_j\delta] \equiv [q_j\beta_j\delta]$ and $[p_j'\alpha_j V_i^\delta] \not\equiv_{n-j} [q_j\beta_j V_i^\delta]$, where α_j or β_j is empty (and neither contain recursive constants).

Without loss of generality assume that $\alpha_j = \epsilon$. Let $r\lambda$ be the entry for p_j' in V_i^δ. There are two cases.

Case 1 $\lambda = \epsilon$. Now consider β_j. First assume that $\beta_j \neq \epsilon$. Let V_{i+1}^δ be V_i^δ except that $q_j\beta_j V_{i+1}^\delta$ is associated with the state p_j' instead of $r\epsilon$ (and throughout the other entries V_{i+1}^δ replaces V_i^δ). Clearly properties 2 and 3 hold for V_{i+1}^δ given that they hold for V_i^δ. Next assume instead that $\beta_j = \epsilon$. Assume that $s\gamma$ is q_j's entry in V_i^δ. There are two subcases. First, $\gamma \neq \epsilon$. Then V_{i+1}^δ is V_i^δ except that $s\gamma$ is associated with p_j' (and throughout all entries V_{i+1}^δ replaces V_i^δ). Second, $\gamma = \epsilon$. If $p_j' < q_j$ in the total order on states V_{i+1}^δ is V_i^δ except that $r\epsilon$ is associated with q_j instead of $s\epsilon$, and if $q_j < p_j'$ then V_{i+1}^δ is V_i^δ except that $s\epsilon$ is associated with p_j' (and in both cases throughout the other entries V_{i+1}^δ replaces V_i^δ). Again clearly properties 2 and 3 both hold for V_{i+1}^δ.

Case 2 $\lambda \neq \epsilon$, and so $\lambda = \lambda' V_i^\delta$. Again consider β_j. If $\beta_j \neq \epsilon$ then as $[p_j'\delta] \equiv q_j\beta_j\delta$ by 3 we know that $[p_j'\delta] \equiv r\lambda'\delta$, and so $r\lambda'\delta \equiv q_j\beta_j\delta$. However $r\lambda' V_i^\delta \not\equiv_{n-j} q_j\beta_j V_i^\delta$ (as $[p_j'\alpha_j V_i^\delta] = r\lambda' V_i^\delta$). Therefore the proof proceeds as before by defining further pairs $r_m\lambda_m'$ and $q_{j+m}\beta_{j+m}$ such that $[r_m\lambda_m'\delta] \equiv [q_{j+m}\beta_{j+m}\delta]$ and $[r_m\lambda_m' V_i^\delta] \not\equiv_{n-(j+m)} [q_{j+m}\beta_{j+m} V_i^\delta]$. Otherwise $\beta_j = \epsilon$. Let $s\gamma$ be the entry for q_j in V_i^δ. If $\gamma = \epsilon$ then we proceed as in case 1 above (with the α and β roles reversed). If $\gamma \neq \epsilon$ then $\gamma = \gamma' V_i^\delta$ where γ' does not contain recursive constants. By 3 for V_i^δ $[q_j\delta] \equiv s\gamma'\delta$ and $[p_j'\delta] \equiv r\lambda'\delta$ and therefore $r\lambda'\delta \equiv s\gamma'\delta$, and also $r\lambda' V_i^\delta \not\equiv_{n-j} s\gamma' V_i^\delta$. Therefore again we define further pairs $r_m\lambda_m'$ and $s_m\gamma_m'$ such that $[r_m\lambda_m'\delta] \equiv [s_m\gamma_m'\delta]$, and $[r_m\lambda_m' V_i^\delta] \not\equiv_{n-(j+m)} [s_m\gamma_m' V_i^\delta]$. As n is finite there can only be finitely many invocations of 3 before V_i^δ is updated according to the first case.

The construction of V_{i+1}^δ updates exactly one entry in V_i^δ which must be of the form $r\epsilon$. The update becomes either non-empty or is replaced by an empty entry from an earlier state in the total order. For each V_i^δ the number of possible different recursive constants V_{i+1}^δ by this construction given that $pX\alpha V_i^\delta \not\equiv_n qY\beta V_i^\delta$ (with n least) is finite. Consequently the set $\{V_{i+1}^\delta : \delta \in \Delta\}$ is finite up to definitional equivalence. Moreover given the regime for updating, there can be at most k^2 updates, and therefore $pX\alpha V_{k^2}^\delta \equiv qY\beta V_{k^2}^\delta$. □

Lemma 1 allows us to reduce an equivalence of the form $pX\alpha \equiv q\beta\delta$ to $pXU\delta \equiv q\beta\delta$. In turn Lemma 2 allows us to reduce $pXU\delta \equiv q\beta\delta$ to $pXUV \equiv q\beta V$ and a family of pairs $[p_i\lambda_i'\delta] \equiv [p_i\delta]$ which have a common suffix. The next result, which is an important corollary of the previous two lemmas, generalises the reduction of $pX\alpha \equiv q\beta\delta$ to the situation $pX\alpha\delta \equiv q\beta\delta$ where there is the common suffix δ. Again we assume that Δ is a finite or infinite family of stack sequences.

Lemma 3 *If $pX\alpha_i\delta_i \equiv q\beta\delta_i$ for all $\alpha_i\delta_i \in \Delta$, and $\beta \in \Gamma^+$ and each α_i does not contain recursive constants, and $\max(pX) < \min(q\beta)$, and $|\beta| \leq M$ then there exists a finite family $\mathcal{U}$ of simple constants and a finite family $\mathcal{V}$ of recursive constants such that for each $\alpha_i\delta_i \in \Delta$ there is a $U \stackrel{\text{def}}{=} (r_1\gamma_1, \ldots, r_k\gamma_k)$ in $\mathcal{U}$ and a $V \stackrel{\text{def}}{=} (q_1\lambda_1, \ldots, q_k\lambda_k)$ in $\mathcal{V}$ such that*

1. $pXUV \equiv q\beta V$, *and*
2. $\forall j \in \mathrm{D}(pX). [p_j\alpha_i V] \equiv r_j\gamma_j V$, *and*
3. $\forall j \in \mathrm{D}(pX\alpha_i) \cup \mathrm{D}(q\beta)$. *if* $\lambda_j = \epsilon$ *then* $[p_j\delta_i] \equiv [q_j\delta_i]$, *and*
4. $\forall j.$ *if* $\lambda_j = \lambda'_j V$ *then* $[p_j\delta_i] \equiv q_j\lambda'_j\delta_i$.

Proof: Suppose $pX\alpha_i\delta_i \equiv q\beta\delta_i$ for all $\alpha_i\delta_i \in \Delta$ and $\beta \in \Gamma^+$ and each α_i does not contain recursive constants, and $\max(pX) < \min(q\beta)$ and $|\beta| \leq M$. By Lemma 1 for each $\alpha_i\delta_i$ there is a simple $U \stackrel{\text{def}}{=} (r_1\gamma_1, \ldots, r_k\gamma_k)$ such that $pXU\delta_i \equiv q\beta\delta_i$ and $\forall j \in \mathrm{D}(pX). [p_j\alpha_i\delta_i] \equiv r_j\gamma_j\delta_i$. By the construction in Lemma 1 we know that there are only finitely many such U (as each component of their definition is drawn from the set $\{q'\gamma' : q\beta \xrightarrow{w} q'\gamma' \text{ for } |w| \leq \max(pX)\}$). Let $U_1, \ldots, U_l$ be the different simple constants. We partition Δ into sets $\Delta_1, \ldots, \Delta_l$ such that for each $\alpha_i\delta_i \in \Delta_t$, with $U_t \stackrel{\text{def}}{=} (r_1\gamma_1, \ldots, r_k\gamma_k)$, $pXU_t\delta_i \equiv q\beta\delta_i$ and $\forall j \in \mathrm{D}(pX). [p_j\alpha_i\delta_i] \equiv r_j\gamma_j\delta_i$. By Lemma 2 for each Δ_t there are finitely many recursive V such that $pXU_tV \equiv q\beta V$ and for each $\alpha_i\delta_i \in \Delta_t$ one of these recursive constants $V \stackrel{\text{def}}{=} (q_1\lambda_1, \ldots, q_k\lambda_k)$ has the property that $[p_j\delta_i] \equiv [q_j\lambda'_j\delta_i]$ for all $j \in \mathrm{D}(q\beta) \cup \mathrm{D}(pXU_t)$ (where if $\lambda_j = \delta V$ then $\lambda'_j = \delta$ and if $\lambda_j = \epsilon$ then $\lambda'_j = \epsilon$). Let $\mathcal{V}_t$ be this finite family of recursive constants. The proof is finished if for each $\alpha_i\delta_i \in \Delta_t$ there is a $V \in \mathcal{V}_t$ such that for all $j \in \mathrm{D}(pX)$. $[p_j\alpha_i V] \equiv q_j\gamma_j V$. Using a similar proof method to that in Lemma 2 we refine this set of recursive constants so that it becomes true. Let $\mathcal{V}_{t0}$ be $\mathcal{V}_t$. Take the least n such that there is an $\alpha_i\delta_i \in \Delta_t$ and $V \stackrel{\text{def}}{=} (q_1\lambda_1, \ldots, q_k\lambda_k) \in \mathcal{V}_{t0}$ with $[p_j\delta_i] \equiv [q_j\lambda'_j\delta_i]$ for all $j \in \mathrm{D}(q\beta) \cup \mathrm{D}(pX\alpha_i)$ such that $[p_j\alpha_i V] \not\equiv_n q_j\gamma_j V$. However we know that $[p_j\alpha_i\delta_i] \equiv q_j\gamma_j\delta_i$. Therefore, by the technique in the proof of Lemma 2 this means that for some j, $[p_jV] \not\equiv_0 [q'\lambda V]$ and $[p_j\delta_i] \equiv [q'\lambda\delta_i]$ and the jth component of V, $q_j\lambda_j$, has the form $r\epsilon$. We now update V. There are two cases. First if $\lambda \neq \epsilon$ then each entry $r\epsilon$ in V is replaced with $q'\lambda V$. If $\lambda = \epsilon$ then replace each entry $r\epsilon$ with the entry for q' (which cannot be $r\epsilon$). All other entries in V remain untouched. Call the resulting constant V'. A small exercise shows that for any α and β if $[p\alpha V] \equiv [q\beta V]$ then $[p\alpha V'] \equiv [q\beta V']$ (and so, in particular, $pXU_tV' \equiv q\beta V'$): this is the reason why all entries $r\epsilon$ are updated at once. Let $\mathcal{V}_{t1}$ be $\mathcal{V}_{t0}$ with V replaced by V'. Now keep repeating the procedure.

As with the argument in Lemma 2 the number of possible updates must be finite (here less than rk^2 where r is the number of constants in $\mathcal{V}_{to}$). □

As we shall see decidability follows from the use of Lemmas 1 and 2 (and their corollary Lemma 3) in tandem.

4 Tableaux

Given a pushdown description and two normed processes $p\alpha$ and $q\beta$, the aim is to show semi-decidability of $p\alpha \sim q\beta$. If $\alpha = \epsilon$ or $\beta = \epsilon$ then checking for decidability is clear. Otherwise the problem reduces to decidability of $p\alpha I \equiv q\beta I$ where I is the initial recursive constant. Therefore, we need to extend the pushdown description with a finite family of stack constants $\mathcal{W}$. As we saw in the previous section we can include all potential simple constants. For the recursive constants we have no such upper bound (and hence the reason for semi-decidability). However, besides the initial constant I, we only need to introduce a finite family (see Lemmas 2 and 3 of the previous section) for pairs pX and $q\beta$, $\beta \in \Gamma^+$, and $|\beta| \leq M$, and for which there is a δ and an α such that $pX\alpha \equiv q\beta\delta$ or $pX\alpha\delta \equiv q\beta\delta$. Therefore we just guess the recursive constants.

We complete the decidability result by presenting a tableau proof system for a-bisimilarity. The proof system is goal directed, and consists of a finite set of rules each of the form

$$\frac{\text{Goal}}{\text{Subgoal}_1 \ \ldots \ \text{Subgoal}_n} \, C$$

where Goal is what currently is to be proved and the subgoals are what it reduces to, and C is a possible side condition on the rule application. Each goal and subgoal has the form $p\alpha = q\beta$ (the proof analogue of $p\alpha \equiv q\beta$) where the constituents are extended normed pushdown processes. Each rule is backwards sound: if all the subgoals are true then so is the goal. As we are dealing with infinite state systems there is also the important notion of when a current goal counts as terminal, for the rules only apply to nonterminals. Terminal goals are classified as either successful or unsuccessful. A *tableau proof* for Goal is a finite proof tree, whose root is Goal and all of whose leaves are successful terminals, and all of whose inner subgoals are the result of an application of one of the rules to the goal immediately above them. If the successful terminals are true it follows that the root goal is also true. We show that $pX\alpha \sim qY\beta$ iff there is a tableau proof for $pX\alpha I = qY\beta I$.

The tableau proof rules are presented in Figure 1. There are two DEC (for "decomposition") rules which introduce simple and recursive constants: their formulation directly reflects the important Lemmas of the previous section. The third rule is UNF, for "unfold": for each transition from $pX\alpha$ there is a corresponding transition from $qY\beta$, and the resulting pairs become subgoals (and vice-versa). A tableau is built from proof steps, possibly interspersed with applications of UNF. A proof step has the form

$$\text{DEC1}\ \frac{pX\alpha\delta = q\beta\delta}{[p_{i1}\alpha V] = r_{i1}\gamma_{i1}V \ldots [p_{il}\alpha V] = r_{il}\gamma_{il}V \quad \Lambda \quad pXUV = q\beta V}\ C1$$

Condition C1:

1. $\beta \in \Gamma^+$ and $|\beta| \leq M$ and $\max(pX) < \min(q\beta)$ and $|\delta| > 1$, and
2. $U \stackrel{\text{def}}{=} (r_1\gamma_1, \ldots, r_k\gamma_k)$ is simple, and $D(pX) = \{i1, \ldots, il\}$, and
3. $V \stackrel{\text{def}}{=} (q_1\lambda_1, \ldots q_k\lambda_k)$ is recursive, and
4. $D(q\beta) \cup D(pX\alpha) = \{i1, \ldots, it\}$, and
5. Λ is $[q_{i1}\lambda'_{i1}\delta] = [p_{i1}\delta] \ldots [q_{it}\lambda'_{it}\delta] = [p_{it}\delta]$, where
6. if $\lambda_{ij} = \epsilon$ then $\lambda'_{ij} = \epsilon$, and if $\lambda_{ij} = \lambda'' V$ then $\lambda'_{ij} = \lambda''$.

$$\text{DEC2}\ \frac{pX\alpha = q\beta\delta}{[p_{i1}\alpha] = r_{i1}\gamma_{i1}\delta \ldots [p_{il}\alpha] = r_{il}\gamma_{il}\delta \quad \Lambda \quad pXUV = q\beta V}\ C2$$

Condition C2:

1. $\beta \in \Gamma^+$ and $|\beta| \leq M$ and $\max(pX) < \min(q\beta)$ and $|\delta| > 1$, and
2. $U \stackrel{\text{def}}{=} (r_1\gamma_1, \ldots, r_k\gamma_k)$ is simple, and $D(pX) = \{i1, \ldots, il\}$, and
3. $V \stackrel{\text{def}}{=} (q_1\lambda_1, \ldots q_k\lambda_k)$ is recursive, and
4. $D(q\beta) = \{i1, \ldots, it\}$, and
5. Λ is $[q_{i1}\lambda'_{i1}\delta] = [p_{i1}\delta] \ldots [q_{it}\lambda'_{it}\delta] = [p_{it}\delta]$, where
6. if $\lambda_{ij} = \epsilon$ then $\lambda'_{ij} = \epsilon$, and if $\lambda_{ij} = \lambda'' V$ then $\lambda'_{ij} = \lambda''$.

$$\text{UNF}\ \frac{pX\alpha = qY\beta}{p_1\alpha_1 = q_1\beta_1 \ \ldots \ p_l\alpha_l = q_l\beta_l}\ C3$$

Condition C3: For any a

1. if $pX\alpha \xrightarrow{a} p'\alpha'$ then $\exists i : 1 \leq i \leq l.\ p'\alpha' = p_i\alpha_i$ and $qY\beta \xrightarrow{a} q_i\beta_i$,
2. if $qY\beta \xrightarrow{a} q'\beta'$ then $\exists i : 1 \leq i \leq l.\ q'\beta' = q_i\beta_i$ and $pX\alpha \xrightarrow{a} p_i\alpha_i$.

Fig. 1. Tableau rules

$$\cfrac{pX\alpha\delta = q\beta\delta}{\ldots [p_i\alpha V] = r_i\gamma_i V \ldots \ \ldots [q_i\lambda'_i\delta] = [p_i\delta] \ldots \ \ \cfrac{pXUV = q\beta V}{\ldots}\ \text{UNF}}\ \text{DEC1}$$

or when DEC1 is not applicable, it has the form

$$\cfrac{pX\alpha = q\beta\delta}{\ldots [p_i\alpha] = r_i\gamma_i\delta \ldots \ \ldots [q_i\lambda'_i\delta] = [p_i\delta] \ldots \ \ \cfrac{pXUV = q\beta V}{\ldots}\ \text{UNF}}\ \text{DEC2}$$

The idea is to repeat proof steps whose roots are themselves leaves of a proof step except when the side conditions for DEC1 and DEC2 do not apply in which case the UNF rule is applied instead. DEC1 takes priority over DEC2, and DEC2 takes priority over UNF. Note that a recursive constant may only appear as a final stack symbol, and that simple constants are only explicitly introduced into processes on the left side of $=$: they can appear on the right hand side of $=$ through the presence of recursive constants, when a process becomes $[q_i V]$.

The conditions for being a terminal node are described in Figure 2. A node

Successful terminals

1. $p\alpha = p\alpha$
2. $p\alpha = q\beta$ and in the proof tree the same equation $p\alpha = q\beta$ occurs above on the path to the root.

Unsuccessful terminals

1. $p\epsilon = q\epsilon$ and $p \neq q$
2. $p\alpha = q\beta$ and $\min(p\alpha) \neq \min(q\beta)$
3. $p\alpha = q\beta$ and $p\alpha \xrightarrow{a}$ but not$(q\beta \xrightarrow{a})$
4. $p\alpha = q\beta$ and $q\beta \xrightarrow{a}$ but not$(p\alpha \xrightarrow{a})$

Fig. 2. Terminal nodes

labelled $p\alpha = q\beta$ in a proof tree is a successful terminal if it is an identity ($q\beta$ is $p\alpha$) or a repeat: that is, there is a node above it on the path to the root also labelled $p\alpha = q\beta$. In the conditions for being an unsuccessful terminal we use the standard notation $r\lambda \xrightarrow{a}$ as an abbreviation for $\exists r'\lambda'. r\lambda \xrightarrow{a} r'\lambda'$. Clearly, if a node labelled $p\alpha = q\beta$ is an unsuccessful terminal then $p\alpha \not\equiv q\beta$.

The tableau proof rules are backwards sound with respect to the approximants $\equiv_n$, and this fact is used in the following soundness result.

Lemma 1 *If there is a tableau proof for* $p\alpha = q\beta$ *then* $p\alpha \equiv q\beta$.

Now the main result which shows completeness of the tableau method.

Theorem 1 $pX\alpha \sim qY\beta$ *iff there is a tableau proof for* $pX\alpha I = qY\beta I$.

Proof: One half follows by Lemma 1 above and Proposition 8 of the previous section: if there is a tableau proof for $pX\alpha I = qY\beta I$ then $pX\alpha \sim qY\beta$. For the other half suppose $pX\alpha \sim qY\beta$. By Proposition 8 $pX\alpha I \equiv qY\beta I$. We now construct a tableau proof for $pX\alpha I = qY\beta I$. First we introduce all the appropriate constants. For each pX and $q\beta$, $\beta \in \Gamma^+$, $|\beta| \leq M$ and where $\max(pX) < \min(q\beta)$, we define finite sets of constants as determined by Lemmas 1, 2 and 3 of the previous section. Now we repeatedly build proof steps that preserve truth until we reach terminals. Lemma 3 of the previous section and the introduction of constants guarantee that if $pX\alpha\delta = q\beta\delta$ is a subgoal with $\beta \in \Gamma^+$ and $|\beta| \leq M$ and $\max(pX) < \min(q\beta)$ and $|\delta| > 1$ then DEC1 is applicable. If this rule is not applicable to $pX\alpha = q\beta\delta$ and $\beta \in \Gamma^+$ and $|\beta| \leq M$ and $\max(pX) < \min(q\beta)$ and $|\delta| > 1$ then DEC2 is applicable by Lemmas 2 and 1 of the previous section, and the introduction of constants. Otherwise the rule UNF is always applicable to a nonterminal subgoal (as any process in a tableau has the form $pX\alpha$ or $p\epsilon$). Clearly, as truth is preserved it is not possible to reach an unsuccessful terminal goal.

The only impediment is the possibility that the proof construction never ends, that we build a proof tree with an infinite path. The rest of the proof shows that this is impossible. Note that because of normedness, for each $k \geq 1$ the set $\{r\delta$: for some $p\alpha$ such that $|\alpha| < k$, $r\delta \equiv p\alpha$ and δ and α contain at most one recursive constant$\}$ is finite.

Let S be the following measure

$$\max(\{|\lambda_i| + M \,:\, V \overset{\text{def}}{=} (q_1\lambda_1, \ldots, q_k\lambda_k) \text{ is recursive}\} \cup \{MG+2\} \cup \{4\})$$

In a goal $p\alpha = q\beta$ we say that $p\alpha$ is a left process and $q\beta$ is a right process. Note the following observations:

1. Any occurrence of a left or right process has at most one recursive constant which can only appear as the final stack symbol.
2. The only way that simple constants can be introduced into a right process is through the UNF rule, in the circumstance that $pX\alpha = qYV$ and $qY \xrightarrow{a} r\epsilon$: this means that in a right process $q\beta U\delta$ where U is simple, $|U\delta| < S$.
3. The only circumstance that DEC1 and DEC2 is not applicable to a nonterminal goal $pX\alpha = q\beta\delta$, $|\beta| \in \Gamma^+$, is when $\max(pX) \not< \min(q\beta)$ and $\delta = \epsilon$ or $\delta = V$ or $\delta = U\delta_1$ and U is simple. In which case $|\beta\delta| < S$.

Suppose $p_1\alpha_1 = q_1\beta_1, \ldots, p_n\alpha_n = q_n\beta_n, \ldots$ is an infinite path of distinct goals in the tableau (with $p_1\alpha_1 = pX\alpha I$ and $q_1\beta_1 = qY\beta I$). Let g_i be the ith goal in this sequence. We show that there must be a repeat goal in this sequence: for some i goal g_i is a terminal. A little notation. Consider the rule that takes g_i to g_{i+1}: if the rule is UNF we say g_{i+1} is an UNF successor of g_i, if the rule is DEC1 or DEC2 then we say it is an l-successor if it is of the form $p_i\alpha V = r_i\gamma_i V$ or $p_i\alpha = r_i\gamma_i\delta$, or an m-successor if it is of the form $[q_i\lambda_i'\delta] = [p_i\delta]$ or an r-successor if it has the form $pXUV = q\beta V$.

The following are true for the sequence $g_1, \ldots, g_n, \ldots$

1. There is an i such that for all $j \geq i$. g_j is not an r-successor from either DEC1 or DEC2 (because the left process of such a goal has the form $pXUV$ and $|XUV| < S$).
2. There is an i such that for all $j \geq i$. g_j is not an l-successor from DEC1 (because the right process of such a goal has the form $r_i\gamma_i V$ and $|\gamma_i V| < S$).
3. There is an i such that for all $j \geq i$. g_j is not an UNF successor. First by 1 above there is an i such that no later goal is an UNF successor via r-successors of DEC1 or DEC2, and by observation 3 earlier DEC1 and DEC2 are not applicable to a goal only when its right process $q\beta$ is such that $|\beta| < S$.

Hence there is a suffix $g_i, \ldots, g_n, \ldots$ of goals such that each goal is an m-successor from DEC1 or DEC2, or an l-successor from DEC2. Clearly, there cannot be $j \geq i$ such that for all $k \geq j$ g_k is an m-successor from DEC1 as each application reduces the right process by at least one stack symbol except when a simple constant is encountered: in which case the stack may temporarily expand but the number of simple constants is reduced by one. (Notice that a recursive constant cannot be "exposed" as an m-successor from either DEC1 or DEC2 because of the side condition $|\delta| > 1$.) Moreover, there must be an i such that for all $j \geq i$ g_j is not an m-successor from DEC1. Consider any sequence $g_i, \ldots, g_{i+k}$ of goals which are m-successors from DEC1 and such that DEC1 is not applicable to g_{i+k}. So g_{i+k-1} has the form $pX\alpha\delta = q\beta\delta$ and g_{i+k} has the form $[q_i\lambda_i'\delta] = [p_i\delta]$: either δ is small (of length less than $M+2$) or δ has the form $\beta_1 U \delta_1$ where U is simple (and $|\beta_1| \leq M$). Hence either $|\beta\delta| < S$ or the right process of g_{i+k} has size less than S. Therefore there is a suffix $g_i, \ldots, g_n, \ldots$ such that each goal is an m-successor from DEC2 or an l-successor from DEC2. However if DEC1 is not applicable to an m-successor from DEC2 then, by reasoning similar to above, either its right process or the right process in the preceeding goal has size less than S. Thus, for some $j \geq i$ for all $k \geq j$ every goal is an l-successor from DEC2. This is impossible. Each application reduces the left process by at least one stack symbol except when a simple constant or a recursive constant is encountered: in the first case the stack may temporarily expand but the number of simple constants is reduced by one and in the second case, whenever a recursive constant is exposed, the left process has size less than S. □

5 Conclusion

We have shown that bisimulation equivalence is decidable for normed pushdown processes. However, no complexity measure is available as the decision procedure essentially relies on Lemmas 2 and 3 of Section 3. Moreover, it is not clear if the proof can be generalised to include unnormed pushdown processes: the main problem is that we are then unable to show completeness of the tableau proof system.

Another area for further work is the long standing issue of decidability of language equivalence for DPDA. The result proved in this paper generalises [20]. However the proof method is very different: [20] uses Valiant's parallel stacking technique whereas the method here relies on congruence and decomposition. Further work is needed to establish whether we can offer new insight into this difficult open problem.

Acknowledgement: The author would like to thank Mojmir Kretinsky whose visit to Edinburgh rekindled the work reported here, and Olaf Burkart and Didier Caucal for comments on an earlier draft.

References

1. Baeten, J., Bergstra, J., and Klop, J. (1987). Decidability of bisimulation equivalence for processes generating context-free languages. *Lecture Notes in Computer Science*, **259**, 94-113.
2. Baeten, J., Bergstra, J., and Klop, J. (1993). Decidability of bisimulation equivalence for processes generating context-free languages. *Journal of Association of Computing Machinery*, **40**, 653-682.
3. Burkart, O., and Steffen, B.(1995). Composition, decomposition, and model checking of pushdown processes. *Nordic Journal of Computing*, **2**, 89-125.
4. Burkart, O., Caucal, D., and Steffen, B. (1994). An elementary decision procedure for arbitrary context-free processes. *Tech. Report* **94-28**, RWTH Aachen.
5. Caucal, D. (1990). Graphes canoniques de graphes algébriques. *Informatique Théorique et Applications (RAIRO)*, **24**,339-352.
6. Caucal, D. (1992). On the regular structure of prefix rewriting. *Theoretical Computer Science*, **106**, 61-86.
7. Caucal, D., and Monfort, R. (1990). On the transition graphs of automata and grammars. *Lecture Notes in Computer Science*, **484**, 311-337.
8. Christensen, S., Hirshfeld, Y., and Moller, F. (1993). Decomposability, decidability and axiomatisability for bisimulation equivalence on basic parallel processes. *Proceedings 8th Annual Symposium on Logic in Computer Science*, IEEE Computer Science Press.
9. Christensen, S., Hirshfeld, Y., and Moller, F. (1993). Bisimulation is decidable for basic parallel processes. *Lecture Notes in Computer Science*, **715**, 143-157.
10. Christensen, S., Hüttel, H., and Stirling, C. (1995). Bisimulation equivalence is decidable for all context-free processes. *Information and Computation*, **121**, 143-148.
11. Groote, J. (1992). A short proof of the decidability of bisimulation for normed BPA processes. *Information Processing Letters*, **42**, 167-171.
12. Groote, J., and Hüttel, H. (1994). Undecidable equivalences for basic process algebra. *Information and Computation*.
13. Hirshfeld, Y. (1994). Deciding equivalences in simple process algebras. *Tech. Report* ECS-LFCS-94-294, Edinburgh University.
14. Hirshfeld, Y., Jerrum, M., and Moller, F. (1994). A polynomial algorithm for deciding bisimilarity of normed context-free processes. *Procs. IEEE 35th Annual Symposium on Foundations of Computer Science*, 623-631.
15. Hopcroft, J., and Ullman, J. (1979). *Introduction to Automata Theory, Languages, and Computation*, Addison-Wesley.
16. Hüttel, H. (1993). Undecidable equivalences for basic parallel processes. *Tech. Report* ECS-LFCS-93-276, Edinburgh University.
17. Hüttel, H., and Stirling, C. (1991). Actions speak louder than words: proving bisimilarity for context free processes. *Proceedings 6th Annual Symposium on Logic in Computer Science*, IEEE Computer Science Press, 376-386.
18. Jančar, P. (1994). Decidability questions for bisimilarity of Petri nets and some related problems. *Lecture Notes in Computer Science*, **775**, 581-594.
19. Muller, D., and Schupp, P. (1985). The theory of ends, pushdown automata, and second-order logic. *Theoretical Computer Science*, **37**, 51-75.
20. Oyamuguchi, M., Honda, N., and Inagaki, Y. (1980). The equivalence problem for real-time strict deterministic languages. *Information and Control*, **45**, 90-115.

The Modal mu-calculus Alternation Hierarchy is Strict

J. C. Bradfield
Laboratory for Foundations of Computer Science
University of Edinburgh, The King's Buildings
EDINBURGH, United Kingdom, EH9 3JZ
email: jcb@dcs.ed.ac.uk

Abstract: One of the open questions about the modal mu-calculus is whether the alternation hierarchy collapses; that is, whether all modal fix-point properties can be expressed with only a few alternations of least and greatest fix-points. In this paper, we resolve this question by showing that the hierarchy does not collapse.

Keywords: temporal logic, mu-calculi, hierarchies, alternation

1 Introduction

The modal mu-calculus, or Hennessy–Milner logic with fix-points, is a popular logic for expressing temporal properties of systems. It was first studied by Kozen in [Koz83], and since then there has been much work on both theoretical and practical aspects of the logic. The feature of the logic that gives it both its simplicity and its power is that it is possible to have mutually dependent minimal and maximal fix-point operators. This makes it simple, as the fix-point is the only non first-order operator, and powerful, as by such nesting one can express complex properties such as 'infinitely often' and fairness. A measure of the complexity of a formula is the *alternation depth*, that is, the number of alternating blocks of minimal/maximal fix-points. Formulae of alternation depth higher than 2 are notoriously hard to understand, and in practice one rarely produces them—not least because they are so hard to understand. It is therefore natural to wonder whether in fact higher alternation depths are needed—it could be the case that this *alternation hierarchy* collapses. Until now, the best result was that we need both min-max and max-min formulae of depth 2, which was proven by Arnold and Niwiński in [ArN90] using automata-theoretic methods and results of Rabin [Rab70].

This question is given additional spice by the consideration of complexity issues. All known algorithms for model-checking modal mu-calculus properties are exponential in the alternation depth d. The natural algorithm, by Emerson and Lei [EmL86], was $O(n^d)$; this has recently been improved to $O(n^{d/2})$ by Long *et al.* [LB+94]. On the other hand, the problem is in NP (due to Emerson and Jutla

[EmJ88], and more directly seen by Stirling's game-theoretic approach [Sti95]), and since the logic is closed under negation, the problem is in NP ∩ co-NP, which suggests quite strongly that it is in fact in P (even if P ≠ NP). If the alternation hierarchy is strict, then we know that algorithms exponential in the alternation depth cannot be made polynomial just by reducing all formulae to alternation depth 3 (say) equivalents. (Of course, if the hierarchy did collapse, we would not necessarily immediately get a polynomial solution, since the reduction might involve a large blow-up in the size of the formula.)

The contribution of this paper is to resolve the question by establishing the strictness of the hierarchy. The technique is slightly unusual, being not at all automata-theoretic; instead, we analyse the descriptive complexity of properties in the modal mu-calculus, and then code suitable arithmetic formulae into a certain transition system in order to achieve the upper bounds. In previous work [Bra96], transferring standard hierarchies allowed us to re-prove Arnold and Niwiński's result, and obtain some other mildly interesting results, such as a Δ^1_2 upper bound on the complexity of modal mu-calculus properties. In this paper, we transfer a similar alternation hierarchy for arithmetic with fix-points, and thereby show the strictness of the modal mu-calculus hierarchy.

The remainder of this paper is thus: in section 2 we introduce the modal mu-calculus, and arithmetic with fix-points, with some of the results on which we rely. In section 3, we establish the non-collapse of the 'simple' alternation hierarchy, which we extend to the real alternation hierarchy in section 4. The technical report version of this paper [Bra96a] contains an appendix giving a summary of the mu-arithmetic hierarchy result that we transfer; unfortunately, page limits forbid its inclusion here.

2 Preliminaries

2.1 Modal mu-calculus

The modal mu-calculus, in positive form, has formulae Φ built up from variables Z by the booleans tt, ff, $\vee$ and $\wedge$, the modal connectives $[K]\Phi$ and $\langle K\rangle\Phi$ (for a set $K \subseteq \mathscr{L}$, where $\mathscr{L}$ is a countable set of *labels*), and the minimal and maximal fix-point connectives $\mu Z.\Phi(Z)$ and $\nu Z.\Phi(Z)$. We also write $[-K]\Phi$ for $[\mathscr{L}-K]\Phi$, and $[-]\Phi$ for $[\mathscr{L}]\Phi$. We further require that the label sets K are recursive (in practice, they are always small finite sets, often singletons, or the complements thereof).

Note that we adopt the convention that the scope of the binding operators μ and ν extends as far as possible. For consistency, we also apply this convention to the $\forall$ and $\exists$ of first-order logic, writing $\forall x\,.\,(\exists y\,.\,P) \vee Q$ rather than the logicians' traditional $\forall x\,[\exists y\,[P] \vee Q]$.

Observe that negation is not in the language, but any closed mu-formula can be negated by using the usual De Morgan dualities—μ and ν are dual by

$\neg\mu Z.\Phi(Z) = \nu Z.\neg\Phi(\neg Z)$. Where necessary, we shall assume that free variables can be negated just by adjusting the valuation. We shall use $\Rightarrow$ etc. freely, though we must ensure that bound variables only occur positively.

Given a labelled transition system $\mathscr{T} = (\mathscr{S}, \mathscr{L}, \longrightarrow)$, where $\mathscr{S}$ is a set of states, $\mathscr{L}$ a set of labels, and $\longrightarrow \subseteq \mathscr{S} \times \mathscr{L} \times \mathscr{S}$ is the transition relation (we write $s \xrightarrow{l} s'$), and given also a valuation $\mathscr{V}$ assigning subsets of $\mathscr{S}$ to variables, the denotation $\|\Phi\|^{\mathscr{T}}_{\mathscr{V}} \subseteq \mathscr{S}$ of a mu-calculus formula Φ is defined in the obvious way for the variables and booleans, for the modalities by

$$\|[K]\Phi\|^{\mathscr{T}}_{\mathscr{V}} = \{\, s \mid \forall s'.\, \forall l \in K \,.\, s \xrightarrow{l} s' \;\Rightarrow\; s' \in \|\Phi\|^{\mathscr{T}}_{\mathscr{V}} \,\}$$

and dually for $\langle K\rangle\Phi$, and for the fix-points by

$$\|\mu Z.\Phi\|^{\mathscr{T}}_{\mathscr{V}} = \bigcap\{\, S \subseteq \mathscr{S} \mid \|\Phi\|^{\mathscr{T}}_{\mathscr{V}[Z:=S]} \subseteq S \,\}$$

$$\|\nu Z.\Phi\|^{\mathscr{T}}_{\mathscr{V}} = \bigcup\{\, S \subseteq \mathscr{S} \mid S \subseteq \|\Phi\|^{\mathscr{T}}_{\mathscr{V}[Z:=S]} \,\}$$

(We shall drop the $^{\mathscr{T}}$ and $_{\mathscr{V}}$ whenever they are obvious.)

It is often useful to think of μZ and νZ as meaning respectively finite and infinite looping from Z back to μZ (νZ) as one 'follows a path of the system through the formula'. Examples of properties expressible by the mu-calculus are 'always P', as $\nu Z.P \wedge [-]Z$, 'eventually P', as $\mu Z.P \vee \langle -\rangle Z$, and 'there is a path along which c happens infinitely often', as $\nu Y.\mu Z.\langle c\rangle Y \vee \langle -c\rangle Z$. (For the latter, we can loop around Y for ever, but each internal loop round Z must terminate.)

There are several notions of alternation. The naive notion is simply to count syntactic alternations of μ and ν, resulting in the following definition: A formula Φ is said to be in the classes $\Sigma^{S\mu}_0$ and $\Pi^{S\mu}_0$ iff it contains no fix-point operators ('S' for 'simple' or 'syntactic'). To form the class $\Sigma^{S\mu}_{n+1}$, take $\Sigma^{S\mu}_n \cup \Pi^{S\mu}_n$, and close under (i) boolean and modal combinators, (ii) $\mu Z.\Phi$, for $\Phi \in \Sigma^{S\mu}_{n+1}$. Dually, to form $\Pi^{S\mu}_{n+1}$, take $\Sigma^{S\mu}_n \cup \Pi^{S\mu}_n$, and close under (i) boolean and modal combinators, (ii) $\nu Z.\Phi$, for $\Phi \in \Pi^{S\mu}_{n+1}$. Thus the examples above are in $\Pi^{S\mu}_1$, $\Sigma^{S\mu}_1$, and $\Pi^{S\mu}_2$ (but not $\Sigma^{S\mu}_2$) respectively. We shall say a formula is *strict* $\Sigma^{S\mu}_n$ if it is in $\Sigma^{S\mu}_n - \Pi^{S\mu}_n$.

However, this simple notion of alternation is not what we are concerned with, since it does not capture the complexity of feedback between fix-points: it does not distinguish these two formulae

$$\Upsilon_1 = \nu Y.\mu Z.\langle -\rangle Y \wedge (P \vee \langle -\rangle Z)$$

$$\Upsilon_2 = \nu Y.\langle -\rangle Y \wedge (\mu Z.P \vee \langle -\rangle Z)$$

—both are in $\Pi^{S\mu}_2 - \Sigma^{S\mu}_2$. To take account of this, we need a stronger definition, for which there is more than one candidate. The most common version is that of Emerson–Lei [EmL86]; however, a more refined notion was used by Niwiński

[Niw86], and since this captures the intuitive notion better than Emerson–Lei, as well as providing a better complexity measure, we shall follow Niwiński. (For an explanation of the differences, see the end of section 4—our results trivially imply the non-collapse of the hierarchy of [EmL86].)

A formula Φ is said to be in the classes $\Sigma_0^{N\mu}$ and $\Pi_0^{N\mu}$ iff it contains no fix-point operators. To form the class $\Sigma_{n+1}^{N\mu}$, take $\Sigma_n^{N\mu} \cup \Pi_n^{N\mu}$, and close under (i) boolean and modal combinators, (ii) $\mu Z.\Phi$, for $\Phi \in \Sigma_{n+1}^{N\mu}$, and (iii) substitution of $\Phi' \in \Sigma_{n+1}^{N\mu}$ for a free variable of $\Phi \in \Sigma_{n+1}^{N\mu}$ provided that no free variable of Φ' is captured by Φ; and dually for $\Pi_{n+1}^{N\mu}$. Now we can distinguish Υ_1 and Υ_2: both are in $\Pi_2^{N\mu}$, but the 'non-alternating' Υ_2 is also in $\Sigma_2^{N\mu}$. (Intuitively, we are allowed to have arbitrary syntactic alternation, as long as the real semantic dependency between the various fix-points is restricted. To take the simplest example, $\mu X_1.\nu X_2.\dots\nu X_{2n}.\mu X_{2n+1}.X_1 \vee X_{2n+1}$ has syntactic alternation depth $2n+1$, but its real alternation depth is just 1, since all we have is an inner minimal fix-point depending on an outer minimal fix-point, all the other fix-points being vacuous. The definition via restricted substitution is the simplest way of capturing this notion.)

The ***(Niwiński) alternation depth*** of a formula Φ is the least n such that $\Phi \in \Sigma_{n+1}^{N\mu}$ and $\Phi \in \Pi_{n+1}^{N\mu}$.

The relationship between the simple and Niwiński hierarchies is that $\Sigma_n^{S\mu} \subseteq \Sigma_n^{N\mu}$, but $\Sigma_2^{N\mu}$ has non-empty intersection with every $\Sigma_n^{S\mu} - \Sigma_{n-1}^{S\mu}$; thus the non-collapse of the simple hierarchy is not sufficient to give the non-collapse of the (Niwiński) alternation hierarchy, which is the real question of interest.

Given a formula $\mu Z.\Phi(Z)$ and a model, the ***approximants*** $\mu^\zeta Z.\Phi$ (for ζ an ordinal) are defined recursively by $\mu^\zeta Z.\Phi = \|\Phi\|_{Z:=S}$ where $S = \bigcup_{\eta<\zeta} \mu^\eta Z.\Phi$, and dually for $\nu Z.\Phi$. We may also write Φ^ζ or Z^ζ for $\mu^\zeta Z.\Phi$. We shall write $Z^{<\zeta}$ for $\bigcup_{\eta<\zeta} Z^\eta$.†

Since mu-calculus formulae are monotonic in their variables, for successor ordinals we have $\mu^{\zeta+1} Z.\Phi = \|\Phi\|_{Z:=\mu^\zeta Z.\Phi}$. Further, by the standard Tarski fix-point theorem we have $\|\mu Z.\Phi\| = \bigcup_{\zeta\in\mathrm{Ord}} \mu^\zeta Z.\Phi$; the smallest κ such that $\|\mu Z.\Phi\| = \bigcup_{\zeta<\kappa} \mu^\zeta Z.\Phi$ is called the ***closure ordinal*** of $\mu Z.\Phi$.

2.2 The arithmetic mu-calculus

In [Lub93] (first presented at LICS '89), Robert Lubarsky studies the logic given by adding fix-point constructors to first-order arithmetic. Precisely, the logic ('mu-arithmetic' for short) has as basic symbols the following: function symbols f, g, h; predicate symbols P, Q, R; first-order variables x, y, z; set variables

† This is the notation introduced in [Mos74]; earlier work, and also work in the modal mu-calculus, uses a different notation, with the effect that their Z^ζ is (equal to) our $Z^{<\zeta}$.

X, Y, Z; and the symbols $\vee, \wedge, \exists, \forall, \mu, \nu, \neg, \in$. (As with the modal mu-calculus, $\neg$ can be pushed inwards to apply only to atomic formulae, by De Morgan duality.)

The language has expressions of three kinds, individual terms, set terms, and formulae. The individual terms comprise the usual terms of first order logic. The set terms comprise set variables and expressions $\mu(x, X).\phi$ and $\nu(x, X).\phi$, where X occurs positively in ϕ. Note that μ binds both an individual variable and a set variable; henceforth we shall write just $\mu X.\phi$, and assume that the individual variable is the lower-case of the set variable. The formulae are built by the usual first-order construction, together with the rule that if τ is an individual term and Ξ is a set term, then $\tau \in \Xi$ is a formula.

This language is interpreted over a structure $\mathcal{M}$ for its first-order part. The semantics of the first-order connectives is as usual; $\tau \in \Xi$ is interpreted naturally; and the set term $\mu X.\phi(x, X)$ is interpreted as the least fix-point of the functional $\mathbf{X} \mapsto \{ m \in \mathcal{M} \mid \mathcal{M} \models \phi(m, \mathbf{X}) \}$ (where $\mathbf{X} \subseteq \mathcal{M}$). As with the modal mu-calculus, we define approximants (and indeed the approximant approach is (of course) essential to Lubarsky's method): X^ζ is now the set $\{ m \in \mathcal{M} \mid \mathcal{M} \models \phi(m, \bigcup_{\xi<\zeta} X^\xi) \}$, and the interpretation of $\mu X.\phi$ is then $\bigcup_{\zeta \in \mathrm{Ord}} X^\zeta$; and dually for the greatest fix-point. Closure ordinals are as for the modal mu-calculus.

Henceforth we shall take $\mathcal{M}$ to be the structure $\mathbf{N}$ of first-order arithmetic with recursive functions and predicates. In particular, let $\langle m, n \rangle$, $(n)_0$ and $(n)_1$ be standard pairing and unpairing functions.

The simplest examples of mu-arithmetic just use least fix-points to represent an inductive definition. For example, $\mu X.x = 0 \vee (x > 1 \wedge (x-2) \in X)$ is the set of even numbers. Of course, the even numbers are also the complement of the odd numbers, so can be expressed as a maximal fix-point $\nu X.x \neq 1 \wedge (x > 1 \Rightarrow (x-2) \in X)$. To produce natural examples involving alternating fix-points is rather difficult, since even one induction is already very powerful, and all natural mathematical objects are simple.

Lubarsky establishes a normal form theorem. The μ-normal form is defined thus: a set term is in μ-normal form if it is a set variable, or of the form $\mu X.\phi$ or $\nu X.\phi$ with ϕ in μ-normal form. A formula is in μ-normal form if it is quantifier-free, or of the form $\tau \in \Xi$ with Ξ in μ-normal form, or of the form $\exists x.\phi$ or $\forall x.\phi$ with ϕ in μ-normal form.

In the presence of a pairing function, as happens in $\mathbf{N}$, it is further possible to shuffle quantifiers and produce a ***pair-normal*** form: a pair-normal formula is either first-order or of the form $\tau \in \Xi$ for pair-normal Ξ, and a pair-normal Ξ is $\mu X.\phi$ where ϕ is either first-order or $\tau' \in \nu Y.\psi$ for pair-normal ψ (and dually). (Thus there is an alternating string of fix-points, followed by a first order formula, which can in fact be restricted to be a boolean combination of Σ_1 and Π_1 formulae.)

Theorem 1. [Lub93] Every formula and set term is semantically equivalent to one in pair-normal form (in a structure with pairing). □

One can define the syntactic alternation classes for arithmetic just as for the modal mu-calculus: First-order formulae are $\Sigma_0^{S\mu}$ and $\Pi_0^{S\mu}$, as are set variables. The $\Sigma_{n+1}^{S\mu}$ formulae and set terms are formed from the $\Sigma_n^{S\mu} \cup \Pi_n^{S\mu}$ formulae and set terms by closing under (i) the first-order connectives and (ii) forming $\mu X.\phi$ for $\phi \in \Sigma_{n+1}^{S\mu}$.

The following crucial lemma is also (taken as obvious) in [Lub93], modulo a technical point to be explained afterwards. It is indeed obvious from the proof of the pair-normal form theorem, but since it is only obvious from the proof, here it is worthwhile to prove the lemma directly—also, we shall use a simpler form of one of its constructions a little later. The following is a slightly condensed version of pp. 298–299 of [Lub93]; refer to the original for more explanation.

Lemma 2. If ϕ is $\Sigma_n^{S\mu}$, it is equivalent to a pair-normal formula that is also $\Sigma_n^{S\mu}$.

Proof. We transform ϕ to pair-normal form by structural induction.

For a set term $\mu X.\phi$, we assume inductively that ϕ is pair-normal; then we are already pair-normal unless ϕ is $\tau \in \mu Y.\psi$. In that case, the translation pairs up X and Y into W in the natural way, so that $m \in X$ iff $\langle 0, m\rangle \in W$ and $n \in Y(m, X)$ iff $\langle 1, \langle m, n\rangle\rangle \in W$ (remember that τ and ψ may depend on the individual variable x as well as the set variable X). Thus we translate the original term into

$$\mu W.((w)_0 = 0 \wedge \langle 1, \langle (w)_1, \tau((w)_1)\rangle\rangle \in W) \vee ((w)_0 = 1 \wedge \psi')$$

where ψ' is obtained from ψ by replacing every '$\rho \in X$' by '$\langle 0, \rho\rangle \in W$', and every '$\rho \in Y$' by '$\langle 1, \langle x, \rho\rangle\rangle \in W$', and then every x by $((w)_1)_0$ and every y by $((w)_1)_1$. This procedure clearly preserves the level in the hierarchy. Next, to obtain pair-normal form, note that ψ' is (if not first-order) of the form $\rho \in \nu Z.\theta$; we can then pull the ν out through the rest of the formula, since $(\rho \in \nu Z.\theta) \wedge \vartheta$ is equivalent to $\rho \in \nu Z.\theta \wedge \vartheta$, etc.; and then repeat until the rest of the formula has been pushed into the inner $\Sigma_0^{S\mu}$ block. This procedure does not change the nesting of fix-points, so preserves the level in the hierarchy. (It may be noted that although Y depends on both x and X, we have only explicitly coded the dependency on x. By standard monotonicity arguments about adjacent fix-points of the same sign, the dependency on X can be ignored.)

For formulae, the booleans are dealt with by the fix-point shuffling just described. For the case $\sigma \in \Xi$, transform to $\langle 0, \sigma\rangle \in \Xi'$, where Ξ' is the construction of the previous paragraph.

For formulae $\exists x\,.\,\phi$, assume that ϕ is $\tau \in \mu Y.\psi$. The existential quantifier is pushed inside the fix-point by a similar construction to that used in the case of set terms: let W be a new variable, and build ψ' from ψ exactly as before. Then the set term

$$\mu W.(w = \langle 0, 0\rangle \wedge \exists x\,.\,\langle 1, \langle x, \tau\rangle\rangle \in W) \vee ((w)_0 = 1 \wedge \psi')$$

contains $\langle 0,0\rangle$ iff $\exists x\,.\,\phi$. Now the case of ϕ being $\tau \in \nu Y.\psi$ is similar; and the case of ϕ first-order is dealt with by adding a dummy fix-point of the appropriate sign.

Similarly for formulae $\forall x\,.\,\phi$.

So we see that the transformation makes no change to the $\Sigma_n^{S\mu}$ level, as claimed. □

Before quoting Lubarsky's main theorem, we need to address one technical point. Lubarsky uses a notion of alternation depth that is even weaker than $\Sigma_n^{S\mu}$, for reasons that are not clear to the present author (perhaps it is required for the mu-calculus over structures with no coding ability at all). Namely, the class Σ_n is closed under μ and under first-order quantifiers, but not under booleans: he has, rather, that if ϕ_1 and ϕ_2 are in $\Sigma_n \cup \Pi_n$, then $\phi_1 \vee \phi_2$ and $\phi_1 \wedge \phi_2$ are in $\Sigma_{n+1} \cap \Pi_{n+1}$ (and also all first-order formulae are $\Sigma_0 \cap \Pi_0$). However, everything in [Lub93] remains true (more simply, if anything) with the $\Sigma_n^{S\mu}$ hierarchy; in any case, the two notions coincide on formulae in pair-normal form. Henceforth we silently substitute $\Sigma_n^{S\mu}$ for the Σ_n of [Lub93].

Lubarsky then proves

Theorem 3. [Lub93] The hierarchy of the sets of integers definable by $\Sigma_n^{S\mu}$ formulae of the arithmetic mu-calculus is a strict hierarchy. □

The theorem is actually that a set of integers is $\Sigma_n^{S\mu}$ definable iff it is Σ_1 over the (least n-reflecting admissible ordinal)-th level of the constructible universe, but all we need is the existence and strictness of the hierarchy. The full paper contains an appendix with a summary of the notions and proof ideas required for this very interesting theorem.

3 Transferring the simple hierarchy

Our aim is to transfer Lubarsky's result to the Niwiński alternation hierarchy for the modal mu-calculus. However, we shall start with the simple hierarchy, since a simple coding trick will then extend it to the Niwiński hierarchy. In order to establish our results, we shall work with a particular class of transition systems.

A *recursively presented transition system (r.p.t.s.)* is a labelled transition system $(\mathscr{S}, \mathscr{L}, \longrightarrow)$ such that $\mathscr{S}$ is (recursively codable as) a recursive set of integers, $\mathscr{L}$ likewise, and $\longrightarrow$ is recursive. Henceforth we consider only recursively presented transition systems, with recursive valuations for the free variables.

The first result is simple:

Theorem 4. For a modal mu-calculus formula $\Phi \in \Sigma_n^{S\mu}$, the denotation $\|\Phi\|$ in any r.p.t.s. is a $\Sigma_n^{S\mu}$ definable set of integers.

Proof. All we have to do is translate the semantics of the modal mu-calculus into arithmetic. We translate $s \in \|\Phi\|$ into a mu-arithmetic formula $\phi(s)$ by induction on Φ. For variables X that were bound in the top-level formula, we translate $s \in \|X\|$ to $s \in X$; for a free variable P of the top-level formula (which has a recursive valuation by assumption), we translate to $P(s)$, where P is the appropriate recursive predicate. The booleans are obvious. For the modal operators, we have $s \in \|[K]\Psi\|$ iff $\forall t \in \mathscr{S}\,.\,\forall a \in K\,.\,(s \xrightarrow{a} t) \Rightarrow \psi$ where ψ is the translation of $t \in \|\Psi\|$, and dually. Finally, for the fix-point operators, we translate $s \in \|\mu X.\Psi\|$ to $s \in \mu X.\psi$, where ψ is the translation of $x \in \|\Psi\|$, and dually.

It follows immediately from the definitions that $s \in \|\Phi\|$ iff $\phi(s)$, and that ϕ has the same $\Sigma^{S\mu}$ complexity as Φ. □

The converse, showing that there are models of the modal mu-calculus with arbitrarily complex mu-arithmetic translations, is conceptually quite straightforward: we just define a suitable (and rather powerful!) transition system to code the evaluation of the target formula.

Theorem 5. Let $\phi(z)$ be a $\Sigma_n^{S\mu}$ formula of mu-arithmetic. There is a r.p.t.s. $\mathscr{T}$ with recursive valuation $\mathscr{V}$ and a $\Sigma_n^{S\mu}$ formula Φ of the modal mu-calculus such that $\phi((s)_0)$ iff $s \in \|\Phi\|^{\mathscr{T}}_{\mathscr{V}}$. (Thus if ϕ is not $\Sigma_{n-1}^{S\mu}$-definable, neither is $\|\Phi\|$.)

Proof. We assume that ϕ is alpha-converted so that all variables are distinct, and if there are any free set variables, we replace them with predicate symbols. Our transition system has as its states tuples of integers, one for each individual term in ϕ. Let s_τ denote the τ component of a state s, for a term τ. We shall construct Φ such that $s \in \|\Phi\|$ iff $\phi(s_z)$ (and in general if ϕ has multiple free individual variables $z_1, \ldots, z_k$, then $s \in \|\Phi\|$ iff $\phi(s_{z_1}, \ldots, s_{z_k})$.)

For every atomic formula $P(\tau)$ occurring in ϕ, we equip the modal mu-calculus with a variable P_τ such that $s \in \mathscr{V}(P_\tau)$ iff $P(s_\tau)$, and similarly for n-ary predicates.

For every individual term τ occurring in ϕ that has the form $f(\tau_1, \ldots, \tau_k)$, we equip $\mathscr{T}$ with a label $f_{(\tau_1,\ldots,\tau_k)}$, and the transitions given by $s \xrightarrow{f_{(\tau_1,\ldots,\tau_k)}} t$ iff $t_\tau = f(s_{\tau_1}, \ldots s_{\tau_k})$ and $t_{\tau''} = s_{\tau''}$ for every $\tau'' \neq \tau$.

For every first-order quantifier $\forall x$ or $\exists x$ in ϕ, we equip $\mathscr{T}$ with a label x and the transitions given by $s \xrightarrow{x} t$ iff $t_\tau = s_\tau$ for every $\tau \neq x$.

This is now sufficient to deal with the first-order part of mu-arithmetic. Before considering the fix-points, let us set down the construction of Φ for the first-order part:

If $\phi(z)$ is $\phi_1 \vee \phi_2$, then Φ is $\Phi_1 \vee \Phi_2$, and dually for $\wedge$. If ϕ is $\forall x\,.\,\psi$, then Φ is $[x]\Psi$, and if ϕ is $\exists x\,.\,\psi$, then Φ is $\langle x\rangle\Psi$.

If ϕ is an atomic formula $P(\tau)$, then Φ is $\langle\tau*\rangle P_\tau$, where $\langle\tau*\rangle\Upsilon$ is defined thus: $\langle x\rangle\Upsilon$ is just Υ, and $\langle f(\tau_1, \ldots \tau_k)*\rangle\Upsilon$ is $\langle\tau_1*\rangle\cdots\langle\tau_k*\rangle\langle f_{(\tau_1,\ldots\tau_k)}\rangle\Upsilon$—that is, we compute the arguments of f and then f. Let $\xrightarrow{\tau*}$ be the corresponding sequence of transitions. (We could, of course, wrap all this computation up into one transition; it makes no difference.)

A simple induction now shows that $s \in \|\Phi\|_{\mathcal{V}}$ iff $\phi(s_z)$.

Thus we have used the transition system to code up all the computation in arithmetic, and the modal connectives to code the first-order quantifiers. To finish the job, we need to translate the fix-point operators of arithmetic into the fix-point operators of the modal mu-calculus.

For every fix-point μX or νX occurring in ϕ, and for every formula $\tau \in X$ in ϕ, we equip $\mathcal{T}$ with a label x_τ (recall that $\mu X.\psi$ is short for $\mu(x, X).\psi$). The transitions are given by $s \xrightarrow{x_\tau} t$ iff $t_x = s_\tau$ and $t_{\tau'} = s_{\tau'}$ for every $\tau' \not\equiv x$. (That is, we copy the value of τ to the 'input variable' x of the fix-point.)

We now complete the translation: if ϕ is $\tau \in X$ for X a set variable, then Φ is $\langle\tau*\rangle\langle x_\tau\rangle X$. If ϕ is $\tau \in \mu X.\psi$, then Φ is $\langle\tau*\rangle\langle x_\tau\rangle\mu X.\Psi$; and similarly for ν.

The simple induction now extends in the obvious way. Since it is a little more complex than the first-order part, we give details.

We add to the inductive hypothesis the clause that if X is a free set variable of ϕ with valuation $\mathbf{X}$, then $s \in \|X\|$ iff $s_x \in \mathbf{X}$. Now if ϕ is $\tau \in X$, then $\phi(s_z)$ iff $\tau \in \mathbf{X}$ iff $\exists t\,.\, t_x = \tau \wedge t_x \in \mathbf{X}$ iff $\exists t\,.\, s \xrightarrow{\tau*} \xrightarrow{x_\tau} t \wedge t_x \in \mathbf{X}$ iff $s \in \|\langle\tau*\rangle\langle x_\tau\rangle X\|$, as required.

For the fix-points themselves, we work by induction on the approximants. Consider the set term $\mu X.\psi$, and suppose by induction that $s \in \mu^\eta X.\Psi$ iff $s_x \in \mu^\eta X.\psi$, for $\eta < \zeta$. Then $s \in \mu^\zeta X.\Psi$ iff $s \in \|\Psi\|_{X:=X^{<\zeta}}$ iff $\psi(s_z, s_x)$ (where X is valued at $\mathbf{X} = X^{<\zeta}$ in arithmetic) iff $s_x \in \mu^\zeta X.\psi$. Thus the modal and arithmetic approximants correspond, and then so do the limits.

Finally, observe that the fix-point structure of ϕ is preserved in the translation to Φ. □

To illustrate this construction, consider the mu-arithmetic definition of the even numbers that was given above; we can rewrite this as

$$\mu(x, X).P(x) \vee (Q(x) \wedge f(x) \in X)$$

where $P(x)$ iff $x = 0$, $Q(x)$ iff $x > 1$, and $f(x) = x - 2$. The individual terms of this formula are x and $f(x)$, so the states of the constructed transition system are pairs (m, n) of integers. We equip the model with two atomic propositions P_x and Q_x such that $\|P_x\| = \{(0, n)\}$ and $\|Q_x\| = \{\,(m, n) \mid m > 1\,\}$. We also have a label f_x such that $(m, n) \xrightarrow{f_x} (m, m - 2)$. Finally, we have a label $x_{f(x)}$ such that $(m, n) \xrightarrow{x_{f(x)}} (n, n)$. The translation into modal logic is then

$$\mu X.P_x \vee (Q_x \wedge \langle f_x\rangle\langle x_{f(x)}\rangle X)$$

and a state (m, n) satisfies this formula just in case m is even.

This theorem, together with the previous theorem, give us non-collapse:

Corollary 6. The simple hierarchy in the modal mu-calculus does not collapse.

Proof. Use the theorem to code an arithmetic strict $\Sigma_n^{S\mu}$ set of integers by a strict $\Sigma_n^{S\mu}$ modal mu-formula Φ on a r.p.t.s. $\mathcal{T}$; by the previous theorem, no

$\Sigma^{S\mu}_{n-1}$ modal formula can have the same denotation in $\mathscr{T}$, and so no $\Sigma^{S\mu}_{n-1}$ modal formula is logically equivalent to Φ. □

Some remarks are in order at this point. Readers who think of the modal mu-calculus as being really about finite systems may be feeling slightly queasy about the transition systems built above—is it not cheating to use infinite (and worse, infinite-branching) systems with arbitrary recursive transition relations? Further, should we not be dealing only with pure sentences, without arbitrary recursive predicates in the logic? To deal with the second point first, the predicates can be easily replaced by transitions coding their characteristic functions. For the first point, note that the modal mu-calculus has the finite model property [StE89], so if a hierarchy is strict on any class of models, it is also strict on the class of finite models. Furthermore, although it looks as if we have relied on the existence of lots of labels, many of these can also be coded away using simple techniques, such those employed in chapter 5 of [Bra91] and in [Bra96]. The only critical labels are those for the first-order variables.

4 The non-collapse of the alternation hierarchy

In order to extend this result to the Niwiński alternation hierarchy, we need to do a little more work along the lines of the normal form theorems. In fact, we shall prove that $\Sigma^{N\mu}_i$ formulae are equivalent (in mu-arithmetic) to $\Sigma^{S\mu}_i$ formulae.

It is possible to define a notion of the Niwiński hierarchy for arithmetic that correctly captures the idea of genuine semantic alternation, but because of the existence of individual variables in arithmetic, the definition is a little complex, and additional minor complexities arise in the subsequent proof. As will become apparent, in the presence of pairing the Niwiński and simple classes are equal, up to logical equivalence, so there is no intrinsic interest in defining it generally. Hence, to avoid unnecessary work, we shall restrict ourselves to formulae of a well-behaved form, sufficient for our purposes. We say that a formula ϕ of mu-arithmetic is *nice* if no set term $\mu X.\psi$ or $\nu X.\psi$ occurring in ϕ contains any free individual variable. Observe that the translation of the modal mu-calculus into mu-arithmetic, given in the proof of Theorem 4, produces only nice formulae. We then define the Niwiński hierarchy $\Sigma^{N\mu}_n$ for nice formulae of mu-arithmetic exactly as for the modal mu-calculus, where the variable capture constraint refers to set variables. To be precise, the $\Sigma^{N\mu}_0 = \Pi^{N\mu}_0$ formulae are the first-order formulae and the $\Sigma^{N\mu}_0 = \Pi^{N\mu}_0$ set terms are the set variables; $\Sigma^{N\mu}_{n+1}$ is formed by taking $\Sigma^{N\mu}_n \cup \Pi^{N\mu}_n$ and closing under (i) first-order connectives and $\in$; (ii) $\mu X.\psi$ for $\psi \in \Sigma^{N\mu}_{n+1}$, provided that ψ has at most x as a free individual variable; (iii) substitution of a $\Sigma^{N\mu}_{n+1}$ set term Ξ for a free set variable of $\psi \in \Sigma^{N\mu}_{n+1}$ provided that no free set variable of Ξ is captured by ψ. Hence the translation takes modal $\Sigma^{N\mu}_n$ to arithmetic $\Sigma^{N\mu}_n$.

Theorem 7. If ϕ is a (nice, by definition) $\Sigma_n^{N\mu}$ formula of mu-arithmetic, it is equivalent to some $\Sigma_n^{S\mu}$ formula, which moreover is nice and has μ as its top-level connective (i.e. is of the form $\sigma \in \mu X.\psi$).

Proof. The proof is firstly by induction on n, and secondly by induction on the construction of formulae according to the rules (i)–(iii) of the alternation hierarchy. The case $n = 0$ is trivial. So assume n, and prove $n + 1$.

The base of the inner induction is the $\Sigma_n^{N\mu}$ and $\Pi_n^{N\mu}$ formulae, which by induction are $\Sigma_n^{S\mu}$ and $\Pi_n^{S\mu}$ respectively. Any first order combination ϕ of such formulae can be made $\Sigma_{n+1}^{S\mu}$ by wrapping a dummy fix-point round it—if ϕ has free variable x, transform it to $x \in \mu X.\phi$ (and then alpha-convert if desired), and if there is more than one free variable, use pairing to code them into one. Similarly, given $\Sigma_{n+1}^{S\mu}$ formulae in the required form, a first-order combination of them can be wrapped in a dummy fix-point to have the required form.

For case (ii), if ϕ is $\Sigma_{n+1}^{N\mu}$, inductively it is equivalent to some $\Sigma_{n+1}^{S\mu}$ formula, and then wrapping a μ round it keeps it in $\Sigma_{n+1}^{S\mu}$ of the desired form.

The non-trivial case is the substitution rule (iii). Let ψ, Ξ be the $\Sigma_{n+1}^{N\mu}$ formula and term such that ϕ is the result of substituting Ξ for the free variable Z of ψ. Inductively, ψ and Ξ are equivalent to formulae $\sigma \in \mu X.\psi_1$ and $\mu Y.\psi_2$ of the required form (and by niceness, the individual variables in σ are exactly the free individual variables of ψ). All we need do now is to combine the inductive generation of X and Y along the lines of the pair normal form theorem. By the side condition of (iii), Ξ contains no reference to any bound set variable of ψ, and by niceness no reference to any individual variable of ψ. We can therefore pull it out to the same level as X. In detail, we use a new variable W, with the intent that $\langle 0, n\rangle \in W \Leftrightarrow n \in X$ and $\langle 1, n\rangle \in W \Leftrightarrow n \in Y$. So we use the formula

$$\langle 0, \sigma\rangle \in \mu W.((w)_0 = 0 \wedge \psi_1') \vee ((w)_0 = 1 \wedge \psi_2')$$

where ψ_1' is formed from ψ_1 by replacing '$\rho \in X$' by '$\langle 0, \rho\rangle \in W$', replacing '$\rho \in Z$' by '$\langle 1, \rho\rangle \in W$', and x by $(w)_1$; and similarly for ψ_2'.

Provided that $\mu X.\psi_1$ and $\mu Y.\psi_2$ are $\Sigma_{n+1}^{S\mu}$, which they are by induction, this formula is also $\Sigma_{n+1}^{S\mu}$, so we are done. □

Corollary 8. The denotation of a modal $\Sigma_n^{N\mu}$ formulae is arithmetic $\Sigma_n^{S\mu}$-definable. □

By combining this result with Theorem 4 and Theorem 5, and the fact that every $\Sigma_n^{S\mu}$ formula is also $\Sigma_n^{N\mu}$, we immediately obtain our desired

Theorem 9. The alternation hierarchy for the modal mu-calculus is strict. □

For those who know only the notion of alternation depth defined in [EmL86], it may be worth explaining the differences between that notion and the one we are using (noted briefly in [Kai95]). In [EmL86], alternation depth is directly defined by an inductive definition on formulae; however, it can easily be cast into our framework. (In fact, the definition of [EmL86] contains a minor error, as noted in [And93]; we assume the corrected version.)

Recall the definition of the classes $\Sigma_n^{N\mu}$; we can define Emerson–Lei versions $\Sigma_n^{EL\mu}$ of these classes by modifying clause (iii) as follows: (iii′) substitution of $\Phi' \in \Sigma_{n+1}^{EL\mu}$ for a free variable of $\Phi \in \Sigma_{n+1}^{EL\mu}$ provided that Φ' is a closed formula. A simple induction now shows the following

Lemma 10. A formula Φ has Emerson–Lei alternation depth $\leq n$ iff $\Phi \in \Sigma_{n+1}^{EL\mu} \cap \Pi_{n+1}^{EL\mu}$, for $n \geq 0$. □

Since it is immediate from the definitions that $\Sigma_n^{S\mu} \subseteq \Sigma_n^{EL\mu} \subseteq \Sigma_n^{N\mu}$, we obtain as a corollary of our results that

Corollary 11. The alternation depth hierarchy of [EmL86] is strict. □

In his thesis [And93], Andersen presents a (somewhat complex) improvement to the direct definition of alternation depth in a way that provides tighter complexity bounds on the algorithm of [EmL86], and better reflects intuition. In fact, Andersen is bringing the direct definition closer to the Niwiński notion: his definition satisfies the "⇒" direction of the above lemma replacing $\Sigma^{EL\mu}$ by $\Sigma^{N\mu}$, and probably also the "⇐" direction, though this remains to be proved. The examples Andersen provides (p. 28) of the difference between the original definition and his improvement also serve as examples of the differences between $\Sigma^{EL\mu}$ and $\Sigma^{N\mu}$; for example,

$$\mu X.\nu Z.\mu U.\nu Y.Y \wedge X$$

is in $\Sigma_2^{N\mu}$, but only in $\Sigma_4^{EL\mu}$.

5 Conclusion

The results of this paper solve the alternation hierarchy problem by a relatively simple reduction to a known hierarchy problem. This is a fairly powerful technique: it will apply to any mu-calculus whose models are powerful enough to allow the coding of arithmetic. There is, however, a drawback: we should like to have simple explicit examples of strict $\Sigma_n^{N\mu}$ modal mu-calculus formulae. Although the arithmetic examples are constructible in principle, the complexity of the proofs in [Lub93] means that the examples are not practically presentable, and so neither are the translations into the modal mu-calculus.

Giacomo Lenzi has recently produced an independent proof of the non-collapse of the (Emerson–Lei, in his case, though the argument should work for Niwiński) alternation hierarchy. The technique is a very delicate topological analysis of the finite models of formulae of a logic closely related to the modal mu-calculus, and it does produce explicit and simple examples of strict formulae—exactly the examples one would expect, in fact. The reader is referred to Lenzi's forthcoming paper [Len96].

Finally, I should like to thank Colin Stirling and other members of the Concurrency Club at the LFCS for valuable discussions and pointers; Robert Lubarsky for helpful additional remarks on his work; and the CONCUR referees for useful suggestions.

6 References

[And93] H. R. Andersen, *Verification of Temporal Properties of Concurrent Systems*, DAIMI PB – 445, Computer Science Dept, Aarhus University (1993).

[ArN90] A. Arnold and D. Niwinski, Fixed point characterization of Büchi automata on infinite trees. *J. Inf. Process. Cybern.*, **EIK 26**, 451–459 (1990).

[Bar75] J. Barwise, *Admissible sets and structures*, Springer-Verlag, Berlin/New York (1975).

[Bra91] J. C. Bradfield, *Verifying Temporal Properties of Systems.* Birkhäuser, Boston, Mass. ISBN 0-8176-3625-0 (1991).

[Bra96] J. C. Bradfield, On the expressivity of the modal mu-calculus. *Proc. STACS '96*, LNCS **1046**, 479–490 (1996).

[Bra96a] J. C. Bradfield, The modal mu-calculus alternation hierarchy is strict. Online via the Web page `http://www.dcs.ed.ac.uk/home/jcb/` or by ftp at `ftp://ftp.dcs.ed.ac.uk/export/jcb/Research/althi.ps.gz`.

[EmJ88] E. A. Emerson and C. Jutla. The complexity of tree automata and logics of programs. Extended version from *FOCS '88.* (1988).

[EmL86] E. A. Emerson and C.-L. Lei, Efficient model checking in fragments of the propositional mu-calculus. *Proc. First IEEE Symp. on Logic in Computer Science* 267–278 (1986).

[Kai95] R. Kaivola, On modal mu-calculus and Büchi tree automata. *Inf. Proc. Letters* **54** 17–22 (1995).

[Koz83] D. Kozen, Results on the propositional mu-calculus. *Theoret. Comput. Sci.* **27** 333–354 (1983).

[Len96] G. Lenzi, A hierarchy theorem for the mu-calculus. To appear in *Proc. ICALP '96.*

[LB+94] D. Long, A. Browne, E. Clarke, S. Jha and W. Marrero, An improved algorithm for the evaluation of fixpoint expressions. *Proc. CAV '94*, LNCS **818** 338–350 (1994).

[Lub93] R. S. Lubarsky, μ-definable sets of integers, *J. Symbolic Logic* **58** 291–313 (1993).

[Mos74] Y. N. Moschovakis, ***Elementary induction on abstract structures***, North-Holland, Amsterdam (1974).

[Niw86] D. Niwiński, On fixed point clones. *Proc. 13th ICALP*, LNCS **226** 464–473 (1986).

[Rab70] M. O. Rabin, Weakly definable relations and special automata, in Y. Bar-Hillel (ed.) *Mathematical Logic and Foundations of Set Theory*, North-Holland, Amsterdam (1970), 1–23.

[RiA74] W. Richter and P. Aczel, Inductive definitions and reflecting properties of admissible ordinals, in Fenstad and Hinman (ed.), *Generalized recursion theory*, North-Holland, Amsterdam 301–381 (1974).

[StE89] R. S. Streett and E. A. Emerson, An automata theoretic decision procedure for the propositional mu-calculus. *Information and Computation* **81** 249–264 (1989).

[Sti95] C. Stirling, Local model checking games. *Proc. Concur '95*, LNCS **962**, 1–11 (1995).

[Tak86] M. Takashashi, The greatest fixed-points and rational omega-tree languages. *Theor. Comput. Sci.* **44** 259–274 (1986).

Bisimulation Collapse and the Process Taxonomy

Olaf Burkart*[1], Didier Caucal**[1] and Bernhard Steffen[2]

[1] IRISA, Campus de Beaulieu, 35042 Rennes, France. (*{burkart,caucal}@irisa.fr*)
[2] Fakultät für Mathematik und Informatik, Universität Passau, Innstraße 33, 94032 Passau, Germany. (*steffen@fmi.uni-passau.de*)

Abstract. We consider the factorization (collapse) of infinite transition graphs wrt. bisimulation equivalence. It turns out that almost none of the more complex classes of the process taxonomy, which has been established in the last years, are preserved by this operation. However, for the class of BPA graphs (i.e. prefix transition graphs of context-free grammars) we can show that the factorization is effectively a regular graph, i.e. finitely representable by means of a deterministic hypergraph grammar. Since finiteness of regular graphs is decidable, this yields, as a corollary, a decision procedure for the finiteness problem of context-free processes wrt. bisimulation equivalence.

1 Introduction

In concurrency theory, process calculi are widely accepted as algebraic description languages for concurrent systems. Their semantics are usually formulated in terms of labelled transition graphs which model the dynamic behaviour together with some notion of behavioural equivalence. Since there is a great choice in the point of view for observing processes, in the last decade a plethora of behavioural equivalences have been suggested in order to capture the various underlying notions of concurrency. However, to be of practical interest decidability of the equivalence at hand is a main concern. Therefore, much research has focused on decision questions for different classes of processes (or transition graphs) with respect to a given equivalence relation.

It is folklore that any reasonable equivalence is decidable for finite-state systems. Moreover, newer results show that notably strong bisimulation equivalence is decidable even for certain classes of infinite-state systems [BBK87, CHS92, CHM93a, Sti96].

In this paper we investigate the structure of transition graphs factorized (collapsed) wrt. bisimulation equivalence, i.e. transition graphs where bisimilar

* Supported by the European Community under HCM grant ERBCHBGCT 920017. Current address: LFCS, University of Edinburgh, JCMB, King's Buildings, Edinburgh EH9 3JZ, UK. (*olaf@dcs.ed.ac.uk*)
** Supported by Esprit BRA 6317 (ASMICS).

states are identified, for different classes of infinite-state systems. It turns out that almost none of the more complex classes, like e.g. BPP and BPA processes, of the process taxonomy, which has been established in the last years, are preserved by this operation. Whereas it is comparatively straightforward to establish that the class of normed BPP graphs is closed by factorization, while this property does not hold for the whole class[1], the treatment of the much more intensely studied class of BPA processes is quite intricate.

Here the normed case has already been solved in [Cau90] showing that also the class of normed BPA processes is closed under bisimulation collapse. We show that this is not true for BPA in general. Rather, the bisimulation collapse of BPA graphs (i.e. prefix transition graphs of context-free grammars) is shown to be a regular graph, i.e. finitely representable by means of a deterministic hypergraph grammar. As our corresponding construction is effective, the well-known decidability of the finiteness of regular graphs yields, as a corollary, the decidability of the finiteness of context-free processes wrt. the bisimulation semantics. This reduction solves the open problem first considered in [MM94], and subsequently in [BG96] where decidability was proved only for certain subclasses of BPA.

The remainder of the paper is organised as follows. Section 2 presents the basic notions and the process taxonomy, which has been established in the last years. In particular, it provides examples closing the remaining separation gaps between the taxonomic classes. The same examples will also be used in the subsequent sections in order to illustrate the power of the bisimulation collapse. Section 3 considers the factorization problem for BPP graphs, while Section 4 presents our main result, the existence of an effective procedure yielding a regular graph for each collapsed BPA graph. Finally, Section 5 gives our conclusions and directions for further research.

2 A Taxonomy of Infinite-State Transition Graphs

In process theory the fundamental notion of *transition graph* is often used to model the behaviour of concurrent programs or processes. However, beyond the finite-state case, only few classes of transition graphs have been considered in greater detail. In this section we summarise known results by presenting a taxonomy for these classes according to their expressive power.

Definition 2.1. A *labelled transition graph* is a triple $\mathcal{T} = (\mathcal{S}, \Sigma, \rightarrow)$ where $\mathcal{S}$ is the set of *vertices* (or *states*), Σ is the set of *transition labels* (or *actions*), and $\rightarrow\, \subseteq \mathcal{S} \times \Sigma \times \mathcal{S}$ is the *transition relation*.
If the transition graph $\mathcal{T}$ possesses a terminal *coroot* $e \in \mathcal{S}$, i.e. e has no outgoing transitions and e is accessible from every vertex $v \in \mathcal{S}$, we say that $\mathcal{T}$ is *normed*. The *norm* of any vertex $v \in \mathcal{S}$ is then defined as the length of the shortest path from v to e.

[1] Nevertheless, Jančar and Esparza [JE96] proved recently that finiteness up to bisimulation is decidable even for the strictly larger class of Petri net transition graphs.

In particular, we are interested in classes of infinite transition graphs which can be finitely represented by labelled rewrite systems.

Definition 2.2. A *labelled rewrite system* is a triple $\mathcal{R} = (V, \Sigma, R)$ where V is an *alphabet* (or set of *nonterminals*), Σ is a set of *labels*, and $R \subseteq V^* \times \Sigma \times V^*$ is a finite set of *rewrite rules*. If the rewrite rules R are of the form $V \times \Sigma \times V^*$ the rewrite system is called *alphabetic*.

In the remainder of the paper, a rewrite rule $(u, a, v) \in R$ is also written as $u \xrightarrow{a} v$. Moreover, we will denote a rewrite system simply by R if V and Σ are clear from the context. Different classes of labelled transition graphs arise now by considering for rewrite systems the following forms of rewritings.

Definition 2.3. Let $\mathcal{R} = (V, \Sigma, R)$ be a labelled rewrite system. The (unrestricted) *rewriting relation* of R is then defined by

$$\underset{R}{\longrightarrow} =_{df} \{ (wuw', a, wvw') \mid (u \xrightarrow{a} v) \in R,\ w, w' \in V^* \},$$

while the *prefix rewriting relation* of R is given by

$$\underset{R}{\longmapsto} =_{df} \{ (uw, a, vw) \mid (u \xrightarrow{a} v) \in R,\ w \in V^* \}.$$

For technical reasons we will consider in our Main Lemma 4.1 also the *suffix rewriting relation* of R defined by

$$\underset{R}{\longrightarrow\!\!\!\!\shortmid} =_{df} \{ (wu, a, wv) \mid (u \xrightarrow{a} v) \in R,\ w \in V^* \},$$

as well as the *prefix reduction relation* of R which is defined by

$$\underset{R}{\Longmapsto} =_{df} \{ (uw, a, v) \mid (u \xrightarrow{a} v) \in R,\ w \in V^* \}.$$

Any of the relations given above can inductively be extended to words over Σ. Moreover, in the case of prefix rewritings we have the following lemma due to Büchi [Büc64].

Proposition 2.4. *The set* $\{ v \mid u \overset{*}{\underset{R}{\longmapsto}} v \}$ *of words reachable by prefix derivation from a given axiom* u *is regular, and a corresponding finite automaton is effectively constructible from* R [2].

Labelled rewrite systems R are a convenient formalism to finitely represent infinite-state processes since each of the rewrite relations $\leadsto_R \subseteq V^* \times \Sigma \times V^*$ given in Definition 2.3 may also be interpreted as a labelled transition system $\mathcal{T}(\leadsto_R) =_{df} (V^*, \Sigma, \leadsto_R)$. Later on, we will also consider *rooted labelled rewrite systems* (R, r), i.e. labelled rewrite systems R together with some axiom $r \in V^*$. The transition graph of (R, r) for any rewrite relation $\leadsto_R$ is then given by $\mathcal{T}(\leadsto_R, r) =_{df} (\{ v \in V^* \mid r \leadsto_R^* v \}, \Sigma, \leadsto_R)$.

[2] Dually, the result holds also if one considers suffix rewriting.

The second device we will use in this paper to generate infinite graphs are *hypergraph grammars*. Let $F = \bigcup_{n \geq 1} F_n$ be a graded set of labels such that $\Sigma \subseteq F_2$. A *hyperarc* of arity n is then a word $As_1 \dots s_n$ labelled by $A \in F_n$ joining the vertices $s_1, \dots, s_n$ in that order. In particular, an ordinary arc $s_1 \xrightarrow{A} s_2$ is the word As_1s_2. Accordingly, a *hypergraph* is a set of hyperarcs, while a graph is a set of (binary) arcs. Finally, we denote by $[G]$ the set of all terminal arcs of a graph G, i.e. $[G] =_{df} \{ As_1s_2 \in G \mid A \in \Sigma \}$.

Definition 2.5. A *(hyper)graph grammar* $\mathcal{G}$ is a quadruple (N, Σ, R, G_0) where

- $N \subseteq F \setminus \Sigma$ is the set of graded *nonterminals*,
- Σ is the set of *terminals*,
- R is a finite set of *rules* of the form $Ax_1 \dots x_n \rhd H$ where $A \in F_n$, H is a finite hypergraph over $\Sigma \cup N$, and $x_1, \dots, x_n$ are distinct vertices of H, and
- G_0 is an initial finite hypergraph over $\Sigma \cup N$.

A graph grammar is said to be *deterministic*, if there is only a single rule for each nonterminal.

Graph grammars can be used to generate infinite graphs by means of graph rewritings. A *graph rewriting* $G \rightarrow_R G'$ consists of replacing a nonterminal hyperarc $X = As_1 \dots s_n$ of G (called the *redex*) by a copy of H where $Ax_1 \dots x_n \rhd H$ is a rule of R such that the vertices s_i and x_i are identified, i.e.

$$G' = (G \setminus \{ X \}) \cup \{ Bg(t_1) \dots g(t_m) \mid Bt_1 \dots t_m \in H \}$$

where g is a matching function mapping x_i to s_i and the other vertices of H injectively to new vertices outside of G. To denote a graph rewriting at redex X we also write $G \rightarrow_{R,X} G'$. Since such a rewriting is context-free, we may define a *complete parallel rewriting* $\Rightarrow_R$ as follows.

$$G \underset{R}{\Rightarrow} G' \quad \text{if} \quad G \underset{R,X_1}{\rightarrow} \circ \dots \circ \underset{R,X_n}{\rightarrow} G'$$

where $\{ X_1, \dots, X_n \}$ is the set of all hyperarcs of G. Henceforth, the grammar $\mathcal{G}$ will be deterministic. The infinite graph $\mathcal{G}^\omega(G_0)$ generated by $\mathcal{G}$ starting from G_0 is then inductively defined by

$$\mathcal{G}^0(G_0) = G_0, \; \mathcal{G}^n(G_0) \underset{R}{\Rightarrow} \mathcal{G}^{n+1}(G_0), \text{ and } \mathcal{G}^\omega(G_0) = \bigcup_{n \geq 0} [\mathcal{G}^n(G_0)].$$

Since $\mathcal{G}$ is deterministic, $\mathcal{G}^\omega(G_0)$ is unique up to graph isomorphism. Finally, we call a graph G *regular* if there exists a graph grammar $\mathcal{G} = (N, \Sigma, R, G_0)$ such that $G = \mathcal{G}^\omega(G_0)$.
Figure 1 shows an example for a deterministic graph grammar with a single rewriting rule, as well as the generated infinite transition graph. Later on, we will need the basic fact that the restriction of a regular graph G to the vertices accessible from a given vertex r is effectively a rooted regular graph.

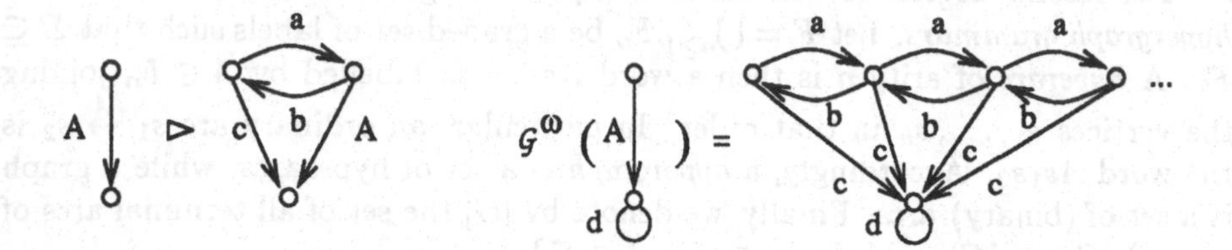

Figure 1. A graph grammar and the generated infinite transition graph.

The classes of infinite-state systems representable by the devices introduced so far can be classified as follows. A transition graph G is said to be a *pushdown process (PDP) graph* (respectively, a *Basic Process Algebra (BPA) graph*) if there exists a rooted rewrite system (respectively, a rooted alphabetic rewrite system) R, r such that G is isomorphic to the prefix transition graph of R accessible from r, i.e. $\mathcal{T}(\underset{R}{\longmapsto}, r)$. Furthermore, a transition graph G is called a *Basic Parallel Process (BPP) graph* if there exists a rooted alphabetic rewrite system R, r such that G is isomorphic to the transition graph of R accessible from r modulo commutation of nonterminals, i.e. $\mathcal{T}(\underset{R}{\longrightarrow}, r)/\equiv$.

Overall, we obtain the taxonomy of classes of infinite-state systems, as depicted in Figure 2. It is known that the class of normed BPA graphs, BPA graphs, PDP graphs, and regular graphs form a strict hierarchy [CM90]. Moreover, the class of PDP graphs coincides with the class of rooted regular graphs of finite degree [Cau92]. On the other side the class of BPP graphs and the strictly larger class of Petri Net transition graphs[3] is incomparable with all the other classes [Chr93]. We complete this picture by providing in Figure 3 examples closing the remaining separation gaps. The same examples will also be used in the subsequent sections in order to illustrate the power of the bisimulation collapse.

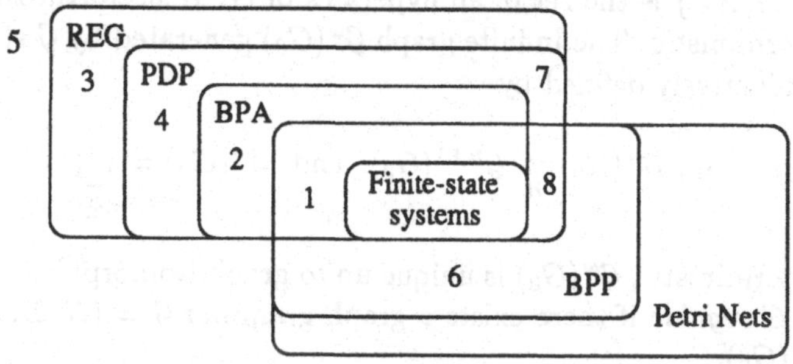

Figure 2. A taxonomy of classes of infinite-state transition graphs.

[3] For a formal definition see e.g. [JE96].

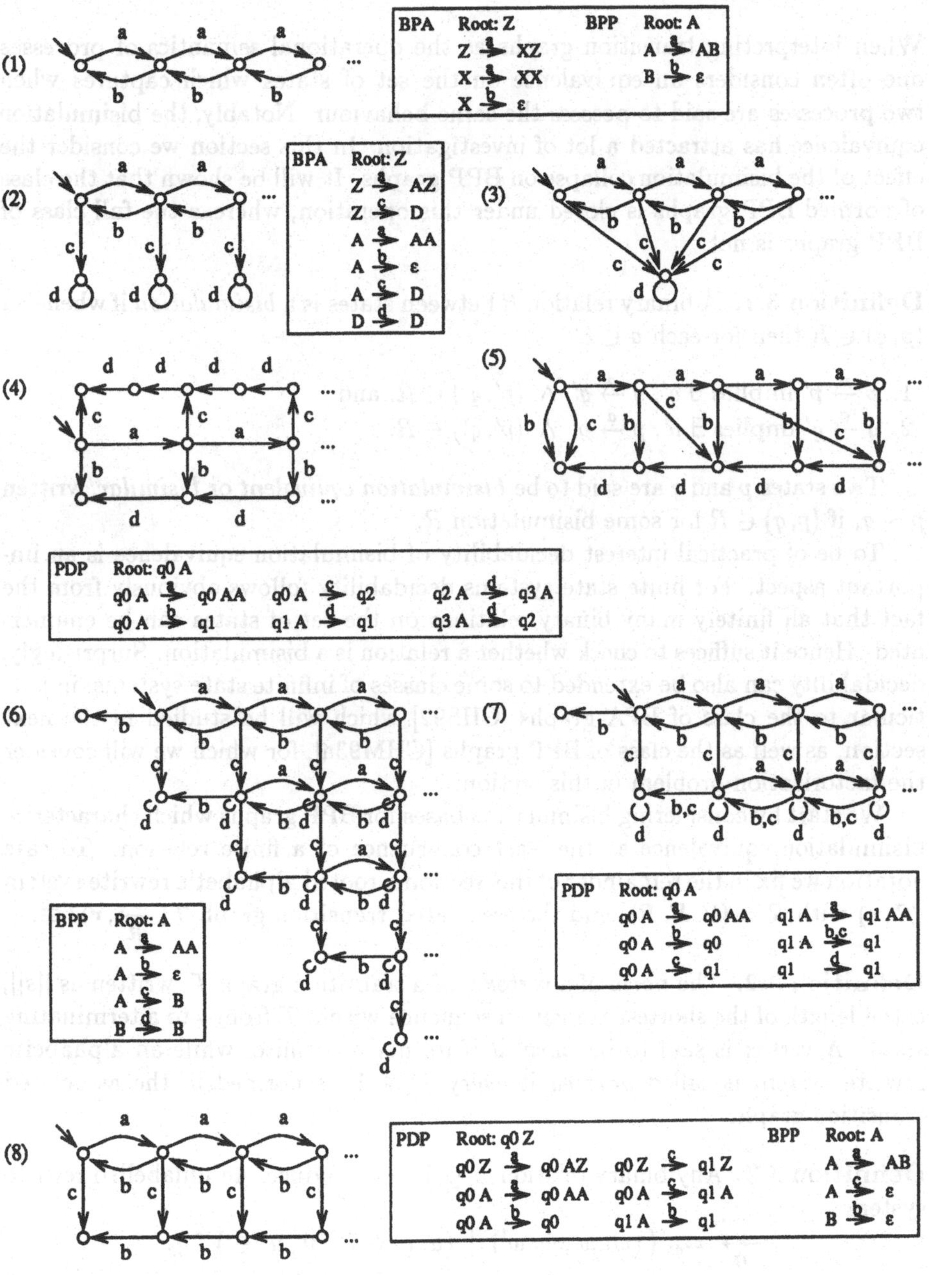

Figure 3. Examples of infinite-state transition graphs.

3 Factorization of BPP graphs

When interpreting transition graphs as the operational semantics of processes one often considers an equivalence on the set of states which captures when two processes are said to possess the same behaviour. Notably, the bisimulation equivalence has attracted a lot of investigation. In this section we consider the effect of the bisimulation collapse on BPP graphs. It will be shown that the class of normed BPP graphs is closed under this operation, whereas the full class of BPP graphs is not.

Definition 3.1. A binary relation R between states is a *bisimulation* if whenever $(p, q) \in R$ then for each $a \in \Sigma$:

1. $p \xrightarrow{a} p'$ implies $\exists\, q'.\ q \xrightarrow{a} q' \ \wedge\ (p', q') \in R$, and
2. $q \xrightarrow{a} q'$ implies $\exists\, p'.\ p \xrightarrow{a} p' \ \wedge\ (p', q') \in R$.

Two states p and q are said to be *bisimulation equivalent* or *bisimilar*, written $p \sim q$, if $(p, q) \in R$ for some bisimulation R.

To be of practical interest decidability of bisimulation equivalence is an important aspect. For finite state systems decidability follows obviously from the fact that all finitely many binary relations on the set of states can be enumerated. Hence it suffices to check whether a relation is a bisimulation. Surprisingly, decidability can also be extended to some classes of infinite state systems, in particular to the class of BPA graphs [CHS92] which will be studied in the next section, as well as the class of BPP graphs [CHM93a], for which we will consider the factorization problem in this section.

We start by considering bisimulation bases for BPP graphs which characterise bisimulation equivalence as the least congruence of a finite relation. To ease notation we fix in the remainder of this section a rooted alphabetic rewrite system $(\mathcal{R}, r)$ with $\mathcal{R} = (V, \Sigma, R)$, and the associated transition graph $\mathcal{T}(\xrightarrow[R]{}, r)/\equiv$.

Definition 3.2. The *norm* of a vertex s of a transition graph $\mathcal{T}$, written as $||s||$, is the length of the shortest transition sequence within $\mathcal{T}$ from s to a terminating state. A vertex is said to be *normed* if its norm is finite, while an alphabetic rewrite system is called *normed* it every $X \in V$ is normed in the associated transition graph.

Definition 3.3. Any binary relation $B \subseteq V \times V^*$ induces an unlabelled rewrite system

$$\xrightarrow[B]{} \ =_{\mathrm{df}} \{\, (wuw', wvw') \mid (u, v) \in B,\ w, w' \in V^* \,\}.$$

The reflexive, symmetric, transitive closure $\leftrightarrow_B^*$ is then always a *congruence relation*, i.e. it is an equivalence relation which additionally satisfies $u \leftrightarrow_B^* v$ implies $xuy \leftrightarrow_B^* xvy$, for all $x, y \in V^*$.

Definition 3.4. A binary relation $B \subseteq V \times V^*$ is called *fundamental* if it satisfies the following three conditions.

– B is *functional*: if $(X,\alpha) \in B$ and $(X,\beta) \in B$ then $\alpha = \beta$.
– B is *factorizing*: $im(B) \subseteq (V_N \setminus dom(B))^*$
– B is *norm-preserving*: if $(X,\alpha) \in B$ then $||X|| = ||\alpha||$.

Since any fundamental relation B is confluent and noetherian each $\alpha \in V^*$ posesses a unique normal form $\alpha \downarrow B$.

Definition 3.5. Let $B \subseteq V \times V^*$ be a fundamental relation of bisimilar vertices which is maximal wrt. inclusion. Then a variable $X \in V$ is called *prime* wrt. bisimilarity if $X \notin dom(B)$.

Theorem 3.6 (Unique Decomposition). *Any normed vertex $\alpha \in V^*$ can be expressed uniquely as a product of primes* [CHM93b].

This unique decomposition property of normed BPP processes implies that bisimulation equivalence for normed BPP graphs can be characterized as the least congruence of a finite fundamental relation, as stated in the following corollary.

Corollary 3.7. *If $\mathcal{R}$ is normed, then there exists a finite* fundamental *relation $B \subseteq V \times V^*$ such that two vertices $\alpha, \beta \in V^*$ are bisimilar iff $\alpha \leftrightarrow^*_B \beta$. Moreover, B can effectively be computed from $\mathcal{R}$.*

Such a fundamental bisimulation base can now be used to reduce the rewrite system under consideration in order to obtain a finite representation for the factor graph of the original system.

Theorem 3.8. *The class of normed BPP graphs is effectively closed under factorization wrt. bisimulation equivalence.*

Proof. Let $\mathcal{R} = (V, \Sigma, R)$ be a labelled rewrite system with root $r \in V^*$, and B be a bisimulation base for $\mathcal{R}$. The factor graph of $\mathcal{T}(\underset{R}{\longrightarrow}, r)/\equiv$ is then isomorphic to the rooted transition graph modulo commutation of $(\mathcal{R}', r')$ where $\mathcal{R}' = (V \setminus dom(B), \Sigma, R'), r' = r \downarrow B$, and $R' = \{(A \overset{a}{\to} \alpha \downarrow B) \mid A \notin dom(B)$ and $(A \overset{a}{\to} \alpha) \in R\}$. □

We close this section by giving an example that this closure property no longer holds for the general case.

Proposition 3.9. *The class of BPP graphs is not closed under factorization wrt. bisimulation equivalence.*

Proof. Consider the unnormed BPP graph (6) of Figure 3 whose factor graph is (7). We will show that the transition graph (7) is not a BPP graph.

Let $s_0, s_1, \dots$ be the vertices in the upper row, and $t_1, t_2, \dots$ be the vertices in the lower row of the graph (7). Since s_0 is terminating it is clearly labelled with ϵ, written as $\epsilon(s_0)$, and the root s_1 must be labelled with a variable. So let wlog. $A_1(s_1)$ and $\gamma_D(t_1) \neq A_1$. Thus we have $A_1(s_1) \xrightarrow{b} \epsilon(s_0), A_1(s_1) \xrightarrow{c} \gamma_D(t_1)$, and $\gamma_D(t_1) \xrightarrow{d} \gamma_D(t_1)$.

Now assume A_1 occurs again in a word labelling some $s_i, i > 1$, i.e. $A_1\alpha_{i-1}(s_i)$. Hence, $A_1\alpha_{i-1}(s_i) \xrightarrow{b} \alpha_{i-1}(s_{i-1})$, and $A_1\alpha_{i-1}(s_i) \xrightarrow{c} \gamma_D\alpha_{i-1}(t_i)$. Moreover, the transition sequence $\alpha_{i-1}(s_{i-1}) \xrightarrow{b^{i-2}} A_1(s_1)$ implies $\gamma_D\alpha_{i-1}(t_i) \xrightarrow{b^{i-2}} \gamma_D A_1(t_2)$. However, this yields a contradiction, since the transition $\gamma_D A_1(t_2) \xrightarrow{c} \gamma_D^2$ is not possible in the graph (7).

Thus we may conclude wlog. $A_2(s_2)$. Applying the same arguments as above we see that also A_2 cannot occur a second time in a labelling of some $s_i, i > 2$. Proceeding with this construction, we obtain an infinite sequence of different alphabetic labels for $s_1, s_2, \ldots$, which is obviously not possible for BPP graphs. □

Although the class of BPP graphs is not closed under factorization wrt. bisimulation, it was recently shown that finiteness up to bisimulation is decidable for the strictly more expressible class of Petri net transition graphs [JE96].

4 Factorization of BPA graphs

Another, practically probably much more important class, the BPA graphs (or context-free processes) has attracted a lot of investigation concerning decidability of bisimulation equivalence [BBK87, Cau90, Gro91, HS91, CHS92, HM94, HJM94, BCS95]. However, only in [Cau90] the structure of the factor graphs wrt. bisimulation has been considered. He has shown that the class of *normed* BPA graphs is effectively closed under factorization by bisimulation. This result does not longer hold for the general unnormed case, as illustrated by the transition graph (2) of Figure 3. Its factorization is the transition graph (3) which in turn is not a BPA graph due to the existence of a vertex with unbounded in-degree. Moreover, it is known that the factorization of PDP graphs already yields graphs which are no longer regular [CM90]. As an example consider the transition graph (4) which has the non-regular graph (5) as its factorization graph.

The main theorem of this paper states that the bisimulation collapse of each (possibly unnormed) BPA graph is effectively a regular graph of finite out-degree. Since the finiteness of regular graphs is decidable, simply by checking that there are no cyclic dependencies in the (hyper)graph grammar, our construction yields, as a corollary, a decision procedure for the finiteness problem of context-free processes wrt. bisimulation [MM94]. It should be noted, however, that our quotient construction is not limited to the case where the resulting quotient is finite.

4.1 The Main Lemma

Key towards the proof of the main result is the observation that the factorization of BPA graphs can be characterised by three rewriting relations. 1) a prefix rewriting relation, capturing the context-free part, 2) a suffix rewriting relation taking care of bisimilar unnormed parts, and 3) a prefix reduction relation, which realizes the required right cancellation.

In order to formalise this idea, let us fix an alphabet V and a label set Σ, as well as finite relations P, Q, R in $V^* \times \Sigma \times V^*$. Moreover, let

$$G_{P,Q,R,r} =_{df} (V^*, \Sigma, \underset{P}{\longmapsto} \cup \underset{Q}{\longrightarrow\!\!\!\!\!|} \cup \underset{R}{\models\!\!\!\Rightarrow}, r)$$

the graph rooted at $r \in V^*$ which is generated by the prefix transitions of P, the suffix transitions of Q, and the prefix reduction transitions of R. Then we can effectively construct a graph grammar generating a transition graph isomorphic to $G_{P,Q,R,r}$, as stated in the following lemma.

Main Lemma 4.1. *For finite relations $P, Q, R \subseteq V^* \times \Sigma \times V^*$, and a root $r \in V^*$, $G_{P,Q,R,r}$ is effectively a regular graph (of finite out-degree).*

Proof. We will construct a deterministic graph grammar $\mathcal{G}$ generating $G_{P,Q,R,r}$ (henceforth only G for short) according to the length of the words denoting the vertices. The key idea is to partition G into a finite graph G_0 plus finitely many isomorphic connected components, each corresponding to a hyperarc in the graph grammar to be constructed. To start with, note that the set V_G of vertices of G is the following rational language:

$$V_G = Dom(P).N^* \cup Im(P).N^* \cup N^*.Dom(Q) \cup N^*.Im(Q) \cup Dom(R).N^* \cup Im(R).$$

Now let m_P (resp. m_Q) be the following length of words in P (respectively in Q):

$$m_P =_{df} \max\{\min\{|u|, |v|\} \mid \exists a\ (u \xrightarrow{a} v) \in P\},$$
$$m_Q =_{df} \max\{\min\{|u|, |v|\} \mid \exists a\ (u \xrightarrow{a} v) \in Q\},$$

and let m_R^1 (resp. m_R^2) be the greatest length of the left hand sides (resp. right hand sides) of R:

$$m_R^1 =_{df} \max\{|u| \mid \exists a\ \exists v\ (u \xrightarrow{a} v) \in R\},$$
$$m_R^2 =_{df} \max\{|v| \mid \exists a\ \exists u\ (u \xrightarrow{a} v) \in R\}.$$

Taking $m_{pre} =_{df} \max(m_P, m_R^1)$, $m_{suf} =_{df} m_Q$ and $M =_{df} \max(m_{pre}+m_{suf}, m_R^2)$, we restrict the vertex set to $V_M =_{df} \{u \in V_G \mid M \leq |u|\}$. Furthermore, any word $u \in V_M$ is decomposed as $u = p_u c_u q_u$ where $|p_u| = m_{pre}$ and $|q_u| = m_{suf}$. Hence every vertex $u \in V_M$ has now the property that prefix and suffix redices do not overlap.
Let us ignore for the moment the prefix reductions of R by considering

$$H =_{df} (V_G, \Sigma, \underset{P}{\longmapsto} \cup \underset{Q}{\longrightarrow\!\!\!\!\!|}),$$

the subgraph of G generated by the prefix transitions of P and the suffix transitions of Q. Let now H_u, for any vertex $u \in V_M$, be the restriction $H_{|\{v \mid |u| \leq |v|\}}$

of H to the vertices of length at least the length of u, and C_u be the connected component of H_u containing u. We then distinguish the *frontier* I_u of C_u

$$I_u =_{df} \{\, v \in V_{C_u} \mid |v| = |u| \,\},$$

and the *border* J_u of C_u

$$J_u =_{df} \{\, v \in V_{C_u} \mid \exists\, a\, \exists\, w, (w \xrightarrow{a} v) \in H \cup H^{-1} \;\wedge\; |w| < |u| < |v| \,\},$$

as depicted in the following Figure.

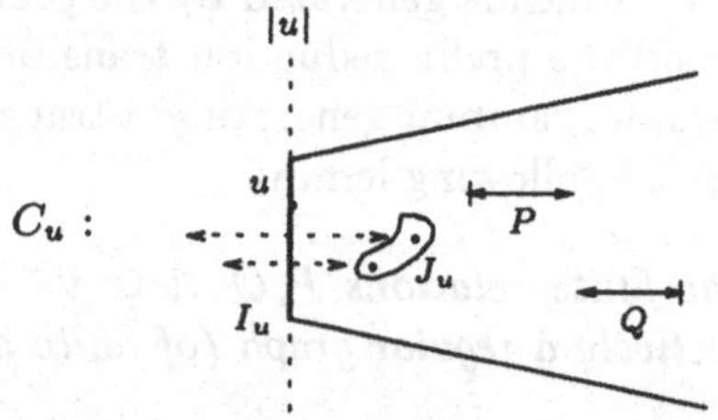

Claim : For any $u \in V_M$, the vertex sets I_u and J_u can effectively be determined.

Proof. We denote by P_0 (resp. Q_0) the unlabelled transitions of $P \cup P^{-1}$ (resp. $Q \cup Q^{-1}$), i.e.

$$P_0 =_{df} \{\, (u,v) \mid \exists\, a,\; u \xrightarrow{a} v\; \in P \cup P^{-1} \,\}, \text{ and}$$
$$Q_0 =_{df} \{\, (u,v) \mid \exists\, a,\; u \xrightarrow{a} v\; \in Q \cup Q^{-1} \,\},$$

which allow to express the connectivity wrt. P (resp. Q). Now we complete P_0 and Q_0 to $\overline{P_0}$, respectively $\overline{Q_0}$, in order to guarantee that the obtained rewrite relations are only applicable to words of length at least M, and, moreover, that the words obtained by rewriting have again length of at least M. Thus we define

$$\overline{P_0} =_{df} \{\, (uw, vw) \mid u\; P_0\; v \quad \text{and} \quad |w| = m_{pre} - min(|u|,|v|) \,\}, \text{ and}$$
$$\overline{Q_0} =_{df} \{\, (wu, wv) \mid u\; Q_0\; v \quad \text{and} \quad |w| = m_{suf} - min(|u|,|v|) \,\}$$

Using $\overline{P_0}$ by prefix and $\overline{Q_0}$ by suffix, we associate now with each $u \in V_M$ the following two finite relations:

$$\langle I_u \rangle =_{df} \{\, (p,q) \mid p_u \overset{*}{\underset{\overline{P_0}}{\longmapsto}} p \;\wedge\; q_u \overset{*}{\underset{\overline{Q_0}}{\longrightarrow\!\!\!\mid}} q \;\wedge\; |u| = |pc_u q| \,\},$$
$$\langle J_u \rangle =_{df} \{\, (p,q) \mid p_u \overset{*}{\underset{\overline{P_0}}{\longmapsto}} p \;\wedge\; q_u \overset{*}{\underset{\overline{Q_0}}{\longrightarrow\!\!\!\mid}} q \;\wedge\; |u| < |pc_u q| \;\wedge$$
$$(p \underset{\overline{P_0}}{\longmapsto} p' \;\wedge\; |p' c_u q| < |u|) \vee (q \underset{\overline{Q_0}}{\longrightarrow\!\!\!\mid} q' \;\wedge\; |pc_u q'| < |u|) \,\}$$

Observe that both relations can effectively be constructed since $\{\, p \mid p_u \overset{*}{\underset{\overline{P_0}}{\longmapsto}} p \,\}$, as well as $\{\, q \mid q_u \overset{*}{\underset{\overline{Q_0}}{\longrightarrow\!\!\!\mid}} q \,\}$ are regular sets c.f. Lemma 2.4.

So overall we have $\{\, pc_u q \mid (p,q) \in \langle I_u \rangle \,\} = I_u$ and $\{\, pc_u q \mid (p,q) \in \langle J_u \rangle \,\} = J_u$. □

The next step in the construction consists of a completion of C_u to the following graph:

$$G_u =_{df} C_u \cup \{\, vw \xrightarrow{a} z \in G \mid v \xrightarrow{a} z \in R \wedge vw \in V_{C_u} \}$$

by adding the R-transitions from the vertices of C_u, as illustrated in the following Figure.

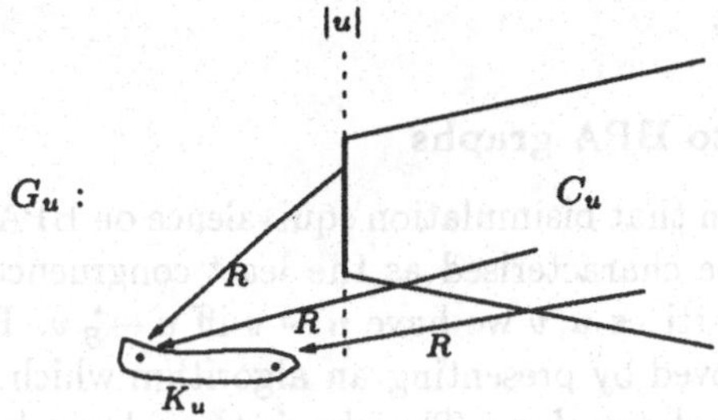

The added vertices are denoted by $K_u =_{df} V_{G_u} - V_{C_u}$. We define an equivalence $\equiv$ on the set V as follows:

$$u \equiv v \quad \text{iff} \quad \langle I_u \rangle \;=\; \langle I_v \rangle \quad \text{and} \quad \langle J_u \rangle \;=\; \langle J_v \rangle$$

Note that if $u \equiv v$ then G_u is isomorphic to G_v. Furthermore, $\equiv$ is of finite index and a set U of representatives is constructible from P, Q, and R. In order to construct the intended graph grammar, we take now a graded alphabet F disjoint of Σ, and to each $u \in U$, we associate a hyperarc $\langle j_u \rangle$ labelled in F such that

$$\begin{array}{lll} & \langle j_u \rangle = f s_1 ... s_n \text{ with } \{s_1, \ldots, s_n\} & = \langle I_u \rangle \cup \langle J_u \rangle \cup K_u \\ \text{and} & s_i \neq s_j & \text{if} \quad i \neq j \\ \text{and} & \langle j_u \rangle(1) \neq \langle j_v \rangle(1) & \text{if} \quad u \neq v \in U. \end{array}$$

Any vertex $v \in V_M$ has a unique representative $u \in U$ with $u \equiv v$, and we consider the hyperarc

$$j_v =_{df} f(s_1 \leftarrow c_v) \ldots (s_n \leftarrow c_v) \quad \text{where } \langle j_u \rangle \;=\; f s_1 \ldots s_n,$$

and, for every $p, q, c \in V$,

$$(p, q) \leftarrow c \;=_{df}\; pcq \quad \text{and} \quad p \leftarrow c \;=_{df}\; p.$$

For any $u \in U$, we construct the terminal transitions T_u of the right-hand side associated to j_u :

$$T_u \;=_{df}\; \{ v \xrightarrow{a} w \in G_u \mid |v| = |u| \quad \text{or} \quad |w| = |u| \}$$

which is the subgraph of G_u consisting of arcs linked to I_u, and we construct the following set N_u of the nonterminal hyperarcs associated to j_u:

$$N_u \;=_{df}\; \{ j_v \mid C_v \text{ is a connected component of } C_u - T_u \}$$

Finally, letting $H_M \;=_{df}\; \{ u \xrightarrow{a} v \in H \mid |u| \geq M \text{ and } |v| \geq M \}$ the restriction of H to the vertices of length at least M, we construct the initial finite hypergraph as

$$G_0 =_{df} G_{\leq M} \cup \{ j_v \mid C_v \text{ is a connected component of } H_M \}$$

Overall, we have constructed the following deterministic graph grammar $\mathcal{G}$:

$$\mathcal{G} =_{\mathrm{df}} (\{\langle j_u\rangle(1)\}_{u\in U}, \Sigma, \{j_u \triangleright T_u \cup N_u\}_{u\in U}, G_0)$$

with the property that, for any $u \in U$, G_u belongs to $\mathcal{G}^\omega(j_u)$, as well as that $\mathcal{G}^\omega(G_0)$ contains G. Thus we have proved that G is effectively a regular graph (of finite out-degree). □

4.2 Application to BPA graphs

In [CHS92] it is shown that bisimulation equivalence on BPA graphs (or context-free processes) can be characterised as the least congruence of a finite relation B, i.e. for any two vertices u, v we have $u \sim v$ iff $u \leftrightarrow_B^* v$. Recently, in [BCS95] this result was improved by presenting an algorithm which allows to effectively compute such a *bisimulation base*. The idea is to exploit a bound on the number of transitions needed to distinguish two nonbisimilar normed vertices for the collection of a finite set of pairs of vertices which is subsequently refined until some fixpoint is reached. In this section we will use these results in conjunction with our Main Lemma 4.1 in order to prove that every BPA graph factorized by bisimulation is effectively a regular graph.

Theorem 4.2. *The factorization of any BPA graph wrt. bisimulation equivalence is effectively a regular graph.*

Proof. We fix a rooted alphabetic rewrite system $\mathcal{R} = (V, \Sigma, \Delta, r)$ with $\Delta \subseteq V \times \Sigma \times V^*$ where the set V of variables is partitioned into the set of *normed* variables $V_N =_{\mathrm{df}} \{X \in V \mid \exists\, w \in \Sigma^*.\ X \stackrel{w}{\rightarrow} \epsilon\}$, and the set of *unnormed* variables $V_U =_{\mathrm{df}} V \setminus V_N$, respectively. Furthermore, let $B \subseteq V^* \times V^*$ be a bisimulation base of $\mathcal{R}$, i.e. for all $\alpha, \beta \in V^*$ we have $\alpha \sim \beta$ iff $\alpha \leftrightarrow_B^* \beta$. Such a bisimulation base can effectively be computed from $\mathcal{R}$ by the algorithm given in [BCS95].

As shown in [CHS92, BCS95] the bisimulation base may be split into two relations B_1 and B_2 such that $B = B_1 \cup B_2$, $B_1 \subseteq V_N \times V_N^+$, and $B_2 \subseteq V_N^* V_U \times V_N^* V_U$. Moreover, the first relation B_1 is *fundamental.*
Our goal is now to construct from $\mathcal{R}$ and B a graph grammar $\mathcal{G}$ and an initial graph G_0 with root r' such that $\mathcal{G}^\omega(G_0, r')$ is isomorphic to $\mathcal{T}(\underset{\Delta}{\longmapsto}, r)/\sim$.

We start by reducing the rewrite rules Δ according to B_1. Since the relation B_1 is functional we obtain $\mathcal{R}' = (V - dom(B_1), \Sigma, \Delta', r \downarrow B_1)$ where

$$(A \stackrel{a}{\rightarrow} \alpha \downarrow B_1) \in \Delta' \quad \text{iff} \quad (A \stackrel{a}{\rightarrow} \alpha) \in \Delta \text{ and } A \notin dom(B_1).$$

This transformation takes care of all bisimulation equivalences obtained by the least congruence of B_1. The second step deals with all pairs of bisimilar vertices contained in the least congruence of the remaining relation $B_2 \downarrow B_1$. Let

$$\begin{aligned}
P &= \{(A, a, \alpha) \mid (A \stackrel{a}{\rightarrow} \alpha) \in \Delta' \quad \text{and} \quad \alpha \in V_N^*\},\\
Q &= \{(\alpha, \$, \beta) \mid (\alpha, \beta) \in B_2 \downarrow B_1\}, \text{ and}\\
R &= \{(A, a, \alpha) \mid (A \stackrel{a}{\rightarrow} \alpha) \in \Delta' \quad \text{and} \quad \alpha \in V_N^* V_U\}.
\end{aligned}$$

By construction, the prefix transitions of P and R generate the prefix transition graph of Δ'. However, using R as a prefix reduction has the benefit that the right-cancellation law for unnormed context-free processes is taken into account, i.e. for any $(A \xrightarrow{a} \alpha) \in \Delta'$ where $\alpha \in V_N^* V_U$, we have

$$A\beta \overset{a}{\underset{\Delta'}{\Longmapsto}} \alpha \quad \text{instead of} \quad A\beta \overset{a}{\underset{\Delta'}{\longmapsto}} \alpha\beta \sim \alpha.$$

Moreover, using Q with suffix rewriting ensures that bisimilar vertices are connected by means of \$ transitions. Lemma 4.1 states now that the transition graph G rooted at r and generated by prefix rewriting of P, suffix rewriting of Q, and prefix reduction of R is regular, i.e. representable by a graph grammar $\mathcal{G}' = (N_{\mathcal{G}'}, \Sigma, R_{\mathcal{G}'}, G'_0)$ such that $G = \mathcal{G}'^{\,\omega}(G'_0)$.

By identifying all vertices in the graph grammar which are connected by \$ transitions one obtains, finally, a graph grammar $\mathcal{G}$ which generates the factorization of $\mathcal{T}(\underset{\Delta}{\longmapsto}, r)$ with respect to bisimulation. □

Since the finiteness of regular graphs is decidable, simply by checking that there are no cyclic dependencies in the (hyper)graph grammar, we obtain the following corollary, which solves the finiteness problem up to bisimulation for arbitrary context-free processes [MM94, BG96].

Corollary 4.3. *It is decidable whether the factorization of a BPA graph with respect to bisimulation equivalence is finite.*

It should be noted, however, that our effective quotient construction is not limited to the case where the resulting quotient is finite.

We close this section by illustrating the construction for the prefix transition graph generated from the root X by the following alphabetic rewrite system [MM94].

$$\Delta_{ex} = \left\{ \begin{array}{l} X \xrightarrow{a} YZ \\ Y \xrightarrow{b} YC \\ Y \xrightarrow{d} \epsilon \\ Z \xrightarrow{c} Z \\ C \xrightarrow{c} \epsilon \end{array} \right\}$$

For Δ_{ex} we have $V_N = \{Y, C\}$, $V_U = \{X, Z\}$, and a bisimulation base $B_{ex} = \{(Z, CZ)\}$. According to the proof of Theorem 4.2 we thus obtain

$$\begin{aligned} P &= \{(Y, b, YC),\ (Y, d, \epsilon),\ (C, c, \epsilon)\}, \\ Q &= \{(Z, \$, CZ)\}, \\ R &= \{(X, a, YZ),\ (Z, c, Z)\}. \end{aligned}$$

The application of Lemma 4.1 then yields $m_P = 1, m_Q = 1, m_R^1 = 1, m_R^2 = 2, m_{pre} = 1, m_{suf} = 1$, and thus $M = 2$. For this example, we hence have only a single frontier $I = \{YZ, CZ\}$ with an empty border $J = \emptyset$. Overall, Figure 4 summarises the prefix transition graph generated from X by Δ_{ex} (1), the associated factor graph (2), the regular graph $G_{P,Q,R,X}$ (3), and the graph grammar generating the factor graph (4).

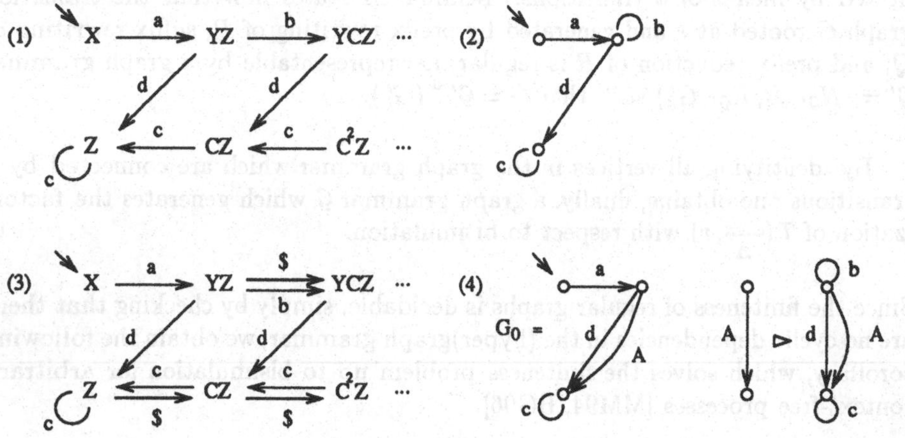

Figure 4. The transition graph, the factor graph, and the construction for Δ_{ex}.

5 Conclusions

In this paper we have considered the factorization problem wrt. bisimulation equivalence for certain classes of infinite-state processes. Our main result states that factor graphs of BPA processes are effectively regular graphs, i.e. finitely representable by a deterministic graph grammar. Since finiteness is trivially decidable for regular graphs, this result yields, as a corollary, a decision procedure for the finiteness up to bisimulation of arbitrary context-free processes thereby improving on already known algorithms for subclasses of BPA [MM94, BG96].

For the class of BPP processes, it turns out that the subclass of normed processes is closed under factorization, which does not longer hold for the general case. Nevertheless, it is possible even for the strictly larger class of Petri net transition graphs to decide equivalence with a given finite-state system, and finiteness up to bisimulation [JM95, JE96]. However, it remains the question whether we can find some reasonable extensions of BPP such that the factor graphs of BPP processes are expressible in this larger class.

References

BBK87. J.C.M. Baeten, J.A. Bergstra, and J.W. Klop. Decidability of Bisimulation Equivalence for Processes Generating Context-Free Languages. In *PARLE '87*, LNCS 259, pages 94–113. Springer, 1987.

BCS95. O. Burkart, D. Caucal, and B. Steffen. An Elementary Bisimulation Decision Procedure for Arbitrary Context-Free Processes. In *MFCS '95*, LNCS 969, pages 423–433. Springer, 1995.

BG96. D.J.B. Bosscher and W.O.D. Griffioen. Regularity for a Large Class of Context-Free Processes is Decidable. Will be presented at ICALP '96, 1996.

Büc64. R. Büchi. Regular Canonical Systems. *Archiv für Mathematische Logik und Grundlagenforschung*, 6:91–111, 1964.

Cau90. D. Caucal. Graphes Canoniques de Graphes Algébriques. *RAIRO*, 24(4):339–352, 1990.

Cau92. D. Caucal. On the Regular Structure of Prefix Rewriting. *Theoretical Computer Science*, 106:61–86, 1992.

CHM93a. S. Christensen, Y. Hirshfeld, and F. Moller. Bisimulation Equivalence is Decidable for all Basic Parallel Processes. In *CONCUR '93*, LNCS 715, pages 143–157. Springer, 1993.

CHM93b. S. Christensen, Y. Hirshfeld, and F. Moller. Decomposability, Decidability and Axiomatisability for Bisimulation Equivalence on Basic Parallel Processes. In *LICS '93*. IEEE Computer Society Press, 1993.

Chr93. S. Christensen. *Decidability and Decomposition in Process Algebras*. PhD thesis, The University of Edinburgh, Department of Computer Science, 1993.

CHS92. S. Christensen, H. Hüttel, and C. Stirling. Bisimulation Equivalence is Decidable for all Context-Free Processes. In *CONCUR '92*, LNCS 630, pages 138–147. Springer, 1992.

CM90. D. Caucal and R. Monfort. On the Transition Graphs of Automata and Grammars. In *Graph-Theoretic Concepts in Computer Science*, LNCS 484, pages 311–337. Springer, 1990.

Gro91. J.F. Groote. A Short Proof of the Decidability of Bisimulation for Normed BPA-Processes. *Information Processing Letters*, 42:167–171, 1991.

HJM94. Y. Hirshfeld, M. Jerrum, and F. Moller. A Polynomial Algorithm for Deciding Bisimilarity of Normed Context-Free Processes. In *FOCS '94*, pages 623–631. IEEE Computer Society Press, 1994.

HM94. Y. Hirshfeld and F. Moller. A Fast Algorithm for Deciding Bisimilarity of Normed Context-Free Processes. In *CONCUR '94*, LNCS 836, pages 48–63. Springer, 1994.

HS91. H. Hüttel and C. Stirling. Actions Speak Louder than Words: Proving Bisimilarity for Context-Free Processes. In *LICS '91*, pages 376–386. IEEE Computer Society Press, 1991.

JE96. P. Jančar and J. Esparza. Deciding Finiteness of Petri Nets up to Bisimulation. Will be presented at ICALP '96, 1996.

JM95. P. Jančar and F. Moller. Checking Regular Properties of Petri Nets. In *CONCUR '95*, LNCS 995, pages 348–362. Springer, 1995.

MM94. S. Mauw and H. Mulder. Regularity of BPA-Systems is Decidable. In *CONCUR '94*, LNCS 836, pages 34–47. Springer, 1994.

Sti96. C. Stirling. Decidability of Bisimulation Equivalence for Normed Pushdown Processes. Will be presented at CONCUR '96, 1996.

On the Expressive Completeness of the Propositional mu-Calculus with Respect to Monadic Second Order Logic

David Janin
LaBRI[1]
Université de Bordeaux I
351, Cours de la Libération
F-33 405 Talence cedex, France
e-mail: janin@labri.u-bordeaux.fr

Igor Walukiewicz
BRICS[2,3]
Department of Computer Science
University of Aarhus
Ny Munkegade
DK-8000 Aarhus C, Denmark
e-mail: igw@mimuw.edu.pl

Abstract. Monadic second order logic (MSOL) over transition systems is considered. It is shown that every formula of MSOL which does not distinguish between bisimilar models is equivalent to a formula of the propositional μ-calculus. This expressive completeness result implies that every logic over transition systems invariant under bisimulation and translatable into MSOL can be also translated into the μ-calculus. This gives a precise meaning to the statement that most propositional logics of programs can be translated into the μ-calculus.

1 Introduction

Transition systems are structures consisting of a nonempty set of *states*, a set of unary relations describing properties of states and a set of binary relations describing *transitions* between states. It was advocated by many authors [28, 3] that this kind of structures provide a good framework for describing behaviour of programs (or program schemes), or even more generally, engineering systems, provided their evolution in time is discrete.

Take as an example an operational semantics of a (scheme of a) programming language, say CCS. It is given in two steps. First one associates with every program a transition system describing all possible executions of the program. This can be done using SOS rules [27] or similar formalism. Next one defines an equivalence relation between transition systems which depends on the intended notion of observable. The meaning of the program is an equivalence class of the associated transition system. Bisimulation relation is often considered to be the finest relation which is interesting in this context [24, 32].

---

[1] Laboratoire Bordelais de Recherche en Informatique (CNRS URA 1304)
[2] Basic Research in Computer Science, Centre of the Danish National Research Foundation.
[3] On leave from: Institute of Informatics, Warsaw University, Banacha 2, 02-097 Warsaw, POLAND

In the setting described above, checking that a modelled system (say a program) has some property amounts to checking that the corresponding transition system has the property. The fact that the meaning of the program is really an equivalence relation and not a transition system itself is reflected in the fact that the properties we are interested in do not distinguish between equivalent systems. This motivates our claim that logics suitable for verification should not distinguish between bisimilar systems. Indeed most of the program logics proposed in the literature have this property.

Since this approach to verification has been suggested [28] a big variety of logics over transition systems has been proposed. New logics were introduced because they were more manageable, more expressive, or represented a better balance between these two kinds of properties. Manageability is concerned with axiomatisations, the complexity of the validity problem, and the complexity of the model checking problem (i.e. a problem of verifying whether a given formula is satisfied in a given transition system). These complexity issues are important especially for computer aided verification. Of course there is no point in considering even very manageable logic if it is not capable of expressing the properties we are interested in.

The question arises: how one does decide which properties are interesting. Of course it is important to list first some example properties which one would like to express (see [15, 12] for such lists), but how can one be sure that we have listed all the properties of potential interest? The solution is to find a "yardstick" which is usually some well established logic. If we can express all the properties from our list in the "yardstick" logic then we know that the set of properties expressible in the logic is complete, in a sense that it is closed under logical operations and contains our interesting properties. This approach was initiated by Kamp [22] who investigated expressive power of propositional temporal logic (PTL) with respect to expressive power of the first order logic over $\langle \omega, \leq \rangle$. This lead him to the discovery of the *until* operator and the proof that PTL with the *until* operator is *expressively complete* with respect to first order logic, i.e.: a class of models is definable by a PTL formula with *until* iff it is definable in the first order logic. PTL is still widely used but it turned out that there are interesting properties which are not expressible in the first order logic and MSOL over $\langle \omega, \leq \rangle$ was proposed as a new yardstick. This choice was particularly useful as it brought new insights and a wealth of automata theoretic methods to the field. The logic expressively complete with respect to MSOL over $\langle \omega, \leq \rangle$ is the μ-calculus of linear time [4].

As noted by Emerson ([12] p. 1026) the situation for branching time logics is not so well understood. Known results are limited to transition systems which are binary trees. For this restricted class of models the yardstick is MSOL theory of the binary tree (*S2S*). It is known that the binary μ-calculus is expressively complete with respect to full *S2S* [26, 13] and CTL* is expressively complete with respect to the fragment of *S2S* where only quantification over paths is allowed [18].

As far as we are aware, the only expressive completeness results dealing with the general case of logics over all transition systems were given by van Benthem [5] and van Benthem and Bergstra [6]. They show that a bisimulation closed class of transition systems is definable in first order logic (resp. in infinitary first order logic) iff it is definable in (system K) modal logic (resp. infinitary modal logic). For these results to hold it is essential that one admits disconnected transition systems. This makes properties like "there is a transition from every node" not closed under bisimulation. These kind of properties also show that these results are not true when restricted only to connected transition systems. Expressive completeness of temporal logic with respect to first order logic over various kinds of orders was investigated among others in [16, 2].

From Gaifman's characterisation of expressive power of first order logic over transition systems [17] it follows that first order logic is not a very interesting logic from a verification point of view. In our opinion the proper yardstick for logics over transition systems should be MSOL, or rather, bisimulation invariant properties expressible in MSOL. This choice is motivated by the fact that it is a very expressive logic, capable of expressing most of the properties considered in the literature. Moreover the set of properties of MSOL is closed under quantification over sets which makes it possible to express for example: path quantification, reachability, least and greatest fixpoints of the properties.

Let us briefly comment why *S2S* is not a good candidate for defining an expressibility standard over transition systems of arbitrary degree. It is of course possible to code every countable transition system into a binary tree but this comes with a price. Any such coding introduces an ordering between siblings which is not available in the original structure. This order allows even a very weak logics over binary trees to express properties of codings not expressible in MSOL over transition systems (see [30] p. 540 for an example).

Finally observe that MSOL over trees of arbitrary degree is very different from monadic second order theory of ω-successors ($S\omega S$). In the later theory even the relation "x is a son of y" is not definable (one would need an infinite formula to do this).

1.1 Synopsis

Our main result is that, every bisimulation closed MSOL definable property of transition systems is definable in the propositional μ-calculus. This shows that among all possible behavioural specification languages whose semantics is expressible in MSOL over transition systems, the μ-calculus is the most expressive one. In particular, this immediately shows that CTL^* and $ECTL^*$ are translatable into the μ-calculus [11] since these logics are easily translatable into MSOL over unwindings of transition systems and formulas resulting from the translation are bisimulation closed, hence invariant under unwinding operation.

Maybe an interesting aspect of this result is that the set of MSOL formulas closed under bisimulation is not recursive (it is even not arithmetical). On the other hand it turns out to be decidable whether a MSOL formula defines a bisimulation closed set of trees. Let us also remark that unlike van Benthem and

Bergstra's results mentioned above our expressibility result also holds when we restrict to connected transition systems or even finite branching trees.

The main tools we will be using are recently developed automata characterisations of the μ-calculus [21] and MSOL [33] over trees. It turns out that there is a more general notion of automata of which both characterisations are special cases. This gives us a common ground to compare the two logics.

The paper is organised as follows. We start with the section introducing transition systems and the bisimulation relation. We also introduce there a notion of ω-expansion which we will need in the main proof. Next we give definitions of MSOL and the μ-calculus. In Section 4 we define a general notion of automaton and give characterisations of MSOL and the μ-calculus in terms of these automata. These characterisations are used in the following section where we prove our main result.

2 Transition systems and bisimulation

Let *Pred* $= \{p, p', \ldots\}$ be a set of unary predicate symbols and let *Rel* $= \{r, r', \ldots\}$ be a set of binary predicate symbols. A *transition system with a source*, simply called *transition system* in the sequel, is a tuple:

$$M = \langle S^M, sr^M, \{r^M\}_{r\in Rel}, \{p^M\}_{p\in Prop}\rangle$$

where: S_M is a nonempty set of *states*; $sr_M \in S$ is a *source*; each r^M is a binary relation on S_M and each p^M is a subset of S^M.

For every $r \in Rel$, let:

$$succ_r^M(s) = \{s' \in S^M \mid (s, s') \in r^M\}$$

Transition system M is called a *transition tree* (or simply a tree) if for every state $s \in M$ there exists a unique path to the root, or more formally there exists a unique sequence $s_0, \ldots, s_n$ such that $s_0 = sr^M$, $s_n = s$ and for every $i = 1, \ldots, n$ we have $(s_i, s_{i+1}) \in r_i^M$ for some $r_i \in Rel$.

Transition systems M and N are called *bisimilar* when there exists a relation $R \subseteq S^M \times S^N$, called a *bisimulation relation*, such that $(sr^M, sr^N) \in R$ and for every $(s,t) \in R$, $p \in Prop$ and $r \in Rel$:

- $s \in p^M$ iff $t \in p^M$,
- whenever $(s, s') \in r^M$ for some s', then there exists t' such that $(t, t') \in r^N$ and $(s', t') \in R$,
- whenever $(t, t') \in r^N$ for some t', then there exists s' such that $(s, s') \in r^M$ and $(s', t') \in R$.

Definition 1 ω-expansion. Given a transition system M, an *ω-indexed path* of M is a sequence u of the form:

$$u = s_0(a_1, r_1, s_1)(a_2, r_2, s_2)\cdots(a_n, r_n, s_n)$$

where $s_0 = sr^M$, $a_i \in \mathbb{N}$ and $(s_{i-1}, s_i) \in r_i^M$ for $i = 1, \ldots, n$.

The *ω-expansion* $\widehat{M}$ of the system M is defined by :

1. $S^{\widehat{M}}$ is the set of ω-indexed paths of M,
2. $sr^{\widehat{M}} = sr^M$,
3. for every $r \in Rel$, every u and $v \in S^{\widehat{M}}$: $(u, v) \in r^{\widehat{M}}$ iff v is an ω-indexed path of the form $u(a, r, s)$, for some a and s,
4. for every $p \in Prop$:

$$p^{\widehat{M}} = \{u(a, r, s) : s \in p^M, \quad u, a, r \text{ arbitrary}\} \cup \{sr^{\widehat{M}} : sr^M \in p^M\}$$

In the rest of this section let us briefly point out how the concept of ω-expansion arises from a general consideration about bisimulation relation.

Definition 2. Given two transition systems M and N, we say that M is an *expansion* of N, denoted $M \succeq N$, when there exists a partial function h : $S_M \rightarrow S_N$ such that :

1. $h(sr^M) = sr^N$,
2. for every $s \in S^M$, $p \in Prop$ and $r \in Rel$:

$$s \in p^M \iff h(s) \in p^N \text{ and } h(succ_r^M(s)) = succ_r^N(h(s))$$

Remark. In [8], with distinct notations and names, Castellani shows that M_1 and M_2 are bisimilar iff there exists N such that $N \preceq M_1$ and $N \preceq M_2$. Intuitively N is a quotient of M_1 and M_2 under bisimulation relation, henceforth a minimal representative. Next fact states that ω-expansions are, in the countable case, maximal representatives of behaviours.

Fact 3. *Considering only transition systems with at most countably many states: for every transition system M we have $M \preceq \widehat{M}$, and, for every transition system N, if M and N are bisimilar then $\widehat{M}$ and $\widehat{N}$ are isomorphic.*

3 Monadic second order logic and the propositional μ-calculus

In this section we will define monadic second order logic (MSOL) and the propositional μ-calculus [23]. Both logics will be interpreted over transition systems of the signature containing only unary symbols from *Prop* and binary symbols from *Rel*. These sets were fixed at the beginning of the previous section. Let $Var = \{X, Y, \ldots\}$ be a countable set of (second order) *variables*.

3.1 MSOL

Monadic second order logic over the signature $\{Rel, Prop\}$ and constant sr can be defined as follows. The set of MSOL formulas is the smallest set containing formulas:

$$p(X), \; r(X, Y), \; X \subseteq Y, \; sr(X)$$

for $p \in Prop$, $r \in Rel$, $X, Y \in Var$; and closed under negation, disjunction and existential quantification. A *sentence* is a formula without free variables.

The definition of the truth of a formula in a given transition system M and a valuation $V : Var \to \mathcal{P}(S^M)$ is defined by induction on the length of the formula:

$$
\begin{array}{ll}
M, V \models p(X) & \text{iff } V(X) \subseteq p^M \\
M, V \models r(X,Y) & \text{iff } V(X) = \{s\}, V(Y) = \{t\} \text{ and } (s,t) \in r^M \\
M, V \models sr(X) & \text{iff } V(X) = \{sr^M\} \\
M, V \models X \subseteq Y & \text{iff } V(X) \subseteq V(Y) \\
M, V \models \alpha \vee \beta & \text{iff } M, V \models \alpha \text{ or } M, V \models \beta \\
M, V \models \neg\alpha & \text{iff not } M, V \models \alpha \\
M, V \models \exists X.\, \alpha(X) & \text{iff there is } T \subseteq S^M \text{ s.t. } M, V[T/X] \models \alpha(X)
\end{array}
$$

We will concentrate here on definability by sentences. Of course it makes no difference for MSOL because the quantification is available, but it will make the difference in the case of the μ-calculus. We write $M \models \varphi$ to mean that the sentence φ is true in M. A sentence φ of MSOL defines a class of transition systems: $\{M : M \models \varphi\}$. A class of transition systems is *MSOL definable* if there exists an MSOL sentence defining this class. A class C of transition systems is *bisimulation closed* if whenever $M \in C$ and M' is bisimilar to M then $M' \in C$. A sentence is *bisimulation invariant* if the class of transition systems it defines is bisimulation closed.

Remark. There exist formulas of MSOL which are not bisimulation invariant. Take for example a formula stating that there is exactly one r–transition from the source. Observe that the problem of checking whether an MSOL formula is bisimulation invariant is not arithmetical because the validity problem is not arithmetical.

3.2 Propositional μ-calculus

The set of the μ-calculus formulas is the smallest set containing $Prop \cup Var$ which is closed under negation, disjunction and the following two formation rules:

- if α is a formula and $r \in Rel$ then $\langle r \rangle \alpha$ is a formula,
- if $\alpha(X)$ is a formula and X occurs only positively (i.e. under even number of negations) in $\alpha(X)$ then $\mu X.\alpha(X)$ is a formula.

Observe that we use relation names in the modalities.

The meaning of a formula α in a transition system M and a valuation $V : Var \to \mathcal{P}(S^M)$ is a set of states, $\|\alpha\|_V^M$, where it is true. It is defined by induction on the length of the formula:

$$
\begin{array}{ll}
\|p\|_V^M & = p^M \\
\|\neg\alpha\|_V^M & = S^M - \|\alpha\|_V^M \\
\|\alpha \vee \beta\|_V^M & = \|\alpha\|_V^M \cup \|\beta\|_V^M \\
\|\langle r \rangle \alpha\|_V^M & = \{s : \exists t.(s,t) \in r^M \wedge t \in \|\alpha\|_V^M\} \\
\|\mu X.\alpha(X)\|_V^M & = \bigcap \{T \subseteq S^M : \|\alpha(X)\|_{V[T/X]} \subseteq T\}
\end{array}
$$

For a sentence φ we write $M, s \models \varphi$ when $s \in \|\varphi\|_V^M$ (the choice of a valuation V is irrelevant as φ is a sentence). A sentence φ of the μ-calculus defines a class of transition systems $\{M : M, sr^M \models \varphi\}$. The class of transition systems is μ-*definable* if there exists a μ-calculus sentence defining this class. It is well known that:

Fact 4. *Every μ-definable class is bisimulation closed.*

Remark. Let us comment on the fact that we consider only definability by sentences. Call a class $\mathcal{C}$, μ-f-definable (μ-formula-definable) if there is a formula φ of the μ-calculus such that:

$$\mathcal{C} = \{M : sr^M \in \|\varphi\|_V^M \text{ for arbitrary } V : \mathit{Var} \to S^M\}$$

There are μ-f-definable classes which are not closed under bisimulation. Consider for example the class defined by the formula $\neg(\langle r \rangle X \wedge \langle r \rangle \neg X)$. This formula defines a class of structures M where there is at most one $s \in S^M$ such that $(sr^M, s) \in r^M$. This class is clearly not bisimulation closed. The μ-f-definability corresponds to definability of frames in modal logic. It is easy to see that the notion of μ-f-definability is not closed under complement. Hence this notion of definability is not interesting from expressive completeness point of view.

4 Automata characterisations

Here we will define automata running on transition systems. Then we will give characterisations of the expressive power of MSOL and the μ-calculus in terms of these automata.

First problem we have to deal with is the description of a transition function. In case of words, a transition function of an automaton with alphabet Σ and states Q is an element of $Q \times \Sigma \to \mathcal{P}(Q)$. In case of binary trees, it is an element from $Q \times \Sigma \to \mathcal{P}(Q \times Q)$. This suggest that for trees of degree less than or equal to κ, a transition function should be an element of $Q \times \Sigma \to \mathcal{P}(Q^\kappa)$. But surely it cannot be an arbitrary such function because MSOL has limited expressive power. The idea is to shift the attention a little. Let us consider the set S of sons of a node. An assignment of states to the elements of S can be seen as a function $m : Q \to \mathcal{P}(S)$, which for each state $q \in Q$ gives a set of elements to which q is assigned. We call such a function a *marking*. The set of markings can be described by a formula with free second order variables $\{Z_q\}_{q \in Q}$ representing the sets of elements assigned q. For example in case of binary trees, S will be always a two element set $\{l, r\}$ and a transition, say, $\delta(q, a) = \{(q_1, q_2), (q_3, q_4)\}$ will be translated into the formula: $(Z_{q_1}(l) \wedge Z_{q_2}(r)) \vee (Z_{q_3}(l) \wedge Z_{q_4}(r))$. This approach extends easily to alternating automata on binary trees [25] but this time formulas obtained in the translation will be arbitrary positive boolean combinations of atomic formulas of the from $Z_{q_i}(l)$ or $Z_{q_i}(r)$. In the case of trees of arbitrary degree the use of formulas to describe markings allows us to abstract from the cardinality of S. By restricting to specific classes of formulas we can control the expressive power of the obtained automata. It turns out that this gives us enough control to characterise the μ-calculus or MSOL over trees. Hence we obtain a common ground to compare the two logics.

Let us proceed with the formal definition of these automata.

Definition 5 Basic formulas. For every finite set $\mathcal{U}$, let $\mathrm{BF}(\mathcal{U})$ be some set of sentences of the first order logic, possibly with the equality predicates, over the signature consisting of unary predicates $\{p\}_{p\in\mathcal{U}}$. A marking of a given set S is a function $m : \mathcal{U} \to \mathcal{P}(S)$. We say that m satisfies a sentence $\varphi \in \mathrm{BF}(\mathcal{U})$ iff φ is satisfied in the structure $\langle S, \{m(p)\}_{p\in\mathcal{U}}\rangle$, i.e., the structure with the carrier S and each predicate $p \in \mathcal{U}$ interpreted as $m(p)$.

An automaton is a tuple:

$$\mathcal{A} = \langle Q, \Sigma_p \subseteq \mathit{Prop}, \Sigma_r \subseteq \mathit{Rel}, q_0 \in Q, \\ \delta : Q \times \mathcal{P}(\Sigma_p) \to \mathrm{BF}(\Sigma_r \times Q), \Omega : Q \to I\!N\rangle \quad (1)$$

where Q is a finite set of states, Σ_p is a *finite* subset of *Prop* and Σ_r is a *finite* subset of *Rel*. Observe that the automaton has two alphabets. One is for examining properties of states and the other is for checking labels of taken transitions.

We find it convenient to give the definition of acceptance in terms of games.

Definition 6 Acceptance. Let M be a transition system and let $\mathcal{A}$ be an automaton as above. We define a game $G(M, \mathcal{A})$ as follows:

- The initial position is a pair (sr^M, q_0).
- If the current position is a pair (s, q) then player I is to move. Let

  $$L(s) = \{p \in \mathit{Prop} : s \in p^M\} \cap \Sigma_p$$

  be a set of relevant propositions holding in s. Player I chooses a marking $m : \Sigma_r \times Q \to \mathcal{P}(\bigcup_{r\in\Sigma_r} \mathit{succ}_r(s))$ such that for every r, q we have $m(r, q) \subseteq \mathit{succ}_r(s)$ and

  $$\langle \bigcup_{r\in\Sigma_r} \mathit{succ}_r(s), \{m(r, q)\}_{(r,q)\in\Sigma_r\times Q}\rangle \models \delta(q_i, L(s))$$

  The marking m becomes the current position.
- If the current position is a marking m then player II chooses some $r \in \Sigma_r$, some automaton state $q \in Q$ and some state $s \in m(r, q)$. The pair (s, q) becomes the current position.

If one of the players cannot make a move then the other player wins. If the play is infinite then as the result we obtain an infinite sequence:

$$(s_0, q_0), m_1, (s_1, q_1), m_2, \ldots$$

Let j be the smallest number appearing infinitely often in the sequence:

$$\Omega(q_0), \Omega(q_1), \ldots$$

Player I wins if j is even, otherwise player II is the winner.

We say that M is *accepted* by $\mathcal{A}$ iff there is a winning strategy for player I in the game $G(M, \mathcal{A})$. A *language* recognised by $\mathcal{A}$ is the class of transition systems accepted by $\mathcal{A}$.

From now on, let $\mathcal{U} = \Sigma_r \times Q$. The following is a reformulation of a result from [21].

Theorem 7. *A class of transition systems is definable by a μ-calculus sentence iff it is a language recognised by an automaton as in (1) with BF($\mathcal{U}$) containing only disjunctions of sentences of the form:*

$$\exists x_1, \ldots, x_k.\ (p_1(x_1) \wedge \ldots \wedge p_k(x_k) \wedge \forall z. p_1(z) \vee \ldots \vee p_k(z)) \tag{2}$$

where $p_i \in \mathcal{U}$ for $i = 1, \ldots, k$.

The goal in [21] was to find the simplest possible form of automaton. Here we will be content with more liberal formalisation. The proof of the fact below can be found in [20], it also follows from [33].

Fact 8. *A class of transition systems is definable by some μ-calculus formula iff it is a language recognised by an automaton as in (1) with BF($\mathcal{U}$) containing only disjunctions of formulas of the form:*

$$\exists x_1, \ldots, x_k.\ (p_1(x_1) \wedge \ldots \wedge p_k(x_k) \wedge \forall z. \beta(z))$$

where $\beta(z)$ is a disjunction of conjunctions of formulas of the form $p(z)$ for $p \in \mathcal{U}$.

Example 1. As an example we construct an automaton equivalent to the μ-calculus formula $\mu X.p \vee \langle r \rangle X$. This automaton is:

$$\langle \{q\}, \{p\}, \{r\}, q, \delta, \Omega \rangle$$

where $\Omega(q) = 1$ and δ is defined by:

$$\begin{aligned} \delta(q, \emptyset) = &\quad \exists x.\ (r, q)(x) \wedge \forall z. true \\ \delta(q, \{p\}) = &\ \forall z.\ true \end{aligned}$$

The following was shown in [33]:

Theorem 9. *A class of trees is definable by a MSOL sentence iff it is a language recognised by an automaton as in (1) with BF($\mathcal{U}$) containing only disjunctions of formulas of the form:*

$$\exists x_1, \ldots, x_k.\ \mathit{diff}(x_1, \ldots, x_k) \wedge p_{i_1}(x_1) \wedge \cdots \wedge p_{i_k}(x_k) \wedge \\ \forall z.\ \mathit{diff}(z, x_1, \ldots, x_k) \Rightarrow \beta(z)$$

where $\beta(z)$ is a disjunction of conjunctions of formulas of the form $p(z)$, for $p \in \mathcal{U}$, and $\mathit{diff}(x_1, \ldots, x_k)$ is a formula stating that the meanings of all the variables are different.

Remark. In the above theorem we can allow arbitrary first or even monadic second order formulas as basic formulas. The set of basic formulas specified above is the smallest set which was shown to be sufficient in [33]. Of course, the simpler the set of basic formulas, the easier would be our task of translating MSOL formulas into μ-calculus formulas.

Because the construction of an automaton equivalent to a given formula is effective and because the emptiness problem for these automata can be shown to be decidable we obtain:

Corollary 10. *MSOL theory of trees is decidable.*

For countably branching trees this corollary is a consequence of Rabin's theorem about decidability of *S2S* [29].

5 Expressive completeness

Theorem 9 together with Fact 8 suggest that there is a very strong connection between the two logics. Basic formulas in case of MSOL automata are more expressive because, for example, they can compare the number of sons with a constant (by the use of existential quantification together with *diff*($\vec{x}$) formula). Intuitively if an MSOL formula is bisimulation closed, an equivalent automaton should not use *diff*($\vec{x}$) formulas, hence it should be equivalent to a μ-calculus formula. A precise argument confirming this intuition must take into account the fact that automata are nondeterministic which means that the automaton may have only runs which use *diff*($\vec{x}$) formulas but nevertheless accept a bisimulation closed set.

Theorem 11 Expressive completeness. *A bisimulation closed class of transition systems is MSOL definable iff it is μ-definable.*

Proof. It is easy to see that every μ-definable class is also MSOL definable. For converse we use the following lemma:

Lemma 12. *For every MSOL sentence φ one can build a μ-calculus sentence $\varphi^\vee$ such that for every transition system M:*

$$M \models \varphi^\vee \quad \textit{iff} \quad \widehat{M} \models \varphi$$

Assume that the lemma was proved. Let φ be a MSOL sentence defining a bisimulation closed class of transition systems. This in particular means that for every transition system M we have: $M \models \varphi$ if and only if $\widehat{M} \models \varphi$. Let $\varphi^\vee$ be the formula given by the lemma above. We have:

$$M \models \varphi \ \text{ iff } \ \widehat{M} \models \varphi \ \text{ iff } \ M \models \varphi^\vee$$

□

Proof of Lemma 12. For every formula ψ of the form:

$$\exists x_1,\ldots,x_l.\ diff(x_1,\ldots,x_l) \land p_1(x_1) \land \cdots \land p_l(x_l) \land \\ \forall z.diff(z,x_1,\ldots,x_l) \Rightarrow \beta(z) \tag{3}$$

we let $\psi^{\vee}$ to be a formula obtained by substituting *true* for *diff* in the above:

$$\exists x_1,\ldots,x_l.\ p_1(x_1) \land \ldots \land p_l(x_l) \land \forall z.\beta(z) \tag{4}$$

For a disjunction $\theta = \psi_1 \vee \ldots \vee \psi_j$ of formulas as in 3 we define: $\theta^{\vee} = \psi_1^{\vee} \vee \ldots \vee \psi_j^{\vee}$.

By Theorem 9 there is an automaton $\mathcal{A} = \langle Q, \Sigma, q, \delta, \Omega \rangle$ accepting the class of tree models of φ. We know that for every $q \in Q$ and $a \in \mathcal{P}(\Sigma_p)$, formula $\delta(q,a)$ is a disjunction of formulas of the form (3). We define the automaton $\mathcal{A}^{\vee}$ which has all the same components as $\mathcal{A}$ but the transition function $\delta^{\vee}$. For every $q \in Q$ and $P \in \Sigma_p$ we let $\delta^{\vee}(q,P) = (\delta(q,P))^{\vee}$.

Observation 1. *The automaton $\mathcal{A}^{\vee}$ accepts M iff $\mathcal{A}$ accepts $\widehat{M}$.*

It is quite easy to see that if M is accepted by $\mathcal{A}^{\vee}$ then $\widehat{M}$ is accepted by $\mathcal{A}$. Conversely, suppose $\widehat{M}$ is accepted by $\mathcal{A}$. We will show that M is accepted by $\mathcal{A}^{\vee}$.

By the definition, $\mathcal{A}$ accepts $\widehat{M}$ iff player I has a winning strategy $\widehat{\sigma}$ in the game $\widehat{G} = G(\widehat{M}, \mathcal{A})$. We define a winning strategy $\sigma^{\vee}$ for player I in the game $G^{\vee} = G(M, \mathcal{A}^{\vee})$. The idea of the strategy is to play simultaneously the games $G^{\vee}$ and $\widehat{G}$ and transfer each move of player II from $G^{\vee}$ to $\widehat{G}$. Then one can consult the strategy $\widehat{\sigma}$ for $\widehat{G}$ and transfer the suggested move of player I back to $G^{\vee}$.

The initial position of $G^{\vee}$ is (sr^M, q_0) and it is also the initial position of $\widehat{G}$.

Assume that each of the players has made k moves. Assume also that the histories of the two plays are respectively:

$$(sr^M, q_0), m^1, (s_1, q_1), \ldots, m^k, (s_k, q_k)$$

for $G^{\vee}$ and

$$(sr^M, q_0), \widehat{m}^1, (u_1, q_1), \ldots, \widehat{m}^k, (u_k, q_k)$$

for $\widehat{G}$, where for every $i = 1\ldots,k$ we have $u_i = u_i'(a_i, r_i, s_i)$ for some ω-indexed path u_i', $a_i \in \mathbb{N}$ and $r_i \in Rel$.

In this position player I is to move. Let $\widehat{m}^{k+1} = \widehat{\sigma}(u_k, q_k)$ be a marking suggested by the strategy $\widehat{\sigma}$. Let us introduce a notation for the two structures

$$\mathcal{M}_{u_k} = \langle \bigcup_{r\in\Sigma_r} succ_r^{\widehat{M}}(u_k), \{\widehat{m}^{k+1}(r,q)\}_{(r,q)\in\Sigma_r\times Q} \rangle$$
$$\mathcal{M}_{s_k} = \langle \bigcup_{r\in\Sigma_r} succ_r^{M}(s_k), \{m^{k+1}(r,q)\}_{(r,q)\in\Sigma_r\times Q} \rangle$$

By definition the marking $\widehat{m}^{k+1} : \Sigma_r \times Q \to \mathcal{P}(succ^{\widehat{M}}(u_k))$ satisfies:

$$\mathcal{M}_{u_k} \models \delta(q_k, L(u_k)) \tag{5}$$

We define $m^{k+1} : \Sigma_r \times Q \to \mathcal{P}(succ^M(s_k))$ by letting:

$$m^{k+1}(r,q) = \{s : u_k(a,r,s) \in \widehat{m}^{k+1}(r,q) \text{ for some } a \in \mathbb{N}\} \tag{6}$$

Let us check that:

$$\mathcal{M}_{s_k} \models \delta^{\vee}(q_k, L(s_k))$$

We know that $\delta(q_k, L(u_k))$ is a disjunction of formulas of the form (3). By definition of $\widehat{M}$ and the fact that $u_k = u'_k(a_k, r_k, s_k)$ we have: $L(u_k) = L(s_k)$. Hence $\delta^{\vee}(q_k, L(s_k)) = (\delta(q_k, L(u_k)))^{\vee}$ by the definition of $\mathcal{A}^{\vee}$.

Assume that $\mathcal{M}_{u_k} \models \psi$ for some disjunct ψ of $\delta(q_k, L(u_k))$. We will show that $\mathcal{M}_{s_k} \models \psi^{\vee}$.

We know that $\psi^{\vee}$ is of the form (4) where each p_j is of the form (r_j, q_j). Let us first check that for every $j = 1, \ldots, l$ there is $s \in m^{k+1}(r_j, q_j)$. For this it is enough to take $u_k(a, r_j, s) \in \widehat{m}^{k+1}(r_j, q_j)$ known to exist by property (5). To see that $\mathcal{M}_{s_k} \models \forall z.\, \beta(z)$ observe that for every $s \in succ_r^M(s_k)$ there is $a \in \mathbb{N}$ such that $\mathcal{M}_{u_k} \models \beta((a, r, s))$. By the fact that β is monotone in predicates $\{p\}_{p \in \Sigma_r \times Q}$ and the definition of m, we obtain: $\mathcal{M}_{s_k} \models \beta(s)$.

Hence taking m is a legal move of player I in the game $G^{\vee}$. After this move we obtain the position:

$$(sr^M, q_0), m^1, (s_1, q_1), \ldots, m^k, (s_k, q_k), m^{k+1}$$

and at the same time in $\widehat{G}$ we obtain the position:

$$(sr^M, q_0), \widehat{m}^1, (u_1, q_1), \ldots, \widehat{m}^k, (u_k, q_k), \widehat{m}^{k+1}$$

with m^{k+1} defined from $\widehat{m}^{k+1}$ by (6). From this position player II chooses some $r_{k+1} \in \Sigma_r$, $q_{k+1} \in Q$ and a state $s_{k+1} \in m^{k+1}(r_{k+1}, q_{k+1})$. The history of the play G becomes:

$$(sr^M, q_0), m^1, (s_1, q_1), \ldots m^k, (s_k, q_k), m^{k+1}, (s_{k+1}, q_{k+1})$$

We make player II in $\widehat{G}$ to choose q_{k+1} and a state $u_k(a_{k+1}, r_{k+1}, s_{k+1}) \in \widehat{m}^{k+1}(r_{k+1}, q_{k+1})$ which exists by (6). We arrive at the position satisfying our initial assumptions so we can repeat the whole argument.

By definition of the strategy player I can always make a move hence he cannot lose in a finite number of steps. If the play is infinite then the result of the play is an infinite sequence:

$$(sr^M, q_0), m_1, (s_1, q_1), \ldots, m_k, (s_k, q_k) \ldots$$

At the same time we know that the corresponding play in the game $\widehat{G}$ has been infinite and its result is:

$$(sr^M, q_0), \widehat{m}_1, (u_1, q_1), \ldots, \widehat{m}_k, (u_k, q_k) \ldots$$

Because in the game $\widehat{G}$ player I used the winning strategy $\widehat{\sigma}$ we know that the smallest integer appearing infinitely often in the sequence $\Omega(q_1), \Omega(q_2), \ldots$ is even. But this implies that player I won in the game $G^\vee$. Hence the strategy we have defined is winning and $\mathcal{A}^\vee$ accepts M.

Function $\delta^\vee$ was defined in such a way that the automaton $\mathcal{A}^\vee$ is of the form required in Fact 8. Hence there is a μ-calculus sentence $\varphi^\vee$ equivalent to $\mathcal{A}^\vee$. □

From Corollary 10 and the fact that the sentence $\varphi^\vee$ from Lemma 12 can be constructed effectively it follows:

Corollary 13. *It is decidable whether a MSOL sentence defines a bisimulation closed set of trees.*

Remark. Analysing the proof of Theorem 11 one can observe that the theorem remains true also when we restrict to finite branching transition systems.

Remark. One may ask what is the meaning of $\widehat{\varphi}$ given in Lemma 12 if φ is not bisimulation invariant. Unfortunately the class defined by $\widehat{\varphi}$ is not so easy to describe and it does not seem to be very interesting. On the other hand we have the following fact.

Fact 14. *Bisimulation closure of a MSOL sentence is not always MSOL definable.*

Let us give an example of such a sentence. Let φ be a sentence saying that every node has exactly one successor and that on the unique path from the source there is exactly one state where a predicate p holds. The bisimulation closure of φ contains all the trees with the property that on every two paths p holds at exactly the same distance from the root. If all such trees are models of some MSOL formula then from the automata characterisation it follows that some tree which does not have this property is also a model of this formula. But this last tree is not bisimilar to a model of φ.

6 Concluding remarks

We have investigated the expressive completeness problem for branching time logics. For this we have introduced a new kind of automata capable of recognising classes of transition systems. The definition of automata has been parametrised by the set of basic formulas. This has given us a common ground to compare expressive power of MSOL and the μ-calculus. The fact that the proof of Theorem 11 is relatively easy suggest that this notion of automata may be an interesting one.

Of course not all properties of potential interest can be expressed in MSOL. Some logics capable of expressing nonregular properties were proposed in the literature (see for example [19, 7]). We think that in this case it is also important to look for some new standards to compare expressive power with.

There is one new area of verification were the need for "yardsticks" seems to be particularly pressing. We have in mind verification with respect to so called non-interleaving semantics [34, 1, 31]. There are good reasons for considering these semantics, as for example, some problems undecidable for transition systems semantics become decidable in this setting [12]. Nevertheless if we consider the number of different non-interleaving semantics and multiply it by the number of logics proposed to date for transition systems semantics we can see that there is a possibility of "problem explosion". That is at some point we may have a big number of incomparable approaches. We think that it would be very useful to find some expressibility standards in this area and we hope that a generalisation of automata presented here may be also a small step in this direction.

References

1. R. Alur, D. Peled, and W. Penczek. Model-checking of causality properties. In *LICS '95*, pages 90–100, 1995.
2. A. Amir. Separation in nonlinear time models. *Information and Computation*, 66:177-203, 1985.
3. A. Arnold. *Finite Transition Systems*. Masson, Prentice-Hall, 1994.
4. B. Banieqbal and H. Barringer. Temporal logic with fixed points. volume 398 of *LNCS*, pages 62–74. Springer-Verlag, 1989.
5. J. Benthem. *Languages in Action: Categories, Lambdas and Dynamic Logic*, volume 130 of *Studies in Logic*. North-Holland, 1991.
6. J. Benthem and J. Bergstra. Logic of transition systems. Report P9308, Programming Research Group, University of Amsterdam, 1993.
7. A. Bouajjani, R. Echahed, and P. Habermehl. On verification problem of nonregular properties of nonregular processes. In *LICS '95*, pages 123–133, 1995.
8. I. Castellani. Bisimulations and abstraction homomorphisms. *Journal of Computer and System Sciences*, 34:210–235, 1987.
9. M. Dam. CTL* and ECTL* as a fragments of the modal μ-calculus. In *CAAP'92*, volume 581 of *LNCS*, pages 145–165, 1992.
10. E. A. Emerson. Temporal and modal logic. In J. Leeuven, editor, *Handbook of Theoretical Computer Science Vol.B*, pages 995–1072. Elsevier, 1990.
11. E. A. Emerson and C. Jutla. Tree automata, mu-calculus and determinacy. In *Proc. FOCS 91*, 1991.
12. J. Esparza and A. Kiehn. On the model checking problem for branching time logics and basic parallel processes. In *CAV '95*, volume 939 of *LNCS*, pages 353–366, 1995.
13. A. Gabbay, A. Pnueli, S. Shelah, and J. Stavi. On the temporal analysis of fairness. In *7th Ann. ACM Symp. on Principles of Programming Languages*, pages 163–173, 1980.
14. D. Gabbay. Expressive functional completeness in tense logic. In *Aspects of Philosophical Logic*, pages 91–117. Reidel, 1981.
15. H. Gaifman. On local and non-local properties. In *Herbrand Symposium, Logic Colloquium'81*, pages 105–135. North-Holland, 1982.
16. T. Hafer and W. Thomas. Computation tree logic CTL* and path quantifiers in the monadic theory of the binary tree. In *14th Internat. Coll. on Automata, Languages and Programming*, volume 267 of *LNCS*, pages 269–279, 1987.
17. D. Harel and D. Raz. Deciding properties of nonregular programs. *SIAM J. Comput*, 22:857–874, 1993.

18. D. Janin. *Propriérés logiques du non-déterminisme et μ-calcul modal.* PhD thesis, LaBRI – Université de Bordeaux I, 1995. Available from `http://www.labri.u-bordeaux.fr/~janin`.
19. D. Janin and I. Walukiewicz. Automata for the μ-calculus and related results. In *MFCS '95*, volume 969 of *LNCS*, pages 552–562, 1995.
20. H. Kamp. *Tense Logic and the Theory of Linear Order.* PhD thesis, University of California, 1968.
21. D. Kozen. Results on the propositional mu-calculus. *Theoretical Computer Science*, 27:333–354, 1983.
22. R. Milner. *Communication and Concurrency.* Prentice-Hall, Englewood Clifs, 1989.
23. D. Muller and P. Schupp. Alternating automata on infinite trees. *Theoretical Computer Science*, 54:267–276, 1987.
24. D. Niwiński. Fixed points vs. infinite generation. In *LICS '88*, pages 402–409, 1988.
25. G. Plotkin. A structural approach to operational semantics. Technical Report DAIMI FN–19, Aarhus University, 1981.
26. A. Pnueli. The temporal logic of programs. In *18th Symposium on Foundations of Computer Science*, pages 46–57, 1977.
27. M. Rabin. Decidability of second-order theories and automata on infinite trees. *Trans. Amer. Math. Soc.*, 141:1–35, 1969.
28. C. S. Stirling. Modal and temporal logics. In S.Abramsky, D.Gabbay, and T.Maibaum, editors, *Handbook of Logic in Comuter Science*, pages 477–563. Oxford University Press, 1991.
29. P. Thiagarajan. A trace based extension of linear time temporal logic. In *LICS*, pages 438–447, 1994.
30. R. van Glabbeek. The linear time – branching time spectrum. In *CONCUR'90*, volume 458 of *LNCS*, pages 278–297, 1990.
31. I. Walukiewicz. Monadic second order logic on tree-like structures. In *STACS '96*, volume 1046 of *LNCS*, pages 401–414, 1996.
32. G. Winskel and M. Nielsen. *Handbook of Logic in Computer Science*, volume 4, chapter Models for Concurrency, pages 1–148. Clarendon Press – Oxford, 1995.

A Facile Tutorial *

Bent Thomsen, Lone Leth and Tsung-Min Kuo

ECRC, Arabellastrasse 17, D-81925, Munich, GERMANY **

Abstract.
The Facile system combines language, compiler and distributed system technology into a programming environment supporting the rapid construction of reliable and sophisticated end-user applications operating in distributed computing environments. In particular, Facile is well suited for construction of systems based on the emerging "mobile agents" principle.
The Facile language combines a predominantly functional programming language, Standard ML (SML), with a model of concurrency based on CCS and its higher order and mobile extensions (CHOCS and the π-calculus). Furthermore, constructs for distributed computing are based on recent results from timed process algebra and true concurrency theory. These models are integrated with the fundamental philosophy of SML that all values in the language are first class values. This means that any value, simple, complex, user defined – even functions, process scripts and communication channels, may be placed in data structures, given as arguments to functions and returned as results of function invocations, or communicated between processes possibly residing on different machines. In addition, Facile brings the notion of strong fully polymorphic typing known from SML into the world of distributed computing. In fact this integration yields the fundamental building blocks for supporting programming of mobile agents in a secure and reliable manner.
Significant components of a number of systems have been implemented in Facile, including Calumet – a cooperative work application that provides a distributed slide presentation; Einrichten – a tele-working application that presents virtual interior design at a distance; and Mobile Service Agents – a mobility application that enables access to agents that operate in an open, distributed environment.
This tutorial presents an overview of the Facile system, introduces the language constructs and goes through several program examples that should enable readers familiar with SML and process algebras, such as CCS and the π-calculus, to construct distributed systems with Facile. Examples are based on the Facile Antigua Release.

---

* This work is partially supported by ESPRIT BRA 8130 LOMAPS.

** New address from July 1st, 1996: Lone Leth and Bent Thomsen, International Computers Limited (ICL), IC-PARC, William Penney Laboratory, Imperial College of Science, Technology and Medicine, London SW7 2AZ, United Kingdom, email: {llt1,bt}@doc.ic.ac.uk

1 Introduction

With the diffusion of communication networks, in particular the development of the Global Information Infrastructure, distributed computing is one of the great challenges and at the same time one of the great opportunities faced by the developers of IT products and services.

The Facile system has been developed to face this challenge and enable industry to speed up the time to market of sophisticated distributed end-user applications.

The defining characteristic of the Facile programming environment is a tight integration between a language with formal foundations and a set of sophisticated "middleware" services. This integration makes it possible for the application programmer to build complex distributed systems while at the same time remaining inside a coherent, integrated framework. Using a special language for distributed programming will make the distance from the programmers mental model to the actual program shorter. It also gives other advantages such as readability, portability, static typing, data flow analysis, program transformations and optimisations.

At the very heart of Facile is a formal model of higher-order concurrent processes. From the beginning, this model has guided the development of the Facile environment, leading to a set of simple but powerful orthogonal features. Additionally, the formal foundation prepares the way for the development of optimisers and analytic tools for Facile programs. Since such tools are noticeably lacking from distributed systems development, this is an extremely important benefit of the Facile environment.

From the perspective of the application programmer Facile is divided into two rough categories of features. The first consists of the parts oriented towards general-purpose programming and the second category builds on the first to support concurrent and distributed programming.

In the first category, Facile brings concepts and techniques from state-of-the-art advanced language research into the toolkit of the programmer. For example, it is very easy to define new complex data types. This is in itself not so impressive. However, in the process of defining a data type the programmer simultaneously defines the constructors that can be used to trivially build instances of that data type. In the reverse direction, traversing and breaking down instances of the type can be programmed using a general, but powerful pattern-matching facility. The net result is that programmers write fewer lines of code and spend less time on the details of manipulating data, instead allowing the programmers to focus on what they are actually trying to do. The pattern matching facility offers a programming style with strong similarities to those found in popular logic programming languages, such as Prolog, without introducing the semantic complexity of backtracking.

Another feature which distinguishes Facile is a strong and flexible type system. This type system permits the construction of complex types and supports fully polymorphic, or generic, functions, but can still automatically infer the types of all values in a program. This has two consequences. First, Facile's strong typing means that any program that passes the type checker is guaranteed not to crash or memory fault at run-time, dramatically increasing the confidence one can have in a Facile program. It is also provided without sacrificing the considerable flexibility that enriches Facile's type system. Second, Facile's type inference means that programmers need not pay for strong type checking with cumbersome type declarations. The system deduces them automatically (and if desired compares them to a specification).

Another key aspect of Facile is that it is a higher-order language. Functions can be defined on the fly, in any scope, and passed to other functions or returned as results. Combined with the polymorphic type system, this allows a concise and expressive programming style that maximises reuse of code and further simplifies manipulation of data structures.

Finally, Facile directly integrates exception handling, and also provides a sophisticated name-management and module system.

Although all of this provides strong motivation for using Facile, the real point where Facile moves decisively ahead of fourth-generation languages is in supporting distribution and concurrency. The challenge that Facile answers is to provide a simple interface to distributed programming that is seamlessly integrated with the features described above.

The Facile programming environment incorporates a number of middleware services. The most important of these is a synchronous message-passing facility that can mediate between very general sets of competing potential connections. Another important service is a preemptive multi-threading system that efficiently supports concurrency. Additional services provide system-wide name management and module exchange.

Each service enters the Facile language via a semantically well-defined set of functions and primitives. For example, the communication metaphor is represented by channels. The programmer can create a channel for any type of value. Two processes that share a channel can then use it for exchanging values or for synchronising. As another example, concurrency is exposed to the programmer using primitives for encapsulating and creating processes. It is simple to create processes running in parallel, even on different machines. The integration of higher-order constructs with the support for distributed computing and communication renders processes mobile. Since processes are treated as first-class entities, it is always possible to transmit a process over a channel to a remote site (while preserving the type safety).

Throughout the integration of the middleware services, key features such as type safety and exception handling are preserved. Low-level details of communication are handled automatically, just as the low-level details of data structures are. For example, data structures passed between heterogeneous machines on a network are transformed as necessary without the need for explicit programmer intervention. This reduces the cognitive load on the programmer and eliminates a category of possible bugs.

In addition to Facile being suitable for constructing reliable transactional or client/server systems, Facile is particularly well suited for programming systems based on the emerging mobile agents principle. This is no coincidence. Since the Facile model of concurrency is based on higher order mobile processes (i.e. processes and communication links as first class objects) this provides the necessary linguistic means for programming mobile agents. In fact the multi-paradigm nature of Facile allows a mixture of styles such as combinations of agent based and client server based applications.

In the following sections we present an overview of the Facile language and give some example programs. Section 2 gives an overview of the Facile programming model. Sections 3, 4 and 5 presents the language constructs for dealing with concurrency, distribution and dynamic connectivity, respectively. Section 6 gives a listing of further readings, and section 7 contain some final remarks and acknowledgements.

2 Programming Model Overview

In this section we give an overview of the Facile programming model and subsequent sections present the language constructs in Facile. The exposition is based on the Facile Antigua Release, the first released implementation of Facile, which modifies the Standard ML of New Jersey implementation.

Facile inherits several good features from Standard ML, such as:

- functions as first-class values, including recursive functions and higher-order functions;
- a strong but flexible type system, supporting polymorphism and polymorphic type inference, that frees the programmer from having to explicitly declare types of expressions;
- a rich set of types, including function types, records, etc., and user-defined datatypes and abstract data types, which may be inductively defined;
- using pattern-matching to define functions on data types;
- a lexical scoping discipline on identifiers;
- elegant exception handling features;
- a sophisticated module system, supporting the modular construction of programs and separate compilation.

Facile enriches Standard ML with primitives for distribution, concurrency and communication over typed channels. The additional data types provided in the language include node identifiers, process scripts and communication channels. All of these are first-class values that can be manipulated in an applicative style and, in particular, be communicated. New nodes and channels can be created dynamically and processes executing a given script can be spawned dynamically on a given node.

The concurrency model of Facile is based on CCS and its higher order and mobile extensions (CHOCS and the π-calculus). Furthermore, constructs for distributed computing are based on recent results from timed process algebra and true concurrency theory.

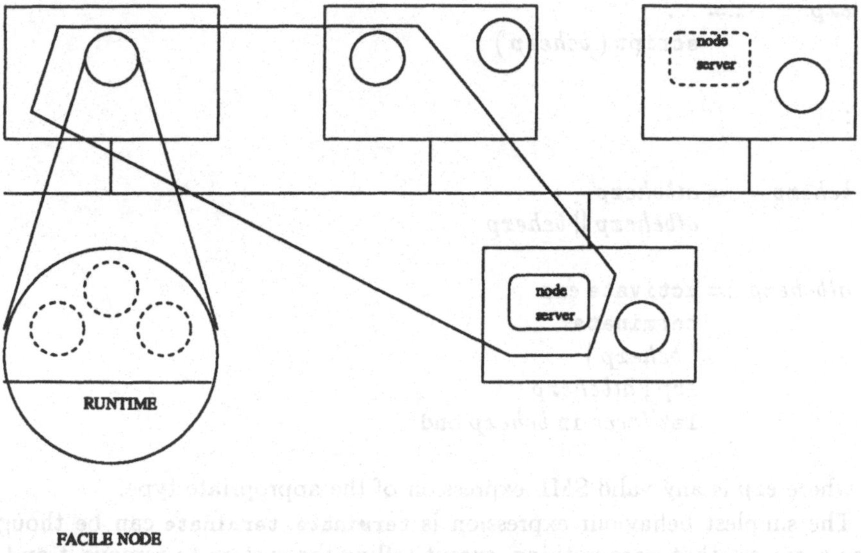

Fig. 1. A Facile system

The basic computational model of Facile consists of one or more nodes or virtual processors, on each of which there are zero or more processes. Processes execute by evaluating expressions in a functional style, and they can communicate values between each other by synchronising over typed channels. Figure 1 shows an example of a Facile system running on a network of workstations. The system is built from two nodes and a node server, illustrated by encapsulating the nodes and the node server. The contents of a Facile node are also shown, namely a number of Facile processes, a heap and a run-time system.

Sequential programming in Facile resembles programming in SML (in particular it resembles programming in SML/NJ version 0.93). We shall not review SML here but refer the reader to the growing list of references such as the book by J.D. Ullman: "Elements of ML Programming", Prentice-Hall International, 1994.

3 Concurrency constructs

Facile extends the SML syntax with behaviour expressions containing constructs that allow the programmer to express parallel composition of processes and to treat process scripts as first class objects:

exp ::= ...
script (*behexp*)

⋮

behexp ::= *atbehexp*
atbehexp || *behexp*

atbehexp ::= **activate** *exp*
terminate
(*behexp*)
exp ; *atbehexp*
let *ldecs* **in** *behexp* **end**

where *exp* is any valid SML expression of the appropriate type.

The simplest behaviour expression is `terminate`. `terminate` can be thought of as a process that does nothing, except telling the system to remove it and to schedule another process to run.

The semicolon operator lets us build behaviour expressions from expressions and other behaviour expressions. The expression is evaluated for its side effects (communications). When evaluation of the expression terminates with a value, the value is discarded and the process continues as described by the behaviour expression.

More complex behaviour expressions can be built using a `let` operation which allows local declarations.

Behaviour expressions need not always end in `terminate`. After evaluating some expressions for their effects, a process can execute a specified script via `activate`. Processes that can execute repeatedly can be defined by making them reactivate a given script.

The concurrent composition construct allows the body of a behaviour expression to consist of several concurrently executing processes. The `||` construct takes two behaviour expressions and indicates that they are to be executed concurrently. The concurrent composition construct extends to more than two behaviour expressions in an obvious way. In general we can write a concurrent composition of a sequence of two or more behaviour expressions separated by `||`, of the form

```
b_1 || b_2 || ... || b_n
```

where `b_1`, `b_2`, ... , `b_n` are behaviour expressions.

The syntactic extension contains constructs similar to those found in many process algebras. However, there are also constructs missing most notably prefixing and restriction. This is deliberate and, as we shall see, this is the point where the integration with SML plays an important role since e.g. prefixing and restriction operators can be constructed using constructs from SML in combination with the concurrency primitives added by Facile.

Before we see how behaviour expressions and expressions complement each other we briefly review the main interfaces to the Facile concurrency primitives which is given as a structure (an SML module) with the following signature:

```
signature FACILE =
  sig
   val channel : unit -> 'la channel
   val equal   : 'a channel *  'a channel -> bool
   val send    : 'a channel *  'a -> unit
   val receive : 'a channel -> 'a
   val sendguard : 'a channel * 'a * (unit -> 'b) -> 'b guard
   val recvguard : 'a channel * ('a -> 'b) -> 'b guard
   val wrapguard : 'a guard * ('a -> 'b) -> 'b guard
   val alternative : 'b guard list -> 'b
   val delay : int -> unit
   val spawn   :  scr -> unit
  end
```

Facile processes interact with the user and with one another by communicating values over channels. Channels are first-class values in Facile, so they can be arguments to functions, results of functions and, in general, they may be manipulated using generic operations like other data values.

Channel values are generated by invoking the function `channel`. It must be applied to a value of unit type. The function `channel` creates a new unique channel and returns a value identifying this new channel.

As a first example of how behaviour expressions and expressions complement each other we show a syntactic fragment that will achieve the effect of restriction:

```
let ch = channel ()
in ...
end
```

where ... is any behaviour expression.

Facile provides two functions, `send` and `receive`, for communicating values to other concurrently executing processes over channels. `send` takes a channel and a value of a type that can be sent on the channel, and returns the unit value. Before it returns the unit value, a call to `send` has the external effect of sending the given value on the specified channel. The `send` function call does not return until there is another process willing to receive the value on the channel. If there is no receiver process, the call to `send` blocks until there is one.

The effect of send prefix, known from many process algebras, is achieved by the following code fragment:

```
send(ch,v);...
```

where ... is any behaviour expression.

receive takes a channel and returns some value — one that is sent by another process on that channel. The function call returns only when another process sends a value on the channel. The value returned can be any value of the type that is transmissible on the channel.

The effect of receive prefix used in many process algebras is achieved by the code fragment below:

```
let x = receive ch
in ...
end
```

where ... is any behaviour expression.

Apart from constructing networks of processes through the parallel construct, Facile allows the programmer to dynamically fork or spawn off a process from within the evaluation of an expression. Here it is important to note that Facile makes a careful distinction between a process (syntactically represented via a behaviour expression) and the code that it executes, i.e., a script. Scripts are first-class values that have type `scr`.

Applying `spawn` to a value of type `scr` (containing a process script) returns the unit value in the invoking process and creates a new process. The new process, which executes as specified by the argument script, is created as an external effect. It is running concurrently with the invoking process and any other processes that already exist.

In Facile there are different ways that one can, for example, create two new processes executing concurrently (say with behaviour *p* and *q*, respectively). One is by spawning first one and then the other, as for example in

```
spawn script( p);
spawn script( q);
```

Another way is by spawning a concurrent composition, e.g.,

```
spawn script( p || q);
```

Which approach to prefer is largely a matter of style and taste. Indeed, one could also have written:

```
spawn script( spawn script( p) ; q );
```

Programmers who prefer to use a functional style, thinking in terms of a system as a main computation that creates various other processes, often prefer the first way. Those that prefer to conceive a system as a composite system of processes may prefer the second way.

One of the main motivations for introducing behaviour expressions and treating process scripts as a primitive data type is to support a style of programming with processes. The idea is to use the functional style to define a wide variety of operations for combining process scripts. One can then use these operations to build a complex script out of simple scripts, and then create a process that runs the complex script. We call such operations *process abstractions*.

Let us try to define a function par: `scr * scr -> scr` describing an operator on process scripts that takes two process scripts and creates a process script describing two concurrent processes, each running one of the argument scripts. That is, if the two argument scripts to the function par were script(*p*) and script(*q*), where *p* and *q* represent two behaviour expressions, the result would behave like the script script(*p* || *q*).

Note, however, that the concurrent composition operator || works only on behaviour expressions. So we need a way to extract the behaviour expressions *p* and *q* from the argument scripts. Pattern matching will not work, since *p* and *q* are not expressions. Therefore we need a way to convert process scripts back into behaviour expressions, i.e., the opposite of what the key word script does. The key word activate allows us to turn scripts into behaviour expressions. A process executing activate script(*b*) is considered the same as one described by the behaviour expression *b*. Note that activate is not a function, and that it must precede an expression of type scr.

The function par can then be defined as follows:

```
- fun par(s1,s2) = script( activate s1 || activate s2);
val par = fn : scr * scr -> scr
```

As defining process scripts and functions on them is an important aspect of Facile programming (especially with process abstractions) it is convenient to have special syntax for this task. The proc key word provides a more convenient and suggestive notation for defining the above process abstraction par.

```
- proc par (s1,s2) = ( activate s1 || activate s2 ) ;
val par = fn : scr * scr -> scr
```

Thus proc is an alternative way to define parametric scripts. As the printed statement from the top-level loop indicates, par is a *function* which takes two scripts as arguments and returns a process script. It is a derived construct in the sense that its effect can be achieved by explicitly using the fun and script key words.

Let us have a look at a simple example involving the script of a process that communicates over channels.

We define a very simple process incrementer that receives an integer on one channel inc, adds one to the received integer and sends the result out on another channel outc. Then the process terminates.

```
- proc incrementer (inc, outc) =
    let val x = receive inc
    in send( outc, x+1);
       terminate
    end;
val incrementer = fn : int channel * int channel -> scr
```

We have actually defined a process script parameterised on the two channel names inc and outc. The body of the script is not executed immediately;

instead, just as in a function definition, a *closure* is created. Let us now instantiate `incrementer` with two integer channels and create a process executing the resulting script. We first create the two integer channels, naming them `in_ch` and `out_ch`.

```
- val in_ch = channel() : int channel;
val in_ch = channel : int channel
- val out_ch = channel() : int channel;
val out_ch = channel : int channel
```

We instantiate `incrementer` with these two channels.

```
- val inc_inst = incrementer(in_ch, out_ch);
val inc_inst = script : scr
```

Then we create a new process executing the instantiated script `inc_inst`. This is called *spawning* a process with a given script.

```
- spawn inc_inst;
val it = () : unit
```

The new process that is spawned executes in parallel with our top-level loop. We can interact with it by communicating with it. Let us send this process an integer, say 6, on the channel `in_ch`.

```
- send(in_ch,6);
val it = () : unit
```

When we send the value 6 on channel `in_ch`, we get back the unit value only when there is another process, such as the one we created earlier, willing to receive a value on that channel. Now, let us try to receive an integer on channel `out_ch`.

```
- val y = receive out_ch;
val y = 7 : int
```

Note that once we receive that integer on channel `out_ch`, the spawned process's ability to send on that channel is exhausted. No value is available on that channel anymore, until we create another process that is willing to send on this channel. So we must warn the Facile user not to repeat the communications given above, e.g. attempting to receive on channel `out_ch`, as the top-level loop will get blocked. There is no graceful way to unblock the top-level loop. For this reason, the Facile user should always be wary of trying to communicate from the top-level loop. One way of "playing safe" is to use the time-out constructs that we shall see later.

It is often the case that a process must be ready to communicate with one of several possible processes — or, more precisely, communicate over one of several possible channels — and consequently select one of several alternative courses of action.

Facile provides an **alternative** operator. This operator allows a process to take one of several courses of action, depending on a communication event.

The **alternative** operator is a function that takes as argument a list of guards. Guards are represented by the predefined type constructor **'a guard** in Facile.

A guard may be created by using the **sendguard** or the **recvguard** function. **sendguard** takes three arguments. The first argument must evaluate to a channel, the second to the value to be sent, the third to a function (the guard continuation). **recvguard** takes two arguments. The first argument must evaluate to a channel, the second to a function (again, the guard continuation).

When **alternative** is applied to a list of guards, all arguments of each guard are evaluated — with the usual strict, call-by-value discipline of SML. A guard with all its arguments evaluated is called a guard value. At this point all the communications specified by the guards are attempted.

If and when one succeeds, the process that invoked **alternative** continues its execution with the continuation of the guard (value) whose communication has been executed. The other guards are discarded. In the case of a **recvguard** the continuation function is applied to the value received while in the case of **sendguard** the continuation is applied to the unit value. The value returned by **alternative** is the result of the invoked continuation.

Here is an example of how **alternative** can be used in modeling a machine that a doorman uses when admitting visitors into a gallery. The machine repeatedly either accepts money or a free pass, and then prints an appropriate message, depending on whether a coin or a pass was entered. It also keeps track of the amount of money fed into it, which the doorman can check periodically.

```
- proc entromat pay free tally (count:int)
  = activate
    alternative
     [ recvguard(pay, fn n => (print "Thank you\n";
                                        entromat pay free tally (count+n))),
       recvguard(free, fn () => (print "Enjoy your free visit\n";
                                        entromat pay free tally count)),
       sendguard(tally, count,
                              fn () => entromat pay free tally count)
     ];
val entromat =
    fn : int channel -> unit channel -> int channel -> int -> scr
```

Note that all the functions appearing as continuations in each guard must return the same type. It is possible to transform a guard from one type to another using the **wrapguard** function. This function takes a guard of type **'a guard** and a function of type **'a -> 'b** and produces a new guard value of type **'b guard**. Remember that each guard carries a continuation function. **wrapguard(g,f)** will compose the function **f** with the continuation function of **g**. Thus the transformation will happen after the synchronisation of the guard **g**.

Facile processes attempting communications on channels for which there are no communication partners will be blocked. This is well known from operating systems where processes may be blocked on communication. Most operating systems provide mechanisms for unblocking processes. Instead of providing mechanisms which directly unblock processes the programmer may safeguard the application by introducing some time-out mechanism on communications.

Facile provides one general primitive function **delay** for programming (weak) time dependent behaviours. The effect of calling **delay** is to suspend the execution of the invoking Facile process for (at least) the number of time units specified by the integer argument. In the current implementation of Facile (the Facile Antigua Release on SunOS) the unit of delay is set to 100 milliseconds. The actual delay duration depends on the accuracy of the machine clock as well as the operating system.

Using the **delay** construct one may define a derived operator **delayguard** as a function:

```
-fun delayguard (time, continuation) =
    let val ch = channel ()
    in spawn script((delay (time);
                     send(ch,());
                     terminate));
        recvguard (ch, continuation)
    end
val delayguard = fn : int * (unit -> 'a) -> 'a guard
- fun time_out_send (ch, v, time_out) =
      alternative [sendguard (ch, v, fn x => ()),
                   delayguard (time_out, fn x => raise EXN_TIMEOUT)]
val time_out_send = fn : 'a channel * 'a * int -> unit
```

delayguard creates a local channel **ch** and spawns a process which waits for a duration no less than **time** (via the call to **delay**), and then sends a signal (**()** value) over the private channel **ch**. The signal can be received (only) by the **recvguard** which proceeds with **continuation**. The net effect is thus to delay **continuation** by **time**. Using delayguards we can, e.g., avoid blocking a process attempting to perform a **send** operation by placing the **send** in an **alternative** with a delayguard.

4 Distributed Programming Constructs

The model of distribution in Facile is loosely based on ideas derived from distributed extensions to CCS. A typical Facile application consists of a collection of nodes. The notion of node corresponds to that of a virtual processor with an address space. Nodes in a Facile system may be thought of as tagged by a node identifier returned by the system upon creation of a new node. Since Facile integrates the SML philosophy of treating denotable objects as first class objects, node identifiers become values that may be manipulated by functions. In particular, node identifiers in combination with the static scoping rules of SML yield a very simple way of controlling access to nodes in a Facile system. Only processes being given explicit access to a node identifier can spawn processes on that node. This is in sharp contrast to most distributed systems where a dynamic interpretation of a string identifier takes place.

In the Facile Antigua Release a node is implemented by a modified SML/NJ system running as a Unix process. The nodes that constitute a Facile application may be dynamically created and may be situated on different workstations on a network. The network can be either a local area network (LAN) or a wide area network (WAN). Each node (potentially) hosts concurrent Facile processes. Processes may be created at specific nodes. It is the choice of the programmer whether to place new processes at specific nodes or place them locally. The Facile Antigua Release does not contain any special syntax for describing distribution. Instead distribution is mainly dealt with through function interfaces and process scripts. The model of concurrency remains essentially unchanged, but the communication model needs a slight adjustment due to potential network failures.

In the following we describe the Facile operators for distributed computing. All operators are placed in a module called `Remote`. The `Remote` structure has the following signature:

```
signature REMOTE =
  sig
    type nodeid
    val node         : string -> nodeid
    val current_node : unit -> nodeid
    val this_node    : unit -> nodeid
    val equal    : nodeid * nodeid -> bool
    val r_channel : nodeid -> '1a channel
    val r_spawn    : nodeid * scr -> unit
    val host_name : nodeid -> string
    val ping : nodeid -> bool
    val kill : nodeid -> unit
  end
```

The function `node` takes as argument a character string identifying a host name and attempts to create a new Facile node on the specified host. If it is successful, it returns a node identifier of type `nodeid`. An exception `EXN_NODE_OUTCOME` is raised upon detecting a failure to complete the operation normally. When exception `EXN_NODE_OUTCOME` is raised it may or may not be the case that a Unix process has been created and it may thus be necessary to check this at the Unix level and take appropriate action.

Distributed applications may require a Facile process to execute on a specific node, maybe because the node possesses special resources, such as a special floating point unit, or maybe because a process driving a user interface operates most efficiently if placed on the same machine as the display. Remote process creation can be done using the function `r_spawn` which takes as arguments a node identifier and a process script, i.e., a value of type `scr`.

The following is a code fragment which illustrates how Facile can be used to create a library of functions that will treat a network of computers as a parallel processor by placing a process on a random node among the available nodes in a system:

```
fun nodes machine_list = map node machine_list
fun random (low,high) : int*int -> int = ...
exception N_th
fun n_th n nil     = raise N_th
  | n_th 1 (h::t) = h
  | n_th n (h::t) = n_th (n-1) t
fun random_spawn node_list scri =
  let val n = random(1,length machine_list)
  in r_spawn(n_th n node_list,scri)
  end
```

The function **nodes** takes as argument a list of machine names and maps the **node** function on this list. **nodes** will return a list of node identifiers and as a side effect start Facile nodes on each machine mentioned in the list. The **random** and **n_th** function indicate functions that respectively generates a random number between **low** and **high** and picks out the n'th element of a list. The **random_spawn** function takes a list of node identifiers and a process script as arguments and randomly places the process script on a node in the system.

The **Remote** structure contains a few more functions that we will describe now. The **current_node** function returns the node identifier of the node hosting the invoking process. The value returned by **current_node** is always interpreted by all build-in functions (that use node identifiers) as the node identifier of the node on which **current_node** was executed.

In contrast, the **this_node** function returns a special constant value of type **nodeid**. This value is always interpreted by all functions that use node identifiers as the current, local node identifier.

The difference between **current_node** and **this_node** is not apparent unless the values returned are transmitted to another node. In that case, the value from **current_node** will correspond to the node identifier of the node on which **current_node** was executed, while the value from **this_node** will correspond to the local node identifier.

One reason for using **this_node** is that it is significantly cheaper to call than **current_node**. Hence if you are not transmitting the result values to other nodes, you should use **this_node** instead of **current_node**.

Node identifiers can be tested for equality using the function **equal**.

The function **host_name**, when applied to a node identifier, returns the string name for the machine where the node is located. **ping**, when applied to a node identifier, returns **true** if the machine where the node is located is up and running and it returns **false** otherwise. **kill** forces a remote node to exit. All processes executing on the node will be terminated. This function may be used to simulate a machine failure. This can be very useful when testing the fault tolerance of a distributed application.

In the Facile Antigua Release a channel has a physical manifestation in the form of a data structure. This data structure is placed in the run-time system on the node where the channel is created (via a call to the `channel` function). All communications over that particular channel will refer to this data structure. Thus processes on two different nodes may end up talking to a third node when communicating over a channel. Since local communication has an optimised implementation it may be desirable to create a channel on a specific node. The function `r_channel` may be used for creating a channel on a remote node. It normally returns a channel identifier, if the node is unreachable the exception `EXN_NODE_OUTCOME` is raised.

The physical reality of distributed programming requires that we adjust the communication model slightly. Failures may occur when Facile processes attempt communications over channels that are shared by processes on different nodes. These failures are reported via exceptions which are raised to the invoker of the corresponding (failed) communication primitive.

The exceptions which can be raised by communication attempts are:

- `EXN_CHANNEL_UNAVAIL` which may be raised by `send`, `receive` and `alternative`. This exception is raised by the run-time system if the node where the channel is located is unreachable. No communication has occurred if this exception is raised.
- `EXN_OUTCOME` which may be raised by `send` or `alternative` applied to one or more `sendguard(s)`. This exception is raised by the run-time system if a failure occurs during the protocol implementing Facile's handshake communication. A communication may or may not have occurred. The protocol guarantees that at most one communication has occurred if an exception is raised.
- `EXN_VALUE` which may be raised by `send` or `alternative` applied to one or more `sendguard(s)` in the case where a message is either too large to be transmitted or where a value is transmitted between heterogeneous nodes for which no conversion is supported. No communication has occurred if this exception is raised.

If a failure is detected in trying to close any branch of an `alternative` expression, the `alternative` expression raises the exception to the invoking process even if some other branch could, or could eventually, have succeeded.

Failure detection is performed on a per-communication basis. Thus it is possible for a retry communication attempt to succeed after the previous attempt raised an exception (e.g. if a partitioned network is repaired).

The following is an abstraction which may be used for retrying a user specified number of communications over a channel:

```
- fun re_send i (ch,v,time) =
    if (i <= 1)
    then timeout_send (ch,v,time)
    else timeout_send (ch,v,time)
          handle EXN_CHANNEL_UNAVAIL => re_send (i-1) (ch,v,time)
               | EXN_TIMEOUT => re_send (i-1) (ch,v,time);
val re_send = fn : int -> 'a channel * 'a * int -> unit
```

For each attempt `re_send` will wait at least the number of time units specified by the `time` parameter.

5 Dynamic Connectivity

As mentioned previously Facile is a strongly typed programming language. In fact Facile brings the polymorphic type system of SML into the world of distributed computing. As long as all activity starts with a common ancestor it is easy to propagate type information throughout the system to guarantee type safety even for communications between distributed systems. However, many distributed systems get created as independent units without a common ancestor and need to become connected later, i.e., a dynamic connection needs to be established between independently created components.

Facile contains constructs which allow for type safe dynamic connectivity between applications which may have been created and compiled independently. These constructs are particularly useful for connecting Facile nodes started from the Unix level, i.e., nodes without a common ancestor. The constructs can also be used for dynamically obtaining new services at run-time.

The constructs discussed here include constructs for storing and retrieving modules (structures) from repositories on a network. Currently the service simulates object persistence by storing modules in Unix files.

The mechanism is based on the principle that applications may store modules by *supplying* them to servers on the network. These modules may be retrieved by other applications by *demanding* them based on an interface specification (a signature). Since signatures are rather weak specifications, several modules may match the same signature. To minimize conflicts between modules matching the same interface a notion of library is introduced. Servers may contain several libraries, and modules matching the same interface can be stored in different libraries.

A library is a logical collection in which any number of modules can be stored (only subject to operating system limitations on the number of files a user may create). Each library is attached to a module server, and a library is identified by a Facile value of the primitive type `library`. New libraries can be created at any point of execution by any Facile process.

The structure `Connect` with the following signature forms the interface to the structure and signature servers and libraries:

```
signature CONNECT =
  sig
    type library
    val new_library : string -> library
    val initial_library : string -> library
    val forget : string -> unit
    val structure_server : string -> unit
    val signature_server : unit -> unit
  end
```

The function **structure_server** creates a new structure server. The function takes a string argument which serves as an identifier for the structure server. The string argument must identify a subdirectory in the current directory or an absolute path name to a directory created somewhere else. The directory is used to store the physical representation of structures. This directory must have been created by the user before the call to **structure_server**.

A structure server is implemented as a special Facile process. When the function **structure_server** is executed it will create a Facile process on the node where the function is executed. Currently there is no way of stopping a structure server from within an application, but if a node dies all the servers created on this node will also die.

A structure server may be unreachable due to network failure or because the node on which it is running has been killed. On re-starts structure servers re-initialise their state from their persistent directory, making the libraries created in previous server incarnations available to their clients together with the structures registered previously.

Each structure server has an initial library which can be obtained by calling **initial_library** with a string argument identifying the server (i.e. the name of the structure server directory). Similarly, new libraries can be created by calling **new_library** with a string argument that identifies the structure server. If the structure server is unreachable these functions will raise the exception **EXN_CONNECT**.

Supplying (storing) a structure is an operation at the module declaration level, i.e., at the same level as declaring structures and signatures. It has the following syntactic form:

sdec ::= **supplying** *exp* **with** *str*

where *exp* must evaluate to a value of type **library**.

Applications can retrieve modules from libraries by specifying a signature. The last module stored matching the interface is sent back after coercion by the signature. Since demanding a structure from a library returns a structure, demanding is a construct at the structure level. It has the following syntax:

str ::= **demanding** *exp* **with** *sign*

where *exp* must evaluate to a value of type **library**.

If there is no structure matching the signature in a library when the command is executed, the execution will block until some other application supplies a matching structure.

The following is a code fragment which illustrates the use of **demanding** and **supplying**.

```
structure exported =
  struct
    datatype user_type = Constructor of ...
    val chan : user_type channel = channel ()
  end
supplying lib with exported
structure application1 =
  struct
    ...
    (receive exported.chan) ...
  end
```

The above code fragment first defines a structure containing a user defined data type `user_type` and a channel of that type within a structure. Then the structure is supplied to the library denoted by `lib`. Now `application1` can use the channel defined in the `exported`structure for receiving data of type `user_type`.

```
structure imported =
  demanding lib with
    sig
      datatype user_type = Constructor of ...
      val chan : user_type channel
    end
structure application2 =
  struct
    ...
    send(imported.chan, imported.Constructor ... )
  end
```

This code fragment may be executed on an independently created node. First it will attempt to retrieve a structure from the library denoted by `lib`. Given that we supplied such a structure above, `application2` will now be able to send data of type `user_type` on the channel locally known as `imported.chan`.

In fact the code fragment given above is the minimal code fragment for establishing a channel connection between two independently created systems. Clearly `supplying` and `demanding` could also be used as a kind of communication media (they actually implement a kind of black board communication media). However, these constructs are heavy weight since they involve a full signature match on each invocation and should therefore only be used to establish the first communication link between two parties. These parties can then use the cheaper channel communication for further exchange of values.

Structures can contain user defined data types, hence an application does not always know the specific signature for a supplied structure. For this purpose there is a mechanism for creating a signature server which can be used to exchange signatures between independently created applications. The signature server is launched by executing the function `signature_server` on a unit argument. Note that no special directory is needed for running the signature server. Signatures are stored under names (identifiers) and retrieved on the basis of lookup for a signature stored under some identifier. Supplying (storing) and demanding (retrieving) a signature has the following syntactic form:

supplying signature *sign* **as** *id*

demanding signature *id*

Supplying a signature with a key (an identifier) that already exists will overwrite the previously supplied signature. Thus demanding a signature will return the last supplied signature under the requested key. If no signature is stored under the requested key `demanding signature` will block until a signature gets supplied under the requested key.

There is no garbage collection procedure for structures supplied to structure servers. However, the Facile Antigua Release provides a function `forget`.

The function `forget` has the following type:

```
val forget = fn : string -> unit
```

Calling the `forget` function has the effect of erasing all structures supplied from the node where the `forget` function is called. Future structure demandings might block.

If one wishes to erase all structures supplied to a structure server by a particular node this could be done by calling the following function:

```
- fun forget_node server node
    = r_spawn(node,script((forget server);terminate));
val forget_node = fn : string -> nodeid -> unit
```

Erasing all structures supplied to a structure server may be done by `map (forget_node server) node_list` provided `node_list` contains identifiers for all nodes in the system.

6 Reading More About Facile

In this tutorial we have tried to take the reader through the main programming constructs in the Facile programming language. For a full description of all constructs and how to configure a Facile system the reader should consult:

Thomsen, B., Leth, L., Prasad, S., Kuo, T.-S., Kramer, A., Knabe, F., Giacalone, A.: "Facile Antigua Release – Programming Guide", Technical report ECRC-93-20, 1993.

For a discussion of the language design and philosophy the reader should consult:

Thomsen, B., Leth, L. and Kuo, T.-M.: "FACILE – from Toy to Tool", To appear in: *ML with Concurrency: Design, Analysis, Implementation, and Application*, Flemming Nielson (Editor), Springer-Verlag, 1996.

Further readings include:

Published papers:

- Giacalone, A., Mishra, P., and Prasad, S.: "Facile: A Symmetric Integration of Concurrent and Functional Programming", in Proc. of 1989 TAPSOFT Conference, LNCS 352, Springer-Verlag, 1989.
- Giacalone, A., Mishra, P., and Prasad, S.: "Facile: A Symmetric Integration of Concurrent and Functional Programming", International Journal of Parallel Programming, Vol. 18, No. 2, 1989.
- Prasad, S., Giacalone, A., Mishra, P.: "Operational and Algebraic Semantics for Facile: A Symmetric Integration of Functional and Concurrent Programming", Proceedings of the 1990 International Colloquium on Automata Languages and Programming, LNCS 443, Springer-Verlag, 1990.
- Glauert, J.: "Asynchronous Mobile Processes and Graph Rewriting", Proceedings of the PARLE'92 Conference, LNCS 605, Springer-Verlag, 1992.
- Knabe, F.: "A Distributed Protocol for Channel-Based Communication with Choice", Proceedings of the PARLE'92 Conference, Poster presentations, LNCS 605, Springer-Verlag, 1992.
- Knabe, F.: "A Distributed Protocol for Channel-Based Communication with Choice", in journal of "Computers and Artificial Intelligence", 1993, volume 12, number 5, pp. 475–490.
- Glauert, J., Leth, L., Thomsen, B.: "A New Process Model for Functions", Chapter 18 in Term Graph Rewriting: Theory and Practice, eds. M. R. Sleep, M. J. Plasmeijer and M. C. van Eekelen, John Wiley & Sons Ltd, 1992. Preliminary version in Proceedings of SEMAGRAPH, 1991.
- Glauert, J., Leth, L., Thomsen, B.: "A New Process Model for Functions", Proceedings of SEMAGRAPH, 1991.
- Thomsen, B., Leth, L., Giacalone, A.: "Some Issues in the Semantics of Facile Distributed Programming", Proceedings of the 1992 REX Workshop on "Semantics: Foundations and Applications", LNCS 666, Springer-Verlag, 1992.
- Cregut, P.: "Safe Dynamic Connection of Distributed Applications", ACM SIGPLAN Workshop on ML and its Applications, 1994.
- Thomsen, B.: "Polymorphic Sorts and Types for Concurrent Functional Programs", Proceedings of the 6th International Workshop on the Implementation of Functional Languages (Ed. J. Glauert), UEA Norwich, UK, 1994.
- Amadio, R. M., Leth, L. and Thomsen, B.: "From a Concurrent λ-calculus to the π-calculus", Proceedings of Fundamentals of Computation Theory, 10th International Conference, FCT'95, Dresden, Germany, August 1995, LNCS 965, Springer Verlag, 1995, pp. 106 – 115.
- Leth, L., and Thomsen, B.: "Some Facile Chemistry", Formal Aspects of Computing (1995) 7:314-328, Springer Verlag, 1995.
- Leth, L., and Thomsen, B.: "Some Facile Chemistry", Formal Aspects of Computing (1995) 7(E):67-110, Springer Verlag Electronic Publications, 1995. (ftp://ftp.cs.man.ac.uk/pub/fac/FACj_7E_pp67-110.ps.Z)
- Thomsen, B., Knabe, F. Leth, L. and Chevalier, P.-Y.: "Mobile Agents set to work" Communications International, July, 1995.

ECRC technical reports:

- Leth, L., Thomsen, B.: "Some Facile Chemistry", Technical report ECRC-92-14, 1992.
- Knabe, F.: "A Distributed Protocol for Channel-Based Communication with Choice", Technical report ECRC-92-16, 1992.
- Thomsen, B., Leth, L., Giacalone, A.: "Some Issues in the Semantics of Facile Distributed Programming", Technical report ECRC-92-32, 1992.
- Thomsen, B.: "Polymorphic Sorts and Types for Concurrent Functional Programs", Technical report ECRC-93-10, 1993.
- Amadio R. M.: "Translating Core Facile", Technical report ECRC-94-3, 1994.
- Talpin, J.-P.: "The Calumet Experiment - Part I: An Implementation of Group-Communication Protocols in Facile", Technical report ECRC-94-4, 1994.
- Leth, L., Thomsen, B.: "Facile Chemistry Revised", Technical report ECRC-94-36, 1994.
- Ahlers, K. H., Kramer, A., Breen, D. E., Chevalier, P.-Y., Crampton, C., Rose, E., Tucheryan, M., Whitaker, R. T. and Greer, D.: "Distributed Augmented Reality for Collaborative Design Applications", Technical report ECRC-95-03, 1995.
- Amadio, R. M., Leth, L. and Thomsen, B.: "From a Concurrent λ-calculus to the π-calculus", Technical report ECRC-95-18, 1995.
- Thomsen, B., Leth, L., Knabe, F. and Chevalier, P.-Y.: "Mobile Agents", Technical report, ECRC-95-21, 1995.
- Borgia, R., Degano, P., Priami, C., Leth, L. and Thomsen, B.: "Understanding Mobile Agents via a non-interleaving semantics for Facile", Technical report, ECRC-96-4, 1996.

7 Final Remarks

Some examples and descriptions in this document have been selected from documents produced by members of the Facile team over the past five years. We greatly acknowledge their contributions.

This document was finalised during the last days of the Facile project at ECRC which terminated its research activities Spring 1996. The ideas and technology of Facile will be taken over by ICL/IC-PARC, and we hope for an even stronger future for the next release of Facile.

Testing Probabilistic Automata

Roberto Segala

Dipartimento di Scienze dell'Informazione
Università di Bologna - Italy

Abstract. We study testing preorders for probabilistic automata and we characterize them in terms of relations that are based on inclusion of trace and failure distributions, i.e., probability distributions over failures and traces that can arise in a probabilistic computation. The novelty of our approach to testing is the use of multiple success actions rather than a single action. This allows us to observe the relative probabilities of different traces within a computation.

We define and characterize two kinds of testing preorders: preorders sensitive to infinite traces, and preorders sensitive to finite traces only. The second kind of preorder is an extension to the probabilistic framework of the testing preorders of De Nicola and Hennessy. We show that under assumptions of finite branching and strong convergence the two kinds of preorders coincide.

1 Introduction

The probabilistic automaton model [13] was introduced as a model for randomized concurrent computation that can be used for the analysis of randomized distributed algorithms [9, 11, 1] and that at the same time has strong mathematical foundations. To achieve the second goal, probabilistic automata are an extension of ordinary labeled transition systems [10], where a transition (s, a, s') is replaced by a triplet $(s, a, \mathcal{P})$ with $\mathcal{P}$ a discrete probability distribution over states.

In [14] several simulation and bisimulation relations, both in their strong and weak form, are defined for probabilistic automata, and in [12] a trace based semantics for probabilistic automata is studied. The results in [14, 12] show that indeed several standard concepts for ordinary labeled transition systems extend to the probabilistic case, thus confirming the original objectives of the probabilistic model.

In this paper we extend the theory of testing [3, 5] to the probabilistic model. Our main objective is to show that it is possible to define a theory of testing for probabilistic automata, and to give alternative characterizations of the may and must relations in terms of some form of probabilistic traces and failures. In particular, the trace distributions of [12] are the alternative characterization of the probabilistic may preorder. We introduce two versions of the testing preorders: one version deals with finite and infinite traces; the other version deals with finite traces only, so that the idea behind the testing preorders of [3] is captured better.

Our main intuition is that we need more success actions rather than a single action w. In fact, since in a probabilistic framework we are interested in observing the relative probabilities of different actions within the same probabilistic computation, we need at least one success action for each action to be observed. We assume that a test has at most countably many distinct success actions. At the end of the paper we show sufficient conditions for the success actions of a test to be finite.

Given a test T for a probabilistic automaton M, i.e., a probabilistic automaton with at most countably many success actions, we denote by H a probabilistic execution of $M\|T$, the parallel composition of M and T. A probabilistic execution is essentially a cycle-free Markov chain obtained by choosing a transition, possibly probabilistically, from each state. We define $W(H)$ to be a vector of probabilities $(p_1, p_2, \ldots)$, where for each i, p_i is the probability of occurrence of action w_i in H. We assume implicitly to have an enumeration of the success actions.

The may preorder is defined as follows: $M_1 \sqsubseteq_{MAY} M_2$ iff for every test T and every probabilistic execution H_1 of $M_1\|T$, there is a probabilistic execution H_2 of $M_2\|T$ such that $W(H_1) \leq W(H_2)$, where the less than or equal to relation is defined componentwise. Our definition is similar to the definition of may testing proposed in [7]. In [7] there is only one success action, and two systems are related by comparing, for each test, the supremums of the probabilities of success. In our case we do not compare supremums because the closure of the set of vectors W does not have a unique maximum element in general. Another consequence of not considering supremums is that our may preorder is sensitive to the presence or absence of limit vectors, while the may preorder of [7] is not.

The must preorder is symmetric to the may preorder. Namely, $M_1 \sqsubseteq_{MUST} M_2$ iff for every test T and every probabilistic execution H_2 of $M_2\|T$, there is a probabilistic execution H_1 of $M_1\|T$ such that $W(H_1) \leq W(H_2)$. Also in this case there is a similarity with the definition in [7]. Our definition states that whenever M_2 passes T with a probability vector W, then it is the case that, resolving the nondeterminism appropriately, M_1 passes T with a probability vector not better than W. Therefore, if M_1 performs always better than some vector W, then M_2 performs always better than W as well.

We show that the may preorder can be characterized alternatively in terms of the trace distribution precongruence of [12], and that the reversed must preorder can be characterized alternatively in terms of the *failure distribution precongruence*, which is a probabilistic generalization of the failure preorder of [2, 6]. The failure distribution precongruence is first defined in this paper and is the coarsest precongruence contained in the failure distribution inclusion preorder. A failure distribution is a probabilistic generalization of the failures of [2, 6], consisting of a probability distribution over failures induced by a probabilistic execution. Of course, as in [2], our characterization of the must preorder holds only for *strongly convergent* systems, i.e., systems that cannot perform infinite internal computation from any point. To deal with the more general case we would need a probabilistic extension of the *divergences* of [2], which we defer to further work.

The characterizations above of our may and must testing preorders are in terms of mathematical objects that include infinite traces. However, especially for decidability issues, it is typical to consider finite traces only. It would be desirable as well to consider only finite vectors of success actions rather than infinite vectors. Therefore, the second part of the paper concentrates on reducing the power of the tests so that the infinite behavior of a probabilistic automaton is not visible.

We define a new kind of trace and failure distributions where all the probability is concentrated on finite traces and failures only. In particular, for each trace and failure distribution there is a limit to the length of the trace and failures that may occur with a non-zero probability (*finite* trace and failure distributions). The related precongruence relations can be characterized again in terms of testing, where for each test there is a maximum number of external actions that can be performed sequentially. These last preorders are based on objects that we can regard as finite, and in our opinion are the relations that express better the testing preorders of [3]. Indeed, if we restrict ourselves to the non probabilistic case, our last testing preorders become the preorders of [3].

The finite preorders enjoy other properties that are valid for ordinary nondeterministic systems. Namely, it is known that the finite behaviors of a system are sufficient to describe the infinite behaviors of the system whenever the system is *finite branching* (finitely many transitions enabled from each state) and strongly convergent. We show that the same property holds in the probabilistic framework. Finally, we impose additional restrictions that allow us to deal only with tests that have finitely many success actions.

The rest of the paper is organized as follows. Section 2 gives an overview of the probabilistic automata of [13], the basic model used in this paper; Section 3 defines the failure distribution precongruence; Section 4 defines our may and must preorders and provides alternative characterizations in terms of trace and failure distributions; Section 5 defines the finite preorders and provides alternative characterizations in terms of finite trace and failure distributions; Section 6 shows sufficient conditions for finite trace and failure distributions to characterize ordinary trace and failure distributions, and for tests to have finitely many success actions.

2 Preliminaries

In this section we give an overview of the probabilistic automata of [13], which appear also in [12].

2.1 Probability Spaces

A *probability space* is a triple $(\Omega, \mathcal{F}, P)$ where Ω is a set, $\mathcal{F}$ is a collection of subsets of Ω that is closed under complement and countable union and such that $\Omega \in \mathcal{F}$, and P is a function from $\mathcal{F}$ to $[0,1]$ such that $P[\Omega] = 1$ and such that for any collection $\{C_i\}_i$ of at most countably many pairwise disjoint elements of $\mathcal{F}$, $P[\cup_i C_i] = \sum_i P[C_i]$. A probability space $(\Omega, \mathcal{F}, P)$ is *discrete* if $\mathcal{F} = 2^{\Omega}$ and for each $C \subseteq \Omega$, $P[C] = \sum_{x \in C} P[\{x\}]$. Given a set X, denote by $Probs(X)$ the set of discrete probability distributions whose sample space is a subset of X and such that the probability of each element is not 0.

The Dirac distribution over an element x, denoted by $\mathcal{D}(x)$, is the probability space with a unique element x.

Throughout the paper we denote a probability space $(\Omega, \mathcal{F}, P)$ by $\mathcal{P}$. As a notational convention, if $\mathcal{P}$ is decorated with indices and primes, then the same indices and primes carry to its elements. Thus, $\mathcal{P}'_i$ denotes $(\Omega'_i, \mathcal{F}'_i, P'_i)$.

The *product* $\mathcal{P}_1 \otimes \mathcal{P}_2$ of two discrete probability spaces $\mathcal{P}_1$, $\mathcal{P}_2$ is the discrete probability space $(\Omega_1 \times \Omega_2, 2^{\Omega_1 \times \Omega_2}, P)$, where $P[(x_1, x_2)] = P_1[x_1]P_2[x_2]$ for each $(x_1, x_2) \in \Omega_1 \times \Omega_2$.

A function $f : \Omega \rightarrow \Omega'$ is said to be a *measurable* function from $(\Omega, \mathcal{F})$ to $(\Omega', \mathcal{F}')$ if for each set C of $\mathcal{F}'$ the inverse image of C, denoted by $f^{-1}(C)$, is an element of $\mathcal{F}$. Let P be a probability measure on $(\Omega, \mathcal{F})$, and let P' be defined on $\mathcal{F}'$ as follows: for each element C of $\mathcal{F}'$, $P'(C) = P(f^{-1}(C))$. Then P' is a probability measure on $(\Omega', \mathcal{F}')$. The measure P' is called the measure *induced* by f, and is denoted by $f(P)$. If $\mathcal{P}$ is a discrete probability space and f is a function defined on Ω, then f can be *extended* to $\mathcal{P}$ by defining $f(\mathcal{P})$ to be the discrete probability space $(f(\Omega), 2^{f(\Omega)}, f(P))$.

2.2 Probabilistic Automata

A labeled transition system, also called an *automaton*, is a state machine with labeled transitions. Each transition leaves from a state and leads to the occurrence of a label, also called an *action*, and to a state. A probabilistic automaton is like an ordinary automaton except that each transition leads to an action and to a probability distribution over states.

Resolving the nondeterminism in an automaton leads to a linear chain of states interleaved with actions, called an *execution* or a *computation*; resolving the nondeterminism in a probabilistic automaton leads to a Markov chain structure since each transition leads probabilistically to more than one state. Such a structure is called a *probabilistic execution*. A probabilistic execution can be visualized as a probabilistic automaton that enables at most one transition from each state (a ***fully probabilistic automaton***). Due to the complex structure of a probabilistic execution, it is convenient to view it as a special case of a probabilistic automaton; in this way the analysis of a probabilistic execution is simplified.

However, nondeterminism could be resolved also using randomization: a scheduler for n processes running in parallel could choose the next process to schedule by rolling an n-side dice; similarly, if some actions model the input of an external environment, the environment could provide the input at random or could provide no input with some non-zero probability. Thus, in a probabilistic execution the transition that leaves from a state may lead to a probability distribution over both actions and states and also over deadlock (no input). This new kind of transition is not part of our informal definition of a probabilistic automaton; yet, it is still convenient to view a probabilistic execution as a probabilistic automaton.

Thus, our definition of a probabilistic automaton allows for a transition to lead to probability distributions over actions and states and over a symbol δ that models deadlock; however, except for the handling of probabilistic executions, we concentrate on *simple probabilistic automata*, which allow only probabilistic choices over states within a transition.

Definition 1. A *probabilistic automaton* M consists of four components:

1. a set $states(M)$ of states,
2. a nonempty set $start(M) \subseteq states(M)$ of start states,
3. an action signature $sig(M) = (ext(M), int(M))$ where $ext(M)$ and $int(M)$ are disjoint sets of *external* and *internal* actions, respectively,

4. a transition relation $trans(M) \subseteq states(M) \times Probs((acts(M) \times states(M)) \cup \{\delta\})$, where $acts(M)$ denotes the set $ext(M) \cup int(M)$ of actions, and δ is a special symbol not in $acts(M)$.

A probabilistic automaton M is *simple* if for each transition $(s, \mathcal{P})$ of $trans(M)$ there is an action a such that $\Omega \subseteq \{a\} \times states(M)$. In such a case a transition can be represented alternatively as $(s, a, \mathcal{P}')$, where $\mathcal{P}' \in Probs(states(M))$, and is called a *simple transition*.

A probabilistic automaton is *fully probabilistic* if it has a unique start state and from each state there is at most one transition enabled. □

Observe that an ordinary automaton is a special case of a probabilistic automaton where each transition leads to a Dirac distribution. We defer the reader to [13] for a comparison with other models.

2.3 Executions and Probabilistic Executions

We now move to the notion of an execution, which is the result of resolving both the nondeterministic and the probabilistic choices in a probabilistic automaton; it corresponds to the notion of an execution for ordinary automata. We introduce also a notion of an extended execution, which we use later to study the probabilistic behavior of a probabilistic automaton.

Definition 2. An *execution* α of a probabilistic automaton M is a (finite or infinite) sequence of alternating states and actions starting with a start state and, if the execution is finite, ending in a state, $\alpha = s_0 a_1 s_1 a_2 s_2 \cdots$, where for each i there exists a probability space $\mathcal{P}$ such that $(s_i, \mathcal{P}) \in trans(M)$ and $(a_{i+1}, s_{i+1}) \in \Omega$. Denote by $fstate(\alpha)$ the first state of α, and, if α is finite, denote by $lstate(\alpha)$ the last state of α. Denote by $exec^*(M)$ and $exec(M)$ the sets of finite and all executions of M, respectively.

An extended execution of M is either an execution of M, or a sequence $\alpha = s_0 a_1 s_1 \cdots a_n s_n \delta$ such that $s_0 a_1 s_1 \cdots a_n s_n$ is an execution of M.

An extended execution α_1 of M is a *prefix* of an extended execution α_2 of M, written $\alpha_1 \leq \alpha_2$, if either $\alpha_1 = \alpha_2$ or α_2 is obtained by extending α_1, i.e., $\alpha_1 = s_0 a_1 s_1 \cdots a_n s_n$ and $\alpha_2 = s_0 a_1 s_1 \cdots a_n s_n a_{n+1} s_{n+1} \cdots$. □

As we said already, an execution is the result of resolving both the nondeterministic and the probabilistic choices in a probabilistic automaton. The result of the resolution of nondeterministic choices only is a fully probabilistic automaton, called a *probabilistic execution*, which is the entity that replaces the executions of ordinary automata. Informally, since in ordinary automata there is no probability left once the nondeterminism is resolved, the executions and probabilistic executions of an ordinary automaton describe the same objects. Before giving the formal definition of a probabilistic execution, we introduce *combined transitions*, which allow us to express the ability to resolve the nondeterminism using probability. Informally, a combined transition leaving from a state s is obtained by choosing a transition that leaves from s probabilistically, and then behaving according to the transition chosen. Among the choices it is possible not to schedule any transition. This possibility is expressed by the term $(1 - \sum_i p_i)$ in the probability of δ in the definition below.

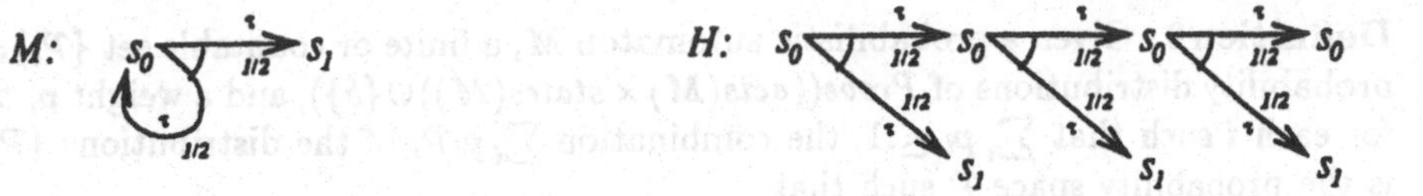

Fig. 1. Probabilistic executions.

There is a strong correspondence between the extended executions of a probabilistic automaton and the extended executions of one of its probabilistic executions. We express this correspondence by means of an operator $\downarrow$ that takes an extended execution α of H and gives back the corresponding extended execution $\alpha\downarrow$ of M, and an operator $\uparrow q_0^H$ that takes an extended execution α of M and gives back the corresponding extended execution $\alpha\uparrow q_0^H$ of H if it exists.

2.4 Events

We now define a probability space $(\Omega_H, \mathcal{F}_H, P_H)$ for a probabilistic execution H, so that it is possible to analyze the probabilistic behavior of a probabilistic automaton once the nondeterminism is resolved. The sample space Ω_H is the set of extended executions of M that represent complete extended executions of H, where an extended execution α of H is complete iff it is either infinite or $\alpha = \alpha'\delta$ and $\delta \in \Omega^H_{lstate(\alpha')}$. For each finite extended execution α of M, let C_α, the *cone* with prefix α, be the set $\{\alpha' \in \Omega_H \mid \alpha \leq \alpha'\}$, and let C_H be the class of cones for H. The probability $\mu_H(C_\alpha)$ of the cone C_α is the product of the probabilities associated with each edge that generates α in H. Formally, if $\alpha = q_0^H a_1 s_1 \cdots s_{n-1} a_n s_n$, then $\mu_H(C_\alpha) \triangleq P^H_{q_0}[(a_1, q_1)] \cdots P^H_{q_{n-1}}[(a_n, q_n)]$, where each q_i is defined to be $q_0^H a_1 s_1 \cdots a_i s_i$, and if $\alpha = q_0^H a_1 s_1 \cdots s_{n-1} a_n s_n \delta$, then $\mu_H(C_\alpha) \triangleq P^H_{q_0}[(a_1, q_1)] \cdots P^H_{q_{n-1}}[(a_n, q_n)] P^H_{q_n}[\delta]$, where each q_i is defined to be $q_0^H a_1 s_1 \cdots a_i s_i$. In [13] it is shown that there is a unique measure $\bar{\mu}_H$ that extends μ_H to the σ-field $\sigma(C_H)$ generated by C_H, i.e., the smallest σ-field that contains C_H. Then, $\mathcal{F}_H$ is $\sigma(C_H)$ and P_H is $\bar{\mu}_H$. With this definition it is possible to show that any union of cones is measurable.

2.5 Convergence

An execution α of a probabilistic automaton M is *divergent* if it is infinite and contains finitely many external actions. An execution α is *convergent* if it is not divergent. A probabilistic automaton M is *strongly convergent* if there are no divergent executions of M. A probabilistic automaton M is *probabilistically convergent* if there are no probabilistic executions of M whose divergent executions have a non-zero probability.

2.6 Parallel Composition

The parallel composition operator for probabilistic automata is defined in the CSP style [6], i.e., by synchronizing two probabilistic automata on their common actions.

Definition 3. Given a probabilistic automaton M, a finite or countable set $\{\mathcal{P}_i\}_i$ of probability distributions of $Probs((acts(M) \times states(M)) \cup \{\delta\})$, and a weight $p_i > 0$ for each i such that $\sum_i p_i \leq 1$, the combination $\sum_i p_i \mathcal{P}_i$ of the distributions $\{\mathcal{P}_i\}_i$ is the probability space $\mathcal{P}$ such that

- $\Omega = \begin{cases} \cup_i \Omega_i & \text{if } \sum_i p_i = 1 \\ \cup_i \Omega_i \cup \{\delta\} & \text{if } \sum_i p_i < 1 \end{cases}$
- $\mathcal{F} = 2^{\Omega}$
- for each $(a, s) \in \Omega$, $P[(a, s)] = \sum_{i \mid (a,s) \in \Omega_i} p_i P_i[(a, s)]$
- if $\delta \in \Omega$, then $P[\delta] = (1 - \sum_i p_i) + \sum_{i \mid \delta \in \Omega_i} p_i P_i[\delta]$.

A pair $(s, \mathcal{P})$ is a *combined transition* of M if there exists a finite or countable family of transitions $\{(s, \mathcal{P}_i)\}_i$ and a set of positive weights $\{p_i\}_i$ with $\sum_i p_i \leq 1$, such that $\mathcal{P} = \sum_i p_i \mathcal{P}_i$. Denote $(s, \mathcal{P})$ by $\sum_i p_i (s, \mathcal{P}_i)$. □

We are now ready to define a probabilistic execution. Informally, a probabilistic execution can be seen as the result of unfolding the transition relation of a probabilistic automaton and then choosing probabilistically a transition from each state.

Definition 4. Let α be a finite execution of a probabilistic automaton M. Define a function $\alpha\frown$ that applied to a pair (a, s) returns $(a, \alpha a s)$, and applied to δ returns δ. Recall from the last paragraph of Section 2.1 that the function $\alpha\frown$ can be extended to discrete probability spaces.

A *probabilistic execution* of a probabilistic automaton M, is a fully probabilistic automaton, denoted by H, such that

1. $states(H) \subseteq exec^*(M)$. Let q range over states of probabilistic executions.
2. $start(H)$ contains a start state of M.
3. for each transition $tr = (q, \mathcal{P})$ of H there is a combined transition $tr' = (lstate(q), \mathcal{P}')$ of M, called the *corresponding combined transition*, such that $\mathcal{P} = q \frown \mathcal{P}'$.
4. each state of H is reachable and enables one transition, where a state q of H is reachable if there is an execution of H whose last state is q.

Denote by $prexec(M)$ the set of probabilistic executions of M. Also, denote by q_0^H the start state of a generic probabilistic execution H, and for each transition $(q, \mathcal{P})$ of H, denote $\mathcal{P}$ by $\mathcal{P}_q^H$.

A *probabilistic execution* is *complete* iff for each state q, $\delta \in \Omega_q^H$ implies that no transition is enabled in M from $lstate(q)$. Denote by $cprexec(M)$ the set of complete probabilistic executions of M.

Example 1. Figure 1 contains an example of a probabilistic execution. The object denoted by H is a probabilistic execution of the probabilistic automaton denoted by M. For notational convenience, in the representation of a probabilistic execution H we do not write explicitly the full names of the states of H since the full names are derivable from the position of each state in the diagram; moreover, whenever a state q enables the transition $(q, \mathcal{D}(\delta))$ we do not draw any arc leaving from the state of the diagram that represents q. □

As outlined in [4], it is not clear how to define a parallel composition operator for general probabilistic automata that extends the CSP synchronization style; thus, we define it only for simple probabilistic automata, and we concentrate on simple probabilistic automata for the rest of this paper. We use general probabilistic automata only for the analysis of probabilistic executions. The reader is referred to [13] for more details.

Definition 5. Two simple probabilistic automata M_1 and M_2 are said to be *compatible* if $int(M_1) \cap acts(M_2) = \emptyset$, and $int(M_2) \cap acts(M_1) = \emptyset$.

The *parallel composition* $M_1 \| M_2$ of two compatible simple probabilistic automata M_1 and M_2 is the simple probabilistic automaton M such that $states(M) = states(M_1) \times states(M_2)$, $start(M) = start(M_1) \times start(M_2)$, $ext(M) = ext(M_1) \cup ext(M_2)$, $int(M) = int(M_1) \cup int(M_2)$, and the transition relation satisfies the following: $((s_1, s_2), a, \mathcal{P}) \in trans(M)$ iff $\mathcal{P} = \mathcal{P}_1 \otimes \mathcal{P}_2$, such that

1. if $a \in acts(M_1)$ then $(s_1, a, \mathcal{P}_1) \in trans(M_1)$, else $\mathcal{P}_1 = \mathcal{D}(s_1)$, and
2. if $a \in acts(M_2)$ then $(s_2, a, \mathcal{P}_2) \in trans(M_2)$, else $\mathcal{P}_2 = \mathcal{D}(s_2)$. □

2.7 Trace Distribution Precongruence

Definition 6. Let H be a probabilistic execution of a probabilistic automaton M. For each extended execution α of M, let $trace(\alpha)$ denote the ordered sequence of external actions of M that appear in α.

Let f be a function from Ω_H to $\Omega = ext(M)^* \cup ext(M)^\omega$ that assigns to each execution of Ω_H its trace. The *trace distribution* of H, denoted by $tdistr(H)$, is the probability space $(\Omega, \mathcal{F}, P)$ where $\mathcal{F}$ is the σ-field generated by the cones C_β, where β is an element of $ext(M)^*$, and $P = f(P_H)$. The fact that f is measurable follows from standard arguments. Denote a generic trace distribution by $\mathcal{D}$. A trace distribution of a probabilistic automaton M is the trace distribution of one of the probabilistic executions of M. □

Given two probabilistic executions H_1 and H_2, it is possible to check whether $tdistr(H_1) = tdistr(H_2)$ just by verifying that $P_{tdistr(H_1)}[C_\beta] = P_{tdistr(H_2)}[C_\beta]$ for each finite sequence of actions β. This follows from standard measure theory arguments.

It is easy to see that trace distributions extend the traces of ordinary automata: the trace distribution of a linear probabilistic execution is a distribution that associates probability 1 to a unique trace. It is easy as well to see that the notion of prefix for traces extends to the probabilistic framework. A trace distribution $\mathcal{D}$ is a *prefix* of a trace distribution $\mathcal{D}'$, denoted by $\mathcal{D} \leq \mathcal{D}'$, iff for each finite trace β, $P_{\mathcal{D}}[C_\beta] \leq P_{\mathcal{D}'}[C_\beta]$. Thus, two trace distributions are equal iff each one is a prefix of the other.

Definition 7. Let M_1, M_2 be two probabilistic automata with the same external actions. The *trace distribution preorder* is defined as follows.

$$M_1 \sqsubseteq_D M_2 \text{ iff } tdistrs(M_1) \subseteq tdistrs(M_2).$$ □

The trace distribution preorder is a direct extension of the trace preorder of ordinary automata; however, it is not a precongruence, as it is shown in [12]. This leads to the following definition.

Definition 8. Let M_1, M_2 be two probabilistic automata with the same external actions. The ***trace distribution precongruence***, denoted by $\sqsubseteq_T$, is the coarsest precongruence that is contained in the trace distribution preorder. □

In [13] the trace distribution precongruence is characterized by means of a ***principal context***, denoted by C_P and represented in Figure 2, in the following sense.

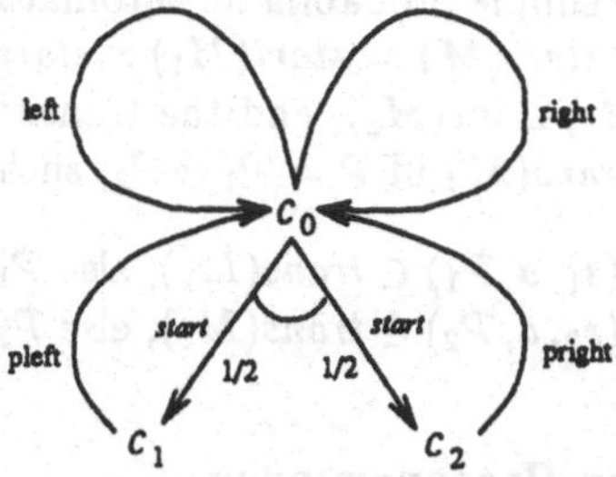

Fig. 2. The principal context.

Proposition 9. $M_1 \sqsubseteq_T M_2$ *iff* $M_1 \| C_P \sqsubseteq_D M_2 \| C_P$. □

3 Failure Distribution Precongruence

In this section we extend to the probabilistic framework the failures of [2]. For each state s of a probabilistic automaton M define $wenabled(s)$ to be the set of actions a that can be performed from s up to internal transitions. A ***failure*** of a probabilistic automaton M is a pair (β, F), where β is a finite trace and F is a set of actions, such that there exists a finite execution α of M with $\beta = trace(\alpha)$ and $F \cap wenabled(lstate(\alpha)) = \emptyset$. Its meaning is that M can produce the external trace β and reach a state from which no action from F can be performed up to internal transitions.

Definition 10. Let H be a probabilistic execution of a probabilistic automaton M. Build a new object H' from H as follows. In every transition $(q, \mathcal{P})$ of H with $\delta \in \Omega$, replace δ with a collection of pairs (q, F), where F is a set of actions of M and $F \cap wenabled(lstate(q)) = \emptyset$, and assign to each pair (q, F) an arbitrary probability p_F so that $\sum p_F = P[\delta]$. In other words, H' is obtained from H by replacing deadlocks with failure sets.

Let f be a function from $\Omega_{H'}$ to $\Omega = ext(M)^* \cup (ext(M)^* \times 2^{acts(M)}) \cup ext(M)^\omega$ that assigns to each execution of $\Omega_{H'}$ its trace or failure as follows:

$$f(\alpha) = \begin{cases} trace(\alpha) & \text{if } trace(\alpha) \in ext(M)^\infty \\ (trace(\alpha), F) & \text{if } lstate(\alpha) = (q, F) \text{ for some } q \\ (trace(\alpha), \emptyset) & \text{if } \alpha \text{ is infinite and } trace(\alpha) \text{ is finite.} \end{cases}$$

A *failure distribution* of H, denoted by $fdistr(H)$, is the probability space $(\Omega, \mathcal{F}, P)$ where $\mathcal{F}$ is the σ-field generated by the cones C_β and $C_{(\beta,F)}$, where β is an element of $ext(M)^*$ and F is a set of actions of M, and $P = f(P_H)$. The fact that f is measurable follows from standard arguments. Denote a generic failure distribution by $\mathcal{F}$. A failure distribution of a probabilistic automaton M is a failure distribution of one of the probabilistic executions of M. Denote by $fdistrs(M)$ the set of failure distributions of M. □

Similar to the case for trace distributions, a failure distribution preorder can be defined as inclusion of failure distributions. Then, the *failure distribution precongruence*, denoted by $\sqsubseteq_F$, is the coarsest precongruence contained in the failure distribution preorder. The principal context characterization is valid also for failure distributions.

Proposition 11. *$M_1 \sqsubseteq_F M_2$ iff $fdistrs(M_1\|C_P) \subseteq fdistrs(M_2\|C_P)$.* □

Observe that a failure distribution as defined so far is not a real extension of the failures of [2] since in a failure distribution the infinite traces may have a non zero probability. Later in the paper we define finite failure distributions, which can be regarded as real extensions of the failures of [2].

4 The Probabilistic May and Must Preorders

Let M be a probabilistic automaton. A *test* for M is a probabilistic automaton T, compatible with M, whose actions include the external actions of M and a collection of at most countably many *success* actions $w_1, w_2, \ldots$. Given a probabilistic execution H of $M\|T$, let $W(H)$ denote the vector $(p_1, p_2, \ldots)$, where each p_i denotes the probability that action w_i occurs in H, i.e., the probability in $\mathcal{P}_H$ of the executions that contain an occurrence of action w_i. Given two probabilistic automata M_1, M_2, define two *testing* preorders as follows.

$$M_1 \sqsubseteq_{MAY} M_2 \text{ iff } \forall_T \forall_{H_1 \in cprexecs(M_1\|T)} \exists_{H_2 \in cprexecs(M_2\|T)} W(H_1) \leq W(H_2),$$
$$M_1 \sqsubseteq_{MUST} M_2 \text{ iff } \forall_T \forall_{H_2 \in cprexecs(M_2\|T)} \exists_{H_1 \in cprexecs(M_1\|T)} W(H_1) \leq W(H_2).$$

The definitions of the may and must preorders differ only in the use of the existential and universal quantifications. They are inspired by the testing preorders of [3] and by the probabilistic preorders of [7, 8]. The may preorder states that for each test T, if there is a possibility that M_1 passes T with a probability vector W, then also M_1 has a possibility to pass T with a probability vector at least W. The must preorder states that for each test T, if there is a possibility that M_2 passes T with a probability vector W, then M_2 has a possibility to pass T with a probability vector at most W.

An alternative definition of the testing preorders can be given as follows. A test is a pair $(T, \bar{W})$, where T is a probabilistic automaton compatible with M whose actions include the external actions of M and a collection of at most countably many *success* actions $w_1, w_2, \ldots$, and $\bar{W}$ is a vector of probabilities. Then,

$$M \text{ MAY } (T, \bar{W}) \text{ iff } \exists_{H \in cprexec(M\|T)}\ \bar{W} \leq W(H),$$
$$M \text{ MUST } (T, \bar{W}) \text{ iff } \nexists_{H \in cprexec(M\|T)}\ W(H) \leq \bar{W},$$

and the testing preorders are defined as

$$M_1 \sqsubseteq_{MAY} M_2 \text{ iff } \forall_{(T,\bar{W})} M_1 \text{ MAY } (T,\bar{W}) \Rightarrow M_2 \text{ MAY } (T,\bar{W}),$$

$$M_1 \sqsubseteq_{MUST} M_2 \text{ iff } \forall_{(T,\bar{W})} M_1 \text{ MUST } (T,\bar{W}) \Rightarrow M_2 \text{ MUST } (T,\bar{W}).$$

A reader may be tempted to replace the non-existential quantification with a universal quantification in the definition of M MUST $(T,\bar{W})$ and to reverse the inequality. That is, M MUST $(T,\bar{W})$ iff $\forall_{H \in cprexec(M\|T)} \bar{W} \leq W(H)$. Such an alternative definition would not work because the closure of the set of vectors W of a probabilistic automaton does not have a unique minimum element in general.

The testing preorders defined so far are equivalent to the trace distribution precongruence and, under the restriction of strong convergence, to the failure distribution precongruence.

Theorem 12. *$M_1 \sqsubseteq_{MAY} M_2$ iff $M_1 \sqsubseteq_T M_2$.*

Proof sketch. $\sqsubseteq_T$ implies $\sqsubseteq_{MAY}$ directly since the vector W is derived from the trace distributions of a probabilistic automaton.

Conversely, let $M_1 \sqsubseteq_{MAY} M_2$, and let $\mathcal{D}$ be a trace distribution of $M_1\|C_P$. Build a test T as follows. The states of T are the symbol δ and all pairs of the form (β, b) where $b \in \{0,1\}$ and β is a finite trace such that $P_{\mathcal{D}}[C_\beta] > 0$. For each state $(\beta, 0)$ there is a transition $(\beta,0) \xrightarrow{w_\beta} (\beta,1)$; for each state $(\beta a, 0)$ there is a transition $(\beta,1) \xrightarrow{a} (\beta a, 0)$; for each finite trace β such that $P_{\mathcal{D}}[\{\beta\}] > 0$ there is a transition $(\beta,1) \xrightarrow{w_{\beta\delta}} \delta$.

For simplicity we assume that there is a probabilistic execution of $M_1\|C_P$ whose set of divergent executions has probability 0 and whose trace distribution is $\mathcal{D}$. The handling of divergences is more complex since we need to detect them by scheduling some additional actions of C_P. Consider now a probabilistic execution H_1 of $M_1\|C\|T$ such that in $W(H_1)$ the probability of occurrence of each action w_β is $P_{\mathcal{D}}[C_\beta]$, and the probability of each action $w_{\beta\delta}$ is $P_{\mathcal{D}}[\{\beta\}]$. Such a probabilistic execution can be built because $\mathcal{D}$ is a trace distribution of $M_1\|C_P$ and because of our simplifying assumption.

From $M_1 \sqsubseteq_{MAY} M_2$, there is a probabilistic execution H_2 of $M_2\|C_P\|T$ such that $W(H_1) \leq W(H_2)$ (we use the test $C_P\|T$ here). Next, we observe that also in $W(H_2)$ the probability of each action w_β is $P_{\mathcal{D}}[C_\beta]$, and the probability of each $w_{\beta\delta}$ is $P_{\mathcal{D}}[\{\beta\}]$, since otherwise we would be able to find events of $\mathcal{F}_{H_2}$ with a probability greater than 1. Therefore, from the construction of T, $\mathcal{D}$ is a trace distribution of $M_2\|C_P$. □

Theorem 13. *If M_1 and M_2 are probabilistically convergent, then $M_1 \sqsubseteq_{MUST} M_2$ iff $M_2 \sqsubseteq_F M_1$.*

Proof sketch. Let $M_1 \sqsubseteq_{MUST} M_2$, and let $\mathcal{F}$ be a failure distribution of $M_2\|C_P$. Build a test T as follows. The states of T are the symbol δ, all pairs of the form (β, b) where $b \in \{0,1\}$ and β is a finite trace such that $P_{\mathcal{F}}[C_\beta] > 0$, all pairs of the form (β, F) and (β, F'), where $P_{\mathcal{F}}[\{(\beta, F)\}] > 0$, and all pairs of the form $(\beta, \emptyset)$ and $(\beta, \emptyset')$, where $P_{\mathcal{F}}[C_\beta] > 0$. In reality some of the pairs $(\beta, \emptyset')$ are not needed; we just include them to keep the construction simple.

For each state $(\beta, 0)$ there is a transition $(\beta, 0) \xrightarrow{w_\beta} (\beta, 1)$; for each state $(\beta a, 0)$ there is a transition $(\beta, 1) \xrightarrow{a} (\beta a, 0)$; for each state (β, F) there is a transition $(\beta, 1) \xrightarrow{w_{\beta F}} (\beta, F)$ and a transition $(\beta, F') \xrightarrow{w'_{\beta F}} \delta$; furthermore, for each $a \in F$, there is a transition $(\beta, F) \xrightarrow{a} (\beta, F')$; finally, for each state (β, F') and each prefix β' of β there is a transition $(\beta', 1) \xrightarrow{w_{\beta F}} (\beta, F')$.

Consider now a complete probabilistic execution H_2 of $M_2 \| C_P \| T$ such that in $W(H_2)$ the probability of each action w_β is $P_{\mathcal{F}}[C_\beta]$, the probability of each $w_{\beta F}$ is $P_{\mathcal{D}}[\{(\beta, F)\}]$, and the probability of each $w'_{\beta F}$ is 0. Such a probabilistic execution can be built because $\mathcal{F}$ is a failure distribution of $M_2 \| C_P$ and M_2 is probabilistically convergent.

From $M_1 \sqsubseteq_{MUST} M_2$, there is a complete probabilistic execution H_1 of $M_1 \| C_P \| T$ such that $W(H_1) \leq W(H_2)$ (we use the test $C_P \| T$). Observe that also in H_1 each action $w'_{\beta F}$ occurs with probability 0, which means that none of the transitions labeled with $w_{\beta F}$ are performed from states different from $(\beta, 1)$ (otherwise $w'_{\beta F}$ would be the only action enabled). Furthermore, from the completeness of H_1, since actions of the form $w_{\beta F}$ continue to be enabled unless one of them occurs, and since M_1 is probabilistically convergent, the probability in H_2 of actions of the form $w_{\beta F}$ plus infinite traces is 1. Thus, we use the probabilistic convergence of M_1 and M_2 to derive $W(H_1) = W(H_2)$, and consequently that $\mathcal{F}$ is a failure distribution of $M_1 \| C_P$.

Conversely, suppose that $M_2 \sqsubseteq_F M_1$, and let H_2 be a complete probabilistic execution of $M_2 \| T$. From $M_2 \sqsubseteq_F M_1$ there is a probabilistic execution H_1 of $M_1 \| T$ such that $W(H_1) = W(H_2)$ and such that all failures are with the set $ext(M_1 \| T)$. Therefore, H_1 is complete. □

From the proof sketches of Theorems 12 and 13 we understand the structure of the *canonical* tests for our preorders, i.e., the minimal tests that are sufficient to characterize the testing preorders. A canonical test for the may preorder is the principal context in parallel with a nondeterministic automaton that has a tree-like structure. In the test all the external actions are interleaved with success actions, and each finite trace β to be observed is marked by a special success action $w_{\beta\delta}$ that leads to a deadlock state. Essentially a test has the structure of a trace distribution, where each success action is used to detect the probability of a specific cone. In this sense our tests are similar to the tests of [3]. The success actions that are interleaved with the external actions are the main difference with respect to [3]; these actions are needed because our testing preorders are sensitive to infinite traces; In the following section we study preorders that are not sensitive to infinite traces, thus removing the interleaved success actions.

The canonical tests for the must preorder are very similar to the canonical tests for the may preorder. The main difference is that the actions that test for finite traces are replaced by gadgets that test for failures. Each gadget is based on two actions: the first success action is used to show that we are testing for a specific failure set F; the second success action becomes enabled only if some action from F occurs after the occurrence of the first success action. Informally, we regard a test as successful if the second success action occurs with probability 0. To make sure that some failure is tested before stopping, the canonical tests have several transitions labeled with the first kind of success actions that lead to states where only success actions of the second kind are enabled. Our canonical tests are similar to the canonical tests of [3]; the main difference is that here, since we must check for several failures, we use success actions also to signal that we are testing a specific failure.

5 Finite Trace and Failure Distributions

We now impose a restriction to trace distributions and failure distributions, namely, that for each trace or failure distribution there is a constant k such that all the probability is concentrated on traces or failures of length at most k. We call the corresponding trace and failure distributions *finite*, and we denote the corresponding precongruence relations by $\sqsubseteq_{Tf}$ and $\sqsubseteq_{Ff}$, respectively. In this case for each test T there must be a number k such that no execution of T contains more than k external actions. We denote the corresponding testing preorders by $\sqsubseteq_{MAYf}$ and $\sqsubseteq_{MUSTf}$.

The principal context characterization changes in this case, since the method of [13] to reduce the branching structure of a distinguishing context does not work any more. The new principal context is represented in Figure 3.

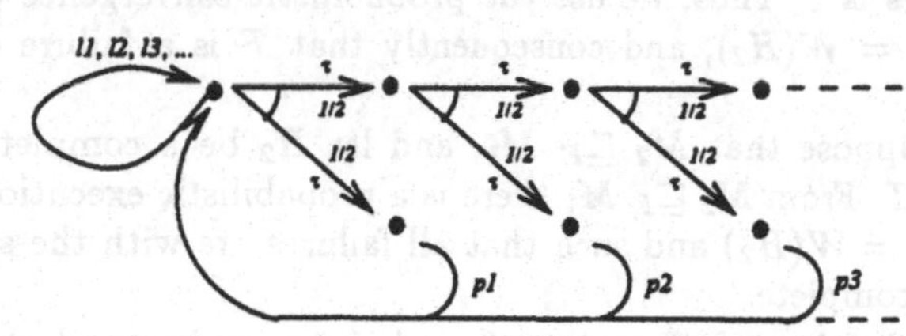

Fig. 3. The principal context for the finite preorders.

Theorem 14. *If M_1 and M_2 are probabilistically convergent, then $M_1 \sqsubseteq_{MAYf} M_2$ iff $M_1 \sqsubseteq_{Tf} M_2$.*

Proof sketch. $\sqsubseteq_{Tf}$ implies $\sqsubseteq_{MAYf}$ directly since the vector W is derived from the finite trace distributions of a probabilistic automaton in parallel with a finite test.

Conversely, let $M_1 \sqsubseteq_{MAYf} M_2$, and let $\mathcal{D}$ be a finite trace distribution of $M_1 \| C_{Pf}$. We build a test T as follows. The states of T are the symbol δ, and all finite traces β such that $P_{\mathcal{D}}[C_\beta] > 0$. For each state βa there is a transition $\beta \xrightarrow{a} \beta a$; for each state β such that $P_{\mathcal{D}}[\{\beta\}] > 0$ there is a transition $\beta \xrightarrow{w_{\beta\delta}} \delta$. The test T is guaranteed to be finite because $\mathcal{D}$ is a finite trace distribution. Then the conclusion is derived as in the proof of Theorem 12, where we do not need to deal with the interleaved success actions and where the probabilistic convergence of M_1 is used to rule out the case of a trace distribution that derives only from probabilistic executions that diverge with a non-zero probability. □

Theorem 15. *If M_1 and M_2 are probabilistically convergent, then $M_1 \sqsubseteq_{MUSTf} M_2$ iff $M_2 \sqsubseteq_{Ff} M_1$.*

Proof sketch. Let $M_1 \sqsubseteq_{MUSTf} M_2$, and let $\mathcal{F}$ be a finite failure distribution of $M_2 \| C_{Pf}$. We build a test T as follows. The states of T are the symbol δ, all finite traces β such that $P_{\mathcal{F}}[C_\beta] > 0$, all pairs of the form (β, F) and (β, F'), where $P_{\mathcal{F}}[\{(\beta, F)\}] > 0$, and all pairs of the form $(\beta, \emptyset)$ and $(\beta, \emptyset')$, where $P_{\mathcal{F}}[C_\beta] > 0$. For each state βa there is a transition $\beta \xrightarrow{a} \beta a$; for each state (β, F) there is a transition $\beta \xrightarrow{w_{\beta F}} (\beta, F)$ and a transition $(\beta, F') \xrightarrow{w_{\beta F'}} \delta$; furthermore, for each $a \in F$, there is a transition $(\beta, F) \xrightarrow{a} (\beta, F')$; finally, for each state (β, F') and each prefix β' of β there is a transition $\beta' \xrightarrow{w_{\beta F}} (\beta, F')$.

The test T is guaranteed to be finite because $\mathcal{F}$ is a finite failure distribution. Then the conclusion is derived as in the proof of Theorem 13, where we do not need to deal with the interleaved success actions.

Conversely, suppose that $M_2 \sqsubseteq_{Ff} M_1$, and let H_2 be a complete probabilistic execution of $M_2 \| T$. From $M_2 \sqsubseteq_{Ff} M_1$ there is a probabilistic execution H_1 of $M_1 \| T$ such that $W(H_1) = W(H_2)$ and such that all failures are with the set $ext(M_1 \| T)$. Therefore, H_1 is complete. □

The canonical tests for the finite testing preorders, beside the structure of the principal context, are essentially finite depth trees without interleaved success actions. These tests are very similar to the tests of [3]. A difference between our testing preorders and those of [3] is that our preorders are totally insensitive to infinite traces, while the must preorder of [3] is partially sensitive to infinite traces if a system is not finite branching.

6 Continuity and Finiteness of Tests

In this section we study sufficient conditions for finite trace and failure distributions to describe infinite failure and trace distributions as well. In the nondeterministic case strong convergence and finite branching are sufficient; here we show that the same holds in the probabilistic case. We describe also additional restrictions that allow us to consider only vectors with finitely many success actions, thus reducing our canonical tests to be really finite.

Before stating the first result, we need to say what we mean by finite branching. In a probabilistic automaton there are two kinds of nondeterminism: the *pure nondeterminism*, which is due to the choice between different transitions, and the *probabilistic nondeterminism*, which is due to the choice of a next state once a transition is chosen. By finite branching we mean that there are finitely many start states and from every state there are finitely many transitions enabled. We do not impose any restriction on the probability distributions associated with each transition.

Theorem 16. *Let M be a probabilistically convergent, finitely branching probabilistic automaton, and let $\mathcal{D}_1, \mathcal{D}_2, \ldots$ be a chain of finite trace distributions of M. Let $\mathcal{D}$ be $\lim_i \mathcal{D}_i$. Then $\mathcal{D}$ is a trace distribution of M.*

Proof sketch. Consider a collection of probabilistic executions $H_1, H_2, \ldots$, with the same start state s_0, such that, for each i, $tdistr(H_i) = \mathcal{D}_{f(i)}$, where f is a monotonic increasing function from naturals to naturals. Such collection of probabilistic executions exists since M has finitely many start states. Consider the set of probability distributions over states that describe what is reached after the first transition in the H_i's. From the finite branching structure of M, the set of distributions over states reachable from s_0 in one transition is compact under the distance $d(\mathcal{P}_1,\mathcal{P}_2) = \sum_{s\in\Omega_1\cup\Omega_2} |P_1[s] - P_2[s]|$. Thus, the distributions reached in the H_i's have at least one accumulation point.

We build the transition relation of a probabilistic execution H inductively as follows. For the first transition of H choose one of the accumulation points described above. For the ith level transitions, assume that the transitions at previous levels are defined. For each $\epsilon > 0$, let $\mathcal{H}_\epsilon$ be the set of probabilistic executions H' that at the first $i-1$ levels are within distance ϵ of the probabilities of the states in H. Each $\mathcal{H}_\epsilon$ is not empty. For each $k \geq 0$, let H'_k be an element of $\mathcal{H}_{1/k}$. Then, from the finite branching structure of M, the first i-level distributions of the H'_is have an accumulation point that at the first $i-1$ levels coincides with the distributions of the states of H. Choose such point for the i-level distribution of H.

Let $\mathcal{D}_H$ denote $tdistr(H)$. We need to show that $\mathcal{D}_H = \mathcal{D}$. To do this we show that for each finite trace β and each $\epsilon > 0$ there is an i such that for each $j \geq i$, $|P_H[C_\beta] - P_{H_j}[C_\beta]| \leq \epsilon$.

First we observe that, from probabilistic convergence, for each fixed length l and for each $\epsilon > 0$ there is a constant $k_{l,\epsilon}$ such that in all probabilistic executions of M the set of executions that at length at least $k_{l,\epsilon}$ have less than l external actions has probability at most ϵ. Thus, we derive that there is a depth k such that in every probabilistic execution of M the probability of β truncated at depth k is within $\epsilon/3$ of its real value. From the construction of H, there are infinitely many H_i's such that the probability of β truncated at level k in H and H_i differ at most by $\epsilon/3$. Thus, there is a minimum number l such that, for $i \geq l$, the probability of β in H and H_i differ at most by ϵ. □

Theorem 17. *Let M be a probabilistically convergent, finitely branching probabilistic automaton, and let $\mathcal{F}_1, \mathcal{F}_2, \ldots$ be a chain of finite failure distributions of M. Let $\mathcal{F}$ be $\lim_i \mathcal{F}_i$. Then $\mathcal{F}$ is a failure distribution of M.*

Proof sketch. Same idea as in Theorem 16 where we extend probabilistic executions with failure sets as well. □

With the results above we derive that in the strongly convergent and finite branching case, finite trace and failure distributions give the same information as general trace and failure distributions. Thus, the general and finite testing preorders coincide.

We conclude this section by stating sufficient conditions for the tests to have only finitely many success actions. Since the success actions are used to study the relative probabilities of different traces, we need to make sure that every finite trace distribution contains finitely many traces with a non-zero probability. This is guaranteed by strong convergence (not by probabilistic convergence) and by the requirement that every transition leads to probability distributions over finitely many states.

7 Concluding Remarks

We have defined a theory of testing for probabilistic automata and we have characterized our testing preorders in terms of trace and failure distributions, which are a probabilistic generalization of the traces and failures of ordinary, nondeterministic, automata. The main idea behind the new theory of testing is that a test is equipped with at most countably many success actions rather than a single action as in [3].

We have defined finite versions of the testing preorders that generalize the testing preorders of [3], and we have characterized the new preorders in terms of finite trace and failure distributions. We have shown that for finite branching and probabilistically convergent systems the finite and general testing preorders coincide. Finally we have given sufficient conditions for distinguishing processes by means of tests with finitely many success actions.

Although we have shown that there is a natural extension of the theory of testing to probabilistic automata and that the characterization in terms of traces and failures extend as well, the underlying theory is not as simple as in the non probabilistic case. In particular we do not know an explicit definition of parallel composition of the trace and failure distribution sets. Studying such definitions would be helpful in understanding better the theory.

References

1. S. Aggarwal. Time optimal self-stabilizing spanning tree algorithms. Technical Report MIT/LCS/TR-632, MIT Laboratory for Computer Science, 1994. Master's thesis.
2. S.D. Brookes, C.A.R. Hoare, and A.W. Roscoe. A theory of communicating sequential processes. *Journal of the ACM*, 31(3):560–599, 1984.
3. R. De Nicola and M. Hennessy. Testing equivalences for processes. *Theoretical Computer Science*, 34:83–133, 1984.
4. H. Hansson. *Time and Probability in Formal Design of Distributed Systems*, volume 1 of *Real-Time Safety Critical Systems*. Elsevier, 1994.
5. M. Hennessy. *Algebraic Theory of Processes*. MIT Press, Cambridge, MA, 1988.
6. C.A.R. Hoare. *Communicating Sequential Processes*. Prentice-Hall International, Englewood Cliffs, 1985.
7. B. Jonsson, C. Ho-Stuart, and W. Yi. Testing and refinement for nondeterministic and probabilistic processes. In *Proceedings of the Symposium on Formal Techniques in Real-Time and Fault-Tolerant Systems*, LNCS 863, pages 418–430, 1994.
8. B. Jonsson and W. Yi. Compositional testing preorders for probabilistic processes. In *Proceedings 10th Annual Symposium on Logic in Computer Science*, San Diego, California. IEEE Computer Society Press, 1995.
9. N.A. Lynch, I. Saias, and R. Segala. Proving time bounds for randomized distributed algorithms. In *Proceedings of the 13th Annual ACM Symposium on Principles of Distributed Computing*, Los Angeles, CA, pages 314–323, 1994.
10. G.D. Plotkin. A structural approach to operational semantics. Technical Report DAIMI FN-19, Computer science Department, Aarhus University, 1981.
11. A. Pogosyants and R. Segala. Formal verification of timed properties of randomized distributed algorithms. In *Proceedings of the 14th Annual ACM Symposium on Principles of Distributed Computing*, Ottawa, Ontario, Canada, pages 174–183, August 1995.
12. R. Segala. A compositional trace-based semantics for probabilistic automata. In *Proceedings of CONCUR 95*, Philadelphia, PA, USA, LNCS 962, pages 234–248, 1995.
13. R. Segala. *Modeling and Verification of Randomized Distributed Real-Time Systems*. PhD thesis, MIT, Dept. of Electrical Engineering and Computer Science, 1995.
14. R. Segala and N.A. Lynch. Probabilistic simulations for probabilistic processes. *Nordic Journal of Computing*, 2(2):250–273, 1995.

Extended Markovian Process Algebra *

Marco Bernardo and Roberto Gorrieri

Università di Bologna, Dipartimento di Scienze dell'Informazione
Mura Anteo Zamboni 7, 40127 Bologna, Italy
E-mail: {bernardo, gorrieri}@cs.unibo.it

Abstract. EMPA enhances the expressiveness of classical process algebras by integrating functional and performance descriptions of concurrent systems. This is achieved by offering, besides passive actions (useful for pure nondeterminism), actions whose duration is exponentially distributed as well as immediate actions (useful for performance abstraction), parametrized by priority levels (hence prioritized choices) and weights (hence probabilistic choices). In order to analyze an EMPA term, from its integrated semantic model (a transition system labeled on both action types and action durations) we derive a functional semantic model (a transition system labeled on action types only) and a performance semantic model (a Markov chain). We show that an integrated analysis, i.e. a notion of equivalence on the integrated semantic model, is not only convenient but also necessary to achieve compositionality.

1 Introduction

The need of integrating the performance modeling and analysis of a concurrent system into the design process of the system itself has been widely recognized (see, e.g., [20, 6]). Unfortunately, it often happens that a system is first fully designed and tested for functionality, and afterwards tested for efficiency. The major drawback is that, whenever the performance is detected to be poor, the system has to be designed again, thereby negatively affecting both the design costs and the delivery at a fixed deadline. Another relevant drawback is that tests for functionality and performance are carried out on two different models of the system, so one has to make sure that these two models are consistent, i.e. they really describe (different aspects of) the same system.

In the last two decades a remarkable effort has been made in order to make existing formal description techniques suitable to support performance modeling and analysis by introducing the concept of time. One of the most mature fields where functional and performance aspects of concurrent systems are both considered is that of generalized stochastic Petri nets (GSPNs) [1], where a zero or exponentially distributed firing delay is associated with each net transition. Functional and performance analyses are carried out separately on two different projected models (a classical Petri net and a Markov chain) obtained from the same integrated model (the GSPN), so we are guaranteed that the projected

* This research has been partially funded by MURST, CNR and LOMAPS n. 8130.

models are consistent. However two problems have to be addressed: (*i*) lack of compositionality, and (*ii*) inability to perform an analysis directly on the integrated model, which can be much more efficient as there is no need of building projected models.

In order to solve the two problems above, in this paper we propose the adoption of a stochastic process algebra that extends the expressiveness of classical process algebras by representing each action as a pair composed of a type and a duration. Such a stochastic process algebra (*i*) naturally supplies compositionality, and (*ii*) allows functional and performance analyses to be carried out both on two consistent projected semantic models (a transition system labeled only on the type of the actions, and a Markov chain) and directly on the integrated semantic model (a transition system labeled on both the type and the duration of the actions) thanks to a suitable integrated equivalence.

The stochastic process algebra is called *Extended Markovian Process Algebra (EMPA)* [3]. Its name stems from the fact that action durations are mainly expressed by means of exponentially distributed random variables (hence Markovian), but it is also possible to express actions having duration zero as well as actions whose duration is unspecified (hence Extended). The restriction to exponentially distributed durations simplifies the performance evaluation, as the performance models are Markov chains. Also, such a restriction affects the semantic treatment, because the memoryless property of the exponential distribution allows us to define an integrated semantics for EMPA through the interleaving approach. For instance, given an action a whose duration is exponentially distributed with rate λ, and an action b whose duration is exponentially distributed with rate μ, consider term $E_1 \equiv <a,\lambda>.<b,\mu>.\underline{0} + <b,\mu>.<a,\lambda>.\underline{0}$ that executes either a followed by b or b followed by a, and term $E_2 \equiv <a,\lambda>.\underline{0} \,\|_{\emptyset}\, <b,\mu>.\underline{0}$ that executes a in parallel with b. Their integrated semantic models are isomorphic:

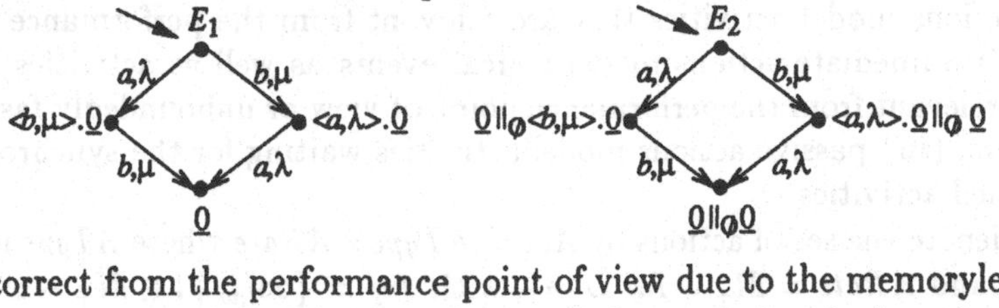

This is correct from the performance point of view due to the memoryless property of the exponential distribution: if E_2 completes a before b, then the residual time to the completion of b is still exponentially distributed with rate μ, so the rate labeling the transition from state $\underline{0} \,\|_{\emptyset}\, <b,\mu>.\underline{0}$ to state $\underline{0} \,\|_{\emptyset}\, \underline{0}$ is μ itself instead of μ conditional on λ.

The paper is organized as follows. In Sect. 2 we introduce EMPA by giving the syntax of terms and the meaning of operators. In Sect. 3 we define the integrated operational interleaving semantics, the functional semantics and the performance semantics. In Sect. 4 we introduce a notion of integrated equivalence in the bisimulation style and we show that it is a congruence: this will prove that the analysis carried out on the integrated semantic model is not only convenient but even necessary for compositionality purposes. In Sect. 5 we present an example showing the expressiveness of EMPA. Finally, in Sect. 6 we report some concluding remarks. [2]

2 Syntax and Informal Semantics

2.1 Actions: Types and Rates

Each action is a pair "$<a, \tilde{\lambda}>$" consisting of the *type* of the action and the *rate* of the action. The rate indicates the speed at which the action occurs from the point of view of an external observer: the rate is used as a concise way to denote the random variable specifying the duration of the action. Depending on the type, like in classical process algebras, actions are divided into *external* and *internal*: as usual, we denote by τ the only internal action type we use. Depending on the rate, actions are divided into:

- *Active actions*, i.e. actions whose rate is fixed, in turn divided into:
  - *Exponentially timed actions*, i.e. actions whose rate λ is a positive real number. Such a number is interpreted as the parameter of the exponential distribution specifying the duration of the action.
  - *Immediate actions*, i.e. actions whose rate $\infty_{l,w}$ is infinite. Such actions have duration zero, and each of them is given a priority level $l \in \mathbb{N}_+$ and a weight $w \in \mathbb{R}_+$.
- *Passive actions*, i.e. actions whose rate (denoted by $*$) is undefined. The duration of a passive action is fixed only by synchronizing it with an active action of the same type.

The classification of actions based on their rates implies that: (*i*) exponentially timed actions model activities that are relevant from the performance point of view, (*ii*) immediate actions model logical events as well as activities that are either irrelevant from the performance point of view or unboundedly faster than the others, (*iii*) passive actions model activities waiting for the synchronization with timed activities.

We denote the set of actions by $Act = AType \times ARate$ where $AType$ is the set of types and $ARate = \mathbb{R}_+ \cup Inf \cup \{*\}$, with $Inf = \{\infty_{l,w} \mid l \in \mathbb{N}_+ \wedge w \in \mathbb{R}_+\}$, is the set of rates. We use $a, b, c, \ldots$ as metavariables for $AType$, $\tilde{\lambda}, \tilde{\mu}, \tilde{\gamma}, \ldots$ for $ARate$, and $\lambda, \mu, \gamma, \ldots$ for $\mathbb{R}_+$.

2.2 Syntax of Terms and Informal Semantics of Operators

Let $Const$ be a set of *constants*, ranged over by $A, B, C, \ldots$, and let $Relab = \{\varphi : AType \longrightarrow AType \mid \varphi(\tau) = \tau \wedge \varphi(AType - \{\tau\}) \subseteq AType - \{\tau\}\}$ be a set of *relabeling functions*.

[2] Due to lack of space, the reader is referred to [3] for an extensive presentation of EMPA as well as proofs of results.

Definition 1. The set $\mathcal{L}$ of *process terms* is generated by the following syntax

$$E ::= \underline{0} \mid <a, \tilde{\lambda}>.E \mid E/L \mid E\backslash H \mid E[\varphi] \mid E + E \mid E \|_S E \mid A$$

where $L, S \subseteq AType - \{\tau\}$ and $H \subseteq AType$. The set $\mathcal{L}$ will be ranged over by $E, F, G, \ldots$. We denote by $\mathcal{G}$ the set of closed and guarded terms of $\mathcal{L}$. ■

In the rest of the section we informally explain the semantics of the operators: the formal semantics will be presented in Sect. 3. Since the *null term* "$\underline{0}$", the *prefix operator* "$<a, \tilde{\lambda}>.\_$", the *functional abstraction operator* "$\_/L$" (the hiding operator of CSP [11]), the *functional relabeling operator* "$\_[\varphi]$", and the *alternative composition operator* "$\_+\_$" are typical of classical process algebras, we concentrate on the two remaining operators.

The *temporal restriction operator* "$\_\backslash H$" prevents the execution of passive actions whose type is in H. Based on this operator, we define the notion of *temporal closure*: a term is temporally closed if it cannot execute passive actions. Thus, the temporal closure property singles out terms that are completely specified from the performance viewpoint.

The *parallel composition operator* "$\_ \|_S \_$" is based on two synchronization disciplines. The synchronization discipline on action types is the same as that of CSP [11]. The synchronization discipline on action rates states that action $<a, \tilde{\lambda}>$ can be synchronized with action $<a, \tilde{\mu}>$ if and only if $\min(\tilde{\lambda}, \tilde{\mu}) = *$, [3] and the rate of the resulting action is given by $\max(\tilde{\lambda}, \tilde{\mu})$ up to normalization (see Sect. 3). In other words, in a synchronization at most one active action can be involved and its rate determines the rate of the resulting action, up to normalization. This choice leads to an intuitive treatment of the synchronization discipline on action rates, as it is based on the client-server paradigm.

2.3 Race Policy

Since several active actions may be simultaneously executable, we need a mechanism for choosing the action to be executed. Like in [1, 8, 10], we adopt the *race policy*: the action sampling the least duration succeeds.

If we consider a state enabling only exponentially timed actions, the race policy establishes that (*i*) the random variable describing the *sojorn time* in that state is the minimum of the exponentially distributed random variables describing the duration of the enabled actions, and (*ii*) the *execution probability* of each enabled action is determined as well by the exponentially distributed random variables describing the duration of the enabled actions. In order to compute the two quantities above, we exploit the property that the minimum of n independent exponentially distributed random variables is an exponentially distributed random variable whose rate is the sum of the n original rates. As a consequence, if n exponentially timed actions $<a_1, \lambda_1>, <a_2, \lambda_2>, \ldots, <a_n, \lambda_n>$ are enabled, then the sojorn time is exponentially distributed with rate $\lambda = \sum_{i=1}^{n} \lambda_i$ and the execution probability of $<a_k, \lambda_k>$, $1 \leq k \leq n$, is given by λ_k / λ.

If we consider instead a state enabling both exponentially timed and immediate actions, the race policy establishes that (*i*) the exponentially timed actions

[3] We assume that $* < \lambda < \infty_{l,w}$ for all $\lambda \in \mathbb{R}_+$ and $\infty_{l,w} \in Inf$.

cannot be executed at all because they cannot sample zero durations, and (*ii*) the sojorn time in that state is zero. Only the enabled immediate actions having the highest priority level are actually executable, and the choice among them is probabilistically made by giving each of them an execution probability proportional to its weight. As a consequence, if n immediate actions $<a_1, \infty_{l,w_1}>$, $<a_2, \infty_{l,w_2}>$, $\ldots$, $<a_n, \infty_{l,w_n}>$ are enabled and no immediate action with higher priority level is enabled, then the execution probability of $<a_k, \infty_{l,w_k}>$, $1 \leq k \leq n$, is given by w_k/w where $w = \sum_{i=1}^{n} w_i$. [4]

Concerning the alternative composition operator, we realize that in its simpler form it expresses a choice between two active actions whose nature is:

- *Prioritized* if the two active actions have different priority levels. The choice is solved *implicitly* if it concerns an exponentially timed action and an immediate action (because the choice is implicitly determined by the race policy), *explicitly* if it concerns two immediate actions having different priority levels (because the priority levels explicitly determine the choice).
- *Probabilistic* if the two active actions have the same priority level. The choice is solved *implicitly* if it concerns two exponentially timed actions (because their execution probabilities are implicitly determined by their durations due to the race policy), *explicitly* if it concerns two immediate actions having the same priority level (because their execution probabilities are explicitly determined by their weights).

Now we turn our attention to passive actions, which cannot be undergone to the race policy since their duration is unspecified. Passive actions that are not synchronized with active actions of the same type result in models that are not temporally closed. Nevertheless, these models could be useful: since passive actions can be safely viewed as actions of a classical process algebra, a choice between two passive actions has a *nondeterministic* nature.
If we consider instead passive actions that do engage in synchronizations, then their execution probability is assigned a value. Whenever n passive actions can be separately synchronized with the same active action, we assume that each of the synchronizations is assigned the same execution probability, given by the execution probability of the active action divided by n. For example, terms $<a, \lambda>.\underline{0} \|_{\{a\}} (<a, *>.\underline{0} + <a, *>.\underline{0})$ and $<a, \lambda>.\underline{0} \|_{\{a\}} (<a, *>.\underline{0} \|_{\emptyset} <a, *>.\underline{0})$ comprise two passive actions that can be separately synchronized with the same active action, and each of the two synchronizations is given probability 1/2.

3 Integrated, Functional and Performance Semantics

The main problem to tackle when defining the semantics for EMPA is that the actions executable by a given term may have different priority levels, and only those having the highest priority level are actually executable. Let us call *potential move* of a given term a pair composed of (*i*) an action executable by the

[4] w and λ above are called the *exit rate* of the corresponding state.

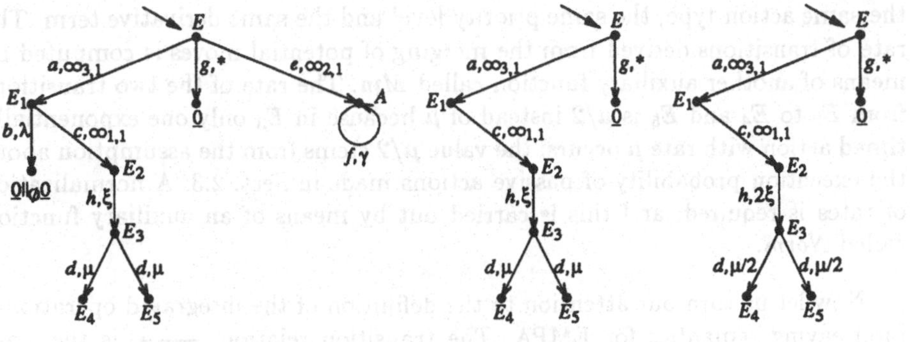

Fig. 1. Integrated interleaving model of term E

term, and (*ii*) a derivative term obtained by executing that action. To solve the problem above, we compute inductively all the potential moves of a given term regardless of priority levels, and then we select those having the highest priority level. This is motivated, in a stochastic framework, by the fact that the actual executability as well as the execution probability of an action depend upon all the actions that are executable at the same time when it is executable: only if we know all the potential moves of a given term, we can correctly determine its transitions and their rates. This is clarified by the following example.

Example 1. Consider term $E \equiv <a, \infty_{3,1}>.E_1 + <g, *>.\underline{0} + <e, \infty_{2,1}>.A$ where $E_1 \equiv <b, \lambda>.(\underline{0} \|_\emptyset \underline{0}) + <c, \infty_{1,1}>.E_2$, $E_2 \equiv <h, \xi>.E_3 + <h, \xi>.E_3$, $E_3 \equiv <d, \mu>.\underline{0} \|_{\{d\}} (<d, *>.\underline{0} \|_\emptyset <d, *>.\underline{0})$, $A \triangleq <f, \gamma>.A$. Suppose we apply to E standard rules for classical process algebras, thereby disregarding priority levels. Then we obtain the labeled transition system (LTS) in Fig. 1(a) where $E_4 \equiv \underline{0} \|_{\{d\}} (\underline{0} \|_\emptyset <d, *>.\underline{0})$ and $E_5 \equiv \underline{0} \|_{\{d\}} (<d, *>.\underline{0} \|_\emptyset \underline{0})$.

Now assume that priority levels are taken into account. Then lower priority transitions must be pruned, thus resulting in the LTS in Fig. 1(b): note that the passive transition has not been discarded. This is obtained by means of an auxiliary function called *Select*.

Finally, consider the rate of the transition from E_2 to E_3 and the rate of the two transitions from E_3 to E_4 and E_5. In the correct semantic model for E, such rates have to be like in Fig. 1(c). The rate of the transition from E_2 to E_3 is $2 \cdot \xi$ instead of ξ because in E_2 two exponentially timed actions with rate ξ occur and the race policy has been adopted. To achieve this, we keep track of the multiplicity [5] of potential moves, and then we construct transitions by using an auxiliary function called *Melt* that merges together those potential moves having

[5] We use "{|" and "|}" as brackets for multisets, "$\_ \oplus \_$" to denote multiset union, $\mathcal{M}u_{fin}(S)$ ($\mathcal{P}_{fin}(S)$) to denote the collection of finite multisets (sets) over set S, and $\pi_i(M)$ to denote the multiset obtained by projecting the tuples in multiset M on their i-th component.

the same action type, the same priority level and the same derivative term. The rate of transitions derived from the merging of potential moves is computed by means of another auxiliary function called *Min*. The rate of the two transitions from E_3 to E_4 and E_5 is $\mu/2$ instead of μ because in E_3 only one exponentially timed action with rate μ occurs: the value $\mu/2$ stems from the assumption about the execution probability of passive actions made in Sect. 2.3. A normalization of rates is required, and this is carried out by means of an auxiliary function called *Norm*. ■

Now let us turn our attention to the definition of the integrated operational interleaving semantics for EMPA. The transition relation $\longrightarrow$ is the least subset of $\mathcal{G} \times Act \times \mathcal{G}$ satisfying the inference rule reported in the first part of Table 1. This rule selects the potential moves having the highest priority level, and then merges together the remaining potential moves having the same action type, the same priority level and the same derivative term. The first operation is carried out through functions $Select : \mathcal{M}u_{fin}(Act \times \mathcal{G}) \longrightarrow \mathcal{M}u_{fin}(Act \times \mathcal{G})$ and $PL : Act \longrightarrow PLSet$, with $PLSet = \{-1\} \cup \mathbb{N}$, which are defined in the third part of Table 1. The second operation is carried out through function $Melt : \mathcal{M}u_{fin}(Act \times \mathcal{G}) \longrightarrow \mathcal{P}_{fin}(Act \times \mathcal{G})$ and partial function $Min : (ARate \times ARate) \multimap ARate$, which are defined in the fourth part of Table 1.

The multiset $PM(E)$ of potential moves of $E \in \mathcal{G}$ is defined by structural induction as the least element of $\mathcal{M}u_{fin}(Act \times \mathcal{G})$ satisfying the rules reported in the second part of Table 1. The normalization of the rates of potential moves resulting from the synchronization of the same active action with several independent or alternative passive actions is carried out through partial function $Norm : (AType \times ARate \times ARate \times \mathcal{M}u_{fin}(Act \times \mathcal{G}) \times \mathcal{M}u_{fin}(Act \times \mathcal{G})) \multimap ARate$ and function $Split : (ARate \times \mathbb{R}_{]0,1]}) \longrightarrow ARate$, which are defined in the fifth part of Table 1. Note that $Norm(a, \tilde{\lambda}, \tilde{\mu}, PM_1, PM_2)$ is defined if and only if $\min(\tilde{\lambda}, \tilde{\mu}) = *$, which is the condition on action rates we have required in Sect. 2.2 in order for a synchronization to be permitted.

Definition 2. The *integrated operational interleaving semantics* of $E \in \mathcal{G}$ is the LTS $\mathcal{I}[\![E]\!] = (\uparrow E, Act, \longrightarrow_E, E)$ where $\uparrow E$ is the set of states reachable from E, and $\longrightarrow_E$ is $\longrightarrow$ restricted to $\uparrow E \times Act \times \uparrow E$. ■

Definition 3. $E \in \mathcal{G}$ is *temporally closed* if and only if $\mathcal{I}[\![E]\!]$ is isomorphic to $\mathcal{I}[\![E \backslash AType]\!]$. We denote by $\mathcal{E}$ the set of temporally closed terms of $\mathcal{G}$. ■

Given a term $E \in \mathcal{G}$, its integrated operational interleaving semantics $\mathcal{I}[\![E]\!]$ fully represents the behavior of E because transitions are decorated by both the action type and the action rate. One can think of obtaining the *functional semantics* $\mathcal{F}[\![E]\!]$ and the *performance semantics* $\mathcal{P}[\![E]\!]$ of E from $\mathcal{I}[\![E]\!]$ by simply dropping action rates and action types, respectively. As a matter of fact, this is the case for the functional semantics.

Definition 4. The *functional semantics* of $E \in \mathcal{G}$ is the LTS $\mathcal{F}[\![E]\!] = (\uparrow E, AType, \longrightarrow_{E,\mathcal{F}}, E)$ where $\longrightarrow_{E,\mathcal{F}}$ is $\longrightarrow_E$ restricted to $\uparrow E \times AType \times \uparrow E$. ■

$$\frac{(\langle a, \tilde{\lambda}\rangle, E') \in Melt(Select(PM(E)))}{E \xrightarrow{a,\tilde{\lambda}} E'}$$

$$PM(\underline{0}) = \emptyset$$

$$PM(\langle a, \tilde{\lambda}\rangle.E) = \{\!|\, (\langle a, \tilde{\lambda}\rangle, E) \,|\!\}$$

$$\begin{aligned} PM(E/L) = {} & \{\!|\, (\langle a, \tilde{\lambda}\rangle, E'/L) \mid (\langle a, \tilde{\lambda}\rangle, E') \in PM(E) \wedge a \notin L \,|\!\} \oplus \\ & \{\!|\, (\langle \tau, \tilde{\lambda}\rangle, E'/L) \mid (\langle a, \tilde{\lambda}\rangle, E') \in PM(E) \wedge a \in L \,|\!\} \end{aligned}$$

$$PM(E \backslash H) = \{\!|\, (\langle a, \tilde{\lambda}\rangle, E' \backslash H) \mid (\langle a, \tilde{\lambda}\rangle, E') \in PM(E) \wedge \neg(a \in H \wedge \tilde{\lambda} = *) \,|\!\}$$

$$PM(E[\varphi]) = \{\!|\, (\langle \varphi(a), \tilde{\lambda}\rangle, E'[\varphi]) \mid (\langle a, \tilde{\lambda}\rangle, E') \in PM(E) \,|\!\}$$

$$PM(E_1 + E_2) = PM(E_1) \oplus PM(E_2)$$

$$\begin{aligned} PM(E_1 \|_S E_2) = {} & \{\!|\, (\langle a, \tilde{\lambda}\rangle, E_1' \|_S E_2) \mid a \notin S \wedge (\langle a, \tilde{\lambda}\rangle, E_1') \in PM(E_1) \,|\!\} \oplus \\ & \{\!|\, (\langle a, \tilde{\lambda}\rangle, E_1 \|_S E_2') \mid a \notin S \wedge (\langle a, \tilde{\lambda}\rangle, E_2') \in PM(E_2) \,|\!\} \oplus \\ & \{\!|\, (\langle a, \tilde{\gamma}\rangle, E_1' \|_S E_2') \mid a \in S \wedge \\ & \qquad (\langle a, \tilde{\lambda}\rangle, E_1') \in PM(E_1) \wedge \\ & \qquad (\langle a, \tilde{\mu}\rangle, E_2') \in PM(E_2) \wedge \\ & \qquad \tilde{\gamma} = Norm(a, \tilde{\lambda}, \tilde{\mu}, PM(E_1), PM(E_2)) \,|\!\} \end{aligned}$$

$$PM(A) = PM(E) \quad \text{if } A \triangleq E$$

$$\begin{aligned} Select(PM) = \{\!|\, & (\langle a, \tilde{\lambda}\rangle, E) \in PM \mid PL(\langle a, \tilde{\lambda}\rangle) = -1 \vee \\ & \forall (\langle b, \tilde{\mu}\rangle, E') \in PM.\, PL(\langle a, \tilde{\lambda}\rangle) \geq PL(\langle b, \tilde{\mu}\rangle) \,|\!\} \end{aligned}$$

$$PL(\langle a, *\rangle) = -1 \qquad PL(\langle a, \lambda\rangle) = 0 \qquad PL(\langle a, \infty_{l,w}\rangle) = l$$

$$\begin{aligned} Melt(PM) = \{ & (\langle a, \tilde{\lambda}\rangle, E) \mid (\langle a, \tilde{\mu}\rangle, E) \in PM \wedge \\ & \tilde{\lambda} = Min \{\!|\, \tilde{\gamma} \mid (\langle a, \tilde{\gamma}\rangle, E) \in PM \wedge PL(\langle a, \tilde{\gamma}\rangle) = PL(\langle a, \tilde{\mu}\rangle) \,|\!\} \} \end{aligned}$$

$$* \; Min \; * = * \qquad \lambda \; Min \; \lambda' = \lambda + \lambda' \qquad \infty_{l,w} \; Min \; \infty_{l,w'} = \infty_{l,w+w'}$$

$$Norm(a, \tilde{\lambda}, \tilde{\mu}, PM_1, PM_2) = \begin{cases} Split(\tilde{\lambda}, 1/(\pi_1(PM_2))(\langle a, *\rangle)) & \text{if } \tilde{\mu} = * \\ Split(\tilde{\mu}, 1/(\pi_1(PM_1))(\langle a, *\rangle)) & \text{if } \tilde{\lambda} = * \end{cases}$$

$$Split(*, \alpha) = * \qquad Split(\lambda, \alpha) = \lambda \cdot \alpha \qquad Split(\infty_{l,w}, \alpha) = \infty_{l,w \cdot \alpha}$$

Table 1. Inductive rules for EMPA integrated interleaving semantics

The definition of the performance semantics requires instead a more careful treatment. Since in EMPA the durations of the actions are mainly expressed by exponentially distributed random variables, it is natural to associate with each term a homogeneous continuous-time Markov chain (HCTMC) [13] acting as a performance model. Since in a HCTMC neither passive transitions nor immediate transitions are allowed, we restrict ourselves to temporally closed terms and, given $E \in \mathcal{E}$, its performance semantics $\mathcal{P}[\![E]\!]$, hereafter called *Markovian semantics* and denoted by $\mathcal{M}[\![E]\!]$, is obtained from $\mathcal{I}[\![E]\!]$ by discarding action types and immediate transitions. Formally, $\mathcal{M}[\![E]\!]$ is represented as a variant of a LTS, called probabilistically rooted labeled transition system (PLTS), in which there is no initial state but a probability mass function that determines for each state the probability that it is the initial state. We report below the definition of PLTS together with a notion of equivalence in the style of [14] that will be used in the following.

Definition 5. A *probabilistically rooted labeled transition system (PLTS)* is a quadruple $(S, U, \longrightarrow, P)$ such that $S, U, \longrightarrow$ are defined as for a LTS, and the *initial state probability function* $P : S \longrightarrow \mathbb{R}_{[0,1]}$ satisfies $\sum_{s \in S} P(s) = 1$. ■

Definition 6. Let $Z_i = (S_i, \mathbb{R}_+ \cup Inf, \longrightarrow_i, P_i)$, $i \in \{1, 2\}$, be two PLTSs. We say that Z_1 is *p-bisimilar* to Z_2 if and only if there exists an equivalence relation $\mathcal{B} \subseteq (S_1 \cup S_2) \times (S_1 \cup S_2)$ such that:

- for each $C \in (S_1 \cup S_2)/\mathcal{B}$ it turns out $\sum_{s \in C \cap S_1} P_1(s) = \sum_{s \in C \cap S_2} P_2(s)$;
- whenever $(s_1, s_2) \in \mathcal{B} \cap (S_1 \times S_2)$, then for each $C \in (S_1 \cup S_2)/\mathcal{B}$ it turns out $Min\{\!|\, \tilde{\lambda} \mid s_1 \xrightarrow{\tilde{\lambda}}_1 s_1' \wedge s_1' \in C \cap S_1 \,|\!\} = Min\{\!|\, \tilde{\lambda} \mid s_2 \xrightarrow{\tilde{\lambda}}_2 s_2' \wedge s_2' \in C \cap S_2 \,|\!\}$. ■

The algorithm to transform $\mathcal{I}[\![E]\!]$ into $\mathcal{M}[\![E]\!]$ is organized in two phases.

1. The first phase drops action types and eliminates all the immediate transitions occurring in $\mathcal{I}[\![E]\!]$. The removal of the immediate transitions and the related states is justified from a stochastic point of view by the fact that the sojorn time in these states is zero.
2. The second phase aggregates states in order to reduce the HCTMC obtained at the end of the previous phase. The aggregation is based on the notion of ordinary lumping [12]: the state space is partitioned in such a way that the rates labeling the transitions from any two states lying in the same class to any class of the partition sum up to the same value.

Due to lack of space, we only show an application of such an algorithm.

Example 2. Consider $E \equiv \langle a, \lambda \rangle.E_1$ where $E_1 \equiv \langle b, \infty_{1,2} \rangle.A + \langle c, \infty_{1,1} \rangle.B$, $A \stackrel{\Delta}{=} \langle e, \mu \rangle.B$, $B \stackrel{\Delta}{=} \langle f, \mu \rangle.A$. The LTS $\mathcal{I}[\![E]\!]$ is reported in Fig. 2(a). To obtain the Markovian semantics of E, we have to eliminate state E_1 together with its immediate transitions. This is carried out by splitting the exponentially timed transition from E to E_1 into two exponentially timed transitions from E to A

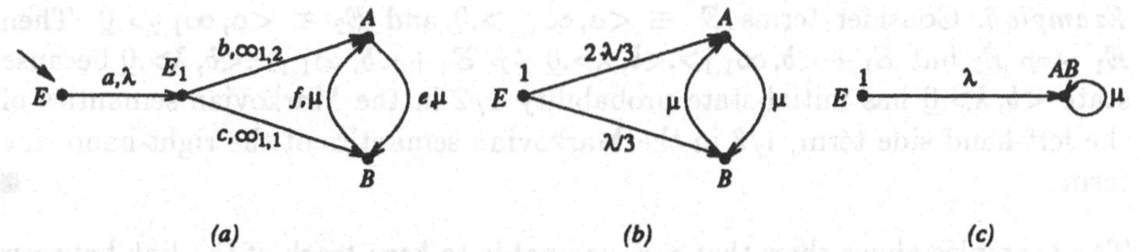

Fig. 2. Markovian model of term E

and B whose rates are $2 \cdot \lambda/3$ and $\lambda/3$, respectively: factors 2/3 and 1/3 are the execution probabilities of the two immediate transitions. The resulting PLTS is reported in Fig. 2(*b*).

Afterwards, we discover that states A and B have the same rate to each of the other states, so they can be ordinarily lumped together. The resulting PLTS is reported in Fig. 2(*c*). Note that the two exponentially timed transitions from E to A and B have been merged into a single transition from E to AB whose rate is the sum of the rates of the two transitions, while the transition from A to B and the transition from B to A have just been merged into a single one from AB to itself. ■

4 Extended Markovian Bisimulation Equivalence

Following the bisimulation style, it is straightforward to define two projected notions of equivalence based on the two projected semantic models.

Definition 7. Let $E_1, E_2 \in \mathcal{G}$. We say that E_1 is *functionally equivalent* to E_2, written $E_1 \sim_F E_2$, if and only if $\mathcal{F}[\![E_1]\!]$ is bisimilar to $\mathcal{F}[\![E_2]\!]$. ■

Definition 8. Let $E_1, E_2 \in \mathcal{E}$. We say that E_1 is *performance equivalent* to E_2, written $E_1 \sim_P E_2$, if and only if $\mathcal{M}[\![E_1]\!]$ is p-bisimilar to $\mathcal{M}[\![E_2]\!]$. ■

A natural candidate notion of equivalence for EMPA may be $\sim_{FP} = \sim_F \cap \sim_P$. However, the examples below show that $\sim_{FP}$ is not a congruence.

Example 3. Consider terms $E_1 \equiv <a, \lambda>.\underline{0} + <b, \mu>.\underline{0}$ and $E_2 \equiv <a, \mu>.\underline{0} + <b, \lambda>.\underline{0}$. Then $E_1 \sim_{FP} E_2$ but $E_1 \|_{\{b\}} \underline{0} \not\sim_P E_2 \|_{\{b\}} \underline{0}$ because the left-hand side term has exit rate λ while the right-hand side term has exit rate μ. Note that the action with type a of E_1 has execution probability $\lambda/(\lambda+\mu)$, while the action with type a of E_2 has execution probability $\mu/(\lambda+\mu)$, and this is not detected by $\sim_{FP}$. ■

Example 4. Consider terms $E_1 \equiv <a, \infty_{1,1}>.\underline{0}$ and $E_2 \equiv <a, \infty_{2,1}>.\underline{0}$. Then $E_1 \sim_{FP} E_2$ but $E_1 + <b, \infty_{1,1}>.\underline{0} \not\sim_F E_2 + <b, \infty_{1,1}>.\underline{0}$ because the left-hand side term can execute an action with type b while the right-hand side term cannot. ■

Example 5. Consider terms $E_1 \equiv <a, \infty_{1,1}>.\underline{0}$ and $E_2 \equiv <a, \infty_{1,2}>.\underline{0}$. Then $E_1 \sim_{FP} E_2$ but $E_1 + <b, \infty_{1,1}>.<b, \lambda>.\underline{0} \not\sim_P E_2 + <b, \infty_{1,1}>.<b, \lambda>.\underline{0}$ because state $<b, \lambda>.\underline{0}$ has initial state probability 1/2 in the Markovian semantics of the left-hand side term, 1/3 in the Markovian semantics of the right-hand side term. ■

The examples above show that $\sim_{FP}$ is unable to keep track of the link between the functional part and the performance part of the actions. This means that to achieve compositionality, it is ***necessary*** to define an equivalence based on the integrated semantic model. Incidentally, this is even ***convenient*** with respect to $\sim_{FP}$, since it avoids the need of building the two projected semantic models and checking them for bisimilarity and p-bisimilarity, respectively.

In order to define an integrated equivalence $\sim_I$ for EMPA in the bisimulation style, we can follow the guideline below:

- Active actions should be treated by following the notion of ***probabilistic bisimulation*** [14], which consists of requiring a bisimulation to be an equivalence relation such that two bisimilar terms have the same aggregated probability to reach the same equivalence class by executing actions of the same type and priority level.
  - For exponentially timed actions, the notion of probabilistic bisimulation must be refined by requiring additionally that two bisimilar terms have identically distributed sojorn times. For example, if we consider terms $E_1 \equiv <a, \lambda>.F + <a, \mu>.G$ and $E_2 \equiv <a, 2 \cdot \lambda>.F + <a, 2 \cdot \mu>.G$, then both transitions labeled with a, λ and $a, 2 \cdot \lambda$ have execution probability $\lambda/(\lambda + \mu)$, and both transitions labeled with a, μ and $a, 2 \cdot \mu$ have execution probability $\mu/(\lambda + \mu)$, but the average sojorn time of E_1 is twice the average sojorn time of E_2. Due to the race policy, requiring that two bisimilar terms have identically distributed sojorn times and the same aggregated probability to reach the same equivalence class by executing exponentially timed actions of the same type amounts to requiring that two bisimilar terms have the same aggregated rate to reach the same equivalence class by executing exponentially timed actions of the same type. For example, it must hold that
$$<a, \lambda>.F + <a, \mu>.F \sim_I <a, \lambda + \mu>.F$$
This coincides with the notion of ***Markovian bisimulation*** [9, 10, 4].
  - For immediate actions, the notion of probabilistic bisimulation must be restated in terms of weights. As a consequence, two bisimilar terms are required to have the same aggregated weight to reach the same equivalence class by executing immediate actions of the same type and priority level. For example, it must hold that
$$<a, \infty_{l,w_1}>.F + <a, \infty_{l,w_2}>.F \sim_I <a, \infty_{l,w_1+w_2}>.F$$
This coincides with the notion of ***direct bisimulation*** [19].
- Passive actions should be treated by following the classical notion of bisimulation [16]. Thus, bisimilar terms are required to have the same passive actions reaching the same equivalence class, regardless of the actual number

of these passive actions. For example, it must hold that

$$<a,*>.F + <a,*>.F \sim_I <a,*>.F$$

Concerning priority levels, it might seem useful to be able to write equations like

$$<a,\lambda>.E + <b,\infty_{l,w}>.F \sim_I <b,\infty_{l,w}>.F$$

$$<c,\infty_{l,w}>.E + <d,\infty_{l',w'}>.F \sim_I <d,\infty_{l',w'}>.F \quad \text{if } l' > l$$

The problem is that the applicability of such equations depends on the context: e.g., terms $(<a,\lambda>.E + <b,\infty_{l,w}>.F) \|_{\{b\}} \underline{0}$ and $(<b,\infty_{l,w}>.F) \|_{\{b\}} \underline{0}$ are not equivalent at all. To solve the problem, we follow the proposal of [2] by introducing a ***priority interpretation operator*** Θ, and considering the language $\mathcal{L}_\Theta$ generated by the following syntax

$$E ::= \underline{0} \mid <a,\tilde{\lambda}>.E \mid E/L \mid E\backslash H \mid E[\varphi] \mid \Theta(E) \mid E + E \mid E \|_S E \mid A$$

whose semantic rules are those reported in Table 1 except that the rule in the first part is replaced by

$$\frac{(<a,\tilde{\lambda}>, E') \in Melt(PM(E))}{E \xrightarrow{a,\tilde{\lambda}} E'}$$

and the following rule for Θ is introduced in the second part

$$PM(\Theta(E)) = Select(PM(E))$$

It is easily seen that EMPA coincides with the set of terms $\{\Theta(E) \mid E \in \mathcal{L}\}$.

To keep the definition of integrated equivalence as simple as possible, we formalize the key concept of *conditional exit rate* in a uniform way for all kinds of action through partial function $ERate : (\mathcal{G}_\Theta \times AType \times PLSet \times \mathcal{P}(\mathcal{G}_\Theta)) \twoheadrightarrow ARate$ defined by $ERate(E,a,l,C) = Min\{\!| \tilde{\lambda} \mid E \xrightarrow{a,\tilde{\lambda}} E' \wedge PL(<a,\tilde{\lambda}>) = l \wedge E' \in C |\!\}$.

Definition 9. An equivalence relation $\mathcal{B} \subseteq \mathcal{G}_\Theta \times \mathcal{G}_\Theta$ is a ***strong extended Markovian bisimulation (strong EMB)*** if and only if, whenever $(E_1, E_2) \in \mathcal{B}$, then for all $a \in AType$, $l \in PLSet$ and $C \in \mathcal{G}_\Theta/\mathcal{B}$ it turns out

$$ERate(E_1,a,l,C) = ERate(E_2,a,l,C)$$ ■

Since the union of all the strong EMBs is a strong EMB as well, we call such a relation the *strong extended Markovian bisimulation equivalence (strong EMBE)*, denoted by $\sim_{EMB}$.

Theorem 10. *$\sim_{EMB}$ is preserved by all the operators as well as by recursive definitions.* ■

Theorem 11. *In $\mathcal{E} \times \mathcal{E}$ it turns out that $\sim_{EMB} \subseteq \sim_{FP}$.* ■

The inclusion above is strict, as one can see by considering the examples below. Additionally, such examples show that $\sim_{EMB}$ cannot abstract from either priority levels or weights of immediate actions; otherwise, the congruence property would not hold.

Example 6. Consider terms E_1 and E_2 of Example 3. Then $E_1 \sim_{FP} E_2$ but $E_1 \not\sim_{EMB} E_2$ because $ERate(E_1,a,0,[\underline{0}]_{\sim_{EMB}}) \neq ERate(E_2,a,0,[\underline{0}]_{\sim_{EMB}})$. ■

Example 7. Consider terms E_1 and E_2 of Example 4. Then $E_1 \sim_{FP} E_2$ but $E_1 \not\sim_{EMB} E_2$ because $ERate(E_1, a, 1, [\underline{0}]_{\sim_{EMB}}) \neq ERate(E_2, a, 1, [\underline{0}]_{\sim_{EMB}})$. If we relax Definition 9 to abstract from the priority level of immediate actions, then $E_1 \sim_{EMB} E_2$ but this new strong EMBE would be closed under neither the alternative composition operator nor the parallel composition operator. For example, $E_1 + {<}b, \infty_{1,1}{>}.\underline{0} \not\sim_{EMB} E_2 + {<}b, \infty_{1,1}{>}.\underline{0}$ and $E_1 \,||_{\emptyset}\, {<}b, \infty_{1,1}{>}.\underline{0} \not\sim_{EMB} E_2 \,||_{\emptyset}\, {<}b, \infty_{1,1}{>}.\underline{0}$ because the left-hand side terms can execute an action with type b while the right-hand side terms cannot. ■

Example 8. Consider terms E_1 and E_2 of Example 5. Then $E_1 \sim_{FP} E_2$ but $E_1 \not\sim_{EMB} E_2$ because $ERate(E_1, a, 1, [\underline{0}]_{\sim_{EMB}}) \neq ERate(E_2, a, 1, [\underline{0}]_{\sim_{EMB}})$. If we relax Definition 9 to consider execution probabilities instead of weights for immediate actions (see the notion of *relative bisimulation* proposed in [19]), then $E_1 \sim_{EMB} E_2$ but this new strong EMBE would be closed under neither the alternative composition operator nor the parallel composition operator. For example, $E_1 + {<}b, \infty_{1,1}{>}.\underline{0} \not\sim_{EMB} E_2 + {<}b, \infty_{1,1}{>}.\underline{0}$ and $E_1 \,||_{\emptyset}\, {<}b, \infty_{1,1}{>}.\underline{0} \not\sim_{EMB} E_2 \,||_{\emptyset}\, {<}b, \infty_{1,1}{>}.\underline{0}$ because the left-hand side terms can execute actions having type a with probability 1/2 while the right-hand side terms can execute actions having type a with probability 2/3. ■

As a matter of fact, it turns out that $\sim_{EMB}$, restricted to the set $\mathcal{E}_{-\tau\infty}$ of terms in $\mathcal{E}$ whose integrated semantic model has no immediate internal transitions, is the coarsest congruence contained in $\sim_{FP}$.

Theorem 12. *Let $E_1, E_2 \in \mathcal{E}_{-\tau\infty}$. Then $E_1 \sim_{EMB} E_2$ if and only if, for all $F \in \mathcal{G}$ and $S \subseteq AType - \{\tau\}$ such that $E_1 + F$, $E_2 + F$, $E_1 \,||_S\, F$, $E_2 \,||_S\, F \in \mathcal{E}_{-\tau\infty}$, it turns out $E_1 + F \sim_{FP} E_2 + F$ and $E_1 \,||_S\, F \sim_{FP} E_2 \,||_S\, F$.* ■

Example 9. Consider terms $E_1 \equiv {<}a, \infty_{1,1}{>}.A$ and $E_2 \equiv {<}a, \infty_{1,1}{>}.B$ where $A \equiv {<}\tau, \infty_{1,1}{>}.A$ and $B \equiv {<}\tau, \infty_{1,2}{>}.B$. Then $E_1 \not\sim_{EMB} E_2$ but there does not exist any context based on the alternative composition operator or the parallel composition operator that distinguishes E_1 and E_2 with respect to $\sim_{FP}$. ■

5 An Example: Dining Philosophers Problem

Suppose we are given n philosophers P_i $(0 \leq i \leq n-1)$ sat at a round table each with a plate in front of him, and n chopsticks C_i $(0 \leq i \leq n-1)$ each shared by two neighbor philosophers and used to get the rice at the center of the table. Let us denote by "$\_ +_n \_$" the sum modulo n, and let $think_i$ be the action type "P_i is thinking", pu_i $(pu_{i+_n 1})$ be "P_i picks up C_i $(C_{i+_n 1})$", eat_i be "P_i is eating", and pd_i $(pd_{i+_n 1})$ be "P_i puts down C_i $(C_{i+_n 1})$". The scenario can be described as follows:

- $DP_n \equiv (P_0 \,||_{\emptyset} \ldots ||_{\emptyset}\, P_{n-1}) \,||_{\{pu_i, pd_i | 0 \leq i \leq n-1\}}\, (C_0 \,||_{\emptyset} \ldots ||_{\emptyset}\, C_{n-1})$
  - $P_i \stackrel{\Delta}{=} {<}think_i, *{>}.({<}pu_i, *{>}.{<}pu_{i+_n 1}, *{>}.P'_i + {<}pu_{i+_n 1}, *{>}.{<}pu_i, *{>}.P'_i)$
    $P'_i \stackrel{\Delta}{=} {<}eat_i, *{>}.{<}pd_i, *{>}.{<}pd_{i+_n 1}, *{>}.P_i$
  - $C_i \stackrel{\Delta}{=} {<}pu_i, *{>}.{<}pd_i, *{>}.C_i$

Since all the actions are passive, the system is purely nondeterministic: this is exactly the same description we would obtain with classical process algebras, so EMPA is a conservative extension of them.

As a naive solution to break the symmetry that may cause deadlock, we could introduce a precedence relation among philosophers by means of the priority levels of immediate actions, thus modifying the specification of P_i as follows:

$$P_i \triangleq <think_i, *>.<pu_i, \infty_{i+1,1}>.<pu_{i+_n 1}, \infty_{i+1,1}>.$$
$$<eat_i, *>.<pd_i, *>.<pd_{i+_n 1}, *>.P_i$$

To solve the problem in a more elegant and fair manner, we could use the randomized distributed algorithm of [15]: P_i flips a fair coin to choose between C_i and C_{i+1}, gets the chosen chopstick as soon as it becomes free, and gets the other chopstick if it is free, otherwise releases the chosen chopstick and flips the coin again. This algorithm can be easily described in EMPA through the weights of immediate actions by modifying the specification of P_i as follows:

$$P_i \triangleq <think_i, *>.P_i'$$
$$P_i' \triangleq <\tau, \infty_{1,1/2}>.<pu_i, *>.(<pu_{i+_n 1}, *>.P_i'' + <pd_i, *>.P_i')+$$
$$<\tau, \infty_{1,1/2}>.<pu_{i+_n 1}, *>.(<pu_i, *>.P_i'' + <pd_{i+_n 1}, *>.P_i')$$
$$P_i'' \triangleq <eat_i, *>.<pd_i, *>.<pd_{i+_n 1}, *>.P_i$$

Now in the system nondeterministic and probabilistic aspects coexist, so EMPA can be viewed as a possible syntactical counterpart of formal models for randomized distributed computations such as those defined in [18].

Finally, by temporally closing the system, with EMPA we can even assess some performance indices like, e.g., the average time during which there is at least one philosopher eating, i.e. the chopstick utilization. The specification of P_i has to be modified as follows:

$$P_i \triangleq <think_i, \lambda_i>.P_i'$$
$$P_i' \triangleq <\tau, \infty_{1,1/2}>.<pu_i, \infty_{1,1}>.(<pu_{i+_n 1}, \infty_{1,1}>.P_i'' + <pd_i, \infty_{1,1}>.P_i')+$$
$$<\tau, \infty_{1,1/2}>.<pu_{i+_n 1}, \infty_{1,1}>.(<pu_i, \infty_{1,1}>.P_i'' + <pd_{i+_n 1}, \infty_{1,1}>.P_i')$$
$$P_i'' \triangleq <eat_i, \mu_i>.<pd_i, \infty_{1,1}>.<pd_{i+_n 1}, \infty_{1,1}>.P_i$$

Observe that actions pu_i and pd_i have been modeled as immediate, because they are irrelevant from the performance evaluation point of view. Thus immediate actions provide a mechanism for *performance abstraction*, in the same way as action type τ provides a mechanism for functional abstraction.

6 Conclusion

In this paper we have proposed the stochastic process algebra EMPA in order to integrate functional and performance aspects in the modeling and analysis of concurrent systems. The development of EMPA has been influenced by the stochastic process algebras MTIPP [8] and PEPA [10], and by the formalism of GSPNs [1]. While designing EMPA, emphasis has been placed on expressiveness and formal semantics.

In particular, in EMPA action durations are mainly expressed by means of exponentially distributed random variables (like in MTIPP and PEPA), but it is also possible to express immediate actions (like in MTIPP) each of which is assigned a priority level and a weight (like in GSPNs), as well as actions whose duration is unspecified (like in classical process algebras). As a consequence, the expressiveness of EMPA is the sum of the expressiveness of a classical process algebra, a probabilistic process algebra (resulting in stratified models of probabilistic processes [7], though also reactive models are expressible via the interplay of immediate and passive actions), a prioritized process algebra (consisting of an extension of the approach proposed in [5]), and an exponentially timed process algebra. The price to pay for this enhanced expressiveness from the point of view of the underlying theory is relatively low: the idea of potential move in the definition of the integrated semantics is quite intuitive, and the notion of equivalence is simple and elegant.

The usefulness of all the features above is illustrated both in the previous section and in [3] by means of examples based on:

- Queueing systems [13]. They are models largely used for performance evaluation purposes whenever the scenario under study can be described by means of the interaction between a population of customers requiring service from a set of servers. In [3] we have stressed the expressiveness of EMPA by representing queueing systems with scalable service rate and with customers requiring different service rates or having different priorities; we have also described queueing systems with forks and joins as well as queueing networks.
- Communication protocols. In [3] the alternating bit protocol has been described by means of EMPA. From the specification we have obtained the integrated semantic model (composed of 302 states), which has been then projected on the functional model (by discarding action rates) and the performance model (composed of only 33 states because many original states had only immediate transitions, and moreover the phase of ordinary lumping has been able to capture the symmetry of the protocol). The projected models have finally been analyzed to detect functional properties (such as the absence of deadlock) as well as performance measures (such as the protocol throughput and the channel utilization).

Finally, we recall that there are several open problems in the field of stochastic process algebras, as listed in [3]. Probably, the most challenging one is the extension to generally distributed durations. It is however important to point out that the limitation to exponentially distributed durations is (*i*) convenient because exponential timing allows for a Markovian analysis without resorting to time-costly simulations, and (*ii*) not so restrictive because many frequently occurring distributions are (or can be approximated by) phase-type distributions [17], and these are expressible in EMPA by means of the interplay of exponentially timed actions and weights of immediate actions.

References

1. M. Ajmone Marsan, G. Balbo, G. Conte, *"A Class of Generalized Stochastic Petri Nets for the Performance Evaluation of Multiprocessor Systems"*, in ACM Trans. on Computer Systems 2:143-172, 1984
2. J. Baeten, J. A. Bergstra, J. W. Klop, *"Syntax and Defining Equations for an Interrupt Mechanism in Process Algebra"*, in Fundamenta Informatica IX:127-168, 1986
3. M. Bernardo, L. Donatiello, R. Gorrieri, *"Integrating Performance and Functional Analysis of Concurrent Systems with EMPA"*, Technical Report UBLCS-95-14, University of Bologna (Italy), September 1995 (revised March 1996), available via anonymous ftp from `ftp.cs.unibo.it:/pub/TR/UBLCS`
4. P. Buchholz, *"Markovian Process Algebra: Composition and Equivalence"*, in Proc. of PAPM '94, Erlangen (Germany), pages 11-30, July 1994
5. R. Cleaveland, M. Hennessy, *"Priorities in Process Algebras"*, in Proc. of LICS '88, Edinburgh (UK), IEEE-CS Press, pages 193-202, July 1988
6. D. Ferrari, *"Considerations on the Insularity of Performance Evaluation"*, in IEEE Trans. on Software Engineering 12(6):678-683, June 1986
7. R. van Glabbeek, S. A. Smolka, B. Steffen, C. M. N. Tofts, *"Reactive, Generative and Stratified Models of Probabilistic Processes"*, in Proc. of LICS '90, Philadelphia (PA), IEEE-CS Press, pages 130-141, 1990
8. N. Götz, U. Herzog, M. Rettelbach, *"Multiprocessor and Distributed System Design: the Integration of Functional Specification and Performance Analysis Using Stochastic Process Algebras"*, in Proc. of PERFORMANCE '93, Rome (Italy), LNCS 729:121-146, September 1993
9. H. Hermanns, M. Rettelbach, *"Syntax, Semantics, Equivalences, and Axioms for MTIPP"*, in Proc. of PAPM '94, Erlangen (Germany), pages 71-87, July 1994
10. J. Hillston, *"A Compositional Approach to Performance Modelling"*, Ph.D. Thesis, University of Edinburgh (UK), March 1994
11. C. A. R. Hoare, *"Communicating Sequential Processes"*, Prentice Hall, 1985
12. J. G. Kemeny, J. L. Snell, *"Finite Markov Chains"*, Springer-Verlag, 1977
13. L. Kleinrock, *"Queueing Systems"*, Wiley, 1975
14. K. G. Larsen, A. Skou, *"Bisimulation through Probabilistic Testing"*, in Information and Computation 94(1):1-28, September 1991
15. D. Lehmann, M. Rabin, *"On the Advantage of Free Choice: A Symmetric and Fully Distributed Solution to the Dining Philosophers Problem"*, in Proc. of POPL '81, pages 133-138, 1981
16. R. Milner, *"Communication and Concurrency"*, Prentice Hall, 1989
17. M. F. Neuts, *"Matrix-Geometric Solutions in Stochastic Models - An Algorithmic Approach"*, John Hopkins University Press, 1981
18. R. Segala, *"Modeling and Verification of Randomized Distributed Real-Time Systems"*, Ph.D. Thesis, MIT, June 1995
19. C. Tofts, *"A Synchronous Calculus of Relative Frequency"*, in Proc. of CONCUR '90, Amsterdam (The Netherlands), LNCS 458:467-480, August 1990
20. Y. Yemini, J. Kurose, *"Towards the Unification of the Functional and Performance Analysis of Protocols, or Is the Alternating-Bit Protocol Really Correct?"*, in Protocol Specification, Testing and Verification II, 1982

Rewriting Logic as a Semantic Framework for Concurrency: a Progress Report*

José Meseguer

SRI International, Menlo Park, CA 94025

Abstract. This paper surveys the work of many researchers on rewriting logic since it was first introduced in 1990. The main emphasis is on the use of rewriting logic as a *semantic framework* for concurrency. The goal in this regard is to express as faithfully as possible a very wide range of concurrency models, each on its own terms, avoiding any encodings or translations. Bringing very different models under a common semantic framework makes easier to understand what different models have in common and how they differ, to find deep connections between them, and to reason across their different formalisms. It becomes also much easier to achieve in a rigorous way the *integration* and *interoperation* of different models and languages whose combination offers attractive advantages. The logic and model theory of rewriting logic are also summarized, a number of current research directions are surveyed, and some concluding remarks about future directions are made.

Table of Contents

1 Introduction

2 Rewriting Logic

3 Models

4 Rewriting Logic as a Semantic Framework for Concurrency
- 4.1 Parallel Functional Programming
- 4.2 Labelled Transition Systems
- 4.3 Grammars
- 4.4 Petri Nets
- 4.5 Gamma and the Chemical Abstract Machine
- 4.6 CCS, LOTOS and the π-Calculus
- 4.7 Concurrent Objects, Actors, and OO Databases
- 4.8 Unity

* Supported by Office of Naval Research Contracts N00014-95-C-0225 and N00014-96-C-0114, National Science Foundation Grant CCR-9224005, and by the Information Technology Promotion Agency, Japan, as a part of the Industrial Science and Technology Frontier Program "New Models for Software Architecture" sponsored by NEDO (New Energy and Industrial Technology Development Organization).

4.9 Concurrent Access to Objects
4.10 Graph Rewriting
4.11 Dataflow
4.12 Neural Networks
4.13 Real-Time Systems

5 Rewriting Logic Languages
5.1 Executable Specification Languages
5.2 Parallel Programming Languages

6 Other Developments and Research Directions
6.1 2-Category Models
6.2 Infinite Computations
6.3 Formal Reasoning, Refinement, and Program Transformation
6.4 Rewriting Logic as a Logical Framework
6.5 Reflection and Strategies
6.6 Avoiding the Frame Problem
6.7 Nondeterminism

7 Concluding Remarks

1 Introduction

Since the first conference paper on rewriting logic in CONCUR'90 [73], dozens of authors in Europe, the US, Japan, and Northern Africa have vigorously advanced the rewriting logic research program in over sixty papers. By a serendipitous coincidence, the first international workshop on rewriting logic will take place in Asilomar, California, the week after CONCUR'96. The time seems somehow ripe for taking stock of the advances that have taken place, and I am very grateful to the organizers of CONCUR'96 for having given me the opportunity and the stimulus to do so.

Although I will try to cover most of the work that I am aware of, my main emphasis in this talk will be on rewriting logic as a *semantic framework* for concurrency. Rewriting logic has many theories and many models. Therefore, the task of providing a semantics is not conceived at all as a search for a *universal model* of concurrency, into which other models can be translated. The goal is very different, namely, to express as faithfully as possible each model on its own terms, avoiding any encodings or translations. In fact, given the wide variety of concurrency models and of concurrency phenomena the search for a universal model seems futile.

Bringing very different models under a common semantic framework has important conceptual and practical advantages. Conceptually, it becomes easier to understand what different models have in common and how they differ, to find deep connections between them, and to reason across their different formalims. In practice, it becomes much easier to achieve in a rigorous way the *integration* and *interoperation* of different models and languages whose combination offers attractive advantages. Section 4 explains how different models of concurrent computation can be naturally represented in rewriting logic. Some of these model representations were known from earlier work [74, 75]; they are briefly reviewed here in an updated form. Others, such as the treatment of simultaneous access to objects, graph rewriting, dataflow, neural networks, and real-time systems are new and are therefore discussed in greater detail.

To place the subject in perspective, the paper begins with a review of rewriting logic and its model theory in Sections 2 and 3. Section 5 surveys the different rewriting logic language implementation efforts in Europe, the US and Japan, including both interpreters and parallel implementations. Section 6 surveys other developments and research directions and the progress made in them. Finally, Section 7 makes some remarks about future directions.

2 Rewriting Logic

A *signature* in (order-sorted) rewriting logic is an (order-sorted) equational theory (Σ, E), where Σ is an equational signature and E is a set of Σ-equations. Rewriting will operate on equivalence classes of terms modulo E. In this way, we free rewriting from the syntactic constraints of a term representation and gain a much greater flexibility in deciding what counts as a *data structure*; for example, string rewriting is obtained by imposing an associativity axiom, and multiset rewriting by imposing associativity and commutativity. Of course, standard term rewriting is obtained as the particular case in which the set of equations E is empty. Techniques for rewriting modulo equations have been studied extensively [31] and can be used to implement rewriting modulo many equational theories of interest.

Given a signature (Σ, E), *sentences* of rewriting logic are sequents of the form

$$[t]_E \longrightarrow [t']_E,$$

where t and t' are Σ-terms possibly involving some variables, and $[t]_E$ denotes the equivalence class of the term t modulo the equations E. A *rewrite theory* $\mathcal{R}$ is a 4-tuple $\mathcal{R} = (\Sigma, E, L, R)$ where Σ is a ranked alphabet of function symbols, E is a set of Σ-equations, L is a set of *labels*, and R is a set of pairs $R \subseteq L \times T_{\Sigma,E}(X)^2$ whose first component is a label and whose second component is a pair of E-equivalence classes of terms, with $X = \{x_1, \ldots, x_n, \ldots\}$ a countably infinite set of variables. Elements of R are called *rewrite rules*.[2] We understand a rule $(r, ([t], [t']))$ as a labelled sequent and use for it the notation $r : [t] \longrightarrow [t']$. To indicate that $\{x_1, \ldots, x_n\}$ is the set of variables occurring in either t or t', we write $r : [t(x_1, \ldots, x_n)] \longrightarrow [t'(x_1, \ldots, x_n)]$, or in abbreviated notation $r : [t(\overline{x})] \longrightarrow [t'(\overline{x})]$.

[2] To simplify the exposition the rules of the logic are given for the case of *unconditional* rewrite rules. However, all the ideas presented here have been extended to conditional rules in [75] with very general rules of the form

$$r : [t] \longrightarrow [t'] \ \textit{if} \ [u_1] \longrightarrow [v_1] \wedge \ldots \wedge [u_k] \longrightarrow [v_k].$$

This increases considerably the expressive power of rewrite theories.

Given a rewrite theory $\mathcal{R}$, we say that $\mathcal{R}$ ***entails*** a sentence $[t] \longrightarrow [t']$, or that $[t] \longrightarrow [t']$ is a *(concurrent) $\mathcal{R}$-rewrite*, and write $\mathcal{R} \vdash [t] \longrightarrow [t']$ if and only if $[t] \longrightarrow [t']$ can be obtained by finite application of the following ***rules of deduction*** (where we assume that all the terms are well formed and $t(\overline{w}/\overline{x})$ denotes the simultaneous substitution of w_i for x_i in t):

1. **Reflexivity**. For each $[t] \in T_{\Sigma,E}(X)$, $\overline{[t] \longrightarrow [t]}$.
2. **Congruence**. For each $f \in \Sigma_n, n \in \mathbb{N}$,

$$\frac{[t_1] \longrightarrow [t'_1] \quad \ldots \quad [t_n] \longrightarrow [t'_n]}{[f(t_1, \ldots, t_n)] \longrightarrow [f(t'_1, \ldots, t'_n)]}.$$

3. **Replacement**. For each rule $r : [t(x_1, \ldots, x_n)] \longrightarrow [t'(x_1, \ldots, x_n)]$ in R,

$$\frac{[w_1] \longrightarrow [w'_1] \quad \ldots \quad [w_n] \longrightarrow [w'_n]}{[t(\overline{w}/\overline{x})] \longrightarrow [t'(\overline{w'}/\overline{x})]}.$$

4. **Transitivity**

$$\frac{[t_1] \longrightarrow [t_2] \qquad [t_2] \longrightarrow [t_3]}{[t_1] \longrightarrow [t_3]}.$$

Rewriting logic is a logic for reasoning correctly about ***concurrent systems*** having ***states***, and evolving by means of ***transitions***. The signature of a rewrite theory describes a particular structure for the states of a system—e.g., multiset, binary tree, etc.—so that its states can be distributed according to such a structure. The rewrite rules in the theory describe which ***elementary local transitions*** are possible in the distributed state by concurrent local transformations. The rules of rewriting logic allow us to reason correctly about which ***general*** concurrent transitions are possible in a system satisfying such a description. Thus, computationally, each rewriting step is a parallel local transition in a concurrent system.

Alternatively, however, we can adopt a logical viewpoint instead, and regard the rules of rewriting logic as ***metarules*** for correct deduction in a ***logical system***. Logically, each rewriting step is a logical ***entailment*** in a formal system.

The computational and the logical viewpoints under which rewriting logic can be interpreted can be summarized in the following diagram of correspondences:

State	$\leftrightarrow$ *Term*	$\leftrightarrow$ *Proposition*
Transition	$\leftrightarrow$ *Rewriting*	$\leftrightarrow$ *Deduction*
Distributed Structure	$\leftrightarrow$ *Algebraic Structure*	$\leftrightarrow$ *Propositional Structure*

The last row of equivalences is actually quite important. Roughly speaking, it expresses the fact that a state can be transformed in a concurrent way only if it is nonatomic, that is, if it is ***composed*** out of smaller state components that can be changed independently. In rewriting logic this composition of a concurrent state is formalized by the ***operations*** of the signature Σ of the rewrite theory $\mathcal{R}$ that axiomatizes the system. From the logical point of view such operations can naturally be regarded as user-definable ***propositional connectives*** stating the particular structure that a given state has. A subtle additional point about the last row of equivalences is that the algebraic structure of a system also involves *equations*. Such equations describe the system's global state as a *concurrent data structure*. As we shall see, such equations can have a dramatic impact on the amount of concurrency available in a system. They work as "data solvents" to loosen up the data structures so that more rewrites can be performed in parallel.

Note that it follows from this discussion that rewriting logic is primarily a logic *of* change—in which the deduction directly corresponds to the change—as opposed to a logic to talk *about* change in a more indirect and global manner such as the different variants of modal and temporal logic. In our view these latter logics support a nonexecutable—as far as the system described is concerned—level of specification above that of rewriting logic. Narciso Martí-Oliet and I are currently studying how these two levels can be best integrated within a unified wide-spectrum approach to the specification, prototyping, and declarative programming of concurrent systems; Ulrike Lechner has independently proposed a two-level integration of this kind as well [56, 55].

3 Models

We first sketch the construction of initial and free models for a rewrite theory $\mathcal{R} = (\Sigma, E, L, R)$. Such models capture nicely the intuitive idea of a "rewrite system" in the sense that they are systems whose states are E-equivalence classes of terms, and whose transitions are concurrent rewritings using the rules in R. By adopting a logical instead of a computational perspective, we can alternatively view such models as "logical systems" in which formulas are validly rewritten to other formulas by concurrent rewritings which correspond to proofs for the logic in question. Such models have a natural *category* structure, with states (or formulas) as objects, transitions (or proofs) as morphisms, and sequential composition as morphism composition, and in them dynamic behavior exactly corresponds to deduction.

Given a rewrite theory $\mathcal{R} = (\Sigma, E, L, R)$, for which we assume that different labels in L name different rules in R, the model that we are seeking is a category $\mathcal{T}_{\mathcal{R}}(X)$ whose objects are equivalence classes of terms $[t] \in T_{\Sigma,E}(X)$ and whose morphisms are equivalence classes of "proof terms" representing proofs in rewriting deduction, i.e., concurrent $\mathcal{R}$-rewrites. The rules for generating such proof terms, with the specification of their respective domains and codomains, are given below; they just "decorate" with proof terms the rules 1–4 of rewriting logic. Note that we always use "diagrammatic" notation for morphism composition, i.e., $\alpha;\beta$ always means the composition of α *followed by* β.

1. **Identities**. For each $[t] \in T_{\Sigma,E}(X)$, $\dfrac{}{[t] : [t] \longrightarrow [t]}$.
2. **Σ-structure**. For each $f \in \Sigma_n$, $n \in \mathbb{N}$,

$$\frac{\alpha_1 : [t_1] \longrightarrow [t'_1] \quad \dots \quad \alpha_n : [t_n] \longrightarrow [t'_n]}{f(\alpha_1, \dots, \alpha_n) : [f(t_1, \dots, t_n)] \longrightarrow [f(t'_1, \dots, t'_n)]}.$$

3. **Replacement.** For each rewrite rule $r : [t(\overline{x}^n)] \longrightarrow [t'(\overline{x}^n)]$ in R,

$$\frac{\alpha_1 : [w_1] \longrightarrow [w'_1] \quad \dots \quad \alpha_n : [w_n] \longrightarrow [w'_n]}{r(\alpha_1, \dots, \alpha_n) : [t(\overline{w}/\overline{x})] \longrightarrow [t'(\overline{w'}/\overline{x})]}.$$

4. **Composition** $\dfrac{\alpha : [t_1] \longrightarrow [t_2] \quad \beta : [t_2] \longrightarrow [t_3]}{\alpha; \beta : [t_1] \longrightarrow [t_3]}$.

Each of the above rules of generation defines a different operation taking certain proof terms as arguments and returning a resulting proof term. In other words, proof terms form an algebraic structure $\mathcal{P}_{\mathcal{R}}(X)$ consisting of a graph with nodes $T_{\Sigma,E}(X)$, with identity arrows, and with operations f (for each $f \in \Sigma$), r (for each rewrite rule), and $\_;\_$ (for composing arrows). Our desired model $\mathcal{T}_{\mathcal{R}}(X)$ is the quotient of $\mathcal{P}_{\mathcal{R}}(X)$ modulo the following equations:[3]

1. **Category**
   (a) *Associativity.* For all α, β, γ, $\quad (\alpha; \beta); \gamma = \alpha; (\beta; \gamma)$.
   (b) *Identities.* For each $\alpha : [t] \longrightarrow [t']$, $\quad \alpha; [t'] = \alpha$ and $[t]; \alpha = \alpha$.
2. **Functoriality of the Σ-algebraic structure.** For each $f \in \Sigma_n$,
   (a) *Preservation of composition.* For all $\alpha_1, \dots, \alpha_n, \beta_1, \dots, \beta_n$,

$$f(\alpha_1; \beta_1, \dots, \alpha_n; \beta_n) = f(\alpha_1, \dots, \alpha_n); f(\beta_1, \dots, \beta_n).$$

   (b) *Preservation of identities.* $\quad f([t_1], \dots, [t_n]) = [f(t_1, \dots, t_n)]$.
3. **Axioms in E.** For $t(x_1, \dots, x_n) = t'(x_1, \dots, x_n)$ an axiom in E, for all $\alpha_1, \dots, \alpha_n$, $\quad t(\alpha_1, \dots, \alpha_n) = t'(\alpha_1, \dots, \alpha_n)$.
4. **Exchange.** For each $r : [t(x_1, \dots, x_n)] \longrightarrow [t'(x_1, \dots, x_n)]$ in R,

$$\frac{\alpha_1 : [w_1] \longrightarrow [w'_1] \quad \dots \quad \alpha_n : [w_n] \longrightarrow [w'_n]}{r(\overline{\alpha}) = r(\overline{[w]}); t'(\overline{\alpha}) = t(\overline{\alpha}); r(\overline{[w']})}.$$

Note that the set X of variables is actually a parameter of these constructions, and we need not assume X to be fixed and countable. In particular, for $X = \emptyset$, we adopt the notation $\mathcal{T}_{\mathcal{R}}$. The equations in 1 make $\mathcal{T}_{\mathcal{R}}(X)$ a category, the equations in 2 make each $f \in \Sigma$ a functor, and 3 forces the axioms E. The exchange law states that any rewriting of the form $r(\overline{\alpha})$—which represents the ***simultaneous*** rewriting of the term at the top using rule r *and* "below," i.e., in the subterms matched by the variables, using the rewrites $\overline{\alpha}$—is equivalent to the sequential composition $r(\overline{[w]}); t'(\overline{\alpha})$, corresponding to first rewriting on top with r and then below on the subterms matched by the variables with $\overline{\alpha}$, and is also equivalent to the sequential composition $t(\overline{\alpha}); r(\overline{[w']})$ corresponding to first rewriting below with $\overline{\alpha}$ and then on top with r. Therefore, the exchange law states that rewriting at the top by means of rule r and rewriting "below" using $\overline{\alpha}$ are processes that are independent of each other and can be done either simultaneously or in any order.

[3] In the expressions appearing in the equations, when compositions of morphisms are involved, we always implicitly assume that the corresponding domains and codomains match.

Since each proof term is a description of a concurrent computation, what these equations provide is an equational theory of *true concurrency* allowing us to characterize when to such descriptions specify the same abstract computation. We will see in Section 4.4 that for Petri nets this notion of true concurrency coincides with the well-known notion of commutative processes of a net.

Since $[t(x_1,\ldots,x_n)]$ and $[t'(x_1,\ldots,x_n)]$ can be regarded as functors $\mathcal{T}_{\mathcal{R}}(X)^n \longrightarrow \mathcal{T}_{\mathcal{R}}(X)$, from the mathematical point of view the exchange law just asserts that r is a *natural transformation*.

Lemma 1. *[75] For each rewrite rule* $r : [t(x_1,\ldots,x_n)] \longrightarrow [t'(x_1,\ldots,x_n)]$ *in* R, *the family of morphisms*

$$\{r([\overline{w}]) : [t(\overline{w}/\overline{x})] \longrightarrow [t'(\overline{w}/\overline{x})] \mid \overline{[w]} \in T_{\Sigma,E}(X)^n\}$$

is a natural transformation $r : [t(x_1,\ldots,x_n)] \Rightarrow [t'(x_1,\ldots,x_n)]$ *between the functors* $[t(x_1,\ldots,x_n)], [t'(x_1,\ldots,x_n)] : \mathcal{T}_{\mathcal{R}}(X)^n \longrightarrow \mathcal{T}_{\mathcal{R}}(X)$.

The category $\mathcal{T}_{\mathcal{R}}(X)$ is just one among many *models* that can be assigned to the rewrite theory $\mathcal{R}$. The general notion of model, called an $\mathcal{R}$-*system*, is defined as follows:

Definition 2. Given a rewrite theory $\mathcal{R} = (\Sigma, E, L, R)$, an $\mathcal{R}$-*system* $\mathcal{S}$ is a category $\mathcal{S}$ together with:

- a (Σ, E)-algebra structure given by a family of functors

$$\{f_{\mathcal{S}} : \mathcal{S}^n \longrightarrow \mathcal{S} \mid f \in \Sigma_n, n \in \mathbb{N}\}$$

  satisfying the equations E, i.e., for any $t(x_1,\ldots,x_n) = t'(x_1,\ldots,x_n)$ in E we have an identity of functors $t_{\mathcal{S}} = t'_{\mathcal{S}}$, where the functor $t_{\mathcal{S}}$ is defined inductively from the functors $f_{\mathcal{S}}$ in the obvious way.
- for each rewrite rule $r : [t(\overline{x})] \longrightarrow [t'(\overline{x})]$ in R a natural transformation $r_{\mathcal{S}} : t_{\mathcal{S}} \Rightarrow t'_{\mathcal{S}}$.

An $\mathcal{R}$-*homomorphism* $F : \mathcal{S} \longrightarrow \mathcal{S}'$ between two $\mathcal{R}$-systems is then a functor $F : \mathcal{S} \longrightarrow \mathcal{S}'$ such that it is a Σ-algebra homomorphism, i.e., $f_{\mathcal{S}} * F = F^n * f_{\mathcal{S}'}$, for each f in Σ_n, $n \in \mathbb{N}$, and such that "F preserves R," i.e., for each rewrite rule $r : [t(\overline{x})] \longrightarrow [t'(\overline{x})]$ in R we have the identity of natural transformations[4] $r_{\mathcal{S}} * F = F^n * r_{\mathcal{S}'}$, where n is the number of variables appearing in the rule. This defines a category $\mathcal{R}$-**Sys** in the obvious way.

A detailed proof of the following theorem on the existence of initial and free $\mathcal{R}$-systems for the more general case of conditional rewrite theories is given in [75], where the soundness and completeness of rewriting logic for $\mathcal{R}$-system models is also proved.

Theorem 3. $\mathcal{T}_{\mathcal{R}}$ *is an initial object in the category* $\mathcal{R}$-**Sys**. *More generally,* $\mathcal{T}_{\mathcal{R}}(X)$ *has the following universal property: Given an* $\mathcal{R}$-*system* $\mathcal{S}$, *each function* $F : X \longrightarrow |\mathcal{S}|$ *extends uniquely to an* $\mathcal{R}$-*homomorphism* $F^{\natural} : \mathcal{T}_{\mathcal{R}}(X) \longrightarrow \mathcal{S}$.

[4] Note that we use diagrammatic order for the *horizontal*, $\alpha * \beta$, and *vertical*, $\gamma;\delta$, composition of natural transformations [67].

4 Rewriting Logic as a Semantic Framework for Concurrency

Regarding the computational uses of rewriting logic, an obvious question to ask is how general and natural rewriting logic is as a *semantic framework* in which to express different languages and models of computation. This section presents concrete evidence for the thesis that a wide variety of models of computation, including concurrent ones, can be naturally and directly expressed as rewrite theories in rewriting logic without any encoding or artificiality. As a consequence, models hitherto quite distant from each other can be naturally unified and interrelated within a common framework.

4.1 Parallel Functional Programming

Parallel functional programming is an important model of parallel computation. A lot of research has been devoted to parallel implementations of functional languages [96] and also to parallel dataflow and reduction architectures supporting them.

We can distinguish between *first-order* functional languages, also called *equational* languages, in which programs are collections of functions defined by Church-Rosser equational theories, and *higher-order* languages that are typically based on some typed or untyped lambda calculus, so that functions can be defined by lambda expressions.

Functional computations, although amenable to parallelization, are nevertheless *determinate*, in the sense that the final result of a functional expression is the unique value—if it exists—computed by the composition of functions described in the expression. The Church-Rosser property is the technical property guaranteeing such determinacy.

By contrast, the rewrite rules in a rewrite theory need nor be Church-Rosser, and may never terminate. Therefore, in general their concurrent execution cannot be understood as the computation of a unique functional value; often not even as the computation of *a* value at all. However, parallel functional programming can be viewed as the special case in which the rewrite rules *are* Church-Rosser. In this way, a seamless integration of parallel functional programming within the more general framework of rewriting logic is naturally achieved. More abstractly, such an integration can be viewed as a conservative embedding of equational logic within rewriting logic [68].

For first-order functional programs the above remarks make clear how they can be regarded as a special case of rewriting logic. However, for higher-order functions, since their formalization is somewhat different, more has to be said. The key observation is that rewriting logic allows rewriting *modulo* equational axioms. We can then take advantage of the different reductions of lambda calculi to first-order equational logic using an equational theory of *explicit substitution* to view lambda calculus reduction as first-order rewriting *modulo* the substitution equations. In fact, in several formalizations congruence modulo substitution exactly corresponds to alpha-conversion equivalence between lambda terms.

The natural inclusion of the lambda calculus within rewriting logic using explicit substitution was pointed out in [75]. An illuminating investigation of parallel computations in the lambda calculus using rewriting logic has been carried out by Laneve and Montanari [52, 53].

Before addressing the case of the lambda calculus, Laneve and Montanari [53] first clarify the exact relationship between the equivalence of rewrites obtained by the equations identifying proof terms in the free model $\mathcal{T}_{\mathcal{R}}(X)$ of a rewrite theory $\mathcal{R}$, and Boudol's notion of permutation equivalence for term rewriting systems using the residual calculus [17]. The theory $\mathcal{R}$ is assumed to have its equational part E empty (syntactic rewriting) and to be such that the rewrite rules are left-linear (no repeated variable occurrences in lefthand sides or rules) and have nonvariable lefthand sides that contain all the variables in their corresponding righthand sides. They prove that both notions of equivalence coincide, and conclude that the equational description in $\mathcal{T}_{\mathcal{R}}(X)$ is considerably simpler than that provided by the residual calculus.

Laneve and Montanari then go on to consider the general case of ***orthogonal, left-normal combinatory reduction systems*** as formalized by Aczel [1], that contain the lambda calculus as a special case. They show that such systems exactly correspond to rewrite theories $\mathcal{R}$ whose equational part E consists of explicit substitution equations. They then prove that the traditional model of parallel rewriting in such systems—generalizing parallel lambda calculus rewriting—exactly corresponds to a quotient of $\mathcal{T}_{\mathcal{R}}(X)$ by a few equations. In this way, they obtain a simple and purely equational theory of equivalence or "true concurrency" between parallel lambda calculus computations that is considerably simpler than that afforded by the heavy machinery of the residual calculus.

4.2 Labelled Transition Systems

A labelled transition system is a poor man's rewrite theory. It is just a rewrite theory $\mathcal{R} = (\Sigma, E, L, R)$ in which Σ consists only of constants, E is empty, and the rules are all of the form $r : a \longrightarrow b$ with a and b some constants in Σ.

Their poverty has two aspects. Firstly, they are very ***low-level***, since the states are unstructured atomic entities so that infinite state spaces need some form of schematic presentation; also, the rules apply only to individual transitions, whereas for general rewrite theories a single rule may cover an infinite number of them. Secondly, and more importantly, ***a labelled transition system can be nondeterministic, but it cannot exhibit concurrency***. The reason for this is the negative side of our motto

Distributed Structure $\leftrightarrow$ *Algebraic Structure*

Since the states are *atomic* entities, they do not have parts that can evolve concurrently. For a system to be concurrent its states must be ***decomposable***. This is what the nonconstant operators in a signature Σ make possible. Petri nets are also low level, automaton-like systems, but they are concurrent precisely because there is a binary multiset union operator composing their distributed states.

4.3 Grammars

Traditional grammars for formal languages are just string rewriting systems. They can be concurrent, because different rewrites may simultaneously transform different substrings. The most general such grammars are Post systems; their parallelism is meant to model that of logical deductions in a formal system. Phrase-structure grammars are more restrictive, because they only involve ground terms in their rewrite rules. Turing machines, viewed as grammars, are even more restrictive. All of them can be naturally viewed as rewrite theories having a signature with $\Sigma_0 = \Delta \uplus \{\lambda\}$ (with λ the empty string), $\Sigma_2 = \{\_\_\}$ (the binary string concatenation operator), and all the other Σ_n are empty. The equational axioms E are in this case the ***associativity*** of string concatenation and the ***identity*** axioms for concatenation with λ. Therefore, $T_{\Sigma,AI} = \Delta^*$, and $T_{\Sigma,AI}(X) = (\Delta \uplus X)^*$. The rules of a rewrite theory for this case must have the form:

$$u_0\, X_{k_1} u_1 \ldots u_{n-1}\, X_{k_n} u_n \longrightarrow v_0\, X_{l_1} v_1 \ldots v_{m-1}\, X_{l_m} v_m$$

with $n, m \in \mathbb{N}$, $u_i, v_j \in \Delta^*$, where the variables $X_{k_i}, X_{l_j} \in X$ could actually be repeated, i.e., we could have $X_{k_i} = X_{k_{i'}}$ with $i \neq i'$ and similarly for the X_l's.

4.4 Petri Nets

Petri nets have a straightforward and very natural expression as rewrite theories. Their distributed states correspond to ***markings***, that is, to finite multisets of basic constants called ***places***. Algebraically they are axiomatized by an ***associative*** and ***commutative*** multiset union operation with ***identity*** the empty multiset and with constants the places. A transition t in a place-transition net is simply a labelled rewrite rule $t : M \longrightarrow M'$ between two multiset markings [75]. Therefore, we can view a net $\mathcal{N}$ as a rewrite theory $\mathcal{N}$ with the above algebraic axiomatization for its markings and with one rewrite rule per transition, so that firing of a transition exactly corresponds to rewriting modulo associativity, commutativity and identity with the corresponding rewrite rule.

In this way, the finite concurrent computations of a net $\mathcal{N}$ are formalized as arrows in the category $\mathcal{T}_{\mathcal{N}}$. Specifically, they exactly correspond to the ***commutative processes*** of $\mathcal{N}$ in the sense of Best and Devillers [11]. This result, showing that the equational theory of true concurrency provided by rewriting logic agrees with more traditional notions of true concurrency in the case of Petri nets, has been proved by Degano, Meseguer and Montanari [28, 29] using an earlier categorical model of Petri net computations denoted $\mathcal{T}[\mathcal{N}]$ [80] that is in fact identical to $\mathcal{T}_{\mathcal{N}}$.

Since Petri nets are in some ways a very simple concurrency model, in practice it is often convenient to specify systems at a higher level, yet using the same basic properties of Petri nets. That is, instead of atomic places one wants to have ***structured data***, perhaps equationally axiomatized by algebraic data types. This is the analogue for Petri nets of what languages like LOTOS provide for process algebras, since in both cases the practical need to support data types is very similar. Rewriting logic offers a very natural framework for giving semantics to different kinds of *algebraic* Petri nets of this kind. For the case of Engelfriet et al.'s higher level Petri nets, called POPs [35, 36], this was pointed out in [75]. Applications of rewriting logic to Petri net algebraic specification have been developed by Battiston, Crespi, De Cindio, and Mauri [8], and also by Bettaz and Maouche [12, 13].

4.5 Gamma and the Chemical Abstract Machine

The Gamma language of Banâtre and Le Mètayer [7], and Berry and Boudol's *chemical abstract machine*, or *cham* [66, 10], share the metaphor of viewing a certain kind of distributed state as a "solution" in which many "molecules" float. Concurrent transitions are then viewed as "reactions" that can occur simultaneously in many points of the solution. This metaphor is a suggestive way of describing the case in which the top-level structure of a system's distributed state is a *multiset*, because the associativity and commutativity axioms enjoyed by multiset union allow the different elements to "float" freely in the expression, so as to come into contact with each other at will. Therefore, both Gamma and the *cham* specify classes of rewrite theories in which the equational axioms $E = ACI$ are the *associativity* and *commutativity* of a multiset union operator $\_,\_$ having the empty multiset, say λ, as its *identity*. This generalizes the place/transition Petri net case by allowing structured elements in the multiset, instead of just atomic places, so that both Gamma and the *cham* could in some sense be regarded as high-level Petri net formalisms.

A Gamma program is essentially a collection of conditional rewrite rules, called *basic reactions*, of the form

$$x_1, \ldots, x_n \longrightarrow A(x_1, \ldots, x_n) \;\; \textit{if} \;\; R(x_1, \ldots, x_n)$$

where the condition R is a boolean expression and A is a multiset expression called the *action*. Typically, concurrent Gamma computations are performed exhaustively until termination is reached.

In the case of the *cham*, there is a common syntax shared by all chemical abstract machines, with each machine possibly extending the basic syntax by additional function symbols. The common syntax is typed, and can be expressed as the following order-sorted signature Ω:

sorts Molecule, Molecules, Solution .
subsorts Solution $<$ *Molecule* $<$ *Molecules* .
op λ : $\longrightarrow$ *Molecules* .
op $\_,\_$: *Molecules Molecules* $\longrightarrow$ *Molecules* .
op $\{|\_|\}$: *Molecules* $\longrightarrow$ *Solution* . `*** membrane operator`
op $\_ \triangleleft \_$: *Molecule Solution* $\longrightarrow$ *Molecule* . `*** airlock operator`

We can describe a *cham* as a rewrite theory $\mathcal{C} = (\Sigma, ACI, L, R)$, with $\Sigma \supseteq \Omega$, together with a partition

$$R = \textit{Reaction} \uplus \textit{Heating} \uplus \textit{Cooling} \uplus \textit{AirlockAx}.$$

The rules in R are subject to certain syntactic restrictions that guarantee an efficient form of matching modulo ACI. See [75] for some more discussion.

4.6 CCS, LOTOS and the π-Calculus

Kokichi Futatsugi, Timothy Winkler and I [78], and in a different later version Narciso Martí-Oliet and I [68], have shown two different ways in which Milner's CCS can be naturally represented in rewriting logic. One representation essentially treats the transitions as rewrite rules, with some syntactic care to record in the term the actions that have been performed. The other representation considers the operational semantics rules of CCS as the rewrite rules of a rewrite theory and provides a more declarative account. In both of them the representation exactly characterizes the legal CCS computations [68]. Another rewriting specification of CCS in a double category model that is a natural generalization of the 2-category models of rewriting logic has been proposed by Gadducci and Montanari [38] and is discussed in Section 6.1.

LOTOS [42] is a specification language combining the two formalisms of algebraic data types and (an extension of) CCS. It is pointed out in [78] that writing an executable specification of LOTOS in rewriting logic that could be used as a LOTOS interpreter is both very natural and straightforward. In fact, an interpreter of this kind has been written by Futatsugi and his collaborators with very good results [86]. The point is that the algebraic and process formalisms—whose relationship seems somewhat unclear in their original LOTOS combination—find what might be called their true semantic home in rewriting logic, where the equational part is accounted for by the equational signature and axioms, and the process part is described by rewrite rules over the corresponding expressions. Viry [102] makes essentially the same observation about the naturalness of rewriting logic as a semantic framework for LOTOS, and also points out that the particular syntactic restrictions imposed by LOTOS make the combined execution of LOTOS equations and LOTOS transition rules very easy by rewriting, because they satisfy the *coherence* property defined in [102].

More recently, Viry [101] has given a very natural specification of the π-calculus in rewriting logic. The realization that the operational semantics of the π-calculus can be naturally described using rewrite rules modulo the associativity and commutativity of a multiset union operator goes back to Milner [84]. However, as in the case of rewriting logic specifications of the lambda calculus discussed in Section 4.1, binding operators become an extra feature that should be accounted for. As for the lambda calculus, the answer given by Viry [102] resides in an equational theory of explicit substitution, so that expressions up to alpha-conversion can be regarded as equivalence classes.

4.7 Concurrent Objects, Actors, and OO Databases

In a concurrent object-oriented system the concurrent state, which is usually called a *configuration*, has typically the structure of a *multiset* made up of objects and messages. Therefore, we can view configurations as built up by a binary multiset union operator which we can represent with empty syntax as

```
subsorts Object Msg < Configuration .
```

```
op __ : Configuration Configuration -> Configuration
                                   [assoc comm id: null] .
```

where the multiset union operator __ is declared to satisfy the structural laws of associativity and commutativity and to have identity null. The subtype declaration

```
subsorts Object Msg < Configuration .
```

states that objects and messages are singleton multiset configurations, so that more complex configurations are generated out of them by multiset union.

An *object* in a given state is represented as a term

$$\langle O : C \mid a_1 : v_1, \ldots, a_n : v_n \rangle$$

where O is the object's name or identifier, C is its class, the a_i's are the names of the object's *attribute identifiers*, and the v_i's are the corresponding *values*. The set of all the attribute-value pairs of an object state is formed by repeated application of the binary union operator _,_ which also obeys structural laws of associativity, commutativity, and identity; i.e., the order of the attribute-value pairs of an object is immaterial.

For example, a bounded buffer whose elements are numbers can be represented as an object with three attributes: a contents attribute that is a list of numbers of length less than or equal to the bound, and attributes in and out that are numbers counting how many elements have been put in the buffer or got from it since the buffer's creation. A typical bounded buffer state can be

```
< B : BdBuff | contents: 9 5 6 8, in: 7, out: 3 >
```

The concurrent behavior of bounded buffers that interact with other objects by put and get messages can then be axiomatized by the rewrite rules

```
(put E in B) < B : BdBuff | contents: Q, in: N, out: M > =>
   < B : BdBuff | contents: E Q, in: N + 1, out: M >
   if (N - M) < bound .

(getfrom B replyto I)
   < B : BdBuff | contents: Q E, in: N, out: M > =>
   < B : BdBuff | contents: Q, in: N, out: M + 1 >
   (to I elt-in B is E) .
```

Then, a configuration such as

```
(put 7 in B1) < B2 : BdBuff | contents: 2 3, in: 7, out: 5 >
< B1 : BdBuff | contents: nil, in: 2, out: 2 >
(getfrom B2 replyto C)
```

(where the buffers are assumed to have a large enough bound) can be rewritten into the configuration

```
< B2 : BdBuff | contents: 2, in: 7, out: 6 >
< B1 : BdBuff | contents: 7, in: 3, out: 2 >
(to C elt-in B2 is 3)
```

by applying concurrently the two rewrite rules[5] for put and get modulo associativity and commutativity.

Intuitively, we can think of messages as "travelling" to come into contact with the objects to which they are sent and then causing "communication events" by application of rewrite rules. In rewriting logic, this travelling is accounted for in a very abstract way by the structural laws of associativity, commutativity, and identity. The above two rules illustrate the ***asynchronous message passing*** communication between objects typical of *Actor systems* [3, 2]. Generalizing slightly the Actor case, the Simple Maude language [62] adopts the following general form of conditional rules for asynchronous message passing interaction between objects

$$
\begin{aligned}
(\dagger)\quad (M)\ \langle O : F \mid atts\rangle & \\
\longrightarrow\ & (\langle O : F' \mid atts'\rangle) \\
& \langle Q_1 : D_1 \mid atts''_1\rangle \ldots \langle Q_p : D_p \mid atts''_p\rangle \\
& M'_1 \ldots M'_q \\
& \textit{if } C
\end{aligned}
$$

Such rules involve at most one object and one message in their lefthand side, where the notation (M) means that the message M is only an optional part of the lefthand side, that is, that we also allow ***autonomous objects*** that can act on their own without receiving any messages. Similarly, the notation $(\langle O : F' \mid atts'\rangle)$ means that the object O—in a possibly different state—is only an optional part of the righthand side, i.e., that it can be omitted in some rules so that the object is then deleted. In addition, p new objects may be created, and q new messages may be generated for $p, q \geq 0$.

Furthermore, the lefthand sides in rules of the form (†) should fit the general pattern

$$M(O)\ \langle O : C \mid atts\rangle$$

where O could be a variable, a constant, or more generally—in case object identifiers are endowed with additional structure—a term. Under such circumstances, an efficient way of realizing rewriting modulo associativity and commutativity by communication is available to us for rules of the form (†), namely we can associate object identifiers with specific addresses in the virtual address space of a parallel machine and can then send messages addressed to an object to its corresponding addres.

The above representation of objects is the one adopted in the Maude language [72, 83, 76]. It assumes, as it is common in many object-oriented systems, that each object has a unique name, different from that of all other objects. In

[5] Note that rewrite rules for natural number addition have also been applied.

fact, by giving appropriate rewrite rules for the creation and deletion of objects [76], it is not hard to ensure that this property is preserved by the rules of an object-oriented system. However, rewriting logic as such is neutral about the treatment of object identity and many other such matters. For example, for purposes of grouping objects in *components* that can be combined with each other to form bigger open systems, Carolyn Talcott adopts instead a more abstract representation of objects as *abstract actors* [100], where objects can be renamed by a form of alpha-conversion to avoid name clashes across components. In two very fine papers [100, 99] she then uses rewriting logic to reason formally about the behavior of actors, including their infinite fair computations.

An important problem in concurrent object-oriented programming to which rewriting logic has been successfully applied is the so-called *inheritance anomaly* [71], that is, the serious difficulties often encountered when trying to integrate object-oriented inheritance and concurrency in a programming language. The problem is that an object such as the bounded buffer described above may not be ready to process certain messages, such as a put when the buffer is full or a get when it is empty. The more or less ad-hoc solutions adopted to deal with this typically do not survive well the passage to subclasses in which more attributes and more methods may have been introduced. Using an order-sorted type structure [40], class inheritance can be naturally supported in rewriting logic; and message redefinition in subclasses can be described by appropriate composition operations between rewrite theories [76]. I used these ideas in [77] to show how the inheritance anomaly can be resolved by adopting a declarative programming style with rewrite rules. A more recent paper by Lechner, Lengauer, Nickl and Wirsing [57] proposes additional rewriting logic techniques to give a somewhat different solution to this problem.

Object interaction need not be asynchronous. In systems different from Actor systems it may involve events in which several objects, with or without the prompting of messages, synchronously participate in a local transition. Rewriting logic can easily specify such synchronous interactions between objects as more general rewrite rules of the form

$$
\begin{aligned}
(\ddagger)\quad & M_1 \ldots M_n\, \langle O_1 : F_1 \mid atts_1\rangle \ldots \langle O_m : F_m \mid atts_m\rangle \\
& \longrightarrow \langle O_{i_1} : F'_{i_1} \mid atts'_{i_1}\rangle \ldots \langle O_{i_k} : F'_{i_k} \mid atts'_{i_k}\rangle \\
& \langle Q_1 : D_1 \mid atts''_1\rangle \ldots \langle Q_p : D_p \mid atts''_p\rangle \\
& M'_1 \ldots M'_q \\
& \mathit{if}\ C
\end{aligned}
$$

where the Ms are message expressions, $i_1, \ldots, i_k$ are different numbers among the original $1, \ldots, m$, and C is the rule's condition. As we shall see later, some particular instances of rules of the form ($\ddagger$) correspond to the UNITY language, graph rewriting, dataflow, and neural net computations for which efficient parallel implementation techniques exist. That is, in some particular cases the cost of synchronization can be quite low, and a direct implementation of the corresponding rules may be the most natural and efficient thing to do. However, in cases where the synchronization and communication demands become quite high, it may be better to consider such synchronous rules as higher level executable specifications of the desired behavior, and to implement them at a lower level by asynchronous message passing. The paper [62] shows that, under quite general assumptions, it is indeed possible to transform synchronous rules of the form (‡) into simpler Actor-like rules of the form (†).

Besides the work already cited, a number of other authors have developed various object-oriented applications of rewriting logic. For example, Lechner, Lengauer, and Wirsing have carried out an ambitious case study investigating the expressiveness of rewriting logic and Maude for object-oriented specification and have explored refinement concepts in [58]; and Wirsing Nickl and Lechner [106] have proposed the rewriting logic-based *OOSpectrum* formalism for formal object-oriented specifications. Wirsing has also been studying the important topic of how to pass from more informal specifications expressed in any of the widely accepted object-oriented design notations to formal specifications in rewriting logic [105]. From a different, (co-)algebraic, perspective, Reichel has found rewriting logic useful in his final coalgebra semantics for objects [91]. The benefits of rewriting logic for execution of, and formal reasoning about, object-oriented ***discrete event simulations*** is another application area currently being investigated by Landauer [51].

Another area where rewriting logic has proved useful is in the specification and programming of ***object-oriented databases.*** Meseguer and Quian [81] have shown how the equational approach to object-oriented databases and bulk data types taken by other database researchers can be extended thanks to the use of rewrite rules to deal with the dynamic aspect of database ***updates***, so that a formal executable specification of all the aspects of an object-oriented database can be achieved. Denker and Gogolla [30] have used Maude to give semantics to the TROLL *light* object-oriented database specification language; this work has the advantage of providing a formal link between rewriting logic and the algebraic approach to information systems proposed by the IS-CORE Group [92, 44]. More recently, Pita and Martí-Oliet [89] have carried out a thorough case study on the application of Maude to the executable specification of a database model for broadcast telecommunication networks.

4.8 Unity

UNITY [19] is an elegant and important theory of concurrent programming with an associated logic to reason about the behavior of concurrent programs that has been developed by K. Many Chandy and Jayadev Misra. As shown in [75] the rewriting logic approach to object-oriented systems yields UNITY's model of computation as a special case in a direct way.

The details are given in [75], but the basic idea is straightforward. In essence a UNITY program is a a set of multiple assignment statements of the form

$$(\star) \quad x_1, \ldots, x_n := exp_1(x_1, \ldots, x_n), \ldots, exp_n(x_1, \ldots, x_n)$$

where the x_i are declared variables, and the $exp_i(x_1, \ldots, x_n)$ are Σ-terms for Σ a fixed many-sorted signature defined on the types of the declared variables. The intuitive meaning of executing such an assignment is that all the variables x_i are *simultaneously* assigned the values that their corresponding expression $exp_i(x_1, \ldots, x_n)$ evaluate to.

Such a program exactly corresponds to a rewrite theory specifying the behavior of a system composed of "variable" objects of the form $\langle x : T \mid val : v \rangle$ with T a type, having only one attribute, namely a value v of type T.

Each multiple assignment ($\star$) yields a corresponding rewrite rule, namely the rule:

$$\langle x_1 : T_1 \mid val : v_1 \rangle \ldots \langle x_n : T_n \mid val : v_n \rangle$$
$$\longrightarrow \langle x_1 : T_1 \mid val : exp_1(\overline{v}) \rangle \ldots \langle x_n : T_n \mid val : exp_n(\overline{v}) \rangle$$

4.9 Concurrent Access to Objects

In an object system there are two kinds of concurrency, ***inter-object*** concurrency, thanks to the concurrent execution of rules of the form (†) or (‡), and ***intra-object*** concurrency. Intra-object concurrency is due to the fact that many rewrites can simultaneously update different parts of an object's internal state; this can typically be due to the concurrency of the different functional data types used in the attributes of an object.

Inter- and intra-object concurrency can be combined to maximize overall concurrency. This can be accomplished through a number of subobjects under an object, to which many tasks of the object can be delegated in parallel. For Maude, this idea of "objects within objects" was suggested in [76] and is also used in [57]. However, even if the message-processing computations of a master object are made very "lightweight" by the object delegating tasks to its subobjects, the fact remains that in the formalization proposed so far *the same object cannot be shared by two simultaneous rewrites*, and therefore such a master object may still become a bottleneck. Therefore, as things stand rewrites involving the same object must be sequentialized, even if by safely sharing the object concurrency would be increased. For example, a flight object in an object-oriented airline reservation database should be accessible by several transaction messages simultaneously. This can be done using the general idea that the equational axioms of a rewrite theory have as their purpose to "loosen" the distributed state of the system in order to make it more concurrent. If we picture the concurrent multiset top structure of an object-oriented system as water in which the objects float, we can imagine each object as an insoluble blob of oil. What we need are "copying" and "emulsifying" axioms that can either duplicate or break the blob of oil into several pieces, so that the pieces can interact concurrently.

Consider first the case of simultaneous reads to the same object. We say that an object O occurs in a *read-only* way in a rewrite rule if the state of the object is the same on both sides of the rule. We would therefore like to share such an object in two simultaneous rewrites. This can be accomplished by adding the following two "copying" equational axioms to our specification[6]

$$\langle O : C \mid atts\rangle = \{O : C \mid atts \mid 0\}$$
$$\{O : C \mid atts \mid n\} = \{O : C \mid atts \mid n+1\}\ [O : C \mid atts]$$

and by transforming the original rules so that each read-only occurrence of an object $\langle O : C \mid atts\rangle$ in a rule is replaced by the sharable read-only variant $[O : C \mid atts]$.

The entities being shared by means of such "copying" axioms do not have to be objects in an object-oriented system. They could for example be places in a Petri net, or any kind of element in a distributed system having a multiset structure. The slightly more general formulation

$$x = \{x \mid 0\}$$
$$\{x \mid n\} = \{x \mid n+1\}\ [x]$$

where x ranges over elements in the multiset, allows this, and yields as a special case the place/transition version of the *contextual nets with positive contexts* model of computation with shared reads proposed by Montanari and Rossi [85]. Specifically, a contextual net transition t with preconditions $a_1, \ldots, a_n$, postconditions $b_1, \ldots, b_m$, and positive context $c_1, \ldots, c_k$ becomes a rewrite rule

$$t : a_1 \ldots a_n\, [c_1] \ldots [c_k] \longrightarrow b_1 \ldots b_m\, [c_1] \ldots [c_k]$$

More generally, one would like to allow simultaneous reads and writes on the same object. This can be accomplished by making the notion of reading or writing local to particular attributes within an object. This is related to the notational convention in object-oriented Maude specifications [83, 76] of not mentioning in a given rule those attributes of an object that are not relevant for that rule. Indeed, let $\overline{a : v}$ denote the attribute-value pairs $a_1 : v_1, \ldots, a_n : v_n$, where the $\overline{a}$ are the attribute identifiers of a given class C having $\overline{s}$ as the corresponding sorts of values prescribed for those attributes. In this context, the v_i can be either terms (with or without variables) or variables of sort s_i. We allow rules where the attributes appearing in the lefthand and righthand side patterns for an object O mentioned in the rule need not exhaust all the object's attributes, but can instead be in any two arbitrary subsets of the object's attributes[7]. We can picture this as follows

$$\ldots \langle O : C \mid \overline{al : vl}, \overline{ab : vb}\rangle \ldots \longrightarrow \ldots \langle O : C \mid \overline{ab : vb'}, \overline{ar : vr}\rangle \ldots$$

---

[6] Where the counting of the read-only copies and their read-only use guarantee coherence, since all the copies must have been "folded back together" in order for the original object to be engaged in a rewrite that changes some of its attributes.

[7] We assume that, as it is usually but not exclusively the case, the class of the object O does not change due to the rewrite; however, it should be possible to extend the present convention to some cases of interest in which the class does change.

where $\overline{al}$ are the attributes appearing only on the *left*, $\overline{ab}$ are the attributes appearing on *both* sides, and $\overline{ar}$ are the attributes appearing only on the *right*. What this abbreviates is a rule of the form

$$\begin{array}{l} \ldots \langle O : C \mid \overline{al : vl}, \overline{ab : vb}, \overline{ar : x}, atts\rangle \ldots \\ \longrightarrow \ldots \langle O : C \mid \overline{al : vl}, \overline{ab : vb'}, \overline{ar : vr}, atts\rangle \ldots \end{array}$$

where the $\overline{x}$ are new "don't care" variables and *atts* matches the remaining attribute-value pairs. The attributes mentioned only on the left are preserved unchanged, the original values of attributes mentioned only on the right don't matter, and all attributes not explicitly mentioned are left unchanged. Therefore, $\overline{al}$ are the *read-only* attributes actually involved in the rewrite, $\overline{ab}$ and $\overline{ar}$ are the *read* attributes, and the remaining attributes are not involved at all.

What we desire is a program transformation that replaces each rule

$$\ldots \langle O : C \mid \overline{al : vl}, \overline{ab : vb}\rangle \ldots \longrightarrow \ldots \langle O : C \mid \overline{ab : vb'}, \overline{ar : vr}\rangle \ldots$$

by the rule

$$\begin{array}{l} \ldots [O : C \mid \overline{al : vl}]\ \{O : C \mid \overline{ab : vb}, \overline{ar : x}\} \ldots \\ \longrightarrow \ldots [O : C \mid \overline{al : vl}]\ \{O : C \mid \overline{ab : vb'}, \overline{ar : vr}\} \ldots \end{array}$$

where $[O : C \mid \overline{al : vl}]$ is the sharable read-only part of the object, and $\{O : C \mid \overline{ab : vb}, \overline{ar : x}\}$ cannot be shared, and where possible additional attributes not involved in the rewrite are are again left implicit by convention.

With adequate equational axioms this allows several rules to simultaneously and coherently access the attributes of an object so that read-only attributes can take part in several simultaneous reads, but write attributes can only be modified by a single rewrite. The axioms in question achieve both "copying" and "emulsifying" effects and are quite simple

$$\begin{array}{l} \langle O : C \mid atts, att's\rangle = \{O : C \mid atts \mid att's \mid 0\} \\ \{O : C \mid atts \mid att's \mid n\} = \{O : C \mid atts \mid att's \mid n + 1\}\ [O : C \mid atts] \\ \{O : C \mid atts \mid att's, att''s \mid n\} = \{O : C \mid atts \mid att''s \mid n + 1\}\ \{O : C \mid att's\} \end{array}$$

What these axioms provide is a precise algebraic specification of what correct simultaneous access to objects should be, so that the concurrency of the system can be increased. They of course are like "magic," in that they give a declarative specification but do not prescribe any particular mechanism. A concrete implementation using for example locks on attributes, or concurrent aggregates [20], can then be judged correct relative to such a specification.

The above axioms are one way of illustrating how algebraic laws can axiomatize coherent simultaneous access to elements of a distributed state. The general method implicit in these examples is to increase the concurrency available in a rewrite theory $\mathcal{R}$ by defining a refinement map $\mathcal{R} \longrightarrow \mathcal{R}^\flat$, where we have added in $\mathcal{R}^\flat$ the additional equational laws that increase concurrency. Section 4.11 will present even simpler axioms for increasing concurrency in dataflow networks. It would be interesting to investigate equational laws for increased concurrency in areas such as coherent distributed memory models, and concurrent database transactions.

4.10 Graph Rewriting

Parallel graph rewriting is a model of computation of great importance. On the one hand, efficient implementations of functional languages often represent expressions as directed acyclic graphs rather than as trees, so that at the implementation level the rewriting taking place is graph rewriting. This case is usually called ***term graph rewriting*** and has been studied extensively (see [97] for a representative collection of papers). However, graph rewriting is a very general model and can express many other computations besides functional ones. The theory of graph grammars and graph transformations (see [33, 94] for recent conferences) considers graph rewriting in this more general sense.

Different mathematical axiomatizations of graph rewriting have been proposed in the literature. The categorical approach using double or single pushouts has been studied quite extensively [33, 94]. However, for our purposes the most convenient axiomatizations are those in which labelled graphs are axiomatized equationally as an algebraic data type in such a way that graph rewriting becomes rewriting modulo the equations axiomatizing the type. Axiomatizations in this spirit include those of Bauderon and Courcelle [9], Corradini and Montanari [26], and Raoult and Voisin [90].

Taking an object-oriented point of view allows a particularly simple axiomatization of graph rewriting in rewriting logic, similar in some respects—although with some notable differences—to the algebraic axiomatization of Raoult and Voisin [90] where graph rewriting is also understood as multiset rewriting. The basic idea is to consider each node of a labelled graph as an ***object*** with two attributes, one the data element labelling the node—which can belong to any desired data type of values—and the other a ***list*** of node names consisting of the immediate neighbors in the graph, that is, nodes to which the node is directly linked. Grouping them in a class *Node*, they have the form

$$\langle a : \mathit{Node} \mid \mathit{val} : v, \mathit{links} : l \rangle$$

An object with this information is essentially what is called a ***hyperedge*** in the terminology of graph grammars [27], except that hyperedge labels are defined as ***unstructured*** atomic elements that cannot be further analyzed, whereas we allow them to be structured data on which a graph rewrite rule can also impose patterns. We therefore treat the commonly occurring case in which all the edges coming out of a node can be naturally formalized by a single hyperedge; however, our treatment can easily be generalized to deal with several hyperedges with a common source node.

In this object-oriented view, a labelled graph is then understood as a ***configuration*** of node objects. Of course, as for other object-oriented systems, we require that different node objects should have different names. In addition, for such a configuration to be really a graph, there should be no "dangling pointers," that is, if a node name appears in the list of neighbors of a node, then there must be a node object with that name present in the configuration. Graph rewrite rules are then a special case of synchronous object-oriented rewrite rules

(‡) that do not involve any messages and that rewrite configurations that are graphs into other configurations that are also graphs.

We illustrate these ideas with an example borrowed from [62], namely a single graph rewrite rule accomplishing the clustering of a two-dimensional image into its set of connected components. We may assume that the image is represented as a two-dimensional array of points, where each point has a unique identifier different from that of any other point, say a nonzero number, if it is a point in the image; points not in the image have the value 0. Figure 1 shows one such image and its two connected components.

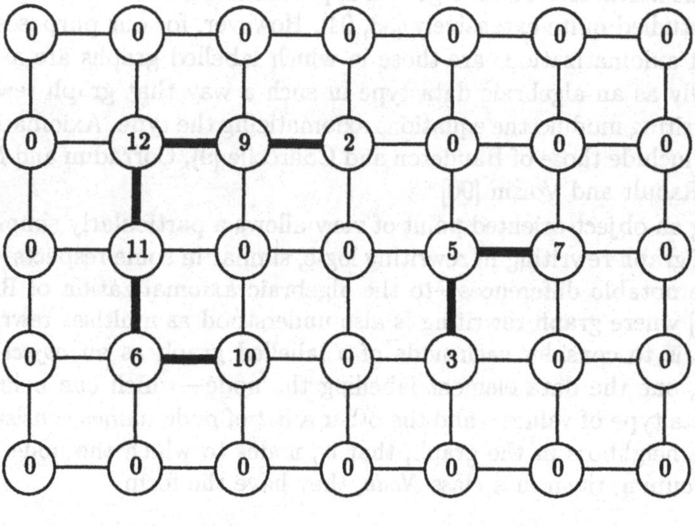

Fig. 1. Image as two-dimensional array.

One way to compute the connected components is to assign to all points in each component the greatest identifier present in the component. In the above example all points in the left component will end up with value 12, and all those in the right component with value 7. This can be accomplished by repeated application of the single rewrite rule in Figure 2, which can be applied concurrently to the data graph. Note that the rule is conditional on the value N_0 being different from 0. The labels a, b, c, d, e identify the same nodes of the graph before and after the rewrite is performed.

Note that only the value in node a may change as a result of applying this rule. Therefore, the remaining nodes act as "read-only" nodes that can be simultaneously read by other matches of the same rule, thus increasing concurrency. The rewriting logic expression of this rule, making the read-only nodes available for other matches, is simply,

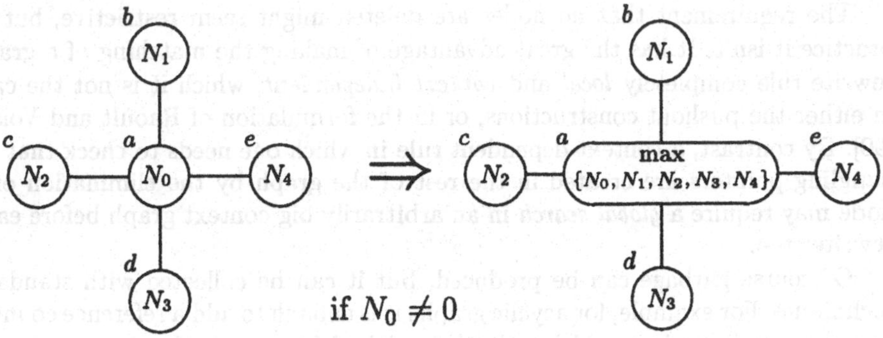

Fig. 2. A graph rewrite rule.

$$\begin{array}{ll} \langle A : Node \mid val : N_0, links : BCDE \rangle \to & \langle A : Node \mid val : max \rangle \\ [B : Node \mid val : N_1] & [B : Node \mid val : N_1] \\ [C : Node \mid val : N_2] & [C : Node \mid val : N_2] \\ [D : Node \mid val : N_3] & [D : Node \mid val : N_3] \\ [E : Node \mid val : N_4] & [E : Node \mid val : N_4] \end{array}$$

$$\textit{if } N_0 \neq 0$$
$$\textit{where } \; max = max(N_0, N_1, N_2, N_3, N_4)$$

In this rule, as it happens, the *topology* of the graph does not change. As explained in [62, 63], rules with this additional property, since they allow efficient data mapping at compile time and do not require any garbage collection, can be implemented in parallel very efficiently. They typically express highly regular parallel computing problems.

In general, however, a graph rewrite rule may change the links between the nodes and may add new nodes, but it is not allowed to remove nodes. In addition, it should not create "dangling pointers," which is guaranteed if the new links added in the righthand side all correspond to nodes appearing in the rule. As usual for object-oriented systems, the rule must also satisfy the additional requirement of never leading to a situation where two objects have the same name. Several simple solutions in the style described in [76] are possible for this. For example, we may assume that, when rules can create new nodes, the values stored in the nodes are actually pairs (v, n) consisting of the actual value v and a natural number n. Then, one of the "write" objects, say A, appearing on the lefthand side with value (v, n) can be used to create k fresh new names $A.n.1, \ldots, A.n.k$ for the k new nodes appearing on the righthand side, where the value of A now becomes $(v', n + 1)$ for an appropriate v'. This will always work, provided that the node names in the initial graph being rewritten are all different and do not involve strings of numbers.

The requirement that no nodes are deleted might seem restrictive, but in practice it isn't. It has the great advantage of making the matching of a graph rewrite rule completely *local* and *context independent*, which it is not the case in either the pushout constructions, or in the formulation of Raoult and Voisin [90]. By contrast, a context-dependent rule in which one needs to check that no dangling pointers are created in the rest of the graph by the elimination of a node may require a *global search* in an arbitrarily big context graph before each rewrite step.

Of course garbage can be produced, but it can be collected with standard techniques. For example, for acyclic graphs it is enough to add a reference counter as a new attribute in a sublclass *RcNode* with objects of the form

$$\langle a : RcNode \mid val : v, rc : n, links : l \rangle$$

and to update the reference count of those nodes in a rule's righthand side whose references have been modified by the rule. Assuming that nodes of the graph with zero reference count become garbage, one can then collect such garbage with rules

$$\langle A : RcNode \mid rc : 0, links : B\, L \rangle\ \langle B : RcNode \mid rc : n \rangle$$
$$\longrightarrow \langle A : RcNode \mid rc : 0, links : L \rangle\ \langle B : RcNode \mid rc : n - 1 \rangle$$

$$\langle A : RcNode \mid rc : 0, links : nil \rangle \longrightarrow null$$

The case of cyclic graphs could be handled with other techniques such as mark-and-sweep that can also be specificed by adequate rules.

4.11 Dataflow

The dataflow model of computation [43] has been thoroughly investigated both at the level of parallel functional languages, and in terms of parallel architectures directly supporting the dataflow model. In fact, it is one of the contending models of parallel computing and parallel architecture. The model is very intuitive. One pictures the computation as a graph in which data flows along edges and is computed in nodes labelled by different functions. The actual functions computed by each node are specified in an associated *data algebra*, which is just an algebraic data type such as the integers, the reals, or some many-sorted data type.

The specification of different variants of dataflow in rewriting logic is very direct. The variants in question have to do with the nature of edges. In *piped* models they are FIFO buffers—of arbitrary or of limited capacity, down to the case of holding a single value—in which data is placed as output of some node and consumed as input to another node. In *tagged* models, edges are instead multisets in which data tagged with a number is placed and consumed. In general, an edge is an object $\langle e : Edge \mid cts : c \rangle$ with just one attribute, namely a list or a multiset data structure.

Nodes are also objects. They contain a list of input edges, one or several output edges, and have a class identifying the functionality of the node. A *state* of the dataflow network is a configuration of edge and node objects. Typically it satisfies the restriction that each edge links exactly two nodes; duplication of data is made explicit by duplicator nodes. However, this restriction could be relaxed. The *firing rules* specifying the concurrent behavior of all networks with the same data algebra exactly correspond to object-oriented rewrite rules in which a node and its input and output edges rewrite together. Intuitively, however, the same edge could simultaneously receive the output of one rewrite and provide one of the inputs to another, so as to maximize the concurrency of the net. The equational axiom allowing simultaneous input and output access to an edge in the piped model is very simple, namely,

$$\langle e : Edge \mid cts : l\,x\rangle = [e : Edge \mid cts : l]_{in}\ [e : Edge \mid cts : x]_{out}$$

The firing rule for a functional node computing a function f of n arguments in the piped model is then

$$\begin{aligned}
&[e_1 : Edge \mid cts : x_1]_{out} \ldots [e_n : Edge \mid cts : x_n]_{out}\\
&\langle a : f \mid inputs : e_1 \ldots e_n, output : e\rangle\\
&[e : Edge \mid cts : l]_{in}\\
&\qquad \longrightarrow [e_1 : Edge \mid cts : nil]_{out} \ldots [e_n : Edge \mid cts : nil]_{out}\\
&\qquad\quad\ \langle a : f \mid inputs : e_1 \ldots e_n, output : e\rangle\\
&\qquad\quad\ [e : Edge \mid cts : f(x_1 \ldots x_n)\,l]_{in}
\end{aligned}$$

where we of course assume that the equations in our rewrite theory axiomatize the data algebra, so as to compute the actual value of $f(x_1 \ldots x_n)$. Similarly, the behavior of a T-gate control node that lets an element from its second input go through when the first input is true, and discards that same element when it is false, is axiomatized by the rules

$$\begin{aligned}
&[e_1 : Edge \mid cts : true]_{out}\ [e_2 : Edge \mid cts : x]_{out}\\
&\langle a : TGate \mid inputs : e_1\,e_2, output : e\rangle\\
&[e : Edge \mid cts : l]_{in}\\
&\qquad \longrightarrow [e_1 : Edge \mid cts : nil]_{out}\ [e_2 : Edge \mid cts : nil]_{out}\\
&\qquad\quad\ \langle a : TGate \mid inputs : e_1\,e_2, output : e\rangle\\
&\qquad\quad\ [e : Edge \mid cts : x\,l]_{in}
\end{aligned}$$

$$\begin{aligned}
&[e_1 : Edge \mid cts : false]_{out}\ [e_2 : Edge \mid cts : x]_{out}\\
&\langle a : TGate \mid inputs : e_1\,e_2, output : e\rangle\\
&[e : Edge \mid cts : l]_{in}\\
&\qquad \longrightarrow [e_1 : Edge \mid cts : nil]_{out}\ [e_2 : Edge \mid cts : nil]_{out}\\
&\qquad\quad\ \langle a : TGate \mid inputs : e_1\,e_2, output : e\rangle\\
&\qquad\quad\ [e : Edge \mid cts : l]_{in}
\end{aligned}$$

The firing rule for a duplicator node (Δ) is also straightforward, namely,

$$[e : Edge \mid cts : x]_{out}$$
$$\langle a : \Delta \mid input : e, outputs : e_1\, e_2\rangle$$
$$[e_1 : Edge \mid cts : l_1]_{in}\, [e_2 : Edge \mid cts : l_2]_{in}$$
$$\longrightarrow [e : Edge \mid cts : nil]_{out}$$
$$\langle a : \Delta \mid input : e, outputs : e_1\, e_2\rangle$$
$$[e_1 : Edge \mid cts : x\, l_1]_{in}\, [e_2 : Edge \mid cts : x\, l_2]_{in}$$

A dataflow network may be embedded in a highly unpredictable environment, such as for example a collection of sensors providing streams of inputs to the network. Such an environment can also be formalized by input nodes and a nondeterministic rewrite rule

$$\langle a : Input \mid output : e\rangle\, [e : Edge \mid cts : l]_{in}$$
$$\longrightarrow \langle a : Input \mid output : e\rangle\, [e : Edge \mid cts : x\, l]_{in}$$

where x is a variable of appropriate type.

Variants in which the FIFO buffer is bounded, as well as the tagged case can be handled with similar firing rules.

4.12 Neural Networks

Artificial neural networks [65] are another important model of parallel computation. They are particularly well-suited for providing massively parallel solutions to pattern recognition problems. They have been around since the early days of cybernetics, but have received renewed attention in recent years due to the many practical applications that have been found for them. The basic idea behind artificial neural networks is very simple: they are networks of computing nodes where each node simulates the behavior of a biological neuron. Each connection has a *weight*, and the neuron has a *threshold* θ that determines whether the stimulus is strong enough to cause its firing; both the weights and the threshold can be changed by training. When all the inputs from the connections with other neurons have been received, if their weighted sum exceeds the threshold, they cause the *firing* of the neuron's response, whose actual value is simulated as a particular function of the weighted sum of inputs minus the threshold. All such firings may happen asynchronously, thus yielding an intrinsically parallel model of computation.

The formalization in rewriting logic is very direct. Neurons can be regarded as objects

$$\langle b : Neuron \mid in(a_1) : (w_1, v_1), \ldots, in(a_n) : (w_n, v_n),$$
$$thld : \theta, function : f, out(c_1) : u_1, \ldots, out(c_m) : u_m\rangle$$

where the $a_1, \ldots, a_n$ are the neurons providing inputs, the $c_1, \ldots, c_m$ those receiving b's output, f is the name of the function governing the firing, the

$w_1, \ldots, w_n$ are the weights of the corresponding input connections, the $v_1, \ldots, v_n$ are either numerical values for the inputs, or the nonnumerical constant *mt* if a particular input has not been received, and the $u_1, \ldots, u_m$ are either *true* or *false* depending on whether the output has being received or not by the corresponding target neuron. The main rewrite rule is the firing rule for neurons, namely,

$$\begin{aligned}
&\langle b : Neuron \mid in(a_1) : (w_1, x_1), \ldots, in(a_n) : (w_n, x_n), \\
&\qquad thld : \theta, function : f, output : o, out(c_1) : true, \ldots, out(c_m) : true\rangle \\
&\to \langle b : Neuron \mid in(a_1) : (w_1, mt), \ldots, in(a_n) : (w_n, mt), \\
&\qquad thld : \theta, function : f, output : f((\Sigma_i x_i w_i) - \theta), \\
&\qquad out(c_1) : false, \ldots, out(c_m) : false\rangle
\end{aligned}$$

where the x_i are all variables of numerical type, and where we of course assume that the equational part of the specification fully axiomatizes all the required numerical computations, including the function f. To allow as much parallelism as possible in a neural network, we should allow all the inputs of a neuron to be received asynchronously and even concurrently, and the output to be similarly received by their targets. This can be accomplished using the techniques for simultaneous access to objects described in Section 4.9 by means of the single rewrite rule

$$\begin{aligned}
&\{a : Neuron \mid out(b) : false\}\ [a : Neuron \mid output(y)] \\
&\{b : Neuron \mid in(a) : (w, mt)\} \\
&\qquad \longrightarrow \{a : Neuron \mid out(b) : true\}\ [a : Neuron \mid output(y)] \\
&\qquad\quad \{b : Neuron \mid in(a) : (w, y)\}
\end{aligned}$$

Training of nets can also be easily formalized by similar rewrite rules, but a few more attributes must be added to each neuron for this purpose. Also, as in the dataflow case, the inputs from an external environment can be formalized by means of nondeterministic rewrite rules involving input nodes.

4.13 Real-Time Systems

The first important research contribution exploring the application of rewriting logic to real-time specification has been the work of Kosiuczenko and Wirsing on *timed rewriting logic* (TRL) [50], an extension of rewriting logic where the rewrite relation is labeled with time stamps. Axioms in TRL are sequents of the form $t \xrightarrow{r} t'$. Their intuitive meaning is that t evolves to t' in time r. The rules of deduction of standard rewriting logic are extended, and are further restricted, with time requirements, to allow only deductions in which all the different parts of a system evolve in the same amount of time. TRL has been shown well-suited for giving object-oriented specifications of complex hybrid systems such as the steam-boiler [87]. In fact, rewriting logic object-oriented specifications in the Maude language have a natural extension to TRL object-oriented specifications in *Timed Maude* [87].

Although it is in some sense possible to regard rewriting logic as a subcase of TRL in which all rules take zero time, Peter Ölveczky and I are currently investigating a different alternative, namely, the suitability of standard rewriting logic for directly specifying real-time systems. This seems an interesting research problem in its own right, and has the advantage of making available for real-time specification the different language tools that have been developed for standard rewriting logic.

A number of frequently used models of real-time computation have a very natural and direct expression in standard rewriting logic. One of the models that Ölveczky and I consider in [88] is *timed automata.* Omitting details about initial states and acceptance conditions, a timed automaton (see, e. g., [6]) consists of

- a finite alphabet Σ,
- a finite set S of states,
- a finite set C of clocks,
- a set $\Phi(C)$ of clock constraints, and
- a set $E \subseteq S \times S \times \Sigma \times 2^C \times \Phi(C)$ of transitions. The tuple $\langle s, s', a, \lambda, \phi \rangle$ represents a transition from state s to state s' on input symbol a. The set $\lambda \subseteq C$ gives the clocks to be reset with this transition, and ϕ is a clock constraint over C.

Given a timed word (i. e. a sequence of tuples $\langle a_i, r_i \rangle$ where a_i is an input symbol and r_i is the time at which it occurs), the automaton starts at time 0 with all clocks initialized to 0. As time advances the values of all clocks change, reflecting the elapsed time; that is, the state of the automaton can change not only by the above transitions, but also by the passage of time, with all the clocks being increased by the same amount. At time r_i the automaton changes state from s to s' using some transition of the form $\langle s, s', a_i, \lambda, \phi \rangle$ reading input a_i, if the current values of the clocks satisfy ϕ. With this transition the clocks in λ are reset to 0, and thus start counting time again.

A timed automaton can be naturally represented in rewriting logic. The time domain and its associated constraints $\Phi(C)$ are equationally axiomatized. Then, the tuple $\langle s, c_1, \ldots, c_n \rangle$ represents an automaton in state s such that the values of the clocks in C are $c_1, \ldots, c_n$. Each transition $\langle s, s', a, \lambda, \phi \rangle$ is then expressed as a rewrite rule

$$a : \langle s, c_1, \ldots, c_n \rangle \longrightarrow \langle s', c'_1, \ldots, c'_n \rangle \ \mathit{if}\ \phi(c_1, \ldots, c_n)$$

where $c'_i = 0$ if $c_i \in \lambda$, and $c'_i = c_i$ otherwise. In addition, a rewrite rule

$$\mathit{tick} : \langle x, c_1, \ldots, c_n \rangle \longrightarrow \langle x, c_1 + r, \ldots, c_n + r \rangle$$

(with r a variable in the time domain) is added to represent the elapse of time. Other real-time models such as *timed transition systems* [41] and *hybrid automata* [5, 4] have similar straightforward formulations within standard rewriting logic [88]. Ölveczky and I are also investigating a translation of TRL into rewriting logic with the purpose of making Timed Maude executable using the Maude interpreter.

5 Rewriting Logic Languages

Several language implementation efforts in Europe, the US, and Japan have adopted rewriting logic as their semantic basis and support either executable rewriting logic specification, or declarative parallel programming in rewriting logic.

5.1 Executable Specification Languages

Rewriting logic is particularly well-suited for the executable specification of systems and languages, including concurrent and distributed ones. As further discussed in Section 6.4, rewriting logic has also very good properties as a logical framework in which many other formal systems can be naturally represented. Several research groups have developed language tools to support formal reasoning and executable specification in rewriting logic.

The ELAN language developed at INRIA Lorraine by Borovanský, C. Kirchner, H. Kirchner, P.-E. Moreau and Vittek [46, 103, 16] has as modules *computational systems*, consisting of a rewrite theory and a *strategy* to guide the rewriting process. This group and their collaborators have developed a very impressive collection of examples and case studies in areas such as logic programming languages, constraint solving, higher-order substitution, equational theorem-proving and other such computational systems [46, 103, 49, 14, 18]. A nice feature of rewriting logic, namely its natural way of dealing with concurrency and interaction, is exploited by Viry to treat input-output for ELAN within the logic itself [101].

Futatsugi and Sawada at Japan's Advanced Institute of Science and Technology in Kanazawa are in a very mature stage of development of their Cafe language [37], which is also based on rewriting logic, contains OBJ as its functional sublanguage, and supports object-oriented specifications. The Cafe language will be the basis of an ambitious research effort involving several research institutions in Japan, Europe and the US, as well as several Japanese industries, to exploit the promising possibilities of rewriting logic for formal methods applications in software engineering.

In our group at SRI, Manuel Clavel, Steven Eker, Patrick Lincoln and I are working on the implementation of an interpreter for Maude [83, 76, 22]. Maude is based on a typed version of rewriting logic that is order-sorted and supports *sort constraints* [79]. It has *functional modules*, that are Church-Rosser and terminating equational theories, *system modules*, that specify general rewrite theories, and *object-oriented modules*, that provide syntactic sugar for object-oriented rewrite theories. These modules can be combined by module composition operations in the OBJ style. Its rewrite engine is highly modular and extensible, so that new matching algorithms for rewriting modulo different equational theories can easily be added and can be efficiently combined with those of other theories [34]. In addition, Maude supports reflective rewriting logic computations, and has flexible evaluation strategies.

5.2 Parallel Programming Languages

Since in general rewriting can take place *modulo* an arbitrary set of structural axioms E, which could be undecidable, some restrictions are necessary in order to use rewriting logic for parallel programming. We have therefore considered two subsets of rewriting logic. The first subset, in which the structural axioms E have algorithms for finding all the matches of a pattern modulo E, gives rise to the Maude language, in the sense that Maude modules are rewriting logic theories in that subset, and can be supported by an interpreter implementation adequate for rapid prototyping, debugging, and executable specification. The second, smaller subset gives rise to Simple Maude [62], a sublanguage meant to be used as a machine-independent parallel programming language. Program transformation techniques can then support passage from general rewrite theories to Maude modules and from them to modules in Simple Maude. Figure 3 summarizes the three levels involved.

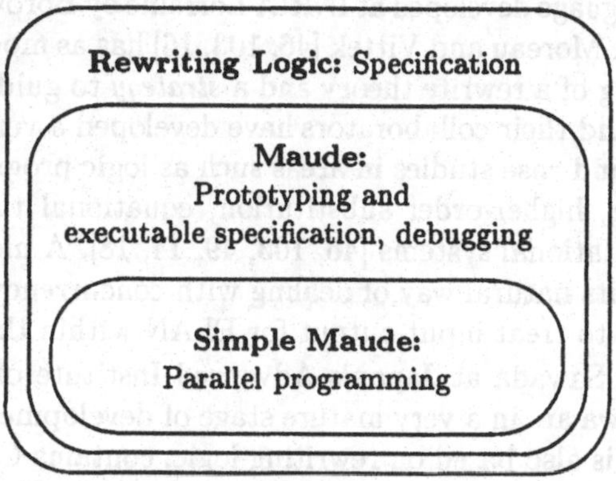

Fig. 3. Maude and Simple Maude as subsets of rewriting logic.

In Simple Maude, three types of rewriting, all of which can be efficiently implemented, are supported. Together, they cover a very wide variety of applications; they are:

Term rewriting. In this case, the data structures being rewritten are *terms*, that is, syntactic expressions that can be represented as labelled trees or acyclic graphs. Functional programming falls within this type of rewriting, that does also support nonconfluent term rewrite rules, and rewriting modulo confluent and terminating structural axioms E. Symbolic computations are naturally expressible using term rewrite rules.

Graph rewriting. In this case, the data structures being rewritten are *labelled graphs*. For general graph rewrite rules, the graph can evolve by rewriting in highly unpredictable ways. A very important subcase is that of graph rewrite rules for which the *topology* of the data graph remains unchanged after rewriting. Many highly regular computations, including many scientific computing applications, cellular automata algorithms, and systolic algorithms, fall within this fixed-topology subclass, for which adequate placement of the data graph on a parallel machine can lead to implementations with highly predictable and often quite low communications costs.

Object-oriented rewriting. This case corresponds to actor-like objects that interact with each other by asynchronous message-passing. Abstractly, the distributed state of a concurrent object-oriented system of this kind can be naturally regarded as a *multiset* data structure made up of objects and messages; the concurrent execution of messages then corresponds to concurrently rewriting this multiset by means of appropriate rewrite rules. In a parallel machine this is implemented by *communication* on a network, on which messages travel to reach their destination objects. Many applications are naturally expressible as concurrent systems of interacting objects. For example, many discrete event simulations, and many distributed AI and database applications can be naturally expressed and parallelized in this way.

The design of Simple Maude seeks to support a very wide range of parallel programming applications in an efficient and natural manner. In this sense Simple Maude is a *multiparadigm* parallel programming language that includes a *functional* facet (the term rewriting case), a *concurrent object-oriented* facet (the object-oriented rewriting case), and a facet supporting *highly regular in-place computations* (the graph rewriting case). By supporting programming and efficient execution of each application in the facet better suited for it, the inadequacies—both in terms of expressiveness and efficiency—of a single-facet language are avoided, while the benefits of each facet are preserved in their entirety.

Patrick Lincoln, Livio Ricciulli and I have developed parallel compilation techniquies and a prototype Simple Maude compiler [63] that generates parallel code for the Rewrite Rule Machine that we are developing at SRI [64]. Our detailed simulation and performance studies with an RRM having 64 SIMD nodes indicate that very high performance—typically with two to three orders of magnitude speedups over the best sequential implementations on advanced workstations for the same problem—can be achieved with this approach to declarative parallel computing with rewrite rules.

At INRIA Lorraine, Viry and C. Kirchner [47] have studied parallel implementation techniques for rewriting on loosely coupled parallel machines and have experimented with their techniques through a particular implementation in a transputer-based machine. Their approach addresses the case called term rewriting in the above classification, and provides new implementation techniques for this case on multicomputers.

Ciampolini, Lamma, Mello, and Stefanelli at the University of Bologna, have designed a parallel programming language called Distributed Logic Objects (DLO) that corresponds to an adequate subset of objec-oriented rewrite theories [21]. They have developed a number of implementation techniques for efficiently executing DLO in multicomputers. In their experience, rewriting logic provides a more attractive approach than stream-based parallel logic programming implementations; they point out that the actor subset of object oriented rewriting chosen in Simple Maude has also in their experience particularly good features for efficient implementation.

6 Other Developments and Research Directions

I include here several research developments that are more topical and can give the reader a more comprehensive view of the entire research program.

6.1 2-Category Models

Lawvere [54] made the seminal discovery that, given an equational theory $T = (\Sigma, E)$ and a Σ-algebra A satisfying E, the assignment to each E-equivalence class $[t(x_1, \ldots, x_n)]$ of its associated functional interpretation in A, $A_{[t]} : A^n \longrightarrow A$ is in fact a product-preserving functor $\hat{A} : \mathcal{L}_T \longrightarrow \mathbf{Set}$, when we view $[t(x_1, \ldots, x_n)]$ as an arrow $[t(x_1, \ldots, x_n)] : n \longrightarrow 1$ and compose such arrows by substitution. That is,

$$m \xrightarrow{([u_1], \ldots, [u_n])} n \xrightarrow{[t]} 1$$

yields as a composition $[t(\overline{u}/\overline{x})] : m \longrightarrow 1$. In fact, choosing canonical set-theoretic products in the targets of such functors and denoting by $\mathbf{Mod}(\mathcal{L}_T, \mathbf{Set})$ the category with objects those functors and morphims natural transformations between them the assignment, $A \mapsto \hat{A}$ becomes an isomorphism of categories

$$\mathbf{Alg}_{\Sigma,E} \cong \mathbf{Mod}(\mathcal{L}_T, \mathbf{Set})$$

where $\mathbf{Alg}_{\Sigma,E}$ is the category of T-algebras.

As pointed out in [74], this situation generalizes very naturally to the case of rewriting logic, where models are algebraic structures on categories instead than on sets. That is, the *ground* on which they exist is the 2-category [67, 45] **Cat**, instead of the category **Set**. Intuitively, $\mathcal{C}$ is a 2-category when the morphisms $\mathcal{C}(A, B)$ between two objects form not just a set, but a category, and the two arrow compositions fit together in a coherent way. In **Cat**, $\mathbf{Cat}(A, B)$ is the category with objects the functors from A to B, and with morphisms the natural transformations between such functors.

Given a rewrite theory $\mathcal{R} = (\Sigma, E, L, R)$ we define a 2-category with 2-products $\mathcal{L}_{\mathcal{R}}$ where the objects are the natural numbers, the category $\mathcal{L}_{\mathcal{R}}(n, 1)$ has as objects E-equivalence classes of terms $[t(x_1, \ldots, x_n)]$, and as morphisms equivalence classes of proof terms $[\alpha] : [t(x_1, \ldots, x_n)] \longrightarrow t'(x_1, \ldots, x_n)]$ with (vertical) composition given by $[\alpha]\ [\beta] = [\alpha; \beta]$. The horizontal composition of proofs

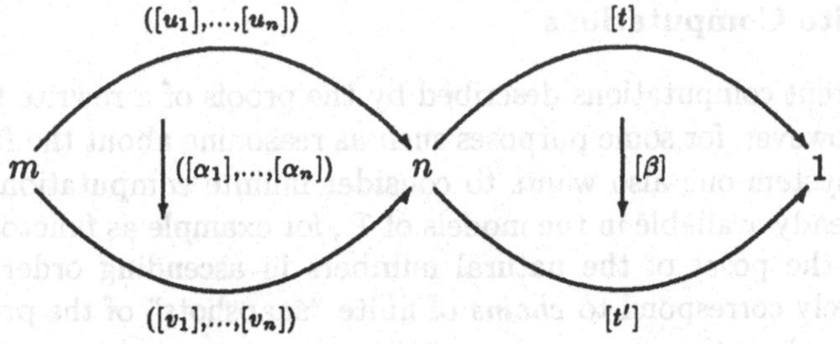

is then given by the proof term $[t(\overline{\alpha}/\overline{x}); \beta(\overline{v}/\overline{x})] : [t(\overline{u}/\overline{x})] \longrightarrow [t'(\overline{v}/\overline{x})]$.

The point is that, as mentioned in [74], $\mathcal{L}_{\mathcal{R}}$ does for $\mathcal{R}$-systems what in the **Set** case $\mathcal{L}_T$ does for T-algebras. That is, given an $\mathcal{R}$-system $\mathcal{S}$ the assignment to each rule $r : [t] \longrightarrow [t']$ in R of a natural transformation $r_{\mathcal{S}} : t_{\mathcal{S}} \Rightarrow t'_{\mathcal{S}}$ between the functors $t_{\mathcal{S}}, t'_{\mathcal{S}} : \mathcal{S}^n \longrightarrow \mathcal{S}$ extends naturally to a 2-product preserving 2-functor $\hat{\mathcal{S}} : \mathcal{L}_{\mathcal{R}} \longrightarrow$ **Cat**, and the assignment $\mathcal{S} \mapsto \hat{\mathcal{S}}$ yields an isomorphism of 2-categories

$$\mathcal{R}\textbf{-Sys} \cong \textbf{Mod}(\mathcal{L}_{\mathcal{R}}, \textbf{Cat})$$

where $\textbf{Mod}(\mathcal{L}_{\mathcal{R}}, \textbf{Cat})$ is the category of canonical 2-product-preserving 2-functors from $\mathcal{L}_{\mathcal{R}}$ to **Cat**.

Therefore, models of rewriting logic have a natural 2-categorical interpretation in which $\mathcal{L}_{\mathcal{R}}$ plays the role of generic model among all the 2-category models of $\mathcal{R}$. This point of view has been further generalized and exploited in Pisa to provide very useful connections with other concurrency theory models. Corradini, Gadducci and Montanari [25] provide a uniform construction for $\mathcal{L}_{\mathcal{R}}$ and for a *sesqui-category* model, similar to $\mathcal{L}_{\mathcal{R}}$ but satisfying fewer equations, that has been proposed by Stell [98]. They associate posets of partial orders of events to both models, and make the important observation that when a rewrite rule is not right linear—that is, when it has a repeated occurrence of a variable in its righthand side—then the poset associated to $\mathcal{L}_{\mathcal{R}}$ is not a prime algebraic domain, whereas the poset of the sesqui-category model is. In this way, the relationship between rewriting logic models and event structures is clarified. What happens is that, when rules are not right linear, $\mathcal{L}_{\mathcal{R}}$ is in a sense too abstract, because what is one event in one proof term may— because of repetition of variables— become several events in a proof term equivalent to it by the exchange axiom; in the sesqui-category model the exchange axiom does not hold, and therefore those computations are considered different.

More recently, Gadducci and Montanari have proposed another generalization of $\mathcal{L}_{\mathcal{R}}$ to a *double category* [45], in which one composes vertically and horizontally square "tiles" instead of just cells. Their model is particularly perspicuous for dealing with *context conditions* required for a rewriting, such as those arising in structural operational semantics presentations. In particular, they give a very elegant categorical semantics of CCS that fits very precisely with its standard operational semantics definiton.

6.2 Infinite Computations

The concurrent computations described by the proofs of a rewrite theory $\mathcal{R}$ are all *finite*. However, for some purposes such as reasoning about the fairness properties of a system one also wants to consider infinite computations. Somehow, they are already available in the models of $\mathcal{R}$, for example as functors $\omega \longrightarrow \mathcal{T}_{\mathcal{R}}$, where ω is the poset of the natural numbers in ascending order. Such functors intuitively correspond to *chains* of finite "snapshots" of the progress of the computation along time.

This viewpoint can be made more abstract by considering adequate notions of equivalence between such chains, since the particular instant chosen for each snapshot should not matter. Sassone, Montanari and I have studied in detail this more abstract notion of infinite computation in the particular case when $\mathcal{R}$ is the rewrite theory of a Petri net [93]. However, the techniques that we have developed, based on the notion of completion by filtered colimits of a category, should extend naturally to the case of rewrite theories.

Talcott has focused on the case of infinite computations for actor systems specified in rewriting logic, to obtain a precise semantic account of their fair computations. Her ideas and results are very elegant; they are discussed in [99].

Yet another, quite interesting approach has been taken by Corradini and Gadducci [24]. They consider rewrite theories with empty set of equations and interpret them in *continuos* cpo algebra models in such a way that not only the terms, but also the proof terms, become endowed with an approximation ordering. They then propose a natural *infinitary* extension of rewriting logic that allows reasoning about infinite computations that are limits of finite ones. Then, they study the soundness and completeness of their infinitary logic in terms of 2-category models in an adequate cpo-enriched 2-category.

6.3 Formal Reasoning, Refinement, and Program Transformation

Although a good amount of formal reasoning about rewriting logic specifications can be carried out within the logic itself—a good example is the formal reasoning about actor systems illustrated by Talcott in [100]—one may want for certain purposes, such as for example to reason about global properties of a system, to use a more abstract formal language to complement the more operational formalization provided by rewriting logic. Modal or temporal logics seem good candidates for this more abstract level of specification. Lechner and Lengauer [56] and more recently Lechner [55] have proposed the modal μ-calculus as that more abstract level of specification. Modal μ-calculus specifications can then be *refined* into more specific ones until reaching a rewriting logic specification. Martí-Oliet and I are also investigating an adequate modal logic for similar purposes.

In fact, the refinement process is also very important at the level of rewriting logic specifications, since it supports program transformations, implementations of more abstract levels by more concrete ones, and important theory composition operations such as the instantiation of parameterized modules. An approach to refinement of rewrite theories by means of maps $\mathcal{R} \longrightarrow \mathcal{Q}$ that can be best understood as 2-functors $\mathcal{L}_{\mathcal{R}} \longrightarrow \mathcal{L}_{\mathcal{Q}}$ between the corresponding Lawvere theories was proposed in [74]. A similar notion has also been proposed and used by Lechner Lengauer and Wirsing in [58]. Yet another recent development that seems promising for reasoning about behavioral satisfaction and that may provide more flexible ways of refining rewriting logic specifications is Diaconescu's notion of *hidden sorted* rewriting logic [32].

Viry has developed a very useful program transformation techniques for rewrite theories using completion methods [102]. His key notion is that of *coherence* between the equational part E and the rules R of a rewrite theory. This property makes very easy the implementation of such a theory by rewriting techniques without having to have an E-matching algorithm. Lincoln, Martí-Oliet and I have studied several program transformation techniques, including coherence completion, to pass from rewrite theories to theories implementable in Maude, and from Maude specifications to efficient parallel programs in Simple Maude [62].

6.4 Rewriting Logic as a Logical Framework

Rewriting logic is like a coin with two inseparable sides: one computational and another logical. A proof term is a concurrent computation and viceversa. The generality and expressiveness of rewriting logic as a semantic framework for concurrent computation has also a logical counterpart. Indeed, rewriting logic is also a promising *logical framework* or *universal logic* in which many different logics and formal systems can be naturally represented and interrelated. Doing justice to this logical side is beyond the scope of this paper, but good evidence, including a good number of examples of logic representations can be found in two joint papers with Martí-Oliet [68, 69]. Additional quite impressive evidence is also provided by research based on the ELAN language [46, 103, 49, 14, 18], that stresses the logical framework applications of rewriting logic.

There is also a very fruitful relationship between rewriting logic and the theory of *reasoning theories* proposed by Giunchiglia, Pecchiari and Talcott [39]. Reasoning theories provide a logic-independent architecture for combining and interoperating different mechanized formal systems. They are closely related to rewrite theories and there are fruitful synergies between both concepts that Carolyn Talcott and I are currently investigating [82].

The work of Levy and Agustí [60, 59, 61] and the more recent work of Schorlemmer [95] explores the relationships between rewriting logic and their general bi-rewriting approach to automated deduction.

6.5 Reflection and Strategies

Intuitively, a logic is reflective if it can represent its metalevel at the object level in a sound and coherent way. Reflection is a very useful property in computing systems and therefore very desirable in a computational logic. Manuel Clavel and I [23] have given general axioms centered around the notion of a *universal theory* that a logic should satisfy to properly be called reflective. We have also shown that rewriting logic is reflective in this precise sense. This opens up very interesting possibilities for rewiting logic languages that will be exploited in Maude [22], ELAN [48], and Cafe.

Reflection is closely connected with the topic of *strategies* that is of outmost importance in rewriting logic to control the rewriting process. Clavel and I have proposed the notion of an *internal strategy language* for a general logic, and have advocated it for rewriting logic [23] as a way of being able to reason formally within the logic about the semantics of strategies. This general idea of expressing strategies with rewrite rules has also been adopted by the most recent work on ELAN [15], and by the Maude system [22].

6.6 Avoiding the Frame Problem

Since rewriting logic is a logic of change whose subject matter is precisely the dynamic changes in context within a system, all the insoluble problems and absurdities that one runs into when trying to formalize change with essentially static logics—the so-called *frame problem*—do not cause any trouble for rewriting logic. Martí-Oliet and I have explained the advantages of rewriting logic for formally representing change, have illustrated those advantages with many examples, and have shown how other logical approaches to dynamic change can be subsumed within rewriting logic [70].

6.7 Nondeterminism

A poset is a poor man's category. Therefore, the different algebraic powerset models of nondeterminism can be understood as categories. In this way, as explained in [75], many models of nondeterminism can be viewed as restricted instances of models of rewrite theories. The relationship between rewriting logic and algebraic models of nondeterminism is further explored in the recent survey on the subject by Meldal and Walicki [104].

7 Concluding Remarks

Thanks to the important contributions of the researchers mentioned in this survey, the rewriting logic research program has advanced to a stage in which more ambitious future tasks can be contemplated.

We can see the outlines of rewriting logic as a wide-spectrum semantic framework. This framework will be complemented at a more abstract level by specifications in some form of temporal or modal logic that can be further refined through formal techniques, first into rewriting logic specifications, and then into efficent declarative programs in subsets for which good parallel implementations exist. Encouraging advances at all the levels of this spectrum have already been made. However, much work remains ahead to tie these levels together, and to develop both formal techniques and well-finished tools supporting all the tasks involved. Tools of this kind include verification tools to mechanically check important properties, sequential and parallel compilers, and tools for program transformation. The area of reflection and strategies seems very important and promising, and will also require much more work.

With tools and methods sufficiently developed, it will become possible to bring these ideas into contact with industrial practice, both for formal methods applications, and for the development of entire software solutions. Areas such as parallel and distributed programming, mobile computing, office automation, hardware verification, parallel symbolic simulation, logical framework uses, and formal software environments would provide very good application opportunities. All this will keep us busy for a while.

Acknowledgments

I very much wish to thank all the researchers who have contributed through their work to the advancement of these ideas. With many of them I have exchanged ideas in person that have enriched and influenced my views, and from all of them I have learned much. I owe a special debt of gratitude to those researchers with whom I am working or have worked most closely on these topics. They include Adel Bouhoula, Manuel Clavel, Steven Eker, Kokichi Futatsugi, Jean-Pierre Jouannaud, Patrick Lincoln, Narciso Martí-Oliet, Peter Ölveczky, Xiaolei Qian, Livio Ricciulli, Carolyn Talcott, and Timothy Winkler. I have also benefited much form conversations with Joseph Goguen, Ugo Montanari and Claude and Hélène Kirchner. Manuel Clavel, Jagan Jagannathan, Patrick Lincoln, Peter Ölveczky, and Carolyn Talcott deserve special thanks for their help reading earlier drafts of this paper. I finally thank again the organizers of CONCUR'96 for giving me the opportunity of presenting these ideas in Pisa, a beautiful city full of dear friends and fond memories.

References

1. Peter Aczel. A general Church-Rosser theorem. Manuscript, University of Manchester, 1978.
2. G. Agha. *Actors.* MIT Press, 1986.
3. G. Agha and C. Hewitt. Concurrent programming using actors. In A. Yonezawa and M. Tokoro, editors, *Object-Oriented Concurrent Programming,* pages 37–53. MIT Press, 1988.
4. R. Alur, C. Courcoubetis, N. Halbwachs, T. A. Henzinger, P.-H. Ho, X. Nicollin, A. Olivero, J. Sifakis, and S. Yovine. The algorithmic analysis of hybrid systems. *Theoretical Computer Science,* 138:3–34, 1995.
5. R. Alur, C. Courcoubetis, T. A. Henzinger, and P.-H. Ho. Hybrid automata: an algorithmic approach to the specification and verification of hybrid systems. In R.L. Grossman, A. Nerode, A.P. Ravn, and H. Rischel, editors, *Workshop on Theory of Hybrid Systems,* pages 209–229. Springer LNCS 739, 1993.
6. Rajeev Alur and David Dill. The theory of timed automata. In J.W. de Bakker, G. Huizing, W. P. de Roever, and G. Rozenberg, editors, *Real-Time: Theory in Practice,* volume 600 of *Lecture Notes in Computer Science,* 1991.

7. J.-P. Banâtre and D. Le Mètayer. The Gamma model and its discipline of programming. *Science of Computer Programming*, 15:55–77, 1990.
8. E. Battiston, V. Crespi, F. De Cindio, and G. Mauri. Semantic frameworks for a class of modular algebraic nets. In M. Nivat, C. Rattray, T. Russ, and G. Scollo, editors, *Proc. of the 3rd International AMAST Conference*, Workshops in Computing. Springer-Verlag, 1994.
9. M. Bauderon and B. Courcelle. Graph expressions and graph rewriting. *Math. Systems Theory*, 20:83–127, 1987.
10. Gérard Berry and Gérard Boudol. The chemical abstract machine. *Theoretical Computer Science*, 96(1):217–248, 1992.
11. E. Best and R. Devillers. Sequential and concurrent behavior in Petri net theory. *Theoretical Computer Science*, 55:87-136, 1989.
12. M. Bettaz and M. Maouche. How to specify nondeterminism and true concurrency with algebraic term nets. In M. Bidoit and C. Choppy, editors, *Recent Trends in Data Type Specification*, pages 164–180. Springer LNCS 655, 1993.
13. M. Bettaz and M. Maouche. Modeling of object based systems with hidden sorted ECATNets. In *Proc. of MASCOTS'95, Durham, North Carolina*, pages 307–311. IEEE, 1995.
14. P. Borovanský. Implementation of higher-order unification based on calculus of explicit substitutions. In M. Bartosek, J. Staudek, and J. Wiedermann, editors, *Proc. SOFTSEM'95*, pages 363–368. Springer LNCS 1012, 1995.
15. P. Borovanský, C. Kirchner, and H. Kirchner. Controlling rewriting by rewriting. To appear in *Proc. 1st Intl. Workshop on Rewriting Logic and its Applications*, ENTCS, North Holland, 1996.
16. P. Borovanský, C. Kirchner, H. Kirchner, P.-E. Moreau, and M. Vittek. ELAN: A logical framework based on computational systems. To appear in *Proc. 1st Intl. Workshop on Rewriting Logic and its Applications*, ENTCS, North Holland, 1996.
17. G. Boudol. Computational semantics of term rewriting systems. In Maurice Nivat and John Reynolds, editors, *Algebraic Methods in Semantics*, pages 169–236. Cambridge University Press, 1985.
18. C. Castro. An approach to solving binary CSP using computational systems. To appear in *Proc. 1st Intl. Workshop on Rewriting Logic and its Applications*, ENTCS, North Holland, 1996.
19. K. Mani Chandy and Jayadev Misra. *Parallel Program Design: A Foundation*. Addison-Wesley, 1988.
20. A. Chien. *Concurrent Aggregates*. MIT Press, 1993.
21. A. Ciampolini, E. Lamma, P. Mello, and C. Stefanelli. Distributed logic objects: a fragment of rewriting logic and its implementation. To appear in *Proc. 1st Intl. Workshop on Rewriting Logic and its Applications*, ENTCS, North Holland, 1996.
22. Manuel G. Clavel, Steven Eker, Patrick Lincoln, and José Meseguer. Principles of Maude. To appear in *Proc. 1st Intl. Workshop on Rewriting Logic and its Applications*, ENTCS, North Holland, 1996.
23. Manuel G. Clavel and José Meseguer. Axiomatizing reflective logics and languages. In Gregor Kiczales, editor, *Proceedings of Reflection'96, San Francisco, California, April 1996*, pages 263–288. Xerox PARC, 1996.
24. A. Corradini and F. Gadducci. CPO models for infinite term rewriting. In *Proc. AMAST'95*, pages 368–384. Springer LNCS 936, 1995.
25. A. Corradini, F. Gadducci, and U. Montanari. Relating two categorical models of term rewriting. In J. Hsiang, editor, *Proc. Rewriting Techniques and Applications, Kaiserslautern*, pages 225–240, 1995.

26. Andrea Corradini and Ugo Montanari. An algebra of graphs and graph rewriting. In D.H. Pitt et al., editor, *Category Theory and Computer Science*, pages 236–260. Springer LNCS 530, 1991.
27. B. Courcelle. Graph rewriting: an algebraic and logic approach. In J. van Leeuwen, editor, *Handbook of Theoretical Computer Science, Vol. B*, pages 193–242. North-Holland, 1990.
28. P. Degano, J. Meseguer, and U. Montanari. Axiomatizing net computations and processes. In *Proc. LICS'89*, pages 175–185. IEEE, 1989.
29. P. Degano, J. Meseguer, and U. Montanari. Axiomatizing the algebra of net computations and processes. To appear in *Acta Informatica*, 1996.
30. G. Denker and M. Gogolla. Translating TROLL *light* concepts to Maude. In H. Ehrig and F. Orejas, editors, *Recent Trends in Data Type Specification*, volume 785 of *LNCS*, pages 173–187. Springer-Verlag, 1994.
31. N. Dershowitz and J.-P. Jouannaud. Rewrite systems. In J. van Leeuwen, editor, *Handbook of Theoretical Computer Science, Vol. B*, pages 243–320. North-Holland, 1990.
32. R. Diaconescu. Hidden sorted rewriting logic. To appear in *Proc. 1st Intl. Workshop on Rewriting Logic and its Applications*, ENTCS, North Holland, 1996.
33. H. Ehrig, H.-J. Kreowski, and G. Rozenberg, editors. *Graph Grammars and their Application to Computer Science*. Springer LNCS 532, 1991.
34. Steven Eker. Fast matching in combination of regular equational theories. To appear in *Proc. 1st Intl. Workshop on Rewriting Logic and its Applications*, ENTCS, North Holland, 1996.
35. J. Engelfriet, G. Leih, and G. Rozenberg. Parallel object-based systems and Petri nets, I and II. Technical Report 90-04,90-05, Dept. of Computer Science, University of Leiden, February 1990.
36. J. Engelfriet, G. Leih, and G. Rozenberg. Net-based description of parallel object-based systems, or POTs and POPs. In J. W. de Bakker, W. P. de Roever, and G. Rozenberg, editors, *Foundations of Object-Oriented Languages, Noordwijkerhout, The Netherlands, May/June 1990*, pages 229–273. Springer LNCS 489, 1991.
37. K. Futatsugi and T. Sawada. Cafe as an extensible specification environment. To appear in *Proc. of the Kunming International CASE Symposium, Kunming, China, November*, 1994.
38. F. Gadducci and U. Montanari. Enriched categories as models of computation. In *Proc. 5th Italian Conference on Theoretical Computer Science, Ravello*, 1995.
39. F. Giunchiglia, C.L. Pecchiari, and C. Talcott. Reasonig theories: towards an architecture for open mechanized reasoning systems. Technical Report 9409-15, IRST, University of Trento, November 1994.
40. Joseph Goguen and José Meseguer. Order-sorted algebra I: Equational deduction for multiple inheritance, overloading, exceptions and partial operations. *Theoretical Computer Science*, 105:217–273, 1992. Originally given as lecture at *Seminar on Types*, Carnegie-Mellon University, June 1983; several draft and technical report versions were circulated since 1985.
41. T.A. Henzinger, Z. Manna, and A. Pnueli. Timed transition systems. In J.W. de Bakker, G. Huizing, W. P. de Roever, and G. Rozenberg, editors, *Real-Time: Theory in Practice*, volume 600 of *Lecture Notes in Computer Science*, 1991.
42. ISO. *IS8807 : Information Processing Systems - Open System Interconnection - LOTOS - A formal description technique based on the temporal ordering of observational behavior*. ISO, February 1989.

43. R. Jagannathan. Dataflow models. In E.Y. Zoyama, editor, *Parallel and Distributed Computing Handbook*, pages 223–238. McGraw Hill, 1996.
44. R. Jungclaus, G. Saake, T. Hartmann, and C. Sernadas, editors. *Object-oriented specification of information systems: the TROLL language.* Technische Universität Braunschweig, Information-Berichte 91-04, 1991.
45. G.M. Kelly and R. Street. Review of the elements of 2-categories. In G.M. Kelly, editor, *Category Seminar, Sydney 1972/73*, pages 75–103. Springer Lecture Notes in Mathematics No. 420, 1974.
46. C. Kirchner, H. Kirchner, and M. Vittek. Designing constraint logic programming languages using computational systems. In V. Saraswat and P. van Hentryck, editors, *Principles and Practice of Constraint Programming: The Newport Papers*, pages 133–160. MIT Press, 1995.
47. C. Kirchner and P. Viry. Implementing parallel rewriting. In B. Fronhöfer and G. Wrightson, editors, *Parallelization in Inference Systems*, pages 123–138. Springer LNAI 590, 1992.
48. H. Kirchner and P.-E. Moreau. Computational reflection and extension in ELAN. To appear in *Proc. 1st Intl. Workshop on Rewriting Logic and its Applications*, ENTCS, North Holland, 1996.
49. H. Kirchner and P.-E. Moreau. Prototyping completion with constraints using computational systems. In J. Hsiang, editor, *Proc. Rewriting Techniques and Applications, Kaiserslautern*, 1995.
50. P. Kosiuczenko and M. Wirsing. Timed rewriting logic, 1995. Working material for the 1995 Marktoberdorf International Summer School "Logic of Computation".
51. C. Landauer. Discrete event systems in rewriting logic. To appear in *Proc. 1st Intl. Workshop on Rewriting Logic and its Applications*, ENTCS, North Holland, 1996.
52. C. Laneve and U. Montanari. Axiomatizing permutation equivalence in the λ-calculus. In H. Kirchner and G. Levi, editors, *Proc. Third Int. Conf. on Algebraic and Logic Programming, Volterra, Italy, September 1992*, volume 632 of *LNCS*, pages 350–363. Springer-Verlag, 1992.
53. C. Laneve and U. Montanari. Axiomatizing permutation equivalence. *Mathematical Structures in Computer Science*, 1994. To appear.
54. F. William Lawvere. Functorial semantics of algebraic theories. *Proceedings, National Academy of Sciences*, 50:869–873, 1963. Summary of Ph.D. Thesis, Columbia University.
55. U. Lechner. Object-oriented specification of distributed systems in the μ-calculus and Maude. To appear in *Proc. 1st Intl. Workshop on Rewriting Logic and its Applications*, ENTCS, North Holland, 1996.
56. U. Lechner and C. Lengauer. Modal μ-Maude. To appear in *Object Orientation with Parallelism and Persistence*, B. Freitag, C.B. Jones, C. Lengauer and H.-J. Schek, editors, Kluwer, 1996.
57. U. Lechner, C. Lengauer, F. Nickl, and M. Wirsing. How to overcome the inheritance anomaly. To appear in *Proc.ECOOP'96*, Springer LNCS, 1996.
58. U. Lechner, C. Lengauer, and M. Wirsing. An object-oriented airport. In E. Astesiano, G. Reggio, and A. Tarlecki, editors, *Recent Trends in Data Type Specification, Santa Margherita, Italy, May/June 1994*, pages 351–367. Springer LNCS 906, 1995.

59. J. Levy. A higher order unification algorithm for bi-rewriting systems. In J. Agustí and P. García, editors, *Segundo Congreso Programación Declarativa*, pages 291–305, Blanes, Spain, September 1993. CSIC.
60. J. Levy and J. Agustí. Bi-rewriting, a term rewriting technique for monotonic order relations. In C. Kirchner, editor, *Proc. Fifth Int. Conf. on Rewriting Techniques and Applications, Montreal, Canada, June 1993*, volume 690 of *LNCS*, pages 17–31. Springer-Verlag, 1993.
61. J.-J. Lévy. Optimal reductions in the lambda calculus. In J. P. Seldin and J. R. Hindley, editors, *To H.B. Curry: Essays on Combinatory Logic, Lambda Calculus and Formalism*, pages 159–191. Academic Press, 1980.
62. Patrick Lincoln, Narciso Martí-Oliet, and José Meseguer. Specification, transformation, and programming of concurrent systems in rewriting logic. In G.E. Blelloch, K.M. Chandy, and S. Jagannathan, editors, *Specification of Parallel Algorithms*, pages 309–339. DIMACS Series, Vol. 18, American Mathematical Society, 1994.
63. Patrick Lincoln, Narciso Martí-Oliet, José Meseguer, and Livio Ricciulli. Compiling rewriting onto SIMD and MIMD/SIMD machines. In *Proceedings of PARLE'94, 6th International Conference on Parallel Architectures and Languages Europe*, pages 37–48. Springer LNCS 817, 1994.
64. Patrick Lincoln, José Meseguer, and Livio Ricciulli. The Rewrite Rule Machine Node Architecture and its Performance. In *Proceedings of CONPAR'94, Linz, Austria, September 1994*, pages 509–520. Springer LNCS 854, 1994.
65. R.P. Lippmann. An introduction to computing with neural nets. *IEEE ASSP Magazine*, pages 4–22, April 1987.
66. The Chemical Abstract Machine. Gérard Berry and Gérard Boudol. In *Proc. POPL'90*, pages 81–94. ACM, 1990.
67. Saunders MacLane. *Categories for the working mathematician.* Springer-Verlag, 1971.
68. Narciso Martí-Oliet and José Meseguer. Rewriting logic as a logical and semantic framework. Technical Report SRI-CSL-93-05, SRI International, Computer Science Laboratory, August 1993. To appear in D. Gabbay, ed., *Handbook of Philosophical Logic*, Oxford University Press.
69. Narciso Martí-Oliet and José Meseguer. General logics and logical frameworks. In D. Gabbay, editor, *What is a Logical System?*, pages 355–392. Oxford University Press, 1994.
70. Narciso Martí-Oliet and José Meseguer. Action and change in rewriting logic. In R. Pareschi and B. Fronhoefer, editors, *Theoretical Approaches to Dynamic Worlds in Artificial Intelligence and Computer Science.* 1996. To be published by Kluwer Academic Publisher.
71. Satoshi Matsuoka and Akinori Yonezawa. Analysis of inheritance anomaly in object-oriented concurrent programming languages. In Gul Agha, Peter Wegner, and Akinori Yonezawa, editors, *Research Directions in Concurrent Object-Oriented Programming*, pages 107–150. MIT Press, 1993.
72. José Meseguer. A logical theory of concurrent objects. In *ECOOP-OOPSLA'90 Conference on Object-Oriented Programming, Ottawa, Canada, October 1990*, pages 101–115. ACM, 1990.
73. José Meseguer. Rewriting as a unified model of concurrency. In *Proceedings of the Concur'90 Conference, Amsterdam, August 1990*, pages 384–400. Springer LNCS 458, 1990.

74. José Meseguer. Rewriting as a unified model of concurrency. Technical Report SRI-CSL-90-02, SRI International, Computer Science Laboratory, February 1990. Revised June 1990.
75. José Meseguer. Conditional rewriting logic as a unified model of concurrency. *Theoretical Computer Science*, 96(1):73–155, 1992.
76. José Meseguer. A logical theory of concurrent objects and its realization in the Maude language. In Gul Agha, Peter Wegner, and Akinori Yonezawa, editors, *Research Directions in Concurrent Object-Oriented Programming*, pages 314–390. MIT Press, 1993.
77. José Meseguer. Solving the inheritance anomaly in concurrent object-oriented programming. In Oscar M. Nierstrasz, editor, *Proc. ECOOP'93*, pages 220–246. Springer LNCS 707, 1993.
78. José Meseguer, Kokichi Futatsugi, and Timothy Winkler. Using rewriting logic to specify, program, integrate, and reuse open concurrent systems of cooperating agents. In *Proceedings of the 1992 International Symposium on New Models for Software Architecture, Tokyo, Japan, November 1992*, pages 61–106. Research Institute of Software Engineering, 1992.
79. José Meseguer and Joseph Goguen. Order-sorted algebra solves the constructor-selector, multiple representation and coercion problems. *Information and Computation*, 103(1):114–158, 1993.
80. José Meseguer and Ugo Montanari. Petri nets are monoids. *Information and Computation*, 88:105–155, 1990.
81. José Meseguer and Xiaolei Qian. A logical semantics for object-oriented databases. In *Proc. International SIGMOD Conference on Management of Data*, pages 89–98. ACM, 1993.
82. José Meseguer and Carolyn Talcott. Reasoning theories and rewriting logic. Manuscript, Stanford University, June 1996.
83. José Meseguer and Timothy Winkler. Parallel programming in Maude. In J.-P. Banâtre and D. Le Mètayer, editors, *Research Directions in High-level Parallel Programming Languages*, pages 253–293. Springer LNCS 574, 1992. Also Technical Report SRI-CSL-91-08, SRI International, Computer Science Laboratory, November 1991.
84. Robin Milner. Functions as processes. *Mathematical Structures in Computer Science*, 2(2):119–141, 1992.
85. U. Montanari and F. Rossi. Contextual nets. *Acta Informatica*, 32:545–596, 1995.
86. K. Ohmaki, K. Futatsugi, and K. Takahashi. A basic LOTOS simulator in OBJ. In *Proceedings of the International Conference of Information Technology Commemorating the 30th Anniversary of the Information Processing Society of Japan (InfoJapan'90)*, pages 497–504. IPSJ, October 1990.
87. Peter Csaba Ölveczky, Piotr Kosiuczenko, and Martin Wirsing. An object-oriented algebraic steam-boiler control specification. In Jean-Raymond Abrial, Egon Börger, and Hans Langmaack, editors, *The Steam-Boiler Case Study Book*. Springer-Verlag, 1996. To appear.
88. Peter Csaba Ölveczky and José Meseguer. Specifying real-time systems in rewriting logic. Paper in preparation.
89. Isabel Pita and Narciso Martí-Oliet. A Maude specification of an object oriented database model for telecomunication networks. To appear in *Proc. 1st Intl. Workshop on Rewriting Logic and its Applications*, ENTCS, North Holland, 1996.
90. J.-C. Raoult and F. Voisin. Set-theoretic graph rewriting. In H.-J. Schneider and H. Ehrig, editors, *Graph Transformations in Computer Science*, pages 312–325. Springer LNCS 776, 1994.

91. H. Reichel. An approach to object semantics based on terminal co-algebras. To appear in *Mathematical Structures in Computer Science*, 1995. Presented at *Dagstuhl Seminar on Specification and Semantics*, Schloss Dagstuhl, Germany, May 1993.
92. G. Saake and A. Sernadas, editors. *Information Systems—Correctness and Reusability*. Technische Universität Braunschweig, Information-Berichte 91-03, 1991.
93. Vladimiro Sassone, José Meseguer, and Ugo Montanari. Inductive completion of monoidal categories and infinite net computations. Submitted for publication.
94. H.-J. Schneider and H. Ehrig, editors. *Graph Transformations in Computer Science*. Springer LNCS 776, 1994.
95. M. Schorlemmer. Bi-rewriting rewriting logic. To appear in *Proc. 1st Intl. Workshop on Rewriting Logic and its Applications*, ENTCS, North Holland, 1996.
96. Wolfgang Schreiner. Parallel functional programming: an annotated bibliography. Technical report, Research Institute for Symbolic Computation, Johannes Kepler University, Linz, Austria, 1993.
97. M. R. Sleep, M. J. Plasmeijer, and M. C. J. D. vanEekelen, editors. *Term Graph Rewriting*. Wiley, 1993.
98. J.G. Stell. Modelling term rewriting systems by sesqui-categories. Technical Report TR94-02, Keele University, 1994. Also in shorter form in Proc. C.A.E.N., 1994, pp. 121–127.
99. C. L. Talcott. An actor rewrite theory. To appear in *Proc. 1st Intl. Workshop on Rewriting Logic and its Applications*, ENTCS, North Holland, 1996.
100. C. L. Talcott. Interaction semantics for components of distributed systems. In *1st IFIP Workshop on Formal Methods for Open Object-based Distributed Systems, FMOODS'96*, 1996.
101. P. Viry. Input/output for ELAN. To appear in *Proc. 1st Intl. Workshop on Rewriting Logic and its Applications*, ENTCS, North Holland, 1996.
102. P. Viry. Rewriting: An effective model of concurrency. In C. Halatsis et al., editors, *PARLE'94, Proc. Sixth Int. Conf. on Parallel Architectures and Languages Europe, Athens, Greece, July 1994*, volume 817 of *LNCS*, pages 648–660. Springer-Verlag, 1994.
103. M. Vittek. *ELAN: Un cadre logique pour le prototypage de langages de programmation avec contraintes*. PhD thesis, Université Henry Poincaré — Nancy I, 1994.
104. M. Walicki and S. Meldal. Algebraic approaches to nondeterminism—an overview. To appear in *Computing Surveys*.
105. M. Wirsing. A formal approach to object-oriented software enginering. To appear in *Proc. 1st Intl. Workshop on Rewriting Logic and its Applications*, ENTCS, North Holland, 1996.
106. M. Wirsing, F. Nickl, and U. Lechner. Concurrent object-oriented design specification in SPECTRUM. Technical report, Institut für Informatik, Universität München, 1995.

Truly Concurrent Constraint Programming

Vineet Gupta * Radha Jagadeesan ** Vijay Saraswat*

Abstract. Concurrent Constraint Programming (CCP) is a powerful computation model for concurrency obtained by internalizing the notion of computation via deduction over (first-order) systems of partial information (constraints). In [SRP91] a semantics for indeterminate CCP was given via sets of bounded trace operators; this was shown to be fully abstract with respect to observing all possible quiescent stores (= final states) of the computation. Bounded trace operators constitute a certain class of (finitary) "invertible" closure operators over a downward closed sublattice. They can be thought of as generated via the grammar: $t ::= c \mid c \rightarrow t \mid c \wedge t$ where c ranges over primitive constraints, $\wedge$ is conjunction and $\rightarrow$ intuitionistic implication.

We motivate why it is interesting to consider as observable a "causality" relation on the store: what is observed is not just the conjunction of constraints deposited in the store, but also the causal dependencies between these constraints — what constraints were required to be present in the computation before others could be generated. We show that the same construction used to give the "interleaving" semantics in [SRP91] can be used to give a true-concurrency semantics provided that denotations are taken to be sets of bounded closure operators, which can be generated via the grammar:

$$k ::= c \mid c \rightarrow k \mid k \wedge k$$

Thus we obtain a denotational semantics for CCP fully-abstract with respect to observing this "causality" relation on constraints. This semantics differs from the earlier semantics in preserving more fine-grained structure of the computation; in particular the Interleaving Law

$$(a \rightarrow P) \parallel (b \rightarrow Q) = (a \rightarrow (P \parallel (b \rightarrow Q))) \,\square\, (b \rightarrow (Q \parallel (a \rightarrow P))) \quad (1)$$

is not verified ($\square$ is indeterminate choice). Relationships between such a denotational approach to true concurrency and different powerdomain constructions are explored.

1 Introduction

Concurrent constraint programming [Sar93, SR90, SRP91] is a simple and powerful model of concurrent computation obtained by internalizing the notion of computation as deduction over (first-order) systems of partial information. The model is characterized by monotonic accumulation of information in a distributed context: multiple agents

* Xerox PARC, 3333 Coyote Hill Road, Palo Alto Ca 94304; {vgupta, saraswat}@parc.xerox.com

** Dept. of Mathematical Sciences,Loyola University-Lake Shore Campus, Chicago, Il 60626; radha@math.luc.edu

work together to produce *constraints* on shared variables. A primitive constraint or *token*, (over a given finite set of variables) is a finitary specification of possibly partial information about the values the variable can take. A typical example of a token is a first order formula over some algebraic structure. Tokens come naturally equipped with an entailment relation: $c_1, \ldots, c_n \vdash c$ holds exactly if the presence of tokens $c_1, \ldots, c_n$ implies the presence of the token c. Thus tokens can combine additively, without any prejudice about their source or origin, to produce other tokens. An *agent* has access to a finite set of variables — the basic operations it may perform are to constrain some subset of variables it has access to by posting a token (A::=c), to check whether a token is entailed by ones that have already been posted and if so, reduce to another agent, perhaps indeterminately ($A ::= \Box_{i \in I} c_i \rightarrow A_i$), to create new variables ($A ::= \exists X.A$), or to reduce to a parallel composition of other agents ($A ::= A_1 \parallel A_2$).

Several authors have investigated the semantic framework of CCP languages [SRP91, dBP91]. It is natural to observe for every agent the final store obtained on executing the agent to quiescence (i.e., the final store). To obtain a compositional analysis, one needs to investigate the nature of interactions across a boundary between a system S and its environment E. (Both S and E should be thought of as consisting of a parallel composition of agents.) Typically, S and E will share some variables V. One may think of S as detecting the presence of some tokens c_1 (on V), producing tokens c_2, and then suspending until more tokens c_3 are produced, and then producing tokens c_4, and so on, until finally it produces a token c_{2n} and quiesces (that is, it reaches a stage in which it is inert unless the environment provides some input). Such interactions may be described by means of the grammar

$$t ::= c \mid c \rightarrow t \mid c \wedge t$$

Each t is called a *trace*; the conjunction of all tokens appearing in t, denoted $|t|$, is called its *bound*. Mathematically, each such t can be taken to describe a certain class of finitary "invertible" closure operators over the lattice generated by the constraint systems, called *bounded trace operators* (bto's). (Recall that a closure operator over a lattice is an operator that is monotone, idempotent and increasing.) The denotation of an agent may then be taken to be the set of all btos that an agent can engage in. [SRP91] shows that program combinators can be defined over such a structure, and in fact such a denotational semantics is fully abstract with respect to observing final stores. Furthermore, it turns out that the semantics of the determinate fragment of CCP can in fact be described by a single closure operator, equivalent to the parallel composition of each of the btos. In what follows, we will call this the "standard model" of CCP.

It is important to point out that the nature of communication in CCP is somewhat different from that in other models of concurrency, such as actors, CCS, CSP, or imperative concurrency. In particular, the lack of "atomicity" of basic actions is already built into this model of CCP[3]. For instance, if a token c is logically equivalent to the conjunction of tokens a and b, the standard model validates the *Law of Non-Atomicity of Tells*

$$a \parallel b = c \tag{2}$$

[3] For the purposes of this paper, CCP refers to "eventual tell" version of CCP [Sar93], rather than the "atomic tell" version for which a similar claim cannot be made.

and the *Law of Non-Atomicity of Asks*

$$a \to b \to A = c \to A \tag{3}$$

1.1 Causal semantics for CCP

Such a development of the semantics of CCP is not fully satisfactory for several reasons.

Interleaving of concurrent actions. The standard model is said to be an "interleaving" model because it validates the Interleaving Law (Law 1), which expresses that a parallel composition of agents can be reduced to a choice between all possible interleavings of its basic actions. In some sense, such a law indicates that the system is operating in "global time", or has a single notion of observer. This seems particularly unnatural in the context of CCP because of the asynchronous, distributed nature of the constraint store, and the notion of communication via information accumulation. There is no need ever for any "system-wide" global-time, or synchronization in an implementation of CCP; multiple agents may detect the presence of constraints in different order; it is therefore surprising that the semantic treatment reflects such a "global" time.

Further, the conflation of parallelism with non-deterministic choice means that it is not possible for CCP compilers to transform input programs soundly using the laws valid in this model, while preserving the "degree of parallelism" of the input program. A natural question that arises then, is the formalization of the notion of "degree of parallelism" and the elaboration of a model which respects this notion. Clearly, such a model would have to be more fine-grained than (make more distinctions than) the standard model because it would have to invalidate the Interleaving Law. However, there are laws satisfied by the standard model which allow for useful compile time optimizations that respect degree of parallelism, e.g. the Law of Immediate Discharge:

$$a \parallel (a \to B) = a \parallel B \tag{4}$$

or the Law of Intermediate Causation:

$$\exists X.[b \to (X \parallel A) \parallel X \to B] = b \to (A \parallel B) \tag{5}$$

(where X is not free in b, A, B). These laws should be preserved by the new model.

More speculatively, we also aim to provide some semantic support to a question faced by a compiler designer: in what order should a compiler carry out a given set of optimizations? Intuitively, an optimization is applicable if and only if an associated precondition is satisfied (e.g., a variable can be put in a register if certain non-aliasing conditions are met); and once an optimization is carried out, certain post-conditions can be asserted based on what that optimization does. So, given two optimizations O_1 and O_2, we hope that causality based semantics can be used to address the question of the dependencies between O_1 and O_2. The results of this paper would be particularly relevant for optimizers that can be written as programs in the cc paradigm — such as the constraint based program analysis techniques, see for example [Hei92].

Modeling application-level causality Another reason for considering a richer semantic model for CCP arises from a class of applications for which CCP is being used.

One of the distinguishing characteristics of CCP is that it combines a powerful and expressive language for concurrent systems with a declarative reading. This makes it particularly attractive for use in modeling (concurrent) physical systems. The Model-based Computing project [FS95] is developing models for reprographics systems (photocopiers) and their components. From these physics-based models, reasoners are used to derive information that can be plugged into standard architectures for tasks such as simulation and scheduling. Each physical component is modeled as a transducer which accepts inputs and control signals, operates in a given set of modes, and produces output signals. Models of assemblies are put together by connecting models of components in the same way as the components are put together to form the assemblies.

In such a context, the task of *scheduling* is to determine the control signals and the inputs which should be supplied to the system so as to *cause* the production of the given output. In other words, given a program P (the system model), and given constraints $o_1, \ldots, o_n$ (on the output variables), it is desired to produce constraints $i_1, \ldots, i_n$ on the input and control variables such that P can coherently (i.e. with the same set of choices for resolving indeterminacy) produce o_1 when run from i_1, o_2 when run from i_2 and so on. Generally one is interested in "minimal" explanations, i.e., the weakest i_j that can produce o_j.

One can recover explanations from the standard semantics as follows. Find t in the denotation of P such that t when run on i_j produces o_j for each j. Note that each t corresponds to a coherent execution of the program. However, in general the standard semantics will not able to provide minimal explanations.

Example 1 Faulty not gates. Consider a not gate that may be arbitrarily be in one of three modes, ok, stuck_at_1 or stuck_at_0:

```
not(Mode, In, Out) ::
  (Mode = ok→Out = not(In)
   [] Mode = stuck_at_1→Out = 1
   [] Mode = stuck_at_0→Out = 0).
```

Intuitively, one may say that for this gate, `Mode = ok` *causes* the output to be the negated version of the input, etc.

Now consider an assembly P of two disconnected not gates `not(M1, X1, Y1)` and `not(M2, X2, Y2)`. An explanation that can be offered for $o_1 = (Y1 = 1)$ and $o_2 = (Y2 = 0)$ are $i_1 = i_2 = (M1 = ok, X1 = 0, M2 = ok, X2 = 1)$.

However, it is quite clear that the corresponding minimal explanations are $i_1 = (M1 = ok, X1 = 0)$ and $i_2 = (M2 = ok, X2 = 1)$; there is no causal relationship between $Y2$ and $O2$, and hence between the two sub-explanations. The standard semantics will however find *one* execution of the system that can answer both queries, and hence produce an *interleaved* answer that does not respect the causality in the program.

1.2 Representing causality: the basic idea

From these considerations we are motivated to find a semantics for CCP that invalidates the Law of Interleaving.

Let us reconsider the basic notion of observation. What is the finer-grain structure in the store that we might observe? Given the discussion of the previous section, a natural idea (e.g., see [MR95]) is to associate a token c in the store with its *causes*, that is, with the tokens b that needed to be supplied by the environment in order to trigger some computation in the program that results in c. Thus the store can be taken to be a collection of such *contexted* tokens c^b, given the (usually implicit) program P. Such an assertion is read as "b causes c", with b the *cause*, and c the *effect*. A *run* of the program generates many such contexted tokens in the store. Given such a collection of contexted tokens ρ, their associated *generated effect* is obtained by simply taking the conjunction of the effects of each assertion in ρ; in this way one may recover the "constraint store" of the usual operational semantics of CCP.

Example 2 Contd. Consider the program P of Example 1, started in the presence of the constraints $\mathtt{M1} = \mathtt{ok}, \mathtt{M2} = \mathtt{ok}, \mathtt{X1} = 0, \mathtt{X2} = 1$. The activation of the behaviour of the two not agents yields the addition of $\mathtt{Y1} = \mathtt{not(X1)}^{\mathtt{M1=ok}}$ and $\mathtt{Y2} = \mathtt{not(X2)}^{\mathtt{M2=ok}}$ to the store. In the presence of the token $\mathtt{X1} = 0$, it should be possible to use the first assertion to derive: $\mathtt{Y1} = 1^{\mathtt{M1=ok,X1=0}}$. Similarly for $\mathtt{Y2} = 0$.

This example also illustrates another important point about the causal execution of agents. What we wish to record in the store are the assumptions *on the environment* that were made in the production of a given token c. Conventionally, only "closed" programs are executed — that is, no interaction with the environment is allowed. In such cases, the resulting store of contexted tokens will contain no more information than can be gleaned from examining the generated effect. The possibility of interesting non-trivial differences arises when we internalize the interactions $c_1, \ldots, c_n$ with the environment by running the program P in parallel with the contexted tokens $c_1^{c_1}, \ldots, c_n^{c_n}$. Intuitively, c^c captures the notion that c is an "external" input. For a collection of tokens $c_1, \ldots, c_n$, define $\Uparrow (c_1, \ldots, c_n)$ to be the set of contexted tokens $c_1^{c_1}, \ldots, c_n^{c_n}$. Thus the execution of the program P "started in the presence of the tokens $\mathtt{M1} = \mathtt{ok}, \mathtt{M2} = \mathtt{ok}, \mathtt{X1} = 0, \mathtt{X2} = 1$ is to be thought of as the execution of the agent $\mathtt{P}, \Uparrow (\mathtt{M1} = \mathtt{ok}, \mathtt{M2} = \mathtt{ok}, \mathtt{X1} = 0, \mathtt{X2} = 1)$.

Another useful way to think of a contexted token b^a is as the assertion "on assumption a, program P produces output b". The tokens that a program is initially started in are "assumed", that is, are taken to depend only on themselves. One may now think of the operational semantics as manipulating tokens tagged with their assumptions, while maintaining the intuitive semantics of assumptions, e.g. as done by an Assumption-based Truth Maintenance System (ATMS) [deK86].

Logic of contexted tokens. Execution of a program is thus taken to yield a store of contexted tokens. However, the actual store that results depends in ways on the syntax of the program that are not crucial. For instance, the contexted store that results on the execution of $\mathtt{a} \parallel \mathtt{a} \rightarrow \mathtt{b}$ (in the presence of no other tokens) is different from that obtained from $\mathtt{a} \parallel \mathtt{b}$, though semantically they should be identical. Indeed, the need to abstract from the concrete syntax is already present in the standard semantics. Two programs A and B are considered behaviorally equivalent for a given initial store c if they produce stores c_1 and c_2 respectively that are equivalent (even if they are syntactically distinct), i.e. they *entail* each other. The entailment relation on tokens relevant there is the primitive relation $\vdash_C$ supplied with the constraint system. Given that the store is now taken to contain contexted tokens, what is the relevant entailment relation?

Let o, p, q range over contexted tokens. Consider the judgement:

$$o_1, \ldots, o_n \vdash o$$

Such a judgement should be taken to hold exactly when it is the case that for any program P, any run of P which satisfies the assertions $o_1, \ldots, o_n$ could also satisfies o. In the following, let Γ, Δ range over multisets of contexted tokens.

From elementary considerations it is clear that the following structural rules should hold:

$$\frac{\Gamma, p, q, \Delta \vdash o}{\Gamma, q, p, \Delta \vdash o} \quad \frac{\Gamma \vdash o}{\Gamma, p \vdash o} \quad \frac{\Gamma, p, p \vdash o}{\Gamma, p \vdash o}$$

Regarding the identity rules, it is clear that any program P should be able to produce b on the assumption a if in fact a entails b in the underlying constraint system. And we should expect that the Cut rule should hold:

$$\frac{a \vdash_C b}{\vdash b^a} \quad \frac{\Gamma \vdash p \quad \Delta, p \vdash o}{\Gamma, \Delta \vdash o}$$

Finally we are left with the rules for inference that involve basic observations. Assume (1) that a process P satisfies all the assertions in Γ together with b^a, (2) $\Gamma \vdash a^{true}$, and that (3) for any process it is the case that if it satisfies Γ, and b^{true}, then it must satisfy o. From (1) and (2) it follows that P can on its own (i.e. assuming only that the environment supplies `true`), produce a. However, from (1), P satisfies b^a; therefore it must be the case that P can, on its own, produce b, and hence P satisfies b^{true}. But then, by (3) P satisfies o. This leads to the validity of the inference rule:

$$\frac{\Gamma \vdash a^{true} \quad \Gamma, b^{true} \vdash o}{\Gamma, b^a \vdash o}$$

Now it remains to consider the conditions under which it can be established that any program P satisfying Γ must satisfy b^a. Assume that for any program P it is the case that if P satisfies Γ and can on its own produce a, then it can on its own produce b. Now assume that Q is a program that satisfies Γ. Now note that if Q satisfies Γ, (Q, a) must also satisfy Γ. Clearly Q, a can on its own produce a. Therefore, by assumption Q, a must on its own be able to produce b. But if Q, a can produce b, then it must be the case that when Q is supplied a by the environment it can produce b. Hence we have:

$$\frac{\Gamma, a^{true} \vdash b^{true}}{\Gamma \vdash b^a}$$

Thus in our analysis, the "internal" logic of causation turns out to be that of intuitionistic implicational logic (over the underlying constraint system).

Denotational semantics. The observations of a program P are thus taken to be the contexted stores generated when P is executed in the presence of different tokens, modulo the equivalence generated by $\vdash$. What should a denotational semantics that respects this notion of observation look like?

To answer this, let us return to the analysis of the interaction between a system S and its environment E, via shared variables V. Instead of thinking of S as engaged in a *sequence* of interactions with E (e.g., detecting the presence of a token c_1 and producing c_2, *and then* detecting the presence of c_3 and producing c_4 and so on), one should now also allow the possibility of *several* such independent interactions with the environment. That is, one should allow for interactions as described by the richer grammar:

$$k ::= c \mid c \rightarrow k \mid k \wedge k$$

Each k is called a *closure*; as before the conjunction of all tokens appearing in k, denoted $|k|$ is called its *bound*. Mathematically, each such k can be taken to describe a certain class of finitary closure operators over the lattice generated by the constraint systems, called *bounded closure operators* (bco's). Intuitively, closure operators allow for parallel branches of causality, whereas trace operators sequentialize these branches. Thus closure operators serve for CCP the role that "pomsets" serve for true concurrency semantics for other languages. (More precisely, multiplicities of tokens are irrelevant in CCP, since conjunction is idempotent. The poset of interest $\leq_R$ can be recovered from the closure operator f by: $a \leq_R b$ iff $f(b)$ entails $f(a)$.) The denotation of an agent may then be taken to be the set of all bco's that an agent can engage in. (In order to define recursion, we will define bco's over constraints rather than tokens; see the next section.) We will show that program combinators can be defined over such a structure, and in fact such a denotational semantics is fully abstract with respect to observing the contexted tokens in the final store. As before, the denotation of a determinate program P is equivalent to the parallel composition of each of the bco's that can be observed of P; interestingly, however, this denotation is identical to that which would be obtained in the standard semantics. Thus, in some sense, the standard analysis of determinate CCP already incorporates an analysis of causality.

Rest of this paper The rest of this paper is concerned with fully developing these notions. We give the precise "causal" operational semantics and develop the denotational semantics along the lines sketched above. We study two kinds of models of indeterminacy, corresponding to must and may testing in the sense of [dNH84], and using the Hoare [Plo76] and the Smyth powerdomain[Smy78] respectively to handle indeterminacy. We establish full abstraction results. In addition, we expose some of the logical character of CCP by presenting two sound and complete proof systems that can be used to establish that an observation lies in the Hoare (resp. Smyth) denotations of a program P.

Related work

Many "true concurrency" semantics, see for example [AH89, BCHK92, vGV87, Gor91, Pra86, Vog92, Win87], which capture causality to varying degrees, have been proposed for other models of concurrency, including process algebras such as CSP and CCS, Petri Nets, and event structures. These semantics have typically generalized interleaving semantics to encode some degree of concurrency, such as "steps" of concurrent actions rather than single actions, and "pomsets" of partially-ordered multisets of actions rather than linear temporal sequences. Note that while our semantics is a sets of closure operators semantics, it does make the early vs. late branching distinction, so $a \rightarrow ((b \rightarrow B) \Box (c \rightarrow C)) \neq (a \rightarrow b \rightarrow B) \Box (a \rightarrow c \rightarrow C)$, unlike [Pra86].

The studies most relevant to the present paper are studies of causality and true concurreny issues in the cc paradigm — see for example, [MR95, MR91, dBGMP94, dBPB95].

[MR95, MR91] propose a framework, based on graph rewriting and occurrence nets, to study true concurrency issues in the cc languages [MR95]. In this paper, we do (essentially) adopt the framework of "contextual agents" of [MR95, MR91] to describe extraction of causality information from the program execution in the operational semantics. Our primary distinct contribution is the logical/denotational analysis of the operational semantics.

[dBPB95] propose a true concurrency framework for a more general class of non-monotonic cc languages. When specialised to monotonic cc languages, their framework yields essentially a "step semantics", where a collection of concurrent actions can be performed at each step. Our work differs from [dBPB95] in the analysis of the process of addition of constraints. [dBPB95] distinguishes different occurrences of the same constraint. This view of separating occurrences of the same constraint is not appropriate for some of our motivating examples, especially the scheduler. In our framework, the process of imposition of constraints is idempotent.

[dBGMP94] adapts the study of the logical structure of domains [Abr91] to CCP. That paper does not directly address issues of causality and true concurrency; however, we acknowledge the methodological influence of their work on our work.

2 Causal Transition System for CCP

cc languages are described parametrically over a *constraint system*. The constraint system determines the pieces of partial information that can be added to the store. For a detailed description, we refer the reader to [SRP91, Sar92]. Briefly, a constraint system C consists of a set D of first order formulas called primitive constraints or *tokens* and an entailment relation $\vdash_C \subseteq Fin(D) \times D$ between them. This relation tells us which tokens follow from which others, and should be decidable and finitary, i.e. the set $Fin(D)$ consists of finite sets of tokens.

Subsets of D closed under $\vdash_C$ are called *constraints*. The set of all constraints, denoted $|D|$, is ordered by inclusion, and forms an algebraic lattice. We will use $\sqcup$ and $\sqcap$ to denote joins and meets of this lattice. Note that this ordering corresponds to the information ordering on tokens, as stronger constraints entail more tokens. We will use $a, b, c \ldots$ to denote tokens, and $u, v, w, \ldots$ to denote constraints. $\bar{a}$ denotes the embedding of a in $|D| : \bar{a} = \{b \in D \mid a \vdash_C b\}$.

The syntax of CCP languages is as follows:

$$\begin{array}{|l|}\hline P ::= a \mid P \parallel P \mid \Box_i a_i \rightarrow P_i \mid \exists X.P \mid g(X) \mid \{D.P\} \\ D ::= \epsilon \mid g(X) :: P, D \\ \hline\end{array}$$

We use the words "agents" and "programs" synonymously in the rest of the paper. Formally, the execution semantics can be given by a transition system. A *configuration* Γ is a multiset of agents. $\sigma(\Gamma)$ denotes the set of tell tokens in Γ. The transition system relates configurations to configurations and is the least relation satisfying the following axioms and inference rules [SRP91]:

$$\Gamma,(P \parallel Q) \longrightarrow \Gamma, P, Q \qquad \frac{\sigma(\Gamma) \vdash_C a_i}{\Gamma, (\Box_{i \in I} a_i \rightarrow P_i) \longrightarrow \Gamma, P_i}$$

$$\Gamma, \exists X.P \longrightarrow \Gamma, P[Y/X] \ (Y \text{ new}) \quad \Gamma, g(X) \longrightarrow \Gamma, P(X) \ \text{ if } g(X) :: P(X) \in D$$

Observing causality. To detect causality information, we will allow our configurations to remember the set of tokens which enabled each agent to be executed, i.e., instead of taking a configuration to be a multiset of agents, we take it to be a multiset of contexted agents P^a. The transition relation may now be defined straightforwardly:

$$\Gamma, (P \parallel Q)^c \longrightarrow \Gamma, P^c, Q^c \qquad \frac{\sigma(\Gamma) \vdash_C a_i}{\Gamma, (\Box_{i \in I} a_i \rightarrow P_i)^c \longrightarrow \Gamma, P_i^{a_i, c}}$$

$$\Gamma, (\exists X.P)^c \longrightarrow \Gamma, P[Y/X]^c \ (Y \text{new}) \qquad \Gamma, g(X)^c \longrightarrow \Gamma, P(X)^c \ \text{ if } g(X) :: P(X) \in D$$

Operational semantics From the transition system, various operational semantics can be defined in the obvious way. Each operational semantics records for a program the contexted store that results when a program is executed in the presence of different assumed tokens. The different operational semantics arise from different treatment of non-termination (should only terminated computations be observed?) and indeterminacy (when are two sets of results equivalent?). For the purposes of this paper we shall focus on the "may" semantics which observes for each program P the results of terminating execution sequences, for all possible assumed tokens. In Section 4 we briefly discuss a similar treatment for "must" semantics, which leads to the Smyth powerdomain.

Note that in order to accomodate hiding, our observations will need to hide all the new variables introduced in the transitions. Thus they will be of the form $\delta V.o$, where $\delta V.o = \exists X_1 \ldots \exists X_n.o$, for all X_i in $\mathbf{var}(o) - V$. As none of these X_i's will occur in $\mathbf{var}(P, c)$, they need not be in the cause of any contexted token in o. Now we can use the law $\exists_X(a^b, c^d) = (\exists_X a)^b, (\exists_X c)^d, (\exists_X a \wedge c)^{\{b,d\}}$ to get the usual contexted tokens. The logical rules for existential quantification of observations are the usual intuitionistic rules for existential quantification. Let $\rho(\Gamma)$ be the multiset of contexted tokens in Γ. Define the *size* of a contexted store o, denoted $||o||$ as the lub of all the tokens occurring in it: $||a|| = a$, $||a^b|| = a \sqcup b$, $||o \wedge o'|| = ||o|| \sqcup ||o'||$ and $||\exists_X o|| = \exists_X ||o||$.

The may semantics may be defined straightforwardly:

$$\mathcal{O}_H[\![P]\!] = \{o \mid P, \Uparrow(||o||) \rightarrow^* \Gamma \not\rightarrow, o = \delta V.\rho(\Gamma), V = \mathbf{var}(P, o)\}$$

3 Causal denotational semantics

A *closure operator* is a function f from constraints to constraints, which is extensive ($f(u) \supseteq u$), idempotent ($f \circ f = f$) and monotone (if $u \supseteq v$ then $f(u) \supseteq f(v)$). An alternative way of presenting a closure operator is as a set of its fixed points, *i.e.* those constraints v such that $f(v) = v$. We recall that the set of fixed points of a closure operator is a set of constraints which is closed under greatest lower bounds (glb's) — any set of constraints A which is closed under glb's can be used to define a closure operator by $f_A(u) = \sqcap\{v \in A \mid v \supseteq u\}$. In the rest of this paper we will use both these representations interchangeably. We will also use the CCP operations on closure operators — thus $a \rightarrow f = \{u \in |D| \mid a \in u \Rightarrow u \in f\}$, and $\exists_X f = \{u \in |D| \mid \exists v \in f, \exists_X u = \exists_X v\}$.

A *bounded closure operator* (bco) is a pair (f, u), where f is a closure operator, and u is a constraint, $u \in f$. The u determines the *domain* of the bco — this is defined as $u \downarrow$, the set of constraints smaller than u. Thus if $(f, u), (g, u)$ are bco's, with $f \cap u \downarrow = g \cap u \downarrow$, then we consider $(f, u) = (g, u)$.

Closure operators are ordered pointwise — thus if for all u, $f(u) \subseteq g(u)$, we define $f \leq g$. In the set representation, this simply becomes $f \leq g$ iff $f \supseteq g$. We will refer to this ordering as the *information ordering*, it is the converse of the usual set ordering. This ordering is extended to bco's — $(f, u) \leq (g, u)$ iff $f \leq g$. Note that we do not compare bco's with different domains, these are regarded as unrelated. The set of all bco's under this ordering now forms a domain, called **Obs**, the carrier set of this domain is denoted as **|Obs|**.

In the rest of this section we define the semantics of cc languages by examining the Hoare powerdomain constructions on this domain[Plo76]. Later in section 4 we will examine the Smyth powerdomain construction. In this paper, we use the representation theorems of [Smy78] to simplify the presentation of the powerdomain constructions. Furthermore, for powerdomain aficionados, we point out that we are technically using the powerdomain constructions with the emptyset, rather than the more traditional ones without the emptyset.

The elements of the Hoare powerdomain on **Obs** are sets S of bco's satisfying the closure condition:

$$(f, u) \in S, g \supseteq f \Rightarrow (g, u) \in S$$

The ordering relation is given by subset inclusion: $S_1 \sqsubseteq S_2 \Leftrightarrow S_1 \subseteq S_2$.

The Hoare powerdomain on **Obs** yields a complete lattice — the least element is the empty set, the greatest element is | **Obs** |, least upper bounds are given by union, and greatest lower bounds are given by intersection.

The semantics of the various programs can be given as follows:

$$\begin{aligned}
\mathcal{H}[\![a]\!] &\stackrel{d}{=} \{(f, u) \in \mathbf{Obs} \mid a \in u, f \supseteq \bar{a} \uparrow\} \\
\mathcal{H}[\![P \parallel Q]\!] &\stackrel{d}{=} \{(f \cap g, u) \in \mathbf{Obs} \mid (f, u) \in \mathcal{H}[\![P]\!], (g, u) \in \mathcal{H}[\![Q]\!]\} \\
\mathcal{H}[\![\square_{i \in I} a_i \rightarrow P_i]\!] &\stackrel{d}{=} \{(u \downarrow, u) \in \mathbf{Obs} \mid \forall i \in I. a_i \notin u\} \\
&\quad \cup \textstyle\bigcup_{i \in I}\{(f, u) \in \mathbf{Obs} \mid a_i \in u, \exists (f_i, u) \in \mathcal{H}[\![P_i]\!], f \supseteq a_i \rightarrow f_i\} \\
\mathcal{H}[\![\exists X.P]\!] &\stackrel{d}{=} \{(f, u) \in \mathbf{Obs} \mid \exists (g, v) \in \mathcal{H}[\![P]\!]. \exists X.g = \exists X.f, \exists_X u = \exists_X v, \\
&\quad g(\exists_X v) = v\}
\end{aligned}$$

Recursive definitions are as usual defined by least fixed points.

Note the extra clause in the definition of $\exists X.P$, which states that $g(\exists X.w) = g(w)$ for all w in the domain of g. This is motivated by the fact that P cannot receive any information about X from the environment, thus any information it uses on X needs to be produced by it. So any observed bco in P which can be a witness for an observation in $\exists X.P$ must use only internally generated X-information, and so it must be the case that on any input X, it must be able to ignore the X information, by generating the same output on $\exists X.w$ as on w.

We note a few interesting facts to give the reader some more intuition about the resulting semantics:

- Let P_i be a collection of processes indexed by i. Let a be a token in the constraint system. Then $\mathcal{H}[\![a \to P_i]\!] \sqsubseteq \mathcal{H}[\![\ \Box_{\ i \in I}\, a \to P_i]\!]$. We justify the inequation by noting that the semantic interpretation of bounded choice in the special case when all the guards are identical is just union. This inequation is characteristic of Hoare powerdomain style semantics — adding more branches to a process moves it up the ordering in the powerdomain.
- Let the process P_1 be defined recursively as $P_1 :: P_1$. Let the process P_2 be defined recursively as $P_2 :: b \parallel P_2$. Then $\mathcal{H}[\![P_1]\!] = \mathcal{H}[\![P_2]\!] = \emptyset$. This indicates the treatment of termination by the semantics — only terminating runs are counted.
- Let P be any process. Consider the processes $P_3 = \ \Box\ [a \to P, a \to P_1]$, and $P_4 = \Box\ [a \to P, a \to P_2]$, where P_1, P_2 are as above. Then $\mathcal{H}[\![P_3]\!] = \mathcal{H}[\![P_4]\!] = \mathcal{H}[\![a \to P]\!]$. This further clarifies termination issues in the Hoare semantics — non-terminating runs are ignored.

Full abstraction We now show that the semantics is fully abstract with respect to the may operational semantics. We first state a lemma showing that if we embed the operational semantics of a program in the Hoare powerdomain in the obvious way, we get the denotational semantics of the program. The proof is by induction on the structure of the program. We use $[\![o]\!]$ to denote the closure operator associated with the observation o[4].

Lemma 1. *For any program P, if $o \in \mathcal{O}_H[\![P]\!]$, then $([\![o]\!], \|o\|) \in \mathcal{H}[\![P]\!]$. Conversely, if $(f, v) \in \mathcal{H}[\![P]\!]$, then there is an $o \in \mathcal{O}_H[\![P]\!]$ such that $\|o\| = v$, and $[\![o]\!] \subseteq f$.*

From this we get the full abstraction theorem for the Hoare semantics —

Theorem 2. *If P, Q are two indeterminate programs, and $\mathcal{H}[\![P]\!] \neq \mathcal{H}[\![Q]\!]$, then there is an input a, such that the possible output contexted stores of $P \parallel a$ and $Q \parallel a$ are different. Conversely, if the set of possible output contexted stores of P and Q are different for some input, then $\mathcal{H}[\![P]\!] \neq \mathcal{H}[\![Q]\!]$.*

3.1 Logical form

We now present the Hoare semantics in a logical form, based on Abramsky's [Abr91]. We observe the properties that are true of the program, by executing the program. These

[4] $[\![a^b]\!] = b \to [\![a]\!]$, where $[\![a]\!] = \{c \in D \mid c \vdash_C a\}$. $[\![o_1 \wedge o_2]\!] = [\![o_1]\!] \cap [\![o_2]\!]$ and $[\![\exists_X o]\!] = \{c \in D \mid \exists b \in [\![o]\!], \exists_X b = \exists_X c\}$

properties are used to construct the denotational semantics of the program. This gives us an alternative presentation of the denotational semantics, and gives a clear connection between the operational and denotational semantics. In this section and the section on logical Smyth semantics, we will consider programs without hiding, due to the standard mismatch between hiding and existential quantification.

Properties are generated by the following syntax:

$$\phi ::= c \mid c \rightarrow \phi \mid \phi \wedge \phi$$

We define the size of a property as the lub of all the constraints occurring in it — $||c|| = c, ||c \rightarrow \phi|| = c \sqcup ||\phi||, ||\phi \wedge \psi|| = ||\phi|| \sqcup ||\psi||$. Note that size is a syntactic property, and can be changed by appending $a \rightarrow a$ to any property (without changing its logical content).

Intuitively, the Hoare semantics of a program consists of all the properties which are satisfied exactly by some execution sequence of the program in some input context. Define an execution sequence of a program P as a sequence $S = (P_0, P_1, P_2, \ldots, P_n)$, where $P_0 = P$, $P_n \not\longrightarrow$ and for each i between 0 and n, $P_i \longrightarrow P_{i+1}$ or $P_{i+1} = P_i, a$, where the a is fed by the environment. An execution sequence $S = (P_0, P_1, P_2, \ldots, P_n)$ satisfies ϕ iff $\delta V(\rho(P_n)) \vdash_{IL} \phi$, all information from the environment is already coded in ϕ, in implications and $||\phi|| = ||\delta V(\rho(P_n))||$. Here $\vdash_{IL}$ denotes Intuitionistic logic implication, which is the logic of determinate cc programs.

In the following, Γ, Γ' represent multisets of agents.

$$\frac{\Gamma, A, B, \Delta \Vdash \phi}{\Gamma, B, A, \Delta \Vdash \phi} \qquad \frac{\Gamma \Vdash \phi \quad \phi \vdash_{IL} \psi \quad ||\phi|| = ||\psi||}{\Gamma \Vdash \psi}$$

$$\frac{c_1, \ldots, c_n \vdash_{IL} \phi \qquad ||\phi|| = ||c_1|| \sqcup \ldots \sqcup ||c_n||}{c_1, \ldots, c_n \Vdash \phi}$$

$$\frac{\Gamma, A, B \Vdash \phi}{\Gamma, (A \parallel B) \Vdash \phi} \qquad \frac{\Gamma \Vdash \phi \quad \Gamma' \Vdash \psi \quad ||\phi|| = ||\psi||}{\Gamma, \Gamma' \Vdash \phi \wedge \psi}$$

$$\frac{\sigma(\Gamma) \vdash c_i \qquad c_i, \Gamma, A_i \Vdash \phi}{\Gamma, \Box_{i \in I} c_i \rightarrow A_i \Vdash \phi} \qquad \frac{\Gamma, c \Vdash \phi}{\Gamma \Vdash c \rightarrow \phi}$$

$$\frac{\forall i \in I. d \not\supseteq c_i \qquad \Gamma \Vdash d}{\Gamma, \Box_{i \in I} c_i \rightarrow A_i \Vdash d} \qquad \frac{\Gamma, A(X) \Vdash \phi \quad g(X) :: A(X)}{\Gamma, g(X) \Vdash \phi}$$

We can now show the theorem that shows the correspondence between the denotation of a process and its logic, its proof is by induction over the structure of programs. The closure operator corresponding to ϕ is defined using the usual CCP definitions.

Theorem 3. *If P is a hiding-free program, $P \Vdash \phi$ iff $([\![\phi]\!], ||\phi||) \in \mathcal{H}[\![P]\!]$, where $[\![\phi]\!]$ is the closure operator corresponding to ϕ.*

4 Causal Must semantics

An alternative causal semantics of cc programs allows us to observe what *must* be true for all runs of the system — this style does not ignore infinite runs of the system, and allows us to observe intermediate results. The formulation is quite similar to the may semantics presented above, so here we will review it briefly.

o is a *must* observation of a program P with context c if either $P, \Uparrow(c) \longrightarrow^* \Gamma \not\longrightarrow$ and $o = \delta V.\rho(\Gamma)$, where $V = \mathbf{var}(P, c)$ or there is an infinite sequence $P, \Uparrow(c) \longrightarrow \Gamma_1 \longrightarrow \Gamma_2 \longrightarrow \ldots$, such that $o = \bigcup_i \{\delta V.\rho(\Gamma_i)\}$. We say that o is minimal for P, c if there is no other must observation o' such that $o \vdash o'$.

$$\mathcal{O}_S[\![P]\!] = \{o \mid \exists c.\, o \text{ is a must observation of } P \text{ in context } c, \text{ and } o \text{ is minimal for } P, c\}$$

This definition allows us to identify two sets of observations which have the same minimal elements, giving us the must tests of [dNH84].

The Smyth powerdomain. The elements of the Smyth powerdomain on **Obs** are sets S of bco's satisfying the condition:

$$(f, u) \in S, g \subseteq f \Rightarrow (g, u) \in S$$

In the Smyth powerdomain, the ordering relation is given by reverse subset inclusion: $S_1 \sqsubseteq S_2 \Leftrightarrow S_1 \supseteq S_2$. The Smyth powerdomain on **Obs** yields a complete lattice — the greatest element is the empty set, the least element is $\mid \mathbf{Obs} \mid$, least upper bounds are given by intersection, and greatest lower bounds are given by union.

The semantics of the various programs can be given as follows:

$$\begin{aligned}
\mathcal{S}[\![a]\!] &\stackrel{d}{=} \{(f, u) \in \mathbf{Obs} \mid f \subseteq a\uparrow, a \in u\} \\
\mathcal{S}[\![P \parallel Q]\!] &\stackrel{d}{=} \mathcal{S}[\![P]\!] \cap \mathcal{S}[\![Q]\!] \\
\mathcal{S}[\![\Box_{i \in I} a_i \rightarrow P_i]\!] &\stackrel{d}{=} \{(f, u) \in \mathbf{Obs} \mid \forall i \in I. a_i \notin u\} \\
&\quad \cup \textstyle\bigcup_{i \in I} \{(f, u) \in \mathbf{Obs} \mid a_i \in u, \exists (f', v) \in \mathcal{S}[\![P_i]\!], f \subseteq a_i \rightarrow f'\} \\
\mathcal{S}[\![\exists X.P]\!] &\stackrel{d}{=} \{(f, u) \in \mathbf{Obs} \mid \exists (g, v) \in \mathcal{S}[\![P]\!]. \exists X.g = \exists X.f, \exists_X u = \exists_X v, \\
&\qquad g(\exists_X v) = v\}
\end{aligned}$$

Recursion occurs via least fixed points. Note that we could have defined parallel composition as in the Hoare semantics, but the result would be the same as above, which corresponds to our operational intuition of must testing.

We note a few interesting facts to give the reader some more intuition about the resulting semantics: we are choosing the same examples as those discussed for the Hoare semantics, and draw the readers attention to the differences.

- Let P_i be a collection of processes indexed by i. Let a be a token in the constraint system. Then $\mathcal{S}[\![a \rightarrow P_i]\!] \sqsupseteq \mathcal{S}[\![\Box_{i \in I} a \rightarrow P_i]\!]$. This can be justified by noting that the semantic interpretation of bounded choice in the special case when all the guards are identical is just union. This inequation (which we note is the exact converse of the one for the earlier semantics) is characteristic of Smyth powerdomain style semantics — adding more branches to a process moves it lower down the ordering in the domain.

- Let the process P_1 be defined recursively as $P_1 :: P_1$. Then $\mathcal{S}[\![P_1]\!] = \mid \mathbf{Obs} \mid$. Let the process P_2 be defined recursively as $P_2 :: a \parallel P_2$. Then $\mathcal{S}[\![P_1]\!] = \mathcal{S}[\![a]\!]$. These examples indicate the treatment of non-termination by the semantics — in effect, the semantics only looks at the store as it evolves, and allows one to observe "intermediate" stores even in an unbounded computation.
- Let P be any process. Consider the process $P_3 = b \rightarrow P \,\square\, b \rightarrow P_1$, where P_1 is as above. Then $\mathcal{S}[\![P_3]\!] = \mathcal{S}[\![b \rightarrow P_1]\!] = \mid \mathbf{Obs} \mid$. This further clarifies the treatment of non–determinism in the Smyth semantics. The intuitive reasoning is as follows: if b is not entailed by the store, neither side does anything to the store. If b is entailed by the store, the minimum guaranteed output is from the P_1 branch, which adds nothing new. This type of minimum guarantee reasoning is typical of Smyth powerdomain style semantics.

Similar to Lemma 2, we get a full abstraction theorem for the Smyth semantics —

Theorem 4. *If P, Q are two indeterminate programs, and $\mathcal{S}[\![P]\!] \neq \mathcal{S}[\![Q]\!]$, then there is a context a, such that the output stores of $P \parallel a$ and $Q \parallel a$ are different. Conversely, if the set of* minimal *output stores of P and Q are different, then $\mathcal{S}[\![P]\!] \neq \mathcal{S}[\![Q]\!]$.*

Smyth semantics in logical form. Intuitively, the Smyth semantics consists of properties that are satisfied by all runs of the program. We define $P \Vdash_u \phi$ to mean that *every* execution sequence of P satifies ϕ, given that the final resting point does not exceed u. Intuitively, u is the second component of the bco's. We extend the definition of an execution trace to extend to infinite runs — this is done by dropping the condition on P_n that $P_n \not\longrightarrow$. Thus the definition now becomes — an execution sequence of a program P is a sequence $P_0, P_1, P_2, \ldots, P_n$, where $P_0 = P$ and for each i between 0 and n, $P_i \longrightarrow P_{i+1}$ or $P_{i+1} = P_i, a$, where the a is fed by the environment. A sequence satisfies ϕ if all interaction with the environment is coded via implications, and $\delta V.(P_n) \vdash_{IL} \phi$.

The syntax of properties is derived from the following grammar:

$$\phi ::= u \mid a \rightarrow \phi \mid \phi \wedge \phi \mid \phi \vee \phi$$

The following deduction rules establish when this is true. Once again Γ stands for a multiset of agents, and $\sigma(\Gamma)$ for the tell tokens in it.

$$\frac{\Gamma \Vdash_u \phi}{\Gamma, P \Vdash_u \phi} \qquad \frac{\sigma(\Gamma) \supseteq v, \quad u \supseteq v}{\Gamma \Vdash_u v}$$

$$\frac{\Gamma, P_1, P_2 \Vdash_u \phi}{\Gamma, (P_1, P_2) \Vdash_u \phi} \qquad \frac{\Gamma \Vdash_u \phi_1 \quad \Gamma \Vdash_u \phi_2}{\Gamma \Vdash_u \phi_1 \wedge \phi_2}$$

$$\frac{\sigma(\Gamma) \vdash_C a \quad \Gamma, A \Vdash_u \phi}{\Gamma, a \rightarrow A \Vdash_u \phi} \qquad \frac{a \in u \quad \Gamma, a \Vdash_u \phi}{\Gamma \Vdash_u a \rightarrow \phi}$$

$$\frac{J = \{i \in I \mid a_i \in u\} \neq \emptyset \qquad \forall i \in J.\, \Gamma, a_i \rightarrow P_i \Vdash_u \phi}{\Gamma, \square_{i \in I} a_i \rightarrow P_i \Vdash_u \phi}$$

$$\frac{\Gamma, A(X) \Vdash_u \phi \;\; (g(X) :: A(X))}{\Gamma, g(X) \Vdash_u \phi} \qquad \frac{\Gamma \Vdash_u \phi_1}{\Gamma \Vdash_u \phi_1 \vee \phi_2}$$

Note that the rules given above are conservative over logical entailment, thus if $\phi \rightarrow \psi$ follows from the constraint system (with standard logical rules), then if $\Gamma \vdash_u \phi$, then $\Gamma \vdash_u \psi$. In particular, the rules are conservative over the logical entailment of the underlying constraint system.

Theorem 5. *For a hiding-free program P, if $P \Vdash_u \phi$, then all execution sequences of P with final resting point below u satisfy ϕ, and conversely.*

The logical semantics of a program can now be defined. Suppose $P \Vdash_u \phi$. Embed ϕ in the Smyth powerdomain as $E_S(\phi)$ using the formulas given for the denotational semantics, treating $\vee$ as set union. Let $\mathcal{E}_S(\phi, u)$ be the subset of $E_S(\phi)$ containing those bco's with second component u. Then the logical semantics is given as the intersections of the embedded sets — $\mathcal{L}_S[\![P]\!] = \bigcup_u \bigcap_\phi \{\mathcal{E}_S(\phi, u) \mid P \Vdash_u \phi\}$. And we get the theorem:

Theorem 6. *For any indeterminate hiding-free* cc *program P, $\mathcal{L}_S[\![P]\!] = \mathcal{S}[\![P]\!]$.*

5 Acknowledgements

We would like to thank Prakash Panangaden, Martin Rinard, Markus Fromherz and Saumya Debray for extensive discussions on the topics discussed in this paper, which led to many insights. Work on this paper was funded by grants from ONR and ARPA, and the second author was also funded by NSF.

References

[Abr91] S. Abramsky. Domain theory in logical form. *Annals of Pure and Applied Logic*, 51:1–77, 1991.

[AH89] L. Aceto and M. Hennessy. Towards action-refinement in process algebras. In *Proceedings, Fourth Annual Symposium on Logic in Computer Science*, pages 138–145. IEEE Computer Society Press, 1989.

[BCHK92] G. Boudol, I. Castellani, Matthew C. Hennessy, and A. Kiehn. A theory of processes with localities. In *Proceedings of International Conference on Concurrency Theory, Volume 630 of Lecture Notes in Computer Science*, pages 108–122, 1992.

[dBGMP94] F. S. de Boer, M. Gabrielli, Elena Marchiori, and Catuscia Palamidessi. Proving concurrent programs correct. In *Proceedings of the 21st ACM SIGPLAN-SIGACT Symposium on Principles of Programming Languages*, pages 98–108, 1994.

[dBP91] F. S. de Boer and Catuscia Palamidessi. A fully abstract model for concurrent constraint programming. In *Proceedings of TAPSOFT/CAAP*, pages 296–319, LNCS 493, 1991.

[dBPB95] F. S. de Boer, Catuscia Palamidessi, and Eike Best. Concurrent constraint programming with information removal. In *Proceedings of the Concurrent Constraint Programming Workshop*, pages 1–13, Venice, 1995.

[deK86] J. deKleer. An assumption based TMS. *Artifical Intelligence*, 28:127–162, 1986.

[dNH84] R. de Nicola and M.C.B. Hennessy. Testing equivalences for processes. *Theoretical Computer Science*, 34:83–133, 1984.

[FS95] Markus Fromherz and Vijay Saraswat. Model-based computing: Using concurrent constraint programming for modeling and model compilation. In *Principles and Practices of Constraint Programming*, volume 976 of *LNCS*, pages 629–635. Springer Verlag, 1995.

[Gor91] Roberto Gorrieri. *Refinement, Atomicity, and Transactions for Process Description Languages*. PhD thesis, University of Pisa, 1991.

[Hei92] N. Heintze. *Set–Based Program analysis*. PhD thesis, Carnegie Mellon University, 1992.

[MR91] Ugo Montanari and Francesca Rossi. True concurrency semantics for concurrent constraint programminmg. In V. Saraswat and K. Ueda, editors, *Proc. of the 1991 International Logic Programming Symposium*, 1991.

[MR95] Ugo Montanari and Francesca Rossi. A concurrent semantics for concurrent constraint programs via contextual nets. In *Principles and Pranctices of Constraint Programming*, pages 3–27, 1995.

[Plo76] G.D. Plotkin. A powerdomain construction. *SIAM J. of Computing*, 5(3):452–487, September 1976.

[Pra86] V.R. Pratt. Modeling concurrency with partial orders. *Int. J. of Parallel Programming*, 15(1):33–71, February 1986.

[Sar92] Vijay A. Saraswat. The Category of Constraint Systems is Cartesian-closed. In *Proc. 7th IEEE Symp. on Logic in Computer Science, Santa Cruz*, 1992.

[Sar93] Vijay A. Saraswat. *Concurrent constraint programming*. Doctoral Dissertation Award and Logic Programming Series. MIT Press, 1993.

[Smy78] M. B. Smyth. Powerdomains. *Journal of Computer and System Sciences*, 16:23–36, February 1978.

[SR90] Vijay A. Saraswat and Martin Rinard. Concurrent constraint programming. In *Proceedings of Seventeenth ACM Symposium on Principles of Programming Languages, San Fransisco*, January 1990.

[SRP91] V. A. Saraswat, M. Rinard, and P. Panangaden. Semantic foundations of concurrent constraint programming. In *Proceedings of Eighteenth ACM Symposium on Principles of Programming Languages, Orlando*, January 1991.

[vGV87] Rob van Glabbeek and Frits Vaandrager. Petri net models for algebraic theories of concurrency. In *Proceedings of PARLE, Volume 259 of the Lecture Notes in Computer Science*, pages 224–242, 1987.

[Vog92] Walter Vogler. *Modular Construction and Partial Order Semantics of Petri Nets*, volume 625 of *LNCS*. Springer-Verlag, 1992. 252 pp.

[Win87] Glynn Winskel. Event structures. In *Petri Nets: Applications and Relationships to Other Models of Concurrency, Volume 255 of Lecture Notes in Computer Science*, pages 325–392, 1987.

Constraints as Processes

Björn Victor[1] * and Joachim Parrow[2] **

[1] Dept. of Computer Systems, Uppsala University,
Box 325, S-751 05 Uppsala, Sweden.

[2] Dept. of Teleinformatics, Royal Institute of Technology,
Electrum 204, S-164 40 Kista, Sweden.

Abstract. We present a compositional encoding of the γ-calculus into the π-calculus. The former, used in the Oz semantics, is a recent small language with equational constraints over logical variables; the latter is a basic calculus of interacting processes. We establish a close correspondence between the reductions in the γ-calculus and its encoding, using weak barbed bisimulation congruence.

1 Introduction

In this paper we shall relate two different strands in the semantics of programming languages. One is the concurrent constraints paradigm where facts about data values combine to resolve goals; the other is the communicating processes paradigm where parallel agents interact through data transmission. We shall use two small semantic calculi which embody these paradigms in a rigorous and tractable format: the γ-calculus for concurrent constraints and the π-calculus for communicating processes. These calculi have been deemed successful as semantic bases for programming languages in their respective areas. Our main result, that the γ-calculus has a natural encoding in the π-calculus, implies that many of the techniques and tools developed for process calculi can be transferred to the concurrent constraints community.

The relevance of the γ-calculus lies in its relationship to Oz [Smo95b, Smo94, Smo95a]. Oz is a real programming language; its performance is comparable to commercial implementations of Lisp or Prolog, it has an extensive programming environment, and it supports important concepts like higher-order functions, object-oriented programming, and concurrent constraints. Its computational model, the Oz calculus [Smo95a], has been inspired by process calculi but analysis methods such as equivalence checking and model checking have not been applied to it. This is partly because the calculus contains elements such as logical variables with no direct counterparts in other calculi. The γ-calculus [Smo94] is a simplified version of the Oz calculus; it retains the concept of logical variable and a primitive form of constraint solving, *elimination*. An example is in the reduction

$$E \wedge x = a \quad \longrightarrow \quad E\{x/a\}.$$

* Work partially supported by ESPRIT BRA project No. 8130: LOMAPS.

** Work partially supported by The Human Capital and Mobility Project EXPRESS.

Here $E \wedge x = a$ is a γ-term, namely a conjunction of a subterm E with the "fact" that x is a; the reduction results in $E\{x/a\}$, which is E where the logical variable x is "eliminated" and replaced by a.

In a process calculus the terms denote processes, called *agents*, interacting by sending data over named ports. The distinctive feature of the π-calculus [MPW92, Mil91] is that the data transmitted are again ports. There is no difference in kind between ports and data, and they are collectively called *names*. The calculus has a considerable expressive power, as witnessed by its use in, e.g., the semantics of the programming language PICT [PRT93] and of object-oriented programming [Wal95]; it can naturally encode higher-order communications [San92] and the λ-calculus [Mil92]. There is a variety of proof methods based on bisimulations [MPW92, San96, San92, San95, PS96], rewrite systems [PS95] and model checking [Dam93, AD96], and automated tools for these are emerging [VM94, FMQ95].

An example π-calculus reduction is the following *interaction*:

$$b(x) \,.\, P \mid \overline{b}\langle a\rangle \,.\, Q \quad \longrightarrow \quad P\{a/x\} \mid Q.$$

Here $b(x) \,.\, P$ is an "input" which receives something for x along b and continues as the subagent P, and $\overline{b}\langle a\rangle \,.\, Q$ is an "output" which transmits a along b and continues as the subagent Q. When combined with the parallel operator "|" they may interact and reduce to $P\{a/x\} \mid Q$, where bound occurrences of x are replaced everywhere in P by a.

At first it may seem a trivial task to encode elimination by interaction, since in both cases the result is a substitution of atomic entities. The difficulty lies in the extent that other reductions are permissible. In the example of elimination above, the subterm E may have other reductions and these are inherited by the whole term $E \wedge x = a$. In this way an elimination can be deferred in favour of reductions where the (not yet eliminated) logical variable x can play a role. In contrast, the π-calculus input $b(x) \,.\, P$ must await its input along b before any reduction within P can occur. No reductions involving names bound by input are possible. Another difference between the calculi is in the conditional construct: in the π-calculus an outermost conditional can always be decided (because the only conditions are equalities between names), while in the γ-calculus the conditions include "undecided" equalities between not yet eliminated logical variables.

We will demonstrate an encoding of the γ-calculus into the π-calculus which is compositional, i.e., the encoding of a term is derived from the encodings of its subterms. The main problem is the treatment of logical variables. We solve it by introducing special *handler* agents, one for each variable, which administer eliminations and resolve conditions. To argue that the encoding is correct relative to the predefined reduction relations we use the concept of *barbed bisimulation congruence*, originally introduced for the π-calculus [MS92a, San92] but equally applicable to the γ-calculus. In essence, two agents (or two terms) are bisimilar if their reductions can mimic indefinitely, and they are congruent if they are bisimilar in all contexts. Our correctness criterion is that two terms are congruent if and only if their encodings are congruent. In short, this means that the encoding is neither too sloppy in that it disregards significant aspects of terms, nor too picky in that it takes insignificant aspects into consideration.

Related work: Smolka [Smo94] inspired our research by relating the γ-calculus to a variant of the π-calculus with variables, equations and an elimination rule. We show that these additions can be dropped. Niehren and Müller [NM95] relate the γ-calculus to the ρ-calculus with equational constraints ($\rho(x = y)$), and observe that the ρ-calculus without constraints ($\rho(\emptyset)$) is a subcalculus both of $\rho(x = y)$ and of the π-calculus. We strengthen their result by formally showing the correspondence between the γ-calculus and π-calculus directly.

Ross [Ros93] gives π-calculus specifications of simplified logic variables and unification, and Li [Li94] gives a π-calculus specification of Prolog, including logic variables and unification, with support for backtracking. Neither of these provide proofs of formal correctness.

The programming languages PICT [PRT93] and Facile [TLP+93] have semantics formulated in π-calculus and CHOCS [Tho90], respectively. They support concurrent, functional and (in the PICT case) object-oriented programming, but not constraints.

Outline: The rest of the paper is structured as follows. In Sections 2 and 3 we give brief introductions to the γ-calculus and the π-calculus. In Section 4 we present our encoding of the γ-calculus in the π-calculus, and in Section 5 we prove that it is correct relative to weak barbed bisimulation. Finally in Section 6 we conclude with some areas for future work.

2 The γ-calculus

The γ-calculus is a simplified version of the Oz calculus, with equational constraints and where search is omitted. In this section we give a brief presentation of its syntax and semantics. For a fuller treatment we refer the reader to [Smo94].

There are three entities in the γ-calculus: *names* (ranged over by $a, b, c, \ldots$), *variables* (ranged over by $x, y, z, \ldots$), and *terms* (ranged over by $E, F, \ldots$). Names and variables are collectively referred to as *references* (ranged over by $u, v, w, \ldots$).

The syntax of the γ-calculus is given by the following BNF equation (the terminology in the equation comes from [Smo94]):

$$
\begin{array}{rll}
E ::= & \top & \textit{null} \\
\mid & E_1 \wedge E_2 & \textit{composition} \\
\mid & \exists u E & \textit{declaration} \\
\mid & u = v & \textit{equation} \\
\mid & u{:}\, \tilde{x}/E & \textit{abstraction} \\
\mid & u\tilde{v} & \textit{application} \\
\mid & \texttt{if } u = v \texttt{ then } E_1 \texttt{ else } E_2 & \textit{conditional} \\
\mid & u{:}\, v & \textit{cell}
\end{array}
$$

We have generalized the syntax from [Smo94] by allowing variables as locations of abstractions and cells. This admits terms like $\exists a, b, c(a{:}\, x/\exists y(x{:}\, y) \wedge ab \wedge bca)$. (The semantics remains the same – only abstractions and cells with names as locations can take part in a reduction using the APPL_γ or EXCH_γ rules which follow.)

Briefly, $\top$ represents an inactive term; each term in a composition can reduce in parallel; a declaration $\exists uE$ introduces a new reference u with scope E; an equation $u = v$ imposes the equality of u and v on all terms; an abstraction $a\colon \tilde{x}/E$ can communicate with an application $a\tilde{v}$, producing the new term $E\{\tilde{v}/\tilde{x}\}$. A cell $a\colon u$ can be seen as holding the value u, and can interact with an application avw, updating the cell's value to w and simultaneously extracting the old value rendering the equation $u = v$. A conditional **if** $u = v$ **then** E_1 **else** E_2 tests whether u and v are equal.

The semantics of the γ-calculus is defined by a structural congruence (Figure 1) and a reduction relation (Figure 2). A reference u is bound in $\exists uE$ and in $v\colon u/E$ (but *not* in $v\colon u$). We use $\text{br}(E)$ to refer to the bound references of P, and $\text{fr}(E)$ for the free references. A substitution $\{\tilde{u}/\tilde{v}\}$ simultaneously replaces each v_i with u_i.

1. $E \equiv_\gamma F$ if E is α-convertible to F
2. Abelian monoid laws for $\wedge$ and $\top$:
   $E \wedge F \equiv_\gamma F \wedge E, E \wedge (F \wedge G) \equiv_\gamma (E \wedge F) \wedge G, E \wedge \top \equiv_\gamma E$
3. $\exists u \top \equiv_\gamma \top$, $\exists u \exists v E \equiv_\gamma \exists v \exists u E$, $\exists u E \wedge F \equiv_\gamma \exists u (E \wedge F)$ if $u \notin \text{fr}(F)$
4. $u = v \equiv_\gamma v = u$

Fig. 1. Structural congruence for γ.

$$\text{STRUCT}_\gamma : \frac{E \equiv_\gamma E' \qquad E' \to_\gamma F' \qquad F' \equiv_\gamma F}{E \to_\gamma F}$$

$$\text{COMP}_\gamma : \frac{E \to_\gamma E'}{E \wedge F \to_\gamma E' \wedge F} \qquad \text{DECL}_\gamma : \frac{E \to_\gamma E'}{\exists uE \to_\gamma \exists uE'}$$

$$\text{APPL}_\gamma : \; a\tilde{u} \wedge a\colon \tilde{x}/E \to_\gamma E\{\tilde{u}/\tilde{x}\} \wedge a\colon \tilde{x}/E \text{ , if } \tilde{u} \text{ free for } \tilde{x} \text{ in } E \text{ and } |\tilde{u}| = |\tilde{x}|$$

$$\text{THEN}_\gamma : \; \mathbf{if}\ u = u\ \mathbf{then}\ E\ \mathbf{else}\ F \to_\gamma E$$

$$\text{ELSE}_\gamma : \; \mathbf{if}\ a = b\ \mathbf{then}\ E\ \mathbf{else}\ F \to_\gamma F \text{ , if } a \neq b$$

$$\text{EXCH}_\gamma : \; a\colon u \wedge avw \to_\gamma a\colon w \wedge u = v$$

$$\text{ELIM}_\gamma : \; \exists x(x = u \wedge E) \to_\gamma E\{u/x\} \text{ , if } x \neq u \text{ and } u \text{ free for } x \text{ in } E$$

Fig. 2. Reduction relation for γ.

An example of a reduction sequence shows that even though variables cannot be used for interaction in the APPL_γ or EXCH_γ rules, they can take part in reductions:

$$\exists x(x = y \wedge \texttt{if } x = y \texttt{ then } E \texttt{ else } E') \overset{\text{ELIM}_\gamma}{\rightarrow_\gamma} \texttt{if } y = y \texttt{ then } E \texttt{ else } E' \overset{\text{THEN}_\gamma}{\rightarrow_\gamma} E$$

3 The π-calculus

In this section we give a brief presentation of the syntax and semantics of the π-calculus. For fuller treatment we refer the reader to, e.g., [Mil91, San92].

There are two entities in the π-calculus: *names* (ranged over by lowercase letters) and *agents* (ranged over by $P, Q, \ldots$). The syntax of the π-calculus is given by the following BNF equation:

$P ::= \mathbf{0}$		*null*
$\mid$	$P_1 \mid P_2$	*composition*
$\mid$	$P_1 + P_2$	*summation*
$\mid$	$(\nu x)P$	*restriction*
$\mid$	$a(\tilde{b}) \,.\, P$	*input*
$\mid$	$\overline{a}\langle\tilde{b}\rangle \,.\, P$	*output*
$\mid$	$[a = b](P_1\,,\,P_2)$	*conditional*
$\mid$	$!\,P$	*replication*
$\mid$	$A(a_1, \ldots, a_k)$	*identifier*

where A ranges over some set of identifiers with associated nonnegative arities k and agent definitions $A(b_1, \ldots, b_k) \overset{def}{=} P$.

Briefly, $\mathbf{0}$ represents an inactive agent; each agent in a composition can execute in parallel; a summation $P_1 + P_2$ offers a choice between the agents P_1 and P_2; a restriction $(\nu b)P$ introduces a new name b with scope P; an input prefix $a(\tilde{b}) \,.\, P_1$ can communicate with an output $\overline{a}\langle\tilde{c}\rangle \,.\, P_2$, reducing to the agent $P_1\{\tilde{c}/\tilde{b}\} \mid P_2$. A conditional $[a = b](P_1\,,\,P_2)$ reads as "*if $a = b$ then P_1 else P_2*" and tests whether a and b are equal; a replication $!\,P$ corresponds to an unbounded number of copies of P in parallel. For convenience we use both replication and recursive definitions although one could be expressed in terms of the other (see [Mil91, section 3]), as long as we use a finite number of identifiers. Note that we include the binary conditional [PS95] whereas in most presentations of the π-calculus there is only the unary form $[x = y]P$. The binary form facilitates our encoding since the γ-calculus has an if-then-else conditional.

We only use guarded summation, i.e., summands must be prefix forms. This admits a definition of the semantics of the π-calculus by the structural congruence in Figure 3 and the reduction relation in Figure 4. Note that the MATCH_π and MISMATCH_π rules have no premises. This format enables us to deduce COMM_π reductions of agents with conditionals in parallel compositions.

A name a is bound in $(\nu a)P$ and in $b(a) \,.\, P$. We use $\text{bn}(P)$ to refer to the bound names of P, and $\text{fn}(P)$ for the free names of P. A substitution $\{\tilde{a}/\tilde{b}\}$ simultaneously replaces each b_i with a_i.

1. $P \equiv_\pi Q$ if P is α-convertible to Q
2. Abelian monoid laws for $+$ and $\mathbf{0}$:
$P + Q \equiv_\pi Q + P, P + (Q + R) \equiv_\pi (P + Q) + R, P + \mathbf{0} \equiv_\pi P$
3. Abelian monoid laws for $\mid$ and $\mathbf{0}$:
$P \mid Q \equiv_\pi Q \mid P, P \mid (Q \mid R) \equiv_\pi (P \mid Q) \mid R, P \mid \mathbf{0} \equiv_\pi P$
4. $(\nu x)\mathbf{0} \equiv_\pi \mathbf{0}, (\nu x)(\nu y)P \equiv_\pi (\nu y)(\nu x)P, (\nu x)P \mid Q \equiv_\pi (\nu x)(P \mid Q)$ if $x \notin \mathrm{fn}(Q)$
5. $!P \equiv_\pi P \mid !P$
6. $A(\tilde{x}) \equiv_\pi P\{\tilde{x}/\tilde{y}\}$ if $A(\tilde{y}) \stackrel{def}{=} P$ and $|\tilde{x}| = |\tilde{y}|$

Fig. 3. Structural congruence for π.

$$\textsc{Struct}_\pi : \frac{P \equiv_\pi P' \quad P' \rightarrow_\pi Q' \quad Q' \equiv_\pi Q}{P \rightarrow_\pi Q}$$

$$\textsc{Match}_\pi : [x = x](P, Q) \rightarrow_\pi P \qquad \textsc{Mismatch}_\pi : [x = y](P, Q) \rightarrow_\pi Q \text{ if } x \neq y$$

$$\textsc{Par}_\pi : \frac{P \rightarrow_\pi P'}{P \mid Q \rightarrow_\pi P' \mid Q} \qquad \textsc{Res}_\pi : \frac{P \rightarrow_\pi P'}{(\nu x)P \rightarrow_\pi (\nu x)P'}$$

$$\textsc{Comm}_\pi : (\cdots + x(\tilde{y}) . P) \mid (\overline{x}\langle\tilde{z}\rangle . Q + \cdots) \rightarrow_\pi P\{\tilde{z}/\tilde{y}\} \mid Q \text{ if } |\tilde{y}| = |\tilde{z}|$$

Fig. 4. Reduction relation for π.

Some notational conventions: $\overline{a}\langle b, \nu c, d\rangle . P$ is shorthand for $(\nu c)\overline{a}\langle b, c, d\rangle . P$; we use an underscore _ to signify a name not used anywhere else; and we often omit trailing $\mathbf{0}$ in inputs and outputs (e.g., $\overline{a}\langle b\rangle$ stands for $\overline{a}\langle b\rangle . \mathbf{0}$).

4 Encoding γ in π

4.1 Handlers

The main difficulty when encoding the γ-calculus is the treatment of variables. As a result of the $\textsc{Elim}_\gamma$ rule a variable can be substituted by another reference. The only mechanism for substitution in the π-calculus is in the interaction between input and output prefixes. Unfortunately we cannot use that mechanism directly to emulate the $\textsc{Elim}_\gamma$ rule. A π-calculus name which can be substituted in an interaction must be bound in an input prefix, and this prefix must reduce in the $\textsc{Comm}_\pi$ rule before the rest of the agent can reduce. In contrast, in the γ-calculus a term can reduce before its variables have been eliminated.

Our solution to this difficulty is to introduce one π-calculus *handler* agent for each reference not bound by abstraction. A handler interacts with its environment (the encoding of the term where the reference occurs) to perform the substitutions corresponding to the ELIM_γ rule, and to report its current *value*. Originally the value of a handler is the corresponding reference, but the value can change as a result of *updates* emanating from γ-calculus equations. The handlers thus collectively contain a global state corresponding to the eliminations in a reduct.

We distinguish between three kinds of handlers. $N(\underline{a})$ is a handler for a name a (the underscore will be explained below). It will not update to another reference and always gives its value as a. A variable x which has been updated to a reference u is handled by $R(\underline{x}, \underline{u})$. When queried for its value or asked to update it will relay the request to the handler for u. A variable x not yet eliminated is handled by $V(\underline{x})$. It gives x as value, and when asked to update to u it changes state to $R(\underline{x}, \underline{u})$. In this way we think of N as standing for "name", V for "variable" and R for "relay" in our encoding.

Since the reference u in $R(\underline{x}, \underline{u})$ may itself be represented by a handler of type R (if u is eliminated after x) the handlers will form a forest. At the root of each tree in the forest sits a handler of type V or N; interior nodes are type R handlers who will relay any queries to its parent. An update of a V root will graft its tree to another tree. Each tree forms an equivalence class of references under the substitutions from ELIM_γ rules. We call such a tree an *equivalence tree*. See Figure 5 for an example of how an update affects the equivalence trees.

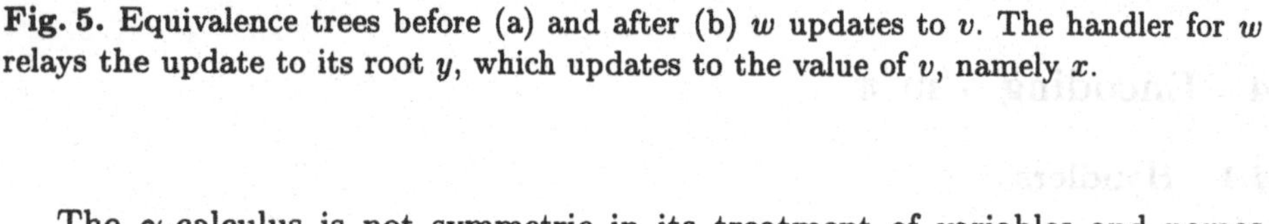

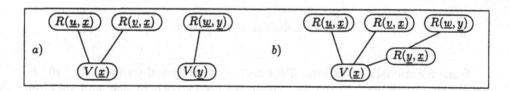

Fig. 5. Equivalence trees before (a) and after (b) w updates to v. The handler for w relays the update to its root y, which updates to the value of v, namely x.

The γ-calculus is not symmetric in its treatment of variables and names — e.g., the ELSE_γ rule only applies when a and b are names — so a handler additionally must report whether its reference is a name. For the same reason it is convenient to let handlers deal with the queries of equality between references that emanate from the conditional terms in the γ-calculus. Such queries can only be resolved in case the references are identical references or distinct names; an equality between distinct variables must be deferred to a later stage.

To let the handlers perform their tasks we introduce, for each γ-calculus reference u, the five π-calculus names u, $u\triangleright$name, $u\triangleright$value, $u\triangleright$update, $u\triangleright$eq, called the *handler interface* names, which we collectively refer to using the notation $\underline{u}$. The symbol $\triangleright$ is part of the names. We use a notation x: (a, b, c) to specify that names a, b, c are transmitted along x in the following explanation.

— u itself is used for the interaction between encodings of applications and abstractions or cells.

— $u\triangleright$name: (a) ascertains that u has the γ-calculus name a as root in its equivalence tree.

— $u\triangleright$value: (c, v) queries u for its value, by passing a π-calculus name c where the value is to be received, and the identity v of the source of the query. The value of a reference is the root of its equivalence tree. The source of the query, v, is used to avoid circular queries.

— $u\triangleright$update: $(\underline{v})$ tells u to update to the reference v. Care must be taken to avoid circular updates.

— $u\triangleright$eq: $(\underline{v}, y, n)$ asks u to decide whether it is in the same equivalence tree as v, and if it is, to signal on y, or if they are both names and not equal, to signal on n.

Finally, note that variables bound by abstraction have no handlers. This is because the APPL$_\gamma$ rule can be emulated with the COMM$_\pi$ rule.

4.2 The Encoding

The definitions of handlers can now be presented in Figure 6 on the next page.

A handler $N(\underline{a})$ never changes state to another type of handler; it can always handle requests and therefore uses replication in its definition. If it is asked to update to some other reference u through $a\triangleright$update$(\underline{u})$ it simply reflects the request and asks u to update a instead. The case where a name is asked to update to another name then results in a divergence, but this is not a problem, since an equation $a = b$ has no computational significance in the γ-calculus. In an equality check $a\triangleright$eq, the other reference is established to be a γ-calculus name, and this name and a itself are compared using a π-calculus conditional, and y or n is signalled appropriately.

The definition of a handler $V(\underline{x})$ is more intricate. When handling $x\triangleright$update$(\underline{u})$ to change into $R(\underline{x}, \underline{u})$, we must make sure the equivalence tree does not become circular; if it did, the handlers would end up relaying requests to each other. This could happen in two cases: (1) if $V(\underline{x})$ is asked to update to itself or to a reference in the same equivalence tree, so we must test for this situation by reading the value of the target u and check if it is x using a π-calculus conditional. Circularity can also occur (2) if two or more variables try to update to each other simultaneously. This can be avoided by not allowing any other variable to update to x while $V(\underline{x})$ is handling an $x\triangleright$update request. This is accomplished by *not* handling $x\triangleright$value requests during update sections, and vice versa, since another variable must read the value of the reference it is updating to. But this means that in the case that x is told to update to itself, $V(\underline{x})$ now cannot respond to its own $x\triangleright$value query. We therefore add a conditional which tests the "un-evaluated" target for equality with x. The case that x is told to update to itself through a number of relay handlers must also be taken care of: the last

$$\underline{u} \equiv u, u\triangleright\mathsf{name}, u\triangleright\mathsf{value}, u\triangleright\mathsf{update}, u\triangleright\mathsf{eq}$$

$$\begin{aligned}
N(\underline{a}) \equiv\ & !\,\overline{a\triangleright\mathsf{name}}\langle\underline{a}\rangle \\
& \mid\ !\,a\triangleright\mathsf{value}(c,_)\,.\,\overline{c}\langle\underline{a}\rangle \\
& \mid\ !\,a\triangleright\mathsf{update}(\underline{u})\,.\,\overline{u\triangleright\mathsf{update}}\langle\underline{a}\rangle \\
& \mid\ !\,a\triangleright\mathsf{eq}(\underline{u},y,n)\,.\,u\triangleright\mathsf{name}(\underline{b})\,.\,[a=b](\overline{y}\,,\,\overline{n})
\end{aligned}$$

$$\begin{aligned}
V(\underline{x}) \stackrel{def}{=}\ & x\triangleright\mathsf{value}(c,_)\,.\,\overline{c}\langle\underline{x}\rangle\,.\,V(\underline{x}) \\
& +x\triangleright\mathsf{update}(\underline{u})\,. \\
& \qquad [x=u]\Big(V(\underline{x})\,,\,\overline{u\triangleright\mathsf{value}}\langle\nu c,x\rangle\,.\,c(\underline{u})\,. \\
& \qquad\qquad [x=u](V(\underline{x})\,,\,R(\underline{x},\underline{u}))\Big) \\
& +x\triangleright\mathsf{eq}(\underline{u},y,n)\,. \\
& \qquad \Big(V(\underline{x}) \\
& \qquad \mid \overline{u\triangleright\mathsf{value}}\langle\nu c,x\rangle\,.\,c(\underline{u})\,.\,[x=u](\overline{y}\,,\,\overline{x\triangleright\mathsf{eq}}\langle\underline{u},y,n\rangle)\Big)
\end{aligned}$$

$$\begin{aligned}
R(\underline{x},\underline{u}) \equiv\ & !\,u\triangleright\mathsf{name}(\underline{a})\,.\,\overline{x\triangleright\mathsf{name}}\langle\underline{a}\rangle \\
& \mid\ !\,x\triangleright\mathsf{value}(c,v)\,.\,[u=v]\Big(\overline{c}\langle\underline{u}\rangle\,,\,\overline{u\triangleright\mathsf{value}}\langle c,v\rangle\Big) \\
& \mid\ !\,x\triangleright\mathsf{update}(\underline{v})\,.\,\overline{u\triangleright\mathsf{update}}\langle\underline{v}\rangle \\
& \mid\ !\,x\triangleright\mathsf{eq}(\underline{v},y,n)\,.\,\overline{u\triangleright\mathsf{eq}}\langle\underline{v},y,n\rangle
\end{aligned}$$

Fig. 6. Definitions of handlers.

relay handler in the chain cannot get a reply to its $x\triangleright\mathsf{value}$ query. This situation is dealt with in the $x\triangleright\mathsf{value}$ case of the R handlers, where the R handler will respond on behalf of the source of the request, which in this case will be $V(\underline{x})$.

The treatment of $x\triangleright\mathsf{eq}$ requests in a $V(\underline{x})$ handler is straightforward: the value of the other reference is read, and if it is x itself, we generate a positive response. Otherwise the request is reiterated, deferring the response until a decision can be reached, i.e., until either both have updated to names, or both are in the same equivalence tree.

The $R(\underline{x},\underline{u})$ handler is almost transparent. On receipt of $u\triangleright\mathsf{name}(\underline{a})$, the relay can repond to $x\triangleright\mathsf{name}$ requests. The $x\triangleright\mathsf{update}$ and $x\triangleright\mathsf{eq}$ requests are simply relayed to the handler for u. The treatment of $x\triangleright\mathsf{value}$ was mentioned above: if the source of the request is the handler of u, it may be in a state where it cannot respond to its own query, so the R handler responds by proxy. If the source was some other reference, the request is relayed.

Given the handling of references, the encoding of γ-calculus terms themselves can be presented in Figure 7 on the following page. Null of the γ-calculus ($\top$) corresponds to null of the π-calculus ($\mathbf{0}$), and $\wedge$ (composition) to $\mid$. Declaration $\exists$ corresponds to restriction ν, with the addition of a handler for the reference being declared.

$$
\begin{aligned}
[\![\top]\!] &= \mathbf{0} \\
[\![E \wedge F]\!] &= [\![E]\!] \mid [\![F]\!] \\
[\![\exists a E]\!] &= (\nu \underline{a})(N(\underline{a}) \mid [\![E]\!]) \\
[\![\exists x E]\!] &= (\nu \underline{x})(V(\underline{x}) \mid [\![E]\!]) \\
[\![u{:}\, \tilde{x}/E]\!] &= !\, u\triangleright\mathsf{name}(\underline{a}) \,.\, a(\tilde{\underline{x}}) \,.\, [\![E]\!] \\
[\![u{:}\, v]\!] &= u\triangleright\mathsf{name}(\underline{a}) \,.\, \mathit{Cell}(\underline{a}, \underline{v}) \\
[\![u\tilde{v}]\!] &= \overline{u\triangleright\mathsf{name}}(\underline{a}) \,.\, \overline{a}\langle \tilde{\underline{v}} \rangle \\
[\![u = v]\!] &= \overline{u\triangleright\mathsf{update}}\langle \underline{v} \rangle \\
[\![\mathtt{if}\ u = v\ \mathtt{then}\ E\ \mathtt{else}\ F]\!] & \\
&= (\nu y, n)(\overline{u\triangleright\mathsf{eq}}\langle \underline{v}, y, n\rangle \mid y \,.\, [\![E]\!] \mid n \,.\, [\![F]\!])
\end{aligned}
$$

$$
\mathit{Cell}(\underline{a}, \underline{u}) \stackrel{\mathit{def}}{=} a(\underline{v}, \underline{w}) \,.\, \Big([\![u = v \wedge a{:}\, w]\!] \Big)
$$

Fig. 7. Encoding of the γ-calculus.

The encoding of a γ-calculus cell ensures that its location is a γ-calculus name, and proceeds according to the π-calculus definition *Cell*. An encoded γ-calculus application must also ensure its location to be a γ-calculus name, and then outputs the vector of references together with their handler interface names. A γ-calculus abstraction is encoded as a replication which first makes sure its location is a γ-calculus name, inputs the references along with their handler interface names, and proceeds as the encoding of the body of the abstraction. The replication is necessary since, in the APPL_γ rule, the abstraction recurs.

4.3 Variants of the encoding

The use of summation (the + operator) in the definition of type V reference handlers can be avoided by using a standard π-calculus technique: we replace the summation of inputs on "selector" names $a_1, \ldots, a_n$, $a_1(\tilde{x}_1) \,.\, P_1 + \cdots + a_n(\tilde{x}_n) \,.\, P_n$, with *one* input on a "contact" name b: $b(a_1, \ldots, a_n) \,.\, (a_1(\tilde{x}_1) \,.\, P_1 \mid \cdots \mid a_n(\tilde{x}_n) \,.\, P_n)$, where $\forall i : \{a_j : j \neq i\} \cap \mathrm{fn}(P_i) = \emptyset$, and replace the "selector" outputs $\overline{a_i}\langle \tilde{c}_i \rangle \,.\, P_i$ with $\overline{b}\langle \nu a_1, \ldots, \nu a_n \rangle \,.\, \overline{a_i}\langle \tilde{c}_i \rangle \,.\, P_i$, with the same restriction on $\mathrm{fn}(P_i)$. This also makes handler interface names more local.

Our encoding introduces divergence in several places. As already mentioned the encoding of a γ-calculus equation $a = b$ causes the handlers for the names a and b to ask each other to update indefinitely. This can easily be avoided by not reflecting update requests to other names. The reiteration of the $\overline{x\triangleright\mathsf{eq}}\langle \underline{u}, y, n\rangle$ request in the definition of $V(\underline{x})$ can also result in a divergence. This can be avoided by "freezing" the request by putting it under a prefix (local to $V(\underline{x})$), which is activated if x is later updated, possibly deciding the condition. Finally, indefinitely iterated checks that a reference is a name, i.e., interactions along

$u\triangleright$name, occur in relay handlers and in abstractions. Again divergence can be avoided if these are modified to only perform the check once. This is enough since whenever the check succeeds it will always continue to succeed — a name can never cease to be a name.

Divergence does not affect the formal correctness proofs to follow, since termination is not among the observables in our notion of correctness. In other words, the fact that a γ-term terminates but its encoding diverges is not considered relevant. This can be construed as a weakness from the point of view of the γ-calculus and Oz programming. By adopting the variants above we can eliminate divergence at the expense of a more complicated encoding. Although we have not carried out all details of the proofs, we strongly conjecture that the correctness results of Section 5 are still valid in these variants.

5 Correctness

In this section we show that our encoding is correct, in the sense that if two γ-calculus terms are behaviourally equivalent, we know that the encodings of these terms into the π-calculus are also equivalent, and vice versa. We also show that γ-calculus reductions correspond to π-calculus reductions in our encoding.

5.1 Free references

As in [Smo94], we assume that there are no free γ-calculus variables at top level of a term. However, free γ-calculus names may still appear. To complete the encoding of terms $[\![\cdot]\!]$, we must add an N handler for each free name. Also there may be more free π-calculus names than there are free γ-calculus names. E.g., for the term $E \equiv a{:}x/ax$, $\mathrm{fr}(E) = \{a\}$, while $\mathrm{fn}([\![E]\!]) = \{\underline{a}\} = \{a, a\triangleright\mathsf{name}, a\triangleright\mathsf{value}, a\triangleright\mathsf{update}, a\triangleright\mathsf{eq}\}$. To correct this and make sure the handler interface names cannot be used improperly by some external agent, we add a restriction on them.

We define a closing operation $\mathcal{V}$ to add the name handlers and the restriction:

Definition 1. If $\mathrm{fr}(E) = \{a_1, \ldots, a_n\}, n \geq 0$,

$$\mathcal{V}(E) \equiv (\nu\tilde{a})(N(\underline{a_1}) \mid \cdots \mid N(\underline{a_n}) \mid [\![E]\!])$$

where $\tilde{a} \equiv \bigcup_{i=1}^{n} \{a_i\triangleright\mathsf{name}, a_i\triangleright\mathsf{value}, a_i\triangleright\mathsf{update}, a_i\triangleright\mathsf{eq}\}$

An example: $E \equiv a{:}x/ax$

$$[\![E]\!] \equiv\ !\,a\triangleright\mathsf{name}(\underline{a}) \,.\, a(\underline{x}) \,.\, a\triangleright\mathsf{name}(\underline{a}) \,.\, \overline{a}\langle\underline{x}\rangle$$

$$\mathcal{V}(E) \equiv (\nu a\triangleright\mathsf{name}, a\triangleright\mathsf{value}, a\triangleright\mathsf{update}, a\triangleright\mathsf{eq})\Big(N(\underline{a}) \mid [\![E]\!]\Big)$$

5.2 Behavioural equivalences

We must define what we mean by two terms or agents being "equivalent". Using the results of Milner and Sangiorgi [MS92a, San92], we propose a version of *barbed bisimulation*, based on the reduction relations of Sections 2 and 3, adding predicates for observability.

Definition 2 Observability in γ-calculus.
$a\tilde{v} \downarrow^a_\gamma$, $a{:}\tilde{x}/E \downarrow^a_\gamma$, $a{:}u \downarrow^a_\gamma$
$(\exists u E) \downarrow^a_\gamma$ if $E \downarrow^a_\gamma$ and $a \neq u$
$(E \wedge F) \downarrow^a_\gamma$ if $E \downarrow^a_\gamma$ or $F \downarrow^a_\gamma$

Definition 3 Observability in π-calculus.
$\bar{a}\tilde{b} \downarrow^a_\pi$, $a(\tilde{b}).P \downarrow^a_\pi$
$(\nu b)P \downarrow^a_\pi$ if $P \downarrow^a_\pi$ and $a \neq b$
$(P \mid Q) \downarrow^a_\pi$ if $P \downarrow^a_\pi$ or $Q \downarrow^a_\pi$
$(P + Q) \downarrow^a_\pi$ if $P \downarrow^a_\pi$ or $Q \downarrow^a_\pi$

The relation $\Rightarrow_\gamma$ is the reflexive and transitive closure of $\rightarrow_\gamma$, and similarly for $\Rightarrow_\pi$ and $\rightarrow_\pi$. We write $E \Downarrow^a_\gamma$ if $E \Rightarrow_\gamma \downarrow^a_\gamma$, and $P \Downarrow^a_\pi$ if $P \Rightarrow_\pi \downarrow^a_\pi$.

We can now define observational equivalences for γ-calculus terms and for π-calculus agents. We start by giving a parameterized definition of weak barbed bisimulation [MS92a, San92]. Let $\Box$ be γ or π.

Definition 4. A symmetric relation $\mathcal{R}$ on $\Box$ expressions is a *weak $\Box$-barbed bisimulation* if for all $(X, Y) \in \mathcal{R}$,

1. if $X \rightarrow_\Box X'$, then $Y \Rightarrow_\Box Y'$ such that $X'\mathcal{R}Y'$
2. if $X \downarrow^a_\Box$, then $Y \Downarrow^a_\Box$.

Two expressions X and Y are *weak $\Box$-barbed bisimilar*, written $X \dot{\approx}_\Box Y$, if $X\mathcal{R}Y$ for some weak $\Box$-barbed bisimulation $\mathcal{R}$.

These definitions of bisimilarity are too weak; e.g, the agents $a\,.\,b\,.\,\mathbf{0}$ and $a\,.\,\mathbf{0}$ are considered weak π-barbed bisimilar. We remedy this by closing under contexts:

Definition 5. Two terms E and F are *weak γ-barbed congruent*, written $E \approx_\gamma F$, if for all γ-calculus contexts $C[\cdot]$, it holds that $C[E] \dot{\approx}_\gamma C[F]$.

In the π-calculus case, we choose to close not under all π-calculus contexts, but only under γ contexts, i.e., contexts occurring in encodings of γ-calculus terms. Formally, these can be defined by introducing term variables; the γ contexts are then encodings of γ terms with one occurrence of a term variable.

Definition 6. Two agents P and Q are *weak π-barbed congruent*, written $P \approx_\pi Q$, if for all γ contexts $C[\cdot]$, it holds that $C[P] \dot{\approx}_\pi C[Q]$.

If arbitrary π-calculus contexts were used in the previous definition, the relation would coincide with weak early bisimulation [San92]. Our congruence is coarser since only contexts corresponding to the γ-calculus are considered. For example, the terms $a{:}\,x/(x=x)$ and $a{:}\,x/\top$ are equivalent in the sense that their encodings have the same reductions and observations in arbitrary γ-calculus contexts. But there is a π-calculus context which distinguishes them, for example $(\overline{a}\langle \underline{u}\rangle \mid \bullet)$. Inserting the encoding of $a{:}\,x/(x=x)$ we will get observations along the interface names in $\underline{u}$, in contrast to when inserting $a{:}\,x/\top$. A similar situation is present in the encoding of the λ-calculus into the π-calculus [Mil92], and indeed it would be unreasonable to expect any encoding to be robust under alien contexts.

We now have definitions of the congruences we will use in the full abstraction theorem below. However, to make the proofs easier, we use the *up-to* $\approx$ technique of [MS92b, San92]. Again we give a parameterized definition. Let $\Box$ be γ or π.

Definition 7. A symmetric relation $\mathcal{R}$ on $\Box$ expressions is a *weak $\Box$-barbed bisimulation up-to* $\approx_\Box$ if for all $(X,Y)\in\mathcal{R}$,

1. if $X \Rightarrow_\Box X'$, then $Y \Rightarrow_\Box Y'$ such that $X' \approx_\Box \mathcal{R} \approx_\Box Y'$
2. if $X \Downarrow^a_\Box$, then $Y \Downarrow^a_\Box$.

Again, we close these bisimilarities under contexts.

Definition 8. Two terms E and F are *weak γ-barbed congruent up-to* $\approx_\gamma$, written $E \approx^+_\gamma F$, if for all γ-calculus contexts $C[\cdot]$, it holds that $(C[E],C[F])\in\mathcal{R}$ for some $\mathcal{R}$ which is a weak γ-barbed bisimulation up-to $\approx_\gamma$.

Definition 9. Two agents P and Q are *weak π-barbed congruent up-to* $\approx_\pi$, written $P \approx^+_\pi Q$, if for all γ contexts $C[\cdot]$, it holds that $(C[P],C[Q])\in\mathcal{R}$ for some $\mathcal{R}$ which is a weak π-barbed bisimulation up-to $\approx_\pi$.

Proposition 10.

1. If $E \approx^+_\gamma F$, then $E \approx_\gamma F$.
2. If $P \approx^+_\pi Q$, then $P \approx_\pi Q$.

Proof. Analogous to Lemma 4.5 in [Mil89].

5.3 Full abstraction

We now have enough machinery to proceed to show full abstraction of the encoding, i.e., that two γ-calculus terms are congruent iff their encodings in the π-calculus are congruent. We omit the proofs because of the limited space available; they are often quite detailed.

Theorem 11. *$E \approx_\gamma F$ iff $\mathcal{V}(E) \approx_\pi \mathcal{V}(F)$.*

In the rest of this section we sketch the proof.

We use straight-forward Lemmas concerning operational correspondence between γ-calculus terms E and their encodings $\mathcal{V}(E)$. The first Lemma says that if a γ-calculus term E can reduce to E', its encoding $\mathcal{V}(E)$ can reduce to an agent congruent to the encoding of E'.

Lemma 12. *$E \rightarrow_\gamma E'$ implies $\mathcal{V}(E) \Rightarrow_\pi \approx_\pi \mathcal{V}(E')$.*

Proof. By induction over reduction rules.

An immediate corollary is the following:

Corollary 13. *$E \Rightarrow_\gamma E'$ implies $\mathcal{V}(E) \Rightarrow_\pi \approx_\pi \mathcal{V}(E')$.*

The next Lemma goes in the other direction: it states that however $\mathcal{V}(E)$ reduces in the π-calculus, it reduces to an agent which is congruent to the encoding of a γ-calculus term to which E can reduce in the γ-calculus.

Lemma 14. *$\mathcal{V}(E) \Rightarrow_\pi P'$ implies $\exists E' : E \Rightarrow_\gamma E'$ and $P' \approx_\pi \mathcal{V}(E')$.*

Proof. By induction on the structure of terms E.

We move on to the observations: if we can observe a on E, we can also observe a on the encoding of E.

Lemma 15. *$E \downarrow_\gamma^a$ implies $\mathcal{V}(E) \Downarrow_\pi^a$.*

Proof. By induction on the structure of terms E.

A corollary of this (and Corollary 13) is the following:

Corollary 16. *$E \Downarrow_\gamma^a$ implies $\mathcal{V}(E) \Downarrow_\pi^a$.*

The other direction is also true: if we can observe a on the encoding of a term E, we can observe it on E itself.

Lemma 17. *$\mathcal{V}(E) \Downarrow_\pi^a$ implies $E \Downarrow_\gamma^a$.*

Proof. By induction on the structure of terms E.

Proposition 18. *$E \approx_\gamma^+ F$ iff $\mathcal{V}(E) \approx_\pi^+ \mathcal{V}(F)$.*

Proof. Using Corollaries 13 and 16 and Lemmas 14 and 17, induction, and the fact that the name handlers and restrictions introduced in $\mathcal{V}$ distribute over γ-calculus contexts.

Now, Theorem 11 is a consequence of Propositions 18 and 10.

6 Conclusion

We have demonstrated a compositional encoding of the γ-calculus into the π-calculus and established its correctness by means of barbed bisimulation congruence. This opens several avenues of further work.

The constraints in the γ-calculus are just equalities between variables and names. In this way γ is equipotent with a special case of the ρ-calculus[NM95]. A natural direction for further work is to investigate other versions of the ρ-calculi and the Oz-calculus. These calculi use constraints over arbitrary data types and although data type encodings in the π-calculus are well understood it is less clear how to deal with constraints over them.

Further the γ-calculus lacks disjunction and failure. An encoding of disjunction could be envisaged with the π-calculus summation operator (which is akin to committed choice in that non selected branches are irrevocably lost) plus a backtracking mechanism. An encoding of failures is straightforward by giving unsatisfiable equations such as $a = b$ a computational content beyond that in our present scheme (where equations merely trigger updates of a global state).

Calculi with concurrent constraints typically come with "computational models" which express how terms represent computational behaviour. In a sense our encoding is such a model, since it dictates how the global state is represented and how it can be updated. The model for the γ-calculus in [Smo94] uses a central store (a "blackboard") for noncritical resources such as abstractions, but effectuates state updates through global substitutions of variables. Our encoding is therefore closer to an implementation, and it might be interesting to compare it with various implementation strategies.

Finally, the equivalence introduced in this paper has not been investigated. As explained in Section 5, our π-calculus congruence is coarser than weak early bisimulation congruence [San92]. Nevertheless the barbed congruence in the γ-calculus is a potential area of further study and presumably many techniques will carry over from the π-calculus.

References

[AD96] R. Amadio and M. Dam. Toward a modal theory of types for the π-calculus. 1996. To appear in the proceedings of FTRTFT'96, Lecture Notes in Computer Science.

[Dam93] M. Dam. Model checking mobile processes. In E. Best, editor, *CONCUR'93, 4th Intl. Conference on Concurrency Theory*, volume 715 of *Lecture Notes in Computer Science*, pages 22–36. Springer-Verlag, 1993. Full version in Research Report R94:01, Swedish Institute of Computer Science, Kista, Sweden.

[FMQ95] G. Ferrari, G. Modoni and P. Quaglia. Towards a semantic-based verification environment for the pi-calculus. In *Proceedings of 5th Italian Conference on Theoretical Computer Science: ICTCS-95*. World Scientific, 1995.

[Li94] B. Li. A π-calculus specification of Prolog. In D. Sannella, editor, *Proceedings of European Symposium on Programming*, volume 788 of *Lecture Notes in Computer Science*, pages 379–393, Edinburgh, 1994. Springer-Verlag.

[Mil89] R. Milner. *Communication and Concurrency*. Prentice Hall, 1989.

[Mil91] R. Milner. The polyadic π-calculus: a tutorial. Technical Report ECS-LFCS-91-180, Laboratory for Foundations of Computer Science, Department of Computer Science, University of Edinburgh, UK, October 1991. Also in *Logic and Algebra of Specification*, ed. F. L. Bauer, W. Brauer and H. Schwichtenberg, Springer-Verlag, 1993.

[Mil92] R. Milner. Functions as processes. *Journal of Mathematical Structures in Computer Science*, 2(2):119–141, 1992.

[MPW92] R. Milner, J. Parrow and D. Walker. A calculus of mobile processes, Parts I and II. *Journal of Information and Computation*, 100:1–77, September 1992.

[MS92a] R. Milner and D. Sangiorgi. Barbed bisimulation. In W. Kuich, editor, *Proc. of 19th International Colloquium on Automata, Languages and Programming (ICALP '92)*, volume 623 of *Lecture Notes in Computer Science*, pages 685–695. Springer-Verlag, 1992.

[MS92b] R. Milner and D. Sangiorgi. The problem of "weak bisimulation up-to". In R. Cleaveland, editor, *CONCUR'92, 3rd Intl. Conference on Concurrency Theory*, volume 630 of *Lecture Notes in Computer Science*. Springer-Verlag, 1992. Revised version available as ftp://ftp.dcs.ed.ac.uk/pub/sad/x.ps.Z, entitled *Techniques of "weak bisimulation up-to"*.

[NM95] J. Niehren and M. Müller. Constraints for free in concurrent computation. In K. Kanchanasut and J.-J. Lévy, editors, *Asian Computing Science Conference on Algorithms, Concurrency and Knowledge (ACSC '95)*, volume 1023 of *Lecture Notes in Computer Science*, Pathumthani, Thailand, 11–13 December 1995. Springer-Verlag.

[PRT93] B. C. Pierce, D. Rémy and D. N. Turner. A typed higher-order programming language based on the pi-calculus. In *Workshop on Type Theory and its Application to Computer Systems, Kyoto University*, July 1993.

[PS95] J. Parrow and D. Sangiorgi. Algebraic theories for name-passing calculi. *Journal of Information and Computation*, 120(2):174–197, 1995.

[PS96] M. Pistore and D. Sangiorgi. A partition refinement algorithm for the π-calculus. 1996. To appear in the proceedings of CAV'96, Lecture Notes in Computer Science.

[Ros93] B. Ross. A π-calculus semantics of logical variables and unification. In S. Purushothaman and A. Zwarico, editors, *Proceedings of First North American Process Algebra Workshop, Stony Brook, 1992, Workshops in Computing*, pages 216–230. Springer-Verlag, 1993.

[San92] D. Sangiorgi. *Expressing Mobility in Process Algebras: First-Order and Higher-Order Paradigms.* PhD thesis, Department of Computer Science, University of Edinburgh, UK, 1992.

[San95] D. Sangiorgi. On the proof method for bisimulation (extended abstract). In J. Wiederman and P. Hájek, editors, *Mathematical Foundations of Computer Science 1995 (MFCS'95)*, volume 969 of *Lecture Notes in Computer Science*, pages 479–488. Springer-Verlag, 1995. Full version available electronically as `ftp://ftp.dcs.ed.ac.uk/pub/sad/bis-proof.ps.z`.

[San96] D. Sangiorgi. A theory of bisimulation for the π-calculus. *Acta Informatica*, 33:69–97, 1996. Earlier version published as Report ECS-LFCS-93-270, University of Edinburgh. An extended abstract appeared in LNCS 715 (Proc. CONCUR'93).

[Smo94] G. Smolka. A foundation for higher-order concurrent constraint programming. In J.-P. Jouannaud, editor, *Proc. 1st International Conference on Constraints in Computational Logics*, volume 845 of *Lecture Notes in Computer Science*, pages 50–72. Springer-Verlag, September 1994. Available as Research Report RR-94-16 from DFKI Kaiserslautern.

[Smo95a] G. Smolka. The definition of Kernel Oz. In A. Podelski, editor, *Constraints: Basics and Trends*, volume 910 of *Lecture Notes in Computer Science*, pages 251–292. Springer-Verlag, 1995.

[Smo95b] G. Smolka. An Oz primer. DFKI Oz documentation series, DFKI, Saarbrücken, Germany, 1995. Available as ftp://ps-ftp.dfki.uni-sb.de-/pub/oz/documentation/Primer.ps.Z.

[Tho90] B. Thomsen. *Calculi for Higher Order Communicating Systems.* PhD thesis, Imperial College, University of London, September 1990.

[TLP+93] B. Thomsen, L. Leth, S. Prasad, T.-S. Kuo, A. Kramer, F. Knabe and A. Giacalone. Facile Antigua release – programming guide. Technical Report ECRC-93-20, ECRC, München, Germany, 1993.

[VM94] B. Victor and F. Moller. The Mobility Workbench — a tool for the π-calculus. In D. Dill, editor, *Computer Aided Verification (Proc. of CAV'94)*, volume 818 of *Lecture Notes in Computer Science*, pages 428–440. Springer-Verlag, 1994.

[Wal95] D. Walker. Objects in the π-calculus. *Journal of Information and Computation*, 116(2):253–271, 1995.

A Calculus of Mobile Agents

Cédric Fournet, Georges Gonthier,
Jean-Jacques Lévy, Luc Maranget, Didier Rémy

INRIA Rocquencourt *
78153 Le Chesnay Cedex, FRANCE
e-mail Cedric.Fournet@inria.fr

Abstract. We introduce a calculus for mobile agents and give its chemical semantics, with a precise definition for migration, failure, and failure detection. Various examples written in our calculus illustrate how to express remote executions, dynamic loading of remote resources and protocols with mobile agents. We give the encoding of our distributed calculus into the join-calculus.

1 Introduction

It is not easy to match concurrency and distribution. Suppose, for instance, that we want to implement a concurrent calculus with CCS-like communication channels and with processes running on different physical sites. If we do not locate channels, we quickly face a global consensus problem for nearly every communication which uses the interconnection network. In a previous work [6], we introduced the join-calculus, an asynchronous variant of Milner's π-calculus with better locality and better static scoping rules. It avoids global consensus and thus may be implemented in a realistic distributed environment. Furthermore, it is shown to have the same expressive power as the π-calculus. In this paper, we extend the join-calculus with explicit locations and primitives for mobility. The new calculus, the Distributed Join-Calculus, allows to express mobile agents moving between physical sites. Agents are not only programs but core images of running processes with their communication capabilities.

The novelty of the distributed join-calculus is the introduction of locations. Intuitively, a location resides on a physical site, and contains a group of processes. We can move atomically a location to another site. We represent mobile agents by locations. Agents can contain mobile sub-agents, this is represented by nested locations. Locations move as a whole with all their sublocations. For these reasons, we organize locations in a tree.

Our calculus also provides a simple model of failure. The crash of a physical site causes the permanent failure of all its locations. More generally, any location can halt, with all its sublocations. The failure of a location can be detected at any other running location, allowing error recovery.

* This work is partly supported by the ESPRIT Basic Research Action 6454 - CONFER.

Our aim is to use this calculus as the core of a distributed programming language. In particular, our operational semantics is easily implementable in a distributed setting with failures. The specification of atomic reduction steps becomes critical, since it defines the balance between abstract features and realistic concerns.

In the spirit of the π-calculus, our calculus treats channel names and location names as first class values with lexical scopes. A location controls its own moves, and can only move towards a location whose name it has received. This provides a sound basis for static analysis and for secure mobility. Our calculus is complete for expressing distributed configurations. In the absence of failure, however, the execution of processes is independent of distribution. This location transparency is essential for the design of mobiles agents, and very helpful for checking their properties.

We present classical examples of distribution and mobility. The basic example is remote procedure call with timeouts. Dynamic loading of remote applications is our second example. Unlike Java applets, we download a process with its active communications, simply by moving its location. The third example, remote execution of a local agent, is the dual case. The last example is a combination of the second and third. The client creates an agent that moves to a server to perform some task; when this task is completed, the agent comes back to the client to report the result. We take this example, which we dub the client-agent-server architecture (CASA), as our paradigm for mobility. We show that causal error recovery can be integrated into this CASA with minimal implementation assumptions.

In section 2, we review related work. In section 3, we give a brief presentation of the join-calculus and recall the basics of the reflexive chemical machine framework. In section 4 and 5, we gradually extend the join-calculus. In section 4, we introduce our location model as a refinement of the reflexive chemical model and present a first set of new primitives aimed at expressing location management and migration. In section 5, we give our final calculus that copes with failure and recovery, discussing various semantical models for failure. In parallel, we develop our main example of the client-agent-server architecture. In section 6, we suggest techniques for formal proofs, we provide an encoding of the distributed calculus into the join-calculus, and we state a full abstraction theorem. Finally, we give directions for future work.

2 Related work

Migration has been investigated mostly for object-oriented languages. Initially used in distributed systems to achieve a better load-balancing, migration evolves to a language feature in Emerald [9] : objects can be *moved* from one machine to another; they can also be *attached* to one another, an object carrying its attached objects as it moves. At the language level, numerous calling conventions such as call-by-move reflect these capabilities, and the use of migration for safety purposes is advocated.

More recently, several languages have been proposed for large-scale distributed programming, with some support for the mobile agent paradigm. For instance, Obliq [5] encodes migration as a combination of remote cloning and aliasing, in a language with a global distributed scope. Examples of applications with large-grain mobility in Obliq can be found in [3]. However, little support is provided for failure recovery. In a functional setting, FACILE [7] provides process mobility from site to site, as the communication of higher-order values. As in this paper, the design choices are discussed in a chemical framework [10].

Mobility and locality already have other meanings in process calculi. Mobility in the π-calculus refers to the communication of channel names on channels [11], whereas locality has been used as a tool to capture spatial dependencies among processes in non-interleaving semantics [4, 14].

The formal model developed for core FACILE [1] is more closely related to our work. In the π_l-calculus, the authors extend the syntax of the π-calculus with locations. Channels are statically located; a location can fail, preventing further communication on its channels; location status can be tested in the language. Due to the properties of the π-calculus, observation with failures become very different from the usual observation, but an encoding of the π_l-calculus in the π-calculus is given and proved adequate. In this paper, we also introduce a distributed calculus as a refinement of a core calculus – the join-calculus –. However, the join-calculus was specifically designed for this purpose, which leads to simpler formal developments, even though our extensions capture both migration and failure.

3 Chemical frameworks

In this section, we introduce key notions for the syntax and semantics of our distributed calculi, we briefly present the join-calculus, and we define observational equivalence. The join-calculus is our basic process calculus. Later in this paper, we extend it by introducing locations, migration, and failure.

3.1 General setting

Our calculus is a name-passing calculus. We assume given an infinite set of port names with arities $\mathcal{N}$ (ports are also called channels). We use lowercase variables x, y, *foo*, *bar*, ... to denote the elements of $\mathcal{N}$. Names obey lexical scoping and can be sent in messages. At present, we only have port names. Later in this paper, we will introduce other values (location names, integers, booleans) and letters u, v, ... will denote values in general.

We assume that names are used consistently in processes, respecting their arities. This could be made precise by using a recursive sort discipline as in the polyadic π-calculus [11, 12]. We assume that all processes are well-sorted.

Notations: We use the following conventions: $\widetilde{v}$ is the tuple $v_1, v_2, \cdots v_n$, $(n \geq 0)$; RR' is the composition of the relations R and R'; R^* is the transitive closure of relation R.

Chemical rules: We present our operational semantics in the chemical abstract machine style of Berry and Boudol [2]. The CHAM provides a precise and convenient way to specify reduction modulo equivalence. It also conveys some intuition about implementation schemes and implementation costs, especially in distinguishing between local and global operations.

As usual, we use two families of chemical rules that operate on multisets of terms (the so-called chemical soups, or chemical solutions): *Structural rules* $\rightleftharpoons$ are reversible ($\rightharpoonup$ is *heating*, $\leftharpoondown$ is *cooling*); they represent the syntactical rearrangements of terms in solution. *Reduction rules* $\longrightarrow$ consume some specific terms in the soup, replacing them by some other terms; they correspond to the basic computation steps.

3.2 The join-calculus and the reflexive chemical machine (RCHAM)

Our starting point is the join-calculus as described in [6]. The join-calculus is as expressive as the asynchronous π-calculus. Furthermore, our calculus is closer to a programming language than the π-calculus. In particular, it can be seen as a concurrent extension of functional programming.

Syntax: Terms of the calculus are processes and definitions:

$$\begin{aligned} P &\stackrel{\text{def}}{=} x\langle\widetilde{v}\rangle \mid \mathbf{def}\ D\ \mathbf{in}\ P \mid P|P \mid \mathbf{0} \\ D &\stackrel{\text{def}}{=} J \triangleright P \mid D \wedge D \mid \mathbf{T} \\ J &\stackrel{\text{def}}{=} x\langle\widetilde{v}\rangle \mid J|J \end{aligned}$$

A process P is the asynchronous emission of a message $x\langle\widetilde{v}\rangle$, the definition of port names, the parallel composition of processes, or the null process. A definition D is made of a few reaction rules $J \triangleright P$ connected by the $\wedge$ operator. Such rules match join-patterns of messages J to trigger their guarded processes. They can be considered as an extension of named functions with synchronization, and obey similar lexical scoping rules:

- The formal parameters $v_1, v_2, \ldots v_n$ received in join-patterns are bound in (each instance of) the corresponding guarded process. They are pairwise distinct.
- Defined port names are recursively bound in the whole defining process **def** D **in** P, that is, in the main process P and in the guarded processes inside definition D.

A name is fresh with regards to a process or a solution when it is not free in them. We write $\{^x/_y\}$ for the substitution of name x for name variable y, and σ for an arbitrary substitution. We assume implicit α-conversion on bound variables to avoid clashes. Received variables $rv[J]$, defined variables $dv[J]$ and $dv[D]$, and free variables $fv[D]$ and $fv[P]$ are formally defined for the full calculus in Figure 2.

Local chemistry A *reflexive solution* $\mathcal{D} \vdash \mathcal{P}$ consists of two parts: $\mathcal{P}$ is a multiset of running processes; $\mathcal{D}$ is a multiset of active rules. Such reaction rules define the possible reductions of processes, while processes can introduce new names and reaction rules. The chemical rules are:

$$\begin{array}{lrcl}
\textbf{str-join} & \vdash P_1|P_2 & \rightleftharpoons & \vdash P_1, P_2 \\
\textbf{str-null} & \vdash \mathbf{0} & \rightleftharpoons & \vdash \\
\textbf{str-and} & D_1 \wedge D_2 \vdash & \rightleftharpoons & D_1, D_2 \vdash \\
\textbf{str-nodef} & \mathbf{T} \vdash & \rightleftharpoons & \vdash \\
\textbf{str-def} & \vdash \mathbf{def}\ D \ \mathbf{in}\ P & \rightleftharpoons & D\sigma_{\mathrm{dv}} \vdash P\sigma_{\mathrm{dv}} \quad (\mathit{range}(\sigma_{\mathrm{dv}})\ \text{fresh}) \\
\\
\textbf{red} & J \triangleright P \vdash J\sigma_{\mathrm{rv}} & \longrightarrow & J \triangleright P \vdash P\sigma_{\mathrm{rv}}
\end{array}$$

The first four structural rules state that $|$ and $\wedge$ are associative and commutative, with units $\mathbf{0}$ and $\mathbf{T}$. The **str-def** rule provides *reflection*, with a static scoping discipline: a defining process can activate its reaction rules, substituting fresh names for its defined variables. Conversely, rules can be frozen on a process, as long as their names are local to that process. The single reduction rule **red** describes the use of active reactions ($J \triangleright P$) to consume join-messages present in the soup and produce a new instance of their guarded process.

In this paper, *the presentation of every chemical rule assumes an implicit context.* In other words, we omit the parts of multisets in chemical solutions that do not change by the effect of the presented rule. For instance, the verbose **str-def** rule is

$$\mathcal{D} \vdash \mathcal{P} \cup \{\mathbf{def}\ D\ \mathbf{in}\ P\} \ \rightleftharpoons\ \mathcal{D} \cup \{D\sigma_{\mathrm{dv}}\} \vdash \mathcal{P} \cup \{P\sigma_{\mathrm{dv}}\}$$

with the side-condition $\sigma_{\mathrm{dv}} : dv[D] \mapsto (\mathcal{N} - fv[\mathcal{P}] - fv[\mathcal{D}] - fv[\mathbf{def}\ D\ \mathbf{in}\ P])$.

Example 1. The simplest process is written $x\langle y\rangle$; it sends a name y on some other name x. In examples, we shall assume the existence of basic values, such as integers, strings, etc. For instance, assuming a printing service has been defined on name *print*, we would write $\mathit{print}\langle 3\rangle$. A program would be of the form

$$\mathbf{def}\ \mathit{print}\langle x\rangle \triangleright \ldots\ \mathbf{in}\ \mathit{print}\langle 3\rangle$$

To print several integers in order, we would need the printer to send back some message upon completion. For that purpose, the printer should be given a *return channel* κ together with every job.

$$\mathbf{def}\ \mathit{print}\langle x,\kappa\rangle \triangleright \ldots \kappa\langle\rangle \ldots\ \mathbf{in}\ \mathbf{def}\ \kappa\langle\rangle \triangleright \mathit{print}\langle 4,\kappa'\rangle\ \mathbf{in}\ \mathit{print}\langle 3,\kappa\rangle$$

In practice, sequential control is so common that it deserves some syntactic sugar to make continuations implicit, as in the language PICT [13]. We write:

$$\mathbf{def}\ \mathrm{print}(x) \triangleright \ldots\ \mathbf{reply\ to}\ \mathrm{print} \ldots\ \mathbf{in}\ \mathrm{print}(3); \mathrm{print}(4)$$

Synchronous names are written "x" and "print" instead of "x" and "*print*" to remind that they also carry an implicit continuation channel κ_{x}. In their definitions, we use fresh names κ_{x}, and we translate:

$$\mathrm{x}(\widetilde{v}) \stackrel{\mathrm{def}}{=} x\langle\widetilde{v}, \kappa_{\mathrm{x}}\rangle \text{ (in join-patterns J)}$$
$$\textbf{reply } \widetilde{V} \textbf{ to } \mathrm{x} \stackrel{\mathrm{def}}{=} \kappa_{\mathrm{x}}\langle\widetilde{V}\rangle \text{ (in guarded processes P)}$$

On the caller's side, we introduce let-bindings, sequences, and nested calls. We use a reserved name κ, and we translate top-down, left-to-right:

$$x\langle\widetilde{V}\rangle \stackrel{\mathrm{def}}{=} \textbf{let } \widetilde{v} = \widetilde{V} \textbf{ in } x\langle\widetilde{v}\rangle$$
$$\textbf{let } \widetilde{u} = \mathrm{x}(\widetilde{V}) \textbf{ in } P \stackrel{\mathrm{def}}{=} \textbf{def } \kappa\langle\widetilde{u}\rangle \triangleright P \textbf{ in } x\langle\widetilde{V}, \kappa\rangle$$
$$\textbf{let } u = v \textbf{ in } P \stackrel{\mathrm{def}}{=} P\{^{u}/_{v}\}$$
$$\textbf{let } \widetilde{u} = \widetilde{V} \textbf{ in } P \stackrel{\mathrm{def}}{=} \textbf{let } u_1 = V_1 \textbf{ in let } u_2 = \ldots \textbf{ in } P \quad \text{(otherwise)}$$
$$\mathrm{x}(\widetilde{V}); P \stackrel{\mathrm{def}}{=} \textbf{def } \kappa\langle\rangle \triangleright P \textbf{ in } x\langle\widetilde{V}, \kappa\rangle$$

3.3 Observation

We choose the observational equivalence framework as a formal basis for reasoning about processes [8, 6]. A first step is to define a reduction relation on processes, as a combination of heating, chemical reduction and cooling:

$$P \to P' \stackrel{\mathrm{def}}{=} \emptyset \vdash \{P\} \quad (\rightleftharpoons^{*} \longrightarrow \rightleftharpoons^{*}) \quad \emptyset \vdash \{P'\}$$

In the definition above, the notation $\emptyset \vdash \{P\}$ stands for a chemical solution that contains no definitions and only one running process P.

Then, our idea of observation is to characterize processes by their capabilities to emit on certain names. Testing one particular name is enough: let "*test*" be that name. We define the *testing predicate* $\Downarrow$ as follows:

$$P \Downarrow \stackrel{\mathrm{def}}{=} \exists P', \quad P \to^{*} (P' \mid \mathit{test}\langle\rangle)$$

Hence, the test succeeds when output on the name *test* is enabled, possibly after some internal reductions took place.

The *observational congruence* is the largest equivalence relation $\approx$ that meets the following requirements:

- $\approx$ is a refinement of $\Downarrow$;
- $\approx$ is a congruence;
- $\approx$ is a weak bisimulation. That is, for all processes P and Q such that $P \approx Q$ holds, we have the following implication:

$$P \to^{*} P' \text{ implies } \exists Q', Q \to^{*} Q' \text{ and } P' \approx Q'$$

This equivalence is as discriminating as the barbed bisimulation congruence, which would test emission on every name x. We refer to [6] for discussion, examples and proof methods.

The above definition of observational congruence is parametric in the reduction relation and in the context syntax. As we refine the calculus, we will apply the same definition to yield refined equivalences.

4 Computing with locations

We now refine the reflexive CHAM to model distributed systems. First, we partition processes and definitions into several *local solutions*. This flat model suffices for representing both local computation on different sites and global communication between them. Then, we introduce some more structure to account for creation and migration of local solutions: we attach *location names* to solutions, and we organize them as a tree of nested locations

4.1 Distributed solutions

A distributed reflexive chemical machine (DRCHAM) is a multiset of CHAMs; we write its global state as several solutions $\mathcal{R}_i \vdash \mathcal{P}_i$ separated by $\|$; our chemical rules do not mention the solutions that are left unchanged. Using this convention, the local solutions evolve internally by the same rules as before. They can also interact with one another by the new reduction:

$$\textbf{comm} \;\; \vdash x\langle\widetilde{v}\rangle \;\|\; J \triangleright P \vdash \;\longrightarrow\; \vdash \;\|\; J \triangleright P \vdash x\langle\widetilde{v}\rangle \qquad (x \in dv[J])$$

This rule states that a message emitted in a given solution on a port name x that is remotely defined can be forwarded to the solution of its definition. Later on, this message can be consumed there using the red rule. This two-step decomposition of global communication reflects what happens at run-time in actual implementations, where message transport and message treatment are distinct operations. We only consider *well-formed* DRCHAMs, where every name is defined in at most one solution. Hence, the transport is deterministic, static, and point-to-point, and synchronization is only done locally on the receiving site during message treatment. As a distributed model of computation, the DRCHAM hides the details of message routing, but not those of synchronization.

4.2 The location tree

In order to compute with locations, we view them both as syntactic definitions and local chemical solutions; we use *location names* to relate the two. The set of location names is denoted by $\mathcal{L}$; we use the letters $a, b, \ldots \in \mathcal{L}$ for location names, and $\varphi, \psi \ldots \in \mathcal{L}^*$ for finite strings of location names.

Running locations are local labeled solutions $\mathcal{R} \vdash_\varphi \mathcal{P}$. We define the sublocation relation as: $\vdash_\varphi$ is a sublocation of $\vdash_\psi$ when ψ is a prefix of φ. In the following, DRCHAMs are multisets of labeled solutions whose labels φ are distinct, prefix-closed, and uniquely identified by their rightmost location name, if any. These conditions ensures that solutions ordered by the sublocation relation form a tree.

Location names are first-class values that statically identify a location. Like port names, they can be created locally, sent and received in messages, and they obey the lexical scoping discipline. To introduce new locations, we extend the syntax of definitions with a new location constructor:

$$D \stackrel{\text{def}}{=} \ldots \mid a[D:P]$$

In the heating direction, the semantics of this new construct is to create a sublocation of the current location containing the unique definition D and the unique running process P. More precisely, we have a new structural rule:

$$\textbf{str-loc} \quad a[D:P] \vdash_{\varphi} \rightleftharpoons \vdash_{\varphi} \parallel \{D\} \vdash_{\varphi a} \{P\} \quad (a \text{ frozen})$$

The side condition means that there are no solutions of the form $\vdash_{\varphi a \psi}$ where ψ is a non-empty label. As the definition D could contain sublocation definitions, this side condition guarantees that D syntactically captures the whole subtree of a sublocations. Such a complete cooling has a "freezing effect" on locations and will be useful later for controlling migration.

All previous chemical rules apply unchanged, except for the explicit labeling of solutions. However, it is worth noticing that **str-def** also applies to defined location names, introducing fresh locations in running processes. In well-formed DRCHAMs, all reaction rules defining one name belong to a single location. To maintain this invariant when we dilute definitions, we constrain the syntax accordingly: in a multiple definition $D \wedge D'$, $dv[D] \cap dv[D']$ contains only port names that are not defined under a sublocation of D or D'.

Example 2. The simplest example of distribution is to send a value to a remote name. For instance, we may assume that the printer is running at location s (the server), while the print request is sent from another location c (the client):

$$\mathrm{print}(x) \triangleright \ldots \vdash_s \quad \parallel \quad \vdash_c \mathrm{print}(3); \ldots$$

The definition of print at location s is in the solution. In particular, it can be used from the client c.

Example 3. Remote procedure call is an abstraction of the previous example: it sends a value x to a remote service f and waits for a result.

$$\begin{aligned} & \mathrm{f}(y) \triangleright \textbf{reply } \mathrm{computation}(y) \textbf{ to } \mathrm{f} \vdash_s \\ \parallel \; & \vdash_c \textbf{def } \mathrm{rpc}(\mathrm{g}, x) \triangleright \textbf{reply } \mathrm{g}(x) \textbf{ to } \mathrm{rpc} \textbf{ in} \ldots \mathrm{rpc}(\mathrm{f}, 3) \ldots \end{aligned}$$

As above, f is visible from both solutions. By contrast, rpc is local to c, and can be considered as part of its communication library. We can also use a more elaborate definition of rpc that handles timeouts:

$$\begin{aligned} & \textbf{def } \mathrm{rpc}(\mathrm{f}, x, \mathit{error}) \triangleright \\ & \quad \textbf{def } \mathit{incall}\langle\rangle \mid \mathit{done}\langle r \rangle \triangleright \textbf{reply } r \textbf{ to } \mathrm{rpc} \\ & \quad \wedge \; \mathit{incall}\langle\rangle \mid \mathit{timeout}\langle\rangle \triangleright \mathit{error}\langle\rangle \\ & \quad \textbf{in } \mathit{incall}\langle\rangle \mid \mathit{done}\langle \mathrm{f}(x) \rangle \mid \mathit{start\_timer}\langle \mathit{timeout}, 3 \rangle \\ & \textbf{in} \ldots \mathrm{rpc}(\mathrm{f}, 3, \mathit{error\_handler}) \ldots \end{aligned}$$

The *incall* message guarantees mutual exclusion between the normal return from the remote call and the timeout error message.

4.3 Migration

We are now ready to extend the syntax of processes with a new primitive for migration, along with a new chemical reduction:

$$P \stackrel{\text{def}}{=} \ \ldots \mid go\langle b, \kappa\rangle$$

$$\textbf{move} \quad a\,[D : P|go\langle b, \kappa\rangle] \vdash_{\varphi} \parallel \vdash_{\psi b} \longrightarrow \vdash_{\varphi} \parallel a\,[D : P|\kappa\langle\rangle] \vdash_{\psi b}$$

Informally, the location a moves from its current position φa in the tree, to a new position ψba just under b. The destination solution $\vdash_{\psi b}$ is identified by its relative name b. Once a arrives, the continuation $\kappa\langle\rangle$ can trigger other computations. In case the rule **str-loc** has been used beforehand to cool down location a into a definition, its side-condition (a frozen) forces all the sublocations of a to migrate at the same time. As a consequence, migration to a sublocation is ruled out, and nested migrations in parallel are confluent.

In the paper, we use the same notation for port names and for primitives like $go\langle\cdot,\cdot\rangle$. We extend the synchronous call convention accordingly for go($\cdot$). Notice, however, that primitives are not first-class names: they cannot be sent as values in messages.

Example 4. Another example of distribution is to download code from a code server *à la Java* for the computation to take place on the local site.

$$\begin{array}{l} \text{load\_applet}(a) \triangleright \textbf{def}\ b[\text{applet}(y) \triangleright \textbf{reply} \ldots \textbf{to}\ \text{applet} \\ \qquad\qquad\qquad\qquad : \text{go}(a); \textbf{reply}\ \text{applet}\ \textbf{to}\ \text{load\_applet}]\ \textbf{in}\ \mathbf{0}\ \vdash_s \\ \parallel \vdash_c \textbf{let}\ \text{f} = \text{load\_applet}(c)\ \textbf{in} \ldots \text{f}(3) \ldots \end{array}$$

This reduces to the same server, and a local copy of the applet:

$$\begin{array}{l} \text{load\_applet}(a) \triangleright \textbf{def}\ b[\text{applet}(y) \triangleright \textbf{reply} \ldots \textbf{to}\ \text{applet} \\ \qquad\qquad\qquad\qquad : \text{go}(a); \textbf{reply}\ \text{applet}\ \textbf{to}\ \text{load\_applet}]\ \textbf{in}\ \mathbf{0}\ \vdash_s \\ \parallel b'[\text{applet}(y) \triangleright \textbf{reply} \ldots \textbf{to}\ \text{applet}] \vdash_c \ldots \text{applet}(3) \ldots \end{array}$$

Assuming that the applet does not include another go primitive, b' remains attached to c and the program behaves as if a fresh copy of the applet had been defined at location c.

4.4 Building our CASA

The opposite of retrieving code is sending computation to a remote server. The client defines the request; the request moves to the server, runs there, and sends the result back to the client:

$$\textbf{def}\ \text{f}(x, s) \triangleright a[\text{go}(s); \textbf{reply} \ldots \textbf{to}\ \text{f} : \mathbf{0}]\ \textbf{in} \ldots \text{f}(3, \text{server}) \ldots$$

In the code above, the remote computation returns a tuple of basic values. In general however, the result might contain arbitrary data allocated during the computation, or even active data (processes with internal state). In the generic CASA, the server cannot just return a pointer to the data; it must also move the data and the code back to the client location. To illustrate this, we consider an agent that allocates and uses a reference cell; new_cell creates a fresh cell and returns its two methods, set for updates and get for access.

```
def c[f(x, s) ▷
      def a[T : go(s);
            let set, get = new_cell(a)
             in set(computation(x)); go(c); reply get to f]
      in ... : 0]
  in ... f(3, server) ...
```

The data is allocated within the agent at location a, upon arrival on the server. It does not need to be pre-allocated, and grows on demand during the computation. Eventually, the agent is repatriated to the client by the go(c) primitive call.

5 Failure and recovery

Modeling failures is the litmus test for a distributed computation formalism. In the absence of failures, locations have only pragmatic significance, and no semantic importance. In fact, it was our incapacity to come up with a simple failure model for the π-calculus that spawned the join-calculus.

In this section we present our failure model, we introduce our two failure management primitives, we show their use in examples, and finally we discuss the choice of our failure model.

5.1 Representing failures

We use a marker $\Omega \notin \mathcal{L}$ to tag failed locations. For every $a \in \mathcal{L}$, εa denotes either a or Ωa, and φ, ψ denote strings of such εa. In the DRCHAM, Ω appears in the location string φ of failed locations $\vdash_\varphi$. We say φ is *dead* if it contains Ω, and *alive* otherwise; the position of the tag indicates where the failure was triggered. In the process syntax, failed locations are frozen as tagged definitions $\Omega a\, [D : P]$; thus the general shape of a location definition is $\varepsilon a\, [D : P]$.

In order to preserve scopes, structural rules are allowed in failed locations, hence the structural rules in Figure 3 are almost unchanged from sections 3–4, except for the obvious generalization of **str-loc** to the failed location syntax.

We model failure by prohibiting reactions inside a failed location or any of its sublocations. More precisely, in Figure 3 we add a side condition to **red**, **comm**, and **move**, that prevents these rules from taking messages (or $go\langle\cdot,\cdot\rangle$ primitives) in a solution with a dead label. Note however that we do not prevent messages or even locations from moving to a failed location, as such deadly moves are unavoidable in an asynchronous distributed setting.

Because failure can only occur in a named location, the top solution $\vdash$ provides a "safe haven" where pervasive definitions, such as the behavior of integers, may be put. Because of this we need to consider two equivalences for the calculus with failures: a "static equivalence" that is a congruence for all but the

$P \stackrel{\text{def}}{=} x\langle\widetilde{v}\rangle$	message		$D \stackrel{\text{def}}{=} J \triangleright P$	local rule
$\mathbf{def}\ D\ \mathbf{in}\ P$	definition		$\mathbf{T}$	inert definition
0	inert process		$D \wedge D$	co-definition
$P\vert P$	composition		$a\,[D : P]$	sub-location
$go\langle a, \kappa\rangle$	migration		$\Omega a\,[D : P]$	dead sub-location
$halt\langle\rangle$	termination		$J \stackrel{\text{def}}{=} x\langle\widetilde{v}\rangle$	message pattern
$fail\langle a, \kappa\rangle$	failure detection		$J\vert J$	join-pattern

Fig. 1. Syntax for the distributed-join-calculus

$$
\begin{array}{llll}
J: dv[x\langle\widetilde{v}\rangle] \stackrel{\text{def}}{=} \{x\} & & rv[x\langle\widetilde{v}\rangle] \stackrel{\text{def}}{=} \{u \in \widetilde{v}\} \\
\quad dv[J \mid J'] \stackrel{\text{def}}{=} dv[J] \cup dv[J'] & & rv[J \mid J'] \stackrel{\text{def}}{=} rv[J] \uplus rv[J'] \\
\\
D: dv[J \triangleright P] \stackrel{\text{def}}{=} dv[J] & & fv[J \triangleright P] \stackrel{\text{def}}{=} dv[J] \cup (fv[P] - rv[J]) \\
\quad dv[\mathbf{T}] \stackrel{\text{def}}{=} dv[\emptyset] & & fv[\mathbf{T}] \stackrel{\text{def}}{=} \emptyset \\
\quad dv[D \wedge D'] \stackrel{\text{def}}{=} dv[D] \cup dv[D'] & & fv[D \wedge D'] \stackrel{\text{def}}{=} fv[D] \cup fv[D'] \\
\quad dv[a\,[D : P]] \stackrel{\text{def}}{=} \{a\} \uplus dv[D] & & fv[a\,[D : P]] \stackrel{\text{def}}{=} \{a\} \cup fv[D] \cup fv[P] \\
\\
P: fv[x\langle\widetilde{v}\rangle] \stackrel{\text{def}}{=} \{x\} \cup \{u \in \widetilde{v}\} & & fv[go\langle a, \kappa\rangle] \stackrel{\text{def}}{=} \{a, \kappa\} \\
\quad fv[0] \stackrel{\text{def}}{=} \emptyset & & fv[halt\langle\rangle] \stackrel{\text{def}}{=} \emptyset \\
\quad fv[P \mid P'] \stackrel{\text{def}}{=} fv[P] \cup fv[P'] & & fv[fail\langle a, \kappa\rangle] \stackrel{\text{def}}{=} \{a, \kappa\} \\
\quad fv[\mathbf{def}\ D\ \mathbf{in}\ P] \stackrel{\text{def}}{=} (fv[P] \cup fv[D]) - dv[D] & &
\end{array}
$$

Well-formed conditions for D: In a scope, location variables can be defined only once; port variables can only appear in the join-patterns of one location (cf. 3.2, 4.2)

Fig. 2. Scopes for the distributed-join-calculus

str-join	$\vdash P_1 \vert P_2 \rightleftharpoons\ \vdash P_1, P_2$	
str-null	$\vdash 0 \rightleftharpoons\ \vdash$	
str-and	$D_1 \wedge D_2 \vdash\ \rightleftharpoons D_1, D_2 \vdash$	
str-nodef	$\mathbf{T} \vdash\ \rightleftharpoons\ \vdash$	
str-def	$\vdash \mathbf{def}\ D\ \mathbf{in}\ P \rightleftharpoons D\sigma_{\text{dv}} \vdash P\sigma_{\text{dv}}$	($range(\sigma_{\text{dv}})$ fresh)
str-loc	$\varepsilon a\,[D : P] \vdash_\varphi\ \rightleftharpoons\ \vdash_\varphi \parallel \{D\} \vdash_{\varphi\varepsilon a} \{P\}$	(a frozen)
red	$J \triangleright P \vdash_\varphi J\sigma_{\text{rv}} \longrightarrow J \triangleright P \vdash_\varphi P\sigma_{\text{rv}}$	(φ alive)
comm	$\vdash_\varphi x\langle\widetilde{v}\rangle \parallel J \triangleright P \vdash\ \longrightarrow\ \vdash_\varphi \parallel J \triangleright P \vdash x\langle\widetilde{v}\rangle$	($x \in dv[J]$, φ alive)
move	$a\,[D : P \vert go\langle b, \kappa\rangle] \vdash_\varphi \parallel \vdash_{\psi\varepsilon b} \longrightarrow\ \vdash_\varphi \parallel a\,[D : P \vert \kappa\langle\rangle] \vdash_{\psi\varepsilon b}$	(φ alive)
halt	$a\,[D : P \vert halt\langle\rangle] \vdash_\varphi \longrightarrow \Omega a\,[D : P] \vdash_\varphi$	(φ alive)
detect	$\vdash_\varphi fail\langle a, \kappa\rangle \parallel \vdash_{\psi\varepsilon a} \longrightarrow\ \vdash_\varphi \kappa\langle\rangle \parallel \vdash_{\psi\varepsilon a}$	($\psi\varepsilon a$ dead, φ alive)

Side conditions: in str-def, σ_{dv} instantiates the port variables $dv[D]$ to distinct, fresh names; in red, σ_{rv} substitutes the transmitted names for the received variables $rv[J]$; "a frozen" means that a has no sublocations in solution; φ is dead if it contains Ω, and alive otherwise.

Fig. 3. The distributed reflexive chemical machine

$\varepsilon a[\cdot : \cdot]$ constructor, and a "mobile equivalence" that is a congruence for the full calculus. The two notions coincide for processes that do not export agents.

5.2 Primitives for failure and recovery

We introduce two new primitives *halt*$\langle\rangle$ and *fail*$\langle\cdot,\cdot\rangle$. A *halt*$\langle\rangle$ at location a can make this location permanently inert (rule **halt** in Figure 3), while *fail*$\langle a, \kappa\rangle$ triggers $\kappa\langle\rangle$ after it detects that a has failed, i.e. that a or one of its parent locations has halted (rule **detect**). Note that the (φ alive) side condition in rules **move** and **comm** are sufficient to prevent all output from a dead location; it is attached to rules **red**, **halt**, and **detect** only for consistency.

In conjunction with the static equivalence, the *halt*$\langle\rangle$ primitive allows us to use the calculus to express the site failure patterns under which we prove an equivalence: a top-level location that does not move can only fail if it executes a *halt*$\langle\rangle$. In addition, *halt*$\langle\rangle$ can be used to encode a "kill" operation, as in

$$\begin{array}{l}\textbf{def } b[\mathit{kill}\langle\rangle \triangleright \mathit{halt}\langle\rangle : \mathit{start\_timer}\langle \mathit{kill}, 5\rangle] \\ \textbf{in let } \mathrm{f} = \mathrm{load\_applet}(b) \textbf{ in} \ldots \mathrm{f}(3) \ldots\end{array}$$

The *fail*$\langle\cdot,\cdot\rangle$ primitive provides a natural guard for error recovery. For example, we can make the CASA more secure as follows:

$$\mathrm{f}(x, s) \triangleright \textbf{def } a[\ldots] \textbf{ in } (\mathrm{fail}(a); \textbf{reply } \mathrm{f}(x, s') \textbf{ to } \mathrm{f})$$

If no error occurs, the agent returns permanently to the client, hence the fail is permanently disabled. Conversely, if the fail triggers then the server must have failed while hosting agent a. As this agent cannot return to the server, a new agent is created and sent to another server. Anyway, we are assured that there is at most one agent at large, and that its action is only completed once (which might be quite important, say if the action is "get a plane ticket"). This would still be true if the client did not know the server location, and the agent moved through several intermediate sites before reaching the server location.

This uniqueness property is difficult to obtain with timeouts only. The *fail*$\langle\cdot,\cdot\rangle$ primitive provides more information than timeouts do. However, timeouts are easier to implement and to model (they are just silent transitions in any bisimulation-based process calculus), so they are a natural complement of *fails*. Indeed, for RPC-like interactions that are asynchronous and without side effects, there is little practical use for the uniqueness property, so a simpler timeout is preferable to a *fail* check.

5.3 Failure models

What does "failure" mean? The most conservative answer, in our message-passing setting, is that when a location fails, *some* messages to, at, or from the location are lost. However it is very hard to do sensible error recovery in such a weak model: it is impossible to issue a replacement b for a failed agent a without running the risk of having a and b interfere through side effects.

Assuming that all messages from a failed agent are lost would solve this. Unfortunately this strong model is not consistent with the **comm** rule and our asynchronous, distributed setting. It would require that the system track and delete all messages issued by a failing location.

A more reasonable requirement would be that a failed location a cannot respond to messages; this can be enforced by blocking output to a from all locations detecting an a failure (or having received messages triggered by that failure-detection). This "weak asynchronous" model can easily be seen to be testing-equivalent to our "strong asynchronous" model (simply delay the failure until all the required output from a leave a); hence we are justified in using the stricter, simpler model in the calculus, but only implementing the weaker one. However, the models do give different interpretations to $a\,[\mathbf{T} : \mathit{halt}\langle\rangle \mid x\langle\rangle \mid x\langle\rangle]$ under bisimulation congruence.

6 Proofs for mobile protocols

The primary purpose of our calculus is to found a core language with enough expressivity for distributed and mobile programming. But locations with their primitives can also be used to model fallible distributed environments, as specific contexts within the calculus. As a result, we can use our observational equivalence to relate precisely the distributed implementations with their specification (i.e. simpler programs and contexts without failures or distribution). In combination with the usual proof methods developed for other process calculi, this should provide a setting for the design and the proof of distributed programs under realistic assumptions.

In this section, we explore this setting through a few simple examples and an internal encoding of locations. The equivalence relation $\approx$ is the observational congruence defined in section 3, applied to the distributed join-calculus of section 5. Due to lack of space, proofs are omitted.

6.1 A sample of equational laws

First, we state several "garbage collection" laws which are useful for simplifying terms in proofs: we have $P \approx 0$ when P resides in a failed location, when it is guarded by patterns of messages that cannot be assembled, or when it has neither free port names nor $\mathit{halt}\langle\rangle$, $\mathit{go}\langle\cdot,\cdot\rangle$ primitives.

Second, some basic laws hold for the $\mathit{go}\langle\cdot,\cdot\rangle$, $\mathit{fail}\langle\cdot,\cdot\rangle$, and $\mathit{halt}\langle\rangle$ primitives. For instance, we have $\mathrm{fail}(a); \mathrm{fail}(b); P \approx \mathrm{fail}(b); \mathrm{fail}(a); P$. Because these primitives are strictly static, the analysis of their local usage yields simplifications of the location tree. The following laws show how to get rid of location b once it has reached its final destination a : when D, P contain neither $\mathit{go}\langle\cdot,\cdot\rangle$ nor $\mathit{halt}\langle\rangle$, the b boundary is irrelevant:

$$\mathbf{def}\ a\,[b\,[D : P] \wedge D' : P']\ \mathbf{in}\ P'' \approx \mathbf{def}\ a\,[b\,[\mathbf{T} : 0] \wedge D \wedge D' : P \mid P']\ \mathbf{in}\ P''$$

When a location is empty, migrations and failure-detections using its name b or its parent's name a cannot be distinguished:

$$\text{def } a\,[b\,[\mathbf{T} : 0] \wedge D : P] \text{ in } P' \approx (\text{def } a\,[D : P] \text{ in } P')\{^a/_b\}$$

6.2 Internal encoding

We present a translation from the distributed join-calculus with all the features introduced in section 4 and section 5, into the simpler join-calculus of section 3. In combination with the encoding of the join-calculus into the π-calculus [6], this provides an alternative definition of migration and failure in the usual setting of process calculi. This also suggests that our distributed extension does not unduly add semantic complexity.

The basic idea is to replace every location construct by a definition that supports an equivalent protocol, and every use of locality information by a message call for this protocol. Once this is done, the structural translation $[\![P]\!]$ of the distributed process P simply makes explicit the side-conditions of the DRCHAM. For instance, we have $[\![x\langle 1\rangle]\!] = \text{ping}(); x\langle 1\rangle$, where ping() checks that the current location is alive before returning, thus mimicking the **comm** rule.

The interface to the encoding of location a consists of two port names. a stands for the location value; h_a provides internal access to the current location. They are sent to the encoding of location primitives (ping, fail, *halt*, go, subloc). The corresponding implementation $\mathcal{E}(\cdot)$ defines these primitives and the top-level location:

```
def subloc(h₀) ▷
    def live⟨p⟩ | poll() ▷ let r = p() in (live⟨p⟩ | reply r to poll)
      ∧ live⟨p⟩ | kill⟨⟩ ▷ dead⟨p⟩
      ∧ dead⟨p⟩ | poll() ▷ let r = p() in
                  dead⟨p⟩ | reply (if r = alive then failed else r) to poll
      ∧ live⟨p⟩ | get() ▷ lock⟨⟩ | reply p to get
      ∧ lock⟨⟩ | poll() ▷ lock⟨⟩ | reply retry to poll
      ∧ lock⟨⟩ | set⟨p⟩ ▷ live⟨p⟩ in
    def here() ▷ reply poll, kill, get, set to here in
    let poll₀, _, _, _ = h₀() in live⟨poll₀⟩ | reply poll, here to subloc in
def ping(h) ▷ let p, _, _, _ = h() in repeat p() until alive; reply  to ping in
def fail(p) ▷ repeat p() until failed; reply  to fail in
def halt⟨h⟩ ▷ let _, kill, _, _ = h() in kill⟨⟩ in
def go(h, p′) ▷ let p, _, get, set = h() in
    def attempt() ▷ if (if p′() = retry then failed else p()) = alive
          then set⟨p′⟩ | reply done to attempt
          else set⟨p⟩ | reply retry to attempt in
    repeat attempt(get()) until done in
def here() ▷
    def top() ▷ reply alive to top ∧ top() ▷ reply retry to top
      ∧ kill⟨⟩ | get() | set⟨p⟩ ▷ 0 in
    reply top, kill, get, set to here in
def start⟨hₛ, ã⟩ ▷ (·) in init⟨start, here, ping, fail, halt, go, subloc⟩
```

$$\begin{aligned}
[\![0]\!]_a &\stackrel{\text{def}}{=} 0 \\
[\![x\langle\widetilde{v}\rangle]\!]_a &\stackrel{\text{def}}{=} \text{ping}(\mathrm{h}_a); x\langle\widetilde{v}\rangle \\
[\![\mathit{fail}\langle a,\kappa\rangle]\!]_a &\stackrel{\text{def}}{=} \text{fail}(a); [\![\kappa\langle\rangle]\!] \\
[\![\mathit{halt}\langle\rangle]\!]_a &\stackrel{\text{def}}{=} \mathit{halt}(\mathrm{h}_a) \\
[\![\mathit{go}\langle b,\kappa\rangle]\!]_a &\stackrel{\text{def}}{=} \text{go}(\mathrm{h}_a, b); [\![\kappa\langle\rangle]\!] \\
[\![P \mid P']\!]_a &\stackrel{\text{def}}{=} [\![P]\!]_a \mid [\![P']\!]_a \\
[\![\text{def } D \text{ in } P]\!]_a &\stackrel{\text{def}}{=} [\![D]\!]_a^L\left(\text{def } [\![D]\!]_a^D \text{ in } ([\![D]\!]_a^P \mid [\![P]\!]_a)\right)
\end{aligned}$$

D	$[\![D]\!]_a^D$	$[\![D]\!]_a^P$	$[\![D]\!]_a^L$
$J \triangleright P$	$[\![J]\!]_a \triangleright [\![P]\!]_a$	0	$(\cdot)$
$b[D:P]$	$[\![D]\!]_b^D$	$[\![D]\!]_b^P \mid [\![P]\!]_b$	$\text{let } b, \mathrm{h}_b = \text{subloc}(\mathrm{h}_a) \text{ in } [\![D]\!]_b^L(\cdot)$
$D \wedge D'$	$[\![D]\!]_a^D \wedge [\![D']\!]_a^D$	$[\![D]\!]_a^P \mid [\![D']\!]_a^P$	$[\![D]\!]_a^L([\![D']\!]_a^L(\cdot))$
$\mathbf{T}$	$\mathbf{T}$	0	$(\cdot)$

In the translation above, we assume that location names in P are pairwise distinct. We omit the formal translation of the syntactic sugar we use for control (symbolic constants, **if then else, repeat until**).

When placed in an arbitrary context, the encoding $\mathcal{E}([\![P]\!]_s)$ exports the *init* message. The context can set up an arbitrary location tree using the location primitives, then starts the translation in some location by providing some valid interface $\mathrm{h}, \widetilde{a}$. To keep things simple, we use a refined sort discipline for the target calculus; the port names h_a and a are given special sorts; $\approx_{local}$ is the restricted congruence over contexts that do not define or sends messages to names of these sorts. In particular, this prevents contexts from accessing our internal representation or otherwise meddling with our protocol. We believe that this limitation can be enforced using "firewall" techniques as in [6].

Theorem 1 *The encoding $\mathcal{E}([\![\cdot]\!]_s)$ is fully-abstract up-to observational congruences $\approx$ in the distributed join-calculus and $\approx_{local}$ in the join-calculus:*

$$\forall P, P', \forall \widetilde{a} \supset (fv[P,P'] \cap \mathcal{L}), \quad P \approx P' \iff \mathcal{E}([\![P]\!]_s) \approx_{local} \mathcal{E}([\![P']\!]_s)$$

As a special case, contexts of the simple join-calculus have the same discriminating power than distributed ones, as long as there is no exchange of location names. This condition automatically holds for simple processes considered as distributed processes, meaning that simple and distributed observation coincide. This is in sharp contrast with the π-calculus with locality [1], where the distributed congruence is strictly finer than the local one, even for local processes.

7 Future work

In this paper, we laid the groundwork for a calculus of distributed processes with mobility and failure, and we investigated the use of process-calculus techniques for proving distributed protocols. In complement, more specific tools are needed (weaker equivalences, fairness). In order to validate our approach, we plan to apply the distributed join-calculus to asynchronous protocols in an unreliable setting, or with security requirements; to this end, we currently experiment with the design and implementation of a high-level programming language founded on our calculus.

Acknowledgments

This work benefited from numerous discussions with Roberto Amadio, Gérard Boudol, Damien Doligez, Florent Guillaume, Benjamin Pierce, Peter Sewell, and David Turner.

References

1. R. Amadio and S. Prasad. Localities and failures. In *14th Foundations of Software Technology and Theoretical Computer Science Conference.* Springer-Verlag, 1994. LNCS 880.
2. G. Berry and G. Boudol. The chemical abstract machine. *Theoretical Computer Science*, 96:217–248, 1992.
3. K. A. Bharat and L. Cardelli. Migratory applications. Technical Report 138, DEC-SRC, February 1996.
4. G. Boudol, I. Castellani, M. Hennessy, and A. Kiehn. A theory of processes with localities. *Formal Aspects of Computing*, 6:165–200, 1994.
5. L. Cardelli. A language with distributed scope. *Computing Systems*, 8(1):27–59, Jan. 1995.
6. C. Fournet and G. Gonthier. The reflexive chemical abstract machine and the join-calculus. In *23rd ACM Symposium on Principles of Programming Languages*, Jan. 1996.
7. A. Giacalone, P. Mishra, and S. Prasad. FACILE: A symmetric integration of concurrent and functional programming. *International Journal of Parallel Programming*, 18(2):121–160, 1989.
8. K. Honda and N. Yoshida. On reduction-based process semantics. *Theoretical Computer Science*, 151:437–486, 1995.
9. E. Jul. *Object Mobility in a Distributed Object-Oriented System.* PhD thesis, University of Washington, Computer Science Department, Dec. 1988.
10. L. Leth and B. Thomsen. Some facile chemistry. Technical Report ECRC-92-14, European Computer-Industry Research Centre, Munich, May 1992.
11. R. Milner. The polyadic π-calculus: a tutorial. In *Logic and Algebra of Specification.* Springer Verlag, 1993.
12. B. C. Pierce and D. Sangiorgi. Typing and subtyping for mobile processes. *Mathematical Structures in Computer Science*, 1995. To appear. A summary was presented at LICS '93.
13. B. C. Pierce and D. N. Turner. Concurrent objects in a process calculus. In *Theory and Practice of Parallel Programming, Sendai, Japan*, Apr. 1995. LNCS 907.
14. D. Sangiorgi. Localities and non-interleaving semantics in calculi for mobile processes. Technical Report ECS–LFCS–94–282, University of Edinburgh, 94. to appear in TCS.

Algebraic Interpretation of Lambda Calculus with Resources

Carolina Lavatelli

LIENS - École Normale Supérieure
45, rue d'Ulm - 75005 PARIS - France
email:lavatel@dmi.ens.fr

Abstract. Lambda calculus with resources λ_r is a non-deterministic refinement of lazy lambda calculus which allows to control argument availability and introduces the possibility of raising deadlocks during evaluation. We apply Lévy's program [18] to λ_r : we give an algebraic interpretation of this calculus in terms of approximants which is adequate w.r.t. the observational semantics of λ_r.

1 Introduction

Scott models of λ-calculus do not allow a direct interpretation of the reduction relation, which is studied through the properties of the local structure of these models. Hyland [15] and Wadsworth [24, 25] followed this approach and showed that denotations of terms are the limit of their approximants. Lévy [18] proceeded the other way round : he showed that the algebraic interpretation of λ-calculus upon the domain of approximants induces a precongruence and yields an adequate semantics. The particularity of this interpretation is that $\lambda x.\Omega$ and Ω are distinguished; that is the observables are the weak head normal forms [4].

The fundamental idea is that any term N in a sequence of reductions of a starting term M can be seen as a *partial or approximate normal form* (or simply *approximant*) of M. The set of approximate normal forms of a term M is obtained by reducing it to some term say L and replacing some of L's subterms (among which redexes) by an added undefined normal form $\perp$. The computational behavior of a term is completely determined by the set of its approximants. In classical λ-calculus : For any term M and context C closing M, $C[M]$ reduces to a value iff there is an approximant A of M such that $C[A]$ reduces to a value. The knowledge of a *unique approximant* of a term is necessary and sufficient to mimic the computational content of a term in a given context. The uniqueness property follows from the *confluence* of λ-calculus, which implies that the set of approximants of a term (completed in a straightforward way) constitutes a *directed* set. So that, any time two different approximants A_1, A_2, are needed to reproduce the behavior of two different occurrences of M in the convergent evaluation of $C[M]$, one can take the least upper bound of A_1 and A_2.

Recently, the study of the connection between elaborated process calculi - such as π calculus - and λ-calculi gave rise to a resource-conscious lambda calculus λ_r, defined by Boudol [6], which is non-deterministic (it is in fact *non-confluent*) and, moreover, introduces the possibility of *deadlock* during evaluation. The main theme of this paper is the study of the notion of approximant in the frame of λ_r, that is, in the absence of confluence[1].

The novel feature of λ_r is to consider arguments as resources for the process of substitution and to provide syntactic means to express the effective use of these resources. Arguments of λ_r are bags of terms $(M_1 \mid \ldots \mid M_n)$, of finite or infinite cardinality. Each M_i is a resource that can be used at most once in the substitution process. In order to do not lose any resource, substitution is explicit in the calculus : (β)-conversion is $(\lambda x.M)P \rightarrow M\langle P/x \rangle$, and, moreover, substitution is accomplished in a delayed manner that makes resources to be consumed only when required for continuing evaluation. For instance,

$$xP_1 \ldots P_k\langle (M_1 \mid \ldots N \ldots \mid M_n)/x \rangle \rightarrow NP_1 \ldots P_k\langle (M_1 \mid \ldots \mid M_n)/x \rangle$$

if no free variable of N is captured. Remark that N disappeared from the remaining resources available for other occurrences of x. The calculus λ_r is non-deterministic since the fetch of resources does not follow any strategy. The fact that bags may be finite is the key feature to allow deadlocks : once all resources of an environment (explicit substitution) are consumed, represented by $\langle \mathbf{1}/x \rangle$, if x occurs at the head position then the evaluation cannot proceed. Normal forms or irreducible terms in λ_r are of two types : abstractions (since we consider a lazy evaluation) and deadlocked terms like $xP_1 \ldots P_n\langle \mathbf{1}/x \rangle$. The standard notion of observation λ_r does not distinguish between deadlock and divergence; the only values are abstractions. Following Morris's schema, the observational semantics (preorder) is defined by : $M \sqsubseteq_r N \iff \forall\ \lambda_r$-context C if $C[M]$ reduces to an abstraction then $C[N]$ reduces to an abstraction too. We build an algebraic interpretation of λ_r in terms of the set of approximants of a term completed straightforwardly, $\downarrow\mathcal{A}(M)$. Our main result says : the knowledge of a *finite* number of approximants of a λ_r-term is necessary and sufficient to mimic the behavior of the term in a given context. Assuming $\oplus$ denote non-deterministic choice in λ_r,

$$\forall M \in \Lambda_r\ C[M]\Downarrow_r \iff \exists A_1, \ldots, A_n \in \downarrow\mathcal{A}(M)\ C[A_1 \oplus \ldots \oplus A_n]\Downarrow_r$$

[1] One of the motivations for introducing non-determinism in lazy lambda calculus comes from domain theory. In fact, models issued from domain equations (or fixed point models for PCF) provide extra means to discriminate expressions than λ-contexts themselves : models are adequate but not fully abstract. Traditionally, from Plotkin [23] to Abramsky/Ong [22, 3] and Boudol [5, 7], lambda calculus is completed with parallel (non-deterministic) facilities in order to be as discriminant as the canonical models. The parallel convergence testing combinator $\mathbf{p}$ in [22, 3] applied to three arguments, $\mathbf{p}MNL$, gives L (which can be further reduced) whenever M or N are convergent. Lambda calculus with parallel composition [7] does not verify the uniqueness of values but it is confluent : it is enough to continue the reduction of any one of the branches. As for lambda calculus with internal choice $\oplus$ [5], even if it is non-confluent, its discriminatory power can be simulated in the calculus with parallel composition (and conversely) [16, 17]. In [13], both parallelism and internal choice are added to the lazy lambda calculus, in a must-testing perspective.

As a corollary, the semantics $\leq$ induced by the algebraic interpretation verifies :

$$\text{(Adequacy)} \quad M \leq N \Rightarrow M \sqsubseteq_r N$$

We should mention the work of Dezani, de Liguoro and Piperno [14]. They define an algebraic semantics for the classical lambda calculus extended with parallel composition and internal choice with a must-convergence criterion and show that it is fully abstract with respect to some filter semantics based upon a type system with intersections and unions. This result is based on an approximation theorem, proved using a variant of Tait's computability technique, which states that a term has a type iff there is an approximant of it with the same type.

The plan of the paper is as follows. In section 2 we present λ_r and its observational semantics and we characterize the induced theory as fully lazy maximal (using the terminology of [3]). Section 3 contains the definition of a new lambda calculus with bags, λ_d, that is λ_r without explicit substitutions. The principal result is that the observational theories of λ_r and λ_d are the same. Our interest for λ_d comes from the fact that it is a good frame to build the approximants in λ_r (i.e. approximants of $M \in \lambda_r$ will be terms of λ_d), since it allows the definition of a strong reduction, necessary to eliminate redexes of the form $xP_1 \ldots P_n\langle Q/x\rangle$. In section 4 we define the notion of approximant for λ_r and show the approximation lemma. As a corollary, we get the adequacy of the algebraic semantics, which fails to be complete.

Some proofs are omitted by lack of space. We refer the interested reader to [17].

2 Lambda Calculus with resources

2.1 Syntax and Evaluation of λ_r

Given a denumerable set Var of variables ranged over by $u, v, w, x, y, z \ldots$ the following grammar defines the syntax of λ_r-terms :

$$(\Lambda_r)\ M ::= x \mid \lambda x.M \mid (MP) \mid M\langle P/x\rangle$$

$$P ::= \mathbf{1} \mid M \mid (P \mid P) \mid M^{\infty}$$

Capital letters $L, M, N, \ldots$ stand for terms of the language, and $P, Q, \ldots$ stand for arguments, called *bags*. We denote by T terms or bags indistinctly. Moreover, $R, S, \ldots$ represent bags or explicit substitution entries $\langle P/x\rangle$. We use $\tilde{R}$ as an abbreviation of $R_1 \ldots R_n$ whenever there is no ambiguity. For sequences composed exclusively of substitution entries we use $\langle\tilde{P}/\tilde{x}\rangle$, or $\rho, \rho' \ldots$ instead of $\langle P_1/x_1\rangle \ldots \langle P_n/x_n\rangle$.

The usual characterization of free and bound variables in lambda calculus is extended as follows : free (bound) variables of arguments P and of substitution entries $\langle P/x\rangle$ are free (bound) variables of P, and free occurrences of x in M are bound in $M\langle P/x\rangle$. Clearly, $fv(\mathbf{1}) = bv(\mathbf{1}) = var(\mathbf{1}) = \emptyset$ and also $fv(P \mid Q) =$

$fv(P) \cup fv(Q)$ and $bv(P \mid Q) = bv(P) \cup bv(Q)$. We note Λ_r^o the set of closed λ_r-terms.

Alpha-conversion $M =_\alpha N$ is the congruence induced by the following clauses :

$$\lambda x.M = \lambda z.M[z/x] \quad \text{with } z \notin var(M)$$
$$M\langle P/x\rangle = (M[z/x])\langle P/z\rangle \quad \text{with } z \notin var(M)$$

where the renaming operation $M[z/x]$ with $z \notin var(M)$ extends the usual one for λ-terms, distributes over parallel composition and applied to a term which comes with a substitution entry gives

$$(M\langle P/y\rangle)[z/x] = \begin{cases} M\langle P[z/x]/y\rangle & \text{if } y = x \\ (M[z/x])\langle P[z/x]/y\rangle & \text{otherwise} \end{cases}$$

The multiset character of bags and the meaning of infinite resources are expressible by means of the following structural equivalence $\equiv$, which is in fact a congruence relation on $\Lambda_r \times \Lambda_r$:

$$(1 \mid P) \equiv P \quad M^\infty \equiv (M \mid M^\infty) \quad (P \mid (Q \mid T)) \equiv ((P \mid Q) \mid T)$$
$$(P \mid Q) \equiv (Q \mid P) \quad P \equiv Q \Rightarrow \begin{cases} MP \equiv MQ \\ M\langle P/x\rangle \equiv M\langle Q/x\rangle \end{cases}$$

The evaluation relation $\rightarrow_r$ of lambda calculus with resources defined in figure 1, corresponds to the weak strategy adopted by Abramsky and Ong for pure lambda calculus : neither the bodies of abstractions, nor the arguments of applications, nor the substitutions entries are evaluated. The rules are split into two parts : the first part formalizes weak (β)-reduction in a calculus with explicit substitutions; the second one establishes a mechanism of *fetch* of resources to perform substitutions in a delayed manner, through an auxiliary relation $\succ$. As is standard, $\xrightarrow{*}_r$ stands for zero or more evaluation steps and $\xrightarrow{+}_r$ stands for one or more evaluation steps. Internal choice can be encoded in λ_r (see [6]) : $(M \oplus N) \stackrel{def}{=} x\langle (M \mid N)/x\rangle$. By commutativity of parallel composition and definition of fetch, one can derive $(M \oplus N) \rightarrow_r M\langle N/x\rangle$ and $(M \oplus N) \rightarrow_r N\langle M/x\rangle$, provided $x \notin var(M, N)$. The results $M\langle N/x\rangle$ and $N\langle M/x\rangle$ are essentially M and N, respectively.

The deterministic version of λ_r, called lambda calculus with multiplicities, is obtained just by accepting only finite or infinite homogeneous bags of the form $(M \mid \ldots \mid M)$. This calculus proved to be very useful in the study of the relationship between π-calculus and λ-calculus (see [21, 8, 9, 10]).

2.2 Observational Semantics of λ_r

We said in the introduction that irreducible terms are of two types : deadlocked terms - with no available resource for the head variable - and abstractions. The

$$(\beta)\ (\lambda x.M)P \rightarrow_r M\langle P/x\rangle \qquad (v)\ (\lambda x.M)\langle P/z\rangle \rightarrow_r \lambda x.(M\langle P/z\rangle)\ (x \notin fv(z,P))$$

$$\frac{N \rightarrow_r N' \ (M =_\alpha N \text{ or } M \equiv N)}{M \rightarrow_r N'} \quad \frac{M \rightarrow_r M'}{MP \rightarrow_r M'P} \quad \frac{M \rightarrow_r M'}{M\langle P/x\rangle \rightarrow_r M'\langle P/x\rangle}$$

$$(\text{fetch})\ \frac{M\langle N/x\rangle \succ M' \quad x \notin fv(N)}{M\langle (N \mid Q)/x\rangle \rightarrow_r M'\langle Q/x\rangle}$$

$$x\langle N/x\rangle \succ N \qquad \frac{M\langle N/x\rangle \succ M'}{MP\langle N/x\rangle \succ M'P} \qquad \frac{M\langle N/x\rangle \succ M' \ (x \neq z \ \&\ z \notin fv(N))}{M\langle P/z\rangle\langle N/x\rangle \succ M'\langle P/z\rangle}$$

Fig. 1. Evaluation in λ_r

values of the calculus are a subset of the irreducible terms. The standard approach of the observational semantics is based on a notion of observation that identifies deadlocked and divergent terms. The only observable terms are abstractions :

$$\mathbb{V}_r = \{\lambda x.M \mid M \in \Lambda_r\}$$

The convergence predicate $\Downarrow_r$ over the closed terms is defined by :

$$M \Downarrow_r V \stackrel{def}{\Longleftrightarrow} V \in \mathbb{V}_r \ \&\ M \stackrel{\star}{\rightarrow}_r V$$

In an abuse of notation, $M\Downarrow_r$ stands for $\exists V, M\Downarrow_r V$, and $M \Downarrow_r^n V$ or simply $M \Downarrow_r^n$ means that the convergent evaluation of M (to V) has length n up to uses of the rule (v). If M does not converge, we say that it diverges, $M \Uparrow_r$ in notation. Contexts are built-up using the constructors of the language plus a constant $[]$. We let $C[M]$ denote the term of Λ_r obtained by replacing in C all occurrences of $[]$ by M. Multiple-hole contexts are made up with constants $[]_i$. We assume that for any such context C there exists n st. $[]_1, \ldots, []_n$ are exactly the constants in C. We write $C[M_1, \ldots, M_n]$ for the term obtained by replacing $[]_i$ by M_i in C. We say that C closes M if the free variables of M are bound in $C[M]$. The testing preorder or observational semantics is defined by :

$$M \sqsubseteq_r N \stackrel{def}{\Longleftrightarrow} \forall C \text{ closing } M, N \ C[M]\Downarrow_r \Rightarrow C[N]\Downarrow_r$$

We write $M \simeq_r N$ whenever $M \sqsubseteq_r N$ and $N \sqsubseteq_r M$. An alternative presentation of $\sqsubseteq_r$ in terms of *applicative contexts* is possible. The syntax is :

$$A ::= [] \mid AP \mid A\langle P/x\rangle$$

We write $M \sqsubseteq_{\mathcal{A}} N$ whenever the implication $A[M]\Downarrow_r \Rightarrow A[N]\Downarrow_r$ holds for any applicative context A closing M and N. The associated equivalence is $\simeq_{\mathcal{A}}$.

Lemma 1. (Context Lemma)[6] $\forall M, N \in \Lambda_r \ \ M \sqsubseteq_r N \iff M \sqsubseteq_{\mathcal{A}} N$

The following inequalities illustrate the nature of the observational semantics :

$$\Omega \sqsubseteq_{\mathcal{A}} M$$
$$MP \sqsubseteq_{\mathcal{A}} M(P \mid Q) \qquad M\langle P/x\rangle \sqsubseteq_{\mathcal{A}} M\langle (P \mid Q)/x\rangle$$
$$M\langle R/x\rangle \simeq_{\mathcal{A}} M \qquad x \notin fv(M)$$
$$(MP)\langle R/x\rangle \simeq_{\mathcal{A}} (M\langle R/x\rangle)P \qquad x \notin fv(P)$$
$$(M\langle P/z\rangle)\langle R/x\rangle \simeq_{\mathcal{A}} (M\langle R/x\rangle)\langle P/z\rangle \quad z \neq x, x \notin fv(P), z \notin fv(R)$$
$$MP \simeq_{\mathcal{A}} My^{\infty}\langle P/y\rangle \quad \text{for } y \notin fv(M) \cup fv(P)$$

2.3 Theory $\simeq_r$

The non-confluence of the evaluation $\rightarrow_r$ inhibits a classification of terms like in pure lambda calculus, where terms are either solvables or unsolvables. Nevertheless, it is possible to define the *functionality order* (or simply *order*) and the *unsolvability order* (or *proper order*) of a term, from which we can deduce some results as the *fully-laziness* of the theory induced by the standard observational preorder. See [22] for the characterization of pure lazy lambda theory and [8] for that of the lambda calculus with multiplicities. We refer the reader to [4] for basic notions of (sensible) λ-theories.

i	Functionality Order i : $M \in \mathrm{O}^r_i$	Unsolvability Order i : $M \in \mathrm{PO}^r_i$
0	$\neg(\exists N \,.\, M \xrightarrow{\star}_r \lambda x.N)$	$M \in \mathrm{O}^r_0 \ \& \ \neg(\exists \boldsymbol{R} \,.\, M \xrightarrow{\star}_r x\boldsymbol{R})$
$n+1$	$\exists F \in \mathrm{O}^r_n \,.\, M \xrightarrow{\star}_r \lambda x.F$	$\exists F \in \mathrm{PO}^r_n \,.\, M \xrightarrow{\star}_r \lambda x.F$
∞	$\forall n \in \mathbb{N} \,.\, M \notin \mathrm{O}^r_n$	$M \in \mathrm{O}^r_\infty$

Strict Unsolvability Order n : $M \in \mathrm{sPO}^r_n$
$\forall k.\ (M \in \mathrm{PO}^r_k \Rightarrow n \geq k)$ & $(M \in \mathrm{O}^r_k \ \& \ M \notin \mathrm{PO}^r_k \Rightarrow k = \infty)$

It is easy to see that $M \in \mathrm{PO}^r_0 \iff M \in \mathrm{sPO}^r_0$ holds for all $M \in \Lambda_r$. Other properties are : Let $M \in \mathrm{PO}^r_0$; then $(M \xrightarrow{\star}_r N \Rightarrow N \in \mathrm{PO}^r_0)$, $(M =_\alpha N \Rightarrow N \in \mathrm{PO}^r_0)$ and $(M\langle P/x\rangle \in \mathrm{PO}^r_0 \ \& \ MP \in \mathrm{PO}^r_0)$. Strictly unsolvable terms are characterized as follows : For any $M \in \Lambda^o_r$, we have $M \in \mathrm{sPO}^r_0$ iff $M\Uparrow_r$.

Theorem 2. (Maximal fully lazy theory) *Let $\mathcal{T}_r$ be the λ_r-theory induced by $\sqsubseteq_r$ and Th be the closure operation with respect to provability in λ_r. The theory $\mathcal{T}_r$ identifies only strictly unsolvable terms of same order :*

(fully lazy) $\forall M \in sPO^r_m \ \forall N \in sPO^r_n \ \ M \sqsubseteq_r N \iff m \leq n$
(maximal) $\forall M, N \in \Lambda_r \ \neg(M \sqsubseteq_r N) \Rightarrow$
$Th(\mathcal{T}_r \cup M \simeq_r N)$ *is not fully lazy or it is inconsistent*

The observation that unsolvable subterms of a given term are not useful more than once in the convergent evaluations of the term motivated us to build a simplification procedure which determines an important class of λ_r-terms in the relation $\sqsubseteq_r$. To be more precise, whatever the convergent evaluation of a term is, at most one unsolvable subterm can be used. As a consequence, all except one unsolvable subterm can be erased or simplified from a term, without affecting its potential convergence ability.

Definition 3. The strict order $M \lesssim N$ is defined by :

$$(\lambda x_1 \ldots x_n.\Omega \mid Q) \lesssim (\lambda x_1 \ldots x_n.\Omega \mid \lambda x_1 \ldots x_m.\Omega \mid Q) \text{ if } n \geq m$$

$$P \lesssim P' \Rightarrow \begin{cases} (MP) \lesssim (MP') \\ M\langle P/x\rangle \lesssim M\langle P'/x\rangle \end{cases}$$

$$M \lesssim N \Rightarrow \begin{cases} (MP) \lesssim (NP) \\ M\langle P/x\rangle \lesssim N\langle P/x\rangle \\ \lambda x.M \lesssim \lambda x.N \end{cases}$$

Lemma 4. [2]
If $M, N \in \Lambda_r$, then $M \lesssim N \Rightarrow M \simeq_r N$

Proof. Let $M \lesssim N$; the first step is to show :

$$(i)\ N \in \mathrm{PO}^r_k \ \Rightarrow \exists h\ M \in \mathrm{PO}^r_h\ \&\ h \geq k$$

$$(ii)\ (N \in \mathrm{O}^r_k\ \&\ N \notin \mathrm{PO}^r_k) \ \Rightarrow\ (M \in \mathrm{O}^r_k\ \&\ M \in \mathrm{PO}^r_k)$$

Moreover, for any applicative context A, $M \lesssim N$ implies $A[M] \lesssim A[N]$. Then, if $A[N]\Downarrow_r$, we have $A[N] \in \mathrm{O}^r_k$ with $k > 0$. By (i) and (ii), we conclude $A[M] \in \mathrm{O}^r_h$, where $h \geq k$. That is, $A[M]\Downarrow_r$.

3 Eliminating Explicit Substitutions

The presence of explicit substitutions in the lambda calculus with resources allows the definition of a delayed substitution mechanism for (β)-conversion that leads to a normalizing evaluation strategy $\rightarrow_r$. That is, from the point of view of convergence, any other way of performing substitution would be less satisfactory. In order to formalize this, we define a lambda calculus with bags λ_d, without explicit substitutions, for which the substitution process is a meta-operation (as in standard lambda calculi) that does not privilege any particular strategy of resource distribution (i.e. (β)-conversion is non-deterministic). The

[2] The property does not hold if we add a convergence testing operator to the language (cf. [11, 17]). In this extended calculus, the number of unsolvable resources that compose a bag is not always irrelevant.

main motivation[3] for introducing such a calculus is that it is a good frame to define an approximant based interpretation of λ_r, as we will see later. We show in particular how to simulate within λ_d the convergence of λ_r and conversely[4].

3.1 Syntax and Evaluation of λ_d

The set of terms of λ_d is the subset of Λ_r without explicit substitutions. Abstractions are the values for the standard observational semantics.

$$\begin{array}{ll} \Lambda_d & M ::= x \mid \lambda x.M \mid (MP) \\ & P ::= \mathbf{1} \mid M \mid (P \mid P) \mid M^\infty \\ \mathbb{V}_d & V ::= \lambda x.M \end{array}$$

Definition 5. (Substitution in λ_d) Let $M, P \in \Lambda_d$. The substitution of P for free occurrences of x in M, written $M\lceil P/x\rceil$, is the subset of Λ_d defined by :

$$\begin{array}{rl} x\lceil P/x\rceil &= \{M \,/\, P \equiv (M \mid Q)\} \cup \{\Omega\} \\ y\lceil P/x\rceil &= \{y\} \\ (\lambda y.M)\lceil P/x\rceil &= \begin{cases} \{\lambda z.M' \,/\, \forall z \;\; z \notin fv(\lambda y.M, P, x) \;\& \\ \qquad M' \in M[z/x]\lceil P/x\rceil\} & \text{if } y \neq x \\ \{\lambda y.M\} & \text{otherwise} \end{cases} \\ (MQ)\lceil P/x\rceil &= \{(M'Q') \,/\, P \equiv (P_1 \mid P_2) \;\& \\ & \qquad M' \in M\lceil P_1/x\rceil \;\&\; Q' \in Q\lceil P_2/x\rceil\} \\ \\ \mathbf{1}\lceil P/x\rceil &= \{\mathbf{1}\} \\ (M \mid Q)\lceil P/x\rceil &= \{(M' \mid Q') \,/\, P \equiv (P_1 \mid P_2) \;\& \\ & \qquad M' \in M\lceil P_1/x\rceil \;\&\; Q' \in Q\lceil P_2/x\rceil\} \\ M^\infty\lceil P/x\rceil &= \{(M_1 \mid \ldots \mid M_k \mid N^\infty) \,/\, P \equiv (P_1 \mid \ldots \mid P_k) \;\& \\ & \qquad M_i \in M\lceil P_i/x\rceil \;\&\; N \in M\lceil \mathbf{1}/x\rceil\} \end{array}$$

Roughly, the substitution process $M\lceil P/x\rceil$ distributes resources in P over M's subterms. Observe that if $z \notin var(M\lceil P/y\rceil)$, then

$$\forall N \in M\lceil P/y\rceil \;\; N[z/x] \in \begin{cases} (M[z/x])\lceil P[z/x]/y\rceil & \text{if } x \neq y, \\ M\lceil P[z/x]/y\rceil & \text{otherwise} \end{cases}$$

---

[3] The calculus λ_d is also interesting because its substitution procedure corresponds exactly to the way environments are dealt with in the denotational interpretations of λ_r given in [17].

[4] A result of this kind was shown by Abadi et al. [1, 12] for weak lambda calculus $\lambda\sigma$ and pure weak lambda calculus, that play the rôles of λ_r and λ_d respectively. They show that the evaluation of a term a in $\lambda\sigma$ ends in a whnf b iff the evaluation of $\sigma(a)$ in the pure calculus ends in a whnf a' verifying $a' = \sigma(b)$, where the function $\sigma(c)$ denotes the term obtained by computing the explicit substitutions of c. Even if the statements are very similar, there is not hope to apply directly the proofs of [1, 12] to our case, since the result for the pure calculus is based on the strong normalization of the calculus of explicit substitutions. In our case, the substitution process must give account of *every* possible distribution of resources. In other words, the calculus λ_d is non-confluent while weak lambda calculus is.

The evaluation relation of terms and the convergence predicate in λ_d are defined in figure 2. Notice that the rules of $\rightarrow_d$ are those of weak λ-calculus, with a non-deterministic β-conversion. It is easy to show that for all $M \in \Lambda_d$, $M \Downarrow_d V$ iff $M \stackrel{\star}{\rightarrow}_d V$. As before, $M \Downarrow_d$ stands for $\exists V\ M \Downarrow_d V$.

$$(\beta)\ \frac{N \in M\lceil P/x \rceil}{(\lambda x.M)P \rightarrow_d N} \qquad \frac{M \rightarrow_d M'}{MP \rightarrow_d M'P}$$

$$\lambda x.M \Downarrow_d \lambda x.M \qquad \frac{M \Downarrow_d \lambda x.M' \quad N \in M\lceil P/x \rceil \quad N \Downarrow_d V}{MP \Downarrow_d V}$$

Fig. 2. Evaluation and Convergence in λ_d

Definition 6. **(Reduction Rules $\rhd_d$)** The relation $\rhd_d \subset \Lambda_d \times \Lambda_d$ is defined by :

$$\frac{N \in M\lceil P/x \rceil}{(\lambda x.M)P \rhd_d N} \qquad \frac{M \rhd_d M'}{MP \rhd_d M'P} \qquad \frac{M \rhd_d M'}{\lambda x.M \rhd_d \lambda x.M'}$$

$$\frac{P \rhd_d P'}{MP \rhd_d MP'} \qquad \frac{M \rhd_d M' \quad P \equiv (M \mid P')}{P \rhd_d (M' \mid P')}$$

Lemma 7. (Normalizing Strategy)

1. $\forall M, N, V \in \Lambda_d,\ M \rhd_d N \rightarrow_d V \Rightarrow \exists W \in \Lambda_d\ M \rightarrow_d W \rhd_d V$
2. $\forall M \in \Lambda_d\ M \stackrel{\star}{\rhd}_d N \stackrel{\star}{\rightarrow}_d V\ \&\ V \in \mathbb{V}_d \Rightarrow \exists W \in \mathbb{V}_d\ M \stackrel{\star}{\rightarrow}_d W \stackrel{\star}{\rhd}_d V$

3.2 Relating λ_r and λ_d

Given a term $M \in \Lambda_r$, we can compute a subset of Λ_d by distributing the explicit substitutions of M, following the meta-process of substitution $\lceil P/x \rceil$:

Definition 8. The transformation $\{\![\,]\!\} : \Lambda_r \rightarrow \mathcal{P}(\Lambda_d)$ is given by :

$$\begin{aligned}
\{\![x]\!\} &= \{x\} \\
\{\![\lambda x.M]\!\} &= \{\lambda x.N \,/\, N \in \{\![M]\!\}\} \\
\{\![MP]\!\} &= \{NQ \,/\, N \in \{\![M]\!\}\ \&\ Q \in \{\![P]\!\}\} \\
\{\![M\langle P/x\rangle]\!\} &= \bigcup N\lceil Q/x \rceil \ \text{ where } N \in \{\![M]\!\}\ \&\ Q \in \{\![P]\!\}
\end{aligned}$$

$$\begin{aligned}
\{\![\mathbf{1}]\!\} &= \{\mathbf{1}\} \\
\{\![(P \mid Q)]\!\} &= \{(P' \mid Q') \,/\, P' \in \{\![P]\!\}\ \&\ Q' \in \{\![Q]\!\}\} \\
\{\![M^\infty]\!\} &= \{(N_1^\infty \mid \ldots \mid N_k^\infty) \,/\, N_i \in \{\![M]\!\}\ \&\ k \in \mathbb{N}\}
\end{aligned}$$

Theorem 9. ***(Convergence Simulation)***

1. Let $M \in \Lambda_d$*. Then* $M\Downarrow_r \iff M\Downarrow_d$.
2. Let $M \in \Lambda_r$*. Then* $M\Downarrow_r \Rightarrow \exists N \in \{\!\![M]\!\!\}\ N\Downarrow_d$.

Proof. The proof is based on the following two properties :

$(\star)\ \forall M, M' \in \Lambda_r\ \ M \xrightarrow{\star}_r M' \Rightarrow \forall N' \in \{\!\![M']\!\!\}\ \exists N \in \{\!\![M]\!\!\}\ N \xrightarrow{\star}_d N'$

$(\star\star)\ \forall M, M', N \in \Lambda_d\ \forall T \in \Lambda_r\ \ M =_\alpha M' \in \{\!\![T]\!\!\}\ \&\ M \xrightarrow{\star}_d N \Rightarrow$
$\exists N', N''\ T \xrightarrow{\star}_r N'\ \&\ N =_\alpha N'' \in \{\!\![N']\!\!\}$

and in the fact that $\{\!\![V]\!\!\}$ for $V \in \mathbb{V}_r$ is made up of values in $\mathbb{V}_d$.

Theorem 10. *1.* $M \overset{\star}{\triangleright}_d N \Rightarrow N \sqsubseteq_r M$
2. $\forall M\ \forall$ *applicatif* $A\ \ (A[M] \Downarrow_r^m \Rightarrow \exists L \in \{\!\![M]\!\!\}\ \exists l \leq m\ A[L] \Downarrow_r^l)$
3. $\forall M \in \Lambda_r\ \forall L\ \ (L \in \{\!\![M]\!\!\} \Rightarrow L \sqsubseteq_r M)$

Proof. 1. Let $M \overset{\star}{\triangleright}_d N$ and A st. $A[N]\Downarrow_d V$. Then $A[M] \xrightarrow{\star}_d V$. By lemma 7, there exists $W \in \mathbb{V}_d$ st. $A[M]\Downarrow_d W$. We showed $N \sqsubseteq_d M$. It is not difficult to prove that this implies $N \sqsubseteq_r M$, using theorem 9(1) twice. Remark that λ_r-contexts can be transformed into equivalent λ_d-contexts : for instance $[\,](x|x)\langle \mathbf{I}/x\rangle$ is equivalent to $(\lambda x.[\,](x|x))\mathbf{I}$.

2. Let A st. $A[M] \Downarrow_r^m V$. By property $(\star)$ above,

$$\forall W \in \{\!\![V]\!\!\}\ \exists N \in \{\!\![A[M]]\!\!\}\ \ N \xrightarrow{\star}_d W$$

By construction of $\{\!\![A[M]]\!\!\}$, there is $L \in \{\!\![M]\!\!\}$ such that $N \in \{\!\![A[L]]\!\!\}$. Then, using property $(\star\star)$,

$$\exists W' \in \Lambda_r\ \ A[L] \xrightarrow{\star}_r W'\ \ \&\ \ W \in \{\!\![W']\!\!\}$$

Since W is an abstraction, W' is also an abstraction, eventually followed by some explicit substitution entries. Then $A[L]\Downarrow_r$.

3. Similar to the proof of the second point. It is enough to exchange M and L. Remark that this is so because for all $L \in \{\!\![M]\!\!\}$, $N \in \{\!\![A[L]]\!\!\}$ implies $N \in \{\!\![A[M]]\!\!\}$, independently of A.

4 Approximants

The goal of this section is to define an algebraic interpretation of the lambda calculus with resources, based on the notion of approximant of a term, such that the induced semantics of λ_r is adequate with respect to the observational preorder. We show how to apply to the calculus with resources, Lévy's program for pure lambda calculus [18]. The only requirement is to deal with a "may testing" observational preorder[5].

[5] Our former intention was to apply the program directly to the calculus with multiplicities, whose principal feature is to be deterministic by construction of its evaluation

Definition 11. (Approximants) The set $\mathcal{L}_r$ of approximants for λ_r is the least subset of Λ_d containing $\lambda x_1 \ldots x_n.\bot$ and $\lambda \boldsymbol{x}.\boldsymbol{x}\boldsymbol{A}_1 \ldots \boldsymbol{A}_s$ whenever $\boldsymbol{A}_i = (A_1 \mid \ldots \mid A_n)$ and $A_j \in \mathcal{L}_r$. Note that bags of approximants only have finite multiplicities.

Direct approximants $\varpi(T) \subseteq \mathcal{L}_r$ of terms and bags $T \in \Lambda_d$ are recursively defined as follows :

$$\varpi(\lambda\tilde{x}.(\lambda y M)P\tilde{R}) = \{\lambda\tilde{x}.\bot\}$$

$$\varpi(\lambda\tilde{x}.yP_1 \ldots P_s) = \{\lambda\tilde{x}.y\varpi(P_1)\ldots\varpi(P_s)\}$$

$$\varpi(P) = \begin{cases} \{\bot\} & \text{if } P = \mathbf{1} \\ \bigcup(M' \mid Q') & \text{if } P = (M \mid Q) \text{ and } M' \in \varpi(M) \;\&\; Q' \in \varpi(Q) \\ \bigcup \varpi(M)^m & \text{if } P = M^\infty \text{ and } m \in \mathbb{N} \end{cases}$$

The set of approximants of a term $M \in \Lambda_r$ is :

$$\mathcal{A}(M) = \bigcup \bigcup \{\varpi(N) \,/\, \exists M' \in \{\!\!\{M\}\!\!\} \; M' \overset{*}{\rhd}_d N\}$$

In order to define the preorder $\leq$ on $\mathcal{L}_r$, induced by $\bot \leq A$, we must say at the same time what is the preorder on the bags of approximants. One of the most restrictive definitions one can think about is $\boldsymbol{A} \leq \boldsymbol{B}$ if $\boldsymbol{A} \equiv (A_1 \mid \ldots \mid A_m)$, $\boldsymbol{B} \equiv (B_1 \mid \ldots \mid B_n)$, and there exists injection $j : [1, m] \to [1, n]$ st. $A_i \leq B_{j(i)}$ for any $i \in [1, m]$. Remark that with this definition, $x(A \mid \bot) \not\leq x(A \mid B)$ holds since resources $\bot$ are considered as any other one. Instead, $x(A \mid \Omega) \sqsubseteq_r x(A \mid B)$. Henceforth, our definition of $\leq$ is the following - which, in particular, verifies $x(A \mid \bot) \leq x(A \mid B)$:

Definition 12. (Preorder $\leq$ on $\mathcal{L}_r$) The preorder $\leq$ on the (bags of) approximants is the least transitive relation verifying :

$$\begin{array}{ll} \bot \leq A & \text{for any } A \in \mathcal{L}_r \\ \lambda x.A \leq \lambda x.B & \text{if } A \leq B \\ x\boldsymbol{A}_1 \ldots \boldsymbol{A}_n \leq x\boldsymbol{B}_1 \ldots \boldsymbol{B}_n & \text{if } \boldsymbol{A}_i \leq \boldsymbol{B}_i \text{ for any } i \end{array}$$

---

rules. But the syntax of λ_m is far too restrictive. Consider $M = (x(\lambda z.yz^1)^2)\langle \mathbf{I}^1/y\rangle$ and try to devise its approximants : it is clear that $\bot$, $x\bot^1$, $x(\lambda z.\bot)^2$, $x(\lambda z.\bot)^1$ and also $x(\lambda z.\mathbf{I}z^1)^1$ are approximants of M. The last term can be explained as follows : one can say that M is better than $(x(\lambda z.yz^1)^1)\langle \mathbf{I}^1/y\rangle$, and, intuitively

$$(x(\lambda z.yz^1)^1)\langle \mathbf{I}^1/y\rangle \rhd_d x((\lambda z.yz^1)^1\langle \mathbf{I}^1/y\rangle) \rhd_d x(\lambda z.y\langle \mathbf{I}^1/y\rangle z^1)^1 \rhd_d x(\lambda z.\mathbf{I}z^1)^1$$

However, if $C = [\,]\langle \lambda v.vv^1/x\rangle$, these approximants A fail to verify $C[A]\Downarrow_m$ while $C[M]\Downarrow_m$. The problem here is that the distribution of $\langle \mathbf{I}/y\rangle$ over the argument $(\lambda z.yz^1)^2$ cannot be done safely without considering this argument as the bag $(\lambda z.yz^1 \mid \lambda z.yz^1)$, so that $(\lambda z.\mathbf{I}z^1 \mid \lambda z.\bot)$ is obtainable by reduction. But the approximant $B = x(\lambda z.\mathbf{I}z^1 \mid \lambda z.\bot)$, which verifies $C[B]\Downarrow_m$, is not a term of the lambda calculus with multiplicities.

where $\boldsymbol{A} \leq \boldsymbol{B}$ iff $\exists A_1, \ldots, A_m \neq \bot$ st.

$$\boldsymbol{A} \equiv (A_1 \mid \ldots \mid A_m \mid \bot \mid \ldots \mid \bot) \;\; \& \;\; \boldsymbol{B} \equiv (B_1 \mid \ldots \mid B_n)$$

and there is an injection $j : [1, m] \rightarrow [1, n]$ st. $A_i \leq B_{j(i)}$.

The main difficulty to overcome is the fact that the set of approximants of a term in λ_r is not directed w.r.t. $\leq$, as it is for pure lambda calculus [18]. For instance, if $M = K \oplus F$, then $\{K, F\} \subseteq \mathcal{A}(M)$ holds but there is no $A \in \mathcal{A}(M)$ st. $K \leq A$ and $F \leq A$. The reason is here the non-confluence of the reduction relation $\rhd_d$. Another kind of example comes from the limited availability of arguments : if $M = (xyy)\langle K/y\rangle$, then $A_1 = xK\bot$ and $A_2 = x\bot K$ are two approximants of M without upper bound in $\mathcal{A}(M)$. It should be clear that the standard syntactic continuity theorem, namely, $C[M]\Downarrow_r$ iff $\exists A \in \mathcal{A}(M)\ C[A]\Downarrow_r$, does not hold for λ_r (th. 5.7 [18]) : because the lambda calculus with resources is not confluent, a unique approximant of a term for a given context does not necessarily exists. Nevertheless, a convergent evaluation of $C[M]$ can be reproduced by taking a different approximant from $\mathcal{A}(M)$ each time M (or a term obtained from M by renamings) appears at head position during the evaluation. Since the evaluation should be of finite length, the number of approximants we need is finite too.

Remark that if we define the intensional preorder $\leq_{\mathcal{L}_r}$ by

$$M \leq_{\mathcal{L}_r} N \overset{def}{\Longleftrightarrow} \mathcal{A}(M) \subseteq \mathcal{A}(N)$$

then it cannot be characterized in terms of $\leq$. Indeed, $\mathcal{A}(M) \subseteq \mathcal{A}(N) \Rightarrow \forall A \in \mathcal{A}(M)\ \exists B \in \mathcal{A}(N)\ A \leq B$ (we make $B = A$), but the reverse implication does not hold. This is so because $\mathcal{A}(M)$ is not downward closed by $\leq$; in particular, there exists $M \in \Lambda_r$ st. $\bot \notin \mathcal{A}(M)$. This is the case, e.g. for $M = \mathbf{I}$. Therefore, we define

$$M \leq_{\mathcal{L}_r} N \overset{def}{\Longleftrightarrow} \downarrow\!\mathcal{A}(M) \subseteq \downarrow\!\mathcal{A}(N)$$

where $\downarrow\!\mathcal{A}(M)$ the least non-empty downset[6] containing $\mathcal{A}(M)$, and this preorder is equivalent to

$$M \leq_{\mathcal{L}_r} N \iff \forall A \in \mathcal{A}(M)\ \exists B \in \mathcal{A}(N)\ A \leq B$$

Lemma 13. *1.* $A \in \overline{\omega}(N) \Rightarrow A \sqsubseteq_r N$
2. $A \leq B \Rightarrow A \sqsubseteq_r B$

Proof. 1. As a corollary of theorem 2, which gives a characterization of the theory induced by $\simeq_r$, one has $\Omega \sqsubseteq_r N$ for all N. The statement holds then because $\sqsubseteq_r$ is a congruence and bags can be augmented without changing the convergence ability of the term.

[6] Non-empty downsets on $(\mathcal{L}_r, \leq)$ are subsets X of $\mathcal{L}_r$ st. $\bot \in X$, and, if $A \in X$ and $B \leq A$, then $B \in X$.

2. The proof is by induction on the derivation of $A \leq B$. The interesting case is $A = yA_1 \ldots A_n \leq yB_1 \ldots B_n$, with $A_i \leq B_i$ for all i. We sketch the proof for $n = 1$. Let A and B be the arguments of y, and suppose w.l.o.g.

$$A = (A_1 \mid \ldots \mid A_k \mid \bot \mid \ldots \mid \bot) \text{ and } B = (B_1 \mid \ldots \mid B_k \mid B')$$

where $A_i \leq B_i$ for any $i = 1, \ldots, k$. By i.h., $C[A_i] \sqsubseteq_r C[B_i]$ whatever the context C is. There are contexts $C_1, \ldots, C_{k+1}$ st.

$$yA = C_1[A_1] \sqsubseteq_r C_1[B_1] = C_2[A_2] \sqsubseteq_r \ldots \sqsubseteq_r C_{k-1}[B_{k-1}] = C_k[A_k] \sqsubseteq_r$$

$$C_{k+1}[B_k] = y(B_1 \mid \ldots \mid B_k \mid \Omega \ldots \mid \Omega) \sim_r y(B_1 \mid \ldots \mid B_k) \sqsubseteq_r yB$$

Definition 14. A context C is *linear* in $[]_i$ if this constant does not occurs in C more than once.

Lemma 15. (Approximation Lemma) *For all λ_r-context C and for all $M \in \Lambda_r$ st. $C[M] \in \Lambda_r^o$, the following holds :*

$$C[M]\Downarrow_r \iff \exists A_1, \ldots, A_n \in \downarrow\mathcal{A}(M)\ C[A_1 \oplus \ldots \oplus A_n]\Downarrow_r$$

Furthermore, if C is linear in $[]$, then $n = 1$.

Proof. All along this proof, we write $\mathbb{A}$ for terms of the shape $A_1 \oplus \ldots \oplus A_n$; the notation $\mathbb{A} \in \downarrow\mathcal{A}(M)$ stands for $\forall i\ A_i \in \downarrow\mathcal{A}(M)$.

We show first the $\Leftarrow$ part: let $C[A_1 \oplus \ldots \oplus A_n]\Downarrow_r$, with $A_i \in \downarrow\mathcal{A}(M)$. Remind that for each A_i there is $B_i \in \mathcal{A}(M)$ st. $A_i \leq B_i$. Moreover, for all i, there exists M_i, N_i st. $B_i \in \overline{\omega}(N_i)$, $M_i \in \{\!\{M\}\!\}$ and $M_i \overset{\star}{\rhd}_d N_i$. By lemma 13, we have $A_i \sqsubseteq_r B_i \sqsubseteq_r N_i$ for any $i = 1, \ldots, n$. Using theorem 10(1), $N_i \sqsubseteq_r M_i$ holds; now, by theorem 10(3) we have $M_i \sqsubseteq_r M$. Then, $A_i \sqsubseteq_r M$ for any $i = 1, \ldots, n$. Since $\sqsubseteq_r$ is a precongruence, $C[M \oplus \ldots \oplus M]\Downarrow_r$. Then $C[M]\Downarrow_r$ as $M \simeq_r M \oplus \ldots \oplus M$.

The $\Rightarrow$ part is a corollary of the following more general statement : Let C be multiple-hole λ_r-context and $M_1, \ldots, M_p \in \Lambda_r$ st. $C[M_1, \ldots, M_p] \in \Lambda_r^o$. Then,

$$C[M_1, \ldots, M_p]\Downarrow_r \Rightarrow \forall i \in [1, p]\ \exists \mathbb{A}_i \in \downarrow\mathcal{A}(M)\ C[\mathbb{A}_1, \ldots, \mathbb{A}_p]\Downarrow_r$$

Furthermore, for any i such that C is linear in $[]_i$, we can take $\mathbb{A}_i = A_i \in \downarrow\mathcal{A}(M_i)$. The notation $C[\tilde{M}]$ stands for $C[M_1, \ldots, M_p]$. In an abuse of terminology, we write $\tilde{\mathbb{A}} \in \downarrow\mathcal{A}(\tilde{M})$ whenever $\mathbb{A}_i \in \downarrow\mathcal{A}(M_i)$ for all i. The general shape of a λ_r-context C is $C_0 C_1 \ldots C_n$ where C_0 is either $[]_i$, or a variable x, or a context $\lambda x.D$, and C_j, $j > 0$, is either a bag of contexts $(D_1^{m_1} \mid \ldots \mid D_q^{m_q})$ or an explicit substitution made up of contexts $\langle D_1^{m_1} \mid \ldots \mid D_q^{m_q}/x\rangle$.

Let $C[M_1, \ldots, M_p]\Downarrow_r^l$ and assume, w.l.o.g., that C is linear in $[]_i$, for $i = k, \ldots, p$, with $0 \leq k \leq p + 1$ (the case $k = p + 1$ corresponds to a context C non-linear in any constant $[]_i$). We proceed by induction on l :

(1) If $l = 0$, $C[\tilde{M}]$ reduces to an abstraction by applying rule (v); that is, $C_1, \ldots, C_n$ are substitution contexts. We have, either $C_0 = \lambda x.D$, or $C_0 = []_i$.

In the first case, we can take $\perp$ as approximant for any M_i. In the second one, M_i must be an abstraction so we can take $\lambda x.\perp$ as approximant of M_i and $\perp$ for any M_j with $i \neq j$.

(2) If $l > 0$, we proceed by cases on C_0 :

(2a) $C_0 = \lambda x.D$: one can define a context C' such that the convergent evaluation is $C[\tilde{M}] \xrightarrow{\star}_r C'[\tilde{M}, \tilde{M}'[z/x]] \Downarrow_r^{l-1}$ where $\tilde{M}' = M_1, \ldots, M_{k-1}$. Essentially by induction, $C'[\tilde{\mathbb{A}}, \tilde{\mathbb{A}}'[z/x]] \Downarrow_r$ for some $\tilde{\mathbb{A}} \in \downarrow\mathcal{A}(\tilde{M})$ and some $\tilde{\mathbb{A}}' \in \downarrow\mathcal{A}(\tilde{M}')$. Define $\mathbb{A}_i'' = \mathbb{A}_i \oplus \mathbb{A}_i'$ for $i = 1, \ldots k-1$, and $\mathbb{A}_i'' = \mathbb{A}_i$ for $i = k, \ldots, p$. Then, $C[\tilde{\mathbb{A}}''] \xrightarrow{\star}_r C'[\tilde{\mathbb{A}}'', (\mathbb{A}_1'' \oplus \ldots \oplus \mathbb{A}_{k-1}'')''[z/x]]$. Since $C'[\tilde{\mathbb{A}}, \tilde{\mathbb{A}}'[z/x]] \sqsubseteq_r C'[\tilde{\mathbb{A}}'', (\mathbb{A}_1'' \oplus \ldots \oplus \mathbb{A}_{k-1}'')[z/x]]$, $C[\tilde{\mathbb{A}}''] \Downarrow_r$ holds.

(2b) $C_0 = []_i$: There are three cases to analyze, depending on M_i. We skip the proof for $M_i = \lambda x.M'$ and for M_i not in normal form (full details can be found in [17]). Assume $M_i = xR_1 \ldots R_q$ and $\tilde{R}$ does not bind the head occurrence of x. Since some R_i are possibly substitution entries, we cannot build the approximant of M_i by a separate reasoning on each R_i. Nevertheless, theorem 10 (2) implies

$$\exists M_i' \in \{\![M_i]\!\} \;\; C[M_1, \ldots, M_i', \ldots, M_p] \Downarrow_r^{l'} \quad \text{where } l' \leq l$$

The general shape of M_i' is $xP_1 \ldots P_t$ where $P_{j+1} = (N_{s_j+1} \mid \ldots \mid N_{s_{j+1}})$ with $1 = s_0 < s_1 \ldots < s_t$, and $s_0 = 1$. We write $\tilde{M}'$ the sequence $M_1, \ldots M_i' \ldots M_p$ and $\tilde{N}$ the sequence $N_{s_0}, \ldots N_{s_1}, \ldots N_{s_t}$. Our starting point is the convergent evaluation of $C[\tilde{M}']$. Let C_j be the first substitution context $\langle (D \mid D')/x \rangle$ among $C_1 \ldots C_n$, and let z be a fresh variable. For the sake of simplicity, we consider the case where α-conversion is not necessary. The convergent evaluation is then

$$C[\tilde{M}'] \xrightarrow{\star}_r D\tilde{P}C_1 \ldots C_{j-1}\langle D'/z \rangle C_{j+1} \ldots C_n[\tilde{M}'] \Downarrow_r^{l''} \quad \text{with } l'' < l$$

We define $C' = DD_1 \ldots D_t C_1 \ldots C_{j-1}\langle D'/z \rangle C_{j+1} \ldots C_n$ where

$$D_{j+1} = ([]_{s_j+p+1} \mid \ldots \mid []_{s_{j+1}+p}) \qquad j = 0, \ldots, t-1$$

In other words, $C[\tilde{M}'] \xrightarrow{\star}_r C'[\tilde{M}', \tilde{N}] \Downarrow_r^{l''}$. One should remark that C' is linear in $[]_j$, $j = k+1, \ldots, s_t + p$. By induction, $C'[\tilde{\mathbb{A}}, B_1, \ldots, B_{s_t}] \Downarrow_r$, with $\tilde{\mathbb{A}} \in \downarrow\mathcal{A}(\tilde{M}')$ and $B_j \in \downarrow\mathcal{A}(N_i)$. Let $\boldsymbol{B}^{j+1} = (B_{s_j+1} \mid \ldots \mid B_{s_{j+1}})$. The term $x\boldsymbol{B}^1 \ldots \boldsymbol{B}^t$ is an approximant of M_i'; by definition, $x\boldsymbol{B}^1 \ldots \boldsymbol{B}^t \in \downarrow\mathcal{A}(M_i)$ as $M_i' \in \{\![M_i]\!\}$. Let $\tilde{\mathbb{A}}' = \mathbb{A}_1, \ldots, (\mathbb{A}_i \oplus x\boldsymbol{B}^1 \ldots \boldsymbol{B}^t), \ldots, \mathbb{A}_p$. Hence,

$$C[\tilde{\mathbb{A}}'] = (\mathbb{A}_i \oplus x\boldsymbol{B}^1 \ldots \boldsymbol{B}^t)C_1 \ldots C_n[\tilde{\mathbb{A}}'] \xrightarrow{\star}_r$$

$$x\boldsymbol{B}^1 \ldots \boldsymbol{B}^t C_1 \ldots C_n[\tilde{\mathbb{A}}'] \xrightarrow{\star}_r C'[\tilde{\mathbb{A}}', B_1, \ldots, B_{s_t}]$$

Since $C'[\tilde{\mathbb{A}}, B_1, \ldots, B_{s_t}] \sqsubseteq_r C'[\tilde{\mathbb{A}}', B_1, \ldots, B_t]$, we conclude $C[\tilde{\mathbb{A}}'] \Downarrow_r$.

(2c) $C_0 = x$: The proof is as for case (2b).

Theorem 16. (Adequacy of the Algebraic Interpretation of λ_r)

$$\forall M, N \in \Lambda_r \;\; M \leq_{\mathcal{L}_r} N \;\Rightarrow\; M \sqsubseteq_r N$$

Proof. Let $M, N \in \Lambda_r$ and C be a λ_r-context closing M and N. Suppose $M \leq_{\mathcal{L}_r} N$ and $C[M]\Downarrow_r$. By the approximation lemma 15, there are $A_1, \ldots, A_n$ in $\downarrow\mathcal{A}(M)$ st. $C[(A_1 \oplus \ldots \oplus A_n)]\Downarrow_r$. By definition of $\leq_{\mathcal{L}_r}$, $A_i \in \downarrow\mathcal{A}(N)$ for any $i = 1, \ldots, n$. We conclude $C[N]\Downarrow_r$ by using the approximation lemma.

The algebraic semantics $\leq_{\mathcal{L}_r}$ is too restrictive to define a fully abstract (or completely adequate) w.r.t. $\sqsubseteq_r$. Many kinds of examples show

$$\neg(M \sqsubseteq_r N \Rightarrow M \leq_{\mathcal{L}_r} N)$$

The first one involves η-conversion (it was already pointed out by Lévy [18], see also [8]) : $x \sqsubseteq_r \lambda y.xy^\infty$ but $\neg(x \leq_{\mathcal{L}_r} \lambda y.xy^\infty)$. The second example arises because $\leq_{\mathcal{L}_r}$ has no maximal element : let $\Xi = (\lambda fx.ff^\infty)(\lambda fx.ff^\infty)^\infty$; then $I \sqsubseteq_r \Xi$ but $\neg(I \leq_{\mathcal{L}_r} \Xi)$. A third problem raised by the definition is that $\leq_{\mathcal{L}_r}$ is sensible to the number of resources in a bag. This not always the case for $\sqsubseteq_r$, as the simplification lemma 4 shows.

References

1. M. Abadi, L. Cardelli, P.-L. Curien, J.-J. Lévy. *Explicit Substitutions.* Journal of Functional Programming, 1. 1991.
2. S. Abramsky . *The Lazy Lambda Calculus.* In D. Turner, editor, Research Topics in Functional Programming. Addison Wesley. 1989.
3. S. Abramsky, L. Ong. *Full Abstraction in the lazy lambda calculus.* Information and Computation, 105(2). 1993.
4. H.P. Barendregt. *The Lambda Calculus.* North-Holland. 1985.
5. G. Boudol. *A Lambda-Calculus for Parallel Functions.* Technical Report 1231, INRIA Sophia-Antipolis. 1990.
6. G. Boudol. *The lambda calculus with multiplicities.* Technical Report 2025, INRIA Sophia-Antipolis. 1993.
7. G. Boudol. *Lambda-calculi for (strict) parallel functions.* Information and Computation, 108(1). 1994.
8. G. Boudol, C. Laneve. *The discriminating power of multiplicities in the λ-calculus.* Information and Computation 126 (1). 1996.
9. G. Boudol, C. Laneve. *Termination, deadlock and divergence in the λ-calculus with multiplicities.* Proceedings of the 11th Conference on the Mathematical Foundations of Programming Semantics, Electronic Notes in Computer Science 1. 1995.
10. G. Boudol, C. Laneve. *λ-Calculus, Multiplicities and the π-Calculus.* Technical Report 2581, INRIA Sophia-Antipolis. 1995.
11. G. Boudol, C. Lavatelli. *Full Abstraction for Lambda Calculus with Resources and Convergence Testing.* CAAP'96. LNCS 1059, Springer-Verlag, Berlin. 1996.
12. P.-L. Curien, T.Hardin, J.-J. Lévy. *Confluence Properties of Weak and Strong Calculi of Explicit Substitutions.* Journal of ACM 43(2). 1996.
13. M. Dezani-Ciancaglini, U. de Liguoro, A. Piperno. *Fully Abstract Semantics for Concurrent λ-calculus.* TACS'94. LNCS 789, Springer-Verlag, Berlin. 1994.
14. M. Dezani-Ciancaglini, U. de Liguoro, A. Piperno. *Filter Models for Conjunctive-Disjunctive λ-calculi.* To appear in TCS.
15. J.M.E. Hyland. *A Syntactic Characterization of the Equality in Some Models for the Lambda Calculus.* Journal of the London Mathematical Society 12. 1976.

16. C. Lavatelli. *Non-deterministic lazy λ-calculus vs. π-calculus.* Technical Report LIENS 93-1. 1993.
17. C. Lavatelli. *Sémantique du lambda-calcul avec ressources.* PhD. Thesis. Université Paris 7. France. Janvier 1996.
18. J.-J. Lévy. *An algebraic interpretation of the $\lambda\beta K$-calculus; and an application of a labelled λ-calculus.* Theoretical Computer Science, 2(1). 1976.
19. G. Longo. *Set Theoretical Models of Lambda Calculus : Theories, expansions and isomorphisms.* Annals of Pure and Applied Logic, 24. 1983.
20. R. Milner, J. Parrow, D. Walker. *A Calculus of Mobile Processes, Parts I and II.* Information and Computation, 100(1). 1992.
21. R. Milner. *Functions as Processes.* Mathematical Structures in Computer Science, 2. 1992.
22. C.-H. Luke Ong. *The Lazy Lambda Calculus/ An Investigation into the Foundations of Functional Programming.* PhD Thesis, Imperial College. 1988.
23. G. Plotkin. *LCF Considered as a Programming Language.* Theoretical Computer Science, 5. 1975.
24. C. Wadsworth. *The relation between computational and denotational properties for Scott D_∞-model of the lambda-calculus.* SIAM Journal on Computing, 5. 1976.
25. C. Wadsworth. *Approximate Reduction and Lambda-Calculus Models.* SIAM Journal on Computing, 7. 1978.

Concurrent Graph and Term Graph Rewriting

A. Corradini

Università di Pisa, Dipartimento di Informatica, Corso Italia 40, 56125 Pisa, Italy
(andrea@di.unipi.it)

Abstract. Graph Rewriting Systems are a powerful formalism for the specification of parallel and distributed systems, and the corresponding theory is rich of results concerning parallelism and concurrency. I will review the main results of the theory of concurrency for the algebraic approach to graph rewriting, emphasizing the relationship with the theory of Petri nets. In fact, graph rewriting systems can be regarded as a proper generalization of Petri nets, where the current state of a system is described by a graph instead of by a collection of tokens. Recently, this point of view allowed for the generalization to graph rewriting of some interesting results and constructions of the concurrent semantics of nets, including processes, unfoldings, and categorical semantics based on pair of adjoint functors.

1 Introduction

The *theory of graph grammars* (or of *graph rewriting systems, GRS*) basically studies a variety of formalisms which extend the theory of formal languages in order to deal with structures more general than strings, like graphs and maps. A graph grammar allows one to describe finitely a (possibly infinite) collection of graphs, i.e., those graphs which can be obtained from a start graph through repeated applications of graph productions. Each production can be applied to a graph by replacing an occurrence of its left-hand side with its right-hand side. The form of graph productions and the mechanisms stating how a production can be applied to a graph and what the resulting graph is, depend on the specific formalism.

The development of this theory, originated in the late sixties, includes many fruitful applications in different areas of computer science: among them we recall data bases, software specification, incremental compilers and pattern recognition (see [5, 24, 25, 23, 28], the proceedings of the international workshops on graph grammars, and the forthcoming Handbook [63]).

Since many (natural or artificial) distributed structures can be represented (at a suitable level of abstraction) by graphs, and graph productions act on those graphs with local transformations, it is quite obvious that graph rewriting systems are potentially interesting for the study of the concurrent transformation of structures. In fact, on the one hand they have been used in various ways for the specification of concurrent and distributed systems, like actor systems (e.g., in [40, 42]), Petri nets (see the references in Sections 5), systems of distributed processes ([16, 68]), and others; on the other hand a rich theory of concurrency has been developed, which includes many results concerning aspects of parallelism and concurrency of graph derivations.

Such contributions can be classified better by looking at the relationship between graph grammars and related areas of Theoretical Computer Science. In fact, in many cases other areas have provided the inspiration for some notions or results that, after a suitable translation in graph rewriting terminology, provided the ground for interesting, original generalizations.

More precisely, in my view, most of the contributions to the theory of concurrency have been originated by considered graph rewriting systems under two different (although certainly related) points of view. The first one, which is by far the most widely adopted in the classical literature of the area, regards graph grammars as a generalization of Chomsky grammars and of Term Rewriting Systems to the rewriting of more complex structures. As a consequence, many notions and results concerning parallelism and concurrency have been developed that recast in this more general setting corresponding notions and results of string grammars and Term Rewriting Systems, exploring properties like confluence, orthogonality of redexes, parallel moves, and so on (see for example [46, 48, 20, 19, 37]). The more general framework also allowed for some generalizations of these notions that exploit the greater expressive power of graph rewriting (for example, the *amalgamated* compositions of productions in the algebraic approach [19]).

The second point of view stresses instead the relationship between graph rewriting systems and other formalisms for the specification of concurrent or distributed systems, and in particular with Petri nets. Petri nets [58, 60] have been the first formal tool proposed for the specification of the behaviour of systems which are naturally endowed with a notion of concurrency. Their success can be measured by the looking not only at the uncountably many practical applications of nets, but also at the development of the theoretical aspects, which range from a complete analysis of the various phenomena arising in simple models of nets to the definition of more expressive (and complex) classes of nets. As a matter of fact, Petri nets have been equipped along the years with rich, formal computation-based semantics, including both interleaving and truly-concurrent models (see, among others, [62, 30]). In many cases such semantics have been defined via well-established categorical techniques, often involving adjunctions between suitable categories [57, 52, 53].

Nets and their semantics are therefore a reference point for any formalism intended to describe concurrent and distributed systems. Since the early eighties various encodings of nets as graph grammars have been proposed. In most cases these encodings provide a one-to-one correspondence between the very basic concepts of the two formalisms; for example firing and step sequences become sequential and parallel graph derivations, respectively; and concurrency, causal dependency, and conflict between two transitions correspond to analogous relations between graph productions. Recently this correspondence has been reconsidered under a new perspective, that has provided a solid ground for a fruitful cross-fertilization of the two fields. The basic idea is to regard Petri nets simply as graph rewriting systems that act on a restricted kind of graphs, namely discrete, labeled graphs (that can be considered as sets of tokens labeled by places). Conversely, graph rewriting systems generalize Petri nets not only because they allow for arbitrary (also non-discrete) graphs, but also because they allow for the specification of context-dependent operations, where part of the state is read but not consumed. This new perspective allowed for recasting and generalizing many semantical notions and results developed for nets to graph rewriting systems, including (deterministic) processes [13], unfoldings [61], and the definition of morphisms and categories of systems [7, 32], that provide the basis for a categorical semantics via adjoint functors [7, 61].

The paper is organized as follows. Section 2 introduces the basic notions of graph rewriting systems, and in particular of the algebraic Double-Pushout (DPO) approach. Section 3 surveys some classical results concerning independence and local confluence of direct derivations, which are the core of the theory of concurrency of graph rewriting. In the last years various contributions have been proposed for providing an event structure semantics for graph grammars: They are summarized in Section 4. Section 5 presents various proposal of encodings of Place/Transition Petri nets as graph grammars, stressing the correspondences among the basic concepts of the two formalisms. Based on this correspondence, many semantic constructions for nets have been generalized to graph grammars: Among them non-sequential processes (discussed in Section 6), and the definition of categories of systems and of semantics based on adjoint functors (in Section 7).

The present tutorial paper is not intended to cover all the literature related to aspects of parallelism and concurrency in graph grammars: It focuses instead on the main contributions to a concurrent semantics for that formalism. For example, I will not consider *parallel* graph grammars (that were defined as a generalization of Lindenmayer-systems), nor *distributed* ones (see [69] for an overview of the different approaches to parallel and distributed graph grammars). Other tutorial presentations concerning the theory of concurrency of graph grammars can be found in [19, 48, 67, 6].

2 Graph Rewriting Systems: Basic notions

A graph grammar (or graph rewriting system) consists of a set of rules that can be applied repeatedly producing (usually) local transformations on a given graph. Sometimes a distinguished start graph is provided, as well as a set of terminal labels (or any other mean to characterize a set of terminal graphs): In this case one would speak more properly of a graph *grammar*, by analogy with Chomsky grammars. Since I'm not interested here in generated languages, I shall disregard start graphs and terminal labels by considering only the set of productions, and I will use "graph grammar" and "graph rewriting system" as synonymous, as well as "production" and "rule".

A graph production usually consists of a triple $p = (L, R, Emb)$, where L and R are two graphs (the *left-* and the *right-hand* sides, respectively), and Emb is some embedding mechanism. Production p can be applied to a given *host* graph G via the following procedure:

a. Find an occurrence of the left-hand side L in G (in some cases suitable application conditions need to be satisfied);
b. Remove a part of the graph G determined by the occurrence of L, obtaining the *context* or *rest* graph D;
c. Embed (a copy of) the right-hand side R into D, by using the embedding mechanism *Emb*, and obtaining the *derived* graph H.

In this case one writes $G \stackrel{p}{\Longrightarrow} H$, and one says that there is a *direct derivation from G to H via p*. The various approaches to graph rewriting differ for one or more of the following aspects of the above general procedure:

1. The kind of graphs that are rewritten;
2. Possible restrictions imposed on the left-hand side of productions;
3. The way an occurrence of L in G is determined, and the corresponding application conditions;
4. The way the context graph D is obtained;
5. The embedding mechanism.

The most successful approaches proposed in literature can be classified in two families, namely the *algebraic* and the *set-theoretical* ones. Although both of them have been initially proposed as generalizations of Chomsky grammars, the theories of the two approaches diverged quite a lot in the last decades.

In fact, in the theory of the set-theoretical approaches [56, 55, 27] most emphasis has been placed on the generating power of various classes of grammars, on the properties of the generated graph languages, and on their decidability; shortly, on the *results* of the generation process. On the contrary, the theory of the algebraic approaches [26, 14, 22] mainly focused on *the generation process itself*, by placing great emphasis on properties of derivation sequences, and studying their transformation and equivalence, also from the concurrent point of view.[1]

This is the reason why, apart from a few exceptions, most of the theory of concurrency for graph grammars has been developed for the algebraic approaches: As a consequence, most of the notions and results presented in the next sections are taken from the corresponding literature.

2.1 The algebraic approaches to graph rewriting

In the algebraic approaches the basic notions of graph rewriting are defined in terms of suitable diagrams in the category of graphs; in particular, a central

[1] There are remarkable exceptions to this rough classification. For example, Hyperedge Replacement grammars [31, 17] (that belongs to the algebraic approach) have been studied deeply from the viewpoint of generative power and decidability properties; on the other hand, Actor Grammars [40] and ESM systems [36] are example of set-theoretical formalisms mainly concerned with concurrency aspects.

role is played by the notion of *gluing* of graphs, characterized as the categorical construction of pushout. The algebraic approaches can be divided in the Double-Pushout (DPO) and the Single-Pushout (SPO) approach [14, 22], that differ by the basic rewriting mechanism that is modeled by a construction involving two pushouts or one pushout, respectively. Actually, both the DPO and the SPO approaches are families of formalisms, because they have been defined for various types of graphs as well as for other kinds of structures.

Let us consider the DPO approach [26, 18, 14], which is certainly the most well-known in the family. Before its algebraic presentation, let me summarize how it could be characterized with respect to the above list of properties:

1. In the original presentation, the graphs considered are directed, labeled multigraphs (i.e., many edges with the same label can connect two nodes).
2. A production has the form $p = (L \xleftarrow{l} K \xrightarrow{r} R)$: That is, the embedding information is provided by a third graph K (the *interface*) and by its *injective* embeddings in L and R. Without loss of generality, K will be considered as a subgraph of L and R. There is no restriction on L.
3. An occurrence of L in G is a graph morphism $g : L \rightarrow G$. Rule p can be applied if the *gluing conditions* [18] are satisfied, that ensure that the context as defined below is a graph.
4. The *context* graph D is obtained by deleting from G the all nodes and edges in $g(L - K)$.
5. The embedding of R in D is obtained by taking their disjoint union, and then by identifying for each node or edge x in K, its images $g(x)$ in G and $r(x)$ in R,

Let us introduce now these concepts in a more formal way.

Given two fixed alphabets Ω_E and Ω_V for edge and vertex labels, respectively, a ***labeled, directed multigraph** (over (Ω_E, Ω_V))*, called simply a ***graph*** in the following, is a tuple $G = \langle E, V, s, t, l_E, l_V \rangle$, where E is a finite set of *edges*, V is a finite set of *vertices*, $s, t : E \rightarrow V$ are the *source* and *target* functions, and $l_E : E \rightarrow \Omega_E$ and $l_V : V \rightarrow \Omega_V$ are the *edge* and the *vertex labeling* functions, respectively. A graph is *discrete* if it has no edges. A *graph morphism* $f : G \rightarrow G'$ is a pair of functions $f = (f_E : E \rightarrow E', f_V : V \rightarrow V')$ which preserve sources, targets, and labels, i.e., such that $f_V \circ t = t' \circ f_E$, $f_V \circ s = s' \circ f_E$, $l'_V \circ f_V = l_V$, and $l'_E \circ f_E = l_E$. A graph morphism f is an *isomorphism* if both f_E and f_V are bijections. The category having labeled graphs over (Ω_E, Ω_V) as objects and graph morphisms as arrow is called (Ω_E, Ω_V)-**Graph**, or simply **Graph** if the alphabets of labels are understood.

The rewriting procedure described above is usually presented via a simple, equivalent categorical construction involving two pushout diagrams in the category of graphs, hence the name "Double-Pushout". It is worth recalling that given two graph morphisms $b : A \rightarrow B$ and $c : A \rightarrow C$, a triple $\langle D, g : B \rightarrow D, f : C \rightarrow D \rangle$ as in Figure 1 (a) is called a *pushout* of $\langle b, c \rangle$ (and D is called its *pushout object*) if [*commutativity property*] $g \circ b = f \circ c$, and [*universal property*] for all graphs D' and graph morphisms $g' : B \rightarrow D'$ and $f' : C \rightarrow D'$, with

$g' \circ b = f' \circ c$, there exists a unique morphism $h : D \to D'$ such that $h \circ g = g'$ and $h \circ f = f'$.

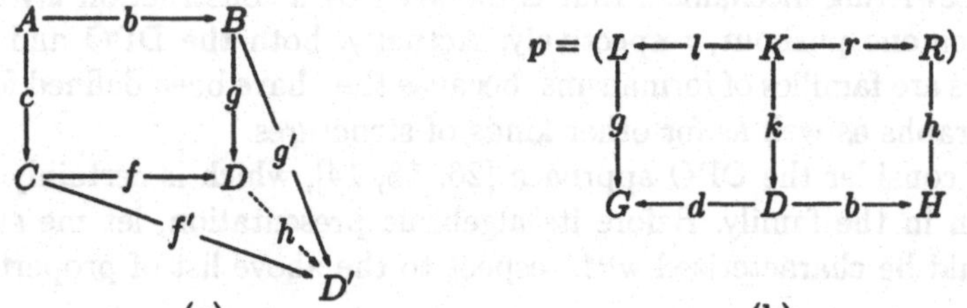

(a) (b)

Fig. 1. (a) Pushout diagram. (b) Graph rewriting via double pushout construction.

Given a *production* p having the form $p = (L \stackrel{l}{\leftarrow} K \stackrel{r}{\rightarrow} R)$ and an *occurrence morphism* $g : L \to G$ as in Figure 1 (b), the context graph D can be characterized as a *pushout complement object* of l and g, i.e., a graph such that $\langle G, g, d \rangle$ becomes a pushout in the left square; such a graph exists if the gluing conditions [18] are satisfied. In this case the derived graph H is characterized as the pushout object of r and k. Therefore we have a *direct derivation from G to H via p and g*, written $G \stackrel{p,g}{\Longrightarrow} H$ if the double-pushout diagram of Figure 1 (b) can be constructed.

This categorical characterization is the basis of the great generality and flexibility of the algebraic approaches. In fact, since the basic notions of production and direct derivation are defined in terms of diagrams and constructions in a category, they have been defined in a uniform way for a wide range of structures, simply by changing the underlying category. Moreover, many results can be proved once and for all using categorical techniques. For example, algebraic approaches (either DPO or SPO) have been defined for various kind of graphs and hypergraphs, relational structures, arbitrary algebras with monadic operators only, algebraic specifications, and others. Furthermore, *High-Level Replacement Systems* [21] have been defined by replacing a specific category of structures with a generic category **C** (satisfying certain properties).

A *graph rewriting system* is a set $\mathcal{R}$ of graph productions. A *derivation* from G to H over $\mathcal{R}$ (shortly $G \Rightarrow^*_{\mathcal{R}} H$), is a finite sequence of direct derivations of the form $G_0 \stackrel{p_1}{\Longrightarrow} G_1 \stackrel{p_2}{\Longrightarrow} \ldots \stackrel{p_n}{\Longrightarrow} G_n = H$, where $p_1, \ldots, p_n$ are in $\mathcal{R}$.

The notion of derivation just introduced is intrinsically sequential, but the categorical framework makes easy the definition of the parallel application of more than one production to a graph, and thus of parallel derivation. Given two productions $p = (L \stackrel{l}{\leftarrow} K \stackrel{r}{\rightarrow} R)$ and $p' = (L' \stackrel{l'}{\leftarrow} K' \stackrel{r'}{\rightarrow} R')$, their *parallel composition* is $p + p' = (L + L' \stackrel{l+l'}{\leftarrow} K + K' \stackrel{r+r'}{\rightarrow} R + R')$, where $+ :$ **Graph** $\times$ **Graph** $\to$ **Graph** is a coproduct functor. Since the coproduct of two graphs (i.e., their disjoint union) is only characterized up to isomorphism, the parallel production $p + p'$ is well defined only if we assume a fixed *choice of coproducts* in the category of graphs [14].

The parallel composition of productions can be iterated in the obvious way, and a ***parallel production*** (over $\mathcal{R}$) is defined inductively as either the empty production $\emptyset : \emptyset \leftarrow \emptyset \rightarrow \emptyset$, or a production $p \in \mathcal{R}$, or the parallel composition of two parallel productions. A ***parallel direct derivation*** is a direct derivation via a parallel production. A ***parallel derivation*** is a sequence of parallel direct derivations.

3 Parallelism and independence in Graph Grammars

I summarize here some basic notions and results of the classical theory of parallelism of the DPO approach on labeled, directed multigraphs, that includes some results that are reminiscent of corresponding results for Term Rewriting Systems (like the Local Church-Rosser and the Parallelism theorems). On these results are based many of the definitions and constructions presented in the next sections.

It is worth stressing here that in a DPO production $p = (L \stackrel{l}{\leftarrow} K \stackrel{r}{\rightarrow} R)$ the interface graph K specifies which items are required to exist for the application of p, and are preserved by it (in fact such items are both in L and in R). This feature can be used to specify a sort of context-dependent rewriting, and shows the greater expressive power of grammars with respect to, for example, Petri nets, that do not have the possibility of specifying the preservation of items. Furthermore, this feature causes some interesting phenomena, like the asymmetric conflicts discussed in Section 4.

Parallel independence. For $i \in \{1,2\}$, let $p_i = (L_i \stackrel{l_i}{\leftarrow} K_i \stackrel{r_i}{\rightarrow} R_i)$ be a production, and let $g_i : L_i \rightarrow G$ be an occurrence morphism satisfying the gluing conditions.

Intuitively, the two alternative direct derivations $G \stackrel{p_1,g_1}{\Longrightarrow} H_1$ and $G \stackrel{p_2,g_2}{\Longrightarrow} H_2$ (as in Figure 2) are parallel independent (of each other), if each of them can still be applied after the other one has been performed. Therefore parallel independence is analogous to the non-overlapping of redexes in the theory of TRSs, or to the concurrent enabling of transitions in Petri net theory, and, as expected, it ensures a local confluence property (see Theorem 3 below).

Interestingly enough, the two direct derivations of Figure 2 can be parallel independent even if the occurrences of their left-hand sides in G, $g_1(L_1)$ and $g_2(L_2)$, are not disjoint. In fact, it is sufficient that neither the first nor the second direct derivation deletes items of G which are also needed by the other one. Since a direct derivation does not delete from the host graph the whole occurrence of its left-hand side, but only those items that are not in the image of the interface, then for parallel independence it is sufficient that the overlapping of the left-hand sides of p_1 and p_2 in G is included in the intersection of the images of the interface graphs K_1 and K_2 in G.

Formally, the two direct derivations of Figure 2 are ***parallel independent*** if $g_1(L_1) \cap g_2(L_2) \subseteq g_1(l_1(K_1)) \cap g_2(l_2(K_2))$. The same property can be formulated

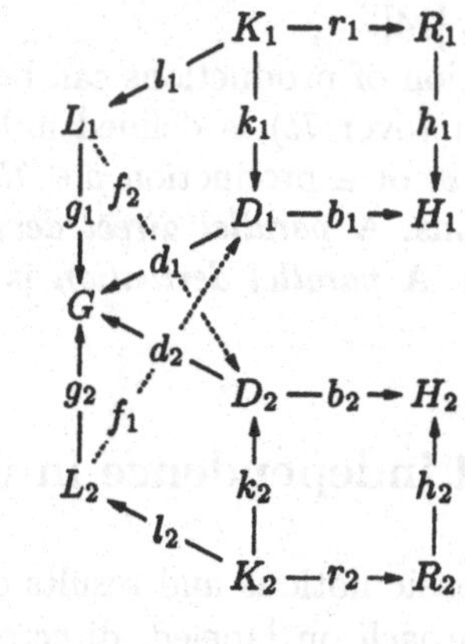

Fig. 2. Parallel independence of direct derivations

in pure categorical terms in the following way, that is applicable to any other instance of the DPO approach: There exist two morphisms $f_2 : L_1 \to D_2$ and $f_1 : L_2 \to D_1$ such that $d_2 \circ f_2 = g_1$ and $d_1 \circ f_1 = g_2$.

Applicability of parallel productions. It is well-known that two non-overlapping redexes can be reduced in parallel (the *parallel moves lemma*, e.g., in [33]), and that two concurrently enabled transitions can be fired together in a step [60]. A similar fact holds for direct derivations: they are parallel independent iff the induced parallel direct derivation can be applied to the host graph.

Proposition 1 (applicability of parallel productions). *Let $p_1 + p_2 = L_1 + L_2 \overset{l_1+l_2}{\leftarrow} K_1 + K_2 \overset{r_1+r_2}{\rightarrow} R_1 + R_2$ be a parallel production, and let $g : L_1 + L_2 \to G$ be an occurrence morphism. For each $i \in \{1,2\}$, let $g_i : L_i \to G$ be the occurrence of the i-th production in G induced by g, defined as $g_i = g \circ in^i_L$ (where $in^i_L : L_i \to L_1 + L_2$ is the coproduct injection).*

Then there is a parallel direct derivation $G \overset{p_1+p_2,g}{\Longrightarrow} H$ (i.e., the occurrence morphism g satisfies the gluing conditions), if and only if for all $i \in \{1,2\}$ the occurrence morphism g_i satisfies the gluing condition, i.e., p_i can be applied at match g_i, say with result H_i, and direct derivations $G \overset{p_1,g_1}{\Longrightarrow} H_1$ and $G \overset{p_2,g_2}{\Longrightarrow} H_2$ are parallel independent.

It is worth stressing here that this property does not hold for the SPO approach, where a parallel production can be applied even if the induced occurrences of the component productions are not parallel independent [51].

Sequential independence. Intuitively, two consecutive direct derivations $G \overset{p_1,g_1}{\Longrightarrow} H_1 \overset{p_2,g_2}{\Longrightarrow} X$ as in Figure 3 are sequentially independent if they may be swapped, i.e., if p_2 can be applied to G, and p_1 to the resulting graph.

Analogously to the case of parallel independence, it is not required that the images of the RHS of the first production and of the LHS of the second production in H_1 (i.e., $h_1(R_1)$ and $g_2(L_2)$) are disjoint. In fact, it is sufficient

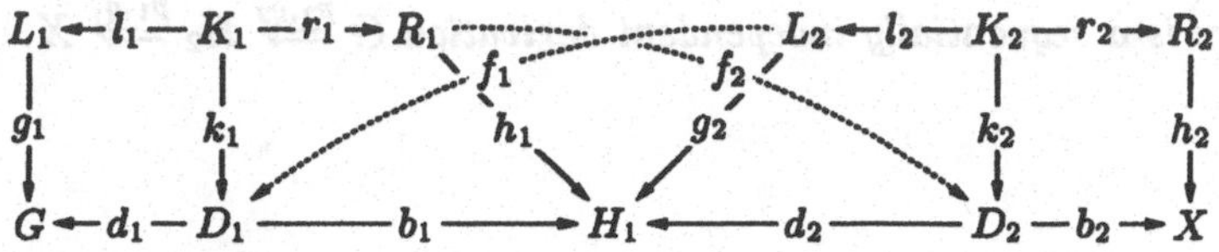

Fig. 3. Sequentially independent derivation.

that the application of p_2 does not delete anything that has been explicitly preserved by the application of p_1, and does not use (neither consuming nor preserving it) any element generated by p_1; this is ensured if the overlapping of R_1 and L_2 in H_1 is included in the intersection of the images of the interface graphs K_1 and K_2 in H_1.

Formally, the two-step derivation of Figure 3 is sequentially independent if $h_1(R_1) \cap g_2(L_2) \subseteq h_1(r_1(K_1)) \cap g_2(l_2(K_2))$ Also this property can be formulated in pure categorical terms in the following way: There exist two morphisms $f_2 : R_1 \to D_2$ and $f_1 : L_2 \to D_1$ such that $d_2 \circ f_2 = h_1$ and $b_1 \circ f_1 = g_2$.

Analysis and Synthesis. Given a parallel direct derivation $G \stackrel{p_1+p_2,g}{\Longrightarrow} X$, we know by Proposition 1 that both p_1 and p_2 are applicable to G at the occurrences induced by g, and that the resulting direct derivations are parallel independent. Because of independence, if there is a direct derivation from G to H_1 via p_1 and g_1, then we can still apply p_2 to H_1 obtaining a direct derivation $H_1 \stackrel{p_2,g_2'}{\Longrightarrow} X'$. Moreover, if the occurrence morphism g_2' is chosen in a "correct" way, then we are sure that X and X' are isomorphic, and exploiting the fact that pushout objects are defined up to isomorphism, we can have that $X = X'$.

All this is amounts to say that there is an *analysis construction* that, given a parallel direct derivation $G \stackrel{p_1+p_2,g}{\Longrightarrow} X$, transforms it in a derivation $G \stackrel{p_1,g_1}{\Longrightarrow} H_1 \stackrel{p_2,g_2'}{\Longrightarrow} X$ (with same starting end ending graphs) which, moreover, is proved to be sequentially independent.

There is also a *synthesis construction*, which is essentially the inverse of analysis. It can be applied to any sequentially independent two-step derivation, and transforms it into a parallel direct derivation between the same start and ending graphs. The explicit analysis and synthesis constructions are quite interesting, because they represent typical examples of the use of categorical techniques for proving properties in the DPO approach; they are reported for example in [46, 21, 14]. The analysis and synthesis constructions provide a *constructive* proof of the Parallelism Theorem.

Theorem 2 (Parallelism). *Given (possibly parallel) productions p_1 and p_2, the following statements are equivalent (see Figure 4):*

1. *There is a parallel direct derivation $G \stackrel{p_1+p_2,g}{\Longrightarrow} X$*
2. *There is a sequentially independent derivation $G \stackrel{p_1,g_1}{\Longrightarrow} H_1 \stackrel{p_2,g_2'}{\Longrightarrow} X$.*

3. There is a sequentially independent derivation $G \overset{p_2,g_2}{\Longrightarrow} H_2 \overset{p_1,g_1'}{\Longrightarrow} X$. □

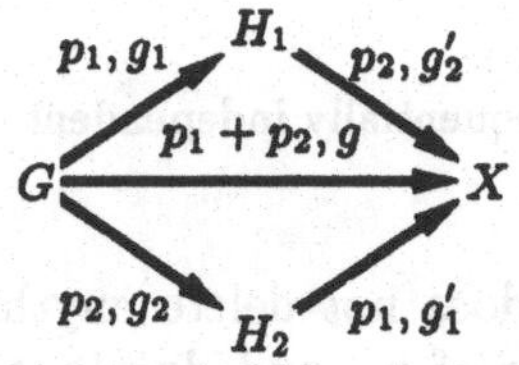

Fig. 4. Local confluence of independent direct derivations.

An easy corollary of the previous results is the following Local Church-Rosser theorem.

Theorem 3 (Local Church-Rosser).

1. *Let* $G \overset{p_1,g_1}{\Longrightarrow} H_1$ *and* $G \overset{p_2,g_2}{\Longrightarrow} H_2$ *be two direct derivations starting from the same graph, as in Figure 4. If they are parallel independent, then there are direct derivations* $H_1 \overset{p_2,g_2'}{\Longrightarrow} X$ *and* $H_2 \overset{p_1,g_1'}{\Longrightarrow} X$.
   Moreover, derivations $G \overset{p_1,g_1}{\Longrightarrow} H_1 \overset{p_2,g_2'}{\Longrightarrow} X$ *and* $G \overset{p_2,g_2}{\Longrightarrow} H_2 \overset{p_1,g_1'}{\Longrightarrow} X$ *are sequentially independent.*
2. *Conversely, if* $G \overset{p_1,g_1}{\Longrightarrow} H_1 \overset{p_2,g_2'}{\Longrightarrow} X$ *is a sequentially independent derivation, then there exists a direct derivation* $G \overset{p_2,g_2}{\Longrightarrow} H_2$ *such that* $G \overset{p_2,g_2}{\Longrightarrow} H_2$ *and* $G \overset{p_1,g_1}{\Longrightarrow} H_1$ *are parallel independent.* □

Shift equivalence. From the concurrency viewpoint it is quite obvious that the three different ways to derive graph X from G in Figure 4 (i.e., by applying first p_1 and then p_2, or first p_2 and then p_1, or both in parallel) should be considered as equivalent. This equivalence is analogous for example to the Lévy- or permutation-equivalence for TRSs, and it is called *shift equivalence* in the framework of algebraic graph grammars.

More precisely, the *shift construction* is defined as a suitable combination of analysis and synthesis. If $\rho = G \overset{p}{\Longrightarrow} H \overset{p_1+p_2}{\Longrightarrow} X$ is a derivation, and $G \overset{p}{\Longrightarrow} H \overset{p_1}{\Longrightarrow} X_1$ (which exists by Proposition 1) is sequentially independent, then we can obtain a derivation $\rho' = G \overset{p+p_1}{\Longrightarrow} X_1 \overset{p_2}{\Longrightarrow} X$ (called a *shift* of ρ) by first applying an analysis and then a synthesis construction. The *shift relation* is the transitive closure of the relation that relates two derivations iff a subderivation of the first is a shift of the corresponding subderivation of the second one, and the *shift equivalence* is its reflexive closure.

Canonical derivations. It has been shown in [46] that the shift relation is well-founded: Intuitively, the shift construction "shifts" the application of a production one step towards the beginning of the derivation, and therefore it decreases a "delay index" that cannot become negative. Moreover, in the same thesis it is shown that the shift relation enjoys a weak form of local confluence (i.e., up to isomorphism). It follows that shift-equivalent classes of graph derivations have canonical representatives (which are unique up to isomorphism). Such representatives are called *canonical derivations*, and are characterized by the fact that each direct derivation is applied as soon as possible. Canonical derivations can be considered as the graph-grammatical counterpart to left-most derivations in Chomsky grammars; moreover they are related to Petri net non-sequential processes [60], which are also standard representatives of firing sequences which differ only for the order of firing of concurrent transitions (see also Section 6).

Other interesting composition operations on productions have been studied in the algebraic theory of graph grammars: The **amalgamated composition** generalizes the parallel composition to non-parallel-independent direct derivations; and the **sequential composition** (formerly called "concurrent production") generalizes the synthesis construction to the case of a non-sequentially-independent two-step derivations (see [14] and the references therein).

4 Event Structure semantics for Graph Grammars

Event Structures [72] are widely accepted as a semantic domain for systems that manifest concurrency and non-determinism. Since the suitability of graph grammars as a formalism for the specification of concurrent and distributed systems is by now well understood, some efforts have been devoted to equip them with an event structure semantics.

The first paper on the topic is [65], where Georg Schied showed how to construct a prime event structure from a *consuming* graph grammar (i.e., a grammar where each production deletes something). He uses a *deterministic* variation of the DPO approach, in the sense that at each direct derivation the derived graph is uniquely determined by the host graph, the applied production and the occurrence morphism. This is achieved by giving to newly created items of the derived graph an identity that is uniquely determined by their generation history. To obtain a prime event structure from the collection of all derivations of a grammar starting from the start graph, he constructs as an intermediate step a *trace language* (defined using the shift-equivalence), and applies general results from [2] to extract the event structure from the trace language.

At the same time, independently, Ugo Montanari, Francesca Rossi, Hartmut Ehrig, Michael Löwe and myself started a joint research activity having the same goal of providing DPO graph grammars with an event structure semantics, but taking into account explicitly the intrinsic non-determinism of the double-pushout construction. In fact, since colimits are characterized up to isomorphism, for a given pair of arrows in the category of graphs there exist in general infinitely many pushout objects, and thus, fixed a production p and an occurrence morphism $g : L \to G$, there are in general infinitely many (isomorphic) graphs H such that $G \overset{p,g}{\Longrightarrow} H$.

To get rid of this undesirable, unbounded non-determinism, the natural way is to consider *abstract* graphs, i.e., isomorphism classes of graphs, and a suitable notion of *abstract* derivations. In [10, 8] we addressed the problem of defining a satisfactory equivalence on graph derivations that could relate derivations differing only for representation details (i.e., for the identity of nodes or edges), and that would be a congruence with respect to the fundamental operations on derivations, like sequential composition and the analysis and synthesis constructions. We showed that the equivalence relating all isomorphic derivations (recall that a derivation is just a diagram in **Graph**) does not satisfy this requirement, and therefore we introduced the equivalence denoted "$\equiv_3$": Two derivations are 3-equivalent if they are isomorphic via a family of isomorphisms such that the isomorphisms relating the start and ending graphs are *standard*. A family of *standard isomorphisms*, introduced in [10], is a family of distinguished isomorphisms, one for each pair of isomorphic graphs, closed under composition; their use in the definition of equivalence $\equiv_3$ ensures that abstract derivations (i.e., 3-equivalent classes of derivations) can be composed sequentially, and therefore that a category of abstract derivation can be defined for a given graph grammar.

This equivalence has been exploited in [11] to construct the event structure associated with a grammar. An interesting result is that the domain of finite configurations of the event structure can be obtained with an elegant construction as follows. First a category of *concatenable derivation traces* is defined, where objects are abstract graphs and arrows are equivalence classes of derivations with respect to the shift and the *abstraction* equivalence (i.e., $\equiv_3$). Then the comma category under the start graph is taken. This category is shown to be a preorder, and the induced partial order is shown to be isomorphic to the domain of the event structure.

A similar result has been obtained earlier [9] for the subclass of *safe* graph grammars, i.e., grammars where each reachable graph has no non-trivial automorphisms. In this simpler case the equivalence on derivations based on isomorphisms was sufficient, and the comma category constructed as above turned out to be a partial order isomorphic to the domain of finite configurations of a prime event structure.

For the SPO approach, an event structure semantics has been proposed by Martin Korff in [42], together with an application to Actor Systems. In a more abstract framework, Richard Banach proposes in [1] a very general categorical construction based on "op-fibrations" that should be applicable to various graph rewriting formalisms. The proposed construction is able to associate an event structure semantics with a variety of graph rewriting approaches.

Asymmetric conflicts in graph grammars. The contributions mentioned above consider prime event structures as an adequate semantic domain for graph rewriting systems. However, not all researchers agree on this. The point is that graph rewriting system manifest a form of asymmetric conflict that cannot be captured by prime event structures.

In fact, suppose that there is an item that is only read by a production p_1 (i.e., it is in the gluing graph K_1) and consumed by another production p_2. Then one would say that these production have some conflicting behavior on the common item. However, they could be safely executed in parallel, with the resulting situation in which the item has been deleted. In this case the resulting effect is the same as executing first p_1 and then p_2, while applying p_2 first (i.e., consuming the item first) makes the application of p_1 not possible anymore. Thus productions p_1 and p_2 manifest a form of *asymmetric conflict*, since they are serializable only in one order. One can also say that there is a *weak dependency* between p_1 and p_2, in the sense that if both are applied, then p_1 cannot be applied after p_2.

Concerning the DPO approach, the classical solution to this problem is simply to forbid the parallel application of weakly dependent rules, and to consider the above situation as a symmetric conflict (this is reflected in the definitions of parallel and sequential independence). The consequence of this assumption in the event structure semantics mentioned above is that, for example, the application of p_2 after p_1, and the application of p_2 alone are represented by two different events. In [15] it is proposed to allow for the synchronized application of weakly dependent productions. Under this assumption a prime event structure semantics is no more suited (in the sense that it cannot express the fact that two events can happen concurrently without allowing for all possible serializations of them): new semantic domains have to be looked for, possibly based on the work by Janicki and Koutny [34, 35], who address similar problems motivated by an analogous phenomenon manifested by Petri nets with inhibitor arcs.

It is worth stressing that in the SPO approach the natural solution is instead to allow for the parallel application of weakly dependent productions. This fact suggests that a prime event structure semantics would not be completely satisfactory for this approach.

Weak dependency situations also occur in non-orthogonal Term Graph Rewriting, as shown with a clear example in [41]. In that paper the authors show that given an *orthogonal* term graph rewriting system, with each normalizable term graph an elementary event structure can be associated, which essentially represents all the possible reduction sequences (including only *needed* redexes) from the graph to its normal form. Clark and Kennaway [3, 4] extend the construction of the prime event structure to the case of left-linear, non-orthogonal term graph rewriting systems, but they stress that in order to get a correct description of the configuration of the system, an asymmetric conflict relation must be imposed on the events.

5 Graph Rewriting Systems and Petri nets

The success of Petri nets as specification formalism for concurrent or distributed systems is due (among other things) to the fact that they can describe in a natural way the evolution of systems whose states have a distributed nature. In fact, thinking for example to Place/Transition nets, a state of the system to be specified is represented by a marking, i.e., a set of tokens distributed among a set of places. Thus the state is intrinsically distributed, and this makes easy the explicit representation of phenomena like ***mutual exclusion, concurrency, sequential composition*** and ***non-determinism.*** Nets and their semantics are therefore a reference point for any formalism intended to describe concurrent and distributed systems, and thus also for graph grammars.

In this section, after recalling the very basic definitions concerning P/T-nets, we review some encodings of nets as graph grammars proposed in literature (see also the tutorial papers [19] and [67]). These encodings are the basis of the cross-fertilization between the two fields, described in the next sections.

A (infinite capacity) ***marked Place/Transition Petri net*** (shortly ***(P/T) net***) [60] is a tuple $N = \langle S, T, F, W, M_0 \rangle$ where S is a set of ***places***; T is a set of ***transitions*** (we require that $S \cap T = \emptyset$); $F \subseteq (S \times T) \cup (T \times S)$ is a relation, called the ***causal dependency relation***; $W : F \to \mathbb{N}^+$ is a ***weight*** function (we consider W as extended canonically to $(S \times T) \cup (T \times S)$ by $W(x, y) = 0$ iff $(x, y) \notin F$); and $M_0 : S \to \mathbb{N}$ is an ***initial marking*** function.

Figure 5 (a) shows a net consisting of only one transition, depicted with the usual conventions: transitions are thick segments, places are circles, the causal dependency relation is represented by directed edges that are labeled by the weight, and the marking M_0 is depicted by drawing $M_0(X)$ tokens (black dots) in each place $X \in S$.

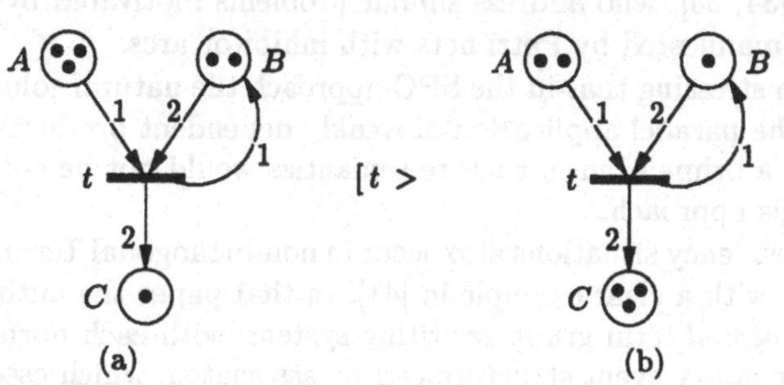

Fig. 5. (a) A marked Place/Transition Petri net. (b) The follower marking after the firing of transition t.

A ***marking*** for a P/T net $\mathbf{N}$ is a function $M : S \to \mathbb{N}$. For each transition $t \in T$, its ***precondition*** $pre(t)$ is the marking defined as $pre(t)(s) = W(s, t)$, and its ***postcondition*** $post(t)$ is the marking defined as $post(t)(s) = W(t, s)$. A transition $t \in T$ is ***enabled at*** M iff $pre(t) \leq M$.[2] If $t \in T$ is a transition which is enabled at marking M then t may ***occur*** (or ***fire***), yielding a ***follower*** marking M' defined as $M' = M - pre(t) + post(t)$. This situation is denoted by $M[t\rangle M'$.

[2] If M and M' are markings, $M \leq M'$, $M + M'$, and $M - M'$ are meant to be computed pointwise. Thus $M \leq M' \Leftrightarrow (\forall s \in S \,.\, M(s) \leq M'(s))$; $(M + M')(s) = M(s) + M'(s)$, and $(M - M')(s) = M(s) - M'(s)$ for all $s \in S$.

In the net of Figure 5 (a) transition t is enabled at marking M_0, and we have that $M_0[t\rangle M_1$, where M_1 is the marking of Figure 5 (b).

To my knowledge, Wileden [70] has been the first one to observe that graph rewriting systems can model the behaviour of Petri nets, but he did not go beyond an informal discussion of this topic.

The first formalization was proposed by Hans-Jörg Kreowski in [47] using the DPO approach, and it is shown in Figure 6.[3] The marked net of Figure 5 (a) is represented in Figure 6 by the graph $Kr(M_0)$ having three kinds of nodes (for transitions, places, and tokens, respectively) and where edges connect either places and transitions (modelling the causal dependency relation) or tokens and places (determining the place where the token lies). Transition t is represented by production $Kr(t)$ (the top row of the figure): The production does not modify the topological structure of the net (nodes and edges corresponding to places, transitions and causal dependency relation are also in the interface), but only deletes and creates the nodes representing tokens (as well as the edges connecting them to places). It is easy to check that the production is applicable to graph $Kr(M_0)$ (the gluing conditions are satisfied), and since the two squares in the figure are pushouts, that $Kr(M_0) \stackrel{Kr(t)}{\Longrightarrow} Kr(M_1)$; moreover, the derived graph $Kr(M_1)$ obviously represents marking M_1, as expected.

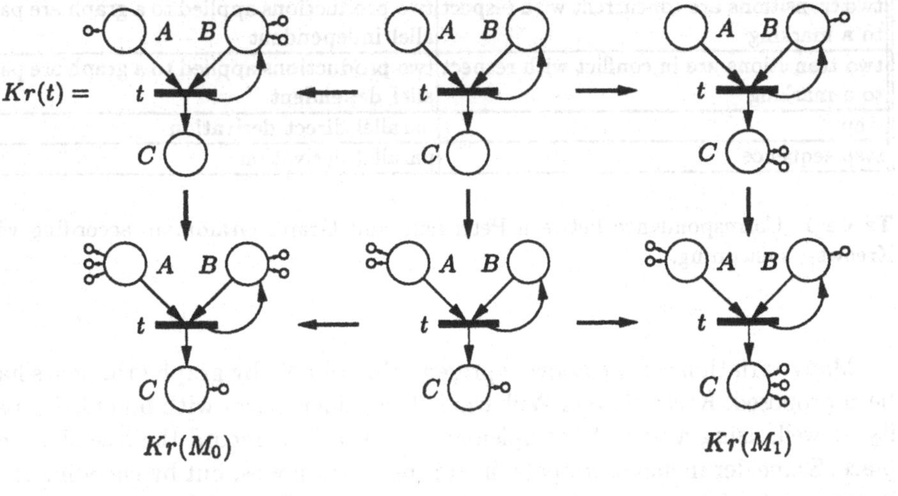

Fig. 6. Encoding of nets as grammars according to Kreowski.

[3] In the same proceedings Reisig [59] considered the relationship between nets and grammars from a different perspective, showing that all non-sequential processes (see Section 6) of a given marked net can be generated by a suitable graph grammar (using the set-theoretical approach). Intuitively, a production in this grammar corresponds to a transition of the net: Its application simulates the firing of the transition, and leaves a copy of the transition in the derived graph.

More in general it can be shown that the production representing a transition can be applied to a graph representing a marked net only if the transition is enabled at that marking, and that the derived graph represents the follower marking. An important point in the proof of this consistency result is that although in general in the DPO approach a production can be applied to a non-injective occurrence morphism, the gluing conditions ensure that such a morphism must be injective on nodes representing tokens; therefore a production requiring two tokens in a place A cannot be applied if there is only one token, even if there is a graph morphism from its left-hand side.[4]

The correspondence between direct derivations and firing of transitions can be extended easily to firing sequences, as well as to steps and step sequences. The correspondence between the very basic concepts of the two formalisms is summarized in Table 1.

PETRI NETS	GRAPH GRAMMARS
places, transitions, tokens	nodes
causal dependency relation, mapping from tokens to places	edges
marked net	labeled graph
transition enabled at a marking	production applicable to a graph
firing	direct derivation
firing sequence	derivation
two transitions are concurrent with respect to a marking	two productions applied to a graph are parallel independent
two transitions are in conflict with respect to a marking	two productions applied to a graph are parallel dependent
step	parallel direct derivation
step sequence	parallel derivation

Table 1. Correspondence between Petri nets and Graph Grammars according with Kreowski's encoding.

Many variations of the above representation of nets by graph grammars have been proposed. Kreowski and Wilharm [49] consider places with bounded capacity as well, using a sort of "complemented tokens" to record the free slots in a place. Schneider in [66] represents the tokens not as nodes, but by encoding them in the labels of the nodes corresponding to places. This is presented as a case study for a variation of the DPO approach, where graphs labeled over objects of a category are used. Choosing a suitable category for labels, it is shown that the follower marking is correctly computed as a pushout in the category of labelled graphs. Moreover, this approach can be extended by allowing *graphs* as labels

[4] This property does not hold true for example in the SPO approach, where there is no structural applicability condition. In this approach, in order to get similar consistency results, one should restrict to injective occurrence morphisms [45].

of places, obtaining a sort of high-level nets that transform graphs instead of multisets of tokens.

A quite different representation of P/T nets (with unary weights) is proposed by Genrich *et al.* in [29], using *Generalized Handle grammars*, that belong to the set-theoretical approaches. Transitions and tokens are represented by nodes, while places only appear as labels of tokens. Directed edges connect transition t to t' if $post(t) \cap pre(t') \neq \emptyset$, and moreover connect all tokens in $pre(t)$ to t and, symmetrically, t to all tokens in $post(t)$. The LHS of a production corresponding to transition t is a "generalized handle", i.e., a set of edges (one for each place in $pre(t)$) having t as common target; similarly, the RHS contains one edge for each place in $post(t)$ with t as common source. The application of this production deletes from the host graph the nodes corresponding to t and to the selected tokens in $pre(t)$, as well as all the incident edges, and inserts a copy of the RHS (i.e., the transition with all postconditions). The embedding relation creates suitable edges that rebuild the correct topology of the net.

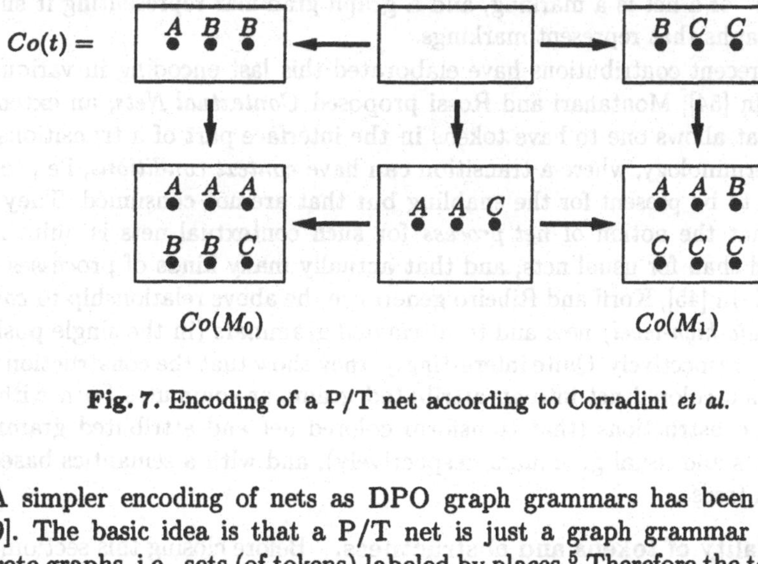

Fig. 7. Encoding of a P/T net according to Corradini *et al.*

A simpler encoding of nets as DPO graph grammars has been proposed in [9]. The basic idea is that a P/T net is just a graph grammar acting on discrete graphs, i.e., sets (of tokens) labeled by places.[5] Therefore the topological structure of the net is not represented at all: It is only recorded in the productions corresponding to the transitions. According to this intuition, the marked net of Figure 5 (a) is represented in Figure 7 by the (discrete) graph $Co(M_0)$ having one node for each token of marking M_0, labeled by the corresponding place. Transition t is represented by production $Co(t)$ (the top row of the figure), that deletes the tokens in the preconditions and creates those in the postconditions of t; note that the interface is the empty graph, as it is reasonable because all the

[5] This simple idea can hardly be considered as original: It seems to belong to the "folklore". For example, the encoding of non-sequential processes in [59] is based on a similar intuition. Also [39] mentions it explicitly.

tokens in the preconditions have to be deleted. Production $Co(t)$ is applicable to graph $Co(M_0)$ with an injective occurrence morphism, and thus the Double-Pushout diagram of Figure 7 can be constructed, showing that $Co(M_0) \stackrel{Co(t)}{\Longrightarrow} Co(M_1)$. As expected, the derived graph $Co(M_1)$ represents marking M_1 of Figure 5 (b). It is worth stressing that the correspondence between concepts of nets and of graph grammars shown in Table 1 is still valid, except for the first three rows that are simplified as follows:

tokens	nodes
places	node labels
marking	discrete, labeled graph

This simpler encoding of nets is in my view more natural than the other ones because it stresses the fact that a net is just a system that rewrites collections of tokens, i.e., markings, exactly like a Term Rewriting System rewrites terms, a Chomsky grammar rewrites strings, and a graph grammar rewrites graphs. Thus the "state" of a net is a marking, and a graph grammar representing it should rewrite graphs that represent markings.

Some recent contributions have elaborated this last encoding in various directions. In [54], Montanari and Rossi proposed *Contextual Nets*, an extension of nets that allows one to have tokens in the interface part of a transitions, or, in their terminology, where a transition can have *context conditions*, i.e., tokens that have to be present for the enabling but that are not consumed. They also showed that the notion of *net process* for such contextual nets is quite more elaborated than for usual nets, and that actually many kinds of processes may be defined. In [45], Korff and Ribeiro generalize the above relationship to *colored* (or *algebraic high-level*) nets and to *attributed* grammars (in the single pushout approach), respectively. Quite interestingly, they show that the construction that transforms a colored net into an attributed grammar commutes both with the *flattening* constructions (that transform colored net and attributed grammars in P/T nets and usual grammars, respectively), and with a semantics based on derivation trees.

Individuality of tokens and abstractness. Before closing this section, it is honest to stress that there is a subtle mismatch between net transitions and the corresponding graph productions, in *all* the encodings I mentioned. In fact, in the initial marking depicted in Figure 5 (a) the three tokens in place A are indistinguishable (i.e., in P/T nets tokens do not have an *identity*): this is formalized in literature by saying that a marking is a *multiset* over the set of places S [60], or, equivalently, that it is an element of the free commutative monoid over S [52]. As a consequence, there is only one possible firing of the transition t from marking M_0. On the contrary the three nodes labeled by A in graph $Co(M_0)$ of Figure 7 do have a distinguished identity, and indeed there are *twelve* different injective morphisms from the left-hand side of production $Co(t)$ to that $Co(M_0)$. The same observation also holds for all the other encodings.

Thus nets are "more abstract" than the corresponding grammars, or, in other words, graph grammars over discrete labeled graphs can be regarded as nets with *individual* tokens, in the sense that the different tokens in the same place can be distinguished. In [45], Korff and Ribeiro put in evidence that analogous differences of abstraction level also hold for the high-level versions of nets and grammars. In fact they show that the derivation tree semantics of a net is isomorphic to some *abstract* derivation tree semantics of the grammar encoding it.

6 Graph Grammar Processes

An *occurrence net* [60] is an acyclic net with unary weights, without forward and backward conflicts (i.e., a place cannot be in the preconditions or in the postconditions of more than one transition). A *non-sequential process* [30] of a P/T net N consists of an occurrence net K together with a net morphism $p : K \to N$ satisfying suitable conditions. Intuitively such a process records a deterministic run of net N: a transition t of K records one specific firing of transition $p(t)$, while a place s of K records the presence of a token on place $p(s)$.

There are two appealing properties of non-sequential processes, in my view. Firstly, a process represents a net computation in a truly-concurrent way as a partial order, therefore more abstractly than firing or step sequences (where a total ordering is imposed). Actually, a process can be regarded as the representative of the class of all firing (or step) sequences that differ only for the order of non-causally related transition firings. The second interesting aspect is that processes are defined in terms of a suitable subclass of nets (occurrence nets) and net morphisms. This homogeneity between systems (nets) and their truly concurrent semantics (processes) is certainly very convenient: On the one hand it confirms the suitability of nets for the specification of concurrent aspects of computing; on the other hand it makes the semantics immediately understandable to anybody familiar with nets.

Given the strong relationship between nets and graph grammars stressed in the previous section, it is not surprising that various kinds of processes have been considered as a truly-concurrent semantics for graph grammars as well. Kreowski and Wilharm [49] define *derivation processes* as partial orders of derivations steps. An equivalence is defined on processes, that essentially relates all processes containing the same derivation steps, disregarding the order and the multiplicity in which they appear. *Complete processes*, i.e., processes that for each pair of independent derivation steps contain the whole Curch-Rosser diamond (as in Figure 4), are shown to be standard representative of equivalence classes. In particular, complete *conflict-free* processes are representatives of shift-equivalence classes of sequential derivations, thus are one-to-one with canonical derivations. Various kind of transformations of derivation processes are considered in [50].

More recently *graph processes* have been proposed by the author in a joint work with Montanari and Rossi [13]. The most interesting feature of our graph processes is, in my opinion, the fact that they enjoy both properties of net processes mentioned above: In particular, they are defined as a special kind of graph grammars, together with a morphism to the original grammar. It was possible to provide such a definition by changing the classical definitions slightly, introducing the so-called *typed graph grammars*: These are standard grammars where all the involved graphs have a morphism to a fixed *type graph*, which plays a role similar to that of the set of places in a net (more formally, all involved graphs belong to the comma category of objects over the type graph). In practice, the type graph can be regarded also as a more structured presentation of the label alphabets for nodes and arcs that are part of the definition of labeled graphs.

A *(deterministic) graph process* for a given grammar $\mathcal{G}$ is an *occurrence grammar* (i.e., a grammar satisfying suitable acyclicity requirements, similar to those for occurrence nets), equipped with a morphism to $\mathcal{G}$. In this framework a graph grammar morphism consists of a graph morphism between the type graphs, and of a function relating the productions that satisfy some obvious commutativity requirements. It is not difficult to check that this definition of graph processes is a proper generalization of net non-sequential processes, provided that nets with individual tokens are considered.

A graph process can be constructed with a simple colimit construction. Given a graph derivation of grammar $\mathcal{G}$, i.e., a sequence of double-pushout diagrams, the corresponding process is obtained simply by taking as type graph the colimit object in category **Graph** of all the diagram, and as productions all the occurrences of productions of $\mathcal{G}$ that appear in the derivation; such productions have morphisms to the type graph given by the colimit injections. Interestingly, processes of *shift-equivalent* derivations are isomorphic, and therefore graph processes are a good candidate as representatives of shift-equivalence classes of derivations.

Various other process-like semantics have been proposed in literature. For example, *concurrent derivations* have been proposed by Korff in [42, 43] as a notion of deterministic processes for grammars in the single-pushout approach (a non-deterministic extension is proposed in [44]). Also concurrent derivations are obtained as colimits of derivation diagrams, and they can be considered as grammars; in particular, their *core graph* corresponds exactly to our type graph. In [61] Ribeiro proposes a notion of non-deterministic unfolding of graph grammars in the SPO approach. Such unfolding is itself a grammar and can be regarded as a non-deterministic process.

A process semantics has been proposed by Janssens for Extended Structure Morphisms systems, which are an evolution of Actor Grammars [40] and are based on the NLC approach to graph rewriting. In [36] the notion of a computation structure is introduced; a computation structure formalizes a rewriting process of an ESM system. The notion may be seen as an improved and generalized version of the computation graphs from [38]. It is shown in [39] that abstract computation structures and concrete configuration graphs form a category that is a natural generalization of the well-known notion of a transition system. The set (or category) of computation structures may be taken as the basic process semantics of an ESM system.

7 Towards a categorical semantics for graph grammars

The previous sections showed that as far as concurrent semantic constructions and results are concerned, the gap between nets and grammars is being filled up quickly. However, with respect to Petri nets and to other formalisms aimed at describing concurrent and distributed systems (like Event Structures, Asynchronous Transition Systems and others [57, 2, 52, 64]) the classical theory of graph grammars still lacks a formal categorical, in-the-large treatment. In the works just referred to, the above mentioned formalisms are equipped with a functorial semantics where the leading idea is to define suitable categories of "systems", and to relate them with pairs of adjoint functors. Such semantics (that I call "in-the-large" because the emphasis is on properties of a whole class of systems, as opposed to the "in-the-small" semantics, which study properties of a single system) are useful to understand the relationships between different formalisms, or also to relate different aspects of the same formalism.

As paradigmatical examples of the use of categories in the semantics of nets, I mention [71] and [52]. In [71] Winskel shows that the event structure semantics of *safe* nets can be given through a chain of adjunctions starting from the category **Safe** of safe nets, through category **Occ** of occurrence nets (this result has been generalized to arbitrary P/T nets in [53]). In other words, this implies that the construction of the event structure of nets can be made *functorial*, i.e., consistent with a reasonable notion of net morphism. Also, in [52] Meseguer and Montanari show that there is an adjunction between the category of P/T nets **Petri** and the category of their computational models **CatPetri**. Intuitively, the free model of a net is a small category, equipped with a suitable algebraic structure, where each arrow is a computation of the net.

The chains of adjunctions mentioned above are just prototypical examples of a general technique in the categorical semantics of concurrency. Other adjuctions relating categories of systems can be found in [2, 53, 64].

As far as graph grammars are concerned, the issue of providing a functorial semantics similar to that of nets has been addressed only very recently. For such semantics, an obvious precondition is the definition of a reasonable notion of *graph grammar morphisms*. Quite surprisingly, such a concept does not appear in the classical literature of the area, but has gained only recently some attention in the community, leading to a number of alternative definitions. All of them are based on the notion of typed graph grammar (already mentioned in Section 6). A grammar is defined as a quadruple $\mathcal{G} = \langle TG, P, \pi, G_0 \rangle$, where TG is the type graph, P is a set of production names, π associates with each production name a production, and G_0 is the start graph. All graphs involved in the grammar belong to the comma category over TG, i.e., are equipped with a morphism to TG in such a way that all resulting diagrams commute.

A morphism of typed graph grammars $h : \mathcal{G} \to \mathcal{G}'$ consists of two components: h_{TG}, that relates in some way the type graphs TG and TG', and h_P that is a function relating the sets of production names. Whatever is the definition of h_{TG} (for which the various proposal differ), it is important that it induces a functor from the comma category over TG to that over TG'. Using this functor one can express natural consistency requirements for morphisms, for example that this functor maps G_0 to (an isomorphic graph of) G'_0, and similarly for left- and right-hand sides of all productions. A very general notion of morphism is proposed in [7], where h_{TG} can be an arbitrary span (i.e., a pair of morphisms with common source) in **Graph**. In [12, 32] h_{TG} is a partial graph morphism from TG to TG', and similarly in [61] but in the opposite direction.

It is worth stressing that the most general definition of graph grammar morphisms was obtained by regarding the definitions of nets (with individual tokens) and of their morphisms as suitable diagrams in the category **Set**, and by considering exactly the same diagrams, but in the category **Graph**, as the corresponding definitions for grammars.

A first contribution to the functorial semantics of grammars is [7], where beside of introducing grammar morphisms, we proposed a semantics for graph grammars borrowing the general outline from [52]. We defined three categories: **GraGra**, having typed graph grammars as objects and grammar morphisms as arrows; **GraTS**, with (typed) graph transition systems as objects; and **GraCat**, having small categories of (typed) graph derivations as objects. The main result is that there exist left adjoint functors TS : **GraGra** $\to$ **GraTS** and C : **GraGra** $\to$ **GraCat** to the forgetful functors U : **GraTS** $\to$ **GraGra** and V : **GraCat** $\to$ **GraGra**, respectively.

In her doctoral thesis [61], Ribeiro defines an unfolding functor from the category of graph grammars to a category of (abstract) *occurrence grammars*, and she shows that it is a right adjoint to a suitable *folding functor*. This result is exploited to prove that the unfolding semantics is compositional with respect to certain operations on grammars defined in terms of limits.

8 Conclusions

In this tutorial paper I revisited various constructions and results concerning concurrency aspects of the theory of graph rewriting systems. Most of them have been developed for the algebraic approaches. I first summarized the basic notions and results that go back to the early seventies, and that can be considered as translations or extensions of parallelism results for Term Rewriting Systems to graph grammars. Then I analyzed in depth the relationships with Petri nets. Through various encodings of nets as grammars a robust link between the two theories is established, that allowed for the study in the graph grammar framework of notions originally developed for nets, including processes, event structure based semantics, and functorial semantics.

Let me add here that various definitions and constructions of Place/Transitions Petri nets and Graph Grammars can be regarded as based on suitable diagrams having the same shape, but belonging to different categories: **Set** and **Graph**, respectively. This is a powerful (although informal) "meta-result" that it should be possible to exploit further for the cross-fertilization of the two fields. For example, for any concept about nets one can try to generalize it to graph grammars simply by isolating the notions based on sets, and by replacing them with the corresponding notions based on graphs. Such a procedure is by no way automatic: the same set-based notion can have many different generalizations to graphs, and the choice of the right one is in general not trivial. However, the categorical framework often narrows the possible choices, making the work easier. Just to mention a possible application of this idea, it would be interesting to explore how the theory of net invariants translates to graph grammars.

Generalizing even further, one may think to nets and grammars as two instantiations of a more abstract theory of concurrent semantics where **Set** and **Graph** are replaced by an arbitrary category **C** satisfying suitable requirements (in the same spirit of High-Level Replacement Systems [21]). However, it is not clear if some relevant constructions can be described in such an abstract framework, neither if there exist other interesting instantiations besides nets and graph grammars.

References

1. R. Banach. DPO Rewriting and Abstract Semantics via Opfibrations. In A. Corradini and U. Montanari, editors, *Proceedings SEGRAGRA'95*, volume 2 of *Electronic Notes in Theoretical Computer Science*. Elsevier Sciences, 1995. `http://www.elsevier.nl/locate/entcs/volume2.html`.
2. M.A. Bednarczyk. *Categories of asynchronous systems*. PhD thesis, University of Sussex, 1988. Report no. 1/88.
3. D. Clark and R. Kennaway. Some Properties of Non-Orthogonal Term Graph Rewriting. In A. Corradini and U. Montanari, editors, *Proceedings SEGRAGRA'95*, volume 2 of *Electronic Notes in Theoretical Computer Science*. Elsevier Sciences, 1995. `http://www.elsevier.nl/locate/entcs/volume2.html`.
4. D. Clark and R. Kennaway. Event Structures and Non-Orthogonal Term Graph Rewriting. *Mathematical Structures in Computer Science*, 1996. To appear.
5. V. Claus, H. Ehrig, and G. Rozenberg, editors. *Proceedings of the 1st International Workshop on Graph-Grammars and Their Application to Computer Science and Biology*, volume 73 of *LNCS*. Springer Verlag, 1979.
6. A. Corradini. Concurrent Computing: From Petri Nets to Graph Grammars. In A. Corradini and U. Montanari, editors, *Proceedings SEGRAGRA'95*, volume 2 of *Electronic Notes in Theoretical Computer Science*. Elsevier Sciences, 1995. `http://www.elsevier.nl/locate/entcs/volume2.html`.
7. A. Corradini, H. Ehrig, M. Löwe, U. Montanari, and J. Padberg. The category of Typed Graph Grammars and its adjunctions with categories of derivations. In *Proceedings of the Fifth International Workshop on Graph Grammars and their Application to Computer Science*, LNCS. Springer Verlag, 1996. To appear.
8. A. Corradini, H. Ehrig, M. Löwe, U. Montanari, and F. Rossi. Abstract Graph Derivations in the Double-Pushout Approach. In H.-J. Schneider and H. Ehrig, editors, *Proceedings of the Dagstuhl Seminar 9301 on Graph Transformations in Computer Science*, volume 776 of *LNCS*, pages 86–103. Springer Verlag, 1994.

9. A. Corradini, H. Ehrig, M. Löwe, U. Montanari, and F. Rossi. An event structure semantics for safe graph grammars. In E.-R. Olderog, editor, *Programming Concepts, Methods and Calculi*, IFIP Transactions A-56, pages 423–444. North-Holland, 1994.
10. A. Corradini, H. Ehrig, M. Löwe, U. Montanari, and F. Rossi. Note on standard representation of graphs and graph derivations. In H.-J. Schneider and H. Ehrig, editors, *Proceedings of the Dagstuhl Seminar 9301 on Graph Transformations in Computer Science*, volume 776 of *LNCS*, pages 104–118. Springer Verlag, 1994.
11. A. Corradini, H. Ehrig, M. Löwe, U. Montanari, and F. Rossi. An Event Structure Semantics for Graph Grammars with Parallel Productions. In *Proceedings of the Fifth International Workshop on Graph Grammars and their Application to Computer Science*, LNCS. Springer Verlag, 1996. To appear.
12. A. Corradini and R. Heckel. A Compositional Approach to Structuring and Refinement of Typed Graph Grammars. In A. Corradini and U. Montanari, editors, *Proceedings SEGRAGRA'95*, volume 2 of *Electronic Notes in Theoretical Computer Science*. Elsevier Sciences, 1995. `http://www.elsevier.nl/locate/entcs/volume2.html`.
13. A. Corradini, U. Montanari, and F. Rossi. Graph processes. *Fundamenta Informaticae*, 1996. to appear.
14. A. Corradini, U. Montanari, F. Rossi, H. Ehrig, R. Heckel, and M. Löwe. Algebraic Approaches to Graph Transformation I: Basic Concepts and Double Pushout Approach. In G. Rozenberg, editor, *The Handbook of Graph Grammars, Volume I: Foundations*. World Scientific, 1996. To appear.
15. A. Corradini and F. Rossi. Synchronized Composition of Graph Grammar Productions. In *Proceedings of the Fifth International Workshop on Graph Grammars and their Application to Computer Science*, LNCS. Springer Verlag, 1996. To appear.
16. P. Degano and U. Montanari. A model of distributed systems based on graph rewriting. *Journal of the ACM*, 34:411–449, 1987.
17. F. Drewes, A. Habel, and H.-J. Kreowski. Hyperedge Replacement Graph Grammars. In G. Rozenberg, editor, *Handbook of Graph Transformations. Vol. I: Foundations*. World Scientific, 1996. To appear.
18. H. Ehrig. Introduction to the Algebraic Theory of Graph Grammars. In V. Claus, H. Ehrig, and G. Rozenberg, editors, *Proceedings of the 1st International Workshop on Graph-Grammars and Their Application to Computer Science and Biology*, volume 73 of *LNCS*, pages 1–69. Springer Verlag, 1979.
19. H. Ehrig. Aspects of Concurrency in Graph Grammars. In H. Ehrig, M. Nagl, and G. Rozenberg, editors, *Proceedings of the 2nd International Workshop on Graph-Grammars and Their Application to Computer Science*, volume 153 of *LNCS*, pages 58–81. Springer Verlag, 1983.
20. H. Ehrig. Tutorial introduction to the algebraic approach of graph-grammars. In H. Ehrig, M. Nagl, G. Rozenberg, and A. Rosenfeld, editors, *Proceedings of the 3rd International Workshop on Graph-Grammars and Their Application to Computer Science*, volume 291 of *LNCS*, pages 3–14. Springer Verlag, 1987.
21. H. Ehrig, A. Habel, H.-J. Kreowski, and F. Parisi-Presicce. Parallelism and Concurrency in High-Level Replacement Systems. *Mathematical Structures in Computer Science*, 1:361–404, 1991.
22. H. Ehrig, R. Heckel, M. Korff, M. Löwe, L. Ribeiro, A. Wagner, and A. Corradini. Algebraic Approaches to Graph Transformation II: Single Pushout Approach and comparison with Double Pushout Approach. In G. Rozenberg, editor, *The Hand-*

book of Graph Grammars, Volume I: Foundations. World Scientific, 1996. To appear.
23. H. Ehrig, H.-J. Kreowski, and G. Rozenberg, editors. *Proceedings of the 4th International Workshop on Graph-Grammars and Their Application to Computer Science*, volume 532 of *LNCS*. Springer Verlag, 1991.
24. H. Ehrig, M. Nagl, and G. Rozenberg, editors. *Proceedings of the 2nd International Workshop on Graph-Grammars and Their Application to Computer Science*, volume 153 of *LNCS*. Springer Verlag, 1983.
25. H. Ehrig, M. Nagl, G. Rozenberg, and A. Rosenfeld, editors. *Proceedings of the 3rd International Workshop on Graph-Grammars and Their Application to Computer Science*, volume 291 of *LNCS*. Springer Verlag, 1987.
26. H. Ehrig, M. Pfender, and H.J. Schneider. Graph-grammars: an algebraic approach. In *Proceedings IEEE Conf. on Automata and Switching Theory*, pages 167–180, 1973.
27. J. Engelfriet and G. Rozenberg. Node Replacement Graph Grammars. In G. Rozenberg, editor, *Handbook of Graph Rewriting, Vol. I: Foundations.* World Scientific, 1996. To appear.
28. G. Engels and G. Rozenberg, editors. *Preliminary Proceedings of the Fifth International Workshop on Graph Grammars and their Application to Computer Science*, 1994.
29. H.J. Genrich, D. Janssens, G. Rozenberg, and P.S. Thiagarajan. Petri nets and their relation to graph grammars. In H. Ehrig, M. Nagl, and G. Rozenberg, editors, *Proceedings of the 2nd International Workshop on Graph-Grammars and Their Application to Computer Science*, volume 153 of *LNCS*, pages 115–129. Springer Verlag, 1983.
30. U. Golz and W. Reisig. The Non-sequential Behaviour of Petri Nets. *Info. and Co.*, 57:125–147, 1983.
31. A. Habel. *Hyperedge replacement: Grammars and languages*, volume 643 of *LNCS*. Springer Verlag, 1992.
32. R. Heckel, A. Corradini, H. Ehrig, and M. Löwe. Horizontal and Vertical Structuring of Graph Transformation Systems. *Mathematical Structures in Computer Science*, 1996. To appear.
33. G. Huet and J-J. Lévy. Computations in Orthogonal Rewriting Systems, I. In J.-L. Lassez and G. Plotkin, editors, *Festschrift in Honor of J. A. Robinson*, pages 395–414. MIT Press, 1991.
34. R. Janicki and M Koutny. Invariant semantics of nets with inhibitor arcs. In *Proceedings CONCUR '91*, volume 527 of *LNCS*. Springer Verlag, 1991.
35. R. Janicki and M Koutny. Structure of concurrency. *Theoret. Comput. Sci.*, 112:5–52, 1993.
36. D. Janssens. ESM systems and the composition of their computations. In *Graph Transformations in Computer Science*, volume 776 of *LNCS*, pages 203–217. Springer Verlag, 1994.
37. D. Janssens, H.-J. Kreowski, G. Rozenberg, and H. Ehrig. Concurrency of node-label-controlled graph transformations. Technical Report 82-38, Antwerp, 1982.
38. D. Janssens, M. Lens, and G. Rozenberg. Computation graphs for actor grammars. *Computer and System Sciences*, 46:60–90, 1993.
39. D. Janssens and T. Mens. Abstract semantics for ESM systems. Technical Report 95-04, University of Antwerp - UIA, dept. of Math. and Comp. Sci., 1995. to appear in Fundamenta Informaticae.

40. D. Janssens and G. Rozenberg. Actor Grammars. *Mathematical Systems Theory*, 22:75–107, 1989.
41. J.R. Kennaway, J.W. Klop, M.R. Sleep, and F.J. de Vries. Event structures and orthogonal term graph rewriting. In M.R. Sleep, M.J. Plasmeijer, and M.C. van Eekele, editors, *Term Graph Rewriting: Theory and Practice*, pages 141–155. Wiley, London, 1993.
42. M. Korff. True Concurrency Semantics for Single Pushout Graph Transformations with Applications to Actor Systems. In *Proceedings International Workshop on Information Systems – Corretness and Reusability, IS-CORE'94*, pages 244–258. Vrije Universiteit Press, 1994. Tech. Report IR-357.
43. M. Korff. *Generalized graph structure grammars with applications to concurrent object-oriented systems.* PhD thesis, Technische Universität Berlin, 1996.
44. M. Korff and L. Ribeiro. Concurrent Derivations as Single Pushout Graph Grammar Processes. In A. Corradini and U. Montanari, editors, *Proceedings SEGRA-GRA'95*, volume 2 of *Electronic Notes in Theoretical Computer Science*. Elsevier Sciences, 1995. `http://www.elsevier.nl/locate/entcs/volume2.html`.
45. M. Korff and L. Ribeiro. An Attributed Graph Transformation Approach to the Behaviour of Algebraic High-Level Nets. In *Proceedings of the Fifth International Workshop on Graph Grammars and their Application to Computer Science*, LNCS. Springer Verlag, 1996. To appear.
46. H.-J. Kreowski. *Manipulation von Graphmanipulationen.* PhD thesis, Technische Universität Berlin, 1977.
47. H.-J. Kreowski. A comparison between Petri nets and graph grammars. In H. Noltemeier, editor, *Proceedings GraphTheoretic Concepts in Computer Science WG80*, volume 100 of *LNCS*, pages 306–317. Springer Verlag, 1981.
48. H.-J. Kreowski. Is parallelism already concurrency? Part 1: Derivations in graph grammars. In H. Ehrig, M. Nagl, G. Rozenberg, and A. Rosenfeld, editors, *Proceedings of the 3rd International Workshop on Graph-Grammars and Their Application to Computer Science*, volume 291 of *LNCS*, pages 343–360. Springer Verlag, 1987.
49. H.-J. Kreowski and A. Wilharm. Net processes correspond to derivation processes in graph grammars. *Theoret. Comput. Sci.*, 44:275–305, 1986.
50. H.-J. Kreowski and A. Wilharm. Is parallelism already concurrency? Part 2: Non-sequential processes in graph grammars. In H. Ehrig, M. Nagl, G. Rozenberg, and A. Rosenfeld, editors, *Proceedings of the 3rd International Workshop on Graph-Grammars and Their Application to Computer Science*, volume 291 of *LNCS*, pages 361–377. Springer Verlag, 1987.
51. M. Löwe. Algebraic approach to single-pushout graph transformation. *Theoret. Comput. Sci.*, 109:181–224, 1993.
52. J. Meseguer and U. Montanari. Petri nets are monoids. *Info. and Co.*, 88:105–155, 1990.
53. J. Meseguer, U. Montanari, and V. Sassone. On the semantics of Petri nets. In *Proceedings CONCUR '92*, volume 630 of *LNCS*, pages 286–301. Springer Verlag, 1992.
54. U. Montanari and F. Rossi. Contextual nets. *Acta Informatica*, 32, 1995. Also as Technical Report TR 4-93, Department of Computer Science, University of Pisa, February 1993.
55. M. Nagl. Set theoretic approaches to graph grammars. In H. Ehrig, M. Nagl, G. Rozenberg, and A. Rosenfeld, editors, *Proceedings of the 3rd International*

Workshop on Graph-Grammars and Their Application to Computer Science, volume 291 of *LNCS*, pages 41–54. Springer Verlag, 1987.

56. Manfred Nagl. *Graph-Grammatiken: Theorie, Anwendungen,Implementierungen.* Vieweg, Braunschweig, 1979.
57. M. Nielsen, G. Plotkin, and G. Winskel. Petri Nets, Event Structures and Domains, Part 1. *Theoret. Comput. Sci.*, 13:85–108, 1981.
58. C.A. Petri. *Kommunikation mit Automaten.* Schriften des Institutes für Instrumentelle Matematik, Bonn. 1962.
59. W. Reisig. A graph grammar representation of nonsequential processes. In H. Noltemeier, editor, *Proceedings Graphtheoretic Concepts in Computer Science WG80*, volume 100 of *LNCS*, pages 318–325. Springer Verlag, 1981.
60. W. Reisig. *Petri Nets: An Introduction.* EACTS Monographs on Theoretical Computer Science. Springer Verlag, 1985.
61. L. Ribeiro. *Parallel Composition and Unfolding Semanics of Graph Grammars.* PhD thesis, Technische Universität Berlin, 1996.
62. G. Rozenberg. Behaviour of Elementary Net Systems. In *Petri Nets: Central Models and Their Properties*, volume 254 of *LNCS*, pages 60–94. Springer Verlag, 1987.
63. G. Rozenberg, editor. *The Handbook of Graph Grammars, Volume I: Foundations.* World Scientific, 1996. To appear.
64. V. Sassone, M. Nielsen, and G. Winskel. Relationships between models of concurrency. In *Proceedings REX '93*, 1993.
65. G. Schied. On relating Rewriting Systems and Graph Grammars to Event Structures. In H.-J. Schneider and H. Ehrig, editors, *Proceedings of the Dagstuhl Seminar 9301 on Graph Transformations in Computer Science*, volume 776 of *LNCS*, pages 326–340. Springer Verlag, 1994.
66. H.-J. Schneider. On categorical graph grammars integrating structural transformations and operations on labels. *Theoret. Comput. Sci.*, 109:257–274, 1993.
67. H.-J. Schneider. Graph Grammars as a Tool to Define the Behaviour of Process Systems: From Petri Nets to Linda. In G. Engels and G. Rozenberg, editors, *Preliminary Proceedings of the Fifth International Workshop on Graph Grammars and their Application to Computer Science*, 1994.
68. H.J. Schneider. Describing distributed systems by categorial graph grammars. In *15th International Workshop on Graph-theoretic Concepts in Computer Science*, volume 411 of *LNCS*, pages 121–135. Springer Verlag, 1990.
69. G. Taentzer. *Parallel and distributed graph transformation: Formal description and application to communication-based systems.* PhD thesis, Technische Universität Berlin, 1996.
70. J.C. Wileden. Relationships between graph grammars and the design and analysis of concurrent software. In V. Claus, H. Ehrig, and G. Rozenberg, editors, *Proceedings of the 1st International Workshop on Graph-Grammars and Their Application to Computer Science and Biology*, volume 73 of *LNCS*, pages 456–463. Springer Verlag, 1979.
71. G. Winskel. Event Structures. In *Petri Nets: Applications and Relationships to Other Models of Concurrency*, volume 255 of *LNCS*, pages 325–392. Springer Verlag, 1987.
72. G. Winskel. An Introduction to Event Structures. In *Linear Time, Branching Time and Partial Order in Logics and Models for Concurrency*, volume 354 of *LNCS*, pages 325–392. Springer Verlag, 1989.

Petri Boxes and Finite Precedence

Raymond Devillers *

Abstract. The paper shows that even the infinite nets arising from the application of the (non-guarded as well as guarded) recursion operator in the Petri Box Calculus exhibit the "finite precedence" property, i.e. each event in a process only has finitely many predecessor events, and each "complete" process only has finitely many events. The techniques used in the paper extensively exploit the labelled tree device introduced in the definition of the general recursion operator, the general properties of the latter, and the S-invariant analysis results obtained in a previous paper.

1 Introduction

The Petri Box Calculus (PBC for short) is a Petri net based theory developed with the aim at easing the compositional definition of the Petri net semantics of various concurrent programming languages [20, 7], following the schema:

Program in a concurrent language $\Rightarrow$ *Box expression* $\Rightarrow$ *Petri Box*

It is composed of two parts: a syntactic domain of Box expressions (a process algebra very much inspired from CCS, but with more general labels and operators) and a semantic domain of Petri Boxes (classes of labelled Petri nets, with the same algebraic structure as Box expressions, which may be used to model the latter but may also be studied for themselves), plus higher level versions of them [22, 5, 19].

The recursion operator generally leads to infinite nets, with a well-defined systematic structure and some peculiarities. Let us consider for instance the model of the expression $(\mu X.(a\|X));b$ exhibited in Figure 1.

This net is infinite to the right, so that transition b has an infinite in-degree and thus needs the completion of the infinitely many a_i's transitions ($i = 0, 1, 2, \ldots$) to occur. Now the semantics of infinite nets has been thoroughly examined in [1, 2], and it was observed that it is possible to allow infinite steps, by firing simultaneously infinitely many concurrent transitions, which then allows to consider evolutions of a system which may not be equivalently obtained by arbitrary interleavings as is usually the case (unless allowing transfinite evolutions). In terms of the process semantics of nets, this amounts to allowing processes with events having infinitely many predecessors, provided the causal chains from the initial situation to them have a bounded length. At that point the special places e_∞ and i_∞ in the figure deserve a special attention; indeed, beside the fact they arise

* Département d'Informatique, Université Libre de Bruxelles, Boulevard du Triomphe, 1050 Bruxelles, Belgium; e-mail address: rdevil@ulb.ac.be.

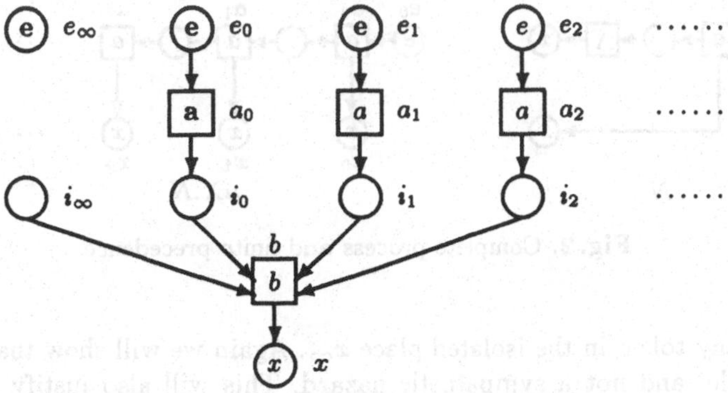

Fig. 1. Petri Box model of $(\mu X.(a\|X));b$

naturally in the theory (see [3]) and are necessary to get a non-ambiguous definition of the recursion operator (in general there are many solutions to the fixpoint equation associated with the operator, and there is no least solution while there is a unique maximal one, sometimes introducing strange places of the kind e_∞, i_∞ [8]), they will have here a special consequence; if these two places were dropped, the result would still be a (non-maximal) solution of the associated fixpoint equation, but then after firing concurrently all the a_i's transition in a row it would be possible to fire b with infinitely many causal predecessors; on the contrary, with these two places, even after concurrently firing all the a_i's, b will still miss the token in i_∞, and there will be no event with infinitely many causes. We shall show in this paper that this is not a fortunate circumstance but the general rule; as a consequence also, interleaving semantics do not lose any interesting evolutions and our results based on S-invariant analyses ([15, 14]) may be applied in all generality; this will also, a posteriori, justify constructions used in [10], where it was implicitely assumed that all events in a process were finitely preceded.

Another observation, different but of the same nature, concerns the terminated evolutions, i.e., such that all the exit places get tokens (in fact exactly one each, from the results of [14], if we start from the natural initial marking which puts one token in each entry place). Let us consider for instance the nets exhibited in Figure 2. Again, $\mu X.N$ is an infinite net, but here the (unique) infinite evolution may not be reduced to a finite succession of steps; the final cut of the corresponding process corresponds to the limit marking with one token in each of the x_i's places; if we dropped the special x_∞ place, which is again not essential to get a valid fixpoint solution of the associated recursive equation, this would lead to a complete process, in the sense that the final cut corresponds to the natural final marking, with one token in each x-place, with infinitely many events (one for each a_i); but with x_∞, which was introduced in order to get the unique maximal fixpoint solution, the situation is more appealing: while the cut only contains terminal conditions, the process is not complete since there will

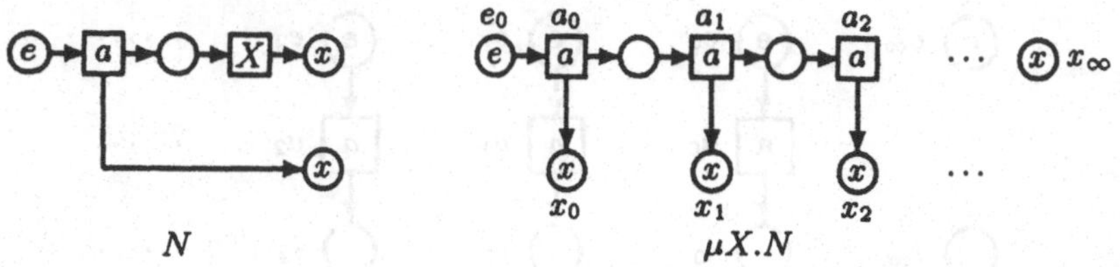

Fig. 2. Complete process and finite precedence

never be any token in the isolated place x_∞. Again we will show that this is the general rule, and not a sympathetic hazard. This will also justify a posteriori another implicit assumption used in the constructions of [10]. For instance, let us assume that a Box B is obtained by putting two component boxes B_1 and B_2 in sequence; one expects that processes of B may be constructed by putting in sequence a complete process of B_1 and any process of B_2, but if the first one is not event-finite, it could happen that the result is not a process.

2 Previous Definitions and Results

2.1 Petri Boxes and their Operators

Petri Boxes are classes of labelled P/T nets. The labels materialize various forms of interfaces allowing to combine Boxes together; places may have $e - x$ labels which are used in control flow (or vertical) operations, empty labels characterizing internal local states; transitions may have hierarchical labels (from some variable name set, plus possibly pending transformations to be applied later), also used for control flow operations, or communication labels (multisets of elementary actions), used in communication (horizontal) operators (between Boxes or with the environment), empty labels characterizing again internal (invisible from outside) transitions. Entry places may not have input transitions, output places may not have output transitions, but each transition must both have input and output places. The equivalence relation, used to define classes of (equivalent) nets constituting a Box, allows to add or drop communication transitions or places with the same label and connectivity. An example of (a representative) of a Box is shown on Figure 3.

Many operators are available to handle Petri Boxes, but horizontal ones will not be considered here since it is clear that they never invalidate the finite precedence property, both for events and for complete evolutions. Indeed, *relabellings* only change the labels of the transitions, and thus do not modify the structure of processes; *restrictions* simply drop some transitions, and this again never introduce new process structures; *synchronisations* only add transitions corresponding to finite steps of original ones (with modified labels), and this never creates infinite precedence if there was none before; *scopings* are simply a particular combination of synchronisations and restrictions. Recently, more general relabelling,

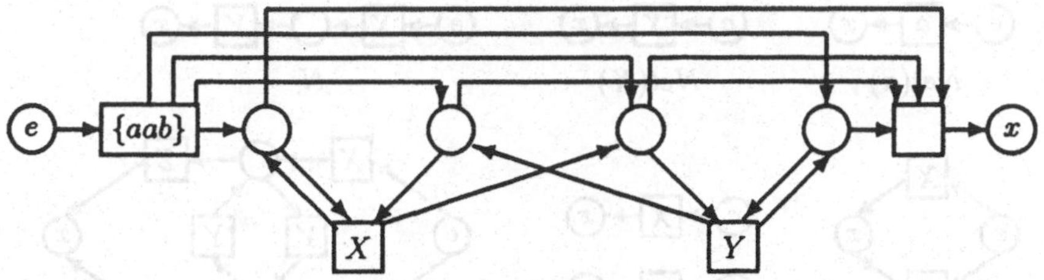

Fig. 3. A Box representative

synchronisation and restriction schemes have been considered [11, 12, 13, 18], but they still stick to the general principles mentionned above, and we shall assume this will still be true for any future extension of the present Petri Box theory.

In the standard Petri Box Calculus, if we forget horizontal operators, all the Boxes which arise in the theory result from putting side by side a *control flow* Box and a finite number of *data* Boxes [7, 5, 6, 21]. The data Boxes considered up to now may be infinite, but they all fulfill the finite precedence condition, both for events and complete evolutions. Of course, the theory is not at all fixed in that respect and other kinds of data Boxes could be introduced in the future in order to cope with other kinds of data structures, but we feel that it is not too restrictive to assume that the finite precedence condition will still be verified for them. Hence, we only have to consider the control flow Boxes.

As far as control flow Boxes are concerned, it has been noticed in [3, 9] that the usual control flow operators (sequence, choice, parallel composition, iteration) may be synthesized through refinements from simple *operative* Boxes ($N_;$, $N_{\Box}$, $N_{\|}$, N_*), shown in Figure 4. More generally, it has been shown in [15] that, in the standard theory, any control flow Box may be expressed as a single (simultaneous) recursion $\mu\{X_i.N_i|i \in I\}N$, meaning that in the net N each X_i-labelled transition has to be replaced (more exactly, refined) by the corresponding net N_i, recursively since the N_i's may themselves exhibit new X_j's, where I is a finite indexing set and each N_i or N is a copy of some basic or operative net (the basic nets, $Net(\alpha)$ and $Net(X)$, are also shown in Figure 4).

The basic and operative nets have some interesting properties in common: they are all finite, do not have side conditions and are covered by 1-conservative S-components (see next subsection). Again however, the theory is not fully fixed: alternate operative Boxes have been proposed for the iteration operator, for instance, and in the future, other operative Boxes could also be introduced in order to synthesize new vertical operators, but we shall assume they will all fulfill the very same constraints.

The recursion operator may be defined as follows (see [3, 8, 9, 15, 21] for more explanations and concrete examples): $\mu\{X_i.N_i|i \in I\}N$ is the labelled net $\tilde{N} = (\tilde{S}, \tilde{T}, \tilde{F}, \tilde{\lambda})$, where

1. the set $\tilde{T}$ of transitions is the set of (finite, nonempty) sequences of the form $\tilde{t} = t_1.t_2 \ldots t_n$ where t_1 is a transition of N, if t_i has a label X_j then t_{i+1}

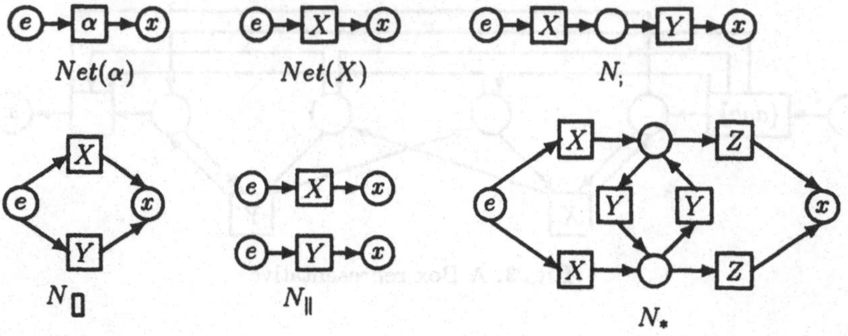

Fig. 4. The basic and operative nets

exists and is a transition of N_j, t_n is the last one if and only if its label does not belong to $\{X_i | i \in I\}$; the label of $\tilde{t}$ is the label of t_n;

2. the set $\tilde{S}$ of places is the set of (possibly infinite) labelled trees of the form schematized in Figure 5;

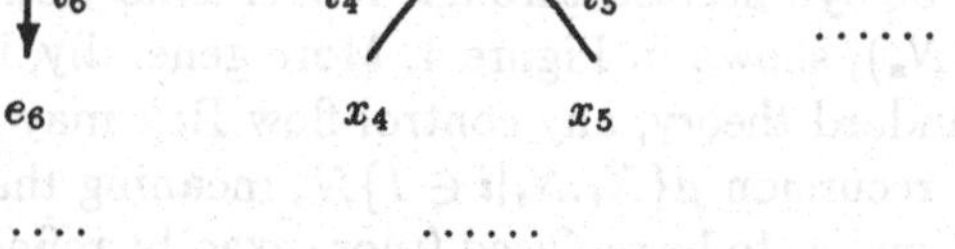

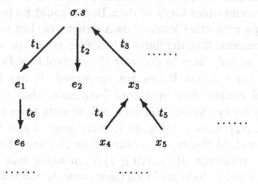

Fig. 5. The general form of a place in a recursive net

the root has a label $\sigma.s$, where σ is a (finite, possibly empty) sequence of transitions $t_1.t_2 \ldots t_n$ where each t_i is a transition with a label in $\{X_i | i \in I\}$, t_1 is a transition of N, and if t_i has a label X_j then t_{i+1}, if it exists, is a transition of N_j; if σ is empty, then s may be any place of N, otherwise it is an internal place of N_i if t_n has a label X_i; for any output transition t of s with a label in $\{X_i | i \in I\}$, there is an arc with label t going down to a node whose label is some (arbitrarily chosen) entry place of N_i, if X_i is the label of t; for any input transition t of s with a label in $\{X_i | i \in I\}$, there is an arc with label t going up from a node whose label is some (arbitrarily chosen) exit place of N_i, if X_i is the label of t; for any node labelled by an entry place e, for any output transition t of e with a label in $\{X_i | i \in I\}$, there is an arc with label t going down to a node whose label is some (arbitrarily chosen)

entry place of N_i, if X_i is the label of t; for any node labelled by an exit place x, for any input transition t of x with a label in $\{X_i | i \in I\}$, there is an arc with label t going up (i.e., arcs are labelled both by a transition name and by a direction, up or down) from a node whose label is some (arbitrarily chosen) exit place of N_i, if X_i is the label of t; the various places of $\tilde{S}$ arise from the various ways to choose σ, s and the labels of the other nodes. The label of the place is the same as the label of s. It may be observed that the (out-) degree of each node of such a tree is always finite, since the basic and operative nets we start from are all finite;
3. the connectivity of the places and transitions is directly driven by their structure: a transition $\sigma'.t$ is an output transition (with weight 1, since all the basic and operative nets are unweighted) of a place of the form explained above if and only if $\sigma' = \sigma.\sigma''$ where σ'' is the succession of the labels of the arcs of some path going down from the root to some place labelled e (or s if σ'' is empty) and t is an output transition of e (or s); similarly, a transition $\sigma'.t$ is an input transition (with weight 1) of a place of the form explained above if and only if $\sigma' = \sigma.\sigma''$ where σ'' is the succession of the labels of the arcs of some 'up'-path from the root to some place labelled x (or s if σ'' is empty) and t is an input transition of x (or s).

This definition may seem complex but, besides its systematic structure, it gives a closed form for the result, and not as limit net to construct through an infinite iteration, as is often the case. The labelled trees used to define the places of the recursive net may be infinitely deep, infinite down paths corresponding to a 'front' unguardedness (i.e., hierarchical transitions are connected to entry places), while infinite up paths correspond to a 'rear' unguardedness (i.e., hierarchical transitions are connected to exit places).

2.2 S-components and S-invariants

An S-component of a net may be defined as a weight function $\nu : S \cup T \rightarrow \{0,1\}$ such that for any $t \in T$ we have $\sum_{s \in {}^\bullet t} \nu(s) = \nu(t) = \sum_{s \in t^\bullet} \nu(s)$ (but other, equivalent, definitions may be found in the literature). A (semi-positive) S-invariant may be defined similarly, but replacing the set $\{0,1\}$ by the set $\mathcal{R}^+$ of nonnegative reals. In the Box domain, an S-component or an S-invariant is said to be 1-conservative if the global weight of all the entry places as well as the global weight of all the exit places is equal to 1: $\sum_{\{s \text{ with label } e\}} \nu(s) = 1 = \sum_{\{s \text{ with label } x\}} \nu(s)$. A transition or a place is covered by an S-component if there is a 1-conservative S-component for which it has a weight 1; it is covered by an S-invariant with weight w if there is a 1-conservative semi-positive S-invariant for which it has a weight w. A net is covered by S-components if each of its places and transitions is so covered; in particular, all the basic and operative Boxes of the standard PBC shown in Figure 4 are covered by S-components. The interest of those coverability properties is that

1. if a transition is covered by an S-component, then it is never enabled concurrently with itself (there is no self-concurrency for it) in any finite evolu-

tion from the natural initial marking which puts one token in each e-place and nothing elsewhere; more generally, if two transitions are simultaneously covered by an S-component, then they are never concurrently enabled, in the same circumstances; hence also, in a corresponding process (see next subsection), no two concurrent events may be labelled by them;

2. if a place is covered by an S-component, then it is 1-safe for any finite evolution from the natural initial marking; more generally, if two places are simultaneously covered by an S-component, then they may never hold tokens simultaneously, in the same circumstances; hence also, in a corresponding process, no two concurrent conditions may be labelled by them;
3. if a place is covered by an S-invariant with weight w, then it is at most $\lfloor w^{-1} \rfloor$-safe for any finite evolution from the natural initial marking.

In [15], a thorough study has been conducted on ways to construct S-components and S-invariants for a constructed Box, from S-components and S-invariants of its components. In particular, it has been shown that in a recursive Box constructed from basic and operative nets covered by S-components:

1. any transition is covered by an S-component; moreover, two distinct transitions may be simultaneously covered by an S-component, unless they are of the form $\sigma.t_1.\sigma_1$ and $\sigma.t_2.\sigma_2$ (σ, σ_1 and/or σ_2 may be empty), where t_1 and t_2 may not be covered simultaneously by an S-component in their original basic or operative Box (like in $N_{\square}$);
2. on the contrary, it may happen that a place (of the form shown in Figure 5) may not be covered by an S-component; this only happens when, from the root, there is a 'down' nonempty path σ_1 leading to a node labelled by a place e_1 and an 'up' path with the very same labelling σ_1 (this may only happen if s in the root has a side condition) leading to a node labelled by a place x_1, such that e_1 and x_1 may not be covered simultaneously by an S-component in their original basic or operative Box (like in $N_{\|}$); as a consequence, if the basic and operative net are pure, i.e., none of them has side conditions, as we assumed, all places are covered by S-components and are 1-safe;
3. in the more general case, when side conditions are allowed, a place may always be covered by an S-invariant with weight $\frac{1}{2}$, so that it is at most 2-safe (and indeed the net exhibited in Figure 3 is 2-safe and occurred in a previous version of the standard Petri Box Calculus); but it may be observed that, if we fix the 'down' part of a labelled-tree-place, it is always possible to choose the 'up' part in such a way that the resulting place may be covered by an S-component (and symmetrically if we fix the 'up' part and let the 'down' part free); as a consequence, any transition always puts and gets tokens from places covered by an S-component, since the output connectivity only fixes (part of) the 'up' part of the concerned places while the input connectivity only fixes (part of) the 'down' part of the concerned places.

2.3 Process Semantics

Processes have been introduced in net theory in order to yield a *true concurrency* semantics of marked nets. A general presentation of the subject may be found in [2], where a special care has been devoted to infinite nets, which is our present concern.

A process for a (possibly weighted) net $N = (S, T, W, M_0)$ is a labelled occurrence net $\pi = (B, E, F, l)$ with some constraints. Let us first recall that an occurrence net is an acyclic net without (in- or out-) branching places ($\forall b \in B : |{}^\bullet b| \leq 1 \geq |b^\bullet|$). Since the occurrence net is acyclic, it naturally defines a partial order between its nodes; two nodes are said concurrent if they are not ordered for it, and the predecessors of a node are all the nodes coming before it (not necessarily immediately) in that order. The elements of B are called the *conditions* of the occurrence net and the elements of E are its *events*. The extra conditions which have to be fulfilled in order to get a representation of some evolution of the original net N are the following:

1. the conditions of π are labelled by places of N, and the events of π are labelled by transitions of N (sort preservation);
2. $\forall e \in E\ \forall s \in S : W(s, l(e)) = |l^{-1}(s) \cap {}^\bullet e|$ and $W(l(e), s) = |l^{-1}(s) \cap e^\bullet|$ (local coherence);
3. $\forall s \in S : M_0(s) = |l^{-1}(s) \cap Min(\pi)|$, where $Min(\pi)$ denotes the set of minimal elements of π with respect to its partial order (initial coherence);
4. for any node of π, the chains from $Min(\pi)$ to it have a bounded length (finite accessibility).

The finite accessibility property implies in particular that any node is accessible from $Min(\pi)$ and that any event may be accessed through a finite sequence of (possibly infinite) steps. Moreover, for each node we may define its *level* (even for events, odd for conditions) as the maximal length (in terms of arcs) of the chains from the minimal elements to it; it may be seen that all elements at the same level are concurrent.

Among the semantical properties carried out by a process, we may recall that if two conditions are concurrent, then there is a finite step sequence corresponding to their predecessors such that the reached marking simultaneously marks the places given by their labels; similarly, if two events are concurrent, then there is a finite step sequence corresponding to their predecessors such that the reached marking concurrently enables the transitions given by their labels.

3 Finite Precedence of Events

We are now ready to prove our first main result:

Theorem 1. *Finite precedence of events*

If $\tilde{N} = \mu\{X_i.N_i | i \in I\}N$ is a recursive Box constructed from a finite set of finite pure nets (N and the N_i's) covered by S-components, then any event of any process of it only has finitely many predecessor events.

Proof: By contraposition: let us assume a process π of $\tilde{N}$ has events with infinitely many predecessor events.
Since each node of π has bounded descending chains, the associated partial order is well-founded and we may consider a minimal such event; let us call it e. Hence, it must have infinitely many direct predecessor events, each one only having finitely many predecessor events (so that we are allowed to apply to them all the results concerning finite evolutions, like the consequences of S-component or S-invariant coverings), and part of the configuration of π looks like exhibited in Figure 6(a) (but notice that we may have more conditions between some e_i's and e).

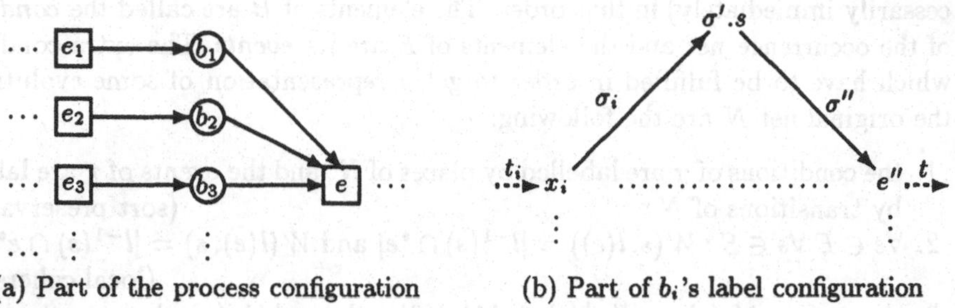
e_1
b_1
e_2
b_2
e_3
b_3
e
$\sigma'.s$
σ_i
σ''
t_i
x_i
e''
t
(a) Part of the process configuration
(b) Part of b_i's label configuration

Fig. 6. Characteristic part of the process.

Let $\sigma.t$ be the label of e; then, from the connectivity rule for recursive nets, the label of each b_i is of the form exhibited in Figure 6(b), with a root labelled $\sigma'.s$ and $\sigma = \sigma'.\sigma''$, and the label of the corresponding e_i is of the form $\sigma'.\sigma_i.t_i$ (but it may happen that σ, σ', σ'' and/or σ_i are empty; notice also that the dashed arcs labelled t and t_i do not belong to the labelled tree: they only indicate how and where the event labels are connected to 'up' and 'down' paths of the condition tree). Moreover, since there are infinitely many b_i's and only finitely many possible values for the prefix σ' of σ, and finitely many possible values for the place s, infinitely many b_i's have the same root label; since we only represented part of the configuration in Figure 6(a), we may even assume without loss of generality that this is the case for all the shown b_i's. In the same spirit, infinitely many e_i's are at the same level since there are only finitely many levels before e, and we may assume without loss of generality that this is the case for all the shown e_i's, which are thus concurrent and all have different labels (since there is no self-concurrency).
Let us consider more carefully the various e_i's and, for each of them, the corresponding 'up'-path $\sigma_i.t_i$, together with the labels of the visited nodes, in the labelled tree associated to b_i; from the same argument as above, infinitely many of these 'up'-paths have the same prefixes, and if we consider the first (from the top) discrepancy between the 'up'-paths

corresponding to e_i and e_j (there must be a discrepancy since the labels of e_i and e_j are different: $\sigma'.\sigma_i.t_i \neq \sigma'.\sigma_j.t_j$), it occurs that:

- it must be at place-nodes of the labelled trees, since if it were at transition-arcs ($\sigma_i'.t_i = \sigma'''.t_i'.\sigma_i''$, $\sigma_j'.t_j = \sigma'''.t_j'.\sigma_j''$ with $t_i' \neq t_j'$, and, in the labelled trees, t_i' and t_j' arrive at nodes with the same label s'), we would have that t_i' and t_j' are covered by a same S-component (since s' is covered), and from what we have seen in subsections 2.2 and 2.3, e_i and e_j could not be concurrent;
- let us thus assume that $\sigma_i'.t_i = \sigma'''.t_i'.\sigma_i''$, $\sigma_j'.t_j = \sigma'''.t_j'.\sigma_j''$ and, in the trees, t_i' arrives at a node labelled x_i' while t_j' arrives at a node labelled $x_j' \neq x_i'$; we may assume that $t_i' \neq t_j'$ since otherwise, e_j also produces a condition b_j' identical to b_j up to the fact that in its label the x_j' is replaced by x_i' (so that b_j' is also absorbed by e; more exactly, e must absorb a condition b_j'' with the same label than b_j', but since the net is 1-safe and e_j is a direct predecessor event of e, these conditions must be the same: $b_j' = b_j''$), and the discrepancy occurs later; moreover, t_i' and t_j' have no common input or output places (otherwise they would be covered by a same S-component and, again, e_i and e_j could not be concurrent) so that x_i' is not an output place of t_j', and x_j' is not an output place of t_i';
- when there is such a discrepancy, since there are again finitely many possibilities for the differing node label, infinitely many pairs (e_k, b_k) continue in the same way (i.e. with a same further common prefix part; we may even have many infinite families continuing each in their own way).

As a consequence, we may assume again without loss of generality that the events e_i have labels with increasing common prefixes:
$\lambda(e_i) = \sigma'.t_1'.\sigma_1'.t_2'.\sigma_2'.\ldots.t_i'.\sigma_i'.t_i''.\sigma_i''$ (the σ_i''s, σ_i'''s may be empty),
and the corresponding b_i's labels have increasing common 'up'-paths as shown in Figure 7(a).

But then, from the definition of the recursion operator, there is also a place $\tilde{s}$ in the recursive net (maybe many in fact, since there may be some flexibility in the choice of the rest of the labelled tree) with the same root, the same 'down'-path $\sigma''.t$ as all the e_i's, and an infinite 'up'-path $\sigma'.t_1'.\sigma_1'.t_2'.\sigma_2'.\ldots.t_i'.\sigma_i'.t_{i+1}'.\sigma_{i+1}'\ldots$, as shown in Figure 7(b); this place is of the same kind as place i_∞ which occurred in Figure 1 in the introduction. A token in this place is also needed by $\lambda(e) = \sigma.t$, and it is not produced by any of the $\lambda(e_i)$'s since they need a node x_i'' where there is one labelled x_i'. Hence, we must have in π, before e, another event producing it; let us call $\tilde{e}$ this event, and $\tilde{b}$ the condition with label $\tilde{s}$, which is an immediate predecessor of e; as usual, $\tilde{s}$ corresponds to an 'up'-path in the labelled tree of the place: let us consider the point where this path joins the infinite one mentioned above; it may thus be expressed as $\sigma'.t_1'.\sigma_1'.\ldots.t_k'.\sigma_k'.\sigma'''.\tilde{\sigma}.\tilde{t}$, where σ''' is a (possibly empty) prefix of $t_{k+1}'.\sigma_{k+1}'$, for some $k \geq 0$ (see Figure 7(b)). Now, it may be

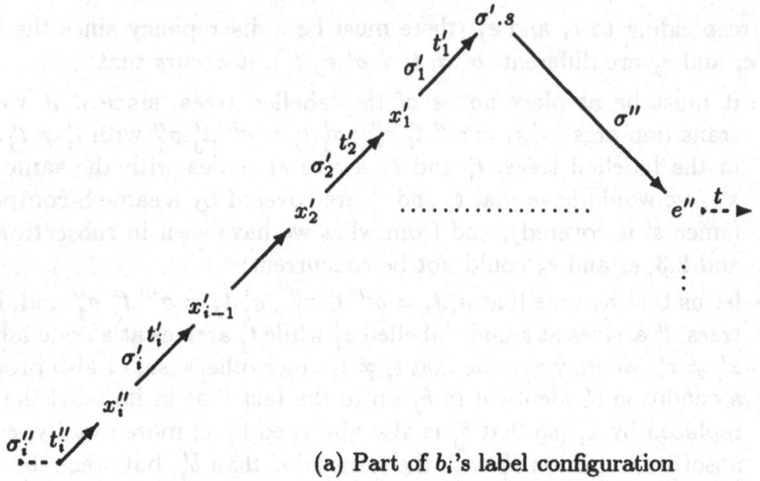

(a) Part of b_i's label configuration

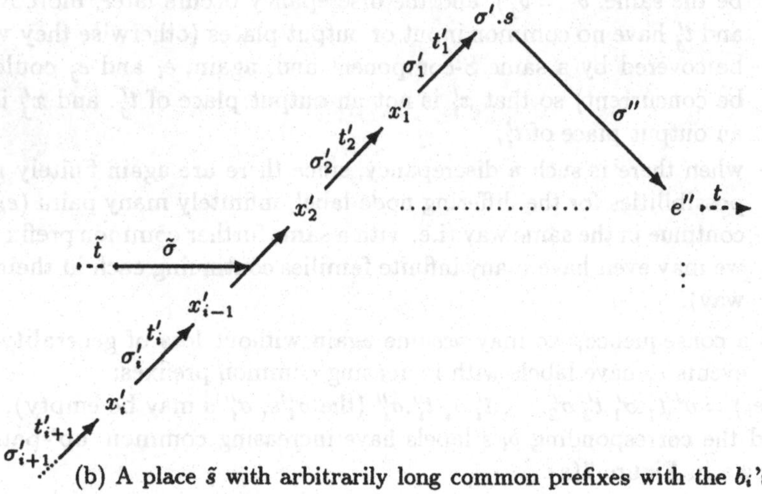

(b) A place $\tilde{s}$ with arbitrarily long common prefixes with the b_i's labels

Fig. 7. Characteristic configurations.

observed that, for any $i > k$:

- $\lambda(e_i)$ and $\lambda(\tilde{e})$ are simultaneously covered by an S-component (for the same reason as above, i.e., the discrepancy occurs at transitions which have a common output place); hence, they may not be concurrent;
- $\tilde{e}$ may not be preceded by infinitely many of such e_i's since it precedes e and the latter is the first one with infinite precedence; hence $\tilde{e}$ precedes almost all those e_i's;
- more precisely, for any $i > k$, there is a place $\tilde{s}_i$ (maybe many) characterized by the configuration exhibited on Figure 8, such that both $\tilde{e}$ and e_i produce a condition with that label, with exactly the same 'down'-part as in $\tilde{s}$.

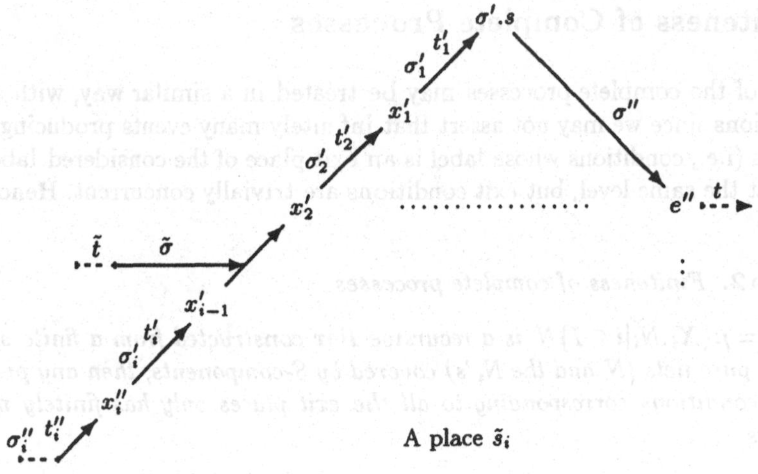

Fig. 8. A characteristic configuration produced by both $\tilde{e}$ and e_i.

The one produced by $\tilde{e}$ must thus be absorbed by a predecessor event of e_i (since no two conditions with the same label may be concurrent from our pureness assumption), but it occurs from the connectivity rule that this event must also absorb a condition with the same label $\tilde{s}$ as $\tilde{b}$, and from our hypotheses no two concurrent conditions may have the same label (see Figure 9).

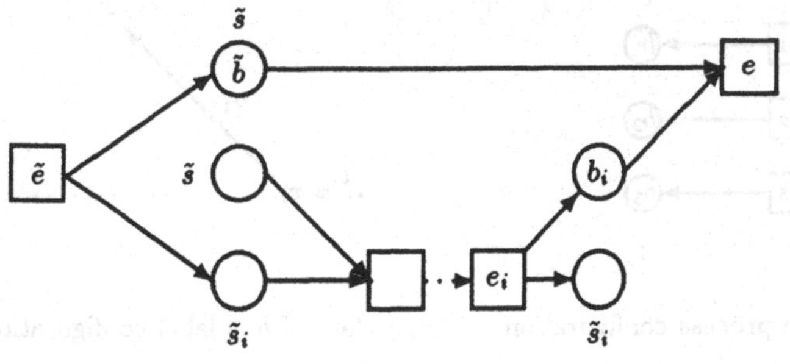

Fig. 9. Characteristic production and absorption configuration.

Hence a contradiction since the examination of the configuration in Figure 9 shows that the two conditions labelled $\tilde{s}$ may not be ordered, while they may not be concurrent either since no two concurrent conditions may have the same label: such a process π may not exist. ■ 1

4 Finiteness of Complete Processes

The case of the complete processes may be treated in a similar way, with some modifications since we may not assert that infinitely many events producing exit conditions (i.e., conditions whose label is an exit place of the considered labelled net) are at the same level, but exit conditions are trivially concurrent. Hence we may state

Theorem 2. *Finiteness of complete processes*

> *If $\tilde{N} = \mu\{X_i.N_i | i \in I\}N$ is a recursive Box constructed from a finite set of finite pure nets (N and the N_i's) covered by S-components, then any process with conditions corresponding to all the exit places only has finitely many events.*

Proof: By contraposition: let us assume there is a process π of $\tilde{N}$ with conditions corresponding to all the exit places of $\tilde{N}$ and infinitely many events. From the coverability result by 1-conservative S-components, it results that all the nodes of π precede one or more conditions labelled by an exit place. Since, from Theorem 1, each event of π only has finitely many predecessors, we must have infinitely many events producing exit conditions. No two of them may have the same label, otherwise they would produce two concurrent (exit) conditions with the same label. The situation may thus be characterized by the schemas exhibited in Figure 10, with $\lambda(e_i) = \sigma_i.t_i$.

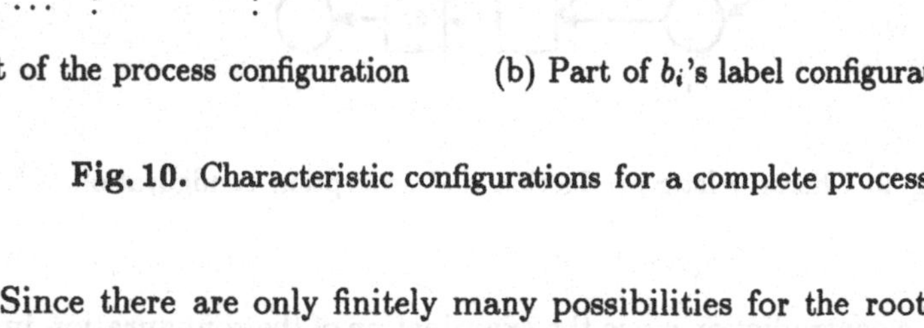

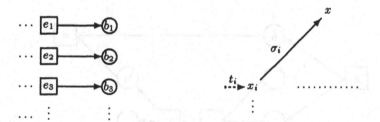

(a) Part of the process configuration (b) Part of b_i's label configuration

Fig. 10. Characteristic configurations for a complete process.

Since there are only finitely many possibilities for the root label x, we may assume without loss of generality that all the b_i's have labels with the same x. Again also, if the labels of e_i and e_j have a common prefix σ, we may assume that in the trees corresponding to b_i and b_j the nodes encountered along the path σ (up to the last but one transition of it) from the root are the same (i.e. they have the same exit place label; indeed, if there is a difference, that means that there are exit places which have common input transitions, and we may modify the b_i's without modifying the connectivity in such a way that we always use the same exit places in such circumstances); moreover, at the discrepancy point ($\lambda(e_i) = \sigma.t_i.\sigma_i''$ and $\lambda(e_j) = \sigma.t_j.\sigma_j''$, with $t_i \neq t_j$), in the corresponding labelled trees, the arcs labelled t_i and t_j go to differently labelled nodes, and more generally they have no common output exit place, otherwise e_i and e_j also produce conditions with the same (exit place) label, which is impossible. Since in each componing net (N or N_i), we only have finitely many transitions, we may construct a series of e_i's with strictly increasing common prefixes: $\lambda(e_i) = \sigma_1'.\sigma_2'.\ldots.\sigma_{i-1}'.\sigma_i''$. Now, combining the above remarks, it occurs that there is an exit place whose tree has an infinite 'up' path $\sigma_1'.\sigma_2'.\ldots.\sigma_{i-1}'.\sigma_i'\ldots$ which is not produced by any of the e_i's. This is illustrated in Figure 11; this place is of the same kind as place x_∞ which occurred in Figure 2 in the introduction .

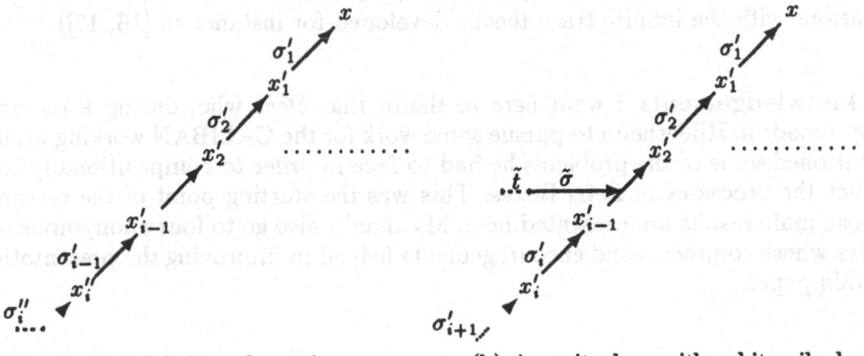

(a) Part of b_i's label configuration

(b) An exit place with arbitrarily long common prefixes with the b_i's

Fig. 11. Characteristic exit configurations.

A condition corresponding to (a token in) this place must be present in the complete process π; hence, we must have in π another event, let us call it $\tilde{e}$, producing this condition; as usual, it corresponds to an 'up'-path in the labelled tree of the place: let us consider the point where this path joins the infinite one mentioned above; it may thus be expressed as $\sigma_1'.\ldots.\sigma_k'.\sigma'''.\tilde{\sigma}.\tilde{t}$, where σ''' is a (possibly empty) prefix of σ_{k+1}', for some $k \geq 0$. Now, it may be observed that, for any $i > k$, e_i and $\tilde{e}$ both produce at least one exit condition with the same label (with the kind of 'skeleton' exhibited in Figure 11(a) plus the same $\tilde{\sigma}$-branch as in Figure 11(b)), which is impossible.

Hence a contradiction: such a process π may not exist. ■ 2

5 Conclusion

We thus have proved the properties we claimed, and we need in order to get a nice, coherent and unambiguous compositional semantics for the box algebra. It is very likely however that our results may be generalised. For instance, we assumed that the basic and operative nets used in the theory are pure; we indeed used this fact in the proofs, through the impossibility to have two concurrent conditions with the same label; but we feel that the property should also be valid when side conditions are allowed (simply the proof should be be technically more involved, or a better argument should be found), so that the finite precedence property would also be valid for the original PBC theory (see [4, 3]), which used a version of the iteration operative Box with a side condition. Also, it should be possible to relax the finiteness assumption of the basic and operative nets, provided some extra conditions are introduced, like their degree-finiteness (or at least the fact that they fulfill themselves the finite precedence properties). Finally, we hope that the kind of results and ideas developed here in a Petri net framework could be of interest in other semantical approaches (in particular, it seems to have strong relations with the infinite trace theory developed for instance in [16, 17]).

Acknowledgements I want here to thank Eike Best who, during a research stay I made in Hildesheim to pursue some work for the CALIBAN working group, mentioned some of the problems he had to face in order to compositionally construct the processes of Petri Boxes. This was the starting point of the research whose main results are presented here. My thanks also go to four anonymous referees whose comments and encouragements helped in improving the presentation of this paper.

References

1. E.Best and R.Devillers: Interleaving and Partial Orders in Concurrency: a Formal Comparison. Proceedings of the IFIP TC2 Working Conference on Formal Description of Programming Concepts-III. M. Wirsing (ed.), North-Holland, pp. 299-323 (1987).
2. E.Best and R.Devillers: Sequential and Concurrent Behaviour in Petri Net Theory. TCS 55, pp. 87-136 (1987).
3. E.Best, R.Devillers and J.Esparza: General Refinement and Recursion Operators for the Petri Box Calculus. Proceedings STACS-93, P. Enjalbert et al. (eds.). Springer-Verlag Lecture Notes in Computer Science Vol. 665, pp. 130-140 (1993).
4. E.Best, R.Devillers and J.Hall: The Box Calculus: a New Causal Algebra with Multi-label Communication. Advances in Petri Nets 1992. Springer-Verlag Lecture Notes in Computer Science Vol. 609, pp.21-69 (1992).
5. E.Best, H.Fleischhack, W.Fraczak, R.P.Hopkins, H.Klaudel and E.Pelz: A High Level Petri Net Semantics of $B(PN)^2$. Proceedings STRICT'95, Workshop in Computing. Springer Verlag (1995).
6. E.Best, H.Fleischhack, W.Fraczak, R.P.Hopkins, H.Klaudel and E.Pelz: A Class of Composable High Level Petri Nets. Proceedings of the International Conference

on Application and Theory of Petri Nets 95. Springer-Verlag Lecture Notes in Computer Science Vol. 935, pp.103-120 (1995).

7. E.Best and R.P.Hopkins: $B(PN)^2$ - A Basic Petri Net Programming Notation. Proceedings of PARLE-93. Springer-Verlag Lecture Notes in Computer Science Vol. 694, pp.379-390 (1993).
8. E.Best and M.Koutny: Solving Recursive Net Equations. Proceedings ICALP'95, Szeged (F.Gecseg and Z.Fülöp, eds.), Springer-Verlag Lecture Notes in Computer Science Vol. 944, pp.605-623 (1995).
9. E.Best and M.Koutny: A Refined View of the Box Calculus. Proceedings of the 16th International Conference on Application and Theory of Petri Nets, Torino (G.De Michelis and M.Diaz, eds), Springer-Verlag Lecture Notes in Computer Science Vol. 935, pp.1-21 (1995).
10. E.Best and H-G.Linde-Göers: Compositional Process Semantics of Petri Boxes. Proceedings of Mathematics of Program Construction 92. Springer-Verlag Lecture Notes in Computer Science Vol. 670 (1993).
11. R.Devillers: Towards a General Relabelling Operator for the Petri Box Calculus. Internal Report LIT-274. Université Libre de Bruxelles (1993).
12. R.Devillers: On a More Liberal Synchronisation Operator for the Petri Box Calculus. Internal Report LIT-281. Université Libre de Bruxelles (1993).
13. R.Devillers: The Synchronisation Operator Revisited for the Petri Box Calculus. Internal Report LIT-290. Université Libre de Bruxelles (1994).
14. R.Devillers: Analysis of General Refined Petri Boxes. Proceedings of the XIIIth International Conference of the Chilean Society of Computer Science (La Serena, Chile), pp. 419-434 (1993).
also in Computer Science 2: Research and Applications (Plenum Publishing), pp.411-428 (1994).
15. R.Devillers: S-invariant Analysis of General Recursive Petri Boxes. Acta Informatica 32, pp.313-345 (1995).
16. V.Diekert: Complex and complex-like traces. MFCS'93. Lecture Notes in Computer Science Vol. 711, pp.68-82 (1993).
17. V.Diekert, P.Gastin and A.Petit: Rational and recognizable complex trace languages. Information and Computation Vol. 116, pp.134-153 (1995).
18. W.Fraczak: Composition Parallèle et Synchronisation de Systèmes à Evénements Discrets. Ph.D. Thesis, Université Paris Sud (Orsay, France) (1996)
19. W.Fraczak, H.Klaudel and E.Pelz: Multi-labeled High Level Nets for a Semantics of $B(PN)^2$. LRI draft report (Orsay, France) (1992)
20. R.P.Hopkins, J.Hall and O.Botti: A Basic-Net Algebra for Program Semantics and its Application to occam. Advances in Petri Nets 1992. Springer-Verlag Lecture Notes in Computer Science Vol. 609, pp. 179-214 (1992).
21. H.Klaudel: Modèles Algébriques, Basés sur les Réseaux de Petri, pour la Sémantique des Langages de Programmation Concurrents. Ph.D. Thesis, Université Paris Sud (Orsay, France) (1995)
22. H.Klaudel and E.Pelz: Algebraic Representation of Data in the PBC. LRI Report 793 (Orsay, France) (1992)

Constrained Properties, Semilinear Systems, and Petri Nets

Ahmed Bouajjani Peter Habermehl

VERIMAG Miniparc-Zirst, Rue Lavoisier, 38330 Montbonnot St-Martin, France.
email: Ahmed.Bouajjani@imag.fr, Peter.Habermehl@imag.fr

Abstract

We investigate the verification problem of two classes of infinite state systems w.r.t. nonregular properties (i.e., nondefinable by finite-state ω-automata). The systems we consider are Petri nets as well as *semilinear systems* including pushdown systems and PA processes. On the other hand, we consider properties expressible in the logic CLTL which is an extension of the linear-time temporal logic LTL allowing two kinds of constraints: *pattern constraints* using finite-state automata and *counting constraints* using Presburger arithmetics formulas. While the verification problem of CLTL is undecidable even for finite-state systems, we identify a fragment called $\mathrm{CLTL}_{\Box}$ for which the verification problem is decidable for pushdown systems as well as for Petri nets. This fragment is strictly more expressive than finite-state ω-automata. We show that, however, the verification problem of semilinear systems (PA processes in particular) is undecidable even w.r.t. LTL formulas. Therefore, we identify another fragment (a restriction of LTL extended with counting constraints) covering a significant class of properties and for which the verification problem is decidable for all PA processes.

1 Introduction

Reasoning about infinite state systems is an important and intensively studied topic in automatic verification and concurrency theory [1, 8, 6, 12, 4, 9, 11]. Several classes of infinite state systems are investigated corresponding to different description formalisms that are, mainly, either process algebras like BPA (context-free processes) [2] and BPP (basic parallel processes) [7], or "*extended*" automata like pushdown systems, Petri nets (vector addition systems with states), and lossy channel systems. Important results have been established on the verification problem of such systems. These results concern behavioural equivalences/preorders testing [8] as well as model checking [1, 6, 12, 4, 11]. Our work follows the latter verification approach. Its originality consists of the consideration of *nonregular* properties. Indeed, as far as we know, all the other works on the subject address the verification of properties expressed in the usual specification logics like propositional temporal logics and μ-calculi, or by means of finite-state ω-automata. However, these formalisms cannot capture some important aspects of the behaviours of infinite state systems. In particular, it is impossible to express in these formalisms properties involving *counting constraints*, i.e., properties comparing *numbers of occurrences of events*. These properties are essential to characterize behaviours of systems involving counting mechanisms. To express such properties, we have proposed in [5, 4] new specification logics combining temporal logics with Presburger arithmetics. In these previous works, we have considered the verification problem of nonregular properties for infinite state systems described in the process algebra PA [3] (subsuming BPA and BPP). We have identified classes of nonregular properties for which the verification problem is decidable for PA or BPA using different specific reductions to the satisfiability problem in Presburger arithmetics.

In this work, we pursue our investigations by considering a more general framework and establishing decidability results for the verification problem concerning larger classes of systems and properties. We propose classes of nonregular properties for which a uniform approach can be applied to reason about the verification problem for different classes of infinite state systems. Roughly speaking, the basic idea is to define properties that can be *decomposed* into ω-regular properties and elementary nonregular properties, e.g., counting constraints on the set of prefixes. Depending on the nature of the system, the ω-regular property and the constraints, this *constrained emptiness problem* is decidable or not, and when it is decidable, different techniques can be applied to establish this fact.

The properties we consider are expressed in the logic CLTL (Constrained Linear Temporal Logic) introduced in [4]. This logic is an extension of the linear-time propositional temporal logic LTL [16] with the ability of expressing ***pattern constraints*** and ***counting constraints*** on computations. Pattern constraints are expressed using finite-state automata and allow to say that the computation since some given point in the past corresponds to some pattern (specified as a regular language). Counting constraints are expressed using Presburger arithmetics formulas and allow to say that the numbers of occurrences of events since some designated points in the past fulfil some arithmetical constraints. CLTL has two sublogics ALTL and PLTL corresponding respectively to the extensions of LTL with either pattern or counting constraints only.

The satisfiability problem of CLTL (as well as PLTL) is highly undecidable (Σ_1^1-complete), and already the verification problem of PLTL is undecidable even for finite-state systems [4]. Therefore, we define a syntactical fragment of CLTL called $\text{CLTL}_\Box$ and its corresponding fragment of PLTL called $\text{PLTL}_\Box$. These fragments are not closed under negation. So, we characterize syntactically the complements of $\text{CLTL}_\Box$ and $\text{PLTL}_\Box$ properties by introducing two other fragments $\text{CLTL}_\Diamond$ and $\text{PLTL}_\Diamond$. Both fragments $\text{CLTL}_\Box$ and $\text{CLTL}_\Diamond$ subsume the logic ALTL which expresses exactly the ω-regular properties. As for $\text{PLTL}_\Box$ and $\text{PLTL}_\Diamond$, they subsume the logic LTL, which means that they can express all the ω-star-free properties [17].

Then, the key result we prove is that $\text{CLTL}_\Diamond$ properties can be decomposed into ω-regular properties and eventuality properties with counting constraints. The same holds for $\text{PLTL}_\Diamond$ with ω-star-free properties instead of ω-regular ones. By this decomposition, the satisfiability problem of a $\text{CLTL}_\Diamond$ formula φ relatively to a system $\mathcal{S}$ reduces to a ***constrained emptiness problem*** as mentioned above. Then, we discuss the decidability of this problem and the techniques that can be applied to solve it, depending on the considered systems and formulas.

We consider two incomparable and fairly general classes of systems that are *semilinear systems* and Petri nets. Semilinear systems are those generating sets of finite traces whose Parikh images are semilinear and effectively constructible (examples are pushdown systems and PA processes). On the other hand, BPP processes, that are semilinear, can also be encoded as Petri nets.

First, we investigate the case of semilinear systems and consider the decision method based on reduction to the nonemptiness problem of semilinear sets. This reduction is possible if the intersection of the ω-language of the considered system with the ω-regular part of the property is semilinear (via Parikh image of its set of prefixes). This is the case for pushdown systems, and hence, we deduce that their verification problem w.r.t. CLTL$_\Box$ is decidable. This result generalizes the one we have established in [4] for BPA processes and a subset of CLTL$_\Box$. This reduction is, however, not possible for all semilinear systems. Indeed, we can show that for PA processes the verification problem is undecidable even for LTL properties. Therefore, we consider another pair of dual fragments, called simple-PLTL$_\Box$ and simple-PLTL$_\Diamond$, and prove that the verification problem of all PA processes w.r.t. simple-PLTL$_\Box$ is decidable. This result generalizes the one we established in [4] for a subset of simple-PLTL$_\Box$.

Then, we consider the case of Petri nets. We show that the constrained nonemptiness problem stated above can be reduced in this case to the reachability problem in Petri nets. Consequently, the verification problem of Petri nets w.r.t. CLTL$_\Box$ is decidable. In particular this fact holds for BPP processes, and thus, answers the question we left open in [4]. Our result extends the one shown in [12] for Petri nets and the linear-time μ-calculus, since we consider a strictly more expressive logic allowing nonregular properties. Moreover, CLTL$_\Box$ allows to express constraints on places of Petri nets by counting their ingoing and outgoing transitions. Then, our result can be considered as a decidability result for a logic on Petri nets markings. In this context, our result is incomparable with the existing results [14, 13].

The paper is organized as follows. In Section 2, we introduce notations and give some preliminary results. In Section 3, we define CLTL. In Section 4, we introduce the fragments of CLTL. In Section 5, we show the decomposition of CLTL$_\Diamond$ properties. In Section 6, we consider the verification problem of semilinear systems and its reducibility to the emptiness problem of semilinear sets. In Section 7, we consider the verification problem of Petri nets. We conclude in Section 8.

2 Preliminaries

2.1 Sequences, languages, projection, and cylindrification

Let Σ be a finite alphabet. We denote by Σ^* (resp. Σ^ω) the set of finite (resp. infinite) sequences over Σ. Let $\Sigma^\infty = \Sigma^* \cup \Sigma^\omega$. A *language* (resp. *$\omega$-language*) is a subset of Σ^* (resp. Σ^ω).

An infinite sequence $\sigma \in \Sigma^\omega$ can be seen as a mapping from $I\!N$ to Σ. Hence, σ is equal to $\sigma(0)\sigma(1)\cdots$. Given i and j with $i \leq j$, we denote by $\sigma(i,j)$ the finite sequence $\sigma(i)\cdots\sigma(j)$ (with $\sigma(i,i) = \sigma(i)$). We denote by $Pref(\sigma)$ the set of finite prefixes of σ, i.e., $Pref(\sigma) = \{\sigma(0,i) : i \geq 0\}$. This notation can be extended to sets of sequences in the obvious way.

Let $\mathcal{P}$ be a finite set of ***atomic propositions***. Then, we consider a set of ***transition labels*** $\Sigma = 2^{\mathcal{P}}$. Let $\Sigma' \supseteq \Sigma$. Then, given a sequence $\sigma' \in (\Sigma')^\omega$, the ***projection*** of σ' on Σ, denoted $\sigma'|_\Sigma$, is the sequence $\sigma \in \Sigma^\omega$ such that, for every $i \geq 0$, $\sigma(i) = \sigma'(i) \cap \mathcal{P}$. Conversely, given a sequence $\sigma \in \Sigma^\omega$, the ***cylindrification*** of σ to Σ', denoted $\widetilde{\sigma}$, is the set of sequences $\sigma' \in (\Sigma')^\omega$ such that $\sigma = \sigma'|_\Sigma$. These definitions are generalized to sets of sequences.

Notice that for every $S \subseteq (\Sigma')^\omega$, $S = \emptyset$ iff $S|_\Sigma = \emptyset$. Moreover, it is clear that projection distributes w.r.t. union (i.e., $(S \cup S')|_\Sigma = S|_\Sigma \cup S'|_\Sigma$). However, projection does not distribute w.r.t. conjunction. Indeed, given $S, S' \in (\Sigma')^\omega$, we have $(S \cap S')|_\Sigma \subseteq S|_\Sigma \cap S'|_\Sigma$, but the converse does not hold in general. Nevertheless, we can show the following fact:

Lemma 2.1 *Let $S, T \subseteq \Sigma^\omega$, and $T' \subseteq (\Sigma')^\omega$ such that $T = T'|_\Sigma$. Then, $S \cap T = (\widetilde{S} \cap T')|_\Sigma$.*

2.2 Finite-state ω-automata

A finite-state Büchi ω-automaton is a tuple $\mathcal{A} = (Q, \Sigma, q_0, \delta, F)$ where (Q, Σ, q_0, δ) is a finite-state labelled transition system (LTS), let us call it $S_\mathcal{A}$, and $F \subseteq Q$ is the set of repeating locations. Given a sequence $\sigma \in \Sigma^\omega$, a run of $S_\mathcal{A}$ over σ is a sequence $\rho \in Q^\omega$ such that $\rho(0) = q_0$, and $\forall i \geq 0$, $(\rho(i), \sigma(i), \rho(i+1)) \in \delta$. Let $\rho \in Q^\omega$ be a run of $S_\mathcal{A}$. We denote by $Inf(\rho)$ the set of locations q such that $\exists^\infty i \in I\!N$ with $\rho(i) = q$. Then, a run ρ is ***accepting*** if $Inf(\rho) \cap F \neq \emptyset$. The ***$\omega$-language*** of $\mathcal{A}$, denoted by $L(\mathcal{A})$, is the set of sequences $\sigma \in \Sigma^\omega$ such that $S_\mathcal{A}$ has an accepting run over σ. Subsets of Σ^ω that are recognizable by finite-state Büchi ω-automata are called ***ω-regular*** languages. The class of ω-regular languages is closed under all boolean operations.

A ***simple ω-regular language*** is an ω-language definable by a finite-state Büchi ω-automaton such that every loop in its transition system is a self-loop. The class of simple ω-regular language is closed under union and intersection but not under complementation.

2.3 Pushdown systems, and PA processes

The definitions of finite-state labelled transition systems and ω-automata can be extended in the usual way to ***pushdown systems*** and ***ω-pushdown automata*** (the Büchi acceptance condition is defined, as in the finite-state case, by means of a set of repeating control locations). Subsets of Σ^ω that are recognizable by pushdown Büchi ω-automata are called ω-context-free languages [10].

A PA process [3] is defined by a finite set of well-guarded recursive equations of the form $X = t$ where X is a process variable, and t is a term constructed from transition labels (actions), process variables, and binary operators: nondeterministic choice "+", sequential composition "·", and merge (or asynchronous parallel) composition "||". BPA processes are PA processes without merge composition.

They generate the same ω-languages as pushdown systems. BPP processes are PA processes with prefixing ("$a \cdot t$") instead of general sequential composition "$\cdot$". They correspond to a subclass of Petri nets and generate a subclass of ω-context sensitive languages incomparable with BPA ω-languages [7]. We mention finally that the classes of PA and Petri nets ω-languages are incomparable.

2.4 Petri nets

A *Petri net* is a tuple $\mathcal{N} = (\mathbf{P}, \mathbf{T}, \mathbf{F}, M_{\mathcal{N}}, \Lambda)$ where $\mathbf{P}$ is a finite set of ***places***, $\mathbf{T}$ is a finite set of ***transitions*** such that $\mathbf{P}$ and $\mathbf{T}$ are disjoint, $\mathbf{F} : (\mathbf{P} \times \mathbf{T}) \cup (\mathbf{T} \times \mathbf{P}) \rightarrow \mathbb{N}$ is the ***flow function***, $M_{\mathcal{N}} : \mathbf{P} \rightarrow \mathbb{N}$ is an ***initial marking***, and $\Lambda : \mathbf{T} \rightarrow \Sigma$ is a labelling function. A ***marking*** M associates a natural number (number of ***tokens***) to each place. A marking is also considered as a vector in $\mathbb{N}^{|\mathbf{P}|}$. We write $M[t\rangle$ if, $\forall p \in P$, $M(p) \geq \mathbf{F}(p,t)$, and we write $M[t\rangle M'$ if $M[t\rangle$ and, $\forall p \in P$, $M'(p) = M(p) - \mathbf{F}(p,t) + \mathbf{F}(t,p)$. Given $a \in \Sigma$, we write $M \xrightarrow{a}$ (resp. $M \xrightarrow{a} M'$) if $\exists t \in \mathbf{T}$ such that $M[t\rangle$ (resp. $M[t\rangle M'$) and $\Lambda(t) = a$. These definitions can be extended to sequences of transitions $\tau \in \mathbf{T}^{\infty}$ and sequences of transition labels $\sigma \in \Sigma^{\infty}$. The ***reachability set*** of $\mathcal{N}$, denoted by $\mathcal{R}(\mathcal{N})$, is the set of markings M such that $\exists \tau \in \mathbf{T}^*$, $M_{\mathcal{N}}[\tau\rangle M$. The ***$\omega$-language*** of $\mathcal{N}$, denoted by $L(\mathcal{N})$, is the set of infinite sequences $\sigma \in \Sigma^{\omega}$ such that $M_{\mathcal{N}} \xrightarrow{\sigma}$. Finally, given a transition $t \in \mathbf{T}$, we denote by $\mathcal{M}_{\infty}(\mathcal{N}, t)$ the set of markings M for which $\exists \tau \in \mathbf{T}^{\omega}$ such that $M[\tau\rangle$ and $\exists^{\infty} i \in \mathbb{N}$ with $\tau(i) = t$.

2.5 Semilinear sets, semilinear languages, and semilinear systems

A ***linear set*** is a subset of $\mathbb{N}^n$ of the form $\{\vec{v} + k_1\vec{u}_1 + \cdots + k_m\vec{u}_m : k_1, \cdots, k_m \in \mathbb{N}\}$ where $n > 0$ and $\vec{v}, \vec{u}_1, \cdots, \vec{u}_m \in \mathbb{N}^n$. A ***semilinear set*** is a finite union of linear sets. Let $\sigma \in \Sigma^*$. For every $a \in \Sigma$, $|\sigma|_a$ is the number of occurrences of a in σ. Let $\Sigma = \{a_1, \cdots, a_n\}$. We denote by $[\sigma]$ the Parikh image of σ, i.e., the vector $(|\sigma|_{a_1}, \cdots, |\sigma|_{a_n})$ of $\mathbb{N}^n$. This notation is generalized to sets of sequences. A set $S \subseteq \Sigma^*$ (resp. $S \subseteq \Sigma^{\omega}$) is a ***semilinear language*** (resp. ***semilinear ω-language***) if the set of vectors $[S]$ (resp. $[Pref(S)]$) is semilinear. A ***semilinear system*** is any system whose ω-language S is semilinear and such that (a representation of) $[Pref(S)]$ is effectively constructible from the representation of the system.

Lemma 2.2 *ω-context-free languages as well as PA ω-languages are semilinear. Petri nets ω-languages are, however, not semilinear.*

For PA processes, the proof uses Parikh's theorem (concerning context-free languages) and the fact that permutation of symbols preserves Parikh image. As for Petri nets, this is a direct consequence of the well known fact that sets of reachable markings are not semilinear in general.

Remark 2.1 The class of semilinear sets are closed under all boolean operations (they correspond exactly to the Presburger arithmetics definable sets). The class of semilinear languages is, however, not closed under intersection (see Section 6).

3 Constrained Linear Temporal Logic

3.1 Syntax and semantics

Recall that $\mathcal{P}$ is a finite set of atomic propositions and that $\Sigma = 2^{\mathcal{P}}$. We use letters $P, Q, \ldots$ to range over elements of $\mathcal{P}$. Let $\mathcal{V}$ be a set of integer valued variables. We use letters $x, y, \ldots$ to range over variables in $\mathcal{V}$. We use also letters $f, g, \ldots$ to range over Presburger arithmetics formulas (the first order logic of natural numbers with addition, subtraction, and the usual ordering). We introduce a set $\mathcal{W}$ of *position variables*, and use letters $u, v, \ldots$ to range over $\mathcal{W}$. We use letters $A, B, \ldots$ to range over deterministic finite-state (Rabin-Scott) automata over Σ. We denote by $L(A)$ the set of sequences in Σ^* accepted by A, by $\overline{A}$ an automaton recognizing $\Sigma^* - L(A)$, and by $A \times B$ an automaton recognizing $L(A) \cap L(B)$. Finally, let π range over the set of *propositional formulas* that are boolean combinations of atomic propositions. Then, the set of formulas of CLTL is defined by:

$$\varphi ::= P \mid \neg\varphi \mid \varphi \vee \varphi \mid \bigcirc\varphi \mid \varphi\mathcal{U}\varphi \mid \tilde{\exists} x.\varphi \mid [x : \pi].\varphi \mid f \mid u.\varphi \mid A^u$$

We define also two sublogics of CLTL obtained by extending LTL by either pattern or counting constraints only. The first logic, called ALTL, corresponds to the set of formulas

$$\psi ::= P \mid \neg\psi \mid \psi \vee \psi \mid \bigcirc\psi \mid \psi\mathcal{U}\psi \mid u.\psi \mid A^u$$

whereas the second logic, called PLTL, corresponds to the set of formulas

$$\psi ::= P \mid \neg\psi \mid \psi \vee \psi \mid \bigcirc\psi \mid \psi\mathcal{U}\psi \mid \tilde{\exists} x.\varphi \mid [x : \pi].\psi \mid f$$

We consider abbreviations as the boolean connectives $\wedge$, $\Rightarrow$, the universal quantification $\tilde{\forall}$, $\Diamond\varphi = true\mathcal{U}\varphi$, $\Box\varphi = \neg\Diamond\neg\varphi$, and $\varphi_1\overline{\mathcal{U}}\varphi_2 = \varphi_1\mathcal{U}(\varphi_1 \wedge \varphi_2)$. We write $[\vec{x} : \vec{\pi}].\varphi$ or $[x_1, \ldots, x_n : \pi_1, \ldots, \pi_n].\varphi$ or $[x_i : \pi_i]_{i=1}^n.\varphi$ for $[x_1 : \pi_1].\cdots[x_n : \pi_n].\varphi$.

CLTL formulas are interpreted on infinite sequences over Σ. The operators $\bigcirc, \mathcal{U}, \Diamond$, and $\Box$, are the *next*, *until*, *eventually*, and *always* operators of LTL; $\overline{\mathcal{U}}$ is a *right-closed until* operator.

The operator $\tilde{\exists}$ is the (rigid) quantification over natural numbers. We distinguish between $\tilde{\exists}$ and the Presburger arithmetics quantifier $\exists$ since they do not have the same scope. The construction "$[x : \pi]$." introduce a *counting variable* x which is associated with the propositional formula π. The variable x counts from the current position the number of occurrences of transition labels satisfying π on the sequence. Then, x can be used in Presburger formulas f to express *counting constraints* (that may involve several counting variables). For instance, the formula $\phi_1 = [x, y : \pi_1, \pi_2].\Box(P \Rightarrow (x \leq y))$ expresses the fact that from now on, whenever P holds, the number of transitions satisfying π_2 is greater than the number of transitions satisfying π_1.

The construction "u." associates the position variable u with the current position on the sequence. The variable u is used as a label allowing to refer to the position associated with it. Then, u can be used to express *pattern constraints* A^u saying that the subsequence since the position u is accepted by the automaton A. For instance, the formula $\phi_2 = u.[x, y : \pi_1, \pi_2].\Box(A^u \Rightarrow (x \leq y))$ expresses the fact that from now on, in every finite subsequence accepted by A, the number of transitions satisfying π_2 is greater or equal than the number of transitions satisfying π_1.

In the formula ϕ_2, the construction "$[x : \pi_1]$." (resp. "u.") binds the variable x (resp. u) in the subformula $\Box(A^u \Rightarrow (x \leq y))$. So, a variable $x \in \mathcal{V}$ may be bound by either $\tilde{\exists}$, or by Presburger quantification, or by the construction "$[x : \pi]$.". A position variable $u \in \mathcal{W}$ can be bound by the construction "u.". We call "$[x : \pi]$." (resp. "u.") the ***reset quantification*** (resp. ***position quantification***). We suppose without loss of generality that each variable is bound at most once. Then, every variable appearing in some formula is either *bound* or *free*. A formula φ is *closed* if all the variables occurring in it are bound, otherwise φ is *open*.

The formal semantics of CLTL is defined using a satisfaction relation $\models$ between sequences in Σ^ω, positions (positive integers), and formulas. Since formulas may be open, the relation is parameterized by a valuation E of the variables in $\mathcal{V}$ (we write $E \models f$ when the evaluation of f under E is true), a ***position association*** θ that associates with each counting or position variable the position where it has been introduced, and a ***propositional formula association*** η that records for each counting variable the propositional formula which is associated with it. Let ξ stands for E, θ, or η. Then, $\mathcal{D}(\xi)$ denotes the domain of ξ; the function ξ such that $\mathcal{D}(\xi) = \emptyset$ is denoted by $\emptyset$. We denote by $\xi[z \leftarrow \kappa]$ the function ξ' such that $\mathcal{D}(\xi') = \mathcal{D}(\xi) \cup \{z\}$, and which associates the value κ with z and coincides with ξ on all the other variables.

Now, let $\sigma \in \Sigma^\omega$. Then, for every $i \geq 0$, every valuation E, every position association θ (such that $\forall z \in \mathcal{D}(\theta)$, $0 \leq \theta(z) \leq i$), every propositional formula association η, and every CLTL formula φ, we define the meaning of $\langle \sigma, i \rangle \models_{(E,\theta,\eta)} \varphi$ inductively on the structure of φ; the definition is given in Table 1. Let φ be a closed formula. It is clear that $\langle \sigma, i \rangle \models_{(E,\theta,\eta)} \varphi$ iff $\langle \sigma, i \rangle \models_{(\emptyset,\emptyset,\emptyset)} \varphi$, and hence, we write simply $\langle \sigma, i \rangle \models \varphi$. We write also $\sigma \models \varphi$, and say that σ ***satisfies*** φ, if $\langle \sigma, 0 \rangle \models \varphi$. Let $[\![\varphi]\!]$ be the set of sequences $\sigma \in \Sigma^\omega$ such that $\sigma \models \varphi$. For every $S \subseteq \Sigma^\omega$, φ is ***satisfiable*** (resp. ***valid***) relatively to S iff $S \cap [\![\varphi]\!] \neq \emptyset$ (resp. $S \subseteq [\![\varphi]\!]$), and φ is ***satisfiable*** (resp. ***valid***) iff it is satisfiable (resp. valid) relatively to Σ^ω. The relative satisfiability (resp. validity) problem is whether a given formula is satisfiable (resp. valid) relatively to a given set of sequences. The relative validity problem is also called verification problem.

3.2 Expressiveness

We can show that ALTL is as expressive as finite-state ω-automata. Indeed, by McNaughton's theorem, every ω-regular language can be defined by an ALTL formula of the form:

$$u. \bigvee_{i=1}^{n} (\Box\Diamond A_i^u \wedge \Diamond\Box B_i^u)$$

On the other hand, for any given closed ALTL formula ψ, we can construct a Büchi ω-automaton which recognizes precisely $[\![\psi]\!]$. This construction generalizes the one given in [19] for LTL formulas by dealing with position quantification

$$
\begin{array}{ll}
\langle\sigma,i\rangle \models_{(E,\theta,\eta)} P & \text{iff } P \in \sigma(i) \\
\langle\sigma,i\rangle \models_{(E,\theta,\eta)} \neg\varphi & \text{iff } \langle\sigma,i\rangle \not\models_{(E,\theta,\eta)} \varphi \\
\langle\sigma,i\rangle \models_{(E,\theta,\eta)} \varphi_1 \vee \varphi_2 & \text{iff } \langle\sigma,i\rangle \models_{(E,\theta,\eta)} \varphi_1 \text{ or } \langle\sigma,i\rangle \models_{(E,\theta,\eta)} \varphi_2 \\
\langle\sigma,i\rangle \models_{(E,\theta,\eta)} \bigcirc\varphi & \text{iff } \langle\sigma,i+1\rangle \models_{(E,\theta,\eta)} \varphi \\
\langle\sigma,i\rangle \models_{(E,\theta,\eta)} \varphi_1 \mathcal{U} \varphi_2 & \text{iff } \exists j.\, i \leq j.\ \langle\sigma,j\rangle \models_{(E,\theta,\eta)} \varphi_2 \text{ and} \\
& \quad \forall k.\, i \leq k < j.\ \langle\sigma,k\rangle \models_{(E,\theta,\eta)} \varphi_1 \\
\langle\sigma,i\rangle \models_{(E,\theta,\eta)} \widetilde{\exists} x.\varphi & \text{iff } \exists k \in \mathbb{N}.\ \langle\sigma,i\rangle \models_{(E',\theta,\eta)} \varphi \text{ where } E' = E[x \leftarrow k] \\
\langle\sigma,i\rangle \models_{(E,\theta,\eta)} [x:\pi].\varphi & \text{iff } \langle\sigma,i\rangle \models_{(E,\theta',\eta')} \varphi \text{ where} \\
& \quad \theta' = \theta[x \leftarrow i] \text{ and } \eta' = \eta[x \leftarrow \pi] \\
\langle\sigma,i\rangle \models_{(E,\theta,\eta)} f & \text{iff } E' \models f \text{ where} \\
& \quad E' = E[x \leftarrow |\{j \in [\theta(x),i] \ :\ \langle\sigma,j\rangle \models \eta(x)\}|]_{x \in \mathcal{D}(\eta)} \\
\langle\sigma,i\rangle \models_{(E,\theta,\eta)} u.\varphi & \text{iff } \langle\sigma,i\rangle \models_{(E,\theta',\eta)} \varphi \text{ where } \theta' = \theta[u \leftarrow i] \\
\langle\sigma,i\rangle \models_{(E,\theta,\eta)} A^u & \text{iff } \sigma(\theta(u),i) \in L(A)
\end{array}
$$

Table 1. Definition of the satisfaction relation

and pattern constraints. It uses mainly the fact that every regular language (pattern constraint) has a finite number of derivatives (left-quotients) w.r.t. finite sequences over Σ.

Using counting constraints, we can express *nonregular* properties, i.e., properties that cannot be expressed by ω-regular automata. For instance, consider the property saying: given an infinite sequence of transitions (events), every a is followed by a b, at each position between an a and the next b, the number of c's is greater or equal than the number of d's, and at b, the numbers of c's and d's are equal. Formally, the property imposes that the sequences between two successive a and b are in the language $\{\sigma \in \Sigma^* \ :\ |\sigma|_c = |\sigma|_d$, and $\forall i \leq |\sigma|, |\sigma(0,i)|_c \geq |\sigma(0,i)|_d\}$. This property can be expressed in PLTL by:

$$\Box(a \Rightarrow [x,y,z:c,d,b].((x \geq y \mathcal{U}\, b) \wedge \Box((b \wedge z = 1) \Rightarrow x = y))) \tag{1}$$

The introduction of counting constraints allows to characterize nonregular languages that can be context-free as in (1), but also context-sensitive when constraints relating more than two counting variables are considered.

The use of pattern constraints allows to constrain the order of appearance of events. Suppose for instance that we want to strengthen the property above by imposing that between two successive a and b, all the c's appear before all the d's. The new property can be expressed by the conjunction of the LTL formula $\Box(a \Rightarrow \Diamond b)$ (every a is followed by a b) with the CLTL formula:

$$u.[x,y:c,d].\,\Box(A^u \Rightarrow (B^u \wedge x = y)) \tag{2}$$

where A and B are finite-state automata such that $L(A) = \Sigma^* a(\Sigma - \{a,b\})^* b$, and $L(B) = \Sigma^* a(\Sigma - \{d\})^*(\Sigma - \{c\})^* b$.

Finally, let us illustrate the use of the $\widetilde{\forall}$ quantification. It allows to relate counting constraints at different positions on the sequence, and express counting constraints on the numbers of occurrences of events in different subsequences. For instance, consider the property saying: every a is followed by a b, and between successive a's and b's the subsequences are in the language $\{\sigma s \sigma' : \sigma, \sigma' \in (\Sigma - \{a,b,s\})^*, |\sigma|_c = |\sigma'|_d\}$. This property can be expressed by the conjunction of the LTL formula $\Box(a \Rightarrow \bigcirc(\neg s\,\mathcal{U}\,(s \wedge \bigcirc(\neg s\,\mathcal{U}\,b))))$ with the PLTL formula:

$$\widetilde{\forall} n.\ \Box(a \Rightarrow [x,y,z : c,d,b].\ \Box((s \wedge x = n) \Rightarrow \Box((b \wedge z = 1) \Rightarrow y = n))) \qquad (3)$$

The variable n in (3) is used to memorize the number of c's between a and s, and then, this number can be compared with the number of d's between s and b.

3.3 Undecidability results

Theorem 3.1 ([4]) *The satisfiability problems of PLTL and CLTL are Σ_1^1-complete. Consequently, the validity problems of PLTL and CLTL, as well as their verification problem for finite-state LTS's, are Π_1^1-complete.*

Actually, we can prove the undecidability of the verification problem for even a very simple class of PLTL formulas corresponding to *counting constraints eventuality properties*, i.e., formulas of the form $[\vec{x} : \vec{\pi}].\ \Diamond f(\vec{x})$. For this kind of formulas, the verification problem for finite-state LTS's is Σ_1^0-complete.

4 The fragments CLTL$_\Box$ and CLTL$_\Diamond$

We introduce hereafter several fragments of CLTL. These fragments are defined so that they do not contain formulas that cause the undecidability of the verification problem, namely the counting constraints eventuality formulas. These fragments are not closed under negation. So, for each of these fragments we introduce another one such that the negation of every formula in the first one is equivalent to a formula in the second one, and vice versa. We discuss the expressiveness of these fragments and consider their satisfiability and validity problems.

4.1 Definitions

We start by defining the most expressive fragments, called CLTL$_\Box$ and CLTL$_\Diamond$. To describe simply the syntactical restrictions corresponding to these fragments, we introduce the *positive form* of CLTL formulas given by:

$$\varphi ::= \widetilde{\exists} x.\varphi \mid \widetilde{\forall} x.\varphi \mid [x : \pi].\varphi \mid f \mid u.\varphi \mid A^u \mid P \mid \neg P \mid \varphi \vee \varphi \mid \varphi \wedge \varphi \mid \bigcirc\varphi \mid \Box\varphi \mid \varphi\,\mathcal{U}\,\varphi \qquad (4)$$

We can prove that every CLTL formula has an equivalent formula in positive normal form. Notice that the positive form of ALTL (resp. PLTL) formulas corresponds to (4) without reset (resp. position) quantification and counting (resp. pattern) constraints.

Now, recall that the verification problem is undecidable as soon as eventuality formulas with counting constraints are considered. Hence, to avoid such formulas, we define the fragment CLTL$_\Box$ obtained by imposing in (4) that the formulas in the right-hand side of $\mathcal{U}$ must be in ALTL (i.e., counting constraints free). We admit also in this fragment $\overline{\mathcal{U}}$-formulas under the same condition. We also forbid in CLTL$_\Box$ the operator $\tilde{\exists}$. The fragment CLTL$_\Diamond$ is defined in such a manner that it characterizes exactly the complements of CLTL$_\Box$ properties. So, CLTL$_\Box$ consists of the set of formulas φ defined by:

$$\varphi ::= \tilde{\forall}x.\varphi \mid [x:\pi].\varphi \mid f \mid u.\varphi \mid A^u \mid P \mid \neg P \mid \varphi \vee \varphi \mid \varphi \wedge \varphi \mid \bigcirc\varphi \mid \Box\varphi \mid \varphi\mathcal{U}\psi \mid \varphi\overline{\mathcal{U}}\psi$$

whereas CLTL$_\Diamond$ consists of the set of formulas φ defined by:

$$\varphi ::= \tilde{\exists}x.\varphi \mid [x:\pi].\varphi \mid f \mid u.\varphi \mid A^u \mid P \mid \neg P \mid \varphi \vee \varphi \mid \varphi \wedge \varphi \mid \bigcirc\varphi \mid \Box\psi \mid \psi\mathcal{U}\varphi \mid \psi\overline{\mathcal{U}}\varphi$$

where, in both definitions, ψ stands for any ALTL formula.

We define in a similar way the fragments of PLTL called PLTL$_\Box$ and PLTL$_\Diamond$ (in this case, the ψ's are required to be LTL formulas). Moreover, we consider the fragments *simple*-PLTL$_\Box$ and *simple*-PLTL$_\Diamond$ obtained from the previous ones by imposing that the ψ's are propositional formulas instead of any LTL formulas.

Proposition 4.1 *For every CLTL$_\Box$ (resp. PLTL$_\Box$, simple-PLTL$_\Box$) closed formula φ, there exists a CLTL$_\Diamond$ (resp. PLTL$_\Diamond$, simple-PLTL$_\Diamond$) closed formula φ' such that $[\![\neg\varphi]\!] = [\![\varphi']\!]$, and conversely.*

4.2 Expressiveness

It is easy to see that the set of ALTL formulas in positive form is a subset of both CLTL$_\Box$ and CLTL$_\Diamond$. Hence, both fragments CLTL$_\Box$ and CLTL$_\Diamond$ can express all the ω-regular properties. However, these fragments obviously do not express the same classes of nonregular properties. For instance, CLTL$_\Box$ allow to express *constrained safety properties* (see (2) for instance), but cannot express their negations (*constrained eventuality properties*) that are CLTL$_\Diamond$ properties.

Similarly, it can be observed that PLTL$_\Box$ and PLTL$_\Diamond$ subsume the logic LTL, and hence, they can express all the *ω-star-free* properties [17]. Moreover, we can show that simple-PLTL$_\Diamond$ expresses all the *simple* ω-regular languages (the definition is given in Section 2.2) whereas simple-PLTL$_\Box$ expresses obviously all their complements (recall that simple ω-regular languages are not closed under complementation). The same duality existing between CLTL$_\Box$ and CLTL$_\Diamond$ concerning nonregular properties exists also between their subfragments. Even restricted, these subfragments allow to capture significant classes of nonregular properties. For instance, the formulas (1) and (3) are in simple-PLTL$_\Box$.

The following picture shows the inclusions between the different logics we consider.

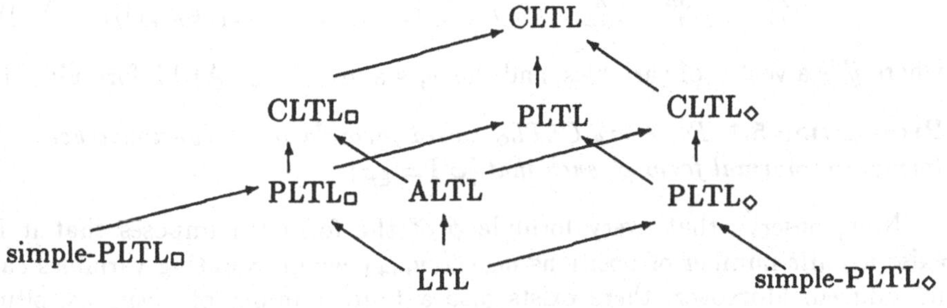

4.3 Satisfiability problem

We can prove in the same manner as Theorem 3.1 the following undecidability result concerning the satisfiability and validity problems of the fragments introduced above.

Theorem 4.1 *The satisfiability (resp. validity) problems of simple-PLTL$_\Box$, PLTL$_\Box$, and CLTL$_\Box$ (resp. simple-PLTL$_\Diamond$, PLTL$_\Diamond$, and CLTL$_\Diamond$) are Σ_1^1-complete (resp. Π_1^1-complete).*

We prove in Section 6 that the validity (resp. satisfiability) problem of CLTL$_\Box$ (resp. CLTL$_\Diamond$) is actually decidable (see Corollary 6.1).

5 Decomposing CLTL$_\Diamond$ properties

We show in this section that every CLTL$_\Diamond$ property can be decomposed (modulo projection) into an ω-regular property and a counting constraints eventuality property (more precisely, every CLTL$_\Diamond$ property is a finite union of projections of sets that are intersections of ω-regular properties with counting constraints eventuality properties).

This decomposition is helpful for reasoning about the (relative) satisfiability problem of CLTL$_\Diamond$, and hence, on the verification problem of CLTL$_\Box$. Indeed, it allows to reduce the satisfiability problem of a CLTL$_\Diamond$ formula φ relatively to a set of sequences S, to a *constrained emptiness problem*: whether there exists a sequence in a set of finite sequences which satisfies some counting constraints. This set of finite sequences is the set of prefixes of sequences that are in the intersection of S (a cylindrification of S actually) with, roughly speaking, the "ω-regular part" of the property expressed by φ. Hence, when the set S is the ω-language of a system, the problem reduces to a *constrained reachability problem* in the product of the considered system with an ω-automaton characterizing the "ω-regular part" of φ. The decidability of this problem is discussed in the next sections depending on the considered classes of systems and properties.

To establish the decomposition property mentioned above, we proceed in several steps. The first one is to put CLTL$_\Diamond$ formulas into a *normal form* which is defined below. Let $\Sigma = \{a_1, \cdots, a_n\}$, and for every $i \in \{1, \cdots, n\}$, let $\pi_i = (\bigwedge_{P \in a_i} P) \wedge (\bigwedge_{P \notin a_i} \neg P)$. We say that a CLTL$_\Diamond$ formula is in *normal form* if it is a disjunction of formulas of the form

$$\widetilde{\exists} \vec{y}.\, u_0.\, [x_i^0 : \pi_i]_{i=1}^n.\, (\psi_0 \wedge (\psi_0' \,\overline{\mathcal{U}}\, (f_0 \wedge \bigcirc u_1.\, [x_i^1 : \pi_i]_{i=1}^n.\, (\psi_1 \wedge (\psi_1' \,\overline{\mathcal{U}}\, (f_1 \wedge \cdots$$
$$\cdots \bigcirc u_m.\, [x_i^m : \pi_i]_{i=1}^n.\, (\psi_m \wedge (\psi_m' \,\overline{\mathcal{U}}\, (f_m \wedge \bigcirc u_{m+1}.\, \psi_{m+1}))) \cdots)))))) \quad (5)$$

where $\vec{y}$ is a vector of variables, and the ψ_j's and ψ_j''s are ALTL formulas. Then:

Proposition 5.1 *For every CLTL$_\Diamond$ closed formula φ, we can construct a closed formula in normal form φ' such that $[\![\varphi']\!] = [\![\varphi]\!]$.*

Now, observe that every formula ϕ of the form (5) imposes that it must exist a *finite* number of positions $u_0, \cdots, u_{m+1}$ where counting variables can be introduced. Moreover, there exists also a finite number of positions, situated just before the u_j's, where counting constraints (on counting variables previously introduced) must be satisfied. Actually, we can construct from ϕ another formula where all the counting variables are introduced at the first position (u_0), and all the counting constraints are checked at the last position (u_{m+1}). For that, we introduce new propositional formulas to distinguish between the different subsequences delimited by successive positions u_j and u_{j+1}. So, for every $j \in \{0, \cdots, m+1\}$, we consider a new atomic proposition at_j, and we define the formula $\lambda_j = \mathrm{at}_j \wedge \bigwedge_{k \neq j} \neg\, \mathrm{at}_k$. Let $\mathcal{P}'$ be the union of $\mathcal{P}$ with the set of the new atomic propositions, and let $\Sigma' = 2^{\mathcal{P}'}$. Then, given a formula ϕ of the form (5), let $\widehat{\phi}$ denote the formula:

$$\widetilde{\exists}\vec{y}.\, u_0.\, [z_i^j : \pi_i \wedge \lambda_j]_{i=1..n}^{j=0..m} \cdot (\psi_0 \wedge ((\psi'_0 \wedge \lambda_0)\overline{\mathcal{U}} \cdots$$
$$\cdots \bigcirc u_m.\, (\psi_m \wedge ((\psi'_m \wedge \lambda_m)\overline{\mathcal{U}}\, ((\bigwedge_{j=0}^{m} f_j[\sum_{\ell=k}^{j} z_i^\ell / x_i^k]_{i=1..n}^{k=0..j}) \wedge$$
$$\bigcirc u_{m+1}.\, (\psi_{m+1} \wedge \Box\lambda_{m+1})))))\cdots))$$

It can be seen that $[\![\phi]\!] = [\![\widehat{\phi}]\!]|_{\Sigma}$. Indeed, notice that the λ_j's are mutually exclusive propositional formulas, and that the counting variables z_i^j are associated with $\pi_i \wedge \lambda_j$. Hence, each variable z_i^j counts the number of occurrences of π_i exactly in the subsequence between u_j (included) and u_{j+1} (excluded). So, we can move every counting constraint f_j to the position u_{m+1} provided each counting variable x_i^k appearing in f_j, for every $k \leq j$, is substituted by the sum $\sum_{\ell=k}^{j} z_i^\ell$.

Now, it can be observed that $\widehat{\phi}$ is equivalent to the conjunction of two formulas, one of them is in ALTL, the other one is a *counting constraints eventuality* formula. Let $\widehat{\phi}^*$ be the ALTL formula:

$$u_0.\, (\psi_0 \wedge ((\psi'_0 \wedge \lambda_0)\overline{\mathcal{U}} \cdots \bigcirc u_m.\, (\psi_m \wedge ((\psi'_m \wedge \lambda_m)\overline{\mathcal{U}} \bigcirc u_{m+1}.\, (\psi_{m+1} \wedge \Box\lambda_{m+1})))\cdots)) \tag{6}$$

and $\widehat{\phi}^\#$ the eventuality formula:

$$[z_i^j : \pi_i \wedge \lambda_j]_{i=1..n}^{j=0..m} \cdot [z : \lambda_{m+1}].\, \Diamond(z = 1 \wedge \overbrace{\exists\vec{y}.\, \bigwedge_{j=0}^{m} f_j[\sum_{\ell=k}^{j} z_i^\ell / x_i^k]_{i=1..n}^{k=0..j}}^{g}) \tag{7}$$

Notice that the global quantification $\widetilde{\exists}\vec{y}$ in $\widehat{\phi}$ has been replaced by a quantification $\exists\vec{y}$ in the Presburger formula g above.

It can be seen that $[\![\widehat{\phi}]\!] = [\![\widehat{\phi}^* \wedge \widehat{\phi}^\#]\!]$. This fact holds since, given a sequence that satisfies $\widehat{\phi}^*$, the positions $u_0, \ldots, u_{m+1}$ are uniquely determined by the truth of the λ_j's. Moreover, the constraint $z = 1$ ensures that the counting constraints of $\widehat{\phi}^\#$ are checked at u_{m+1}. Actually, we could replace the constraint $z = 1$ by $z \geq 1$ since after u_{m+1}, all the counting variables, except z, are frozen due to the fact that λ_{m+1} is continuously true.

Then, since $[\![\phi]\!] = [\![\widehat{\phi}]\!]|_{\Sigma}$ and $[\![\widehat{\phi}]\!] = [\![\widehat{\phi}^* \wedge \widehat{\phi}^\#]\!]$, we obtain the following fact:

Theorem 5.1 *Let φ be a CLTL$_\Diamond$ closed formula and let $\bigvee_{i=1}^{\ell} \phi_i$ be a formula in normal form which is equivalent to φ. Then, we have $[\![\varphi]\!] = \bigcup_{i=1}^{\ell}([\![\widehat{\phi}_i^*]\!] \cap [\![\widehat{\phi}_i^\#]\!])|_{\Sigma}$.*

By Theorem 5.1, Lemma 2.1, and the fact that projection preserves nonemptiness:

Corollary 5.1 *Let $S \subseteq \Sigma^\omega$, φ a CLTL$_\Diamond$ closed formula, and $\bigvee_{i=1}^{\ell} \phi_i$ a formula in normal form equivalent to φ. Then, φ is satisfiable relatively to S if and only if $\bigcup_{i=1}^{\ell}(\widetilde{S} \cap [\![\widehat{\phi}_i^*]\!] \cap [\![\widehat{\phi}_i^\#]\!]) \neq \emptyset$.*

6 Reasoning about semilinear systems

We address the relative satisfiability problem of CLTL$_\Diamond$ formulas and show the conditions of its reducibility to the emptiness problem of semilinear sets. Then we exhibit classes of semilinear systems and properties whose verification problem is (i) decidable by reduction to emptiness of semilinear sets, (ii) not reducible to emptiness of semilinear sets but still decidable, or (iii) undecidable.

First we need to introduce some notations. Let f be a Presburger formula with n free variables. We denote by $\langle\!| f |\!\rangle$ the set of valuations (vectors in $\mathbb{N}^n$) satisfying f. It is well known that for every Presburger formula f, the set $\langle\!| f |\!\rangle$ is semilinear.

Let $S \subseteq \Sigma^\omega$, φ a CLTL$_\Diamond$ closed formula, and $\bigvee_{i=1}^{\ell} \phi_i$ a formula in normal form equivalent to φ (by Proposition 5.1). Then, by Corollary 5.1, we have $S \cap [\![\varphi]\!] \neq \emptyset$ iff $\exists i \in \{1, \ldots, \ell\}, \widetilde{S} \cap [\![\widehat{\phi}_i^*]\!] \cap [\![\widehat{\phi}_i^\#]\!] \neq \emptyset$, i.e., $\widehat{\phi}_i^\#$ is satisfiable relatively to $\widetilde{S} \cap [\![\widehat{\phi}_i^*]\!]$. Let g_i be the Presburger formula expressing the counting constraints in $\widehat{\phi}_i^\#$ (see 7). Then, $\widetilde{S} \cap [\![\widehat{\phi}_i^*]\!] \cap [\![\widehat{\phi}_i^\#]\!] \neq \emptyset$ iff there exists a finite prefix of some sequence σ in $\widetilde{S} \cap [\![\widehat{\phi}_i^*]\!]$, say $\sigma(0, j)$, whose Parikh image satisfies g_i, i.e., $[\sigma(0, j)] \in \langle\!| g_i |\!\rangle$. Hence:

$$S \cap [\![\varphi]\!] \neq \emptyset \text{ iff } \exists i \in \{1, \ldots, \ell\}. \, [Pref(\widetilde{S} \cap [\![\widehat{\phi}_i^*]\!])] \cap \langle\!| g_i |\!\rangle \neq \emptyset. \tag{8}$$

This fact allows to reduce relative satisfiability of CLTL$_\Diamond$ formulas to nonemptiness of semilinear sets provided the considered set S and formula φ are such that all the $(\widetilde{S} \cap [\![\widehat{\phi}_i^*]\!])$'s are semilinear ω-languages (semilinear sets being closed under intersection).

Now, recall that the $\widehat{\phi}_i^*$'s are ALTL formulas. Thus, all the $[\![\widehat{\phi}_i^*]\!]$'s are ω-regular languages. Moreover, it can be seen from (6) that, if φ is a PLTL$_\Diamond$, the $\widehat{\phi}_i^*$'s are actually LTL formulas, and thus, the $[\![\widehat{\phi}_i^*]\!]$'s are in this case ω-star-free languages. Finally, it is easy to show that when φ is in simple-PLTL$_\Diamond$, the $[\![\widehat{\phi}_i^*]\!]$'s are simple ω-regular languages. Indeed, if the ψ_i's and the ψ_i''s in (6) are propositional formulas, then roughly speaking, each set $[\![\widehat{\phi}_i^*]\!]$ corresponds to a union of ω-languages of the form $a_0 b_0^* a_1 b_1^* \cdots a_n b_n^\omega$, that are clearly simple ω-regular.

Then, since all the ω-regular languages are semilinear, and since the emptiness problem of semilinear sets is decidable, we obtain the following result.

Theorem 6.1 *Let C be a class of ω-languages over Σ such that: for every $\Sigma' \supseteq \Sigma$, for every $S \in C$, and for every ω-regular (resp. ω-star-free, simple ω-regular) language R over Σ', $\widetilde{S} \cap R$ is semilinear. Then, the satisfiability problem of CLTL$_\Diamond$ (resp. PLTL$_\Diamond$, simple-PLTL$_\Diamond$) closed formulas relatively to ω-languages in C is decidable, and consequently, the validity problem of CLTL$_\Box$ (resp. PLTL$_\Box$, simple-PLTL$_\Box$) relatively to C is decidable.*

We deduce from Theorem 6.1 several decidability results depending on which class of ω-languages we consider. First of all, let us address the problem of *satisfiability* and *validity* of, respectively, $CLTL_{\Diamond}$ and $CLTL_{\Box}$. Then, by taking $\mathcal{C} = \{\Sigma^\omega\}$ we obtain by Theorem 6.1:

Corollary 6.1 *The satisfiability (resp. validity) problem of* $CLTL_{\Diamond}$ *(resp.* $CLTL_{\Box}$*) closed formulas is decidable.*

Now, let us address the *verification problem* of semilinear systems. We start by considering the case of pushdown systems. These systems generate ω-context-free languages that are semilinear (see Lemma 2.2). The class of ω-context-free languages is clearly closed under cylindrification, and it is also closed under intersection with ω-regular languages [10]. Then, by Theorem 6.1:

Corollary 6.2 *The satisfiability (resp. validity) problem of* $CLTL_{\Diamond}$ *(resp.* $CLTL_{\Box}$*) closed formulas relatively to* ω*-context-free languages is decidable. In particular, the verification problem of pushdown systems w.r.t.* $CLTL_{\Box}$ *closed formulas is decidable.*

This decidability result, however, does not hold for the whole class of semilinear systems. Indeed, we can encode the halting of a 2-counter machine as the nonemptiness of the intersection of an ω-star-free language R with a semilinear (actually a PA) ω-language S.

Proposition 6.1 ([4]) *The satisfiability problem of LTL formulas relatively to PA* ω*-languages is undecidable. Consequently, the verification problem of PA w.r.t. LTL is undecidable.*

As a consequence of Theorem 6.1 and Proposition 6.1, the class of semilinear ω-languages is not closed under intersection with ω-star-free languages. Actually, we can give a direct proof of this fact by showing that even the intersection of a BPP ω-language with an ω-regular one can be nonsemilinear, and this holds as soon as we consider *nonsimple* ω-regular languages definable by automata having loops with two control locations [4]. This means that the verification problem of BPP processes w.r.t. $CLTL_{\Box}$ formulas cannot be reduced to the emptiness problem of semilinear sets. We show in the next section that, nevertheless, this problem is decidable (since we will show that it is decidable for Petri nets and BPP corresponds to a subclass of Petri nets). Now, if we restrict ourselves to *simple* ω-regular languages, we can prove that:

Proposition 6.2 *The class of PA* ω*-languages is closed under intersection with simple* ω*-regular languages.*

Then, using Theorem 6.1, Proposition 6.2, and the fact that the class of semilinear ω-languages is closed under cylindrification, we obtain the following result:

Corollary 6.3 *The satisfiability (resp. validity) problem of simple-*$PLTL_{\Diamond}$ *(resp. simple-*$PLTL_{\Box}$*) closed formulas relatively to PA* ω*-languages is decidable. Consequently, the verification problem of PA processes w.r.t. simple-*$PLTL_{\Box}$ *closed formulas is decidable.*

7 Reasoning about Petri nets

We consider now the satisfiability problem of CLTL$_\Diamond$ closed formulas relatively to Petri nets. Recall that these systems are not semilinear (see Lemma 2.2), and thus, the problem we consider cannot be tackled as in the previous section by reduction to the emptiness problem of semilinear sets. Nevertheless, we show that it is decidable by reduction to the reachability problem in Petri nets.

Let $\mathcal{N}$ be a Petri net, φ a CLTL$_\Diamond$ closed formula, and $\bigvee_{i=1}^{\ell} \phi_i$ a formula in normal form equivalent to φ. By Corollary 5.1, we have $L(\mathcal{N}) \cap [\![\varphi]\!] \neq \emptyset$ iff $\exists i \in \{1, \ldots, \ell\}, \widetilde{L(\mathcal{N})} \cap [\![\widehat{\phi}_i^*]\!] \cap [\![\widehat{\phi}_i^\#]\!] \neq \emptyset$, where $\widetilde{L(\mathcal{N})}$ as well as the $\widehat{\phi}_i^*$'s and the $\widehat{\phi}_i^\#$ are defined over a new alphabet Σ'. Let us fix $i \in \{1, \ldots, \ell\}$ and focus on the problem $\widetilde{L(\mathcal{N})} \cap [\![\widehat{\phi}_i^*]\!] \cap [\![\widehat{\phi}_i^\#]\!] \neq \emptyset$.

The net $\mathcal{N}$ can be transformed straightforwardly into a net $\widetilde{\mathcal{N}}$ over Σ' such that $L(\widetilde{\mathcal{N}}) = \widetilde{L(\mathcal{N})}$. We denote by g_i the counting constraint involved in $[\![\widehat{\phi}_i^\#]\!]$. Then, by definition of $[\![\widehat{\phi}_i^\#]\!]$, we have

$$\widetilde{L(\mathcal{N})} \cap [\![\widehat{\phi}_i^*]\!] \cap [\![\widehat{\phi}_i^\#]\!] \neq \emptyset \text{ iff } \exists \sigma \in Pref(L(\widetilde{\mathcal{N}}) \cap [\![\widehat{\phi}_i^*]\!]).\ [\sigma] \models g_i \tag{9}$$

Recall that $\widehat{\phi}_i^*$ is an ALTL formula, and that we can effectively construct a finite-state Büchi ω-automaton $\mathcal{A} = (\mathcal{S}_\mathcal{A}, F)$ such that $L(\mathcal{A}) = [\![\widehat{\phi}_i^*]\!]$. Let $\widetilde{\mathcal{N}} \times \mathcal{S}_\mathcal{A}$ be the product net of $\widetilde{\mathcal{N}}$ and the net obtained from $\mathcal{S}_\mathcal{A}$ by considering each control location as a place. Moreover, let $\mathbf{T}_\infty$ be the set of transitions in $\widetilde{\mathcal{N}} \times \mathcal{S}_\mathcal{A}$ that involve a transition of $\mathcal{S}_\mathcal{A}$ having as target some repeating location in F. Then, $L(\widetilde{\mathcal{N}}) \cap [\![\widehat{\phi}_i^*]\!]$ is the set of infinite sequences over Σ' generated by sequences of transitions in $\widetilde{\mathcal{N}} \times \mathcal{S}_\mathcal{A}$ including infinitely often transitions in $\mathbf{T}_\infty$. Thus, $Pref(L(\widetilde{\mathcal{N}}) \cap [\![\widehat{\phi}_i^*]\!])$ is the set of finite sequences over Σ' generated by sequences of transitions in $\widetilde{\mathcal{N}} \times \mathcal{S}_\mathcal{A}$ reaching markings from which there are infinite sequences of transitions including infinitely often transitions in $\mathbf{T}_\infty$. The set of such markings is actually semilinear and effectively constructible using the result proved in [18]:

Lemma 7.1 *Let $\mathcal{N}$ be a Petri net, and t one of its transitions. Then, the set $\mathcal{M}_\infty(\mathcal{N}, t)$ is semilinear and can be effectively constructed.*

Let us denote by $\mathcal{L}_\infty$ the semilinear set $\bigcup_{t \in \mathbf{T}_\infty} \mathcal{M}_\infty(\widetilde{\mathcal{N}} \times \mathcal{S}_\mathcal{A}, t)$. Then, by (9):

$$\widetilde{L(\mathcal{N})} \cap [\![\widehat{\phi}_i^*]\!] \cap [\![\widehat{\phi}_i^\#]\!] \neq \emptyset \text{ iff } \exists \sigma \in (\Sigma')^*.\ \exists M \in \mathcal{L}_\infty.\ M_{\widetilde{\mathcal{N}} \times \mathcal{S}_\mathcal{A}} \xrightarrow{\sigma} M \text{ and } [\sigma] \models g_i \tag{10}$$

To deal with counting constraints, we extend the net $\widetilde{\mathcal{N}} \times \mathcal{S}_\mathcal{A}$ by new places encoding the counting variables in g_i. Each such a place is associated with some label in Σ', say a, and counts the number of times the transitions of $\widetilde{\mathcal{N}} \times \mathcal{S}_\mathcal{A}$ labelled by a are fired. Let $\mathbf{P}^\#$ be the set of the new places, and $\widetilde{\mathcal{N}}_\mathcal{A}^\#$ the net resulting from this extension. Clearly, $\langle\!|g_i|\!\rangle$ is a semilinear subset of $\mathbb{N}^d$ where $d = |\mathbf{P}^\#|$. Let $\langle\!|g_i|\!\rangle'$ (resp. $\mathcal{L}'_\infty$) be the set of all markings of $\widetilde{\mathcal{N}}_\mathcal{A}^\#$ whose projections on $\mathbf{P}^\#$ (resp. the places of $\widetilde{\mathcal{N}} \times \mathcal{S}_\mathcal{A}$) are in $\langle\!|g_i|\!\rangle$ (resp. $\mathcal{L}_\infty$). The sets $\langle\!|g_i|\!\rangle'$ and $\mathcal{L}'_\infty$

are semilinear and can be constructed easily from the original ones. Moreover, the class of semilinear sets being closed under intersection, the set $\mathcal{L}'_\infty \cap \llparenthesis g_i \rrparenthesis'$ is also semilinear. Then, we obtain from (10) the following fact:

$$\widetilde{L(\mathcal{N})} \cap [\![\widehat{\phi}_i^*]\!] \cap [\![\widehat{\phi}_i^\#]\!] \neq \emptyset \text{ iff } \exists \sigma \in (\Sigma')^*. \exists M \in (\mathcal{L}'_\infty \cap \llparenthesis g_i \rrparenthesis'). M_{\widetilde{\mathcal{N}}^*_{\mathcal{A}}} \xrightarrow{\sigma} M \quad (11)$$

We have reduced the nonemptiness problem we are interested in to the reachability problem of a semilinear set in Petri nets, i.e., whether there is a reachable marking in some given semilinear set of markings. We can prove that this problem is reducible to the reachability problem in Petri nets (i.e., whether a given marking is reachable), which is decidable [15]: First of all, notice that given two nets $\mathcal{N}_1$ and $\mathcal{N}_2$ with the same number of places, the problem whether $\mathcal{R}(\mathcal{N}_1) \cap \mathcal{R}(\mathcal{N}_2) \neq \emptyset$ is reducible to the reachability problem in Petri nets. Indeed, we can add to $\mathcal{N}_1$ and $\mathcal{N}_2$ transitions clearing simultaneously, token by token, places in both nets with the same index, and then, $\mathcal{R}(\mathcal{N}_1) \cap \mathcal{R}(\mathcal{N}_2) \neq \emptyset$ iff the empty marking is reachable. Now, given a *linear* set $\mathcal{L}$, we can construct easily a net $\mathcal{N}_\mathcal{L}$ such that $\mathcal{R}(\mathcal{N}_\mathcal{L}) = \mathcal{L}$. Then, assuming that $\mathcal{L}$ is a set of markings of some net $\mathcal{N}$, by the remark above, the problem $\mathcal{R}(\mathcal{N}) \cap \mathcal{L} \neq \emptyset$ is reducible to the reachability problem in Petri nets. Obviously, this can be generalized to semilinear sets.

Lemma 7.2 *Let $\mathcal{N}$ be a Petri net, and $\mathcal{L}$ a semilinear set of markings of $\mathcal{N}$. Then, the problem $\mathcal{R}(\mathcal{N}) \cap \mathcal{L} \neq \emptyset$ is decidable.*

Then, by (11) and Lemma 7.2, we deduce the following result:

Theorem 7.1 *The satisfiability problem of CLTL$_\diamond$ closed formulas relatively to Petri nets is decidable. Consequently, the verification problem of Petri nets w.r.t. CLTL$_\square$ closed formulas is decidable.*

8 Conclusion

We have addressed the verification problem of nonregular properties for two incomparable classes of infinite state systems: semilinear systems including pushdown systems and PA processes, and Petri nets.

Our main results are that the verification problems of pushdown systems as well as Petri nets w.r.t. CLTL$_\square$ formulas are decidable. This logic is strictly more expressive than the linear-time μ-calculus and allows the expression of nonregular properties like constrained safety properties.

$\models$	LTL	ALTL	PLTL	CLTL	simple-PLTL$_\square$	PLTL$_\square$	CLTL$_\square$
Finite-state LTS	yes	yes	no	no	yes	yes	yes
Pushdown syst.	yes	yes	no	no	yes	yes	yes
PA processes	no	no	no	no	yes	no	no
Petri nets	yes	yes	no	no	yes	yes	yes

Table 2. Decidability of the verification problem

To establish these results, we have reduced the relative satisfiability problem of CLTL$_\Diamond$ (the dual fragment of CLTL$_\Box$) to a constrained emptiness problem. Then, we have tackled the latter problem either by reduction to the emptiness problem of semilinear sets or by reduction to the reachability problem of Petri nets. We have shown also that the verification problem of semilinear systems is in general undecidable for LTL (ω-star-free properties). Nevertheless, we have shown that this problem is decidable for all PA processes and simple-PLTL$_\Box$ which allows to express significant nonregular properties (like (1) and (3)). We summarize these results in Table 2.

References

1. P. Abdulla and B. Jonsson. Verifying Programs with Unreliable Channels. In *LICS'93.* IEEE, 1993.
2. J. Baeten, J.A. Bergstra, and J.W. Klop. Decidability of Bisimulation Equivalence for Processes Generating Context-Free Languages. T.R. CS-R8632, 1987. CWI.
3. J.A. Bergstra and J.W. Klop. Process Theory based on Bisimulation Semantics. In *REX School/Workshop on Linear Time, Branching Time and Partial Order in Logics and Models for Concurrency*, 1988. LNCS 354.
4. A. Bouajjani, R. Echahed, and P. Habermehl. On the Verification Problem of Nonregular Properties for Nonregular Processes. In *LICS'95.* IEEE, 1995.
5. A. Bouajjani, R. Echahed, and P. Habermehl. Verifying Infinite State Processes with Sequential and Parallel Composition. In *POPL'95.* ACM, 1995.
6. O. Burkart and B. Steffen. Pushdown Processes: Parallel Composition and Model Checking. In *CONCUR'94*, 1994. LNCS 836.
7. S. Christensen. *Decidability and Decomposition in Process Algebra.* PhD thesis, University of Edinburgh, 1993.
8. S. Christensen and H. Hüttel. Decidability Issues for Infinite State Processes - A Survey. *Bull. of the EATCS*, 51, 1993.
9. S. Christensen, H. Hüttel, and C. Stirling. Bisimulation Equivalence is Decidable for all Context-Free Processes. *Information and Computation*, 121, 1995.
10. R.S. Cohen and A.Y. Gold. Theory of ω-Languages. I: Characterizations of ω-Context-Free Languages. *J.C.S.S.*, 15, 1977.
11. J. Esparza and A. Kiehn. On the Model Checking Problem for Branching Time Logics and Basic Parallel Processes. In *CAV'95.* LNCS 939, 1995.
12. Javier Esparza. On the Decidability of Model-Checking for Several Mu-calculi and Petri Nets. In *CAAP'94.* LNCS 787, 1994.
13. R. Howell, L. Rosier, and H.C. Yen. A Taxonomy of Fairness and Temporal Logic Problems for Petri Nets. *T.C.S.*, 82, 1991.
14. P. Jancar. Decidability of a Temp. Logic Problem for Petri Nets. *T.C.S.*, 74, 1990.
15. E. Mayr. An Algorithm for the General Petri Net Reachability Problem. *SIAM J. on Comput.*, 13, 1984.
16. A. Pnueli. The Temporal Logic of Programs. In *FOCS'77.* IEEE, 1977.
17. W. Thomas. Star-Free Regular Sets of ω-Sequences. *Inform. and Cont.*, 42, 1979.
18. R. Valk and M. Jantzen. The Residue of Vector Sets with Applications to Decidability Problems in Petri Nets. *Acta Informatica*, 21, 1985.
19. M.Y. Vardi and P. Wolper. An Automata-Theoretic Approach to Automatic Program Verification. In *LICS'86.* IEEE, 1986.

Linear Constraint Systems as High-Level Nets *

Eike Best
Institut für Informatik, Universität Hildesheim, Marienburger Platz 22,
D-31141 Hildesheim, Germany. Email: e.best@informatik.uni-hildesheim.de

Catuscia Palamidessi
DISI, Università di Genova, Via Dodecaneso, 35,
I-16146 Genova, Italy. Email: catuscia@disi.unige.it

Abstract. Linear constraint systems are simple deductive systems based on the main underlying idea of linear logic: hypotheses represent physical resources which are consumed by the entailment relation. For such systems, we define back-and-forth translations into a class of high-level Petri nets. Using the specific properties of that class of nets, and previous results about the complexity of the reachability problem for such nets, we examine the complexity of the entailment problem for finitely generated linear constraint systems and we show that it is NP-complete.

1 Introduction

Constraint programming is one of the most successful paradigms for processing declarative information. One of the reasons of its success is that it leads quite naturally to a model for concurrency, as shown in [16, 17]. In this model, agents interact via a *shared store* containing all the information generated by the system. The basic communication actions are the *tell*, which updates the store by adding new information (i.e. a new constraint), and the *ask*, which tests whether the store entails a certain constraint. The ask can be successful, in which case the agent proceeds, or unsuccessful, in which case the agent suspends (waits for the other agents to enrich the store). Concerning the tell, there are two variants: the *atomic tell*, which blocks if the new constraint makes the store inconsistent, and the *eventual tell*, which just adds a constraint without any consistency check. It is relatively easy to prove that the first mechanism leads to a concurrent paradigm which is strictly more expressive [3]. Intuitively this is because the atomic tell is a test-and-set action, which cannot be simulated by test (ask) and set (eventual tell) separately. On the other hand, the particular kind of test-and-set performed by the atomic tell is not very suitable for distributed systems. In fact the test for consistency depends on the *global* content of the store, hence only one such action can be performed at a time.

In [4] we have proposed a concurrent constraint paradigm aimed to combine expressiveness and parallelism. The idea is to allow a test-and-set action (*get*) which tests (part of) the store for entailment, like the ask, but, when successful,

* This work is supported by the HCM project EXPRESS.

it removes from the store the entailing information. This is similar to the interaction mechanism used in Linda [12, 6], where the store is seen as a *blackboard* in which agents add and remove information. However, in Linda there is no structure on the information, i.e. the tokens of information are essentially unrelated (apart from the relation given by variable instantiation). On the contrary, our paradigm assumes an underlying inference mechanism which allows for some deductive processing of information at the level of the store.

The standard notion of constraint system is based on the laws of classical logic, and does not support naturally the get operation. For instance, the entailment relation is monotonic, i.e. if a constraint c entails a constraint d, then also c plus c', for any c', entails d. Thus the notion of *entailing information* as it is here is not suitable to our purposes. One could define it as "the minimal information which entails ...", but also the concept of minimality is not natural here, since c plus c is regarded as equivalent to c. In order to model naturally the get operation, therefore, it is convenient to adopt a notion of constraint system based on a logic like linear logic, where items of information are seen as physical resources which are *consumed* by the entailment relation, and where the notion of entailing information, as we need it, is primitive.

Linear constraint systems are simple deduction systems which are to linear logic as constraint systems are to classical logic. Technically, the main difference is that an element (of a system) is defined as a multiset of constraints, instead than a set. The following example, from [4], illustrates the main idea.

Example 1. Let $available(x)$ denote the situation in which the theater place number x is available, and let $mpc(y)$ denote the fact that Mr. y makes a phone call to reserve a theater place. Then we want to have an inference of the form

$$\{available(x), mpc(y)\} \vdash booked(x, y)$$

where $booked(x, y)$ means that Mr. y has booked place x. Now, assume that the price of a place is \$50. If a person has booked a place, and he has the money to pay for it, then he can take the place:

$$\{booked(x, y), has(y, \$50)\} \vdash takes(y, x).$$

If we have, say, two places available with numbers 1 and 2, then the initial situation is $\{available(1),\ available(2)\}$. Now, suppose that Mr. A and Ms. B want to go to the theater, make phone calls, and have \$50 to pay the place. The store becomes $\{available(1),\ available(2),\ mpc(A),\ mpc(B),\ has(A, \$50),\ has(B, \$50)\}$. The two possible final stores, nondeterministically generated by the inference system, are $\{takes(A, 1), takes(B, 2)\}$ or $\{takes(A, 2), takes(B, 1)\}$. If a third person Ms. C makes now a phone call, she cannot reserve a place, because there are no places available anymore.

The reason why constraint systems in literature are only a subset of classical logic is that, for practical uses, it is essential that the entailment relation is decidable and that it is computed efficiently. Two questions which then arise, about the notion of linear constraint system, are:

Under what conditions the entailment problem is decidable and "not too hard"?, and

Does the definition of entailment lead to a natural distributed model, i.e. does it present some natural degree of parallelism?

In this paper we investigate these two aspects.

We attack the problem by using the formalism of Petri nets, which are particularly convenient for our purposes, since they represent a natural model of distributed computation, and complexity questions about them have been extensively investigated. Moreover, the relationship between linear logic and Petri nets has been investigated in [5, 8], albeit not focussing on constraint systems. The main idea is to regard constraints as tokens, and entailment as transitions. A similar interpretation was considered also in [13], where it was shown that (standard) constraint systems can be naturally modeled as Contextual Nets. Note that in the standard notion of entailment there is no "consumption of resources", hence the standard model of Petri Nets (where a transition consumes its pre-condition and generates its post-conditions) is more suited for linear constraint systems rather than for standard constraint systems. In the above mentioned work, in fact, the authors propose an enrichment of Petri Nets with the notion of *context*, i.e. a condition which must be present for the transition, but it is not consumed by it.

We prove that there is a complete correspondence between a particular class of high-level nets and a class of linear constraint systems which we call *finitely generated*. By using this correspondence, and previous results about the complexity of the reachability problem, we prove that the entailment problem in such systems is NP-complete.

The paper is organized as follows. In Section 2 we recall the notion of linear constraint system and we define the property of being finitely generated. In Section 3 we recall the definition of high-level net, we illustrate it with an example, and show the correspondence with ordinary Petri Nets. Furthermore we define the class of T-out-sequential, quasi-elementary high-level nets, and we prove that for this class of nets the reachability problem is NP-complete (by using previous results about T-out-sequential Petri nets). In Section 4 we define the translation from finitely generated linear systems into this class of nets and vice versa. In Section 5 we prove the NP-completeness of the entailment relation in such constraint systems. In Section 6 we discuss linear constraint system with variables, and an alternative translation into high-level nets. This section also describes a benefit of the high-level (as opposed to a low-level) translation; in this way, the distributed character and the structure of the constraint system can be be preserved almost one-to-one. Section 7 concludes.

2 Linear constraint systems

Before introducing the notion of linear constraint system, it is worth recalling the notion of standard constraint system. Actually in literature this notion has been formalized in various ways, which differ for degree of abstraction. We illustrate here the notion of Saraswat, Rinard and Panangaden [17], which is the most abstract we know of, and which is closely related to the notion of *information system* by Scott [18].

Definition 1. [17]

- A ***basic constraint system*** is a pair $\langle B, \vdash_B \rangle$ where B is a set of ***basic constraints***, c, d ..., and the ***basic entailment relation*** $\vdash_B \subseteq \mathcal{P}_f(B) \times B$ (where $\mathcal{P}_f(B)$ is the set of the finite subsets of B) satisfies:
  (i) if $c \in s$ then $s \vdash_B c$,
  (ii) if $s \vdash_B c_1, \ldots, s \vdash_B c_n$, and $\{c_1, \ldots, c_n\} \vdash_B c$, then $s \vdash_B c$.
- The constraint system induced by $\langle B, \vdash_B \rangle$ is a pair $\langle \mathcal{P}_c(B), \vdash \rangle$ where $\mathcal{P}_c(B)$ is the set of subsets of B closed under entailment, i.e. $\mathcal{P}_c(B) = \{s \subseteq B \mid$ if $s' \subseteq s$ and $s' \vdash_B c$ then $c \in s\}$, and $\vdash \subseteq \mathcal{P}_c(B) \times \mathcal{P}_c(B)$ is defined by $s \vdash s'$ iff for any $c \in s'$ there exists $s'' \subseteq s$ such that $s'' \vdash_B c$.

It can be proved that $\langle \mathcal{P}_c(B), \vdash \rangle$ is an algebraic lattice with ordering relation given by the inverse of $\vdash$. If we regard B as a set of propositions, and $c \vdash_B d$ as an axiom stating that proposition c implies proposition d, then we can consider the algebraic elements of $\mathcal{P}_c(B)$ as particular propositional formulas on B (the formulas obtained by conjunction of basic propositions), modulo logical equivalence. Conjunction corresponds to the join operator. In other words, this construction can be considered (limited to the algebraic part) as a subset of the classical propositional calculus, subset in the sense that certain operators, like disjunction and negation, are usually not expressible.

In [17] this construction is further enriched with the addition of logical variables and (a weak form of) existential quantifier. This is done by means of ***cylindrification operators*** and ***diagonal elements***, and by imposing (some of) the axioms of cylindrical algebras. The resulting system can be regarded (still limited to the algebraic part) as a subset of a weak form of first order logic; subset in the same sense as above, and weak in the sense that not all the laws of first order logic hold here.

We illustrate now the notion of ***linear constraint system***, as defined in [4]. For the sake of simplicity, we do not consider here the mechanism of variable instantiation (or else we assume that the basic entailment relation is closed under variable instantiation). In Section 6 we discuss this mechanism.

As announced in the introduction, the aim is to model a constraint as a physical resource, which can be produced in several copies and each copy of which disappears once it is consumed, i.e. used as a hypothesis in the entailment relation. In order to represent the idea that the same resource can have multiple copies, it is natural to define the elements of the constraint system to be multisets instead than sets. Furthermore the underlying logic must be modified. The derivation of a (basic) constraint by the entailment relation ***consumes the hypothesis***, hence, if the derivation of a constraint uses twice the same information, then this information must be represented twice in the hypothesis. Therefore the entailment relation must be defined from multisets of constraints to constraints.

In the following, $\mathcal{M}(X)$ and $\mathcal{M}_f(X)$ stand for the set of multisets and for the set of finite multisets of a set X, respectively; $\oplus$ is the multiset sum, $\ominus$ is the multiset difference. We refer to the appendix for the formal definition of these notions.

Definition 2. [4]

- A *basic linear constraint system* is a pair $\langle B, \vdash_B \rangle$ where B is a set of *basic constraints* and the *basic entailment relation* $\vdash_B \subseteq \mathcal{M}_f(B) \times B$ satisfies:
  (i) $\{c\} \vdash_B c$,
  (ii) if $\mu_1 \vdash_B c_1, \ldots, \mu_n \vdash_B c_n$ and $\{c_1, \ldots, c_n\} \vdash_B d$, then $\mu_1 \oplus \ldots \oplus \mu_n \vdash_B d$.
- The *linear constraint system* induced by $\langle B, \vdash_B \rangle$ is the structure $\langle \mathcal{M}(B), \vdash \rangle$, where $\vdash \subseteq \mathcal{M}(B) \times \mathcal{M}(B)$ is the minimal relation such that

$$\text{if} \quad \forall i \in I.\ \mu_i \vdash_B c_i \quad \text{then} \quad \bigoplus_{i \in I} \mu_i \vdash \bigoplus_{i \in I} \{c_i\}.$$

Note that we cannot define the elements of a constraint system to be multisets closed under entailment. In fact if we take a definition like in 1, then a set of constraints and its closure are not equivalent, because they represent different sets of resources.

A linear constraint system does not have all the properties as a constraint system; it is not a complete algebraic lattice and not even a lattice (for instance it does not necessarily have a minimum element). However it is a preorder, and therefore can be transformed into a partial order by factorising it with respect to the associated equivalence relation.

Lemma 3. *$\vdash$ is a preorder on $\mathcal{M}(S) \times \mathcal{M}(S)$.*

Proof

Reflexivity. Assume $\mu = \bigoplus_{i \in I} \{c_i\}$. By Definition 2 (i) we have that for each $i \in I$, $\{c_i\} \vdash_B c_i$ holds. Hence by definition $\bigoplus_{i \in I} \{c_i\} \vdash \bigoplus_{i \in I} \{c_i\}$ holds.

Transitivity. Assume $\mu \vdash \mu'$ and $\mu' \vdash \mu''$. We have to show that $\mu \vdash \mu''$. Assume $\mu'' = \bigoplus_{i \in I} \{c_i\}$. Then there exist a collection of multisets $\{\mu'_i \mid i \in I\}$ such that $\mu' = \bigoplus_{i \in I} \mu'_i$ and for each $i \in I$, $\mu'_i \vdash_B c_i$ holds. Let, for $i \in I$, $\mu'_i = \bigoplus_{j \in J_i} \{d_{ij}\}$. We have that there exists a collection of multisets $\{\mu_{ij} \mid j \in J_i\}$ such that $\mu = \bigoplus_{i \in I} \bigoplus_{j \in J_i} \mu_{ij}$ and for each $i \in I, j \in J_i$, $\mu_{ij} \vdash_B d_{ij}$ holds. By Definition 2 (ii), we get that for each $i \in I$, $\bigoplus_{j \in J_i} \mu_{ij} \vdash_B c_i$ holds. Hence by definition we obtain $\bigoplus_{i \in I} \bigoplus_{j \in J_i} \mu_{ij} \vdash \bigoplus_{i \in I} \{c_i\}$. ∎

The relation $\vdash$ is generally infinite, even when B is finite, and even when restricted to $\mathcal{M}_f(B)$ modulo equivalence. Of course, from a practical point of view we are mainly interested in linear constraint systems which have a decidable and "not too hard" entailment relation. To this end, we introduce the notion of *finitely generated* linear constraint systems. We will show that for this class of systems the entailment relation is in fact decidable and NP complete. Intuitively, a linear constraint systems is finitely generated if the basic entailment relation is obtained by starting from a finite relation and closing it up with respect to Conditions (i) and (ii) of Definition 2.

Definition 4. A linear constraint system is *finitely generated* if its base is a pair $\langle B, \vdash_B \rangle$ where B is a finite set, and $\vdash_B$ is defined by the following inductive system, for some finite $\vdash_0 \subseteq \mathcal{M}_f(B) \times B$:

$$(1)\ \frac{}{\{c\} \vdash_B c} \quad (2)\ \frac{\mu \vdash_0 c}{\mu \vdash_B c} \quad (3)\ \frac{\mu_1 \vdash_B c_1, \ldots, \mu_n \vdash_B c_n,\ \{c_1, \ldots, c_n\} \vdash_B d}{\mu_1 \oplus \ldots \oplus \mu_n \vdash_B d}$$

We conclude this section by showing a property of finitely generated constraint systems, which will be useful for studying the correspondence with high-level nets.

Definition 5. Let $\langle B, \vdash_B \rangle$ be a basic constraint system finitely generated by $\vdash_0$. Define $\rightsquigarrow$ as the relation induced by the following rule:

$$\frac{\mu \in \mathcal{M}_f(B),\ \{c_1, \ldots, c_n\} \vdash_0 d}{\{c_1, \ldots, c_n\} \oplus \mu \rightsquigarrow \{d\} \oplus \mu}$$

Proposition 6. *Let $\langle \mathcal{M}(B), \vdash \rangle$ be a finitely generated linear constraint system with generating relation $\vdash_0$. Let μ and μ' be two finite multisets of B. Then $\mu \vdash \mu'$ if and only if $\mu \rightsquigarrow^* \mu'$, where $\rightsquigarrow^*$ is the reflexive and transitive closure of $\rightsquigarrow$.*

Proof The if part is easy. To prove the only-if part, we use the following lemma:

Lemma 7. *Let μ, μ' be two finite multisets of B, let $c \in B$, and assume that $\mu \vdash_B c$. Then $\mu \oplus \mu' \rightsquigarrow^* \{c\} \oplus \mu'$ holds.*

Proof By induction on the definition of $\vdash_B$. There are three cases, depending whether $\mu \vdash_B c$ is obtained from Rule (1), Rule (2) or Rule (3) respectively.

(1) In this case $\mu = \{c\}$. Just observe that $\{c\} \oplus \mu' \rightsquigarrow^0 \{c\} \oplus \mu'$.

(2) In this case $\mu \vdash_0 c$. Then $\mu \oplus \mu' \rightsquigarrow \{c\} \oplus \mu'$ holds by definition.

(3) In this case there exist $\mu_1, \ldots, \mu_n$, $c_1, \ldots, c_n$ such that $\mu_1 \vdash_B c_1, \ldots, \mu_n \vdash_B c_n$, $\{c_1, \ldots, c_n\} \vdash_B c$, and $\mu = \mu_1 \oplus \ldots \oplus \mu_n$. By inductive hypothesis we have
- for any finite multisets $\mu'_1, \ldots \mu'_n$, for any $i \in \{1, \ldots, n\}$, $\mu_i \oplus \mu'_i \rightsquigarrow^* \{c_i\} \oplus \mu'_i$ holds, and
- for any finite multiset μ'', $\{c_1, \ldots, c_n\} \oplus \mu'' \rightsquigarrow \{c\} \oplus \mu''$ holds.

Then define, for $i \in \{1, \ldots, n\}$, $\mu'_i = \mu_{i+1} \oplus \ldots \oplus \mu_n \oplus \{c_1, \ldots, c_{i-1}\} \oplus \mu'$, and $\mu'' = \mu'$. We have that, for each $i \in \{1, \ldots, n\}$, $\mu_i \oplus \ldots \oplus \mu_n \oplus \{c_1, \ldots, c_{i-1}\} \oplus \mu' \rightsquigarrow^* \mu_{i+1} \oplus \ldots \oplus \mu_n \oplus \{c_1, \ldots, c_i\} \oplus \mu'$, and $\{c_1, \ldots, c_n\} \oplus \mu' \rightsquigarrow^* \{c\} \oplus \mu'$. Finally, apply the transitivity of $\rightsquigarrow^*$. ■

We prove now Proposition 6. Let $\mu' = \{c_1, \ldots, c_n\}$. Then there are $\mu_1, \ldots, \mu_n$ such that $\mu = \mu_1 \oplus \ldots \oplus \mu_n$ and $\mu_1 \vdash_B c_1, \ldots, \mu_n \vdash_B c_n$. By previous lemma we have, for each $i \in \{1, \ldots, n\}$, $\mu_i \oplus \ldots \oplus \mu_n \oplus \{c_1, \ldots, c_{i-1}\} \rightsquigarrow^* \mu_{i+1} \oplus \ldots \oplus \mu_n \oplus \{c_1, \ldots, c_i\}$. Hence apply the transitivity of $\rightsquigarrow^*$. ■

3 High-level Petri nets

Rather than use the full power of Pr/T-nets [1, 10], colored nets [11] or algebraic nets [15, 19], we consider a somewhat restricted model: M-nets [2].

Let $x, y, z, \ldots$ (letters near the end of the alphabet) be variables and let $a, b, c, \ldots$ (letters near the beginning of the alphabet) be values. A *high-level net*, for our present purpose, is a structure $N = (S, T, \iota)$. As usual, S is the set of places and T is the set of transitions (satisfying $S \cap T = \emptyset$). The function ι associates:

– With every place $s \in S$ a nonempty set of values (its *type*).

– With every pair (s, t) and (t, s) (with $s \in S$ and $t \in T$) a possibly empty multiset of variables.

– With every transition t a predicate involving variables from the set $Var(t)$, where $Var(t)$ is defined as the set of variables occurring in a multiset $\iota(s, t)$ or $\iota(t, s')$, for some $s, s' \in S$. Function ι may be considered to satisfy these properties:

$$s \neq s' \Rightarrow \iota(s) \cap \iota(s') = \emptyset \quad \text{and} \quad t \neq t' \Rightarrow Var(t) \cap Var(t') = \emptyset,$$

since it follows from standard high-level net theory that they are no restriction of generality; they can always be forced to be true, provided enough values and variables are available in the universe.

A *marking* M of N is a function associating with every place s a finite multiset $M(s)$ on $\iota(s)$. A *binding of t*, where t is a transition, is a function σ associating a value with every variable in $Var(t)$.[2] A binding of t is *legal* if variables get assigned values from the types of the places they correspond to, i.e. if x is a variable occurring in $\iota(s, t)$ or in $\iota(t, s)$, then $\sigma(x) \in \iota(s)$. In what follows we will tacitly assume all bindings to be legal. A (legal) binding σ of t is *enabling (for t)* if the predicate $\iota(t)$ evaluates to *true* under σ. A marking M *activates t under σ (or 'in mode σ')* if σ enables t and, moreover, for all (s, t), the multiset of values $\iota(s, t)[\sigma]$ (i.e., σ applied to every individual element of $\iota(s, t)$) is a sub-multiset of $M(s)$. If M activates t in mode σ then t may *occur in mode σ*, yielding a successor marking M' which is calculated as follows: for every place s,

$$M'(s) \;=\; (M(s) \ominus (\iota(s, t)[\sigma])) \oplus (\iota(t, s)[\sigma]).$$

Figure 1 exemplifies the notions just defined. The net on the left-hand side of this figure is $(\{s_1, s_2, s_3\}, \{t\}, \iota)$ with

$$\begin{array}{ll} \iota(s_1) = \{0,1\} & \iota(s_2, t) = \{u\} \\ \iota(s_2) = \{2,3,4\} & \iota(t, s_2) = \emptyset \\ \iota(s_3) = \{5\} & \iota(s_3, t) = \emptyset \\ \iota(s_1, t) = \{x, x, z\} & \iota(t, s_3) = \{y\} \\ \iota(t, s_1) = \emptyset & \iota(t) = (z{=}0 \wedge u{=}3 \wedge y{=}5). \end{array}$$

The same net is also shown on the right-hand side of the figure. The marking M on the left-hand side is $M(s_1) = \{0, 1, 1\}$, $M(s_2) = \{2, 2, 3\}$ and $M(s_3) = \{5\}$, while the marking M' (of the same net) on the right-hand side is $M'(s_1) = \emptyset$, $M'(s_2) = \{2, 2\}$ and $M'(s_3) = \{5, 5\}$. Consider four bindings for t:

$$\begin{array}{ll} \sigma_1 : x{=}0, z{=}1, u{=}3, y{=}0 & \sigma_3 : x{=}0, z{=}0, u{=}3, y{=}5 \\ \sigma_2 : x{=}0, z{=}1, u{=}3, y{=}5 & \sigma_4 : x{=}1, z{=}0, u{=}3, y{=}5. \end{array}$$

The first binding σ_1 is not legal because the value of y is not in the type of the corresponding place. The second binding is legal but not enabling for t because

[2] In the following, we use standard notation relating to bindings and substitutions; thus, if X is some object then $X[\sigma]$ denotes X where σ is applied (elementwise or otherwise) to X.

the predicate does not evaluate to *true* (due to z being bound to 1 rather than 0). The third binding σ_3 is legal and enabling for t, but the marking M on the left-hand side does not activate t in mode σ_3 (due to there being insufficiently many tokens 0 on place s_1). Finally, σ_4 is legal, enabling for t, and such that t is activated by M in mode σ_4. Thus, t can occur in mode σ_4 starting from M. If it does, then the marking M' shown on the right-hand side of the figure is obtained after its occurrence.

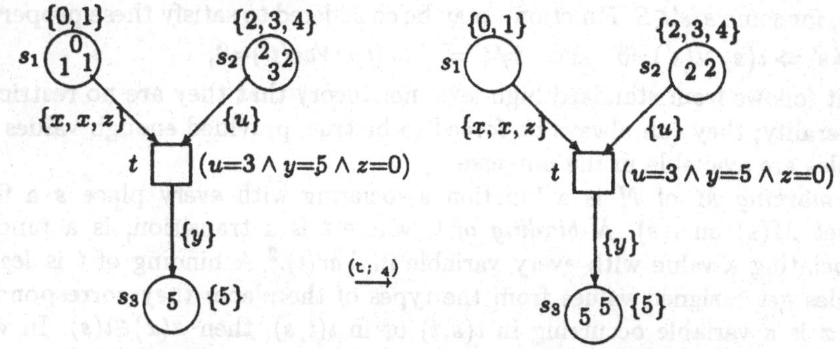

Fig. 1. Illustrating some basic notions of high-level nets

Next, we define the unfolding of a high-level net into a place/transition net. A (weighted) place/transition net is a triple (S,T,W) where S and T are sets as above and W is a function from $(S{\times}T)\cup(T{\times}S)$ to attaching a weight (possibly 0) to every arc. Let $N=(S,T,\iota)$ be a high-level net as defined above. The *unfolding* of N, $U(N)$, is a place/transition net $U(N)=(S_u,T_u,W_u)$ defined as follows:

- $S_u=\{s_v \mid s{\in}S \text{ and } v{\in}\iota(s)\}$.
- $T_u=\{t_\sigma \mid t{\in}T \text{ and } \sigma \text{ is an enabling binding of } t\}$.
- $W_u(s_v,t_\sigma)=|\,\iota(s,t)[\sigma]|_v\,|$ and $W_u(t_\sigma,s_v)=|\,\iota(t,s)[\sigma]|_v\,|$.[3]

Moreover, a marking M of N corresponds to a marking M_u of $U(N)$, which is a function from places to natural numbers as usual, in a unique and canonical way, namely as $M_u(s_v)=|\,M(s)|_v\,|$ for all $s_v\in S_u$. Figure 2 shows the unfolding corresponding to the net on the left-hand side of Figure 1.[4] Note that transition t of Figure 1 has been split into t_1 and t_2. This is due to the fact that t has exactly two enabling bindings which are discriminated by $x{=}0$ and $x{=}1$, respectively, namely $x{=}0, z{=}0, u{=}3, y{=}5$ and $x{=}1, z{=}0, u{=}3, y{=}5$. It is left to the reader to compute the unfolding of the net shown on the right-hand side of Figure 1.[5] It should be added that every place/transition system can be interpreted canonically as a special high-level system (the specialisation consists

[3] Compare the appendix for the notion of the restriction $\mu|_v$ of a multiset μ.
[4] Arc weights greater than 1 have been indicated explicitly.
[5] Hint: the structure of the net is the same, the only difference is in the marking.

in that every place type is a singleton and every transition predicate has precisely one enabling binding); however for historical reasons it is not usual to view place/transition nets in this way.

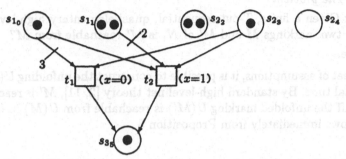

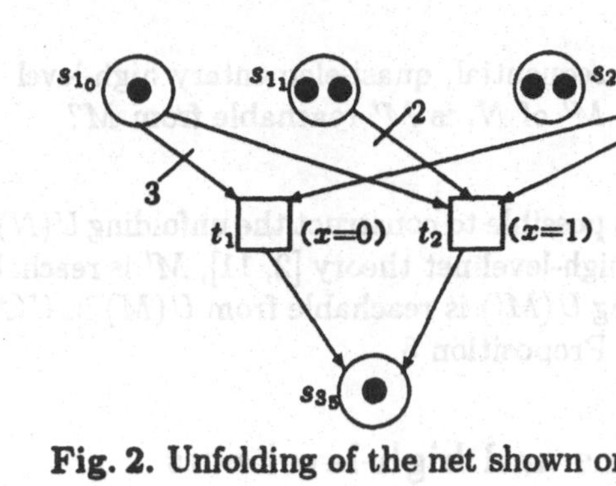

Fig. 2. Unfolding of the net shown on the left-hand side of Figure 1

We are interested in certain classes of high-level nets and place/transition nets. Let a place/transition net (S, T, W) be called *T-out-sequential* if for all $t \in T$, $\sum_{s \in S} W(t, s) = 1$ and *T-in-sequential* if for all $t \in T$, $\sum_{s \in S} W(s, t) = 1$. T-out-sequential nets are the class of interest in connection with linear constraint programming while T-in-sequential nets are the class of nets used for translating BPP (Basic Parallel Processes) of process algebra [7, 9].

Proposition 8. *The problem*

REACH-1: Given a finite T-out-sequential place/transition net N and two markings M and M' of N, is M' reachable from M?

is NP-complete.

Proof Let $N'=(S, T, W')$ be the reverse of $N=(S, T, W)$, i.e. $W'(t, s)=W(s, t)$ and $W'(s, t)=W(t, s)$ for all $s \in S$ and $t \in T$. From the transition rule of place/transition nets [14] it follows that M' is reachable from M in N iff M is reachable from M' in N'. Moreover, N' is a T-in-sequential net. Reachability in T-in-sequential nets has been shown to be NP-complete in [9]. The NP-completeness of REACH-1 follows immediately. ■

The definition of being T-out-sequential can be lifted to high-level nets. Let $N = (S, T, \iota)$ be a high-level net. Then N is called T-out-sequential if for all transitions t there is exactly one place s' with $|\iota(t, s')| = 1$ while for all the other places, $|\iota(t, s)| = 0$. It is clear that if N is T-out-sequential then so is its unfolding $U(N)$.[6] However, the previous proposition cannot be transferred immediately because it may be the case that an exponential number of transitions is created in the unfolding of a (T-out-sequential) high-level net. Hence we consider nets with the following property. A high-level net is called *quasi-elementary* if every transition has exactly one enabling binding.[7] Note that via its interpretation as

[6] Note that this happens to be the case in Figures 1 and 2.

[7] The weaker property of having a polynomially bounded number of enabling bindings

a high-level net, every place/transition net is always quasi-elementary. A high-level net is *finite* iff S is finite, T is finite and all place types $\iota(s)$, for $s \in S$, are finite sets. If N is finite then so is its unfolding $U(N)$.

Corollary 9. *The problem*

REACH-2: Given a finite, T-out-sequential, quasi-elementary high-level net N and two markings M and M' of N, is M' reachable from M?

is NP-complete.

Proof By the set of assumptions, it is possible to construct the unfolding $U(N)$ of N in polynomial time. By standard high-level net theory [2, 11], M' is reachable from M in N iff the unfolded marking $U(M')$ is reachable from $U(M)$ in $U(N)$. The result follows immediately from Proposition 8. ■

4 Linear constraint systems and high-level nets

This section has two parts. First we define a translation from finitely generated linear constraint systems to high-level Petri nets (Section 4.1). Then we define a converse translation from quasi-elementary T-out-sequential high-level nets into linear constraint systems (Section 4.2). The two translations are not converses of each other. For instance, starting out with an arbitrary net N satisfying the conditions, deriving the linear constraint system $C(N)$, and then deriving back a net $N(C(N))$, will always end up with a one-place net even if the original one had more places than that.

4.1 Translating a linear constraint system into a high-level net

Let a finitely generated linear constraint system $C = \langle \mathcal{M}(B), \vdash \rangle$ be given and let $\vdash_0 \subseteq \mathcal{M}_f(B) \times B$ be its generating relation. We associate a high-level net $N = N(C)$ with C as follows. N has exactly one place, say s, with type B. For every element of $\vdash_0$ there is a transition t. Suppose $(\{c_1, \dots, c_n\}, d) \in \vdash_0$. Then the corresponding transition t has the following connections: $\iota(s,t) = \{x_1, \dots, x_n\}$, where the x_i's are variables occurring with the same multiplicities as specified by the multiset $\{c_1, \dots, c_n\}$, i.e. if c_i is the same value as c_j then x_i is the same variable as x_j. Moreover, $\iota(t,s) = \{y\}$. Finally, $\iota(t) = ((\forall i, 1 \le i \le n{:}\, x_i = c_i) \wedge (y = d))$.

Example 2. Let $B = \{a, \mathit{true}, \mathit{false}\}$ and

$$\vdash_0 = \{ (\{a,a\}, \mathit{false}), (\emptyset, \mathit{true}), (\{\mathit{false}\}, a), (\{\mathit{false}\}, \mathit{true}), (\{\mathit{false}\}, \mathit{false}) \}.$$

We do not show the relation $\vdash$, i.e. we do not give the system $C = \langle \mathcal{M}(B), \vdash \rangle$ generated by $\vdash_0$ explicitly.[8] The net $N(C)$ corresponding to this system has one place with a value set of size three and five transitions corresponding to the five members of $\vdash_0$. It is shown (with initial marking $\{a, a\}$, which is not specified

is sufficient for the next corollary, but in the following, we will be interested only in nets for which this number is actually 1. The number 0 is uninteresting because transitions with no enabling bindings are dead.

[8] Note that $\vdash$ is infinite, and $\vdash_B$ too.

by the construction) in Figure 3. To verify Proposition 10 below, the reader may check that with this initial marking (for example) transition t_1 is enabled, and after occurrence of t_1, t_3 is enabled and can occur yielding $\{a\}$, and that the inference system allows a corresponding deduction $\{a,a\} \vdash \{a\}$.

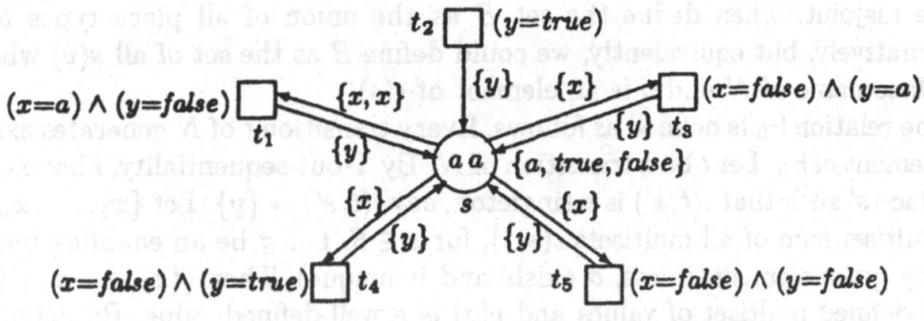

Fig. 3. A net $N(C)$ arising from the construction defined in the text

Note that any high-level net $N(C)$ arising from the above construction is finite, T-out-sequential and quasi-elementary. It is finite because there is only one place with (by assumption) finite type B, and moreover, there are $\mid \vdash_0 \mid$ transitions (where by assumption, $\vdash_0$ is a finite relation). It is T-out-sequential because, by construction, every transition t has exactly one output arc with label $\iota(t,s) = \{y\}$, i.e. a singleton set. It is quasi-elementary because every predicate of a transition specifies exactly the (only) enabling binding of that transition. Moreover, every multiset μ of B is at the same time also a marking of s, and therefore (since s is the only place) also a marking of $N(C)$. Furthermore:

Proposition 10. *Let μ and μ' be two multisets on B. Then $\mu \vdash \mu'$ in C iff μ' is reachable from μ in $N(C)$.*

Proof ($\Rightarrow$:) Assume $\mu \vdash \mu'$ in C. By Proposition 6($\Rightarrow$),

$$\mu = \mu_0 \rightsquigarrow \mu_1 \rightsquigarrow \ldots \rightsquigarrow \mu_m = \mu'$$

for some $m \geq 0$. For every $1 \leq j \leq m$, multiset μ_j arises from multiset μ_{j-1} by an application of some member, say $(\{c_1,\ldots,c_n\}, d)$, of $\vdash_0$ by the inference rule defined in Definition 5. According to that rule, $\{c_1,\ldots,c_n\}$ is a submultiset of μ_{j-1}. This implies, by the construction of $N(C)$, that the transition, say t_j, which corresponds to $(\{c_1,\ldots,c_n\}, d)$ is activated at marking μ_{j-1} in mode σ_j assigning to the variables $x_1,\ldots,x_n$ and y of t_j the values $c_1,\ldots,c_n$ and d, respectively. Hence t_j can occur in mode σ_j at marking μ_{j-1}, and the marking obtained after the occurrence of t_j is $(\mu_{j-1} \ominus \{c_1,\ldots,c_n\}) \oplus \{d\}$, which, by Definition 5, coincides with μ_j. Inductively, this proves that μ' is reachable from μ in $N(C)$.

($\Leftarrow$:) All arguments of part ($\Rightarrow$:) can be reverted using Proposition 6($\Leftarrow$) instead of ($\Rightarrow$). ∎

4.2 Translating a high-level net into a linear constraint system

Let a finite, T-out-sequential, quasi-elementary high-level net N be given. We associate a linear constraint system $C(N)$ with N as follows. Assume (without loss of generality) that all values occurring in N are different from *true* and *false*. Assume further, again without loss of generality, that the place types of N are disjoint. Then define the set B as the union of all place types of N. (Alternatively, but equivalently, we could define B as the set of all $s(v)$ where s is a place name of N and v is an element of $\iota(s)$.)

The relation $\vdash_0$ is defined as follows. Every transition t of N generates exactly one element of $\vdash_0$. Let t be a transition of N. By T-out-sequentiality, t has exactly one place s' such that $\iota(t,s')$ is a singleton, say $\iota(t,s') = \{y\}$. Let $\{x_1,\ldots,x_n\}$ be the multiset sum of all multisets $\iota(s,t)$, for $s \in S$. Let σ be an enabling binding of t (by quasi-elementariness, σ exists and is unique). Then $(\{x_1,\ldots,x_n\})[\sigma]$ is a well-defined multiset of values and $y[\sigma]$ is a well-defined value. By definition, let $((\{x_1,\ldots,x_n\})[\sigma], y[\sigma]) \in \vdash_0$.

Example 3. Let N be the net shown in Figure 2. Then $C(N)$ is the linear constraint system generated by the following set B and relation $\vdash_0$:

$$B = \{0,1,2,3,4,5,\mathit{true},\mathit{false}\} \text{ and } \vdash_0 = \{\,(\{0,0,0,3\},5),(\{0,1,1,3\},5)\}.$$

The two pairs of $\vdash_0$ come from the two transitions t_1 and t_2 of Figure 2. In order to check Proposition 11 below, consider, the inference $\{0,1,1,2,2,3,5\} \vdash \{2,2,5,5\}$ coming from the second pair in $\vdash_0$. This corresponds to the occurrence of transition t_2 in the initial marking shown in Figure 2.

Note that any constraint system $C(N)$ arising from this construction is finitely generated. The set B of $C(N)$ is finite since, by assumption, all place types of N are finite. The relation $\vdash_0$ has only finitely many elements as a consequence of the sets T (of N) and B (of $C(N)$) being finite.

Let M be a marking of N associating a multiset of values with every place s of N. From M we construct a multiset $\mu(M)$ of B as the multiset sum of all $M(s)$, for all places s. Then:

Proposition 11. *Let M and M' be two markings of N. Then M' is reachable from M in N iff $\mu(M) \vdash \mu(M')$ in $C(N)$.*

Proof (⇒:) Assume M' can be reached from M in N. By the transition rule for high-level nets,

$$M = M_0 \stackrel{(t_1,\sigma_1)}{\longrightarrow} M_1 \stackrel{(t_2,\sigma_2)}{\longrightarrow} \ldots \stackrel{(t_m,\sigma_m)}{\longrightarrow} M_m = M'$$

where $M_{j-1} \stackrel{(t_j,\sigma_j)}{\longrightarrow} M_j$ means that t_j is activated in mode σ_j at M_{j-1} and M_j is the successor marking of M_{j-1} after occurrence of t_j in mode σ_j.[9] Suppose $\{x_1,\ldots,x_n\}$ and $\{y\}$ are the relevant multisets of t_j used in constructing the corresponding element of $\vdash_0$ (which generates $C(N)$). Then this element is

$$(\{x_1,\ldots,x_n\}[\sigma_j], y[\sigma_j]) \;=\; (\{c_1,\ldots,c_n\}, d).$$

[9] Actually we could omit the modes at this point since they are uniquely determined by quasi-elementariness.

By the fact that M_{j-1} activates t_j we get $\{c_1, \ldots, c_n\} \subseteq \mu(M_{j-1})$. Moreover, $\mu(M_j) = (\mu(M_{j-1}) \ominus \{c_1, \ldots, c_n\}) \oplus \{d\}$ because of the way M_j is calculated from M_{j-1} by the transition rule of high-level nets. Hence this inference rule can be applied and yields $\mu(M_j) \rightsquigarrow (\mu(M_{j-1})$. Inductively, we get $\mu(M) \rightsquigarrow \ldots \rightsquigarrow \mu(M')$, and an appeal to Proposition 6($\Leftarrow$) yields $\mu(M) \vdash \mu(M')$ as required.

($\Leftarrow$:) All arguments of part ($\Rightarrow$:) can be reverted using Proposition 6($\Rightarrow$) instead of ($\Leftarrow$) and ignoring all applications of rule $(\emptyset, true) \in \vdash_0$. ■

5 NP-completeness of linear entailment

We now show that the entailment problem in a finitely generated linear constraint system is NP-complete.

Proposition 12. *The problem*

ENTAIL: Given a finitely generated linear constraint system $\langle \mathcal{M}(B), \vdash \rangle$ and two finite multisets μ and μ' of B, does $\mu \vdash \mu'$?

is NP-complete.

Proof The proof is done in two steps: ENTAIL is NP-hard and ENTAIL is a member of NP.

NP-hardness is shown by reduction from the problem REACH-1. Let an instance of REACH-1, i.e. a finite T-out-sequential place/transition net $N = (S, T, W)$ and two markings M and M' of N, be given. To check whether M' is reachable from M in N, first turn N into a (quasi-elementary) high-level net, then apply the construction defined in Section 4.2[10] and finally check whether or not $\mu(M) \vdash \mu(M')$ in the resulting linear constraint system. By Proposition 11 this yields 'yes' if and only if M' is reachable from M in N. Hence the NP-hardness of REACH-1 implies the NP-hardness of ENTAIL.

Membership in NP is shown by reduction to the problem REACH-2. Let an instance of ENTAIL, i.e. a finitely generated linear constraint system $C = \langle \mathcal{M}(B), \vdash \rangle$ and two finite multisets μ and μ' of B, be given. A nondeterministic polynomial-time algorithm to test whether or not $\mu \vdash \mu'$ can be defined as follows. First apply the construction defined in Section 4.1 to obtain a quasi-elementary T-out-sequential high-level net $N(C)$ from C,[11] then apply the polynomial-time nondeterministic algorithm, which exists by the fact that REACH-2 is in NP, to check whether or not μ' is reachable from μ in $N(C)$. By Proposition 10, this is the case if and only if $\mu \vdash \mu'$ in C. Hence the fact that REACH-2 is in NP implies that ENTAIL is in NP. ■

6 Translating constraint systems with variables

In example 1, inference involves instantiation of variables in the relation $\vdash$. We did not introduce this mechanism in previous chapters; however the constraint

[10] Both constructions can be done in polynomial time.

[11] This is again a polynomial-time construction.

system in example 1 can be transformed into a constraint system of the kind treated before by considering its relation $\vdash$ as a schema for representing $\vdash_0$: the pairs in $\vdash_0$ are obtained by instantiating the pairs of $\vdash$ on all possible elements of the domain (possibly typed, i.e. parted in places and persons). If the domain is finite, also $\vdash_0$ is finite.

When we have extra structure on the constraint system, such as the predicate-variable-structure of example 1, it can be reasonable to define a slightly different kind of translation into high-level nets. It may be the case that such a translation represents more realistically the distributed nature of the inference system. For instance, for the translation of example 1, instead of having a single place we could attach a different place to every predicate, having as value sets the range of individuals it applies to. A net of this type corresponding to example 1 is shown in Figure 4. Note that it satisfies the property of being T-out-sequential.

In translating example 1 into the net shown in Figure 4, we have assumed that there exist two (finite) sets $\mathbf{A} = \{1, 2, \ldots\}$ of theater places and $\mathbf{P} = \{A, B, \ldots\}$ of persons. The typed of places $s_1, \ldots, s_5$ in Figure 4 are constructed from these sets in a fashion appropriate to the predicates defined in example 1. The initial marking is M_0 shown in the following table:

$M_0 : s_1 \mapsto \{1,2\}$	$s_2 \mapsto \emptyset$	$s_3 \mapsto \emptyset$	$s_4 \mapsto \emptyset$	$s_5 \mapsto \emptyset$
$M_1 : s_1 \mapsto \{1,2\}$	$s_2 \mapsto \{A, B\}$	$s_3 \mapsto \emptyset$	$s_4 \mapsto \{A, B\}$	$s_5 \mapsto \emptyset$
$M_2 : s_1 \mapsto \emptyset$	$s_2 \mapsto \emptyset$	$s_3 \mapsto \{(1, A), (2, B)\}$	$s_4 \mapsto \{A, B\}$	$s_5 \mapsto \emptyset$
$M_2' : s_1 \mapsto \emptyset$	$s_2 \mapsto \emptyset$	$s_3 \mapsto \{(1, B), (2, A)\}$	$s_4 \mapsto \{A, B\}$	$s_5 \mapsto \emptyset$
$M_3 : s_1 \mapsto \emptyset$	$s_2 \mapsto \emptyset$	$s_3 \mapsto \emptyset$	$s_4 \mapsto \emptyset$	$s_5 \mapsto \{(A, 1), (B, 2)\}$
$M_3' : s_1 \mapsto \emptyset$	$s_2 \mapsto \emptyset$	$s_3 \mapsto \emptyset$	$s_4 \mapsto \emptyset$	$s_5 \mapsto \{(A, 2), (B, 1)\}$.

M_0 corresponds to the initial store specified in example 1, and transitions t_2 and t_3 model the making of phone calls and earning money, respectively (alternatively, the set of persons having made phone calls and having earned fifty dollars could be coded into the initial marking). Moreover, it can be checked that the two changes of the store specified in that example correspond to two occurrence sequences in the net, namely, in abbreviated form,

$$M_0 \xrightarrow{t_2,t_3} M_1 \xrightarrow{t_1,t_1} M_2 \xrightarrow{t_4,t_4} M_3 \text{ and } M_0 \xrightarrow{t_2,t_2,t_3,t_3} M_1 \xrightarrow{t_1,t_1} M_2' \xrightarrow{t_4,t_4} M_3',$$

respectively, leading to the same final stores specified above.

7 Conclusion

We have defined the notion of finitely generated linear constraint systems and we have shown that there is a complete correspondence between these systems and the class of T-out-sequential, quasi-elementary high-level nets. This interpretation allows to study the parallelism implicit in the notion of entailment, and its complexity: by using known results of Petri-net theory, we have proved that the entailment problem is NP-complete.

It is worth noting that this result depends critically on the nature of the generating entailment relation, i.e. on the property of inferring one single constraint at the time. Another natural way of defining the basic entailment relation

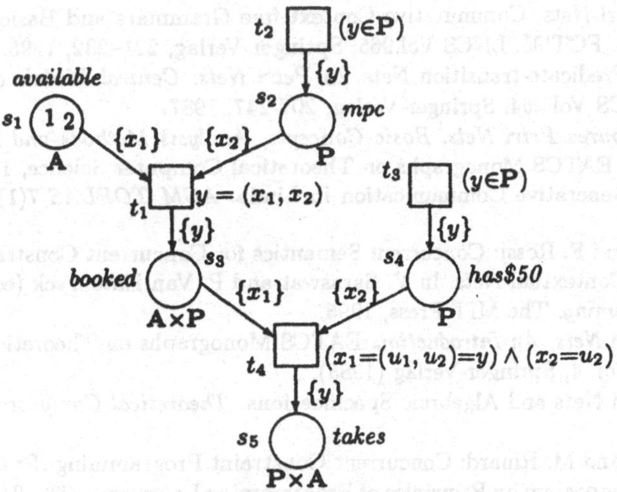

Fig. 4. A net corresponding to example 1

would be as a relation from multiset to multisets, thus obtaining something similar to the concept of multiset rewriting. However, in this case the translation into T-out-sequential nets would not have been possible, and NP-completeness (probably) would not hold.

Acknowledgments. We are indebted to Raymond Devillers and four anonymous reviewers for comments.

References

1. B. Baumgarten: *Petri-Netze. Grundlagen und Anwendungen.* BI-Verlag, 1990.
2. E. Best, H. Fleischhack, W. Frączak, R.P. Hopkins, H. Klaudel and E. Pelz: A Class of Composable High Level Petri Nets. Proc. of 16th ICPN, LNCS Vol.935, Springer Verlag, 103–120, 1995.
3. F.S. de Boer and C. Palamidessi: Embedding as a Tool for Language Comparison. *Information and Computation* 108(1):128–157, 1994.
4. F.S. de Boer, C. Palamidessi and E. Best: Concurrent Constraint Programming with Information Removal. Proc. First Intl. Workshop on Concurrent Constraint Programming, Venice, 1–13, May 1995.
5. C. Brown and D. Gurr: A Categorical Linear Framework for Petri Nets. Proc. Fifth Annual IEEE Symposium on Logic in Computer Science, Philadelphia, IEEE Comput. Soc. Press, 208–218, 1990.
6. N. Carriero and D. Gelernter: Linda in Context. *Comm. ACM* 32(4):445–458, 1989.
7. S. Christensen, Y. Hirshfeld and F. Moller: Bisimulation Equivalence is Decidable for Basic Parallel Processes. Proc. CONCUR'93, LNCS Vol.715, Springer Verlag, 143-175, 1993.
8. U. Engberg and G. Winskel: Petri Nets as Models of Linear Logic. Proc. 15th Colloquium on Trees in Algebra and Programming, LNCS Vol.431, Springer-Verlag, 147–161, 1990.

9. J. Esparza: Petri Nets, Commutative Context-free Grammars and Basic Parallel Processes. Proc. FCT'95, LNCS Vol.965, Springer Verlag, 221–232, 1995.
10. H.J. Genrich: Predicate-transition Nets. In *Petri Nets: Central Models and their Properties*, LNCS Vol.254, Springer-Verlag, 207-247, 1987.
11. K. Jensen: *Coloured Petri Nets. Basic Concepts, Analysis Methods and Practical Use.* Volume 1. EATCS Monographs on Theoretical Computer Science, 1992.
12. D. Gelernter: Generative Communication in Linda. *ACM TOPLAS* 7(1):80–112, 1985.
13. U. Montanari and F. Rossi: Concurrent Semantics for Concurrent Constraint Programming via Contextual Nets. In V. Saraswat and P. Van Entenryck (eds) *Constraint Programming.* The MIT Press, 1995.
14. W. Reisig: *Petri Nets. An Introduction.* EATCS Monographs on Theoretical Computer Science Vol. 4, Springer-Verlag (1985).
15. W. Reisig: Petri Nets and Algebraic Specifications. *Theoretical Computer Science* 80, 1-34, 1991.
16. V.A. Saraswat and M. Rinard: Concurrent Constraint Programming. Proc. seventeenth ACM Symposium on Principles of Programming Languages, 232–245, ACM, New York, 1990.
17. V.A. Saraswat, M. Rinard, and P. Panangaden: Semantics Foundations of Concurrent Constraint Programming. Proc. eighteenth ACM Symposium on Principles of Programming Languages, ACM, New York, 1991.
18. D. Scott: Domains for Denotational Semantics. Proc. ICALP, Springer Verlag, 1982.
19. J. Vautherin: Parallel Systems Specification with Colored Petri Nets and Algebraic Specification. LNCS Vol. 266, Springer-Verlag, 1987.

A Multisets

In this appendix we recall some basic notions about multisets. Given a set X, a multiset of elements of X is a mapping $\mu: X \rightarrow$ where is the set of natural numbers. We sometimes use extensional notation: for instance, the multiset μ such that $\mu(a) = 2$, $\mu(b) = 1$ and $\mu(c) = 0$ for $c \notin \{a, b\}$, will be represented by $\mu = \{a, a, b\}$. We denote by $\mathcal{M}(X)$ the set of the multisets on X, and by $\mathcal{M}_f(X)$ the set of the *finite* multisets on X, i.e. those multisets μ for which the set $\{a \in X \mid \mu(a \neq 0)\}$ is finite. If μ is finite then the number $|\mu| = \sum_{a \in X} \mu(z)$ is well-defined; it is called the *cardinality* of μ. A useful notion is *multiset inclusion*, denoted by $\subseteq$, and defined as $\mu' \subseteq \mu$ iff $\forall a \in X. \mu'(a) \leq \mu(a)$.
The *multiset sum* is a (total) function $\oplus: \mathcal{M}(X) \times \mathcal{M}(X) \rightarrow \mathcal{M}(X)$ defined as

$$(\mu \oplus \mu')(a) = \mu(a) + \mu'(a).$$

The *multiset difference* is a (partial) function $\ominus : \mathcal{M}(X) \times \mathcal{M}(X) \rightarrow \mathcal{M}(X)$. If $\mu' \subseteq \mu$ then $\mu \ominus \mu'$ is defined by putting, for each $a \in X$,

$$(\mu \ominus \mu')(a) = \mu(a) - \mu'(a).$$

Let $b \in X$ and μ a multiset. The *restriction* $\mu|_b$ is defined as the multiset

$$\mu|_b(a) = \begin{cases} \mu(a) & \text{if } a = b \\ 0 & \text{if } a \neq b. \end{cases}$$

A Space-Efficient On-the-fly Algorithm for Real-Time Model Checking

Thomas A. Henzinger[1]* Orna Kupferman[2] Moshe Y. Vardi[3]

[1] UC Berkeley, EECS Department, Berkeley, CA 94720-1770, U.S.A.
Email: tah@eecs.berkeley.edu URL: http://www.eecs.berkeley.edu/~tah

[2] Bell Laboratories, 600 Mountain Avenue, Murray Hill, NJ 07974, U.S.A.
Email: ok@research.att.com

[3] Rice University, Department of Computer Science, Houston, TX 77251-1892, U.S.A.
Email: vardi@cs.rice.edu URL: http://www.cs.rice.edu/~vardi

Abstract. In temporal-logic model checking, we verify the correctness of a program with respect to a desired behavior by checking whether a structure that models the program satisfies a temporal-logic formula that specifies the behavior. The main practical limitation of model checking is caused by the size of the state space of the program, which grows exponentially with the number of concurrent components. This problem, known as the state-explosion problem, becomes more difficult when we consider *real-time model checking*, where the program and the specification involve quantitative references to time. In particular, when use timed automata to describe real-time programs and we specify timed behaviors in the logic TCTL, a real-time extension of the temporal logic CTL with clock variables, then the state space under consideration grows exponentially not only with the number of concurrent components, but also with the number of clocks and the length of the clock constraints used in the program and the specification. Two powerful methods for coping with the state-explosion problem are *on-the-fly* and *space-efficient* model checking. In on-the-fly model checking, we explore only the portion of the state space of the program whose exploration is essential for determining the satisfaction of the specification. In space-efficient model checking, we store in memory the minimal information required, preferring to spend time on reconstructing information rather than spend space on storing it. In this work we develop an *automata-theoretic* approach to TCTL model checking that combines both methods. We suggest, for the first time, a PSPACE on-the-fly model-checking algorithm for TCTL.

1 Introduction

While *program verification* was always a desirable, but never an easy task, the advent of concurrent programming has made it significantly more necessary and difficult. The first step in program verification is to come up with a *formal specification* of the program. *Temporal logics* can describe a temporal ordering of events and have been adopted as a powerful tool for specifying and verifying concurrent programs [Pnu77, MP92]. In temporal logic *model checking*, we verify that a program meets a desired behavior by checking that a mathematical model of the program satisfies a temporal logic formula that specifies the behavior [CE81, QS81]. Temporal logics come in two varieties: *linear* and *branching* [Lam80]. In linear temporal logics, formulas are interpreted over infinite words and describe the behavior of each of the infinite computations of a program. In branching temporal logics, formulas are interpreted over infinite trees and describe the behavior of the possible computations of a nondeterministic program.

* Supported in part by the ONR YIP award N00014-95-1-0520, by the NSF CAREER award CCR-9501708, by the NSF grant CCR-9504469, by the AFOSR contract F49620-93-1-0056, and by the ARPA grant NAG2-892.

The development of concurrent programs that must meet rigid *real-time* constraints has brought with it a need for *real-time temporal logics* that enable quantitative reference to time [EMSS90, AH92]. Formulas of real-time temporal logics are interpreted over *timed structures* (infinite words or infinite trees in which a time stamp is associated with every position), and their syntax includes, in addition to qualitative temporal operators (such as "eventually"), also explicit time references (such as "within 4 time units"). Early research on real-time temporal logics considered *discrete time*, where time stamps are *integers*. It turned out that model-checking methods for untimed temporal logics can be extended quite easily to handle discrete time [Eme92, AH93]. Present research on real-time temporal logics focuses on *dense time*, where time stamps are *reals* [Alu91, AFH96]. There, model checking becomes significantly more complex. For example, while the model-checking problem is PSPACE-complete for the linear temporal logic LTL [SC85], it is undecidable for its real-time extension TLTL [AH94].

We can still define real-time temporal logics with a dense-time domain for which model checking is decidable. Such a logic is TCTL, the real-time extension of the branching temporal logic CTL. The branching nature and the limited syntax of TCTL circumvent the difficulties that make TLTL model checking undecidable and yet enables the specifications of many interesting real-time properties. Nevertheless, model checking for TCTL is hard. Indeed, while the model-checking problem for CTL can be solved in linear time [CES86], it is PSPACE-complete for TCTL [ACD93]. This means that methods that cope with the computational limitations of CTL model checking become even more essential when we turn to consider TCTL model checking.

The main computational limitation of CTL model checking is caused by the size of the program. In particular, in a concurrent setting, the state space of the program grows exponentially with the number of its concurrent components. This issue, known as the *state-explosion* problem, is one of the most challenging issues in the area of computer-aided verification and is the subject of active research. Two powerful methods for coping with the state explosion problem are *on-the-fly* model checking and *space-efficient* model checking. In on-the-fly model checking, we explore only a portion of the state space of the program; namely, the portion whose exploration is essential for determining the satisfaction of the specification [FMJJ92]. On-the-fly model-checking is strongly related to *local* model-checking, where we check whether a specific state of the program satisfies a specification [SW89]. The motivation for space-efficient algorithms comes from the fact that space, rather than time, is the computational bottleneck of model checking. Accordingly, in space-efficient model checking, we store in memory the minimal information required, preferring to spend time on reconstructing information rather than spend space on storing it. In this work we develop an automata-theoretic approach to TCTL model checking that combines both methods and suggests, for the first time, a PSPACE on-the-fly model-checking algorithm for TCTL.

We can view temporal-logic formulas as describing languages (of infinite words or trees). ***Automata on infinite objects*** also describe languages. Like temporal logics, they come in two varieties: automata on infinite words (*word automata*, for short) and automata on infinite trees (*tree automata*). The automata-theoretic approach to temporal logic uses the theory of automata as a unifying paradigm for program specification and verification [VW94, BVW94]. In this paradigm, both the program and the specification are translated to (or are given as) automata. Linear temporal logic formulas correspond to word automata and branching temporal logic formulas correspond to tree automata. Then, questions about programs and their specifications can be reduced to questions about automata. More specifically, questions such as satisfiability of specifications and correctness of programs with respect to their specifications can be reduced to questions such as nonemptiness and containment of automata. These reductions yield clean and optimal algorithms and are helpful in implementing model-checking methods [CVWY92].

In the automata-theoretic approach to CTL model checking, we translate a formula ψ to a tree *hesitant alternating automaton* (HAA) $\mathcal{A}_\psi$ of size linear in the length of ψ. For checking whether a program P satisfies ψ, we check the nonemptiness of the product of $\mathcal{A}_\psi$ and P.

This product is a word HAA over a 1-letter alphabet and its nonemptiness can be tested in linear time, matching the known bound. Moreover, the special structure of HAA enables us to check their nonemptiness in efficient space and leads to an on-the-fly model-checking algorithm for CTL that needs space linear in the length of ψ but only polylogarithmic in the size of P [BVW94]. So, for model checking of untimed temporal logics, the automata-theoretic approach combines on-the-fly methods and space efficiency.

The automata-theoretic counterpart for describing languages of timed objects are *timed automata* [AD94]. Timed automata use finitely many real-valued *clocks* to keep track of timing constraints, and serve as the common way of modeling the behavior of real-time programs. The automata-theoretic approach to CTL cannot be easily extended to handle TCTL. The reason is TCTL's dense time domain which requires models with infinitely many states. It was shown, however, in [AD94], that each real-time program induces a finite quotient of the infinite state space. More precisely, it partitions the infinite time domain of clock valuations into finitely many *regions*, each of which can be viewed as a set of clock constraints (e.g., $2 < clock_1 < 3$; $clock_2 = 1$). This finite quotient enables us to place the problem of TCTL model checking in the framework of untimed automata. In fact, the automata we use are the same alternating automata used for CTL model checking. Given a TCTL formula ψ and a real-time program $\mathcal{U}$, we construct a 1-letter word HAA $\mathcal{D}_{\psi,\mathcal{U}}$ such that the language of $\mathcal{D}_{\psi,\mathcal{U}}$ is not empty iff $\mathcal{U}$ satisfies ψ.

Several model-checking algorithms for TCTL are studied in the literature [ACD93, HNSY94, LL95, SS95]. All these algorithms use the finite quotient of the state space suggested in [AD94]. They differ in how they explore the finite-state structure it induces. In [ACD93], a bottom-up labeling algorithm is used. This basic algorithm gains two optimizations in [HNSY94]. There, the algorithm uses a symbolic presentation of the state space and it tries to reduce the state space by integrating regions together. Typically, regions whose clock values are indistinguishable by the clock constraints in the program and the formula are integrated into a single *zone*. More work on reducing the state space is done in [SS95], adopting the minimization algorithm of [YL93]. The model-checking algorithm TMC, suggested in [SS95], combines top-down and bottom-up reasoning. The algorithm TMC works on-the-fly and explores only a portion of the program checked, but, unlike our algorithm, TMC maintains this portion all along its execution. Thus, the best bound to its complexity is exponential space. Maintenance of this portion and the bottom-up reasoning in [HNSY94, YL93, SS95] are essential, however, for obtaining zones that are as coarse as possible.

The simple combinatorial structure that emerges from our automata-theoretic approach offers several advantages. First, automata separate the logical and the algorithmic components of the model-checking problem. The translation to automata handles the logic, and the nonemptiness test handles the algorithmics. This separation makes both components simple and enables us to identify the exact complexity of the model checking problem. Second, using *Libi alternating automata* (LAA), which are HAA augmented with a fairness condition [KV95], we can restrict path quantification in TCTL to range only over computations of the program that diverge (i.e., in which time always proceed), and we can extend our method to fair-TCTL. Both extensions do not exist in the algorithm TMC. Most importantly, as the nonemptiness test for LAA combines on-the-fly and space efficiency, so does our model-checking algorithm. Thus, we explore only the part of the program whose exploration is essential for determining the satisfaction of ψ, and we do so in space polynomial in the program and in ψ (assuming a binary encoding of the clock constraints).

Optimization is incorporated into the automata-theoretic framework by integrating several transitions of the automaton into a single transition. This achieves only part of the minimization achieved by the algorithm TMC, but enables a pure top-down reasoning, which is the key to our space efficiency. In addition, we point on a subset of TCTL for which our top-down reasoning obtains zones that are as coarse as possible.

2 Definitions

2.1 Timed Structures and Timed Words

We model real-time programs by *timed structures*. Timed structures extend traditional Kripke structures by labeling each transition with a nonnegative real number denoting its duration. Formally, a timed structure is a tuple $K = \langle AP, W, R, w^0, \sigma \rangle$, where

- AP is a finite set of atomic propositions,
- W is a set of states,
- $R \subseteq W \times \mathbb{R} \times W$ is a transition relation (for simplicity, we denote by $\mathbb{R}$ the set of all non negative real numbers),
- $w^0 \in W$ is an initial state,
- $\sigma : W \rightarrow 2^{AP}$ maps to each state a set of atomic propositions true in the state.

A *path* in K is an infinite sequence of pairs $\langle w_0, \delta_0 \rangle, \langle w_1, \delta_1 \rangle, \ldots$, such that for all $i \geq 0$, we have $\langle w_i, \delta_i, w_{i+1} \rangle \in R$. A *timed word* is an infinite sequence $\tau \in (2^{AP} \times \mathbb{R})^\omega$. We sometimes refer to a timed word as a function $\tau : \mathbb{N} \rightarrow 2^{AP} \times \mathbb{R}$ and use $\tau_1(i)$ and $\tau_2(i)$ to refer to the i'th event and duration, respectively, in τ. A timed word τ *diverges* iff for all $r \in \mathbb{R}$, there exists an $i \in \mathbb{N}$ such that $r \leq \sum_{j=0}^{i} \tau_2(i)$. Note that each path in a timed structure induces a timed word: the timed word τ^π induced by τ has $\tau^\pi(i) = \langle \sigma(w_i), \delta_i \rangle$ for all $i \in \mathbb{N}$. We say that the path π diverges iff τ^π diverges.

2.2 Linear Timed Automata

We model real-time programs by *linear timed automata*. We now define linear timed automata and the timed structures induced by them.

Given a set C of clocks, a *clock environment* $\mathcal{E} : C \rightarrow \mathbb{R}$ assigns to each clock a nonnegative real value. Given a clock environment $\mathcal{E}$, a set $S \subseteq C$ of reset clocks and a time delay $\delta \in \mathbb{R}$, we define $progress(\mathcal{E}, S, \delta)$ as the clock environment $\mathcal{E}'$ where for all $c \in C$, we have

$$\mathcal{E}'(c) = \begin{cases} 0 & \text{if } c \in S, \\ \mathcal{E}(c) + \delta & \text{if } c \notin S. \end{cases}$$

For two clock environments $\mathcal{E}$ and $\mathcal{E}'$, we say that $\mathcal{E} < \mathcal{E}'$ iff for every clock $c \in C$, we have $\mathcal{E}(c) < \mathcal{E}'(c)$. For a set C of clocks, a formula in $guard(C)$ is one of the following:

- **true**, **false**, or $c \sim v$, where $c \in C$, $v \in \mathbb{N}$[4], and $\sim \in \{\geq, >, \leq, <\}$,
- $\theta_1 \vee \theta_2$ or $\theta_1 \wedge \theta_2$, where θ_1 and θ_2 are formulas in $guard(C)$.

A *linear timed automaton* is a tuple $\mathcal{U} = \langle AP, C, L, E, P, inv, l^0 \rangle$, where

- AP is a finite set of atomic propositions,
- C is a finite set of clocks,
- L is a finite set of locations,
- $E : L \rightarrow 2^{guard(C) \times 2^C \times L}$ is a nondeterministic transition function,
- $P : L \rightarrow 2^{AP}$ is a labeling function,
- $inv : L \rightarrow guard(C)$ is an invariance function,
- $l^0 \in L$ is an initial location.

[4] As we can multiply all clock values by the same factor [AD94], using $\mathbb{N}$, rather then $\mathbb{Q}$, does not reduce the expressive power of the automata.

A *position* of $\mathcal{U}$ is a pair $\langle l, \mathcal{E}\rangle \in L \times \mathbb{R}^C$. That is, a position describes a location and a clock environment. Given a position $\langle l, \mathcal{E}\rangle$ and a time delay $\delta \in \mathbb{R}$, we say that the position $\langle l', \mathcal{E}'\rangle$ is a *δ-successor* of $\langle l, \mathcal{E}\rangle$ iff there exists a triple $\langle \theta, S, l'\rangle \in E(l)$ such that the following hold:

1. $progress(\mathcal{E}, \emptyset, \delta) \models \theta$,
2. for every $0 \leq \delta' < \delta$, we have $progress(\mathcal{E}, \emptyset, \delta') \models inv(l)$,
3. $\mathcal{E}' = progress(\mathcal{E}, S, \delta)$.

Linear timed automata run on timed words. A *run* r of a linear timed automaton on a timed word is an infinite sequence of positions. Thus, $r \in (L \times \mathbb{R}^C)^\omega$. We sometimes refer to a run as a function $r : \mathbb{N} \to L \times \mathbb{R}^C$. Given a timed word $\tau : \mathbb{N} \to 2^{AP} \times \mathbb{R}$, a run r of $\mathcal{U}$ on τ satisfies the following. For every $i \geq 0$, let $r(i) = \langle l_i, \mathcal{E}_i\rangle$. Then,

- $l_0 = l^0$ and $\mathcal{E}_0$ assigns to all clocks 0,
- for every $i \geq 0$, we have $P(l_i) = \tau_1(i)$,
- for every $i \geq 0$, we have $\langle l_{i+1}, \mathcal{E}_{i+1}\rangle$ is a $\tau_2(i)$-successor of $\langle l_i, \mathcal{E}_i\rangle$.

We say that $\mathcal{U}$ *accepts* a timed word τ iff there exists a run of $\mathcal{U}$ on τ. The *language* of $\mathcal{U}$ is the set of all timed words that $\mathcal{U}$ accepts. Each linear timed automaton induces a timed structure. Formally, the *timed structure of* $\mathcal{U}$ is

$$K_{\mathcal{U}} = \langle AP, L \times \mathbb{R}^C, R, \langle l^0, 0^{|C|}\rangle, \sigma\rangle,$$

where R and σ are defined as follows:

- $\langle\langle l, \mathcal{E}\rangle, \delta, \langle l', \mathcal{E}'\rangle\rangle \in R$ iff $\langle l', \mathcal{E}'\rangle$ is a δ-successor of $\langle l, \mathcal{E}\rangle$,
- for all states $\langle l, \mathcal{E}\rangle \in L \times \mathbb{R}^C$, we have $\sigma(\langle l, \mathcal{E}\rangle) = P(l)$.

Note that the state set of $K_{\mathcal{U}}$ is infinite and that $K_{\mathcal{U}}$ may have an infinite branching degree. It is easy to see that a timed word is accepted by $\mathcal{U}$ iff it is induced by a path in $K_{\mathcal{U}}$.

2.3 The Real-time Branching Temporal Logic TCTL

We specify properties of timed structures using real-time temporal logics. We consider here TCTL, the real-time extension of the branching temporal logic CTL [ACD93]. Formulas of TCTL are defined with respect to the sets AP and $C_{\mathcal{U}}$ of the program's atomic propositions and clocks, respectively, and a set C_ψ of specification clocks. Atomic formulas of TCTL refer to the satisfaction of atomic propositions and put constraints on the values of the clocks. In addition to the Boolean operators $\neg$, $\vee$, and $\wedge$, TCTL allows the time operators U ("until") and $\tilde{U}$ ("dual until"), and the reset quantifier $c.\varphi$, which resets a specification clock c. For example, if p and q are atomic propositions in a linear timed automaton $\mathcal{U}$ with a clock x, then the TCTL formula

$$ApU((x > 5) \wedge (z.A(qU(z = 3))))$$

uses a specification clock z and asserts that in all computations of $\mathcal{U}$, the atom p hold until a point where the value of the clock x is bigger than 5 and the atom q holds along the first 3 time units of all the computations that start at this point. We consider TCTL formulas in a positive normal form in which negation may apply to atomic propositions only. Given $AP, C_{\mathcal{U}}$, and C_ψ, a formula of TCTL is one of the following:

- **true**, **false**, p or $\neg p$, where $p \in AP$,
- $c \sim v$, where $c \in C_{\mathcal{U}} \cup C_\psi$, $v \in \mathbb{N}$, and $\sim \in \{\geq, >, \leq, <\}$,
- $\varphi_1 \vee \varphi_2$, $\varphi_1 \wedge \varphi_2$, $E\varphi_1 U\varphi_2$, $A\varphi_1 U\varphi_2$, $E\varphi_1\tilde{U}\varphi_2$, or $A\varphi_1\tilde{U}\varphi_2$, where φ_1 and φ_2 are TCTL formulas,
- $c.\varphi$, where $c \in C_\psi$ and φ is a TCTL formula.

The reset quantifier $c.\varphi$ *binds* all free occurrences of c in φ. By renaming clocks we can make sure that no occurrence of a clock in φ is bound to more than one clock. A formula is *closed* if each non-binding occurrence of a specification clock is bound to exactly one clock. We denote by $cl(\psi)$ the set of all subformulas of ψ. It is easy to see that the size of $cl(\psi)$ is bounded by the length of ψ.

TCTL formulas are interpreted over the states of a timed structure $K = \langle AP, W, R, w_0, \sigma\rangle$ and a clock environment $\mathcal{E} : C \to \mathbb{R}$. For $\delta \in \mathbb{R}$, we write $\mathcal{E} + \delta$ to denote the clock environment that maps a clock c to $\mathcal{E}(c) + \delta$. We write $\mathcal{E}[c := 0]$ to denote the clock environment that maps c to 0 and maps every other clock c' to $\mathcal{E}(c')$. Consider a path $\langle w_0, \delta_0\rangle, \langle w_1, \delta_1\rangle \ldots$, in K. Given $\{j, i\} \subseteq \mathbb{N}$ and $\{\delta', \delta\} \subseteq \mathbb{R}$ with $\delta' \le \delta_j$ and $\delta \le \delta_i$, we say that $(j, \delta') < (i, \delta)$ iff $j < i$, or $j = i$ and $\delta' < \delta$.

We use $w, \mathcal{E} \models \varphi$ to indicate that a formula φ holds at state w with clock environment $\mathcal{E}$ (with respect to a given timed structure K). The relation $\models$ is defined inductively as follows:

- For all w and $\mathcal{E}$, we have $w, \mathcal{E} \models$ **true** and $w, \mathcal{E} \not\models$ **false**.
- For $p \in AP$, we have $w, \mathcal{E} \models p$ iff $p \in \sigma(w)$ and $w, \mathcal{E} \models \neg p$ iff $p \notin \sigma(w)$.
- For $c \in C$, $v \in \mathbb{N}$, and $\sim\, \in \{\ge, >, \le, <\}$, we have $w, \mathcal{E} \models c \sim v$ iff $\mathcal{E}(c) \sim v$.
- $w, \mathcal{E} \models \varphi_1 \vee \varphi_2$ iff $w, \mathcal{E} \models \varphi_1$ or $w, \mathcal{E} \models \varphi_2$.
- $w, \mathcal{E} \models \varphi_1 \wedge \varphi_2$ iff $w, \mathcal{E} \models \varphi_1$ and $w, \mathcal{E} \models \varphi_2$.
- $w, \mathcal{E} \models E\varphi_1 U \varphi_2$ iff there exists a diverging path $\langle w_0, \delta_0\rangle, \langle w_1, \delta_1\rangle \ldots$ in K with $w_0 = w$ such that there exist $i \ge 0$ and $0 \le \delta \le \delta_i$ such that $w_i, (\mathcal{E} + \delta + \sum_{j=0}^{i-1} \delta_j) \models \varphi_2$ and for all $(j, \delta') < (i, \delta)$, we have $w_j, (\mathcal{E} + \delta' + \sum_{k=0}^{j-1} \delta_k) \models \varphi_1 \vee \varphi_2$.
- $w, \mathcal{E} \models A\varphi_1 U \varphi_2$ iff for every diverging path $\langle w_0, \delta_0\rangle, \langle w_1, \delta_1\rangle \ldots$ in K with $w_0 = w$, there exist $i \ge 0$ and $0 \le \delta \le \delta_i$ such that $w_i, (\mathcal{E} + \delta + \sum_{j=0}^{i-1} \delta_j) \models \varphi_2$ and for all $(j, \delta') < (i, \delta)$, we have $w_j, (\mathcal{E} + \delta' + \sum_{k=0}^{j-1} \delta_k) \models \varphi_1 \vee \varphi_2$.
- $w, \mathcal{E} \models E\varphi_1 \tilde{U} \varphi_2$ iff there exists a diverging path $\langle w_0, \delta_0\rangle, \langle w_1, \delta_1\rangle \ldots$ in K with $w_0 = w$ and for every $i \ge 0$ and $0 \le \delta \le \delta_i$ such that $w_i, (\mathcal{E} + \delta + \sum_{j=0}^{i-1} \delta_j) \not\models \varphi_2$, there exists (j, δ') such that $(j, \delta') < (i, \delta)$ and $w_j, (\mathcal{E} + \delta' + \sum_{k=0}^{j-1} \delta_k) \models \varphi_1 \wedge \varphi_2$.
- $w, \mathcal{E} \models A\varphi_1 \tilde{U} \varphi_2$ iff for every diverging path $\langle w_0, \delta_0\rangle, \langle w_1, \delta_1\rangle \ldots$ in K with $w_0 = w$ and for every $i \ge 0$ and $0 \le \delta \le \delta_i$ such that $w_i, (\mathcal{E} + \delta + \sum_{j=0}^{i-1} \delta_j) \not\models \varphi_2$, there exists (j, δ') such that $(j, \delta') < (i, \delta)$ and $w_j, (\mathcal{E} + \delta' + \sum_{k=0}^{j-1} \delta_k) \models \varphi_1 \wedge \varphi_2$.
- $w, \mathcal{E} \models c.\varphi$ iff $w, \mathcal{E}[c := 0] \models \varphi$.

Note that path quantification in TCTL ranges over diverging paths only. Note also that the semantics of the until operator and its duality requires either φ_1 or φ_2 to be satisfied until the satisfaction of φ_2. As explained in [HNSY94], this meets our expectations of the dense-time domain. Thus, the formula $z.A(z \le 4)U(z > 4)$ is always valid and, similarly, the dual formula $z.A(z > 4)\tilde{U}(z \le 4)$ is not satisfiable.

For a timed structure K and a TCTL formula ψ, we say that $K \models \psi$ iff $w_0, \mathcal{E}_0 \models \psi$, where $\mathcal{E}_0$ denotes the clock environment that assigns 0 to all clocks. The *model-checking* problem for TCTL is defined as follows: given a closed TCTL formula ψ and a linear timed automaton $\mathcal{U}$, determine whether $K_{\mathcal{U}} \models \psi$.

3 The Model-Checking Method

Given a TCTL formula ψ and a linear timed automaton $\mathcal{U}$, we are going to solve the model-checking problem as follows.

1. Define the set Υ of clock regions induced by ψ and $\mathcal{U}$ [AD94].

2. Define the function *reg_succ* : $\Upsilon \rightarrow \Upsilon$, that maps a clock region to its (unique) successor clock region [AD94].
3. Construct a 1-letter alternating automaton $\mathcal{D}_{\psi,\mathcal{U}}$ on infinite words. Each state in this untimed automaton is associated with a subformula φ of ψ, a location l of $\mathcal{U}$, and a clock region π from Υ. Intuitively, the language of a state $\langle \varphi, l, \pi \rangle$ is nonempty iff φ is satisfied in all states $\langle l, \mathcal{E} \rangle$ of the timed structure $K_{\mathcal{U}}$ for which the clock environment $\mathcal{E}$ is in π.
4. Check $\mathcal{D}_{\psi,\mathcal{U}}$ for nonemptiness.

We describe our method in two steps. First, in Section 3.4, we ignore the fact that path quantification in TCTL range only over computations that diverge. Then, in Section 3.5, we extend our method to handle path quantification correctly. We now define regions, the function *reg_succ*, and alternating automata.

3.1 Regions and Region Successors

Given a TCTL formula ψ and a linear timed automaton $\mathcal{U}$, let C_ψ and $C_{\mathcal{U}}$ be the set of clocks in ψ and $\mathcal{U}$, respectively. We assume that C_ψ and $C_{\mathcal{U}}$ are disjoint and denote their union by C. The clocks in C run through infinitely many clock environments. We can partition the infinitely many clock environments to finitely many equivalent classes such that all clock environments of the same class are indistinguishable by formulas in *guard*(C) that are clock constraints in either ψ or $\mathcal{U}$. It was proven in [AD94] that a sufficient condition for two environment clocks to be indistinguishable is agreement on the integral parts of all clocks values and agreement on the ordering of the fractional parts of all clock values. This leads to the following definition of *regions*. For $x \in \mathbb{R}$, let $\lfloor x \rfloor$ and $\langle x \rangle$ denote the integer and the fractional parts of x, respectively. Also, for each $c \in C$, let v_c be the largest integer v for which $x \sim v$ is a subformula of some clock constraint in ψ or $\mathcal{U}$. We define an equivalent relation $\approx \subseteq \mathbb{R}^{|C|} \times \mathbb{R}^{|C|}$. For two clock environments $\mathcal{E}$ and $\mathcal{E}'$, we have that $\mathcal{E} \approx \mathcal{E}'$ iff the following hold:

1. For all $c \in C$, either $\lfloor \mathcal{E}(c) \rfloor = \lfloor \mathcal{E}'(c) \rfloor$, or $\mathcal{E}(c) > v_c$ and $\mathcal{E}'(c) > v_c$.
2. For all $\{c, d\} \subseteq C$ with $\mathcal{E}(c) \leq v_c$ and $\mathcal{E}(d) \leq v_d$, we have that $\langle \mathcal{E}(c) \rangle \leq \langle \mathcal{E}(d) \rangle$ iff $\langle \mathcal{E}'(c) \rangle \leq \langle \mathcal{E}'(d) \rangle$.
3. For all $c \in C$ with $\mathcal{E}(c) \leq v_c$, we have $\langle \mathcal{E}(c) \rangle = 0$ iff $\langle \mathcal{E}'(c) \rangle = 0$.

We now define a region as an equivalent class of the relation $\approx$. Let Υ denote the set of all regions induced by ψ and $\mathcal{U}$ and let *rep* : $\Upsilon \rightarrow \mathbb{R}^{|C|}$ map each region to a representative clock environment in it. We represent a region π by *rep*(π). A clock environments $\mathcal{E}$ then belongs to π iff $\mathcal{E} \approx$ *rep*(π). We sometime represent a region also by a finite set of clock constraints (e.g., $[x = 1; 2 < z < 3]$). A clock environment $\mathcal{E}$ then belongs to π iff it satisfies all its clock constraints. Following the definition of regions, the constraints that represent π specify the integral part of all clocks, the order among the fractional parts, and whether they are equal to 0.

Lemma 1. [AD94] *The number of regions in* Υ *is bounded by* $|C|! \cdot 2^{|C|} \cdot \prod_{c \in C}(2v_c + 2)$.

For a region π and a formula $\varphi \in$ *guard*(C), we say that π satisfies φ (denoted $\pi \models \varphi$) iff *rep*(π) satisfies φ. Note that by the definition of regions, π satisfies φ iff all clock environments in π satisfy φ.

Each region has a unique successor region. Intuitively, the successor of a region π is obtained from π by letting time pass. The function *reg_succ* : $\Upsilon \rightarrow \Upsilon$ maps a region π to its successor region. For a region π and a clock environment $\mathcal{E}$, we have that $\mathcal{E} \in$ *reg_succ*(π) iff *rep*$(\pi) \not\approx \mathcal{E}$, *rep*$(\pi) < \mathcal{E}$, and for every clock environment $\mathcal{E}'$ with *rep*$(\pi) < \mathcal{E}' < \mathcal{E}$, we have $\mathcal{E}' \approx$ *rep*(π) or $\mathcal{E}' \approx \mathcal{E}$. So, for example, if π has a clock constraint $c = v$, for $v \neq v_c$, its successor has a clock constraint $v < c < v+1$. If $v = v_c$, then the successor region has a clock constraint $c > v$, reflecting the fact that once c is bigger than v_c, we are no longer interested in how much it is bigger.

Example 1. Consider the TCTL formula $\psi = z.A(q \vee (1 < z < 3))U(p \wedge q)$ and the linear timed automaton $\mathcal{U}$ appearing in the figure below.

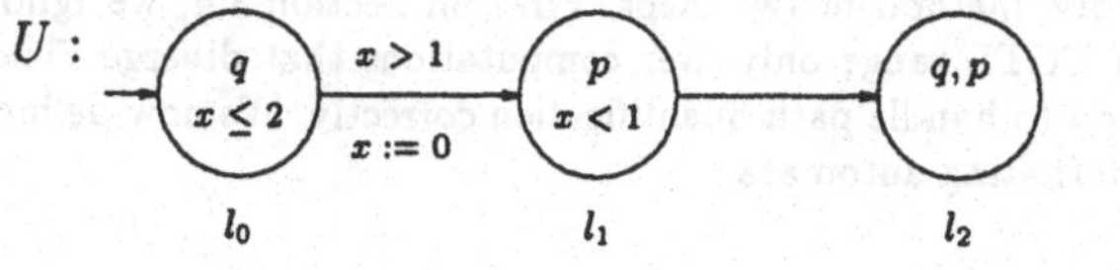

The corresponding set Υ of regions, appearing in the figure below, is of size 59.

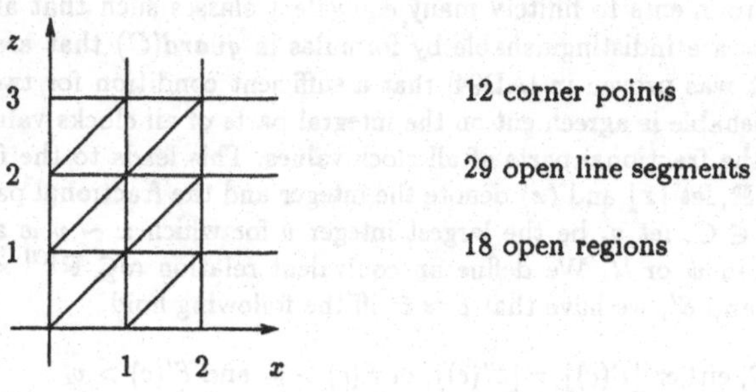

Below are two chains of successive regions in Υ.

- $\pi_0 : [x = z = 0] \rightsquigarrow \pi_1 : [0 < x = z < 1] \rightsquigarrow \pi_2 : [x = z = 1] \rightsquigarrow \pi_3 : [1 < x = z < 2] \rightsquigarrow \pi_4 : [x = z = 2] \rightsquigarrow \ldots$
- $\pi_5 : [x = 0; 1 < z < 2] \rightsquigarrow \pi_6 : [0 < x < 1; 1 < z < 2; \langle x \rangle < \langle z \rangle] \rightsquigarrow \pi_7 : [0 < x < 1; z = 2] \rightsquigarrow \pi_8 : [0 < x < 1; 2 < z < 3; \langle z \rangle < \langle x \rangle] \rightsquigarrow \pi_9 : [x = 1; 2 < z < 3] \rightsquigarrow \ldots$

3.2 Alternating Automata

For an introduction to the theory of automata on infinite words see [Tho90]. *Alternating automata* on infinite words generalize nondeterministic automata and were first introduced in [MS87]. Consider a nondeterministic word automaton with a set Q of states and a transition function M. The function M maps an automaton state $q \in Q$ and an input letter $\sigma \in \Sigma$ to a set of states. Each such state suggests a nondeterministic choice for the automaton's next state. For a given set X, let $\mathcal{B}^+(X)$ be the set of positive Boolean formulas over X (i.e., Boolean formulas built from elements in X using $\wedge$ and $\vee$, where we also allow the formulas **true** and **false** and, as usual, $\wedge$ has precedence over $\vee$). We can represent the transition function M using $\mathcal{B}^+(Q)$. For example, $M(q, \sigma) = \{q_1, q_2\}$ can be written as $M(q, \sigma) = q_1 \vee q_2$.

In nondeterministic automata, $M(q, \sigma)$ is a disjunction. In alternating automata, $M(q, \sigma)$ can be an arbitrary formula from $\mathcal{B}^+(Q)$. We can have, for instance, a transition $M(q, \sigma) =$

$(q_1 \wedge q_2) \vee q_3$. Thus, several "copies" of the automaton may be sent to the same suffix of the input word. Formally, an *alternating automaton* is a tuple $\mathcal{A} = \langle \Sigma, Q, \delta, q_0, \alpha \rangle$, where Σ is the input alphabet, Q is a finite set of states, $\delta : Q \times \Sigma \to \mathcal{B}^+(Q)$ is a transition function, $q_0 \in Q$ is an initial state, and α is an acceptance condition (a condition that defines subset of Q^ω). If $|\Sigma| = 1$, then we call $\mathcal{A}$ a 1-letter automaton. For a set $Y \subseteq X$ and a formula $\theta \in \mathcal{B}^+(X)$, we say that Y *satisfies* θ iff assigning **true** to elements in Y and assigning **false** to elements in $X \setminus Y$ satisfies θ. A *run* of an alternating automaton $\mathcal{A}$ over an input word $\sigma_0 \cdot \sigma_1 \cdots$ is a tree labeled by elements of Q. The root of the tree is labeled by q_0 and the labels of a node and its children have to satisfy the transition function. That is, if a node x of level i (that is, the path from the root to x is of length i) is labeled q and $\delta(q, \sigma_i) = \theta$, then there is a possibly empty set $Y = \{q_1, q_2, \ldots, q_n\} \subseteq Q$ such that the following hold:

- Y satisfies θ, and
- for all $1 \leq j \leq n$, the node x has a child labeled with q_j.

For example, if $\delta(q_0, \sigma_0) = (q_1 \wedge q_2) \vee q_3$, then possible runs of $\mathcal{A}$ start in a tree with root q_0 and either two children, q_1 and q_2, or a single child q_3. Note that if $\theta =$ **true**, then x need not have successors. Also, we can not have a run with $\theta =$ **false**. Note also that each infinite path in the run corresponds to a sequence in Q^ω. The run is accepting if all its infinite paths satisfy the acceptance condition. An automaton is *nonempty* if it accepts some word.

A *hesitant alternating automaton* (HAA) on words [BVW94] is an alternating automaton $\mathcal{A} = \langle \Sigma, Q, \delta, q_0, \alpha \rangle$ where $\alpha = \langle G, B \rangle$ with $G \subseteq Q$ and $B \subseteq Q$ and δ satisfies the following. First, as in *weak alternating automata* [MSS86], there exists a partition of Q into disjoint sets Q_i, and a partial order $\leq$ on the collection of the Q_i's such that for every $q \in Q_i$ and $q' \in Q_j$ for which q' occurs in $\delta(q, \sigma)$ for some $\sigma \in \Sigma$, we have $Q_j \leq Q_i$. Thus, transitions from a state in Q_i lead to states in either the same Q_i or a lower one. We call this condition the *weakness condition*. In addition, each set Q_i is classified as either *transient*, *existential*, or *universal*, such that for each set Q_i and for all $q \in Q_i$ and $\sigma \in \Sigma$, the following hold:

1. If Q_i is a transient set, then $\delta(q, \sigma)$ contains no elements of Q_i.
2. If Q_i is an existential set, then $\delta(q, \sigma)$ only contains *disjunctively related* elements of Q_i (i.e., if the transition function is rewritten in disjunctive normal form, there is at most one element of Q_i in each disjunct).
3. If Q_i is a universal set, then $\delta(q, \sigma)$ only contains *conjunctively related* elements of Q_i (i.e., if the transition function is rewritten in conjunctive normal form, there is at most one element of Q_i in each conjunct).

We call this condition the *hesitation condition*. It follows that every infinite path of a run of a HAA ultimately gets trapped either within some existential or within some universal set Q_i. For a path ρ, we denote by $inf(\rho)$ the set of states that ρ visits infinitely often. A path ρ satisfies an acceptance condition $\alpha = \langle G, B \rangle$ if and only if either Q_i is an existential set and $inf(\rho) \cap G \neq \emptyset$, or Q_i is a universal set and $inf(\rho) \cap B = \emptyset$. Note that the acceptance condition of HAA combines the Rabin and the Streett acceptance conditions: existential sets refer to the Rabin condition $\{\langle G, \emptyset \rangle\}$ and universal sets refer to the Streett condition $\{\langle B, \emptyset \rangle\}$. The number of sets in the partition of Q is defined as the *depth* of $\mathcal{A}$.

Theorem 2. [BVW94]

(1) *The 1-letter nonemptiness problem for HAA can be solved in linear time.*

(2) *The 1-letter nonemptiness problem for HAA of size n and depth m can be solved in space $O(m \log^2 n)$.*

The restricted structure of HAA suggests an automata-based model-checking algorithm that combines on-the-fly methods with space efficiency [BVW94]. Essentially, HAA enable on-the-fly model-checking since their transition function depends only on the current states and input. They enable space efficiency since their nonemptiness can be checked in efficient space. We now show that the model-checking problem for TCTL can also be placed in the framework of HAA.

3.3 Region Positions and Region-Position Successors

Let $\mathcal{U} = \langle AP, C_{\mathcal{U}}, L, E, P, inv, l^0 \rangle$ be a linear timed automaton. Given a TCTL formula ψ, let Υ and *reg_succ* be defined as above. For $\pi \in \Upsilon$ and a set S of clocks, we denote by $\pi[S := 0]$ the region obtained from π by reseting all clocks in S. That is, $\pi[S := 0]$ contain the clock environment $progress(rep(\pi), S, 0)$. Also, let π_0 denote the region where all clocks are set to 0. We define a *region position* of the automaton $\mathcal{U}$ as a pair $\langle l, \pi \rangle \in L \times \Upsilon$. When we say that $\mathcal{U}$ is in region position $\langle l, \pi \rangle$, we mean that $\mathcal{U}$ is in location l and that its clock environment is in π. We say that a region position $\langle l, \pi \rangle$ is *admissible* iff π satisfies $inv(l)$.

We know that the automaton $\mathcal{U}$ can be only in admissible region positions. Moreover, when $\mathcal{U}$ is in region position $\langle l, \pi \rangle$, we know what its possible futures are: the automaton $\mathcal{U}$ can either take an *edge transition* and move to another location, possibly resetting some clocks, or take a *time transition* and stay in l while the values of the clocks change and meet the successor region. We now define a function $succ : L \times \Upsilon \to 2^{L \times \Upsilon}$ that, given $\langle l, \pi \rangle$, returns the set of region positions reachable from $\langle l, \pi \rangle$ by either a time or an edge transition. Thus, $\langle l', \pi' \rangle$ is in $succ(\langle l, \pi \rangle)$ iff it is admissible and either $l' = l$ and $\pi' = reg\_succ(\pi)$, or there exists $\langle \theta, S, l' \rangle \in E(l)$ such that π satisfies θ and $\pi' = \pi[S := 0]$.

Example 2. Consider ψ and $\mathcal{U}$ from Example 1. Below is a partial definition of $succ : L \times \Upsilon \to 2^{L \times \Upsilon}$.

- $succ(\langle l_0, \pi_0 \rangle) = \{\langle l_0, \pi_1 \rangle\}$. The only possible next location is l_1. Since π_0 does not satisfy its guard, no edge transition is enabled.
- $succ(\langle l_0, \pi_3 \rangle) = \{\langle l_0, \pi_4 \rangle, \langle l_1, \pi_5 \rangle\}$. Here, both transitions are enabled.
- $succ(\langle l_1, \pi_5 \rangle) = \{\langle l_1, \pi_6 \rangle, \langle l_2, \pi_5 \rangle\}$.
- $succ(\langle l_1, \pi_6 \rangle) = \{\langle l_1, \pi_7 \rangle, \langle l_2, \pi_6 \rangle\}$.
- $succ(\langle l_1, \pi_7 \rangle) = \{\langle l_1, \pi_8 \rangle, \langle l_2, \pi_7 \rangle\}$.
- $succ(\langle l_1, \pi_8 \rangle) = \{\langle l_2, \pi_8 \rangle\}$. Here, as π_9 does not satisfy $inv(l_1)$, a time transition is not enabled.

3.4 The Construction of $\mathcal{A}_{\psi,\mathcal{U}}$

We now describe a construction of $\mathcal{A}_{\psi,\mathcal{U}}$ that ignores the fact that path quantification in TCTL ranges only over computations that diverge. Given ψ and $\mathcal{U}$, we define the HAA $\mathcal{A}_{\psi,\mathcal{U}} = \langle \{a\}, Q, \delta, q_0, \alpha \rangle$, where

- $Q \subseteq cl(\psi) \times L \times \Upsilon$ and $\langle \varphi, l, \pi \rangle \in Q$ iff $\langle l, \pi \rangle$ is admissible (recall that $cl(\psi)$ is the set of all subformulas of ψ).
- $q_0 = \langle \psi, l^0, \pi_0 \rangle$ (if $\langle l^0, \pi_0 \rangle$ is not admissible then the language of $\mathcal{A}_{\psi,\mathcal{U}}$ is clearly empty).
- The transition function δ is given below.
  - $\delta(\langle p, l, \pi \rangle, a) = \begin{cases} \textbf{true} \text{ if } p \in P(l), \\ \textbf{false} \text{ otherwise.} \end{cases}$
  - $\delta(\langle \neg p, l, \pi \rangle, a) = \begin{cases} \textbf{true} \text{ if } p \notin P(l), \\ \textbf{false} \text{ otherwise.} \end{cases}$

- $\delta(\langle c \sim v, l, \pi\rangle, a) = \begin{cases} \textbf{true} \text{ if } \pi \models c \sim v, \\ \textbf{false} \text{ otherwise.} \end{cases}$
- $\delta(\langle \varphi_1 \vee \varphi_2, l, \pi\rangle, a) = \delta(\langle \varphi_1, l, \pi\rangle, a) \vee \delta(\langle \varphi_2, l, \pi\rangle, a)$.
- $\delta(\langle \varphi_1 \wedge \varphi_2, l, \pi\rangle, a) = \delta(\langle \varphi_1, l, \pi\rangle, a) \wedge \delta(\langle \varphi_2, l, \pi\rangle, a)$.
- $\delta(\langle E\varphi_1 U \varphi_2, l, \pi\rangle, a) = \delta(\langle \varphi_2, l, \pi\rangle, a) \vee (\delta(\langle \varphi_1, l, \pi\rangle, a) \wedge \bigvee_{(l',\pi') \in succ((l,\pi))} \langle E\varphi_1 U \varphi_2, l', \pi'\rangle)$.
- $\delta(\langle A\varphi_1 U \varphi_2, l, \pi\rangle, a) = \delta(\langle \varphi_2, l, \pi\rangle, a) \vee (\delta(\langle \varphi_1, l, \pi\rangle, a) \wedge \bigwedge_{(l',\pi') \in succ((l,\pi))} \langle A\varphi_1 U \varphi_2, l', \pi'\rangle)$.
- $\delta(\langle E\varphi_1 \tilde{U} \varphi_2, l, \pi\rangle, a) = \delta(\langle \varphi_2, l, \pi\rangle, a) \wedge (\delta(\langle \varphi_1, l, \pi\rangle, a) \vee \bigvee_{(l',\pi') \in succ((l,\pi))} \langle E\varphi_1 \tilde{U} \varphi_2, l', \pi'\rangle)$.
- $\delta(\langle A\varphi_1 \tilde{U} \varphi_2, l, \pi\rangle, a) = \delta(\langle \varphi_2, l, \pi\rangle, a) \wedge (\delta(\langle \varphi_1, l, \pi\rangle, a) \vee \bigwedge_{(l',\pi') \in succ((l,\pi))} \langle A\varphi_1 \tilde{U} \varphi_2, l', \pi'\rangle)$.
- $\delta(\langle c.\varphi, l, \pi\rangle, a) = \delta(\langle \varphi, l, \pi[\{c\} := 0]\rangle, a)$.

– The acceptance condition is $\alpha = \langle G, B\rangle$, where G consists of all triples $\langle \varphi, l, \pi\rangle \in Q$ for which φ is of the form $E\varphi_1 \tilde{U} \varphi_2$ and B consists of all triples $\langle \varphi, l, \pi\rangle \in Q$ for which φ is of the form $A\varphi_1 U \varphi_2$. Thus, an accepting run of $\mathcal{A}_{\psi,\mathcal{U}}$ may get trapped in a set associated with a $\tilde{U}$-formula, but may not get trapped in a set associated with an U-formula.

We define a partition of Q into disjoint sets as follows. Each formula $\varphi \in cl(\psi)$ induces a set $Q_\varphi = \{\varphi\} \times L \times \mathcal{T}$ in the partition. The partial order over the sets is defined by $Q_{\varphi_1} \leq Q_{\varphi_2}$ iff $\varphi_1 \in cl(\varphi_2)$. Since each transition of the automaton from a state associated with φ leads to states associated with formulas in $cl(\varphi)$, the weakness condition holds. We classify the sets as follows.

1. Sets Q_φ for φ of the form $p, \neg p, c \sim v, \varphi_1 \vee \varphi_2, \varphi_1 \wedge \varphi_2$, or $c.\varphi$ are transient.
2. Sets Q_φ for φ of the form $E\varphi_1 U \varphi_2$ or $E\varphi_1 \tilde{U} \varphi_2$ are existential.
3. Sets Q_φ for φ of the form $A\varphi_1 U \varphi_2$ or $A\varphi_1 \tilde{U} \varphi_2$ are universal.

It is easy to see that the hesitation condition holds too.

As in the automata for CTL [BVW94], disjunctions and conjunctions in ψ are handled by the existential and universal branching, respectively, of alternating automata. The until operator and its duality are handled by partitioning them to requirements on the present (current location) and requirements on the future (successor locations). The acceptance condition then takes care of requirements that are repeatedly postponed to the future.

Example 3. Consider ψ and $\mathcal{U}$ from Example 1. Below are some transitions of $\mathcal{A}_{\psi,\mathcal{U}}$. Let $\varphi = A(q \vee (1 < z < 3))U(p \wedge q)$.

– $\delta(\langle \psi, l_0, \pi_0\rangle, a) = \delta(\langle \varphi, l_0, \pi_0\rangle, a) = \textbf{false} \vee (\textbf{true} \wedge \langle \varphi, l_0, \pi_3\rangle) = \langle \varphi, l_0, \pi_1\rangle$.
– $\delta(\langle \varphi, l_0, \pi_1\rangle, a) = \langle \varphi, l_0, \pi_2\rangle$.
– $\delta(\langle \varphi, l_0, \pi_2\rangle, a) = \langle \varphi, l_0, \pi_3\rangle$.
– $\delta(\langle \varphi, l_0, \pi_3\rangle, a) = \langle \varphi, l_1, \pi_5\rangle$.
– $\delta(\langle \varphi, l_1, \pi_5\rangle, a) = \langle \varphi, l_1, \pi_6\rangle \wedge \langle \varphi, l_2, \pi_5\rangle$.
– $\delta(\langle \varphi, l_1, \pi_6\rangle, a) = \langle \varphi, l_1, \pi_7\rangle \wedge \langle \varphi, l_2, \pi_6\rangle$.
– $\delta(\langle \varphi, l_1, \pi_7\rangle, a) = \langle \varphi, l_1, \pi_8\rangle \wedge \langle \varphi, l_2, \pi_7\rangle$.
– $\delta(\langle \varphi, l_1, \pi_8\rangle, a) = \langle \varphi, l_2, \pi_5\rangle$.
– $\delta(\langle \varphi, l_2, \pi_5\rangle, a) = \delta(\langle \varphi, l_2, \pi_6\rangle, a) = \delta(\langle \varphi, l_2, \pi_7\rangle, a) = \delta(\langle \varphi, l_2, \pi_8\rangle, a) = \textbf{true}$.

This partial definition suffices to see that there exists a run of $\mathcal{A}_{\psi,\mathcal{U}}$ in which all copies eventually reach **true**. Thus, $\mathcal{A}_{\psi,\mathcal{U}}$ is nonempty.

3.5 Handling Divergence and Fairness

Path quantification in TCTL ranges only over paths that diverge. Consider an infinite sequence $\gamma = \pi_0, \pi_1, \ldots$ of regions. Divergence of γ is defined with respect to the sequence

$\gamma' = rep(\pi_0), rep(\pi_1), \ldots$ of clock environments. We say that γ diverges iff γ' satisfies the following: for every clock c, either c is reset infinitely often or eventually always $c > v_c$, where v_c is the largest constant with which c is compared. This can be specified using the generalized Büchi fairness condition: a sequence of region diverges iff for every clock $c \in C_{\mathcal{U}}$, the sequence visits infinitely often a region with either $c = 0$ or $c > v_c$.

In order to perform *fair* model checking, HAA were extended in [KV95] to *Libi Alternating Automata* (LAA). A LAA is an HAA extended with a generalized Büchi fairness condition $\beta \subseteq 2^Q$; i.e., β is a set of subsets of the state-space of the LAA (the version presented in [KV95] uses a Rabin fairness condition). For a run of a LAA with an acceptance condition α and a fairness condition $\beta = \{F_1, \ldots, F_n\}$, a path ρ that gets trapped within a set Q_i is accepted by the run iff either Q_i is an existential set, in which case ρ satisfies α and for all $1 \leq i \leq n$, we have $inf(\rho) \cap F_i \neq \emptyset$, or Q_i is a universal set, in which case ρ satisfies α or there exists $1 \leq i \leq n$ for which $inf(\rho) \cap F_i = \emptyset$. It is shown in [KV95] that the time and space complexities of the 1-letter nonemptiness problem for HAA apply also to LAA.

We now use LAA in order to range path quantification only over computations that diverge. Given ψ and $\mathcal{U}$, let $\mathcal{A}_{\psi,\mathcal{U}} = \langle\{a\}, Q, \delta, q_0, \alpha\rangle$ be the HAA defined in Section 3.4. We define the LAA $\mathcal{D}_{\psi,\mathcal{U}} = \langle\{a\}, Q', \delta', q_0, \alpha', \beta\rangle$, where

- $Q' = Q \cup (\{E\mathbf{true}, A\mathbf{false}\} \times L \times \Upsilon)$. The new states constitute two new sets. An existential set $Q_E = \{E\mathbf{true}\} \times L \times \Upsilon$, and a universal set $Q_A = \{A\mathbf{false}\} \times L \times \Upsilon$. The task of these sets will get clearer after the definition of α, δ, and β.
- For $\alpha = \langle G, B\rangle$, we have $\alpha' = \langle G \cup Q_E, B \cup Q_A\rangle$.
- The new states are sinks. Thus,
  - $\delta'(\langle E\mathbf{true}, l, \pi\rangle, a) = \bigvee_{\langle l',\pi'\rangle \in succ(\langle l,\pi\rangle)} \langle E\mathbf{true}, l', \pi'\rangle$.
  - $\delta'(\langle A\mathbf{false}, l, \pi\rangle, a) = \bigwedge_{\langle l',\pi'\rangle \in succ(\langle l,\pi\rangle)} \langle A\mathbf{false}, l', \pi'\rangle$.

  In addition, we change δ as follows.
  - $\delta'(\langle E\varphi_1 U\varphi_2, l, \pi\rangle, a) = \delta(\langle E\varphi_1 U\varphi_2, l, \pi\rangle, a) \wedge \bigvee_{\langle l',\pi'\rangle \in succ(\langle l,\pi\rangle)} \langle E\mathbf{true}, l', \pi'\rangle$.
  - $\delta'(\langle A\varphi_1 U\varphi_2, l, \pi\rangle, a) = \delta(\langle A\varphi_1 U\varphi_2, l, \pi\rangle, a) \vee \bigwedge_{\langle l',\pi'\rangle \in succ(\langle l,\pi\rangle)} \langle A\mathbf{false}, l', \pi'\rangle$.
  - $\delta'(\langle E\varphi_1 \tilde{U}\varphi_2, l, \pi\rangle, a) = \delta(\langle E\varphi_1 \tilde{U}\varphi_2, l, \pi\rangle, a) \wedge \bigvee_{\langle l',\pi'\rangle \in succ(\langle l,\pi\rangle)} \langle E\mathbf{true}, l', \pi'\rangle$.
  - $\delta'(\langle A\varphi_1 \tilde{U}\varphi_2, l, \pi\rangle, a) = \delta(\langle A\varphi_1 \tilde{U}\varphi_2, l, \pi\rangle, a) \vee \bigwedge_{\langle l',\pi'\rangle \in succ(\langle l,\pi\rangle)} \langle A\mathbf{false}, l', \pi'\rangle$.

  By the definition of α', if we ignore the fact that $\mathcal{D}_{\psi,\mathcal{U}}$ is a LAA, a copy of the automaton conjunctively sent to a state in Q_E has no significance, it is just like conjuncting a formula with **true**. In a dual way, a copy disjunctively sent to a state in Q_A has no significance either. In LAA, however, these copies are significant. The copy sent to a state in Q_E is guaranteed to accept iff it can continue with a computation that satisfies β. In a dual way, the copy sent to a state in Q_A is guaranteed to reject iff some computation it continues with satisfies β.
- The fairness condition β holds in computations that diverge. For every clock $c \in C_{\mathcal{U}}$, let

$$F_c = \{\langle\varphi, l, \pi\rangle : \pi \models (c = 0) \vee (c > v_c)\}.$$

  Then, $\beta = \{F_c : c \in C_{\mathcal{U}}\}$.

It follows that whenever $\mathcal{D}_{\psi,\mathcal{U}}$ is in a state associated with an existential formula and a location $\langle l, \pi\rangle$, it makes sure that there exists a path starting in $\langle l, \pi\rangle$ that diverges. Similarly, whenever $\mathcal{D}_{\psi,\mathcal{U}}$ is in a state associated with a universal formula and no path that starts in $\langle l, \pi\rangle$ diverges, it does not require satisfaction of the formula. This at first seems too weak, as we want more; we want quantification to range only over diverging paths. To see that it is not too weak, observe that as long as we keep visiting an existential or universal state, we keep sending copies of $\mathcal{D}_{\psi,\mathcal{U}}$ to states in Q_E and Q_A. Consider for example a state associated with the formula $A\varphi_1 U\varphi_2$. Each computation of $\mathcal{D}_{\psi,\mathcal{U}}$ either reaches a region position from which there are no diverging computations (and then, and only then, it can chose the Q_A disjunct), or a region position that satisfies φ_2 (and then, and only then, it can chose the φ_2 disjunct), or continues to visit $A\varphi_1 U\varphi_2$ forever. In the third case, if a path of $K_{\mathcal{U}}$ does not diverge, then it does not satisfy β. Therefore, the fact that it gets trapped in the set $Q_{A\varphi_1 U\varphi_2}$ (and hence does not satisfy α) does not prevent $\mathcal{D}_{\psi,\mathcal{U}}$ from accepting. The explanation is dual for the other cases.

In the definition above, we use β to restrict path quantification to range over paths that diverge. We can add to β more sets (e.g. $\{\langle\varphi, l, \pi\rangle : grant \in P(l)\}$) and restrict path quantification further (in the above example, to paths that diverge and visit a state labeled with *grant* infinitely often). Thus, like fair-CTL of [CES86], we can handle fair-TCTL, where the input linear timed automaton is augmented with fairness constraints.

Theorem 3.

(1) *The size of* $\mathcal{D}_{\psi,\mathcal{U}}$ *is bounded by* $|\psi| \cdot |L| \cdot |C|! \cdot 2^{|C|} \cdot \prod_{c\in C}(2v_c + 2)$.
(2) *The depth of* $\mathcal{D}_{\psi,\mathcal{U}}$ *is bounded by* $|\psi|$.
(3) *The automaton* $\mathcal{D}_{\psi,\mathcal{U}}$ *is nonempty iff* $K_{\mathcal{U}} \models \psi$.

Theorems 3 and 2 imply the following theorem.

Theorem 4. *Given a linear timed automaton* $\mathcal{U}$ *and a TCTL formula* ψ*, checking whether* $K_{\mathcal{U}} \models \psi$ *can be done either*

(1) *in time* $O(|\psi| \cdot |L| \cdot |C|! \cdot 2^{|C|} \cdot \prod_{c\in C}(2v_c + 2)))$, *or*
(2) *in space* $O(|\psi| \cdot \log^2(|\psi| \cdot |L| \cdot |C|! \cdot 2^{|C|} \cdot \prod_{c\in C}(2v_c + 2)))$.

We note that as the time and space bounds given in Theorem 2 are not obtained simultaneously, so are the above bounds for the TCTL model-checking problem. In particular, the time complexity of our space-efficient algorithm requires more time than the bound in (1).

3.6 Some Optimizations

The bound given in Theorem 4 captures worst-case complexity. In practice, the set of reachable states in $\mathcal{D}_{\psi,\mathcal{U}}$ may be considerably smaller than $|cl(\psi) \times L \times \Upsilon|$. First, not all positions $\langle l, \pi\rangle$ are admissible. Second, as our algorithm works on-the-fly, it does not consider triples that are not relevant for the satisfaction of ψ. In addition, we suggest here an optimization that minimizes the reachable state space further.

Consider a linear timed automaton $\mathcal{U}$. Recall that in each region position, the automaton takes either an edge or a time transition. Practically, it is often the case that only after taking several time transitions one of the following happens: $\mathcal{U}$ is able to take an edge transition (e.g., when all edge transitions are guarded with a lower bound on some clock), or $\mathcal{U}$ reaches a region position whose region satisfies subformulas of ψ that refer to clock values. We would like to integrate these successive time transitions into a single transition.

For $\varphi \in cl(\psi)$ and a region position $\langle l, \pi\rangle$, we define the set $sat(\langle\varphi, l, \pi\rangle)$ of "relevant" clock constraints that π satisfies. A formula θ is in $sat(\langle\varphi, l, \pi\rangle)$ iff $\pi \models \theta$ and either

1. $\theta \in cl(\varphi)$ is of the form $c \sim v$ for $c \in C$, or
2. $\theta \in guard(C)$ and there exist a transition $\langle\theta, S, l'\rangle \in E(l)$ for some S and l'.

Let $post_l : \Upsilon \rightarrow 2^{\Upsilon}$ be the transitive closure of *reg_succ* when restricted to regions π for which the region position $\langle l, \pi\rangle$ is admissible. That is, the region π' is in $post_l(\pi)$ iff there exists $i > 0$ such that $\pi' = reg\_succ^i(\pi)$ and for all $0 \leq j \leq i$ the pair $\langle l, reg\_succ^j(\pi)\rangle$ is admissible. Given a set $\Upsilon' \subseteq post_l(\pi)$ for some π and l, let $\min\Upsilon'$ denote the region π' for which there exists no

$\pi'' \in \Upsilon'$ with $\pi' \in post_l(\pi'')$. That is, if $\mathcal{U}$ is in region position $\langle l, \pi \rangle$, time passes, and no clocks are reset, then $\min \Upsilon'$ is the first region in Υ' that $\mathcal{U}$ meets.

We can now define a function $opt\_succ : cl(\psi) \times L \times \Upsilon \rightarrow 2^{L \times \Upsilon}$ that, given a formula φ and a region position $\langle l, \pi \rangle$, returns the set of positions reachable from $\langle l, \pi \rangle$ either by an edge transition or by successive time transitions that lead to the first region in which there is a change in satisfaction of relevant clock constraints. Formally, a position $\langle l', \pi' \rangle$ is in $opt\_succ(\langle \varphi, l, \pi \rangle)$ iff it is admissible and either

1. there exists $\langle \theta, S, l' \rangle \in E(l)$ such that $\pi \models \theta$ and $\pi' = \pi[S := 0]$, or
2. $l' = l$ and $\pi' = \min(post_l(\pi) \cap \{\pi'' : sat(\langle \varphi, l, \pi'' \rangle) \neq sat(\langle \varphi, l, \pi \rangle)\})$.

Thus, in *opt_succ* we integrate together time transitions that go through regions that are equivalent from "the point of view" of the current state of $\mathcal{D}_{\psi,\mathcal{U}}$. Now, whenever a transition $\delta(\langle \varphi, l, \pi \rangle, a)$ contains a disjunction or a conjunction over $succ(\langle l, \pi \rangle)$, we replace it with a disjunction or conjunction over $opt\_succ(\langle \varphi, l, \pi \rangle)$. Some comments about the saving obtained by this integration are in order. Consider the linear timed automaton $\mathcal{U}$ below and assume we model check it with respect to a formula without specification clocks.

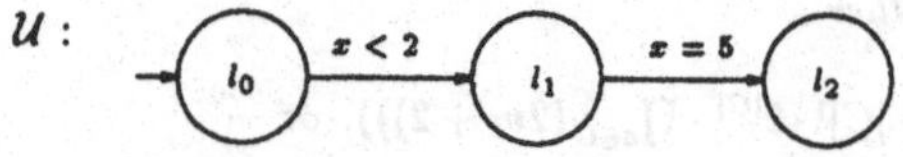

We can split $\mathbb{R}$ into the following four zones.

$$[0 \leq x < 2] \rightsquigarrow [2 \leq x < 5] \rightsquigarrow [x = 5] \rightsquigarrow [x > 5].$$

Each zone forms an equivalence class in the sense that for every location l of $\mathcal{U}$ and two regions π and π' of the same zone, the behavior of $\mathcal{U}$ from the region position $\langle l, \pi \rangle$ is identical to its behavior from the region position $\langle l, \pi' \rangle$. Our algorithm does not achieve such a coarse split of $\mathbb{R}$. Instead, it refines the zone $[0 \leq x < 2]$ into its four regions

$$[x = 0] \rightsquigarrow [0 < x < 1] \rightsquigarrow [x = 1] \rightsquigarrow [1 < x < 2].$$

In this sense, the algorithm in [HNSY94] and the algorithm TMC in [SS95] are more efficient than our algorithm. Why can not we integrate the four regions into a single zone as well? To answer this question, consider the linear timed automaton $\mathcal{U}'$ below.

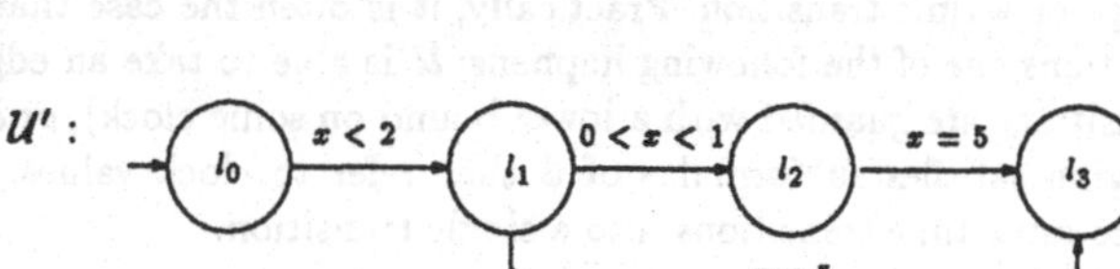

For $\mathcal{U}'$, the coarsest split of $\mathbb{R}$ into zones equals the split that our algorithm suggests for $\mathcal{U}$. Indeed, we cannot couple together any two regions. When we perform a pure top-down reasoning about $\mathcal{U}$ and $\mathcal{U}'$ (that is, reasoning without look ahead), we discover the difference between them only in location l_1. Therefore, when we integrate regions together, we must get ready to every possible future, in particular to one that requires the split of the zone $[0 \leq x < 2]$. The optimal split performed by [HNSY94, SS95] must involve also some bottom-up reasoning, which increases worst-case space complexity.

From the example, the reader can grasp that the saving achieved by our optimization is quite poor with respect to guards that are upper bounds ($c < v$ or $c \leq v$); there, we can not integrate time transitions. The saving is more significant with respect to guards that are lower bounds ($c > v$ or $c \geq v$); there, we can integrate all the time transitions up to the lower bound. Finally, the saving is optimal (that is, achieves the same coarse split as in [HNSY94, SS95]) with respect to guards that are tight bounds ($c = v$). In particular, it follows that our algorithm is optimal for model checking of the subset of TCTL in which all guards (in both the linear timed automaton and the formula) are tight bounds.

4 Discussion

In this work we suggested a space-efficient on-the-fly algorithm for TCTL model checking. We showed that there is a trade-off between worst-case space efficiency and optimization of the state space by integrating several regions into a zone. The measure for this trade-off is the amount of look-ahead on the input linear timed automaton allowed to the model-checking algorithm. The algorithm in [HNSY94] performs pure bottom-up reasoning (i.e., reasoning with complete look-ahead), and achieves maximal zones. Our algorithm performs pure top-down reasoning (i.e., reasoning without look ahead), and achieves space efficiency. The algorithm TMC in [SS95] combines the two savings; it proceeds on-the-fly to save space, but restricts the look-ahead to only part of the input. Naturally, for each of the algorithms we can contract problems for which the algorithm performs better than the other algorithms. It remains to be seen how the algorithms perform in practice.

Our algorithm is based on an automata-theoretic framework to TCTL model checking. One may wonder why our framework is purposeful for model checking and does not attempt to serve the satisfiability problem. The satisfiability problem for TCTL is undecidable [ACD93]. Hence, a comprehensive automata-theoretic framework for TCTL should involve tree automata for which the nonemptiness problem is undecidable. Such an automata-theoretic framework would contribute significantly to our understanding of real-time temporal logics and would provide a clear explanation to the computational gap between the satisfiability and the model-checking problem of TCTL.

References

[ACD93] R. Alur, C. Courcoubetis, and D. Dill. Model-checking in dense real-time. *Information and Computation*, 104(1):2–34, May 1993.

[AD94] R. Alur and D. Dill. A theory of timed automata. *Theoretical Computer Science*, 126(2):183–236, 1994.

[AFH96] R. Alur, T. Feder, and T.A. Henzinger. The benefits of relaxing punctuality. *Journal of the ACM*, 43(1):116–146, 1996.

[AH92] R. Alur and T.A. Henzinger. Logics and models of real time: a survey. In J.W. de Bakker, K. Huizing, W.-P. de Roever, and G. Rozenberg, editors, *Real Time: Theory in Practice*, Lecture Notes in Computer Science 600, pages 74–106. Springer-Verlag, 1992.

[AH93] R. Alur and T. Henzinger. Real-time logics: Complexity and expressiveness. *Information and Computation*, 104(1):35–77, May 1993.

[AH94] R. Alur and T.A. Henzinger. A really temporal logic. *Journal of the ACM*, 41(1):181–204, 1994.

[Alu91] R. Alur. *Techniques for Automatic Verification of Real-time Systems*. PhD thesis, Stanford University, 1991.

[BVW94] O. Bernholtz, M.Y. Vardi, and P. Wolper. An automata-theoretic approach to branching-time model checking. In D. L. Dill, editor, *Computer Aided Verification, Proc. 6th Int. Conference*, volume 818 of *Lecture Notes in Computer Science*, pages 142–155, Stanford, June 1994. Springer-Verlag.

[CE81] E.M. Clarke and E.A. Emerson. Design and synthesis of synchronization skeletons using branching time temporal logic. In *Proc. Workshop on Logic of Programs*, volume 131 of *Lecture Notes in Computer Science*, pages 52–71. Springer-Verlag, 1981.

[CES86] E.M. Clarke, E.A. Emerson, and A.P. Sistla. Automatic verification of finite-state concurrent systems using temporal logic specifications. *ACM Transactions on Programming Languages and Systems*, 8(2):244–263, January 1986.

[CVWY92] C. Courcoubetis, M.Y. Vardi, P. Wolper, and M. Yannakakis. Memory efficient algorithms for the verification of temporal properties. *Formal Methods in System Design*, 1:275–288, 1992.

[Eme92] E.A. Emerson. Real time and the μ-calculus. In J.W. de Bakker, K. Huizing, W.-P. de Roever, and G. Rozenberg, editors, *Real Time: Theory in Practice*, Lecture Notes in Computer Science 600, pages 176–194. Springer-Verlag, 1992.

[EMSS90] E.A. Emerson, A.K. Mok, A.P. Sistla, and J. Srinivasan. Quantitative temporal reasoning. In *Proc. 2nd Workshop on Computer Aided Verification*, volume 531 of *Lecture Notes in Computer Science*, pages 136–145. Springer-Verlag, 1990.

[FMJJ92] J.-C. Fernandez, L. Mounier, C. Jard, and T. Jeron. On-the-fly verification of finite transition systems. *Formal Methods in System Design*, 1:251–273, 1992.

[HNSY94] T.A. Henzinger, X. Nicollin, J. Sifakis, and S. Yovine. Symbolic model checking for real-time systems. *Information and Computation*, 111:193–244, 1994.

[KV95] O. Kupferman and M.Y. Vardi. On the complexity of branching modular model checking. In *Proc. 6th Conferance on Concurrency Theory*, pages 408–422, Philadelphia, August 1995.

[Lam80] L. Lamport. Sometimes is sometimes "not never" - on the temporal logic of programs. In *Proceedings of the 7th ACM Symposium on Principles of Programming Languages*, pages 174–185, January 1980.

[LL95] F. Laroussinie and K. G. Larsen. Compositional model checking of real time systems. In *Proc. 6th Conferance on Concurrency Theory*, pages 27–41, Philadelphia, August 1995.

[MP92] Z. Manna and A. Pnueli. *The Temporal Logic of Reactive and Concurrent Systems: Specification*. Springer-Verlag, Berlin, January 1992.

[MS87] D.E. Muller and P.E. Schupp. Alternating automata on infinite trees. *Theoretical Computer Science*, 54,:267–276, 1987.

[MSS86] D.E. Muller, A. Saoudi, and P.E. Schupp. Alternating automata, the weak monadic theory of the tree and its complexity. In *Proc. 13th Int. Colloquium on Automata, Languages and Programming*. Springer-Verlag, 1986.

[Pnu77] A. Pnueli. The temporal logic of programs. In *Proc. 18th IEEE Symposium on Foundation of Computer Science*, pages 46–57, 1977.

[QS81] J.P. Queille and J. Sifakis. Specification and verification of concurrent systems in Cesar. In *Proc. 5th International Symp. on Programming*, volume 137, pages 337–351. Springer-Verlag, Lecture Notes in Computer Science, 1981.

[SC85] A.P. Sistla and E.M. Clarke. The complexity of propositional linear temporal logic. *J. ACM*, 32:733–749, 1985.

[SS95] O.V. Sokolsky and S.A. Smolka. Local model checking for real-time systems. In *Computer Aided Verification, Proc. 7th Int. Workshop*, Lecture Notes in Computer Science 939, pages 211–224, Liege, July 1995.

[SW89] C. Stirling and D. Walker. Local model checking in the modal mu-calculus. In *Proc. 15th Col. on Trees in Algebra and Programming*. Lecture Notes in Computer Science, 1989.

[Tho90] W. Thomas. Automata on infinite objects. *Handbook of Theoretical Computer Science*, pages 165–191, 1990.

[VW94] M.Y. Vardi and P. Wolper. Reasoning about infinite computations. *Information and Computation*, 115(1):1–37, November 1994.

[YL93] M. Yannakakis and D. Lee. An efficient algorithm for minimizing real-time transition systems. In C. Courcoubetis, editor, *Computer Aided Verification, Proc. 5th Int. Workshop*, volume 697 of *Lecture Notes in Computer Science 697*, pages 210–224, Elounda, Crete, June 1993. Lecture Notes in Computer Science, Springer-Verlag.

State Equivalences for Rectangular Hybrid Automata*

Thomas A. Henzinger[1] and Peter W. Kopke[2]

[1] Department of Electrical Engineering and Computer Sciences, University of California, Berkeley, CA 94720

[2] Department of Computer Science, Cornell University, Ithaca, NY 14853

Abstract. Three natural equivalence relations on the infinite state space of a hybrid automaton are language equivalence, simulation equivalence, and bisimulation equivalence. When one of these equivalence relations has a finite quotient, certain model checking and controller synthesis problems are decidable. When bounds on the number of equivalence classes are obtained, bounds on the running times of model checking and synthesis algorithms follow as corollaries.

We characterize the time-abstract versions of these equivalence relations on the state spaces of *rectangular hybrid automata* (RHA), in which each continuous variable is a clock with bounded drift. These automata are useful for modeling communications protocols with drifting local clocks, and for the conservative approximation of more complex hybrid systems. Of our two main results, one has positive implications for automatic verification, and the other has negative implications. On the positive side, we find that the (finite) language equivalence quotient for RHA is coarser than was previously known by a multiplicative exponential factor. On the negative side, we show that simulation equivalence for RHA is equality (which obviously has an infinite quotient).

Our main positive result is established by analyzing a subclass of timed automata, called *one-sided timed automata* (OTA), for which the language equivalence quotient is coarser than for the class of all timed automata. An exact characterization of language equivalence for OTA requires a distinction between synchronous and asynchronous definitions of (bi)simulation: if time actions are silent, then the induced quotient for OTA is coarser than if time actions (but not their durations) are visible.

1 Introduction

A *hybrid automaton* consists of a finite automaton interacting with a dynamical system on $\mathbb{R}^n$ [ACHH93, NOSY93]. Hybrid automata are used to model embedded controllers and other systems that consist of interacting discrete and

* This research was supported in part by ONR Young Investigator award N00014-95-1-0520, by NSF CAREER award CCR-9501708, by NSF grant CCR-9504469, by Air Force Office of Scientific Research contract F49620-93-1-0056, by ARPA grant NAG2-892, and by the U.S. Army Research Office through the Mathematical Sciences Institute of Cornell University, Contract Number DAAL03-91-C-0027.

continuous components. If the continuous dynamics are fixed, one can ask when two vectors $\mathbf{x}, \mathbf{y} \in \mathbb{R}^n$ are distinguishable by some hybrid automaton from a given class. The purpose of this exercise is to find finite quotients of the infinite state space $\mathbb{R}^n$ so that algorithmic verification can be performed. For example, if every continuous variable moves uniformly at slope 1 (as in *timed automata*), then there is a finite bisimulation equivalence quotient on $\mathbb{R}^n$ [AD94]. It follows that verification and control problems for timed automata can be solved using finite-state methods.

We consider *time-abstract* distinguishability, in which the durations of time delays are not taken into account. The opposite approach, *timed* distinguishability, leads to a sterile theory in which, relative to any interesting class of hybrid automata, no two states are equivalent. Moreover, any specific timing constraint that is required of a system can (and should) be specified by the introduction of a clock variable that enforces the constraint [Hen95]. Thus it is unnecessary to burden the semantics by the introduction of infinitely many time actions.

We consider three types of time-abstract distinguishability, or, dually, three types of equivalence: language equivalence, simulation equivalence[3], and bisimulation equivalence. Each equivalence relation $\equiv$ has a direct connection to a temporal logic $TL_{\equiv}$ (bisimulation equivalence corresponds to the full branching-time logic CTL* [BCG88]; simulation equivalence corresponds to the universal fragment of CTL* [BBLS92]; language equivalence corresponds to linear temporal logic). When the quotient of $\equiv$ is finite (and computable) for a class $\mathcal{C}$ of hybrid automata, the model checking problem for $TL_{\equiv}$ and the controller synthesis problem for invariance are decidable on the class $\mathcal{C}$ [Hen96]. Moreover, when the number of equivalence classes is determined, upper bounds on the running times of the model checking and controller synthesis algorithms are obtained.

We distinguish between two models of each equivalence. Hybrid automata have time actions and discrete actions. In the *synchronous model*, time actions are visible, while in the *asynchronous model*, time actions are silent. Thus in the synchronous model of simulation, discrete actions must be matched by discrete actions and time actions must be matched by time actions, while in the asynchronous model, each discrete action may be matched by a silent time action followed by a matching discrete action. Language equivalence is inherently asynchronous. However, it is profitable to consider both models of (bi)simulation, because asynchronous (bi)simulation equivalence may be coarser than synchronous (bi)simulation equivalence; and so the subtle distinction is necessary for a precise analysis.[4] We therefore study five different equivalence relations.

We are interested in *rectangular hybrid automata (RHA)*, in which each continuous variable x is a clock with bounded drift, and therefore follows a nondeterministic differential equation of the form $\frac{dx}{dt} \in [a, b]$. Rectangular hybrid automata are useful for modeling distributed communication protocols [HW95], and for approximating nonlinear hybrid systems [HH95].

---

[3] Two states are *simulation equivalent* if each simulates the other.

[4] It has come to our attention that the two models of bisimulation are introduced independently in [TY96].

Two well-studied classes of hybrid automata are *timed automata* [AD94] and *linear hybrid automata (LHA)* [ACH+95]. In a timed automaton, every continuous variable x is a precise clock, and therefore satisfies the differential equation $\frac{dx}{dt} = 1$. In a linear hybrid automaton, the first derivatives of the continuous variables satisfy linear relationships. Linearity allows many properties of LHA to be analyzed symbolically [AHH96]. Rectangular hybrid automata are an intermediate class, more general than timed automata, but less general than linear hybrid automata. For timed automata, all five equivalence relations coincide (with a relation called *region equivalence*, which considers two vectors to be equivalent if their components (1) have the same integer parts, and (2) their fractional parts have the same relative ordering). For linear hybrid automata, each of the five equivalence relations degenerates to equality on $\mathbb{R}^n$. The intermediate class of rectangular hybrid automata is amenable to automatic verification because even though RHA are more general than timed automata, their language equivalence quotient is still finite [PV94]. On the other hand, the synchronous bisimulation quotient for RHA is known to be infinite [Hen95]. Our goal is to elucidate the relationships between the five equivalence relations for the class of rectangular hybrid automata: we determine which quotients are finite, and provide bounds on the number of equivalence classes.

We develop two main results, which we discuss throughout the remainder of this introduction. The first shows that language equivalence for RHA is coarser than was previously known by a multiplicative exponential factor. We therefore obtain an improved model checking algorithm for linear temporal logic on RHA. The second shows that, contrary to a previous conjecture [HHK95], both the synchronous and asynchronous simulation equivalence relations (and hence also both bisimulation equivalence relations) for RHA degenerate to equality. In fact, equality is the only synchronous simulation already in three dimensions (i.e., when $n = 3$). It follows that symbolic algorithms, such as those implemented in HyTech [HHWT95, AHH96], need not terminate when applied to universal CTL* properties of RHA.

Language Equivalence for Rectangular Hybrid Automata. Rectangular hybrid automata generalize timed automata, yet incur no complexity penalty for several decision problems [HKPV95]. In particular, the language emptiness problem for RHA is PSPACE-complete, due to the existence of a language-preserving translation from rectangular hybrid automata into timed automata. Examining this translation, we find that the clocks of the resulting timed automata have a special property: each clock is constrained in only one direction. We study these *one-sided timed automata (OTA)*, which have two sets of clocks: upper-bounded clocks are constrained by guards only from above, while lower-bounded clocks are constrained by guards only from below. We show that for OTA, language equivalence and asynchronous simulation equivalence coincide, and are coarser than region equivalence by a multiplicative factor of 2^n. Since two states of a hybrid automaton are language equivalent if they are translated to language equivalent states of a one-sided timed automaton, we obtain a new sufficient condition for language equivalence for RHA as a corollary. For symbolic

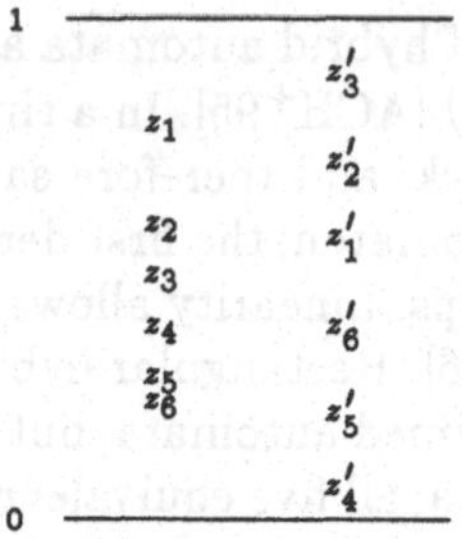

Fig. 1. Vectors **z** and **z**′ are one-sided region equivalent

model checkers, such as HyTech, Kronos [DY95], and UppAal [LPY95], our results may be applied to obtain better bounds on performance. For enumerative model checking, we obtain better algorithms, because we reduce the number of equivalence classes that must be enumerated.

We illustrate by an example the increased compaction of the state space on rectangular hybrid automata given by our main positive result. Consider the class $\mathcal{C}$ of all rectangular hybrid automata with three continuous variables, each a clock drifting between slopes 1 and 2. Consider the 3-vectors $\mathbf{y} = (0.4, 0.3, 0.25)$ and $\mathbf{y}' = (0.25, 0.3, 0.4)$. The translation of RHA into OTA maps a 3-vector of drifting clock values into a 6-vector of three upper-bounded clock values and three lower-bounded clock values. The former are obtained by doubling the drifting clock values, while the latter coincide with the drifting clock values. Thus the 3-vector $\mathbf{y}$ translates into the 6-vector $\mathbf{z} = (0.8, 0.6, 0.5, 0.4, 0.3, 0.25)$, and the 3-vector $\mathbf{y}'$ translates into $\mathbf{z}' = (0.5, 0.6, 0.8, 0.25, 0.3, 0.4)$, where the first three components represent upper-bounded clock values, and the last three components represent lower-bounded clock values. See Figure 1. The two 6-vectors are not equivalent with respect to the class of all timed automata, because $z_1 > z_2$ while $z'_1 < z'_2$. To see this, consider a timed automaton T that has an edge e guarded by the predicate $x_1 \geq 1 \geq x_2$, where x_i denotes the value of the ith clock variable. After a delay of duration $\delta \in \mathbb{R}_{\geq 0}$, where $1 - z_2 \geq \delta \geq 1 - z_1$, the vector $\mathbf{z}$ is transformed into the vector $\mathbf{z} + \delta\mathbf{1}$, which satisfies $z_1 + \delta \geq 1 \geq z_2 + \delta$. But for every duration $\delta' \in \mathbb{R}_{\geq 0}$, vector $\mathbf{z}'$ does not satisfy $z'_1 + \delta' \geq 1 \geq z'_2 + \delta'$. Thus the edge e with its guard $x_1 \geq 1 \geq x_2$ distinguishes between $\mathbf{z}$ and $\mathbf{z}'$. However, no one-sided timed automaton has such a guard, which constrains clocks of the same type (in this case, upper-bounded) both from above and from below. Our results enable us to deduce that $\mathbf{y}$ and $\mathbf{y}'$ are language equivalent with respect to $\mathcal{C}$, because $\mathbf{z}$ and $\mathbf{z}'$ are language equivalent with respect to the class of one-sided timed automata. This equivalence does not depend on the relative order of lower-bounded clocks, nor upon the relative order of upper-bounded clocks, but only on the relative order of the lower-bounded clocks with respect to the upper-bounded clocks.

Simulation Equivalence of Rectangular Hybrid Automata. A structural explanation for the finiteness of the language equivalence quotient of RHA was sought in [HHK95]. It was there shown that every 2D RHA has a finite synchronous simulation equivalence quotient (and therefore a finite asynchronous simulation equivalence quotient). It was conjectured that this result generalized to RHA of arbitrary dimension. We disprove this conjecture, showing that, in fact, the only synchronous simulation on three-dimensional RHA is equality. Asynchronous simulation equivalence relation is equality in four or more dimensions (we do not know if the asynchronous simulation equivalence quotient is finite or infinite in three dimensions).

The remainder of the paper is organized as follows. Section 2 provides definitions and previous results. Section 3 presents an analysis of one-sided timed automata. In Section 4 the results of Section 3 are applied to the language equivalence problem for rectangular hybrid automata, and then the synchronous and asynchronous simulation equivalence relations for RHA are characterized. Section 5 summarizes our results; a tabulation is given in Figure 7. We have omitted most of the proofs from the conference version of this paper. Full proofs may be found in [HK96].

2 Definitions and Previous Results

Fix a positive integer n. A *rectangle* B is a closed subset of $\mathbb{R}^n$ that is the cartesian product of (possibly unbounded) intervals on $\mathbb{R}$, all of whose finite endpoints are integers. We write B_i for the projection of B on the ith coordinate, so that $B = \prod_{i=1}^{n} B_i$.

For a closed interval $I \subseteq \mathbb{R}$ and a number $x \in \mathbb{R}$, define *closest*(x, I) to be the closest point to x lying in I. So if $x \in I$, then *closest*$(x, I) = x$; if $x \leq \min I$ then *closest*$(x, I) = \min I$; and if $x \geq \max I$ then *closest*$(x, I) = \max I$. A *guarded command* is a triple $g = (B, U, F)$, where the *guard* B and the *reset* F are rectangles, and $U \subseteq \{1, \ldots, n\}$ is the *update set*. The guarded command g defines a binary relation $jump_g$ on $\mathbb{R}^n$ by $(\mathbf{x}, \mathbf{x}') \in jump_g$ iff (1) $\mathbf{x} \in B$, (2) for each $i \in U$, $x'_i \in F_i$, and (3) for each $i \notin U$, $x'_i = closest(x_i, F_i)$. Thus the guarded command g may act on $\mathbf{x}$ iff $\mathbf{x}$ satisfies the guard. The result of the action is to reassign each coordinate $i \in U$ nondeterministically to a value in F_i, and to reassign each coordinate $i \notin U$ to the closest value in F_i. In particular, if $F = B$, then the coordinates $i \notin U$ are left unchanged. The set of all guarded commands is denoted $\mathcal{G}_n$.

Rectangular Hybrid Automata. An n-dimensional *rectangular hybrid automaton A* [HKPV95] over the alphabet Σ consists of a directed multigraph (V_A, E_A), an n-dimensional compact (closed and bounded) rectangle act_A with positive endpoints called the *activity rectangle*, and two edge labeling functions $guard_A : E \to \mathcal{G}_n$ and $event_A : E_A \to \Sigma$.[5] When only one automaton is under consideration, we omit the subscript on the components of A.

[5] There is one important difference between the model of RHA we present and the one used in [HKPV95]. Our automata have a constant activity rectangle, and therefore

A *state* of A is a pair $(v, \mathbf{x})$ consisting of a discrete part $v \in V_A$ and a continuous part $\mathbf{x} \in \mathbb{R}^n$; the *state space* of A is $V_A \times \mathbb{R}^n$. The automaton A defines a labeled transition system on its state space as follows. The *time action* $\stackrel{time}{\rightarrow}$ is defined by $(v, \mathbf{x}) \stackrel{time}{\rightarrow} (v', \mathbf{x}')$ iff (1) $v' = v$ and (2) either $\mathbf{x}' = \mathbf{x}$ or $\frac{\mathbf{x}'-\mathbf{x}}{t} \in act_A$ for some $t \in \mathbb{R}_{>0}$. Therefore as time passes, the continuous state of A follows a trajectory satisfying the nondeterministic differential equation $\frac{d\mathbf{x}}{dt} \in act_A$. For $\sigma \in \Sigma$, the *discrete action* $\stackrel{\sigma}{\rightarrow}$ is defined by $(v, \mathbf{x}) \stackrel{\sigma}{\rightarrow} (v', \mathbf{x}')$ iff there exists an edge $e = (v, v') \in E_A$ such that $event(e) = \sigma$ and $(\mathbf{x}, \mathbf{x}') \in jump_{guard(e)}$. A discrete action $\stackrel{\sigma}{\rightarrow}$ is thus only enabled in vertex v when the continuous state satisfies the guard of an edge e with source v and event σ, and the resulting continuous state is obtained by applying the guarded command of e.

A *run of A beginning at* $(v, \mathbf{x})$ is a finite sequence

$$(v^0, \mathbf{x}^0) \stackrel{time}{\rightarrow} (v^1, \mathbf{x}^1) \stackrel{\sigma_1}{\rightarrow} \cdots \stackrel{time}{\rightarrow} (v^{2k-1}, \mathbf{x}^{2k-1}) \stackrel{\sigma_k}{\rightarrow} (v^{2k}, \mathbf{x}^{2k})$$

of alternating time actions and discrete actions, where $(v^0, \mathbf{x}^0) = (v, \mathbf{x})$. This run *generates* the string $\sigma_1\sigma_2 \cdots \sigma_k \in \Sigma^*$. The language $L_A(v, \mathbf{x})$ of state $(v, \mathbf{x})$ is the set of strings $\overline{\sigma} \in \Sigma^*$ that are generated by runs of A beginning at $(v, \mathbf{x})$.

One-sided Timed Automata. A *timed automaton* is a rectangular hybrid automaton T such that act_T is the singleton $\{(1, 1, \ldots, 1)\}$ consisting of the vector $\mathbf{1}$ with all components equal to 1. Thus each coordinate of the continuous state of a timed automaton moves deterministically and uniformly at slope 1 as time passes. We say that coordinate i is an *upper-bounded clock* if for each edge $e \in E_T$, if $guard(e) = (B, U, F)$, then B_i (which is an interval) is unbounded from below. This means that the ith coordinate of the continuous state of T is constrained by guards only from above. We say that coordinate j is a *lower-bounded clock* if for each edge $e \in E_T$, if $guard(e) = (B, U, F)$, then B_j is unbounded from above. This means that the jth coordinate of the continuous state of T is constrained by guards only from below. The timed automaton T is *upper-bounded* (resp. *lower-bounded*) if each coordinate is an upper-bounded (resp. lower-bounded) clock. The timed automaton T is *one-sided* if every coordinate is either an upper-bounded clock or a lower-bounded clock.

Every n-dimensional rectangular hybrid automaton can be translated into a $2n$-dimensional one-sided timed automaton with the same language. The mapping from $\mathbb{R}^n$ to $\mathbb{R}^{2n}$ is uniform among all RHA with the same activity rectangle, and therefore allows characterizations of language equivalence for one-sided timed automata to yield sufficient conditions for language equivalence for the class of rectangular hybrid automata with a fixed activity rectangle.

---

correspond to the *initialized* RHA of [HKPV95]. Three other differences appear in order to simplify the presentation; they do not materially affect our results. First, we have restricted attention to closed rectangles. Second, we have not included vertex invariants in the definition. Third, we have slightly generalized the reset mechanism.

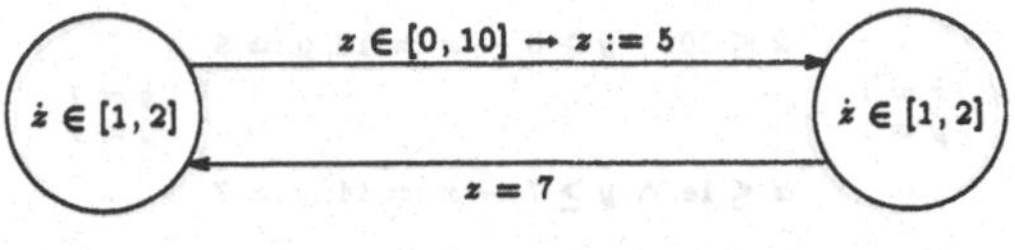

Fig. 2. A rectangular automaton A

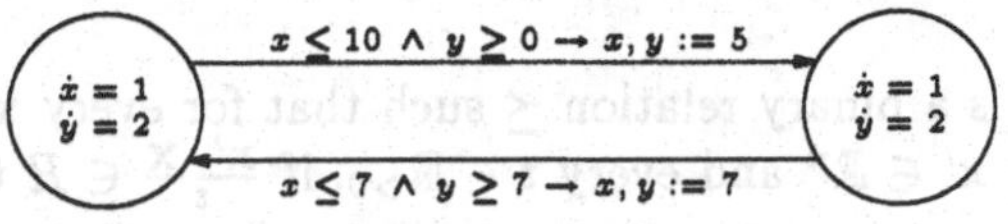

Fig. 3. The one-sided, constant-slope automaton M_A

Theorem 1 [HKPV95] *Let $R \subseteq \mathbb{R}^n$ be a compact rectangle. For every vector $\mathbf{z} \in \mathbb{R}^n$, there exist vectors $\mathbf{x}, \mathbf{y} \in \mathbb{R}^n$ such that for every rectangular hybrid automaton A with $act_A = R$, there exists a $2n$-dimensional one-sided timed automaton T_A such that for every vertex v, $L_A(v, \mathbf{z}) = L_{T_A}(v, (\mathbf{x}, \mathbf{y}))$.*

Proof Outline. Given A, we define an RHA M_A in which each continuous variable has constant slope. The automaton M_A essentially acts in the same way as the subset construction for finite automata, giving bounds on all possible behaviors of A. Each continuous variable z with $\dot{z} \in [a, b]$ is replaced by two variables x and y, where $\dot{x} = a$ and $\dot{y} = b$, which give exact lower and upper bounds on the possible values for z. Testing if $z \in [c, d]$ is equivalent to testing if $x \leq d \wedge y \geq c$, and then resetting x and y to the closest points in $[c, d]$.[6] Thus in M_A, x is only bounded from above, and y is only bounded from below. The constant-slope automaton M_A is transformed into a one-sided timed automaton by first dividing each guard and reset for x by a, and for y by b, and then multiplying all guards and resets by the least common multiple of all of the slopes. An example is given in Figures 2, 3, and 4. □

Equivalences for Rectangular Hybrid Automata.

Language Equivalence. Let C be a class of n-dimensional rectangular hybrid automata. We that say two vectors $\mathbf{x}, \mathbf{u} \in \mathbb{R}^n$ are *language equivalent with respect to C*, and write $\mathbf{x} \approx^{C}_{\text{lang}} \mathbf{u}$, iff for every automaton $A \in C$, and every vertex $v \in V_A$, $L_A(v, \mathbf{x}) = L_A(v, \mathbf{u})$. Define $\mathbf{x} \preceq^{C}_{\text{lang}} \mathbf{u}$ iff for every automaton $A \in C$, and every vertex $v \in V_A$, $L_A(v, \mathbf{x}) \subseteq L_A(v, \mathbf{u})$.

Simulation Equivalence. Let C be a class of n-dimensional rectangular hybrid automata, each having the same activity rectangle R. Let G be the set of guarded commands appearing in some automaton in C. A *synchronous simulation* on $\mathbb{R}^n$

[6] It is for this reason that the generalized reset mechanism is introduced: it simplifies the translation from RHA into timed automata.

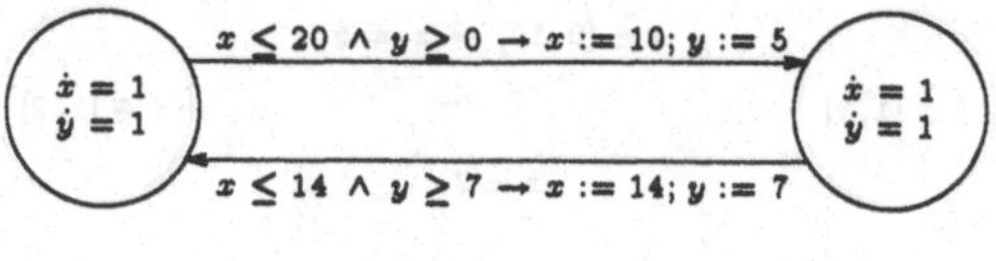

Fig. 4. The one-sided timed automaton T_A

with respect to $\mathcal{C}$ is a binary relation $\preceq$ such that for every $\mathbf{x}, \mathbf{u} \in \mathbb{R}^n$, if $\mathbf{x} \preceq \mathbf{u}$ then (1) for every $\mathbf{x}' \in \mathbb{R}^n$ and every $t \in \mathbb{R}_{>0}$, if $\frac{\mathbf{x}'-\mathbf{x}}{t} \in R$ then either $\mathbf{x}' \preceq \mathbf{u}$ or there exist a $t' \in \mathbb{R}_{>0}$ and a $\mathbf{u}' \in \mathbb{R}^n$ such that $\mathbf{x}' \preceq \mathbf{u}'$ and $\frac{\mathbf{u}'-\mathbf{u}}{t'} \in R$, and (2) for every $\mathbf{x}' \in \mathbb{R}^n$ and every guarded command $g \in G$, if $(\mathbf{x}, \mathbf{x}') \in jump_g$ then there exists a $\mathbf{u}' \in \mathbb{R}^n$ such that $\mathbf{x}' \preceq \mathbf{u}'$ and $(\mathbf{u}, \mathbf{u}') \in jump_g$. The largest synchronous simulation on $\mathbb{R}^n$ with respect to $\mathcal{C}$ is denoted by $\preceq^{\mathcal{C}}_{\mathsf{syn}}$. If $\mathbf{x} \preceq^{\mathcal{C}}_{\mathsf{syn}} \mathbf{u}$, we say $\mathbf{u}$ *synchronously simulates* $\mathbf{x}$ with respect to $\mathcal{C}$. If $\mathbf{x} \preceq^{\mathcal{C}}_{\mathsf{syn}} \mathbf{u}$, then every time action with source $\mathbf{x}$ can be matched by a time action with source $\mathbf{u}$, and every immediate application of a guarded command to $\mathbf{x}$ can be matched by the immediate application of the same guarded command to $\mathbf{u}$. It follows that if $\mathbf{x} \preceq^{\mathcal{C}}_{\mathsf{syn}} \mathbf{u}$, then $\mathbf{x} \preceq^{\mathcal{C}}_{\mathsf{lang}} \mathbf{u}$. We write $\mathbf{x} \approx^{\mathcal{C}}_{\mathsf{syn}} \mathbf{u}$ if $\mathbf{x} \preceq^{\mathcal{C}}_{\mathsf{syn}} \mathbf{u}$ and $\mathbf{u} \preceq^{\mathcal{C}}_{\mathsf{syn}} \mathbf{x}$. This equivalence relation is known as *synchronous simulation equivalence* with respect to $\mathcal{C}$.

For asynchronous simulations, time is folded into the application of guarded commands. For a guarded command g, define the binary relation $delayed^R_g$ on $\mathbb{R}^n$ by $(\mathbf{x}, \mathbf{x}') \in delayed^R_g$ iff there exists an $\mathbf{x}'' \in \mathbb{R}^n$ such that (1) $(\mathbf{x}'', \mathbf{x}') \in jump_g$ and (2) either $\mathbf{x}'' = \mathbf{x}$ or there exists a time $t > 0$ such that $\frac{\mathbf{x}''-\mathbf{x}}{t} \in R$. An *asynchronous simulation* on $\mathbb{R}^n$ with respect to $\mathcal{C}$ is a binary relation $\preceq$ such that for every $\mathbf{x}, \mathbf{u} \in \mathbb{R}^n$, if $\mathbf{x} \preceq \mathbf{u}$ then for every $\mathbf{x}' \in \mathbb{R}^n$ and every guarded command $g \in G$ with $(\mathbf{x}, \mathbf{x}') \in delayed^R_g$, there exists a $\mathbf{u}' \in \mathbb{R}^n$ such that $\mathbf{x}' \preceq \mathbf{u}'$ and $(\mathbf{u}, \mathbf{u}') \in delayed^R_g$. The largest asynchronous simulation on $\mathbb{R}^n$ with respect to $\mathcal{C}$ is denoted by $\preceq^{\mathcal{C}}_{\mathsf{asyn}}$. If $\mathbf{x} \preceq^{\mathcal{C}}_{\mathsf{asyn}} \mathbf{u}$, we say $\mathbf{u}$ *asynchronously simulates* $\mathbf{x}$ with respect to $\mathcal{C}$. If $\mathbf{x} \preceq^{\mathcal{C}}_{\mathsf{asyn}} \mathbf{u}$, then every guarded command executable by $\mathbf{x}$ after an unspecified waiting period can be matched by $\mathbf{u}$. It follows that if $\mathbf{x} \preceq^{\mathcal{C}}_{\mathsf{asyn}} \mathbf{u}$, then $\mathbf{x} \preceq^{\mathcal{C}}_{\mathsf{lang}} \mathbf{u}$. We write $\mathbf{x} \approx^{\mathcal{C}}_{\mathsf{asyn}} \mathbf{u}$ if $\mathbf{x} \preceq^{\mathcal{C}}_{\mathsf{asyn}} \mathbf{u}$ and $\mathbf{u} \preceq^{\mathcal{C}}_{\mathsf{asyn}} \mathbf{x}$. This equivalence relation is known as *asynchronous simulation equivalence* with respect to $\mathcal{C}$. Notice that every synchronous simulation is an asynchronous simulation. Therefore if $\mathbf{x} \preceq^{\mathcal{C}}_{\mathsf{syn}} \mathbf{u}$, then $\mathbf{x} \preceq^{\mathcal{C}}_{\mathsf{asyn}} \mathbf{u}$. Hence asynchronous simulation equivalence is at least as coarse as synchronous simulation equivalence.

Bisimulation Equivalence. A *synchronous* (resp. *asynchronous*) *bisimulation* with respect to $\mathcal{C}$ is a symmetric synchronous (resp. asynchronous) simulation with respect to $\mathcal{C}$. The largest synchronous (resp. asynchronous) bisimulation on $\mathbb{R}^n$ with respect to $\mathcal{C}$ is denoted by $\cong^{\mathcal{C}}_{\mathsf{syn}}$ (resp. $\cong^{\mathcal{C}}_{\mathsf{asyn}}$), and called *synchronous bisimulation equivalence* (resp. *asynchronous bisimulation equivalence*). Bisimulation equivalence is at least as fine as simulation equivalence, and it is finer if simulation equivalence is not a simulation.

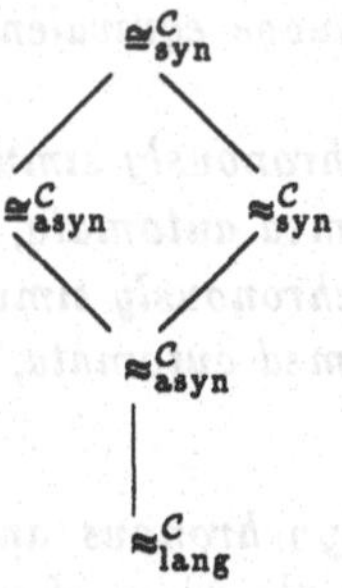

Fig. 5. Lattice of equivalence relations

Figure 5 depicts the relative coarseness of each of the five equivalence relations with respect to C. Language equivalence is the coarsest, and synchronous bisimulation equivalence is the finest.

Equivalences with Respect to the Class of Timed Automata. The ceiling or floor of a vector $\mathbf{x}$ is taken coordinatewise, so $\lceil \mathbf{x} \rceil = (\lceil x_1 \rceil, \lceil x_2 \rceil, \ldots, \lceil x_n \rceil)$. Recall that the *region equivalence relation* on $\mathbb{R}^n$ is defined by $\mathbf{x} \cong_{\text{reg}} \mathbf{x}'$ iff $\lceil \mathbf{x} \rceil = \lceil \mathbf{x}' \rceil$, $\lfloor \mathbf{x} \rfloor = \lfloor \mathbf{x}' \rfloor$, and for each $k, \ell \in \{1, \ldots, n\}$, $\lfloor x_k - x_\ell \rfloor = \lfloor x'_k - x'_\ell \rfloor$. That is, (1) each x_k and x'_k must have the same integer part, and both or neither must be an integer, and (2) the fractional parts of x_k and x_ℓ must be ordered in the same way as the fractional parts of x'_k and x'_ℓ.

Theorem 2 [AD94] *With respect to the class of timed automata, all five equivalence relations (language equivalence, and synchronous and asynchronous simulation and bisimulation equivalence) coincide with region equivalence.*

3 One-sided Timed Automata

We begin the analysis of one-sided timed automata by first considering automata whose clocks are all of the same type.

3.1 Upper-bounded Timed Automata

Every guard B appearing in an upper-bounded timed automaton is of the form $\prod_{i=1}^{n}(-\infty, q_i]$, where each $q_i \in \mathbb{Z} \cup \{\infty\}$. It follows that $\mathbf{x} \in B$ iff $\mathbf{x} \leq \mathbf{q}$ coordinatewise. Thus for any guarded command $g = (B, U, F)$, the domain of $jump_g$ is $\{\mathbf{x} \in \mathbb{R}^n \mid \mathbf{x} \leq \mathbf{q}\}$. It follows that $\mathbf{x} \approx^{UA}_{\text{lang}} \mathbf{x}'$ implies $\lceil \mathbf{x}' \rceil = \lceil \mathbf{x} \rceil$, where UA is the class of upper-bounded timed automata. The converse is also true, but in fact a much stronger statement can be made.

Proposition 1 *For all* $\mathbf{x}, \mathbf{x}' \in \mathbb{R}^n$, *the following four conditions are equivalent:*

- *clock vectors* $\mathbf{x}$ *and* $\mathbf{x}'$ *are language equivalent with respect to the class of upper-bounded timed automata,*
- *clock vectors* $\mathbf{x}$ *and* $\mathbf{x}'$ *are synchronously simulation equivalent with respect to the class of upper-bounded timed automata,*
- *clock vectors* $\mathbf{x}$ *and* $\mathbf{x}'$ *are asynchronously simulation equivalent with respect to the class of upper-bounded timed automata,*
- $\lceil \mathbf{x} \rceil = \lceil \mathbf{x}' \rceil$.

In two or more dimensions, the synchronous and asynchronous bisimulation equivalence relations with respect to the class of upper-bounded timed automata coincide with region equivalence.

3.2 Lower-bounded Timed Automata

Every guard B appearing in a lower-bounded timed automaton is of the form $\prod_{j=1}^{n}[p_j, \infty)$, where each $p_j \in \mathbb{Z} \cup \{-\infty\}$. It follows that $\mathbf{y} \in B$ iff $\mathbf{y} \geq \mathbf{p}$ coordinatewise. Thus for any guarded command $g = (B, U, F)$, the domain of $jump_g$ is $\{\mathbf{y} \in \mathbb{R}^n \mid \mathbf{y} \geq \mathbf{p}\}$. But since for any $\mathbf{y}$ there is a $t \geq 0$ such that $\mathbf{y} + t\mathbf{1} \geq \mathbf{p}$, the domain of $delayed_g$ is $\mathbb{R}^n$. This proves 1) below.

Proposition 2 *1. Language equivalence, asynchronous simulation equivalence, and asynchronous bisimulation equivalence with respect to the class of lower-bounded timed automata coincide with the universal relation* $\mathbb{R}^n \times \mathbb{R}^n$.
2. Clock vectors $\mathbf{y}, \mathbf{y}' \in \mathbb{R}^n$ *are synchronously simulation equivalent with respect to the class of lower-bounded timed automata iff* $\lfloor \mathbf{y} \rfloor = \lfloor \mathbf{y}' \rfloor$.
3. In two or more dimensions, synchronous bisimulation equivalence with respect to the class of lower-bounded timed automata coincides with region equivalence.

3.3 One-sided Timed Automata

Let T be an $(n + m)$-dimensional one-sided timed automaton with n upper-bounded clocks and m lower-bounded clocks. After suitable rearrangement, we can assume that coordinates 1 through n are upper-bounded clocks and that coordinates $n+1$ through $n+m$ are lower-bounded clocks. Then for each guarded command $guard_T(e) = (B, U, F)$, it follows that the guard B is of the form

$$\prod_{i=1}^{n}(-\infty, q_i] \times \prod_{j=1}^{m}[p_j, \infty),$$

where each $q_i \in \mathbb{Z} \cup \{\infty\}$ and each $p_j \in \mathbb{Z} \cup \{-\infty\}$. So we represent guards B of one-sided timed automata by pairs of vectors $(\mathbf{q}, \mathbf{p}) \in (\mathbb{Z} \cup \{\infty\})^n \times (\mathbb{Z} \cup \{-\infty\})^m$. We call such guards and the guarded commands they comprise *one-sided*. We write a vector $\mathbf{u} \in \mathbb{R}^{n+m}$ as the pair $(\mathbf{x}, \mathbf{y})$, where $\mathbf{x} = (u_1, \ldots, u_n) \in \mathbb{R}^n$ and $\mathbf{y} = (u_{n+1}, \ldots, u_{n+m}) \in \mathbb{R}^m$. We use the notational convention that i ranges over $\{1, \ldots, n\}$ and j ranges over $\{1, \ldots, m\}$.

Definition 1 The binary relation $\preceq_1$ on $\mathbb{R}^{n+m}$ is defined by $(\mathbf{x},\mathbf{y}) \preceq_1 (\mathbf{x}',\mathbf{y}')$ iff $\lceil \mathbf{x}' \rceil \leq \lceil \mathbf{x} \rceil$ and $\forall i.\forall j.\ \lfloor y'_j - x'_i \rfloor \geq \lfloor y_j - x_i \rfloor$. □

Put $(\mathbf{x},\mathbf{y}) \approx_1 (\mathbf{x}',\mathbf{y}')$ iff $(\mathbf{x},\mathbf{y}) \preceq_1 (\mathbf{x}',\mathbf{y}')$ and $(\mathbf{x}',\mathbf{y}') \preceq_1 (\mathbf{x},\mathbf{y})$. The difference between region equivalence and $\approx_1$-equivalence is that the latter only considers the relative order of fractional parts of upper-bounded clocks with respect to the fractional parts of lower-bounded clocks. The relative order of the fractional parts of two different lower-bounded clocks (or two different upper-bounded clocks) is irrelevant to $\approx_1$-equivalence.

Lemma 1 *For all* $(\mathbf{x},\mathbf{y}),(\mathbf{x}',\mathbf{y}') \in \mathbb{R}^{n+m}$, $(\mathbf{x},\mathbf{y}) \preceq_1 (\mathbf{x}',\mathbf{y}')$ *iff for every one-sided guarded command* g, $(\mathbf{x},\mathbf{y}) \in \mathrm{dom}\ \mathit{delayed}_g$ *implies* $(\mathbf{x}',\mathbf{y}') \in \mathrm{dom}\ \mathit{delayed}_g$.

Synchronous Analysis. It is not the case that $(\mathbf{x},\mathbf{y}) \preceq_1 (\mathbf{x}',\mathbf{y}')$ implies that for every one-sided guarded command g, $(\mathbf{x},\mathbf{y}) \in \mathrm{dom}\ \mathit{jump}_g$ implies $(\mathbf{x}',\mathbf{y}') \in \mathrm{dom}\ \mathit{jump}_g$. For this we need the additional condition that $\lfloor \mathbf{y}' \rfloor \geq \lfloor \mathbf{y} \rfloor$.

Definition 2 The binary relation $\preceq_2$ on $\mathbb{R}^{n+m}$ is defined by $(\mathbf{x},\mathbf{y}) \preceq_2 (\mathbf{x}',\mathbf{y}')$ iff $(\mathbf{x},\mathbf{y}) \preceq_1 (\mathbf{x}',\mathbf{y}')$ and $\lfloor \mathbf{y}' \rfloor \geq \lfloor \mathbf{y} \rfloor$. □

Proposition 3 *The relation* $\preceq_2$ *is the largest synchronous simulation on* $\mathbb{R}^{n+m}$ *with respect to the class of one-sided timed automata.*

Asynchronous Analysis. It turns out that synchronous simulation equivalence is more discriminating than asynchronous simulation equivalence. The latter coincides with language equivalence.

Proposition 4 *The relation* $\preceq_1$ *is the largest asynchronous simulation on* $\mathbb{R}^{n+m}$ *with respect to the class of one-sided timed automata.*

Proof. We show that $\preceq_1$ is an asynchronous simulation. For a vector $\mathbf{z}$ and a number t, write $\mathbf{z}+t$ for $\mathbf{z}+t\mathbf{1}$. Suppose $(\mathbf{x},\mathbf{y}) \preceq_1 (\mathbf{u},\mathbf{v})$ and $((\mathbf{x},\mathbf{y}),(\mathbf{x}',\mathbf{y}')) \in \mathit{delayed}_g$. There exists a $t \geq 0$ such that $((\mathbf{x}+t,\mathbf{y}+t),(\mathbf{x}',\mathbf{y}')) \in \mathit{jump}_g$. Let h be any one-sided guarded command with guard $(\lceil \mathbf{x}+t \rceil, \lfloor \mathbf{y}+t \rfloor)$. Then $(\mathbf{x},\mathbf{y}) \in \mathrm{dom}\ \mathit{delayed}_h$. By Lemma 1, $(\mathbf{u},\mathbf{v}) \in \mathrm{dom}\ \mathit{delayed}_h$ as well. Therefore there exists a time $t' \geq 0$ such that $(\mathbf{u}+t',\mathbf{v}+t') \in \mathrm{dom}\ \mathit{jump}_h$. It follows that $(\mathbf{x}+t,\mathbf{y}+t) \preceq_2 (\mathbf{u}+t',\mathbf{v}+t')$. Therefore there exists a $(\mathbf{u}',\mathbf{v}')$ such that $((\mathbf{u}+t',\mathbf{v}+t'),(\mathbf{u}',\mathbf{v}')) \in \mathit{jump}_g$ and $(\mathbf{x}',\mathbf{y}') \preceq_2 (\mathbf{u}',\mathbf{v}')$. Immediately from the definitions follow $((\mathbf{u},\mathbf{v}),(\mathbf{u}',\mathbf{v}')) \in \mathit{delayed}_g$ and $(\mathbf{x}',\mathbf{y}') \preceq_1 (\mathbf{u}',\mathbf{v}')$. □

Theorem 3 *For all* $(\mathbf{x},\mathbf{y}),(\mathbf{x}',\mathbf{y}') \in \mathbb{R}^{n+m}$, *the following are equivalent:*

- *clock vectors* $(\mathbf{x},\mathbf{y})$ *and* $(\mathbf{x}',\mathbf{y}')$ *are language equivalent with respect to the class of one-sided timed automata,*
- *clock vectors* $(\mathbf{x},\mathbf{y})$ *and* $(\mathbf{x}',\mathbf{y}')$ *are asynchronously simulation equivalent with respect to the class of one-sided timed automata,*
- *1.* $\lceil \mathbf{x} \rceil = \lceil \mathbf{x}' \rceil$, *and*

2. $\forall i \in \{1,\ldots,n\}. \forall j \in \{1,\ldots,m\}. \lfloor y_j - x_i \rfloor = \lfloor y'_j - x'_i \rfloor$.

Clock vectors $(\mathbf{x},\mathbf{y}),(\mathbf{x}',\mathbf{y}') \in \mathbb{R}^{n+m}$ *are synchronously simulation equivalent with respect to the class of one-sided timed automata iff they are asynchronously simulation equivalent and* $\lceil \mathbf{y} \rceil = \lceil \mathbf{y}' \rceil$. *Synchronous and asynchronous bisimulation equivalence with respect to the class of one-sided timed automata coincide with region equivalence.*

Size of the Language Equivalence Quotient. The coarseness of an equivalence relation on $\mathbb{R}^n$ is measured by the number of equivalence classes per unit volume. Let *Regions*(n) be the number of region equivalence classes on n dimensions where all clocks are constrained to lie in the interval $(0,1)$, and let *OneSidedRegions*(n) be the number of language equivalence classes for one-sided timed automata with $n/2$ upper-bounded clocks and $n/2$ lower-bounded clocks, where all clocks are constrained to lie in the interval $(0,1)$, as defined by Theorem 1. These classes are called *regions* and *one-sided regions* respectively. While the region equivalence of $(\mathbf{x},\mathbf{y})$ and $(\mathbf{x}',\mathbf{y}')$ requires that the relative ordering of the fractional parts of each pair of coordinates be identical for the two vectors, one-sided region equivalence only requires the same relative ordering of the fractional parts of pairs of coordinates for which one is a lower-bounded clock and one is an upper-bounded clock. It follows that one-sided region equivalence is considerably coarser than region equivalence.

Figure 6 illustrates the difference between regions and one-sided regions. Any one of the following four conditions bars the vectors $(\mathbf{x},\mathbf{y})$ and $(\mathbf{x}',\mathbf{y}')$ from being region equivalent: (1) $x_1 > x_2$ but $x'_1 = x'_2$, (2) $y_1 > y_2$ but $y'_1 < y'_2$, (3) $x_3 > x_4$ but $x'_3 < x'_4$, and (4) $y_1 > x_4$ but $y'_1 = x'_4$. However, the relative order of the fractional parts of two upper-bounded clocks (or two lower-bounded clocks) is irrelevant to one-sided region equivalence. Therefore (1), (2), and (3) do not prevent the one-sided region equivalence of the two vectors. Nor does condition (4) prevent it, because $\lfloor y_1 - x_4 \rfloor = \lfloor y'_1 - x'_4 \rfloor$. The two vectors are in fact one-sided region equivalent.

Using characterizations of *Regions*(n) and *OneSidedRegions*(n) in terms of Stirling numbers of the second kind (see, e.g., [GKP89]), we show that, while the number of one-sided regions is still exponential, it is less than the number of regions by a multiplicative exponential factor.

Theorem 4 $\frac{\mathit{Regions}(2n)}{\mathit{OneSidedRegions}(2n)} = \Omega(2^n)$.

Proof. Let S^n_k be the number of ways to partition a set of n elements into k subsets. Each region in $(0,1)^{2n}$ defines a partition of $\{1,\ldots,2n\}$ into k subsets, where each subset defines a set of coordinates with the same value, and a permutation of the partition classes, giving the relative ordering of these values. Therefore

$$\mathit{Regions}(2n) = \sum_{k=1}^{2n} S^{2n}_k \, k!.$$

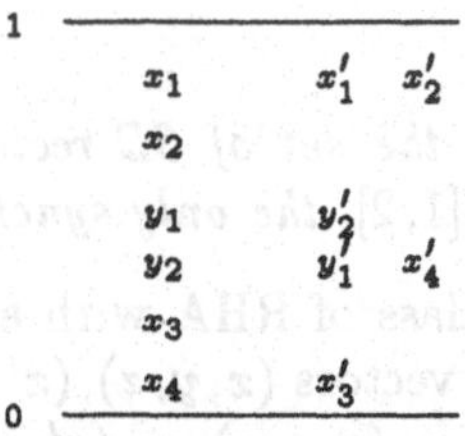

Fig. 6. Vectors $(\mathbf{x}, \mathbf{y})$ and $(\mathbf{x}', \mathbf{y}')$ are one-sided region equivalent but not region equivalent

Each one-sided region with an upper-bounded clock having the highest value determines a partition of the upper-bounded clocks into k subsets, and a permutation thereof. The upper-bounded clock partition is interleaved with a partition of the lower-bounded clocks into k or $k-1$ subsets. The same analysis applies if a lower-bounded clock has the highest value. It follows that

$$\begin{aligned} OneSidedRegions(2n) &= 2\sum_{k=1}^{n}(S_k^n)^2 k!^2 + 2\sum_{k=2}^{n} S_k^n S_{k-1}^n k!(k-1)! \\ &\le 4(\sum_{k=1}^{n} S_k^n k!)^2 \\ &= 4 Regions(n)^2. \end{aligned}$$

Therefore $OneSidedRegions(2n) = O(Regions(n)^2)$. Since every pair of n-dimensional regions can be used to form a distinct $2n$-dimensional region by placing one "on top" of the other, $\frac{Regions(2n)}{Regions(n)^2} \ge \binom{2n}{n}$. Now $\binom{2n}{n} = \frac{(2n)!}{n!^2}$, $(2n)! = \Omega((\frac{2n}{e})^{2n})$, and $n! = O(n(\frac{n}{e})^n)$. So

$$\frac{Regions(2n)}{OneSidedRegions(2n)} = \Omega(\frac{(2n)!}{n!^2}) = \Omega(\frac{(\frac{2n}{e})^{2n}}{n^2(\frac{n}{e})^{2n}}) = \Omega(\frac{2^{2n}}{n^2}) = \Omega(2^n). \square$$

4 Rectangular Hybrid Automata

Combining Theorems 1 and 3, we obtain the following sufficient condition for the language equivalence of two vectors with respect to the class of rectangular hybrid automata with fixed activity rectangle R.

Corollary 1 *Let* $R = \prod_{k=1}^{n}[a_k, b_k]$, *and let* $\lambda = lcm(a_1, b_1, \ldots, a_n, b_n)$. *For all* $\mathbf{x}, \mathbf{x}' \in \mathbb{R}^n$, *if*

- $\forall i \in \{1, \ldots, n\}. \lceil x_i \frac{\lambda}{a_i} \rceil = \lceil x'_i \frac{\lambda}{a_i} \rceil$, *and*
- $\forall i, j \in \{1, \ldots, n\}. \lfloor x_j \frac{\lambda}{b_j} - x_i \frac{\lambda}{a_i} \rfloor = \lfloor x'_j \frac{\lambda}{b_j} - x'_i \frac{\lambda}{a_i} \rfloor$,

then $\mathbf{x}$ ***and*** $\mathbf{x}'$ ***are language equivalent with respect to the class of rectangular hybrid automata with activity rectangle*** R.

Synchronous analysis.

Theorem 5 *With respect to the set of 3D rectangular hybrid automata with activity rectangle* $\{1\} \times \{1\} \times [1,2]$, *the only synchronous simulation is equality.*

Proof Outline. Let C be the class of RHA with activity rectangle $\{1\}^2 \times [1,2]$. It suffices to show that for all vectors $(x,y,z), (x',y',z')$ in the unit cube $[0,1]^3$, $(x,y,z) \preceq^{C}_{\mathrm{syn}} (x',y',z')$ implies $(x,y,z) = (x',y',z')$. First we show that for every n, if $x \leq \frac{1}{2^n}$ and $x' > \frac{1}{2^n}$ then $(x,y,z) \not\preceq^{C}_{\mathrm{syn}} (x',y',z')$ and $(x',y',z') \not\preceq^{C}_{\mathrm{syn}} (x,y,z)$. Call this statement $1(n)$. We prove the analogous results for y $(2(n))$ and z $(3(n))$ simultaneously by induction. The induction step requires care: rather than proving that $1(n) \wedge 2(n) \wedge 3(n)$ implies $1(n+1) \wedge 2(n+1) \wedge 3(n+1)$, it is necessary to prove $1(n+1) \wedge 2(n+1) \wedge 3(n)$ implies $1(n+2) \wedge 2(n+2) \wedge 3(n+1)$. The key fact is that if $z \geq 2y$ and $z' < 2y'$, then $(x,y,z) \not\preceq^{C}_{\mathrm{syn}} (x',y',z')$. This follows from $2(1)$. Second, we extend these results from numbers of the form $\frac{1}{2^n}$ to every dyadic rational $\frac{k}{2^n} \in [0,1]$. The theorem then follows from the density of the dyadic rationals. Full details are contained in [HK96]. □

Asynchronous analysis. Since every time predecessor of a point simulates that point, equality is not the only asynchronous simulation with respect to the class of RHA with a given activity rectangle. Nevertheless, asynchronous simulation equivalence coincides with equality. The proof of the next theorem is similar to the proof of Theorem 5, but it is slightly more complicated due to the lack of synchrony.

Theorem 6 *With respect to the class of 4D rectangular hybrid automata with activity rectangle* $\{1\}^3 \times [1,2]$, *asynchronous simulation equivalence coincides with equality.*

5 Summary

A summary of our results is given in Figure 7. All of the results are new, except those in the column regarding the class of timed automata [AD94]. In the four columns regarding subclasses of timed automata, exact characterizations of each of the five equivalence relations are given. Our main results relate to rectangular hybrid automata. First, language equivalence is finite, and a sufficient condition for language equivalence, superior by a multiplicative exponential factor to previously-known conditions, is derivable from the language equivalence relation that is displayed for one-sided timed automata. Second, the only synchronous simulation in three dimensions is equality, and asynchronous simulation equivalence in four dimensions is equality. Finally, our results suggest that simulation equivalence can be a more useful approximation to language equivalence than bisimulation equivalence. Indeed, for all of the subclasses of timed automata that we consider, synchronous bisimulation equivalence is finer than language equivalence. Moreover, except in the case of lower-bounded timed automata, the same can be said for asynchronous bisimulation equivalence.

	Upper-bounded Timed Automata	Lower-bounded Timed Automata	One-Sided Timed Automata	Timed Aut.	RHA
Lang. Equiv.	$\lceil x \rceil = \lceil x' \rceil$	universal relation	1. $\lceil x \rceil = \lceil x' \rceil$ 2. $\forall i. \forall j.$ $\lfloor y_j - x_i \rfloor = \lfloor y'_j - x'_i \rfloor$	region equiv.	finite quotient (Cor. 1)
Asynch. Sim. Equiv.	$\lceil x \rceil = \lceil x' \rceil$	universal relation	1. $\lceil x \rceil = \lceil x' \rceil$ 2. $\forall i. \forall j.$ $\lfloor y_j - x_i \rfloor = \lfloor y'_j - x'_i \rfloor$	region equiv.	equality
Synch. Sim. Equiv.	$\lceil x \rceil = \lceil x' \rceil$	$\lfloor y \rfloor = \lfloor y' \rfloor$	1. $\lceil x \rceil = \lceil x' \rceil$ 2. $\forall i. \forall j.$ $\lfloor y_j - x_i \rfloor = \lfloor y'_j - x'_i \rfloor$ 3. $\lfloor y \rfloor = \lfloor y' \rfloor$	region equiv.	equality
Asynch. Bisim. Equiv.	region equivalence	universal relation	region equivalence	region equiv.	equality
Synch. Bisim. Equiv.	region equivalence	region equivalence	region equivalence	region equiv.	equality

Fig. 7. Summary of results

References

[ACH+95] R. Alur, C. Courcoubetis, N. Halbwachs, T.A. Henzinger, P.-H. Ho, X. Nicollin, A. Olivero, J. Sifakis, and S. Yovine. The algorithmic analysis of hybrid systems. *Theoretical Computer Science*, 138:3–34, 1995.

[ACHH93] R. Alur, C. Courcoubetis, T.A. Henzinger, and P.-H. Ho. Hybrid automata: an algorithmic approach to the specification and verification of hybrid systems. In R.L. Grossman, A. Nerode, A.P. Ravn, and H. Rischel, editors, *Hybrid Systems I*, Lecture Notes in Computer Science 736, pages 209–229. Springer-Verlag, 1993.

[AD94] R. Alur and D.L. Dill. A theory of timed automata. *Theoretical Computer Science*, 126:183–235, 1994.

[AHH96] R. Alur, T.A. Henzinger, and P.-H. Ho. Automatic symbolic verification of embedded systems. *IEEE Transactions on Software Engineering*, 22(3):181–201, 1996.

[BBLS92] S. Bensalem, A. Bouajjani, C. Loiseaux, and J. Sifakis. Property-preserving simulations. In G. von Bochmann and D.K. Probst, editors, *CAV 92: Computer-aided Verification*, Lecture Notes in Computer Science 663, pages 260–273. Springer-Verlag, 1992.

[BCG88] M.C. Browne, E.M. Clarke, and O. Grümberg. Characterizing finite Kripke structures in propositional temporal logic. *Theoretical Computer Science*, 59:115–131, 1988.

[DY95] C. Daws and S. Yovine. Two examples of verification of multirate timed automata with Kronos. In *Proceedings of the 16th Annual Real-time Systems Symposium*, pages 66–75. IEEE Computer Society Press, 1995.

[GKP89] R. Graham, D. Knuth, and O. Patashnik. *Concrete Mathematics*. Addison-Wesley Publishing Company, 1989.

[Hen95] T.A. Henzinger. Hybrid automata with finite bisimulations. In Z. Fülöp and F. Gécseg, editors, *ICALP 95: Automata, Languages, and Programming*, Lecture Notes in Computer Science 944, pages 324–335. Springer-Verlag, 1995.

[Hen96] T.A. Henzinger. The theory of hybrid automata. In *Proceedings of the Eleventh Annual Symposium on Logic in Computer Science*. IEEE Computer Society Press, 1996.

[HH95] T.A. Henzinger and P.-H. Ho. Algorithmic analysis of nonlinear hybrid systems. In P. Wolper, editor, *CAV 95: Computer-aided Verification*, Lecture Notes in Computer Science 939, pages 225–238. Springer-Verlag, 1995.

[HHK95] M.R. Henzinger, T.A. Henzinger, and P.W. Kopke. Computing simulations on finite and infinite graphs. In *Proceedings of the 36rd Annual Symposium on Foundations of Computer Science*, pages 453–462. IEEE Computer Society Press, 1995.

[HHWT95] T.A. Henzinger, P.-H. Ho, and H. Wong-Toi. HyTech: the next generation. In *Proceedings of the 16th Annual Real-time Systems Symposium*, pages 56–65. IEEE Computer Society Press, 1995.

[HK96] T.A. Henzinger and P.W. Kopke. State equivalences for rectangular hybrid automata. Technical Report CSD-TR-96-1588, Cornell University, 1996.

[HKPV95] T.A. Henzinger, P.W. Kopke, A. Puri, and P. Varaiya. What's decidable about hybrid automata? In *Proceedings of the 27th Annual Symposium on Theory of Computing*, pages 373–382. ACM Press, 1995.

[HW95] P.-H. Ho and H. Wong-Toi. Automated analysis of an audio control protocol. In P. Wolper, editor, *CAV 95: Computer-aided Verification*, Lecture Notes in Computer Science 939, pages 381–394. Springer-Verlag, 1995.

[LPY95] K.G. Larsen, P. Pettersson, and W. Yi. Compositional and symbolic model checking of real-time systems. In *Proceedings of the 16th Annual Real-time Systems Symposium*, pages 76–87. IEEE Computer Society Press, 1995.

[NOSY93] X. Nicollin, A. Olivero, J. Sifakis, and S. Yovine. An approach to the description and analysis of hybrid systems. In R.L. Grossman, A. Nerode, A.P. Ravn, and H. Rischel, editors, *Hybrid Systems I*, Lecture Notes in Computer Science 736, pages 149–178. Springer-Verlag, 1993.

[PV94] A. Puri and P. Varaiya. Decidability of hybrid systems with rectangular differential inclusions. In D.L. Dill, editor, *CAV 94: Computer-aided Verification*, Lecture Notes in Computer Science 818, pages 95–104. Springer-Verlag, 1994.

[TY96] S. Tripakis and S. Yovine. Analysis of timed systems based on time-abstracting bisimulations. In *CAV 96: Computer-aided Verification*, Lecture Notes in Computer Science. Springer-Verlag, 1996.

Verifying Abstractions of Timed Systems

Serdar Taşıran* Rajeev Alur** Robert P. Kurshan** Robert K. Brayton*

Abstract. Given two descriptions of a real-time system at different levels of abstraction, we consider the problem of proving that the refined representation is a correct implementation of the abstract one. To avoid the complexity of building a representation for the refined system in its entirety, we develop a compositional framework for the implementation check to be carried out in a module-by-module manner using assume-guarantee style proof rules. On the algorithmic side, we show that the problem of checking the existence of timed simulation relations, a sufficient condition for correct implementation, is decidable. We study state homomorphisms as a way of specifying a correspondence between two modules. We present an algorithm for checking if a given mapping is a homomorphism preserving timed behaviors. We have implemented this check in the verifier COSPAN, and applied our method to the compositional verification of an asynchronous queue circuit.

1 Introduction

We address the problem of refinement for real-time systems such as control protocols and asynchronous circuits. We want to prove that, of the two given representations of a system, the more refined one "implements" the more abstract one. By doing so, one would be assured that the properties proved about the abstract description continue to hold in the refined version. This scenario may arise either because the design is being carried out in a top-down fashion by refining the system iteratively, or because the system is too complex and an abstraction of the system needs to be used to verify properties. This work addresses the following two problems: proving that one timed system is an abstraction of the other, and developing a compositional verification framework so that this proof can be carried out modularly.

Typically, a model of a system is described as a collection of coordinating components. The aim of compositional verification is to decompose the problem of verifying refinement into subproblems so that a monolithic representation for the system does not have to be built. Performing verification in this way has the important benefit of scaling with the increasing complexity of real-time systems encountered in practice. With this goal, in Section 2 we present a model for real-time systems. Defining timed language inclusion as the weakest notion for "implementation", we prove compositionality properties and show the soundness of an assumption-guarantee paradigm for modular verification in Section 3. To prove that a refined system with two components A and B implements an abstraction consisting of two components C and D, the compositionality principle asserts that it suffices to prove A implements C and B implements D, separately, while the stronger assumption-guarantee rule asserts that it suffices to prove that

* Department of Electrical Engineering and Computer Sciences, University of California at Berkeley. Supported by SRC under contract DC-324-026.

** Computing Sciences Research Center, Bell Laboratories, Murray Hill, NJ.

(1) the composition of A and D implements C, and (2) the composition of B and C implements D. Note the circularity in the assumption-guarantee rule. Its correctness requires that the processes involved are nonblocking in the sense that they are willing to accept any inputs and do not block the progress of time.

While the relation of timed language inclusion is a natural choice for abstraction relation, it was proved in [AD94] that language containment is undecidable for non-deterministic systems. Since abstract descriptions often involve non-determinism, we propose timed simulation relations as a sufficient condition for implementation. In Section 4 we prove that it is decidable (in EXPTIME) to check whether such a relation exists between two systems.

In Section 5, we investigate homomorphisms, which are restricted forms of simulation relations, as an alternative way of specifying and verifying timed abstractions. This approach requires the user to specify a correspondence between the locations of the abstract and refined versions, but is computationally more feasible, and is a generalization of the existing homomorphism checks supported by the system COSPAN. We present an algorithm for checking if a given mapping between the locations of two timed systems implies inclusion of timed languages. Our algorithm is implemented in COSPAN. We used this algorithm and assumption-guarantee style reasoning to verify abstractions of an asynchronous queue circuit. The algorithm and the results of the experiments are presented in Section 5.

Related research. In recent years, many tools have been developed to support verification of real-time systems (for instance, KRONOS [DOY94], ORBITS [Rok93], timed COSPAN [AK96] and UPPAAL [LPY95]). These tools consider the problem of model checking, that is, verifying that a mathematical model of a system satisfies its specification. The problem of proving refinements of timed systems has been considered only in the context of manual proofs (see, for instance, [AL91, Sha92, LA92]).

We have emphasized compositionality and modularity. Compositionality means that the implementation relation is a congruence with respect to parallel composition, and is exhibited by any reasonable formalism. Modularity makes explicit distinction between which variables are updated by the system and which are updated by the environment so as to support assume-guarantee style reasoning (an example of such a framework is I/O automata [LT87]). Assume-guarantee style proof rules for untimed systems have been proposed by many researchers (for instance, [GL94, AL93, AH96]). When the rule is symmetric and involves circularity, it is necessary to require that a process is nonblocking [LT87, AH96]. In the case of timed systems, these issues have been considered for timed I/O automata in [GSSL94]. Our framework uses synchronous composition and a much simpler definition of nonblocking without resorting to games.

For timed systems, a variety of implementation relations can be considered. Timed language containment is undecidable [AD94]. Timed bisimulation is decidable [Č92], but is not appropriate for refinements. Time-abstract simulation is considered in [HHK95], but does not preserve timed properties. As far as we know, there is no previous study of timed simulations.

The use of simulation mappings or homomorphisms to prove refinements is common in the literature (see, for instance, [Kur94, Sha92, AL91, LT87]). Among automated tools, COSPAN provides support to check whether the user-supplied mappings actually define a homomorphism. Our work generalizes this to checking the preservation of timed behaviors.

2 Timed Abstractions

Notation. Let X be a finite set of real-valued variables. An X-valuation Φ assigns a nonnegative real value $\Phi(x)$ to each variable $x \in X$. Let Φ be an X-valuation. For a real number $\delta \geq 0$, $\Phi + \delta$ denotes the X-valuation that assigns the value $\Phi(x)+\delta$ to each variable x, and $\mathbf{0}$ denotes the X-valuation that assigns the value 0 to all $x \in X$. For a subset $Y \subseteq X$, $\Phi[Y := 0]$ denotes the X-valuation that assigns the value 0 to each $x \in Y$ and the value $\Phi(x)$ to each $x \notin Y$. An X-predicate φ is a positive Boolean combination of constraints of the form $x \diamond k$, where k is a nonnegative integer constant, $x \in X$ is a variable, and $\diamond$ is one of the binary comparison relations: $\leq, \geq, =$. We write $\Phi \models \varphi$ if the valuation Φ satisfies the formula φ. Note that the set of X-valuations satisfying the X-predicate φ is closed.

Let P be a finite set of variables, each ranging over a finite type. A P-valuation $\mathbf{f}$ is an assignment of values to variables in P. For a P-valuation $\mathbf{f}$ and a subset $Q \subseteq P$, $\mathbf{f}(Q)$ denotes the Q-valuation obtained by the restriction of $\mathbf{f}$ to the variables in Q. A P-event is a pair $\langle \mathbf{f}, \mathbf{f}' \rangle$ consisting of P-valuations $\mathbf{f}$ and $\mathbf{f}'$ denoting the old and the new values of the variables in P. A P-predicate χ is a subset of P-events. While writing P-predicates as formulas, we use primed variables to refer to the updated values. For instance, the P-predicate $p' \neq p$ is the set of all P-events $\langle \mathbf{f}, \mathbf{f}' \rangle$ such that $\mathbf{f}'(p) \neq \mathbf{f}(p)$. We use *stutter*$(P)$ as an abbreviation for the predicate $\wedge_{p \in P}\, p' = p$.

With these conventions, we proceed to define timed processes as a model for real-time systems. All real-time systems that can be specified in the S/R language of COSPAN can be described as timed processes.

Timed processes. A *timed process* A is a tuple $\langle S, S_0, O, I, X, \alpha, \mu, E \rangle$, where

- S is the finite (nonempty) set of locations.
- $S_0 \subseteq S$ is the nonempty set of initial locations.
- X is the finite set of real-valued variables, called *clocks*.
- O is the finite set of output variables, each ranging over a finite type. An *output* of A is a O-valuation.
- I is the finite set of input variables, each ranging over a finite type. It is required that I and O are disjoint. An *input* of A is an I-valuation, an *input-event* is an I-event, and an *input-predicate* is a I-predicate. An *observation* of A is a $(I \cup O)$-valuation, and an *observation-event* of A is a $(I \cup O)$-event.
- α is the invariant function that assigns the X-predicate $\alpha(s)$ to each location $s \in S$. A *state* σ of A is a pair $\langle s, \Phi \rangle$ containing the location $s \in S$ and the X-valuation $\Phi \in \alpha(s)$. The set of all states is denoted Σ_A. The state $\langle s, \Phi \rangle$ is initial if $s \in S_0$ and $\Phi(x) = 0$ for all $x \in X$.
- μ is the output function that assigns the output $\mu(s)$ to each location $s \in S$.

– E is the finite set of edges. Each edge e is a tuple $\langle s, t, \varphi, \chi, Y\rangle$ consisting of the source location s, the target location t, the X-predicate φ, the input-predicate χ, and the set $Y \subseteq X$ of clocks to be reset. It is required that (1) E contains the edge $\langle s, s, true, stutter(I), \emptyset\rangle$ for each location s, and (2) for given source and target locations, there is at most one edge between them.

Consider a state $\sigma = \langle s, \Phi\rangle$ of the timed process A and a positive time increment δ. The process A can *wait* for δ in state σ, written $wait(\sigma, \delta)$, iff for all $0 \leq \delta' < \delta$, $(\Phi + \delta') \models \alpha(s)$. A *timed event* γ of the timed process A is a tuple $\langle \delta, \mathbf{f}, \mathbf{f}'\rangle$ consisting of a positive real-valued increment δ and the observation-event $\langle \mathbf{f}, \mathbf{f}'\rangle$. Such an event means that the process can wait for the time period δ and then update its output variables from $\mathbf{f}(O)$ to $\mathbf{f}'(O)$ while the environment is updating the input variables from $\mathbf{f}(I)$ to $\mathbf{f}'(I)$. The set of all timed events of A is denoted Γ_A.

The timed process A gives a labeled transition system over the state-space Σ_A with the labels Γ_A. For states $\sigma = \langle s, \Phi\rangle$ and $\tau = \langle t, \Theta\rangle$ in Σ_A, and a timed event $\gamma = \langle \delta, \mathbf{f}, \mathbf{f}'\rangle$ in Γ_A, define $\sigma \xrightarrow{\gamma} \tau$ iff $\mathbf{f}(O) = \mu(s)$, $\mathbf{f}'(O) = \mu(t)$, $wait(\sigma, \delta)$, and there exists an edge $\langle s, t, \varphi, \chi, Y\rangle$ such that $(\Phi + \delta) \models \varphi$, $\langle \mathbf{f}, \mathbf{f}'\rangle \models \chi$, and $\Theta = (\Phi + \delta)[Y := 0]$. We write $\sigma \xrightarrow{\gamma}$ if $\sigma \xrightarrow{\gamma} \tau$ for some τ.

Proposition 1 (Closure under stuttering). *For $\gamma = \langle \delta, \mathbf{f}, \mathbf{f}'\rangle$, if $\sigma \xrightarrow{\gamma} \tau$ then for every $0 < \delta' < \delta$, there exists σ' with $\sigma \xrightarrow{\gamma'} \sigma'$ and $\sigma' \xrightarrow{\gamma''} \tau$ where $\gamma' = \langle \delta', \mathbf{f}, \mathbf{f}\rangle$ and $\gamma'' = \langle \delta - \delta', \mathbf{f}, \mathbf{f}'\rangle$.*

Example. Figure 1 depicts a timed process representing an inertial delay buffer with non-deterministic delay between d_{min} and d_{max}. According to the inertial delay model, an input pulse must have duration at least d_{min} to be reflected at the output, and any input pulse of duration more than d_{max} has to create a corresponding pulse at the output. Note that any logic gate with inertial delay can be modeled as a delayless logic gate followed by an inertial delay buffer. Observe that, in our model of timed processes, a process spends nonzero time in each location and transitions are instantaneous. The enabling condition on a transition can refer to the old (unprimed) as well as the new (primed) values of the inputs, this makes the use of transient (zero-time) states unnecessary.

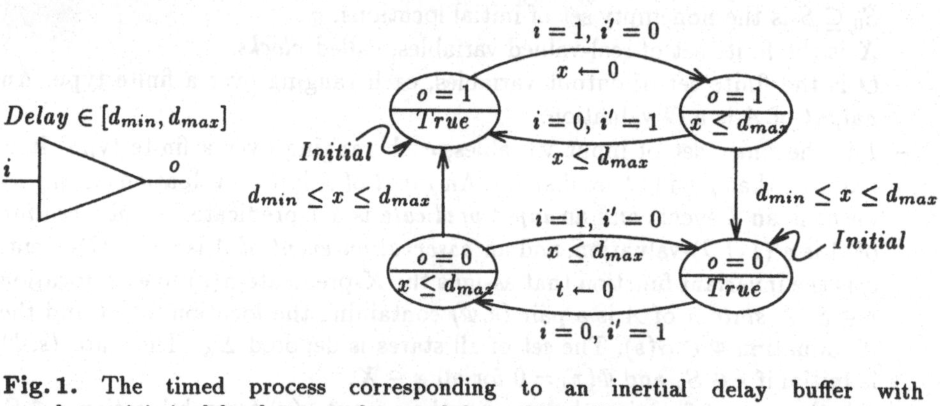

Fig. 1. The timed process corresponding to an inertial delay buffer with non-deterministic delay between d_{min} and d_{max}. The self loops on states corresponding to the stuttering edges have not been shown.

Timed language. A *timed event sequence* $\overline{\gamma} = \gamma_0, \gamma_1, ..., \gamma_{k-1}$ is a finite sequence of timed events $\gamma_i = \langle \delta_i, \mathbf{f}_i, \mathbf{f}'_i \rangle$ such that $\mathbf{f}_{i+1} = \mathbf{f}'_i$ for $0 \leq i < k-1$. For such a timed event sequence, define $\Delta_0 = 0$ and $\Delta_i = \sum_{j=0}^{i-1} \delta_j$ for $1 \leq i \leq k$. Each such $\overline{\gamma}$ uniquely defines a function $F_{\overline{\gamma}}$ from the closed interval $[0, \Delta_k]$ to the observations given by $F_{\overline{\gamma}}(t) = \mathbf{f}_i$ for $t \in [\Delta_i, \Delta_{i+1})$ and $F_{\overline{\gamma}}(\Delta_k) = \mathbf{f}'_{k-1}$.

A *run* of A on a timed event sequence $\overline{\gamma}$ is a sequence of states $\sigma_0, \sigma_1, \sigma_2, ..., \sigma_k$ such that $\sigma_0 \xrightarrow{\gamma_0} \sigma_1 \xrightarrow{\gamma_1} \sigma_2 \xrightarrow{\gamma_2} ... \xrightarrow{\gamma_{k-1}} \sigma_k$ in A. The timed event sequence $\overline{\gamma}$ is called a *trace* of A if there exists a run in A on $\overline{\gamma}$ starting from an initial state. The *timed language* of a process A, denoted $\mathcal{L}(A)$, is the set of traces of A.

Timed abstraction relations. Consider two timed processes $A = \langle S^A, S_0^A, O^A, I^A, X^A, \alpha^A, \mu^A, E^A \rangle$ and $B = \langle S^B, S_0^B, O^B, I^B, X^B, \alpha^B, \mu^B, E^B \rangle$. The timed process A is *comparable* to B iff $O^B \subseteq O^A$ and $I^B \subseteq I^A$.

Suppose A is comparable to B. Then, a *timed simulation relation* from A to B is a binary relation $\Omega \subseteq \Sigma_A \times \Sigma_B$ among the states of the two processes such that for every $(\sigma, \tau) \in \Omega$ and for every timed event γ in Γ_A if $\sigma \xrightarrow{\gamma} \sigma'$ then there exists $\tau' \in \Sigma_B$ such that $\tau \xrightarrow{\gamma} \tau'$ and (σ', τ') is in Ω. The timed simulation relation Ω is said to be *initialized* iff for every initial state σ of A, there exists an initial state τ of B with $(\sigma, \tau) \in \Omega$. If the timed process A is comparable to the timed process B, and an initialized timed simulation relation from A to B exists, then A is said to *timed-simulate* B, written $A \preceq_S B$.

Let A be comparable to B. A is said to *timed-implement* B iff for every trace $\overline{\gamma}^A$ of A, there exists $\overline{\gamma}^B$ in $\mathcal{L}(B)$ assigning the same values to the input and output variables of B at all times, i.e., $F_{\overline{\gamma}^A}(I^B \cup O^B) = F_{\overline{\gamma}^B}$. Timed implementation is denoted by $A \preceq_L B$ and is also referred to as the *language inclusion* relation.

Proposition 2 (Preorder). *The relations $\preceq_S$ and $\preceq_L$ are reflexive and transitive.*

The two timed processes are *timed simulation equivalent*, written $A \cong_S B$, iff both $A \preceq_S B$ and $B \preceq_S A$. It follows that the relation $\cong_S$ is an equivalence relation. Similarly, the timed language equivalence $\cong_L$ is the equivalence induced by $\preceq_L$. Timed simulation is a stronger requirement than timed implementation.

Proposition 3 (Languages and simulation). *If $A \preceq_S B$, then $A \preceq_L B$.*

Composition of timed processes. The key operator to build complex processes from simpler ones is parallel composition. Consider two timed processes $A = \langle S^A, S_0^A, O^A, I^A, X^A, \alpha^A, \mu^A, E^A \rangle$ and $B = \langle S^B, S_0^B, O^B, I^B, X^B, \alpha^B, \mu^B, E^B \rangle$. We assume that the clocks X^A and X^B are disjoint (this can be achieved by renaming). The two timed processes A and B are *composable* iff their output variables O^A and O^B are disjoint. For two such composable timed processes, their parallel composition $A \parallel B$ is the timed process with the following components:

- The set S of locations equals $S^A \times S^B$.
- The set S_0 of initial locations equals $S_0^A \times S_0^B$.

- The set O of output variables equals $O^A \cup O^B$.
- The set I of input variables equals $(I^A \cup I^B) \setminus O$.
- The set X of clock variables equals $X^A \cup X^B$.
- For every $s \in S^A$ and $t \in S^B$, the invariant $\alpha(\langle s,t\rangle)$ equals the conjunction $\alpha^A(s) \wedge \alpha^B(t)$.
- For every $s \in S^A$ and $t \in S^B$, the output $\mu(\langle s,t\rangle)$ equals $\mu^A(s) \cup \mu^B(t)$.
- For every edge $e = \langle s,t,\varphi,\chi,Y\rangle$ in E^A and $e' = \langle s',t',\varphi',\chi',Y'\rangle$ in E^B, the set E contains the edge $\langle\langle s,s'\rangle,\langle t,t'\rangle,\varphi\wedge\varphi',\chi'',Y\cup Y'\rangle$, where the I-event $\langle \mathbf{f},\mathbf{f}'\rangle$ is in χ'' iff $\langle \mathbf{f}\cup\mu^B(t),\mathbf{f}'\cup\mu^B(t')\rangle \models \chi$ and $\langle \mathbf{f}\cup\mu^A(s),\mathbf{f}'\cup\mu^A(s')\rangle \models \chi'$.

First observe that the parallel composition operator is commutative and associative:
Proposition 4. *$A \parallel B \cong_S B \parallel A$, and $A \parallel (B \parallel C) \cong_S (A \parallel B) \parallel C$.*
The composed process is an implementation of each component:
Proposition 5. *$A \parallel B \preceq_S A$.*
Both the timed equivalence relations are congruences with respect to the composition operator $\parallel$:
Proposition 6 (Compositionality). *If $A \preceq_S B$ then $A \parallel C \preceq_S B \parallel C$; if $A \preceq_L B$ then $A \parallel C \preceq_L B \parallel C$.*
The compositionality principle tells us that to prove that $A \parallel B$ is a timed refinement of $C \parallel D$ it suffices to show separately that A is a timed refinement of C and B is a timed refinement of D.

3 Modularity

In this section, we examine assumption-guarantee style reasoning principles for the abstraction relations. It is not clear if such principles hold for the simulation preorder, however, for the language preorder, with certain restrictions, a simple and powerful modularity principle can be obtained.

A timed process $A = \langle S, S_0, O, I, X, \alpha, \mu, E\rangle$ is said to be *nonblocking* iff for all states σ in Σ_A,
(1) $\sigma \xrightarrow{\gamma}$ for some timed event γ, and
(2) if $\sigma \xrightarrow{\gamma}$ for some timed event $\gamma = \langle \delta,\mathbf{f},\mathbf{f}'\rangle$ then $\sigma \xrightarrow{\langle\delta,\mathbf{g},\mathbf{g}'\rangle}$ for all $\mathbf{g}$ and $\mathbf{g}'$ with $\mathbf{g}(O) = \mathbf{f}(O)$ and $\mathbf{g}'(O) = \mathbf{f}'(O)$.

The intuition behind this definition is that a non-blocking process should be able to generate a trace no matter what the sequence of input events is. The execution of a nonblocking timed process can be viewed operationally as follows. Consider the timed process in state $\sigma = \langle s, \Phi\rangle$ with output $\mathbf{f} = \mu(s)$. The process chooses a timed delay δ' such that $wait(\sigma,\delta')$, and simultaneously, the environment chooses a time delay δ''. Let δ be the minimum of δ' and δ''. The next observable event happens after a delay of δ. The timed process decides to update its output from $\mathbf{f}$ to $\mathbf{f}'$. The environment decides to update the input from $\mathbf{g}$ to $\mathbf{g}'$ independently. The timed process updates its state to $\sigma' = \langle s', \Phi'\rangle$ with $\mu(s') = \mathbf{f}'$ by choosing an appropriate edge. Such an update always exists due to the nonblocking requirement. Thus, while the update of outputs is independent of the update of inputs, the update of internal variables (i.e., the location and the clocks) depends on it.

Proposition 7 (Closure under composition). *If A and B are nonblocking, then so is $A \parallel B$.*

The following assumption-guarantee rule is useful in modular reasoning.

Proposition 8 (Assumption-Guarantee). *For nonblocking timed processes, if $A \parallel D \preceq_L C$ and $C \parallel B \preceq_L D$ then $A \parallel B \preceq_L C \parallel D$.*

Observe the apparent circularity in the rule: to prove that $A \parallel B$ is a refinement of $C \parallel D$, it suffices to prove that (1) A is a refinement of C assuming that the environment behaves like D, and (2) B is a refinement of D assuming that the environment behaves like C. The proof relies on the fact that all processes are nonblocking. Let us note a few observations before we give a detailed proof. First, the rule is incorrect if we remove the requirement of nonblocking. Second, the rule is incorrect if we replace $\preceq_L$ by the simulation preorder $\preceq_S$. Third, recall that we have required all X-predicates to be closed, (i.e. all invariants labeling the locations are conjunctions of non-strict inequalities). If we allow predicates that define open sets (e.g. invariants of the form $x < 5$), the rule fails again. In the proof below, we show that a timed process cannot force infinitely many transitions within a finite interval (the so-called condition of non-Zenoness). This does not hold automatically with open invariants. In this case, the nonblocking requirement needs to be strengthened by replacing requirement (1) in the definition of nonblocking using games. In [GSSL94], such a framework is developed for (asynchronous) timed I/O automata. However, that complicates the development considerably (indeed, the proof that the nonblocking requirement is preserved under composition runs many pages in [GSSL94]).

Proof. The proof is by contradiction. Assume that there exists a timed event sequence $\overline{\gamma} = \gamma_0, \gamma_1, ..., \gamma_{n-1}$ in $\mathcal{L}(A \parallel B)$ and not in $\mathcal{L}(C \parallel D)$. Let $\overline{\gamma_k} = \gamma_0, \gamma_1, ..., \gamma_{k-1}$, where $k < n$ be the longest prefix of $\overline{\gamma}$ that is a trace of $C \parallel D$. Let $\tau_0 \xrightarrow{\gamma_0} \tau_1 \xrightarrow{\gamma_1} ... \xrightarrow{\gamma_{k-1}} \tau_k$ be in $C \parallel D$. Since $\overline{\gamma} \in \mathcal{L}(A \parallel B)$, we have a run in $A \parallel B$ of the form $\sigma_0 \xrightarrow{\gamma_0} ... \xrightarrow{\gamma_{k-1}} \sigma_k \xrightarrow{\gamma_k} ... \xrightarrow{\gamma_{n-1}} \sigma_n$. Let $\sigma_i = \langle \sigma_i^A, \sigma_i^B \rangle$ and $\tau_i = \langle \tau_i^C, \tau_i^D \rangle$ for all i. From the above, we have

$$\langle \sigma_0^A, \tau_0^D \rangle \xrightarrow{\gamma_0} \langle \sigma_1^A, \tau_1^D \rangle \xrightarrow{\gamma_1} ... \xrightarrow{\gamma_{k-1}} \langle \sigma_k^A, \tau_k^D \rangle \text{ in } A \parallel D$$

and

$$\langle \tau_0^C, \sigma_0^B \rangle \xrightarrow{\gamma_0} \langle \tau_1^C, \sigma_1^B \rangle \xrightarrow{\gamma_1} ... \xrightarrow{\gamma_{k-1}} \langle \tau_k^C, \sigma_k^B \rangle \text{ in } C \parallel B$$

The partitioning of the input and output variables of the processes in Figure 2 will be useful in the rest of the proof. Let σ_k^A, σ_k^B, τ_k^C and τ_k^D be denoted by $\boldsymbol{a}$, $\boldsymbol{b}$, $\mathbf{c}$ and $\boldsymbol{d}$ respectively. Also let $\gamma_k = \gamma = \langle \delta, \mathbf{f}, \mathbf{f}' \rangle$. We have $\langle \boldsymbol{a}, \boldsymbol{b} \rangle \xrightarrow{\gamma} \langle \boldsymbol{a}', \boldsymbol{b}' \rangle$ for some $\langle \boldsymbol{a}', \boldsymbol{b}' \rangle \in \Sigma_{A \parallel B}$ since $\overline{\gamma}$ is in the language. Consider $\langle \boldsymbol{a}, \boldsymbol{d} \rangle \in \Sigma_{A \parallel D}$ and $\langle \mathbf{c}, \boldsymbol{b} \rangle \in \Sigma_{C \parallel B}$. From the above, A and B can select an increment of δ at states $\boldsymbol{a}$ and $\boldsymbol{b}$ respectively. The rest of the proof splits into two cases.

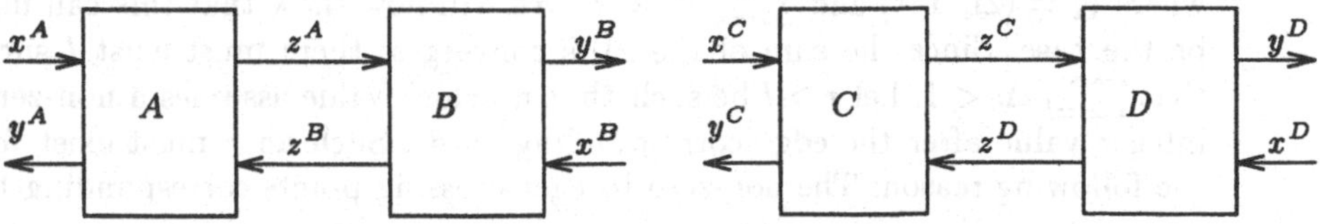

Fig. 2. The partitioning of the input and output variables.

Case 1. C and D can both select time increments of δ or greater in states $\boldsymbol{c}$ and $\boldsymbol{d}$. In this case, letting the environment choose the inputs x^A and x^B according to γ_k, we have

(I) $\langle \boldsymbol{a}, \boldsymbol{d}\rangle \xrightarrow{\langle \delta, \mathbf{g}, \mathbf{g}'\rangle} \langle \boldsymbol{a}'', \boldsymbol{d}'\rangle$ for some $\boldsymbol{a}''$ and $\boldsymbol{d}'$ such that g and g′ agree with f and f′ on x^A, y^A and z^A respectively. Thus $\gamma_0, \gamma_1, ..., \gamma_{k-1}, \langle \delta, \mathbf{g}, \mathbf{g}'\rangle$ is a trace of $A \parallel D$, and since $A \parallel D \preceq_L C \parallel D$, it is a trace of $C \parallel D$.

(II) $\langle \boldsymbol{c}, \boldsymbol{b}\rangle \xrightarrow{\langle \delta, \mathbf{h}, \mathbf{h}'\rangle} \langle \boldsymbol{c}', \boldsymbol{d}''\rangle$ for some $\boldsymbol{c}'$ and $\boldsymbol{d}''$ such that h and h′ agree with f and f′ on x^B, y^B and z^B respectively. We conclude that $\gamma_0, \gamma_1, ..., \gamma_{k-1}$, $\langle \delta, \mathbf{h}, \mathbf{h}'\rangle$ is a trace of $C \parallel D$ by a similar reasoning.

(I) and (II), together with the fact that C and D are nonblocking imply that $\gamma_0, \gamma_1, ..., \gamma_{k-1}, \gamma_k$ is a trace of $C \parallel D$, which contradicts our assumption that $\gamma_0, \gamma_1, ..., \gamma_{k-1}$ is maximal.

Case 2. Either C or D can not select a time increment of δ or greater in states $\boldsymbol{c}$ and $\boldsymbol{d}$. Let δ^C and δ^D be the largest increments that C and D can select and let Δ_0 be the minimum of δ^C and δ^D. Since $\Delta_0 < \delta$, for $\theta_0 = \langle \Delta_0, \mathbf{f}, \mathbf{f}\rangle$, we have $\langle \boldsymbol{a}, \boldsymbol{b}\rangle \xrightarrow{\theta_0} \langle \boldsymbol{a}_0^*, \boldsymbol{b}_0^*\rangle$ for some $\langle \boldsymbol{a}_0^*, \boldsymbol{b}_0^*\rangle$. Then,

(I) $\langle \boldsymbol{a}, \boldsymbol{d}\rangle \xrightarrow{\langle \Delta_0, \mathbf{g}_0, \mathbf{g}_0'\rangle} \langle \boldsymbol{a}_0, \boldsymbol{d}_0\rangle$ for some $\boldsymbol{a}_0$ and $\boldsymbol{d}_0$ such that $\mathbf{g}_0$ and $\mathbf{g}_0'$ agree with f on x^A, y^A and z^A. With a similar reasoning to (I) in Case 1, we have that $\gamma_0, \gamma_1, ..., \gamma_{k-1}, \langle \Delta_0, \mathbf{g}_0, \mathbf{g}_0'\rangle$ is a trace of $C \parallel D$.

(II) $\langle \boldsymbol{c}, \boldsymbol{b}\rangle \xrightarrow{\langle \Delta_0, \mathbf{h}_0, \mathbf{h}_0'\rangle} \langle \boldsymbol{c}_0, \boldsymbol{b}_0\rangle$ for some $\boldsymbol{c}_0$ and $\boldsymbol{b}_0$ such that $\mathbf{h}_0$ and $\mathbf{h}_0'$ agree with f on x^B, y^B and z^B. From this, we obtain $\gamma_0, \gamma_1, ..., \gamma_{k-1}, \langle \Delta_0, \mathbf{h}_0, \mathbf{h}_0'\rangle$ as a trace of $C \parallel D$.

From (I) and (II), we derive that $\gamma_0, \gamma_1, ..., \gamma_{k-1}, \theta_0$ is a trace of $C \parallel D$.
Note that $\overline{\gamma_k}$ is equivalent modulo stuttering to $\gamma_0, \gamma_1, ..., \gamma_{k-1}, \theta_0, \gamma_k^{(0)}$, where $\gamma_k^{(0)} = \langle \delta - \Delta_0, \mathbf{f}, \mathbf{f}'\rangle$. It suffices to show that the latter is a trace of $C \parallel D$ to obtain a contradiction.
Consider $\overline{\phi_0} = \gamma_0, \gamma_1, ..., \gamma_{k-1}, \theta_0$ and some run of $C \parallel D$ on this trace. Let $\langle \boldsymbol{c}_0^*, \boldsymbol{d}_0^*\rangle$ be the state reached at the end of this run. We can replace $\overline{\gamma_k}$ by ϕ_0, and $\boldsymbol{a}$, $\boldsymbol{b}$, $\boldsymbol{c}$ and $\boldsymbol{d}$ with $\boldsymbol{a}_0^*$, $\boldsymbol{b}_0^*$, $\boldsymbol{c}_0^*$ and $\boldsymbol{d}_0^*$ and repeat the argument in the proof so far. If it is the case that it is possible to select a time increment of $\delta - \Delta_0$ at states $\boldsymbol{c}_0^*$ and $\boldsymbol{d}_0^*$, we conclude similarly that $\gamma_0, \gamma_1, ..., \gamma_{k-1}, \theta_0, \gamma_k^{(0)}$ is a trace of $C \parallel D$, which contradicts the maximality of $\gamma_0, \gamma_1, ..., \gamma_{k-1}, \theta_0$. Otherwise, we can obtain $\theta_1 = \langle \Delta_1, \mathbf{f}, \mathbf{f}\rangle$ such that $\Delta_1 < \delta - \Delta_0$ and $\gamma_0, \gamma_1, ..., \gamma_{k-1}, \theta_0, \theta_1$ is a trace of $C \parallel D$. Then, the whole argument can be repeated again. If the process terminates after finitely many repetitions, we obtain $\gamma_0, \gamma_1, ..., \gamma_{k-1}, \theta_0, \theta_1, ..., \theta_m, \gamma_k^{(m)}$, where $\gamma_k^{(m)} = \langle \delta - \sum_{i=0}^{m} \Delta_i, \mathbf{f}, \mathbf{f}'\rangle$, which is equivalent modulo stuttering to $\overline{\gamma_k}$, the contradiction we sought. Otherwise, we must have an infinite sequence $\gamma_0, \gamma_1, ..., \gamma_{k-1}, \theta_0, \theta_1, \theta_2, \theta_3, ...$ where $\theta_i = \langle \Delta_i, \mathbf{f}, \mathbf{f}\rangle$ and $\sum_{i=0}^{\infty} \Delta_i < \delta$. We will now show that this can not be the case. Since the sum of the Δ_i's converges, there must exist l such that $\sum_{i=l}^{\infty} \Delta_i < 1$. Let $r > l$ be such that no clock value assumes a non-zero integer value after the edge corresponding to θ_r. Such an r must exist for the following reason: The non-zero integer crossing points corresponding to

a clock must be separated by 1 time unit, so there can not be more than one such crossing per clock after θ_r. But there are a finite number of clocks, therefore only finitely many such points, which means there is a last one. We argue that after θ_r, the same set of clock predicates of the form $x \diamond k$ are satisfied. This is because no clocks cross integer boundaries other than 0, and the clocks that get reset after θ_r satisfy $0 < x \leq 1$ on all edges after θ_r. Let us choose any $q > r$. By the preceding argument, Δ_q could have been increased to $\sum_{i=q}^{\infty} \Delta_i$, which contradicts the maximality of Δ_q.

4 Decidability of Timed Simulation

A language inclusion check between non-deterministic timed processes is undecidable in the general case[3] while [Č92] has proved that computing timed bisimulation is decidable. We have shown the existence of a timed simulation relation is a sufficient condition for language inclusion. In the following, we will show that the problem of checking the existence of a timed simulation relation is decidable. We achieve this by converting this check to a finite check on the finitely many equivalence classes of an equivalence relation defined on $\Sigma_{A\|B}$. Our argument generalizes that of [Č92] for the decidability of bisimulations.

Preliminaries. Let A be a timed process and for each $x \in X$ let K_x denote the integer such that $x \diamond K_x$ appears in an X-predicate on some edge of A. Also let $Fr(x) = x - \lfloor x \rfloor$, the fractional part of x. The region equivalence [AD94] relation is defined as follows: **f** and Φ are equivalent iff for all $x \in X$, either both $\Phi(x)$ and $\Theta(x)$ are larger than K_x, or the following hold

- $\lfloor \Phi(x) \rfloor = \lfloor \Theta(x) \rfloor$, and
- For all $x' \in X$ such that $\Phi(x') \leq K_{x'}$, $Fr(\Phi(x)) \geq Fr(\Phi(x'))$ iff $Fr(\Theta(x)) \geq Fr(\Theta(x'))$, and
- $Fr(\Phi(x)) = 0 \Leftrightarrow Fr(\Theta(x)) = 0$.

We write $\langle s, \Phi \rangle \equiv \langle t, \Theta \rangle$ iff $s = t$ and Φ and Θ are region equivalent. The following lemma will enable us to pick an arbitrary representative of an equivalence class in the rest of the paper.

Lemma 9. *If* $\langle s, \Phi \rangle \overset{\langle \delta, \mathbf{f}, \mathbf{f}' \rangle}{\rightarrow} \langle t, \Phi' \rangle$ *and* $\langle s, \Phi \rangle \equiv \langle s, \Theta \rangle$*, then* $\langle s, \Theta \rangle \overset{\langle \delta', \mathbf{f}, \mathbf{f}' \rangle}{\rightarrow} \langle t, \Theta' \rangle$ *for some* $\delta' > 0$ *and* Θ' *such that* $\langle s, \Phi' \rangle \equiv \langle s, \Theta' \rangle$.

Simulation relations and equivalence classes of $\equiv$. The following theorem stipulates that any simulation relation can be extended to one consisting of equivalence classes of $\equiv$.

[3] The halting problem for non-deterministic 2-counter machines can be reduced to the language inclusion problem in a similar manner to [AD94]. There are two key differences from [AD94]: the non-halting computations of the 2-counter machine are encoded as finite strings and accepting states of automata are mimicked by using output variables. The details of the reduction are too lengthy to present here.

Theorem 10. *Let Ω be a timed simulation from A to B and let X^A and X^B be the clocks of A and B. Define*

$$\Omega' = \{\langle \sigma^A, \sigma^B \rangle \mid \langle \sigma^A, \sigma^B \rangle \equiv \langle \tau^A, \tau^B \rangle \text{ for some } \langle \tau^A, \tau^B \rangle \in \Omega \}$$

where $\equiv$ is interpreted over $X^A \cup X^B$. Then, Ω' is a timed simulation relation from A to B. Furthermore, if Ω is initialized, then so is Ω'.

Theorem 10 is important, because it implies that the maximal timed simulation relation consists of a union of equivalence classes of $\equiv$. In the following, we will develop machinery to show that given A and B, the problem of deciding if a timed simulation from A to B exists can be converted to a condition on the equivalence classes of $\equiv$ which can be checked in finitely many steps. From this we will infer that the problem is decidable.

Symbolic simulations. For timed processes A and B, let $\mathcal{EQ}_{A\|B}$ be the set of equivalence classes of $\equiv$ on $\Sigma_{A\|B}$. With $\mathcal{EQ}(\sigma^A, \sigma^B)$, denote the equivalence class that the state $\langle \sigma^A, \sigma^B \rangle \in \Sigma_{A\|B}$ belongs to, where $\sigma^A \in \Sigma_A$ and $\sigma^B \in \Sigma^B$. For $\langle \sigma^A, \sigma^B \rangle$, assume that $u_0, u_1, \ldots, u_k$ are the fractional parts of clock values of σ^A and σ^B in ascending order. Let k_A be such that u_{k_A} is the largest fractional part of a clock value of σ^A. Define

$$Times(\langle \sigma^A, \sigma^B \rangle) = \{(1-u_i) \mid k_A \leq i \leq k\} \cup \{(1-0.5(u_i+u_{i+1})) \mid k_A \leq i \leq k\}$$

with the convention that $u_{k+1} = 1$. If we imagine the fractional parts of clocks ordered on the real line and if we also include the mid-points between each two adjacent fractional parts, *Times* consists of the distances between these points and the next integer point.

We say that $\mathcal{X} \subseteq \mathcal{EQ}_{A\|B}$ is a *symbolic simulation* from A to B iff for each $\mathcal{EQ}(\sigma^A, \sigma^B) \in \mathcal{X}$ the following condition is satisfied. For every timed event $\gamma = \langle t, \mathbf{f}, \mathbf{f}' \rangle$, if $\sigma^A \xrightarrow{\gamma} \tau^A$ such that $t \in Times(\langle \sigma^A, \sigma^B \rangle)$, if $\sigma^A \xrightarrow{\gamma} \tau^A$, then

(1) $\sigma^B \xrightarrow{\gamma} \tau^B$ for some τ^B such that $\mathcal{EQ}(\tau^A, \tau^B) \in \mathcal{X}$, and
(2) If A can wait in σ^A for time t, then so can B in state σ^B.

Note that, by Lemma 9, the conditions above are independent of what representative is chosen for each equivalence class.

Theorem 11. *Given $\mathcal{X} \subseteq \mathcal{EQ}_{A\|B}$ let $\mathcal{R}_\mathcal{X} = \{\langle \sigma^A, \sigma^B \rangle \mid \mathcal{EQ}(\sigma^A, \sigma^B) \in \mathcal{X}\}$. $\mathcal{R}_\mathcal{X}$ is a timed simulation relation from A to B iff $\mathcal{X}$ is a symbolic simulation from A to B.*

Proof. The ($\Rightarrow$) direction is straightforward. We will prove the ($\Leftarrow$) direction. Suppose that $\mathcal{X}$ is a symbolic simulation from A to B. Let $\langle \sigma^A, \sigma^B \rangle \in \mathcal{R}_\mathcal{X}$ and let $\sigma^A \xrightarrow{\gamma} \tau^A$ for some timed event $\gamma = \langle t, \mathbf{f}, \mathbf{f}' \rangle$. We need to show that there exists a τ^B such that $\sigma^B \xrightarrow{\gamma} \tau^B$ and $\langle \tau^B, \tau^B \rangle \in \mathcal{R}_\mathcal{X}$. If $t \in Times(\langle \sigma^A, \sigma^B \rangle)$ the claim holds by the definition of a symbolic simulation. Otherwise, let t_{max} be the largest element of $Times(\langle \sigma^A, \sigma^B \rangle)$. We will denote the latter with *Times* in the rest of the proof. There are two cases.

(I) $t \leq t_{max}$. Then, $p < t < q$ for some p and q in *Times*. One of p and q has the form $1 - 0.5(u_i + u_{i+1})$ (call this one r) and the other has the form $1 - u_j$, for some i and j. Let $\sigma^A = \langle s^A, \Phi^A \rangle$ and $\sigma^B = \langle s^B, \Phi^B \rangle$. Define $\theta = \langle r, \mathbf{f}, \mathbf{f}' \rangle$, i.e., the time increment in γ replaced with r. $\sigma^A \xrightarrow{\theta} \tau^A$, since r and t are both less than $1 - u_{k_A}$, which means that the same timing predicates are satisfied by Φ^A, $\Phi^A + t$ and $\Phi^A + r$. By the fact that $\mathcal{X}$ is a symbolic simulation, and $r \in Times$, $\sigma^B \xrightarrow{\theta} \tau^B$ for some τ^B such that $\langle \tau^A, \tau^B \rangle \in \mathcal{R}_{\mathcal{X}}$. We claim that $\sigma^B \xrightarrow{\gamma} \tau^B$, which will imply the desired result. This claim follows from the fact that $\Phi^B + t$ satisfies the same clock predicates as $\Phi^B + r$, since no clock value crosses an integer value between these two clock valuations.

(II) $t > t_{max}$. Let us consider all points in time when a clock of A takes on an integer value as A waits for time t starting from state σ^A. Clearly there must be a finite number of such points since t is finite and there are a finite number of clocks. More precisely, let $\sigma_1^A, \sigma_2^A, ..., \sigma_k^A$ be the maximal sequence of states such that (1) σ_i^A is reached from σ^A by waiting for time δ_i, and has some clock with an integer value, and (2) $\sigma_k^A \xrightarrow{\langle \delta, \mathbf{f}, \mathbf{f}' \rangle} \tau^A$, where $\delta = t - \delta_k$. We will prove the original claim in $(\Leftarrow)$ by induction on k. The case where $k = 0$ follows from (I). Let us assume that the claim holds for k. We will show that the claim holds for $k+1$. Consider $\sigma_1^A, \sigma_2^A, ..., \sigma_k^A, \sigma_{k+1}^A$. Since $\mathcal{X}$ is a symbolic simulation, and since A can wait for δ_1 at σ^A to reach σ_1^A, B can wait at σ^B for δ_1 to reach σ_1^B such that $\mathcal{EQ}(\sigma_1^B, \sigma_1^B) \in \mathcal{X}$. Applying the induction assumption to the transition $\sigma_1^A \xrightarrow{\langle t - \delta_1, \mathbf{f}, \mathbf{f}' \rangle} \tau^A$, we conclude that there exists τ^B such that $\sigma_1^B \xrightarrow{\langle t - \delta_1, \mathbf{f}, \mathbf{f}' \rangle} \tau^B$. Thus, at state σ^B, B can wait for a total of t and take a transition to τ^B, such that $\mathcal{EQ}(\tau^A, \tau^B) \in \mathcal{X}$, i.e., $\langle \tau^A, \tau^B \rangle \in \mathcal{R}_{\mathcal{X}}$ as desired.

Thus, the problem of checking whether a timed process A timed-simulates another process B can be reduced to computing the maximal symbolic simulation relation over the equivalence classes $\mathcal{EQ}_{A \| B}$. For this purpose, any of the existing algorithms for computing simulation (eg. see [KS90, HHK95]) can be adopted to obtain an algorithm with complexity polynomial in the size of $\mathcal{EQ}_{A \| B}$. The size of $\mathcal{EQ}_{A \| B}$ is polynomial in the number of locations and exponential in the number of clocks and the size of binary encodings of the clock constraints. This gives an exponential algorithm for checking timed simulation:

Theorem 12. *Given two timed processes A and B, the problem of checking whether A timed-simulates B is solvable in* EXPTIME.

We conjecture that EXPTIME is also a lower bound for this problem.

5 Verification Using Homomorphisms

In this section, we propose homomorphisms as an alternative way of proving timed refinement. Homomorphisms can roughly be viewed as mappings from the locations of one process to those of the other which conserve the transition structure. There are several reasons for exploring this alternative approach.

First, the algorithm of the previous section is computationally expensive, and we do not yet have good heuristics to proceed with an implementation. Second, the tool COSPAN already supports the use of homomorphisms for proving refinements for untimed systems, and thus, for us it is natural to generalize this to timed systems. Third, homomorphisms capture the user's intuition of the correspondence between the two levels, and it is desirable to make use of this knowledge[4].

For a timed process $A = \langle S, S_0, O, I, X, \alpha, \mu, E \rangle$, let A_{ut} denote the untimed transition structure obtained by removing all the clocks and the timing constraints. More precisely, let $A_{ut} = \langle S, S_0, O, I, E_{ut} \rangle$, where $\langle s, t, \chi \rangle \in E_{ut}$ iff $\langle s, t, \varphi, \chi, Y \rangle \in E$ for some φ and Y. The states of A_{ut} are locations in S and the events of A_{ut} are observation events of A. The runs of A_{ut} are called the untimed runs of A. A mapping $h : S^A \to S^B$ is said to ***preserve untimed behavior*** iff for each run $s_0 \xrightarrow{\theta_0} s_1 \xrightarrow{\theta_1} \cdots \xrightarrow{\theta_{k-1}} s_k$ of A_{ut} with $s_0 \in S_0^A$, $h(s_0) \xrightarrow{\theta_0} h(s_1) \xrightarrow{\theta_1} \cdots \xrightarrow{\theta_{k-1}} h(s_k)$ is a run of B_{ut} with $h(s_0) \in S_0^B$. The mapping h preserves untimed behavior iff h is a state homomorphism from the reachable locations of A_{ut} to B_{ut} (see [Kur94] for the definition of homomorphisms for untimed systems). h is a mapping to be supplied by the user capturing the intuition regarding the correspondence of locations at different levels. The syntax of S/R, the input language of COSPAN, allows specifications of such maps. The verifier COSPAN checks, using either an on-the-fly depth-first-search or a BDD-based symbolic search of the product of the two processes, whether the user-supplied mapping h preserves untimed behavior. Let us generalize this to timed behavior.

A mapping $h : S^A \to S^B$ is said to ***preserve timed behavior*** iff for each run $\langle s_0, \Phi_0 \rangle \xrightarrow{\gamma_0} \langle s_1, \Phi_1 \rangle \xrightarrow{\gamma_1} \cdots \xrightarrow{\gamma_{k-1}} \langle s_k, \Phi_k \rangle$ of A starting from an initial state, there exist $\Theta_0, \ldots, \Theta_k$ such that $\langle h(s_0), \Theta_0 \rangle \xrightarrow{\gamma_0} \langle h(s_1), \Theta_1 \rangle \xrightarrow{\gamma_1} \cdots \xrightarrow{\gamma_{k-1}} \langle h(s_k), \Theta_k \rangle$ is a run of B that starts from an initial state. Note that, since there is at most one edge between two locations, if there exist such $\Theta_0, \ldots, \Theta_k$, then they are uniquely determined. It is easy to show that

Proposition 13. *If $h : S^A \to S^B$ preserves timed behavior, then $A \preceq_L B$.*

Observe that for a mapping to preserve timed or untimed behavior, it must map initial locations to initial locations. We restrict our attention to such mappings.

The remaining part of this section describes a method for checking if a given mapping h preserves timed behavior. This is achieved by converting the problem to an untimed homomorphism check, which can then be performed by a tool such as COSPAN [Kur94]. The basic idea is to construct an untimed transition structure $\mathcal{R}$ in the fashion of the region automaton of [AD94]. This approach has the added advantage that we use the homomorphism checking in COSPAN as a black-box, and thus, we can use either an on-the-fly DFS or a BDD-based symbolic search.

The untimed process $\mathcal{R}$ has no outputs and the same inputs as A, with an additional input specifying the location of B. For notational convenience, an input event of $\mathcal{R}$ will be given as an input event of A together with the old and

[4] A user-given simulation relation has these properties as well, but is harder to specify.

new locations of B, s^B and t^B, denoted as $\langle \mathbf{f} + s^B, \mathbf{f}' + t^B \rangle$. The location of $\mathcal{R}$ keeps track of the location of A and the equivalence class of the clock valuations of A and B. Let $[\Phi]$ denote the equivalence class of $\equiv$ that Φ belongs to. The locations $S^{\mathcal{R}}$ of $\mathcal{R}$ are given by

$$\{\langle s^A, [\Phi^A, \Phi^B] \rangle \mid s^A \in S^A \text{ and } \Phi^A \text{ and } \Phi^B \text{ are } X^A \text{ and } X^B \text{ valuations}\} \cup \{Bad\}$$

The initial locations of $\mathcal{R}$ are all locations of the form $\langle s_0^A, [0,0] \rangle$ where $s_0^A \in S_0^A$.

Consider a sequence of (untimed) observation events $\overline{\gamma'} = \gamma'_0, \gamma'_1, \ldots, \gamma'_{k-1}$ where $\gamma'_i = \langle \mathbf{f}_i, \mathbf{f}'_i \rangle$. Note that there are many timed event sequences $\overline{\gamma} = \gamma_0, \gamma_1, \ldots, \gamma_{k-1}$ such that for all i, $\gamma_i = \langle \delta_i, \mathbf{f}_i, \mathbf{f}'_i \rangle$ for some $\delta_i > 0$. Imagine a run of timed processes A and B on $\overline{\gamma}$, where $\overline{s} = s_0^B, s_1^B, \ldots, s_k^B$ is such that s_i^B is the location of B after timed event γ_i. Each location that $\mathcal{R}$ can reach on $\overline{\gamma'}$ and $\overline{s}$ corresponds to some such $\overline{\gamma}$ and carries the information about the location that A reaches and the equivalence classes that the clock values of A and B are in.

$\mathcal{R}$ has an edge from $\langle s^A, [\Phi^A, \Phi^B] \rangle$ to $\langle t^A, [\Theta^A, \Theta^B] \rangle$ on observation event $\gamma' = \langle \mathbf{f} + s^B, \mathbf{f}' + t^B \rangle$ iff for some timed event $\gamma = \langle \delta, \mathbf{f}, \mathbf{f}' \rangle$ we have (1) $\langle s^A, \Phi^A \rangle \xrightarrow{\gamma} \langle t^A, \tilde{\Theta}^A \rangle$ and (2) $\langle s^B, \Phi^B \rangle \xrightarrow{\gamma} \langle t^B, \tilde{\Theta}^B \rangle$ for some $[\tilde{\Theta}^A, \tilde{\Theta}^B] = [\Theta^A, \Theta^B]$. $\mathcal{R}$ has a transition to location *Bad* from $\langle s^A, [\Phi^A, \Phi^B] \rangle$ on γ' if for some γ as above (1) holds for some $\tilde{\Theta}^A$ and (2) does not hold for any $\tilde{\Theta}^B$. *Bad* has a self-loop on all observation events.

By Lemma 9, the choice of the representatives from equivalence classes is immaterial. Also note that, since clock predicates on edges cannot distinguish clock valuations belonging to the same equivalence class, one need only consider values of δ that lead to distinct equivalence classes, i.e., different $[\Phi^A + \delta, \Phi^B + \delta]$.

Theorem 14. *Let h be a mapping from A to B and let $h' : (S^{\mathcal{R}} \setminus \{Bad\}) \to S^B$ given by $h'(\langle s^A, [\Phi^A, \Phi^B] \rangle) = h(s^A)$. h preserves timed behavior iff, assuming that the location of B is specified by h' at all times, (1) h' preserves untimed behavior and (2)Bad is unreachable in $\mathcal{R}$.*

Proof.($\Rightarrow$) Assume that h preserves timed behavior. Let $\overline{\gamma'} = \gamma'_0, \gamma'_1, \ldots, \gamma'_{k-1}$ be a sequence of observation events for A. We show by induction on the length of $\overline{\gamma'}$ that conditions (1) and (2) of the theorem are not violated by any run on $\overline{\gamma'}$. If $k = 0$, then both claims hold trivially. Assume that we have the desired properties for k. Consider $k+1$. By the induction assumptions on (1) and (2), observe that all runs of $\mathcal{R}$ on $\gamma'_0, \gamma'_1, \ldots, \gamma'_{k-1}$ where the location of B is given by h' must have the form $t_0, \ldots, t_k$ where $t_i = \langle s_i, [\tilde{\Phi}_i, \tilde{\Theta}_i] \rangle$. Let us take one such run. By the construction of $\mathcal{R}$ we can find runs $\langle s_0, \Phi_0 \rangle \xrightarrow{\gamma_0} \langle s_1, \Phi_1 \rangle \xrightarrow{\gamma_1} \ldots \xrightarrow{\gamma_{k-1}} \langle s_k, \Phi_k \rangle$ of A, and $\langle h(s_0), \Theta_0 \rangle \xrightarrow{\gamma_0} \langle h(s_1), \Theta_1 \rangle \xrightarrow{\gamma_1} \ldots \xrightarrow{\gamma_{k-1}} \langle h(s_k), \Theta_k \rangle$ of B such that $[\Phi_i, \Theta_i] = [\tilde{\Phi}_i, \tilde{\Theta}_i]$ for $1 \leq i \leq k$ where $\gamma_i = \langle \delta_i, \mathbf{f}_i, \mathbf{f}'_i \rangle$ for all i. Now consider γ'_k. If $\mathcal{R}$ has a transition on γ'_k, then there must exist $\gamma_k = \langle \delta_k, \mathbf{f}_k, \mathbf{f}'_k \rangle$ such that $\langle s_k, \Phi_k \rangle \xrightarrow{\gamma_k} \langle s_{k+1}, \Phi_{k+1} \rangle$. Let us pick any such transition. Since h preserves timed behavior and since h and $\gamma_0, \ldots, \gamma_{k-1}$ uniquely determine B's run up to $\langle h(s_k), \Theta_k \rangle$, we must have $\langle h(s_k), \Theta_k \rangle \xrightarrow{\gamma_k} \langle h(s_{k+1}), \Theta_{k+1} \rangle$. Thus, conditions (1) and (2) are satisfied for k as well.

($\Leftarrow$) Assume (1) and (2). Let $\gamma_0, \gamma_1, \ldots, \gamma_{k-1}$ be a timed event sequence, where $\gamma_i = \langle \delta_i, \mathbf{f}_i, \mathbf{f}'_i \rangle$ for all i. We will proceed by induction on k. For $k = 0$, ($\Leftarrow$) holds by the fact that initial locations are mapped to initial locations by h. Assume that ($\Leftarrow$) holds for k. Consider $k+1$. Let $\langle s_0, \Phi_0 \rangle \xrightarrow{\gamma_0} \langle s_1, \Phi_1 \rangle \xrightarrow{\gamma_1} \ldots \langle s_k, \Phi_k \rangle \xrightarrow{\gamma_k} \langle s_{k+1}, \Phi_{k+1} \rangle$ be a run of A. By the induction assumption there exist $\Theta_0, \ldots, \Theta_k$ such that $\langle h(s_0), \Theta_0 \rangle \xrightarrow{\gamma_0} \langle h(s_1), \Theta_1 \rangle \xrightarrow{\gamma_1} \ldots \xrightarrow{\gamma_{k-1}} \langle h(s_k), \Theta_k \rangle$ is a run of B. Then, by (2) and the construction of $\mathcal{R}$, $t_0 \xrightarrow{\gamma'_0} t_1 \xrightarrow{\gamma'_1} \ldots \xrightarrow{\gamma'_{k-1}} t_k$ is in $\mathcal{R}$, where $\gamma'_i = \langle \mathbf{f}_i, \mathbf{f}'_i \rangle$ and $t_i = \langle s_i, [\Phi_i, \Theta_i] \rangle$ for all i, and the location of B is specified by h'. Since $\langle s_k, \Phi_k \rangle \xrightarrow{\gamma_k} \langle s_{k+1}, \Phi_{k+1} \rangle$ in A, by the construction of $\mathcal{R}$, $t_k \xrightarrow{\gamma'_k} t_{k+1}$ for some t_{k+1}, while the location of B changes to $h(s_{k+1})$ from $h(s_k)$. By (2), *Bad* is unreachable from t_k in this case. Then, by the construction of $\mathcal{R}$ and (1), there must exist Θ_{k+1} such that $\langle h(s_k), \Theta_k \rangle \xrightarrow{\gamma_k} \langle h(s_{k+1}), \Theta_{k+1} \rangle$, which is what was required.

The size of $\mathcal{R}$ is exponential in the number of clocks in A and B and the constants used in the timing predicates, and linear in $|S_A \times S_B|$. The complexity of checking (1) and (2) in the theorem is then linear in the reachable part of $\mathcal{R}$.

Implementation and Modular Verification Example. We have implemented an algorithm within the COSPAN [Kur94] system to construct $\mathcal{R}$ from A and B. COSPAN supports timing verification and homomorphism checks (see [AK96] for an overview). Our implementation integrates these two capabilities. Given $\mathcal{R}$ and B, conditions (1) and (2) of Theorem 14 can be checked simultaneously by COSPAN by an on-the-fly search. If (1) fails, this points to the fact that h does not preserve untimed behavior in the reachable parts of A and B. If (2) fails, on the other hand, then B can not follow A due to timing constraints.

We applied the assumption-guarantee reasoning paradigm and the homomorphism checking algorithm described above to the verification of an asynchronous circuit: the Seitz queue element given in Figure 3. The Seitz queue element is a self-timed circuit that constitutes one stage of a FIFO queue. It was studied in detail in [Rok93]. The functioning of this circuit depends critically on the ranges of gate delays: if the deviation of the gate delays from the specified values exceeds 20%, the circuit does not function correctly [Rok93]. We model each gate by a timed process. Each such process involves one clock, except for gates marked "H" which can pass one hazardous pulse (see [Rok93]), which involve two clocks each. This is not necessarily the most efficient way of modeling this circuit. The main purpose of this example was to demonstrate the techniques that we proposed for assumption-guarantee reasoning and homomorphism checks.

The circuit can be viewed as consisting of four blocks. The block marked "input stage" is responsible for passing on to the rest of the circuit the request for new data to be read in, and signaling an acknowledge to the requester when the queue element is ready to receive the data. Similarly, "output stage" signals a request for passing on the data to the circuit connected to "reqout", and when this request is acknowledged and data passed on, signals to the rest of the circuit that new data can be read in. The "center left" and "center right" stages are responsible for storing the input data and passing it to the output, and isolating

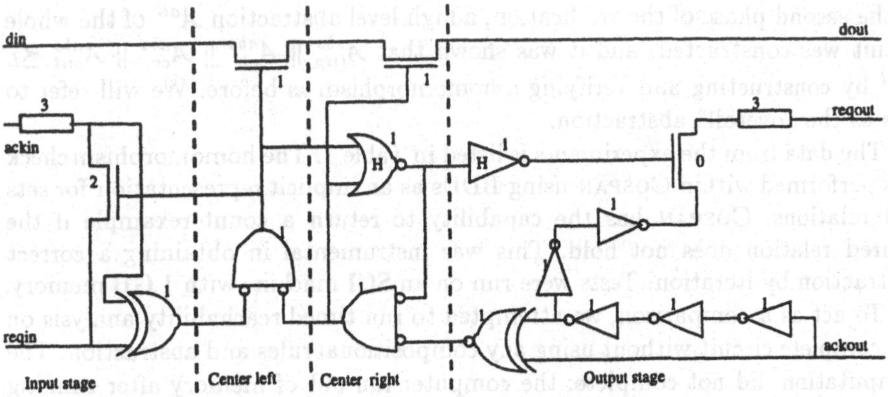

Fig. 3. The Seitz queue element. The delay for each component is indicated next to it.

the stored data from the data that is requested to be input. The timed process for each block consisted of the composition of the timed processes for its gates. Let $\mathcal{A}_{inp}$, $\mathcal{A}_{cl}$, $\mathcal{A}_{cr}$ and $\mathcal{A}_{out}$ be the timed processes describing the input, center left, center right and output stages respectively.

The verification consisted of two phases. In the first phase, an abstraction for each circuit block was constructed by hand. Let these be denoted by $\mathcal{A}_{inp}^{abs}$, $\mathcal{A}_{cl}^{abs}$, $\mathcal{A}_{cr}^{abs}$ and $\mathcal{A}_{out}^{abs}$. These abstractions described the qualitative functioning of each block, and hid the information about particular signals. In other words, the abstract processes encapsulated the "interface timing behavior" of each block. Untimed state homomorphisms were specified and it was verified as described above that each circuit block is an implementation of its abstraction. For this, we used the assumption-guarantee rule of Proposition 8. For each block, we showed that $\mathcal{A} \preceq_L \mathcal{A}^{abs}$ in the context of the abstractions of the rest of the circuit blocks. For instance, for the input stage we showed

$$\mathcal{A}_{inp} \parallel \mathcal{A}_{cl}^{abs} \parallel \mathcal{A}_{cr}^{abs} \parallel \mathcal{A}_{out}^{abs} \;\preceq_L\; \mathcal{A}_{inp}^{abs} \parallel \mathcal{A}_{cl}^{abs} \parallel \mathcal{A}_{cr}^{abs} \parallel \mathcal{A}_{out}^{abs} \qquad (1)$$

Since the state space of the composition of the abstractions was too big, we actually showed

$$\mathcal{A}_{inp} \parallel \mathcal{A}_{inp}^{env} \;\preceq_L\; \mathcal{A}_{inp}^{abs} \parallel \mathcal{A}_{inp}^{env} \qquad (2)$$

where $\mathcal{A}_{inp}^{env}$ is a timed process that incorporates the information about $\mathcal{A}_{cl}^{abs} \parallel \mathcal{A}_{cr}^{abs} \parallel \mathcal{A}_{out}^{abs}$ that is necessary for proving (2). We then verified

$$\mathcal{A}_{cl}^{abs} \parallel \mathcal{A}_{cr}^{abs} \parallel \mathcal{A}_{out}^{abs} \;\preceq_L\; \mathcal{A}_{inp}^{env} \qquad (3)$$

With some manipulation, we can infer (1) from (2) and (3) by Propositions 5 and 6. The same methodology was used for each of the circuit blocks. In some cases, when checking the equivalent of (3) it was possible to "free" some of the processes on the left hand side, i.e., disregard their transition structures and consider them as processes that pose no restriction on their inputs and outputs. This was useful in reducing the computation involved in checking (3). The conclusion from the first phase was that

$$\mathcal{A}_{inp} \parallel \mathcal{A}_{cl} \parallel \mathcal{A}_{cr} \parallel \mathcal{A}_{out} \;\preceq_L\; \mathcal{A}_{inp}^{abs} \parallel \mathcal{A}_{cl}^{abs} \parallel \mathcal{A}_{cr}^{abs} \parallel \mathcal{A}_{out}^{abs}$$

In the second phase of the verification, a high level abstraction $\mathcal{A}^{all}$ of the whole circuit was constructed, and it was shown that $\mathcal{A}^{abs}_{inp} \parallel \mathcal{A}^{abs}_{cl} \parallel \mathcal{A}^{abs}_{cr} \parallel \mathcal{A}^{abs}_{out} \preceq_L \mathcal{A}^{all}$ by constructing and verifying a homomorphism as before. We will refer to this as the "overall" abstraction.

The data from the experiments is listed in Table 1. The homomorphism check was performed within COSPAN using BDDs as an implicit representation for sets and relations. COSPAN has the capability to return a counterexample if the desired relation does not hold. This was instrumental in obtaining a correct abstraction by iteration. Tests were run on an SGI machine with 1 GB memory.

To act as a comparison, we attempted to run timed reachability analysis on the complete circuit without using any compositional rules and abstraction. The computation did not complete: the computer ran out of memory after running for several hours.

	Num. of clocks	Largest timing constant	Num. of loc.s of $\mathcal{R}$ (in thousands)	BDD nodes (in thousands)	CPU time (seconds)
Input	6	32	.24	15	39
Input (Env)	3	12	6	13	15
Center Left	11	22	18	131	403
Center Right	11	22	19	142	4879
Center (Env)	3	32	.12	7	30
Output	8	22	478	235	1029
Output (Env)	3	12	4.9	15	16
Overall	9	32	101	262	8115

Table 1. (Env) denotes the verification corresponding to equation (3). The same environment abstraction was used for both center blocks. Since timing constants must be integers, a 20% variation in a gate delay of k is represented by specifying the delay to be between $5k$ and $6k$.

6 Conclusion and Future Work

We proposed a framework for hierarchical reasoning about real-time systems. Our framework supports modular and compositional verification rules. We proved that the problem of checking for timed simulation relations is decidable. On the application side, we generalized the notion of state homomorphisms to timed processes, and gave an algorithm to check if a given map between the locations of two processes preserves timed behavior. The proposed algorithm was implemented in COSPAN, and as a case study, we dealt with the Seitz queue circuit.

Our experience was that it can be difficult to specify a correct homomorphism and one usually has to go through several iterations. Therefore, it would be valuable to have the capability to check for timed simulation relations without the user needing to provide the relation. The only concern is that such an algorithm may be too complex. Heuristics can be devised for certain application domains.

The verification method described in Section5 combines the region automaton approach for timing verification and homomorphism checking for the verification of abstractions. In principle, other methods for performing these tasks could be combined in a similar fashion, and may yield more efficient algorithms.

We believe that our work will be useful in applications such as asynchronous circuits and hardware software co-design, where abstract descriptions of systems necessarily include timing information.

References

[AD94] R. Alur and D.L. Dill. A theory of timed automata. *Theoretical Computer Science*, 126:183–235, 1994.

[AH96] R. Alur and T.A. Henzinger. Reactive modules. In *Proceedings of the 11th IEEE Symposium on Logic in Computer Science*, 1996.

[AK96] R. Alur and R.P. Kurshan. Timing analysis in COSPAN. In *Hybrid Systems III*, LNCS 1066, pages 220-231, Springer-Verlag, 1996.

[AL91] M. Abadi and L. Lamport. An old-fashioned recipe for real time. In *Real-Time: Theory in Practice, REX Workshop*, LNCS 600, pages 1–27. Springer-Verlag, 1991.

[AL93] M. Abadi and L. Lamport. Composing specifications. *ACM TOPLAS*, 15(1):73–132, 1993.

[DOY94] C. Daws, A. Olivero, and S. Yovine. Verifying ET-LOTOS programs with KRONOS. In *Formal Description Techniques VII, Proceedings of FORTE'94*, pages 227–242, 1994.

[GL94] O. Grümberg and D.E. Long. Model checking and modular verification. *ACM Transactions on Programming Languages and Systems*, 16(3):843–871, 1994.

[GSSL94] R. Gawlick, R. Segala, J. Sogaard-Andersen, and N. Lynch. Liveness in timed and untimed systems. In *Automata, Languages, and Programming, Proceedings of the 21st ICALP*, LNCS 820, pages 166–177, Springer-Verlag 1994.

[HHK95] M.R. Henzinger, T.A. Henzinger, and P.W. Kopke. Computing simulations on finite and infinite graphs. In *Proceedings of the 36th IEEE Symposium on Foundations of Computer Science*, pages 453–462, 1995.

[KS90] P. Kanellakis and S.A. Smolka. CCS expressions, finite state processes, and three problems of equivalence. *Information and Computation*, 86(1):43–68, 1990.

[Kur94] R.P. Kurshan. *Computer-aided Verification of Coordinating Processes: the automata-theoretic approach.* Princeton University Press, 1994.

[LA92] N.A. Lynch and H. Attiya. Using mappings to prove timing properties. *Distributed Computing*, 6:121–139, 1992.

[LPY95] K. Larsen, P. Pettersson, and W. Yi. Compositional and symbolic model-checking of real-time systems. In *Proceedings of the 16th IEEE Real-Time Systems Symposium*, 1995.

[LT87] N.A. Lynch and M. Tuttle. Hierarchical correctness proofs for distributed algorithms. In *Proceedings of the Seventh ACM Symposium on Principles of Distributed Computing*, pages 137–151, 1987.

[Rok93] T. Rokicki. *Representing and modeling digital circuits.* PhD thesis, Stanford University, 1993.

[Sha92] A.U. Shankar. A simple assertional proof system for real-time systems. In *Proceedings of the 13th IEEE Real-Time Systems Symposium*, pages 167–176, 1992.

[Č92] K. Čerāns. Decidability of bisimulation equivalence for parallel timer processes. In *Proceedings of the Fourth Workshop on Computer-Aided Verification*, LNCS 663, pages 302–315, Springer-Verlag, 1992.

Towards Automatic Temporal Logic Verification of Value Passing Process Algebra Using Abstract Interpretation*

Alessandro Fantechi[1], Stefania Gnesi[2], Diego Latella[3]

[1] Universita' di Firenze, Dipartimento di Sistemi e Informatica, Via S.Marta 3, 50139 Firenze - email:fantechi@dsi.ing.unifi.it

[2] C.N.R., Istituto di Elaborazione dell'Informazione, Via S. Maria 46, 56126 Pisa - email:gnesi@iei.pi.cnr.it

[3] C.N.R, Istituto CNUCE, Via S. Maria 36, 56126 Pisa - email:d.latella@cnuce.cnr.it

Abstract. In this paper we present an abstract model of process semantics, Abstract Trace Semantics, which is built on top of an abstract interpretation for (the Abstract Data Types part of) LOTOS. We use it as a model for an abstract interpretation of a linear time temporal logics. Both Abstract Trace Semantics and the abstract interpretation of the satisfiability relation are proven correct w.r.t. their concrete counterparts. The main advantage of the proposed approach is that it makes automatic model checking applicable also to full *value passing* process algebras. Currently, model checking is applied only to process algebraic specifications where only synchronization is supported (or, equivalently, value passing is restricted to data types which must be finite). By means of abstract interpretation we can reduce the infinite branching of labeled transition systems, which is due to infinite data types, to finite branching. In this way we can completely automate the verification that a formula is satisfied by a process in the abstract domain. When the formula is satisfied by the process in the abstract domain, then the correctness theorem guarantees that indeed the formula holds for the process.

1 Introduction

In [13] a technique for the *automatic* derivation of an abstract interpretation domain for (the Abstract Data Types part of) LOTOS specifications has been defined. The abstract interpretation domain is composed of (finite) approximations of the *sets of possible values* of LOTOS data expressions. In this paper we present an abstract model of process semantics, Abstract Trace Semantics,

* The work presented in this paper has been partially funded by "Progetto Coordinato C.N.R.: Metodologie e Strumenti di Analisi, Verifica e Validazione per Sistemi Software Affidabili."

which is built on top of the above mentioned abstract interpretation domain. This model is an abstraction of Trace Semantics [15] which is a model suitable for linear time temporal logics. Consequently, we give an abstract interpretation of the satisfiability relation for a simple linear temporal logic of processes using Abstract Trace Semantics. The abstract interpretation of the satisfiability relation is proven sound: whenever its result is positive it is guaranteed that the formula is satisfied by the process. We think that our model is attractive because, when combined with *automatic* model checking by means of the derivation of a finite state automaton for the abstract traces of processes, it opens the way for completely automatic partial verification of FULL LOTOS specifications. Currently, automatic verification via model checking is usually confined to BASIC LOTOS specifications [8, 14], i.e. specifications without abstract data types. This is so because of the extra "infinity dimension" which comes up from abstract data types. On the other hand, current approaches to the application of abstract interpretation to process verification usually require that the abstract domain is built by means of "ad hoc" techniques [4, 6].

In Section 2 the notation used in this paper will be briefly outlined. Section 3 shortly introduces our sample process algebra, with its Trace Semantics. The abstract semantics of specifications is discussed in Section 4. Section 5 introduces the simple temporal logic used in this paper. Its abstract interpretation is given in Section 6. A final discussion can be found in Section 7. A detailed version of the present paper is available [10], where all formal definitions and detailed transformational proofs can be found.

2 Notation

In this paper we use a *FunMath*-like notation [3], as specified below. Function application is denoted simply by juxtaposition and it is left-associative. Double square brackets $[\![\_]\!]$ are used for syntactical arguments. The *domain* of the function f, i.e. the set of values in which f is defined, is denoted by $\mathcal{D}f$; its range is denoted by $\mathcal{R}f$. The set of the subsets of X is denoted by $\wp X$. Furthermore, standard set theory notation will also be used freely.

Curried functions are used: for a function $f : \Theta_1 \times \Theta_2 \rightarrow \Theta_3$ its curried version f' is defined as $f' : \Theta_1 \rightarrow \Theta_2 \rightarrow \Theta_3$ with $f'ab = f(a, b)$. Θ_1, Θ_2, Θ_3 denote type variables, so that $\_'$ is *polymorphic*. In this paper $\Theta, \Theta_1, \ldots, \Theta'$, etc. stand for type variables in polymorphic function definitions.

Partial application provides a natural way for dealing with higher-order functions. This is possible also for infix operators. So, for instance $(+3)$ is the function which for each number n returns the number $n + 3$. Function composition is denoted by $\circ$: $(f \circ g)x = f(gx)$. Function extension is denoted by $\_[\_/\_]$:

$$\begin{aligned}
&\textbf{def}\ \ _[_/_] \quad : \quad (\Theta_1 \rightarrow \Theta_2) \rightarrow \Theta_1 \rightarrow \Theta_2 \rightarrow \Theta_1 \rightarrow \Theta_2 \\
&\textbf{with}\ f[v_2/v_1]v = v_2,\ \textbf{if}\ v = v_1 \\
&\qquad\qquad\qquad\quad = fv,\ \textbf{otherwise}
\end{aligned}$$

An n-tuple denotes a function with domain $\{0, \ldots, n-1\}$ for n in Nat. For example $(a, (3, 4), c)$ denotes the function of type $\{0, 1, 2\} \rightarrow \{a, (3, 4), c\}$ such that:

$(a,(3,4),c)0 = a$, $(a,(3,4),c)1 = (3,4)$ and $(a,(3,4),c)2 = c$. Given a set T, the set of n-tuples over T is denoted by T^n. For $n = 0$ we have $T^0 = \{\epsilon\}$ where ϵ is the empty tuple, i.e. the tuple with empty domain. $T^* = \bigcup_{n \geq 0} T^n$ is the set of all finite *traces* over T. Given a trace σ, the trace obtained by shifting σ by j steps ahead, for j in Nat, is denoted by $\sigma^{j\cdot\cdot}$ and it is obviously defined as $\sigma^{j\cdot\cdot} = \sigma \circ (+j)$. Modeling tuples as functions helps in keeping the notation for tuple/trace manipulation functions relatively simple.

The notation $x : X.E$ denotes typed lambda abstraction, i.e. the function which maps x (in X) to E. X is an expression denoting a type. Universal and existential quantifiers are defined as follows:

$$\mathbf{def}\,\forall \;:\; (\Theta \to Bool) \to Bool \;\; \mathbf{with}\; (\forall\, g) = (\mathcal{R}g = \{\mathbf{t}\})$$

$$\mathbf{def}\,\exists \;:\; (\Theta \to Bool) \to Bool \;\; \mathbf{with}\; (\exists\, g) = (\mathbf{t} \in (\mathcal{R}g))$$

So, $\forall(x : X.Px)$ can be read as the more common notation $\forall x \in X.Px$ but formally it is the application of function $\forall$ to function (abstraction) $x : X.Px$.

The above notation leads to all formulas, including logic ones, being treated in a uniform way, that is, as functions.

3 The Process Algebra

In this paper, we shall consider a process algebra which is essentially a small subset of the LOTOS specification language [1]. We choose LOTOS only for definiteness reasons since the technique we propose here can be applied to any process algebra which includes a mechanism for the specification of abstract data types. We consider a simple subset since this keeps the treatment of our technique reasonably simple: considering the full language would not add any conceptual improvement.

A LOTOS specification consists of an *abstract data types specification* part and a *behaviour* part. Here we will not go into the details on syntax and semantics of the abstract data type part, for which we refer to [1, 13].

Let Ga denote the (countable) set of LOTOS *Gates Identifiers*. Let moreover Va be the set of *Values* defined via the abstract data type part of the specification. It is assumed that for each value in Va, its *sort* is uniquely defined. The abstract syntax of the *behaviour expressions* follows:

$$\mathrm{B ::= stop} \mid (g!\mathrm{e;B}) \mid (g?\mathrm{x{:}S;B}) \mid (\mathrm{B}[\,]\mathrm{B}) \mid (\mathrm{B}|G|\mathrm{B})$$

The behaviour expression *stop* denotes the process which performs no action. The *action prefix* process $g?x : S; B$ can be engaged in any action (g, v) where $g \in Ga$ and $v \in Va$ is of sort S. After such an action occurred the process behaves like B_v. B_v is the instance of B obtained by substituting v for all the (free) occurrences of x. The process $g!e; B$ can be engaged in the action (g, v) where $g \in Ga$ and $v = \mathcal{V}[\![e]\!]\xi$ is the value of value expression e in a proper environment ξ. As stated above we will leave out the definition of $\mathcal{V}$ here. The *choice* process $B_1[\,]B_2$ behaves either like B_1 or like B_2. $B_1|G|B_2$ can perform any action which can be performed by B_1 or B_2 provided that such an action does not involve a gate $g \in G \subset Ga$. If instead gate $g \in G$ is involved, then the action can be performed only if both processes can perform it. Moreover they must perform it simultaneously, i.e. they have to synchronize on the gates in G. In the sequel, the syntactic category of behaviour expressions will be denoted by *Bex* ; *Vex* will denote the syntactic category of value expressions. In Fig. 1 there is an example of a behaviour expression and an abstract data type definition which we shall take as a working example in the sequel. Process $DM2$ computes the parity function $m2$ on any positive natural number n received as a request on gate RQ, returns the result $m2(n)$ on gate RS and stops. Moreover, if the input value is 0 the process may non-deterministically return 0 on gate $BLOB$ and stop (we have included in the functions specification also the zero- and one-tests, which will be useful later in the paper).

```
process DM2[RQ,RS,BLOB]:=
 RQ?x: Nat; RS!m2(x);stop
 []
 RQ!0; BLOB!0; stop
where
 (* Abstract Data Type Definition Part *)
 type SP_type is
 sorts Nat, Bool
 constructors
  0    :-->Nat          (* constructors for Natural Numbers *)
  s    :Nat-->Nat
  t,f  :Bool            (* constructors for Boolean Values  *)
 functions
  m2:Nat-->Nat        is_0:Nat-->Bool    is_1:Nat-->Bool
  m2(0)       = 0     is_0(0)     = t    is_1(0)        = f
  m2(s(0))    = s(0)  is_0(s(x))  = f    is_1(s(0))     = t
  m2(s(s(x))= m2(x)                      is_1(s(s(x)))  = f

 (* other, standard functions on Natural Numbers and Booleans ... *)
```

Fig. 1. A sample behaviour expression and abstract data type definition

The semantics we choose here for our process algebra is *Trace Semantics*. A process is represented by the set of its traces. A trace is a sequence of actions the process engages up to some moment in time. The choice of Trace Semantics is motivated by the fact that it is simple and suitable as a model for linear time temporal logic. It must anyway be pointed out that Trace Semantics is weak in the sense that, for instance, it does not allow us to reason about liveness properties of processes. Despite such limitations, we anyway chose traces since the main purpose of this paper is to show the key conceptual ideas about how abstract interpretation could help in verification via temporal logic, rather than to present an effective tool which is useful for practical purposes.

In the following we shall give the Trace Semantics of the process algebra above in a denotational style. Before giving the formal definition of the Trace Semantics interpretation function $\mathcal{T}$ we need a number of auxiliary notions, which we introduce below.

Actions are pairs (*gate*, *value*), i.e. $Act = Ga \times Va$. We let $Tr = Act^*$ be the set of *Traces*, with σ ranging over it, and $Env = Ide \rightarrow Va$ denote the domain of *environments*, i.e. mappings from *(Value-)Identifiers* to *Values*.

Besides function $\mathcal{V}$ mentioned before, we assume a function, $\mathcal{S}$, which gives the *sort* of its data value argument. Also $\mathcal{S}$ is part of the LOTOS standard (static) semantics and then its definition will be left out here.

In the definition of the traces of the parallel composition of two processes we will use the notation $\mathcal{E}(S)$ for the set of all the elements of the sequences in set S. We recall that sequences are functions of natural numbers, so the set of elements of sequence σ is its range $\mathcal{R}\sigma$.

$$\mathbf{def}\, \mathcal{E}(\_) \ : \ \wp(\Theta^*) \rightarrow \wp\Theta \ \ \mathbf{with}\, \mathcal{E}(S) \ = \ \{x \mid \exists(\sigma : S.x \in (\mathcal{R}\sigma)\}$$

We use a *chop* operator, $\bowtie$. Essentially for sets of actions S_0 and S_1 and set of gates G, the set of "compound actions" $S_0 \bowtie_G S_1$ is built in the following way. If the same action occurs in both sets and its gate identifier belongs to G, then a compound action is created as a pair in which both elements are the action itself; otherwise, if an action occurs in S_0 (S_1) *and* its gate identifier does *not* belong to G, then a compound action is generated having such action as left (right) component, and a $\surd$ as the right (left) one. For example, we have that $\{(a,1),(b,2),(a,3),(d,1)\} \bowtie_{\{a\}} \{(a,3),(c,4),(d,1)\}$ is equal to the set $\{((a,3),(a,3)),((b,2),\surd),(\surd,(c,4)),(\surd,(d,1)),((d,1),\surd)\}$.

Given set V and given an object $\surd$ such that $\surd \notin V$, we let $\mathcal{L}V$ denote the set $\{(v,\surd) \mid v \in V\} \cup \{(\surd,v) \mid v \in V\} \cup \{(v,v) \mid v \in V\}$. The formal definition of the chop operator follows:

$$\begin{array}{ll} \mathbf{def}\ \_\bowtie\_\,\_ & : \ (\wp(Ga \times \Theta)) \times (\wp Ga) \times (\wp(Ga \times \Theta)) \rightarrow \wp(\mathcal{L}(Ga \times \Theta)) \\ \mathbf{with}\ S_0 \bowtie_G S_1 = & \{((g,v),\surd) \mid g \notin G \wedge (g,v) \in S_0\} \cup \\ & \{(\surd,(g,v)) \mid g \notin G \wedge (g,v) \in S_1\} \cup \\ & \{((g,v),(g,v)) \mid g \in G \wedge (g,v) \in S_0 \cap S_1\} \end{array}$$

Finally, two more functions, U and F, are used in the definition of the Abstract Trace Semantics. Function U below is used for recovering traces from sequences of "compound actions", by "unlabeling" them: $((a,3),(c,4),(c,10))$ is the sequence obtained as $U(((a,3),(a,3)),(\surd,(c,4)),((c,10),\surd))$.

$$\begin{array}{ll} \mathbf{def}\ U & : \ (\mathcal{L}\Theta)^* \rightarrow \Theta^* \\ \mathbf{with}\ U\sigma j & = \sigma j1, \mathbf{if}\ j \in \mathcal{D}\sigma \wedge \sigma j0 = \surd \\ & = \sigma j0, \mathbf{if}\ j \in \mathcal{D}\sigma \wedge \sigma j0 \neq \surd \end{array}$$

Notice that for a sequence σ and for $j \in \mathcal{D}\sigma$, σj is the *j-th* element of σ and if it is itself a sequence, as in the case above, that $\sigma j0$ is the first component of such an element. Similarly $U\sigma j$ is the *j-th* element of the sequence $U\sigma$.

Function F acts as a filter w.r.t. $\surd$. For $j \in \{0,1\}$ Fj deletes all the elements of its argument σ whose j-th component is $\surd$:

$$\begin{array}{ll} \textbf{def } F & : \{0,1\} \rightarrow (\mathcal{L}\Theta)^* \rightarrow (\mathcal{L}\Theta)^* \\ \textbf{with } Fj\epsilon & = \epsilon \\ \quad Fj(v \succ \sigma) & = v \succ (Fj\sigma), \textbf{if } vj \neq \surd \\ & = (Fj\sigma), \textbf{otherwise} \end{array}$$

We have that $F1(((a,3),(a,3)),(\surd,(c,4)),((b,2),\surd))$ is equal to the sequence $(((a,3),(a,3)),(\surd,(c,4)))$.

We are now ready for giving the formal definition of the Trace Semantics interpretation function $\mathcal{T}$:

Definition 1. Trace Semantics Interpretation Function

$$\begin{array}{ll} \textbf{def } \mathcal{T} & : Bex \rightarrow Env \rightarrow (\wp Tr) \\ \textbf{with } \mathcal{T}[\![stop]\!]\xi & = \{\epsilon\} \\ \quad \mathcal{T}[\![g!e;B]\!]\xi & = \{\sigma \mid \sigma 0 = (g, \mathcal{V}[\![e]\!]\xi) \wedge \sigma^{1..} \in \mathcal{T}[\![B]\!]\xi\} \cup \{\epsilon\} \\ \quad \mathcal{T}[\![g?x:S;B]\!]\xi & = \{\sigma \mid \exists (v : \mathcal{V}a.\mathcal{S}[\![v]\!] = S \wedge \sigma 0 = (g,v) \wedge \\ & \qquad \sigma^{1..} \in \mathcal{T}[\![B]\!]\xi[v/x])\} \cup \{\epsilon\} \\ \quad \mathcal{T}[\![B_0[\,]B_1]\!]\xi & = \mathcal{T}[\![B_0]\!]\xi \cup \mathcal{T}[\![B_1]\!]\xi \\ \quad \mathcal{T}[\![B_0|G|B_1]\!]\xi & = \{U\sigma \mid \sigma \in (\mathcal{E}(\mathcal{T}[\![B_0]\!]\xi) \bowtie_G \mathcal{E}(\mathcal{T}[\![B_1]\!]\xi))^* \\ & \qquad \wedge U(F0\sigma) \in \mathcal{T}[\![B_0]\!]\xi \wedge U(F1\sigma) \in \mathcal{T}[\![B_1]\!]\xi\} \end{array}$$

The first and second equations in the above definition are straightforward. In the third equation, the binding of x to v, for computing the traces of B, is taken care of by the "new" environment $\xi[v/x]$.

The semantics of parallel composition is given in essentially the same style as in [16] and resembles the temporal semantics given to LOTOS in [9]. For generating the traces of the parallel composition of B_0 with B_1 with synchronization on G, we first of all build all possible traces of compound actions from the set $S_0 \bowtie_G S_1$, where S_j is the set of the elements of the traces of B_j. From the above set we take only those traces which can be projected (via functions U and F) into the traces of B_0 and B_1. Finally we "clean up" these traces via the unlabeling function U.

The Trace Semantics of expression B is given by applying $\mathcal{T}[\![B]\!]$ to the empty environment ξ_e, i.e. the environment whose domain is empty. It is intended that B does not contain free occurrences of variables (i.e. any data variable x is within the scope of some $?x : S\_$ construct).

Definition 2. Trace Semantics

$$\textbf{def } T : Bex \rightarrow Tr \textbf{ with } T[\![B]\!] = \mathcal{T}[\![B]\!]\xi_e$$

The following result can be proven, by induction on the structure of B, in a similar way as in [16].

Theorem 3. *$T[\![B]\!]$ is the set of traces defined by the standard operational semantics of LOTOS.*

4 Abstract Interpretation of Behaviour Expressions

The key point of the Abstraction Procedure presented in [13] is to statically and *automatically* compute information on the possible values which LOTOS value expressions can evaluate to in a given specification. Abstract interpretation is used for finitely approximating the sets of those values. The level of uncertainty present in those approximations is determined by the amount of information on both the "data flow" and the behaviour of functions defined in the Abstract Data Type part of a specification which can be deduced by a static analysis of the text of the specification. In our example function $m2$ is defined on Nat. The set $\{0, s(0), s(s(\bot))\}$ can be chosen as a representation for Nat, where 0 and $s(0)$ are exactly represented and $s(s(\bot))$ represents $s(s(0)), s(s(s(0))), s(s(s(s(0))))$... Notice that the above representation is finite (it contains only three elements) and complete (every term in Nat is represented). Also, it is an abstraction of Nat (the term $s(s(\bot))$ intuitively stands for any natural number greater than 1). Moreover, it gives 0 and $s(0)$ a "special status" of distinguished elements; this is because those two terms are the only terms which occur explicitly in the text of the process definition. Starting from $\{0, s(0), s(s(\bot))\}$ we can use its power set as an abstraction for $\wp Nat$. We must keep in mind that the elements of such an abstract domain, i.e. the abstract terms, are just approximations of sets on natural numbers in the sense that not all sets are exactly represented. Some of them are only approximated by terms which represent sets in which the former are included. The empty set, i.e. the bottom of the abstract domain, denotes the undefined value, i.e. a computation which definitely fails to terminate. Any other abstract term denotes computations which may terminate and it gives information on the set of the possible values they can yield.

The abstract version $f^{\mathcal{A}}$ of a function f is a function which gives information on the possible outcomes of f when applied to sets of possible input values. $f^{\mathcal{A}}$ is defined on abstract terms and is then a finite function. Finally, the information on the possible values of value expressions is obtained via an abstract evaluation function $\widetilde{\mathcal{V}}$, which maps LOTOS value expressions into abstract terms. Both the abstract domain and the abstract version of functions are computed *automatically* from the input FULL LOTOS specification.

In the table below the abstract versions $is\_0^{\mathcal{A}}$, $is\_1^{\mathcal{A}}$ and $m2^{\mathcal{A}}$ of functions is_0, is_1 and $m2$ of our sample specification are given.

	$\emptyset$	$\{0\}$	$\{s(0)\}$	$\{s(s(\bot))\}$	$\{0, s(0)\}$	$\{0, s(s(\bot))\}$	$\{s(0), s(s(\bot))\}$	$\{0, s(0), s(s(\bot))\}$
$is\_0^{\mathcal{A}}$	$\emptyset$	$\{\mathtt{t}\}$	$\{\mathtt{f}\}$	$\{\mathtt{f}\}$	$\{\mathtt{t},\mathtt{f}\}$	$\{\mathtt{t},\mathtt{f}\}$	$\{\mathtt{f}\}$	$\{\mathtt{t},\mathtt{f}\}$
$is\_1^{\mathcal{A}}$	$\emptyset$	$\{\mathtt{f}\}$	$\{\mathtt{t}\}$	$\{\mathtt{f}\}$	$\{\mathtt{t},\mathtt{f}\}$	$\{\mathtt{f}\}$	$\{\mathtt{t},\mathtt{f}\}$	$\{\mathtt{t},\mathtt{f}\}$
$m2^{\mathcal{A}}$	$\emptyset$	$\{0\}$	$\{s(0)\}$	$\{0, s(0)\}$	$\{0, s(0)\}$	$\{0, s(0)\}$	$\{0, s(0)\}$	$\{0, s(0)\}$

It is interesting to point out the kind of *don't know* information provided by the abstract version of predicates. This information is represented by the abstract term $\{\mathtt{t}, \mathtt{f}\}$. So, for instance, $is\_0^{\mathcal{A}}(\{0, s(0), s(s(\bot))\}) = \{\mathtt{t}, \mathtt{f}\}$ means that no information can be statically inferred on the behaviour of the test on 0 when no information is available on the argument which the test is applied to, except that it is a natural number. On the other hand, from $is\_0^{\mathcal{A}}(\{s(0), s(s(\bot))\}) = \{\mathtt{f}\}$ we know that the test on 0 will yield $\mathbf{f}$ on any number greater than 0. This kind of uncertainty, once generated by means of an abstract evaluation of what textually occurs in the LOTOS specification is propagated through the abstractions of the functions. Finally, it is worth noting that $m2^{\mathcal{A}}(\{0, s(0), s(s(\perp))\}) = \{0, s(0)\}$ essentially tells us which is the range of $m2$.

4.1 Abstract Trace Semantics

The Abstract Trace Semantics of a behaviour expression is a set of abstract traces. These abstract traces are traces from which it must be possible to recover all the traces in the Trace Semantics of the behaviour expression. Notice that we do not require that the traces of the Trace Semantics be *the only ones* which can be generated from the abstract ones, but only that *all of them* can indeed be generated. In this sense we can speak of the set of abstract traces as being an *approximation* of the set of concrete ones.

Abstract traces $\widetilde{Tr} = (\widetilde{Act})^*$ are traces made out of abstract actions. An abstract action is a pair (*gate, abstract value*), i.e. $\widetilde{Act} = Ga \times \widetilde{Va}$. Abstract values have been briefly discussed above. They are defined in [13], where their domain is called ABS; here we rename it $\widetilde{Va}$, just for notational uniformity. We let $\tilde{\sigma}$ range over $\widetilde{Tr}$. $\widetilde{Env} = Ide \rightarrow \widetilde{Va}$ denotes the domain of abstract environments.

Before giving the formal definition of the Abstract Trace Semantics interpretation function $\widetilde{\mathcal{T}}$ we discuss in some detail how we deal with parallel composition and the implications on the abstract semantics of action-prefix.

Let us first consider $\widetilde{\mathcal{T}}[\![g!e; B]\!]\rho$ and, for the sake of simplicity, let us assume e is a variable x. A straightforward definition of $\widetilde{\mathcal{T}}[\![g!x; B]\!]\rho$ could have been the following:

$$\widetilde{\mathcal{T}}[\![g!x; B]\!]\rho = \{\tilde{\sigma} \mid \tilde{\sigma}0 = (g, \widetilde{\mathcal{V}}[\![x]\!]\rho) \wedge \tilde{\sigma}^{1\cdot\cdot} \in \widetilde{\mathcal{T}}[\![B]\!]\rho\} \cup \{\epsilon\}$$

Such a definition would not work when using it in conjunction with parallel composition. We show this by means of an example. Suppose we want to compute $\widetilde{\mathcal{T}}[\![g!x_1; B_1|\{g\}|g!x_2; B_2]\!]\rho$, under the assumption $\rho x_1 = \{0, s(s(\perp))\}$, $\rho x_2 = \{s(0), s(s(\perp))\}$. Any non-empty trace $\tilde{\sigma}$ in $\widetilde{\mathcal{T}}[\![g!x_1; B_1]\!]\rho$ would start with the abstract event $(g, \{0, s(s(\perp))\})$ and continue with some abstract trace. As it will be made clear and formalized later, such an abstract trace would represent traces starting with actions (g, v) where v is one of the *possible values* of x in the particular context ρ, that is any natural number different from 1. Similarly, non-empty traces of $g!x_2; B_2$ will start with events involving values greater than or equal to 1. According to the LOTOS standard semantics, if synchronization takes place, it will happen on any of those values which *both* x_1 and x_2 can evaluate to. Moreover, there is also the possibility that synchronization will *not* take place, because the actual value of x_1 is different from that of x_2. Using our abstract interpretation function $\widetilde{\mathcal{V}}$ we could easily express a correct approximation of the set of values on which synchronization may take place as $\widetilde{\mathcal{V}}[\![x_1]\!]\rho \cap \widetilde{\mathcal{V}}[\![x_2]\!]\rho$, that is $\{s(s(\perp))\}$, which represents the set of all values greater than 1. This would be fine since it safely represents what the LOTOS semantics requires when synchronization occurs in the parallel composition of the two behaviour expressions. Unfortunately there is a technical problem: after synchronization has taken place, the *new* abstract value for both x_1 and x_2 must be recorded in some environment for the rest of the computation. In other words the abstract traces of *both* B_1 and B_2 must be computed using an environment ρ' such that $\rho' x_1 = \rho' x_2 = \{s(s(\perp))\}$. The problem is that the environment used for the computation for the abstract traces of, say, B_1 in $g!x_1; B_1$ is ρ, which is *different* from ρ'. The constraint imposed by the synchronization is obviously not known "at the moment" of computing $\widetilde{\mathcal{T}}[\![g!x_1; B_1]\!]\rho$ but it will be imposed when computing the traces of the parallel composition. In other words parallel composition should "modify" the environment ρ into ρ' (notice that this holds also for "output" action-prefix, as in our example). On the other hand, the compositionality of definition of $\widetilde{\mathcal{T}}$ requires that when the traces of the parallel composition are computed, the traces of B_1 have already been computed, by using ρ, and they are no longer easily "accessible" for modification. One possible solution could be to redefine the semantic domain of traces in order to make them parameterized on synchronization values. We found it easier to adopt a solution which we shall illustrate by means of the same example. We define $\widetilde{\mathcal{T}}[\![g!x_1; B_1]\!]\rho$ in such a way that it contains all prefixes of the traces in the following set:

$$\begin{array}{l}\{\widetilde{\sigma} \mid \widetilde{\sigma}0 = (g, \{0, s(s(\perp))\}) \wedge \widetilde{\sigma}^{1\cdots} \in \widetilde{\mathcal{T}}[\![B_1]\!]\rho[\{0, s(s(\perp))\}/x_1]\} \cup \\ \{\widetilde{\sigma} \mid \widetilde{\sigma}0 = (g, \{0\}) \wedge \widetilde{\sigma}^{1\cdots} \in \widetilde{\mathcal{T}}[\![B_1]\!]\rho[\{0\}/x_1]\} \cup \\ \{\widetilde{\sigma} \mid \widetilde{\sigma}0 = (g, \{s(s(\perp))\}) \wedge \widetilde{\sigma}^{1\cdots} \in \widetilde{\mathcal{T}}[\![B_1]\!]\rho[\{s(s(\perp))\}/x_1]\}\end{array}$$

that is, we *add* to the traces generated by using the abstract value of x_1, $\widetilde{\mathcal{V}}[\![x_1]\!]\rho$, all those traces generated by considering non-empty abstract values included in $\widetilde{\mathcal{V}}[\![x_1]\!]\rho$. First of all notice that this results only in introducing redundancy to the Abstract Trace Semantics of behaviour expressions while keeping it correct w.r.t. Trace Semantics. This will be guaranteed by a theorem shown later in this section. Intuitively, in our example we are adding to the traces starting by any natural number different from 1 those starting by 0 and those starting by any natural different from 0 or 1 (and with proper continuations). As long as we are interested in properties of *all* traces of a process, which *is* the case of *linear* temporal logics, the soundness of the abstract satisfiability relation (which we shall define later) will not be hampered. The nice advantage of adding all these extra-traces is that now the definition of the abstract semantics of parallel composition looks very much like that of the Trace Semantics. In fact, with respect to data values, synchronization at the abstract level is not represented by the intersection of the abstract values but exactly by equality, as in the concrete case. In our working example, for $\widetilde{\mathcal{T}}[\![g!x_2; B_2]\!]\rho$ we get all the prefixes of the traces in the following set:

$$\begin{array}{l}\{\widetilde{\sigma} \mid \widetilde{\sigma}0 = (g, \{s(0), s(s(\perp))\}) \wedge \widetilde{\sigma}^{1\cdots} \in \widetilde{\mathcal{T}}[\![B_2]\!]\rho[\{s(0), s(s(\perp))\}/x_2]\} \cup \\ \{\widetilde{\sigma} \mid \widetilde{\sigma}0 = (g, \{s(0)\}) \wedge \widetilde{\sigma}^{1\cdots} \in \widetilde{\mathcal{T}}[\![B_2]\!]\rho[\{s(0)\}/x_2]\} \cup \\ \{\widetilde{\sigma} \mid \widetilde{\sigma}0 = (g, \{s(s(\perp))\}) \wedge \widetilde{\sigma}^{1\cdots} \in \widetilde{\mathcal{T}}[\![B_2]\!]\rho[\{s(s(\perp))\}/x_2]\}\end{array}$$

and then in the parallel composition only traces starting with $(g, \{s(s(\bot))\})$ (and proper continuations) will appear.

The case in which synchronization does not take place is covered by the fact that Trace Semantics is prefix closed.

Up to now, we considered only the case in which the value expression involved in an action prefix is just a variable. In order to extend the above reasoning to the case in which we have a general expression e, we have to use the notion of constrained environments for abstract values. Given an expression e, whose abstract value is a under the abstract environment ρ, we are interested in all those abstract environments ψ which bind all variables occurring in e to non-empty abstract values which are smaller than or equal to the values they are bound to by ρ, and such that the value of e under ψ is still a. We write it as $\psi \preceq_e^a \rho$, to be read as "ψ constrained by a via e under ρ":

$$
\begin{array}{ll}
\textbf{def } \_\preceq_{\_}^{\_}\_ : & \widetilde{Env} \to Vex \to \widetilde{Va} \to \widetilde{Env} \to Bool \\
\textbf{with } \psi \preceq_e^a \rho = \widetilde{\mathcal{V}}[\![e]\!]\psi = a \wedge & \\
& \forall (x : Ide\, .(x \in Var[\![e]\!] \Rightarrow \emptyset \subset \psi x \subseteq \rho x) \wedge \\
& \qquad (x \notin Var[\![e]\!] \Rightarrow \psi x = \rho x))
\end{array}
$$

where $Var[\![e]\!]$ denotes the set of *variables* of value expression $e \in Vex$. The following example will clarify the meaning of $\psi \preceq_e^a \rho$. Let's suppose we add the following definition to the abstract data types part of our sample specification:

```
eq: Nat x Nat --> Bool
 eq(0,0)          = t
 eq(0,s(x))       = f
 eq(s(x),0)       = f
 eq(s(x),s(y)) = eq(x,y)
```

The abstraction procedure produces the function [4] $eq^{\mathcal{A}}$ such that $eq^{\mathcal{A}}(x,y)$ evaluates to $\{\mathtt{t}\}(resp.\{\mathtt{t},\mathtt{f}\})$ if x and y are equal and they both evaluate to $\{0\}$ or $\{s(0)\}(resp.\{s(s(\bot))\})$. Otherwise, $eq^{\mathcal{A}}(x,y)$ evaluates to $\{\mathtt{f}\}$. Let now ρ be the abstract environment defined only on x and y and such that $\rho\ x = \{0, s(0)\}$ and $\rho\ y = \{0, s(0), s(s(\bot))\}$. The only environments ψ such that $\psi \preceq_{eq(x,y)}^{\{\mathtt{t}\}} \rho$ are ψ_1 and ψ_2 which are defined only on x and y and such that: $\psi_1 x = \psi_1 y = \{0\}$ and $\psi_2 x = \psi_2 y = \{s(0)\}$.

The formal definition of the Abstract Trace Semantics interpretation function $\widetilde{\mathcal{T}}$ follows:

---

[4] We give the values of $eq^{\mathcal{A}}$ only for singletons, since $eq^{\mathcal{A}}(a_1 \cup a_2) = eq^{\mathcal{A}}(a_1) \cup eq^{\mathcal{A}}(a_2)$ as discussed in [13].

Definition 4. Abstract Trace Semantics Interpretation Function

$$\begin{array}{ll}
\textbf{def}\ \widetilde{\mathcal{T}} & : Bex \rightarrow \widetilde{Env} \rightarrow (\wp \widetilde{Tr}) \\
\textbf{with}\ \widetilde{\mathcal{T}}[\![stop]\!]\rho & = \{\epsilon\} \\
\widetilde{\mathcal{T}}[\![g!e; B]\!]\rho & = \{\widetilde{\sigma} \mid \exists (a : \widetilde{V}a, \psi : \widetilde{Env}.\widetilde{\sigma}0 = (g,a) \wedge \emptyset \subset a \subseteq \widetilde{\mathcal{V}}[\![e]\!]\rho \wedge \\
& \quad \widetilde{\sigma}^{1..} \in \widetilde{\mathcal{T}}[\![B]\!]\psi \wedge \psi \preceq_e^a \rho)\} \cup \{\epsilon\} \\
\widetilde{\mathcal{T}}[\![g?x : S; B]\!]\rho & = \{\widetilde{\sigma} \mid \exists (a : \widetilde{V}a \setminus \emptyset . S[\![a]\!] = S \wedge \widetilde{\sigma}0 = (g,a) \wedge \\
& \quad \widetilde{\sigma}^{1..} \in \widetilde{\mathcal{T}}[\![B]\!]\rho[a/x])\} \cup \{\epsilon\} \\
\widetilde{\mathcal{T}}[\![B_0 [\!] B_1]\!]\rho & = \widetilde{\mathcal{T}}[\![B_0]\!]\rho \cup \widetilde{\mathcal{T}}[\![B_1]\!]\rho \\
\widetilde{\mathcal{T}}[\![B_0|G|B_1]\!]\rho & = \{U\sigma \mid \widetilde{\sigma} \in (\mathcal{E}(\widetilde{\mathcal{T}}[\![B_0]\!]\rho) \bowtie_G \mathcal{E}(\widetilde{\mathcal{T}}[\![B_1]\!]\rho))^* \wedge \\
& \quad U(F0\widetilde{\sigma}) \in \widetilde{\mathcal{T}}[\![B_0]\!]\rho \wedge U(F1\widetilde{\sigma}) \in \widetilde{\mathcal{T}}[\![B_1]\!]\rho\}
\end{array}$$

The Abstract Trace Semantics of an expression B is given by applying $\widetilde{\mathcal{T}}[\![B]\!]$ to the empty abstract environment ρ_e.

Definition 5. Abstract Trace Semantics

$$\textbf{def}\ \widetilde{\mathcal{T}} : Bex \rightarrow \widetilde{Tr}\ \textbf{with}\ \widetilde{\mathcal{T}}[\![B]\!] = \widetilde{\mathcal{T}}[\![B]\!]\,\rho_e$$

As an example, the set of the abstract traces of process $DM2$ produced by this semantics is composed by all and only the prefixes of the following sequences

$((RQ, \{0\}), (BLOB, \{0\}))$
$((RQ, \{0\}), (RS, \{0\}))$
$((RQ, \{s(0)\}), (RS, \{s(0)\}))$
$((RQ, a_1), (RS, a_2))$ where
$a_1 \in \{\{s(s(\perp))\}, \{0, s(0)\}, \{0, s(s(\perp))\}, \{s(0), s(s(\perp))\}, \{0, s(0), s(s(\perp))\}\}$
$a_2 \in \{\{0\}, \{s(0)\}, \{0, s(0)\}\}$

4.2 Correctness of the Abstract Trace Semantics

In this section $\widetilde{\mathcal{T}}$ is shown correct with respect to the concrete trace semantics $\mathcal{T}$. In [13] a notion of correctness has been formalized by means of a relation $\mathcal{C}$ such that $a\ \mathcal{C}\ v$ if and only if $v \in (\gamma\ a)$, where $\gamma\ a$ is the set of concrete values represented by abstract value a.

In this section we extend function γ to traces (γ_t) and relation $\mathcal{C}$ to traces ($\mathcal{C}_t$), sets of traces ($\mathcal{C}_s$) and environments ($\mathcal{C}_{env}$). These extensions are straightforward.

Definition 6. Trace Concretization Function

$$\begin{array}{ll}
\textbf{def}\ \gamma_t & : \widetilde{Tr} \rightarrow (\wp Tr) \\
\textbf{with}\ \gamma_t\ \epsilon & = \{\epsilon\} \\
\gamma_t\ ((g,a) \succ \widetilde{\sigma}) & = \{\sigma \mid \sigma\ 0 = (g,v) \wedge v \in (\gamma\ a) \wedge \sigma^{1..} \in (\gamma_t\ \widetilde{\sigma})\}
\end{array}$$

Definition 7. Correctness Relations

$$\textbf{def}\ \_\ \mathcal{C}_t\ \_\ :\ \widetilde{Tr} \rightarrow Tr \rightarrow Bool\ \textbf{with}\ \tilde{\sigma}\ \mathcal{C}_t\ \sigma\ = (\sigma \in (\gamma_t\ \tilde{\sigma}))$$
$$\textbf{def}\ \_\ \mathcal{C}_s\ \_\ :\ (\wp\widetilde{Tr}) \rightarrow (\wp Tr) \rightarrow Bool\ \textbf{with}\ \tilde{A}\ \mathcal{C}_s\ A\ = \forall(\sigma : A.\exists(\tilde{\sigma} : \tilde{A}.\tilde{\sigma}\ \mathcal{C}_t\ \sigma))$$
$$\textbf{def}\ \_\ \mathcal{C}_{env}\ \_\ :\ \widetilde{Env} \rightarrow Env \rightarrow Bool\ \textbf{with}\ \rho\ \mathcal{C}_{env}\xi\ = \forall(x : Ide.(\rho\ x)\ \mathcal{C}\ (\xi\ x))$$

The following theorem establishes the correctness of the Abstract Trace Semantics. Its proof is carried out by induction on the structure of B.

Theorem 8. *Correctness of Abstract Trace Semantics*

$$\forall(B : Bex, \rho : \widetilde{Env}, \xi : Env.\rho\ \mathcal{C}_{env}\ \xi\ \Rightarrow\ \tilde{\mathcal{T}}[\![B]\!]\rho\ \mathcal{C}_s \mathcal{T}[\![B]\!]\xi)$$

5 The Temporal Logic

In this paper we consider an extremely simple linear temporal logic. Again, the reason for such a choice is to achieve simplicity in the presentation of the basic ideas on how verification based on temporal logic can benefit from abstract interpretation. The abstract syntax of the *logic formulas* follows:

$$\mathrm{L} ::= P@\mathrm{g} \mid \mathrm{L} \wedge \mathrm{L} \mid \neg\, \mathrm{L} \mid \Box\, \mathrm{L}$$

The logic we consider is composed by a set of atomic formulas which serve the purpose of stating properties of messages exchanged through gates. The formula $P@g$ means that predicate P is true of the current value on gate g. Predicate P is assumed defined in the abstract data type part of the LOTOS specification at hand. So, when applying the technique presented in this paper, the first step for the user is to extend with such predicates the abstract data type part of the specification to verify. Such a requirement is there only for pragmatic reasons and indeed a different specification language for atomic predicates could be used. The logics has only one temporal operator, namely *forever* ($\Box$). Usual abbreviations are: $L_1 \vee L_2 \equiv \neg(\neg L_1 \wedge \neg L_2), L_1 \Rightarrow L_2 \equiv \neg L_1 \vee L_2$ and $\diamond L \equiv \neg\Box\neg L$. In the sequel, the syntactic category of logic formulas will be denoted by *Lex*. In this paper we assume the standard satisfiability relation for traces ($\models$). The formal definition of $\sigma \models L$ is given in the usual way, i.e. by induction on the structure of the logic formula L. Moreover, for all behaviour expressions B, $B \ ||\!\models L$ iff $\sigma \models L$ for all traces σ of B. Going back to our sample specification $DM2$ we have for instance that $DM2 \ ||\!\models \Box(true@BLOB \Rightarrow is\_0@BLOB)$ and $DM2 \ ||\!\models \Box(\neg is\_1@BLOB)$. All the details about the definition of the satisfiability relations can be found in [10].

6 Abstract Interpretation of the Temporal Logic

In this section we give an abstract interpretation of temporal logic formulas and we state the main result of this work, namely *soundness* of this interpretation: if the abstract interpretation of the satisfiability relation applied to a behaviour expression and a logic formula gives {t} as result, then it is guaranteed that the formula is satisfied by the expression[5].

6.1 Abstract Interpretation of First Order Logics Operators

We remind the reader that the abstract domain of boolean values $\widetilde{Bool}$ is {∅, {t}, {f}, {t, f}}. The following definitions of the abstract versions of the basic logic operators (¬, ∧, etc.) show how the "don't know" information {t, f} is propagated through them. Correctness w.r.t. their concrete versions is proven in [10] where it is also shown that some useful properties, like *De Morgan* and duality of quantifiers, are preserved by the abstract interpretation.

Definition 9. Abstract Propositional Operators

	∅	{t}	{f}	{t,f}
$\tilde{\neg}$	∅	{f}	{t}	{t,f}

$\tilde{\wedge}$	∅	{t}	{f}	{t,f}	$\tilde{\vee}$	∅	{t}	{f}	{t,f}	$\tilde{\Rightarrow}$	∅	{t}	{f}	{t,f}
∅	∅	∅	{f}	∅		∅	{t}	∅	∅		∅	{t}	∅	∅
{t}	∅	{t}	{f}	{t,f}		{t}	{t}	{t}	{t}		∅	{t}	{f}	{t,f}
{f}	{f}	{f}	{f}	{f}		∅	{t}	{f}	{t,f}		{t}	{t}	{t}	{t}
{t,f}	∅	{t,f}	{f}	{t,f}		∅	{t}	{t,f}	{t,f}		∅	{t}	{t,f}	{t,f}

Definition 10. Abstract Quantifiers

$$
\begin{array}{lll}
\textbf{def } \tilde{\forall} : & (Va \rightarrow \widetilde{Bool}) \rightarrow \widetilde{Bool} & \\
\textbf{with } \tilde{\forall} f = \emptyset & \textbf{, if } \{\emptyset\} \subseteq (\mathcal{R}\ f) \subseteq \{\emptyset, \{t\}, \{t,f\}\} \\
\quad = \{t\} & \textbf{, if } (\mathcal{R}\ f) = \{\{t\}\} \\
\quad = \{f\} & \textbf{, if } \{\{f\}\} \subseteq (\mathcal{R}\ f) \\
\quad = \{t,f\} & \textbf{, if } \{\{t,f\}\} \subseteq (\mathcal{R}\ f) \subseteq \{\{t\}, \{t,f\}\}
\end{array}
$$

$$
\begin{array}{lll}
\textbf{def } \tilde{\exists} : & (Va \rightarrow \widetilde{Bool}) \rightarrow \widetilde{Bool} & \\
\textbf{with } \tilde{\exists} f = \emptyset & \textbf{, if } \{\emptyset\} \subseteq (\mathcal{R}\ f) \subseteq \{\emptyset, \{f\}, \{t,f\}\} \\
\quad = \{t\} & \textbf{, if } \{\{t\}\} \subseteq (\mathcal{R}\ f) \\
\quad = \{f\} & \textbf{, if } (\mathcal{R}\ f) = \{\{f\}\} \\
\quad = \{t,f\} & \textbf{, if } \{\{t,f\}\} \subseteq (\mathcal{R}\ f) \subseteq \{\{f\}, \{t,f\}\}
\end{array}
$$

[5] Notice that in the abstract interpretation community the word *safety* is commonly used instead of *soundness*; here we prefer *soundness* in order not to generate confusion with the meaning of *safety* in the temporal logics context.

6.2 Abstract Interpretation of the Temporal Logic Formulas

The definition of the abstract satisfiability relation for a single abstract trace is given below. Informally $\tilde{\sigma} \,\tilde{\models}\, P@g = \{\mathtt{t}\}(\mathit{resp}.\{\mathtt{t},\mathtt{f}\},\emptyset)$ if and only if $\tilde{\sigma}$ has at least one element, the gate of its first element is g and the abstract version $P^{\mathcal{A}}$ of P evaluates to $\{\mathtt{t}\}(\mathit{resp}.\{\mathtt{t},\mathtt{f}\},\emptyset)$ when applied to the abstract value component of such a first element. In all other cases, it gives $\{\mathtt{f}\}$. The definition of $\tilde{\models}$ follows the usual recursion pattern for formulas built by means of logical as well as temporal operators.

Definition 11. Trace Abstract Satisfiability Relation

$$
\begin{array}{ll}
\textbf{def } \_\tilde{\models}\_ & : \widetilde{Tr} \to Lex \to \widetilde{Bool} \\
\textbf{with } \tilde{\sigma} \,\tilde{\models}\, P@g & = \{\mathtt{t}\}, \textbf{if} \\
& \quad (0 \in \mathcal{D}\tilde{\sigma}) \wedge \exists(a : \widetilde{Va}.\tilde{\sigma}\,0 = (g,a) \wedge (P^{\mathcal{A}}\,a = \{\mathtt{t}\})) \\
& = \{\mathtt{f}\}, \textbf{if} \\
& \quad (0 \notin \mathcal{D}\tilde{\sigma}) \vee \\
& \quad \exists(a : \widetilde{Va}, g' : Ga \setminus \{g\}.\tilde{\sigma}\,0 = (g',a)) \vee \\
& \quad \exists(a : \widetilde{Va}.\tilde{\sigma}\,0 = (g,a) \wedge (P^{\mathcal{A}}\,a = \{\mathtt{f}\})) \\
& = \{\mathtt{t},\mathtt{f}\}, \textbf{if} \\
& \quad (0 \in \mathcal{D}\tilde{\sigma}) \wedge \\
& \quad \exists(a : \widetilde{Va}.\tilde{\sigma}\,0 = (g,a) \wedge (P^{\mathcal{A}}\,a = \{\mathtt{t},\mathtt{f}\})) \\
& = \emptyset, \textbf{if} \\
& \quad (0 \in \mathcal{D}\tilde{\sigma}) \wedge \exists(a : \widetilde{Va}.\tilde{\sigma}\,0 = (g,a) \wedge (P^{\mathcal{A}}\,a = \emptyset)) \\
\tilde{\sigma} \,\tilde{\models}\, L_1 \wedge L_2 & = (\tilde{\sigma} \,\tilde{\models}\, L_1) \tilde{\wedge} (\tilde{\sigma} \,\tilde{\models}\, L_2) \\
\tilde{\sigma} \,\tilde{\models}\, \neg L & = \tilde{\neg}(\tilde{\sigma} \,\tilde{\models}\, L) \\
\tilde{\sigma} \,\tilde{\models}\, \Box L & = \tilde{\forall}(j : \mathcal{D}\tilde{\sigma}.\tilde{\sigma}^{j\cdot\cdot} \,\tilde{\models}\, L)
\end{array}
$$

where $P^{\mathcal{A}} : \widetilde{Va} \to \widetilde{Bool}$ is the abstract version of $P : Va \to Bool$. $P^{\mathcal{A}}$ is generated by the Abstraction Procedure defined in [13] applied to P.

Definition 12. Behaviour Expressions Abstract Satisfiability Relation

$$\textbf{def}\ \_\,\widetilde{|\!|\!\models}\,\_ : Bex \to Lex \to \widetilde{Bool}\ \textbf{with}\ B \,\widetilde{|\!|\!\models}\, L = \tilde{\forall}(\tilde{\sigma} : \tilde{T}[\![B]\!].\tilde{\sigma} \,\tilde{\models}\, L)$$

For instance, we have $DM2 \,\widetilde{|\!|\!\models}\, \Box(\mathit{true}@BLOB \;\Rightarrow \mathit{is\_0}@BLOB) = \{\mathtt{t}\}$ and $DM2 \,\widetilde{|\!|\!\models}\, \Box(\neg \mathit{is\_1}@BLOB) = \{\mathtt{t}\}$.

6.3 Correctness of the Abstract Satisfiability Relations

In this section we show the main theorem of the present paper, namely soundness of the behaviour expression abstract satisfiability relation. The following is the core lemma, i.e. correctness of the trace satisfiability relation. The proof is done by induction on the structure of L [10].

Lemma 13. *Correctness of the Trace Abstract Satisfiability Relation*

$$\forall(\tilde{\sigma} : \widetilde{Tr}, L : Lex.((\tilde{\sigma} \,\tilde{\models}\, L = \{\mathtt{t}\}) \Rightarrow \forall(\sigma : (\gamma_t \tilde{\sigma}).\sigma \models L) \wedge \\ (\tilde{\sigma} \,\tilde{\models}\, L = \{\mathtt{f}\}) \Rightarrow \forall(\sigma : (\gamma_t \tilde{\sigma}).\neg(\sigma \models L)))$$

The correctness theorem for the abstract satisfiability relation for processes follows easily from Lemma 13 and Theorem 8:

Theorem 14. *Correctness of the Behaviour Expression Abstract Satisfiability Relation*

$$\forall(B : Bex, L : Lex.(B \,\widetilde{|||\!\!\models}\, L = \{\mathtt{t}\}) \Rightarrow (B \,|||\!\!\models\, L))$$

7 Conclusions and Future Work

The abstract interpretation proposed in this paper can help in finding a representation for value passing process algebra terms which is finite state. In the present paper, for the sake of notational simplicity, we have not dealt with recursion. Recursion can be dealt with in the standard way, by means of fixpoint semantics. On the other hand, its interplay with parallel composition may make processes infinite states. In this case the use of the approach proposed in this paper is not sufficient any longer. It might be interesting, then, to investigate on its integration with the one proposed in [7], in which abstract interpretation is used in the above mentioned circumstances.

For simplicity we considered only an extremely simple temporal logic, which, for instance, lacks the possibility of distinguishing between finite and infinite traces. The introduction of a *next* operator would be sufficient to that purpose, provided an interpretation domain stronger than Trace Semantics is chosen. However, difficulties arise for the definition of a denotational semantics of a process algebra including the parallel composition operator, using a stronger interpretation domain (like maximal traces), as shown in [11]. In this case, an operational semantics should be used [5].

In this paper we have been concerned only with the *correctness* of the abstraction. A very important issue which we did not cover is *quality* of abstraction and, as an extreme, its *optimality*. We leave this for further study, just pointing out here that the data abstraction procedure described in [13] is not always optimal as well. One possibility could be to show optimality of the Abstract Trace Semantics *relative* to the quality of the data abstraction procedure. In any case, from a more practical point of view, we think it is worth to first better study the quality of the data abstraction procedure. The most promising way for increasing it seems to be one of defining suitable heuristics based also on methodological considerations concerning the style in which specifications are written.

We just started an implementation effort of the ideas presented in this paper based on the abstract interpreter described in [12] and the model checker proposed in [2].

References

1. T. Bolognesi and E. Brinksma. Introduction to the ISO specification language LOTOS. *Computer Networks and ISDN Systems*, 14:25–59, 1987.
2. A. Bouali, S. Gnesi, S. Larosa. The integration Project for the JACK Environment. Bulletin of the EATCS, n.54, October 1994, pages 207-223.
3. R. Boute. Funmath illustrated: A declarative formalism and application examples. Technical Report Declarative Systems Series n.1, Univerity of Nijmegen, july 1993.
4. E.M.Clarke, O.Grumberg, D.E.Long. Model Checking and Abstraction. ACM TOPLAS, 16(5), 1994, pages 1512–1542.
5. R. Cleaveland and J. Riely. Testing-based Abstractions for Value-Passing Systems. *Concur '94: Concurrency Theory, Lecture Notes in Computer Science* 836, pages 415-432. Springer-Verlag, 1994.
6. D.Dams, O.Grumberg, R.Gerth. Automatic Verification of Abstract Interpretation of Reactive Systems: Abstractions Preserving "CTL*, CTL*, CTL*. IFIP Transactions A-56, Conference on Programming Concepts, Methods and Calculi (PROCOMET'94), E. Olderog (ed.), North Holland, 1994.
7. N. De Francesco, A. Fantechi, S. Gnesi, P.Inverardi. Model Checking of non-finite state processes by Finite Approximations. TACAS'95, Lecture Notes in Computer Science 1019, Springer-Verlag.
8. P. van Eijk. The Lotosphere Integrated Tool Environment. 4th International Conference on Formal Description Techniques (FORTE '91), North-Holland, 1991, pp. 473-476.
9. A. Fantechi, S. Gnesi, C. Laneve. An Expressive Temporal Logic for Basic LOTOS 2nd International Conference on Formal Description Techniques (FORTE '89), North-Holland, 1990, pp. 261-276.
10. A. Fantechi, S. Gnesi, D. Latella. Temporal Logics Verification of LOTOS Specifications Using Abstract Interpretation. CNUCE Internal Report C94-19, Oct. 1994. Available from anonymous ftp as pub/fantechi/repC94-19.ps at rep1.iei.pi.cnr.it.
11. A. Fantechi, S. Gnesi, G. Ristori. Compositionality and Bisimulation: a negative result. Information Processing Letters, vol. 39, July 1991, pp.109-114.
12. F. Fiore and F. Giannotti. An abstract interpreter for the specification language LOTOS. 7h International Conference on Formal Description Techniques - FORTE '94, 1994.
13. F. Giannotti and D. Latella. Gate splitting in LOTOS specifications using abstract interpretation. *Science of Computer Programming*, (23):127–149, 1994.
14. S. Gnesi, E. Madelaine, G. Ristori. An Exercise in Protocol Verification. LOTOSPHERE - Software Development using LOTOS - Results of the LotoSphere Project; Kluwer Academic Publishers, 1995.
15. C.A.R. Hoare. A model for Communicating Sequential Processes. Technical Monograph Prg-22, Computing laboratory, University of Oxford, 1981.
16. R. Langerak. Transformations and Semantics for LOTOS. Ph. D. Thesis - University of Twente 1992

Modelling and Verification of Distributed Algorithms

Wolfgang Reisig

Humboldt University of Berlin, Germany

Abstract. Distributed Algorithms are frequently published in informal or semiformal representations and are often informally verified. Formal approaches frequently extend classical algorithmic concepts. This yields frequently clumsy and unnecessarily compilated representations.
We suggest integrated representation- and verification concepts, tailored for Distributed Algorithms. They respect and exploit basic characteristic features of Distributed Algorithms, such as local causes and effects of actions, and synchronization of control strands.
The approach aims at an optimal compromize of technical simplicity and conceptual adequacy for a wide class of Distributed Algorithms, in analogy to the simplicity and adequacy of Pascal and Hoare Logic for a wide class of sequential algorithms. A number of case studies shows the adequacy of the approach.

1 Elementary Petri Net Models of Distributed Algorithms

Here we consider Distributed Algorithms with two characteristic properties: firstly, the number of partners (processes, actors) and the topology of message lines is fixed, and secondly, the algorithms are governed by control rather than by values. Such algorithms can adequately be modelled by a variant of *elementary net systems* (en-systems), a well known class of Petri Nets. In our case, each place carries at most one token; loops will however be treated as usual in *place / transition nets*. Furthermore, each action is either *progressing* or *quiescent*, and some actions are assumed to be *fair*.

As a motivating example we consider an asymmetric mutual exclusion algorithm, as given in [4]. Fig. 1.1 shows a Petri Net representation of this algorithm. Essentially, it consists of a *writer* process (left cycle) and a *reader* process (right cycle). Each process has a local *flag* "...detached" that can be observed (tested) by its partner process. A shared variable is furthermore assumed, but not explicitly modelled. Whenever prepared to update the shared variable, the writer (at *prep1*) will eventually execute this update, i.e. reach its critical state *writing*. The reader is guaranteed less: Whenever *pending* (i.e. wanting to read the shared variable) at *pend1*, the reader will eventually reach its critical state *reading* or the writer will again update the shared variable.

Testing of flags is typically modelled by help of loops. Notice that *writer involved* is just the complement of *writer detached*, i.e. *writer involved* allows to test the *absence* of *writer detached*.

The algorithm should not enforce the writer to update the shared variable infinitely often. Rather, the writer may remain *producing* after finitely many updates.

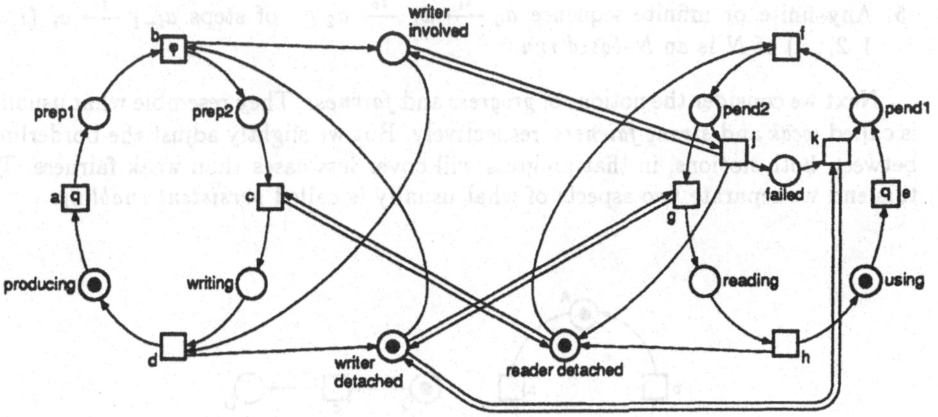

Fig. 1.1. es-net N_1: Owicki / Lamport's Asymmetrical Mutex Algorithm

This is indicated by the inscription q ("quiescent") of the action a. Hence, this action may eventually remain enabled forever, in contrast to the actions b, c and d.

The reader likewise should not be enforced to strive at reading infinitely often. Hence the action e is assumed as quiescent, in contrast to f, g, h, j and k.

Finally, the action b is assumed to be *fair*. Details of this concept will be given later.

2 Elementary System Nets

A lot of Distributed Algorithms (among them the Mutex Algorithm of Fig. 1.1) reveal a class of Petri Nets that have not been identified in the literature so far: One-safe place / transition nets with quiescent and fair transitions. This class is worth being named by its own, and we have chosen the term *elementary system nets*, in accordance with *advanced system nets*, to be considered in Chapter 6.

As usual we write a net N as $N = (P, T, F)$. We employ standard notations such as ${}^\bullet x$ and $x^\bullet$, denoting the *pre-set* and the *post-set* of $x \in P \cup T$ or $x \subseteq P \cup T$, respectively. Due to the intended use of nets, the elements of P and T will be called *local states* and *actions*, respectively. We employ the usual graphical representation of nets, depicting elements of P, T and F as circles, squares and arcs, respectively.

Enabledness and occurrence of actions are defined as follows:

Definition 1. Let $N = (P, T, F)$ be a net.

1. Any subset $a \subseteq P$ of local states is called a (global) *state* of N.
2. An action $t \in T_\Sigma$ is *enabled in* $a \subseteq P$ iff ${}^\bullet t \subseteq a$ and $(t^\bullet \setminus {}^\bullet t) \cap a = \emptyset$.
3. Let $a \subseteq P$ and $t \in T$. Then $\text{eff}(a,t) := (a \setminus {}^\bullet t) \cup t^\bullet$ is the *effect of t's occurrence on a*.
4. Let $t \in T$ be enabled at $a \subseteq P$. Then $(a, t, \text{eff}(a,t))$ is a *step of N*, written $a \xrightarrow{t} \text{eff}(a,t)$.

5. Any finite or infinite sequence $a_0 \xrightarrow{t_1} a_1 \xrightarrow{t_2} a_2 \ldots$ of steps $a_{i-1} \xrightarrow{t_i} a_i$ $(i = 1, 2, \ldots)$ of N is an *N-based run*.

Next we consider the notions of *progress* and *fairness*. They resemble what usually is called *weak* and *strong fairness*, respectively. But we slightly adjust the borderline between both notions, in that progress will cover less cases than weak fairness. To this end we separate two aspects of what usually is called *persistent enabling*.

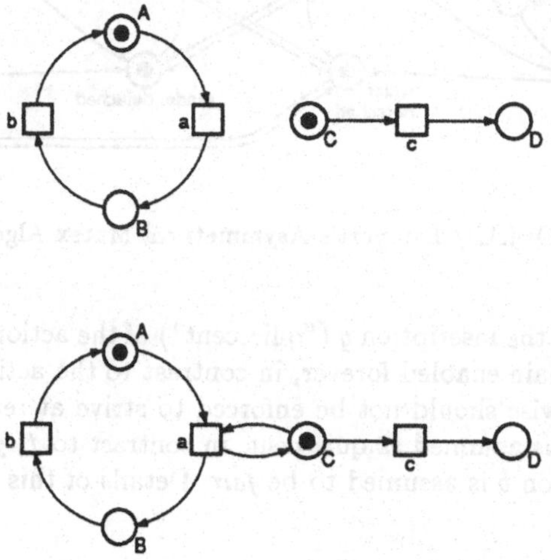

Fig. 2.1. es-nets N_2 and N_3

As a technical example, compare the two es-nets N_2 and N_3 in Fig. 2.1. Representing a state $\{a_1, \ldots, a_n\}$ just as $a_1 \ldots a_n$, the infinite run

$$w = AC \xrightarrow{a} BC \xrightarrow{b} AC \xrightarrow{a} \ldots$$

is a run of both es-nets N_2 and N_3 in Fig. 2.1, with the respective action c not occurring in w. For both N_2 and N_3, the action c is usually said to be *persistently enabled* in w. However, w and c are quite differently related in N_2 and N_3: They are entirely detached in N_2, hence c could lightly occur during the course of w. As c does *not* occur in w we say that w *neglects progress* of c. In contrast, w infinitely often employs a precondition of c in N_3 (i.e. the local state C). This prevents c to occur at any state of w. Thus w does not just neglect progress of c. It is questionable to denote c persistently enabled in this run. Rather there is *conflict* between a and c whenever the state AC is taken in w. And this conflict is always solved in favour of a. Therefore, w is said to be *unfair* to c, i.e. to *neglect fairness* of c. This observation motivates the following definition.

Definition 2. Let $N = (P, T, F)$ be a net, let $t \in T$ and let $w = a_0 \xrightarrow{t_1} a_1 \xrightarrow{t_2} \ldots$ be a finite or infinite N-based run.

1. w ***neglects progress for*** t iff some state a_i enables t and for no index $j > i$ holds: $t_j \in ({}^\bullet t)^\bullet$.
2. w ***neglects fairness for*** t iff t occurs finitely often in w and is infinitely often enabled in w.
3. w ***respects progress or fairness for*** t iff w does not neglect progress or fairness, respectively, for t.

The above distinctions of progress and fairness are quite intuitive: *Progress* of an action a in a run w refers to the *enabledness* of a: Whenever the preconditions of a all hold, then either a will eventually occur or some competing action b will occur, affecting some of a's preconditions. In contrast, *fairness* of a refers to the decision of *conflict* between a and some competing actions: Infinitely many decisions must not always refuse a. Consequently, each finite run respects fairness of each action. And if an infinite run w respects fairness of an action a, then w also respects progress of a.

Implementation strategies for progress and fairness are quite different: The implementation of progress does not require any book-keeping of previous conflict decisions, in contrast to the implementation of fairness.

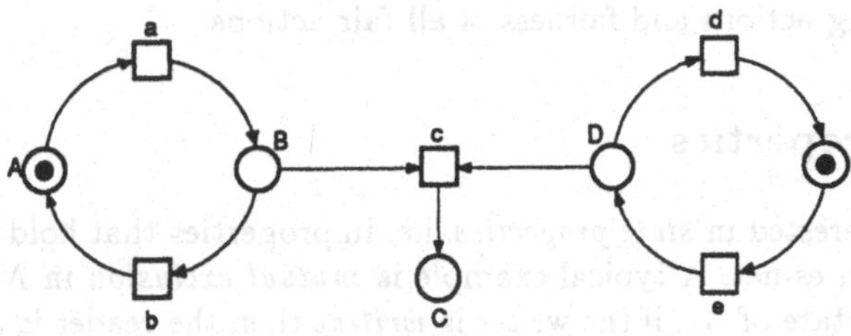

Fig. 2.2. es-net N_4: action c is not conflict reduced

Another consequence of the above definition deserves attention: Fairness is sensitive against arbitrarily interleaved concurrent actions. For example, in the es-net N_4 of Fig. 2.2, the infinite run

$$w_1 = AE \xrightarrow{a} BE \xrightarrow{d} BD \xrightarrow{b} AD \xrightarrow{e} AE \xrightarrow{a} \ldots$$

infinitely often enables the action c, whereas

$$w_2 = AE \xrightarrow{a} BE \xrightarrow{b} AE \xrightarrow{d} AD \xrightarrow{e} AE \xrightarrow{a} \ldots$$

does not. Both w_1 and w_2 respect progress of c, and w_2 also respects fairness, whereas w_1 neglects fairness of c.

This observation is intuitively not satisfactory, because the i-th occurrence of b and d are mutually independent. Their order in w_1 and w_2 is arbitrarily chosen, and should not govern any relevant properties of runs. Fortunately, experience shows that Distributed Algorithms usually stick to a quite restricted case: Fairness is assumed for an action a only if a is *conflict reduced*, i.e. competes with at most *one* further enabled action at a time. Swapping mutually independent actions in concurrent runs does not affect fairness in this case.

Nets that describe *elementary* Distributed Algorithms, are called *elementary system nets* and are defined as follows:

Definition 3. A net $N = (P, T, F)$ is called an *elementary system net* (es-net, for short) iff

1. a state $a \subseteq P$ is distinguished, called the *initial state of* Σ.
2. each action $t \in T$ is denoted as either *progressing* or *quiescent*.
3. some progressing actions are distinguished as *fair*.

In the graphical representation of an es-net each place of the initial state is inscribed with a token. Quiescent and fair actions are inscribed with "q" and "φ", respectively. The nets N_1, and N_4 (Fig. 1.1 and Fig. 2.2, respectively) are typical examples.

Behaviour of es-nets is now defined as follows:

Definition 4. Let N be an es-net.
A N-based run w is a *run of* N iff w begins at the initial state of N, respects progress of all progressing actions and fairness of all fair actions.

3 State Properties

Here we are interested in *state properties*, i.e. in properties that hold in all reachable states of a given es-net. A typical example is *mutual exclusion* in N_1 (Fig. 1.1): At each reachable state of N_1, if the writer is *writing* then the reader is not *reading* and vice versa, if the reader is *reading* then the writer is not *writing*.

This kind of properties is usually described in terms of *state formulas*: A state formula is a propositional expression where each atom is a local state. An atom p holds in a global state a iff $p \in a$. For example, the formula

$$p \equiv \neg(writing \wedge reading) \tag{1}$$

describes mutual exclusion of N_1. Then

$$N_1 \models p \tag{2}$$

states that p is valid in N_1, i.e. p holds in each reachable state of N_1. This brings about the following Definition:

Definition 5. Let $N = (P, T, F)$ be a net. Then

1. each local state $p \in P$ is a state formula of N, and
2. if p and q are state formulas of N, then $\neg p$ and $p \wedge q$ are state formulas of N.

Validity of state formulas is defined as can be expected:

Definition 6. Let $N = (P, T, F)$ be a net, let p, q be state formulas of N and let $a \subseteq P$ be a state. Then $a \models p$ ("a is a p-state") is inductively defined as follows:
$a \models p$ iff $p \in a$, for $p \in P$,
$a \models \neg p$ iff not $a \models p$,
$a \models p \wedge q$ iff $a \models p$ and $a \models q$.
Furthermore $N \models p$ ("p holds in N") iff each reachable state of N is a p-state.

Of course, we apply the usual propositional conventions such as $p \vee q$, $p \rightarrow q$ etc.

The problem remains as to *prove* the validity of a state formula, p. A nearby idea was to visit all reachable states a and to test $a \models p$ (e.g. by checking for $a = \{a_1, \ldots, a_n\}$ whether $(a_1 \wedge \ldots \wedge a_n) \rightarrow p$ is a propositional tautology). *Assertional reasoning* is frequently more efficient: One proves that p holds initially and for each transition t one shows, by considering t and p only, that each step formed $a \xrightarrow{t} b$ preserves p. The well known technique of *place invariants* is an example for assertional reasoning. Place invariants don't yield state formulas, but integer equations. However, valid state formulas can be derived from those equations.

$\underline{N}$	a	b	c
A	-1	1	
B	1	-1	
C			-1
D			1

	i
A	1
B	1
C	
D	

	a_N
A	1
B	
C	1
D	

Fig. 3.1. Matrix, place invariant and initial state of N_2 and N_3 (entries with value 0 are skipped)

In order to construct a place invariant of an es-net N, a matrix $\underline{N}$ is constructed, with local states and actions of N taken as row- and column-indices, respectively. The arcs of N are represented as entries in the matrix. Fig. 3.1 shows an example. Intuitively formulated, each entry $\underline{N}(p, t)$ shows the effect to the token load of the local state p upon occurrence of the action t. Notice that loops vanish: N_2 and N_3 have equal matrices. Now, each integer solution of the linear equational system $\underline{N}^{\tau} \cdot i = 0$ is a *place invariant of* N, (e.g. i in Fig. 3.1). Each place invariant i is canonically associated its *characteristic equation.* This equation is formed

$$i_1 \cdot p_1 + \ldots + i_k \cdot p_k = m \tag{3}$$

where $p_1, \ldots, p_k$ are the places of the net, now taken as variables ranging over $\{0, 1\}$, and $i_j = i(p_j)$ is the value of the place invariant i at the index place p_j ($j = 1, \ldots, k$). Furthermore, m is the value of the inner product $i \cdot a_N$ (i.e. $\Sigma_{j=1,\ldots,k} i(k) \cdot a_N(k)$) of the place invariant i and the initial state a_N of N. As an example, the place invariant i of the es-nets N_2 and N_3, as given in Fig. 3.1, yields the equation $1 \cdot A + 1 \cdot B + 0 \cdot C + 0 \cdot D = 1 \cdot 1 + 1 \cdot 0 + 0 \cdot 1 + 0 \cdot 0$, i.e. shortly

$$A + B = 1. \tag{4}$$

Each state $a \subseteq P$ can be considered as a *valuation* of the variables $p \in P$ occurring in a characteristic equation, by $a(p) = 1$ if $p \in a$ and $a(p) = 0$, otherwise. The fundamental property of the place invariant formalism then says that each reachable state solves the characteristic equation of a place invariant.

As an example, the above equation (4) implies for each reachable state a of Σ_2 and Σ_3: If $A \in a$ then $B \notin a$ and vice versa, if $B \in a$ then $A \notin a$.

Identifying the truth values *true* and *false* with the integer values 1 and 0, we get the validity of the formulas $A \rightarrow \neg B$ and $B \rightarrow \neg A$ for all reachable states a of Σ_2 and Σ_3.

In the forthcoming Fig. 3.2, typical place invariants are i_1 and i_2, with $i_1(C) = i_1(D) = i_1(F) = 1$, $i_2(G) = i_2(K) = i_2(L) = 1$, and $i(x) = 0$ for all other cases. The characteristic equations then are

$$C + D + F = 1, \text{ and} \tag{5}$$

$$G + K + L = 1. \tag{6}$$

Though useful in many cases, place invariants do not suffice for *all* the relevant state properties of Distributed Algorithms that are modelled as es-nets. N_1 provides an example: The mutual exclusion property (3) in Chapter 3, i.e. $\neg(writing \wedge reading)$, certainly fails when all loops of N_1 are skipped. But the place invariants are not affected by this transformation, as was shown above.

The technique of *traps* applies frequently in the presence of loops. This well known technique is likewise an example for assertional reasoning. A trap is a subset $Q \subseteq P$ of places, such that each action t that removes a token from Q (i.e. $t \in Q^\bullet$) also augments a token to Q (i.e. $t \in {}^\bullet Q$), or shortly

$$Q^\bullet \subseteq {}^\bullet Q \tag{7}$$

If Q carries initially a token (i.e. $Q \cap a_N \neq \emptyset$) then Q carries a token at each reachable state. Taking again the local states of a net as variables ranging over $\{0,1\}$, a trap $Q = \{q_1, \ldots, q_n\}$ is assigned its *characteristic inequality*

$$q_1 + \ldots + q_n \geq 1 \tag{8}$$

It is obvious that each valuation of each reachable state solves (8), provided the initial state does.

The characteristic equations of place invariants and the characteristic inequalities of traps can be combined (i.e. be added or subtracted), thus deriving new equations or inequalities that hold in all reachable states.

As an example, it is quite easy to prove mutual exclusion for N_1 in this way: Fig. 3.2 re-names the local states of N_1 and outlines the trap $\{C, F, G, K\}$: Each arrow leaving the trap is boldfaced, together with a corresponding arrow entering the trap. The characteristic inequality of this trap is

$$C + F + G + K \geq 1 \tag{9}$$

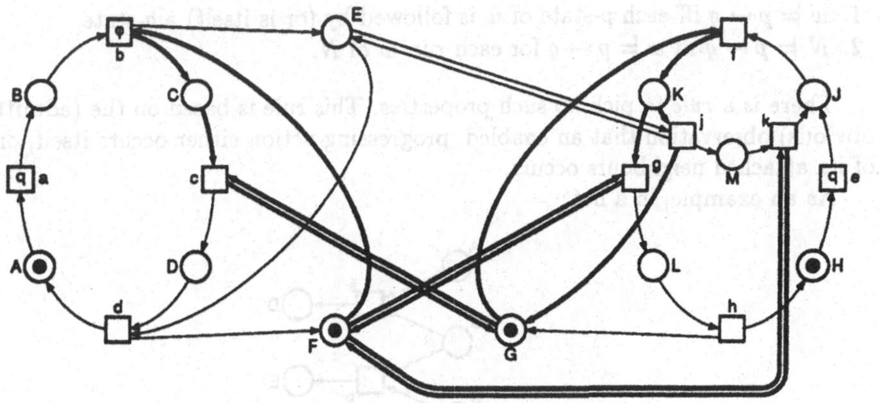

Fig. 3.2. Trap $\{C, F, G, K\}$ in the mutex algorithm N_1

Subtraction of this inequality from the sum of the above characteristic equations (5) and (6) then yields

$$D + L \leq 1 \tag{10}$$

In logical terms, this inequality implies

$$\neg(D \wedge L),$$

hence mutual exclusion of N_1.

Not each valid state formula can be proven by combination of characteristic equations and inequalities of place invariants and traps. But experience shows this usually fits for Distributed Algorithms.

4 Progress Properties

This Chapter provides techniques to formulate and to prove *progress properties.* As discussed in Chapter 1, two progress properties of N_1 are decisive: The *prepared* writer will become *writing*, and the *pending* reader will become *reading* in case the writer eventually remains *producing*.

In accordance with other formalisms such as UNITY, a progress property is written $p \mapsto q$ ("p leads to q"), with state formulas p and q. The above properties (in the representation of Fig. 3.2) then read

$$B \mapsto D \text{ and } J \mapsto (D \vee L). \tag{11}$$

Validity of a formula $p \mapsto q$ in an es-net N is defined as follows:

Definition 7. Let N be an es-net, let p, q be state formulas of N, and let w be a run of N.

1. $w \models p \mapsto q$ iff each p-state of w is followed by (or is itself) a q-state.
2. $N \models p \mapsto q$ iff $w \models p \mapsto q$ for each run w of N.

There is a *rule* to pick up such properties. This rule is based on the (admittedly obvious) observation that an enabled, progressing action either occurs itself, or one of its attached neighbours occurs.

As an example, in a net

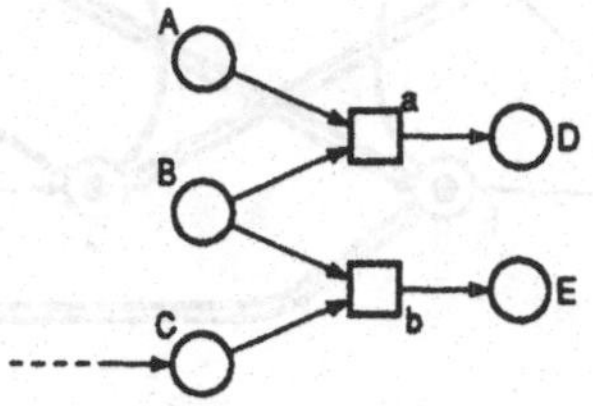

(12)

the state $\{A, B\}$ enables the progressing action a; hence either a or b occurs eventually. So the formula $AB \mapsto (D \vee AE)$ holds in this net. More generally, in the net

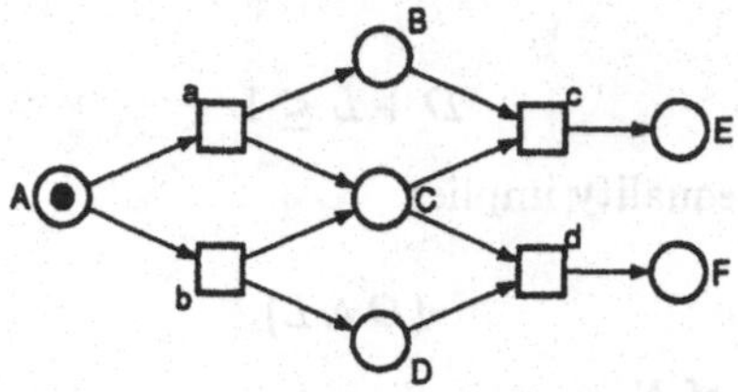

(13)

the formula $BC \mapsto E$ holds because of the valid state formula $B \rightarrow \neg D$.

The core arguments of (12) and (13) are captured in the following Definition:

Definition 8. Let $N = (P, T, F)$ be an es-net and let $Q = \{q_1, \ldots, q_n\} \subseteq P$.

1. Q is *progress prone* iff Q enables at least one progressing action of N.
2. Q *prevents an action* $t \in T$ iff for ${}^\bullet t = \{p_1, \ldots, p_m\}$ holds: The state formula $(q_1 \wedge \ldots \wedge q_n) \rightarrow \neg(p_1 \wedge \ldots \wedge p_m)$ holds in N.
3. $U \subseteq T$ is a *change set of* Q iff $U \neq \emptyset$ and Q prevents each $t \in Q^\bullet \setminus U$.

As an example, in the net (13), BC is progress prone, whereas BD is not. BC furthermore prevents d, hence $\{c\}$ is a change set of BD.

The pick-up rule for progress is now captured in a Theorem. For the sake of convenience, a set $Q = \{q_1, \ldots, q_n\}$ of logical atoms denotes the formula $q_1 \wedge \ldots \wedge q_n$:

Theorem 9. *Let $N = (P, T, F)$ be an es-net, let $Q \subseteq P$ be progress prone and let $U \subseteq T$ be a change set of Q. Then*

$$\Sigma \models Q \mapsto \bigvee_{u \in U} \mathrm{eff}(Q, u).$$

This Theorem in fact allows to "pick up" the formula $AB \mapsto (D \vee AE)$ in (12) and $BC \mapsto E$ with change set $\{c\}$ in (13). But the progress formulas (11) of the net in Fig. 3.2 cannot be picked up this way immediately. Rather, those properties can be gained by *combining* picked up properties. In fact, progress properties can be combined by help of the following Theorem:

Theorem 10. *Let N be an es-net, and let p and q be state formulas of N.*

1. *If $N \models p \rightarrow q$ then $N \models p \mapsto q$*
2. *If $N \models p \mapsto q$ and $N \models q \mapsto r$ then $N \models p \mapsto r$*
3. *If $N \models p \mapsto r$ and $N \models q \mapsto r$ then $N \models (p \vee q) \mapsto r$.*

The transitivity of $\mapsto$ can graphically be depicted by $p \mapsto q \mapsto r$, and a disjunctive formula $p \mapsto (q_1 \vee \ldots \vee q_n)$ by

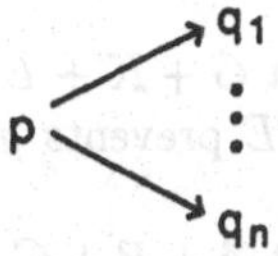

(14)

Both representations are combined in the *proof graph* (in [4] called "proof lattice")

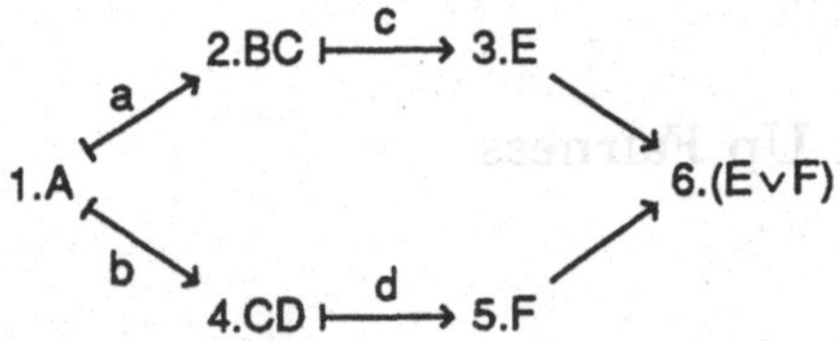

(15)

that shows $A \mapsto (E \vee F)$ for the net (13). Its nodes are numbered and decorated by the actions that cause the respective step. Implications $p \rightarrow q$ are included due to Theorem 10.1.

A more involved proof graph is shown in Fig. 4.1, proving the second part of (11), i.e. $J \mapsto (D \vee L)$ of the net in Fig. 3.2.

The forward branching arcs of each node are justified by Theorem 9 together with the following propositions:

Node 1: the place invariant $H + J - G = 0$ implies $J \rightarrow G$;
node 2: trivial;
node 3: place invariant $A + B + C + D = 1$;
node 4: invariant $A + B - F = 0$ implies $A \rightarrow F$;
node 5: invariant $A + B - F = 0$ implies $B \rightarrow F$;
node 6: invariant $C + D - E = 0$ implies $C \rightarrow E$;
node 7: trivial;
node 8: A prevents b by invariant $A + B + C + D = 1$, F prevents j by invariant $F + E = 1$ and K prevents k by invariant $H + J + K + L + M = 1$;
node 9: F prevents j by invariant $F + E = 1$ and K prevents k by invariant $H + J + K + L + M = 1$;

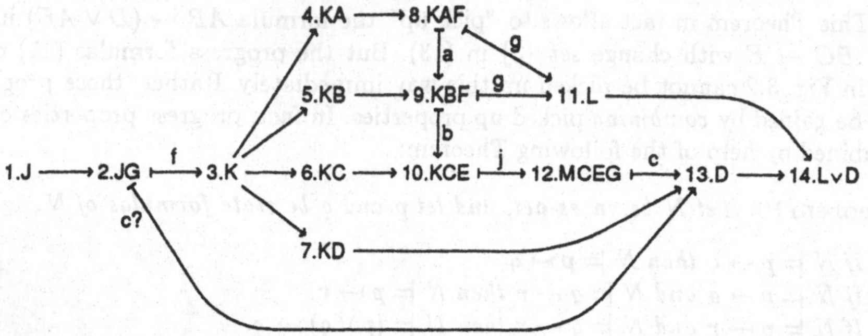

Fig. 4.1. Proof graph of the reader's evolution property

node 10: K prevents c by invariant $G+K+L=1$, C prevents d by invariant $A+B+C+D=1$ and E prevents g by invariant $E+F=1$;
node 11: trivial;
node 12: C prevents d by invariant $A+B+C+D=1$, M prevents j by invariant $H+J+K+L+M=1$, M prevents f by invariant $H+J+K+L+M=1$ and E prevents k by invariant $E+F=1$;
node 13: trivial.

5 How to Pick Up Fairness

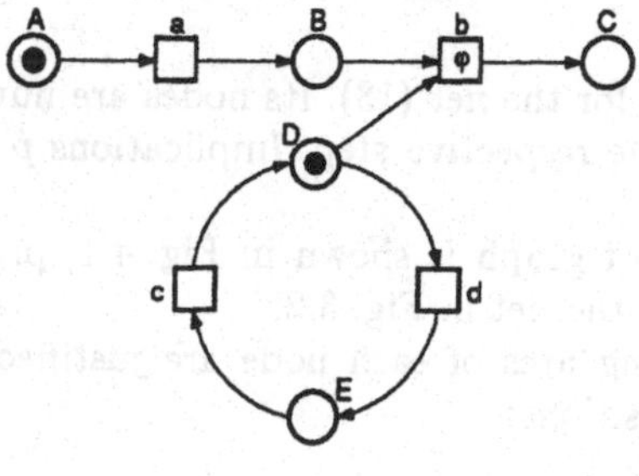

Fig. 5.1. In this net holds $B \mapsto C$

The first property of (11), i.e. $N_1 \models B \mapsto D$, cannot be proven by help of the so far derived techniques: $N_1 \models BF \mapsto C$ cannot be picked up. Theorem 9 only yields $N_1 \models BF \mapsto (C \vee L \vee J)$. Hence a pick up rule is required that exploits the assumption of fairness. Such a rule will be derived in the sequel. As a technical example, each run of the net N in Fig. 5.1 respects progress of the action a, hence the local state B will eventually be reached. Afterwards, b is infinitely often enabled and hence will occur because b is assumed to be fair. The crucial property to be proven is $B \mapsto C$.

Most distributed algorithms require fairness for quite a restricted kind of actions t only: The pre-set $\bullet t$ of t has only *one* forward branching place p, the *conflict place* of t. Hence each action conflicting with t is linked to t along p. A quite simple, yet powerful rule then allows to pick up progress for fair and *conflict reduced* actions.

Definition 11. A transition $t \in T$ of a net $N = (P, T, F)$ is *conflict reduced* iff for at most one $p \in \bullet t$ holds: $p^\bullet \neq \{t\}$. Then p is called the *conflict place* of t.

For example, the action b in N_1 is conflict reduced (with conflict place *writer detached*) whereas action c in N_4 is not. Fairness of conflict reduced actions is apparently robust against swapping independent occurrences of actions in runs. Progress for fair and conflict reduced actions can be picked up as follows:

Theorem 12. *Let* $N = (P, T, F)$ *be an es-net and let* $t \in T$ *be conflict reduced and fair, with conflict place* p. *For* $Q := \bullet t \setminus \{p\}$ *assume furthermore* $N \models Q \mapsto p$. *Then* $N \models Q \mapsto t^\bullet$.

Now, $B \mapsto D$ holds in Fig. 5.1 due to the proof graph

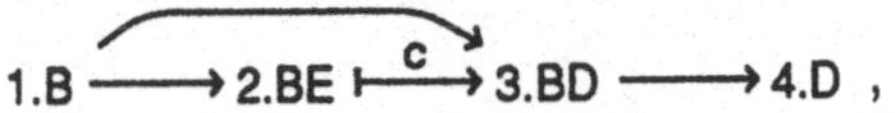

$$1.\text{B} \longrightarrow 2.\text{BE} \overset{c}{\longmapsto} 3.\text{BD} \longrightarrow 4.\text{D} , \tag{16}$$

where nodes 1 and 2 are justified by the place invariant $D + E = 1$. Node 3 is trivial.

Hence $B \mapsto C$ according to the above Theorem.

This theorem can now be used for proving evolution of the writer, in Fig. 1.1, i.e. $B \mapsto D$ in the version of Fig. 3.2. The conflict place of b is F. Furthermore, $B \rightarrow F$ holds according to the place invariant $A + B - F = 0$. Hence $B \mapsto CE$ according to Theorem 12.

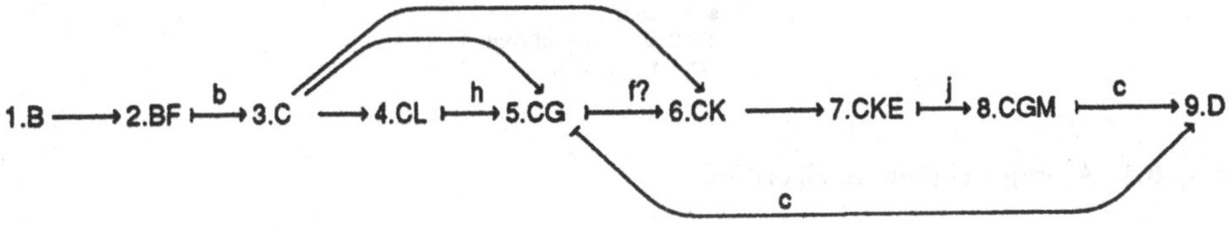

Fig. 5.2. Proof graph of the writer's evolution property

The complete proof graph for $B \mapsto D$ is shown in Fig. 5.2. Its nodes are justified as follows:

Node 1: place invariant $A + B - F = 0$;
node 2: Theorem 12;
node 3: place invariant $L + G + K = 1$;
node 4: L prevents c by place invariant $L + G + K = 1$;
node 5: trivial;
node 6: place invariant $C + D - E = 0$;
node 7: K prevents c by place invariant $G + K + L = 1$, E prevents g by place invariant $E + F = 1$ and C prevents d by place invariant $A + B + C + D = 1$;
node 8: M prevents f by place invariant $H + J + K + L + M = 1$ and C prevents k by place invariant $C + D + F = 1$.

6 Advanced Petri Net Models of Distributed Algorithms

Here we consider Distributed Algorithms that are to run on *any* network of computing agents: Neither the number of agents, nor the topology of message lines are fixed. Such an algorithm can adequately be modelled by a *symbolic* high level Petri Net.

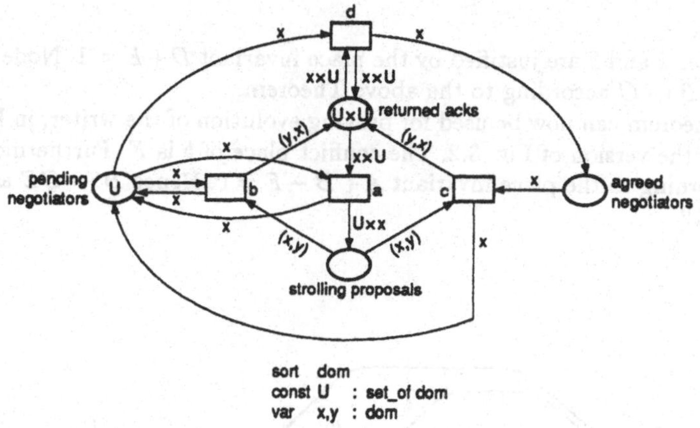

Fig. 6.1. A simple consensus algorithm

As a motivating example we consider a *consensus algorithm*, in fact a variant of [2]. Fig. 6.1 shows a symbolic high level Petri Net representation of a simple version of this algorithm. It assumes a set U of *negotiators* which are to communicate messages to the other negotiators, aimed at a joint contract that eventually all negotiators agree upon. A message sent from a negotiator u to a negotiator v is represented as a tuple (v, u), i.e. the receiver is followed by the sender. A message (u, v) is either a *proposal* of v that is sent to u but not yet received by u (hence strolling), or an *acknowledgement*, received by u from v. As Fig. 6.1 indicates, all negotiators are initially pending and all acknowledgements are *returned*. In this situation, any negotiator u may send a proposal to all negotiators: The action a occurs in the mode $x = u$. As a shorthand we write $x \times U$ and $U \times x$ for $\{x\} \times U$ and $U \times \{x\}$, respectively. Hence $u \times U$ denotes the set of all pairs (u, y) with $y \in U$. Upon receiving a proposal (u, v), a negotiator u reads its contents and returns an acknowledgement (v, u) to its sender, v: Action b occurs in the mode $x = u$ and $y = v$, or action c occurs in this mode. In any case, the receiver v gets *pending*. Finally, each *pending* negotiator u may turn *agreed*, provided acknowledgements have been returned for all messages sent out by u: Action d occurs in mode $x = u$. Obviously at any time, a negotiator is either *pending* or *agreed*, and for each pair (u, v) of negotiators, there is either a *strolling proposal* (v, u) or a *returned acknowledgement* (u, v). The algorithm does not guarantee that the negotiators ever are together agreed. However, the algorithm guarantees *stability*: In case eventually all negotiators are together *agreed* then no proposal is strolling and no further proposal will be generated.

An advanced version of this algorithm is shown in Fig. 6.2: Each negotiator u is associated a set $N(u) \subseteq U$ of *neighboured* negotiators. u communicates only with neighbours and is not aware of any negotiator in $U \setminus N(u)$. Upon sending out proposals, u each time nondeterministically selects a subset $V \subseteq N(u)$ of neighbours: An occurrence mode of the action a fixes a negotiator u for the variable x and a set $V \subseteq N(u)$ of neighbours of u for the variable Y. Let $N := \bigcup\{(u, v) \mid u \in U \wedge v \in N(u)\}$ be the set of all acknowledgements. Initially, they are all *returned*.

This algorithm guarantees stability, too: In each reachable state of this net, *agreed* $= U$ implies *strolling proposals* $= \emptyset$. This property will now be proven by help of *symbolic place invariants* and *symbolic weighted traps*. Technical details of symbolic place invariants have been discussed in [5], among others. Symbolic, weighted traps will formally be presented in [9]. Here we just show how those techniques work for the example of Fig. 6.2.

Fig. 6.3 shows the matrix $\underline{N}$ of the net of Fig. 6.2, together with the initial state a_N and two symbolic place invariants, i_1 and i_2. The entries of $\underline{N}$ represent the arc inscriptions of N (in analogy to Fig. 3.1). The entries of the matrix, as well as the entries of the vectors a_N, i_1 and i_2, are *terms*. U and N are *constant symbols* for a set and a pair of sets, respectively, of negotiators. x and y are variables for negotiators and Y is a variable for sets of negotiators. Each element $u \in U$ or subset $V \subseteq U$ of negotiators can canonically be conceived as a *multiset* $\widetilde{u} : U \to \mathbb{Z}$ or $\widetilde{V} : U \to \mathbb{Z}$ with $\widetilde{u}(u) = 1$, $\widetilde{V}(u) = 1$ for $u \in V$ and $\widetilde{u}(v) = \widetilde{V}(v) = 0$ for all other elements v of N. Each term can therefore be considered as representing a multiset, and in fact we will do so in the sequel. As a consequence of this assumption there is a sum and a product of terms: Addition of terms σ and τ is defined symbolically, with $\sigma + \tau = \tau + \sigma$ and $\sigma - \sigma = 0$. The product $\sigma \cdot \tau$ of σ and τ is defined as substitution of σ into τ, linearly extended to multisets σ. For the variables x and z this yields e.g. $x \cdot z = x$, $-x \cdot z = -x$ and for the variable w, ranging over pairs, we get e.g. $(y, x) \cdot w = (y, x)$ and $-(x, y) \cdot w^{-1} = -(x, y)^{-1} = -(y, x)$. And due to the linear extension of the product, $(Y \times x) \cdot w^{-1} = (Y \times x)^{-1} = x \times Y$. As a further example, in the course of showing that i_2 is in fact a place invariant, we get for the inner product of the a-indexed column a of $\underline{N}$ with i_2 : $\mathrm{a} \cdot i_2 = 0 \cdot 0 + 0 \cdot 0 - (x \times Y) \cdot w + (Y \times x) \cdot w^{-1} = -x \times Y + (Y \times x)^{-1} = -x \times Y + x \times Y = 0$. Furthermore, $a_N \cdot i_1 = U$ and $a_N \cdot i_2 = N$. In analogy to Chapter 3 we derive characteristic equations of place invariants, which for i_1 is

$$pending + agreed = U \tag{17}$$

and for i_2

$$acks + proposals = N. \tag{18}$$

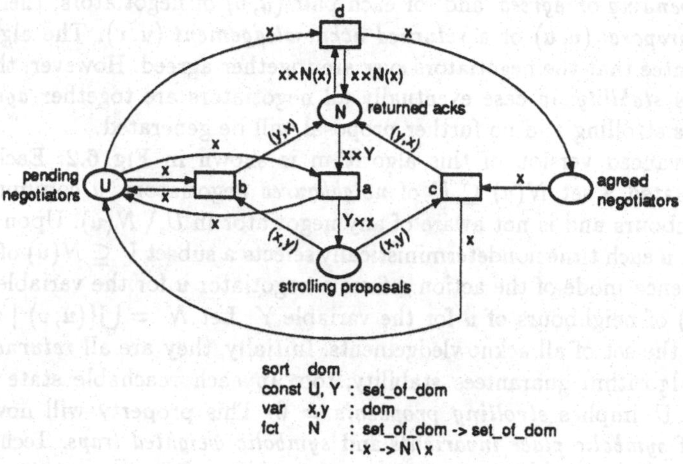

Fig. 6.2. An advanced consensus algorithm

	a	b	c	d	a_N	i_1	i_2
pending			x	$-x$	U	z	
agreed			$-x$	x		z	
acks	$-x \times Y$	(y,x)	(y,x)		N		w
proposals	$Y \times x$	$-(x,y)$	$-(x,y)$				w^{-1}

Fig. 6.3. Matrix, initial state and two place invariants to Fig. 6.2

The notion of *traps* can likewise be lifted to symbolic high-level nets: Each place can be *weighted* for this purpose. As an example, let $ack : U \to \mathcal{P}(U \times U)$ be defined by $ack(u) = u \times N(u)$. Hence *ack* assigns each negotiator u its set of acknowledgements. Then $ack(pending)$ returns the acknowledgements of all negotiators that reside at *pending*. With this weight function the set

$$Q = \{acks, ack(pending)\} \tag{19}$$

is a trap for the set $N = ack(U)$ of all acknowledgements: N resides initially at Q (as $a_N(acks) = U$) and each action that removes an acknowledgement (u, v) from Q also returns (u, v) to Q: The actions b and c add to $acks$ and leave $pending$ unchanged. The action d removes $ack(x) = x \times N(x)$ from both $acks$ and $ack(pending)$ and returns $ack(x)$ to $acks$. Finally, the action a removes $ack(x) = x \times N(x)$ from $pending$ and $x \times Y$ from $acks$, where Y is a subset of $N(x)$. And a returns $ack(x)$ to $pending$. This yields the characteristic inequality

$$acks + ack(pending) \geq N. \tag{20}$$

Now we apply ack to the equation (17):

$$ack(pending) + ack(agreed) = ack(U) = N \tag{21}$$

and subtract (20) from the sum of (18) and (21):

$$ack(agreed) + proposals \leq N. \tag{22}$$

Obviously,

$$agreed = U \text{ implies } ack(agreed) = ack(U) = N; \tag{23}$$

hence with (22) and (23) we get

$$ack(agreed) = U \text{ implies } proposals = \emptyset. \tag{24}$$

This just states the above discussed stability of the algorithm.

Acknowledgements

This paper reports some aspects of sustained effort on settling an adequate basis for fundamental Distributed Algorithms. This effort started in 1988 with the "Sonderforschungsbereich 342" at the Technical University of Munich, together with the EC-based projects DEMON and CALIBAN. It is still going on at the Humboldt University of Berlin ([3], [6]–[10]) now supported by the projects "Distributed Algorithms", "Consensus Algorithms" and "Petri Net Applications", all granted by the "Deutsche Forschungsgemeinschaft".

People involved include, among others, Jörg Desel, Dominik Gomm, Ekkart Kindler, Sibylle Peuker, Tobias Vesper, Hagen Völzer and Rolf Walter. Eike Best draw my attention to an example in his monography [1] which is based on [2] and inspired us with the consensus algorithm in Fig. 6.1 and Fig. 6.2. Many thanks to all of them.

References

1. E. Best: Semantik. Vieweg-Verlag Braunschweig (1995)
2. E. W. Dijkstra: Finding the Correctness Proof of a Concurrent Program. Proc. Koninklijke Nederlandse Akademie van Wetenschappen, Vol 81/2, pp 207–215 (June 1978)
3. E. Kindler: Modularer Entwurf verteilter Systeme mit Petrinetzen. Edition Versal, Bertz-Verlag (1995)
4. S. Owicki, L. Lamport: Proving liveness properties of concurrent programs. ACM Transactions on Programming Languages and Systems 4, pp 455–495 (1982)
5. W. Reisig: Petri Nets and Algebraic Specifications. Theoretical Computer Science 80, pp 1–34 (1991)
6. W. Reisig: Correctness Proofs of Distributed Algorithms. in: K. P. Birman et al (eds): Theory and Practice in Distributed Systems. LNCS 938, pp 164–177, Springer-Verlag (1995)
7. W. Reisig: Petri Net Models of Distributed Algorithms. in: J. van Leeuven (ed): Computer Science Today: Recent Trends and Developments. LNCS 1000, pp 441–454, Springer-Verlag (1995)
8. W. Reisig: Interleaved Progress, Concurrent Progress and Local Progress. Proceedings of the DIMACS Workshop on Partial Order Methods in Verification. D. Peled, G. Holzmann, V. Pratt (eds), American Mathematical Society (to appear)
9. W. Reisig: Distributed Algorithms: Modelling and Analysis with Petri Nets. Monography (to appear)
10. R. Walter: Petrinetzmodelle verteilter Algorithmen. Edition Versal, Bertz-Verlag (1995)

An Algorithmic Approach for Checking Closure Properties of ω-Regular Languages

Doron Peled[1] and Thomas Wilke[2]* and Pierre Wolper[3]

[1] Bell Laboratories, 700 Mountain Avenue, Murray Hill, NJ 07974, USA
doron@research.att.com

[2] DIMACS, Rutgers University, Piscataway, NJ 08855-1179, USA
wilke@dimacs.rutgers.edu

[3] Université de Liège, Institut Montefiore, B28, 4000 Liège, Belgium
pw@montefiore.ulg.ac.be

Abstract. In concurrency theory, there are several examples where the interleaved model of concurrency can distinguish between execution sequences which are not significantly different. One such example is sequences that differ from each other by stuttering, i. e., the number of times a state can adjacently repeat. Another example is executions that differ only by the ordering of independently executed events. Considering these sequences as different is semantically rather meaningless. Nevertheless, specification languages that are based on interleaving semantics, such as linear temporal logic (LTL), can distinguish between them. This situation has led to several attempts to define languages that cannot distinguish between such equivalent sequences. In this paper, we take a different approach to this problem: we develop algorithms for deciding if a property cannot distinguish between equivalent sequences, i. e., is *closed* under the equivalence relation. We focus on properties represented by regular languages, ω-regular languages, or propositional LTL formulae and show that for such properties there is a wide class of equivalence relations for which determining closure is decidable, in fact in PSPACE. Hence, checking the closure of a specification is no more difficult than checking satisfiability of a temporal formula. Among the closure properties we are able to handle, one finds trace closedness, stutter closedness and projective closedness, for all of which we are also able to prove a PSPACE lower bound. Being able to check that a property is closed under an equivalence relation has an immediate application in state-space exploration based verification. Indeed, the knowledge that the specification does not distinguish between equivalent execution sequences allows constructing a reduced state space where it is sufficient that at least one sequence per equivalence class is represented.

1 Introduction

In the total order model of concurrency, the atomic actions of the various processes are *interleaved* into totally ordered executions. If two actions are *inde-*

* This author is supported by a DIMACS postdoctoral fellowship funded by NSF award 91-19999 and the New Jersey Commission on Science and Technology.

pendent, they will be interleaved in both possible ways, but will appear in each execution in a specific, though arbitrary, order. Distinguishing between sequences that differ from each other only by the order of concurrently executed events is artificial and mostly meaningless. It is thus usual and useful to group such sequences into equivalence classes. A well-known way of doing this is the concept of *traces* due to Mazurkiewicz [10]: a trace is a set of interleaving sequences that can be obtained from each other by successively commuting independent adjacent actions. Traces are equivalence classes, and sequences belonging to the same trace are said to be *trace equivalent*. Unfortunately, most common specification languages, such as linear-time temporal logic [16] (LTL), naturally allow the specification of properties that are not trace closed, i. e., that can distinguish between trace equivalent sequences. One will usually not specify such properties, but since they can be expressed, every property should be treated as if it might not be trace closed. To work around this, several attempts have been made in the past to define logics that can only define trace-closed properties, e.g., ISTL [5, 15], TrPTL [19] and TLC [1]. None of these logics is completely satisfying: they lack simplicity and/or cannot express all relevant properties. A full practical and complete solution to the problem has not been given.

Another equivalence that is useful in studying concurrent systems is *stutter equivalence*: a pair of sequences are considered to be equivalent if they differ in at most the number of times a state may adjacently repeat [9]. Although next-time operator free linear-time temporal logic formulas are naturally stutter closed, i. e. cannot distinguish between stutter equivalent sequences, the use of a next-time operator does not preclude stutter closure and can be convenient. Finally, projective equivalence [12] is an extension of stutter equivalence that requires stutter equivalence of various projections of a sequence.

One context in which knowing that a property is closed is valuable is that of *partial-order verification algorithms* [22, 4, 26, 13, 14]. These algorithms proceed by checking a property on a reduced state space obtained by only exploring selected interleaving sequences. The reduction is based on the observation that it is not necessary to explore different interleavings that vary from each other only by the relative order of occurrence of independent (concurrent) transitions. Since it is guaranteed that at least one sequence is selected out of each equivalence class for trace equivalence [13] or stuttering equivalence [22, 14], one needs to ensure that the checked property is closed with respect to the equivalence relation exploited. If the property is not closed, one has to be more restrictive as to which transitions can be viewed as independent, with the consequence that a smaller reduction is obtained. Thus, being able to check whether a property is closed for a given equivalence relation is important for achieving good partial-order reductions. Recognizing projective closedness can also be used for improving the throughput of partial-order reduction [13, 12]. Projective properties are also preserved by sequential consistent [8] implementations of cache protocols [12].

In this paper, we study the problem of determining whether a property is closed under various equivalence relations, including what we will call concurrency relations, namely, trace equivalence, stutter equivalence, and projective equivalence [12]. We exhibit sufficient conditions that the equivalence relation should satisfy in order for the problem to be decidable for regular and ω-regular properties and hence also for linear-time temporal logic properties [23]. In the case of regular languages, we only assume that the equivalence relation is generated by a sequential relation [20], that is, by a relation 'recognized' by a finite automaton; in the case of ω-regular languages, we assume that the equivalence relation is what we call a "piecewise extension" (see Definition 10) of an equivalence relation on finite words generated by a sequential relation.

We first show how closure under an equivalence relation generated from a sequential relation can be decided for finite word languages. We obtain a polynomial time decision procedure for languages represented by deterministic automata and show that the problem is in PSPACE when non-deterministic automata are used as a representation. Furthermore, we obtain a matching lower bound for each of the concurrency relations. Extending the decision procedure to ω-regular languages is more difficult, but is achieved by using the characterization of ω-regular languages in terms of congruences [2]. Furthermore, the problem remains in PSPACE both for languages specified by non-deterministic automata and by LTL formulae, with the matching lower bound still holding for each of the concrete relations we consider.

The case of trace equivalence for ω-regular languages was also dealt with in [3]. There, the authors prove that it is decidable whether a regular ω-language is trace closed. However, the decision procedure that is suggested by their proof has worst-case space complexity at least exponential.

2 The Concurrency Relations

We recall the notions of trace, stutter, and projective equivalence, which will also be referred to as *concurrency relations*. We also introduce the notion of the limit extension of an equivalence relation. This allows us to view the infinite versions of the concurrency relations as uniform extensions of the corresponding finite versions.

2.1 The Limit Extension

Throughout this paper, Σ stands for a finite alphabet and Σ^∞ for $\Sigma^* \cup \Sigma^\omega$. The prefix order on Σ^∞ is denoted by $\sqsubset$.

Definition 1 (limit extension). The *limit extension* $\sim^{\lim} \subseteq \Sigma^\omega \times \Sigma^\omega$ of an equivalence relation $\sim \subseteq \Sigma^* \times \Sigma^*$ is defined as follows: $\alpha \sim^{\lim} \beta$ holds iff

- for every $u \in \Sigma^*$ such that $u \sqsubset \alpha$ there exist $v, v' \in \Sigma^*$ such that $v \sqsubset \beta$ and $uv' \sim v$, and
- for every $u \in \Sigma^*$ such that $u \sqsubset \beta$ there exist $v, v' \in \Sigma^*$ such that $v \sqsubset \alpha$ and $uv' \sim v$.

Recall that an equivalence relation $\sim$ on Σ^* is called a congruence relation if $uv \sim u'v'$ whenever $u \sim u'$ and $v \sim v'$.

Lemma 2. *If $\sim$ is a congruence relation on Σ^*, then $\sim^{\lim}$ is an equivalence relation on Σ^ω.*

Proof. The relation $\sim^{\lim}$ is a binary relation on Σ^ω, which is obviously reflexive and symmetric. Assume $\alpha \sim^{\lim} \beta \sim^{\lim} \gamma$ and let $u \sqsubset \alpha$. By definition of $\sim^{\lim}$, there exist $v \sqsubset \beta$ and v' such that $uv' \sim v$. On the other hand, since $\beta \sim^{\lim} \gamma$, there exist $w \sqsubset \gamma$ and w' such that $vw' \sim w$. Thus $uv'w' \sim w$, since $\sim$ is a congruence relation. Symmetrically, for $u \sqsubset \gamma$ we can find v, v', w, w' such that $w \sqsubset \alpha$ and $uv'w' \sim w$. Hence $\alpha \sim^{\lim} \gamma$. So $\sim^{\lim}$ is also transitive and thus an equivalence relation. □

2.2 Finite and Infinite Traces

A *dependency relation* is a reflexive and symmetric relation $D \subseteq \Sigma \times \Sigma$. The pair (Σ, D) is also called a *dependency graph.*

For two words $u, v \in \Sigma^*$, write $u \overset{1}{\equiv} v$ if there exist words w_1, w_2, and letters a, b such that $(a, b) \notin D$, $u = w_1abw_2$ and $v = w_1baw_2$. That is, u is the same as v or is obtained from v by exchanging the order of two adjacent independent letters. Let $\equiv$ be the transitive and reflexive closure of the relation $\overset{1}{\equiv}$. We say that u and v are *trace equivalent* [10] over (Σ, D) iff $u \equiv v$. That is, u is trace equivalent to v iff it can be obtained from it by repeatedly commuting adjacent independent letters.

As in [6], the infinite words α and β are said to be *trace equivalent* if $\alpha \equiv^{\lim} \beta$.

2.3 Stutter and Projective Equivalence

The *stutter removal* operator $\natural\colon \Sigma^\infty \mapsto \Sigma^\infty$ maps every word x to the word that is obtained from x by replacing every maximal finite substring of identical characters by a single copy of the character. For instance, $\natural(aabbbcaa) = abca$ and $\natural(aabbbc^\omega) = abc^\omega$. Words x and y are said to be *stutter equivalent* if $\natural x = \natural y$.

Let Σ_1 and Σ_2 be finite alphabets and $\Sigma = \Sigma_1 \times \Sigma_2$. The definitions below can be easily generalized to an n-component alphabet $\Sigma = \Sigma_1 \times \Sigma_2 \times \ldots \times \Sigma_n$. As usual, we identify the elements of Σ^∞ with elements of $\Sigma_1^\infty \times \Sigma_2^\infty$ in the natural way, e. g., we identify $(a_1, b_1)(a_2, b_2)$ with (a_1a_2, b_1b_2).

For each pair $c = (a, b) \in \Sigma$, let $c|_1 = a$ and $c|_2 = b$. For each word $x = c_1c_2c_3 \ldots \in \Sigma^\infty$, define the *projection* $x|_i$ $(i \in \{1, 2\})$ of x on the ith component to be $\natural(c_1|_ic_2|_ic_3|_i \ldots)$.

Notice that the projection operator also removes stuttering. Consider, for example, the word $u = (a_1, b_3)(a_1, b_5)(a_2, b_5)(a_9, b_5)$. Then $u|_1 = a_1a_2a_9$, and $u|_2 = b_3b_5$.

Words x and y are called *projective equivalent* if $x|_1 = y|_1$ and $x|_2 = y|_2$.

The following Lemma can be proved quite easily from the definitions of stutter and projective equivalence.

Lemma 3. *Both stutter and projective equivalence over infinite words are limit extensions of the corresponding equivalence relation over finite words.*

2.4 The Closure Problem

Given an equivalence relation $\sim$ over a set M and a subset $M' \subseteq M$, it is said that M' is *saturated* by $\sim$ if M' is a union of equivalence classes of $\sim$. In that case, we will say that M' is *$\sim$-closed* or *closed under* $\sim$. In particular, we will say that a language is trace closed (with respect to a given dependency alphabet), stutter closed, or projective if it is saturated by the corresponding trace, stutter, or the projective equivalence relation, respectively.

Given an alphabet Σ, a class $\mathcal{L}$ of languages of finite or infinite words over Σ, and an equivalence relation $\sim$ on, respectively, Σ^* or Σ^ω, the *closure problem* is to determine whether a given language $L \in \mathcal{L}$ is $\sim$-closed.

The term 'closure problem' can be explained as follows. Given an equivalence relation on Σ, the mapping $L \mapsto \{x \mid \exists y\,(x \sim y \wedge y \in L)\}$ defines a closure operator on the set of all languages over Σ. The closure problem is to determine whether the closure of a given language L is L itself.

We are mainly interested in those closure problems where $\sim$ is one of the concurrency relations and $\mathcal{L}$ is the class of regular or ω-regular languages, or LTL definable properties. Recall that every LTL definable property is ω-regular [25].

3 The Closure Problem for Finite Words

We will prove that the closure problem is decidable for the set of regular languages of finite words over a given alphabet Σ and every equivalence relation that is generated by a sequential relation, i. e., a relation recognizable by a finite automaton in the sense we define below. In fact, we will show that, under these assumptions, the closure problem is in PSPACE. The finite version of all the concurrency relations we introduced in the previous section fit these assumptions. In addition, we show that, for these relations, the closure problems are PSPACE-hard and hence obtain a tight characterization of their complexity.

Let \$ be a symbol not belonging to the alphabet Σ, write $\Sigma_\$$ for $\Sigma \cup \{\$\}$ and $x \downarrow \Sigma$ for the *canonic projection* $\Sigma_\$^\infty \to \Sigma^\infty$ (the one erasing the symbol \$, not to be confused with the projection defined in Sect. 2). For a binary relation R on Σ^*, let $R_\$$ be the relation that, for $(u,v) \in R$, contains $(u\,\$^{|v|-|u|}, v)$ if $|u| \leq |v|$ and $(u, v\,\$^{|u|-|v|})$ otherwise. Note that any two words that are related by $R_\$$ have the same length, and recall that we identify every pair in $R_\$$ with a word over $\Sigma_\$ \times \Sigma_\$$, and $R_\$$ itself with a language over $\Sigma_\$ \times \Sigma_\$$.

Definition 4 [20]. A binary relation R on Σ^* is said to be *sequential* if $R_\$$ (viewed as a language) is regular.

We say that an equivalence relation $\sim$ is *generated* by a relation $\overset{1}{\sim}$ if $\sim$ is the reflexive, symmetric, transitive closure of $\overset{1}{\sim}$, that is, if $\sim$ is the smallest equivalence relation containing $\overset{1}{\sim}$.

The proof of the following lemma is straightforward:

Lemma 5. *Let $L \subseteq \Sigma^*$ and $\sim$ an equivalence relation on Σ^* generated by a symmetric relation $\overset{1}{\sim}$. Then L is not $\sim$-closed iff there exist words $u, v \in \Sigma^*$ such that $u \overset{1}{\sim} v$, $u \in L$, and $v \notin L$.*

For regular languages, it is immediate to extract from Lemma 5 a decision procedure that checks whether for a fixed equivalence relation $\sim$, generated by a sequential relation $\overset{1}{\sim}$, a given regular language L is $\sim$-closed. We assume the regular languages L are given by finite automata A, and, w. l. o. g., that $\overset{1}{\sim}$ is symmetric. (Note that the symmetric closure of a sequential relation is itself sequential). We build an automaton B accepting $R_\$$, where R is the relation containing all the pairs (u, v) that satisfy exactly the conditions of Lemma 5. The automaton B can be obtained as the product of three automata:

1. an automaton that checks that the first component of a given input belongs to $L\,\$^*$;
2. an automaton that checks that the second component of a given input does not belong to $L\,\$^*$; and
3. an automaton that checks that a given input belongs to $\overset{1}{\sim}_\$$ (viewed as a language).

If the automaton A is deterministic, the first and the second automaton can be chosen to be of size $O(|A|)$. If A is non-deterministic, the second automaton has size $O(2^{|A|})$. The third automaton is the automaton that recognizes $\overset{1}{\sim}_\$$ and has a fixed size.

Given that the non-emptiness problem for finite automata can be checked in linear time, we have the following results:

Theorem 6. *Let $\sim$ be an equivalence relation generated by a sequential relation, and consider the closure problem for $\sim$ with respect to languages represented by deterministic or non-deterministic finite automata, where $|A|$ stands for the size of an input automaton A.*

1. *The closure problem is decidable in time $O(|A|)$ for deterministic automata.*
2. *The closure problem is decidable in time $O(2^{|A|})$ for non-deterministic automata.*

An automaton for the complement of a language given by a non-deterministic automaton can be exponentially bigger. However, it need not be constructed to check the emptiness of the automaton B described above. We actually have:

Theorem 7. *Let $\sim$ be an equivalence relation generated by a sequential relation. The closure problem for $\sim$ and languages represented by non-deterministic finite automata is in PSPACE.*

Sketch of Proof. What pushes the complexity of our procedure up is that we have to check for nonacceptance by the automaton describing the language. However, it is well known that checking for the existence of a word not accepted by a non-deterministic automaton can be done in PSPACE. Basically, one does a non-deterministic search through the state-space of the deterministic version of the automaton. Since all one needs to remember is the current state, the procedure is in NPSPACE and hence in PSPACE. This procedure can easily be combined with a search through the other components of our automaton, yielding an overall PSPACE procedure. □

Returning to the concurrency equivalence relations presented in Sect. 2, it is enough to show that each one of the three equivalence relations is generated by a sequential relation. Trace equivalence $\equiv$ is already defined to be the transitive closure of a sequential relation, namely $\overset{1}{\equiv}$. Stutter equivalence is generated by the sequential relation $\{(uav, uaav) \mid u, v \in \Sigma^*, a \in \Sigma\}$. Projective equivalence is generated by the sequential relation that relates

- $u(a,b)v$ with $u(a,b)(a,b)v$,
- $u(a_1,b_1)(a_1,b_2)(a_2,b_3)v$ with $u(a_1,b_1)(a_2,b_2)(a_2,b_3)v$, and
- $u(a_1,b_1)(a_2,b_1)(a_3,b_2)v$ with $u(a_1,b_1)(a_2,b_2)(a_3,b_2)v$,

for $u, v \in \Sigma^*$, $a_1, a_2, a_3 \in \Sigma_1$, and $b_1, b_2, b_3 \in \Sigma_2$.
To sum up:

Corollary 8. *The closure problem for trace, stutter, and projective equivalence with respect to languages represented by non-deterministic finite automata is in PSPACE.*

Next, we will complement this result by proving a matching lower bound.

Theorem 9. *The closure problem for trace, stutter, and projective equivalence with respect to languages represented by non-deterministic finite automata is PSPACE-hard.*

Sketch of Proof. For every language $L \subseteq \Gamma^*$ accepted by a deterministic polynomial space Turing machine M, we can construct a polynomial time computable function $f: x \mapsto A_x$ that associates with every $x \in \Gamma^*$ a finite automaton A_x over Σ such that

- if $x \notin L$ then $L(A_x) = \Sigma^*$, and
- if $x \in L$ then $L(A_x) = \Sigma^* \setminus \{u\}$ for some $u \in ab\Sigma^*$. (The word u encodes the accepting computation of M on x, prefixed by ab).

This construction is similar to the one given in [7]. If we choose $(a,b) \notin D$, we have that $x \in L$ iff $L(A_x)$ is not trace closed. Similarly, we have that $x \in L$ iff $L(A_x)$ is not stutter-closed, or is not projective. This means that the complements of the problems in question are PSPACE-hard, and, hence, that so are the problems themselves. □

Note that, in general, not every equivalence relation on Σ^* is generated by a sequential relation. Moreover, the $\sim$-closure of a regular language is not necessarily regular again. Consider, for instance, the case where $\Sigma = \{a, b\}$, $\sim$ is the trace equivalence relation with respect to the dependency alphabet $D = \{(a,a),(b,b)\}$, and L is the regular set $(ab)^*$. In this case, the $\sim$-closure of L is the set of strings which have as many occurrences of a as occurrences of b. But this set is not regular.

4 The Closure Problem for Infinite Words

We prove that the closure problem is decidable for the set of regular languages of infinite words for a large class of equivalence relations. These relations are "piecewise extensions" (see next definition) of relations that are generated by sequential relations. In fact, we show that the closure problem is in this case in PSPACE. The infinite versions of the concurrency relations from Sect. 2 are all particular instances of this.

Definition 10 (piecewise extension). Let $\sim$ be a binary relation on Σ^* (not necessarily an equivalence relation). We define the relations $\sim^\omega$ and $\sim^{\omega *}$ on Σ^ω.

We write $\alpha \sim^\omega \beta$ if there exist decompositions $\alpha = u_0u_1u_2\ldots$ and $\beta = v_0v_1v_2\ldots$ such that $u_i \sim v_i$ for every $i \geq 0$. The relation $\sim^{\omega *}$ is the transitive closure of $\sim^\omega$, and it is called the *piecewise extension* of $\sim$.

It is easy to see that the relation $\sim^{\omega *}$ is an equivalence relation, provided that $\sim$ is reflexive and symmetric.

We denote the *syntactic congruence of a language* $L \subseteq \Sigma^\omega$ by $\approx_L$ (see [2]). It is a relation on finite words that is defined as follows: $u \approx_L v$ holds iff

- $xuyz^\omega \in L \leftrightarrow xvyz^\omega \in L$, for $x, y \in \Sigma^*$ and $z \in \Sigma^+$, and
- $x(uy)^\omega \in L \leftrightarrow x(vy)^\omega \in L$, for $x, y \in \Sigma^*$ with $uy \neq \varepsilon$ and $vy \neq \varepsilon$.

We will use the following property of the syntactic congruence, which is an immediate consequence of Lemma 2.2 in [2] and Proposition 2.3 in [11].

Proposition 11 [2, 11]. *Let $\sim$ be a congruence relation on Σ^* and $L \subseteq \Sigma^\omega$ an ω-regular language. Then L is closed under $\sim^{\omega *}$ iff $\sim \subseteq \approx_L$.*

We have:

Theorem 12. *Let $\sim$ be a congruence relation on Σ^* generated by a reflexive, symmetric relation $\stackrel{1}{\sim}$ and $L \subseteq \Sigma^\omega$ an ω-regular language. Then L is closed under $\sim^{\omega *}$ iff L is closed under $\stackrel{1}{\sim}^\omega$.*

Proof. For the non-trivial direction, assume L is not closed under $\sim^{\omega *}$. Then, according to Proposition 11, the syntactic congruence $\approx_L$ of L is not saturated by $\sim$, i.e., there exists an equivalence class of $\approx_L$ that is not closed under $\sim$. Hence, by Lemma 5, there are finite words u, v such that $u \stackrel{1}{\sim} v$ but $u \not\approx_L v$. So there exist x, y, z such that

- $xuyz^\omega \in L$ and $xvyz^\omega \notin L$, or

– $x(uy)^\omega \in L$ and $x(vy)^\omega \notin L$, where $uy \neq \varepsilon$ and $vy \neq \varepsilon$.

But $xuyz^\omega \overset{1}{\sim}{}^\omega xvyz^\omega$, as well as $x(uy)^\omega \overset{1}{\sim}{}^\omega x(vy)^\omega$. Thus, L is not $\overset{1}{\sim}{}^\omega$-closed. □

It follows from Theorem 12 that an ω-regular language L is closed under $\sim^{\omega *}$ iff there exists no word $(\alpha, \beta) \in (\Sigma_\$ \times \Sigma_\$)^\omega$ such that $\alpha \downarrow \Sigma \in L$, $\beta \downarrow \Sigma \notin L$, and $(\alpha, \beta) \in (\overset{1}{\sim}_\$)^\omega$, where $(\overset{1}{\sim}_\$)^\omega$ stands for the ω iteration of the relation $\overset{1}{\sim}_\$$, viewed as a language of finite words.

We can now use an algorithm similar to the one in Sect. 3 to solve the closure problem for regular ω-languages and the piecewise extension $\sim^{\omega *}$ of a congruence relation $\sim$ that is generated by a sequential relation $\overset{1}{\sim}$. W. l. o. g., we can assume that $\overset{1}{\sim}$ is reflexive and symmetric, since the reflexive, symmetric closure of a sequential relation is, again, sequential.

One has to check the emptiness of an automaton obtained as the product of the following three automata:

1. an automaton that checks that the canonic projection on Σ of the first component of the input is in L;
2. an automaton that checks that the canonic projection on Σ of the second component of the input is not in L;
3. an automaton that checks that the input can be decomposed into infinitely many factors that are all elements of $\overset{1}{\sim}_\$$ (when viewed as a language).

The first automaton can be directly obtained from a Büchi automaton A for a given language L and has size $O(|A|)$; the second automaton can be constructed in the same way from a Büchi automaton for the complement of L. Using the results of [18], this yields the following complexity result.

Theorem 13. *Let $\sim$ be a congruence relation on Σ^* that is generated by a sequential relation. The closure problem for $\sim^{\omega *}$ with respect to languages represented by Büchi automata is in PSPACE.*

Sketch of Proof. Similarly to the proof of Theorem 7, we use the fact that checking nonacceptance by a Büchi automaton can be done in PSPACE [18, 24]. □

If we can now show that trace, stutter and projective equivalences are piecewise extensions of congruence relations generated by sequential relations, we can apply our algorithm to obtain the desired decidability (and complexity) results.

We first mention the following straightforward statement.

Lemma 14. *If $\sim$ is a congruence relation, then $\sim^{\omega *} \subseteq \sim^{\lim}$.*

A congruence relation $\sim$ is called *left cancellative* if $v \sim w$ whenever $uv \sim uw$. Trace, stutter, and projective equivalences are easily shown to be left cancellative. The following theorem, which is a generalization of a result concerning trace equivalence in [3], gives the converse of Lemma 14 for left cancellative congruences.

Theorem 15. *Let $\sim$ be a left cancellative congruence relation. Then $\sim^{\lim} = \sim^{\omega*}$.*

Proof. In view of Lemma 14, we only have to show $\sim^{\lim} \subseteq \sim^{\omega*}$.

Assume $\alpha \sim^{\lim} \beta$. We will show that there are decompositions $\alpha = u_0 u_1 u_2 \ldots$ and $\beta = v_0 v_1 v_2 \ldots$ and an infinite sequence of words $w_0, w_1, w_2 \ldots$ such that

$$v_j \sim w_{2j} w_{2j+1}, \quad \text{and} \qquad (1)$$

$$u_j \sim w_{2j-1} w_{2j}, \quad \text{for } j \geq 0, \qquad (2)$$

where w_{-1} is the empty word ε. This implies $\alpha \sim^{\omega} w_0 w_1 w_2 \ldots \sim^{\omega} \beta$, which means $\alpha \sim^{\omega*} \beta$.

We will give an inductive definition for the u_i, v_i, and w_i. In step 0, we choose an arbitrary non-empty finite prefix $u_0 \sqsubset \alpha$, and set $w_0 = u_0$. In step $2i+1$, for $i \geq 0$, we will define v_i and w_{2i+1}; and in step $2i$, for $i \geq 1$, we will define u_i and w_{2i}.

We assume that before each step, (1) and (2) hold for words thus far defined; we have to make sure that the words to be defined in a new step don't lead to a violation of (1) or (2).

We describe only the steps $2i+1$; the description for the others is symmetric. Since (1) and (2) hold for words thus far defined, we have $u_0 u_1 \ldots u_i \sim w_0 w_1 \ldots w_{2i}$, where $u_0 u_1 \ldots u_i$ is a prefix of α, and $v_0 v_1 \ldots v_{i-1} \sim w_0 w_1 \ldots w_{2i-1}$, where $v_0 v_1 \ldots v_{i-1}$ is a prefix of β. Since $\alpha \sim^{\lim} \beta$, it follows from Definition 1 that there are finite non-empty strings y and z, such that $y \sqsubset \beta$ and $u_0 u_1 \ldots u_i z \sim y$. We choose y to be long enough such that $v_0 v_1 \ldots v_{i-1}$ is a proper prefix of it. Let $x \in \Sigma^+$ be the string such that $y = v_0 v_1 \ldots v_{n-1} x$. Hence $w_0 w_1 \ldots w_{2i} z \sim u_0 u_1 \ldots u_i z \sim v_0 v_1 \ldots v_{i-1} x \sim w_0 w_1 \ldots w_{2i-1} x$. Set $v_i = x$ and $w_{2i+1} = z$. Then, since $\sim$ is cancellative, $v_i = x \sim w_{2i} w_{2i+1}$, i.e., (1) holds for $j = i$. □

From Theorems 13 and 15 we have:

Corollary 16. *Let $\sim$ be a left cancellative congruence relation generated by a sequential relation. The closure problem for the limit extension of $\sim$ with respect to languages represented by Büchi automata is in PSPACE.*

Since the finite version of each concurrency relation is a left-cancellative congruence, and the infinite version of each concurrency relation is the limit extensions of its finite version, the previous corollary allows us to state.

Theorem 17. *The closure problem for trace, stutter and projective equivalence with respect to languages represented by Büchi automata is in PSPACE.*

It is now straightforward to adapt the proof of Theorem 9 to obtain:

Theorem 18. *The closure problem for trace, stutter and projective equivalence with respect to languages represented by Büchi automata is PSPACE-hard.*

5 The Closure Problem for LTL Properties

We focus now on the closure problem for the concurrency relations with respect to languages defined by LTL formulae. At first glance, it looks like this problem is harder than the closure problem for languages represented by Büchi automata. The reason is that there is an inherent exponential explosion in the conversion from LTL to Büchi automata [25]. However, we show that for the class of equivalence relations we are interested in, the problem is still in PSPACE, even when the property is described using an LTL formula. Notice that a propositional LTL formula φ uses a set of propositions Γ and that the corresponding alphabet of the language described by φ is $\Sigma = 2^{\Gamma}$. Notice also that projective closedness is defined with respect to a partition of Γ into two sets Γ_1 and Γ_2 of propositions; the alphabets Σ_1 and Σ_2 are 2^{Γ_1} and 2^{Γ_2}, respectively, and every $c \in \Sigma$ is identified with the letter $(c \cap \Gamma_1, c \cap \Gamma_2)$ from $\Sigma_1 \times \Sigma_2$ (see [12]).

Theorem 19. *Let $\sim$ be a congruence relation on Σ^* that is generated by a sequential relation. The closure problem for $\sim^{\omega*}$ with respect to languages represented by LTL formulae is in PSPACE.*

Sketch of Proof. LTL formulae can be translated to Büchi automata [25]. The translation incurs an exponential blowup. However, as we did in the case of the automaton for the complement language in the proof of Theorem 13, it is not necessary to construct the automaton for a formula φ. Instead, one can conduct a search through its states, provided that each state and the successor relation between states can be calculated in time polynomial in the size of φ. Moreover, the complement of the automaton for φ is merely an automaton for $\neg\varphi$, eliminating the doubly exponential blowup in translating and complementing. □

Theorem 20. *The closure problem for trace, stutter, and projective equivalence with respect to languages defined by LTL formulae is PSPACE-hard.*

Proof. Let $\sim$ be an arbitrary non-trivial concurrency relation. We will reduce the satisfiability problem for LTL formulas to the complement of the closure problem for $\sim$. Recall that LTL satisfiability is PSPACE-complete [17] and that PSPACE is closed under complementation.

As explained in the sketch of the proof of Theorem 9, there exist $a, b \in \Sigma$ such that $ab\Sigma^\omega$ is not $\sim$-closed. In fact, for such a and b and an arbitrary non-empty set $L \subseteq \Sigma^\omega$, abL is not $\sim$-closed.

Let ψ be a formula that defines $ab\Sigma^\omega$. Take, for instance,

$$\psi = \bigwedge_{p \in a} p \wedge \bigwedge_{p \in \Gamma \setminus a} \neg p \wedge \bigcirc\Big(\bigwedge_{p \in b} p \wedge \bigwedge_{p \in \Gamma \setminus b} \neg p\Big).$$

Consider the function that maps a given LTL formula ϕ to $\eta = \bigcirc \bigcirc \phi \wedge \psi$. Clearly, this mapping is computable in polynomial time. Thus to conclude the proof, we only have to show that ϕ is satisfiable iff the set defined by η is not $\sim$-closed.

Assume first ϕ is not satisfiable. Then $\bigcirc\bigcirc\phi$ is not satisfiable, and thus η is not satisfiable. So the set defined by η, the empty set, is $\sim$-closed. Assume now that ϕ is satisfiable, and let L be the set of ω-words that satisfy ϕ. Then abL is the set defined by η, and, as we have argued above, η is thus not $\sim$-closed. □

Notice that the proof of Theorem 20 is general and can easily be adapted for a large class of equivalence relations.

6 Application of Recognizing Equivalence Closedness

6.1 Model-Checking Applications

Partial-order reduction methods is a generic name for a family of algorithms for generating a reduced state space of a concurrent program [22, 4, 26, 14]. These algorithms are used for model-checking properties of concurrent programs. They are based on a modified depth-first search, where at each state in the search only a subset of the transitions that can be taken (i. e., are *enabled*) are chosen. The main observation in these algorithms is that for most purposes, there is no need to distinguish between program execution sequences that are equivalent. Hence, a state space that includes at least one sequence per equivalence class can replace the full state space of a program.

However, most specification formalisms for sequences, e.g., temporal logics or Büchi automata, can specify properties that can distinguish between sequences that are trace equivalent. Although partial-order reductions are applicable also for such non-closed properties, the amount of reduction achieved typically degrades. The reason for this is that the correctness of the reduction is maintained by adding more dependencies to the system, forcing the property to become trace closed under a bigger dependency relation. These dependencies are usually added pessimistically, e.g., adding dependencies among all transitions that can potentially affect the truth of the checked property [22], or among subsets of such transitions, after applying some LTL rewriting rules [13].

The results of this paper offer an interesting alternative: check that the formula to be verified is trace closed and use the partial-order technique without any additional dependencies. Note that the property to be checked will usually be trace closed. If the checked property is not closed, one can use our algorithm to guide the partial-order reduction algorithms as to which dependencies are needed to be added in order for the property to be checked reliably.

Checking for stutter equivalence is also important for similar applications. For instance, in the partial-order reduction methods of [22, 14], the reduction algorithm guarantees to generate at least one execution sequence from each stutter equivalence class. Hence, it is only usable for stutter-closed formulae. In [22, 14], this condition is enforced by restricting oneself to LTL formulae not containing the next-time operator. The decision procedure we have developed in this paper offers a more flexible alternative.

6.2 State-Based and Transition-Based Specifications

The above decision procedure, applied to trace equivalence, is based on a specification that expresses properties as sequences of atomic transitions. However, in most cases, the specification is given with respect to sequences of *states*, interpreted over a set of boolean *propositions*. We show how to change our decision procedure, when additional knowledge about the relation between the transitions and the propositions used in the specification is given.

Let Γ be a set of propositions. Each state is a subset of Γ. Each transition τ from a set of transitions Δ induces a relation $\delta(\tau) \subseteq 2^{\Gamma} \times 2^{\Gamma}$, which restricts the way the transition τ may change the propositions in Γ. We say that a sequence of transitions in $\rho \in \Delta^{\omega}$ *conforms* with a sequence of states $\sigma \in 2^{\Gamma^{\omega}}$ iff for each $i > 0$, $(\sigma(i-1), \sigma(i)) \in \delta(\rho(i))$. It is easy to see that the language $C \subseteq (\Delta \times 2^{\Gamma})^{\omega}$ that recognizes pairs of conforming sequences is ω-regular.

Our modified decision procedure will check whether the checked property L can distinguish between sequences that conform with sequences of transitions that are trace equivalent.

We check the emptiness of the intersection of the following five automata over $2^{\Gamma} \times \Delta \times \Delta \times 2^{\Gamma}$. Each word of the automata is a quadruple $w = (\sigma_1, \rho_1, \rho_2, \sigma_2)$. The five automata are as follows:

(1) Checks that the first word σ_1 is in L;
(2) Checks that the fourth word σ_2 is in the complement $\overline{L}$ of L;
(3) Checks that the pair (ρ_1, ρ_2) consists of infinitely many factors, such that each factor consists of a pair of words that are related by $\stackrel{1}{\equiv}$.
(4) Checks that ρ_1 conforms with σ_1.
(5) Checks that ρ_2 conforms with σ_2.

7 Conclusions

Being trace closed or stutter closed is a natural property of specifications for concurrent systems. Yet, many specification languages can specify properties that violate it, e.g., LTL and finite automata recognizable languages. We have proposed an algorithm for a family of equivalence relations, including trace, stutter and projective equivalence, which decides closedness for regular and ω-regular languages, and LTL specifications. This allows exploiting the simplicity of such languages, while using the decision procedure to restrict the specifications to closed ones.

Furthermore, it is perfectly realistic to expect to be able to use our algorithm in the context of verification tools that use partial-order state space reductions. Indeed, it involves no other construction than those routinely used in model-checking, and has the same complexity in terms of the LTL formula, namely PSPACE-complete.

References

1. Alur, R., Peled, D., Penczek, W.: Model-checking of causality properties. In Proc. 10th IEEE Symposium on Logic in Computer Science, San Diego, California (1995) 90–100.
2. Arnold, A.: A syntactic congruence for rational ω-languages. Theoretical Computer Science **39** (1985) 333–335.
3. Diekert, V., Gastin, P., Petit, A.: Rational and recognizable trace languages. Information and Computation **116** (1995) 134–153.
4. Godefroid, P.: Using partial orders to improve automatic verification methods. In Proc. 2nd Workshop on Computer Aided Verification, New Brunswick, NJ. Lect. Notes in Comput. Sci., vol. 531, Springer (1990) 176–185.
5. Katz, S., Peled, D.: Verification of distributed programs using representative interleaving sequences. Distributed Computing **6** (1992) 107–120.
6. Kwiatkowska, M. Z.: Event fairness and non-interleaving concurrency. Formal Aspects of Computing **1** (1989) 213–228.
7. Kozen, D.: Lower bounds for natural proof systems. 18th IEEE Symposium on Foundations of Computer Science, Providence, Rhode Island (1977) 254–266.
8. Lamport, L.: How to make a multiprocessor computer that correctly executes multiprocess programs. IEEE Transactions on Computers **28** (1979) 690–691.
9. Lamport, L.: What good is temporal logic? In Proc. IFIP Congr. on Information Processing, Elsevier (1983) 657–668.
10. Mazurkiewicz, A.: Trace theory. In Proc. Advances in Petri Nets 1986, Bad Honnef, Germany. Lect. Notes in Comput. Sci., vol. 255, Springer (1987) 279–324.
11. Pécuchet, J.-P.: Etude Syntaxique des parties reconnaissable de mots infinis. In Automata, Languages, and Programming: 13th Intern. Coll. Rennes, France. Lect. Notes in Comput. Sci., vol. 226, Springer (1986) 294–303.
12. Peled, D.: On projective and separable properties. In Proc. Colloquium on Trees in Algebra and Programming, Edinburgh, Scotland. Lect. Notes in Comput. Sci., vol. 787, Springer (1994) 291–307.
13. Peled, D.: All from One, One from All: on Model Checking using representatives, In Proc. 5th International Conference on Computer Aided Verification, Elounda, Greece, Lect. Notes in Comput. Sci., vol. 697, Springer (1993) 409–423.
14. Peled, D.: Combining partial-order reductions with on-the-fly model-checking. Formal Methods in System Design **8** (1996) 39–64.
15. Peled, D., Pnueli, A.: Proving partial-order properties. Theoretical Computer Science **126** (1994) 143–182.
16. Pnueli, A.: The temporal logic of programs. In Proc. 18th IEEE Symposium on Foundation of Computer Science, Providence, Rhode Island (1977) 46–57.
17. Sistla, A. P., Clarke, E. M.: The complexity of propositional linear temporal logics. Journal of the ACM **32** (1985) 733–749.
18. Sistla, A. P., Vardi, M. Y., Wolper, P.: The complementation problem for Büchi automata with applications to temporal logic. Theoretical Computer Science **49** (1987) 217–237.
19. Thiagarajan, P. S.: A trace based extension of linear time temporal logic. In Proc. 10th IEEE Symposium on Logic in Computer Science, Paris, France (1994) 438–447.
20. Thomas, W.: Automata and quantifier hierarchies: formal properties of finite automata and applications. In Proc. of LITP Spring School on Theoretical Com-

puter Science, J. E. Pin, ed. Lect. Notes in Comput. Sci., vol. 386, Springer (1989) 104–119.

21. Thomas, W.: Automata on infinite objects. In Handbook of Theoretical Computer Science, vol. B, J. van Leeuwen, ed., Elsevier, Amsterdam (1990) 133–191.
22. Valmari, A.: A stubborn attack on state explosion. Formal Methods in System Design **1** (1992) 297–322.
23. Vardi, M. Y., Wolper, P.: Automata-theoretic techniques for modal logics of programs. J. Comput. System Sci. **32** (1986) 182–221.
24. Vardi, M. Y., Wolper, P.: Reasoning about infinite computations. Information and Computation **115** (1994) 1–37.
25. Wolper, P.: Temporal logic can be more expressive. Information and Control **56** (1983) 72–99.
26. Wolper, P., Godefroid, P.: Partial-order methods for temporal verification. In Proc. CONCUR, 4th Conference on Concurrency Theory, Hildesheim, Germany. Lect. Notes in Comput. Sci., vol. 715, Springer (1993) 233–246.

Towards Automata for Branching Time and Partial Order *

Michaela Huhn and Peter Niebert

Institut für Informatik, Universität Hildesheim, Germany
[huhn|niebert]@informatik.uni-hildesheim.de

Abstract. In this work we develop an automata framework for partial order structures with branching, for which we use trace systems. The aim is to investigate the prospects of *decidable* partial order logics of branching time, derivable from an automata framework.
On the one hand we define automata for trace systems directly, which combine asynchronous automata for linear time with tree automata. On the other hand we develop a branching generalisation of Mazurkiewicz trace theory, which links branching concurrent behaviour with tree automata directly: the idea is to generalise *interleaving sequences* for partially ordered runs to *interleaving trees* for trace systems. This development can also be used for partial order reduction methods in model checking for branching time.
The latter approach also exposes a problem for the *specification* of branching time and concurrent behaviour: the distinction between nondeterministic choice and parallelism cannot be maintained completely in the presence of *confusion*, a notion known from Petri net theory. We discuss several possible ways of coping with this problem.
Also on the automata side there are a few surprises. In particular the emptiness problem is decidable as desired, but turns out to be co-NP-complete.

1 Introduction

Automata theoretic methods have turned out to be a very useful and systematic approach to computer aided verification of reactive systems. The idea is to represent behaviour properties as (recognisable) languages, which can be specified by automata. Then, using automata theoretic constructions, such properties can be verified automatically. The first systematic account of the machinery was given in [VW86] for linear time temporal logics. Meanwhile this scheme has been transferred to many other semantics, in particular to branching time (tree automata, see e.g. [BVW94]) and to Mazurkiewicz traces (asynchronous automata [Zie89, Thi94]).
Automata for Mazurkiewicz traces are of special interest to automatic verification, because this notion combines the standard automata theoretic framework with the notion of partial order semantics. Partial order semantics have proven to be successful in mastering the state explosion problem resulting from the parallel composition of many components. See e.g. [Pel93], where linear time model checking is optimised for certain linear time temporal properties, which are robust against Mazurkiewicz

* Part of this work was financially supported by the Human Capital and Mobility Cooperation Network "EXPRESS" (Expressivity of Languages for Concurrency).

equivalence. The results of [NP95, Thi95] imply that Peled's work can be embedded into the automata framework using asynchronous automata. More generally, Thiagarajan gives a trace based generalisation of linear temporal logics which can be translated to asynchronous automata [Thi94].
On the other hand, there is strong interest in branching time model checking, especially for CTL, for which model checking is possible with effort linear in both the size of the model and the CTL formula (in contrast to linear time model checking, which requires an effort exponential in the size of the formula).
The question arises, to what extent it is possible to combine both branching time and partial order semantics to get the best from both worlds. A lot of such semantic models exist, e.g. event structures [Win87] or concurrent transition systems [Sta89]. There also have been several definitions of branching logics on such models [Pen92, MT90], but no such attempt has yet lead to a logic known to be decidable, while some are known to be undecidable.
The motivation for this work is to lay a basis for the combination of partial order methods with branching semantics in *logical specifications* by the definition of an appropriate automaton model. Using an automaton model we can more easily expose problems which are otherwise hidden in the logical framework. On such a basis one may define logics (translatable to the automata and thus decidable) like a trace based generalisation of CTL and optimise branching time model checking for formulae which are robust against a branching version of Mazurkiewicz equivalence.
As semantic framework for the representation of concurrent behaviour we use trace systems[2] [Ma88], because these are language oriented and thus suitable for the definition of automata. Trace systems are equivalent to prime event structures [Win87] with certain additional properties concerning the labelling as explained in the next section. On these systems we will define a common generalisation of Zielonka's asynchronous automata and tree automata.
In an alternative approach we develop a branching Mazurkiewicz trace theory as a rigorous generalisation of the linear case, where linear traces and interleaving sequences (or words) are generalised to trace systems and interleaving trees. We get interleaving trees as *sequentialised* representatives of trace behaviours. In particular we derive a Mazurkiewicz equivalence on trees via exchange operations on choices corresponding to the exchange operation on letters in the linear case. This approach allows the specification of trace systems via tree automata, and the comparison of tree automata with asynchronous tree automata, similar to the linear case.
However there are some problems in this generalisation for both approaches: A specific difficulty of branching partial order models lies in the ordering of independent choices: Whereas an action cannot be disabled or enabled by an independent action, the *choice* of an independent system component may very well be influenced by an independent action. This problem is known in Petri net theory as confusion[GLT79]. It is a problem for branching time because one aim of the partial order approach is to treat nondeterminism (choice) and parallelism differently - and this is also crucial for decidability: the source of undecidability in frameworks like [Pen92] is the treatment of parallelism like choice (cf. also proposition 23). However with confusion

[2] Mazurkiewicz originally uses the name *trace structure*. We follow [KP95] in our terminology.

this distinction cannot always be maintained, i.e. there is some kind of choice in the order in which independent actions are taken.
The confusion free case is of course ideal, because the problem just disappears and everything works fine. For example free choice nets [DE95] do not produce confusion! The question remains what can be done, when this restriction is unacceptable. We do not address this problem formally, but propose to look at partial behaviours, where the order of confused actions is resolved and thus reduce one behaviour of the general kind to a set of behaviours with resolved confusion. This would means to trade confusion against branching.
For the presentation we stick to automata over finite behaviours, because there already all problems specific to the framework are present. Even for the confusion free case things are not quite like we would expect: In the linear case asynchronous automata were introduced by [Zie89] for which the emptiness problem is linear in the size of the global state space (which is the same complexity as for word automata). In the branching case there is a surprise: the emptiness problem for branching asynchronous automata over free choice trace behaviours is *co-NP-complete* already for the simplest non-trivial concurrent alphabet, whereas tree automata as the corresponding sequential acceptors have a polynomial emptiness problem. These results and proofs shed light on the intrinsic complexity of the combination of independent branching and communication. We believe this to be independent of the concrete framework.
The rest of the paper is organised as follows: In section 2 we introduce trace systems. In section 3 we develop a branching Mazurkiewicz theory, discuss the problem of confusion and show that interleaving trees give an alternative, *sequential* representation of trace systems. In section 4 we define branching asynchronous automata, for which we analyse the emptiness problem in section 5. In section 6 we investigate the relation of our automata over trace systems to automata over interleaving trees. In the conclusions we give some hints on the connection of our results to model checking. Due to lack of space most of the proofs can only be sketched, more detailed proofs can be found in the full version [HN96] of this paper.

2 Trace Systems

In this section we define a representation of concurrent branching behaviour, which are called *trace systems* (or *trace structures*, as they are also called) [Ma88]. The essential underlying concept of this representation is that of Mazurkiewicz traces, which is a linear time partial order model.
Trace systems (or closely related formalisms) as representation of concurrent behaviour has been well studied, see in particular [RT91, NW95]. Trace systems have also been used as model in [Pen92] to define the branching time partial order logic CTL_P, which has an undecidable satisfiability problem.
Trace systems are capable of representing prime event structures [Win87] with two additional assumptions on the labelling [RT91]: the labelling must be *deterministic* (i.e. two simultaneously enabled and conflicting events must carry a different action label) and *context independent* (i.e. the action names determine precisely, whether two adjacent events can be commuted, so that a Mazurkiewicz dependency relation can be defined).

Since the first assumption seems to imply, that nondeterministic behaviour cannot be represented in trace systems, we should answer the question: ***are trace systems a branching time model?*** No – and yes! Two different trees can be distinguished by a single sequence, so there is no difference between linear time and branching time w.r.t. ***distinguishability.*** But there is a difference concerning ***definability*** in terms of properties or sets of behaviours: while with branching time we directly specify sets of trees, with linear time we specify sets of sequences and thus indirectly trees having only allowed sequences. Besides the restriction to deterministic behaviour can be technically handled by using an enriched alphabet with several copies a_1, a_2 of each action letter a, so e.g. $a + a$ can be represented deterministically by $a_1 + a_2$.
The second assumption means, that the action names used represent the communication structure. As a typical example, the behaviour of safe Petri nets can be modelled in trace systems, where the action names uniquely identify transitions.

Definition 1 (concurrent alphabet, trace). We assume a *concurrent alphabet* (Σ, I) where Σ is an action alphabet and I is an irreflexive, symmetric relation over Σ, called *independence relation.* $D = \Sigma^2 - I$ is called *dependence relation.* We will use both relations, depending on which one is more convenient. $(\Sigma^*, \circ, \varepsilon)$ denotes the free monoid over Σ. Let $\sim_I$ be the least congruence on Σ^* such that $ab \sim_I ba$ if $a\, I\, b$. The equivalence classes are known as *Mazurkiewicz traces* and are denoted by $[w]$, where w is a (representative) member of the class. As usual, a prefix relation is defined on $\Sigma^*/\sim_I$ by $[v] \preceq [w]$ iff there exists a u such that $[vu] = [w]$. Two traces $[v], [w]$ are called *consistent*, iff there exists a trace $[u]$, such that $[v], [w] \preceq [u]$, otherwise they are called *inconsistent.*

Definition 2 (event equivalence). We define the *enabling congruence* $\bowtie_I$ on Σ^+ to be the least equivalence satisfying:
i) if $ua, uba \in \Sigma^+$ and $a\, I\, b$ then $ua \bowtie_I uba$,
ii) if $u \sim_I u'$ then $u'a \bowtie_I ua$.

Where we consider traces rather than words, we will also write $([u], a) \bowtie_I ([v], a)$ iff $ua \bowtie_I va$, which is justified by the second part of the definition.
This equivalence was originally defined in [NW95] to identify events in translating trace systems into event structures: each equivalence class represents one event. Here we use it mainly to talk about confusion.

Definition 3 (Σ-tree, synchronization tree, trace system). A Σ-tree T is a nonempty, prefix closed subset $T \subseteq \Sigma^*$.
A Σ-tree T' is a subtree of T iff $T' \subseteq T$.
A set $T \subseteq \Sigma^*$ is *I-consistent* iff $v \in T$ and $v \sim_I w$ implies $w \in T$.
A set $T \subseteq \Sigma^*$ is called *I-diamond closed* iff $ua, v \in T$ and $ua \bowtie_I va$ implies $va \in T$.
A (Σ, I)-*synchronisation tree* T is a nonempty, prefix closed, I-consistent, I-diamond closed subset T of Σ^*.
For a (Σ, I)-synchronization tree T we call $\widetilde{T} = T/\sim_I$ a *trace system* and we call the equivalence classes of $\widetilde{T}$ *configurations.*

We use trace systems, because the representation is simple and well suited for the definition of (tree) acceptors. Merely for simplicity here we stick to the deterministic framework.

3 A Branching Mazurkiewicz Trace Theory

In Mazurkiewicz trace theory words are considered as serialisations of traces. Moreover, the equivalence $\sim_I$ on words is generated by simple exchange operations. We look for a representation of trace systems by *interleaving trees* that correspond to interleaving sequences of the linear time case in the following sense:

a) A trace system can be reconstructed from its interleaving trees, ideally from a single interleaving tree.
b) The different interleaving trees that represent the same (part of a) system behaviour form an equivalence class which is generated by simple exchange operations.
c) Nodes in a tree represent configurations, and configurations in different branches are incompatible (i.e. the source of branching is choice, never interleaving).
d) The generalisation is conservative, i.e. in the case without branching where a trace system essentially reduces to a trace, the corresponding interleaving trees reduce to interleaving sequences.

3.1 Confusion: independence meets choice

In the case of general trace systems it is sometimes impossible to represent the complete behaviour in a single interleaving tree (i.e. there exist trace systems, which are not representable by any single interleaving tree satisfying the requirements), as the following example shows:

Example 1. Let $\Sigma = \{a, b, c, d\}$, $a\ I\ b$ (all other pairs are dependent), and let $\widetilde{T} = \{[\varepsilon], [a], [b], [ab], [ac], [bd]\}$. This trace system and a Petri net with this behaviour are depicted below. It is not representable by an interleaving tree, because that one would either have to begin with a or b (to have both a and b at the root would violate condition (c)), in which case either $[bd]$ or $[ac]$ could not be represented in the tree (contradicting (a))!

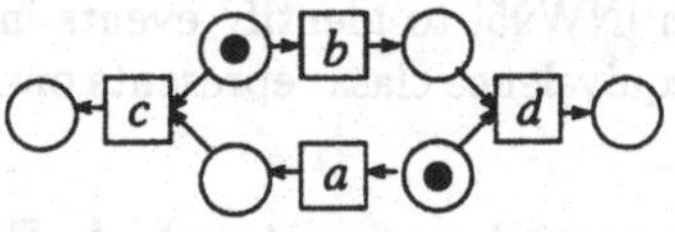

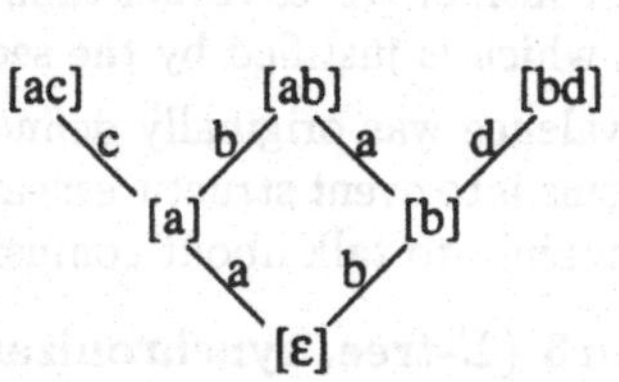

Even if we simplify the example by omitting the d transition, there is a problem: in that case we can start with a postponing the choice between b and c. Thus we get an sequential object because the choices are orderable, but the configuration $[b]$ is not present in any interleaving tree also containing $[ac]$.

This problem results from *confusion*, a notion known from Petri net theory (cf. [GLT79]): a place with a token belongs to both an enabled transition (say a) and a transition, which is not yet, but can be enabled (say d), (or conversely a transition, which is not enabled anymore, but was enabled previously).
Since confusion in Petri net theory is defined on nets (i.e. syntax), and we deal with models here, we choose our own presentation:

Definition 4 (confusion). For a trace system $\widetilde{T}$ a pair $([u], a)$ with $[ua] \in \widetilde{T}$ is called *confusion* iff there exist v, b such that $([u], a) \bowtie_I ([v], a)$, $[vb] \in \widetilde{T}$, $a\, D\, b$, but $[ub] \notin \widetilde{T}$. The pair $([v], b)$ is called *witness* of the confusion of $([u], a)$.
A trace system is *confusion free*, iff there exists no confusion for it.

Independent of the framework we propose we consider this an important problem for the combination of partial order and branching time: the notion of choice from interleaving semantics does not fit precisely to the partial order case.
There are several possible ways to attack this problem:

i) One can consider (in terms of the example) a and b actually as dependent, so that in confused situations parallelism is replaced by interleaving.
ii) One can restrict the systems admitted to the confusion free case, e.g. to free choice Petri nets (cf. [DE95]).
iii) Another, maybe unorthodox approach is to distinguish two levels of choices, and to treat them separately: to consider confusions (and their resolution by the order in which confused, independent transitions are taken) as high level choices and simultaneously enabled dependent transitions as standard or low level choices.

The first approach is considered in [NP95]. In systems with a lot of confusion this can result in a completely interleaved view, and if we use a specification formalism that coincides with tree automata in the sequential case, we immediately obtain an undecidable satisfiability problem (cf. proposition 23). Hence for our considerations this approach is not appropriate.
Nevertheless from a model checking point of view both orders in which a and b can occur must be considered, i.e. at such confused situations partial order reduction methods necessarily fail and an interleaving view at the behaviour is inevitable. The question is, how this look is to be taken without harm.
Whenever the second approach is possible, the problem is completely eliminated, and the system behaviour can be represented faithfully by a single interleaving tree. We will only consider this case in our investigations below, but it serves as the bases for the third possibility also.
The third approach might mean, that one could use automata with two levels of branching also, but we do not know about this. Instead we propose to, for instance by treating only the standard (low level) choices in a branching time fashion and the high level (confusion) choices in a *linear time* fashion! Concretely we would allow to represent a complete behaviour using several nonequivalent interleaving trees, or behaviours with resolved confusion. Automata specifying interleaving trees thus define behaviours such that *all* interleaving trees are accepted by the automaton. This approach would put us somewhere between the standard linear and branching time, depending on the degree of confusion. For the confusion free case it is completely branching time (because the system is essentially represented by one interleaving tree), for the completely confused case mentioned for the first approach it can be completely linear time!

3.2 Interleaving trees

With the above considerations and problems in mind we turn to the formal definition of interleaving trees. We have two alternative definitions:

Definition 5 (interleaving tree, version 1).
A (Σ, I)-interleaving tree T is a maximal subtree of some (Σ, I)-synchronisation tree T', such that for all $ua, ub \in T$ we have $a\ D\ b$. An interleaving tree T is confusion free, iff the corresponding synchronisation tree is.

While the previous definition captures the spirit of interleaving trees well, we can also define them without reference to (Σ, I) synchronisation trees:

Definition 6 (interleaving tree, version 2).
A Σ-tree (prefix closed subset of Σ^*) T is called (Σ, I) *interleaving tree* iff

i) $ua, ub \in T$ implies $a\ D\ b$,
ii) if $uv_1, uv_2 \in T$, and w such that $[w] \preceq [v_1]$, and $[w]$ and $[v_2]$ are compatible, then there exists v_2' such that $uv_2' \in T$, $v_2 \preceq v_2'$, and $[w] \preceq [v_2']$,

An interleaving tree T is confusion free iff for all $ua, ub, w \in T$ with $[v] \preceq [w]$ and $ua \bowtie_I va$ also $ub \bowtie_I vb$.

By condition (i) the labellings of edges starting at the same node are dependent, as in the first definition. Condition (ii) is a kind of diamond closure property on interleaving trees.
For illustration of the definition see figure 1.
The conciseness property demanded as condition (c) of our informal requirements holds in a very strong sense:

Lemma 7. *Let T be an interleaving tree, $u, v \in T$ such that $[u] \preceq [v]$. Then already u is a prefix of v.*

We assign configurations to nodes u of an arbitrary *(Σ, I)-synchronisation tree T* by mapping them to traces $[u]$. Next we lift this assignment to trees: the set of all *configurations covered* by a tree T is denoted by $[T] = \{[u];\ \exists v \in T.[u] \prec [v]\}$.
$[T]$ is in fact a trace system and the mapping $[.]$ induces an equivalence on interleaving trees.

Proposition 8. *Let T be an (Σ, I)-interleaving tree. Then $[T]$ is a trace system. T is confusion free iff $[T]$ is. For every confusion free trace system $\widetilde{T}$ there exists an interleaving tree T' such that $[T'] = \widetilde{T}$.*

Proof. $[T]$ is by definition prefix closed and obviously I-diamond closed (cf. lemma 7). Confusion freeness is obviously inherited.
For the converse direction we inductively build a tree T' with nodes u such that $[u] \in \widetilde{T}$: during the construction we extend T' at leaves u such that $[u]$ is not maximal in $\widetilde{T}$ with children $ub_1, ..., ub_l$, where $\{b_1, ..., b_l\}$ is a maximal group of pairwise dependent actions such that $[ub_i] \in \widetilde{T}$. Confusion freeness implies that the constructed tree covers all configurations of $\widetilde{T}$.

Definition 9 (exchange operation). Let T be an interleaving tree, $v \in T$ such that $a_1, ..., a_k$ are the labels of the outgoing edges at v. Assume that at all nodes va_i the edges are labelled identically by $b_1, ..., b_l$ and $a_i\ I\ b_j$ for all i, j, and let T_{ij} denote the subtree beginning at va_ib_j in T.

We construct a tree T' by taking all $u \in T$ where $v \not\leq u$. We take v, but then we add the edges $b_1, ..., b_l$ getting nodes $vb_1, ..., vb_l$, and for each such vb we identically add edges labelled $a_1, ..., a_k$ and finally attach to each node $vb_j a_i$ the subtree T_{ij}. For two trees T, T' such that T' can be obtained from T by an exchange operation we write $T \rightsquigarrow_I T'$. To obtain an equivalence relation on trees we define $\sim_I$ to be the transitive (and inherently reflexive and symmetric) closure of $\rightsquigarrow_I$.

Proposition 10.

i) If T is an interleaving tree, and $T \rightsquigarrow_I T'$ then T' is also an interleaving tree with $[T] = [T']$.

ii) For any two confusion free interleaving trees T and T' we have $T \sim_I T'$ iff $[T] = [T']$.

Proof. The proof of (i) is straight forward by a case analysis concerning the position of nodes of interest with respect to the position of the transformation.
The "⇒ direction of (ii) follows by induction from (i). The "⇐" direction of (ii) is proved by constructing a transformation sequence from T' to T, where the construction is guided by a properly defined *distance* $dist(T, T')$: either $dist(T, T') = 0$ in which case $T = T'$ or a distance reducing transformation is possible. The idea is to start to make the trees similar from the root to the leaves. The transformation uses a sorting process, which is based on lemma 11.

Lemma 11. *Let T be a finite confusion free interleaving tree with $ab \in T$, $a\ I\ b$, then there exists a (confusion free) interleaving tree T' with $T \sim_I T'$ such that $b \in T$.*

Note that this lemma strongly depends on confusion freeness.

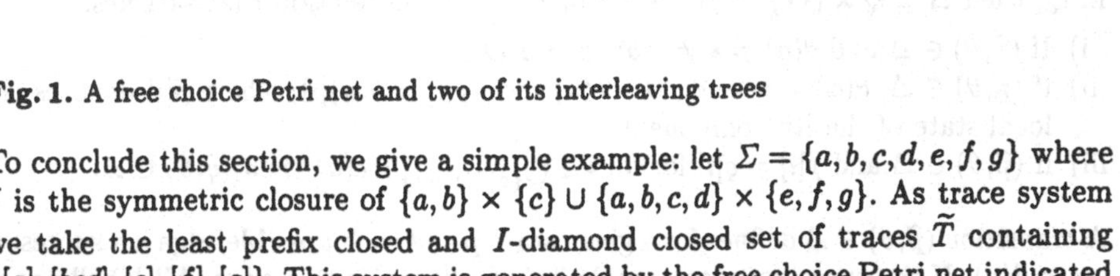

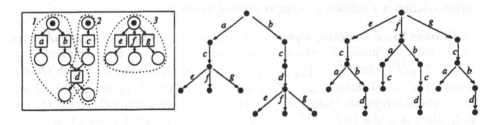

Fig. 1. A free choice Petri net and two of its interleaving trees

To conclude this section, we give a simple example: let $\Sigma = \{a, b, c, d, e, f, g\}$ where I is the symmetric closure of $\{a, b\} \times \{c\} \cup \{a, b, c, d\} \times \{e, f, g\}$. As trace system we take the least prefix closed and I-diamond closed set of traces $\widetilde{T}$ containing $\{[a], [bcd], [e], [f], [g]\}$. This system is generated by the free choice Petri net indicated in figure 1. Below the net, two of the interleaving trees are drawn. Note that the two interleaving trees are of different size, and that the order of postponed actions after an (independent) branching need not always be the same.

4 Branching Asynchronous Automata

In this section we define automata accepting trace systems. Our aim is to join the concepts of sequential tree automata [Tho90] and linear asynchronous automata [Zie89] (which accept trace languages). Asynchronous automata consist of subcomponents called *locations*, each handling a subset Σ_i of the alphabet Σ.
The *locations* of asynchronous automata are used to present dependency. Usually a tuple $(\Sigma_1, ..., \Sigma_K)$ of local alphabets is given such that $\Sigma = \bigcup_{i=1}^{K} \Sigma_i$ and $a\ D\ b$ iff there exists a location i with $a, b \in \Sigma_i$. Such a presentation is possible for any (Σ, I): Consider (Σ, D) as an undirected, unlabelled graph with nodes Σ and edges from D, then any set of cliques $\Sigma_1, ... \Sigma_K$ covering the graph satisfies the previous condition. Each location i with its local state space Q_i is assumed to take part in all letters $a \in \Sigma_i$. The global transition relation for letter a depends only on the local states of locations for which $a \in \Sigma_i$. As for any *pair* of dependent actions there is a common location i, this component will control the order, in which these actions are taken. Whereas transitions labelled with independent actions may be performed "concurrently".
For the branching case we have to deal with choices of pairwise dependent actions. In order to connect the alternatives of such a choice we need a location for each *group* of pairwise dependent actions encompassing them. This is achieved by taking all *maximal* cliques in (Σ, D) as locations. This motivates the following definition:

Definition 12 (maximal location presentation). For (Σ, I) let $\{\Sigma_1, ..., \Sigma_K\}$ be the set of all maximal cliques in the undirected graph (Σ, D). Then we say that $(\Sigma_1, ... \Sigma_K)$ is a *maximal location presentation* of (Σ, I), and let $loc(a) = \{i |\ a \in \Sigma_i\}$ denote the set of locations *participating in a*.

As representation for branching transitions in the automata we use functions θ mapping *directions* (elements of Σ) to successor states. Thus the nondeterministic *transition relation* is a relation between states and functions:

Definition 13. A *branching asynchronous automaton* (abbreviated *BrAsynA*), over (Σ, I) with the maximal location presentation $(\Sigma_1, ..., \Sigma_K)$, is a structure $\mathcal{A} = (\widetilde{Q}, \Delta, Q_{init}, \widetilde{F})$ where $\widetilde{Q} = \prod_{i \in Loc} Q_i$ is the global state space and each Q_i is a finite set of i-local states. $Q_{init} \subseteq \widetilde{Q}$ is a set of *global* initial states and $\widetilde{F} \subseteq \widetilde{Q}$ is a set of *global* acceptance states. Let "$*$" be a dummy state originally not contained in $\widetilde{Q}$, then $\Delta \subseteq \widetilde{Q} \times (\{*\} \cup \widetilde{Q})^{\Sigma}$ is a global transition relation that satisfies:

i) If $(\widetilde{p}, \theta) \in \Delta$ and $\theta(a) \neq * \neq \theta(b)$ then $a\ D\ b$,
ii) if $(\widetilde{p}, \theta) \in \Delta$, $\theta(a) \neq *$, and $i \notin loc(a)$ then $\widetilde{p}[i] = \theta(a)[i]$, where $\widetilde{p}[i]$ denotes the local state of the ith component,
iii) if $(\widetilde{p}, \theta) \in \Delta$ and $\widetilde{p}[i] = \widetilde{q}[i]$ for all $i \in \bigcup_{\{a | \theta(a) \neq *\}} loc(a)$ then $(\widetilde{q}, \theta) \in \Delta$.

A transition $(\widetilde{p}, \theta) \in \Delta$ defines for a given state $\widetilde{p}$ and each possible edge a a successor state $\theta(a)$. If the successor state equals "$*$", $(\widetilde{p}, \theta)$ omits this edge. All labellings of edges for which θ defines a successor state $\widetilde{q} \in \widetilde{Q}$ have to be pairwise dependent, and condition (ii) and (iii) say that transitions respect localities.
BrAsynAs define sets (languages) of trace systems:

Definition 14 (run of a *BrAsynA*). Let $\widetilde{T}$ be a trace system, $\mathcal{A}$ a *BrAsynA*. A run ρ of $\mathcal{A}$ over $\widetilde{T}$ is a map $\rho : \widetilde{T} \longrightarrow \widetilde{Q}$ such that: $\rho([\varepsilon]) \in Q_{init}$, and for each *maximal* set *Next* of indexed actions which satisfies $[ua] \in \widetilde{T}$ for all $a \in Next$ and if $a, b \in Next$ then $a\ D\ b$, there exists a transition $(\widetilde{p}, \theta) \in \Delta$ such that

$$a \in Next \text{ iff } \theta(a) \neq *, \rho([u]) = \widetilde{p}, \text{ and } \rho([ua]) = \theta(a) \text{ for all } a \in Next.$$

ρ is an *accepting run* of $\mathcal{A}$ over $\widetilde{T}$ iff for every maximal $[u] \in \widetilde{T}$ we have $\rho([u]) \in \widetilde{F}$. A trace system $\widetilde{T}$ is accepted by a *BrAsynA* $\mathcal{A}$ iff there exists an accepting run of $\mathcal{A}$ over $\widetilde{T}$. The set (language) of trace systems accepted by $\mathcal{A}$ is called $\mathcal{L}(\mathcal{A})$.

$\mathcal{A}$ works as follows: $\mathcal{A}$ starts in an initial state at the empty trace. At each step it selects a maximal bunch *Next* of pairwise dependent indexed actions that lead to successors of a configuration $[u] \in \widetilde{T}$ which is actually investigated by $\mathcal{A}$. Then a suitable transition $(\widetilde{p}, \theta)$ from Δ is chosen such that the state $\widetilde{p}$ equals the current state and the labels of the (non-dummy) outgoing edges of θ matches *Next* properly. Now θ determines the states corresponding to the *Next*-successors of $[u]$.[3] In case of a confusion free trace system $\widetilde{T}$ the construction always yields a well-defined run if it is possible to find at each node from $\widetilde{T}$ an matching transition from Δ.

5 The Emptiness Problem

Before we can state the theorem we define a property of concurrent alphabets, which says something about their communication structure: what makes a concurrent alphabet complex is the *combination* of *independent branching* and communication.

Definition 15. A concurrent alphabet (Σ, I) is said to be *complex* iff there exist four actions $a, a', b, b' \in \Sigma$, such that $a\ D\ a'$, $b\ D\ b'$, $a, a'\ I\ b, b'$, and a, a', b, b' belong to the same strongly connected component in the undirected graph (Σ, D).

The emptiness problem for automata over finite trees is known to be polynomial in the size of the state space (if the out-degree is bounded) and in fact linear in the size of the transition relation; for branching asynchronous automata we obtain:

Theorem 16. *The emptiness problem for BrAsynAs over confusion free trace systems over a complex concurrent alphabet (Σ, I) is co-NP-hard (in the size of the global state space), over non complex alphabets it is in P. At least for the case of a maximal location presentation (Σ_1, Σ_2) it is in co-NP.*

Here we only show co-NP-hardness in detail, the other proofs are sketched and will be presented in the full version of the paper.
As yet we were only able to show containment in co-NP for special cases (lacking a general construction), hence the restriction. However, we strongly believe:

[3] In general this procedure may not yield a well-defined mapping from configurations of $\widetilde{T}$ to states of $\mathcal{A}$. In the case of confusion it may be *unavoidable* to reach the same configuration via different θs that assign different states to it in order to cover all configurations.

Conjecture 17. The emptiness problem is in co-NP for *BrAsynAs* over an arbitrary fixed alphabet (Σ, I).

Proof (part 1: non complex alphabet). For a non complex (Σ, D) the dependence graph splits into several disjoint strongly connected components and so do the automata, such that the emptiness problem can be solved independently for each component, and the results can be polynomially combined. Now for each component $\Sigma' \subseteq \Sigma$ the non-complex condition and confusion freeness implies, that at each configuration of a trace system there really is at most one location in $(\Sigma', D \cap \Sigma' \times \Sigma')$, where *branching* takes place, while the other locations are either blocked or perform a *sequence* of actions. Such trace systems can be represented by (sorted) interleaving trees, where non branching sequences of actions are taken as early as possible. Then an easy construction allows us to reduce the emptiness problem of *BrAsynAs* over this alphabet to the (polynomial) emptiness problem of tree automata accepting exactly such sorted interleaving trees.

Proof (part 2:co-NP-hardness). Let a, a', b, b' be as required. For an easier presentation of the proof method let us first assume that there exists a single $c \in \Sigma$ connecting these independent parts: $a, a'\ D\ c\ D\ b, b'$. The generalisation to arbitrary complex alphabets is explained at the end. So we now we have two locations $\{a, a', c\} \subseteq \Sigma_1$ and $\{b, b', c\} \subseteq \Sigma_2$. For simplicity let us further assume that $\Sigma = \Sigma_1 \cup \Sigma_2$. For the case of more than two locations the other locations will not play a role.
We use a reduction of 3SAT [GJ79]: for any finite set of clauses $C = \{C_1, ..., C_m\}$, each consisting of three literals, we construct a *BrAsynA* $\mathcal{A}_C$ with a number of global states and transitions polynomial in $|C|$, such that C is satisfiable iff $\mathcal{L}(\mathcal{A}) \neq \emptyset$.
Let $\{P_1, ..., P_k\}$ be the propositions occurring either positively or negatively in some clause C_i of C. Clearly $k \leq 3 \cdot m$.
Location 1 keeps track of clauses and location 2 keeps track of possible valuations. $Q_1 = \{start, accept, reject, C_1, ..., C_m, P_1, ..., P_k, \overline{P_1}, ..., \overline{P_k}\} \uplus B_1$, where B_1 is a set of auxiliary states and $|B_1| < m$. Similarly $Q_2 = \{start, accept, reject, P_1?, ..., P_k?, P_1, ..., P_k, \overline{P_1}, ..., \overline{P_k}\} \uplus B_2$, $|B_2| < k$. We set $Q_{init} = \{(start, start)\}$, $\widetilde{F} = \{(accept, accept)\}$. The intuitive meaning of the states is: clauses stand for themselves, literals stand for an according valuation of their variable, the states $P_i?$ stand for the variable P_i, for which we have not set a value yet.
The transition relation will yield runs consisting of three stages: independent branching, independent guessing, joint comparison. For location 1 - the clause automaton - the first "branching" stage independently builds up a fixed binary tree such that at the leaves we have exactly the states C_i, representing the clauses. For the inner nodes the auxiliary states from B_1 are used, and all edges are labelled with a or a'. Similarly for location 2 - the valuation automaton - we will branch along a fixed binary tree with b or b' edges, such that at the leaves we have all the states $P_i?$.
For the second - guessing - stage in location 1 we provide for each clause C_i transitions $C_i \xrightarrow{a} P_j$ (or $C_i \xrightarrow{a} \overline{P_j}$), where P_j,$\overline{P_j}$ is one of the literals in C_i. Thus we guess the literal that serves as witness for the satisfiability of C_i. Similarly in location 2 we provide transitions from $P_i?$ to either P_i or $\overline{P_i}$ along a single b edge - here we try to guess a proper truth value for P_i.
"After" the first two stages we have reached a combination of $m \cdot k$ global branches. Now we compare the guesses from location 1 and 2: Therefore we provide joint

transitions along a single edge c for each possible combination of local states either to $(accept, accept)$ or to $(reject, reject)$. The global states, which we have to take into account, are pairs of literals: $(P_i, \overline{P_i}) \xrightarrow{c} (reject, reject)$ and $(\overline{P_i}, P_i) \xrightarrow{c} (reject, reject)$ (wrong guess implies rejection), but $(P_i, P_i) \xrightarrow{c} (accept, accept)$ and $(\overline{P_i}, \overline{P_i}) \xrightarrow{c} (accept, accept)$ (agreement). For each other pair of literals, which consists of two different propositions, e.g. $(P_i, \overline{P_j})$, with $i \neq j$, we also have a transition to $(accept, accept)$ (don't care).
Now it is easy to construct an accepting run over a trace behaviour (actually only depending on m and k), from a valuation satisfying C and vice versa.
Thus C is satisfiable iff $L(\mathcal{A}_C) \neq \emptyset$. Adding up all states and transitions of $\mathcal{A}_C$, we clearly have a polynomial (in fact quadratic) reduction.
For more general complex alphabets (Σ, I) the locations 1 and 2 may not be directly connected by a single c, so the transitions in the communication phase may have to be substituted by a chain of communications in connecting the locations 1 and 2.

Proof (part 3: containment in co-NP for the two-location case). Although for *tree-automata* the emptiness problem is polynomial, it is instructive to look at a co-NP procedure for this case first (which can be generalized to *BrAsynAs*). The key observation is that if there exists a tree T with an accepting run ρ, then there exists also a "non redundant" tree T' with run ρ' such that for any state q all subtrees t_u beginning at some node u with $\rho'(u) = q$ are identical, and that no state is ever visited twice on the same path. Thus an NP algorithm for the non-emptiness of tree automata works by guessing (such a non redundant tree and run represented by) an initial state, a total order on the set of states (proving noncircularity) and for each state *the next transition* or no transition at all. Checking, whether the guess represents a tree with an accepting run is obviously polynomial.
The same technique does not work without modification for *BrAsynAs*: it is not always possible to exchange a sub-system beginning at a certain configuration $[u]$ with another one without interfering with diamond closure requirements, etc. But the construction can be refined in a hierarchical process (from more global to more local views of the trace system), which is rather complicated. Therefore we restricted the theorem on the case of two locations, i.e. $\Sigma = \Sigma_1 \cup \Sigma_2$.
For the case of two locations, confusion free trace systems can be cut into pieces of concurrent branching in turn with *global events* (for which no concurrent event exists). In a trace system $\widetilde{T}$ with a run ρ we will call the configurations $[u]$ and $[ua]$ and the states $\rho([u])$ and $\rho([ua])$ before and after a global event a *pre-global* and *post-global* configurations and states. The initial configuration is post-global and the maximal configurations are pre-global in this sense.
Then we can lift the above tree-automata construction hierarchically to *BrAsynAs*: on the level of post-global configurations everything works as in the sequential case. On the non post-global states after a post-global state (q_1, q_2) the local automata work independently (as tree automata with start states q_i and final states P_i), until a cross product $P_1 \times P_2$ of pre-global states is reached.
Thus the NP-procedure for checking non-emptiness of *BrAsynAs* for the case of 2 locations essentially[4] works as follows: For the global level guess a set of post-global

[4] a bit of refinement is necessary w.r.t. the locations participating in global events.

states with a total order and a post-global start state, guess a set of pre-global states and for each such state an appropriate global transition; for the local level guess for each post-global state (q_1, q_2) a total order on each local state space and for each local state guess local transition.
To check, whether these guesses yield a trace system with an accepting run of a trace system, we have to check that the local transitions respect the local orderings, and for each post-global state (q_1, q_2) we have to calculate the set of last (w.r.t. the local orders) states reachable via the local branches, check that these are pre-global and either final or that the transition chosen for them leads to post-global states respecting the global order (w.r.t. (q_1, q_2)). All this checking is easily seen to be of an effort polynomial in the number of states.
Although it is not at all straightforward, the hierarchical approach showing up in the case of 2 components seems to be extendable for arbitrary alphabets.

Note that the above proof of part 2 can be refined to give the following corollary: We merely have to modify the construction of the reduction to replace the non-deterministic choices of literals by manifest differences in the trace system. This can be achieved by using additional states and a unary coding of the literals in lengths of a branches. Instead of guessing a literal then the automaton reads it off.

Corollary 18. *If (Σ, D) is nontrivial, the emptiness problem is co-NP-hard even for deterministic BrAsynAs.*

6 Connection to Tree Automata

The introduction of interleaving trees in section 3 raises the question, how *BrAsynAs* are linked to tree automata running over interleaving trees. For the linear case it is well known, that linear asynchronous automata can naturally be interpreted as word automata by ignoring the independence information: The word automaton works on the *global state space* and a *sequential* run always gives a transition for the action that occurs *next* in the word[5]. The initial, the final states, and the transition relation are taken from the linear asynchronous automaton. This word automaton accepts exactly those words that are representatives of a trace accepted by the asynchronous automaton.
Thus the accepted word language is robust against Mazurkiewicz equivalence, i.e. if a word is accepted, then so are all $\sim_I$-equivalent ones. Zielonka's theorem [Zie89] says even more: any recognisable, $\sim_I$-robust language is accepted also by an asynchronous automaton.
In the branching case we will look at trees that are *serialisations* of confusion free trace systems, i.e. trees where all edges starting at one node are labelled with dependent actions. Therefore ignoring the independence information gives us a tree automaton analogous to the linear case.

Definition 19 (run of a *BrAsynA* as tree automaton). Let $\mathcal{A}$ be a *BrAsynA* and T a synchronisation tree. Then a map $\rho : T \to \widetilde{Q}$ is called *run* of $\mathcal{A}$ over T

[5] and may not select a transition for an action with a later positioning in the word which is independent from all actions in between.

iff $\rho(\epsilon) \in Q_{init}$, and if $Next = \{a | ua \in T\}$ then there exists a transition $(\widetilde{p}, \theta) \in \Delta$ such that $a \in Next$ iff $\theta(a) \neq *$, and $\rho(u) = \widetilde{p}$, and $\rho(ua) = \theta(a)$ for all $a \in Next$.

The tree automaton derived from a *BrAsynA* $\mathcal{A}$ works on the global state space of $\mathcal{A}$ and because Δ contains only transitions with dependent choices, the tree automaton $\mathcal{A}$ will only accept trees where all edges starting at one node are dependent. The idea works well (i) for *deterministic BrAsynAs*, and (ii) if the class of trees is restricted to interleaving trees:

Proposition 20. *Let $\mathcal{A}$ be a BrAsynA and T an interleaving tree. If $\mathcal{A}$ accepts $[T]$, then it also accepts T as tree automaton. If $\mathcal{A}$ is deterministic, the converse holds also, i.e. if it accepts T as a tree automaton, then it also accepts $[T]$ as BrAsynA.*

Unfortunately, this property does not hold for the general, nondeterministic case. The reason is, that in different parts of the tree we may choose different transitions for the "same" choice. This is a drawback, because it is also well known, that deterministic tree automata working from the root are less expressive than nondeterministic ones. The second restriction required above has the following reason:

Proposition 21. *The set of all interleaving trees over (Σ, I) is not recognisable if there is $a, a', b \in \Sigma$ with $a, a' \; I \; b$.*

The proposition is shown by the well known pumping-argument.
Hence we cannot expect any kind of definition, which would give us a tree automaton accepting exactly the representative interleaving trees of a trace system language. This difference to the linear case actually already came up in section 3: whereas each word is a representative of a trace not every tree can be interpreted as representative of a (confusion free) trace system.
Now the question may be raised, whether we should have avoided using *BrAsynAs* with the difficult emptiness problem from the beginning. However, proposition 20 together with corollary 18 imply:

Proposition 22. *Given (Σ, D) such that there exist $a, b, c \in \Sigma$ with $a \; I \; b$ and $a \; D \; c \; D \; b$, the set of tree-automata $\mathcal{A}$, such that there exists no interleaving tree accepted by $\mathcal{A}$, is co-NP-hard.*

With this *co-NP-hardness* result one might ask more rigorously, why we did not stick to (Σ, I)-synchronisation trees in the first place. But that was our starting point (in analogy to interpreting standard branching time logics over trace systems), tree automata running over (Σ, I)-synchronisation trees have an undecidable emptiness problem!

Proposition 23. *Given a complex (Σ, I) (such that there exist $a, a', b, b', c \in \Sigma$ with $a, a' \; I \; b, b'$ and $a, a' \; D \; c \; D \; b, b'$), the set of tree-automata $\mathcal{A}$, such that there exists no (confusion free or not) (Σ, I)-synchronisation tree accepted by $\mathcal{A}$, is Π^0_1-complete.*

Proof. The construction used here is found in many similar settings (e.g. [Pen92]). We use the independent letters a and b to encode a two-dimensional grid and use letter c for decorating the vertices of the grid (with unary coding). The decorated

grid is used to represent computations of Turing machines, where the one direction represents positions on the tape, while the other direction represents computation steps. For an arbitrary TM and an initially empty tape we can effectively construct a tree automaton that accepts exactly those (Σ, I)-synchronisation trees, that represent halting computations of the TM. Of course it might accept other Σ-trees as well, but that does not matter.
Note that the construction can be modified to yield confusion free synchronisation trees if desired: for this we use auxiliary local a' and b' steps branching off the grid, before the joint actions c are allowed.

7 Conclusions

We have been successful in developing an automata framework and a Mazurkiewicz theory for confusion free trace systems. Even for the confusion free case the complexity of the emptiness problem has turned out to be surprisingly high.
Opposed to our motivation of improving efficiency, this might lead to the premature conclusion, that it is a bad idea to take this combination. However the situation for model checking is a bit different from the general emptiness problem.
Since we have presented only finitary structures, we have to think in analogies here: a "model" would a kind of I-respecting transition system, which unfolds into a finite (confusion free) (Σ, I)-synchronisation tree – or equivalently a trace system.
For instance it might be given as a safe free choice Petri net. The model checking problem is, whether this tree or trace system belongs to the language defined by a tree automaton or a *BrAsynA*. Algorithmically we can attack this problem (among other possibilities) by transforming the transition system into a tree automaton accepting exactly the interleaving trees of that trace system (and no non interleaving trees at all). Then we can combine this automaton with an appropriate specification automaton (derived from a deterministic *BrAsynA*) to yield the language intersection. The model satisfies the specification iff the resulting automaton has a non-empty language of arbitrary trees (which inherently are interleaving trees). This is of polynomial effort.
Moreover this approach is very interesting with respect to partial order reductions: we can apply partial order reductions to the model before transforming it to a tree automaton – then accepting then only some of the interleaving trees of the original system. This tree automaton can be significantly smaller than the one obtained without reductions, but since the specifying tree automaton (derived from a deterministic *BrAsynA*) does not distinguish equivalent interleaving trees, the result of the emptiness test will not be changed by the reduction.
Unfortunately this approach does not seem to work for non-deterministic *BrAsynAs*, while deterministic *BrAsynAs* are strictly less expressive. Thus from a practical point of view it would be interesting to look at alternative definitions of automata, which allow (more) non-determinism, but still cannot distinguish equivalent interleaving trees.
An obvious field for future research is to try to extend the class of models, on which the results apply by using a special treatment for confusion, as was indicated in section 3. Since such an approach may be highly non standard, the usefulness in terms of expressibility of interesting properties is almost of primary interest here.

Acknowledgement

We thank Madhavan Mukund, Wojciech Penczek, Barbara Sprick and P.S. Thiagarajan for discussions on the subject. In particular the abstract idea for "interleaving trees" arose in discussions with Wojciech Penczek during the preparation of [NP95] and P.S. Thiagarajan suggested an improved definition of confusion.

References

[BVW94] Orna Bernholtz, Moshe Y. Vardi, and Pierre Wolper. An automata-theoretic approach to branching-time model checking. In *CAV 94*, LNCS 818, pp 142–153, 1994.

[DE95] Jörg Desel and Javier Esparza. *Free choice Petri nets.* Cambridge tracts in theoretical computer science 40, Cambridge University Press, 1995

[GJ79] M.R. Garey and D.S. Johnson. *Computers and Intractability.* Freeman, NY 1979.

[GLT79] H.J. Genrich and K. Lautenbach and P.S. Thiagarajan. Elements of general net theory. In *Net Theory and Applications*, LNCS 84, pages 21–159, 1979.

[GKPP95] R. Gerth, R. Kuiper, D. Peled, and W. Penczek. A partial order approach to branching time logic model checking. In *Israeli Symp. on Theoretical Comp. Sci.*, 1995.

[HN96] Michaela Huhn and Peter Niebert. *Towards automata for branching time and partial order.* Report HIB 16/96. Institute for Informatics, Univ. Hildesheim. 1996.

[KP95] Ruurd Kuiper and Wojciech Penczek. Traces and Logic. In V. Diekert and G. Rozenberg (eds.): *The Book of Traces*, World Scientific, Singapore, 1995, 307-390

[Ma88] Antoni Mazurkiewicz. Basic notions of trace theory. LNCS 354, pp 285–363, 1988

[MT90] Madhavan Mukund and P. S. Thiagarajan. An axiomatisation of well branching prime event structures. Internal Report TCS-90-2, Inst. of Mathematical Sciences, SPIC Science Foundation, Madras 600 113, India, September 1990.

[NP95] Peter Niebert and Wojciech Penczek. On the connection of partial order logics and partial order reduction methods. Report 95-15, TU Eindhoven, CS Dept, 1995.

[NW95] M. Nielsen and G. Winskel. Models for concurrency. in S. Abramsky, D.M Gabbay, T.S.E. Maibaum (eds.): *Handbook of Logic in Computer Science*, Volume 4 Semantic Modelling, pages 1-148, Oxford University Press 1995.

[Pel93] Doron Peled. All from one, one for all: on model checking using representatives. In *Computer Aided Verification*, LNCS 697, 1993.

[Pen92] Wojciech Penczek. On undecidability of propositional temporal logics on trace systems. Information Processing Letters 43, 147–153, 1992

[RT91] B. Rozoy and P.S. Thiagarajan. Event structures and trace monoids, Theoretical Computer Science 91, 285-313, 1991.

[Sta89] E.W. Stark. Concurrent transition systems. In *Theoretical Computer Science* 64: 221-269,1989.

[Thi94] P.S. Thiagarajan. A trace based extension of Linear Time Temporal Logic. In *Proc. of the 9th annual IEEE Symposium on Logic in Computer Science (LICS)*, 1994.

[Thi95] P.S. Thiagarajan. A trace consistent subset of PTL. In *CONCUR '95*, LNCS 962, 1995.

[Tho90] Wolfgang Thomas. Automata on infinite objects. In J. v. Leeuwen (ed.), *Handbook of Theoretical Computer Science*, vol. B, ch. 4, pages 133–191. Elsevier, 1990.

[VW86] Moshe Y. Vardi and Pierre Wolper. An automata-theoretic approach to automatic program verification. In *1st IEEE Symp. Logic in Comp. Sci. (LICS)*, p. 332–344, 1986.

[Win87] Glynn Winskel. Event structures. In *Advances in Petri Nets*, LNCS 255, 1987.

[Zie89] Wieslaw Zielonka. Safe executions of recognisable trace languages by asynchronous automata. In *Logic at Botik*, LNCS 363, pages 278–289, 1989.

Asynchronous Cellular Automata for Pomsets Without Auto-concurrency *

Manfred Droste[1] and Paul Gastin[2]

[1] Institut für Algebra, Technische Universität Dresden, D-01062 Dresden,
droste@math.tu-dresden.de

[2] LITP, IBP, Université Paris 7, 2 place Jussieu, F-75251 Paris Cedex 05,
Paul.Gastin@litp.ibp.fr

Abstract. This paper extends to pomsets without auto-concurrency the fundamental notion of asynchronous cellular automata (ACA) which was originally introduced for traces by Zielonka. We generalize to pomsets the notion of asynchronous mapping introduced by Zielonka and we show how to construct a deterministic ACA from an asynchronous mapping. Our main result generalizes Büchi's theorem for a class of pomsets without auto-concurrency which satisfy a natural axiom. This axiom ensures that an asynchronous cellular automaton works on the pomset as a concurrent read owner write machine. More precisely, we prove the equivalence between non deterministic ACA, deterministic ACA and monadic second order logic for this class of pomsets.

1 Introduction

In a distributed system, some events may occur concurrently, meaning that they may occur in any order or simultaneously or even that their executions may overlap. This is the case in particular when two events use independent resources. On the other hand, some events may causally depend on each other. For instance, the receiving of a message must follow its sending. Therefore, a distributed behavior may be abstracted as a pomset, that is a set of events together with a partial order which describes causal dependencies of events and with a labeling function. In this paper, we mainly deal with pomsets without auto-concurrency : concurrent events must have different labels. These pomsets are called semi-words in [12, 3]. For studies how general pomsets can be used to represent parallel processes and how they can be composed, we refer the reader e.g. to [11, 7].

There are several ways to describe the behaviors of a system. For instance, logic formulas are suited for specification purposes. Depending on the properties we have to express, we can use various logics such as the temporal logic, the first order logic or the (monadic) second order logic. On the other hand, transition systems are often used to give more operational descriptions. On this paper, we will concentrate on these two kinds of descriptions of systems.

* This research was partly carried out during a stay of the second author in Dresden.

When dealing with distributed systems, it is natural to look for transition systems which faithfully reflect the concurrency. For instance, Petri nets are a widely studied class of such transition systems. Asynchronous cellular automata (ACA) form another fundamental class of transition systems with built-in concurrency. They were introduced for traces by Zielonka [14, 15]. Mazurkiewicz introduced traces in order to describe the behaviors of one-safe Petri nets [8, 9]. A trace is a pomset where the partial order is dictated by a static dependence relation over the actions of the system.

The primary aim of this work is to generalize the notion of ACA so that they can work on pomsets without auto-concurrency. There are several possible definitions for such ACA. In Section 3, we give a natural definition of ACA which intuitively run over the Hasse diagrams of pomsets. We also discuss possible alternative definitions.

Asynchronous mappings prove to be a basic tool to construct ACA for traces [15, 2]. In Section 4, we give a definition of asynchronous mappings for general pomsets. We prove that a pomset language recognized by an asynchronous mapping can be accepted by a *deterministic* ACA.

The rest of this paper is devoted to the equivalence between ACA and monadic second order (MSO) logic for pomsets. We prove in Section 5 that from a (non deterministic) ACA one can construct a MSO formula which defines precisely the pomset language accepted by the automaton. We do not know whether the converse holds in general. In Section 6, we prove the converse for the special subclass of pomsets for which the ACA works as a concurrent read owner write (CROW) machine. These pomsets are called CROW-pomsets. More precisely, from a MSO formula we construct a *deterministic* ACA which accepts precisely the CROW-pomsets defined by the formula. Therefore, for CROW-pomsets, we have the equivalence between MSO logic, deterministic ACA and non deterministic ACA. This result is crucial since it opens the way of model checking for distributed systems whose behaviors are described as CROW-pomsets.

Note that the CROW assumption for pomsets is satisfied for a large class of systems. For instance, a stably concurrent automaton $\mathcal{A}$ [6] defines dynamic dependencies between actions of a system, whence it generalizes the static dependencies on actions used for traces. With the computation sequences of a stably concurrent automaton $\mathcal{A}$, one can associate dependence orders [1]. These dependence orders are pomsets which generalize traces but are special cases of pomsets without auto-concurrency. Under the assumption that the automaton $\mathcal{A}$ is stably concurrent and forwardly weakly preserves dependency, these dependence orders satisfy the CROW axiom. Therefore, as a consequence of our results, we obtain a new, Zielonka-type characterization of the recognizable languages of concurrency monoids studied in [6].

We do not give all proofs in this extended abstract. They will appear in a full version of this paper.

2 Preliminaries

2.1 Pomsets

Let Σ be an alphabet. A pomset over Σ is (an isomorphism class of) a finite labeled partial order $t = (V, \leq, \lambda)$ where V is a finite set of vertices, $\leq$ is the partial order on V and $\lambda : V \longrightarrow \Sigma$ is the labeling function.

Let $s = (V_s, \leq_s, \lambda_s)$ and $t = (V_t, \leq_t, \lambda_t)$ be two pomsets. We say that s is a prefix of t, denoted by $s \preceq t$ if V_s is a downward closed subset of V_t (i.e. $(u \leq_t v \wedge v \in V_s) \Longrightarrow u \in V_s$ for all $u, v \in V_t$) and $\leq_s$ and λ_s are the restrictions of $\leq_t$ and λ_t to V_s. The prefix order relation is a partial order on the set of pomsets. In the following, we will identify a downward closed subset of vertices with the corresponding prefix of the pomset. Let $s_1 = (V_{s_1}, \leq_{s_1}, \lambda_{s_1})$ and $s_2 = (V_{s_2}, \leq_{s_2}, \lambda_{s_2})$ be two prefixes of a pomset $t = (V_t, \leq_t, \lambda_t)$. Then, $V_{s_1} \cup V_{s_2}$ is downward closed and the corresponding prefix of t will be denoted by $s_1 \cup s_2$.

Let $t = (V, \leq, \lambda)$ be a pomset. The downward closure of a vertex v is denoted by $\downarrow v = \{u \in V \mid u \leq v\}$. The strict downward closure of a vertex v is denoted by $\Downarrow v = \downarrow v \setminus \{v\}$. Since $\downarrow v$ and $\Downarrow v$ are downward closed subsets of V, we will identify these sets to the corresponding prefixes of t.

Let $\Sigma_1, \ldots, \Sigma_n$ be pairwise disjoint alphabets and let $\Sigma = \Sigma_1 \dot\cup \cdots \dot\cup \Sigma_n$. Intuitively, we can view $[n] = \{1, \ldots, n\}$ as a set of labels of sequential processes and $\Sigma_1, \ldots, \Sigma_n$ as the sets of actions of these sequential processes. Let $p : \Sigma \longrightarrow [n]$ be the mapping which associates with each letter $a \in \Sigma$ the process $p(a) \in [n]$ which executes the letter a, i.e. $a \in \Sigma_{p(a)}$.

Let $t = (V, \leq, \lambda)$ be a pomset. We say that a vertex v covers a vertex u, denoted by $u \longrightarrow\!\!\!\!\!< v$, if $u < v$ and there is no vertex w such that $u < w < v$. We say that two vertices $u, v \in V$ are concurrent, denoted by $u \parallel v$, if $u \not\leq v$ and $u \not\geq v$. We may see the covering relation as the description of the interactions between the processes. More precisely, we consider that an event $v \in V$ reads the states of the processes $p \circ \lambda(\{u \mid u \longrightarrow\!\!\!\!\!< v\})$ and writes in the process $p \circ \lambda(v)$. We will not allow concurrent writes, therefore two concurrent events $u \parallel v$ must write in different process $p \circ \lambda(u) \neq p \circ \lambda(v)$. This leads to the following definition.

A $(\Sigma_1, \ldots, \Sigma_n)$-pomset is a pomset $t = (V, \leq, \lambda)$ for which $\lambda^{-1}(\Sigma_i)$ is totally ordered for all $1 \leq i \leq n$. The set of $(\Sigma_1, \ldots, \Sigma_n)$-pomsets will be denoted by $\mathbb{P}(\Sigma_1, \ldots, \Sigma_n)$. Note that with this notation the set $\mathbb{P}(\Sigma)$ is the set of words over Σ. Another special case which will come into play later is when the sets $\Sigma_1, \ldots, \Sigma_n$ are all singletons.

For $A \subseteq \Sigma$, we denote by $\partial_A(t) = \downarrow\lambda^{-1}(A)$ the least prefix of a pomset t which contains all letters from A. Note that $\partial_A(t) = \bigcup_{v \mid \lambda(v) \in A} \downarrow v$. For $a \in \Sigma$ and $i \in [n]$, we will use the following simplified notations : $\partial_a(t) = \partial_{\{a\}}(t)$ and $\partial_i(t) = \partial_{\Sigma_i}(t)$.

Note that if $\lambda^{-1}(A)$ is totally ordered then $\partial_A(t)$ is either empty or has exactly one maximal vertex. In particular, if t is a $(\Sigma_1, \ldots, \Sigma_n)$-pomset then $\partial_i(t)$ is either empty or has exactly one maximal vertex.

2.2 Traces

We recall now basic definitions for Mazurkiewicz traces which will be needed in this paper. The reader is referred to [5] for a general presentation of traces. Our presentation is not the classical one but is more adequate in our context. Basically, a trace is a pomset which satisfies additional requirements. We consider a reflexive and symmetric relation $\Delta \subseteq \Sigma \times \Sigma$ over the alphabet. Intuitively, two dependent actions must be ordered while two independent actions may occur concurrently. More precisely, a trace over a dependence alphabet (Σ, Δ) is a pomset $t = (V, \leq, \lambda)$ such that for all $u, v \in V$

1. $(\lambda(u), \lambda(v)) \in \Delta \Longrightarrow u \not\parallel v$
2. $u \prec v \Longrightarrow (\lambda(u), \lambda(v)) \in \Delta$.

The set of traces over (Σ, Δ) will be denoted by $\mathbb{M}(\Sigma, \Delta)$.

We will now define recognizable trace languages. A trace automaton is a quadruple $\mathcal{A} = (Q, T, I, F)$ where Q is a finite set of states, $I \subseteq Q$ is the set of initial states, $F \subseteq Q$ is the set of final states and $T \subseteq Q \times \Sigma \times Q$ is the set of transitions which verifies the diamond property : for all $(a, b) \in \Sigma \times \Sigma \setminus \Delta$ and $q, q', q'' \in Q$, if $(q, a, q') \in T$ and $(q', b, q'') \in T$ then there exists some $\bar{q}' \in Q$ such that $(q, b, \bar{q}') \in T$ and $(\bar{q}', a, q'') \in T$. A word $w = a_1 \cdots a_n \in \Sigma^*$ is accepted by $\mathcal{A}$ if there is a run $q_0, a_1, q_1, \ldots, a_n, q_n$ such that $q_0 \in I$, $q_n \in F$ and $(q_{i-1}, a_i, q_i) \in T$ for all $1 \leq i \leq n$. Note that a linearization of a pomset may be identified with a word of Σ^*. A trace $t \in \mathbb{M}(\Sigma, \Delta)$ is accepted by $\mathcal{A}$ if some linear extension of t is accepted by $\mathcal{A}$. Note that, thanks to the diamond property of a trace automaton, if some linear extension of a trace is accepted by $\mathcal{A}$ then all linear extensions of t are accepted by $\mathcal{A}$. A trace language $L \subseteq \mathbb{M}(\Sigma, \Delta)$ is recognizable if it is the set of traces accepted by some trace automaton.

3 Asynchronous Cellular Automata

Definition 3.1. A $(\Sigma_1, \ldots, \Sigma_n)$-ACA (asynchronous cellular automata) is a tuple

$$\mathcal{A} = ((Q_i)_{i \in [n]}, (\delta_{a,J})_{a \in \Sigma, J \subseteq [n]}, F)$$

where

1. for all $i \in [n]$, Q_i is a finite set of local states for process i,
2. for all $a \in \Sigma$ and $J \subseteq [n]$, $\delta_{a,J} : \prod_{i \in J} Q_i \longrightarrow \mathcal{P}(Q_{p(a)})$ is a transition function,
3. and $F \subseteq \bigcup_{J \subseteq [n]} \prod_{i \in J} Q_i$ is the set of accepting states.

The automaton is deterministic if all the transition functions are deterministic, i.e. if $|\delta_{a,J}((q_i)_{i \in J})| \leq 1$ for all $a \in \Sigma$, $J \subseteq [n]$ and $(q_i)_{i \in J} \in \prod_{i \in J} Q_i$.

In order to explain how a $(\Sigma_1, \ldots, \Sigma_n)$-ACA accepts a $(\Sigma_1, \ldots, \Sigma_n)$-pomset, we need to introduce first some new notations. Let $t = (V, \leq, \lambda)$ be a $(\Sigma_1, \ldots, \Sigma_n)$-pomset and let $v \in V$ be a vertex in t. We define the write domain of v by $W(v) = p \circ \lambda(v)$ and the read domain of v as the set of processes of vertices covered by v : $R(v) = p \circ \lambda(\{u \in V \mid u \prec v\})$. A process i is maximal in t if $\lambda(v) \in \Sigma_i$ for some maximal vertex v of t. The set of maximal processes of t is denoted by $\max(t)$.

Intuitively, in order to perform an event v, the ACA reads the states of the processes in $R(v)$ and according to its transition functions determines the new state of the process $W(v)$. At the end of its run, the ACA collects the states of the maximal processes to decide whether the run is accepted or rejected. The formal definition is given below.

Note that if $i \in R(v)$ then $\partial_i(\Downarrow v)$ is non empty, whence has only one maximal vertex which will be identified with $\partial_i(\Downarrow v)$ in Definition 3.2. Similarly, if $i \in \max(t)$ then $\partial_i(t)$ is non empty and will also be identified with its maximum vertex.

Definition 3.2. A run of a $(\Sigma_1, \ldots, \Sigma_n)$-ACA $\mathcal{A}$ over a $(\Sigma_1, \ldots, \Sigma_n)$-pomset $t = (V, \leq, \lambda)$ is a mapping $r : V \longrightarrow \bigcup_{i \in [n]} Q_i$ such that for all $v \in V$,

$$r(v) \in \delta_{\lambda(v), R(v)} \left(r(\partial_i(\Downarrow v))_{i \in R(v)} \right)$$

The run r is accepted if its final maximal state $f(r) = r(\partial_i(t))_{i \in \max(t)}$ is in the accepting set F.

A $(\Sigma_1, \ldots, \Sigma_n)$-pomset t is accepted by $\mathcal{A}$ if there is some accepting run of $\mathcal{A}$ on t. The set of $(\Sigma_1, \ldots, \Sigma_n)$-pomsets accepted by $\mathcal{A}$ is denoted by $L(\mathcal{A})$.

The covering of pomsets by the chains formed by the fixed sequential processes is crucial in the definition of asynchronous cellular automata. It allows to use a fixed number of local states and to determine the read and write domains of the actions using the labeling and the covering relation. The weakest covering is when each Σ_i is a singleton. In this case we have a set of local states per letter as in the asynchronous cellular automata for traces [15, 2]. Note that, even with this trivial covering, our definition is not the same as that of Zielonka for traces. Mainly, in our definition, a run of the ACA is over the Hasse diagram of the pomset whereas with Zielonka's ACA for traces, a run is in fact over the dependence graph of the trace. A dependence graph is an intermediary representation of a trace between its Hasse diagram and its partial order. This intermediary representation is possible thanks to the existence of a static dependence relation over actions. More precisely, our definition of ACA for pomsets and that of Zielonka for traces differ in three respects. First, Zielonka's definition uses a global initial state which in our case is coded in the transition functions. Second, our transition functions only read the states of the processes covered by the current action whereas in Zielonka's definition a fixed set of processes is read even if the last executions of some of these processes are far below the current action. Third, we only read the states of maximal processes to determine whether a run is successful whereas in Zielonka's definition the states of all processes are collected globally to decide acceptance.

Remark 3.3. As discussed below, one could give several alternative definitions of accepting runs. One of these variants corresponds precisely to asynchronous cellular automata for traces. In fact, these differences are not crucial and we will see in Sections 4 and 6 that under some assumptions they are equivalent. In particular, this is true for traces.

1. First, one can change the set of processes read by transition functions. In the definition above, a transition only reads the processes covered by the current vertex. On the contrary, one can allow to read all processes which occur in the past of the current vertex by using $R_{\text{occur}}(v) = p \circ \lambda(\Downarrow v)$ instead of $R(v)$. For traces, we use the trivial covering of Σ by singletons and we identify processes with letters of Σ. Then, we consider a fixed dependence (symmetric and reflexive) relation D_{trace} on Σ and we use $D_{\text{trace}}(v)$ instead of $R(v)$. This static approach enforces the use of an initial state $\bot$. Indeed, for some $a \in D_{\text{trace}}(v)$, the prefix $\partial_a(\Downarrow v)$ may be empty and thus cannot be identified with a vertex of the trace. Thus we define $r(1) = \bot$ where 1 denotes the empty trace.
2. Second, one can change the acceptance condition. In the definition above, we only read the final state of the maximal processes. One can read the final state of all occurring processes by using $f_{\text{occur}}(r) = r(\partial_i(t))_{i \in p \circ \lambda(V)}$ instead of $f(r)$. For traces, we read the final state of all processes by using $f_{\text{trace}}(r) = r(\partial_a(t))_{a \in \Sigma}$ instead of $f(r)$. Again we need the initial state $\bot$ and the convention $r(1) = \bot$.

4 Asynchronous mapping

The domain of an asynchronous mapping must be a prefix closed subset of pomsets, that is a subset $\mathbb{Q}$ of pomsets such that for all pairs of pomsets s and t, if $s \preceq t$ and $t \in \mathbb{Q}$ then $s \in \mathbb{Q}$. For instance, $\mathbb{P}(\Sigma_1, \ldots, \Sigma_n)$ and $\mathbb{M}(\Sigma, \Delta)$ are prefix closed sets of pomsets.

Definition 4.1. Let $\mathbb{Q}$ be a prefix closed set of pomsets and let S be a finite set. A mapping $\sigma : \mathbb{Q} \longrightarrow S$ is asynchronous if for all $t = (V, \leq, \lambda) \in \mathbb{Q}$,

1. for all vertices $v \in V$, the value $\sigma(\downarrow v)$ is uniquely determined by $\sigma(\Downarrow v)$ and $\lambda(v)$.
2. for all prefixes t_1, t_2 of t, the value $\sigma(t_1 \cup t_2)$ is uniquely determined by $\sigma(t_1)$ and $\sigma(t_2)$.

A language $L \subseteq \mathbb{Q}$ is recognized by an asynchronous mapping $\sigma : \mathbb{Q} \longrightarrow S$ if $L = \sigma^{-1}(\sigma(L))$.

Remark 4.2. The definition of asynchronous mappings is valid for arbitrary pomsets and does not depend on the existence of sequential processes $(\Sigma_1, \ldots, \Sigma_n)$ in the pomsets. The definition of asynchronous cellular automata requires at least that each set of vertices labeled with the same letter forms a chain. This simple and weak property is not even required for asynchronous mappings.

Proposition 4.3. *Let $\mathbb{Q} \subseteq \mathbb{P}(\Sigma_1, \ldots, \Sigma_n)$ be a prefix closed set of $(\Sigma_1, \ldots, \Sigma_n)$-pomsets. Let $L \subseteq \mathbb{Q}$ be a language of $(\Sigma_1, \ldots, \Sigma_n)$-pomsets recognized by some asynchronous mapping $\sigma : \mathbb{Q} \longrightarrow S$. Then there exists a deterministic $(\Sigma_1, \ldots, \Sigma_n)$-asynchronous cellular automaton $\mathcal{A}$ such that $L(\mathcal{A}) \cap \mathbb{Q} = L$.*

We do not give the proof of this result here. It follows the same ideas as the corresponding one for traces.

Prop. 4.3 holds also for the alternative definitions of accepting runs discussed in Rem. 3.3.

Note that, for trace languages, the converse of Proposition 4.3 is also true and all alternative definitions of ACA are equivalent. Indeed, it is easy to show that a trace language accepted by an ACA is a recognizable trace language, whatever alternative chosen for accepting runs. Moreover, if L is a recognizable trace language, the existence of an asynchronous mapping which recognizes L was proven in [2]. Finally, as mentioned above, from this asynchronous mapping one can easily get an ACA which accepts L, whatever alternative chosen for accepting runs.

The equivalence between alternative definitions of accepting runs will be extended to a more general class of pomsets in Section 6. On the other hand, in the general setting of $\mathbb{P}(\Sigma_1, \ldots, \Sigma_n)$, the converse of Proposition 4.3 is still open.

5 From ACA to MSOL

In this section, we will define monadic second order (MSO) formulas and their interpretations over pomsets. We will then prove that for all ACA $\mathcal{A}$ (deterministic or not), there exists a MSO formula which defines the language accepted by $\mathcal{A}$.

Let Σ be a finite alphabet. The MSO language over Σ that we consider consists of the unary predicates $(P_a)_{a \in \Sigma}$, a binary predicate R, first order variables $x, y, z, \ldots$, monadic second order variables $X, Y, Z, \ldots$, boolean connectives $\neg, \vee, \wedge, \longrightarrow, \longleftrightarrow$ and quantifiers $\exists, \forall$. A sentence is a formula without free variables. For instance, the following formulas are first order and MSO sentences respectively.

$$\varphi_1 :: \exists x(P_a(x) \wedge \forall y(R(x,y) \longrightarrow \neg P_b(y)))$$

$$\varphi_2 :: \exists X \exists Y (\forall x(x \in X \vee x \in Y) \wedge \exists x\, x \in X \wedge \exists y\, y \in Y$$
$$\wedge \forall x \forall y(x \in X \wedge y \in Y \longrightarrow \neg R(x,y) \wedge \neg R(y,x))$$

A pomset $t = (V, \leq, \lambda)$ can be seen as an interpretation of this MSO language as follows: the domain is the set V of vertices, i.e. first order variables range over vertices and MSO variables range over sets of vertices; for all $a \in \Sigma$ $P_a(x)$ means $\lambda(x) = a$ and $R(x,y)$ means $x \leq y$. We say that a pomset t satisfies a sentence φ, denoted by $t \models \varphi$, when φ is true for the interpretation defined by t. The set of pomsets which satisfy a sentence φ is denoted by $L(\varphi)$. For instance,

$L(\varphi_1)$ is the set of pomsets which have a vertex labeled by a with no vertex labeled by b above and $L(\varphi_2)$ is the set of non connected pomsets.

Note that the language defined by a formula can contain pomsets with auto-concurrency (concurrent vertices with the same label). We do not need to put restrictions on the pomsets defined by a formula because all restrictions we need can be described by MSO formulas. For instance the set $\mathbb{P}(\Sigma_1, \dots, \Sigma_n)$ of $(\Sigma_1, \dots, \Sigma_n)$-pomsets is defined by the formula

$$\varphi_{(\Sigma_1,\dots,\Sigma_n)} :: \forall x \forall y (p \circ \lambda(x) = p \circ \lambda(y) \longrightarrow (x \leq y \vee y \leq x)).$$

We are now ready to state

Theorem 5.1. *Let $\Sigma = \Sigma_1 \dot\cup \cdots \dot\cup \Sigma_n$ and let $\mathcal{A}$ be a possibly non deterministic $(\Sigma_1, \dots, \Sigma_n)$-ACA. There exists a MSO formula φ over Σ such that*

$$L(\varphi) = L(\mathcal{A}).$$

We do not give the proof of this result here. It is quite similar to the usual ones. The formula codes the existence of an accepting run of the automaton.

Remark 5.2. Clearly, Theorem 5.1 holds also for the alternative definitions of accepting runs described in Remark 3.3.

6 From MSOL to deterministic ACA

The converse of Theorem 5.1 is an open problem. In this section, we prove that this converse holds for the special subclass of $(\Sigma_1, \dots, \Sigma_n)$-pomsets for which the ACA works as a Concurrent Read Owner Write (CROW) machine. More precisely, we consider n processes whose sets of actions are $\Sigma_1, \dots, \Sigma_n$ respectively. Each process has a memory which can be read by all actions but can be written by its own actions only (Owner Write). We allow concurrent reads of memories but no concurrent writes. As quoted in Section 2.1, this restriction is already enforced by the very definition of $(\Sigma_1, \dots, \Sigma_n)$-pomsets. Without further restrictions, two concurrent events may respectively read from and write to the same location. This is the case when there exist two concurrent events $y \parallel z$ such that z writes in the memory of some process i ($p \circ \lambda(z) = i$) and y reads the memory of this process i ($p \circ \lambda(x) = i$ for some $x \prec y$). This motivates the following definition.

Definition 6.1. A $(\Sigma_1, \dots, \Sigma_n)$-pomset $t = (V, \leq, \lambda)$ satisfies the Concurrent Read Owner Write (CROW) axiom if $\forall x, y, z \in V$,

$$x \prec y \wedge x < z \wedge y \parallel z \quad \Longrightarrow \quad p \circ \lambda(x) \neq p \circ \lambda(z) \qquad (1)$$

The set of $(\Sigma_1, \dots, \Sigma_n)$-pomsets which satisfy the CROW axiom is denoted by $\mathbb{CROW}(\Sigma_1, \dots, \Sigma_n)$.

Theorem 6.2. *Let $\Sigma = \Sigma_1 \dot\cup \cdots \dot\cup \Sigma_n$ and let φ be a MSO formula over Σ. There exists a deterministic $(\Sigma_1, \ldots, \Sigma_n)$-ACA $\mathcal{A}$ such that*

$$L(\varphi) \cap \mathbb{CROW}(\Sigma_1, \ldots, \Sigma_n) = L(\mathcal{A}) \cap \mathbb{CROW}(\Sigma_1, \ldots, \Sigma_n).$$

In order to prove this theorem, one can use an induction on the structure of the formula. Disjunction and existential quantification are easily dealt with when non deterministic ACA are allowed. On the other hand, complement is easy for deterministic ACA. Whence the core of such an approach is the determinization of ACA. For this problem, starting from a non deterministic ACA $\mathcal{A}$, one can directly construct an asynchronous mapping which accepts the language $L(\mathcal{A})$ and then use Proposition 4.3. This construction is similar to that of [10] and uses the asynchronous time stamping of Zielonka [15, 2] but the proofs are more involved. In particular, it is known that for traces Zielonka's ν mapping is asynchronous by itself [2, 4] but this is not the case for $\mathbb{CROW}(\Sigma_1, \ldots, \Sigma_n)$-pomsets. Here we give a simpler proof which uses Zielonka's theorem. For this, we first map CROW-pomsets into traces by simply changing the labeling.

Let $\Sigma' = \Sigma \times \mathcal{P}([n])$ be a new set of labels and for all $i \in [n]$, let $\Sigma'_i = \Sigma_i \times \mathcal{P}([n])$ be the associated new processes. We define an embedding g from $\mathbb{P}(\Sigma_1, \ldots, \Sigma_n)$ into $\mathbb{P}(\Sigma'_1, \ldots, \Sigma'_n)$ by $g(V, \leq, \lambda) = (V, \leq, \lambda')$ where for all $v \in V, \lambda'(v) = (\lambda(v), R(v))$. Note that g is well defined, since for all $i \in [n]$, $\lambda'^{-1}(\Sigma'_i)$ is totally ordered. Let Δ' be the dependence relation defined on Σ' by

$$\Delta' = \{((a, A), (b, B)) \mid p(a) = p(b) \vee p(a) \in B \vee p(b) \in A\}.$$

Proposition 6.3.

$$\mathbb{CROW}(\Sigma_1, \ldots, \Sigma_n) = g^{-1}(\mathbb{M}(\Sigma', \Delta'))$$

Proof. We first prove that $\mathbb{CROW}(\Sigma_1, \ldots, \Sigma_n) \subseteq g^{-1}(\mathbb{M}(\Sigma', \Delta'))$. Let $t = (V, \leq, \lambda) \in \mathbb{CROW}(\Sigma_1, \ldots, \Sigma_n)$ and let $g(t) = (V, \leq, \lambda')$. Let $x, y \in V$ and assume that $x \prec y$. Then, $p \circ \lambda(x) \in R(y)$ and it follows $(\lambda'(x), \lambda'(y)) \in \Delta'$. Now, let $y, z \in V$ and assume that $(\lambda'(y), \lambda'(z)) \in \Delta'$. If $p \circ \lambda(y) = p \circ \lambda(z)$ then $y \not\parallel z$ since t is a $(\Sigma_1, \ldots, \Sigma_n)$-pomset. Otherwise, we have for instance $p \circ \lambda(z) \in R(y)$. Hence, there exists $x \in V$ such that $x \prec y$ and $p \circ \lambda(x) = p \circ \lambda(z)$. Therefore, x and z must be ordered. Since $x < z$ would contradict the CROW-axiom, it follows $z \leq x$, whence $z < y$. Therefore, $g(t) \in \mathbb{M}(\Sigma', \Delta')$ (see Section 2.2) and it follows $t \in g^{-1}(\mathbb{M}(\Sigma', \Delta'))$.

Conversely, let $t = (V, \leq, \lambda) \in g^{-1}(\mathbb{M}(\Sigma', \Delta'))$ and let $g(t) = (V, \leq, \lambda')$. Let $x, y, z \in V$ be such that $x \prec y \wedge x < z \wedge y \parallel z$. By definition, $p \circ \lambda(x) \in R(y)$ and $(\lambda'(y), \lambda'(z)) \notin \Delta'$. Therefore, $p \circ \lambda(z) \notin R(y)$ and it follows $p \circ \lambda(x) \neq p \circ \lambda(z)$.

Proposition 6.4. *Let φ be a MSO formula over Σ. There exists a MSO formula φ' over Σ' such that*

$$L(\varphi) \cap \mathbb{CROW}(\Sigma_1, \ldots, \Sigma_n) = g^{-1}(L(\varphi') \cap \mathbb{M}(\Sigma', \Delta'))$$

Proof. (sketch) Let φ be a MSO formula over Σ. Let φ' be the MSO formula over Σ' obtained from φ by substituting to atomic formulas of the form $x \in P_a$ the disjunction $\bigvee_{J\subseteq[n]} x \in P_{(a,J)}$:

$$\varphi' = \varphi\left[x \in P_a \Big/ \bigvee_{J\subseteq[n]} x \in P_{(a,J)}\right].$$

The proposition follows easily using Proposition 6.3.

Proposition 6.5. *Let $\mathcal{A}'$ be a (deterministic) $(\Sigma_1',\dots,\Sigma_n')$-ACA. There exists a (deterministic) $(\Sigma_1,\dots,\Sigma_n)$-ACA $\mathcal{A}$ such that $L(\mathcal{A}) = g^{-1}(L(\mathcal{A}'))$.*

Proof. (sketch) Let $\mathcal{A}' = ((Q_i)_{i\in[n]}, (\delta'_{a',J})_{a'\in\Sigma',J\subseteq[n]}, F)$ be a $(\Sigma_1',\dots,\Sigma_n')$-ACA. For all $a \in \Sigma$ and $J \subseteq [n]$, let $\delta_{a,J} = \delta'_{(a,J),J}$. We claim that $\mathcal{A} = ((Q_i)_{i\in[n]}, (\delta_{a,J})_{a\in\Sigma,J\subseteq[n]}, F)$ is the required $(\Sigma_1,\dots,\Sigma_n)$-ACA. Note first that if $\mathcal{A}'$ is deterministic then so is $\mathcal{A}$. Now, let $t = (V,\leq,\lambda) \in \mathbb{P}(\Sigma_1,\dots,\Sigma_n)$ and let $g(t) = (V,\leq,\lambda')$. For all $v \in V$, we have $R'(v) = p\circ\lambda'(\{u \mid u \prec\!\!\cdot\, v\}) = p\circ\lambda(\{u \mid u \prec\!\!\cdot\, v\}) = R(v)$. Therefore $\delta'_{\lambda'(v),R'(v)} = \delta'_{(\lambda(v),R(v)),R(v)} = \delta_{\lambda(v),R(v)}$.

Let $r : V \longrightarrow \bigcup_{i\in[n]} Q_i$. It follows that r is an accepting run of $\mathcal{A}'$ on $g(t)$ if and only if r is an accepting run of $\mathcal{A}$ on t, that is,

$$g(L(\mathcal{A})) \subseteq L(\mathcal{A}') \quad\text{and}\quad g^{-1}(L(\mathcal{A}')) \subseteq L(\mathcal{A}).$$

The proposition follows.

Proof of Theorem 6.2: Let φ be a MSO formula over Σ. By Proposition 6.4, there exists a MSO formula φ' over Σ' such that

$$L(\varphi) \cap \mathbb{CROW}(\Sigma_1,\dots,\Sigma_n) = g^{-1}(L(\varphi') \cap \mathbb{M}(\Sigma',\Delta')).$$

The language $L(\varphi') \cap \mathbb{M}(\Sigma',\Delta')$ is a recognizable trace language [13]. Hence [15, 2], there exists an asynchronous mapping σ from $\mathbb{M}(\Sigma',\Delta')$ into a finite set which recognizes $L(\varphi') \cap \mathbb{M}(\Sigma',\Delta')$. By Proposition 4.3, there exists a deterministic $(\Sigma_1',\dots,\Sigma_n')$-ACA $\mathcal{A}'$ such that $L(\mathcal{A}') \cap \mathbb{M}(\Sigma',\Delta') = L(\varphi') \cap \mathbb{M}(\Sigma',\Delta')$. It follows by Proposition 6.5 that there exists a deterministic $(\Sigma_1,\dots,\Sigma_n)$-ACA $\mathcal{A}$ such that $L(\mathcal{A}) = g^{-1}(L(\mathcal{A}'))$. Finally, applying Proposition 6.3 we obtain

$$\begin{aligned}
L(\mathcal{A}) \cap \mathbb{CROW}(\Sigma_1,\dots,\Sigma_n) &= g^{-1}(L(\mathcal{A}')) \cap g^{-1}(\mathbb{M}(\Sigma',\Delta')) \\
&= g^{-1}(L(\mathcal{A}') \cap \mathbb{M}(\Sigma',\Delta')) \\
&= g^{-1}(L(\varphi') \cap \mathbb{M}(\Sigma',\Delta')) \\
&= L(\varphi) \cap \mathbb{CROW}(\Sigma_1,\dots,\Sigma_n)
\end{aligned}$$

As a corollary of Theorems 5.1 and 6.2 we obtain that MSO formulas, non deterministic $(\Sigma_1,\dots,\Sigma_n)$-ACA and deterministic $(\Sigma_1,\dots,\Sigma_n)$-ACA have the same expressive power for $\mathbb{CROW}(\Sigma_1,\dots,\Sigma_n)$-pomsets.

Theorem 6.6. *Let $L \subseteq \mathbb{CROW}(\Sigma_1, \ldots, \Sigma_n)$. The following are equivalent:*

1. *L is definable by a MSO formula,*
2. *there exists a non deterministic $(\Sigma_1, \ldots, \Sigma_n)$-ACA $\mathcal{A}$ such that*
$$L = L(\mathcal{A}) \cap \mathbb{CROW}(\Sigma_1, \ldots, \Sigma_n)$$
3. *there exists a deterministic $(\Sigma_1, \ldots, \Sigma_n)$-ACA $\mathcal{A}$ such that*
$$L = L(\mathcal{A}) \cap \mathbb{CROW}(\Sigma_1, \ldots, \Sigma_n)$$

Remark 6.7. Finally, we come back to the alternative definitions of accepting runs discussed in Remark 3.3. As a corollary of previous results, we obtain that these alternatives are equivalent for CROW-pomsets. The question whether the same equivalence holds for general pomsets is still open.

7 Conclusion

We believe that the CROW axiom is really natural if one sees an ACA as an abstract representation of a parallel machine where each process writes in its own memory and can read the memories of other processes. In this case, we have proved that deterministic ACA are closed under the boolean operations and have the same expressive power as the MSOL. Since emptiness for ACA is decidable when restricted to $\mathbb{CROW}(\Sigma_1, \ldots, \Sigma_n)$ pomsets, we can use ACA to perform model checking : to check whether an implementation (an ACA) $\mathcal{A}$ satisfies a specification (a MSO formula) φ, one computes the deterministic ACA $\mathcal{B}$ such that $L(\varphi) \cap \mathbb{CROW}(\Sigma_1, \ldots, \Sigma_n) = L(\mathcal{B}) \cap \mathbb{CROW}(\Sigma_1, \ldots, \Sigma_n)$ and then checks for emptiness $L(\mathcal{A}) \cap \overline{L(\mathcal{B})} \cap \mathbb{CROW}(\Sigma_1, \ldots, \Sigma_n)$.

On the other hand, ACA may be seen as an abstract representation of distributed systems communicating asynchronously. In this setting, the covering relation $x \prec y$ can denote a message sent by x to y. If the communication is asynchronous, the process $p(x)$ may perform some actions concurrently to the reception (y) of the message sent (x). In this case, the CROW axiom is not natural anymore. Therefore, an important open problem is to know whether the properties proved in this paper for CROW-pomsets also hold in a more general setting.

Finally, we would like to point out that both the definition of asynchronous mappings and of MSOL can be extended without any change to pomsets with auto-concurrency. It would be very interesting to find a general model of ACA which allows auto-concurrency. Note that it is possible with our ACA to cope with bounded auto-concurrency by suitably relabeling auto-concurrent vertices.

References

1. F. Bracho, M. Droste, and D. Kuske. Dependence orders for computations of concurrent automata. In *Proceedings of STACS'95*, number 900 in Lecture Notes in Computer Science, pages 467–478. Springer Verlag, 1995. Full version to appear in Theoret. Comp. Science.

2. R. Cori, Y. Métivier, and W. Zielonka. Asynchronous mappings and asynchronous cellular automata. *Information and Computation*, 106:159–202, 1993.
3. V. Diekert. A partial trace semantics for petri nets. *Theoretical Computer Science*, 113:87–105, 1994. Special issue of ICWLC 92, Kyoto (Japan).
4. V. Diekert and A. Muscholl. Construction of asynchronous automata. In G. Rozenberg and V. Diekert, editors, *Book of Traces*, pages 249–267. World Scientific, Singapore, 1995.
5. V. Diekert and G. Rozenberg, editors. *Book of Traces*. World Scientific, Singapore, 1995.
6. M. Droste and D. Kuske. Logical definability of recognizable and aperiodic languages in concurrency monoids. In *Proceedings of CSL'95*, Lecture Notes in Computer Science. Springer Verlag, 1996. to appear.
7. J.L. Gischer. The equational theory of pomsets. *Theoretical Computer Science*, 61:199–224, 1988.
8. A. Mazurkiewicz. Concurrent program schemes and their interpretations. Tech. rep. DAIMI PB 78, Aarhus University, 1977.
9. A. Mazurkiewicz. Trace theory. In W. Brauer et al., editors, *Advances in Petri Nets'86*, number 255 in Lecture Notes in Computer Science, pages 279–324. Springer Verlag, 1987.
10. A. Muscholl. On the complementation of Büchi asynchronous cellular automata. In S. Abiteboul and E. Shamir, editors, *Proceedings of the 21st International Colloquium on Automata, Languages and Programming (ICALP'94)*, number 820 in Lecture Notes in Computer Science. Springer Verlag, 1994.
11. V.R. Pratt. Modelling concurrency with partial orders. *J. of Parallel Programming*, 15:33–71, 1987.
12. P.H. Starke. Processes in petri nets. *EIK*, 17:389–416, 1981.
13. Wolfgang Thomas. On logical definability of trace languages. In V. Diekert, editor, *Proceedings of a workshop of the ESPRIT BRA No 3166: Algebraic and Syntactic Methods in Computer Science (ASMICS), 1989*, Report TUM-I9002, Technical University of Munich, pages 172–182, 1990.
14. W. Zielonka. Notes on finite asynchronous automata. *R.A.I.R.O. — Informatique Théorique et Applications*, 21:99–135, 1987.
15. W. Zielonka. Safe executions of recognizable trace languages by asynchronous automata. In A. R. Meyer et al., editors, *Proceedings of the Symposium on Logical Foundations of Computer Science (Logic at Botik'89)*, number 363 in Lecture Notes in Computer Science, pages 278–289. Springer Verlag, 1989.

Action Refinement and Property Inheritance in Systems of Sequential Agents

Michaela Huhn*

Institut für Informatik, Universität Hildesheim, Germany
huhn@informatik.uni-hildesheim.de

Abstract. For systems of sequential agents the fundamental relations between events - *causality and conflict* - are naturally connected to a global dependency relation on the system's alphabet. *Action refinement* as a strictly hierarchical approach to system design should preserve this connection. Then it can be guaranteed that also more complex temporal properties of the refined system are inherited from the abstract level. The behaviour of a system of sequential agents is given in terms of synchronisations structures, a location-based subclass of prime event structures. The action refinement operator inherits causality and conflict according to the dependency relation. To express temporal properties of the systems we use νTrPTL, a linear time temporal logic for Mazurkiewicz traces. The logical framework, based on local modalities and fixpoints, allows to define refinement transformation on formulae. Under certain constraints on the refinement function, satisfaction of a formula for the abstract system turns out to be equivalent to satisfaction of the transformed formula for the refined system.

1 Introduction

In a top-down design methodology, a system specification will be incrementally enriched with details. *Action refinement* - the substitution of actions by more complex subsystems - is a technique that often is proposed for this purpose, see e.g. [GG89, GMM90, DD93, Vog93, GGR94, AH94]. Action refinement does not preserve equivalence of behaviours for many equivalence notions defined for distributed systems on interleaving models. So much work was done on action refinement on partial order models, in particular on event structures [Win86]. To take advantage of hierarchical design, design decisions already taken on the abstract level should be kept. Therefore all work mentioned above uses strict inheritance of the fundamental relations between action occurrences in event based models, namely *causality* and *conflict*: If two abstract actions occurrences are causally ordered then all actions that occur in the refinement of one of these actions are in causal ordering with the actions from the other refinement. The same applies to conflict. Strict inheritance of causality and conflict is appropriate in a very general setting where the actions are just uninterpreted names.

* Part of this work was financially supported by the Human Capital and Mobility Cooperation Network "EXPRESS" (Expressivity of Languages for Concurrency).

But often the structuring of the system into components is fixed already in an early stage of system design. The structure may be imposed by physical distribution of the components and is kept during the various phases of system development. This information is neglected if causality and conflict are inherited strictly which has been shown unsatisfactory in case studies, see e.g. [GG91]. Hence in [JPZ91] and [Weh94] it was suggested to parameterise inheritance of causality by a global dependency relation as it is known from trace theory [Maz88]. In terms of trace theory, this kind of parameterised action refinement corresponds to the substitution of actions by trace languages. But trace substitution does not preserve I-diamond-closure of trace structures.
In the work presented here we consider systems consisting of a fixed set of sequential agents executing actions from a fixed alphabet. In this setting it is quite natural to refine a synchronising action a by a parallel composition of local refinements - one for each agent participating in a. A similar idea was presented in [AH94] for CCS where the associated actions a and $\bar{a}$ may be refined differently. Now consider two sequential components A and B that can choose between communication via two different ports named a and b, written as $(a+b) \parallel_{\{a,b\}} (a+b)$ in a TCSP-like syntax. The two abstract events a and b are in conflict. When implementing the system we may decide that on port a component A will play the role of a sender, whereas on port b B will do so. Thus for A the communication on a is refined into *prepare_data*$_a$*; transmit*$_a$ and B participates only in *transmit*$_a$. b will be refined vice versa. By term substitution we get

$$(\mathit{prepare\_data}_a; \mathit{transmit}_a + \mathit{transmit}_b) \parallel (\mathit{transmit}_a + \mathit{prepare\_data}_b; \mathit{transmit}_b)$$

prepare_data$_a$ and *prepare_data*$_b$ are independent actions. Taking the natural assumption into account that independent actions will not prevent each other from occurrence we expect that the resulting system contains three runs as shown in example 1: Besides the successful execution of the refinements of a and b a deadlock may occur if A chooses *prepare_data*$_a$ and simultaneously B starts with *prepare_data*$_b$. In opposite to that, action refinement as defined in [JPZ91, Weh94] would give us just the two successful executions of the refinement.
Thus we parameterise inheritance of causality *and* conflict by a dependency relation derived from the distribution. We define action refinement on synchronisation structures [Ram95] where causality is generated by the sequentiality of the components and all conflicts originate from local conflicts. The domain of synchronisation structures is not left by refinement (see proposition 4). We characterise a class of refinement functions for which our refinement operator preserves the linear time structure of the system (see theorem 6), in the sense that all runs of the refined system are refinements of abstract runs.

Now one should remember that hierarchical design claims to preserve structural design decisions made on the abstract level. So the question arises: Which *temporal* properties does the abstract system impose on the refined system via action refinement? We cannot hope (or even desire) that the same properties should hold on both levels. So what is conceivable is a relation or transformation of logical properties, which is determined by the refinement function. We will not address the question of inheritance of properties in its full generality, but rather we will give one positive solution to the following scheme: the refinement operator *Ref* on synchronisation structures will induce syntactical transformations $\mathcal{R}ef$ on formulae such that the following correspondence holds:

$$\begin{array}{ccc} \mathcal{H} & \models & \varphi \\ \downarrow & \Updownarrow & \downarrow \\ Ref(\mathcal{H}) & \models & \mathcal{R}ef(\varphi) \end{array} \qquad (1)$$

A positive solution to this scheme supports 'a priori' verification in system design, but its usefulness depends much on the expressiveness of the logic used. Moreover, $\mathcal{R}ef$ is not uniquely determined (even on the semantical level) by this scheme. There may indeed be several transformations achieving this goal, but giving formulae of different strength. What we demonstrate here, is that this scheme can be achieved for an expressive logic under fairly weak assumptions on the refinement function.

To obtain a solution, two preliminaries seem necessary: The refinement function itself should ensure proper inheritance of causality and conflict, e.g. partners in a synchronisation must not be added or lost in the refinement.

Secondly, the operators of the temporal logic used to express the properties should be as close as possible to the fundamental relations between events in the system model. Therefore, we have chosen νTrPTL [Nie95] which is a fixpoint variant of trace-based linear time temporal logic (TrPTL) suggested by Thiagarajan [Thi94, Thi95]. νTrPTL is based on localised modalities $\langle a \rangle_i$ (*next a for agent i*) which exactly correspond to the definition of local transitions of agent i in a synchronisation structure. Similar to the μ-calculus (see e.g. [Sti92]) all other operators are derived from the modalities by using fixpoints.

For strongly connected formulae, a syntactic subset of νTrPTL, a sequence of modalities $\langle a_1 \rangle_{i_1} \langle a_2 \rangle_{i_2} \ldots \langle a_n \rangle_{i_n}$ corresponds to a chain of causal successors in the model. Action refinement substitutes a sequence of causal successors by a tree-like structure. But when the refinement function preserves causal connections, in the refined system there is still a causal ordering from initial actions in the refinement of a_1 to all final actions in the refinement of a_n. This suggests to substitute a modality $\langle a \rangle_i$ by an appropriate sequence of modalities describing a causal chain through $ref(a)$. These are described by regular expressions called ***skeletons*** that allow us to deal also with infinite (but regular) refinements.

We give a class of refinement functions for which the proposed correspondence holds for sequential refinement transformations on arbitrary strongly connected formulae. Moreover, the correspondence (1) coincides with an refinement extension of *run trace equivalence* as defined in [GKP92].

In section 2 synchronisation structures and action refinement are introduced. Section 3 and 4 are concerned with the logic νTrPTL and refinement transformations on formulae. We finish with some concluding remarks. For lack of space all proofs are omitted. We refer the interested reader to [Huh96] where also an application of the theory can be found.

2 Synchronisation Structures and Action Refinement

We consider a model for distributed systems where a system is built as a parallel composition of a fixed set of sequential processes called *agents* (see e.g. [Thi95, Ram95]). The agents or locations are taken from a set $Loc = \{1, \ldots K\}$. The behaviour of each agent is represented as a 'tree-like' structure where branches represent choices and actions occurring on the same path are ordered by causality. The system executes actions of a *distributed alphabet* $\tilde{\Sigma} = (\Sigma_1, \ldots, \Sigma_K)$ where the sets Σ_i may overlap in *joint* actions. The set of agents participating in a is denoted by $loc(a) = \{i \mid a \in \Sigma_i\}$. $\Sigma = \bigcup_i \Sigma_i$ denotes the system's alphabet. Actions $a, b \in \Sigma$ are called *dependent*, denoted by $a\,D\,b$, if $loc(a) \cap loc(b) \neq \emptyset$, otherwise a and b are *independent*, $a\,I\,b$. The system behaviour is modelled by synchronisation structures, a subclass of labelled prime event structures that corresponds to a product of transition systems with common local states [Ram95].

Definition 1. A $\tilde{\Sigma}$*-synchronisation structure* (*SynS*) is a triple $\mathcal{E} = \langle E, \leq, l\rangle$ where

- E is a set of events,
- $\leq \subseteq E \times E$ is a partial order called *causality*,
- $l : E \to \bigcup_{i \in Loc} \Sigma_i$ is a *labelling function*, such that the following holds:
  Let $E_i \triangleq \{e' \in E \mid l(e') \in \Sigma_i\}$ and $\leq_i \triangleq \leq \cap (E_i \times E_i)$, then
  i) $\{e' \mid e' \leq e\} \cap E_i$ is totally ordered by $\leq$ for all $e \in E, i \in Loc$,
  ii) $\leq = (\bigcup_{i \in Loc} \leq_i)^*$.

ES_{syn} denotes the domain of synchronisation structures. The conditions on $\leq$ ensure that every agent i (executing the events E_i) is sequential and causality is generated by the dependency relation D on the event labels. We extend the notion of dependency on events by $e\,D\,f$ iff $l(e)\,D\,l(f)$, and also we use $loc(e) \triangleq loc(l(e))$ and $loc(\mathcal{E}) \triangleq \bigcup_{e \in E} loc(e)$ for the set of agents that are active in $\mathcal{E}$. $\langle E_i, \leq_i, l_i\rangle$ is ordered by $\leq_i$ like a tree and gives the branching behaviour of the sequential agent i. Events $e, e' \in E_i$ that are not ordered by $\leq_i$ are in *local conflict*. In our system model all conflicts will be induced by local conflicts. So e and e' are in *global conflict*, denoted by $e \# e'$, iff there exist $f \leq e$ and $f' \leq e'$ such that f and f' are in local conflict. Thus the notion of conflict is derived from causality and labelling. Events e and e' that are neither ordered by $\leq$ nor are in conflict are called *concurrent* events, denoted by $e\,co\,e'$, formally $co = E \times E - (\leq \cup \leq^{-1} \cup \#)$.
Events labelled with joint actions are interpreted as synchronisations of the participating agents. $e \leq e'$ implies that there must be at least an indirect communication from the agents executing e to those executing e' via a sequence of synchronisations in between. By $e \lessdot f$ ($e \lessdot_i f$) we denote that e is a *direct predecessor* of f w.r.t. $\leq$ ($\leq_i$). e is an i*-maximal* (i-minimal) event of E if e is maximal (minimal) w.r.t. $\leq_i$.
By $\downarrow_X Y = \{e' \in X \mid \exists e \in Y \,.\, e' \leq e\}$ we denote the *downward closure* of Y in the partially ordered set $(X, \leq)$. If X is obvious it is omitted. $\downarrow e$ abbreviates $\downarrow_E \{e\}$. A *SynS* is *finitary* if $\downarrow e$ is finite for all e. As we only consider *SynS*s

as models of computations we restrict ourselves to finitary *SynS*s. For a given *SynS* $\mathcal{E} = \langle E, \leq, l \rangle$ a subset $c \subseteq E$ is called ***conflict-free*** iff c contains no pair of conflicting events. A downward-closed, conflict-free, finite subset c of E is called a *configuration*. Often we are not only interested in the set of events in a configuration c, but in the substructure $\mathcal{E}|_c = \langle c, \leq_c, l_c \rangle$ where $\leq_c = \leq |_{c \times c}$ and $l_c = l|_c$, the restriction of $\mathcal{E}$ on c. $c_\emptyset$ is the empty configuration $\langle \emptyset, \emptyset, \emptyset \rangle$.
The ***global successor relation*** on configurations, $c \xrightarrow{a} d$, is defined by $d = c \oplus \{e\}$ where $e \in E$ and $l(e) = a$. We write $c \longrightarrow d$ if there exists an a such that $c \xrightarrow{a} d$. $\longrightarrow^*$ denotes the transitive closure of $\longrightarrow$. $\langle Con(\mathcal{E}), \longrightarrow^* \rangle$, where $Con(\mathcal{E})$ is the set of configurations of $\mathcal{E}$, is called the ***configuration structure*** of $\mathcal{E}$. A maximal $\longrightarrow^*$-directed subset ρ of $Con(\mathcal{E})$ is called a ***run*** of the *SynS* $\mathcal{E}$ and ***Runs***$(\mathcal{E})$ denotes the set of all runs of $\mathcal{E}$.
In the logic we want to assign propositions to configurations that express atomic predicates on a system state. For simplicity we restrict ourselves to one particular local proposition for each agent denoted by $\surd_i$ that is fundamental to refinement. $\surd_i$ indicates ***successful termination*** of agent i. An ***interpretation of a SynS*** $\mathcal{E}$ is a mapping $\mathrm{I} : \{\surd_i \mid i \in Loc\} \rightarrow 2^E$. From the interpretation on $\mathcal{E}$ we derive the interpretation for configurations by $\mathrm{I} : \{\surd_i \mid i \in Loc\} \rightarrow 2^{Con(\mathcal{E})}$ where $c \in \mathrm{I}(\surd_i)$ iff $e \in \mathrm{I}(\surd_i)$ for the i-maximal event e in c. A configuration c with $c \in \mathrm{I}(\surd_i)$ for all $i \in loc(c)$ is called ***terminated***. If a maximal configuration c is not i-terminated for some $i \in loc(c)$, we say agent i is in a ***local deadlock*** at c. $\mathcal{E}_\mathrm{I}$ denotes an interpreted *SynS* from the domain $ES_{syn,\mathrm{I}}$.
The ***i-view*** of a configuration c is defined as $\downarrow^i c = \downarrow (c \cap E_i)$, i.e. the least configuration that coincides with c on the i-events. Two configurations are ***i-equivalent***, $c \equiv_i d$, iff $\downarrow^i c = \downarrow^i d$. The view is extended to sets of agents by $\downarrow^L c = \downarrow (c \cap \bigcap_{i \in L} E_i)$.
The ***local successor relation***, $c \xrightarrow{a}_i d$, is given by $\exists c', d' \,.\, c \equiv_i c' \wedge c' \xrightarrow{a} d' \wedge d' \equiv_i d$ where $i \in loc(a)$. For a *SynS* $\mathcal{E}$ we define the set of ***causal chains*** $ch(\mathcal{E}) \triangleq \{(i_1, e_1)(i_2, e_2) \ldots \mid \forall n \; e_n \in E \wedge e_1 \in E_{i_1} \wedge e_1 <_{i_2} e_2 <_{i_3} \ldots\}$. We say a causal chain $(i_1, e_1) \ldots (i_n, e_n)$ leads from a configuration c to d if $c \xrightarrow{e_1}_{i_1} \ldots \xrightarrow{e_n}_{i_n} d$. If $s(i,e)$ leads from c to d then $s(i,e)$ also leads from c to d' if $d' \equiv_i d$. We use $ch_{i \rightarrow j}(\mathcal{E})$ to denote the *maximal* causal chains from an i-minimal event to a j-terminated event in $\mathcal{E}$. Causal chains are sequences of consecutive events. Often we are interested in the sequence of labels of a causal chain: $l((i_1, e_1)(i_2, e_2) \ldots) \triangleq (i_1, l(e_1))(i_2, l(e_2)) \ldots$.

Example 1. Let $\Sigma_1 = \{a_1, a_2, b_2\}$ and $\Sigma_2 = \{a_2, b_1, b_2\}$ be the alphabets for a 2-agent system. $\mathcal{E}_\mathrm{I}$ gives the behaviour of the process algebraic expression $(a_1 a_2 + b_2) \parallel (b_1 b_2 + a_2)$ where the synchronisation set is $\{a_2, b_2\}$. If both agents choose corresponding branches, both will terminate, otherwise both agents will end in a local deadlock. (The figure shows $Con(\mathcal{E})$, $\leq$ is depicted as $\rightarrow$, and event identities are omitted as they are uniquely determined by the labels.)

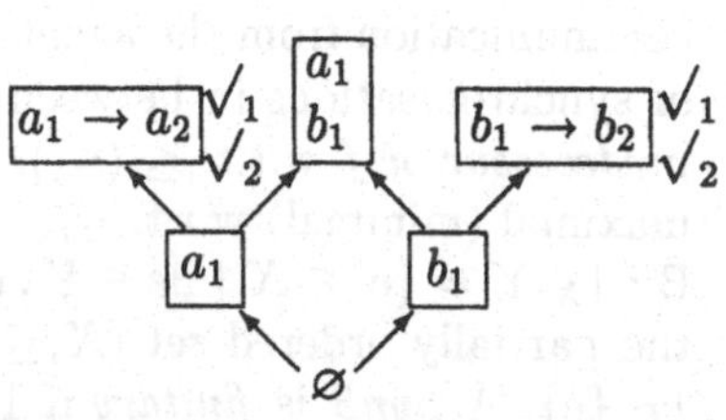

SynSs $\mathcal{E}_{\mathrm{I}}$ and $\mathcal{F}_{\mathrm{J}}$ are *isomorphic*, $\mathcal{E}_{\mathrm{I}} \cong \mathcal{F}_{\mathrm{J}}$, if there exists a bijection from E to F that preserves causality, labelling, and interpretation. The notion of isomorphism is extended to runs in the obvious manner.

2.1 Semantic Action Refinement

Now we consider semantic *action refinement* - the substitution of actions by processes - for synchronisation structures. On each level of abstraction, actions are seen as indivisible atomic entities. When using action refinement, the actions from the abstract level are substituted by more complex subsystems yielding a low-level system. Thus we will replace events by *SynSs* according to a refinement function that determines a low level behaviour for each action a.

Definition 2. $ref : \Sigma \to ES_{syn,\mathrm{I}}$ is called *refinement function* if $loc(a) = loc(ref(a)) = loc(\downarrow e)$ for all events e in $ref(a) \cap \bigcup_{i \in loc(a)} \mathrm{I}_{ref(a)}(\surd_i)$.

The condition on refinement functions ensures that exactly the agents that participate in an abstract action a will take part in each terminating execution of the refinement of a. Moreover, if i and j synchronise on a, each j-terminated execution of $ref(a)$ contains at least an indirect communication between i and j. Thus *ref* preserves communications. Empty refinements are excluded implicitly. In our setting a joint action may be refined differently for different agents, thus the refinement of a joint action can be seen as the parallel composition of 'local' refinement functions ref_i. A refinement function is called *run finite* if all runs $\rho \in Runs(ref(a))$ are finite for all $a \in \Sigma$.
The refined system shall be again a *SynS*. In particular all conflicts have to originate from local conflicts. Thus conflict and causality is only inherited if the events of the refinements are dependent. Technically, the refinement proceeds in two steps: At first we will refine a *SynS* by replacing each a-labelled event by a disjoint copy of some run of $ref(a)$. This would be sufficient if all actions are refined by conflict-free *SynSs*. But when the refinement contains choices, for each branch a different copy of the causal successors of that refinement is needed because simple event replacement does not yield a prime event structure.
Therefore the events of the refined system are built in a second step from pre-configurations that contain the complete history. This part of the construction is similar to a construction in [Vaa89]. Let $ref(a) = \langle E_{ref(a)}, \leq_{ref(a)}, l_{ref(a)} \rangle$ for each $a \in \Sigma$. The event replacement is achieved by:
The *pre-refinement* $\mathcal{E}[ref] = \langle E^{ref}, \leq^{ref}, l^{ref} \rangle$ of a *SynS* $\mathcal{E} = \langle E, \leq l \rangle$ w.r.t. *ref* is defined as:

- $E^{ref} \triangleq \{(e, e') \mid e \in E \wedge e' \in E_{ref(l(e))}\}$
- $\leq^{ref}$ is the transitive closure of $\sqsubseteq^D$, where $\sqsubseteq^D$ is given by

$$(e, e') \sqsubseteq^D (f, f') :\Leftrightarrow$$
$$e = f \text{ and } e' \leq_{ref(l(e))} f'$$
$$\text{or } e < f \text{ and } l_{ref(l(e))}(e') \, D \, l_{ref(l(f))}(f'),$$

- $l^{ref}(e, e') \triangleq l_{ref(l(e))}(e')$.

An event $(e,e') \in E[ref]$ is called *i-complete* if $e' \in \mathrm{I}_{ref(l(e))}(\surd_i)$, i.e. e' is a final event of the refinement of e.

If *ref* contains choices $\mathcal{E}[ref]$ will not be a *SynS* because $\downarrow e \cap E_i^{ref}$ may not be totally ordered. Therefore we build *pre-configurations* from which we get a different copy for each causal successor of a refinement containing choices:
A *proving sequence* $(e_1,e'_1),\ldots,(e_n,e'_n)$ is a sequence of distinct events $(e_1,e'_1),\ldots,(e_n,e'_n) \in E^{ref}$ such that for all $1 \le k,j \le n$ and all $(e,e') \in E^{ref}$:

- $k \neq j \Longrightarrow \neg(e_k,e'_k) \,\#^{ref}\, (e_j,e'_j)$, (conflict-freeness)
- $(e,e') <^{ref} (e_k,e'_k) \Longrightarrow$
  $\exists j < k \,.\, (e_j,e'_j) <^{ref} (e_k,e'_k) \wedge ((e,e') = (e_j,e'_j) \vee (e,e') \,\#^{ref}\, (e_j,e'_j))$,
  (left-closed up to conflicts)
- $(e_j,e'_j) <_i^{ref} (e_k,e'_k) \wedge e_j \neq e_k \Longrightarrow$
  $\exists l, j \le l < k \,.\, (e_j,e'_j) \le_i^{ref} (e_l,e'_l) <_i^{ref} (e_k,e'_k) \wedge (e_l,e'_l)$ is *i*-complete.
  (continuation after successful termination of a refinement)

By the last condition an *i*-deadlock in a refinement has no causal successors. For a proving sequence $(e_1,e'_1),\ldots,(e_n,e'_n)$ the set $x = \{(e_1,e'_1),\ldots,(e_n,e'_n)\}$ is called a *pre-configuration* of $\mathcal{E}[ref]$. A pre-configuration x is *complete prime* if x contains a unique maximal element w.r.t. $\le^{ref}|_x$.

Definition 3 (semantic refinement). The *refinement of* $\mathcal{E}$, denoted by $Ref(\mathcal{E}_\mathrm{I})$, due to the refinement function *ref*, is the *SynS* $\mathcal{F} = \langle F, \le_\mathcal{F}, l_\mathcal{F}\rangle$ where

$$F = \{x \mid x \text{ is a complete prime pre-configuration of } \mathcal{E}[ref]\},$$
$$\le_\mathcal{F} = \subseteq,$$
$$l_\mathcal{F}(x) = l^{ref}(e) \text{ where } e \text{ is the maximal element of } x.$$

Finally, the *refinement of the interpretation* I is given by $Ref(\mathrm{I}) : \{\surd_i \mid i \in Loc\} \to \mathbf{2}^{E_{Ref(\mathcal{E})}}$ where $x \in Ref(\mathrm{I})(\surd_i)$ iff $e \in \mathrm{I}_\mathcal{E}(\surd_i)$ and $e' \in \mathrm{I}_{ref(l(e))}(\surd_i)$ for the maximal event (e,e') in x.

Example 2. Let $\Sigma_1 = \{a,b,a_1,a_2,b_2\}$, $\Sigma_2 = \{a,b,a_2,b_1,b_2\}$, and $\mathcal{F}_\mathrm{I} = \langle\{e,f\},\varnothing,\{(e,a),(f,b)\}\rangle$. We assume that both locations are terminated at the final configurations. $e \,\#\, f$ because a and b are joint actions. We refine a by $\boxed{a_1 \to a_2}\ {}^{\surd_1}_{\surd_2}$ and b by $\boxed{b_1 \to b_2}\ {}^{\surd_1}_{\surd_2}$. Then the refined *SynS* is shown in example 1. The abstract conflict leads to a deadlock on the refined level because now both agents may start independently.

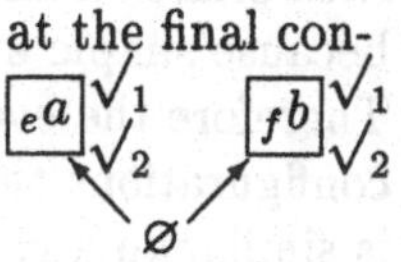

Proposition 4. *Let $\mathcal{E}_\mathrm{I}$ be a SynS and ref a refinement function. Then $Ref(\mathcal{E}_\mathrm{I}) = \langle F, \le_\mathcal{F}, l_\mathcal{F}\rangle$ is a SynS.*

Thus also on the refined level all conflicts originate in local conflicts. Standard action refinement can be retrieved as a special case by choosing $loc(a') = loc(a)$ for all actions a' in $ref(a)$. As shown in example 2 in general

$$Runs(Ref(\mathcal{E}_\mathrm{I})) \neq \bigcup_{\rho \in Runs(\mathcal{E}_\mathrm{I})} Ref(\mathcal{E}_\mathrm{I}|_\rho)$$

because $Con(Ref(\mathcal{E}_I))$ is I-diamond-closed whereas $\bigcup_{\rho \in Runs(\mathcal{E}_I)} Con(Ref(\mathcal{E}_I|\rho))$ may be not.
A refinement function is *deadlock-free* if for all $a \in \Sigma$ and $i \in loc(a)$ every i-maximal e in $ref(a)$ is i-terminated, i.e. $e \in \mathrm{I}_{ref(a)}(\surd_i)$. But even if a deadlock-free system is refined by a deadlock-free refinement the resulting system may contain deadlocks. The refinements of different actions that are in conflict on the abstract level may interfere, as shown in example 2.

Proposition 5. *Let $\mathcal{E}_I$ be a deadlock-free SynS and ref a deadlock-free refinement function. If $Ref(\mathcal{E}_I)$ is the refinement of $\mathcal{E}_I$ due to ref, then $Ref(\mathcal{E}_I)$ is deadlock-free iff for all configurations c, $c \xrightarrow{a} d, c \xrightarrow{b} d'$ in $Con(\mathcal{E}_I)$ and $a\, D\, b$ implies $l(e_1)\, D\, l(f_1)$ for all minimal events e_1 of $ref(a)$ and f_1 of $ref(b)$.*

Thus the interference of refinements of conflicting events is prevented if on the refined level we still find at least one agent to whom the choice between the refinements is local. We say *ref does not introduce interference deadlocks* on $\mathcal{E}_I$ if *ref* satisfies the preliminaries of prop. 5. Then we get:

Theorem 6. *Let $\mathcal{E}_I$ a SynS and ref a refinement function that does not introduce interference deadlocks on $\mathcal{E}_I$. Then*

$$Runs(Ref(\mathcal{E}_I)) = \bigcup_{\rho \in Runs(\mathcal{E}_I)} Ref(\mathcal{E}_I|\rho).$$

3 The Logic νTrPTL

In this section we introduce syntax and semantics of a linear time logic for location based systems. In system specifications temporal logics are used to express temporal requirements on the system behaviour. We use νTrPTL which is based on modalities and will take local views into account. Sequences of νTrPTL-modalities describe causal chains which makes this logic well-suited for action refinement as defined in section 2.1. νTrPTL was examined in [Nie95] and is an extension of TrPTL (see [Thi94]) by fixpoints. It allows a uniform refinement translation of formulae. Linear time operators like "U_i" (*local Until*), "F_i" (*local eventually*) and "G_i" (*local always*) can be defined as derived operators similar to ([Lar88]) e.g. a local Until can be expressed by $\phi\, U_i\, \psi \equiv \mu X.(\psi)_i \vee ((\phi)_i \wedge \bigvee_{a \in \Sigma_i} \langle a \rangle_i X)$ meaning that in the i-view there is a finite sequence of Σ_i-actions leading to a state where ψ holds and on the way always ϕ is satisfied.

Definition 7 (syntax of νTrPTL). Let $\tilde{\Sigma}$ be a distributed alphabet, and $\mathbf{V}$ a set of propositional variables. Then

- $\surd_i, \neg\surd_i \in \nu\mathrm{TrPTL}$ and $\mathbf{V} \subseteq \nu\mathrm{TrPTL}$,
- for all $\phi, \psi \in \nu\mathrm{TrPTL} \Rightarrow \phi \vee \psi, \phi \wedge \psi \in \nu\mathrm{TrPTL}$,
- for all $\phi \in \nu\mathrm{TrPTL}$, $a \in \Sigma_i$, $X \in \mathbf{V} \Rightarrow (\phi)_i, \langle a \rangle_i \phi, [a]_i \phi, \mu X.\phi, \nu X.\phi \in \nu\mathrm{TrPTL}$.

The notion of *free* and *bound* variables is defined w.r.t. the binding operators μ and ν. $\phi[X/\psi]$ denotes the formula where all free occurrences of X in ϕ are substituted by ψ. A formula is *closed* if all variables are bound. Negation is restricted to atomic propositions, hence the least and greatest fixpoint of the function associated with a formula always exist (Tarski's fixpoint theorem). However, the logic is closed under negation, because for every operator we find a *dual* one in νTrPTL. $not(\phi)$ denotes the negation of ϕ. σ will range over $\{\mu, \nu\}$. The basic propositions T (true) and F (false) abbreviate $\nu X.X$ and $\mu X.X$.
Informally, the operator $(.)_i$ gives the local view of agent i on the system. $\langle a\rangle_i\phi$ means: *Next a in the local view of agent i.* Therefore i must be able to perform an a-action next, but its partners are still allowed to execute some preparatory actions independently from i before synchronising in a. $\langle . \rangle_i$ is the localised version of the $\langle . \rangle$-operator in the propositional μ-calculus [Sti92]: A formula $[a]_i\phi$ means that after all possibilities to execute a in the local view of i ϕ holds. In particular, $[a]_i\phi$ is satisfied in configurations without a-successor.
The *valuation function* $v : \mathbf{V} \to \mathbf{2}^{Con(\mathcal{E}_\mathrm{I})}$ assigns sets of configurations to variables and is used in the evaluation of formulae containing free variables.

Definition 8 (semantics of νTrPTL). The *semantics of a formula* ϕ w.r.t. an interpretation I, a valuation v, and a given run ρ is the set of configurations $c \in \rho$ that satisfies ϕ, denoted by $[\![\phi]\!]_v^{(\rho,\mathrm{I})}$:

- $[\![\surd_i]\!]_v^{(\rho,\mathrm{I})} = \mathrm{I}(\surd_i)\big|_\rho$, $\qquad [\![\neg\surd_i]\!]_v^{(\rho,\mathrm{I})} = \rho - [\![\surd_i]\!]_v^{(\rho,\mathrm{I})}$,
- $[\![\phi \wedge \psi]\!]_v^{(\rho,\mathrm{I})} = [\![\phi]\!]_v^{(\rho,\mathrm{I})} \cap [\![\psi]\!]_v^{(\rho,\mathrm{I})}$, $\qquad [\![\phi \vee \psi]\!]_v^{(\rho,\mathrm{I})} = [\![\phi]\!]_v^{(\rho,\mathrm{I})} \cup [\![\psi]\!]_v^{(\rho,\mathrm{I})}$,
- $[\![X]\!]_v^{(\rho,\mathrm{I})} = v(X)\big|_\rho$ for $X \in \mathbf{V}$,
- $[\![(\phi)_i]\!]_v^{(\rho,\mathrm{I})} = \{c \mid \downarrow^i c \in [\![\phi]\!]_v^{(\rho,\mathrm{I})}\}$,
- $[\![\mu X.\phi]\!]_v^{(\rho,\mathrm{I})} = \bigcap\{A \mid [\![\phi]\!]_{v[X/A]}^{(\rho,\mathrm{I})} \subseteq A\}$
  where $v[X/A](Y) \triangleq v(Y)$ for all $Y \neq X$ and $v[X/A](X) \triangleq A$,
- $[\![\nu X.\phi]\!]_v^{(\rho,\mathrm{I})} = \bigcup\{A \mid A \subseteq [\![\phi]\!]_{v[X/A]}^{(\rho,\mathrm{I})}\}$,
- $[\![\langle a\rangle_i\phi]\!]_v^{(\rho,\mathrm{I})} = \{c \in \rho \mid \exists d \in \rho \,.\, c \xrightarrow{a}_i d \text{ and } \downarrow^{loc(a)} d \in [\![\phi]\!]_v^{(\rho,\mathrm{I})}\}$,
- $[\![[a]_i\phi]\!]_v^{(\rho,\mathrm{I})} = \{c \in \rho \mid \forall d \in \rho \,.\, c \xrightarrow{a}_i d \Rightarrow \downarrow^{loc(a)} d \in [\![\phi]\!]_v^{(\rho,\mathrm{I})}\}$.

I and v are omitted if clear from the context. Alternatively we use the *satisfaction relation* $\rho, c \models_\mathrm{I} \phi$ to denote $c \in [\![\phi]\!]_v^{(\rho,\mathrm{I})}$. The semantics of closed formulae do not depend on v.[2] An interpreted *SynS* $\mathcal{E}_\mathrm{I}$ satisfies a formula ϕ, denoted by $\mathcal{E}_\mathrm{I} \models \phi$, if $\rho, c_\varnothing \models \phi$ for all runs ρ of $\mathcal{E}_\mathrm{I}$. A νTrPTL-formula is *guarded* iff every free occurrence of a fixpoint variable in the body of the fixpoint lies within the range of a modality. We note that every formula can be transformed into an equivalent guarded formula.

Example 3. The formula $\phi = [a_1]_1[a_2]_1\surd_2$ is satisfied in the system $\mathcal{E}_\mathrm{I}$ shown in example 1. But also the formula $\psi = [a_1]_1(\langle b_1\rangle_2\mathrm{T} \vee \langle a_2\rangle_2\mathrm{T})$ holds for $\mathcal{E}_\mathrm{I}$ because the configuration c containing the 1-local action a_1 is 1-equivalent to $c_\varnothing$.

[2] As usual, statements on νTrPTL-formulae refer to the subset of closed formulae.

Definition 9. The *type* of a formula gives the set of locations the formula *directly* refers to. The *type* $A \subseteq Loc$ of a formula $\phi \in \nu\text{TrPTL}$ is given by:

- $\phi \in \mathbf{V}$ implies $\text{type}(\phi) = \emptyset$,
- $\text{type}(\surd_i) = \text{type}(\neg\surd_i) = \text{type}((\psi)_i) = \text{type}(\langle a\rangle_i\psi) = \text{type}([a]_i\psi) = \{i\}$,
- $\text{type}(\phi \vee \psi) = \text{type}(\phi) \cup \text{type}(\psi)$, $\text{type}(\phi \wedge \psi) = \text{type}(\phi) \cup \text{type}(\psi)$,
- $\text{type}(\sigma X.\psi) = \text{type}(\psi[X/\sigma X.\psi])$.

Now we define a proper subset of νTrPTL for which a sequence of modalities will keep along a causal chain, i.e. the evaluation of a modality brings us "a step forward" on some causal chain and a change of the local view will not lead to a jump "back into the past". Thus formulae like ψ from example 3 are excluded:

Definition 10. A formula ϕ is *[strongly] connected*, $\phi \in \nu\text{TrPTL}^{con}$, iff

- $\phi \in \{\surd_i, \neg\surd_i \mid i \in Loc\} \cup \mathbf{V}$,
- $\phi = (\psi)_i$ and ψ is [strongly] connected and $\text{type}(\psi) \subseteq \{i\}$,
- $\phi = \langle a\rangle_i\psi$ or $\phi = [a]_i\psi$, ψ is [strongly] connected and $\text{type}(\psi) \subseteq loc(a)$ [and $\text{type}(\psi) \subseteq \{k\}$ with $k \in loc(a)$],
- $\phi = \psi \wedge \psi'$ or $\phi = \psi \vee \psi'$, and ψ, ψ' are [strongly] connected.
- $\phi = \sigma X.\psi$ and ψ is [strongly] connected and $\psi[X/\surd_k]$ is [strongly] connected for all $k \in \text{type}(\psi)$.

If $\langle a\rangle_i\phi$ is connected then type $\phi \subseteq loc(a)$. For a strongly connected formula the type of each subformula is at most a singleton $k \in loc(a)$. Note that for νTrPTL^{con} the localisation $(.)_i$ becomes obsolete: all localisation operators can be eliminated from connected formulae without changing the semantics.
We are able to characterise configurations by strongly connected formulae: $c \in \rho$ iff $\rho, c_\emptyset \models \bigwedge_{i \in loc(c)} \langle a_1 \ldots a_{n_i}\rangle_i \mathrm{T}$ where $a_1, \ldots, a_{n_i}$ are the labels of the events $e_1 \lessdot_i \ldots \lessdot_i e_{n_i}$ from $E_i \cap c$.
If ϕ is connected and subformulae $\psi = \sigma X.\psi'$ of ϕ have a singleton type then ϕ can be transformed into an equivalent strongly connected formula.

4 Action Refinement and νTrPTL

Action refinement as introduced in section 2.1 substitutes high level actions by low level processes. Now we are interested in the inheritance of temporal properties. In νTrPTL, actions are addressed in modalities. Temporal formulae satisfied by the abstract system will not be satisfied in the refined system in general, simply because the system's alphabet is changed by action refinement. However, in the context of a top-down design methodology it is reasonable to ask which temporal properties of the refined system are already determined by the abstract system. We consider refinement transformations on strongly connected νTrPTL- formulae for which the following correspondence holds:

$$\begin{array}{ccc} \mathcal{H} & \models & \varphi \\ \downarrow & \Updownarrow & \downarrow \\ Ref(\mathcal{H}) & \models & \mathcal{R}ef_A(\varphi) \end{array}$$

If an abstract model $\mathcal{H}$ satisfies a temporal property ϕ, the "refined" formula $\mathcal{R}ef_{\mathcal{A}}(\phi)$ will hold on the refined model $Ref(\mathcal{H})$ (inheritance from the abstract to the concrete level). As the trivial refinement transformation that maps all abstract formulae on T (*true*) enjoys these inheritance property we require also a correspondence in the other direction. We concentrate on refinement transformations for νTrPTL^{con} where a modality $\langle a \rangle_i$ is transformed into a bunch of modalities corresponding to *causal chains* through the refinement of a.

The informal meaning of a formula like $\langle a \rangle_i \phi$ is: "in the i-view a is possible next and afterwards ϕ holds". When going to the concrete level an abstract action a is substituted by its refinement and the corresponding informal translation of the formula is "in the i-view a causal chain representing an execution of $ref(a)$ is possible and afterwards the refinement of ϕ holds." This translation still allows several transformations of a modality into bunches of modalities on the concrete level because even in a finite conflict free refinement there may be several causal chains from the i-minimal to a j-terminated event. We will use regular expressions to describe causal chains through the different runs of $ref(a)$.

The set of *regular expressions* over an alphabet Γ, denoted by $Reg(\Gamma)$, is given by: $\varnothing, \hat{a} \in Reg(\Gamma)$ for $\hat{a} \in \Gamma$, and if $\alpha, \beta \in Reg(\Gamma)$, then $\alpha + \beta, \alpha\beta, \alpha^* \in Reg(\Gamma)$. The language associated with α is denoted by $L(\alpha)$ and defined as usual

$$L(\varnothing) = \varnothing, \qquad L(\alpha + \beta) = L(\alpha) \cup L(\beta), \qquad L(\alpha^*) = L(\alpha)^*,$$
$$L(\hat{a}) = \{\hat{a}\}, \qquad L(\alpha\beta) = L(\alpha) \cdot L(\beta),$$

where $L_1 \cdot L_2$ denotes language concatenation, $L^* = \bigcup_{n \in \mathbb{N}} L^n$ denotes iteration (Kleene's star), and ε is the empty word.

Definition 11 ((i→j)-skeleton). Let α be a regular expression over $\{(i,a) \mid a \in \Sigma, i \in loc(a)\}$. Then α is called a *$(i \to j)$-skeleton* of $\mathcal{E} = \langle E, \leq, l \rangle$ iff

- If $w \in L(\alpha)$ then there exists a causal chain $s \in ch(\mathcal{E})_{i \to j}$ and $l(s) = w$.
- If f is j-terminated in $\mathcal{E}$ and $\downarrow f \cap E_i \neq \varnothing$ then there exists a causal chain $s(i_n, f) \in ch(\mathcal{E})_{i \to j}$ such that $l(s(i_n, f)) \in L(\alpha)$.

ref is called *regularly decomposable* iff for each a and $i, j \in loc(a)$ there is a regular expression α that is a $(i \to j)$-skeleton for $ref(a)$.

The alphabet of skeletons consists of pairs (i, a). The first component $i \in Loc$ determines the agent for whom a shall be a local successor. For each j-terminated configuration c of $\mathcal{E}$ containing an $(i \to j)$-causal chain, an $(i \to j)$-skeleton contains a word that corresponds to the labelling of an $(i \to j)$-causal chain in c. Skeletons do not represent local deadlocks or non-terminating runs in $\mathcal{E}$.For finite refinement functions all skeletons can be chosen starfree.

We call a collection $\mathcal{A}$ of skeletons *a family of skeletons due to ref* if $\mathcal{A}$ contains an $(i \to j)$-skeleton α of $ref(a)$ for each $a \in \Sigma$ and $i, j \in loc(a)$. For a family of skeletons we define $\mathcal{A}(ref(a)_{i \to j}) \triangleq \{\alpha \in \mathcal{A} \mid \alpha \text{ is a } (i \to j)\text{-skeleton of } ref(a)\}$.

Definition 12 (refinement transformation on formulae). Let *ref* be a refinement function and $\mathcal{A}$ a family of skeletons due to *ref*. Then a transformation

$\mathit{ref}_{\mathcal{A}}$ on strongly connected formulae is defined as follows:

$$\begin{aligned} (\neg)\surd_i[\mathit{ref}_{\mathcal{A}}] &= (\neg)\surd_i, & X[\mathit{ref}_{\mathcal{A}}] &= X \text{ for } X \in \mathbf{V}, \\ (\phi \wedge \psi)[\mathit{ref}_{\mathcal{A}}] &= \phi[\mathit{ref}_{\mathcal{A}}] \wedge \psi[\mathit{ref}_{\mathcal{A}}], & (\phi \vee \psi)[\mathit{ref}_{\mathcal{A}}] &= \phi[\mathit{ref}_{\mathcal{A}}] \vee \psi[\mathit{ref}_{\mathcal{A}}], \\ (\phi)_i[\mathit{ref}_{\mathcal{A}}] &= (\phi[\mathit{ref}_{\mathcal{A}}])_i, & \sigma X.\phi[\mathit{ref}_{\mathcal{A}}] &= \sigma X.(\phi[\mathit{ref}_{\mathcal{A}}]), \end{aligned}$$

$$(\langle a\rangle_i\phi)[\mathit{ref}_{\mathcal{A}}] = \bigvee_{\alpha\in\mathcal{A}(\mathit{ref}(a)_{i\to j})} \langle\alpha\rangle(\phi[\mathit{ref}_{\mathcal{A}}]) \quad \text{if type}(\phi) \subseteq \{j\},$$

$$([a]_i\phi)[\mathit{ref}_{\mathcal{A}}] = \bigwedge_{\alpha\in\mathcal{A}(\mathit{ref}(a)_{i\to j})} [\alpha](\phi[\mathit{ref}_{\mathcal{A}}]) \quad \text{if type}(\phi) \subseteq \{j\}.$$

In a second step the extended modalities are substituted by local modalities:

$$\begin{aligned} &\mathcal{T}((\neg)\surd_i) = (\neg)\surd_i, & &\mathcal{T}(\phi \vee \psi) = \mathcal{T}(\phi) \vee \mathcal{T}(\psi), \\ &\mathcal{T}(X) = X, & &\mathcal{T}(\phi \wedge \psi) = \mathcal{T}(\phi) \wedge \mathcal{T}(\psi), \\ &\mathcal{T}((\phi)_i) = (\mathcal{T}(\phi))_i, & &\mathcal{T}(\sigma X.\phi) = \sigma X.\mathcal{T}(\phi), \\ &\mathcal{T}(\langle\varepsilon\rangle\phi) = \mathcal{T}(\phi), & &\mathcal{T}([\varepsilon]\phi) = \mathcal{T}(\phi), \\ &\mathcal{T}(\langle(i,a)\rangle\phi) = \langle a\rangle_i\mathcal{T}(\phi), & &\mathcal{T}([(i,a)]\phi) = [a]_i\mathcal{T}(\phi), \\ &\mathcal{T}(\langle\alpha\cdot\beta\rangle\phi) = \mathcal{T}(\langle\alpha\rangle\langle\beta\rangle\phi), & &\mathcal{T}([\alpha\cdot\beta]\phi) = \mathcal{T}([\alpha][\beta]\phi), \\ &\mathcal{T}(\langle\alpha+\beta\rangle\phi) = \mathcal{T}(\langle\alpha\rangle\phi \vee \langle\beta\rangle\phi), & &\mathcal{T}([\alpha+\beta]\phi) = \mathcal{T}([\alpha]\phi \wedge [\beta]\phi), \end{aligned}$$

$$\left.\begin{aligned} \mathcal{T}(\langle\alpha^*\rangle\phi) &= \mathcal{T}(\mu X.\phi \vee \langle\alpha\rangle X) \\ \mathcal{T}([\alpha^*]\phi) &= \mathcal{T}(\nu X.\phi \wedge [\alpha]X) \end{aligned}\right\} \text{ where } X \text{ is a fresh variable not occurring in } \phi.$$

The ***logical refinement transformation*** $\mathcal{R}\mathit{ef}_{\mathcal{A}}$ of a formula ϕ derived from a family of skeletons $\mathcal{A}$ due to a refinement function *ref* is given by:

$$\mathcal{R}\mathit{ef}_{\mathcal{A}}(\phi) = \mathcal{T}(\phi[\mathit{ref}_{\mathcal{A}}]).$$

By $\mathit{ref}_{\mathcal{A}}$ a modality is substituted by skeletons α representing causal chains in $\mathit{ref}(a)$. As the agent for whom the local view shall be taken is encoded in the skeleton we omit the index of the modalities. Next the extended modalities containing regular expressions are translated into νTrPTL-modalities.
In case of infinite refinements where the skeletons contain the Kleene's star operator a fixpoint formula is introduced. $\langle\alpha^*\rangle\phi$ is transformed into "after a finite number of executions of α ϕ holds" whereas $[\alpha]\phi$ is transformed "after each number of executions of α ϕ holds".
We note that $\mathcal{R}\mathit{ef}_{\mathcal{A}}(\phi)$ is connected of type j if ϕ is a strongly connected formula of type j. In case of $\mathit{ref} = \mathit{id}_{\Sigma}$, $\mathcal{R}\mathit{ef}_{\mathcal{A}}$ is the identity on νTrPTL, too.

Correspondence Results

Not every refinement transformation as defined above is appropriate to establish the desired correspondence $\mathcal{H} \models \phi$ iff $\mathit{Ref}(\mathcal{H}) \models \mathcal{R}\mathit{ef}_{\mathcal{A}}(\phi)$. In particular, we get two obvious restrictions on *ref* and the selection of a suitable family of skeletons due to *ref*, respectively. Firstly, a sequence of concrete modalities may allow at most one decomposition into refinement sequences. Secondly, all runs of $\mathit{ref}(a)$ must be represented in the skeletons for $\mathit{ref}(a)$.

Example 4. Consider a system $\mathcal{E}$ over $\Sigma_1 = \{a, b\}$ with a single a-labelled event. Obviously $\mathcal{E} \not\models \langle b \rangle_1 \mathrm{T}$. We refine a by a and b by a then $\mathit{Ref}(\mathcal{E}) \cong \mathcal{E}$, but $\mathcal{E} \models \langle a \rangle_1 \mathrm{T}$ which is the refinement of $\langle b \rangle_1 \mathrm{T}$.

Definition 13 (distinctness). Let *ref* be a refinement function and $\mathcal{A}$ a family of skeletons due to *ref*. Then $\mathcal{A}$ is called *distinct* w.r.t. *ref* iff the following holds:

- If $\alpha \in \mathcal{A}(\mathit{ref}(a)_{i \to j})$ then $\alpha \neq \varnothing$ for all $a \in \Sigma$ and $i, j \in \mathit{loc}(a)$.
- Let $w \in L(\alpha)$, $\alpha \in \mathcal{A}(\mathit{ref}(a)_{i \to j})$, and $\mathit{Ref}(\mathcal{E})$ be a refinement due to *ref*. Let $\mathit{Init}(\mathcal{E})$ denote the minimal events of $\mathcal{E}$. If in $\mathit{Ref}(\mathcal{E})$ there is a causal chain s from $c_\varnothing$ to d with $l(s) = w$ then $d \in \mathit{Con}(\mathit{Ref}(\mathit{Init}(\mathcal{E}))$ and moreover, $d \cong d'$ for some $d' \in \mathit{Con}(\mathit{ref}(b))$ and some $b \in \Sigma$ implies $a = b$ and d' is a j-terminated configuration of $\mathit{Con}(\mathit{ref}(a))$.

The problem with example 4 is avoided if a set of *distinct* skeletons is selected: By the first condition each agent participating in a terminates at least once in $\mathit{ref}(a)$. The second condition ensures that a causal chain labelled by a word from a skeleton describes exactly a complete sequential path through the refinement of a uniquely determined action. In particular cases are excluded where a causal chain labelled by a word from the skeleton of $\mathit{ref}(a)$ builds a part of a causal chain leading through the refinement of b. Not every refinement function may allow to select a distinct family of skeletons (see example 4). A restriction similar to distinctness can be found in [GGR94] to achieve the coincidence of semantic and syntactic (the substitution of actions by terms) action refinement for a TCSP-like process algebra.

As a skeleton for $\mathit{ref}(a)$ leads from initial to terminated events in $\mathit{ref}(a)$ two kinds of runs are ignored: In a distinct family of skeletons we do not find a representative for either a deadlocking or an infinite branch in the refinement. Thus, in general the refined formulae will not hold on a refined run containing a deadlock introduced by *ref* or an non-terminating (infinite) refinement. Thus for the moment we only consider deadlock-free, run finite refinement functions to obtain the desired result.

Theorem 14. *Let $\mathcal{E}_\mathrm{I}$ be a SynS, ref a deadlock-free, run finite refinement function that does not introduce interference deadlocks, and $\mathcal{A}$ a distinct family of skeletons due to ref. If ϕ is strongly connected then*

$$\mathcal{E}_\mathrm{I} \models \phi \qquad \textit{iff} \qquad \mathit{Ref}(\mathcal{E}_\mathrm{I}) \models \mathcal{R}\mathit{ef}_{\mathcal{A}}(\phi).$$

The theorem is proven by an adoption of the proof of the correspondence between bisimulation and Hennessy-Milner-logic as given in [Mil89] chap. 10. The proof is based on a behavioural equivalence between systems w.r.t. a refinement function:

Definition 15 (refinement run equivalence). $\mathcal{E}_\mathrm{I}$ and $\mathcal{F}_\mathrm{J}$ are *refinement run equivalent* w.r.t. a deadlock-free, run finite refinement function *ref*, denoted $\mathcal{E}_\mathrm{I} \sim_{\mathit{ref\ run}} \mathcal{F}_\mathrm{J}$, iff

- For each run $\rho \in Runs(\mathcal{E}_I)$ there is a run $\varrho \in Runs(\mathcal{F}_J)$ such that $\varrho \cong \rho'$ for some $\rho' \in Runs(Ref(\mathcal{E}_I|_\rho))$.
- For each run $\varrho \in Runs(\mathcal{F}_J)$ there is a run $\rho \in Runs(\mathcal{E}_I)$ such that $\varrho \cong \rho'$ for some $\rho' \in Runs(Ref(\mathcal{E}_I|_\rho))$.

Refinement run equivalence guarantees for all runs in the abstract system a counterpart in the low level system and vice versa. For identity refinement $\sim_{ref\ run}$ coincides with run trace equivalence as defined in [GKP92]. Theorem 14 is a corollary of the slightly more general theorem:

Theorem 16. *Let $\mathcal{E}_I$ and $\mathcal{F}_J$ be two systems that are refinement run equivalent w.r.t. a deadlock-free, run finite refinement function ref, and $\mathcal{A}$ a distinct family of skeletons due to ref. If ϕ is strongly connected then*

$$\mathcal{E}_I \models \phi \qquad \textit{iff} \qquad \mathcal{F}_J \models \mathcal{R}ef_{\mathcal{A}}(\phi).$$

Now let us reconsider refinements introducing deadlocks or infinite runs:
Let *ref* be a refinement function and $\mathcal{E}_I$ a *SynS*. A run $\varrho \in Runs(Ref(\mathcal{E}_I))$ is called *faithful* if there is a run $\rho \in Runs(\mathcal{E}_I)$ such that $\varrho \in Runs(Ref(\mathcal{E}_I|_\rho))$ and for all $e \in \rho$ there is a $x \in \varrho$ such that $x = \downarrow(e, e')$ where $(e, e') \in \mathcal{E}_I[ref]$.
Thus in a faithful run ϱ all abstract events e from an abstract run ρ are represented by refinements. The subset of faithfully refined runs of $Ref(\mathcal{E}_I)$ is denoted $Runs_{faithful}(Ref(\mathcal{E}_I))$. We use $Ref(\mathcal{E}_I)_{faithful} \models \phi$ if $\varrho, c_\varnothing \models \phi$ for all $\varrho \in Runs_{faithful}(Ref(\mathcal{E}_I))$. Thus we get the following corollary of theorem 14:

Corollary 17. *Let $\mathcal{E}_I$ be a SynS, ref a refinement function, and $\mathcal{A}$ a distinct family of skeletons due to ref. If ϕ is strongly connected then*

$$\mathcal{E}_I \models \phi \qquad \textit{iff} \qquad Ref(\mathcal{E}_I)_{faithful} \models \mathcal{R}ef_{\mathcal{A}}(\phi).$$

Corollary 17 states that properties from νTrPTL^{con} are inherited on the faithful runs of $Ref(\mathcal{E}_I)$ for any refinement function.

Equivalence induced by refinement transformations on νTrPTL

νTrPTL and a refinement transformation induces an equivalence on synchronisation structures. For a given refinement function *ref* and a family of skeletons we call two *SynS*s $\mathcal{E}_I$ and $\mathcal{F}_J$ are called $\mathcal{R}ef_{\mathcal{A}}$*-equivalent*, denoted $\mathcal{E}_I \sim^{\mathcal{R}ef_{\mathcal{A}}} \mathcal{F}_J$, iff $\mathcal{E}_I \models \phi \iff \mathcal{F}_J \models \mathcal{R}ef_{\mathcal{A}}(\phi)$ for all strongly connected formulae $\phi \in \nu$TrPTL^{con}. From theorem 16 we know that $\sim_{ref\ run} \subseteq \sim^{\mathcal{R}ef_{\mathcal{A}}}$ for distinct families of skeletons $\mathcal{A}$.
The equivalence depends on the selected family of skeletons (see [Huh96] for an example). The reason for this lies in definition 13 where the unique decomposition by skeletons is only required for *SynS*s that are refinements due to *ref*. Thus we have to extend this requirement to arbitrary *SynS*s over the refined alphabet:

Definition 18. A distinct family $\mathcal{A}$ of skeletons due to a refinement function *ref* is called *sufficiently complete* if for each $a \in \Sigma$ and all conflict-free *SynS* $\mathcal{E}_I$ with $loc(\mathcal{E}) = loc(a)$

$$\mathcal{E}_I \models \mathcal{R}ef_{\mathcal{A}}\langle a\rangle_i(\surd_j \wedge \bigwedge_{b\in\Sigma_j}[b]_j\mathrm{F}) \text{ for all } i,j \in loc(a) \text{ iff}$$

$$\mathcal{E}_I \cong d \text{ for some terminated configuration } d \in Con(ref(a)).$$

A sufficiently complete family of skeletons ensures that not only some sequential paths through $ref(a)$ are executed but the complete *distributed* refinement of a is executed when $\mathcal{R}ef_{\mathcal{A}}(\bigwedge_{j\in loc(a)}\langle a\rangle_j\mathrm{T})$ is satisfied.
For sufficiently complete, distinct families of skeletons we get a result analogous to theorem 5.1 in [GKP92]. The restriction to systems with a finite number of runs is necessary even in case of identity refinement and one agent systems.

Theorem 19. *Let* $\mathcal{E}_I, \mathcal{F}_J \in ES_{syn,I}$, *Runs*$(\mathcal{F}_J)$ *be finite, and* $\mathcal{A}$ *be a sufficiently complete, distinct family of skeletons due to ref. If* $\mathcal{E}_I \models \phi \iff \mathcal{F}_J \models \mathcal{R}ef_{\mathcal{A}}(\phi)$ *for all strongly connected* $\phi \in \nu$TrPTL *then* $\mathcal{E}_I \sim_{ref\ run} \mathcal{F}_J$.

5 Conclusions

We have shown that for the specific framework of systems of sequential agents two antagonist issues in formal specification can be brought together: Action refinement as a hierarchical design methodology that changes the observable behaviour of the system and 'a priori' verification by using temporal logic formulae. Using the dependency information from the distributed alphabet it is possible to find refinement transformations on formulae that mimic the action refinement on the models by substituting a modality $\langle a\rangle_i$ by sequences of modalities that describe causal chains through the refinement of a.
We mention two other approaches to the preservation of temporal properties known from the literature, namely [CGL92] and [BBLS92]. Both approaches consider branching time logics on interleaving semantics. A main focus in [BBLS92] and [CGL92] is the relation between *structural correspondences* of the transition graphs - given by some kind of homomorphism relating the two *state* spaces - and the preservation of properties. In that, these approaches are more general then our approach because the structural correspondence which is preliminary for theorem 16 is rather specific to our setting. On the other hand we aimed to link the inheritance of properties to action refinement. Thus in our setting the structural correspondence between two systems is established by the refinement function and therefore it is a spin off of the top-down design approach.

Acknowledgement: I am grateful to P. Niebert, H. Wehrheim, U. Goltz, H.-D. Ehrich, P.S. Thiagarajan, and G. Denker for many fruitful discussions and encouragement. I thank the referees for their valuable suggestions.

References

[AH94] Luca Aceto and Matthew Hennessy. Adding action refinement to a finite process algebra. *Information and Computation*, 115:179–247, 1994.

[BBLS92] S. Bensalem, A. Bouajjani, C. Loiseaux, and J. Sifakis. Property preserving simulations. In *Computer Aided Verification*, *LNCS* 663, pages 260–273, 1992.

[CGL92] Edmund M. Clarke, Orna Grumberg, and David E. Long. Model checking and abstraction. In *Proceedings of the 19th Annual ACM Symposium on Principles of Programming Languages (POPL 92)*, 1992.

[DD93] Philippe Darondeau and Pierpaolo Degano. Refinement of actions in event structures and causal trees. *Theoretical Computer Science*, 118:21–48, 1993.

[GG89] R. v. Glabbeek and U. Goltz. Refinement of actions in causality based models. In *Stepwise Refinement of Distributed Systems*, *LNCS* 430, p. 267–300, 1989.

[GG91] Ursula Goltz and Norbert Götz. Modelling a simple communication protocol in a language with action refinement, 1991.

[GGR94] U. Goltz, R. Gorrieri, and A. Rensink. On syntactic and semantic action refinement. In *Theoretical Aspects of Computer Software*, *LNCS* 789, 1994.

[GKP92] Ursula Goltz, Ruurd Kuiper, and Wojciech Penczek. Propositional temporal logics and equivalences. In *CONCUR'92*, *LNCS* 630, pages 222– 236, 1992.

[GMM90] Roberto Gorrieri, Sergio Marchetti, and Ugo Montanari. A^2CCS: atomic actions for CCS. *Theoretical Computer Science*, pages 203–223, 1990.

[Huh96] Michaela Huhn. On semantic and logical refinement of actions. Technical Report 15/96, Universität Hildesheim, Institut für Informatik, 1996.

[JPZ91] W. Janssen, M. Poel, and J. Zwiers. Actions systems and action refinement in the development of parallel systems. In *Concur'91*, *LNCS* 527, p. 298–316, 1991.

[Lar88] Kim G. Larsen. Proof systems for Hennessy-Milner Logic with recursion. In *Trees in Algebra and Programming, CAAP*, *LNCS* 299, pages 215–230, 1988.

[Maz88] A. Mazurkiewicz. Basic notions of trace theory. In *Linear Time, Branching time and Partial Order in Logics and Models for Concurrency*, *LNCS* 354, pages 280–323, 1988.

[Mil89] Robin Milner. *Communications and Concurrency.* 1989.

[Nie95] Peter Niebert. A ν-calculus with local views for systems of sequential agents. In *MFCS*, *LNCS* 969, 1995.

[Ram95] R. Ramanujam. A local presentation of synchronizing systems. In *Structure in Concurrency Theory (STRICT)*, pages 264–279, 1995.

[Sti92] Colin Stirling. Modal and temporal logics. In *Handbook of Logic in Computer Science.* 1992.

[Thi94] P.S. Thiagarajan. A trace based extension of Linear Time Temporal Logic. In *Proc. of the 9th Ann. IEEE Symp. on Logic in Computer Science* , 1994.

[Thi95] P.S. Thiagarajan. A trace consistent subset of PTL. In *CONCUR '95*, *LNCS* 962, pages 438– 452, 1995.

[Vaa89] Frits Vaandrager. A simple definition for parallel composition of prime event structures. Cs-r8903, CWI, 1989.

[Vog93] Walter Vogler. Bisimulation and action refinement. *Theoretical Computer Science*, 114:173–200, 1993.

[Weh94] Heike Wehrheim. Parametric action refinement. In *Concepts, Methods and Calculi*, volume A-56 of *IFIP Transactions*, pages 247 – 266, 1994.

[Win86] Glynn Winskel. Event structures. In *Petri Nets: Applications and Relationships to Other Models of Concurrency*, *LNCS* 255, pages 325–392, 1986.

A Calculus for Concurrent Objects

Paolo Di Blasio[1] and Kathleen Fisher[2] *

[1] Dipartimento di Informatica e Sistemistica
Università "La Sapienza", via Salaria 113, 00198 Roma
diblasio@dis.uniroma1.it

[2] Computer Science Department
Stanford University, Stanford, CA 94305
kfisher@cs.stanford.edu

Abstract. This paper presents an imperative and concurrent extension of the functional object-oriented calculus described in [FHM94]. It belongs to the family of so-called prototype-based object-oriented languages, in which objects are created from existing ones via the inheritance primitives of object extension and method override. Concurrency is introduced through the identification of objects and processes. To our knowledge, the resulting calculus is the first concurrent object calculus to be studied. We define an operational semantics for the calculus via a transition relation between configurations, which represent snapshots of the run-time system. Our static analysis includes a type inference system, which statically detects *message-not-understood* errors, and an effect system, which guarantees that synchronization code, specified via guards, is side-effect free. We present a subject reduction theorem, modified to account for imperative and concurrent features, and type and effect soundness theorems.

1 Introduction

In the past few years, the desire to bring the benefits of object-oriented programming (modularity, re-usability and incremental design) to multiprocessor environments has led to a significant interest in concurrent object-oriented programming. The fact that objects seem to provide a suitable abstraction for concurrent programming has further encouraged research in this area. Various languages have been designed, some from scratch (*e.g.* POOL [Ame89] and ABCL [Yon90]), and others by adding concurrent features to existing object-oriented languages (*e.g.* concurrent C++ [CGH89] and Eiffel[Car93]). Despite this broad interest, the most effective combination of the object-oriented and concurrent paradigms has not yet emerged.

Considerable effort has been spent in developing theoretical frameworks for studying this issue. To date, there have been two main approaches to such studies: actor languages and process algebras. The actor model [Agh86] can easily

* Supported in part by a Fannie and John Hertz Foundation Fellowship and NSF Grant CCR-9303099.

represent concurrent objects [Agh90] and has been used as a foundation for designing various concurrent object-oriented languages (*e.g.* ABCL [Yon90] and [FA93]). Theoretical research using this model has focused on semantics and equational theories (*e.g.* [AMS92, Tal96]). The process algebra approaches to modeling concurrent object-oriented systems [PT94, Vas94, Nie92, KY94, Jon93] are often extensions of the π-calculus, obtained by adding objects and functional constructs. Researchers adopting this approach have paid particular attention to typing issues (*c.f.* [Vas94, KY94]).

Both the actor and the process algebra approaches suffer from not directly supporting objects, a lack which makes some object-oriented features quite difficult to represent in these frameworks. In contrast, functional object-oriented calculi [AC94, FHM94] already have primitives for object-oriented features and so are a convenient starting point for studying concurrent object-oriented systems. Despite the naturalness of adding concurrency to such calculi, this approach has not been extensively investigated. To our knowledge, Cardelli's object-based language for distributed computation Obliq [Car95] is the only existing language that adopts this philosophy. Except for its sequential imperative core [AC95], however, no formal study of Obliq's semantics or its types has been carried out.

The general goal of this research is to establish theoretical foundations for concurrent object-oriented programming, focusing on the development of intuitive semantics and sound type systems. As a first step towards this goal, we present an imperative and concurrent extension of the calculus in [FHM94]. We believe that one of the contributions of this work is to introduce a new direction for the design of formal systems for studying concurrent object-oriented programming, that of adding concurrency primitives to object calculi.

The rest of the paper is organized as follows. In Section 2, we describe our extended language, focusing on the design choices we made in defining our calculus. In Section 3 we present an example program-fragment to illustrate our language. Section 4 describes an operational semantics for the language, and Section 5 presents its static type system. Section 6 contains the technical results of the paper, including a subject reduction theorem, modified to account for imperative and concurrent features. Type soundness follows as a corollary. Section 7 concludes with some notes on future work.

2 The language: an overview

In this section, we give an overview of our concurrent object-calculus, focusing on the design choices we made in its development.

Typing. The usefulness of static type systems in increasing the reliability and readability of programs, in detecting compile-time type errors, and in providing useful compile-time information is widely recognized. Hence, we chose to define a static type system for our calculus. Reassuringly, only straightforward modifications to the type system of the functional object calculi of [FHM94] were required. One such modification was the incorporation of an effect system [LG88] to insure that the guards we use to define synchronization code are side-effect free (See below). The potential to leverage prior work in this fashion is one of the appeals of designing concurrent object-oriented calculi by extending sequential functional ones.

Prototype-based calculus. The object model of our calculus uses a prototype-based approach to represent inheritance. In other words, new objects are created from existing ones via the inheritance primitives of object extension and method override. A consequence of this approach is that the methods of each object are embedded in the object itself, which is important for managing method lookup when objects are physically distributed on a network. In our syntax the expression $\langle\rangle$ creates an empty object, $\langle ob \longleftarrow\!\!+\ m = method\rangle$ extends object *ob* with new method *m* whose code is specified in *method*, and $\langle ob \longleftarrow m = method\rangle$ replaces *ob*'s *m*-method with new code *method.* We adopt these inheritance primitives instead of the more complex operators defined in Obliq (*e.g. clone*) because Obliq's operators can be encoded.

Processes as objects. Objects represent a suitable and appealing abstraction for the notion of a process, so we introduce concurrency by identifying objects and processes. It is hoped that this unification might simplify the process of writing concurrent code. More definitely, it allows us to use our object primitives to create and activate processes, thus reducing the number of primitives in the calculus.

Communication mechanisms. Concurrent object-oriented languages that unify the notions of object and process use three kind of communication: synchronous, asynchronous and eager invocation [WKH92]. In our calculus, we chose to directly support synchronous and asynchronous method invocation because both are interesting and neither is encodable in the other without adding more syntax. We do not directly provide eager invocation because it can be derived via an encoding of future variables as objects. In our syntax, expression $ob \Leftarrow_a m(arg)$ sends message *m* asynchronously with argument *arg* to object *ob*. The corresponding synchronous invocation is $ob \Leftarrow_s m(arg)$.

Synchronization constraints. In a concurrent object-oriented language, at any given time an object may only be able to respond to a subset of its entire set of messages without losing its internal integrity. For example, a buffer object cannot meaningfully respond to a *put* message if its internal storage is full. Instead, it must wait until a *get* message causes some of its space to become free. Such restrictions on the availability of methods are called *synchronization constraints* because they affect the order in which methods are executed. Code that controls method availability is called *synchronization code* [MY93]. We use guards for this purpose, because they provide one of the most natural ways to define synchronization code and they require minimal additional syntax. (See [Yon90] for another use of guards.) In our language, each method consists of a guard and a method body, i.e., each *method* has the form *when*(*g*) *body*. To insure that guards behave properly, our static analysis guarantees that guards return boolean values and cause no side effects.

Protection. A crucial point in the calculus is the distinction between *self* and *non-self-inflicted* operations. According to the definitions introduced in [Car95], method overriding $\langle ob \leftarrow m = method \rangle$ and invocation $ob \Leftarrow m(arg)$[3] are *self-inflicted* iff *ob* is the same object as the *self*-parameter of the current method. Otherwise the operation is *non-self-inflicted*[4]. Method overriding has different semantics in these two cases. In the self-inflicted case, $\langle ob \leftarrow m = method \rangle$ replaces the method *m* of the object *ob*. This operation is the only way to update the state of an object in our calculus. The non-self-inflicted overriding has a cloning semantics, meaning that we first create a copy of the object *ob* and then replace the *m* method with the new *method*[5]. There are two reasons for these choices. First, we want to provide a form of protection against external writing operations. By insuring that only self-inflicted operations can modify their host object, we can safeguard internal invariants of objects. Secondly, the cloning semantics allows us to support *depth inheritance* (via method overriding)[6].

Serialized objects. As we will formalize in Section 4, an object can be in either an idle or a busy state. Non-self-inflicted operations can be executed only if their target object is in the idle state. This restriction gives each object a serialized structure: at any time a given object is involved in at most one thread of computation. This single-threadedness helps maintain object invariants, since we are guaranteed that once an object starts a computation, it will not be interrupted by an outside request until it has finished its computation. Self-inflicted operations do not have to wait for their target object to become idle. The methods of an object need to be able to access other host object methods without immediately causing deadlock. This freedom maintains the single-threadedness of objects, since self-inflicted operations continue in the same thread.

As can be seen from the preceding paragraphs, the notion of self-infliction is an important concept. Unfortunately, whether an operation is self-inflicted or not can generally only be determined at run-time. Currently, our type system does not approximate this distinction. We leave this question to future work.

3 Example: a buffer and a producer

To provide some intuition for this calculus, we give example producer and one-slot buffer objects. A more complete version can be found in [DF96]. As we will see formally in the next section, the language consists of the untyped λ-calculus extended with the object primitives described above. As a notational convenience, we adopt the following syntactic conventions. We write $\langle m_1 = when(e_1)e'_1, \ldots, m_k = when(e_k)e'_k \rangle$ for $\langle \ldots \langle \langle \rangle \leftarrow\!\!+ m_1 = when(e_1)e'_1 \rangle \ldots \leftarrow\!\!+ m_k = when(e_k)e'_k \rangle$. If we have a method invocation with no parameters, we write $e_1 \Leftarrow m$ instead of $e_1 \Leftarrow m(nil)$, where *nil* is a constant with type **unit**. We introduce the semicolon operator $e_1; e_2$ as syntactic sugar for $((\lambda z.\, \lambda x.\, x)e_1)e_2$, which has the expected meaning for sequencing as our semantics reflects call-by-value evaluation. Finally, we use integer constants and their related operations.

[3] The symbol $\Leftarrow$ indicates either synchronous and asynchronous method invocation.
[4] Note that self-inflicted method extension is prevented by the type system.
[5] Non-self-inflicted method extension has the same semantics.
[6] Width inheritance is obtained via object extension.

The following code creates an empty one-slot buffer object:

$$\begin{aligned} \textit{buffer} = \langle\ x &= \lambda \textit{self}.\,\lambda \textit{arg}.\,0,\\ \textit{size} &= \lambda \textit{self}.\,\lambda \textit{arg}.\,0,\\ \textit{put} &= \textit{when}(\lambda \textit{self}.(\textit{self} \Leftarrow_s \textit{size}) = 0)\\ &\quad \lambda \textit{self}.\,\lambda v.\langle\langle \textit{self} \leftarrow x = \lambda s.\,\lambda a.\,v\rangle \leftarrow \textit{size} = \lambda s.\,\lambda a.\,1\rangle,\\ \textit{get} &= \textit{when}(\lambda \textit{self}.(\textit{self} \Leftarrow_s \textit{size}) = 1)\\ &\quad \lambda \textit{self}.\,\lambda \textit{arg}.\langle \textit{self} \leftarrow \textit{size} = \lambda s.\,\lambda a.\,0\rangle;\ \textit{self} \Leftarrow_s x\ \rangle \end{aligned}$$

Both guards and method bodies occasionally need to access other methods of their host object. To grant this access, we write them as functions from a *self* parameter to their actual code. The operational semantics binds these parameters to the host object when the corresponding methods are invoked.

The x method represents the storage of the buffer. The *size* method indicates whether or not the buffer is full by storing either a 0 (for empty) or a 1 (for full). Both of these methods have constantly *true* guards, which we omit for clarity. The *put* method is only available if the buffer is currently empty, which its guard checks by comparing its current size to 0. When available, *put* stores a new value into the buffer's storage x and sets the *size* to 1. Finally, the *get* method, which is only available if the buffer is full, sets the current *size* to 0 and returns the value contained in the storage x.

When an object is created, it is associated with an address generated by the system. Future interactions with that object occur via the generated address, which may be thought of as the name of the object. For expository purposes, we will assume that the name generated for the above *buffer* object is *buff*.

We may write a producer object that interacts with the *buff* object as follows:

$$\textit{producer} = \langle m = \lambda \textit{self}.\,\lambda \textit{arg}.((\lambda y.\ \textit{buff} \Leftarrow_a \textit{put}(y))(\textit{value\_prod}()))\ ;\ \textit{self} \Leftarrow_a m\rangle$$

Invoking a producer object's m method causes a non-terminating computation to start. During each iteration of this computation, the producer gets a new value by calling the function *value_prod* and then stores this value in the buffer by asynchronously sending *buff* the message *put*. We will assume the name generated for the *producer* object is *prod*.

We illustrate the computational behavior of our objects using the following simplified evaluation rule that reflects the operational semantics defined precisely below:

$$\langle m_1 = \textit{when}(e'_1)e_1, \ldots, m_k = \textit{when}(e'_k)e_k\rangle \Leftarrow m_i \ \longrightarrow \\ e_i\ \langle m_1 = \textit{when}(e'_1)e_1, \ldots, m_k = \textit{when}(e'_k)e_k\rangle$$

This rule allows us to evaluate a message send by retrieving the appropriate method body from the object and applying it to the entire object itself.

Using the rule above and call-by-value β-reduction, we may evaluate the message send $\textit{prod} \Leftarrow_a m$, assuming $\textit{value\_prod}() \longrightarrow v_1$:

$$\begin{aligned} \textit{prod} \Leftarrow_a m &\longrightarrow (\lambda \textit{self}.\,\lambda \textit{arg}.((\lambda y.\ \textit{buff} \Leftarrow_a \textit{put}(y))(\textit{value\_prod}()))\ ;\ \textit{self} \Leftarrow_a m)\,\textit{prod}\,\textit{nil}\\ &\longrightarrow ((\lambda y.\ \textit{buff} \Leftarrow_a \textit{put}(y))(\textit{value\_prod}()))\ ;\ \textit{prod} \Leftarrow_a m)\\ &\longrightarrow (\textit{buff} \Leftarrow_a \textit{put}(v_1))\ ;\ \textit{prod} \Leftarrow_a m\\ &\longrightarrow \textit{prod} \Leftarrow_a m \end{aligned}$$

The asynchronous method invocation $\textit{buff} \Leftarrow_a \textit{put}(v_1)$ (a non-self-inflicted operation) is put in the queue of pending messages, and the computation continues, sending again message m to the object *prod*. When the buffer is free to receive the message $put(v_1)$, it evaluates the guard for the method *put*. If this evaluation returns true, then the $put(v_1)$ message is removed from the queue and the method body is executed. Otherwise, the message remains in the queue. The *put* method reduces as follows:

$$\begin{aligned} buff \Leftarrow_a put(v_1) &\longrightarrow (\lambda self.\, \lambda v. \langle\langle self \leftarrow\!\!\!+\, x = \lambda s.\, \lambda a.\, v\rangle \leftarrow size = \lambda s.\, \lambda a.\, 1\rangle)\; buff\, v_1 \\ &\longrightarrow \langle\langle buff \leftarrow\!\!\!+\, x = \lambda s.\, \lambda a.\, v_1\rangle \leftarrow size = \lambda s.\, \lambda a.\, 1\rangle \\ &\longrightarrow \langle buff \leftarrow size = \lambda s.\, \lambda a.\, 1\rangle \\ &\longrightarrow buff \end{aligned}$$

This evaluation overrides the methods x and *size* (both self-inflicted operations), so the object *buff* now has the following structure, modulo α-conversion:

$$\begin{aligned} buff : \langle\; x &= \lambda self.\, \lambda arg.\, v_1, \\ size &= \lambda self.\, \lambda arg.\, 1, \quad put \;=\; \ldots, \quad get \;=\; \ldots\;\rangle \end{aligned}$$

4 Operational Semantics

We formalize the operational semantics of the calculus as a transition relation on *configurations*, which can be thought of as global snapshots of the run-time system. A configuration contains the collection of all created objects and all pending messages. Formally, a *configuration* $\langle\!\langle \alpha \mid \mu \rangle\!\rangle$ consists of an *object soup* α, containing run-time objects, and a collection of *pending asynchronous messages* μ. More precisely, μ is a finite map from integers to pending messages. As a notational simplification, we use a single collection of pending messages instead of having a smaller queue for each object.

An *object* is represented at run-time as a triple $(a, \eta_a, [S_a])$, where a is the object's *address*, η_a is its *method table*, and S_a its *state*. A method table is a partial function from the set of method names M to guarded expressions of the form $when(e_2)e_3$. The state S_a can be either idle ($[I]$) or busy ($[te_a]$), in which case the expression te_a represents the remaining computation. An object passes from the idle to a busy state in response to either a synchronous or an asynchronous method invocation. At the end of the resulting computation, it returns to the idle state.

4.1 Formal Language Specification

In this section, we introduce the notation needed to formally describe the operational semantics of the calculus.

Language expressions:

$$\begin{aligned} e \;::=&\; x \mid c \mid a \mid \lambda x.e \mid e_1 e_2 \mid \langle\rangle \mid e_1 \Leftarrow_a m(e_2) \mid e_1 \Leftarrow_s m(e_2) \\ &\mid \langle e_1 \leftarrow\!\!\!+\, m = when(e_2)e_3\rangle \mid \langle e_1 \leftarrow m = when(e_2)e_3\rangle \\ te \;::=&\; gs(e,a) \mid ret(e,a) \mid ga(e,c) \mid nonret(e) \end{aligned}$$

In the set of expressions e, x is a variable, c is a constant symbol, a is an object address, $\lambda x.e$ is a lambda abstraction, and $e_1 e_2$ is function application. The remaining syntactic forms are the object primitives described in Section 2. All expressions e except a may occur in source programs. The top-level expressions te appear as the states of busy objects in object triples. They allow us to determine if the expression we are reducing corresponds to a guard evaluation or to a method body application and further, if the reduction is in response to a synchronous or an asynchronous invocation. (We will see an example of this in the next section, where these top-level expressions are explained in more detail.)

To describe transitions internal to an object, we need to uniquely decompose each non-value expression into a reduction context filled with a redex. With this intent, we define values, redexes and reduction contexts.

Values: $v ::= x \mid c \mid a \mid \lambda x.e$

Top Values: $tv ::= gs(v,a) \mid ret(v,a) \mid ga(v,c) \mid nonret(v)$

Redexes: $e_{rdx} ::= v_1 v_2 \mid \langle\rangle \mid v_1 \Leftarrow_a m(v_2) \mid v_1 \Leftarrow_s m(v_2) \mid \langle v_1 \leftarrow\!\!+ m = when(e)v_2\rangle \mid \langle v_1 \leftarrow m = when(e)v_2\rangle$

Inner Reduction Contexts:

$$\begin{aligned} r_{in} ::= \; & \square \mid r_{in}e \mid v\, r_{in} \\ & \mid r_{in} \Leftarrow_a m(e) \mid v \Leftarrow_a m(r_{in}) \mid r_{in} \Leftarrow_s m(e) \mid v \Leftarrow_s m(r_{in}) \\ & \mid \langle r_{in} \leftarrow\!\!+ m = when(e)e_1\rangle \mid \langle v \leftarrow\!\!+ m = when(e)r_{in}\rangle \\ & \mid \langle r_{in} \leftarrow m = when(e)e_1\rangle \mid \langle v \leftarrow m = when(e)r_{in}\rangle \end{aligned}$$

Top Reduction Contexts:

$$r_{top} ::= gs(r_{in}, a) \mid ret(r_{in}, a) \mid ga(r_{in}, c) \mid nonret(r_{in})$$

The reduction contexts identify which subexpression of a given expression is to be evaluated next. These contexts correspond to the standard call-by-value reduction strategy. Because we have two forms of expressions, we need two forms of reduction contexts: inner and top. The following lemma tells us that local computation inside objects is deterministic.

Lemma 1 Unique Decomposition. *Given an expression te, then either te is a top value or there exists a unique* (r_{top}, e_{rdx}) *such that* $te = r_{top}[e_{rdx}]$.

4.2 Reduction Rules

In this section we define the transition relation $\longmapsto$ between configurations. We describe in detail the rules for evaluating asynchronous, non-self-inflicted invocations and method override because these rules illustrate the key concepts of the transition system. The other rules are similar to these or are straightforward and can be found in Appendix A. Although this transition relation describes an interleaving semantics for the calculus, a straightforward modification produces a truly concurrent semantics.

Asynchronous, Non-Self-Inflicted Reductions. These rules describe the computation that results when an object a sends object b the message m asynchronously. The first rule says that the execution of an asynchronous method invocation proceeds by putting the message in the pending queue. The constant *nil* is returned to a to reflect the fact that the message has been placed in the queue. Integer i serves as the name or index of the pending message.

$(\Leftarrow_a)$ *non-self-inflicted* $\quad i$ is fresh.

$$\langle\!\langle\, \alpha, (a, \eta, [r_{top}[b \Leftarrow_a m(v)]]) \mid \mu \,\rangle\!\rangle \longmapsto \langle\!\langle\, \alpha, (a, \eta, [r_{top}[nil]]) \mid \mu, i : b \Leftarrow_a m(v) \,\rangle\!\rangle$$

When object b is in the idle state and there is a pending message m in μ for b, then b evaluates its guard for m within top-level expression ga according to the rule (μ):

(μ) $\quad \eta(m) = when(e)v$

$$\langle\!\langle\, \alpha, (b, \eta, [I]) \mid i : b \Leftarrow_a m(v'), \mu \,\rangle\!\rangle \longmapsto \langle\!\langle\, \alpha, (b, \eta, [ga(e\,b, i)]) \mid i : b \Leftarrow_a m(v'), \mu \,\rangle\!\rangle$$

The top-level expression ga stores the index of the message send from the queue. This information is needed so that the proper message send will be removed from the queue when the method body starts its evaluation.

If the guard evaluates to *true*, rule (μ-*true*) directs object b to start evaluating the method body for m within the top-level expression *nonret*. This rule also removes the message send at index i from the queue, since that message send is now being executed. This rule illustrates the role of the top-level expressions. If we simply had value *true* not wrapped by ga as the state of object b, we would not have enough information to figure out the new state for b.

(μ-*true*) $\quad \eta(m) = when(e)v$

$$\langle\!\langle\, \alpha, (b, \eta, [ga(true, i)]) \mid i : b \Leftarrow_a m(v'), \mu \,\rangle\!\rangle \longmapsto \langle\!\langle\, \alpha, (b, \eta, [nonret(v\,b\,v')]) \mid \mu \,\rangle\!\rangle$$

Finally, when the body of the method has been evaluated to a value, rule (*nonret*) returns object b to the idle state and throws away the resulting value. Note that if we simply had value v'' as the state of object b, we would not have enough information to determine that v'' is the result of an asynchronous method invocation and hence should be thrown away.

(*nonret*) $\quad \langle\!\langle\, \alpha, (b, \eta, [nonret(v'')]) \mid \mu \,\rangle\!\rangle \longmapsto \langle\!\langle\, \alpha, (b, \eta, [I]) \mid \mu \,\rangle\!\rangle$

Method Override Reductions. There are two different rules for evaluating the method override operation, one for self-inflicted and one for non-self-inflicted operations. In the self-inflicted case, we simply replace the guard and body of the method m in the method table of a:

$(\leftarrow)$ *self-inflicted*

$$\langle\!\langle\, \alpha, (a, \eta, [r_{top}[\langle a \leftarrow m = when(e)v \rangle]]) \mid \mu \,\rangle\!\rangle \longmapsto$$
$$\langle\!\langle\, \alpha, (a, \eta[m] := when(e)v, [r_{top}[a]]) \mid \mu \,\rangle\!\rangle$$

Note that because this operation is self-inflicted, we do not wait for a to become idle before performing the update. The notation $\eta[m] := when(e)v$ stands for the function η' that is just like η except that it maps m to $when(e)v$. This operation returns the address of the modified object as its result. In the non-self-inflicted case, we must wait for b to enter the idle state before performing a method override requested by object a:

$(\leftarrow)$ *non-self-inflicted* $\quad b'$ is a fresh address

$$\langle\!\langle\, \alpha, (a, \eta, [r_{top}[\langle b \leftarrow m = when(e)v \rangle]]), (b, \eta', [I]) \mid \mu \,\rangle\!\rangle \longmapsto$$
$$\langle\!\langle\, \alpha, (a, \eta, [r_{top}[b']]), (b, \eta', [I]), (b', \eta'[m] := when(e)v, [I]) \mid \mu \,\rangle\!\rangle$$

This rule first clones object b to create a new object b' and then replaces b''s m

method with the new guard and body. The address of the new object is returned. Note that we cannot clone object b if it is busy. To see this point, suppose we create b' while b is executing e. If we put b' in the idle state, we can violate the integrity of b', because we do not complete the pending computation e, which could be responsible for restoring some invariant for b'. On the other hand, if we clone the state of b as well, we execute the pending computation e twice, potentially causing unwanted side-effects.

5 Type and Effect System

For the most part, the type system presented here is similar to the one defined in [FHM94]. The most novel parts are the effect system and the rules for typing asynchronous method invocation and guards. Because of space considerations, we present only the main ideas here. A complete presentation is in [DF96]

Pro Types. The type of an object is called a *pro type*, short for *prototype*. The following type expression:

$$pro\,t.\langle m_1 : \tau_1 \to \tau_1', \ldots, m_k : \tau_k \to \tau_k' \rangle$$

defines a type t with the property that any expression e of this type is an object such that for $1 \le i \le k$, the result of $e \Leftarrow_s m_i(e_i)$ is a value of type τ_i', if e_i is of type τ_i. Keyword *pro* is a type binding operator. When bound type variable t appears in the types $\tau_1 \ldots \tau_k, \tau_1' \ldots \tau_k'$, it refers to the entire type. Thus, when we say $e \Leftarrow_s m_i(e_1)$ has type τ_i', we mean type τ_i' with any free occurrences of t in τ_i' replaced by the type $pro\,t.\langle m_1 : \tau_1 \to \tau_1', \ldots, m_k : \tau_k \to \tau_k' \rangle$. Thus, *pro types* are a special form of recursive type.

As an example of this kind of type, we may give the one-slot buffer object considered above the type:

$$\begin{aligned} buff : pro\,t.\langle\, & x : unit \to int,\ size : unit \to int, \\ & put : int \to t,\ \ get : unit \to int \rangle \end{aligned}$$

Effects. Our static analysis includes an effect system [LG88] that ensures that the evaluation of guards is side-effect free. This guarantee is important because the guard for a method may be invoked an arbitrary number of times before its corresponding body is allowed to proceed. Since this number is a property of how the system orders pending messages, it is undesirable for guards to produce any observable effects.

We formalize this requirement by adding *pure* and *impure* effects to our static analysis. Only those expressions with *pure* effect will be permitted in guards because such expressions are guaranteed to produce no observable effects. Although a finer analysis of effects is possible, for our current purposes this coarse division suffices. The effect expressions include the constants *pure* and *impure*, and $\epsilon_1 \vee \epsilon_2$, which is impure if either ϵ_1 or ϵ_2 is impure.

Typing and Effecting Rules. We describe in detail only the rule for typing asynchronous method invocation. More rules can be found in Appendix B.

$$(pro \Leftarrow_a) \qquad \frac{\Gamma \vdash e_1 : \tau \,\&\, \epsilon_1 \qquad \Gamma \vdash e_2 : [\tau/t]\tau_1 \,\&\, \epsilon_2}{\Gamma \vdash e_1 \underset{a}{\Leftarrow} m(e_2) : \mathit{unit} \,\&\, \mathit{impure}}$$

$$\text{where } \tau = \mathit{prot}.\langle R \,|\, m : (\tau_1 \xrightarrow{\epsilon} \tau_2) \,\&\, \epsilon' \rangle$$

The first hypothesis of this rule requires e_1 to be an object that has at least a method m with type $\tau_1 \rightarrow \tau_2$ plus other possible methods represented by R. The second hypothesis forces the type of the parameter e_2 to be the same as the argument type of the method m, once we have substituted τ for any free variables t in τ_1. This substitution reflects the recursive structure of *pro* types. The type of the expression $e_1 \Leftarrow_a m(e_2)$ is *unit*, because the asynchronous method invocation does not return any result. The effect is impure because we modify the queue of pending messages.

The latent effect of a method occurs whenever that method is executed. We discuss the effect portions of this rule in detail to illustrate how we track such effects. Because of call-by-value semantics, the body of the method m has the syntactic form $\lambda \mathit{self}.\, e$. Effect ϵ' records the latent effect of e, visible when we first reduce the method body by applying it to its host object and a parameter p: $(\lambda \mathit{self}.\, e)\, a\, p$. In other words, the expression $([a/\mathit{self}]e)p$ reduces to $(\lambda \mathit{arg}.\, e')\, p$ producing an effect ϵ'. Then $[p/\mathit{arg}]e'$ reduces to a value producing the effect ϵ.

6 Main Results

In this section we present subject reduction, side-effect freeness for guards, and type soundness theorems. We prove these results for programs, which are closed, address-free terms typeable in the empty context. Given a program e, its possible computations originate from the following *initial configuration*:

$\langle\!\langle (\mathit{main}, \eta, [I]) \mid \mu \rangle\!\rangle$ where $\eta(\mathit{begin}) = \lambda \mathit{self}.\, \lambda \mathit{arg}.\, e$ and $\mu(1) = \mathit{main} \Leftarrow_a \mathit{begin}$

which contains one object, whose address is *main*, with a method *begin* storing the program and one message pending that invokes method *begin* of *main*.

We let g and its decorated variants range over configurations. A ***computation sequence*** is a finite sequence of transitions of the form $[g_i \longmapsto g_{i+1} \mid i < n]$, for some natural number n, where g_0 is an initial configuration.

Using techniques similar to those of [Har94], we prove a subject reduction theorem by extending typing judgments to type object addresses and method tables. With this intent, we extend our contexts to contain typing assumptions for object addresses:

$$\Gamma ::= \ldots \mid \Gamma, a : \tau$$

where τ is a closed *pro* type. (See Appendix B for formal definitions of context and judgment.) We use Λ to indicate the projection of the context Γ onto the set of object addresses A. More formally, $a : \tau \in \Lambda$ iff $a : \tau \in \Gamma$ and $a \in A$. To state our subject reduction theorem, we need the following definitions.

Definition 2. A *method table* η_a *of an object* a *is typeable in* Γ if when $\Lambda(a) = prot.\langle R \,|\, \mathbf{m} : \tau \,\&\, \epsilon\rangle$ and $\forall m_i \in dom(\eta_a)$, $1 \le i \le k$, $\eta_a(m_i) = when(e_i)v_i$, then the judgments

$$\Gamma, r : T \rightarrow \{\mathbf{m}\} \vdash v_i : [prot.\langle r\,t \,|\, \mathbf{m} : \tau \,\&\, \epsilon\rangle/t](t \xrightarrow{\epsilon_i} \tau_i) \,\&\, pure$$

and

$$\Gamma, r : T \rightarrow \{\mathbf{m}\} \vdash e_i : prot.\langle r\,t \,|\, \mathbf{m} : \tau \,\&\, \epsilon\rangle \xrightarrow{pure} bool \,\&\, pure,$$

are both derivable.

In this definition $\mathbf{m} : \tau \,\&\, \epsilon$ is an abbreviation for $m_1 : \tau_1 \,\&\, \epsilon_1, \ldots, m_k : \tau_k \,\&\, \epsilon_k$.

ObjAddr(α) stands for the set of addresses of objects contained in α.

Definition 3. An *object soup* α *is typeable in* Γ if $dom(\Lambda) = ObjAddr(\alpha)$ and $\forall a \in ObjAddr(\alpha)$, the method table η_a is typeable in Γ and if a is busy with state e_a, there exist type τ_a and effect ϵ_a such that the judgment $\Gamma \vdash e_a : \tau_a \,\&\, \epsilon_a$ is derivable.

Definition 4. A *pending queue* μ *is typeable in* Γ if $\forall i \in dom(\mu)$, there exist type τ_i and effect ϵ_i such that the judgment $\Gamma \vdash \mu(i) : \tau_i \,\&\, \epsilon_i$ is derivable.

Definition 5. A *configuration* $\langle\!\langle\, \alpha \mid \mu \,\rangle\!\rangle$ *is typeable in* Γ if α and μ are typeable in Γ.

In proving subject reduction, we are not interested in showing that the types of top-level expressions are preserved by reduction. Indeed, the types of these expressions are trivially preserved as they are always *unit* (see the typing rules in the Appendix B). Instead, we are interested in preserving the types of the expressions that occur one level below the top expressions. For example, if the state of object a is $e_a \equiv ret(r_{in}[e_{rdx}], b)$ then $r_{in}[e_{rdx}]$ is a's one-level-down expression. If after one reduction step we have $e'_a \equiv ret(r_{in}[e'], b)$, then we want to prove that $r_{in}[e']$ has whatever type we gave to $r_{in}[e_{rdx}]$. Moreover, note that subject reduction holds only for objects whose states before and after a transition are related. In particular, if an object passes through an idle state or transitions from evaluating a guard to evaluating a method body, then the types of its state before and after the transition will be unrelated. This makes sense, since the computations before and after such a transition are not connected.

Definition 6. If $\langle\!\langle\, \alpha \mid \mu \,\rangle\!\rangle \longmapsto \langle\!\langle\, \alpha' \mid \mu' \,\rangle\!\rangle$ via some transition rule T with $a \in ObjAddr(\alpha)$, we say that the states of a in α and α' are *related* if a is busy in α and α', and T is neither (μ-true) nor ($\Leftarrow_s$-true) on object a.

We order effects as follows: $pure \le impure$. The notation $\epsilon' \le \epsilon$ means that if ϵ is *pure* then ϵ' is *pure* as well.

Definition 7. Given a transition $g \longmapsto g'$ with $g = \langle\!\langle\, \alpha \mid \mu \,\rangle\!\rangle$ and $g' = \langle\!\langle\, \alpha' \mid \mu' \,\rangle\!\rangle$ typeable in Γ and Γ' respectively, we say that g and g' are *compatible* if:

- α and α' are compatible, that is, for all objects a whose states e_a and e'_a in α and α' are related, there exist type τ_a and effects ϵ_a and ϵ'_a such that the judgments $\Gamma \vdash r_{in}[e_{rdx}]_a : \tau_a \ \& \ \epsilon_a$[7] and $\Gamma' \vdash r_{in}[e_{rdx}]'_a : \tau_a \ \& \ \epsilon'_a$, with $\epsilon'_a \leq \epsilon_a$ are both derivable;
- μ and μ' are compatible, that is, $\forall\, i \in dom(\mu) \cap dom(\mu')$, there exists type τ and effect ϵ such that the judgments $\Gamma \vdash \mu(i) : \tau \ \& \ \epsilon$ and $\Gamma' \vdash \mu'(i) : \tau \ \& \ \epsilon$ are derivable.

Theorem 8 Subject Reduction. *Given a computation sequence $[g_i \longmapsto g_{i+1} \mid i < n]$, if g_0 is typeable in some context Γ_0, then $\forall i < n$, there exist contexts Γ, Γ_i, Γ_{i+1}, with $\Gamma_{i+1} \equiv \Gamma_i, \Gamma$, such that g_i and g_{i+1} are typeable in Γ_i and Γ_{i+1}, respectively, and are compatible.*

Side-effect freeness for guards and type soundness follow as corollaries of the previous theorem under the same hypothesis.

Corollary 9 Effect Freeness. *Guard evaluation is side-effect free.*

Definition 10. We define the *error* expressions of an object soup α to be those expressions of the forms (where r_c can be either r_{in} or r_{top}):
- $r_c[v_1\, v_2]$ where $v_1 \neq \lambda x.e$ for some e;
- $r_c[v_1 \Leftarrow m(v_2)]$ where v_1 is not an object address a such that $a \in ObjAddr(\alpha)$ and $\eta_a(m)$ exists.
- $r_c[v_1 \leftarrow m = when(e) v_2]$ where v_1 is not an object address a such that $a \in ObjAddr(\alpha)$ and $m \in dom(\eta_a)$.
- $r_c[v_1 \leftarrow\!\!+\ m = when(e) v_2]$ where v_1 is not an object address a such that $a \in ObjAddr(\alpha)$ and $m \notin dom(\eta_a)$.

Corollary 11 Type Soundness. *Given a computation sequence $[g_i \longmapsto g_{i+1} \mid i < n]$, if g_0 is typeable in some context Γ_0, then for every configuration $g_i = \langle\!\langle\, \alpha_i \mid \mu_i \,\rangle\!\rangle$ and for every busy object $a \in ObjAddr(\alpha_i)$, e_a is not an error expression of the object soup α_i.*

Type soundness, which follows from Theorem 8, guarantees that the type system statically detects all expressions that can reduce to the following error expressions: applying a non-functional value to an argument, sending an object a message for which it has no defined method (*message not understood* error), overriding a method which has not been defined, and extending an object with a method it already has.

7 Conclusions

We have presented what we believe is the first typed, prototype-based calculus for concurrent objects. We have described an operational semantics using a

[7] Note that if e_a is typeable in Γ, then its one-level down expression $r_{in}[e_{rdx}]_a$ is typeable in Γ as well.

transition system between configurations and have given a type and effect system. We have proven the soundness of our static analysis with respect to the operational semantics via a subject reduction theorem.

This work is intended as a starting point for studying the theoretical foundations of concurrent object-oriented programming. In the following, we briefly describe some issues we intend to investigate further. Our current type system does not support subtyping because subtyping is unsound in pure prototype-based calculi [FM94]. This problem has been solved for the sequential version of our calculus [FM95], and we believe this solution will carry over to our concurrent setting. A second research direction focuses on method availability. Our type soundness theorem demonstrates that the type system we have given detects "message not understood" errors at compile time, in the sense that no object will ever receive a message for which it has no method defined. However, the theorem does not ensure that the method in question is available (by virtue of having a *true* guard) when its execution is required. Although method unavailability is not a problem for asynchronous method invocation, it can cause deadlock in the synchronous case. Addressing this problem requires additional analysis to account for the communication behavior of objects. Such analyses may be done by modeling communication behaviors as process algebra expressions in the style of [NN93, Nie93]. Finally, we would like to investigate the equational theory of our calculus by defining an observational semantics in the style of [AMS92].

Acknowledgment. We are grateful to Carolyn Talcott and Anna Patterson for insightful discussions and carefully reading a draft of this paper.

References

[AC94] M. Abadi and L. Cardelli. A theory of primitive objects: untyped and first order systems. In *Proc. of TACS'94*, 1994.

[AC95] M. Abadi and L. Cardelli. An imperative object calculus: basic typing and soundness. In *Proc. of second ACM-SIGPLAN workshop on state in programming Languages*, 1995.

[Agh86] G. Agha. Actors: a model of concurrent computation in distributed systems. *MIT Press*, Cambridge, Mass., 1986.

[Agh90] G. Agha. Concurrent object-oriented programming. In *Communication ACM* 33(9), 1990.

[Ame89] P. America. Issue in the design of a parallel object-oriented language. In *Formal Aspects of Computing*, 1, 366-411, 1989.

[AMS92] G. Agha, I. Mason, S. Smith, and C. Talcott. Towards a theory of actor computation. In *Proc. of CONCUR'92*, 1992.

[Car93] D. Caromel. Towards a method of concurrent object-oriented programming. In *Communication of ACM*, 36(9), 1993.

[Car95] L. Cardelli. A language with distributed scope. In *Computing Systems*, 8(1):27–59, 1995.

[CGH89] R. Chandra, A. Gupta, and J. Hennessy. COOL: A language for parallel programming. In *Proc. 2nd workshop on programming languages and compilers for parallel computing*, IEEE CS, 1989.

[DF96] P. Di Blasio and K. Fisher. A calculus for concurrent objects. Stanford University, Technical Note STAN-CS-TN-96-35, 1996.

[FA93] S. Frolund and G. Agha. A language framework for multi-object coordination. In *Proc. of ECOOP'93*, 1993.

[FHM94] K. Fisher, F. Honsell, and J.C. Mitchell. A lambda calculus of objects and method specialization. In *Nordic J. Computing (*formerly *BIT)*, 1:3–37, 1994. Preliminary version appeared in *Proc. IEEE Symp. on Logic in Computer Science*,, 26–38, 1993.

[FM94] K. Fisher and J.C. Mitchell. Notes on typed object-oriented programming. In *Proc. Theoretical Aspects of Computer Software*, pages 844–885. Springer LNCS 789, 1994.

[FM95] K. Fisher and J.C. Mitchell. A delegation-based object calculus with subtyping. In *Proc. 10th Int'l Conf. Fundamentals of Computation Theory (FCT'95)*, pages 42–61. Springer LNCS 965, 1995.

[Har94] R. Harper. A simplified account of polymorphic references. In *Information Processing Letters* 51(4), 1994.

[Jon93] C. Jones. A pi-calculus semantics for an object-based design notation. In *Proc. of CONCUR'93*, 1993.

[KY94] N. Kobayashi and A. Yonezawa. Type theoretic foundations for object-oriented concurrent programming. In *Proc. of OOPSLA'94*, 1994.

[LG88] J. Lucassen and D. Gifford. Polymorphic effect systems. In *Proc. of POPL'88*, 1988.

[MY93] S. Matsuoka and A. Yonezawa. Analysis of inheritance anomaly in object-oriented concurrent programming languages. In *Research Directions in Concurrent Object-Oriented Programming*, MIT Press, 1993.

[Nie92] O. Nierstrasz. Towards an object calculus. In *Proc. of the ECOOP'91 Workshop on Object-Based Concurrent Computing*, 1992.

[Nie93] O. Nierstrasz. Regular types for active objects. In *Proc. of OOPSLA'93*, 1993.

[NN93] F. Nielson and H. Nielson. From CML to process algebra. In *Proc. of CONCUR'93*, 1993.

[PT94] B. Pierce and D. Turner. Concurrent objects in a process calculus. In *Proc. of Theory and Practice of Parallel Programming*, 1994.

[Tal96] C. Talcott. Interaction semantics for components of distributed systems. In *Proc. of FMOODS96*, 1996.

[Vas94] V. T. Vasconcelos. Typed concurrent objects. In *Proc. ECOOP'94*, 1994.

[WKH92] B. Wyatt, K. Kavi, and S. Hufnagel. Parallelism in object-oriented languages: A survey. In *IEEE Software*, 1992.

[Yon90] A. Yonezawa. ABCL: An object-oriented concurrent system. *MIT Press*, Cambridge, Mass., 1990.

A Operational Semantics

The following rules complete the ones in section 4.2.

(λ) $\quad \langle\!\langle\, \alpha, (a, \eta, [r_{top}[(\lambda x.\, e)v]]) \mid \mu \,\rangle\!\rangle \longmapsto \langle\!\langle\, \alpha, (a, \eta, [r_{top}[[v/x]e]]) \mid \mu \,\rangle\!\rangle$

$(\langle\rangle)$ $\quad \langle\!\langle\, \alpha, (a, \eta, [r_{top}[\langle\rangle]]) \mid \mu \,\rangle\!\rangle \longmapsto \langle\!\langle\, \alpha, (a, \eta, [r_{top}[a']]), (a', \eta', [I]) \mid \mu \,\rangle\!\rangle$

where $dom(\eta') = \emptyset$ and $a' \notin ObjAddr(\alpha)$.

$(\leftarrow\!\!+)$ ***non-self-inflicted***

$$\langle\!\langle\, \alpha, (a, \eta, [r_{top}[\langle b \leftarrow\!\!+ m = when(e)v\rangle]]), (b, \eta', [I]) \mid \mu \,\rangle\!\rangle \longmapsto$$
$$\langle\!\langle\, \alpha, (a, \eta, [r_{top}[b']]), (b, \eta', [I]), (b', \eta'[m] := when(e)v, [I]) \mid \mu \,\rangle\!\rangle$$

where $b' \notin ObjAddr(\alpha)$.

$(\Leftarrow_a)$ ***self-inflicted***

$$\langle\!\langle\, \alpha, (a, \eta, [r_{top}[a \Leftarrow_a m(v')]]) \mid \mu \,\rangle\!\rangle \longmapsto \langle\!\langle\, \alpha, (a, \eta, [r_{top}[(\lambda x.\, nil)(v\, a\, v')]]) \mid \mu \,\rangle\!\rangle$$

where $\eta(m) = when(e)v$.

$(\mu\text{-}false)$

$$\langle\!\langle\, \alpha, (a, \eta, [ga(false, i)]) \mid i : a \Leftarrow_a m(v'), \mu \,\rangle\!\rangle \longmapsto$$
$$\langle\!\langle\, \alpha, (a, \eta, [I]) \mid i : a \Leftarrow_a m(v'), \mu \,\rangle\!\rangle$$

$(\Leftarrow_s)$ ***self-inflicted***

$$\langle\!\langle\, \alpha, (a, \eta, [r_{top}[a \Leftarrow_s m(v')]]) \mid \mu \,\rangle\!\rangle \longmapsto \langle\!\langle\, \alpha, (a, \eta, [r_{top}[v\, a\, v']]) \mid \mu \,\rangle\!\rangle$$

where $\eta(m) = when(e)v$.

The next four rules share the condition that $\eta_b(m) = when(e)v$.

$(\Leftarrow_s)$ ***non-self-inflicted***

$$\langle\!\langle\, \alpha, (a, \eta_a, [r_{top}[b \Leftarrow_s m(v')]]), (b, \eta_b, [I]) \mid \mu \,\rangle\!\rangle \longmapsto$$
$$\langle\!\langle\, \alpha, (a, \eta_a, [r_{top}[b \Leftarrow_s m(v')]]), (b, \eta_b, [gs(e\, b, a)]) \mid \mu \,\rangle\!\rangle$$

$(\Leftarrow_s\text{-}true)$

$$\langle\!\langle\, \alpha, (a, \eta_a, [r_{top}[b \Leftarrow_s m(v')]]), (b, \eta_b, [gs(true, a)]) \mid \mu \,\rangle\!\rangle \longmapsto$$
$$\langle\!\langle\, \alpha, (a, \eta_a, [r_{top}[b \Leftarrow_s m(v')]]), (b, \eta_b, [ret(v\, b\, v', a)]) \mid \mu \,\rangle\!\rangle$$

$(\Leftarrow_s\text{-}false)$ $\quad \langle\!\langle\, \alpha, (b, \eta_b, [gs(false, a)]) \mid \mu \,\rangle\!\rangle \longmapsto \langle\!\langle\, \alpha, (b, \eta_b, [I]) \mid \mu \,\rangle\!\rangle$

$(\Leftarrow_s\text{-}ret)$

$$\langle\!\langle\, \alpha, (a, \eta_a, [r_{top}[b \Leftarrow_s m(v')]]), (b, \eta_b, [ret(v'', a)]) \mid \mu \,\rangle\!\rangle \longmapsto$$
$$\langle\!\langle\, \alpha, (a, \eta_a, [r_{top}[v'']]), (b, \eta_b, [I]) \mid \mu \,\rangle\!\rangle$$

B Type and Effect System

Effects $\quad \epsilon ::= pure \mid impure \mid \epsilon_1 \vee \epsilon_2$

Types $\quad \tau ::= t \mid \tau_1 \xrightarrow{\epsilon} \tau_2 \mid pro\, t.R \mid bool \mid unit \mid int$

Rows $\quad R ::= r \mid \langle\rangle \mid \langle R \mid m : \tau \,\&\, \epsilon \rangle \mid \lambda t.\, R \mid R\tau$

Kinds $\quad kind ::= T \mid \kappa \qquad \kappa ::= \{\mathrm{m}\} \mid T \to \{\mathrm{m}\}$

Contexts $\quad \Gamma ::= \epsilon \mid \Gamma, x : \tau \mid \Gamma, t : T \mid \Gamma, r : \kappa \mid \Gamma, a : \tau$

Judgments $\quad \Gamma \vdash *$ well-formed context $\quad \Gamma \vdash e : \tau \,\&\, \epsilon$ term has type and effect
$\Gamma \vdash \tau : T$ well-formed type $\quad \Gamma \vdash R : \kappa$ row has kind

Rules for assigning types to terms

We present only the rules concerning objects. The complete set is in [DF96].

(*addr projection*)

$$\frac{\begin{array}{c}\Gamma \vdash * \\ a : \tau \in \Gamma\end{array}}{\Gamma \vdash a : \tau \ \&\ pure}$$

(*empty object*)

$$\frac{\Gamma \vdash *}{\Gamma \vdash \langle\rangle : prot.\langle\!\langle\rangle\!\rangle \ \&\ impure}$$

(*pro* $\Leftarrow_s$)

$$\frac{\begin{array}{c}\Gamma \vdash e_1 : \tau \ \&\ \epsilon_1 \\ \Gamma \vdash e_2 : [\tau/t]\tau_1 \ \&\ \epsilon_2\end{array}}{\Gamma \vdash e_1 \Leftarrow_s m(e_2) : [\tau/t]\tau_2 \ \&\ \epsilon_1 \vee \epsilon_2 \vee \epsilon' \vee \epsilon}$$

$$\text{where } \tau = prot.\langle\!\langle R \,|\, m : (\tau_1 \xrightarrow{\epsilon} \tau_2) \ \&\ \epsilon' \rangle\!\rangle$$

(*pro ext*)

$$\frac{\begin{array}{l}\Gamma \vdash e_1 : prot.\langle\!\langle R \,|\, \ell : \sigma \rangle\!\rangle \ \&\ \epsilon_1 \\ \Gamma, t : T \vdash R : \{\ell, m\} \\ \Gamma, r : T \to \{\ell, m\} \vdash e_2 : prot.\langle\!\langle rt \,|\, \ell : \sigma, m : (\tau_1 \xrightarrow{\epsilon} \tau_2) \ \&\ \epsilon' \rangle\!\rangle \xrightarrow{pure} bool \ \&\ pure \\ \Gamma, r : T \to \{\ell, m\} \vdash e_3 : [prot.\langle\!\langle rt \,|\, \ell : \sigma, m : (\tau_1 \xrightarrow{\epsilon} \tau_2) \ \&\ \epsilon' \rangle\!\rangle/t](t \xrightarrow{\epsilon'} \tau_1 \xrightarrow{\epsilon} \tau_2) \ \&\ \epsilon_3\end{array}}{\Gamma \vdash \langle e_1 \leftarrow\!\!+ m{=}when(e_2)e_3 \rangle : prot.\langle\!\langle R \,|\, \ell : \sigma, m : (\tau_1 \xrightarrow{\epsilon} \tau_2) \ \&\ \epsilon' \rangle\!\rangle \ \&\ impure}$$

(*pro ov*)

$$\frac{\begin{array}{l}\Gamma \vdash e_1 : prot.\langle\!\langle R \,|\, \ell : \sigma, m : (\tau_1 \xrightarrow{\epsilon} \tau_2) \ \&\ \epsilon' \rangle\!\rangle \ \&\ \epsilon_1 \\ \Gamma, r : T \to \{\ell, m\} \vdash e_2 : prot.\langle\!\langle rt \,|\, \ell : \sigma, m : (\tau_1 \to \tau_2) \ \&\ \epsilon' \rangle\!\rangle \xrightarrow{pure} bool \ \&\ pure \\ \Gamma, r : T \to \{\ell, m\} \vdash e_3 : [prot.\langle\!\langle rt \,|\, \ell : \sigma, m : (\tau_1 \xrightarrow{\epsilon} \tau_2) \ \&\ \epsilon' \rangle\!\rangle/t](t \xrightarrow{\epsilon'} \tau_1 \xrightarrow{\epsilon} \tau_2) \ \&\ \epsilon_3\end{array}}{\Gamma \vdash \langle e_1 \leftarrow m{=}when(e_2)e_3 \rangle : prot.\langle\!\langle R \,|\, \ell : \sigma, m : (\tau_1 \xrightarrow{\epsilon} \tau_2) \ \&\ \epsilon' \rangle\!\rangle \ \&\ impure}$$

Rules to assigning types to top level expressions.

(*exp gs*)

$$\frac{\begin{array}{c}\Gamma \vdash e : bool \ \&\ pure \\ \Gamma \vdash a : \tau \ \&\ pure\end{array}}{\Gamma \vdash gs(e, a) : unit \ \&\ pure}$$

(*exp ret*)

$$\frac{\begin{array}{c}\Gamma \vdash e : \tau_1 \ \&\ \epsilon \\ \Gamma \vdash a : \tau_2 \ \&\ pure\end{array}}{\Gamma \vdash ret(e, a) : unit \ \&\ \epsilon \vee pure}$$

(*exp ga*)

$$\frac{\begin{array}{c}\Gamma \vdash e : bool \ \&\ pure \\ \Gamma \vdash c : int \ \&\ pure\end{array}}{\Gamma \vdash ga(e, c) : unit \ \&\ pure}$$

(*exp nonret*)

$$\frac{\Gamma \vdash e : \tau \ \&\ \epsilon}{\Gamma \vdash nonret(e) : unit \ \&\ \epsilon}$$

Refinement in Interworkings

S. Mauw and M.A. Reniers

Department of Mathematics and Computing Science, Eindhoven University of Technology, P.O. Box 513, NL–5600 MB Eindhoven, The Netherlands.
sjouke@win.tue.nl, michelr@win.tue.nl

Abstract. Interworkings is a graphical language for displaying the interaction between system components. In this paper we give a formal semantics for Interworkings based on process algebra. A notion of refinement on Interworkings will be defined.

1 Introduction

The Interworking language (IW) is a graphical formalism for displaying the communication behaviour of system components. It was developed in order to support the informal diagrams used at Philips Kommunikations Industrie (Nürnberg) which were used for requirements specification and design.

One of the reasons for developing an explicit language was that it showed very hard to maintain a large collection of diagrams by hand. Several problems were encountered. First of all, manually drawing and updating large diagrams is an expensive activity. Secondly, diagrams that are linked to each other must be updated consistently. Therefore, consistency checks are needed. Thirdly, the relation between the diagrams in a collection is only implicit. Some diagrams describe successive behaviour of one part of the system, other diagrams define the concurrent behaviour of different parts of the system, while still others describe the same behaviour of the same part of the system, but from a different level of abstraction. Thus, diagrams may be a refinement of other diagrams. Finally, there existed different interpretations of the meaning of even simple Interworkings.

In order to solve above mentioned problems, a tool set was developed [10] and a formal semantics was proposed [9]. The semantics are given via a translation into process algebra [4, 3, 2].

The proposed semantics does not consider the notion of refinement between Interworkings. Furthermore, it has some minor shortcomings. The purpose of this paper is to extend and improve upon the semantics treated in [9] such that refinement can be defined. Thereto, we will extend the process algebra used and the bisimulation model. We will prove soundness and completeness of our theory and derive some useful properties.

The Interworking language is a member of a large class of similar graphical notations, most of which are only informally defined, such as Signal Sequence Charts, Use Cases, Information Flow Diagrams, Message Flow and Arrow Diagrams. Interworkings are similar to Message Sequence Charts [5], which are standardized by the International Telecommunication Union (ITU). The main difference is that Interworkings describe synchronous communication, whereas Message Sequence Charts describe asynchronous communication. The semantics of MSC as described in [7, 6] is also very similar to the semantics of IW.

This paper is organized as follows. In Sect. 2 we give a short introduction to the Interworking language and the Interworking operators. Section 3 contains a formal definition of the Interworking operators and several properties. Complete proofs can be found in [8]. The Interworking refinement is defined in Sect. 4.

Acknowledgements. We would like to thank Thijs Winter and Mark van Wijk for cooperating on a preliminary, although never published, version of Interworkings with refinement. Furthermore, we thank Jos Baeten, Twan Basten, Loe Feijs, Hans Mulder, Jan Gerben Wijnstra and the anonymous referees for their criticism.

2 Interworkings

In this section, we will explain the graphical Interworking language and two ways of composing Interworkings, namely the Interworking-sequencing and the Interworking-merge. Although Interworkings can also be expressed in a textual notation, we will not discuss this.

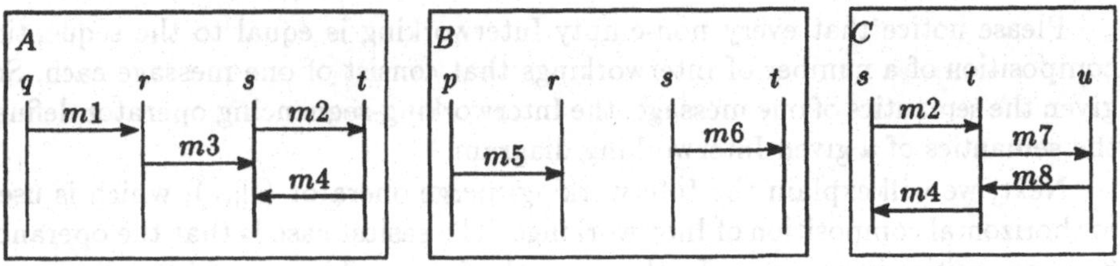

Fig. 1. Interworkings *A*, *B* and *C*

Figure 1 shows a collection of three Interworkings, named *A*, *B* and *C*. Interworking *C*, for instance, describes the communication between three entities, called *s*, *t* and *u*. Every entity is represented by a vertical axis. Along one axis, time runs from top to bottom, but there is no global time ordering assumed. Messages exchanged between entities are represented by arrows. The interpretation of Interworking *C* is simple: first *s* sends message *m*2 to *t*, then *t* sends *m*7 to *u*, next, *u* sends *m*8 to *t*, and finally *t* sends *m*4 to *s*. Due to the time ordering per entity axis, the messages in Interworking *C* are totally ordered.

Interworking *B* shows two unrelated messages *m*5 and *m*6. Although *m*6 is drawn above *m*5, they may occur in any order. In Interworking *A* messages *m*1 and $m2$ are not related, but they have to occur before $m3$, which in turn occurs before $m4$.

In practice, Interworking diagrams may become very large. Therefore, composition and decomposition techniques are introduced that help to keep the size of an Interworking manageable. For vertical composition of Interworkings we introduce the Interworking-sequencing operator ($\circ_{\mathrm{iw}}$). Applying this operator means that the operands are simply concatenated below each other, taking care that common entities are linked in the right way. Interworking D from Fig. 2 is simply the vertical composition of Interworkings A and B ($A \circ_{\mathrm{iw}} B$).

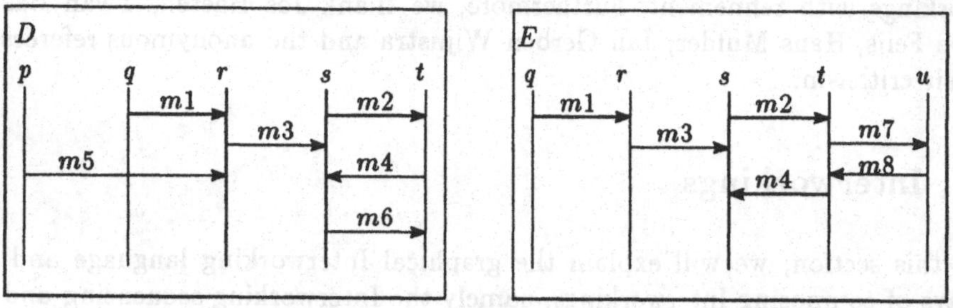

Fig. 2. Interworkings D ($= A \circ_{\mathrm{iw}} B$) and E ($= A \parallel_{\mathrm{iw}} C$)

Please notice that every non-empty Interworking is equal to the sequential composition of a number of Interworkings that consist of one message each. So, given the semantics of one message, the Interworking-sequencing operator defines the semantics of a given Interworking diagram.

Next, we will explain the Interworking-merge operator ($\parallel_{\mathrm{iw}}$), which is used for horizontal composition of Interworkings. The easiest case is that the operands have no entities in common. In this case, the Interworkings are simply put next to each other. In the case that the merged Interworkings have entities in common we will interpret this as an overlap between the Interworkings that should not be duplicated. The common entities of the operands are identified. Likewise, the messages between the common instances of the operands are identified.

Interworking E from Fig. 2 is the horizontal composition of the Interworkings A and C ($A \parallel_{\mathrm{iw}} C$). The common entities are s and t. Notice that the communication behaviour between s and t from A is exactly equal to the communication behaviour between s and t from C.

In case that the communication behaviour between the common entities is not equal for both operands, this is considered as an inconsistency. It indicates that in the description of a part of the system assumptions are made about another part of the system, which are not met.

Among other things, the tool set described in [10] can be used to compose Interworkings both horizontally and vertically. It will report all inconsistencies with respect to horizontal composition. The next section contains a formal treatment of Interworking-sequencing and Interworking-merge operators. The tools also support the refinement of Interworkings. This notion will be explained in Sect. 4.

3 Process Algebra for Interworkings

3.1 Basic Process Algebra with Deadlock and Empty Process

We will give a brief introduction to the process algebra $BPA_{\delta\varepsilon}(A)$ [2, 3]. This process algebra will be our starting point towards the more complex algebras which are introduced in the following sections. The parameter A of the process algebra represents the set of atomic actions. Besides the atomic actions from the set A, the process algebra has the additional constants δ and ε, which represent *deadlock* and the *empty process*, respectively. The process deadlock is incapable of executing any actions and can moreover not terminate successfully. The empty process can also execute no actions, but it terminates successfully. The set of the atomic actions and the deadlock constant is denoted by A_δ.

From these constants more complex processes can be built by using the operators $+$ and $\cdot$. The $+$ is called ***alternative composition*** and $\cdot$ is called ***sequential composition***. The process $x + y$ can execute either process x or process y, but not both. The process $x \cdot y$ starts executing process x, and upon termination thereof starts the execution of process y. These operators are axiomatized by the axioms from Table 1. In these axioms the variables x, y and z denote arbitrary processes. In order to reduce the number of brackets in processes we have the following priorities on operators: $\cdot$ binds stronger than all other operators and $+$ binds weaker than all other operators.

Table 1. Axioms of $BPA_{\delta\varepsilon}(A)$

$x + y = y + x$	$\delta + x = x$
$(x + y) + z = x + (y + z)$	$\delta \cdot x = \delta$
$x + x = x$	$x \cdot \varepsilon = x$
$(x + y) \cdot z = x \cdot z + y \cdot z$	$\varepsilon \cdot x = x$
$(x \cdot y) \cdot z = x \cdot (y \cdot z)$	

To the process algebra $BPA_{\delta\varepsilon}(A)$ we associate a structured operational semantics in the form of the term deduction system $T(BPA_{\delta\varepsilon}(A))$ in Table 2. For the deduction rules in this table we require that $a \in A$ and that x, y, and z are arbitrary processes. A deduction rule is of the form $\frac{H}{C}$ where H is a set of ***hypotheses*** and C is the ***conclusion***. The formula $x \xrightarrow{a} x'$ expresses that the process x can perform an action a and thereby evolves into the process x'. The

Table 2. Structured operational semantics of $BPA_{\delta\varepsilon}(A)$ $(a \in A)$

$$\frac{}{\varepsilon\downarrow} \qquad \frac{x\downarrow}{x+y\downarrow} \qquad \frac{y\downarrow}{x+y\downarrow} \qquad \frac{x\downarrow, y\downarrow}{x\cdot y\downarrow}$$

$$\frac{}{a \xrightarrow{a} \varepsilon} \qquad \frac{x \xrightarrow{a} x'}{x+y \xrightarrow{a} x'} \qquad \frac{y \xrightarrow{a} y'}{x+y \xrightarrow{a} y'} \qquad \frac{x \xrightarrow{a} x'}{x\cdot y \xrightarrow{a} x'\cdot y} \qquad \frac{x\downarrow, y \xrightarrow{a} y'}{x\cdot y \xrightarrow{a} y'}$$

formula $x\downarrow$ expresses that process x has an option to terminate immediately and successfully. For a formal definition of term deduction systems we refer to [2].

Definition 1 (Bisimulation). A symmetric relation R on closed $BPA_{\delta\varepsilon}(A)$ terms is a *bisimulation relation*, if and only if, for every pair $(p,q) \in R$ and $a \in A$, the following conditions hold:

1. if $p \xrightarrow{a} p'$, then there exists a closed $BPA_{\delta\varepsilon}(A)$ term q' such that $q \xrightarrow{a} q'$ and $(p',q') \in R$,
2. if $p\downarrow$, then $q\downarrow$.

The closed $BPA_{\delta\varepsilon}(A)$ terms x and y are *bisimilar*, notation $x \leftrightarrow y$, if and only if there exists a bisimulation relation R relating them.

Finally, we would like to mention the following well-known result from literature, e.g. [3]. The process algebra $BPA_{\delta\varepsilon}(A)$ is a sound and complete axiomatization of bisimulation equivalence on closed $BPA_{\delta\varepsilon}(A)$ terms. This result will be used in the following sections when relating the extended process algebras to $BPA_{\delta\varepsilon}(A)$.

3.2 Interworking-sequencing and Interworking-merge

In this section, we will extend the process algebra $BPA_{\delta\varepsilon}(A)$ from the previous section. First, we will instantiate the parameter A of $BPA_{\delta\varepsilon}(A)$ by the actual atomic actions occurring in Interworkings. Next, we define the Interworking-sequencing operator $\circ_{\mathrm{iw}}$, and the E-Interworking merge operator $\|_{\mathrm{iw}}^{E}$. We will extend the process descriptions with sets of entities and call them entity-labeled processes. Finally, we define the Interworking-merge on these extended processes.

The Entity Function and the Interworking-sequencing. In an Interworking diagram there are two types of objects: entities and messages. Entities come from a set *EID* and messages from a set *MID*. We use $c(i,j,m)$ to denote the sending of message m from entity i to entity j. Thus, parameter A from $BPA_{\delta\varepsilon}(A)$ will be instantiated by $\{c(i,j,m) \mid i,j \in EID, m \in MID\}$.

We want to determine for each process description which entities are actively involved in it. Thereto, we define the entity function E (see Table 3).

Table 3. Active entities of an Interworking ($i, j \in EID$, $m \in MID$, $a \in A$)

$E(\varepsilon)$	$= \emptyset$	$E(a \cdot x)$	$= E(a) \cup E(x)$
$E(\delta)$	$= \emptyset$	$E(x + y)$	$= E(x) \cup E(y)$
$E(c(i, j, m))$	$= \{i, j\}$		

The Interworking-sequencing of two processes x and y ($x \circ_{\mathrm{w}} y$) is their parallel execution with the restriction that the right-hand process may execute an action only if the entities of that action are disjoint from the entities of the left-hand process. The Interworking-sequencing operator is similar to the ***weak sequential composition*** operator from [11].

The axiomatization of $\circ_{\mathrm{w}}$ is basically the one presented in [9], but extended with axioms for the empty process (see Table 4). We use the two auxiliary operators $\mathbf{L}\circ_{\mathrm{w}}$ and $\mathbf{R}\circ_{\mathrm{w}}$. The process $x \, \mathbf{L}\circ_{\mathrm{w}} \, y$ behaves like the process $x \circ_{\mathrm{w}} y$ with the restriction that the first action to be executed must originate from process x. The process $x \, \mathbf{R}\circ_{\mathrm{w}} \, y$ also behaves like the process $x \circ_{\mathrm{w}} y$ but this time with the restriction that the first action to be executed must be from process y. In this case, the first action from y can only be executed if it is not blocked by any of the actions from x. The operator $\surd$ is used to obtain a proper treatment of the empty process (i.e., we want $\varepsilon \circ_{\mathrm{w}} \varepsilon = \varepsilon$).

Table 4. Axioms of Interworking-sequencing ($a \in A_\delta$)

$x \circ_{\mathrm{w}} y$	$= x \, \mathbf{L}\circ_{\mathrm{w}} \, y + x \, \mathbf{R}\circ_{\mathrm{w}} \, y + \surd(x) \cdot \surd(y)$	
$\varepsilon \, \mathbf{L}\circ_{\mathrm{w}} \, x$	$= \delta$	
$a \cdot x \, \mathbf{L}\circ_{\mathrm{w}} \, y$	$= a \cdot (x \circ_{\mathrm{w}} y)$	
$(x + y) \, \mathbf{L}\circ_{\mathrm{w}} \, z$	$= x \, \mathbf{L}\circ_{\mathrm{w}} \, z + y \, \mathbf{L}\circ_{\mathrm{w}} \, z$	
$x \, \mathbf{R}\circ_{\mathrm{w}} \, \varepsilon$	$= \delta$	
$x \, \mathbf{R}\circ_{\mathrm{w}} \, a \cdot y$	$= a \cdot (x \circ_{\mathrm{w}} y)$	if $E(a) \cap E(x) = \emptyset$
$x \, \mathbf{R}\circ_{\mathrm{w}} \, a \cdot y$	$= \delta$	if $E(a) \cap E(x) \neq \emptyset$
$x \, \mathbf{R}\circ_{\mathrm{w}} \, (y + z)$	$= x \, \mathbf{R}\circ_{\mathrm{w}} \, y + x \, \mathbf{R}\circ_{\mathrm{w}} \, z$	
$\surd(\varepsilon)$	$= \varepsilon$	
$\surd(a \cdot x)$	$= \delta$	
$\surd(x + y)$	$= \surd(x) + \surd(y)$	

The structured operational semantics of the Interworking-sequencing and the auxiliary operators is given in Table 5.

The E-Interworking Merge. The axiomatization of the S-Interworking merge as presented in [9] uses the auxiliary operators left S-Interworking merge $\lfloor\!\lfloor^{S}_{\mathrm{iw}}$ and synchronization Interworking-merge $|^{S}_{\mathrm{iw}}$ with S a set of atomic actions. We

Table 5. Structured operational semantics of Interworking-sequencing ($a \in A$)

$$\frac{x\downarrow,\ y\downarrow}{x \circ_{\mathrm{iw}} y \downarrow} \qquad \frac{x \xrightarrow{a} x'}{x \circ_{\mathrm{iw}} y \xrightarrow{a} x' \circ_{\mathrm{iw}} y} \qquad \frac{y \xrightarrow{a} y',\ E(a) \cap E(x) = \emptyset}{x \circ_{\mathrm{iw}} y \xrightarrow{a} x \circ_{\mathrm{iw}} y'}$$

$$\frac{x\downarrow}{\surd(x)\downarrow} \qquad \frac{x \xrightarrow{a} x'}{x \,\mathbf{L}\!\circ_{\mathrm{iw}} y \xrightarrow{a} x' \circ_{\mathrm{iw}} y} \qquad \frac{y \xrightarrow{a} y',\ E(a) \cap E(x) = \emptyset}{x \,\mathbf{R}\!\circ_{\mathrm{iw}} y \xrightarrow{a} x \circ_{\mathrm{iw}} y'}$$

will use similar auxiliary operators only now labeled with a set of entities instead of a set of atomic actions. This set represents the entities on which communication actions must synchronize. The process $x \parallel^E_{\mathrm{iw}} y$ is the parallel execution of the processes x and y with the restriction that the processes must synchronize on all atomic actions which are defined on entities from the set E. The process $x \mathbin{|\!\!\lfloor}^E_{\mathrm{iw}} y$ behaves like the process $x \parallel^E_{\mathrm{iw}} y$ with the restriction that the first action must come from process x and that action cannot synchronize with an action from y. The process $x \mid^E_{\mathrm{iw}} y$ behaves as the process $x \parallel^E_{\mathrm{iw}} y$ with the restriction that the first action to be executed must be a synchronization. Again we will use the termination operator $\surd$ to make sure that the E-Interworking merge behaves correctly for empty processes (Interworkings), i.e., $\varepsilon \parallel^E_{\mathrm{iw}} \varepsilon = \varepsilon$ for all $E \subseteq EID$. The definition of the E-Interworking merge operator is given in Table 6. Recall that the axioms for the termination operator are given in Table 4.

Table 6. Axioms of E-Interworking merge ($a, b \in A_\delta$)

$x \parallel^E_{\mathrm{iw}} y$	$= x \mathbin{|\!\!\lfloor}^E_{\mathrm{iw}} y + y \mathbin{|\!\!\lfloor}^E_{\mathrm{iw}} x + x \mid^E_{\mathrm{iw}} y + \surd(x) \cdot \surd(y)$	
$\varepsilon \mathbin{|\!\!\lfloor}^E_{\mathrm{iw}} x$	$= \delta$	
$a \cdot x \mathbin{|\!\!\lfloor}^E_{\mathrm{iw}} y$	$= a \cdot (x \parallel^E_{\mathrm{iw}} y)$	if $E(a) \not\subseteq E$
$a \cdot x \mathbin{|\!\!\lfloor}^E_{\mathrm{iw}} y$	$= \delta$	if $E(a) \subseteq E$
$(x + y) \mathbin{|\!\!\lfloor}^E_{\mathrm{iw}} z$	$= x \mathbin{|\!\!\lfloor}^E_{\mathrm{iw}} z + y \mathbin{|\!\!\lfloor}^E_{\mathrm{iw}} z$	
$\varepsilon \mid^E_{\mathrm{iw}} x$	$= \delta$	
$x \mid^E_{\mathrm{iw}} \varepsilon$	$= \delta$	
$a \cdot x \mid^E_{\mathrm{iw}} b \cdot y$	$= a \cdot (x \parallel^E_{\mathrm{iw}} y)$	if $a \equiv b \wedge E(a) \subseteq E$
$a \cdot x \mid^E_{\mathrm{iw}} b \cdot y$	$= \delta$	if $a \not\equiv b \vee E(a) \not\subseteq E$
$(x + y) \mid^E_{\mathrm{iw}} z$	$= x \mid^E_{\mathrm{iw}} z + y \mid^E_{\mathrm{iw}} z$	
$x \mid^E_{\mathrm{iw}} (y + z)$	$= x \mid^E_{\mathrm{iw}} y + x \mid^E_{\mathrm{iw}} z$	

Table 7 presents the structured operational semantics of the E-Interworking merge and the auxiliary operators introduced. The process algebra consisting of all operators and axioms introduced so far is called IW_ε. The term deduction system $T(IW_\varepsilon)$ consists of the deduction rules of Tables 2, 5 and 7.

Table 7. Structured operational semantics of E-Interworking merge ($a \in A$)

$\dfrac{x\downarrow, y\downarrow}{x \parallel^{E}_{\mathrm{iw}} y \downarrow}$	$\dfrac{x \xrightarrow{a} x', y \xrightarrow{a} y', E(a) \subseteq E}{x \parallel^{E}_{\mathrm{iw}} y \xrightarrow{a} x' \parallel^{E}_{\mathrm{iw}} y'}$	$\dfrac{x \xrightarrow{a} x', E(a) \not\subseteq E}{x \parallel^{E}_{\mathrm{iw}} y \xrightarrow{a} x' \parallel^{E}_{\mathrm{iw}} y}$
$\dfrac{y \xrightarrow{a} y', E(a) \not\subseteq E}{x \parallel^{E}_{\mathrm{iw}} y \xrightarrow{a} x \parallel^{E}_{\mathrm{iw}} y'}$	$\dfrac{x \xrightarrow{a} x', E(a) \not\subseteq E}{x \,⌊\!⌊^{E}_{\mathrm{iw}}\, y \xrightarrow{a} x' \parallel^{E}_{\mathrm{iw}} y}$	$\dfrac{x \xrightarrow{a} x', y \xrightarrow{a} y', E(a) \subseteq E}{x \mid^{E}_{\mathrm{iw}} y \xrightarrow{a} x' \parallel^{E}_{\mathrm{iw}} y'}$

It turns out that bisimulation equivalence is a congruence for the function symbols in the signature of IW_ε. Furthermore, IW_ε is a sound and complete axiomatization of bisimulation equivalence on closed IW_ε terms. In [8] these results are proven in more detail. These proofs are based on the meta-theory presented in [2, 12].

The Interworking-merge. Now that we have given the axioms and structured operational semantics of the E-Interworking merge we will define the Interworking-merge operator. The Interworking-merge of two processes is their parallel execution with the restriction that the processes must synchronize on all atomic actions which are defined on the common entities of the processes. For the Interworking-merge operator it is necessary to determine the common entities of the operands. The entities of an operand cannot be obtained from the process term representing it (as was done in [9]), since empty entities are not represented in the process term. Therefore, we label every process term by a set of entity names over *EID*. For an Interworking x, this set represents the entities of the Interworking (including the empty entities). An Interworking with a dynamical behaviour denoted by x over the entities from E is denoted by $\langle x, E\rangle$. Such a tuple $\langle x, E\rangle$ will be called an entity-labeled process.

On entity-labeled processes we define the operators Interworking-sequencing and Interworking-merge. The set of all entity-labeled processes is called *LP*. The definition of the Interworking-sequencing on entity-labeled processes is straightforward. As was done in [9] the Interworking-merge is expressed in terms of the E-Interworking merge operator and the common entities of the operands. Technically speaking, we can axiomatize the Interworking-merge without using the E-Interworking merge. But, to stay as close as possible to the existing axiomatization of the Interworking-merge, we use the E-Interworking merge. The axioms for entity-labeled processes are given in Table 8 for $E, F \subseteq EID$. The extension of IW_ε with entity-labeled processes is denoted by IWE_ε.

Next, we define a structured operational semantics of entity-labeled processes. In order to make a clear distinction between the transition relation and termination predicate on non-labeled processes and on entity-labeled processes,

Table 8. Axioms of entity-labeled processes

$\langle x, E\rangle \mathbin{q_{\mathrm{w}}} \langle y, F\rangle = \langle x \mathbin{q_{\mathrm{w}}} y, E \cup F\rangle$	$\langle x, E\rangle \parallel_{\mathrm{iw}} \langle y, F\rangle = \langle x \parallel_{\mathrm{iw}}^{E\cap F} y, E \cup F\rangle$

we denote the latter by $\overset{a}{\Rrightarrow}$ and $\Downarrow$, respectively. The structured operational semantics of entity-labeled processes is related directly to the structured operational semantics of non-labeled processes as expressed in Table 9 (s, t represent entity-labeled processes). Thereto, two auxiliary functions π_{p} and π_{e} are introduced for entity-labeled processes. Intuitively, $\pi_{\mathrm{p}}(s)$ denotes the process-part of s, and $\pi_{\mathrm{e}}(s)$ denotes the entity-part of s.

Table 9. Structured operational semantics of entity-labeled processes ($a \in A$)

$\pi_{\mathrm{p}}(\langle x, E\rangle) = x$	$\pi_{\mathrm{e}}(\langle x, E\rangle) = E$
$\pi_{\mathrm{p}}(s \mathbin{q_{\mathrm{w}}} t) = \pi_{\mathrm{p}}(s) \mathbin{q_{\mathrm{w}}} \pi_{\mathrm{p}}(t)$	$\pi_{\mathrm{e}}(s \mathbin{q_{\mathrm{w}}} t) = \pi_{\mathrm{e}}(s) \cup \pi_{\mathrm{e}}(t)$
$\pi_{\mathrm{p}}(s \parallel_{\mathrm{iw}} t) = \pi_{\mathrm{p}}(s) \parallel_{\mathrm{iw}}^{\pi_{\mathrm{e}}(s)\cap\pi_{\mathrm{e}}(t)} \pi_{\mathrm{p}}(t)$	$\pi_{\mathrm{e}}(s \parallel_{\mathrm{iw}} t) = \pi_{\mathrm{e}}(s) \cup \pi_{\mathrm{e}}(t)$

$$\frac{\pi_{\mathrm{p}}(s) \xrightarrow{a} y}{s \overset{a}{\Rrightarrow} \langle y, \pi_{\mathrm{e}}(s)\rangle} \qquad \frac{\pi_{\mathrm{p}}(s)\downarrow}{s \Downarrow}$$

Definition 2 (Entity bisimulation). A symmetric relation R on closed *LP* terms is an ***entity bisimulation relation***, if and only if, for every pair $(s, t) \in R$ and $a \in A$, the following conditions hold:

1. if $s \overset{a}{\Rrightarrow} s'$, then there is a closed *LP* term t' such that $t \overset{a}{\Rrightarrow} t'$ and $(s', t') \in R$,
2. if $s \Downarrow$, then $t \Downarrow$,
3. $\pi_{\mathrm{e}}(s) = \pi_{\mathrm{e}}(t)$.

The closed *LP* terms s and t are ***entity bisimilar***, notation $s \underline{\leftrightsquigarrow} t$, if and only if there exists an entity bisimulation relation R relating them.

It is also possible to define entity bisimulation in terms of bisimulation of the process-parts and set equality of the entity-parts.

Lemma 3. *For closed LP terms s and t we have*

$$s \underline{\leftrightsquigarrow} t \quad \text{iff} \quad \pi_{\mathrm{p}}(s) \underline{\leftrightarrow} \pi_{\mathrm{p}}(t) \text{ and } \pi_{\mathrm{e}}(s) = \pi_{\mathrm{e}}(t) \tag{1}$$

Proof. Suppose that $s \underline{\leftrightsquigarrow} t$. Then there exists an entity bisimulation relation R on closed *LP* terms that relates s and t. Then the relation $R' = \{(\pi_{\mathrm{p}}(p), \pi_{\mathrm{p}}(q)) \mid (p, q) \in R\}$ is a bisimulation relating $\pi_{\mathrm{p}}(s)$ and $\pi_{\mathrm{p}}(t)$. From the definition of entity bisimulation we also obtain $\pi_{\mathrm{e}}(s) = \pi_{\mathrm{e}}(t)$.

Next, suppose that $\pi_p(s) \leftrightarrow \pi_p(t)$ and $\pi_e(s) = \pi_e(t)$. Then there exists a bisimulation relation R that relates $\pi_p(s)$ and $\pi_p(t)$. Then the relation $R' = \{(\langle p, E\rangle, \langle q, E\rangle) \mid (p, q) \in R, E \subseteq EID\}$ is an entity bisimulation relating s and t. Hence, $s \leftrightsquigarrow t$. □

Theorem 4 (Congruence). ***Entity bisimulation equivalence is a congruence for the function symbols in the signature of*** IWE_ε ***which are defined on LP terms.***

Proof. Suppose $s_1 \leftrightsquigarrow s_2$ and $t_1 \leftrightsquigarrow t_2$. By Lemma 3 we have (1) $\pi_p(s_1) \leftrightarrow \pi_p(s_2)$, (2) $\pi_e(s_1) = \pi_e(s_2)$, (3) $\pi_p(t_1) \leftrightarrow \pi_p(t_2)$, and (4) $\pi_e(t_1) = \pi_e(t_2)$.

From (1) and (3) and the fact that $\leftrightarrow$ is a congruence for $\triangleleft_w$ on closed IW_ε terms, it follows that $\pi_p(s_1 \triangleleft_w t_1) = \pi_p(s_1) \triangleleft_w \pi_p(t_1) \leftrightarrow \pi_p(s_2) \triangleleft_w \pi_p(t_2) = \pi_p(s_2 \triangleleft_w t_2)$. From (2) and (4) we obtain $\pi_e(s_1 \triangleleft_w t_1) = \pi_e(s_1) \cup \pi_e(t_1) = \pi_e(s_2) \cup \pi_e(t_2) = \pi_e(s_2 \triangleleft_w t_2)$. Hence, by Lemma 3, $s_1 \triangleleft_w t_1 \leftrightsquigarrow s_2 \triangleleft_w t_2$.

From (2) and (4) we have that $\pi_e(s_1) \cap \pi_e(t_1) = \pi_e(s_2) \cap \pi_e(t_2)$. From (1) and (3) and the fact that $\leftrightarrow$ is a congruence for $\|_{iw}^{E}$ on closed IW_ε terms, it follows that $\pi_p(s_1 \|_{iw} t_1) = \pi_p(s_1) \|_{iw}^{\pi_e(s_1) \cap \pi_e(t_1)} \pi_p(t_1) \leftrightarrow \pi_p(s_2) \|_{iw}^{\pi_e(s_2) \cap \pi_e(t_2)} \pi_p(t_2) = \pi_p(s_2 \|_{iw} t_2)$. From (2) and (4) we obtain that $\pi_e(s_1 \|_{iw} t_1) = \pi_e(s_1) \cup \pi_e(t_1) = \pi_e(s_2) \cup \pi_e(t_2) = \pi_e(s_2 \|_{iw} t_2)$. Hence, by Lemma 3, $s_1 \|_{iw} t_1 \leftrightsquigarrow s_2 \|_{iw} t_2$. □

Theorem 5 (Soundness). ***The process algebra*** IWE_ε ***is a sound axiomatization of bisimulation equivalence on closed*** IW_ε ***terms. The process algebra*** IWE_ε ***is a sound axiomatization of entity bisimulation on closed LP terms.***

Proof. For the first proposition observe that we did not add any axioms relating closed IW_ε terms. We will prove the second proposition. Since entity bisimulation is a congruence for the closed terms of *LP* (Theorem 4) we only have to show that the axioms from Table 8 are sound. Thereto, we provide a bisimulation relation for each axiom. For both axioms relate the left-hand side to the right-hand side and additionally relate each term to itself. □

Theorem 6 (Conservativity). ***The process algebra*** IWE_ε ***is a conservative extension of the process algebra*** IW_ε***.***

Proof. The proof of this theorem uses the approach of [12]. The conservativity follows from the following observations:

1. bisimulation is definable in terms of predicate and relation symbols only,
2. IW_ε is a complete axiomatization of bisimulation on closed IW_ε terms,
3. IWE_ε is a sound axiomatization of bisimulation on closed IW_ε terms (see Theorem 5),
4. $T(IW_\varepsilon)$ is pure, well-founded and in path format, and
5. $T(IWE_\varepsilon)$ is in path format. □

Definition 7 (Basic terms). *Basic LP terms* are defined inductively by:

1. if x is a closed IW_ε term and $E \subseteq EID$, then $\langle x, E\rangle$ is a basic *LP* term
2. no other closed *LP* terms are basic *LP* terms

Theorem 8 (Elimination). *For every closed LP term s there exists a basic LP term t such that $IWE_\varepsilon \vdash s = t$.*

Proof. This theorem is proven with induction on the structure of a closed *LP* term. First, consider the case $s \equiv \langle x, E\rangle$ (x a closed IW_ε term and $E \subseteq EID$). Then s is a basic *LP* term. Next, consider the case $s \equiv s_1 \,\varsigma_{\rm w}\, s_2$ (s_1, s_2 closed *LP* terms). Then we have by induction that there exist basic *LP* terms t_1, t_2 such that $s_1 = t_1$ and $s_2 = t_2$. From the definition of basic *LP* terms we then also have the existence of closed IW_ε terms x_1, x_2 and $E_1, E_2 \subseteq EID$ such that $t_1 \equiv \langle x_1, E_1\rangle$ and $t_2 \equiv \langle x_2, E_2\rangle$. Then we derive $s \equiv s_1 \,\varsigma_{\rm w}\, s_2 = t_1 \,\varsigma_{\rm w}\, t_2 \equiv \langle x_1, E_1\rangle \,\varsigma_{\rm w}\, \langle x_2, E_2\rangle = \langle x_1 \,\varsigma_{\rm w}\, x_2, E_1 \cup E_2\rangle$ which is a basic *LP* term. Finally, consider the case $s \equiv s_1 \,\|_{\rm iw}\, s_2$ (s_2, s_2 closed *LP* terms). Again by induction and the definition of basic *LP* terms, we have the existence of closed IW_ε terms x_1, x_2 and $E_1, E_2 \subseteq EID$ such that $s_1 = \langle x_1, E_1\rangle$ and $s_2 = \langle x_2, E_2\rangle$. Then we derive $s \equiv s_1 \,\|_{\rm iw}\, s_2 = \langle x_1, E_1\rangle \,\|_{\rm iw}\, \langle x_2, E_2\rangle = \langle x_1 \,\|_{\rm iw}^{E_1 \cap E_2}\, x_2, E_1 \cup E_2\rangle$ which is a basic *LP* term. □

Theorem 9 (Completeness). *The process algebra IWE_ε is a complete axiomatization of entity bisimulation on closed LP terms.*

Proof. By the elimination theorem (Theorem 8) we only have to prove this theorem for basic *LP* terms. Let $\langle x, E_1\rangle$ and $\langle y, E_2\rangle$ be basic *LP* terms such that $\langle x, E_1\rangle \,\underline{\leftrightsquigarrow}\, \langle y, E_2\rangle$. By Lemma 3 we have $x \,\underline{\leftrightarrow}\, y$ and $E_1 = E_2$. Since IW_ε is a complete axiomatization of bisimulation equivalence on closed IW_ε terms, we have $x = y$, and hence $\langle x, E_1\rangle = \langle y, E_2\rangle$. □

The proofs of the following properties can be found in [8]. The Interworking-sequencing is commutative under the assumption that the active entities of the operands are disjoint. Furthermore, it is associative. The Interworking-merge is both commutative and associative. The Interworking-merge as defined in [9] did not have the associativity property. This difference is a direct consequence of our decision to maintain the entities of an Interworking statically.

Proposition 10 (Commutativity of $\varsigma_{\rm w}$ and $\|_{\rm iw}$). *For closed IW_ε terms x, y, closed LP terms s, t and a set of entities E we have*

$$x \,\varsigma_{\rm w}\, y = y \,\varsigma_{\rm w}\, x \quad \text{if } E(x) \cap E(y) = \emptyset \tag{2}$$

$$s \,\varsigma_{\rm w}\, t = t \,\varsigma_{\rm w}\, s \quad \text{if } E(\pi_{\rm p}(s)) \cap E(\pi_{\rm p}(t)) = \emptyset \tag{3}$$

$$x \,\|_{\rm iw}^{E}\, y = y \,\|_{\rm iw}^{E}\, x \tag{4}$$

$$s \,\|_{\rm iw}\, t = t \,\|_{\rm iw}\, s \tag{5}$$

Proposition 11 (Associativity of $\varsigma_{\rm w}$ and $\|_{\rm iw}$). *For closed IW_ε terms x, y, z, closed LP terms s, t, u and sets of entities E_1, E_2, E_3 we have*

$$(x \,\varsigma_{\rm w}\, y) \,\varsigma_{\rm w}\, z = x \,\varsigma_{\rm w}\, (y \,\varsigma_{\rm w}\, z) \tag{6}$$

$$(s \,\varsigma_{\rm w}\, t) \,\varsigma_{\rm w}\, u = s \,\varsigma_{\rm w}\, (t \,\varsigma_{\rm w}\, u) \tag{7}$$

$$(x \,\|_{\rm iw}^{E_1 \cap E_2}\, y) \,\|_{\rm iw}^{(E_1 \cup E_2) \cap E_3}\, z = x \,\|_{\rm iw}^{E_1 \cap (E_2 \cup E_3)}\, (y \,\|_{\rm iw}^{E_2 \cap E_3}\, z) \tag{8}$$

$$(s \,\|_{\rm iw}\, t) \,\|_{\rm iw}\, u = s \,\|_{\rm iw}\, (t \,\|_{\rm iw}\, u) \tag{9}$$

4 Algebraic Definition of Interworking Refinement

Interworking refinement is the replacement of one entity by a number of entities such that the behaviour of the refining Interworking is identical, in a sense to be made precise shortly, to the original Interworking. It is used for enabling a top-down design strategy. In this way, a system can be viewed from the right level of abstraction. Figure 3 shows an example of such a refinement. Interworking A is a refinement of Interworking B, because A contains entities $q1$ and $q2$ that refine the bahaviour of entity q from B.

The relation between the entities in both Interworkings is given by a partial mapping $f : EID \hookrightarrow EID$ from entities to entities. An entity e from $rng(f)$ is refined by the set of all entities e' satisfying $f(e') = e$. If Interworking s is an f-refinement of Interworking t, i.e., s refines t with respect to the entity mapping f, we denote this by $s \sqsubseteq_f t$. The mapping f is partial in order to distinguish between an entity p which is not refined at all ($p \notin rng(f)$) and an entity p which is refined by (amongst others) an entity p ($f(p) = p$).

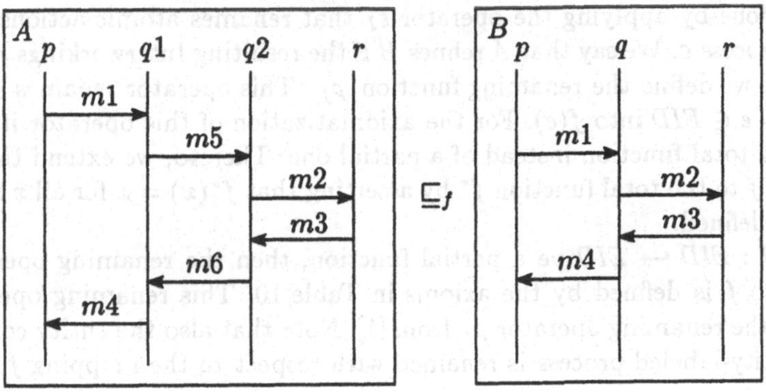

Fig. 3. Interworking refinement ($f(q1) = f(q2) = q$)

The intuition is that the external behaviour of a single entity within the Interworking t can be refined into, or implemented by, the collective behaviour of a number of entities within the Interworking s. Besides the singular refinement discussed above, it is also allowed to consider a number of refinements at the same time. An example of such a multiple refinement is given in Fig. 4. The entity p is refined by the entities $p1$ and $p2$, and the entity q is refined by the entities $q1$ and $q2$.

In the following, we will give the formal definitions involved with Interworking refinement. The operational view basic to the definition of $A \sqsubseteq_f B$ is as follows (see Fig. 3). First, we rename all refining entities of A (i.e. $q1$ and $q2$) that occur in messages of A into the refined entity q. For this purpose, we will define the

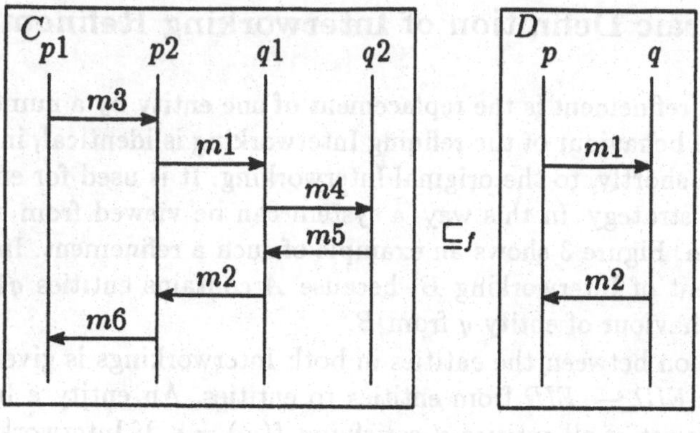

Fig. 4. Multiple refinement ($f(p1) = f(p2) = p$, $f(q1) = f(q2) = q$)

renaming function ρ_f. After this step, all messages between entities $q1$ and $q2$ will become message that are internal to entity q. Now, we remove all these internal messages from the renamed Interworking A and from Interworking B. This is done by applying the operator ε_I that renames atomic actions into the empty process ε. We say that A refines B if the resulting Interworkings are equal,

First, we define the renaming function ρ_f. This operator renames all occurrences of $e \in EID$ into $f(e)$. For the axiomatization of this operator it is easier to have a total function instead of a partial one. Thereto, we extend the partial function f to the total function f^* by asserting that $f^*(x) = x$ for all x for which f is not defined.

Let $f : EID \hookrightarrow EID$ be a partial function, then the renaming operator ρ_f related to f is defined by the axioms in Table 10. This renaming operator resembles the renaming operator ρ_f from [1]. Note that also the entity component of an entity-labeled process is renamed with respect to the mapping f.

Table 10. Entity renaming function on processes ($a \in A$, $i, j \in EID$, $m \in MID$)

$\rho_f(\varepsilon)$	$= \varepsilon$	$\rho_f(a \cdot x)$	$= \rho_f(a) \cdot \rho_f(x)$
$\rho_f(\delta)$	$= \delta$	$\rho_f(x + y)$	$= \rho_f(x) + \rho_f(y)$
$\rho_f(c(i,j,m))$	$= c(f^*(i), f^*(j), m)$	$\rho_f(\langle x, E\rangle)$	$= \langle \rho_f(x), \{f^*(e) \mid e \in E\}\rangle$

Let E be a set of entities. Then the set of all internal actions with respect to the entities from E, notation $Int(E)$, is defined as follows:

$$Int(E) = \{c(i,i,m) \mid i \in EID, m \in MID\} \tag{10}$$

Let I be a set of atomic actions, then we can define the operator ε_I (see [13]) that renames atomic actions from I into ε as in Table 11.

Table 11. Renaming atomic actions into ε ($I \subseteq A$, $a \in A_\delta$)

$\varepsilon_I(\varepsilon) = \varepsilon$		$\varepsilon_I(x+y) = \varepsilon_I(x) + \varepsilon_I(y)$	
$\varepsilon_I(a \cdot x) = \varepsilon_I(x)$	if $a \in I$	$\varepsilon_I(\langle x, E\rangle) = \langle \varepsilon_I(x), E\rangle$	
$\varepsilon_I(a \cdot x) = a \cdot \varepsilon_I(x)$	if $a \notin I$		

Let $f : EID \hookrightarrow EID$ be a refinement mapping, the f-refinement relation on entity-labeled processes is then defined as follows:

$$s \sqsubseteq_f t \quad \text{iff} \quad \varepsilon_{Int(rng(f))}(\rho_f(s)) = \varepsilon_{Int(rng(f))}(t) \tag{11}$$

Next, we extend this notion of refinement with a fixed mapping to a notion of refinement which abstracts from this mapping. This is called *entity refinement*. Interworking s is an entity refinement of Interworking t, notation $s \sqsubseteq t$ if and only if there exists a refinement mapping f such that $s \sqsubseteq_f t$. This is formally expressed as follows:

$$s \sqsubseteq t \quad \text{iff} \quad \exists_{f:EID \hookrightarrow EID} \; s \sqsubseteq_f t \tag{12}$$

Example 1. As an illustration of this algebraic definition of refinement, the refinement relation between the Interworkings in Fig. 4 is computed. Semantically the Interworkings are represented by

$$C = \langle c(p1,p2,m3) \circ_w c(p2,q1,m1) \circ_w c(q1,q2,m4) \circ_w c(q2,q1,m5) \\ \circ_w c(q1,p2,m2) \circ_w c(p2,p1,m6), \{p_1,p_2,q_1,q_2\}\rangle \tag{13}$$

$$D = \langle c(p,q,m1) \circ_w c(q,p,m2), \{p,q\}\rangle \tag{14}$$

Elimination of the $\circ_w$ yields the following equations

$$C = \langle c(p1,p2,m3) \cdot c(p2,q1,m1) \cdot c(q1,q2,m4) \cdot c(q2,q1,m5) \\ \cdot c(q1,p2,m2) \cdot c(p2,p1,m6), \{p1,p2,q1,q2\}\rangle \tag{15}$$

$$D = \langle c(p,q,m1) \cdot c(q,p,m2), \{p,q\}\rangle \tag{16}$$

The refinement mapping f is given by $f(p1) = f(p2) = p$ and $f(q1) = f(q2) = q$. First, we rename the entities of Interworking C according to f.

$$\rho_f(C) = \langle c(p,p,m3) \cdot c(p,q,m1) \cdot c(q,q,m4) \cdot c(q,q,m5) \cdot c(q,p,m2) \\ \cdot c(p,p,m6), \{p,q\}\rangle \tag{17}$$

The set of actions which should be removed is given by

$$Int(rng(f)) = \{c(p,p,m), c(q,q,m) \mid m \in MID\} \tag{18}$$

Removing these actions from the Interworkings $\rho_f(C)$ and D results in the following equations

$$\varepsilon_{Int(rng(f))}(\rho_f(C)) = \langle c(p,q,m1) \cdot c(q,p,m2), \{p,q\}\rangle \tag{19}$$

$$\varepsilon_{Int(rng(f))}(D) = \langle c(p,q,m1) \cdot c(q,p,m2), \{p,q\}\rangle \tag{20}$$

We can conclude that Interworking C is an f-refinement of Interworking D.

For the entity refinement relation we have the following properties.

Proposition 12 (Reflexivity). *For all closed entity-labeled processes s we have*

$$s \sqsubseteq s \tag{21}$$

Proof. We have to show that there exists a partial mapping f such that $s \sqsubseteq_f s$. Take the mapping f with empty domain. Then s is an f-refinement of s. □

Proposition 13 (Transitivity). *For all closed entity-labeled processes s, t, u we have*

$$s \sqsubseteq t \text{ and } t \sqsubseteq u \quad \text{implies} \quad s \sqsubseteq u \tag{22}$$

Proof. Let F be some set and let $f : F \hookrightarrow F$ be a partial function. For all $G \subseteq F$ the extension of f with respect to G, notation f^G, is, for all $x \in F$, defined by

$$f^G(x) = \begin{cases} f(x) & \text{if } x \in dom(f) \\ x & \text{if } x \notin dom(f) \wedge x \in G \\ \text{undefined} & \text{if } x \notin dom(f) \wedge x \notin G \end{cases} \tag{23}$$

Suppose that there exist $f, g : EID \hookrightarrow EID$ such that $s \sqsubseteq_f t$ and $t \sqsubseteq_g u$. Then define $h = g^{rng(f)} \circ f^{dom(g)}$. It is our claim that $s \sqsubseteq_h u$. The proof of this claim is omitted. □

We do not have that the relation $\sqsubseteq$ is anti-symmetrical. This is due to the treatment of internal actions. Consider, for example, the Interworkings $s = \langle c(p,p,m), \{p\}\rangle$ and $t = \langle c(p,p,n), \{p\}\rangle$. Then we have $s \sqsubseteq t$ and $t \sqsubseteq s$, but we do not have $s = t$. For Interworkings without internal communications we do have antisymmetry of entity refinement. So, for Interworkings without internal communication the entity refinement relation is a partial ordering. For the more general class of Interworkings entity refinement is a pre-order.

5 Conclusions

We have given a semantics of Interworkings in which we solved some problems encountered in a former semantics and which allows a definition of entity refinement. The reformulation of the semantics has the following benefits. First, it is now possible to express an empty Interworking. Its semantics is simply the empty process. Next, by extending the processes to entity-labeled processes, the Interworking-merge became an associative operator. Further, we have solved an anomaly described in [8]. We will explain this in short and refer to [8] for an example.

Consider Interworkings A and B, where B is an exact copy of A with the difference that B has one extra entity e without any behaviour. In the old semantics there was no distinction between A and B. However, there is a good reason to make a distinction between these. Suppose there is an Interworking C

that contains entity e such that there is a message to e. Now consider placing A, respectively B in parallel with C. Intuitively, A and C can be merged consistently with respect to entity e, whereas B and C cannot. This is because the communication behaviour of e in B is different from the behaviour of e in C.

A refinement check was already implemented in the Interworking ToolSet based upon an informal explanation by means of examples. The formal definitions provided in this paper seem to correspond well to the existing implementation.

References

1. J.C.M. Baeten and J.A. Bergstra. Global Renaming Operators in Concrete Process Algebra. *Information and Computation*, 78(3):205–245, 1988.
2. J.C.M. Baeten and C. Verhoef. Concrete Process Algebra. In S. Abramsky, D.M. Gabbay, and T.S.E. Maibaum, editors, *Handbook of Logic in Computer Science, volume IV: Semantic Modelling*, pages 149–268. Oxford University Press, 1995.
3. J.C.M. Baeten and W.P. Weijland. *Process Algebra*. Cambridge Tracts in Theoretical Computer Science 18. Cambridge University Press, Cambridge, 1990.
4. J.A. Bergstra and J.W. Klop. Process Algebra for Synchronous Communication. *Information & Control*, 60(1/3):109–137, 1984.
5. ITU-TS. *ITU-TS Recommendation Z.120: Message Sequence Chart (MSC)*. ITU-TS, Geneva, 1994.
6. ITU-TS. *ITU-TS Recommendation Z.120 Annex B: Algebraic semantics of Message Sequence Charts*. ITU-TS, Geneva, 1995.
7. S. Mauw and M.A. Reniers. An Algebraic Semantics of Basic Message Sequence Charts. *The Computer Journal*, 37(4):269–277, 1994.
8. S. Mauw and M.A. Reniers. Empty Interworkings and Refinement - Semantics of Interworkings Revised. Computing science report 95-12, Department of Computing Science, Eindhoven University of Technology, 1995.
9. S. Mauw, M. van Wijk, and T. Winter. A Formal Semantics of Synchronous Interworkings. In O. Færgemand and A. Sarma, editors, *SDL'93 Using Objects*, Proc. Sixth SDL Forum, pages 167–178, Darmstadt, 1993. Elsevier, Amsterdam.
10. S. Mauw and T. Winter. A Prototype Toolset for Interworkings. *Philips Telecommunication Review*, 51(3):41–45, 1993.
11. A. Rensink and H. Wehrheim. Weak Sequential Composition in Process Algebras. In B. Jonsson and J. Parrow, editors, *CONCUR'94: Concurrency Theory*, volume 836 of *Lecture Notes in Computer Science*, pages 226–241. Springer-Verlag, 1994.
12. C. Verhoef. A General Conservative Extension Theorem in Process Algebra. In E.-R. Olderog, editor, *Programming Concepts, Methods and Calculi (PROCOMET '94)*, volume 56 of *IFIP Transactions A*, pages 149–168. North-Holland, 1994.
13. J.L.M. Vrancken. *Studies in Process Algebra, Algebraic Specifications and Parallelism*. PhD thesis, University of Amsterdam, 1991.

Equivalences of Statecharts*

Andrea Maggiolo-Schettini[1], Adriano Peron[2] and Simone Tini[1]

[1] Dipartimento di Informatica, Università di Pisa, Corso Italia 40, 56125 Pisa, Italy.
[2] Dipartimento di Matematica e Informatica, Università di Udine, Viale delle Scienze 206, 33100 Udine, Italy.

Abstract. We present a new semantics of Statecharts that excludes failures and a compositional formulation of this semantics based on Labelled Transition Systems (LTS). We consider a hierarchy of LTS equivalences and we study their congruence properties w.r. to statechart operators.

1 Introduction

Statecharts are a specification language for reactive systems, introduced originally in [4]. The Statecharts formalism belongs to the family of synchronous languages including also, for instance, Esterel [2] and Argos [6]. Statecharts are finite state machines having the appeal of visual formalisms such as state-transition diagrams and Petri nets, but unlike either of these, they offer facilities of hierarchical structuring of states and modularity, which allow high level description and stepwise development. Now when dealing with large specifications, conciseness is an important issue. It may be useful to be able to substitute specifications with equivalent more concise ones. In general, one wants to be able to interchange subsystems proved to be behaviourally equivalent. In the case of statecharts, one is interested in considering equivalent two statecharts that do not differ as regards input-output sequences of signals and their causal dependencies. We define a new semantics of statecharts that differs from the one defined in [8] insofar as in our case the semantics of a statechart is always defined. Next, following [9] (see also [10]), we represent statecharts by terms and we give a compositional semantics of statecharts by translating statechart terms into labelled transition systems (LTS). The agreement of the two semantics can be proved. Then we define equivalence of two statecharts as isomorphism of the respective LTS's. As this equivalence is too strong, we consider LTS equivalences studied in [3] and we investigate their congruence properties with respect to statechart and-composition and or-composition.

2 Statechart terms

Statecharts are a visual specification formalism which enriches state-transition diagrams by a tree-like structuring of states (leaves of such trees are called

* Research partially supported by Esprit BRA 8130 LOMAPS.

basic states), explicit representation of parallelism and communication among parallel components. States are either of type "and", called *and-states*, or of type "or", called *or-states*. An or-state has a privileged immediate substate called the *default* state. The graphical convention is that states are depicted as boxes and the box of a substate of another state is drawn inside the area of the box of that state; and-states are depicted as boxes whose area is partitioned by dashed lines and each element of the partition is a parallel component of the state. A default state is marked by a dangling arrow. The statechart z_1 of Fig.1 consists of an and-state, state 7, having two or-states, 3 and 6, as components. States 1 and 2 are the basic substates of state 3 and state 1 is the default substate. A transition t between two states is labelled by a set of positive and negative signals (the *trigger* of t) and a set of communicated positive signals (the *action* of t). (We do not consider transitions that cross "borders" of states, i.e. the source and the target state of a transition are both immediate substates of the same or-state.)

In [8]statecharts have been endowed with a "step-semantics" which enforces causality, synchrony hypothesis and global consistency (for a review of statecharts semantic variants we refer to [1]). In the semantics of [8], under some circumstances, statecharts may fail, and this does not have a wholly convincing interpretation. In order to fulfill the requirements mentioned and avoid failures, we modify that semantics. The general idea of Statechart semantics is that an environment prompts the statechart with (pure) signals which are related to a discrete time domain. The statechart is supposed to evolve from an initial configuration by "reacting" to the set of signals communicated by the environment at the first instant of time or in the absence of certain signals in the environment (this is represented by negative signals). Reacting means performing a set of transitions called a *step*. In [8] a step is a maximal set of transitions that are *relevant* in the initial configuration, *triggered* by the communicated signals, and *consistent*. A transition is relevant if its source state is in the configuration. Given a set of signals, a transition is triggered if its positive triggering signals belong to the set and the negative ones do not. Two transitions are consistent if they belong to parallel components. In our semantics, in addition, transitions in a step must also be *compatible*, namely must be such that in the action of one there is no signal appearing negated in the trigger of the other (in the opposite case the execution of the former prevents the execution of the latter). When performed, a transition communicates signals instantaneously, which can (instantaneously) enable new (relevant and compatible) transitions (an instantaneous chain reaction). So, the set of transitions in the step are triggered either by signals communicated by the environment or by signals communicated by transitions in the same step, provided that the triggering of each transition can be causally justified starting from signals communicated by the environment (causality). The maximality of the step enforces the synchrony hypothesis, while the global consistency follows from the fact that any transition of the step is triggered by the whole set of signals communicated in the step. So, a configuration is reached from which a new reaction can start at the next instant, triggered by a new set of signals.

Following [9], statecharts are formally represented by terms. Terms are constructed from basic terms (corresponding to basic states) by means of two operations (or-composition and and-composition).

We assume we have sets of names $\mathcal{N}$ for states, $\mathcal{T}$ for transitions, Π for (positive) signals. For all $e \in \Pi$, $\overline{e}$ denotes the negation of e; $\overline{\Pi}$ denotes the set $\{\overline{e} | e \in \Pi\}$. We have that for all $e \in \Pi : \overline{\overline{e}} = e$, and, in general, for $Y \subseteq \Pi \cup \overline{\Pi}$: $\overline{Y} = \{\overline{y} | y \in Y\}$.

Definition 1. The algebra SA of (statechart) terms is defined as follows:

1. $p = [n : \emptyset; \emptyset]$ is a term for every $n \in \mathcal{N}$ (*basic term*).
2. If $p_1, \ldots, p_k$ are terms ($k \geq 1$), $T \subseteq \mathcal{T} \times \{1, \ldots, k\} \times 2^{\Pi \cup \overline{\Pi}} \times 2^{\Pi} \times \{1, \ldots, k\}$ and $n \in \mathcal{N}$, then $p = [n : \{p_1, \ldots, p_k\}; T]$ is a term (the *or-composition* of $p_1, \ldots, p_k$, an *or-term*).
3. If p_1, p_2 are terms and $n \in \mathcal{N}$, then $p = [n : \{p_1, p_2\}]$ is a term (the *and-composition* of p_1, p_2, an *and-term*).
4. There are no other terms.

For instance, the statechart z_1 of Fig.1 is represented by $p = [7 : \{p_3, p_6\}]$, with $p_3 = [3 : \{p_1, p_2\}; \{\langle t_1, 1, \{a\}, \{b\}, 2\rangle\}]$, $p_6 = [6 : \{p_4, p_5\}; \{\langle t_2, 4, \{b\}, \{c\}, 5\rangle\}]$, where $p_1 = [1 : \emptyset; \emptyset]$, $p_2 = [2 : \emptyset; \emptyset]$, $p_4 = [4 : \emptyset; \emptyset]$, $p_5 = [5 : \emptyset; \emptyset]$.

For $p = [n : \emptyset; \emptyset]$ or $p = [n : \{p_1, \ldots, p_k\}; T]$ or $p = [n : \{p_1, p_2\}]$, we define $root(p) = n$.
Let $states : SA \longrightarrow 2^{\mathcal{N}}$ be the function with $states([n : \emptyset; \emptyset]) = \{n\}$; $states([n : \{p_1, \ldots, p_k\}; T]) = \{n\} \cup \bigcup_{1 \leq i \leq k} states(p_i)$; $states([n : \{p_1, p_2\}]) = \{n\} \cup \bigcup_{1 \leq i \leq 2} states(p_i) - \{root(p_i) | i \in \{1, 2\}, p_i \text{ an and-term}\}$.
Let $trans : SA \longrightarrow 2^{\mathcal{T}}$ be the function with $trans([n : \emptyset; \emptyset]) = \emptyset$, $trans([n : \{p_1, \ldots, p_k\}; T]) = \bigcup_{1 \leq i \leq k} trans(p_i) \cup \{t | \langle t, i, A, B, j\rangle \in T\}$; $trans([n : \{p_1, p_2\}]) = trans(p_1) \cup trans(p_2)$.
For any $t \in trans(p)$ there is a subterm $p' = [n : \{p_1, \ldots, p_k\}; T]$ of p with $\langle t, i, A, B, j\rangle \in T$.
We denote by $in(t)$ the state $root(p_j)$ (the *target* of t), by $out(t)$ the state $root(p_i)$ (the *source* of t), by $ev(t)$ the set A (the *trigger* of t), by $act(t)$ the set B (the *action* of t).
For $T \subseteq \mathcal{T}$ we denote by $actions(T)$ the set $\bigcup_{t \in T} act(t)$.
For a term p and $i, j \in states(p)$ (with $i \neq j$), we write $i \prec j$ if there exists a subterm p' such that $root(p') = i$ and $j \in states(p')$.
For simplicity, we shall consider only terms without duplication of names of states and transitions.

We introduce now the notions of *configuration* and *default configuration* for a statechart term. A configuration is a maximal set of states fulfilling the requirement that if an or-state (resp. an and-state) is in the configuration, exactly one (resp. all) of its immediate substates is in it. A default configuration is a configuration where the substate of an or-state in the configuration is the default state. For a term p, $config(p) \subseteq 2^{states(p)}$ is inductively defined as follows:

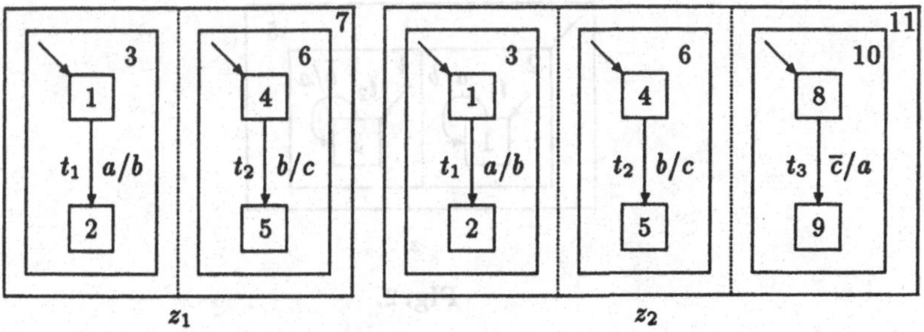

Fig. 1.

1. If p is a basic term $config(p) = \{\{root(p)\}\}$.
2. If $p = [n : \{p_1, \ldots, p_k\}; T]$, $config(p) = \{\{n\} \cup C \mid C \in config(p_i), 1 \leq i \leq k\}$.
3. If $p = [n : \{p_1, p_2\}]$, $config(p) = \{(\{n\} \cup C_1 \cup C_2) \cap states(p) \mid C_1 \in config(p_1) \wedge C_2 \in config(p_2)\}$.

For a term p, $default(p) \subseteq states(p)$ is inductively defined as follows:

1. If p is a basic term $default(p) = \{root(p)\}$.
2. If $p = [n : \{p_1, \ldots, p_k\}; T]$, $default(p) = \{n\} \cup default(p_1)$.
3. If $p = [n : \{p_1, p_2\}]$, $default(p) = (\{n\} \cup default(p_1) \cup default(p_2)) \cap states(p)$.

We introduce now the notions of consistency, compatibility, relevance, triggering and enabling. For a term p, two transitions $t_1, t_2 \in trans(p)$ are *orthogonal*, written $t_1 \perp t_2$, iff there exists a subterm $p' = [n : \{p_1, p_2\}]$ and either $t_1 \in trans(p_1)$ and $t_2 \in trans(p_2)$ or $t_1 \in trans(p_2)$ and $t_2 \in trans(p_1)$.
For a term p, $Consistent : 2^{trans(p)} \longrightarrow 2^{trans(p)}$ is the function such that

$$Consistent(T) = \{t \mid t \in trans(p) \wedge \forall t' \in T : t \perp t'\};$$

$Compatible : 2^{states(p)} \longrightarrow 2^{trans(p)}$ is the function such that

$$Compatible(T) = \{t \mid t \in trans(p) \wedge \forall t' \in T : act(t) \cap \overline{ev(t')} = \emptyset\};$$

$Relevant : 2^{states(p)} \longrightarrow 2^{trans(p)}$ is the function such that

$$Relevant(C) = \{t \mid out(t) \in C\};$$

$Triggered : 2^{\Pi} \longrightarrow 2^{trans(p)}$ is the function such that

$$Triggered(\sigma) = \{t \in trans(p) \mid ev(t) \cap \Pi \subseteq \sigma \wedge \overline{ev(t) \cap \overline{\Pi} \cap \sigma = \emptyset}\};$$

$Enabled : 2^{states(p)} \times 2^{\Pi} \times 2^{trans(p)} \longrightarrow 2^{trans(p)}$ is the function such that $Enabled(C, \sigma, T) = Relevant(C) \cap Consistent(T) \cap Triggered(\sigma \cup actions(T)) \cap Compatible(T)$.
A set of transitions $T \subseteq trans(p)$ is *inseparable* in $C \in config(p)$ for $\sigma \subseteq \Pi$ iff, for any $T' \subset T$, $Enabled(C, \sigma, T') \cap (T - T') \neq \emptyset$.
An inseparable set contains only causally justified transitions.
For a term p, $Step : 2^{states(p)} \times 2^{\Pi} \longrightarrow 2^{2^{trans(p)}}$ is the function such that
$Step(C, \sigma) = \{T \subseteq trans(p) \mid T$ inseparable in C for $\sigma, Enabled(C, \sigma, T) = T\}$.

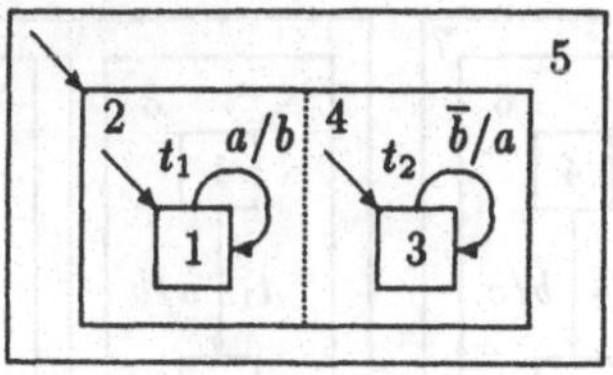

z

Fig. 2.

The function *Step* gives all the possible steps from a given configuration and with a given environment. (Note that the maximality of each step is guaranteed by the condition $Enabled(C, \sigma, T) = T$.) For a configuration C and $\sigma \subseteq \Pi$, the configuration reached from C by $T \in Step(C, \sigma)$, denoted by $Next(C, T)$, is the set $C - \{s \in states(p) | out(t) \prec s \text{ for some } t \in T\} \cup (\bigcup_{t \in T} default(p) | root(p) = in(t))$.
In [8] the function *Enabled* is defined as follows: $Enabled(C, \sigma, T) = Consistent(T) \cap Relevant(C) \cap Triggered(\sigma \cup actions(T))$. As an example, we see the consequences of our definition of set of enabled transitions in the case of the statechart z of Fig.2. Let us assume that in the initial configuration z receives signal a and not signal b. While in the semantics of [8] only $\{t_1\}$ would be a step, in our semantics both $\{t_1\}$ and $\{t_2\}$ are steps. We believe that it is reasonable that the system may choose between performing t_1 and performing t_2 (performing both transitions would violate global consistency) without disfavoring transitions triggered by a negated signal, as is implied by [8]. Moreover, if in the initial configuration z receives neither signal a nor signal b, following the semantics of [8] the statechart fails, because there is no solution of the equation $T = Enabled(C, \sigma, T)$. Instead we allow it to execute step $\{t_2\}$. For our choice we have an intuitive explanation. We can interpret names of signals as names of shared boolean variables. A transition having a signal in its trigger (resp. action) reads (resp. writes) the corresponding variable. So, in order to be enabled, transitions compete for these shared variables. Readings may be concurrent and the same holds for writings (this because only one value can be written). On the other hand, whenever a variable has been read, a writing that changes the value of the variable is not allowed (in the same step). This guarantees that all transitions in a step read the same value in a variable.

Note that our approach differs also from that of Esterel and Argos. In fact we assign a meaning to specifications that in Esterel and Argos would be statically rejected.

As in [8], we give a procedure to compute a step:

Procedure Step-Construction(C, σ)
$T := \emptyset$;
while $T \subset Enabled(C, \sigma, T)$ **do**
  begin

choice $t \in Enabled(C, \sigma, T) - T$;
$T := T \cup \{t\}$
end
end

The procedure cannot fail because for a set T of consistent and compatible transitions T is always included in $Enabled(C, \sigma, T)$, and therefore the procedure will always terminate successfully. This is not true for the procedure given in [8] that in the case of the example of Fig.2 causes a failure for an input that does not include signals a and b. In a manner analogous to that of [8], it can be proved that a set T of transitions is an inseparable solution to the equation $T = Enabled(C, \sigma, T)$ if and only if T is constructible, in the sense that it can be obtained by a sequence of choices of transitions $t \in Enabled(C, \sigma, T) - T$ in the procedure. Notice that all steps in the semantics of [8] are steps also in our semantics, but not viceversa.

3 From statechart terms to LTS's

In this section we associate a Labelled Transition System (LTS) with each statechart term in a syntax directed way. As usual, a LTS is a tuple $\langle Q, \Sigma, q_0 \longrightarrow \rangle$, where Q is the set of states, Σ is the set of labels, $q_0 \in Q$ is the initial state and $\longrightarrow \subseteq Q \times \Sigma \times Q$ is the set of transitions. We denote by L the set of LTS's and write $q \xrightarrow{\sigma} q'$ for $(q, \sigma, q') \in \longrightarrow$. With $q \not\longrightarrow$ we mean that there is no $q' \in Q$ such that $q \xrightarrow{\sigma} q'$ for $\sigma \in \Sigma$. With $q \Longrightarrow q'$ we mean that $q \longrightarrow \ldots \longrightarrow q'$.

We follow the idea of [9] of constructing LTS's with states representing configurations and transitions representing steps, but we shall use more structured labels. Here, as we want to have compositions of LTS's corresponding with compositions of statechart terms, we consider in general, LTS's with states representing configurations (non necessarily reachable by steps) and transitions that represent substeps (namely subsets of steps), possibly empty substeps. If we have $p = [n : \{p_1, p_2\}]$, the union of a step T_1 of p_1 and T_2 of p_2 is not, in general, a step of p. As an example, if a transition $t_1 \in T_1$ is triggered by $\overline{a}$ and a is the action of the transition $t_2 \in T_2$, then there is no step of p containing both t_1 and t_2. In general, a step of p is the union of a substep of p_1 and a substep of p_2. A label of a LTS describes the environments that are compatible with taking the corresponding substep, and carries information about the completeness of that substep.

An *LTS-label* is a tuple $\langle Y, Z, R, F \rangle$, where $Y \subseteq \Pi$, $Z \subseteq \Pi \cup \overline{\Pi}$ and $R, F \subseteq 2^{\Pi \cup \overline{\Pi}} \times 2^{\Pi}$. We denote with $events(R)$ the set $\bigcup_{\langle A,B \rangle \in R} A \cup B$, and we require that $events(R) \cap \overline{events(R)} = \emptyset$, $Z \cap \overline{Z} = \emptyset$, $events(R) \cap Y = \emptyset$, $events(R) \cap Z = \emptyset$, $Y \cap \overline{Z} = \emptyset$. We denote by $\mathcal{L}$ the set of LTS-labels.

Component Y keeps trace of transitions (more precisely it contains their actions) that could be consistently performed together with the substep considered (so giving a step) but are not included in the substep to allow a possible composition with transitions triggered by the negation of signals in Y. Component Z contains signals that are not communicated in the environment and would trigger other consistent transitions. The relations R and F describe the causality relationships between signals triggering a transition and signals belonging to its action. In particular, the former relation allows us to determine the causal relationships of signals involved in transitions in the considered substep, whereas the latter allows us to determine whether a transition that is not included in the step for possible composition is actually triggered.

For a transition t, the function $lab : T \times \mathcal{N} \times 2^{\Pi \cup \overline{\Pi}} \times 2^{\Pi} \times \mathcal{N} \longrightarrow \mathcal{L}$ such that $lab(\langle t, i, A, B, j\rangle) = \langle \emptyset, \emptyset, \{\langle A, \{b\}\rangle | b \in B - A\}, \emptyset\rangle$ if $B - A \neq \emptyset$ and $lab(\langle t, i, A, B, j\rangle) = \langle \emptyset, \emptyset, \{\langle A, \emptyset\rangle\}, \emptyset\rangle$ otherwise, gives the label for the step $\{t\}$. Note that each signal in the action is caused by the trigger.
The function $neg : T \times N \times 2^{\Pi \cup \overline{\Pi}} \times 2^{\Pi} \times N \longrightarrow 2^{\mathcal{L}}$ such that $neg(\langle t, i, A, B, j\rangle) = \{\langle B', \emptyset, \emptyset, \{\langle A, \{b\}\rangle | b \in B' - A, B' \neq \emptyset\}\rangle | B' \subseteq B\} \cup \{\langle \emptyset, A', \emptyset, \emptyset\rangle | A' \subseteq A, A' \neq \emptyset\}$, gives the labels of the empty substeps of the step $\{t\}$. The former set in the definition of *neg* takes into account the cases where t is not performed (even if enabled) to allow possible and- compositionality. The latter set takes into account the cases where t is not performed as it is not triggered. In order to consistently compose substeps belonging to different and-components of a statechart term, we need a notion of consistency for labels. Two labels are consistent when their componentwise union is a description of environments.
Two LTS-labels $v_1 = \langle Y_1, Z_1, R_1, F_1\rangle$ and $v_2 = \langle Y_2, Z_2, R_2, F_2\rangle$ are *consistent* if for all $e \in \overline{Y_1} \cup \overline{Z_1} \cup events(R_1)$ it is the case that $\overline{e} \notin \overline{Y_2} \cup \overline{Z_2} \cup events(R_2)$.

Proposition 2. *The componentwise union of two consistent labels v_1 and v_2, denoted as $v_1 \oplus v_2$, belongs to $\mathcal{L}$. If $v_1, v_2, v_3 \in \mathcal{L}$ are pairwise consistent labels, then $((v_1 \oplus v_2) \oplus v_3) = (v_1 \oplus (v_2 \oplus v_3))$ are labels.*

We give the syntax driven construction of a LTS. To the and-composition of terms, the product of their LTS's corresponds (pairs of their LTS transitions are composed only if their labels are consistent). The absence of transitions from a state of the LTS is interpreted as the lack of whatsoever step from the corresponding configuration, and, instead, an empty substep (which can be possibly completed to a step) is represented by a loop labelled by a tuple $\langle Y, Z, \emptyset, F\rangle$. Note that, when we construct the LTS for an or-term p, we must take into account that an empty substep is due to the lack of both the execution of a transition at the highest level and transitions of subterms of p.

Definition 3. The function $\psi : SA \longrightarrow L$ is s.t. $\psi(p) = \langle Q_p, \Sigma_p, q_{0p}, \longrightarrow_p\rangle$, where $Q_p = config(p)$, $q_{0p} = default(p)$ and Σ_p and $\longrightarrow_p$ are defined inductively as follows:

1. Assume $p = [n : \emptyset; \emptyset\}]$. Then, we have that $\Sigma_p = \emptyset$ and $\longrightarrow_p = \emptyset$.
2. Assume $p = [n : \{p_1, \ldots, p_k\}; T]$ with $p_i \in SA$ and $\psi(p_i) = \langle Q_i, \Sigma_i, q_{0_i}, \longrightarrow_i\rangle$, where $Q_i = \{q_{0_i}, \ldots, q_{g_i}\}$, $1 \leq i \leq k$. For any $q_{h_i} \in Q_i$, if $\langle t, i, A, B, j\rangle \in T$ we have $\{n\} \cup q_{h_i} \xrightarrow{v}_p \{n\} \cup q_{0_j}$, where $v = lab(\langle t, i, A, B, j\rangle)$ (a step

formed by a transition at higher level). Moreover, if $q_{h_i} \xrightarrow{v_i}_i q_{m_i}$, with $v_i = \langle Y_i, Z_i, R_i, F_i \rangle$ and $R_i \neq \emptyset$, then we have $\{n\} \cup q_{h_i} \xrightarrow{v_i}_p \{n\} \cup q_{m_i}$ (a substep in a subterm of p). Assume now $T_i = \{\langle t, i, A, B, j \rangle \in T | t \in \mathcal{T}, A \in 2^{\Pi \cup \overline{\Pi}}, B \in 2^{\Pi}, j \in \{1, \ldots, k\}\} = \{l_1, \ldots, l_{f_i}\}$, for $1 \leq i \leq k$. Assume also $v_h \in neg(l_h)$, $1 \leq h \leq f_i$, with $v_1, \ldots, v_{f_i}$ pairwise consistent, and $v = v_1 \oplus \ldots \oplus v_{f_i}$. If $q_{h_i} \xrightarrow{v_i}_i q_{h_i}$, $v_i = \langle Y_i, Z_i, R_i, F_i \rangle$, $R_i = \emptyset$ and v and v_i are consistent, we have $\{n\} \cup q_{h_i} \xrightarrow{v'}_p \{n\} \cup q_{h_i}$, where $v' = v \oplus v_i$ (an empty substep). Instead, if there is no v_i such that $q_{h_i} \xrightarrow{v_i}_i q_{m_i}$, for any q_{m_i}, we have $\{n\} \cup q_{h_i} \xrightarrow{v}_p \{n\} \cup q_{h_i}$ (an empty substep). Finally, if there are no t, A, B, j such that $\langle t, i, A, B, j \rangle \in T$ and $q_{h_i} \xrightarrow{v_i}_i q_{h_i}$, $v_i = \langle Y_i, Z_i, R_i, F_i \rangle$, $R_i = \emptyset$ we have $\{n\} \cup q_{h_i} \xrightarrow{v_i}_p \{n\} \cup q_{h_i}$ (an empty substep).
3. Assume $p = [n : \{p_1, p_2\}]$ with $p_i \in SA$, $\psi(p_i) = \langle Q_i, \Sigma_i, q_{0_i}, \longrightarrow_i \rangle$, where $Q_i = \{q_{0_i}, \ldots, q_{f_i}\}$, $1 \leq i \leq 2$. Assume $q_{h_i} \xrightarrow{v_i}_p q_{m_i}$, $1 \leq i \leq 2$, with v_1 consistent with v_2. For $v = (v_1 \oplus v_2)$ we have $(\{n\} \cup q_{h_1} \cup q_{h_2}) \cap states(p) \xrightarrow{v}_p (\{n\} \cup q_{m_1} \cup q_{m_2}) \cap states(p)$ (with q_{h_i} nonnecessarily different from q_{m_i}, $i = 1, 2$). If $q_{h_1} \not\longrightarrow_1$ and $q_{h_2} \xrightarrow{v}_2 q_{m_2}$, then we have also $(\{n\} \cup q_{h_1} \cup q_{h_2})) \cap states(p) \xrightarrow{v}_p (\{n\} \cup q_{h_1} \cup q_{m_2}) \cap states(p)$, and similarly exchanging the roles of p_1 and p_2.

In Fig.3.c we show the LTS for the statechart z_1 of Fig.1. In particular, Fig.3.a and Fig.3.b show the LTS's for the subterms rooted in the states 3 and 6, respectively. The LTS's we construct differ from the ones in [9] because we assume a different semantics, and in general, LTS transitions represent substeps and transition labels take into account how substeps could be completed to steps. Consider, as an example, the statechart z_1 in Fig.1. In the LTS we construct from the corresponding term (Fig.3.c), from the configuration $\{1, 3, 4, 6, 7\}$ we have a transition representing step $\{t_1, t_2\}$ and a transition representing substep $\{t_1\}$. Consider now the statechart z_2 of Fig.1 obtained by adding another component to the statechart z_1. In the corresponding LTS there will be a transition representing a step $\{t_1, t_3\}$ obtained by completing the substep $\{t_1\}$. We consider now how causal orders on signals involved by the set of transitions in a substep can be recovered from the component R of the LTS transition label. From a label we can obtain a set of different causal orders reflecting the different ways in which signals can be produced. Then we introduce a notion of compatibility between a label and an environment via causal orders obtained from the label. An environment is compatible with a causal order if it contains the positive occurrences of the minimal signals (w.r. to the given order) and does not contain the negative minimal signals.

Definition 4. Given a label $v = \langle Y, Z, R, F \rangle$, a *causal order* $\leq_R$ over $events(R) \cup \{\lambda\}$ (with $\lambda \notin \Pi$) is the transitive closure of a relation $S \subseteq events(R) \cup \{\lambda\} \times events(R)$ satisfying the following conditions:

1. the transitive closure of S has no circularities
2. if $\langle \lambda, b \rangle \in S$, then $\langle \emptyset, \{b\} \rangle \in R$

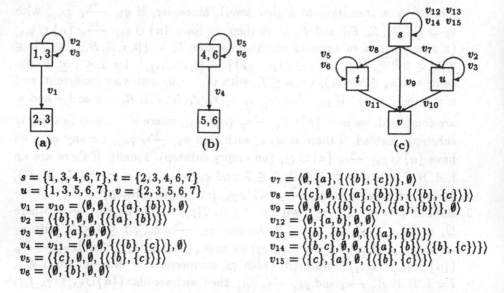

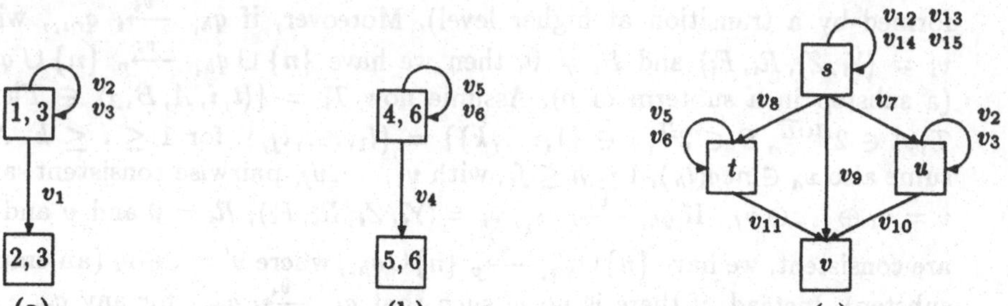

(a) (b) (c)

$s = \{1,3,4,6,7\}, t = \{2,3,4,6,7\}$
$u = \{1,3,5,6,7\}, v = \{2,3,5,6,7\}$
$v_1 = v_{10} = \langle \emptyset, \emptyset, \{\langle \{a\}, \{b\} \rangle\}, \emptyset \rangle$
$v_2 = \langle \{b\}, \emptyset, \emptyset, \{\langle \{a\}, \{b\} \rangle\} \rangle$
$v_3 = \langle \emptyset, \{a\}, \emptyset, \emptyset \rangle$
$v_4 = v_{11} = \langle \emptyset, \emptyset, \{\langle \{b\}, \{c\} \rangle\}, \emptyset \rangle$
$v_5 = \langle \{c\}, \emptyset, \emptyset, \{\langle \{b\}, \{c\} \rangle\} \rangle$
$v_6 = \langle \emptyset, \{b\}, \emptyset, \emptyset \rangle$

$v_7 = \langle \emptyset, \{a\}, \{\langle \{b\}, \{c\} \rangle\}, \emptyset \rangle$
$v_8 = \langle \{c\}, \emptyset, \{\langle \{a\}, \{b\} \rangle\}, \{\langle \{b\}, \{c\} \rangle\} \rangle$
$v_9 = \langle \emptyset, \emptyset, \{\langle \{b\}, \{c\} \rangle, \langle \{a\}, \{b\} \rangle\}, \emptyset \rangle$
$v_{12} = \langle \emptyset, \{a, b\}, \emptyset, \emptyset \rangle$
$v_{13} = \langle \{b\}, \{b\}, \emptyset, \{\langle \{a\}, \{b\} \rangle\} \rangle$
$v_{14} = \langle \{b, c\}, \emptyset, \emptyset, \{\langle \{a\}, \{b\} \rangle, \langle \{b\}, \{c\} \rangle\} \rangle$
$v_{15} = \langle \{c\}, \{a\}, \emptyset, \{\langle \{b\}, \{c\} \rangle\} \rangle$

Fig. 3.

3. if $A \subseteq events(R)$ is a maximal set such that $\forall a \in A : \langle a, b \rangle \in S$, then $\langle A, \{b\} \rangle \in R$.

We denote by $\leq_v$ the set of all the causal orders $\leq_R$.

A similar notion of causal order $\leq_F$ can be introduced also over $events(F)$ (defined analogously with $events(R)$). The way we define causality is different from the approach of [9] regardless of the semantics that is assumed. The way we define the relation $\leq_R$ reflects causality correctly. This is sometimes not the case in the costruction of [9]. Actually, consider the statechart of Fig.4 where signal c, emitted by transition t, is caused by both the signals a and b. Now, the LTS of [9] would have a transition for the step $\{t, t'\}$ with a label saying that a causes c and c causes b, whereas, as we have observed, signal a is not sufficient to cause transition t.

Given a causal order $\leq_R$ over a set of signals $\sigma' \subseteq \Pi \cup \overline{\Pi}$, a set of signals $\sigma \subseteq \Pi$ *causally justifies* σ' if for any causal chain $a_1 \leq_R \ldots \leq_R a_n$, with $a_i \in \sigma'$, $1 \leq i \leq n$, and a_1 minimal (w.r.t. to $\leq_R$), $a_1 \in \sigma$ iff $a_1 \in \Pi$. An LTS-label $v = \langle Y, Z, R, F \rangle$ is *compatible* with a set $\sigma \subseteq \Pi$ if $(Z \cap \Pi) \cap \sigma = \emptyset$, $(\overline{Z} \cap \Pi) \subseteq \sigma$ and there exists a causal order $\leq_R$ such that σ causally justifies $events(R)$.

Finally, we discriminate between LTS transitions which represent full steps and substeps to be completed to steps and we state the correctness of our construction with respect to the semantics defined in the previous section. The proof will appear in the full version of the paper.

Definition 5. Given a label $v = \langle Y, Z, R, F \rangle$ compatible with a set $\sigma \in \Pi$, a LTS transition $q \xrightarrow{v} q'$ is a *LTS transition step* if $\overline{a} \in events(R)$ for any $a \in Y$

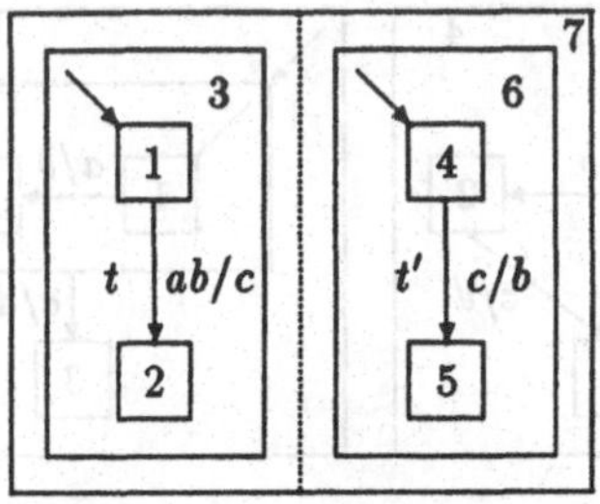

Fig. 4.

such that $(\sigma \cup events(R)) \cap \Pi$ justifies a for some causal order $\leq_F$.

Proposition 6. *There exists a step T with environment σ from a configuration q to a configuration q' iff there exists a LTS transition step $q \xrightarrow{v} q'$ for some LTS-label $v = \langle Y, Z, R, F \rangle$ compatible with σ with $R = \{\langle A, \{b\}\rangle | A = ev(t) \wedge b \in Act(t), t \in T\}$.*

We can observe that from our LTS's we derive LTS's in agreement with Pnueli and Shalev's semantics by simply pruning step transitions with non-empty first component of the transition label.

Note that in [5] Huizing, Gerth and de Roever give a compositional (denotational) semantics for Statecharts without restricting transitions from crossing border of states but also without assuming global consistency.

4 Equivalences of statechart terms

In [3] a hierarchy of well known equivalence notions defined on LTS's is presented. We consider a representative for each level of this hierarchy and we study congruence properties w.r. to statechart operators. The strongest equivalence we consider is isomorphism.

Given $s = \langle Q, \Sigma, q_0, \longrightarrow \rangle \in L$, the set of reachable states of s is $Q^r = \{q_0\} \cup \{q | q \in Q \wedge q_0 \Longrightarrow q\}$.

Definition 7. Two LTS's $s_1 = \langle Q_1, \Sigma_1, q_{0_1}, \longrightarrow_1 \rangle$ and $s_2 = \langle Q_2, \Sigma_2, q_{0_2}, \longrightarrow_2 \rangle$ are *isomorphic*, written $s_1 \equiv s_2$, iff there exists a bijection $f : Q_1^r \longrightarrow Q_2^r$ such that $f(q_{0_1}) = q_{0_2}$ and $q_1 \xrightarrow{\sigma} q_1'$ iff $f(q_1) \xrightarrow{\sigma} f(q_1')$.
Two terms $p, p' \in SA$ are *$\approx$-equivalent*, written $p \approx p'$, iff $\psi(p) \equiv \psi(p')$.

In Fig.5 two $\approx$-equivalent statecharts are shown.

Theorem 8. *$\approx$-equivalence is a congruence w.r. to the operators of SA.*

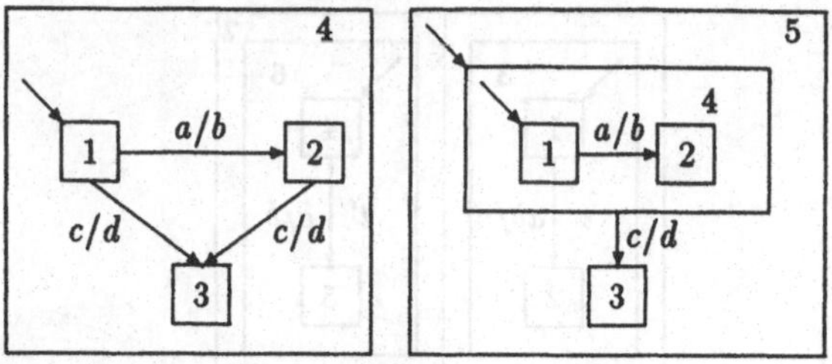

Fig. 5. ≈-equivalent statecharts.

Proof. 1. We assume $\hat{p} = [n : \{p, p_1\}]$, $\hat{p'} = [n' : \{p', p_1\}]$ with $p, p', p_1 \in SA$ and $p \approx p'$ and we prove that $\hat{p} \approx \hat{p'}$. We consider the LTS's $\psi(p) =< Q_p, \Sigma_p, q_{0p}, \longrightarrow_p>$; $\psi(p') =< Q_{p'}, \Sigma_{p'}, q_{0p'}, \longrightarrow_{p'}>$; $\psi(p_1) =< Q_1, \Sigma_1, q_0, \longrightarrow_1>$; $\psi(\hat{p}) =< Q_{\hat{p}}, \Sigma_{\hat{p}}, q_{0\hat{p}}, \longrightarrow_{\hat{p}} >$; $\psi(\hat{p'}) =< Q_{\hat{p'}}, \Sigma_{\hat{p'}}, q_{0\hat{p'}}, \longrightarrow_{\hat{p'}}>$. Let $f : Q^r_p \longrightarrow Q^r_{p'}$ a bijection that gives the isomorphism between $\psi(p)$ and $\psi(p')$. It is easy to see that the map $g : Q^r_{\hat{p}} \longrightarrow Q^r_{\hat{p'}}$ such that

$$g((\{n\} \cup q \cup q') \cap states(\hat{p})) = (\{n'\} \cup f(q) \cup q') \cap states(\hat{p'}) \text{ with } q \in Q^r_p,\ q' \in Q^r_1$$

is a bijection such that $g(q_{0\hat{p}}) = q_{0\hat{p'}}$. Assume now that $q \xrightarrow{v}_{\hat{p}} q'$ with $q, q' \in Q^r_{\hat{p}}$ and $q = (\{n\} \cup q_1 \cup q_2) \cap states(\hat{p})$, $q' = (\{n\} \cup q'_1 \cup q'_2) \cap states(\hat{p})$ with $q_1, q'_1 \in Q^r_p$ and $q_2, q'_2 \in Q^r_1$. We prove that $g(q) \xrightarrow{v} g(q')$. We have one of the following cases:

- There is an LTS-transition from both the configurations q_1 and q_2: $q \xrightarrow{v}_{\hat{p}} q' \Leftrightarrow (q_1 \xrightarrow{v_1}_p q'_1) \wedge (q_2 \xrightarrow{v_2}_1 q'_2) \wedge (v = v_1 \oplus v_2) \Leftrightarrow$ $(f(q_1) \xrightarrow{v_1}_{p'} f(q'_1)) \wedge (q_2 \xrightarrow{v_2}_1 q'_2) \wedge (v = v_1 \oplus v_2) \Leftrightarrow$ $((\{n'\} \cup f(q_1) \cup q_2) \cap states(\hat{p'}) \xrightarrow{v}_{\hat{p'}} (\{n'\} \cup f(q'_1) \cup q'_2) \cap states(\hat{p'}) \Leftrightarrow$ $g(q) \xrightarrow{v}_{\hat{p'}} g(q')$.
- There is an LTS-transition from configuration q_1 (and not from q_2): $q \xrightarrow{v}_{\hat{p}} q' \Leftrightarrow (q_1 \xrightarrow{v_1}_p q'_1) \wedge (q_2 \not\longrightarrow_1) \Leftrightarrow$ $(f(q_1) \xrightarrow{v}_{p'} f(q'_1)) \wedge (q_2 \not\longrightarrow_1) \Leftrightarrow$ $(\{n'\} \cup f(q_1) \cup q_2) \cap states(\hat{p'}) \xrightarrow{v}_{\hat{p'}} (\{n'\} \cup f(q'_1) \cup q_2) \cap states(\hat{p'}) \Leftrightarrow$ $g(q) \xrightarrow{v}_{\hat{p'}} g(q')$.
- There is an LTS-transition from configuration q_2 (and not from q_1): analogous to the previous case.

The converse implication (i.e. $g(q) \xrightarrow{v}_{\hat{p'}} g(q')$, for $q, q' \in Q^r_{\hat{p}}$, implies $q \xrightarrow{v}_{\hat{p}} q'$) can be dealt with by analogous arguments.

2. We assume $\hat{p} = [n : \{p_1 \ldots, p_{i-1}, p_i, p_{i+1}, \ldots, p_k\}; T]$ and $\hat{p'} = [n' : \{p_1, \ldots, p_{i-1}, p'_i, p_{i+1}, \ldots, p_k\}; T]$ with $p_i \approx p'_i$, and we prove that $\hat{p} \approx \hat{p'}$. We consider the LTS's $\psi(p_j) =< Q_{p_j}, \Sigma_{p_j}, q_{0p_j}, \longrightarrow_{p_j}>$, for $1 \leq j \leq k$; $\psi(p'_i) =< Q_{p'_i}, \Sigma_{p'_i}, q_{0p'_i}, \longrightarrow_{p'_i}>$; $\psi(\hat{p}) =< Q_{\hat{p}}, \Sigma_{\hat{p}}, q_{0\hat{p}}, \longrightarrow_{\hat{p}}>$; $\psi(\hat{p'}) =< Q_{\hat{p'}}, \Sigma_{\hat{p'}}, q_{0\hat{p'}},$

$\longrightarrow_{\hat{p}'}>$. Let us suppose that $f : Q^r_p \longrightarrow Q^r_{p'}$ is the bijection that gives the isomorphism between $\psi(p)$ and $\psi(p')$. It is easy to see that the mapping $g : Q^r_{\hat{p}} \longrightarrow Q^r_{\hat{p}'}$ such that:

$$g(\{n\} \cup q) = \{n'\} \cup q \text{ for } q \in Q^r_{p_j} \text{ with } 1 \leq j \leq k,\ j \neq i$$
$$g(\{n\} \cup q) = \{n'\} \cup f(q) \text{ for } q \in Q^r_{p_i}$$

is a bijection such that $g(q_{0\hat{p}}) = q_{0\hat{p}'}$. Assume now that $q \xrightarrow{v}_{\hat{p}} q'$ with $q, q' \in Q^r_{\hat{p}}$ and $q = \{n\} \cup q_1$, $q' = \{n\} \cup q'_1$ with $q_1, q'_1 \in \bigcup_{1 \leq j \leq k} Q^r_{p_j}$. We prove that $g(q) \xrightarrow{v}_{\hat{p}'} g(q')$. We have one of the following cases:

- If $q_1, q'_1 \notin Q^r_{p_i}$, then
  $q \xrightarrow{v}_{\hat{p}} q' \Leftrightarrow g(q) \xrightarrow{v}_{\hat{p}'} g(q')$ (by definition of g).
- If $q_1 \notin Q^r_{p_i}$ and $q'_1 \in Q^r_{p_i}$, then
  $\{n\} \cup q_1 \xrightarrow{v}_{\hat{p}} \{n\} \cup q'_1$ implies $q'_1 = q_{0p_i}$. So, $g(q) = \{n'\} \cup q_1$ and $g(q') = \{n'\} \cup f(q_{0p_i}) = \{n'\} \cup q_{0p'_i}$. Then $g(q) \xrightarrow{v}_{\hat{p}'} g(q')$.
- If $q_1 \in Q^r_{p_i}$ and $q'_1 \notin Q^r_{p_i}$, then
  $q \xrightarrow{v}_{\hat{p}} q' \Leftrightarrow \{n\} \cup q_1 \xrightarrow{v}_{\hat{p}} \{n\} \cup q'_1 \Leftrightarrow$
  $\{n\} \cup f(q_1) \xrightarrow{v}_{\hat{p}} \{n\} \cup q'_1 \Leftrightarrow g(q) \xrightarrow{v}_{\hat{p}'} g(q')$.
- If $q_1, q'_1 \in Q^r_{p_i}$, then
  $q \xrightarrow{v}_{\hat{p}} q' \Leftrightarrow \{n\} \cup q_1 \xrightarrow{v}_{\hat{p}} \{n\} \cup q'_1 \Leftrightarrow$
  $\{n\} \cup f(q_1) \xrightarrow{v}_{\hat{p}'} \{n\} \cup f(q'_1) \Leftrightarrow g(q) \xrightarrow{v}_{\hat{p}'} g(q')$.

The converse implication (i.e. $g(q) \xrightarrow{v}_{\hat{p}'} g(q')$, for $q, q' \in Q^r_{\hat{p}}$, implies $q \xrightarrow{v}_{\hat{p}} q'$) can be dealt with by analogous arguments. □

In Def.7, an isomorphism is a function which preserves labels of transitions. The following proposition shows that if we considered bijections which preserve the set of causal orders associated with labels we would define the same equivalence.

Proposition 9. *For two labels $v_1 = \langle Y_1, Z_1, R_1, F_1 \rangle$ and $v_2 = \langle Y_2, Z_2, R_2, F_2 \rangle$, $\leq_{v_1} = \leq_{v_2}$ iff $R_1 = R_2$.*

This is a direct consequence of the way we construct the relation R of a label when definining the LTS corresponding to a term. Actually, if we define *lab* such that $lab(\langle t, i, A, B, j \rangle) = \langle \emptyset, \emptyset, \{\langle A, B \rangle\}, \emptyset \rangle$, it is easy to see that Prop.9 would not hold anymore. In particular a bijection that preserves causal orders would define an equivalence weaker than a bijection that preserves labels. An example of two statecharts equated by the weaker equivalence and not equated by the stronger one is given in Fig.6.

We consider now bisimulation, which is an equivalence weaker than isomorphism, and we prove that it too is a congruence.

Definition 10. Two LTS's $s_1 = \langle Q_1, \Sigma_1, q_{0_1}, \longrightarrow_1 \rangle$ and $s_2 = \langle Q_2, \Sigma_2, q_{0_2}, \longrightarrow_2 \rangle$ are *bisimilar*, written $s_1 \equiv_{BIS} s_2$, if there exists a relation $\mathcal{S} \subseteq Q^r_1 \times Q^r_2$ with

1. $q_{0_1} \mathcal{S} q_{0_2}$.

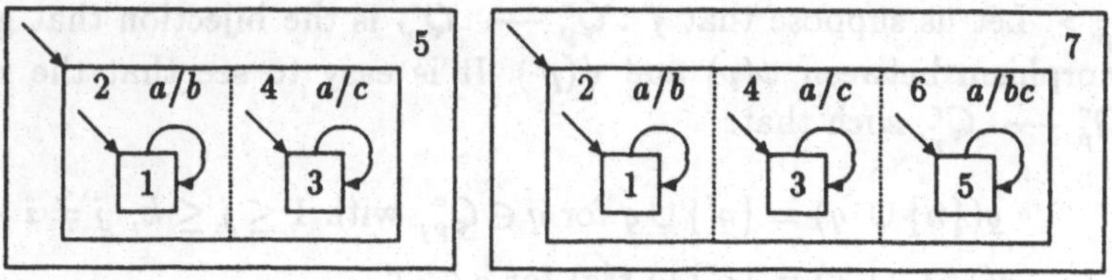

Fig. 6.

2. $\forall q_1 \in Q_1, q_2 \in Q_2 | q_1 \mathcal{S} q_2, \forall \sigma_1 \in \Sigma_1, \sigma_2 \in \Sigma_2$:
   (a) $q_1 \xrightarrow{\sigma_1}_1 q_1' \Longrightarrow \exists q_2' \in Q_2 | (q_2 \xrightarrow{\sigma_1}_2 q_2') \wedge (q_1' \mathcal{S} q_2')$;
   (b) $q_2 \xrightarrow{\sigma_2}_2 q_2' \Longrightarrow \exists q_1' \in Q_1 | (q_1 \xrightarrow{\sigma_2}_1 q_1') \wedge (q_1' \mathcal{S} q_2')$.

Terms p, p' are *$\approx_{BIS}$-equivalent*, written $p \approx_{BIS} p'$, iff $\psi(p) \equiv_{BIS} \psi(p')$.

Theorem 11. *$\approx_{BIS}$-equivalence is a congruence w.r. to SA operators.*

Proof. (Sketch) Assume $p_i \in SA$ with $\psi(p_i) = \langle Q_i, \Sigma_i, q_{0_i}, \rightarrow_i \rangle$, for $1 \leq i \leq 3$, and assume $p_1 \approx_{BIS} p_2$ for a relation $\mathcal{S} \subseteq Q_1^r \times Q_2^r$. Now take $p = [n : \{p_1, p_3\}]$ and $p' = [n : \{p_2, p_3\}]$ and assume $\psi(p) = \langle Q_p, \Sigma_p, q_{0_p}, \rightarrow_p \rangle$ and $\psi(p') = \langle Q_{p'}, \Sigma_{p'}, q_{0_{p'}}, \rightarrow_{p'} \rangle$. Following the line of the proof of Th.8 it can be proved that $\psi(p) \approx_{BIS} \psi(p')$ with a relation $\overline{\mathcal{S}} \subseteq Q_p^r \times Q_{p'}^r$ defined as follows:

$$(\{n\} \cup q_1 \cup q_3) \cap states(p) \overline{\mathcal{S}} (\{n\} \cup q_2 \cup q_3) \cap states(p') \text{ iff } q_1 \mathcal{S} q_2 \text{ for } q_i \in Q_i^r, 1 \leq i \leq 3.$$

Now assume $p = [n : \{p_1, \ldots, p_{i-1}, p_i, p_{i+1}, \ldots, p_k\}; T]$, $p' = [n : \{p_1, \ldots, p_{i-1}, p_i', p_{i+1}, \ldots, p_k\}; T]$ with $p_j, p_i' \in SA$, and $\psi(p_j) = \langle Q_j, \Sigma_j, q_{0_j}, \rightarrow_j \rangle$, $\psi(p_i') = \langle Q_i', \Sigma_i', q_{0_i}', \rightarrow_i' \rangle$, for $1 \leq j \leq k$. Assume $p_i \approx_{BIS} p_i'$ for a relation $\mathcal{S} \subseteq Q_i^r \times Q_i'^r$. Following the line of the proof of Th.8 it can be proved that $\psi(p) \approx_{BIS} \psi(p')$ with a relation $\overline{\mathcal{S}} \subseteq Q_p^r \times Q_{p'}^r$ defined as follows:

$$\{n\} \cup q \; \overline{\mathcal{S}} \; \{n\} \cup q' \text{ iff } q \; \mathcal{S} \; q' \text{ for } q \in Q_i^r \text{ and } q = q' \text{ otherwise.} \square$$

The 2-equivalence, which appears in the hierarchy of [3] at a lower level than bisimulation, fails to be a congruence for both the operations.

Definition 12. Two LTS's $s_1 = \langle Q_1, \Sigma_1, q_{0_1}, \rightarrow_1 \rangle$ and $s_2 = \langle Q_2, \Sigma_2, q_{0_2}, \rightarrow_2 \rangle$ are *2-equivalent*, written $s_1 \equiv_2 s_2$, if $q_{0_1} \equiv_2 q_{0_2}$, where $q_{0_1} \equiv_0 q_{0_2}$ in any case and $q_{0_1} \equiv_{n+1} q_{0_2}$ iff:

1. $q_{0_1} \stackrel{\sigma_1}{\Longrightarrow}_1 q \Rightarrow \exists q' | q_{0_2} \stackrel{\sigma_1}{\Longrightarrow}_2 q' \wedge q \equiv_n q'$;
2. $q_{0_2} \stackrel{\sigma_2}{\Longrightarrow}_2 q' \Rightarrow \exists q | q_{0_1} \stackrel{\sigma_2}{\Longrightarrow}_1 q \wedge q \equiv_n q'$.

Two terms p_1 and p_2 are *$\approx_2$-equivalent*, written $p_1 \approx_2 p_2$ iff $\psi(p_1) \equiv_2 \psi(p_2)$.

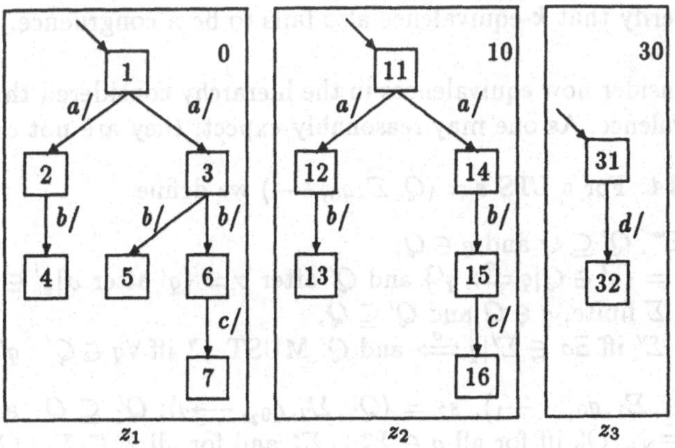

Fig. 7.

Theorem 13. *The $\approx_2$-equivalence is a congruence neither w. r. to or-compositon nor w.r. to and-composition.*

Proof. Let p_1, p_2 and p_3 be the terms representing the statecharts z_1, z_2 and z_3 of Fig.7, respectively. It is easy to verify that $\psi(p_1) \approx_2 \psi(p_2)$. Assume $\psi(p_1) = \langle Q_1, \Sigma_1, q_{0_1}, \longrightarrow_1\rangle$ and $\psi(p_2) = \langle Q_2, \Sigma_2, q_{0_2}, \longrightarrow_2\rangle$ and note that $\{0,1\} \xrightarrow{v}_1 \{0,3\}$, $\{10,11\} \xrightarrow{v}_2 \{10,14\}$, with $v = \langle \emptyset, \emptyset, \langle\{a\}, \emptyset\rangle, \emptyset\rangle$ and $\{0,3\} \approx_1 \{10,14\}$ holds (there is no transition from the state $\{0,5\}$ of p_1). Consider now the terms $p = [40 : \{p_1, p_3\}]$ and $p' = [40 : \{p_2, p_3\}]$ and assume $\psi(p) = \langle Q_p, \Sigma_p, q_{0p}, \longrightarrow_p\rangle$ and $\psi(p') = \langle Q_{p'}, \Sigma_{p'}, q_{0p'}, \longrightarrow_{p'}\rangle$. The products of $\psi(p_1)$ by $\psi(p_3)$ and of $\psi(p_2)$ by $\psi(p_3)$ do not preserve the trace equivalence of the (sub-)LTS's rooted in the states $\{0,3\} \in Q_1^r$ and $\{10,14\} \in Q_2^r$. Now, $q_{0p} \xrightarrow{v}_p s$ and $q_{0p'} \xrightarrow{v}_{p'} s'$ with $s = \{40,30,0,31,3\}$ and $s' = \{40,30,10,31,14\}$ but $s \approx_1 s'$ does not hold. In fact, the state $\{40,30,0,31,5\}$ of p has now a self loop labelled by $\langle\emptyset, \{d\}, \emptyset, \emptyset\rangle$ whereas there is no transition with this label from the state $\{40,30,10,31,15\}$ of p'. Moreover it is easy to verify that there is no state s'' of p' such that $q_{0p'} \xrightarrow{v}_{p'} s''$ and $s \approx_1 s''$.
Consider now the terms $p = [40 : \{p_1, p_3\}; T]$ and $p' = [40 : \{p_2, p_3\}; T]$ with $p_3 = [30 : \emptyset; \emptyset]$ and $T = \{\langle t, 1, \{d\}, \emptyset, 2\rangle\}$. Also in this case the trace equivalence of the (sub-)LTS's rooted in the states $\{0,3\} \in Q_1^r$ and $\{10,14\} \in Q_2^r$ is not preserved. In fact, the state $\{40,0,5\}$ of p has now a self loop labelled by $\langle\emptyset, \{d\}, \emptyset, \emptyset\rangle$ whereas there is no transition with this label from the state $\{40,10,15\}$ of p'. So, states $s = \{40,0,3\}$ and $s' = \{40,10,14\}$ fail to satisfy $s \approx_1 s'$. Now, it is easy to verify that there is no state s'' of p' such that $q_{0p'} \xrightarrow{v}_{p'} s''$ and $s \approx_1 s''$ (with $q_{0p'}$ the initial state of $\psi(p')$). □

k-equivalence (for $k > 2$), which can be defined by analogy with 2-equivalence, lies in the hierarchy of [3], in between bisimulation and 2-equivalence. It is not difficult to verify that k-equivalence also fails to be a congruence.

Let us consider now equivalences in the hierarchy considered that are coarser than 2-equivalence. As one may reasonably expect, they are not congruences.

Definition 14. For a LTS $s = \langle Q, \Sigma, q_0, \longrightarrow \rangle$ we define

1. for $\sigma \in \Sigma^*$, $Q' \subseteq Q$ and $q \in Q$,
   q after $\sigma = \{q' \in Q | q \stackrel{\sigma}{\Longrightarrow} q'\}$ and Q' after $\sigma = \{q'$ after $\sigma | q' \in Q'\}$
2. for $\Sigma' \subseteq \Sigma$ finite, $q \in Q$ and $Q' \subseteq Q$,
   q MUST Σ' iff $\exists \sigma \in \Sigma' | q \stackrel{\sigma}{\Longrightarrow}$ and Q' MUST Σ' iff $\forall q \in Q' : q'$ MUST Σ'.

For $s_1 = \langle Q_1, \Sigma_1, q_{0_1}, \longrightarrow_1 \rangle$, $s_2 = \langle Q_2, \Sigma_2, q_{0_2}, \longrightarrow_2 \rangle$, $Q_1' \subseteq Q_1$ and $Q_2' \subseteq Q_2$, we have $Q_1' \equiv_{NK} Q_2'$ iff for all $\sigma \in \Sigma_1^* \cup \Sigma_2^*$ and for all $\Sigma \subseteq \Sigma_1 \cup \Sigma_2$

$$(Q_1' \text{ after } \sigma) \text{ MUST } \Sigma \Leftrightarrow (Q_2' \text{ after } \sigma) \text{ MUST } \Sigma.$$

The LTS's s_1 and s_2 are *$\equiv_{NK}$-equivalent*, written $s_1 \equiv_{NK} s_2$, iff $q_{0_1} \equiv_{NK} q_{0_2}$. Two terms p and p' are *$\approx_{NK}$-equivalent*, written $p \approx_{NK} p'$, iff $\psi(p) \equiv_{NK} \psi(p')$.

Assume that a chain of reactions takes statecharts z_1 and z_2 to sets of configurations C and C', respectively. For $\approx_{NK}$-equivalence we require that if a set of signals is sufficient to cause a reaction in all configurations of C, the same holds for C', and viceversa. Statecharts z_1 and z_2 of Fig.8 are not discriminated by $\approx_{NK}$-equivalence but are discriminated by $\approx_2$-equivalence.

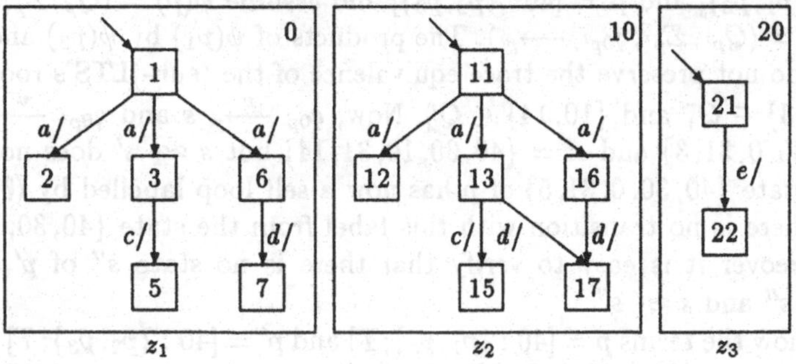

Fig. 8.

Theorem 15. *$\approx_{NK}$-equivalence is not a congruence w.r. to SA operators.*

Proof. Let p_1, p_2 and p_3 be terms representing the statecharts z_1, z_2 and z_3 of Fig.8, respectively. It is easy to verify that $\psi(p_1) \approx_{NK} \psi(p_2)$. Consider now the terms $p = [40 : p_1; p_3]$ and $p' = [40 : p_2; p_3]$ and assume $\sigma = \langle \emptyset, \emptyset, \langle \{a\}, \emptyset \rangle, \emptyset \rangle$ and $\Sigma = \{\langle \emptyset, \{e\}, \emptyset, \emptyset \rangle, \langle \emptyset, \emptyset, \langle \{d\}, \emptyset \rangle, \emptyset \rangle\}$. If q_{0p} and $q_{0p'}$ are the initial states of $\psi(p)$

and $\psi(p')$, respectively, then $q_{0p'}$ after σ MUST Σ holds true, whereas q_{0p} after σ MUST Σ does not.
Consider now the terms $p = [40 : \{p_1, p_3\}; T]$ and $p' = [40 : \{p_2, p_3\}; T]$ with $p_3 = [30 : \emptyset, \emptyset]$ and $T = \{\langle t, 1, \{e\}, \emptyset, 2\rangle\}$. Also in this case if q_{0p} and $q_{0p'}$ are the initial states of $\psi(p)$ and $\psi(p')$, respectively, then $q_{0p'}$ after σ MUST Σ holds true, whereas q_{0p} after σ MUST Σ does not. □

Finally, at the bottom of the hierarchy, we have a class of equivalences of which trace equivalence is a representative. It is easy to verify that trace equivalence is not a congruence w.r.t. to statechart operators.

5 Conclusions

We have proposed an interpretation of statecharts similar to that of [8] but without failures, and we have given both a declarative semantics and an operational one in terms of LTS's inspired by [9]. Then we have considered a hierarchy of LTS equivalences and studied congruence properties with respect to statechart operators. Future work includes axiomatization of these equivalences.

References

1. von der Beeck, M.: A Comparison of Statecharts Variants, Lecture Notes in Computer Science 863, Springer, Berlin, 1994, pp. 128–148.
2. Berry, G., Gonthier, G.: The ESTEREL Synchronous Programming Language: Design, Semantics, Implementation, Science of Computer Programming 19 (1992), pp. 87-152.
3. De Nicola, R.: Extensional Equivalences for Transition Systems, Acta Informatica 24 (1987), pp. 211-237.
4. Harel, D.: Statecharts: A Visual Formalism for Complex Systems, Science of Computer Programming 8 (1987), pp. 231–274.
5. Huizing, C., Gerth, R., de Roever, W. P.: Modelling Statecharts Behaviour in a Fully Abstract Way, Lecture Notes in Computer Science 299, Springer, Berlin, 1988, pp. 271-294.
6. Maraninchi, F.: Operational and Compositional Semantics of Synchronous Automaton Composition, Lecture Notes in Computer Science 630, Springer, Berlin, 1992, pp. 550-564.
7. Harel, D., Pnueli, A., Schmidt, J., P., Sherman, R.: On the Formal Semantics of Statecharts, Proc. 2nd IEEE Symposium on Logic in Computer Science, IEEE CS Press, New York, 1987, pp. 54–64.
8. Pnueli, A., Shalev, M.: What is a Step: On the Semantics of Statecharts, Lecture Notes in Computer Science 525, Springer, Berlin, 1991, pp. 244–464.
9. Uselton, A.C., Smolka, S.A.: A Compositional Semantics for Statecharts using Labeled Transition System, Lecture Notes in Computer Science 836, Springer, Berlin, 1994, pp. 2–17.
10. Uselton, A.C., Smolka, S.A.: A Process Algebraic Semantics for Statecharts via State Refinement, Proceedings of IFIP Working Conference on Programming Concepts, Methods and Calculi, 1994, pp. 267–286.

Modular Verification for Shared-Variable Concurrent Programs

Jürgen Dingel

School of Computer Science
Carnegie Mellon University
Pittsburgh, PA 15213, USA
E-mail: jurgend@cs.cmu.edu

Abstract. We propose a specification language for shared-variable concurrent programs based on Morgan's specification statement [Mor89]. A denotational semantics is given in terms of transition traces (sequences of pairs of states) following [Bro93]. A context-sensitive notion of approximation between specifications is presented which permits modular verification through stepwise program transformation. We argue that the resulting framework also supports program development through stepwise refinement.

1 Introduction

In the quest for tractable verification methods for concurrent systems, assumption-commitment reasoning has received a lot of attention, e.g., [Jon83, Pnu85, AL93, GL91]. In this approach, proofs are split into two parts: First, it is shown that a component of the overall system satisfies a certain property under the assumption that its environment behaves in a certain way. Then, this environment assumption is discharged by proving that the actual environment does indeed meet the assumption. Proofs become modular. This allows reuse of parts of a verification effort if some components of the system are replaced, and, most importantly, provides a powerful tool to deal with the complexity inherent in concurrent systems. Automatic verification methods like model checking constitute a very interesting and rewarding domain of application. There, researchers find themselves in a constant struggle to strike an appropriate balance between expressivity on the one hand and computational complexity on the other. In [GL91], assumption-commitment arguments are introduced into the model-checking setting. Using this approach, a typical line of reasoning goes as follows: Suppose that M and M' are finite state machines and that we want to show that their parallel composition $M \| M'$ satisfies some temporal logic property φ. Furthermore, suppose that the state machine corresponding to $M \| M'$ is too large for model checking techniques to be applicable directly, but that we were able to verify the following simpler relationships:

$$M \preceq A \qquad\qquad A \| M' \preceq A' \qquad\qquad M \| A' \models \varphi$$

where A and A' are assumptions given in terms of finite state machines (tableaux) and $M \preceq A$ expresses that the two machines are homomorphic, that is, that A can simulate M. In other words, M discharges assumption A, M' under assumption A discharges assumption A', and M under assumption A' satisfies the desired formula. The approach to assumption-commitment reasoning as developed in [GL91] allows us to conclude that $M \| M' \models \varphi$.

This paper transfers some of these ideas from finite state machines to shared-variable concurrent programs and uses them for a formal framework supporting compositional reasoning about these kinds of programs. We choose a specification-oriented framework which serves as a uniform device for the description of both abstract properties and concrete computational processes. The semantics is based on transition traces (sequences of pairs of states) which provide an elegant and robust denotational model of fair concurrent computation with shared memory as demonstrated in [Bro93]. We argue that transition traces constitute a powerful specification device and give rise to a useful notion of context-sensitive approximation which supports modular verification in the form of assumption-commitment reasoning. It seems that research on concurrency has so far been dominated by mostly operational methods. We think of our work as providing another indication that, with respect to reasoning about concurrent systems, a combination of denotational and operational methods is very promising.

The next section will introduce the syntax and semantics of our specification language, the language of partial programs. Section 3 will present various notions of approximation which form the basis of a modular verification framework described in Section 4. Further applications are presented in Section 5 and Section 6 concludes and outlines further research.

2 Syntax and semantics of partial programs

We want to be able to describe a single transition in very general terms like "the value of x does not change" or "the value of y at the end of the transition is greater than at the beginning of the transition". We adopt Morgan's specification statement [Mor89] to achieve this. The most basic partial program statement is of the form $V : [P, Q]$, where V is a set of variables and P and Q are assertions. It is meant to describe a single atomic transition, which transforms a state satisfying P into one satisfying Q by just changing the variables in V. A random assignment which may set x to any natural number can thus be described abstractly by $\{x\} : [tt, x \geq 0]$. To be able to refer to the values a variable held initially, i.e., at the beginning of the transition, we reserve zero-subscripted variables $\vec{x}_0$ in Q. The meaning of the assignment statement `x:=x+1`, for example, is thus captured by $\{x\} : [tt, x = x_0{+}1]$. More complex partial programs can be built using sequential and parallel composition, disjunction, conjunction, iteration, and hiding. Partial programs are ranged over by S,T.

$$S ::= V : [P, Q] \mid S_1; S_2 \mid S_1 \vee S_2 \mid S_1 \wedge S_2 \mid [\![S_1 \,\|\, S_2]\!] \mid S^* \mid S^\omega \mid$$
$$\mathbf{new}\ Id = n\ \mathbf{in}\ S\ \mathbf{end}$$

Partial contexts, ranged over by E,F, are partial programs with exactly one hole.

$$E ::= [\,] \mid S;E \mid E;S \mid S \vee E \mid E \vee S \mid S \wedge E \mid E \wedge S \mid [\![S \,\|\, E]\!] \mid [\![E \,\|\, S]\!] \mid$$
$$E^* \mid E^\omega \mid \mathbf{new}\ Id = n\ \mathbf{in}\ E\ \mathbf{end}$$

In [Bro93], the so-called *transition traces* form the basic tool to describe the behaviour of a command. Let $s_i \in \Sigma$ denote states, that is, mappings from the finite set of program variables *Var* to values. A transition trace is a possibly infinite sequence of the form $(s_0, s_0')(s_1, s_1')\ldots(s_n, s_n')\ldots$, and thus represents a possible "interactive" computation of a command in which state-changes made by the command (from s_i to s_i') are punctuated by state-changes made by its environment (from s_i' to s_{i+1}). In [Bro93] the meaning $\mathcal{T}$ of a command is given by a set of transition traces. To achieve full abstraction, trace sets are closed under two conditions: stuttering and mumbling. These closure conditions correspond, respectively, to reflexivity and transitivity of the $\rightarrow^*$ relation in a conventional operational semantics. We will also use transition traces to describe the behaviour of partial programs. However, in contrast with [Bro93], we have to adopt a more restrictive mumbling closure condition, because we want to be able to interpret linear temporal logic (LTL) formulae over denotations of programs. The context-insensitive semantics $\mathcal{T}^S$ maps partial programs to sets of transition traces closed under stuttering and restricted mumbling. Given a set U of traces, the closure under stuttering and restricted mumbling $U^\dagger$ denotes the smallest set which contains U and satisfies:

Stuttering: If $\alpha\beta \in U^\dagger$ then $\alpha(s,s)\beta \in U^\dagger$ and

Mumbling: if $\alpha(s,s)(s,s')\beta \in U^\dagger$ or $\alpha(s,s')(s',s')\beta \in U^\dagger$ then $\alpha(s,s')\beta \in U^\dagger$.

This restricted mumbling condition ensures that all intermediate states are always observable and is crucial for a sensible interpretation of liveness properties over denotations of programs. The semantics is defined compositionally in terms of operations on closed sets of traces. The concatenation $U_1; U_2$ and the infinite iteration operation U^ω are defined as

$$U_1; U_2 = \{\alpha\beta | \alpha \in U_1 \wedge \beta \in U_2\}^\dagger \qquad U^\omega = \{\alpha_0 \ldots \alpha_n \ldots | \alpha_i \in U\}^\dagger.$$

U^* denotes the smallest set containing U and the empty trace, closed under stuttering, mumbling and concatenation. The definition of the fair merge operation modeling fair parallel composition requires a little more work. Given a set T, let T^∞ denote $T^* \cup T^\omega$. Given $\alpha, \beta \in \Sigma^\infty$, let $\alpha\|\beta$ be the set of all traces built by fairly interleaving α and β. One way to define $\alpha\|\beta$ formally is:

$$\begin{aligned} \alpha\|\beta &= \{\gamma | (\alpha, \beta, \gamma) \in \mathit{fairmerge}\} \\ \mathit{fairmerge} &= (L^* R R^* L)^\omega \cup (L \cup R)^* A \\ L &= \{s, \epsilon, s) | s \in \Sigma\} \qquad R = \{\epsilon, s, s) | s \in \Sigma\} \\ A &= \{(\alpha, \epsilon, \alpha) | \alpha \in \Sigma^\infty\} \cup \{(\epsilon, \beta, \beta) | \beta \in \Sigma^\infty\} \end{aligned}$$

where concatenation is extended to sets and triples of traces in the obvious way: $AB = \{\alpha\beta | \alpha \in A \wedge \beta \in B\}$ and $(\alpha_1, \alpha_2, \alpha_3)(\beta_1, \beta_2, \beta_3) = (\alpha_1\beta_1, \alpha_2\beta_2, \alpha_3\beta_3)$. Fair interleaving of closed sets of traces can now be defined by:

$$U_1 \| U_2 = \bigcup \{\alpha_1 \| \alpha_2 \mid \alpha_1 \in U_1 \wedge \alpha_2 \in U_2\}^\dagger.$$

For more details on the above definitions see [Bro93]. The treatment of local variables requires some notation. The trace $\langle x = n \rangle \alpha$ is like α except that x has value n in the first state and that the value of x is "retained across points of interference". Formally, if α is of form $(s_0, s_0')(s_1, s_1')\ldots(s_i, s_i')$ then $\langle x = n \rangle \alpha$ is

$$([s_0 \mid x = n], s_0')([s_1 \mid x = s_0'(x)], s_1')\ldots([s_i \mid x = s_{i-1}'(x)], s_i')$$

where $[s \mid x = n]$ is the state which assigns n to x and is like s otherwise. The trace $\alpha\backslash x$ on the other hand describes a computation like α except that it never changes the value of x. That is, $\alpha\backslash x$ is

$$(s_0, [s_0' \mid x = s_0(x)])(s_1, [s_1' \mid x = s_1(x)]) \ldots (s_i, [s_i' \mid x = s_i(x)]).$$

Given a set of program variables $V \subseteq Var$, its complement $Var - V$ is denoted by $\overline{V}$. $\mathcal{P}^{\dagger}((\Sigma \times \Sigma)^{\infty})$ stands for the set of all closed subsets over $(\Sigma \times \Sigma)^{\infty}$.

Definition 1. The semantic function $\mathcal{T}^S : S \to \mathcal{P}^{\dagger}((\Sigma \times \Sigma)^{\infty})$ is defined by

$$\begin{aligned}
\mathcal{T}^S\,[V : [P, Q]] &= \{(s, s') \mid (s, s') \models P[\vec{x}_0/\vec{x}] \wedge Q \wedge \textstyle\bigwedge_{x \in \overline{V}} x = x_0\}^{\dagger} \\
\mathcal{T}^S\,[S_1; S_2] &= \mathcal{T}^S\,[S_1]\,;\mathcal{T}^S\,[S_2] \\
\mathcal{T}^S\,[S_1 \wedge S_2] &= \mathcal{T}^S\,[S_1] \cap \mathcal{T}^S\,[S_2] \\
\mathcal{T}^S\,[S_1 \vee S_2] &= \mathcal{T}^S\,[S_1] \cup \mathcal{T}^S\,[S_2] \\
\mathcal{T}^S\,[S_1 \parallel S_2] &= \mathcal{T}^S\,[S_1] \parallel \mathcal{T}^S\,[S_2] \\
\mathcal{T}^S\,[S^*] &= (\mathcal{T}^S\,[S\,])^* \\
\mathcal{T}^S\,[S^{\omega}] &= (\mathcal{T}^S\,[S\,])^{\omega} \\
\mathcal{T}^S\,[\texttt{new x=n in } S \texttt{ end}] &= \{\alpha\backslash x \mid \langle x = n\rangle\alpha \in \mathcal{T}^S\,[S\,]\}^{\dagger}
\end{aligned}$$

where $(s, s') \models Q$ iff replacing the variables with zero-subscripts in Q by their values in s and replacing the variables without zero-subscripts in Q by their values in s' makes Q true. □

The traces of **new x=n in** S **end** do not change the value of x and are obtained by executing S under the assumption that x is set to n initially and that the environment cannot change the value of x. Let $sp(S, B)$ be the strongest postcondition of statement S with respect to initial states B. $\{B\}$ denotes $\emptyset : [B, B]$, the stuttering step satisfying B. The programming language considered in [OG76, Bro93] is embedded into the language of partial programs through the following abbreviations. Note how the **await** statement is implemented using busy waiting.

skip	$\equiv$	$\{tt\}$
Id:=e	$\equiv$	$Id : [tt, Id = e[Id_0/Id]]$
if B **then** S_1 **else** S_2 **fi**	$\equiv$	$\{B\}; S_1 \vee \{\neg B\}; S_2$
while B **do** S **od**	$\equiv$	$(\{B\}; S)^*; \{\neg B\} \vee (\{B\}; S)^{\omega}$
await B **then** S **end**	$\equiv$	$\{Id_1, \ldots, Id_n\} : [B, sp(S, B)] \vee \{\neg B\}^{\omega}$ where S is Id_1:=$e_1; \ldots; Id_n$:=e_n
if B **then** S **fi**	$\equiv$	**if** B **then** S **else skip fi**
await B	$\equiv$	$\{B\} \vee \{\neg B\}^{\omega}$
case x of $e_1 : S_1 \mid \ldots \mid e_n : S_n$ **end**	$\equiv$	**if x=**e_1 **then** S_1 **else** ... **if x=**e_n **then** S_n **fi** ... **fi**.

Achieving context-sensitivity: We want to be able to express that, for example, every transition made by a program S_1 in a context E can be matched by a program S_2 in the same context. Thus, we need to be able to distinguish transitions made by the program from transitions made by its environment. To this end, we tag the transitions appropriately — an idea already used, for instance, in [BKP84]. A *tagged transition* is of the form $(s, t, s') \in \Sigma \times \{p, e\} \times \Sigma$ where the tag t indicates whether the transition was made by the program or its environment. Tagged transitions with $t = p$ are called *program transitions*. *Environment transitions* have $t = e$. A tagged transition trace consisting only of program transitions is called a *program trace*. A trace consisting only of environment transitions is called an *environment trace*. The closure conditions have to be modified only slightly to account for tagged traces: Given a set U of tagged traces, the closure under stuttering and mumbling $U^\dagger$ is the smallest set which contains U and satisfies:

Stuttering: If $\alpha\beta \in U^\dagger$ then $\alpha(s,p,s)\beta \in U^\dagger$ and $\alpha(s,e,s)\beta \in U^\dagger$ and

Mumbling: 1. if $\alpha(s,t,s)(s,t',s')\beta \in U^\dagger$ then $\alpha(s,t',s')\beta \in U^\dagger$ and

2. if $\alpha(s,t,s')(s',t',s')\beta \in U^\dagger$ then $\alpha(s,t,s')\beta \in U^\dagger$.

The definition of $\mathcal{T}^S$ is easily adapted to account for tags. To retain the syntactic distinction between a program S and its context E, S is enclosed in angle brackets $\langle \_ \rangle$ when placed into E: $E[\langle S\rangle]$. The set of *tagged partial programs*, denoted by TS, comprises all partial programs containing at most one subprogram in angle brackets. A context-sensitive semantic map $\mathcal{T}^{SE}$ on tagged partial programs can now be defined such that subprograms inside angle brackets map to program traces and subprograms outside angle brackets to environment traces. The operations on traces and sets of traces are defined as before.

Definition 2. The semantic function $\mathcal{T}^{SE} : TS \to \mathcal{P}^\dagger((\Sigma \times \{p,e\} \times \Sigma)^\infty)$ is defined as $\mathcal{T}_e^{SE}[\_]$ where $\mathcal{T}_t^{SE}[\_]$ for $t \in \{p,e\}$ is given by

$$\begin{aligned}
\mathcal{T}_e^{SE}[\langle S\rangle] &= \mathcal{T}_p^{SE}[S] \\
\mathcal{T}_t^{SE}[V:[P,Q]] &= \{(s,t,s') \mid (s,s') \models P[\vec{x}_0/\vec{x}] \wedge Q \wedge \textstyle\bigwedge_{x\in\overline{V}} x = x_0\}^\dagger \\
\mathcal{T}_t^{SE}[S_1;S_2] &= \mathcal{T}_t^{SE}[S_1];\mathcal{T}_t^{SE}[S_2] \\
\mathcal{T}_t^{SE}[S_1 \wedge S_2] &= \mathcal{T}_t^{SE}[S_1] \cap \mathcal{T}_t^{SE}[S_2] \\
\mathcal{T}_t^{SE}[S_1 \vee S_2] &= \mathcal{T}_t^{SE}[S_1] \cup \mathcal{T}_t^{SE}[S_2] \\
\mathcal{T}_t^{SE}[S_1 \| S_2] &= \mathcal{T}_t^{SE}[S_1] \,\|\, \mathcal{T}_t^{SE}[S_2] \\
\mathcal{T}_t^{SE}[S^*] &= (\mathcal{T}_t^{SE}[S])^* \\
\mathcal{T}_t^{SE}[S^\omega] &= (\mathcal{T}_t^{SE}[S])^\omega \\
\mathcal{T}_t^{SE}[\texttt{new x=n in } S \texttt{ end}] &= \{\alpha\backslash x \mid \langle x = n\rangle\alpha \in \mathcal{T}_t^{SE}[S]\}^\dagger.
\end{aligned}$$

□

Note how the mumbling conditions prevent $\mathcal{T}^{SE}$ from distinguishing, for example, **skip**; $\langle S\rangle$, $\langle S\rangle$; **skip** and $\langle S\rangle$. $\mathcal{T}^{SE}$ coincides with $\mathcal{T}^S$ on untagged partial programs, but is finer grained on tagged partial programs. Let $S_1 \sqsubseteq_{\mathcal{T}^{SE}} S_2$ abbreviate $\mathcal{T}^{SE}[S_1] \subseteq \mathcal{T}^{SE}[S_2]$ and equivalently for $\mathcal{T}^S$.

Proposition 3. *1)* $S_1 \sqsubseteq_{\mathcal{T}^{SE}} S_2$ *iff* $S_1 \sqsubseteq_{\mathcal{T}^S} S_2$.
2) $E[\langle S_1\rangle] \sqsubseteq_{\mathcal{T}^{SE}} E[\langle S_2\rangle]$ *implies* $E[S_1] \sqsubseteq_{\mathcal{T}^S} E[S_2]$.
3) $E[S_1] \sqsubseteq_{\mathcal{T}^S} E[S_2]$ *does not imply* $E[\langle S_1\rangle] \sqsubseteq_{\mathcal{T}^{SE}} E[\langle S_2\rangle]$.

Proof: 1) and 2) follow directly from the definitions. For 3) consider the following counterexample: Let S and S_1 be **while tt do skip od**, let E be $[\,]\|S$, and S_2 be **skip**. Then, $E[S_1] \sqsubseteq_{\mathcal{T}^S} E[S_2]$ but $E[\langle S_1\rangle] \not\sqsubseteq_{\mathcal{T}^{SE}} E[\langle S_2\rangle]$. ■

3 Approximation

A very natural notion of approximation arises through trace inclusion. This was already considered in [Bro93] and used to validate several natural laws of concurrent programming, such as $C \,\|\, \texttt{skip} \sqsubseteq_{\mathcal{T}} C$ and $C_1 \,\|\, [C_2 \,\|\, C_3] \sqsubseteq_{\mathcal{T}} [C_1 \,\|\, C_2] \,\|\, C_3$. Due to the replacement of assignment by the more powerful specification statement, partial programs allow us to express very general properties. Trace inclusion can be used to establish these properties for more concrete programs.

Example 1. Let U_1 be the trace set $\{(s, s') \mid s'(x) = s(x) \wedge s, s' \in \Sigma\}^\infty$. This characterizes all finite and infinite computations that never change the value of x. This property is easily expressed by the partial program $S_1 \equiv \text{inv}\{x\}^\infty$ where $\text{inv}V$ abbreviates $V : [tt, tt]$. More precisely, $U_1 = \mathcal{T}^S\,[\![S_1]\!]$. Since U_1 contains all other possible transitions, a program T does not change x iff $T \sqsubseteq_{\mathcal{T}^S} S_1$. For instance, let

$T_1 \equiv$ `s:=0;while y>0 do s:=s+x;y:=y-1 od` $\quad T_2 \equiv$ `y:=1;x:=y`.

Then, $T_1 \sqsubseteq_{\mathcal{T}^S} S_1$, whereas $T_2 \not\sqsubseteq_{\mathcal{T}^S} S_1$. □

Partial programs have a rich algebraic theory. Note, for instance, that trace inclusion is a *congruence*. This is due essentially to the compositional definition of $\mathcal{T}^S$ in terms of monotone operations on trace sets. Moreover, parallel compositions can be "unrolled" using a variant of Milner's expansion theorem [Mil89]. Additionally, trace inclusion between specification statements can be characterized logically. Let A and B range over specification statements.

Proposition 4.

$$E[S_1] \sqsubseteq_{\mathcal{T}^S} E[S_2] \quad \textit{if} \quad S_1 \sqsubseteq_{\mathcal{T}^S} S_2$$
$$[\textstyle\bigvee_i A_i; S_i \,\|\, \bigvee_j B_j; T_j] =_{\mathcal{T}^S} \bigvee_i A_i; [S_i \,\|\, \bigvee_j B_j; T_j] \vee \bigvee_j B_j; [\bigvee_i A_i; S_i \,\|\, T_j]$$
$$V_1 : [P_1, Q_1] \sqsubseteq_{\mathcal{T}^S} V_2 : [P_2, Q_2] \quad \textit{iff} \quad P_1[\vec{x}_0/\vec{x}] \wedge Q_1 \wedge \textstyle\bigwedge_{x \in \overline{V_1}} x = x_0 \Rightarrow P_2[\vec{x}_0/\vec{x}] \wedge Q_2 \wedge \bigwedge_{x \in \overline{V_2}} x = x_0$$

See [Din96] for a more complete set of rules which also make use of the regular expression-like shape of partial programs.

3.1 Context-sensitive approximation on partial programs

Trace set inclusion between two programs is a rather strong property since it expresses that the behaviour of one program in *every* possible context can also be exhibited by the other program in the same context. Typically, we want to reason about a program in a fixed context and thus it suffices to show approximation with respect to that particular context. So, one would like to parameterize the approximation relation with information about the context. In [Lar87] Larsen demonstrates how this can be done for CCS and bisimulation. Let I range over state predicates. A possibly infinite trace $\alpha \equiv (s_0, s_0') \ldots (s_i, s_i') \ldots$ is called *interference-free*, *i-free*(α) for short, if $s_j = s_{j-1}'$ for all $0 < j < \textit{length}(\alpha)$. The projection function fst returns the first state of a trace, that is, $\text{fst}(\alpha) = s_0$. Similarly for tagged traces.

Definition 5. $S_1 \leq_E^I S_2$ iff for all $\alpha \in \mathcal{T}^{SE}\ [E[\langle S_1 \rangle]]$,

$$\text{if i-free}(\alpha) \text{ and fst}(\alpha) \models I \text{ then } \alpha \in \mathcal{T}^{SE}\ [E[\langle S_2 \rangle]].$$

$S_1 \leq_E S_2$ is short for $S_1 \leq_E^{tt} S_2$ and $S_1 \leq S_2$ is short for $S_1 \leq_E S_2$ for all E. □

Intuitively, $S_1 \leq_E^I S_2$ if E and I cause S_1 to exhibit only transitions that can be matched by S_2. In other words, E and I cannot force S_1 to go beyond what S_2 can do. Let $\alpha \lceil t$ denote the subtrace of α consisting of the transitions tagged with t, that is, $((s_0, t_0, s_0')\alpha)\lceil t_0 = (s_0, s_0')(\alpha \lceil t_0)$ and $(s_0, t_0, s_0')\alpha \lceil t = \alpha \lceil t$ if $t_0 \neq t$.

Lemma 6. *Let* $\alpha \in \mathcal{T}^{SE}\ [E[\langle S_1 \rangle]]$. *Then,* $\alpha \in \mathcal{T}^{SE}\ [E[\langle S_2 \rangle]]$ *iff* $\alpha \lceil p \in \mathcal{T}^S\ [S_2]$.

The above lemma provides us with an alternative characterization of approximation.

Corollary 7. $S_1 \leq_E^I S_2$ *iff for all* $\alpha \in \mathcal{T}^{SE}\ [E[\langle S_1 \rangle]]$, *if i-free*$(\alpha)$ *and fst*$(\alpha) \models I$ *then* $\alpha \lceil p \in \mathcal{T}^S\ [S_2]$.

Approximation based on trace inclusion turns out to be a special case of context-sensitive approximation.

Proposition 8. $S_1 \leq S_2$ *iff* $S_1 \sqsubseteq_{\mathcal{T}^S} S_2$.

Proof: Let $S_1 \not\leq S_2$. Thus, there exist E and an interference-free trace α such that $\alpha \in \mathcal{T}^{SE}\ [E[\langle S_1 \rangle]] - \mathcal{T}^{SE}\ [E[\langle S_2 \rangle]]$. With Lemma 6 this implies $\alpha \lceil p \in \mathcal{T}^S\ [S_1] - \mathcal{T}^S\ [S_2]$ and thus, $S_1 \not\sqsubseteq_{\mathcal{T}^S} S_2$. To show the implication from left to right we assume that $\alpha \in \mathcal{T}^S\ [S_1] - \mathcal{T}^S\ [S_2]$. Note that, since we assume the set of program variables *Var* to be finite, α can expect only finitely many different variables to be changed by the environment. Following the full abstraction proof in [Bro93], α can be used to construct a context E_α such that there exists an interference-free $\alpha' \in \mathcal{T}^{SE}\ [E_\alpha[\langle S_1 \rangle]]$ with $\alpha' \lceil p = \alpha$. Again, with Lemma 6 this implies $\alpha' \notin \mathcal{T}^{SE}\ [E_\alpha[\langle S_2 \rangle]]$ and thus, $S_1 \not\leq S_2$. ■

Proposition 9. $S_1 \leq_E^I S_2$ *implies* $E[S_1] \leq_{[]}^I E[S_2]$.

Example 2. The transition traces of $T_2 \equiv$ `x:=1;x:=x+1` are not contained in those of $T_2' \equiv$ `x:=1;x:=2` because the environment may change the value of x after the first assignment to something other than 1. For example, the traces of the form $([s|x=0],[s|x=1])([s|x=0],[s|x=1])$ are possible for T_2 but not for T_2'. Thus, $T_2 \not\sqsubseteq_{\mathcal{T}^S} T_2'$. However, if the two programs run in isolation, i.e., in the empty environment `[]`, then every interference-free trace of T_2 is also possible for T_2'. Since this holds for any initial state we have $T_2 \leq_{[]} T_2'$. Moreover, since $T_2' \sqsubseteq_{\mathcal{T}^S} T_2$ the converse also holds using Proposition 8. Thus, $T_2 =_{[]} T_2'$. Moreover, let $E_2 \equiv$ `x:=2;[[]||y:=1]` and $F_2 \equiv$ `[[]||y:=1||x:=1]`. Again, we have $T_2 =_{E_2} T_2'$ and $T_2 =_{F_2} T_2'$, illustrating the fact that an environment which concurrently changes the value of x to something other than 1 is needed to tell the two programs apart. □

Example 3. Consider the following programs and let E_3 and E'_3 be `[[] || S]` and `[[] || S']` respectively.

```
T3  ≡  while tt do
         await rdy; rdy:=false;
         case cmd of
           "inc" : x:=x+1 |
           "dec" : x:=x-1 |
           "res" : x:=0 |
           "foo" : while tt do x:=x+1 od
         end;
         done:=true
       od
```

```
T3' ≡  while tt do
         await rdy; rdy:=false;
         case cmd of
           "inc" : x:=x+1 mod 10 |
           "dec" : if x>0 then x:=x-1 fi |
           "res" : x:=0
         end;
         done:=true
       od
```

```
S ≡
cmd:="res";
done:=ff; rdy:=tt; await done;
cmd:="inc";
done:=ff; rdy:=tt; await done;
cmd:="dec";
done:=ff; rdy:=tt; await done
```

```
S' ≡
new c=x in
  [({c, cmd} : [tt, cmd = "res" ∧ c = 0] ∨
    {c, cmd} : [c < 9, cmd = "inc" ∧ c = c0 + 1] ∨
    {c, cmd} : [c > 0, cmd = "dec" ∧ c = c0 − 1]);
   done:=ff; rdy:=tt; await done]^∞
end.
```

T_3 and T'_3 provide a service to the environment by "executing" the current command *cmd*. Although the possible behaviours of the two programs are different, the contexts E_3 and E'_3 prevent both from ever exhibiting these distinguishing behaviours and a difference will never be observed, that is, $T_3 =_{E_3}^{\neg rdy} T'_3$ and $T_3 =_{E'_3}^{\neg rdy} T'_3$. Note that the transition system of T_3 when viewed as a reactive system has an *infinite* state space. More precisely, there are contexts such that T_3 in these contexts can set its variables to infinitely many values. T'_3 on the other hand, can set its variables to only finitely many values in any environment. □

A partial program is called *sequential* if it does not contain a parallel composition. We can give a weakest precondition semantics to sequential partial programs. Following [Mor89], the weakest precondition of $V : [P, Q]$ with respect to a state predicate R is given by

$$wp(V : [P,Q], R) = P \wedge (\forall x \in V.Q \Rightarrow R)[\bar{x}/\bar{x}_0].$$

The remaining sequential constructs are characterized by Dijkstra's well-known weakest precondition semantics [Dij76]. In Section 4 we will need the following proof rules.

Proposition 10.

$$S'_1 \leq_E^{I'} S'_2 \quad \textit{if} \quad S_1 \leq_E^I S_2 \textit{ and } S'_1 \sqsubseteq_{\mathcal{T}^S} S_1 \textit{ and } S_2 \sqsubseteq_{\mathcal{T}^S} S'_2 \textit{ and } I' \Rightarrow I$$

$$S_1 \| S_2 \leq_E^I S'_1 \| S'_2 \quad \textit{if} \quad S_1 \leq_{E[[] \| S_2]}^I S'_1 \textit{ and } S_2 \leq_{E[S_1 \| []]}^I S'_2$$

$$S_1 \leq_{S;E}^I S_2 \quad \textit{iff} \quad S_1 \leq_E^{I'} S_2 \textit{ and } I \Rightarrow wp(S, I') \textit{ where } S \textit{ is sequential}$$

We currently work on extending this proposition to a proof system for context-sensitive approximation [Din96].

3.2 Approximation on contexts

We extend approximation to contexts. Consider the contexts `x:=1;y:=2;[]` and `y:=2;x:=1;[]`. Both establish the same precondition for the program to be placed in the hole, and thus any program should behave the same in both of them. Consequently, we would like to identify these contexts. Note that here we cannot resort to a relation based on trace inclusion, since it would fail to identify the above two contexts.

Definition 11. E_1 strongly approximates E_2, $E_1 \lessapprox E_2$ for short, if for all state predicates I, and partial programs S_1 and S_2 we have that $S_1 \leq^I_{E_1} S_2$ implies $S_1 \leq^I_{E_2} S_2$. Two program contexts are strongly equivalent, $E_1 \approx E_2$, if $E_1 \lessapprox E_2$ and $E_2 \lessapprox E_1$. □

Intuitively, E_1 strongly approximates E_2 if whenever E_1 causes the behaviour of a partial program S_1 in some initial state I to be included in that of S_2, then E_2 will do the same.

Example 4. With respect to the example above, we have

$$\mathtt{x:=1;y:=2;[]} \approx \mathtt{y:=2;x:=1;[]}.$$

Moreover, for instance,

$$\mathtt{[]} \,\|\, \mathtt{x:=1} \,\|\, \mathtt{x:=2} \lessapprox \mathtt{[[]} \,\|\, \mathtt{x:=1;x:=2]}.$$

The converse does not hold because starting in initial states with $x = 0$, for example, the context on the left has the ability to decrement x whereas the context on the right always increments x. More precisely,

$$\mathtt{y:=x;z:=x} \leq^{x=0}_{\mathtt{[[]\|x:=1;x:=2]}} y : [tt, y = x_0]; z : [tt, z \geq y_0], \text{ but}$$
$$\mathtt{y:=x;z:=x} \not\leq^{x=0}_{\mathtt{[[]\|x:=1\|x:=2]}} y : [tt, y = x_0]; z : [tt, z \geq y_0].$$

Consider Example 3. We have $E_3' \lessapprox E_3$. □

This example suggests that strong approximation is governed by some helpful laws. We now isolate some of them. A context is called *sequential* if its hole is not in the scope of a parallel composition. The first pair of contexts in Example 4 suggests that in sequential contexts the input-output behaviour of a subprogram suffices to determine its effect on the rest of the context. Consider the refinement calculi for sequential programs as developed by Back, Morgan and Morris [Bac88, Mor94, Mor87]. There, a sequential program C is refined by another C', $C'\,ref_{seq}\,C$ for short, iff $wp(C, R) \Rightarrow wp(C', R)$ for all state predicates R. Using the weakest precondition semantics described above, we adopt this notion of refinement for sequential partial programs. The following proposition constitutes an incomplete set of valid rules where Rules S-SEQ-1 and S-PAR are inspired by Example 4.

Proposition 12.

S-SEQ-1: $E_1[S_1; E_2] \lessapprox E_1[S_2; E_2]$ *iff* $S_2\ ref_{seq}\ S_1$ *where* E_1, S_1, S_2 *sequential*
S-SEQ-2: $E_1[S_1; E_2] \lessapprox E_1[S_2; E_2]$ *if* $S_2 \sqsubseteq_{\mathcal{T}^s} S_1$
S-SEQ-3: $E_1[S; E_2] \approx E_1[E_2]$ *if* $S =_{\mathcal{T}^s} \{tt\}^*$
S-PAR: $E_1[E_2 \,\|\, S_1] \lessapprox E_1[E_2 \,\|\, S_2]$ *if* $S_2 \sqsubseteq_{\mathcal{T}^s} S_1$

On first sight, Definition 11 seems too extensional to be useful, because it does not provide us with an obvious efficient method to determine whether a given context approximates another one or not. However, the above proposition shows that both refinement for sequential programs and transition trace inclusion imply approximation of certain contexts.

Example 5. Consider the three contexts given in Example 2. Let

$$E_5 \equiv Var: [tt, tt]^\infty; \texttt{[[]} \,\|\, Var: [tt, x = x_0 \vee x = 1]^\infty\texttt{]}.$$

Using Proposition 12 we can show that E_5 is less than all three of those contexts. For $\texttt{[]} \,\|\, \texttt{y:=1} \,\|\, \texttt{x:=1}$, for example, we reason as follows: $E_5 \lessapprox Var : [tt, tt]^\infty; \texttt{[[]} \,\|\, \texttt{y:=1} \,\|\, \texttt{x:=1]} \lessapprox \texttt{skip; [[]} \,\|\, \texttt{y:=1} \,\|\, \texttt{x:=1]} \lessapprox \texttt{[]} \,\|\, \texttt{y:=1} \,\|\, \texttt{x:=1}$ using S-PAR, S-SEQ-2, S-SEQ-3. Consider Example 3. $E_3' \lessapprox E_3$ can be deduced with $S \sqsubseteq_{\mathcal{T}^S} S'$ and S-PAR. The remaining approximations in Example 4 are shown similarly using S-SEQ-1 and S-PAR. □

Strong approximation on two contexts requires them to induce approximating behaviours for the *same* initial state. This, in general, rules out the possibility to relate, for example, $E \equiv \texttt{[]} \,\|\, \mathrm{inv}\{x\}^\omega$ and $S; E$ for nontrivial S. Sometimes, however, approximation between partial programs is insensitive to the initial state. For example, $\texttt{x:=1;x:=x+1} \leq_E^I \texttt{x:=1;x:=2}$ holds for any initial state I. Consequently, E can be prefixed with any partial program S without destroying the approximation: $\texttt{x:=1;x:=x+1} \leq_{S;E}^I \texttt{x:=1;x:=2}$ for all I and S.

Definition 13. E_1 weakly approximates E_2, $E_1 \lesssim E_2$ for short, if for all partial programs S_1 and S_2 we have that $S_1 \leq_{E_1} S_2$ implies $S_1 \leq_{E_2} S_2$. Two program contexts are weakly equivalent, $E_1 \sim E_2$, if $E_1 \lesssim E_2$ and $E_2 \lesssim E_1$. □

Note that strong approximation implies weak approximation.

Proposition 14.

W-SEQ: $E_1 \lesssim E_2[E_1]$ *if E_2 is sequential*

W-PAR: $E_1 \,\|\, V : [tt, tt]^\infty \lesssim E_2[E_1] \,\|\, V : [tt, tt]^\infty$ *if E_2 is sequential*

The intuition for W-SEQ is given above. For W-PAR the argument is similar except that now the embedding of E_1 into the sequential context E_2 occurs under the scope of a parallel composition with the program $V : [tt, tt]^\infty$. Thus, the execution of parts of E_1 may be interleaved with transitions from $V : [tt, tt]^\infty$. However, this interaction is harmless, because, informally, E_2 cannot cause $V : [tt, tt]^\infty$ to "do anything it already could not do on its own". If V is $\emptyset$, W-SEQ arises from W-PAR as a special case.

3.3 Application to LTL model checking

We consider the linear time temporal logic *without* the next time operator to achieve invariance under stuttering and to allow for formulae to be interpreted over finite and infinite traces. Let $s_0 s_1 \ldots \models_{LTL} \psi$ denote that the sequence of states $s_0 s_1 \ldots$ satisfies the LTL formula ψ.

Definition 15. Let $\alpha \equiv (s_0, s_1)(s_1, s_2)\ldots$ be a possibly infinite, interference-free transition trace, and let ψ be a LTL-formula. α satisfies ψ, $\alpha \models \psi$ for short, if $s_0 s_1 \ldots \models_{LTL} \psi$. S satisfies ψ in initial states I, $(S, I) \models \psi$ for short, if

$$\text{for all } \alpha \in \mathcal{T}^S\,[S]\,.\ \text{if i-free}(\alpha) \text{ and } \mathrm{fst}(\alpha) \models I \text{ then } \alpha \models \psi.$$

If $(S, tt) \models \psi$, we write $S \models \psi$. □

Since it is based on inclusion of traces, approximation preserves LTL properties.

Proposition 16. *If $S_1 \leq^I_{[]} S_2$ and $(S_2, I) \models \psi$ then $(S_1, I) \models \psi$.*

Example 6. The behaviour of the programs T_3 and T_3' in Example 3 could be described with the following first-order LTL formula ψ:

$$\forall\, n.\mathsf{G}(\ rdy \Rightarrow (cmd = \text{'res'} \Rightarrow \mathsf{F}(done \wedge x = 0)) \wedge \\ ((cmd = \text{'inc'} \wedge x = n) \Rightarrow \mathsf{F}(done \wedge x = n+1)) \wedge \\ ((cmd = \text{'dec'} \wedge x = n \wedge n > 0) \Rightarrow \mathsf{F}(done \wedge x = n-1))))$$

Once we know that $(E_3[T_3'], \neg rdy) \models \psi$ and $T_3 \leq^{\neg rdy}_{E_3} T_3'$ we can conclude that $(E_3[T_3], \neg rdy) \models \psi$. In other words, it suffices to prove the specification for the finite state program T_3' to conclude that the infinite state program T_3 satisfies the same specification. □

4 Assumption-commitment reasoning

We now demonstrate how our framework supports assumption-commitment reasoning through the following program transformation strategy: Let S_0 be some partial program and I some initial states. Suppose we want to find a more abstract partial program S_n such that $S_0 \leq^I_{[]} S_n$. We carry out the following iterative process: If S_i contains a subprogram T_i, that is, $S_i = E_i[T_i]$ for some E_i, which can be abstracted further, we find a more abstract program T_i' and a context E_i' such that: 1) $T_i \leq^I_{E_i'} T_i'$, that is, T_i approximates T_i' with respect to context E_i' and initial states I. 2) $E_i' \lessapprox E_i$, that is, the assumptions placed on the environment in form of E_i' are met by the actual context E_i. If the approximation between T_i and T_i' holds for any initial state, that is, if $T_i \leq_{E_i'} T_i'$, then the environment assumptions can be weakened since it suffices for E_i' to weakly approximate E_i, that is, $E_i' \lesssim E_i$. Then, let S_{i+1} be $E_i[T_i']$. With Proposition 9 we have $E_i[T_i] \leq^I_{[]} E_i[T_i']$ for all $0 \leq i < n$. Since $E_i[T_i'] \equiv S_{i+1} \equiv E_{i+1}[T_{i+1}]$, transitivity implies $S_0 \leq^I_{[]} S_n$.

Example 7. Consider the program S.

$S \;\equiv\; E$[`rdy:=ff;` [$S_1 \,\|\, S_2$]]

```
S1 ≡ while tt do
       done:=ff; T1;
       rdy:=tt;
       await done; T3
     od

S2 ≡ while tt do
       await rdy;
       T2; rdy:=ff;
       done:=tt
     od
```

Assuming that neither the environment E nor any of the T_i change the values of *rdy* or *done*, the three subprograms T_i will be scheduled sequentially in ascending order. Formally,

```
rdy:=ff; [S1 || S2]  =E  rdy:=ff;
                          while tt do
                            done:=ff; T1; rdy:=tt; T2; rdy:=ff; done:=tt; T3
                          od
```

if $[[] \,\|\, \mathrm{inv}\{rdy, done\}^\infty] \lesssim E$ and $T_i \sqsubseteq_{\mathcal{T}^S} \mathrm{inv}\{rdy, done\}^\infty$ for $i = 1, 2, 3$. □

The next examples are more involved and require several steps of transformation. Note that given $S_0 \leq^{I}_{[]} S_n$, Proposition 16 guarantees that every LTL property satisfied by S_n also holds for S_0.

Example 8. Consider the following programs.

```
S1 ≡ while tt do                      S2 ≡ while tt do
        done:=ff;                             await rdy;
T1 ≡    {a,b} : [tt, a ≥ 0 ∧ b ≥ 0];  T2 ≡    new tmpa=a, tmpb=b in
        rdy:=tt;                                while tmpa>0 and tmpb>0 do
        await done;                               tmpa:=tmpa-1; tmpb:=tmpb-1 od
T3 ≡    x:=b                                    if tmpb=0 then b:=a fi;
     od                                       end;
                                              rdy:=ff; done:=tt
S  ≡ E[rdy:=ff; [S1 || S2]]              od.
```

S_2 provides a service to S_1 by computing the maximum of a and b and storing it in b. Suppose that E is of form U_1; `[[] ||` U_2`]`. We want to show that S sets the flag *done* infinitely often and that each time *done* is set, b is the maximum of a and b assuming that U_1 always terminates and does not set *done* and that U_2 does not modify a, b, *rdy* or *done*. Formally, if

$$U_1 \sqsubseteq_{\mathcal{T}S} Var : [tt, \neg done]^* \quad \text{and} \quad U_2 \sqsubseteq_{\mathcal{T}S} \text{inv}\{a, b, rdy, done\}^\infty$$

then

$$(S, \neg done) \models \mathsf{GF}\, done \wedge \mathsf{G}(done \Rightarrow b = max(a, b)).$$

1) Assuming that U_2 does not change the values of *rdy* or *done*, we can resort to Example 7 to replace the parallel subprogram $S_1 \| S_2$ by a sequential one. Let F_1 be $[] \| \text{inv}\{rdy, done\}^\infty$. Then,

$$\texttt{rdy:=ff; [}S_1 \| S_2\texttt{]} =_{F_1} \texttt{rdy:=ff; } E_1\texttt{[}T_2\texttt{]}$$

where E_1 is

$$\texttt{while tt do done:=ff; } T_1 \texttt{; rdy:=tt; []; rdy:=ff; done:=tt; } T_3 \texttt{ od.}$$

To discharge the environment assumption we first show that U_2 does not change *rdy* or *done*, that is,

$$U_2 \sqsubseteq_{\mathcal{T}S} \text{inv}\{a, b, rdy, done\}^\infty \sqsubseteq_{\mathcal{T}S} \text{inv}\{rdy, done\}^\infty.$$

Then, weak approximation between F_1 and E is established as follows:

$$\begin{array}{lllr} F_1 \equiv [] \| \text{inv}\{rdy, done\}^\infty & \lesssim & U_1; \texttt{[}[] \| \text{inv}\{rdy, done\}^\infty\texttt{]} & \text{W-SEQ} \\ & \lesssim & U_1; \texttt{[}[] \| U_2\texttt{]} \;\equiv\; E & \text{S-PAR.} \end{array}$$

Thus, $\texttt{rdy:=ff; [}S_1 \| S_2\texttt{]} =_E \texttt{rdy:=ff; } E_1[T_2]$ and with Proposition 9

$$S \equiv E[\texttt{rdy:=ff; [}S_1 \| S_2\texttt{]}] =_{[]} E[\texttt{rdy:=ff; } E_1[T_2]].$$

2) Assuming that the environment does not change the values of a or b, an interference-free execution of T_2 consists of a finite number of stuttering steps followed by a transition after which b is the maximum of the values of a and b. (The last step may or may not be a stuttering step). In other words, under the above assumption, T_2 behaves the same as $b : [tt, b = max(a_0, b_0)]$. Formally,

$$T_2 =_{F_2} b : [tt, b = max(a_0, b_0)]$$

where F_2 is $[] \| \text{inv}\{a, b\}^\infty$. U_2 does not change a or b, that is,

$$U_2 \sqsubseteq_{\mathcal{T}S} \text{inv}\{a, b, rdy, done\}^\infty \sqsubseteq_{\mathcal{T}S} \text{inv}\{a, b\}^\infty.$$

The environment assumption is discharged with $F_2 \lesssim U_1$, `[rdy:=ff;` $E_1 \| U_2$`]`:

$$F_2 \equiv \Box \,\|\, \mathrm{inv}\{a,b\}^\infty \lesssim \texttt{rdy:=ff}; E_1 \,\|\, U_2 \qquad \text{W-PAR, S-PAR}$$
$$\lesssim U_1; [\texttt{rdy:=ff}; E_1 \,\|\, U_2] \text{ W-SEQ}$$

Note that E_1 is sequential. Thus,

$$T_2 =_{U_1;[\texttt{rdy:=ff};E_1 \| U_2]} b : [tt, b = max(a_0, b_0)]$$

which implies with Proposition 9

$$E[\texttt{rdy:=ff}; E_1[T_2]] =_{\Box} E[\texttt{rdy:=ff}; E_1[b : [tt, b = max(a_0, b_0)]]].$$

3) Putting the final equations from 1) and 2) together, we get

$$S =_{\Box} E[\texttt{rdy:=ff}; E_1[b : [tt, b = max(a_0, b_0)]]]$$

from which the desired result can easily be shown. □

Example 9. Let S be the following implementation of Peterson's mutual exclusion algorithm

```
S      ≡  S_init; E[S1 || T1]            S_init  ≡  x:=ff;y:=ff;s:=1;        E ≡ □ || U
S1     ≡  while tt do                    T1      ≡  while tt do
            (* non-critical *);                        (* non-critical *);
            {x,s} : [tt, x ∧ s = 1];                   {y,s} : [tt, y ∧ s = 2];
            await not(y) or not(s=1);                  await not(x) or not(s=2);
            cs:=tt; (* critical *)                     ct:=tt; (* critical *)
            cs:=ff; x:=ff                              ct:=ff; y:=ff
          od                                         od
```

where U does not modify x, y, s, cs or ct, i.e., $U \sqsubseteq_{\mathcal{T}^S} \mathrm{inv}\{x, y, s, cs, ct\}^\infty$. We want to establish that S_1 and T_1 can never be in their critical region at the same time:

$$(S, \neg cs \wedge \neg ct) \models \mathsf{G}\neg(cs \wedge ct)$$

1) A suitable chain of approximations for S_1 is

$$S_1 =_{\mathcal{T}^S} S_2 \leq_{F_2} S_3 \leq_{F_3}^{I_3} S_4 \leq_{F_4}^{I_4} S_5 \text{ where}$$

$$\begin{array}{lcl}
S_2 & \equiv & (\{x,s\} : [tt, x \wedge s = 1]; (\{\neg y \vee s \neq 1\} \vee \{y \wedge s = 1\}^\omega); \texttt{cs:=tt}; \texttt{cs:=ff}; \texttt{x:=ff})^\omega \\
F_2 & \equiv & \Box \,\|\, T_1 \,\|\, \mathrm{inv}\{x,y,s\}^\omega \\
S_3 & \equiv & (\{x,s\} : [tt, x \wedge s = 1]; \{\neg y \vee s \neq 1\}; \texttt{cs:=tt}; \texttt{cs:=ff}; \texttt{x:=ff})^\omega \\
F_3 & \equiv & \Box \,\|\, \overline{\{x\}} : [tt, (s = s_0 \vee s = 2) \wedge (\neg y_0 \Rightarrow (y \Rightarrow s = 2))]^\omega \\
I_3 & \equiv & \neg x \wedge \neg y \\
S_4 & \equiv & (\{x,s\} : [tt, x \wedge s = 1]; cs : [x \wedge (\neg y \vee s = 2), cs \wedge x \wedge (\neg y \vee s = 2)]; \texttt{cs:=ff}; \texttt{x:=ff})^\omega \\
F_4 & \equiv & \Box \,\|\, \mathrm{inv}\{cs\}^\omega \\
I_4 & \equiv & \neg cs \\
S_5 & \equiv & (\overline{\{ct\}} : [tt, \neg cs] \vee cs : [x \wedge (\neg y \vee s = 2), cs \wedge x \wedge (\neg y \vee s = 2)])^\omega.
\end{array}$$

The first approximation expresses that S_2 does not deadlock in any initial state and partial context F_2 and can thus be replaced by the deadlock-free program S_3. The second approximation says that if the initial state satisfies $\neg x \wedge \neg y$ and if the environment does not modify x, does not change s to any value other than 2, and does not change y from *false* to *true* without also setting s to 2, then all interference-free executions of S_3 are such that whenever S_3 is in its critical section, x must be set and either must y be false or $s = 2$. Finally, the third approximation expresses that if execution starts in a state with $\neg cs$ and the environment leaves cs invariant, then S_4 never changes the value of ct, and only sets cs if x is set and either y is false or $s = 2$.

2) Each of the environment assumptions expressed in F_2, F_3 and F_4 can be discharged in the actual environment with S-PAR as in the previous example,

that is,

$$F_i \lessapprox E[\square \,\|\, T_1] \text{ for } i = 2, 3, 4.$$

Thus, all of the above approximations also hold for $E[\square \,\|\, T_1]$. Therefore,

$$S_1 \leq^{I_3 \wedge \neg cs}_{E[\square \,\|\, T_1]} S_5.$$

3) Using a symmetric argument we can show that

$$T_1 \leq^{I_3 \wedge \neg ct}_{E[S_1 \,\|\, \square]} T_5$$

where $T_5 \equiv (\overline{\{cs\}} : [tt, \neg ct] \vee ct : [y \wedge (\neg x \vee s = 1), ct \wedge y \wedge (\neg x \vee s = 1)])^{\omega}$.

4) With the final approximations from 2) and 3) above, Proposition 10 allows us to conclude

$$S_1 \,\|\, T_1 \leq^{I_3 \wedge \neg cs \wedge \neg ct}_{E} S_5 \,\|\, T_5.$$

Again, with Proposition 10 and $\{x, y\} : [tt, I_3]; E \lessapprox S_{init}; E$, we get

$$S_1 \,\|\, T_1 \leq^{\neg cs \wedge \neg ct}_{S_{init};E} S_5 \,\|\, T_5.$$

5) Using Proposition 4, $S_5 \,\|\, T_5$ can further be simplified by $S_5 \,\|\, T_5 \sqsubseteq_{\mathcal{T}^S} S_6$ where

$$\begin{aligned} S_6 \equiv (\{cs\} : [tt, \neg ct] \vee \{ct\} : [tt, \neg cs] \vee \\ cs : [x \wedge (\neg y \vee s = 2), cs \wedge x \wedge (\neg y \vee s = 2)] \vee \\ ct : [y \wedge (\neg x \vee s = 1), ct \wedge y \wedge (\neg x \vee s = 1)])^{\omega}. \end{aligned}$$

6) Assuming that cs and ct are false initially, and that the environment does not change x, y or s, it is easy to show that along every interference-free trace in S_6, cs and ct cannot simultaneously be true. To see this, first observe that no transition in S_6 can set both cs and ct simultaneously. Without loss of generality, assume that s is a state in which cs is set. Then, s also satisfies $x \wedge (\neg y \vee s = 2)$. However, for ct to be set next, s must also meet $y \wedge (\neg x \vee s = 1)$ which is impossible. Thus,

$$S_6 \leq^{\neg cs \wedge \neg ct}_{\square \,\|\, \mathrm{inv}\{x,y,s\}^{\omega}} Var : [tt, \neg(cs \wedge ct)]^{\omega}.$$

Since E does not change x, y, or s, that is, $\square \,\|\, \mathrm{inv}\{x, y, s\} \lessapprox \square \,\|\, U \equiv E$, we obtain

$$S_6 \leq^{\neg cs \wedge \neg ct}_{E} Var : [tt, \neg(cs \wedge ct)]^{\omega}.$$

Proposition 10 then implies

$$S_6 \leq^{\neg cs \wedge \neg ct}_{S_{init};E} Var : [tt, \neg(cs \wedge ct)]^{\omega}.$$

7) From 4), 5), and 6) we get

$$S_1 \,\|\, T_1 \leq^{\neg cs \wedge \neg ct}_{S_{init};E} S_5 \,\|\, T_5 \leq^{\neg cs \wedge \neg ct}_{S_{init};E} S_6 \leq^{\neg cs \wedge \neg ct}_{S_{init};E} Var : [tt, \neg(cs \wedge ct)]^{\omega}.$$

Transitivity and Proposition 9 imply

$$S \equiv S_{init}; E[S_1 \,\|\, T_1] \leq^{\neg cs \wedge \neg ct}_{\square} S_{init}; E[Var : [tt, \neg(cs \wedge ct)]^{\omega}]$$

from which the desired result easily follows with Proposition 16. □

Before we conclude this section, we want to return to the introduction and validate how closely our theory corresponds to the one presented in [GL91]. To this end, we recast the derivation presented in the introduction in our setting. We will overload the notation and assume that M, M', A and A' also make sense in our framework. For example, M denotes both a finite state machine and a corresponding partial program. The fact that the system will satisfy A' if M' can assume that its environment will meet A is expressed as $M' \leq_{\square \| A} A'$. Simulation ensures that a machine satisfies a property without any environment assumptions, and therefore corresponds to trace inclusion with respect to $\mathcal{T}^S$. $M \preceq A$ is thus translated into $M \sqsubseteq_{\mathcal{T}^S} A$. Given that $M \| A' \models \varphi$, $M \| M' \models \varphi$ can now be derived using the same kind of reasoning as in the above examples: $M \sqsubseteq_{\mathcal{T}S} A$ implies $\Box \| A \lessapprox \Box \| M$. Therefore, $M' \leq_{\Box \| M} A'$, which implies $M \| M' \leq_{\Box} M \| A'$ with together with $M \| A' \models \varphi$ and Proposition 16 gives us $M \| M' \models \varphi$.

5 Other applications

Stepwise Refinement: In [Din96] transition traces are used to work towards a refinement calculus for concurrent programs with shared memory. The idea is to start out with the specification itself and successively refine it until it contains sufficient detail to be implemented directly. Each refinement step is performed using transformation rules which preserve the properties of the refined system. The calculus is based on the following notion of refinement. S_1 refines S_2 with respect to initial states I, S_1 *ref* S_2 (*mod* I) for short, iff $S_1 \leq_{\Box}^{I} S_2$. S_1 *ref* S_2 iff S_1 *ref* S_2 (*mod tt*). Refinement is reflexive and transitive and preserves LTL properties. Proposition 9 implies that approximation entails refinement, that is, $S_1 \leq_E^I S_2$ implies $E[S_1]$ *ref* $E[S_2]$ (*mod* I). Examples for the formal derivation of programs from specifications can be found in [Din96].
Automatic verification: Example 3 illustrates two points. First, our framework supports the replacement of subprograms with large (possibly infinite) state spaces by subprograms with smaller (possibly finite) state spaces. Secondly, partial programs are expressive enough to conveniently capture typical underlying environment assumptions. Besides being useful conceptually, this may be beneficial to existing verification approaches like global model checking for instance, where in the absence of a reachability analysis the replacement of a subprogram with a large state space by one with a smaller state space can be crucial for the generation of a tractable transition relation.

6 Conclusion and Further Work

We have proposed a denotational framework for the specification and modular verification of fair, shared-variable concurrent programs. In contrast to related approaches, e.g. [Jon83, Sti88, Stø91], it is specification-oriented, that is, specifications are distinguished from programs not by the kind of semantic properties they define, but rather by the amount of information they provide towards implementation. The resulting framework resembles compositional approaches to model checking [GL91] which considers finite state systems. This makes our approach more general, but also less amenable to automatic verification methods. One of the major advantages of our approach is that it builds on the rich theories in [Bro93, Mor94] which means that a lot of useful properties and results are directly available to us. Context-sensitive approximation, for instance, could readily be extended to finer levels of granularity by following [Bro93] and allowing for assignments to be treated as non-atomic. Moreover, [AL93], which is cast in a much more general setting, might be helpful for extending our work.

The most important focus for further work will be the development of a proof system with which approximations $S_1 \leq_E^I S_2$ could be formally derived. This

would also allow the development of a refinement calculus for shared-variable concurrent programs.
Acknowledgments: We thank Steve Brookes, Ernst-Rüdiger Olderog and Wil Janssen for helpful discussions and the anonymous referees for their comments.

References

[AL93] M. Abadi and L. Lamport. Composing specifications. *ACM Transactions on Programming Languages and Systems*, 15:73–132, 1993.

[Bac88] R.J.R. Back. A calculus of refinements for program derivations. *Acta Informatica*, 25:593–624, 1988.

[BKP84] H. Barringer, R. Kuiper, and A. Pnueli. Now you may compose temporal logic specifications. In *Sixteenth Annual ACM Symposium on Theory of Computing*, pages 51–63. ACM, April 1984.

[Bro93] S. D. Brookes. Full abstraction for a shared-variable parallel language. In *Proceedings 8th Annual IEEE Symposium on Logic in Computer Science*. IEEE Computer Society Press, June 1993.

[Dij76] E. W. Dijkstra. *A discipline of programming*. Prentice Hall, 1976.

[Din96] J. Dingel. Towards a theory for shared-variable concurrent programming. Thesis proposal, Carnegie Mellon University, 1996.

[GL91] O. Grumberg and D. Long. Model checking and modular verification. In *CONCUR '91*, LNCS 527. Springer Verlag, 1991.

[Jon83] C. B. Jones. Specification and design of (parallel) programs. In *IFIF '83*, 1983.

[Lar87] K. G. Larsen. A context dependent equivalence between processes. *Theoretical Computer Science*, 49(2):185–216, 1987.

[Mil89] Robin Milner. *Communication and Concurrency*. Prentise Hall International, 1989.

[Mor87] J.M. Morris. A theoretical basis for stepwise refinement and the programming calculus. *Science of Computer Programming*, 9(3):287–306, December 1987.

[Mor89] C. Morgan. The specification statement. *ACM Transactions on Programming Languages and Systems*, 10(3), January 1989.

[Mor94] C. Morgan. *Programming from specifications*. Prentice Hall, 1994.

[OG76] S.S. Owicki and D. Gries. An axiomatic proof technique for parallel programs. *Acta Informatica*, 6:319–340, 1976.

[Pnu85] A. Pnueli. In transition from global to modular temporal reasoning about programs. In K.R. Apt, editor, *Logics and Models of Concurrent Systems*, NATO ASI F13, pages 123–144. Springer Verlag, 1985.

[Sti88] C. Stirling. A generalization of Owicki-Gries' Hoare logic for a concurrent while language. *Theoretical Computer Science*, 89:347–359, 1988.

[Stø91] K. Stølen. A method for the development of totally correct shared-state parallel programs. In *CONCUR '91*. Springer Verlag, 1991.

The Impact of Hardware Models on Shared Memory Consistency Conditions *

Jerry James and Ambuj Singh

Department of Computer Science
University of California at Santa Barbara
Santa Barbara, CA 93106

Abstract. Shared memory systems provide a contract to the programmer in the form of a *consistency condition*. The conditions of atomic memory and sequential consistency provide the illusion of a single memory module, as in the uniprocessor case. Weaker conditions improve performance by sacrificing the simple programming model. Consistency conditions are formulated without reference to details of the hardware on which programs execute. We define the notion of a *hardware model*, a set of limitations on the communication network (e.g., message delay assumptions) and processing nodes (e.g., amount of available memory). We examine the effects of several models on a representative set of consistency conditions. In each model, we show how the conditions are related, and show that some are not appropriate for that model. Our study is carried out through *relatively complete* implementations, state machines which exactly capture the possible behaviors of all implementations in a given model. In addition to elucidating properties of the consistency conditions, these state machines can be used in proofs of correctness, when a particular hardware model is assumed.

1 Introduction

Distributed and parallel systems are difficult to program correctly, due to their nondeterministic nature. In the message passing paradigm, the programmer must also explicitly manage any shared data, as well as provide needed load balancing services and fault tolerance. An attractive alternative is to implement a shared memory abstraction in software on top of a message passing layer (i.e., *distributed shared memory*, or DSM [7]). A DSM system provides a contract to the programmer in the form of a *consistency condition*. *Strong* consistency conditions, such as atomic memory [18] and sequential consistency [17], make the shared memory behave like a single memory module. That is, shared memory accesses appear to occur atomically, as in the uniprocessor case. Such systems ease the programmer's burden, but efficiency is a major concern. For example, it is known that neither atomic memory nor sequential consistency can be implemented without some blocking [6].

* This research was supported in part by NSF grants CCR-9223094 and CCR-9505807.

The simple programming model of the strong conditions was sacrificed in the development of *weak* consistency conditions (e.g., causal memory [3] and processor consistency [2, 12]), in an attempt to achieve greater efficiency. Weak consistency conditions introduce a new problem, however; they are frequently unable to support common concurrent programming methods [5]. A class of *hybrid* consistency conditions (e.g., [1, 4]) have been developed which combine two or more conditions in an attempt at reaping the benefits of both.

All shared memory consistency conditions have been formulated without regard to the capabilities of any particular distributed system, for full generality. This paper examines the effects of introducing assumptions about the nature of the system (called a *hardware model*) into several consistency conditions, and the relationships of the conditions to each other under such assumptions. In particular, we examine the effects of changes in the communication network (e.g., message delay assumptions) and the processing nodes (e.g., amount of available memory). We give a clear formulation of each consistency condition for each model we study, and we show how the various conditions are related. We also show that some conditions are not appropriate for some models; that is, they collapse into a stronger condition.

We conduct our study with *relatively complete* implementations. These are state machines which capture all possible behaviors of all implementations in a particular hardware model. The state machines are a useful tool for studying consistency conditions due to this exact matching of behavior. A state machine which captures anything less is unsuitable, since it corresponds to something stronger than the consistency condition under study. A state machine which captures anything more is also unsuitable, because it does not implement the required consistency condition. These relatively complete implementations are useful in constructing proofs of correctness. If a program is written with respect to a hardware model M, then proving that it executes correctly on a relatively complete implementation in M is equivalent to showing that it executes correctly on any implementation in M. Since the behaviors of a program in a model are, in general, a proper subset of those allowed by the formal consistency condition, stronger results can be proved with the relatively complete implementation than with the formal condition.

In addition to use in proving program correctness, relatively complete implementations can be used in proving shared memory implementation correctness. This is done by showing that the possible behaviors of a proposed implementation are included in the possible behaviors of a relatively complete implementation. A proof of behavior inclusion, coupled with a proof of correctness for the relatively complete implementation, yields the desired correctness proof. Behavior inclusion can be proved using the theory of trace inclusion [21] for I/O automata [20], which develops refinements and forward and backward simulations as proof tools.

In related work, Gibbons and Merritt [11] use I/O automata to define a base memory system supporting per-variable consistency, or cache consistency. The actions of this automaton are later restricted to support release consistency [10]. They establish that release consistency behaves as sequential consistency in the absence of data races. The implementations that we develop are similar in spirit, but based on a different set of primitives closer to the machine architecture.

Pratt and Gupta have developed a theory of concurrency based on the algebra of Chu spaces [13, 14, 23]. In this theory, a duality exists between schedules (sequences of events) and automata (state-based structures). This is similar in spirit to our construction of relatively complete implementations, since the possible behaviors of an automaton are captured by the schedule which is its dual, and conversely. However, this theory does not readily permit one to make model restrictions, as we do in this paper. Furthermore, we are interested in viewing concurrency at two levels: at the level of shared memory operations, and at the level of message-based communication. The Chu space approach only lets us examine one level at a time in a convenient fashion.

2 Consistency Conditions

2.1 Shared Memory System

We view a ***shared memory system*** as the composition of three kinds of automata: a ***network*** N, a ***shared memory implementation*** I, and a ***program*** P. They are related as shown in Fig. 1. Each has possibly infinite state, and special ***input*** and ***output*** actions for communicating with its environment (i.e., they are I/O automata [20]). In this case, the output actions of each automaton are the input actions of some other automaton, and conversely.

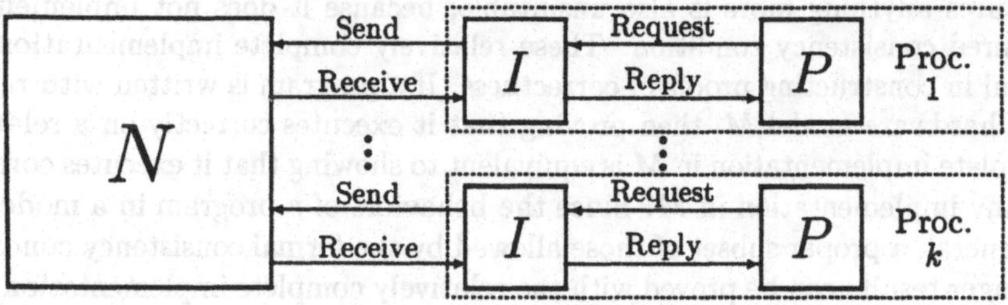

Figure 1. Shared memory system

The network N is a set of k ***processors***, $p_1, p_2, \ldots, p_k$, connected by communication channels. *Send* input actions direct the network to transmit a message from one implementation automaton to another. On delivery, the network generates a *Receive* output action. We assume that the network automaton generates exactly one *Receive* action for each *Send* action, and that messages are received uncorrupted by the designated recipient. We further assume that network N provides FIFO delivery of messages, unless stated otherwise. The primary effect of the network is to specify a delay for each message; that is, an amount of time which passes between the sending and the receiving of each message.

One copy of the shared memory implementation I executes on each processor in the network. Each interacts with the network via *Send* and *Receive* actions, and also interacts with the program automaton executing on the same processor via *Receive* and *Request* actions. The purpose of I is to provide a shared memory abstraction to the program. That abstraction is in the form of a finite set of ***locations***, each of which has an associated ***value***, initially $\perp$.

The program P is specified by a text written in some programming language. One copy of P (called a ***process***) executes on each processor in the network, and generates one *Request* action for each shared memory operation. For each such *Request*, a matching *Reply* action is eventually generated by the implementation running on the same processor. Each *Request* and its matching *Reply* form a shared memory ***operation***. In this paper, we restrict our attention to read and write operations. Read operations are denoted by $R_i(x)v$, which indicates that process p_i read value v from shared memory location x. Write operations are denoted by $W_i(x)v$, which indicates that process p_i wrote value v to location x. We assume that there is a total order on the operations of a process p_i, defined by the program text of P; this is the ***program order of process*** i ($\xrightarrow{i}$).

A ***run*** of the system consists of a record of all internal and external actions and states of all the automata, where each of them began in an initial state, and the states evolve according to each automaton's specification. An ***execution*** is a run with the internal states of the network and program automata excluded; that is, it consists of the *Send, Receive, Request*, and *Reply* actions of a run. A ***shared memory history*** is the external actions of all program automata from some execution; i.e., *Request* and *Reply* actions. A local history H_i is the events of a history H which occur on process p_i. Each execution corresponds to a history, the history embedded in it. A history is said to be *complete* if every *Request* event has a matching *Reply* event; i.e., there are no pending operations. In the sequel, we only consider complete histories. We assume that there is a ***global time model*** [18] for the system, so that runs, executions, and histories are labeled with a time for each event. We do not, however, assume that there is a global clock available to any of the automata.

2.2 Partial Orders

We define memory consistency conditions in terms of ***serializations*** and ***linearizations*** of histories. We say that S is a serialization of a history H if S defines a total order on all the operations of H, and each read operation in S returns the value of the most recent write operation to that location. If o_1 precedes o_2 in S, we write $o_1 \xrightarrow{S} o_2$. We say that L is a linearization of H if L is a serialization of H and if o_1 precedes o_2 in global time in H, then o_1 precedes o_2 in L ($o_1 \xrightarrow{L} o_2$).

In specifying consistency conditions, we sometimes refer to subhistories. For example, given a history H, we denote all the write operations in H as H_w. We write H_{i+w} to denote all the operations of process p_i together with all write operations in H. Finally, we write $H|_x$ to refer to all operations on location x.

In addition to the orderings defined above (program order $\xrightarrow{i}$, serialization order $\xrightarrow{S}$, and linearization order $\xrightarrow{L}$), we are interested in the following orderings:

- $\xrightarrow{wi}$ = writes-into or writes-before order. If o_1 is a write operation on location x, and o_2 reads the value written by o_1 to x, then $o_1 \xrightarrow{wi} o_2$. To make this ordering meaningful, we assume that all write operations to a particular location have a unique value.
- $\xrightarrow{co}$ = causal order = $(\xrightarrow{wi} \cup (\cup_{1 \leq i \leq k} \xrightarrow{i}))^+$; i.e., the transitive closure of the union of writes-into order and all the program orders.
- $\xrightarrow{gt}$ = global time order. If operation o_1 ends before operation o_2 begins in global time, then $o_1 \xrightarrow{gt} o_2$. Note that $(\exists i :: o_1 \xrightarrow{i} o_2) \Rightarrow o_1 \xrightarrow{gt} o_2$.

2.3 Consistency Conditions

To facilitate our study of the effects of hardware models on shared memory consistency conditions, we chose a diverse set of conditions, from the very strong (atomic memory) to the very weak (pipelined RAM). Fig. 2 shows the relationships of the chosen conditions to each other, when viewed as sets of histories. Processor consistency, which is denoted as PCG, is shown in bold for emphasis. This condition, as we explain below, is the intersection of PRAM and CC, or cache consistency. A brief description of each condition follows.

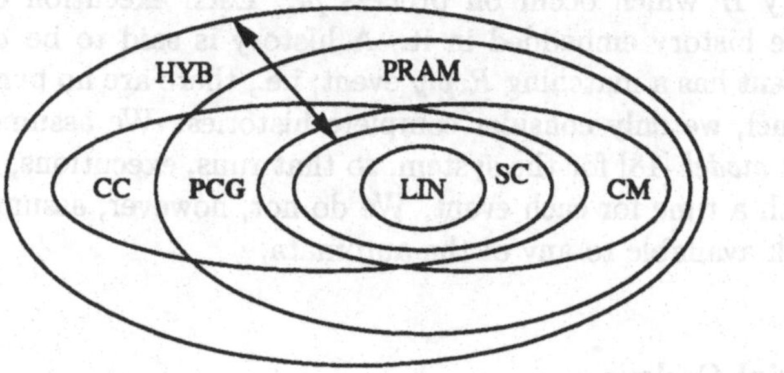

Figure 2. Consistency condition relationships

Atomic memory (linearizability) Linearizability, or atomic consistency, was first described for atomic variables in [18] and extended to arbitrary objects in [15]. The condition requires that all processes agree on the order of all operations, and that order must be consistent with the global time order $\xrightarrow{gt}$.

LIN: There is a linearization L of H.

Sequential consistency Sequential consistency was first defined in [17]. It requires that some serialization S of H exists which preserves each local program order $\xrightarrow{i}$. Another way of stating this requirement is that all processes agree on the order of all operations. This condition is weaker than linearizability, since the global time order $\xrightarrow{gt}$ need not be preserved.

SC: There is a serialization S of H such that $(\exists i :: o_1 \xrightarrow{i} o_2) \Rightarrow o_1 \xrightarrow{S} o_2$.

Cache consistency (coherence) Cache consistency, or memory coherence, guarantees that accesses to any given memory location appear in the same order everywhere [12]. Processes may disagree on the order of two accesses to two different locations, however.

CC: For each memory location x, there is a serialization S_x of $H|_x$ such that
$(\forall o_1, o_2 \in H|_x :: (\exists i :: o_1 \xrightarrow{i} o_2) \Rightarrow o_1 \xrightarrow{S_x} o_2)$.

That is, a cache consistent history H, restricted to a variable x, is sequentially consistent. In general, though, H itself is not sequentially consistent. For example, consider the history of Fig. 3. It is cache consistent since the following serializations exist:

$$S_x : R_2(x)\bot \;\; W_1(x)1$$
$$S_y : R_1(y)\bot \;\; W_2(y)1$$

However, it is not sequentially consistent; otherwise, at least one of the read operations would return 1.

$$P_1 : \boxed{W(x)1}\ \boxed{R(y)\bot}$$
$$P_2 : \boxed{W(y)1}\ \boxed{R(x)\bot}$$

Figure 3. Cache consistent history

Causal Memory Causal memory [3] preserves the causal order. Once a write w becomes visible at p_i, all writes which may have influenced w are also visible at p_i.

CM: For each process p_i, there is a serialization S_i of H_{i+w} such that
$(\forall o_1, o_2 \in H_{i+w} :: o_1 \xrightarrow{co} o_2 \Rightarrow o_1 \xrightarrow{S_i} o_2)$.

Pipelined RAM Pipelined RAM, or PRAM [19], is a very weak consistency condition. It does not provide any guarantees about the relative order of operations between pairs of process histories, but only that write operations are seen by other processes in the order in which they are invoked.

PRAM: For each process p_i, there is a serialization S_i of H_{i+w} such that
$(\forall o_1, o_2 \in H_{i+w} :: (\exists i :: o_1 \xrightarrow{i} o_2) \Rightarrow o_1 \xrightarrow{S_i} o_2)$.

Processor consistency Processor consistency was first described by Goodman [12], but later researchers put varying interpretations on his definition (see, e.g. [2, 9, 10, 22]). We use the interpretation of [2], in which the set of processor consistent histories is the intersection of the coherent and the PRAM histories.

PCG: For each process p_i, there is a serialization S_i of H_{i+w} such that,

- if o_1 and o_2 are operations in H_{i+w} and $(\exists j :: o_1 \xrightarrow{j} o_2)$, then $o_1 \xrightarrow{S_i} o_2$;
- for each location x, all write operations to x appear in the same order in every serialization (i.e., $S_i|_x = S_j|_x$).

Hybrid consistency Hybrid consistency [4, 8] divides all accesses into *strong* and *weak* varieties. The strong accesses are sequentially consistent. The weak accesses are not ordered, except by the strong accesses they lie between.

HYB: For each process p_i, there exists a serialization S_i of H, such that:

- for all j, if $op_1 \xrightarrow{j} op_2$ and at least one of op_1 and op_2 is strong, then $op_1 \xrightarrow{S_i} op_2$;
- if $op_1 \xrightarrow{S_i} op_2$ and op_1 and op_2 are strong, then $(\forall j :: op_1 \xrightarrow{S_j} op_2)$;
- if $op_1 \xrightarrow{i} op_2$, then $op_1 \xrightarrow{S_i} op_2$.

In Fig. 2, hybrid consistency is shown as encompassing all other consistency conditions, but with an arrow leading to sequential consistency. This reflects the fact that hybrid consistency is equivalent to sequential consistency when all operations are strong, but is weaker than all other conditions we study when all operations are weak.

3 Hardware Models

We are interested in ascertaining the impact of various hardware models on shared memory consistency conditions. Let $\mathcal{N}$ represent the set of all network automata, and let $\mathcal{I}^C$ represent the set of all shared memory implementations which provide consistency condition C; i.e., the implementations that are correct for C. A hardware restriction can often be expressed as a predicate over members of these sets; for example, in a synchronous system, the network automaton has a constant message delay. A *hardware model* M^C is a pair of sets $\langle \mathsf{N}, \mathsf{I} \rangle$, where $\mathsf{N} \subseteq \mathcal{N}$ and $\mathsf{I} \subseteq \mathcal{I}^C$, where Nand Iare identified by some predicate. We omit

Model	Description
$\langle \mathcal{N}, \mathcal{I} \rangle$	All networks, all implementations
$\langle \mathsf{N}_A, \mathcal{I} \rangle$	Asynchronous networks, all implementations
$\langle \mathsf{N}_A, \mathsf{I}_E \rangle$	Asynchronous networks, encapsulated implementations
$\langle \mathsf{N}_B, \mathsf{I}_D \rangle$	Bounded networks, deterministic implementations

Figure 4. Presented models

the superscript when the consistency condition is clear from context. In this paper, we explore the models of Fig. 4. The sets appearing in those models are as follows:

- With the full set $\mathcal{N}$ of networks, no information about message send time can be deduced from message arrival time. In particular, a network is simply an automaton that delivers one message for every one that is sent. This includes automata which deliver messages *before* they are sent. The need for such a strange network is described below. Two more realistic sets of networks are the *asynchronous* networks N_A, those with a positive, unbounded network delay, and the *bounded delay* networks N_B, those with a positive, bounded network delay).
- In general, implementations may use an unbounded amount of memory. We examine the set I_B of *bounded memory* implementations.
- Implementations are generally free to copy shared variables to any number of processors, and to use control messages (i.e., messages independent of any shared memory value). We examine the set I_E of *encapsulated* implementations, where neither variable caching nor control messages are allowed.
- Implementations can make random choices in the general case. We examine the set I_D of *deterministic* implementations, which cannot make such choices.

The tools we use to make our study of hardware models are *relatively complete implementations*, which capture all possible behaviors of all implementations in a given model. A state machine which captures anything less is unsuitable, since it corresponds to a stronger condition than the consistency condition under study. A state machine which captures anything more is not an implementation of the consistency condition. The notion of relative completeness is thus the only useful one for studying consistency conditions as state machines.

The possible behaviors of an implementation are those which occur in any execution of some program on the implementation. In particular, we restrict our attention to histories.

Definition 3.1. The *possible histories* $H(N, I, P)$ of a shared memory system $\langle N, I, P \rangle$ is the set of all histories which correspond to some run of $\langle N, I, P \rangle$.

A relatively complete implementation with respect to a model M is one that appears in the model (i.e., it is correct), and whose possible behaviors include all possible behaviors of all implementations in M. In particular, given a history

H corresponding to any run of some system in M, H is a possible history of the same program on a relatively complete implementation, given a suitable choice of network.

Definition 3.2. Let $M = \langle \mathsf{N}, \mathsf{I} \rangle$ be a model for consistency condition C. Implementation I is ***relatively complete*** for C with respect to M iff $I \in \mathsf{I}$ and $(\exists N \in \mathsf{N} :: (\forall N' \in \mathsf{N}, I' \in \mathsf{I}, P :: H(N', I', P) \subseteq H(N, I, P)))$.

In other words, choose any network $N' \in \mathsf{N}$, any implementation $I' \in \mathsf{I}$, and any program P. There exists a network N such that P on N and the relatively complete implementation I generates all histories that P generates on N' and I'. A relatively complete implementation of cache consistency is given in the appendix for the model $\langle \mathsf{N}_A, \mathcal{I} \rangle$.

By viewing both models and consistency conditions as sets of histories, we can produce a picture such as that in Fig. 5. Relatively complete implementations are state machines which capture the entire set of histories in the intersection of the model and the consistency condition (the shaded portion of the left figure). In some cases, a model does not constrain the consistency condition at all. In that case, a relatively complete implementation captures *all* behaviors allowed by the consistency condition (as in the right figure). We call such implementations *complete*.

Definition 3.3. An implementation I of consistency condition C is ***complete*** in model $M = \langle \mathsf{N}, \mathsf{I} \rangle$ if it is relatively complete in M and:
$(\forall H \in C :: (\exists N \in \mathsf{N}, P :: H \in H(N, I, P)))$.

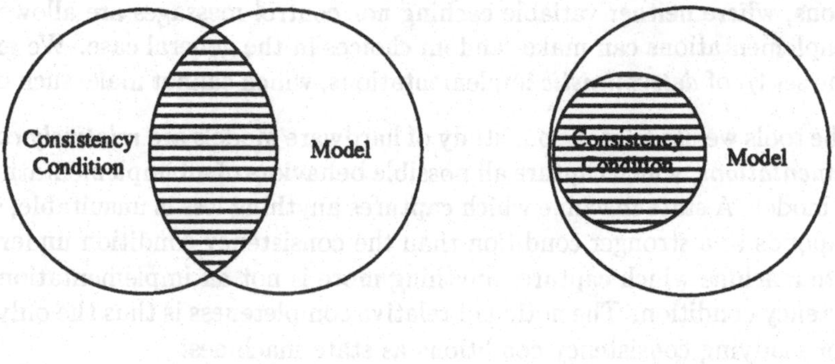

Figure 5. Relatively complete and complete implementations

In the following sections, we consider several hardware models, and investigate how the chosen consistency conditions are related in those models. We do so by determining whether relatively complete implementations exist for each consistency condition. We expect that the hardware independent picture of Fig. 2 will change in a constrained fashion. Some sets may vanish when a consistency condition is insupportable in a given model. Some sets may collapse together, so

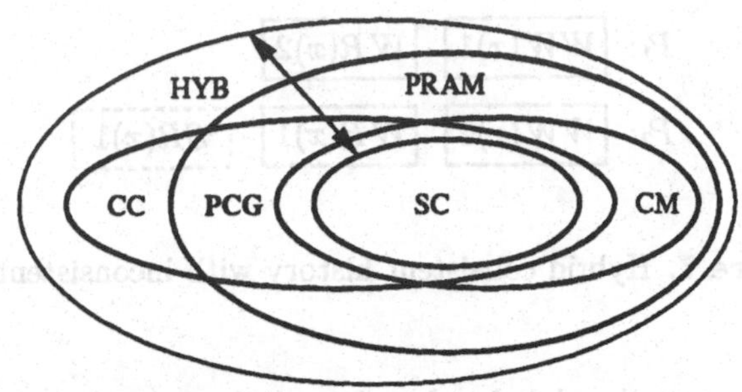

Figure 6. All networks, all implementations

that two consistency conditions are equivalent in a model. However, we expect inclusion relationships to be preserved; e.g., sequential consistency will never be a proper subset of linearizability in any model. In some cases, it may be impossible to produce a relatively complete implementation.

Due to space limitations, we give only some of the results of our study. The full paper [16] contains the proofs and relatively complete implementation constructions for each model. Here we simply show the existence or non-existence of relatively complete implementations for a few models, although we also give one relatively complete implementation in the appendix. We note that the ability to make random choices seems critical. That is, all of the models for which we have been able to prove nonexistence contain deterministic implementations. We also note that, with the exception of linearizability, complete implementations only exist for the full set of networks. In particular, this means that reasoning with the formal definitions for these consistency conditions is equivalent to reasoning with state machines on networks which can deliver messages into the past. Such behavior is necessary to deal with histories in which a read operation returns a value that is written after the read operation terminates. All conditions we study, except linearizability, allow histories of this nature.

The figures that follow show inclusion of consistency conditions. We use a heavy solid border to indicate the existence of a complete implementation. A light solid border indicates the existence of a relatively complete implementation. A dashed border indicates that no relatively complete implementation exists. When a consistency condition is not implementable in a given model, it is simply omitted from the figure. We give results for several models, and conclude with remarks on general proof techniques for relatively complete implementations.

3.1 Model $\langle \mathcal{N}, \mathcal{I} \rangle$

This model places no resource bounds on the implementation or the network. As Fig. 6 shows, all but two of the consistency conditions we study have complete implementations. The two exceptions are linearizability and hybrid consistency. Linearizability has vanished, since it cannot be supported in this model. It

$$P_1: \boxed{WW(x)1} \quad \boxed{WR(x)2}$$

$$P_2: \boxed{WW(x)2} \quad \boxed{WR(x)1} \quad \vdots\!\boxed{SR(x)1}\!\vdots$$

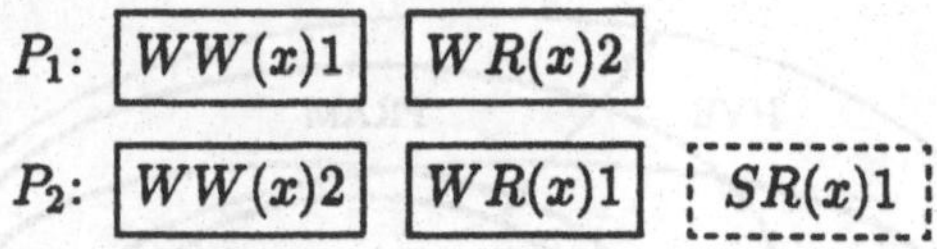

Figure 7. Hybrid consistent history with inconsistent read

places restrictions on the global order of operations; however, such restrictions cannot be enforced, since the arrival of a message gives no information about its sending.

Hybrid consistency has a relatively complete implementation, but no complete implementation. Some hybrid consistent histories cannot be allowed by any correct implementation, since the addition of a single read operation yields an inconsistent history. For example, consider the history of Fig. 7, where weak operations are prefixed with a 'W' and strong operations with an 'S'. After the four weak operations have completed, the history so far is hybrid consistent, since the following serializations exist:

$$S_1 : WW_1(x)1 \ \ WR_2(x)1 \ \ WW_2(x)2 \ \ WR_1(x)2$$
$$S_2 : WW_2(x)2 \ \ WR_1(x)2 \ \ WW_1(x)1 \ \ WR_2(x)1$$

However, when the strong read operation executes, it cannot return a consistent value. In order for P_2 to respect its own program order, the operation must return 1. But in that case, there is no serialization S_1 which respects P_1's program order. No correct implementation can allow the history of Fig. 7, since it may be unable to preserve correctness later on.

The problem exhibited here is that hybrid consistency implies eventual consistency; that is, each memory location is eventually made coherent across processes. Another way of viewing this is that, out of any set of concurrent write operations to the same location, one write operation must be seen last by all processes. In this way, future read operations can return a consistent value. Hence, we need consider only hybrid consistent histories in which every data race has the same winner on all processes.

3.2 Model $\langle N_A, \mathcal{I} \rangle$

This model is the same as the previous one, except that we have replaced the arbitrary message delay feature of the network with an asynchronous network. That is, messages are not delivered before they are sent, but the delay is unbounded. Fig. 8 shows that linearizability has reappeared, and has a complete implementation. All other consistency conditions have relatively complete implementations in this model. See the appendix for a relatively complete implementation of cache consistency in this model.

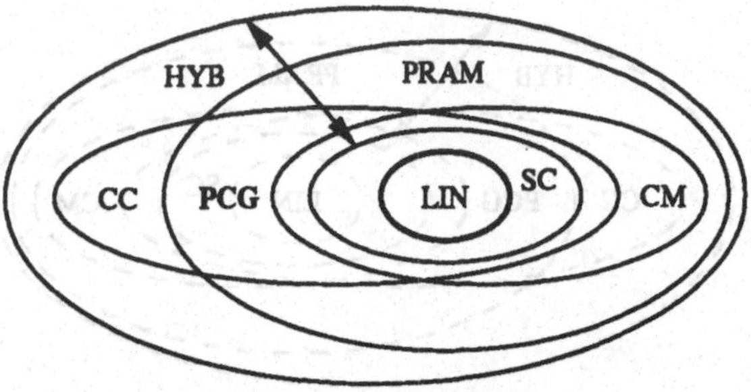

Figure 8. Asynchronous networks, all implementations

3.3 Model $\langle N_A, I_E \rangle$

In this model, we restrict our attention to encapsulated implementations. The fact that only one copy exists gives us coherence by default for all the consistency conditions we study. Thus, we see in Fig. 9 that cache consistency is now the weakest condition. Furthermore, since processor consistency is that part of PRAM which is coherent, PRAM has collapsed into processor consistency; the two conditions are equivalent. This means that there are no incomparable conditions in this model. Note also that linearizability still has a complete implementation in this restricted model. Somewhat surprisingly, the picture is the same for several other models, including $\langle N_A, I_B \rangle$ (asynchronous networks with bounded memory implementations), and $\langle N_B, \mathcal{I} \rangle$ (bounded delay networks with all implementations).

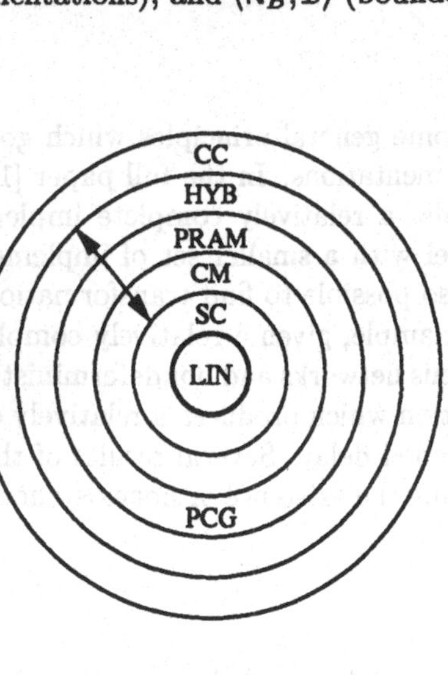

Figure 9. Asynchronous networks, encapsulated implementations

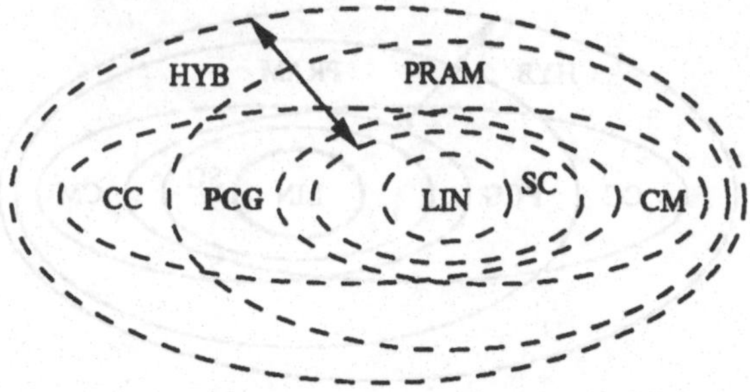

Figure 10. Bounded delay networks, deterministic implementations

3.4 Model $\langle N_B, I_D \rangle$

We introduce both a network with bounded message delays, and deterministic implementations in this model. This model is apparently very severe, as there are no relatively complete implementations for *any* of the consistency conditions we study, as shown in Fig. 10. The proofs of nonexistence are all similar. Introducing determinism into the implementations does not restrict the set of possible histories over all implementations. That is, given a history on some implementation which makes random choices, there is a deterministic implementation on which the same history is possible. The proofs are constructed by demonstrating a set of possible histories for the model such that any given deterministic implementation cannot realize all histories in the set.

3.5 Other Models

It is possible to find some general principles which govern the existence of relatively complete implementations. In the full paper [16], we prove several such theorems. For example, a relatively complete implementation I is relatively complete for any model with a smaller set of implementations, so long as I is still in the set. It is also possible to find transformations from one implementation to another. For example, given a relatively complete implementation for a model with asynchronous networks and nondeterministic implementations, there is a simple transformation which produces a relatively complete implementation for networks with bounded delay. Several results of this nature can be proven, easing the task of proving the existence or nonexistence of these state machines.

4 Conclusion

Our study of hardware models and their impact on shared memory consistency conditions has produced a number of results. In some models, certain consistency conditions collapse to stronger conditions, which shows that they are inappropriate for that model. We also saw that relatively complete implementations do not exist in some models; the implication is that any implementation is actually implementing something stronger than its nominal consistency condition.

Another implication of this work is that a program may be correct with respect to a consistency condition C and model $\mathcal{M}$, but incorrect with respect to C and a weaker model $\mathcal{M}'$. Weaker models allow more histories, just like weakening the consistency condition. Since some models are unrealistic (in particular, the full set of networks), this means that some programs may be correct with respect to all real implementations, but not correct with respect to the abstract consistency condition.

We have also noted that relatively complete implementations, which are state machines, may be useful in constructing proofs of correctness. A program which is correct with respect to a relatively complete implementation is correct with respect to any implementation in the same model. Implementations can also be proven correct by showing that their possible behaviors are contained in the possible behaviors of a relatively complete implementation; e.g., by using refinements or forward and backward simulations.

We proposed several features of the hardware model which can be varied. There are other features that may also be of interest, such as network topology, communication channel features (e.g., FIFO channels, flush channels, etc.), multi-threaded programs, and even progress conditions on the implementations. Studying these topics may lead to further insights into the impact of hardware variations on shared memory consistency conditions.

References

1. AGRAWAL, D., CHOY, M., LEONG, H. V., AND SINGH, A. K. Mixed consistency: A model for parallel programming. In *PODC '94* (Los Angeles, CA, USA, 14–17 Aug. 1994), pp. 101–10.
2. AHAMAD, M., BAZZI, R., JOHN, R., KOHLI, P., AND NEIGER, G. The power of processor consistency. In *SPAA '93* (Velen, Germany, June 1993), pp. 251–60.
3. AHAMAD, M., NEIGER, G., BURNS, J. E., KOHLI, P., AND HUTTO, P. W. Causal memory: Definitions, implementation and programming. *Dist. Comput. 9*, 1 (Aug. 1995), 37–49.
4. ATTIYA, H., AND FRIEDMAN, R. A correctness condition for high-performance multiprocessors. In *STOC '92* (Victoria, British Columbia, Canada, 4–6 May 1992), pp. 679–90.
5. ATTIYA, H., AND FRIEDMAN, R. Limitations of fast consistency conditions for distributed shared memories. *Inf. Process. Lett. 57*, 5 (Mar. 1996), 243–8.
6. ATTIYA, H., AND WELCH, J. L. Sequential consistency versus linearizability. *ACM Trans. Comput. Syst. 12*, 2 (May 1994), 91–122.
7. ESKICIOGLU, M. R. A comprehensive bibliography of distributed shared memory. *Op. Sys. Review 30*, 1 (Jan. 1996), 71–96.
8. FRIEDMAN, R. Implementing hybrid consistency with high-level synchronization operations. *Dist. Comput. 9*, 3 (Dec. 1995), 119–29.
9. GHARACHORLOO, K., ADVE, S. V., GUPTA, A., HENNESSY, J. L., AND HILL, M. D. Specifying system requirements for memory consistency models. Tech. Rep. CSL-TR-93-594, Computer System Laboratory, Stanford University, 1993. Also University of Wisconsin-Madison Computer Sciences Technical Report #1199.

10. Gharachorloo, K., Lenoski, D., Laudon, J., Gibbons, P., Gupta, A., and Hennessy, J. Memory consistency and event ordering in scalable shared-memory multiprocessors. In *ISCA '90* (Seattle, WA, USA, 28–31 May 1990), pp. 15–26. See revision in Stanford University tech. report CSL-TR-93-568.
11. Gibbons, P. B., and Merritt, M. Specifying nonblocking shared memories. In *SPAA '92* (San Diego, CA, USA, 29 June–1 July 1992), pp. 306–15.
12. Goodman, J. R. Cache consistency and sequential consistency. Tech. Rep. 1006, Computer Sciences Department, University of Wisconsin-Madison, Feb. 1991.
13. Gupta, V. *Chu Spaces: A Model of Concurrency*. PhD thesis, Stanford University, Aug. 1994.
14. Gupta, V., and Pratt, V. Gates accept concurrent behavior. In *FOCS '93* (Palo Alto, CA, USA, 3–5 Nov. 1993), pp. 62–71.
15. Herlihy, M. P., and Wing, J. M. Linearizability: A correctness condition for concurrent objects. *ACM Trans. Program. Lang. Syst. 12*, 3 (July 1990), 463–92.
16. James, J., and Singh, A. K. The impact of hardware models on shared memory consistency conditions. Tech. Rep. TRCS96-12, Computer Science Department, University of California at Santa Barbara, 1996.
17. Lamport, L. How to make a multiprocessor computer that correctly executes multiprocess programs. *IEEE Trans. Comput. 28*, 9 (Sept. 1979), 690–1.
18. Lamport, L. On interprocess communication, parts I and II. *Dist. Comput. 1*, 2 (Apr. 1986), 77–101.
19. Lipton, R. J., and Sandberg, J. S. PRAM: A scalable shared memory. Tech. Rep. CS-TR-180-88, Department of Computer Science, Princeton University, Sept. 1988.
20. Lynch, N. A., and Tuttle, M. R. Hierarchical correctness proofs for distributed algorithms. In *PODC '87* (Vancouver, British Columbia, Canada, 10–12 Aug. 1987), pp. 137–51.
21. Lynch, N. A., and Vaandrager, F. Forward and backward simulations. *Inf. Comput. 121*, 2 (Sept. 1995), 214–233.
22. Mosberger, D. Memory consistency models. *Op. Sys. Review 27*, 1 (Jan. 1993), 18–26.
23. Pratt, V. The second calculus of binary relations. In *MFCS '93* (Gdansk, Poland, 30 Aug.–3 Sept. 1993), A. M. Borzyszkowski and S. Sokolowski, Eds., Springer-Verlag, pp. 142–155.

Appendix: Relatively Complete Implementation of CC

The model in which this example is given is $\langle \mathsf{N}_A, \mathcal{I} \rangle$, asynchronous networks with the full set of implementations. In this model, some consistency conditions (e.g., processor consistency and hybrid consistency) have very complex relatively complete implementations. We present a relatively complete implementation for cache consistency, or coherence, as it is simple enough to grasp easily, but not completely trivial. The implementation is not intended to be realistic, but is supposed to capture all possible behaviors of all implementations in the model.

The example is shown in Fig. 11. Each processor in the network caches the entire shared memory space in a variable M. The basic idea is that, associated with each memory location $M[x]$, there is a current value $M[x].cur$ and a queue of waiting values $M[x].q$. Each write operation is assigned a timestamp, and

Write(x,v):

Advance timestamp of $M[x].cur$ arbitrarily.
$M[x].cur := v$
Broadcast the write with its timestamp.

Read(x):

Return $M[x].cur$

On receiving a write message $W(x, v)$ with timestamp t:

Enqueue $\langle v, t\rangle$ on $M[x].q$.

Apply (executed arbitrarily often):

If there is an x with a nonempty queue $M[x].q$, then
Dequeue $\langle v, t\rangle$ from $M[x].q$.
If t is greater than the timestamp of x, assign $\langle v, t\rangle$ to $M[x].cur$.

Figure 11. Relatively complete implementation of cache consistency

the writes to each location are ordered by timestamp, with ties broken using process ID. If an arriving write message bears a lower timestamp than the value already in that location, then the new write is considered as "overwritten" and is never read. Old values may accumulate in a queue, until the Apply function is executed. Also note that the broadcast function necessarily provides FIFO ordering of messages. This implementation is correct, since all processes see the writes to a given variable x in the same order. That order is the timestamp order, with ties broken by process ID (which we did not show in the pseudocode, but is easily added).

To prove relative completeness for this implementation, we need to characterize the possible behaviors of all implementations in the given model. In this case, the model only disallows histories in which a writes-into relation goes backward in time; that is, one in which a read operation returns a value which has not yet been written. Intersecting this set with the set of cache consistent histories gives us the set of cache consistent histories which do not read from the future.

The network N we choose is the totally random FIFO network which does not deliver messages before they are sent. Now, given any program P and a history for it on some implementation in the model, we need to give an execution of our implementation which produces the same history. This is done by considering the collection of coherence orders S_x for each variable x. We construct an execution so that the timestamp assigned to each write to variable x corresponds to its position in S_x. We then adjust the arrival times of messages according to the read operations of each process. Finally, we only execute Apply when it is necessary; i.e., when a write from some other process is to be read. The detailed proof is given in the full paper [16].

Synchronous Development of Asynchronous Systems*

Clemens Fischer**, Wil Janssen***

University of Oldenburg

Abstract. Formal specifications of communicating systems should describe an abstract view of a system and hide unnecessary implementation details. A problematic implementation detail is the kind of communication used in an open or distributed system. We argue that *synchronous* communication is easier to use and to analyse and should be prefered over *asynchronous* communication at early stages of software development. Therefore we present a new class of systems that have the same semantics both with synchronous and with asynchronous communication. Such systems can be developed and verified on the basis of synchronous communication without losing an efficient asynchronous implementation. As formal framework we use CSP and develop a unified theory of asynchronous and synchronous communication in the style of [JJH90].
Our approach generalises the 'delay insensitive circuits approach' where integrated circuits are developed without assumptions on wire delays. Hence, it can be applied to a wide range of applications from IC design to telecommunication systems.

1 Introduction

Over the last decade the theory for specification and design of synchronously communicating systems has become well developed [Hoa85, Old91, Zwi89, BB87]. Synchronous specification languages such as CSP [Hoa85] have a fully understood semantics and nice algebraic properties. Much work has also been done on the transformational design of synchronously communicating systems, such as the work in the ProCoS project where one transformationally designs synchronously operating (OCCAM) programs for trace based specifications and a mixed terms language [Old91, Rös94].

Besides having a well-developed theory, synchronous languages have the advantage that they are relatively easy to use from the point of view of the *specifier*.

* This research was partially supported by the German Ministry for Education and Research (BMBF) as part of the project UniForM under grant No. FKZ 01 IS 521 B3.

** University of Oldenburg, FB Informatik, P.O. Box 2503, 26111 Oldenburg, Germany. E-mail: fischer@informatik.uni-oldenburg.de

*** Telematics Research Centre, P.O.Box 589, 7500 AN Enschede, The Netherlands. E-mail: janssen@trc.nl

Properties can be specified by components and parallel composition basically corresponds to conjunction of properties. Moreover, the coupling between different components is rather tight, leading to a simpler operational view of the system.

When contrasted with *asynchronous* systems where communications are delayed in unbounded buffers we have that asynchronous specifications are much more difficult to understand. Messages are buffered and therefore the coupling between different components is less clear. It is not easy to have an overall view of all buffered messages or to ensure that the right message is received at the right time. Such problems are a well-known source of errors in, for example, communication protocols. The book by Belina, Hogrefe, and Sarma [BHS91] contains a nice example thereof, although the authors never intended to do so.

Though synchronous systems are easier to develop and to understand than asynchronous systems, the implementation architectures one has to aim at are usually of an asynchronous nature. Unless one is aiming at OCCAM programs or strongly coupled parallel architectures the communication primitives available are asynchronous. In the field of unclocked integrated circuits, asynchronicity can be helpful to handle variability in signal delays. This has led to much interest in the notion of *delay insensitive circuits* [Ver94].

In this paper we present a theory for the characterisation and design of asynchronous systems. As a starting point we have taken the unified theory for synchronous and asynchronous communication as introduced by [JJH90] who model an asynchronous subset of CSP by combining normal CSP processes with input and output buffers. These ideas are slightly simplified and on the basis of that we characterise when synchronous specifications can be used in an asynchronous setting while preserving their semantics. Such systems are called *desynchronisable.*

By such a characterisation we obtain a mean to develop asynchronous systems in a synchronous fashion. This is an approach worth while as it has been observed by several researchers that asynchronous systems often behave in a rather "synchronised way" despite their asynchronous implementations. For integrated circuits this is obviously the case: as wires can only buffer a single signal components are still tightly coupled. But also in distributed networks this is often the case. Many algorithms for distributed systems can be analysed in a global, sequential fashion, as has been shown in the work on so-called *communication closed* or *layered systems* [EF82, SdR94, JPZ91].

As the general characterisation of desynchronisability is rather difficult we also present a simpler yet sufficient condition for desynchronisability, called *absolute desynchronisability.* Informally spoken, a system P is absolutely desynchronisable if $P \parallel Q$ is desynchronisable given that Q is absolutely desynchronisable as well. The class of delay insensitive circuits as defined in [Ver94] is shown to be a special case of absolutely desynchronisable systems.

This paper is based on the Master's Thesis of Clemens Fischer [Fis95] where the core of this theory was developed in the setting of the ProCoS specification language SL. In this paper we use CSP as a formal language. We assume the reader has a reasonable knowledge of CSP and its semantics, though notation will be explained when necessary. We refer to [Hoa85] for more details. In the next section some notation and definitions needed in the rest of the paper are introduced. Then, in section 3 we define asynchronous CSP in the style of [JJH90]. In the sections following we characterise desynchronisable systems and absolutely desynchronisable systems and relate them to delay insensitive circuits. We illustrate the definitions with the example of a Centralised Two-Phase Commit protocol and end with some conclusions and a discussion of ideas to be studied in future.

2 Preliminaries

We use CSP as it is defined in [Hoa85]. The alphabet of a CSP process P is denoted by $\alpha(P)$. We assume here that the alphabet consists of input and output communications only. The set of channels of P is denoted by $\alpha\_ch(P)$, i.e., $\alpha\_ch(P) =_{df} \{c \mid \exists v \bullet c.v \in \alpha(P)\}$. The set $inch(P)$ consists of all input channels of P, i.e., all channels c that occur as an input communication (denoted by $c?x$) in P. Analogously $outch(P)$ denotes the set of output channels, i.e., all channels c that occur as an output communication (denoted by $c!e$) in P. Note that $inch(P)$ and $outch(P)$ are not necessarily disjoint (e.g., $P =_{df} c?x \rightarrow Stop \parallel c!47 \rightarrow Stop$; $inch(P) = \{c\} = outch(P)$). *Stop* is the process that deadlocks immediately. *Chaos* is the most unreliable process.

$Comm(C) =_{df} \{c.v \in \alpha(P) \mid c \in C\}$ is the set of communications on a set of channels $C \subseteq \alpha\_ch(P)$.

The *interface* Δ_P of P is the tuple $\Delta_P = (inch(P), outch(P))$. An interface Δ_P is called *simple* if $inch(P) \cap outch(P) = \emptyset$. A process is called *simple* if the interface is simple. The set of communications over an interface Δ_P is

$$Comm(\Delta_P) =_{df} Comm(inch(P) \cup outch(P)) \ .$$

The projection of a trace $tr \in Comm(\Delta_P)^*$ on a set of channels C is denoted by $(tr \downarrow C) \in Comm(C)^*$.

The semantics of a process P is a tuple $(\alpha(P), failures\,[\![P]\!], divergences\,[\![P]\!])$ where $failures\,[\![P]\!]$ is a set of pairs $(tr, \mathcal{R})$ and $divergences\,[\![P]\!]$ the set of traces after which P may diverge. The pair $(tr, \mathcal{R})$ denotes a trace tr of P and a set $\mathcal{R} \subseteq \alpha(P)$ of communications which P can refuse after tr. Let $traces\,[\![P]\!]$ denote the set of traces of P. The process P/tr (P after tr) is P after engaging in tr. P/tr is undefined if $tr \notin traces\,[\![P]\!]$.

The refinement relation on processes is denoted by $\sqsubseteq$. The relation $P \sqsubseteq Q$ (P is refined by Q) holds if $\Delta_P = \Delta_Q$, $failures\,[\![Q]\!] \subseteq failures\,[\![P]\!]$ and $divergences\,[\![Q]\!] \subseteq divergences\,[\![P]\!]$ (intuition: P is less deterministic than Q).

Definition 2.1 (Pipelining). Two processes P and Q with $outch(P) = inch(Q)$ and $inch(P) \cap outch(Q) = \emptyset$ can by joined together by

$$P \gg Q =_{df} (P \parallel Q) \setminus Comm(outch(P))$$

('\' is the concealment operator from CSP. It removes all observations from the set $Comm(outch(P))$.) □

Let 'first(tr)' denote the first communication of a trace and 'tail(tr)' the rest, e.g. first($a.b.c.d$) = a and tail($a.b.c.d$) = $b.c.d$.

Definition 2.2 (Buffer). A simple buffer with input channel c and output channel c' is

$Buff_{c,c'} =_{df} Buff_{c,c'}(\varepsilon)$ (ε is the empty trace) where

$$Buff_{c,c'}(\varepsilon) =_{df} c?x \rightarrow Buff_{c,c'}(x)$$

$$Buff_{c,c'}(s) =_{df} \quad c?x \rightarrow Buff_{c,c'}(s.x) \quad \Box c'!\,\text{first}(s) \rightarrow Buff_{c,c'}(\text{tail}(s)) \qquad \text{where } s \neq \varepsilon.$$

We define a buffer for every set of channels C:

$$Buffer_C =_{df} \Big\|_{\{c \in C\}} Buff_{c,c'}$$

$Buffer_P$ buffers all *input* communications of P:

$$Buffer_P =_{df} Buffer_{\Delta_P} =_{df} Buffer_{inch(P)}$$

□

3 The asynchronous subset of CSP

We model asynchronous communication by explicit introduction of a buffer between two directly connected communication partners. Therefore we define the operator "$\sim$" that introduces a buffer for any input channel of a process. Figure 1 gives a connection diagram for two asynchronous processes.

We have to rename the input channels of P, i.e., we mark the channels between $Buffer_P$ and P with a dash. Hence, the process P' is the same process as the simple process P with all *input* channel names decorated with a dash. We use this notation also for sequences of communications (traces) and sets of channels or communications over simple interfaces.

Definition 3.1 (Operator for Asynchrony). Let P be a process with a simple interface.

$$\widetilde{P} =_{df} (Buffer_P \gg P')$$

The operator "$\sim^{vis}$" is the same as "$\sim$", but leaves channels between $Buffer_P$ and P' visible. $\widetilde{P}^{vis} =_{df} (Buffer_P \parallel P')$ □

The operator "$\sim^{vis}$" is useful for proofs and preparatory lemmas.
We apply "$\sim$" and "$\sim^{vis}$" only to simple processes. A summary of some important facts about "$\sim$" and "$\sim^{vis}$" is given in the following lemmas.

Lemma 3.2 (Connection of $\widetilde{P}$ and $\widetilde{P}^{vis}$). *Let* $In =_{df} Comm(inch(P))$.

$$failures\,[\![\widetilde{P}]\!] = \left\{(tr \downarrow \alpha\_ch(P), \mathcal{R}) \;\middle|\; (tr, \mathcal{R} \cup In') \in failures\,[\![\widetilde{P}^{vis}]\!]\right\}$$

$$divergences\,[\![\widetilde{P}]\!] = \left\{tr \downarrow \alpha\_ch(P) \;\middle|\; tr \in divergences\,[\![\widetilde{P}^{vis}]\!]\right\}$$

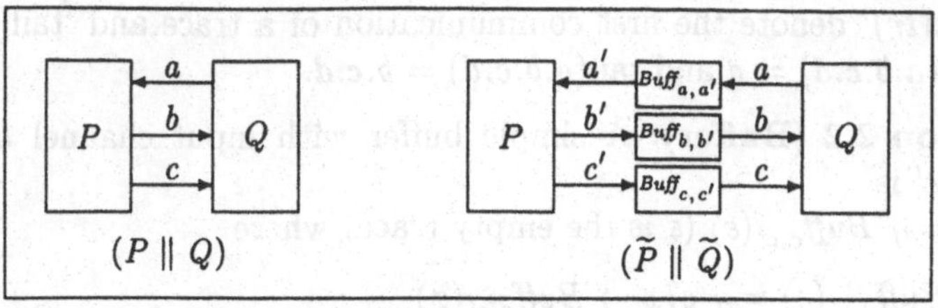

Figure 1. Example for the channels introduced by "$\sim$"

Proof-Sketch. Definition of concealment ([Hoa85, p. 131, 128]). Note that hiding the primed channels between $Buffer_P$ and P does not introduce new divergences. □

Lemma 3.3. *"$\sim$" is monotonic w.r.t. $\sqsubseteq$, i.e., $P \sqsubseteq Q \Longrightarrow \widetilde{P} \sqsubseteq \widetilde{Q}$.*

Proof. $\|$ is monotonic $\Rightarrow$ "$\sim vis$" is monotonic $\overset{\text{Lemma 3.2}}{\Longrightarrow}$ "$\sim$" is monotonic. □

The heart of this section is the definition of the asynchronous subset of CSP.

Definition 3.4 (Asynchronous process).
A process P is called asynchronous iff there exists a process Q with $\widetilde{Q} = P$. □

A simple consequence of this definition is the so called 'Foam Rubber Wrapper Postulate' ([Mol86, Udd84]):

Theorem 3.5 (Foam Rubber Wrapper Postulate).
A process P is asynchronous iff $\widetilde{P} = P$.

Proof. "$\sim$" is idempotent and monotonic. □

We now have a closer look at the effect of the buffer in an asynchronous process aiming at a different characterisation of asynchrony in terms of a simple reorder on traces. As an example take

$$A =_{df} (a? \to b? \to fa! \to sb! \to Stop \Box b? \to a? \to fb! \to sa! \to Stop) \ .$$

A accepts $a.b$ and sends $fa.sb$ ('first a, second b') or accepts $b.a$ and sends $fb.sa$ ('first b, second a'). Now look at $\widetilde{A}^{vis}$. The traces $a.a'.b.b'.fa.sb$ and $b.b'.a.a'.fb.sa$ happen if $Buffer_A$ is always emptied immediately. This idea leads to

$$traces\,[\![P]\!] \subseteq traces\,[\![\widetilde{P}]\!] \tag{1}$$

for all simple P. But messages can also be reordered

$$a.b.b'.a'.fb.sa,\ b.a.a'.b'.fa.sb \in traces\,[\![\widetilde{A}^{vis}]\!]$$

and delayed $a.b.a'.b'.fa.sb,\ b.a.b'.a'.fb.sa \in traces\,[\![\widetilde{A}^{vis}]\!]$. Remember that the primed communications happen between the buffer and the process. The communication a is sent to the buffer before b in $a.b.b'.a'$. Therefore the trace $a.b$

is visible in the interface of $\widetilde{A}$. But a' is taken after b' out of the buffer. For this reason the state of A' is determined by $b'.a'$.

Hence, the information whether a or b happens first gets lost by the buffer. Also the order of input and output communications can change. E.g.

$$B =_{df} (a? \to b! \to Stop \Box b! \to a? \to Stop)$$

We have $a.b.a' \in traces [\![\widetilde{B}^{vis}]\!]$.

The important fact is that these two effects characterise asynchronous processes. To prove this theorem we introduce names for the traces on $inch \cup outch$ ('global trace') and $inch' \cup outch$ ('local trace'). The global trace is the one we observe in $\widetilde{P}$ whereas the local trace controls the state of P' in $\widetilde{P}$.

Definition 3.6. Let $u \in traces [\![\widetilde{P}^{vis}]\!]$. The trace $u \downarrow \alpha\_ch(P)$ is called a *global trace.* A trace $s \in \alpha(P)^*$ with $s' = (u \downarrow (inch(P)' \cup outch(P))$ is a *corresponding local trace* of P. □

E.g. $a.b.fb.sa$ is a global and $b.a.fb.sa$ a corresponding local trace of A.

Note that $traces [\![\widetilde{P}]\!]$ consists of all global traces and $traces [\![P]\!]$ of all local traces. The next definition introduces the relation 'reorder' to model the difference between global and local traces of the same length. The idea comes from [Udd84, Def. 4.0]. The name 'reorder' is used in [JJH90].

Definition 3.7 (Reorder). Let e and s be traces from a simple interface $\Delta = (inch, outch)$. The relation $e \sqsubset_\Delta s$ holds iff

$$e \sqsubset_\Delta s =_{df} |\, s \,| = |\, e \,| \wedge$$
$$\exists u \in Comm(\Delta)^* \bullet \begin{pmatrix} (u \downarrow inch \cup inch') \in traces [\![Buffer_\Delta]\!] \wedge \\ e = (u \downarrow inch \cup outch) \wedge \\ s' = (u \downarrow inch' \cup outch) \end{pmatrix}$$

($|\, s \,|$ is the length of the trace s.) □

E.g. $a.b.fb.sa \sqsubset_{\Delta_A} b.a.fb.sa$ and $a.b \sqsubset_{\Delta_B} b.a$. Reorder catches the effects we presented in the example above. Note that the difference between global and local trace is only caused by the buffer. Therefore no process P is used in the definition.

The example is also helpful to understand the following characterisation of reorder. In principle, it is just an application of properties of $Buffer_\Delta$.

Lemma 3.8 (Characterisation of reorder). *Reorder is the smallest relation* $\sqsubset_\Delta$ *on* $Comm(\Delta)^*$ *with the following properties:*

1. $in.x \sqsubset_\Delta x.in$ *for all* $in \in Comm(inch)$ *and* $x \in Comm(\Delta)$ *with* $\mathrm{chan}(x) \neq \mathrm{chan}(in)$. *(*$\mathrm{chan}(x)$ *is the channel of the communication* x.*)*
2. $\sqsubset_\Delta$ *is a preorder, i.e.,* $\sqsubset_\Delta$ *is reflexive and transitive.*
3. $\sqsubset_\Delta$ *respects concatenation:* $e_1 \sqsubset_\Delta s_1 \wedge e_2 \sqsubset_\Delta s_2 \Longrightarrow e_1.e_2 \sqsubset_\Delta s_1.s_2$. □

This lemma is helpful to check $e \sqsubset_\Delta s$: Take s and move input communications before output communications and interchange input communications on different channels aiming at e. This is the reason for the name 'reorder'.

Note that the set *traces* $[\![\widetilde{P}]\!]$ is downwards closed with respect to reorder, and that the divergences of $\widetilde{P}$ are the downwards closure of *divergences* $[\![P]\!]$.

We need the following technical lemma for a lot of proofs. It can be skipped at first reading. The proof is a straightforward but lengthy calculation in the semantics of CSP using Lemma 3.2.

Lemma 3.9 (Semantics of P and $\widetilde{P}$).
Let P be a simple process and $In =_{df} Comm(inch(P))$.

$$failures\,[\![\widetilde{P}]\!] = \left\{ (tr, \mathcal{R}) \;\middle|\; \begin{array}{l} \exists (s, \mathcal{R}_S) \in failures\,[\![P]\!], tin \in In^*, \mathcal{R}_B \subseteq In' \bullet \\ \quad \left(\begin{array}{l} tr \sqsubset_{\Delta_P} s.tin \wedge \mathcal{R} \cup In' = \mathcal{R}_S{}' \cup \mathcal{R}_B \wedge \\ \forall c'.v \in \mathcal{R}_B \bullet \text{first}(tin \downarrow c) \neq c'.v \end{array} \right) \end{array} \right\}$$
$$\cup \{(tr, \mathcal{R}) \mid \exists s \in divergences\,[\![P]\!] \bullet tr \sqsubset_{\Delta_P} s \wedge \mathcal{R} \subset \alpha(P)\}$$

Explanation: For every $(tr, \mathcal{R}) \in failures\,[\![\widetilde{P}]\!]$ there is a corresponding local trace-refusal pair $(s, \mathcal{R}_S)$ from P. After executing the global trace tr and the local trace s there may be some communications left in $Buffer_P$. This is represented by the trace tin. $\mathcal{R}_B$ is a corresponding refusal set of $Buffer_P$; i.e. $((tr \downarrow In).(s \downarrow In)', \mathcal{R}_B) \in failures\,[\![Buffer_P]\!]$. Hence, the relation $tr \sqsubset_{\Delta_P} s.tin$ holds. ($tr \sqsubset_{\Delta_P} s$ is not true, because tr may be longer than s.)

If follows from the definition of "$\|$" ([Hoa85]) that $\mathcal{R}'_S \cup R_B$ is a refusal set of $\widetilde{P}^{vis}$. Hence, with Lemma 3.2 we have $\mathcal{R} \cup In' = \mathcal{R}_S{}' \cup \mathcal{R}_B$.

The restriction $\forall c'.v \in \mathcal{R}_B \bullet \ldots$ reflects the fact that $Buffer_P$ cannot refuse a communication that is stored as first communication of the corresponding channel. Note that $Buffer_P$ cannot refuse any communication from In, hence $\mathcal{R}_B \subseteq In'$ (and $\mathcal{R} \subseteq Comm(outch(P))$). □

Now everything has been prepared for the desired characterisation of asynchronous processes.

Theorem 3.10 (Characterising asynchronous processes with reorder).
A process P is asynchronous iff

1. *P can refuse input communications only in the case of divergence.* $(s, \mathcal{R}) \in failures\,[\![P]\!] \Longrightarrow \mathcal{R} \subseteq Comm(outch(P)) \vee s \in divergences\,[\![P]\!]$ **and**
2. *any state of P that can be reached by a trace s can be reached with any trace $e \sqsubset_{\Delta_P} s$:*

$$s \in traces\,[\![P]\!] \wedge e \sqsubset_{\Delta_P} s \Longrightarrow P/e \sqsubseteq P/s$$

Proof-Sketch. Note that 2. is equivalent to

$$(s, \mathcal{R}) \in failures\,[\![P]\!] \wedge e \sqsubset_{\Delta_P} s \Longrightarrow (e, \mathcal{R}) \in failures\,[\![P]\!]$$
$$s \in divergences\,[\![P]\!] \wedge e \sqsubset_{\Delta_P} s \Longrightarrow e \in divergences\,[\![P]\!]$$

because of 3.8.3 and the definition of $\sqsubseteq$. Hence, "$\Rightarrow$" follows from Lemma 3.9.

To prove "$\Leftarrow$", we have to show $\widetilde{P} = P$. We only consider non-divergent P. The trace *tin* from Lemma 3.9 must be empty because of 1. Therefore $P \sqsubseteq \widetilde{P}$ holds. To prove $\widetilde{P} \sqsubseteq P$, consider a trace-refusal pair $(tr, \mathcal{R}) \in failures\,[\![\widetilde{P}]\!]$ and $s, \mathcal{R}_S, tin$ and $\mathcal{R}_B$ from Lemma 3.9. Because of 1. we again have $tin = \varepsilon$ and $\mathcal{R}_B = In'$. From 1. follows $\mathcal{R}_S \subseteq Comm(outch(P))$. Hence, $\mathcal{R}_S = \mathcal{R}$ holds. With 2. we conclude $(tr, \mathcal{R}) \in failures\,[\![P]\!]$. □

Other definitions of asynchrony

Our definition of asynchronous communication differs slightly from [JJH90]. There not only the input channels but also the output channels are buffered:

$$\widetilde{P}^{[JJH90]} =_{df} Buffer_P \gg P'' \gg (\|_{c \in outch(P)}\ Buff_{c',c})$$

(The process P'' is P with primed input and output channels.)

This reflects the intuition that an asynchronous process can *send* messages without interaction with its environment. We did not follow this idea because of the following example.

Example 3.11.
$$C =_{df} (a? \to c! \to C \Box b? \to c! \to C)$$
$$D =_{df} (a! \to c? \to D \Box b! \to c? \to D)$$

The process D can send a or b to C and waits for c from C. This behaviour does not change using asynchronous communication: $(D \parallel C) = (\widetilde{D} \parallel \widetilde{C})$. Following the definition from [JJH90] this relation does not hold.

$$(\widetilde{C}^{[JJH90]} \parallel \widetilde{D}^{[JJH90]}) \neq (C \parallel D)$$

because $\widetilde{D}^{[JJH90]}$ can refuse to do $a!$ or $b!$ but D cannot.

This problem has something to do with a fundamental difference between the theories of asynchronous and synchronous communication. An appropriate semantics for a synchronous language must contain readiness information (which communication can take place next) ([Old91, OH86]) or refusal information (which communication cannot take place next) ([Hoa85, OH86]). But these concepts are not appropriate for asynchronous languages. Take for example D from above and

$$E =_{df} (a! \to c? \to E \sqcap b! \to c? \to E)$$

($\sqcap$ denotes internal nondeterministic choice). Using synchronous communication these processes can be distinguished because D leaves the choice between a or b up to the environment whether E decides between a and b without interference of the environment. But using asynchronous communication this difference does not make sense because an asynchronous environment cannot distinguish between D and E. Hence, there is no external nondeterminism but only internal nondeterminism when asynchronous communication is used. Therefore other semantic models have been developed for asynchronous languages, like quiescent traces ([CM84, Jon85, Jon88, Vaa91]) or trace based approaches ([dBH92, dBKPR91]).

As we argue for a development process starting with synchronous communication and aiming at asynchronous communication we need a uniform semantic framework for both communication schemas and thus have to consider a failure semantics for asynchronous communication. Fortunately, this model is consistent with a quiescent trace semantics, i.e., if $P \sqsubseteq Q$ holds in our model this is also true for a quiescent trace semantics but not vice versa ([Fis95]).

4 Desynchronisable Systems

We restrict ourselves to a special kind of process in this section, called ***system***, where every channel occurs as input and output channel.

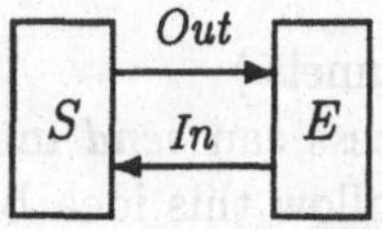

Fig. 2: A System

A ***system*** is a process term of the form $S \parallel E$ where S and E have simple interfaces Δ_S and Δ_E respectively, and $\mathit{outch}(S) = \mathit{inch}(E)$ and $\mathit{inch}(S) = \mathit{outch}(E)$. We use the standard system $S \parallel E$. We write $\mathit{In} =_{df} \mathit{Comm}(\mathit{inch}(\Delta_S))$ and $\mathit{Out} =_{df} \mathit{Comm}(\mathit{outch}(\Delta_S))$.

We stated already the guiding idea for the rest of this paper in the Example 3.11. Our interest lies in systems that fulfill the equation

$$(S \parallel E) = (\widetilde{S} \parallel \widetilde{E}), \tag{2}$$

i.e., it does not matter whether $S \parallel E$ is executed on a synchronous architecture or on an asynchronous one. Such systems $S \parallel E$ are called ***desynchronisable.*** They are very useful for the design aiming at an asynchronous architecture: It is not necessary to develop asynchronous processes S and E, it suffices to develop a desynchronisable system. Hence all verification and validation work can be done more easily for $S \parallel E$ with a usually much smaller state space than $\widetilde{S} \parallel \widetilde{E}$. Nevertheless $S \parallel E$ can directly be implemented on top of an asynchronous architecture.

The intuition behind S and E can be that: S is the process to develop and E is a model for the environment of S, i.e., E describes the assumptions about the environment we make. But this intuitive difference between S and E is not important for the theory. Hence, S and E are arbitrary processes in the sequel. This view is also useful for the design of closed systems, e.g. two communicating processes implementing a given protocol.

The rest of this section is organised as follows. After the definition of desynchronisability and a basic theorem we develop a characterisation with help of reorder, much like we did for asynchronous processes.

We assume only non-divergent processes from now on. Note that $\widetilde{P}$ is divergence free if P is.

Definition 4.1. A system $(S \parallel E)$ is ***desynchronisable*** iff $(S \parallel E) = (\widetilde{S} \parallel \widetilde{E})$ holds. □

E.g. $C \parallel D$ (Example 3.11) is desynchronisable. We start with the investigation of

$$(\widetilde{S} \parallel \widetilde{E}) \sqsubseteq (S \parallel E) \tag{3}$$

From *traces* $[\![P]\!] \subseteq$ *traces* $[\![\widetilde{P}]\!]$ it follows immediately that

$$traces\,[\![S \parallel E]\!] \subseteq traces\,[\![\widetilde{S} \parallel \widetilde{E}]\!] \ .$$

But (3) does not hold in general because $S \parallel E$ refuses a communication if S or E can refuse; but in $\widetilde{S} \parallel \widetilde{E}$ refusals on *In* are controlled only by E and refusals on *Out* only by S.

Hence, (3) holds if S never refuses a communication on *In* offered by E and E never refuses a communication on *Out* offered by S after a trace $tr \in traces\,[\![S \parallel E]\!]$. We call such systems *sender dominated.*

For the definition we need the set $Next_P(tr)$ describing all possible communications that can follow after *tr*.

$$Next_P(tr) =_{df} \{cm \mid tr.cm \in traces\,[\![P]\!]\}$$

Definition 4.2. A system $S \parallel E$ *communicates sender dominated* iff

$$\forall (tr, \mathcal{R}_S) \in failures\,[\![S]\!], (tr, \mathcal{R}_E) \in failures\,[\![E]\!] \bullet$$
$$(\mathcal{R}_S|_{In} \subseteq (In - Next_E(tr)) \wedge \mathcal{R}_E|_{Out} \subseteq (Out - Next_S(tr)))$$

$\mathcal{R}_S \subseteq (In - Next_E(tr))$ states that S cannot refuse any communication from E. As this must only hold for all input communications we restrict $\mathcal{R}_S$ to *In*. $(X|_Y =_{df} X \cap Y.)$ □

Lemma 4.3. *For sender dominated communicating systems* $(\widetilde{S} \parallel \widetilde{E}) \sqsubseteq (S \parallel E)$ *holds.* □

We can now summarise our considerations in the desired theorem about desynchronisable systems. The proof is a lengthy calculation with Lemma 3.9.

Theorem 4.4 (Desynchronisable Systems).
Let E and S communicate sender dominated. The system $E \parallel S$ is desynchronisable if

$$\forall\, tr \in (In \cup Out)^*, tin \in In^*, tout \in Out^*, (e, \mathcal{R}_E) \in failures\,[\![E]\!],$$
$$(s, \mathcal{R}_S) \in failures\,[\![S]\!] \bullet$$
$$\left(\begin{array}{l} tr \sqsubset_S s.tin \wedge tr \sqsubset_E e.tout \wedge \\ (\forall c \in inch(S) \bullet (\text{first}(tin \downarrow c) \in \mathcal{R}_S)) \wedge \\ (\forall c \in inch(E) \bullet (\text{first}(tout \downarrow c) \in \mathcal{R}_E)) \end{array}\right) \Longrightarrow \begin{array}{r} (4) \\ (5) \\ (6) \end{array}$$
$$(tr, \mathcal{R}_S|_{Out} \cup \mathcal{R}_E|_{In}) \in failures\,[\![S \parallel E]\!] \tag{7}$$

Explanation: (4), (5) and (6) represent a trace, refusal pair from $\widetilde{S} \parallel \widetilde{E}$ (compare lemma 3.9), in detail:

(4): *tr* is a global trace of *s* and *e*. *tin* is the contents of Buffer_S in $\widetilde{S}$ after the global trace *tr* and the local trace *s*. Analogously *tout* is the contents of Buffer_E.

(5): The concealment of the channels c' in $\widetilde{S}$ removes observations where a channel c' is enabled (communication on local channels happen immediately), i.e., Buffer_S and S' both do not refuse to communicate on c'.
first$(tin \downarrow c)$ is the first communication in $\mathit{Buff}_{c,c'}$. Either $\mathit{Buff}_{c,c'}$ is empty (first$(\varepsilon) =_{df} \varepsilon$) and Buffer_S refuses to communicate on c' or S' from $\widetilde{S}$ refuses the communication on c'. Hence the state of $\widetilde{S}$ after the global trace *tr* and the local trace *s* is stable. (6) analogous.

(7): $\mathcal{R}_S|_{Out}$ $(\mathcal{R}_E|_{In})$ is a refusal set from $\widetilde{S}$ $(\widetilde{E})$. Hence, $(tr, \mathcal{R}_S|_{Out} \cup \mathcal{R}_E|_{In})$ must be an element from *failures* $[\![S \parallel E]\!]$ □

5 Absolutely Desynchronisable Systems

Theorem 4.4 is not useful for the *compositional design* of desynchronisable systems, i.e., desynchronisability cannot be checked separately for S and E. We aim at simpler and at least partly compositional conditions for desynchronisability. The condition we cannot check compositionally is sender dominated communication. (Have a close look at the definition to see why.) But this is the only condition we have to check globally for $S \parallel E$.

We call the new class of processes which can be combined to desynchronisable systems (if communicating sender dominated) *absolutely desynchronisable.* Intuitively a process S is absolutely desynchronisable if it is not sensitive to possible reorder of communications from *traces* $[\![S]\!]$.

Definition 5.1 (absolutely desynchronisable). Let S be a simple process. S is *absolutely desynchronisable* iff for all $t \in \mathit{traces}\,[\![S]\!]$, $(s, \mathcal{R}) \in \mathit{failures}\,[\![S]\!]$ and $tin \in In^*$, $tout \in Out^*$ the following condition holds:

$$\Big((t.tout \sqsubset_{\Delta_S} s.tin) \wedge (\forall c \in inch(S) \bullet \mathrm{first}(tin \downarrow c) \in \mathcal{R})\Big)$$
$$\Longrightarrow (t.tout, \mathcal{R}) \in \mathit{failures}\,[\![S]\!]$$ □

E.g. C and D (Example 3.11) are absolutely desynchronisable.

Note that all asynchronous processes are absolutely desynchronisable (see Theorem 3.10). Note that we quantify t only over *traces* $[\![S]\!]$ in Definition 5.1 and not over all traces like in Theorem 4.4. This is the important fact to prove in the next theorem. (A slight adaption of the proof can be found in [Fis95].)

Theorem 5.2. *A sender dominated communicating system $S \parallel E$ where S and E are absolutely desynchronisable is desynchronisable.* □

This theorem justifies our definition of absolute desychronisabilty. We need the following simplification of Definition 5.1 in the sequel.

Lemma 5.3. *S is absolutely desynchronisable if for all $tr \in traces\,[\![S]\!]$, $in \in In$ and $x \in (In \cup Out)$ with* $\mathbf{chan}(x) \neq \mathbf{chan}(in)$ *the following condition holds.*

$$(S/(tr.x.in)) \sqsubseteq (S/(tr.in.x)) \;\wedge\; \forall \mathcal{R} \bullet ((tr.x, \mathcal{R}) \in failures\,[\![S]\!] \Rightarrow in \notin \mathcal{R})$$

□

The preconditions of this lemma are easy to check. One only has to look at all states where a communication on an input channel *in* and on a different channel x can follow. The state that can be reached by $in.x$ must also be reachable by $x.in$ and *in* is not disabled by x. This can be used to construct an algorithm for proving absolute desynchronisability.

The theorem is used in [Fis95] to calculate the maximal buffer length of a system. This information is necessary for an implementation with bounded buffers.

6 Example: Two-Phase Commit

A typical example of a protocol in a distributed system is the so-called *Two-Phase Commit Protocol* (TPC). It is a special case of the class of consensus algorithms [BHG87, RH90]. The idea is that we have a coordinator connected to n participants which have to vote globally on a decision to be taken, in this case to COMMIT or to ABORT. Every participant can either vote YES or NO meaning that he is willing to COMMIT or not willing, respectively. Only if all participants vote YES the decision will be to COMMIT, otherwise the decision will be to ABORT. The simplest implementation of this protocol is that the coordinator, when triggered by a request message, requests all participants to vote, gathers the votes and decides accordingly and finally sends the decision to all participants. Such a protocol can very nicely be formalised in a synchronous way.

Example 6.1.

$$\begin{aligned}
TPC &=_{df} C \,\|\, P_1 \,\|\, P_2 \,\|\, \cdots \,\|\, P_n \,\|\, Env,\\
C &=_{df} (Request \,|||\, Vote);\ Decide;\ Inform;\ C,\\
P_i &=_{df} Request_i;\ Vote_i;\ Inform_i;\ P_i,\\
Env &=_{df} Req! \rightarrow Inf?x \rightarrow Env,
\end{aligned}$$

$$\begin{aligned}
Request &=_{df} Req? \rightarrow \|_i (Req_i! \rightarrow Skip),\\
Vote &=_{df} \|_i (Vote_i?(v_i) \rightarrow Skip),\\
Decide &=_{df} \textbf{if } \wedge_i\, v_i = \text{YES} \textbf{ then } dec := \text{COMMIT} \textbf{ else } dec := \text{ABORT},\\
Inform &=_{df} \left(\|_i (Inf_i!(dec) \rightarrow Skip)\right);\ (Inf!(dec) \rightarrow Skip),\\
Request_i &=_{df} Req_i? \rightarrow Skip,\\
Vote_i &=_{df} Vote_i!\text{YES} \rightarrow Skip \sqcap Vote_i!\text{NO} \rightarrow Skip,\\
Inform_i &=_{df} Inf_i?(dec_i) \rightarrow Skip.
\end{aligned}$$

To show that this system is desynchronisable use $S =_{df} C$ and $E =_{df} Env \parallel \left(\|_i P_i\right)$. (Note that $\alpha(P_i) \cap \alpha(P_j) = \emptyset$ for $i \neq j$. Hence, S and E have simple interfaces.) Lemma 5.3 is helpful to show that S and E are absolutely desynchronisable. Sender dominated communication of S and E follows from the definition. Hence, *TPC* is desynchronisable.

7 Delay insensitive circuits

The class of absolutely desynchronisable systems described in Lemma 5.3 happens to be a generalisation of so called delay insensitive circuits. An integrated circuit is called *delay insensitive* if its correctness does not depend on assumptions about delays in the connecting wires or response times ([Ver94, MFR85, Udd84]).

Following [Ver94] communication via wires in integrated circuits is modeled by isochronic and anisochronic communication. Isochronic communication is the same as sender dominated synchronous communication, i.e., a communication happens at the same time for sender and receiver but a message to a receiver that is not ready to communicate leads to *Chaos*. Anisochronic communication is asynchronous communication with maximal buffer length one. An attempt to put a communication into a full buffer leads to *Chaos*. Note that in the literature ([MFR85, Udd84]) the terms 'asynchronous' and 'synchronous' are often used for 'anisochronic' and 'isochronic', respectively.
We define wires and anisochronic communication in our model.

Definition 7.1 (Wire).

$$Wire_{in,out} =_{df} in?x \rightarrow (in?x \rightarrow Chaos \,\Box\, out!x \rightarrow Wire_{in,out}) \qquad \Box$$

Definition 7.2 (Operator for anisochronic communication).

$$\tilde{P} =_{df} (\|_{c \in inch(P)}\ Wire_{c,c'}) \gg P' \qquad \Box$$

Definition 7.3 (Delay insensitive). A system $S \parallel E$ is *delay insensitive* iff

$$(\vec{S} \parallel \vec{E}) = (S \parallel E) \qquad \Box$$

Note that delay insensitive systems are desynchronisable.

The next theorem is useful to check whether a system is delay insensitive. It is a special case of Lemma 5.3.

Theorem 7.4. *Let S and E be processes that fulfill the conditions from Lemma 5.3. Let S and E never send a message twice over the same channel:*

$$\forall tr \in traces\,[\![S \parallel E]\!], cm_1, cm_2 \in \alpha(S) \bullet$$
$$\mathbf{chan}(cm_1) = \mathbf{chan}(cm_2) \Longrightarrow tr.cm_1.cm_2 \notin traces\,[\![S \parallel E]\!]$$

Then $S \parallel E$ is delay insensitive if S and E communicate sender dominated. $\Box$

The conditions from Lemma 5.3 reflect the **JTU-Rules** $\mathcal{X}, \mathcal{Y}'$ and $\mathcal{Z}$ ([Ver94, p. 42]). The additional condition from Theorem 7.4 reflects **JTU-Rules** $\mathcal{W}$. The JTU-Rules ('Jan Tijmen Udding') where first presented in [Udd84] to describe delay insensitive processes.

8 Conclusion and Outlook

We presented the new class of desynchronisable systems which do not change their behaviour whether executed on synchronous or on asynchronous communication media. Desynchronisable systems can be composed from absolutely desynchronisable processes which are a generalisation of delay insensitive circuits.

We see three major topics for further studies. The first question is: What happens if asynchronous communication is introduced on hidden channels? E.g. let C_S be a set of input channels of S and C_E be some input channels of E.

$$\Big(S \parallel E\Big) \setminus (C_S \cup C_E) \stackrel{?}{=} \Big((Buffer_{C_S} \gg S') \parallel (Buffer_{C_E} \gg E')\Big) \setminus (C_S \cup C_E) \quad (8)$$

Here only channels from C_S are primed in S' (E' analogously).

Equation (8) is obviously true for a desynchronisable system $S \parallel E$. But (8) can even hold for non sender dominated communicating systems because different refusal sets do not necessarily matter in (8).

These ideas could be important for the development of an ISO/OSI layer. Take for example the system in Fig. 2. The processes S and E are service access

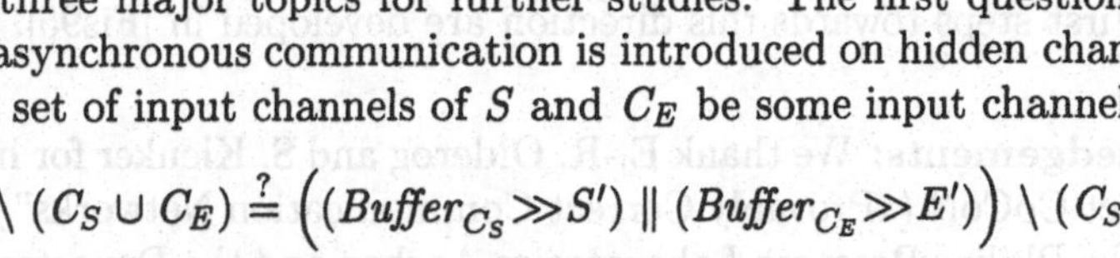

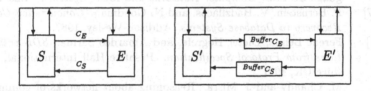

Figure 2. Connection diagram for an OSI layer

points of some layer. The channels C_E and C_S connect S and E, but we are not interested in the communications on C_S and C_E. We just want S and E to provide a certain service for the environment.

An other topic for further studies is the sequential ***compositional design*** of desynchronisable systems. Assume we have n systems $P_i \parallel Q_i$ that are desynchronisable. If P_i and Q_i must terminate after the same traces obviously also the system

$$(P_1;\ P_2;\ \ldots;\ P_n) \parallel (Q_1;\ Q_2;\ \ldots;\ Q_n)$$

is desynchronisable. Thus we want to develop desynchronisable systems from small desynchronisable building blocks. We could apply this idea to "develop" the Two-Phase Commit example from desynchronisable components, thus showing its desynchronisability in a different, indirect way. By showing $Request \parallel (\parallel_i Request_i)$, $Vote \parallel (\parallel_i Vote_i)$, $Decide \parallel (\parallel_i Skip)$ and so on are all desynchronisable, using sender domination and absolute desynchronisability of the components, we could conclude that TCP is desynchronisable.

Unfortunately we cannot state such a theorem in our theory yet because the operator "$\tilde{}$" has not been defined for sequential processes — i.e., those with the termination symbol "✓" in the alphabet — as "✓" is neither an input nor an output communication. (Note that this problem does not occur in the example in section 6.)

The third question that should be addressed in future is the transformation of non desynchronisable systems into desynchronisable ones using methods from [KT96]. First steps towards this direction are developed in [Fis95].

Acknowledgements: We thank E.-R. Olderog and S. Kleuker for helpful hints. The project CoCoN ("Provably Correct Communication Networks") carried out between the Philips Research Laboratories Aachen and the Department of Computer Science at the University of Oldenburg provided an inspiring atmosphere for the development of the ideas presented here.

References

[BB87] T. Bolognesi and E. Brinksma. Introduction to the ISO specification language LOTOS. *Computer Networks and ISDN Systems*, 14:25–59, 1987.

[BHG87] P. Bernstein, V. Hadzilacos, and N. Goodman. *Concurrency Control and Recovery in Database Systems.* Addison-Wesley, 1987.

[BHS91] Ferenc Belina, Dieter Hogrefe, and Amardeo Sarma. *SDL with Applications from Protocol Specification.* Prentice Hall International, Hertfordshire UK, 1991.

[CM84] M. Chandy and J. Misra. Reasoning about networks of communicating processes. In INRIA Advanced Nato Study Institute on Logics and Models for Verification and Specification of Concurrent Systems, Nice , France, 1984.

[dBH92] F. de Boer and J. Hooman. The real-time behaviour of asynchronously communicating processes. In J. Vytopil, editor, *Formal Techniques in Real-Time and Fault-Tolerant Systems*, volume 571 of *LNCS*, pages 451–472. Springer-Verlag, 1992.

[dBKPR91] Frank S. de Boer, J. N. Kok, Catuscia Palamidessi, and J.J.M.M. Rutten. The failure of failures in a paradigm for asynchronous communication. In *Proceedings of CONCUR 1991*, volume 527 of *LNCS*, Amsterdam, 1991.

[EF82] T. Elrad and N. Francez. Decomposition of distributed programs into communication closed layers. *Science of Computer Programming*, 2:155–173, 1982.

[Fis95] Clemens Fischer. Transformation von synchronen SL-Spezifikationen von Telekommunikationssystemen in asynchrone SL-Spezifikationen. Master's thesis, Univ. Oldenburg, 1995.

[Hoa85] C.A.R. Hoare. *Communicating Sequential Processes.* Prentice/Hall International, 1985.

[JJH90] He Jifeng, Mark B. Josephs, and C.A.R. Hoare. A theory of synchrony and asynchrony. In M. Broy and C. B. Jones, editors, *Proceedings of the IFIP Working Conference on Programming Concepts and Methods*, pages 459–478, North-Holland, 1990. Elsevier.

[Jon85] Bengt Jonsson. A model and proof system for asynchronous networks. In *Proc. of the 4th ACM SIGACT-SIGOPS Symposium on Principles of Distributed Computing*, pages 49–58, 1985.

[Jon88] Bengt Jonsson. A fully abstract trace model for dataflow networks. Research Report 88016, Swedish Institute of Computer Science, 1988.

[JPZ91] W. Janssen, M. Poel, and J. Zwiers. Action systems and action refinement in the development of parallel systems. In *Proceedings of CONCUR '91, LNCS 527*, pages 298–316. Springer-Verlag, 1991.

[KT96] S. Kleuker and H. Tjabben. The incremental development of correct specifications for distributed systems. In M.-C. Gaudel and J. Woodcock, editors, *Industrial Benefit and Advances in Formal Methods (FME'96)*, volume 1051 of *LNCS*, pages 479–498, 1996.

[MFR85] Charles E. Molnar, Ting-Pien Fang, and Frederick U. Rosenberger. Synthesis of delay-insensitive modules. In Henry Fuchs, editor, *1985 Chapel Hill Conference on Very Large Scale Integration*, pages 67–86. Computer Science Press, 1985.

[Mol86] Charles E. Molnar. Introduction to asynchronous systems. In *Proceedings New Frontiers in Computer Science Conference*, pages 83–93, Santa Monica, 1986. Citicorp/TTI.

[OH86] E.-R. Olderog and C.A.R. Hoare. Specification-oriented semantics for commuicating processes. *Acta Informatica*, 23:9–66, 1986.

[Old91] E.-R. Olderog. *Nets, Terms and Formulas.* Cambridge University Press, Cambridge, 1991.

[RH90] M. Raynal and J.-M. Helary. *Synchronization and control of distributed systems and programs.* John Wiley & Sons, 1990.

[Rös94] Stephan Rössig. *A Transformational Approach to the Design of Communicating Systems.* Berichte aus dem fachbereich informatik, Universität Oldenburg, 1994.

[SdR94] F. Stomp and W.-P. de Roever. A principle for sequential reasoning about distributed systems. *Formal Aspects of Computing*, 6(6):716–737, 1994.

[Udd84] Jan Tijmen Udding. *Classification and Composition of Delay-Insensitive Circuits.* PhD thesis, Eindhoven University of Technology, 1984.

[Vaa91] F. W. Vaandrager. On the relationship between process algebra and input/output automata. In *Proceedings of Logic in Computer Science*, pages 387–398. IEEE, 1991.

[Ver94] Tom Verhoeff. *A Theory of Delay-Insensitve Systems.* PhD thesis, Eindhoven University of Technology, 1994.

[Zwi89] J. Zwiers. *Compositionality, Concurrency and Partial Correctness, LNCS 321.* Springer-Verlag, 1989.

Author Index

Samson Abramsky 1
Rajeev Alur 546
Roberto Amadio 147
Marco Bernardo 315
Eike Best 498
Michele Boreale 163
Ahmed Bouajjani 481
Julian Bradfield 233
Robert Brayton 546
Olaf Burkart 247
Ilaria Castellani 147
Didier Caucal 247
Rance Cleaveland 34
Andrea Corradini 438
Raymond Devillers 465
Paolo Di Blasio 655
Jürgen Dingel 703
Manfred Droste 627
Alessandro Fantechi 563
Clemens Fischer 735
Kathleen Fisher 655
Cédric Fournet 406
Paul Gastin 627
Stefania Gnesi 563
Georges Gonthier 406
Roberto Gorrieri 315
Vineet Gupta 66, 373
Peter Habermehl 481
Thomas Henzinger 514, 530
Thomas Hildebrandt 84
Michaela Huhn 611, 639
Radha Jagadeesan 66, 373
Jerry James 719
David Janin 263
Wil Janssen 735
Peter Kopke 530
Tsung-Min Kuo 278
Orna Kupferman 514
Robert Kurshan 546
Diego Latella 563
Carolina Lavatelli 422
Lone Leth 278
Jean-Jacques Lévy 406
Huimin Lin 50
Gerald Lüttgen 34
Andrea Maggiolo-Schettini 687
Luc Maranget 406
Sjouke Mauw 671
José Meseguer 331
Faron Moller 195
Vaidhyanathan Natarajan 34
Uwe Nestmann 179
Peter Niebert 611
Catuscia Palamidessi 498
Joachim Parrow 389
Doron Peled 596
Adriano Peron 687
Anna Philippou 131
Benjamin Pierce 179
Andrew Pitts 18
John Power 115
Wolfgang Reisig 579
Didier Rémy 406
Michel Reniers 671
Joshua Ross 18
Davide Sangiorgi 147
Vijay Saraswat 66, 373
Vladimiro Sassone 84
Roberto Segala 299
Ambuj Singh 719
Bernhard Steffen 247
Colin Stirling 217
Serdar Taşıran 546
Bent Thomsen 278
Simone Tini 687
Moshe Vardi 514
Björn Victor 389
David Walker 131
Igor Walukiewicz 263
Thomas Wilke 596
Glynn Winskel 98
Pierre Wolper 596

Lecture Notes in Computer Science

For information about Vols. 1–1053

please contact your bookseller or Springer-Verlag

Vol. 1054: A. Ferreira, P. Pardalos (Eds.), Solving Combinatorial Optimization Problems in Parallel. VII, 274 pages. 1996.

Vol. 1055: T. Margaria, B. Steffen (Eds.), Tools and Algorithms for the Construction and Analysis of Systems. Proceedings, 1996. XI, 435 pages. 1996.

Vol. 1056: A. Haddadi, Communication and Cooperation in Agent Systems. XIII, 148 pages. 1996. (Subseries LNAI).

Vol. 1057: P. Apers, M. Bouzeghoub, G. Gardarin (Eds.), Advances in Database Technology — EDBT '96. Proceedings, 1996. XII, 636 pages. 1996.

Vol. 1058: H. R. Nielson (Ed.), Programming Languages and Systems – ESOP '96. Proceedings, 1996. X, 405 pages. 1996.

Vol. 1059: H. Kirchner (Ed.), Trees in Algebra and Programming – CAAP '96. Proceedings, 1996. VIII, 331 pages. 1996.

Vol. 1060: T. Gyimóthy (Ed.), Compiler Construction. Proceedings, 1996. X, 355 pages. 1996.

Vol. 1061: P. Ciancarini, C. Hankin (Eds.), Coordination Languages and Models. Proceedings, 1996. XI, 443 pages. 1996.

Vol. 1062: E. Sanchez, M. Tomassini (Eds.), Towards Evolvable Hardware. IX, 265 pages. 1996.

Vol. 1063: J.-M. Alliot, E. Lutton, E. Ronald, M. Schoenauer, D. Snyers (Eds.), Artificial Evolution. Proceedings, 1995. XIII, 396 pages. 1996.

Vol. 1064: B. Buxton, R. Cipolla (Eds.), Computer Vision – ECCV '96. Volume I. Proceedings, 1996. XXI, 725 pages. 1996.

Vol. 1065: B. Buxton, R. Cipolla (Eds.), Computer Vision – ECCV '96. Volume II. Proceedings, 1996. XXI, 723 pages. 1996.

Vol. 1066: R. Alur, T.A. Henzinger, E.D. Sontag (Eds.), Hybrid Systems III. IX, 618 pages. 1996.

Vol. 1067: H. Liddell, A. Colbrook, B. Hertzberger, P. Sloot (Eds.), High-Performance Computing and Networking. Proceedings, 1996. XXV, 1040 pages. 1996.

Vol. 1068: T. Ito, R.H. Halstead, Jr., C. Queinnec (Eds.), Parallel Symbolic Languages and Systems. Proceedings, 1995. X, 363 pages. 1996.

Vol. 1069: J.W. Perram, J.-P. Müller (Eds.), Distributed Software Agents and Applications. Proceedings, 1994. VIII, 219 pages. 1996. (Subseries LNAI).

Vol. 1070: U. Maurer (Ed.), Advances in Cryptology – EUROCRYPT '96. Proceedings, 1996. XII, 417 pages. 1996.

Vol. 1071: P. Miglioli, U. Moscato, D. Mundici, M. Ornaghi (Eds.), Theorem Proving with Analytic Tableaux and Related Methods. Proceedings, 1996. X, 330 pages. 1996. (Subseries LNAI).

Vol. 1072: R. Kasturi, K. Tombre (Eds.), Graphics Recognition. Proceedings, 1995. X, 308 pages. 1996.

Vol. 1073: J. Cuny, H. Ehrig, G. Engels, G. Rozenberg (Eds.), Graph Grammars and Their Application to Computer Science. Proceedings, 1994. X, 565 pages. 1996.

Vol. 1074: G. Dowek, J. Heering, K. Meinke, B. Möller (Eds.), Higher-Order Algebra, Logic, and Term Rewriting. Proceedings, 1995. VII, 287 pages. 1996.

Vol. 1075: D. Hirschberg, G. Myers (Eds.), Combinatorial Pattern Matching. Proceedings, 1996. VIII, 392 pages. 1996.

Vol. 1076: N. Shadbolt, K. O'Hara, G. Schreiber (Eds.), Advances in Knowledge Acquisition. Proceedings, 1996. XII, 371 pages. 1996. (Subseries LNAI).

Vol. 1077: P. Brusilovsky, P. Kommers, N. Streitz (Eds.), Multimedia, Hypermedia, and Virtual Reality. Proceedings, 1994. IX, 311 pages. 1996.

Vol. 1078: D.A. Lamb (Ed.), Studies of Software Design. Proceedings, 1993. VI, 188 pages. 1996.

Vol. 1079: Z. W. Raś, M. Michalewicz (Eds.), Foundations of Intelligent Systems. Proceedings, 1996. XI, 664 pages. 1996. (Subseries LNAI).

Vol. 1080: P. Constantopoulos, J. Mylopoulos, Y. Vassiliou (Eds.), Advanced Information Systems Engineering. Proceedings, 1996. XI, 582 pages. 1996.

Vol. 1081: G. McCalla (Ed.), Advances in Artificial Intelligence. Proceedings, 1996. XII, 459 pages. 1996. (Subseries LNAI).

Vol. 1082: N.R. Adam, B.K. Bhargava, M. Halem, Y. Yesha (Eds.), Digital Libraries. Proceedings, 1995. Approx. 310 pages. 1996.

Vol. 1083: K. Sparck Jones, J.R. Galliers, Evaluating Natural Language Processing Systems. XV, 228 pages. 1996. (Subseries LNAI).

Vol. 1084: W.H. Cunningham, S.T. McCormick, M. Queyranne (Eds.), Integer Programming and Combinatorial Optimization. Proceedings, 1996. X, 505 pages. 1996.

Vol. 1085: D.M. Gabbay, H.J. Ohlbach (Eds.), Practical Reasoning. Proceedings, 1996. XV, 721 pages. 1996. (Subseries LNAI).

Vol. 1086: C. Frasson, G. Gauthier, A. Lesgold (Eds.), Intelligent Tutoring Systems. Proceedings, 1996. XVII, 688 pages. 1996.

Lecture Notes in Computer Science

For information about Vols. 1–1053

please contact your bookseller or Springer-Verlag

Vol. 1087: C. Zhang, D. Lukose (Eds.), Distributed Artificial Intelliegence. Proceedings, 1995. VIII, 232 pages. 1996. (Subseries LNAI).

Vol. 1088: A. Strohmeier (Ed.), Reliable Software Technologies – Ada-Europe '96. Proceedings, 1996. XI, 513 pages. 1996.

Vol. 1089: G. Ramalingam, Bounded Incremental Computation. XI, 190 pages. 1996.

Vol. 1090: J.-Y. Cai, C.K. Wong (Eds.), Computing and Combinatorics. Proceedings, 1996. X, 421 pages. 1996.

Vol. 1091: J. Billington, W. Reisig (Eds.), Application and Theory of Petri Nets 1996. Proceedings, 1996. VIII, 549 pages. 1996.

Vol. 1092: H. Kleine Büning (Ed.), Computer Science Logic. Proceedings, 1995. VIII, 487 pages. 1996.

Vol. 1093: L. Dorst, M. van Lambalgen, F. Voorbraak (Eds.), Reasoning with Uncertainty in Robotics. Proceedings, 1995. VIII, 387 pages. 1996. (Subseries LNAI).

Vol. 1094: R. Morrison, J. Kennedy (Eds.), Advances in Databases. Proceedings, 1996. XI, 234 pages. 1996.

Vol. 1095: W. McCune, R. Padmanabhan, Automated Deduction in Equational Logic and Cubic Curves. X, 231 pages. 1996. (Subseries LNAI).

Vol. 1096: T. Schäl, Workflow Management Systems for Process Organisations. XII, 200 pages. 1996.

Vol. 1097: R. Karlsson, A. Lingas (Eds.), Algorithm Theory – SWAT '96. Proceedings, 1996. IX, 453 pages. 1996.

Vol. 1098: P. Cointe (Ed.), ECOOP '96 – Object-Oriented Programming. Proceedings, 1996. XI, 502 pages. 1996.

Vol. 1099: F. Meyer auf der Heide, B. Monien (Eds.), Automata, Languages and Programming. Proceedings, 1996. XII, 681 pages. 1996.

Vol. 1100: B. Pfitzmann, Digital Signature Schemes. XVI, 396 pages. 1996.

Vol. 1101: M. Wirsing, M. Nivat (Eds.), Algebraic Methodology and Software Technology. Proceedings, 1996. XII, 641 pages. 1996.

Vol. 1102: R. Alur, T.A. Henzinger (Eds.), Computer Aided Verification. Proceedings, 1996. XII, 472 pages. 1996.

Vol. 1103: H. Ganzinger (Ed.), Rewriting Techniques and Applications. Proceedings, 1996. XI, 437 pages. 1996.

Vol. 1104: M.A. McRobbie, J.K. Slaney (Eds.), Automated Deduction – CADE-13. Proceedings, 1996. XV, 764 pages. 1996. (Subseries LNAI).

Vol. 1105: T.I. Ören, G.J. Klir (Eds.), Computer Aided Systems Theory – CAST '94. Proceedings, 1994. IX, 439 pages. 1996.

Vol. 1106: M. Jampel, E. Freuder, M. Maher (Eds.), Over-Constrained Systems. X, 309 pages. 1996.

Vol. 1107: J.-P. Briot, J.-M. Geib, A. Yonezawa (Eds.), Object-Based Parallel and Distributed Computation. Proceedings, 1995. X, 349 pages. 1996.

Vol. 1108: A. Díaz de Ilarraza Sánchez, I. Fernández de Castro (Eds.), Computer Aided Learning and Instruction in Science and Engineering. Proceedings, 1996. XIV, 480 pages. 1996.

Vol. 1109: N. Koblitz (Ed.), Advances in Cryptology – Crypto '96. Proceedings, 1996. XII, 417 pages. 1996.

Vol. 1110: O. Danvy, R. Glück, P. Thiemann (Eds.), Partial Evaluation. Proceedings, 1996. XII, 514 pages. 1996.

Vol. 1111: J.J. Alferes, L. Moniz Pereira, Reasoning with Logic Programming. XXI, 326 pages. 1996. (Subseries LNAI).

Vol. 1112: C. von der Malsburg, W. von Seelen, J.C. Vorbrüggen, B. Sendhoff (Eds.), Artificial Neural Networks – ICANN 96. Proceedings, 1996. XXV, 922 pages. 1996.

Vol. 1113: W. Penczek, A. Szałas (Eds.), Mathematical Foundations of Computer Science 1996. Proceedings, 1996. X, 592 pages. 1996.

Vol. 1114: N. Foo, R. Goebel (Eds.), PRICAI'96: Topics in Artificial Intelligence. Proceedings, 1996. XXI, 658 pages. 1996. (Subseries LNAI).

Vol. 1115: P.W. Eklund, G. Ellis, G. Mann (Eds.), Conceptual Structures: Knowledge Representation as Interlingua. Proceedings, 1996. XIII, 321 pages. 1996. (Subseries LNAI).

Vol. 1116: J. Hall (Ed.), Management of Telecommunication Systems and Services. XXI, 229 pages. 1996.

Vol. 1117: A. Ferreira, J. Rolim, Y. Saad, T. Yang (Eds.), Parallel Algorithms for Irregularly Structured Problems. Proceedings, 1996. IX, 358 pages. 1996.

Vol. 1118: E.C. Freuder (Ed.), Principles and Practice of Constraint Programming — CP 96. Proceedings, 1996. XIX, 574 pages. 1996.

Vol. 1119: U. Montanari, V. Sassone (Eds.), CONCUR '96: Concurrency Theory. Proceedings, 1996. XII, 751 pages. 1996.

Vol. 1120: M. Deza. R. Euler, I. Manoussakis (Eds.), Combinatorics and Computer Science. Proceedings, 1995. IX, 415 pages. 1996.

Vol. 1121: P. Perner, P. Wang, A. Rosenfeld (Eds.), Advances in Structural and Syntactical Pattern Recognition. Proceedings, 1996. X, 393 pages. 1996.

Vol. 1122: H. Cohen (Ed.), Algorithmic Number Theory. Proceedings, 1996. IX, 405 pages. 1996.

Vol. 1123: L. Bougé, P. Fraigniaud, A. Mignotte, Y. Robert (Eds.), Euro-Par'96. Parallel Processing. Proceedings, 1996, Vol. I. XXXIII, 842 pages. 1996.

Vol. 1124: L. Bougé, P. Fraigniaud, A. Mignotte, Y. Robert (Eds.), Euro-Par'96. Parallel Processing. Proceedings, 1996, Vol. II. XXXIII, 926 pages. 1996.

Vol. 1125: J. von Wright, J. Grundy, J. Harrison (Eds.), Theorem Proving in Higher Order Logics. Proceedings, 1996. VIII, 447 pages. 1996.

Vol. 1126: J.J. Alferes, L. Moniz Pereira, E. Orlowska (Eds.), Logics in Artificial Intelligence. Proceedings, 1996. IX, 417 pages. 1996. (Subseries LNAI).

Vol. 1129: J. Launchbury, E. Meijer, T. Sheard (Eds.), Advanced Functional Programming. Proceedings, 1996. VII, 238 pages. 1996.